D1243799

# HOLLYWOOD SONG

REF
ML
128
.M7
B6
1995
v.2

# HOLLYWOOD SONG

## THE COMPLETE FILM & MUSICAL COMPANION

### Volume Two: Films M–Z

## KEN BLOOM

LIBRARY
FLORIDA KEYS COMMUNITY COLLEGE
5901 COLLEGE ROAD
KEY WEST, FL 33040

Facts On File®

AN INFOBASE HOLDINGS COMPANY

**HOLLYWOOD SONG: THE COMPLETE FILM MUSICAL COMPANION**

Copyright © 1995 by Ken Bloom

All rights reserved. No part of this book may be reproduced or utilized in any form or by any means, electronic or mechanical, including photocopying, recording, or by any information storage or retrieval systems, without permission in writing from the publisher. For information contact:

Facts On File, Inc.
460 Park Avenue South
New York NY 10016

**Library of Congress Cataloging-in-Publication Data**

Bloom, Ken.
Hollywood song : the complete film musical companion / Ken Bloom.
p.  cm.
Vol. 2: Films M–Z
ISBN 0-8160-2002-7 (set). — ISBN 0-8160-2668-8 (v. 1). — ISBN 0-8160-2667-X (v. 2). — ISBN 0-8160-3231-9 (v. 3).
1. Motion picture music—Bibliography.  2. Songs, English—United States—Indexes.  I. Title.
ML128.M7B6  1995
016.7821′4′0973—dc20                    90-22261

Facts On File books are available at special discounts when purchased in bulk quantities for businesses, associations, institutions or sales promotions. Please call our Special Sales Department in New York at 212/682-2244 or 800/322-8755.

Text design by Catherine Rincon Hyman
Jacket design by Soloway/Mitchell
Printed in the United States of America

VB COM 10 9 8 7 6 5 4 3 2 1

This book is printed on acid-free paper.

*To*

*Russell Metheny and*

*Carl Weaver,*

*both of whom taught me*

*a lot and cared a lot*

# CONTENTS

# ACKNOWLEDGMENTS

The compilation and research of this book was a huge undertaking. It couldn't have been completed without the help of many dedicated people. Although I take the responsibility for any errors in *Hollywood Song*, I would like to share any success with many friends and coworkers who helped me.

First and foremost I would like to thank the many dedicated professionals at the various studios where I researched this project. I'm proud to report that no studio turned down my requests, and only one limited my access to their records. While researching the thousands of pieces of paper and cue sheets I grew to appreciate the tremendous work these music and legal departments undertake.

The first studio that allowed me access to their records was Paramount. I want to especially thank Ridge Walker for his enthusiasm and continued support. He and his staff taught me a lot about the music end of motion picture production and helped me get a foothold in the mountain of documents in the Paramount archives. Ridge and his excellent staff, Marc Miller, David Robles, and Charlee Hutton have my utmost respect and gratitude.

Special thanks also to Danny Gould at Warner Brothers and Susan de Christofaro of Twentieth Century-Fox who generously went out of their way to accommodate my requests. Thanks also to Carol Besso at Disney; Julian Bratolyubov, Mark Porter, and Terry Wolff at Universal; Andrew Velcoff and Cathy Manolis at Turner; Jill Coplan at Republic; Monica Ciafardini at Columbia; Steve Pena and Laurence Zwisohn at Twentieth Century-Fox. They were all helpful and kind.

My admiration and thanks to the professionals at the Academy of Motion Picture Arts and Sciences Margaret Herrick Library whose staff is too numerous to mention but who all are experts in both the history of the motion picture industry and in human interaction. They create a uniquely gracious atmosphere for the researcher and movie buff. Thanks too for special understanding to Ruth Spencer of the American Film Institute library.

Thanks to my parents, George and Florence Bloom, whom I can never repay for their love and support.

Thanks to Barry Kleinbart for helping me in California and for being such a close friend.

Thanks to my friends Harry Bagdasian, Kenny Bennett, Bari Biern Sedar, David Bishop, Adrian Bryan-Brown, Hap Erstein, Paul Ford, Sheila Formoy, Kit Grover, Karen Hopkins, Pat Jacobs, Ken Kantor, Paul Newman, Ezio Petersen, Guy Riddick, David Rose, Bill Rudman, Berthe Schuchat, Scott Sedar, Mike Shuster, David Simone, Robert Sixsmith, Bijou Spialek, Joseph Weiss, Max Woodward, Helene Blue, Denis Peshkov, Arthur Siegel, John Thornton, Doug Schulkind, Deborah Brody and Ellen Zeisler who saw me through the good times and bad and listened to me grouse. Thanks to old and new friends in L.A.: Denny Martin Flinn, Barbara Flinn, Ken Olfson, and Michael Shoop.

I'm blessed with a terrific agent, Heide Lange of Greenburger Associates, who deserves a paragraph of her own, and here it is. Thanks Heide for your encouragement, good advice, and friendship.

I'm sure I have forgotten to thank many individuals who helped me compile the enormous amount of material that has gone into making this book. If I have forgotten to thank you please accept my apologies and send your name to me care of Facts On File.

Ken Bloom
New York City

# INTRODUCTION

This second volume of the *American Song* series (the first was on musical theater) includes data on songs from almost 7,000 American and foreign films. I attempted to track down all American made films and foreign films distributed in major release by American companies, unproduced films for which songs or scores were written, films in which instrumental pieces were later given lyrics, and silent films which had songs written for them.

Volumes 1 and 2 list all movies alphabetically. Volume 3 contains a chronological listing of titles and complete indexes to personnel and songs.

Most books on Hollywood musicals exclude rock musicals and cowboy pictures. Usually, short subjects are ignored, as are documentaries. I decided that to exclude any picture of any type would be presumptuous. After all, great songs have been written for rock pictures and for cowboy films. I decided to include all films except concert films, which usually do not have music written especially for them. Some concert films do have original songs—for example, *Woodstock*—and those are included. Cartoons are usually included under a generic heading (for example, "Popeye films"), since I couldn't always ascertain which songs were written for which cartoons. Warner Brothers, Disney, and MGM cartoon cue sheets, however, do exist on a film by film basis, and their songs are listed under the film's title.

No films are included if they were produced for video or went straight to video without a release. Films are also omitted if they contained a vocal but the song was not written for the film. For example, films containing only a vocal of a popular tune or public domain standard are excluded.

No information has been included unless it has been verified by programs, sheet music, censorship forms, reviews, scripts, publicity materials, production company records, demo discs, recording and dubbing schedules, publishers' files, ASCAP or BMI lists, or by the composers or lyricists themselves.

Since viewing all the films made by American studios is impossible, and since many prints are incomplete, I used the motion picture companies' cue sheets as my primary source. Songs may have been deleted from prints after the initial road-show engagements or excised from television prints. But the cue sheets list the songs as they appeared in the films' initial release. For many early films, cue sheets do not exist or are incomplete. In the early thirties cue sheets were pretty much standardized and their quality and reliability were improved.

I didn't make a list of possible films and then look for those cue sheets. Instead in all but one instance (Columbia), I went through every available cue sheet. I also researched all available complementary records. I estimate that I examined over 15,000 cue sheets.

Cue sheets divide music cues into four categories: Background Vocals, Visual Vocals, Background Instrumentals, and Visual.

Here is how the categories work.

**TITLE:** The title of the film at its initial release is used. Previous titles, alternate titles, and foreign titles are included in the Notes section. If a date in parentheses follows a film's title, it means another film shared the same title. It does not mean the second film had original songs.

**STUDIO:** For the most part films are credited to releasing companies, not production companies. Thus Goldwyn pictures may be credited under United Artists or MGM.

**YEAR:** Year of initial release is used. However, dates differ according to various sources. I tried to be as exact as possible, but sometimes a film might open on a limited basis in December for the holiday market and receive broad distribution the next year. Some films are released simply to accommodate contractual obligations and then withdrawn till a later date.

**MUSIC SCORE:** This category includes the composers of the background instrumental scores.

**COMPOSER, LYRICIST:** When the majority of a score's songs are written by the same people, I have listed them under these headings instead of repeating their names beside their song titles. Any variations appear after the song in question.

**CHOREOGRAPHER:** This credit does not often appear on films that obviously have dancing. I tried to include as many as I could find.

**PRODUCER:** In the early thirties, usually the head of production or head of the studio was listed as Producer. I ignored this credit and usually credited the Associate Producer as the Producer. Later Producers received credit under that title. Some studio heads like Darryl Zanuck did directly oversee a few releases, and they are credited as Producers.

**SCREENWRITER, DIRECTOR:** These are the official credits according to what appears on the screen. Naturally many uncredited writers and even directors work on films but they are not included unless they did major work. For example, although many writers worked on *The Wizard of Oz*, only those with screen credit are listed. If a writer was credited with Additional Dialogue, in credits, I included him or her under the screenplay credits. If more than one director worked on a film, the Notes section indicates this.

**SOURCE:** These categories include the original source material upon which the film is based. These are the official sources, not including uncredited or ill disguised stealing of plots. I did not usually list if a film was a remake or a musicalization under these headings. That information appears under notes. If I list Musical under Source that means stage musical.

**CAST:** All stars are listed, as well as selected character actors and supporting players. If singing voices are dubbed, the dubbers are credited in the Notes section.

**SONGS:** This category includes all songs written expressly for the film. Songs that are interpolated and operatic arias are listed in the Notes section. Exceptions include interpolations with additional music or lyrics written expressly for the production.

**NOTES:** This heading includes miscellaneous information, such as other films in which a song appears, alternate titles, a song written but not used for a film, etc.

Ken Bloom
New York City

# PART TWO

# FILMS M–Z

# M

**3554 ✦ MA AND PA KETTLE AT WAIKIKI**
Universal, 1952

**Producer(s)**   Goldstein, Leonard
**Director(s)**   Sholem, Lee
**Screenwriter(s)**   Henley, Jack; Clork, Harry; Ullman, Elwood

**Cast**   Kilbride, Percy; Main, Marjorie; Smith, Loring; Nelson, Lori; Palmer, Byron; Gilmore, Lowell; Johnson, Russell; Hilo Hattie; Albertson, Mabel

**Song(s)**   Maui La (C/L: Koki, Sam); Kaleponi Hula (C/L: Mossman, Bina)

**3555 ✦ MACAO**
RKO, 1952

**Composer(s)**   Styne, Jule
**Lyricist(s)**   Robin, Leo

**Producer(s)**   Gottlieb, Alex
**Director(s)**   von Sternberg, Josef
**Screenwriter(s)**   Schoenfeld, Bernard C.; Rubin, Stanley

**Cast**   Mitchum, Robert; Russell, Jane; Bendix, William; Gomez, Thomas; Grahame, Gloria; Dexter, Brad; Ashley, Edward; Ahn, Philip; Sokoloff, Vladimir

**Song(s)**   Ocean Breeze; You Kill Me; One for My Baby (C: Arlen, Harold; L: Mercer, Johnny); Talk to Me Tomorrow [1]

**Notes**   [1] Not used.

**3556 ✦ MACKENNA'S GOLD**
Columbia, 1969

**Musical Score**   Jones, Quincy

**Producer(s)**   Foreman, Carl; Tiomkin, Dimitri
**Director(s)**   Thompson, J. Lee
**Screenwriter(s)**   Foreman, Carl
**Narrator(s)**   Jory, Victor

**Cast**   Peck, Gregory; Sharif, Omar; Savalas, Telly; Sparv, Camilla; Wynn, Keenan; Newmar, Julie; Cassidy, Ted; Cobb, Lee J.; Massey, Raymond; Meredith, Burgess; Quayle, Anthony; Robinson, Edward G.; Wallach, Eli; Ciannelli, Eduardo; Garfield, John, Jr.

**Song(s)**   Old Turkey Buzzard (C: Jones, Quincy; L: Douglass, Freddie)

**Notes**   No cue sheet available.

**3557 ✦ MACKINAC ISLAND**
Metro–Goldwyn–Mayer, 1944

**Producer(s)**   FitzPatrick, James A.

**Cast**   FitzPatrick, James A.

**Song(s)**   Lilac Time on Mackinac Island (C/L: Kirk, Lesley)

**Notes**   A FitzPatrick Traveltalk short.

**3558 ✦ MACUMBA LOVE**
United Artists, 1960

**Musical Score**   Simonetti, Enrico

**Producer(s)**   Fowley, Douglas
**Director(s)**   Fowley, Douglas
**Screenwriter(s)**   Graham, Norman

**Cast**   Reed, Walter; Rodann, Ziva; Wellman Jr., William; Wilkinson, June; de Souza, Ruth

**Song(s)**   To Market (C/L: Graham, Norman); Pay What You Can (C/L: Riggs, Charlton); Dance Calinda (C/L: Donaldson, H.C.)

**Notes**   No cue sheet available.

**3559 ✦ MAD ABOUT MEN**
United Artists, 1954

**Musical Score**   Frankel, Benjamin
**Composer(s)**   Frankel, Benjamin
**Lyricist(s)**   Frankel, Benjamin

**Producer(s)**   Box, Betty E.
**Director(s)**   Thomas, Ralph
**Screenwriter(s)**   Blackmore, Peter

**Cast**   Johns, Glynis; Sinden, Donald; Crawford, Anne; Rutherford, Margaret

**Song(s)**   I Can't Resist Men; Maria the Matador's Mother; Sing Hey Sing Ho

## 3560 ✦ MAD ABOUT MUSIC
Universal, 1938

**Composer(s)** McHugh, Jimmy
**Lyricist(s)** Adamson, Harold

**Producer(s)** Pasternak, Joe
**Director(s)** Taurog, Norman
**Screenwriter(s)** Manning, Bruce; Jackson, Felix

**Cast** Durbin, Deanna; Patrick, Gail; Marshall, Herbert; Moran, Jackie; Treacher, Arthur; Frawley, William; Parrish, Helen; Cappy Barra's Harmonica Band; The Vienna Boys Choir

**Song(s)** I Love to Whistle [1]; Chapel Bells; A Serenade to the Stars

**Notes** Remade as THE TOY TIGER (1956). [1] Also in HI, BEAUTIFUL.

## 3561 ✦ MADAME BOVARY
Metro–Goldwyn–Mayer, 1949

**Musical Score** Rozsa, Miklos
**Choreographer(s)** Donohue, Jack

**Producer(s)** Berman, Pandro S.
**Director(s)** Minnelli, Vincente
**Screenwriter(s)** Ardrey, Robert
**Source(s)** *Madame Bovary* (novel) Flaubert, Gustave

**Cast** Jones, Jennifer; Heflin, Van; Jourdan, Louis; Kent, Christopher; Lockhart, Gene; Allenby, Frank; Cooper, Gladys; Abbott, John; Morgan, Henry; Zucco, George; Corby, Ellen; Mason, James

**Song(s)** Dreams (C: Rozsa, Miklos; L: Katz, William); Chanson Populaire (C: Rozsa, Miklos; L: Ardrey, Robert)

## 3562 ✦ MADAME BUTTERFLY
Paramount, 1932

**Director(s)** Gering, Marion
**Screenwriter(s)** Lovett, Josephine; March, Joseph Moncure
**Source(s)** "Madame Butterfly" (story) Long, John Luther

**Cast** Grant, Cary; Ruggles, Charles; Pichel, Irving; Eddy, Helen Jerome; Sidney, Sylvia

**Song(s)** My Flower of Japan (C/L: Rainger, Ralph; Harling, W. Franke)

## 3563 ✦ MADAME ROSA
Atlantic Releasing, 1978

**Musical Score** Sarde, Philippe

**Producer(s)** Danon, Raymond
**Director(s)** Mizrahi, Moshe
**Screenwriter(s)** Mizrahi, Moshe
**Source(s)** *La Vie Devant Soi* (novel) Ajar, Emile

**Cast** Signoret, Simone; Dauphin, Claude; Ben Youb, Samy; Jabboir, Gabriel; Costa-Gavras

**Song(s)** Partition Musicale (C/L: Sarde, Philipe; Rostaing, Hubert)

**Notes** No cue sheet available.

## 3564 ✦ MADAME X (1937)
Metro–Goldwyn–Mayer, 1937

**Musical Score** Snell, Dave

**Producer(s)** McGuinness, James Kevin
**Director(s)** Wood, Sam
**Screenwriter(s)** Meehan, John
**Source(s)** *Madame X* (play) Bisson, Alexandre

**Cast** George, Gladys; Beal, John; William, Warren; Owen, Reginald; Henry, William

**Song(s)** You're Setting Me on Fire (C: Donaldson, Walter; L: Wright, Bob; Forrest, Chet); Farewell Song (C: Snell, Dave; L: Yaconelli, Z.)

## 3565 ✦ MADAME X (1966)
Universal, 1966

**Musical Score** Skinner, Frank

**Producer(s)** Hunter, Ross
**Director(s)** Rich, David Lowell
**Screenwriter(s)** Holloway, Jean
**Source(s)** *Madame X* (play) Bisson, Alexandre

**Cast** Turner, Lana; Forsythe, John; Montalban, Ricardo; Meredith, Burgess; Bennett, Constance; Dullea, Keir

**Song(s)** Swedish Rhapsody (C/L: Wildman, Charles)

**Notes** No cue sheet available. The song may be an instrumental.

## 3566 ✦ MADAM SATAN
Metro–Goldwyn–Mayer, 1930

**Musical Score** Stothart, Herbert
**Composer(s)** Stothart, Herbert
**Lyricist(s)** Grey, Clifford
**Choreographer(s)** Prinz, LeRoy

**Producer(s)** De Mille, Cecil B.
**Director(s)** De Mille, Cecil B.
**Screenwriter(s)** MacPherson, Jeanie; Unger, Gladys; Janis, Elsie

**Cast** Johnson, Kay; Denny, Reginald; Roth, Lillian; Young, Roland; Peterson, Elsa; Boyd, Irwin; MacDonald, Wallace; Marsh, Vera

**Song(s)** Each Little Sin; Live and Love Today (C: King, Jack; L: Janis, Elsie); This Is Love; Low Down (C: King, Jack; L: Janis, Elsie); We're Going Somewhere; Cat Walk; Ballet Mechanique (Inst.); Auction Number (C: King, Jack; L: Janis, Elsie); Meet Madame; All I Know Is You Are in My Arms (C: King, Jack; L: Janis, Elsie)

**Notes**   There is also a vocal of "It Ain't Gonna Rain No Mo'" by Wendall Hall. This film has great character names. They include Call of the Wild, Fish Girl, Confusion, Miss Conning Tower, Little Rolls Riding Hood, Electricity and Spider Girl.

## 3567 ✦ MAD DOG COLL
Columbia, 1961

**Producer(s)**   Schreiber, Edward
**Director(s)**   Balaban, Burt
**Screenwriter(s)**   Schreiber, Edward
**Source(s)**   material by Lieberman, Leo

**Cast**   Chandler, John; Doubleday, Kay; Hayward, Brooke; Nephew, Neil; Orbach, Jerry; Savalas, Telly; Gardenia, Vincent

**Song(s)**   Mad Dog Coll (C: Phillips, Stu; L: Trush, Eddie B.)

**Notes**   No cue sheet available.

## 3568 ✦ MADE FOR EACH OTHER
Twentieth Century–Fox, 1971

**Musical Score**   Martin, Trade

**Producer(s)**   Townshend, Roy
**Director(s)**   Bean, Robert B.
**Screenwriter(s)**   Taylor, Renee; Bologna, Joseph

**Cast**   Taylor, Renee; Bologna, Joseph; Sorvino, Paul; Dukakis, Olympia; Zorich, Louis

**Song(s)**   In My Own Kind of Way (C/L: Martin, Trade); Heavy Guitar (C/L: Martin, Trade)

## 3569 ✦ MADE IN HEAVEN
Lorimar, 1987

**Musical Score**   Isham, Mark

**Producer(s)**   Gideon, Raynold; Evans, Bruce A.; Blocker, David
**Director(s)**   Rudolph, Alan
**Screenwriter(s)**   Evans, Bruce A.; Gideon, Raynold

**Cast**   Hutton, Timothy; McGillis, Kelly; Stapleton, Maureen; Wedgeworth, Ann; Gammon, James; Winningham, Mare; Murray, Don; Daly, Timothy; Rasche, David; Plummer, Amanda; Pugh, Willard; Young, Neil; Ocasek, Ric; Robbins, Tom

**Song(s)**   We've Never Danced (C/L: Young, Neil)

**Notes**   No cue sheet available.

## 3570 ✦ MADE IN PARIS
Metro–Goldwyn–Mayer, 1966

**Musical Score**   Stoll, George; Van Eps, Robert
**Choreographer(s)**   Winters, David

**Producer(s)**   Pasternak, Joe
**Director(s)**   Sagal, Boris
**Screenwriter(s)**   Roberts, Stanley

**Cast**   Ann-Margret; Jourdan, Louis; Crenna, Richard; Adams, Edie; Everett, Chad; McGiver, John; Count Basie and His Octet; Mongo Santamaria and His Band; Lopez, Trini

**Song(s)**   Made in Paris (C: Bacharach, Burt; L: David, Hal); Paris Lullaby (C: Fain, Sammy; L: Webster, Paul Francis); My True Love (Inst.) (C: Skelton, Red); Skol Sister (Inst.) (C: Jones, Quincy); Goof Proof (Inst.) (C: Jones, Quincy)

**Notes**   There is also a vocal of "You Gotta See Mama Ev'ry Night" by Billy Rose and Con Conrad.

## 3571 ✦ MADEMOISELLE
La Strada, 1982

**Composer(s)**   Weiss, George David; Murolo, Giuseppe; Bologna, Pino
**Lyricist(s)**   Weiss, George David; Murolo, Giuseppe; Bologna, Pino

**Producer(s)**   Bologna, Pino
**Director(s)**   Murolo, Giuseppe
**Screenwriter(s)**   Weiss, George David; Murolo, Giuseppe; Firestone, Russell

**Cast**   Weiss, George David; Monts, Susan; Cordes, Kathryn; Pappalardo, Michael A.; Murolo, Giuseppe

**Song(s)**   Imagine (C/L: Weiss, George David; Murolo, Giuseppe); Mademoiselle (C/L: Weiss, George David; Murolo, Giuseppe); Every Little Thing; Say It Like It Is; E Vuo Ebbene A'mme (C: Weiss, George David; L: Faccenna, A.; Petrini, L.; Weiss, George David); Pain (C/L: Weiss, George David)

**Notes**   No cue sheet available.

## 3572 ✦ MADEMOISELLE FRANCE

See REUNION IN FRANCE.

## 3573 ✦ THE MAD GENIUS
Warner Brothers, 1931

**Director(s)**   Curtiz, Michael
**Screenwriter(s)**   Grubb, J.; Thew, Alexander; Thew, Harvey
**Source(s)**   "The Idol" (story) Brown, Martin

**Cast**   Barrymore, John; Marsh, Marian; Cook, Donald; Myers, Carmel; Butterworth, Charles; Alberni, Luis; Luguet, Andre; Karloff, Boris; Darro, Frankie; Madison, Mae

**Song(s)**   Our Love (C/L: Mendoza [3]); "Original Song" [2] (C/L: Mendoza [3]); You've Got that Thing [1] (C/L: Porter, Cole)

**Notes** [1] Not written for this movie. Originally in Broadway musical PARIS. [2] Not titled on cue sheet. [3] Possibly David Mendoza.

## 3574 ✦ THE MAD GHOUL
Universal, 1943

**Musical Score** Salter, Hans J.

**Producer(s)** Pivar, Ben
**Director(s)** Hogan, James
**Screenwriter(s)** Kraly, Hans

**Cast** Zucco, George; Bruce, David; Ankers, Evelyn; Armstrong, Robert; Bey, Turhan; McGraw, Charles; Stone, Milburn; Hobart, Rose; Tombes, Andrew; Richards, Addison

**Song(s)** Our Love Will Live [1] (C: Tchaikovsky, Peter I.; L: Carter, Everett); All for Love [2] (C: von Beethoven, Ludwig; L: Carter, Everett)

**Notes** [1] Based on a piano concerto. [2] Based on the "Minuet in G."

## 3575 ✦ MADISON AVENUE
Twentieth Century–Fox, 1962

**Musical Score** Sukman, Harry

**Producer(s)** Humberstone, H. Bruce
**Director(s)** Humberstone, H. Bruce
**Screenwriter(s)** Corwin, Norman
**Source(s)** *The Build-Up Boys* (novel) Kirk, Jeremy

**Cast** Andrews, Dana; Parker, Eleanor; Crain, Jeanne; Albert, Eddie; St. John, Howard; Daniell, Henry; Freeman, Kathleen; White, David

**Song(s)** The Milk Song (C/L: Harris, Harry)

## 3576 ✦ MADLY IN LOVE
United Artists, 1982

**Musical Score** Zambrini, Bruno
**Composer(s)** Castellano; Pipolo; Rossini, Giacomo
**Lyricist(s)** Castellano; Pipolo; Rossini, Giacomo

**Producer(s)** Cecchi Gori, Vittorio; Cecchi Gori, Mario
**Director(s)** Castellano; Pipolo
**Screenwriter(s)** Castellano; Pipolo

**Cast** Celentano, Adriano; Muti, Ornella; Celi, Adolfo

**Song(s)** Crazy Movie (C/L: Zambrini, Bruno); Cotto, Cottissimo; Conigliette; Ancora Conigliette

## 3577 ✦ MAD MAX BEYOND THUNDERDOME
Warner Brothers, 1985

**Musical Score** Jarre, Maurice

**Producer(s)** Miller, George
**Director(s)** Miller, George; Oglivie, George
**Screenwriter(s)** Hayes, Terry; Miller, George

**Cast** Gibson, Mel; Turner, Tina; Buday, Helen; Thring, Frank; Spence, Bruce; Grubb, Robert; Rossitto, Angelo

**Song(s)** We Don't Need Another Hero (Thunderdome) (C/L: Britten, Terry; Lyle, Graham); One of the Living (C/L: Knight, Holly)

**Notes** No cue sheet available.

## 3578 ✦ MADONNA OF AVENUE 'A'
Warner Brothers, 1929

**Director(s)** Curtiz, Michael
**Screenwriter(s)** Doyle, Ray; Powers, Francis

**Cast** Costello, Dolores; Dresser, Louise; Withers, Grant; Russell, William; Gerrard, Douglas; Hoffman, Otto; Moran, Lee

**Song(s)** My Madonna (C: Silvers, Louis; Fisher, Fred; L: Rose, Billy)

**Notes** No cue sheet available.

## 3579 ✦ THE MADONNA'S SECRET
Republic, 1946

**Producer(s)** Auer, Stephen
**Director(s)** Theile, William
**Screenwriter(s)** Foote, Bradbury; Thiele, William

**Cast** Lederer, Francis; Patrick, Gail; Ashley, Edward; Rutherford, Ann

**Song(s)** Thirsty Little Butterfly (C/L: Newman, Albert)

## 3580 ✦ THE MAD ROOM
Columbia, 1969

**Musical Score** Grusin, Dave

**Producer(s)** Maurer, Norman
**Director(s)** Girard, Bernard
**Screenwriter(s)** Girard, Bernard; Martin, A.Z.
**Source(s)** *Ladies in Retirement* (play) Denham, Reginald; Percy, Edward

**Cast** Stevens, Stella; Winters, Shelley; Ward, Skip; Cole, Carol; Darden, Severn; Garland, Beverly; Burns, Michael

**Song(s)** Open My Eyes (C/L: Rundgren, Todd); Wildwood Blues (C/L: Rundgren, Todd; Mooney, Thom; Antoni, Robert Stewkey; Van Osten, Carson)

## 3581 ✦ THE MADWOMAN OF CHAILLOT
Warner Brothers, 1969

**Musical Score** Lewis, Michael J.

**Producer(s)** Landau, Ely
**Director(s)** Forbes, Bryan
**Screenwriter(s)** Anhalt, Edward
**Source(s)** *The Madwoman of Chaillot* (play) Giradoux, Jean

**Cast** Hepburn, Katharine; Boyer, Charles; Dauphin, Claude; Evans, Edith; Gavin, John; Kaye, Danny; Henreid, Paul; Homolka, Oscar; Leighton, Margaret; Masina, Giuletta; Newman, Nanette; Chamberlain, Richard; Brynner, Yul; Pleasence, Donald; Gravet, Fernand; Heath, Gordon

**Song(s)** The Lonely Ones (C: Lewis, Michael J.; L: King, Gil); Before We Say Goodbye [1] (C: Lewis, Michael J.; L: Stillman, Al)

**Notes** [1] Sheet music only.

## 3582 ✦ MAGIC BOY
### Metro–Goldwyn–Mayer, 1964

**Musical Score** Funamura, Toru

**Producer(s)** Okawa, Hiroshi
**Director(s)** Yamamoto, Sanae
**Screenwriter(s)** Muramatsu, Dohei

**Song(s)** Magic Boy (C: Spielman, Fred; L: Torre, Janice)

**Notes** Animated cartoon.

## 3583 ✦ THE MAGIC CHRISTIAN
### Commonwealth United Entertainment, 1969

**Producer(s)** Weinstein, Henry T.; Unger, Anthony
**Director(s)** McGrath, Joseph
**Screenwriter(s)** Southern, Terry; McGrath, Joseph; Sellers, Peter; Chapman, Graham; Cleese, John
**Source(s)** The Magic Christian (novel) Southern, Terry

**Cast** Sellers, Peter; Starr, Ringo; Attenborough, Richard; Harvey, Laurence; Frey, Leonard; Lee, Christopher; Milligan, Spike; Welch, Raquel; Jeans, Isabel; Hyde-White, Wilfrid; Culver, Roland; Brynner, Yul; Polanski, Roman; Graves, Peter; Jacques, Hattie; Middleton, Guy; Price, Dennis; Cleese, John

**Song(s)** Come and Get It (C/L: McCartney, Paul); Rock of Ages (C/L: Tom; Pete; Mike); Something in the Air (C/L: Keene, John); Unidentified (C: Thorne, Ken; L: McGrath, Joe)

**Notes** There is also a vocal of "Mad About the Boy" by Noel Coward.

## 3584 ✦ THE MAGIC GARDEN OF STANLEY SWEETHEART
### Metro–Goldwyn–Mayer, 1970

**Producer(s)** Poll, Martin
**Director(s)** Horn, Leonard
**Screenwriter(s)** Westbrook, Robert T.
**Source(s)** The Magic Garden of Stanley Sweetheart (novel) Westbrook, Robert T.

**Cast** Gillin, Linda; Greer, Michael; Hull, Dianne; Near, Holly; Racimo, Victoria; Maggart, Brandon; Johnson, Don

**Song(s)** Nobody Knows (C: Legrand, Michel; L: Bergman, Alan; Bergman, Marilyn); Magic Mountain (C/L: Goldstein, Jerry; War); Time to Make a Turn (C/L: Wiegand, Larry); Funny How It Happens (C/L: Styner, Jerry); Sweet Gingerbread Man (C: Legrand, Michel; L: Bergman, Alan; Bergman, Marilyn); Happy Together (C/L: Gordon, Alan; Bonner, Garry); Water (C/L: Lucas, David); Sound of Love (C/L: Gibb, Barry; Gibb, Robin; Gibb, Maurice); Peace on Earth (C/L: Schwartz, Bernie); Tell Me a Story (C/L: Lucas, David)

## 3585 ✦ THE MAGICIAN OF LUBLIN
### Cannon, 1979

**Musical Score** Jarre, Maurice

**Producer(s)** Golan, Menahem; Globus, Yoram
**Director(s)** Golan, Menahem
**Screenwriter(s)** White, Irving S.; Golan, Menahem; Gross, Joseph; Dana, Barbara; Patinkin, Sheldon
**Source(s)** The Magician of Lublin (novel) Singer, Isaac Bashevis

**Cast** Arkin, Alan; Fletcher, Louise; Perrine, Valerie; Winters, Shelley; Jacobi, Lou; Berlinger, Warren; Ophir, Shai K.; Whelchel, Lisa

**Song(s)** The Magician of Lublin (C: Jarre, Maurice; L: Webster, Paul Francis)

**Notes** No cue sheet available.

## 3586 ✦ MAGIC NIGHT
### United Artists, 1932

**Composer(s)** Posford, George
**Lyricist(s)** Marvell, Holt

**Producer(s)** Wilcox, Herbert
**Director(s)** Wilcox, Herbert
**Screenwriter(s)** Marvell, Holt; Posford, George

**Cast** Neagle, Anna; Buchanan, Jack; Currie, Clive; Kendall, William; Bland, Joyce; Carrick, Herbert; Malo, Gino

**Song(s)** Goodnight Vienna; Just Heaven; Living in Clover; Marching Song; Dear Little Waltz; My Pretty Flower

**Notes** No cue sheet available. This is a British and Dominions film, titled GOODNIGHT VIENNA in Great Britain.

## 3587 ✦ THE MAGIC OF LASSIE
### International Picture Show Company, 1978

**Composer(s)** Sherman, Robert B.; Sherman, Richard M.
**Lyricist(s)** Sherman, Robert B.; Sherman, Richard M.

**Producer(s)** Wrather, Bonita Granville; Beaudine Jr., William
**Director(s)** Chaffey, Don

**Screenwriter(s)** Holloway, Jean; Sherman, Robert B.; Sherman, Richard M.

**Cast** Stewart, James; Rooney, Mickey; Roberts, Pernell; Zimbalist, Stephanie; Sharrett, Michael; Faye, Alice; Evans, Gene; Mazurki, Mike; Lussier, Robert; Davies, Lane

**Song(s)** When You're Loved; That Home Town Feeling; Brass Rings and Day Dreams; I Can't Say Good Bye; Nobody's Property; Travelin' Music; There'll Be Other Friday Nights; A Rose Is Not a Rose; Banjo Song; Thanksgiving Prayer

**Notes** No cue sheet available.

## 3588 ✦ MAGIC TOWN
### RKO, 1948

**Musical Score** Webb, Roy

**Producer(s)** Riskin, Robert
**Director(s)** Wellman, William A.
**Screenwriter(s)** Riskin, Robert

**Cast** Stewart, James; Wyman, Jane; Smith, Kent; Sparks, Ned; Ford, Wallace; Toomey, Regis; Doran, Ann; Meek, Donald; Ballantine, E.J.

**Song(s)** My Book of Memory (C: Westendorf, A.; L: Heyman, Edward); Magic Town [1] (C/L: Torme, Mel; Wells, Robert)

**Notes** [1] Used instrumentally only.

## 3589 ✦ THE MAGIC WORLD OF TOPO GIGIO
### Columbia, 1965

**Musical Score** Trovajoli, Armando

**Director(s)** De Rico, Luca
**Screenwriter(s)** Faustinelli, Mario; Stagnaro, Guido; Perego, Maria
**Voices** Mazzulo, Peppino

**Cast** Roveri, Ermanno; Colnaghi, Ignazio; Milani, Federica

**Song(s)** The Daughter of the King (C/L: Rossi, Aldo); The Butterfly (C/L: Rossi, Aldo)

**Notes** No cue sheet available. Topo Gigio is a puppet who achieved fame on the "Ed Sullivan Show." Mario Perego is the puppeteer.

## 3590 ✦ THE MAGNIFICENT LIE
### Paramount, 1931

**Director(s)** Viertel, Berthold
**Screenwriter(s)** Raphaelson, Samson; Lawrence, Vincent
**Source(s)** *Laurels and the Lady* (novel) Merrick, Leonard

**Cast** Chatterton, Ruth; Bellamy, Ralph; Boyer, Charles; Erwin, Stuart; Hardy, Sam

**Song(s)** He Say Go I Say No (C/L: Rainger, Ralph); Just One More Chance [1] (C: Johnston, Arthur; L: Coslow, Sam)

**Notes** [1] Also in COUNTRY MUSIC HOLIDAY, LEMON DROP KID (1934) and THIS RECKLESS AGE.

## 3591 ✦ THE MAGNIFICENT MATADOR
### Twentieth Century–Fox, 1955

**Musical Score** Kraushaar, Raoul

**Producer(s)** Alperson, Edward L.
**Director(s)** Boetticher, Budd
**Screenwriter(s)** Lang, Charles

**Cast** O'Hara, Maureen; Quinn, Anthony; Rojas, Manuel; Denning, Richard; Gomez, Thomas; Albright, Lola; Caruso, Anthony

**Song(s)** Magnificent Matador (C: Alperson Jr., Edward L.; L: Herrick, Paul)

## 3592 ✦ MAGNIFICENT OBSESSION
### Universal, 1954

**Musical Score** Skinner, Frank

**Producer(s)** Hunter, Ross
**Director(s)** Sirk, Douglas
**Screenwriter(s)** Blees, Robert

**Cast** Wyman, Jane; Hudson, Rock; Moorehead, Agnes; Rush, Barbara; Kruger, Otto; Palmer, Gregg; Cavanaugh, Page

**Song(s)** Magnificent Obsession (1) [1] (C: Karger, Fred; L: Laine, Frankie); Magnificent Obsession (2) [1] (C: Skinner, Frank; L: Herbert, Frederick)

**Notes** No cue sheet available. [1] Most likely written for exploitation only.

## 3593 ✦ THE MAGNIFICENT SHOWMAN

See CIRCUS WORLD.

## 3594 ✦ MAGOO'S ARABIAN NIGHTS

See 1001 ARABIAN NIGHTS.

## 3595 ✦ MA, HE'S MAKING EYES AT ME
### Universal, 1940

**Producer(s)** Sanford, Joseph G.
**Director(s)** Schuster, Harold
**Screenwriter(s)** Grayson, Charles; Hartmann, Edmund L.

**Cast** Brown, Tom; Mooore, Constance; Carle, Richard; Nagel, Anne; Cowan, Jerome; Risdon, Elizabeth; Feld, Fritz; Williams, Larry

**Song(s)** Unfair to Love (C: Skinner, Frank; L: Lerner, Sam)

**Notes** No cue sheet available. There is also a vocal of "Ma, He's Making Eyes at Me" by Con Conrad and Sidney Clare and "A Lemon in the Garden of Love" by Richard Carle and M.E. Rourke.

## 3596 ✦ MAHOGANY
### Paramount, 1975

**Musical Score** Masser, Michael
**Choreographer(s)** Jhenkins, Jho

**Producer(s)** Cohen, Rob; Ballard, Jack
**Director(s)** Gordy, Berry
**Screenwriter(s)** Byrum, John
**Source(s)** (story) Amber, Toni

**Cast** Ross, Diana; Williams, Billy Dee; Perkins, Anthony; Aumont, Jean-Pierre; Richards, Beah; Foch, Nina; Mell, Marisa

**Song(s)** Do You Know Where You're Going To (C: Masser, Michael; L: Goffin, Gerry); She's the Ideal Girl (C/L: Jackson, Jermaine; Daniels, Don); Devil in the Bottle (C/L: David, Bobby); If You Move You Lose (C/L: Polk, Hersholt C.); Put Out This Fire Cause My Mama Told Me Not to Fall in Love (C/L: Askey, Gil); Let's Go Back to Day One (C/L: Holloway, Patricia; L: Jones, Gloria)

## 3597 ✦ MAID TO ORDER
### New Century/Vista, 1987

**Musical Score** Delerue, Georges

**Producer(s)** Jaffe, Herb; Engelberg, Mort
**Director(s)** Jones, Amy
**Screenwriter(s)** Jones, Amy; Howze, Perry; Howze, Randy

**Cast** Sheedy, Ally; D'Angelo, Beverly; Ontkean, Michael; Perrine, Valerie; Shawn, Dick; Skerritt, Tom; Clayton, Merry; Phoenix, Rainbow

**Song(s)** I'm on My Own Now (C/L: Jones, Ralph; Haiche, Claudette)

**Notes** No cue sheet available.

## 3598 ✦ MAIL TRAIN
### Twentieth Century–Fox, 1941

**Musical Score** Levy, Louis

**Producer(s)** Black, Edward
**Director(s)** Forde, Walter
**Screenwriter(s)** Orton, J.O.C.; Guest, Val
**Source(s)** characters by Priwin, Hans W.

**Cast** Harker, Gordon; Sim, Alastair; Calvert, Phyllis; Chapman, Edward

**Song(s)** Jungle Lullaby [1] (C/L: Noel, Art; Pelosi, Don)

**Notes** A British film distributed by Fox. Originally titled INSPECTOR HORNLEIGH GOES TO IT. [1] Not written for this film.

## 3599 ✦ THE MAIN EVENT
### Warner Brothers, 1979

**Musical Score** Melvoin, Michael

**Producer(s)** Peters, Jon; Streisand, Barbra
**Director(s)** Zieff, Howard
**Screenwriter(s)** Parent, Gail; Smith, Andrew

**Cast** Streisand, Barbra; O'Neal, Ryan; Sand, Paul; Mayo, Whitman; D'Arbanville, Patti

**Song(s)** The Body Shop (C/L: Michalski, George; Oosterveen, Niki); The Main Event (C/L: Jabara, Paul; Roberts, Bruce); Fight (C/L: Jabara, Paul; Esty, Bob)

## 3600 ✦ MAIN STREET TO BROADWAY
### Metro–Goldwyn–Mayer, 1953

**Musical Score** Ronell, Ann
**Composer(s)** Ronell, Ann
**Lyricist(s)** Ronell, Ann

**Producer(s)** Cowan, Lester
**Director(s)** Garnett, Tay
**Screenwriter(s)** Raphaelson, Samson

**Cast** Norton, Tom; Murphy, Mary; Sundberg, Clinton; De Camp, Rosemary; Bankhead, Tallulah; Barrymore, Ethel; Barrymore, Lionel; Berg, Gertrude; Booth, Shirley; Calhern, Louis; Durocher, Leo; Emerson, Faye; Hammerstein II, Oscar; Harrison, Rex; Logan, Joshua; Martin, Mary; Moorehead, Agnes; Palmer, Lilli; Rodgers, Richard; Shriner, Herb; van Druten, John; Wilde, Cornel; Hayes, Helen

**Song(s)** There's Music in You (C: Rodgers, Richard; L: Hammerstein II, Oscar); Just a Girl; Blue New York [1]

**Notes** [1] Used instrumentally only.

## 3601 ✦ MAISIE GETS HER MAN
### Metro–Goldwyn–Mayer, 1942

**Musical Score** Hayton, Lennie
**Choreographer(s)** Dare, Danny

**Producer(s)** Ruben, J. Walter
**Director(s)** Del Ruth, Roy
**Screenwriter(s)** Reinhardt, Betty; McCall Jr., Mary C.
**Source(s)** characters by Collison, Wilson

**Cast** Sothern, Ann; Skelton, Red; Gorcey, Leo; Jenkins, Allen; Meek, Donald; Corrigan, Lloyd; Catlett, Walter; Feld, Fritz; Ragland, Rags

**Song(s)** Cookin' with Gas [1] (C: Hayton, Lennie; L: Edens, Roger)

**Notes** Released internationally as SHE GOT HER MAN. [1] Footage actually filmed for PANAMA HATTIE (1942) but not used in that film.

## 3602 ◆ MAISIE GOES TO RENO
### Metro–Goldwyn–Mayer, 1944

**Musical Score** Hayton, Lennie; Snell, Dave
**Composer(s)** Fain, Sammy
**Lyricist(s)** Freed, Ralph
**Choreographer(s)** Lee, Sammy

**Producer(s)** Haight, George
**Director(s)** Beaumont, Harry
**Screenwriter(s)** McCall Jr., Mary C.
**Source(s)** characters by Collison, Wilson

**Cast** Sothern, Ann; Hodiak, John; Drake, Tom; Linden, Marte; Cavanagh, Paul; Gardner, Ava

**Song(s)** Panhandle Pete; This Little Song Went to Battle [1]

**Notes** Released internationally as YOU CAN'T DO THAT TO ME. [1] Not used.

## 3603 ◆ MAJOR DUNDEE
### Columbia, 1965

**Musical Score** Amfitheatrof, Daniele

**Producer(s)** Bresler, Jerry
**Director(s)** Peckinpah, Sam
**Screenwriter(s)** Fink, Harry Julian; Paul, Oscar; Peckinpah, Sam

**Cast** Heston, Charlton; Harris, Richard; Hutton, Jim; Coburn, James; Anderson Jr., Michael; Berger, Senta; Adorf, Mario; Peters, Brock; Oates, Warren; Johnson, Ben; Armstrong, R.G.; Pickens, Slim

**Song(s)** Major Dundee March (C: Amfitheatrof, Daniele; L: Washington, Ned); Laura Lee (C: Wood, Forrest; L: Sullivan, Liam); To Be with You (C: Amfitheatrof, Daniele; L: Stillman, Al)

**Notes** No cue sheet available.

## 3604 ◆ MAJOR LEAGUE
### Paramount, 1989

**Musical Score** Howard, James Newton
**Composer(s)** Howard, James Newton

**Producer(s)** Chesser, Chris; Smith, Irby
**Director(s)** Ward, David S.
**Screenwriter(s)** Ward, David S.

**Cast** Sheen, Charlie; Berenger, Tom; Bernsen, Corbin; Whitton, Margaret; Gammon, James; Uecker, Bob

**Song(s)** Most of All You (L: Bergman, Alan; Bergman, Marilyn); How Can the Girl Refuse (L: Ballard, Glen)

**Notes** Also used are the records "Cryin' Shame" by Lyle Lovett; "U.S. Male" by Philip Kennard and Ron Aniello; "Oh You Angel" by Ron Aniello and Philip Kennard; "Burn On" by Randy Newman and "Wild Thing" by Chip Taylor.

## 3605 ◆ MAKE A WISH
### RKO, 1937

**Composer(s)** Straus, Oscar; Alter, Louis
**Lyricist(s)** Webster, Paul Francis

**Producer(s)** Gross, Edward
**Director(s)** Neumann, Kurt
**Screenwriter(s)** Berg, Gertrude; Schubert, Bernard; Snell, Earle

**Cast** Breen, Bobby; Rathbone, Basil; Claire, Marion; Forbes, Ralph; Armetta, Henry; Errol, Leon; Meek, Donald

**Song(s)** Make a Wish; Music in My Heart; Old Man Rip; My Campfire Dreams (C: Alter, Louis); Birchlake Forever

**Notes** No cue sheet available. Alter is co-credited with lyrics on copyright cards, not music.

## 3606 ◆ MAKE BELIEVE BALLROOM
### Columbia, 1949

**Producer(s)** Richmond, Ted
**Director(s)** Santley, Joseph
**Screenwriter(s)** Duffy, Albert; De Wolf, Karen

**Cast** Courtland, Jerome; Randell, Ron; Jergens, Adele; Laine, Frankie; Jimmy Dorsey and His Orchestra; Cole, Nat "King"; Ray McKinley and His Band; Gene Krupa and His Band; Jarvis, Al; Harvey, Paul; Barnet, Charlie; Hunt, Pee Wee; Starr, Kay; The Sportsmen; Smith, Jack; Harper, Toni

**Song(s)** Make Believe Ballroom (C/L: Mercer, Johnny; Rene, Leon; Jarvis, Al); Little Miss In-Between (C/L: Roberts, Allan; Lee, Lester); Hamburger Heaven (C/L: Roberts, Allan; Lee, Lester); The Way the Twig Is Bent (C/L: Roberts, Allan; Fisher, Doris); It's a Blue World [1] (C/L: Forrest, Chet; Wright, Bob)

**Notes** The segments of Ray McKinley and his band playing "Comin' Out" and Gene Krupa and his band playing "Disc Jockey Jump" are from other pictures. There are also vocals of "Candy Store Blues" by Herb Jeffries, Eddie Beal and Nick Castle (also in MANHATTAN ANGEL); "The Trouble with Me Is You" by Roy Alfred and Marvin Fisher; "I'm the Lonesomest Gal in Town" by Albert Von Tilzer and Lew Brown (also in the Universal picture SOUTH SEA SINNER); "Sunny Side of the Street" by Jimmy McHugh and Dorothy Fields and the instrumentals

"Disc Jockey Jump" by Gene Krupa and Gerry Mulligan and "Comin' Out" by Ray McKinley. [1] Also in MUSIC IN MY HEART and SING WHILE YOU DANCE.

## 3607 ✦ MAKE MINE LAUGHS
### RKO, 1942

**Musical Score**   Rose, Gene; Webb, Roy

**Producer(s)**   Bilson, George
**Director(s)**   Fleischer, Richard
**Screenwriter(s)**   Yates, Hal

**Cast**   Bolger, Ray; Shirley, Anne; Day, Dennis; Davis, Joan; Haley, Jack; Errol, Leon; Langford, Frances; Frankie Carle and His Orchestra; LaMouret, Robert; Viera, Manuel and Marita; Rosario and Antonio; Freddie Fisher and His Schnickelfritz Band; The Titans; Dell, Myrna; Granger, Dorothy; Lamb, Gil

**Song(s)**   Who Killed Vaudeville [4] (C: Fain, Sammy; L: Yellen, Jack); Poor Little Fly on the Wall [3] (C/L: Fisher, Fred); Moonlight Over the Islands [1] (C: Pollack, Lew; L: Greene, Mort); Did You Happen to Find a Heart (C: Pollack, Lew; L: Magidson, Herb); La Morena de Mi Copla [2] (C/L: Castallanos, C.)

**Notes**   [1] Also in BAMBOO BLONDE and THE JUDGE STEPS OUT. [2] Also in PAN AMERICANA. [3] Also in SEVEN DAYS ASHORE. [4] Also in GEORGE WHITE'S SCANDALS (1945).

## 3608 ✦ MAKE MINE MUSIC
### Disney, 1946

**Producer(s)**   Grant, Joe
**Director(s)**   Kinney, Jack; Geronimi, Clyde; Luske, Hamilton; Cormack, Bob; Meador, Josh
**Screenwriter(s)**   Brightman, Homer; Huemer, Dick; Kinny, Dick; Wasbridge, John; Okeb, Tom; Shaw, Dick; Gurney, Eric; Holland, Sylvia
**Voices**   Eddy, Nelson; Shore, Dinah; Goodman, Benny; Andrews Sisters, The; Colonna, Jerry; Russell, Andy; Holloway, Sterling; Riabouchinska and Lichine; The Pied Pipers; The King's Men; Ken Darby Chorus

**Song(s)**   Make Mine Music (C/L: Darby, Ken; Daniel, Eliot); Franastan [1] (C: Wolcott, Charles; L: Gilbert, Ray)

**Notes**   This consists of many short cartoons. There are THE MARTINS & THE COYS, BLUE BAYOU, ALL THE CATS JOIN IN, WITHOUT YOU, CASEY AT THE BAT, TWO SILHOUETTES, PETER & THE WOLF, AFTER YOU'VE GONE, JOHNNY FEDORA and THE WHALE WHO WANTED TO SING AT THE MET. Songs are listed under their respective cartoon titles. However, the credits are intermixed here since they aren't differentiated on the credit sheets. [1] Not used.

## 3609 ✦ MAKE WAY FOR TOMORROW
### Paramount, 1937

**Musical Score**   Antheil, George

**Producer(s)**   McCarey, Leo
**Director(s)**   McCarey, Leo
**Screenwriter(s)**   Delmar, Vina
**Source(s)**   *The Years Are So Long* (novel) Lawrence, Josephine; (play) Leary, Helen; Leary, Nolan

**Cast**   Moore, Victor; Bondi, Beulah; Bainter, Fay; Mitchell, Thomas; Hall, Porter; Read, Barbara; Lockhart, Gene; Beavers, Louise; Gombell, Minna

**Song(s)**   Make Way for Tomorrow [1] (C: Coslow, Sam; Schwartz, Jean; L: Coslow, Sam; Robin, Leo)

**Notes**   Originally titled THE YEAR'S ARE SO LONG. There are brief vocal renditions of "When a St. Louis Woman Comes Down to New Orleans" by Arthur Johnston, Sam Coslow and Gene Austin; "Let Me Call You Sweetheart" by Leo Friedman, Harold Rossiter and Beth Slater Whitson and "M-O-T-H-E-R" by Theodore Morse. Leo Robin wrote a poem for the production called "Are You Afraid." It is not known if it was used or not. [1] Used instrumentally only.

## 3610 ✦ MAKING IT
### Twentieth Century–Fox, 1971

**Musical Score**   Fox, Charles
**Composer(s)**   Fox, Charles
**Lyricist(s)**   Gimbel, Norman

**Producer(s)**   Ruddy, Albert S.
**Director(s)**   Erman, John
**Screenwriter(s)**   Bart, Peter
**Source(s)**   *What Can You Do?* (novel) Leigh, James

**Cast**   Tabori, Kristoffer; Mason, Marlyn; Balaban, Bob; Pressman, Lawrence; Latham, Louise; Fiedler, John; Miller, Denny; Merande, Doro; Van Patten, Joyce; Troupe, Tom

**Song(s)**   Morning Song; The All American

## 3611 ✦ MAKING LOVE
### Twentieth Century–Fox, 1982

**Musical Score**   Rosenman, Leonard
**Composer(s)**   Jones, Mickey
**Lyricist(s)**   Jones, Mickey

**Producer(s)**   Adler, Allen; Melnick, Daniel
**Director(s)**   Hiller, Arthur
**Screenwriter(s)**   Sandler, Barry

**Cast**   Ontkean, Michael; Jackson, Kate; Hamlin, Harry; Hiller, Wendy; Hill, Arthur; Olson, Nancy; Dukakis, John; Kiser, Terry

**Song(s)**   Let the Goodbyes Begin; I'll Be Yours; Take Me Higher (C/L: Hornsby, Bruce; Hornsby, Jon); It's Your Love (C/L: Hornsby, Bruce; Hornsby, Jon);

Making Love (C: Bacharach, Burt; L: Sager, Carole Bayer; Robertson, Bruce)

## 3612 ✦ MAKING THE GRADE
### MGM/UA–Cannon, 1984

**Musical Score**  Poledouris, Basil
**Composer(s)**  Lee, Jerry
**Lyricist(s)**  Sinnamon, Shandi

**Producer(s)**  Quintano, Gene
**Director(s)**  Walker, Dorian
**Screenwriter(s)**  Quintano, Gene

**Cast**  Nelson, Judd; Lee, Jonna; Jump, Gordon; Olkewicz, Walter; Lacey, Ronald

**Song(s)**  Living on the Edge; Double Trouble

**Notes**  No cue sheet available.

## 3613 ✦ MALCOLM X
### Warner Brothers, 1972

**Musical Score**  The Last Poets; Holiday, Billie; Ellington, Duke; Slim and Slam

**Producer(s)**  Worth, Marvin; Perl, Arnold
**Screenwriter(s)**  Perl, Arnold
**Source(s)**  *Autobiography of Malcolm X* (autobiography) Haley, Alex; Malcolm X
**Narrator(s)**  Jones, James Earl

**Song(s)**  Niggers Are Afraid of Revolution (C/L: Ben Hassen, Omar)

**Notes**  A documentary on Malcolm X. "Strange Fruit" by Lewis Allen and "God Bless the Child" by Billie Holiday and Arthur Herzog Jr. are also used.

## 3614 ✦ MALIBU HIGH
### Crown International, 1979

**Musical Score**  Myland, Steve

**Producer(s)**  Foldes, Lawrence D.
**Director(s)**  Berwick, Irv
**Screenwriter(s)**  Buckley, John; Singer, Tom

**Cast**  Lansing, Jill; Taylor, Stuart; Johnson, Katie; Taylor, Tammy; Howard, Garth

**Song(s)**  Lovely but Deadly (C/L: Myland, Steve)

**Notes**  No cue sheet available.

## 3615 ✦ MAMA STEPS OUT
### Metro–Goldwyn–Mayer, 1937

**Musical Score**  Ward, Edward
**Composer(s)**  Wright, Bob; Forrest, Chet
**Lyricist(s)**  Wright, Bob; Forrest, Chet

**Producer(s)**  Emerson, John
**Director(s)**  Seitz, George B.

**Screenwriter(s)**  Loos, Anita
**Source(s)**  *Ada Beats the Drum* (play) Kirkpatrick, John

**Cast**  Kibbee, Guy; Brady, Alice; Furness, Betty; Morner, Stanley [1]; Lockhart, Gene

**Song(s)**  Burnt Fingers; Be Careful of My Heart

**Notes**  [1] Name changed to Dennis Morgan when he left for Warner Brothers after this film.

## 3616 ✦ MAMBO
### Paramount, 1955

**Musical Score**  Rota, Nino; Lavagnino, Angelo Francesco
**Composer(s)**  Noriega, Bernardo
**Lyricist(s)**  Dunham, Katherine
**Choreographer(s)**  Dunham, Katherine

**Producer(s)**  De Laurentiis, Dino; Ponti, Carlo
**Director(s)**  Rossen, Robert
**Screenwriter(s)**  Piovene, Guido; Perilli, Ivo; De Concini, Ennio; Rossen, Robert

**Cast**  Mangano, Silvana; Rennie, Michael; Gassman, Vittorio; Winters, Shelley; Dunham, Katherine

**Song(s)**  Baiao Faz Balancar (Back to Bahia) [1]; Caboclo Do Mato (It Wasn't the Red Wine) [1]; New Love New Wine; Boogie in Brazil (Boogie Big Ballet) (L: Stone, Wilson); Mambo [2] (C/L: David, Mack; Stone, Wilson); Washerwoman [2] (C/L: Morales, Obdulio; Sunshine, Marion)

**Notes**  [1] English lyrics by Wilson Stone. [2] Sheet music only.

## 3617 ✦ MAME
### Warner Brothers, 1974

**Composer(s)**  Herman, Jerry
**Lyricist(s)**  Herman, Jerry
**Choreographer(s)**  White, Onna

**Producer(s)**  Fryer, Robert; Cresson, James
**Director(s)**  Saks, Gene
**Screenwriter(s)**  Zindel, Paul
**Source(s)**  *Mame* (musical) Herman, Jerry; Lawrence, Jerome; Lee, Robert E.

**Cast**  Ball, Lucille; Arthur, Beatrice [3]; Preston, Robert; Connell, Jane [3]; Davison, Bruce; Furlong, Kirby; Cook, Doria; McGiver, John; Van Patten, Joyce

**Song(s)**  St. Bridget; It's Today; Open a New Window; The Man in the Moon; My Best Girl; We Need a Little Christmas; Mame; Loving You [1]; Bosom Buddies [2]; Gooch's Song; If He Walked Into My Life

**Notes**  [1] Written for film. The remainder of the score came from the musical. [2] Not in British prints. [3] From Broadway cast.

## 3618 ✦ MAMMY
### Warner Brothers, 1930

**Composer(s)** Berlin, Irving
**Lyricist(s)** Berlin, Irving

**Producer(s)** Morosco, Walter
**Director(s)** Curtiz, Michael
**Screenwriter(s)** Rigby, Gordon; Jackson, Joseph
**Source(s)** *Mr. Bones* (play) Berlin, Irving; Gleason, James

**Cast** Jolson, Al; Moran, Lois; Dresser, Louise; Sherman, Lowell; Bosworth, Hobart; Marshall, Tully; Lewis, Mitchell; Fields, Stanley; Curtis, Jack; Cooke, Ray

**Song(s)** Here We Are; (Across the Breakfast Table) Looking at You; Let Me Sing and I'm Happy; To My Mammy; In the Morning [1]; Knights of the Road [2]

**Notes** The following songs, not written for the film, also receive vocal performances: "When You and I Were Young Maggie" by J.A. Butterfield and George W. Johnson; "Yes, We Have No Bananas" by Frank Silver and Irving Conn, sung to the tune of "Miserere" from Verdi's IL TROVATORE; "Asleep in the Deep" by Arthur J. Lamb and H.W. Petri; "Pretty Baby" by Gus Kahn, Tony Jackson and Egbert Van Alstyne; "Oh, Dem Golden Slippers" and "Why Do They All Take the Night Boat to Albany" by Jean Schwartz, Joseph Young and Sam Lewis; "Swanee River" by Stephen Foster; "You Made Me Love You" by James V. Monaco and Joseph McCarthy; "Who Paid the Rent for Mrs. Rip Van Winkle" by Alfred Bryan and Fred Fisher; "My Mammy" by Sam Lewis and Joe Young originally in Broadway musical SINBAD and "Oh How I Miss You Tonight" by Benny Davis, Joe Burke and Mark Fisher. [1] Instrumental use only. [2] Not in cue sheets.

## 3619 ✦ A MAN ABOUT THE HOUSE
### Twentieth Century–Fox, 1948

**Producer(s)** Black, Edward
**Director(s)** Arliss, Leslie
**Screenwriter(s)** Perry, John
**Source(s)** *A Man About the House* (play) Young, Francis Brett

**Cast** Moore, Kieron; Johnston, Margaret; Gray, Dulcie; Middleton, Guy; Aylmer, Felix; Braithwaite, Lilian

**Song(s)** Core Ngrato [1] (C: Cardillo, S.; L: Cordiferro, R.)

**Notes** [1] Also in AVANTI! (United Artists).

## 3620 ✦ MAN ABOUT TOWN (1939)
### Paramount, 1939

**Composer(s)** Hollander, Frederick
**Lyricist(s)** Loesser, Frank
**Choreographer(s)** Prinz, LeRoy

**Producer(s)** Hornblow Jr., Arthur
**Director(s)** Sandrich, Mark
**Screenwriter(s)** Ryskind, Morrie; Scott, Allan; Myers, Zion

**Cast** Benny, Jack; Lamour, Dorothy; Arnold, Edward; Anderson, Eddie "Rochester"; Jeans, Isabel; Malneck, Matty; Harris, Phil; Woolley, Monty; Clive, E.E.

**Song(s)** That Sentimental Sandwich; Fidgety Joe (C: Malneck, Matty); Strange Enchantment [4]; The Dunes of Doorma [1] (C: Rainger, Ralph; L: Robin, Leo); Bluebirds in the Moonlight [1] [3] (C: Rainger, Ralph; L: Robin, Leo); Don't Cry Little Cloud [1] (C: Malneck, Matty); A Love Letter [1]; Man About Town [1] [5]; Love with a Capital "You" [1] [2]; Petty Girl Routine [1]

**Notes** [1] Not used. [2] Not used in COLLEGE SWING. Also not used in THE BIG BROADCAST OF 1938. Later used in $1,000 A TOUCHDOWN. [3] Not used for PARIS HONEYMOON or CAFE SOCIETY. Used in GULLIVER'S TRAVELS. [4] This was a rewrite of the Ralph Freed and Hollander song "Jungle Love." [5] Published though not used.

## 3621 ✦ MAN ABOUT TOWN (1947)
### RKO/Societe Nouvelle Pathe Cinema Picture, 1947

**Composer(s)** Van Parys, Georges
**Lyricist(s)** Van Parys, Georges

**Producer(s)** Clair, Rene
**Director(s)** Clair, Rene
**Screenwriter(s)** Pirosh, Robert

**Cast** Chevalier, Maurice; Perier, Francois; Derrien, Marcelle; Robin, Dany; Sertilange, Christiane

**Song(s)** Place Pigalle (C/L: Alstone, M.; Pirosh, Robert; Chevalier, Maurice); Par Le P'Tit Bout de la Lorgnette (C/L: Clair, Rene; Van Parys, Georges); Le Jongleur; Piano des Voisino; Le P'Tit Cour de Ninon (C/L: Millandy; Beccucci); Pour Les Amants (C/L: Clair, Rene; Van Parys, Georges); Petit Fleur de Mon Amour; Ce Ne Vaut Pas L'Amour (C/L: Perfignan)

**Notes** Titled in French: LE SILENCE EST D'OR. This is a French/American co-production.

## 3622 ✦ A MAN A WOMAN AND A BANK
### Avco Embassy, 1979

**Musical Score** Conti, Bill

**Producer(s)** Bennett, John B.; Samuelson, Peter
**Director(s)** Black, Noel
**Screenwriter(s)** Gideon, Raynold; Evans, Bruce A.; Margolin, Stuart

**Cast** Sutherland, Donald; Adams, Brooke; Mazursky, Paul; Magicovsky, Allan

**Song(s)** When You Smile at Me (C/L: Conti, Bill; Hill, Dan)

**Notes** No cue sheet available.

## 3623 ✦ THE MAN BEHIND THE GUN
Warner Brothers, 1953

**Musical Score** Buttolph, David

**Producer(s)** Sisk, Robert
**Director(s)** Feist, Felix E.
**Screenwriter(s)** Twist, John
**Source(s)** "City of Angels" (story) Buckner, Robert

**Cast** Scott, Randolph; Wymore, Patrice; Wesson, Dick; Carey, Philip; Romay, Lina; Roberts, Roy

**Song(s)** Some Sunday Morning [1] (C: Heindorf, Ray; Jerome, M.K.; L: Koehler, Ted); Adios Mi Amor (C/L: Amaral, Nestor)

**Notes** [1] Also in SAN ANTONIO.

## 3624 ✦ A MAN BETRAYED
Republic, 1936

**Producer(s)** Berke, William
**Director(s)** Auer, John H.
**Screenwriter(s)** McGowan, Dorrell; McGowan, Stuart

**Cast** Nugent, Eddie; Hughes, Kay; Hughes, Lloyd; Wray, John; Maxwell, Edwin; Burnette, Smiley; Gleason, Pat

**Song(s)** Sunshine for Sale [1] (C: Styne, Jule; L: Barzman, Sol)

**Notes** Reedited as WHEEL OF FORTUNE. [1] Also in GRANDPA GOES TO TOWN.

## 3625 ✦ A MAN CALLED DAGGER
Metro–Goldwyn–Mayer, 1966

**Musical Score** Allen, Steve

**Producer(s)** Horwitz, Lewis M.
**Director(s)** Rush, Richard
**Screenwriter(s)** Peatman, James; Weekley, Robert S.

**Cast** Murray, Jan; Moore, Terry; Langdon, Sue Ane; Mantee, Paul; Arthur, Maureen; Stone, Leonard; O'Neil, Eileen; Keil, Richard

**Song(s)** A Man Called Dagger (C: Allen, Steve; L: Kaye, Buddy)

## 3626 ✦ THE MAN CALLED FLINTSTONE
Columbia, 1966

**Musical Score** Nichols, Ted
**Composer(s)** Goodwin, Doug
**Lyricist(s)** Goodwin, Doug

**Producer(s)** Hanna, William; Barbera, Joseph
**Director(s)** Hanna, William; Barbera, Joseph
**Screenwriter(s)** Allen, R.S.; Bullock, Harvey
**Voices** Blanc, Mel; Reed, Alan

**Song(s)** Spy Type Guy; The Man Called Flintstone (C/L: McCarthy, John); Team Mates (C/L: McCarthy, John); Happy Sounds of Paree; Tickle Toddle

**Notes** Animated feature.

## 3627 ✦ A MAN CALLED GANNON
Universal, 1969

**Musical Score** Grusin, Dave
**Composer(s)** Grusin, Dave
**Lyricist(s)** Bergman, Alan; Bergman, Marilyn

**Producer(s)** Christie, Howard
**Director(s)** Goldstone, James
**Screenwriter(s)** Kearney, Gene; Chase, Borden; Beauchamp, D.D.
**Source(s)** *Man Without a Star* (novel) Linford, Dee

**Cast** Franciosa, Anthony; Sarrazin, Michael; West, Judi

**Song(s)** A Smile, A Mem'ry and an Extra Shirt; A Man Called Gannon [1]

**Notes** A remake of MAN WITHOUT A STAR (1955). [1] Lyric written for exploitation only.

## 3628 ✦ MANDALAY
Warner Brothers–First National, 1934

**Producer(s)** Presnell, Robert
**Director(s)** Curtiz, Michael
**Screenwriter(s)** Parker, Austin; Kenyon, Charles

**Cast** Francis, Kay; Cortez, Ricardo; Oland, Warner; Talbot, Lyle; Donnelly, Ruth; Littlefield, Lucien; Owen, Reginald; Girardrot, Etienne

**Song(s)** When Tomorrow Comes (C: Fain, Sammy; L: Kahal, Irving); Old Infantry Song (C: Traditional; L: Uncredited special lyrics)

## 3629 ✦ MANDINGO
Paramount, 1975

**Musical Score** Jarre, Maurice

**Producer(s)** De Laurentiis, Dino
**Director(s)** Fleischer, Richard
**Screenwriter(s)** Wexler, Norman
**Source(s)** *Mandingo* (novel) Onstott, Kyle; *Mandingo* (play) Kirkland, Jack

**Cast** Mason, James; Norton, Ken; George, Susan; King, Perry; Sykes, Brenda

**Song(s)** Born in This Time (C: Jarre, Maurice; L: Harris, "Hi Tide")

## 3630 ◆ MAN FROM CHEYENNE
Republic, 1941

**Composer(s)**    Nolan, Bob
**Lyricist(s)**    Nolan, Bob

**Producer(s)**    Kane, Joseph
**Director(s)**    Kane, Joseph
**Screenwriter(s)**    Miller, Winston

**Cast**    Rogers, Roy; Hayes, George "Gabby"; Storm, Gale; Payne, Sally; Carver, Lynne; Haade, William; Seay, James; Ingraham, Jack; Sons of the Pioneers

**Song(s)**    Home Again in Ol' Wyomin' (C/L: Spencer, Tim); Happy Cowboy [1]; Long About Sundown (C/L: Spencer, Tim; Spencer, Glenn); You Ain't Heard Nothin' Till You Hear Him Roar; My Old Pal, Pal of Mine; When a Cowboy Starts a Courtin' (C/L: Spencer, Tim)

**Notes**    [1] Also in STRICTLY IN THE GROOVE (Universal).

## 3631 ◆ THE MAN FROM DOWN UNDER
Metro–Goldwyn–Mayer, 1943

**Musical Score**    Snell, Dave

**Producer(s)**    Leonard, Robert Z.; Dull, Orville O.
**Director(s)**    Leonard, Robert Z.
**Screenwriter(s)**    Root, Wells; Seller, Thomas

**Cast**    Laughton, Charles; Barnes, Binnie; Carlson, Richard; Reed, Donna; Charlot, Andre; Cavanaugh, Robert

**Song(s)**    'E Pinched Me (C/L: Brent, Earl)

**Notes**    Note the inclusion of Andre Charlot (one of the greatest British stage producers) as Father Antoine.

## 3632 ◆ MAN FROM FRISCO
Republic, 1944

**Musical Score**    Skiles, Marlin

**Producer(s)**    Cohen, Albert J.
**Director(s)**    Florey, Robert
**Screenwriter(s)**    Bright, John; Ripley, Clements; Hill, Ethel; Manoff, Arnold

**Cast**    O'Shea, Michael; Shirley, Anne; Walker, Ray; Lockhart, Gene; Bond, Tommy; Duryea, Dan; Shoemaker, Ann; Batchelor, Stephanie; Warwick, Robert; Murray, Forbes

**Song(s)**    Rotary Song (C/L: Menoff, Arnold; Darby, Ken)

## 3633 ◆ THE MAN FROM LARAMIE
Columbia, 1955

**Producer(s)**    Goetz, William
**Director(s)**    Mann, Anthony
**Screenwriter(s)**    Yordan, Philip; Burt, Frank

**Cast**    Stewart, James; Kennedy, Arthur; Crisp, Donald; O'Donnell, Cathy; Nicol, Alex; MacMahon, Aline; Ford, Wallace; Elam, Jack

**Song(s)**    Laramie (C/L: Herbert, Frederick; Hughes, Arnold); The Man from Laramie (C: Lee, Lester; L: Washington, Ned)

**Notes**    No cue sheet available.

## 3634 ◆ MAN FROM MONTANA
Universal, 1941

**Composer(s)**    Rosen, Milton
**Lyricist(s)**    Carter, Everett

**Producer(s)**    Cowan, Will
**Director(s)**    Taylor, Ray
**Screenwriter(s)**    Cohen, Bennett R.

**Cast**    Brown, Johnny Mack; Knight, Fuzzy

**Song(s)**    The Western Trail [3]; Call of the Range [2]; Bananas Make Me Tough [1]

**Notes**    There is also a vocal of "Little Joe, the Wrangler" by Frank Loesser and Frederick Hollander. This song is also in DESTRY RIDES AGAIN (1939); LITTLE JOE, THE WRANGLER and THE OLD TEXAS TRAIL. [1] Also in THE LAWLESS BREED. [2] Also in BEYOND THE PECOS, FRONTIER LAW and GUNMAN'S CODE. [3] Also in RUSTLER'S ROUND-UP (1946).

## 3635 ◆ MAN FROM MUSIC MOUNTAIN (1938)
Republic, 1938

**Composer(s)**    Marvin, Johnny; Rose, Fred; Autry, Gene
**Lyricist(s)**    Marvin, Johnny; Rose, Fred; Autry, Gene

**Producer(s)**    Ford, Charles E.
**Director(s)**    Kane, Joseph
**Screenwriter(s)**    Burbridge, Betty; Ward, Luci

**Cast**    Autry, Gene; Burnette, Smiley; Hughes, Carol; Miller, Ivan; Payne, Sally; Cassidy, Edward; Kelly, Lew; Chase, Howard; Marvin, Frankie

**Song(s)**    Love Burning Love; There's a Little Deserted Town; I'm Beginning to Care; All Nice People (C/L: Burnette, Smiley); She Works Third Tub at the Laundry (C/L: Burnette, Smiley); Man From Music Mountain [1] (C: Tinturin, Peter; L: Lawrence, Jack); Goodbye Pinto

**Notes**    No cue sheet available. [1] Added verse has lyric by Eddie Cherkose.

## 3636 ◆ MAN FROM MUSIC MOUNTAIN (1943)
Republic, 1943

**Composer(s)**    Spencer, Tim
**Lyricist(s)**    Spencer, Tim

**Producer(s)**   Grey, Harry
**Director(s)**   Kane, Joseph
**Screenwriter(s)**   Cheney, J. Benton; Ropes, Bradford

**Cast**   Rogers, Roy; Brady, Pat; Terry, Ruth; Kelly, Paul; Gillis, Ann; Cleveland, George; Taliaferro, Hal; Sons of the Pioneers; Novello, Jay

**Song(s)**   King of the Cowboys; After the Rain; Wine, Woman and Song; I'm Thinking Tonight of My Blue Eyes (C/L: Marcotte, Don; Carter, A.P.); Smiles Are Made of the Sunshine [2] (C/L: Gilbert, Ray; Scott, M.); I'm Beginning to Care [1] (C/L: Autry, Gene; Marvin, Johnny; Rose, Fred); Roses on the Trail (C/L: Unknown)

**Notes**   No cue sheet available. [1] From THE MAN FROM MUSIC MOUNTAIN (1938). [2] M. Scott not credited on sheet music.

### 3637 ✦ MAN FROM OKLAHOMA
Republic, 1945

**Choreographer(s)**   Ceballos, Larry

**Producer(s)**   Gray, Louis
**Director(s)**   McDonald, Frank
**Screenwriter(s)**   Butler, John K.

**Cast**   Rogers, Roy; Trigger; Hayes, George "Gabby"; Evans, Dale; Bob Nolan and the Sons of the Pioneers

**Song(s)**   I'm Gonna Have a Cowboy Weddin' [2] (C: Vincent, Nat; L: Sweet, Milo); I'm Beginning to See the Light (C/L: Ellington, James; Hodges, George); For You and Me [1] (C: Kent, Walter; L: Gannon, Kim); Draggin' the Wagon (C/L: Forster, Gordon); The Martins and the Coys (C/L: Weems, Ted; Camaron, Al); Skies Are Bluer (C: Green, Sanford; L: Carroll, June); Prairie Mary (C: Baer, Abel; L: Tobias, Charles); I Know a Girl Named Mary (C/L: Scott, Morton); Cherro-Cherro-Cherrokee (C/L: Forster, Gordon); Man from Oklahoma (C: Green, Sanford; L: Carroll, June)

**Notes**   [1] Also in HITCH HIKE TO HAPPINESS and SWINGIN' ON A RAINBOW. [2] Also in YOUNG BILL HICKOK.

### 3638 ✦ MAN FROM RAINBOW VALLEY
Republic, 1956

**Musical Score**   Glickman, Mort

**Producer(s)**   Gray, Louis
**Director(s)**   Springsteen, R.G.
**Screenwriter(s)**   Burbridge, Betty

**Cast**   Hale, Monte; Booth, Adrian; The Sagebrush Serenaders; Outlaw - The Wild Horse

**Song(s)**   The Man in the Moon is a Cowhand [1] (C/L: Rogers, Roy); Rhythm Roundup (C/L: Spencer, Glenn); Ridin' Down the Trail [2] (C: Feuer, Cy; L: Cherkose, Eddie); Ghost Town Jamboree (C/L: Spencer, Glenn)

**Notes**   This may be an incomplete cue sheet. [1] Also in SHINE ON HARVEST MOON (1938). [2] Also in ROUGH RIDERS ROUND-UP.

### 3639 ✦ MAN FROM THE DINERS' CLUB
Columbia, 1963

**Musical Score**   Phillips, Stu

**Producer(s)**   Bloom, Bill
**Director(s)**   Tashlin, Frank
**Screenwriter(s)**   Blatty, William Peter [1]

**Cast**   Kaye, Danny; Williams, Cara; Hyer, Martha; Savalas, Telly; Sloane, Everett; Stevens, Kay; Caine, Howard

**Song(s)**   Man from the Diners' Club (C: Lawrence, Steve; L: Lehman, Johnny)

**Notes**   [1] Billed as Bill Blatty.

### 3640 ✦ MANHATTAN ANGEL
Columbia, 1948

**Producer(s)**   Katzman, Sam
**Director(s)**   Dreifuss, Arthur
**Screenwriter(s)**   Derr, Albert

**Cast**   Jean, Gloria; White, Patricia; Lloyd, Jimmy; Hall, Thurston; Hall, Dolores; Baker, Benny; Hicks, Russell; Sues, Leonard; Baker, Fay

**Song(s)**   It's a Wonderful Feeling (C/L: Bergman, Dewey; Segal, Jack); I'll Take Romance [1] (C: Oakland, Ben; L: Hammerstein II, Oscar); Naughty Aloysius (C/L: Bilder, Robert); Candy Store Blues [1] [2] (C/L: Jeffries, Herb; Castle, Nick; Beal, Eddie)

**Notes**   [1] Not written for this picture. [2] Also in MAKE BELIEVE BALLROOM.

### 3641 ✦ MANHATTAN COCKTAIL
Paramount, 1928

**Composer(s)**   Schertzinger, Victor
**Lyricist(s)**   Schertzinger, Victor

**Director(s)**   Arzner, Dorothy
**Screenwriter(s)**   Doherty, Ethel

**Cast**   Carroll, Nancy; Lukas, Paul; Tashman, Lilyan; Arlen, Richard; O'Shea, Danny

**Song(s)**   Another Kiss [1]; Gotta Be Good

**Notes**   [1] The song was not on the cue sheet but on sheet music only. Later might have been in THE LAUGHING LADY.

### 3642 ✦ MANHATTAN MELODRAMA
Metro–Goldwyn–Mayer, 1934

**Musical Score**   Axt, William

**Producer(s)**   Selznick, David O.
**Director(s)**   Van Dyke, W.S.

**Screenwriter(s)**    Garrett, Oliver H.P.; Mankiewicz, Joseph L.

**Cast**    Gable, Clark; Powell, William; Loy, Myrna; Carrillo, Leo; Pendleton, Nat; Sidney, George; Jewell, Isabel; Ross, Shirley; Rooney, Mickey

**Song(s)**    The Bad in Every Man [1] (C: Rodgers, Richard; L: Hart, Lorenz); Manhattan Melodrama [1] [2] (C: Rodgers, Richard; L: Hart, Lorenz)

**Notes**    [1] Same music. [2] Cut. The music was originally used for the song "Prayer" which was not used in HOLLYWOOD PARTY. The music finally became the basis for the pop song "Blue Moon."

### 3643 ✦ MANHATTAN MERRY-GO-ROUND
Republic, 1937

**Composer(s)**    Tinturin, Peter
**Lyricist(s)**    Lawrence, Jack

**Producer(s)**    Sauber, Harry
**Director(s)**    Riesner, Charles F.
**Screenwriter(s)**    Sauber, Harry

**Cast**    Regan, Phil; Carrillo, Leo; Dvorak, Ann; Geva, Tamara; Gleason, James; Ted Lewis and His Orchestra; Kay Thompson and Her Ensemble; DiMaggio, Joe; Armetta, Henry; Burnette, Smiley; Louis Prima and His Band; Jackson, Selmer; Olsen, Moroni; Kane, Eddie; The Lathrops; Rosalean and Seville; Autry, Gene

**Song(s)**    Vaudeville Montage (C/L: Colombo, Alberto); All Over Nothing at All; Have You Ever Been in Heaven; Mama I Wanna Make Rhythm [1] (C/L: Kent, Walter; Bryon, Richard; Jerome, Jerome); I Owe You; Chinese Rhythm [3] (C/L: Mills, Irving; Calloway, Cab; White, Harry); Round Up Time in Reno [2] (C/L: Owens, Jack); I'm a Musical Magical Man (C: Chaplin, Saul; L: Cahn, Sammy)

**Notes**    There is also a vocal of "Minnie the Moocher" by Cab Calloway, Clarence Gaskill and Irving Mills. [1] Also in TENTH AVENUE KID and the Columbia picture BEAUTIFUL BUT BROKE. [2] Gene Autry also credited on sheet music. Jack Lawrence and Autry also credited by ASCAP. [3] Irving Mills credit very doubtful.

### 3644 ✦ MANHATTAN PARADE
Warner Brothers, 1932

**Director(s)**    Bacon, Lloyd
**Screenwriter(s)**    Lord, Robert; Branch, Houston
**Source(s)**    *She Means Business* (play) Shipman, Samuel

**Cast**    Lightner, Winnie; Butterworth, Charles; Miller, Walter; Smith, Joe; Dale, Charles; Grandstedt, Greta; Watson, Bobby; Moore, Dickie; Alberni, Luis; Middleton, Charles; McDowell, Claire; Walters, Polly; Pendleton, Nat

**Song(s)**    I Love a Parade [1] (C: Arlen, Harold; L: Koehler, Ted); Temporarily Blue (C: Arlen, Harold; L: Koehler, Ted); I'm Happy When You're Jealous (C: Ruby, Harry; L: Kalmar, Bert)

**Notes**    No cue sheet available. [1] From the COTTON CLUB PARADE revue.

### 3645 ✦ MANHATTAN SERENADE
Metro–Goldwyn–Mayer, 1930

**Composer(s)**    Alter, Louis

**Director(s)**    Lee, Sammy
**Screenwriter(s)**    Farnham, Joe

**Cast**    Hackett, Raymond; Doran, Mary; The Brox Sisters; McKinney, Nina Mae; Kahn, Cy; The Cheer Leaders

**Song(s)**    Manhattan Serenade (L: Johnson, Howard); What Does It Mean When the Owl Says—Whoo (L: Trent, Jo); Harlem Heaven (L: Reisner, Charles)

**Notes**    Short subject.

### 3646 ✦ MAN HUNT
RKO, 1956

**Musical Score**    Vaars, Henry

**Producer(s)**    Bachmann, J.G.
**Director(s)**    Cummings, Irving
**Screenwriter(s)**    Praskins, Leonard; Mintz, Sam

**Cast**    Durkin, Junior; Henry, Charlotte; Reid, Mrs. Wallace; Vinton, Arthur; Carle, Richard

**Song(s)**    Let the Chips Fall Where They May (C: Vaars, Henry; L: Dunham, "By"); Mi Chiquita (C/L: Gonzales-Gonzales, Pedro)

### 3647 ✦ MANHUNT IN THE JUNGLE
Warner Brothers–First National, 1958

**Musical Score**    Jackson, Howard
**Composer(s)**    Jackson, Howard
**Lyricist(s)**    Torres, Enrique

**Producer(s)**    Francis, Cedric
**Director(s)**    McGowan, Tom
**Screenwriter(s)**    Merwin Jr., Sam; Crump, Owen
**Source(s)**    *Man Hunting in the Jungle* (book) Dyott, George M.

**Cast**    Hughes, Robin; Alvarez, Luis; Wilson, James; Montoro, Jorge; Symmes, John B.; Manzuelas, Natalie; Ryan, James; McClosky, Richard

**Song(s)**    Amazon; Tomando Pisco; Triste Melodia

### 3648 ✦ THE MAN I LOVE (1929)
Paramount, 1929

**Producer(s)**    Selznick, David O.
**Director(s)**    Wellman, William A.
**Screenwriter(s)**    Mankiewicz, Herman J.

**Cast**  Arlen, Richard; Brian, Mary; Baclanova, Olga; Oakie, Jack; Green, Harry; O'Malley, Pat

**Song(s)**  Celia (C: Whiting, Richard A.; L: Robin, Leo)

### 3649 ✦ THE MAN I LOVE (1947)
Warner Brothers–First National, 1947

**Producer(s)**  Albert, Arnold
**Director(s)**  Walsh, Raoul
**Screenwriter(s)**  Turney, Catherine
**Source(s)**  *Night Shift* (novel) Wolff, Maritta

**Cast**  Lupino, Ida [1]; Alda, Robert; King, Andrea; Vickers, Martha; Bennett, Bruce; Hale, Alan; Moran, Dolores; Ridgely, John; Stevens, Craig; McGuire, Don

**Notes**  No original songs. Vocals include "The Man I Love" by George and Ira Gershwin; "Why Was I Born" by Jerome Kern and Oscar Hammerstein II (written for stage show SWEET ADELINE and in the movie version of that show); "If I Could Be with You (One Hour Tonight)" by James P. Johnson and Henry Creamer; "Bill" by Jerome Kern, Oscar Hammerstein II and P.G. Wodehouse (from stage musical SHOW BOAT); "Body and Soul" by Johnny Green, Robert Sour, Frank Eyton, Edward Heyman and Howard Dietz (from Broadway revue THREE'S A CROWD. Also in film HER KIND OF MAN). [1] Dubbed by Peg LaCentra.

### 3650 ✦ THE MAN I MARRY
Universal, 1936

**Musical Score**  Previn, Charles
**Composer(s)**  Actman, Irving
**Lyricist(s)**  Loesser, Frank

**Producer(s)**  Paul, Val
**Director(s)**  Murphy, Ralph
**Screenwriter(s)**  Clork, Harry

**Cast**  Nolan, Doris; Whalen, Michael

**Song(s)**  I Know I'm in Harlem; Old Homestead [1]

**Notes**  [1] Not used.

### 3651 ✦ MAN IN THE ATTIC
Twentieth Century–Fox, 1954

**Musical Score**  Friedhofer, Hugo

**Producer(s)**  Jacks, Robert L.
**Director(s)**  Fregonese, Hugo
**Screenwriter(s)**  Presnell Jr., Robert; Lyndon, Barre
**Source(s)**  *The Lodger* (novel) Belloc-Lowndes, Marie

**Cast**  Palance, Jack; Smith, Constance; Palmer, Byron; Bavier, Frances; Williams, Rhys

**Song(s)**  You're in Love [1] (C: Newman, Lionel; L: Daniel, Eliot)

**Notes**  A remake of the THE LODGER (1944). [1] Also in GENTLEMEN PREFER BLONDES.

### 3652 ✦ MAN IN THE DARK
Universal, 1965

**Producer(s)**  Blakeley, Tom
**Director(s)**  Comfort, Lance
**Screenwriter(s)**  Kelly, James; Miller, Peter

**Cast**  Sylvester, William; Shelley, Barbara; Shepherd, Elizabeth

**Song(s)**  Concerto (C/L: Hart, Peter); Blind Corner (C/L: Butcher, Stan; Cordell, Syd); Where Ya Going (C/L: Butcher, Stan; Cordell, Syd); The Princess and the Disc Jockey Bounce (C/L: Fahey, Brian)

**Notes**  No cue sheet available.

### 3653 ✦ MAN IN THE SADDLE
Columbia, 1951

**Composer(s)**  Duning, George

**Producer(s)**  Scott, Randolph; Brown, Harry Joe
**Director(s)**  De Toth, Andre
**Screenwriter(s)**  Gamet, Kenneth
**Source(s)**  *Man in the Saddle* (novel) Haycox, Ernest

**Cast**  Scott, Randolph; Ford, Tennesse Ernie; Drew, Ellen; Leslie, Joan; Knox, Alexander; Mitchell, Cameron; Sully, Frank; Kirkwood, James

**Song(s)**  Man in the Saddle (C: Lewis, Harold; L: Murphy, Ralph)

### 3654 ✦ MANNEQUIN (1938)
Metro–Goldwyn–Mayer, 1937

**Musical Score**  Ward, Edward

**Producer(s)**  Mankiewicz, Joseph L.
**Director(s)**  Borzage, Frank
**Screenwriter(s)**  Hazard, Lawrence

**Cast**  Crawford, Joan; Tracy, Spencer; Curtis, Alan; Morgan, Ralph; Gorcey, Leo; Philips, Mary; O'Shea, Oscar; Risdon, Elizabeth

**Song(s)**  Always and Always [1] (C: Ward, Edward; L: Wright, Bob; Forrest, Chet)

**Notes**  [1] Also in HER CARDBOARD LOVER.

### 3655 ✦ MANNEQUIN (1987)
Twentieth Century–Fox, 1987

**Musical Score**  Levay, Sylvester

**Producer(s)**  Levinson, Art
**Director(s)**  Gottlieb, Michael
**Screenwriter(s)**  Rugoff, Edward; Gottlieb, Michael

**Cast**  McCarthy, Andrew; Cattrall, Kim; Getty, Estelle; Spader, James; Bailey, G.W.; Taylor, Meshach; Vinovich, Stephen; Newman, Phyllis

**Song(s)**  Nothing's Gonna Stop Us Now (C/L: Hammond, Albert; Warren, Diane); In My Wildest

Dreams (C/L: Crewe, Bob; Corbetta, Jerry; Caffey, Charlotte); Do You Dream About Me (C/L: Warren, Diane)

**Notes**   No cue sheet available.

## 3656 ✦ MAN OF A THOUSAND FACES
### Universal, 1937

**Musical Score**   Skinner, Frank

**Producer(s)**   Arthur, Robert
**Director(s)**   Pevney, Joseph
**Screenwriter(s)**   Campbell, R. Wright; Goff, Ivan; Roberts, Ben

**Cast**   Cagney, James; Malone, Dorothy; Greer, Jane; Smith, Roger; Rambeau, Marjorie; Backus, Jim; Lovsky, Celia; Leary, Nolan; Evans, Robert J.

**Song(s)**   Meet Me at the Fair [1] (C: Rosen, Milton; L: Herbert, Frederick)

**Notes**   [1] Also in MEET ME AT THE FAIR.

## 3657 ✦ MAN OF IRON
### United Artists, 1982

**Musical Score**   Korzynski, Andrzej

**Director(s)**   Wajda, Andrzej
**Screenwriter(s)**   Scibor-Rylski, Aleksander

**Cast**   Radziwilowicz, Jerzy; Janda, Krystyna; Opania, Marian; Byrska, Irena

**Song(s)**   Ballad of Janek Wisneiwski (C/L: Korzynski, Andrzej); To My Daughter (C/L: Peitrzyk, Maciej; Kasprzyk, Krzysztof)

**Notes**   No cue sheet available.

## 3658 ✦ MAN OF LA MANCHA
### United Artists, 1972

**Composer(s)**   Leigh, Mitch
**Lyricist(s)**   Darion, Joe
**Choreographer(s)**   Lynne, Gillian

**Producer(s)**   Hiller, Arthur
**Director(s)**   Hiller, Arthur
**Screenwriter(s)**   Wasserman, Dale
**Source(s)**   *Man of La Mancha* (musical) Wasserman, Dale; Darion, Joe; Leigh, Mitch

**Cast**   O'Toole, Peter [1]; Loren, Sophia; Coco, James; Andrews, Harry; Castle, John; Blessed, Brian; Richardson, Ian

**Song(s)**   It's All the Same; I Am I Don Quixote; Dulcinea; I'm Only Thinking of Him; I Like Him; Barber's Song; Golden Helmet; Little Bird; The Impossible Dream; Hail Knight of the Woeful Countenance; Aldonza; The Psalm

**Notes**   All songs are from the Broadway original. [1] Dubbed by Simon Gilbert.

## 3659 ✦ MAN OF THE EAST
### United Artists, 1972

**Musical Score**   De Angelis, Guido; De Angelis, Aurilio

**Producer(s)**   Bulgarelli, Enzo
**Director(s)**   Clucher, E.B.
**Screenwriter(s)**   Barboni, Enzo

**Cast**   Hill, Terrence; Somer, Yanti; Walcott, Gregory; Carey, Harry; Barto, Dominic; Pizzuti, Riccardo

**Song(s)**   Don't Lose Control (C/L: De Angelis, Guido; De Angelis, Aurilio); Jesus Come (C/L: De Angelis, Guido; De Angelis, Aurilio)

## 3660 ✦ MAN OF THE FAMILY

See TOP MAN.

## 3661 ✦ MAN OF THE FRONTIER

See RED RIVER VALLEY (1936).

## 3662 ✦ MAN OF THE MOMENT
### United Artists, 1955

**Musical Score**   Green, Philip
**Composer(s)**   Green, Philip
**Lyricist(s)**   Fishman, Jack

**Producer(s)**   Rank, J. Arthur
**Director(s)**   Carstairs, John Paddy
**Screenwriter(s)**   Sylvaine, Vernon; Carstairs, John Paddy

**Cast**   Wisdom, Norman; Morris, Lana; Lee, Belinda

**Song(s)**   Man of the Moment; Yodelee Yodelay (C: Traditional); Beware (C/L: Wisdom, Norman); Dream for Sale (C/L: Groves, Arthur; Carroll, Peter)

## 3663 ✦ MAN OF THE PEOPLE
### Metro–Goldwyn–Mayer, 1937

**Musical Score**   Ward, Edward

**Producer(s)**   Hubbard, Lucien
**Director(s)**   Marin, Edwin L.
**Screenwriter(s)**   Dolan, Frank

**Cast**   Calleia, Joseph; Mitchell, Thomas; Rice, Florence; Healy, Ted; Doucet, Catherine

**Song(s)**   Molchi Grust Molchi [1] (C: Beresofsky; L: Frenkel, Z.; Wright, Bob; Forrest, Chet); Let Me Day Dream [2] (C: Donaldson, Walter; L: Wright, Robert; Forrest, Chet)

**Notes**   [1] English lyrics by Wright and Forrest. [2] Sheet music only.

## 3664 ✦ MAN OF THE WEST
United Artists, 1958

**Musical Score** Harline, Leigh

**Producer(s)** Mirisch, Walter
**Director(s)** Mann, Anthony
**Screenwriter(s)** Rose, Reginald
**Source(s)** (novel) Brown, Will C.

**Cast** Cooper, Gary; London, Julie; Cobb, Lee J.; Lord, Jack

**Song(s)** Man of the West [1] (C/L: Troup, Bobby)

**Notes** [1] Used instrumentally only.

## 3665 ✦ MAN ON FIRE
Metro–Goldwyn–Mayer, 1957

**Musical Score** Raksin, David

**Producer(s)** Siegel, Sol C.
**Director(s)** MacDougall, Ranald
**Screenwriter(s)** MacDougall, Ranald

**Cast** Crosby, Bing; Stevens, Inger; Fickett, Mary; Marshall, E.G.; Broderick, Malcolm; Seymour, Anne

**Song(s)** Man on Fire (C: Fain, Sammy; L: Webster, Paul Francis)

## 3666 ✦ THE MAN ON THE FLYING TRAPEZE
Paramount, 1935

**Director(s)** Bruckman, Clyde
**Screenwriter(s)** Harris, Ray; Cunningham, Jack; Vernon, Bobby; Hardy, Sam

**Cast** Fields, W.C.; Apfel, Oscar; Howard, Kathleen; Brian, Mary; Sutton, Grady; Littlefield, Lucien; Brennan, Walter

**Song(s)** The Man on the Flying Trapeze [1] (C: Traditional; L: Seymour, Tot; Lawnhurst, Vee)

**Notes** [1] Song not used in picture. Written for exploitation only.

## 3667 ✦ MANPOWER
Warner Brothers–First National, 1941

**Musical Score** Deutsch, Adolph
**Composer(s)** Hollander, Frederick
**Lyricist(s)** Loesser, Frank

**Producer(s)** Wallis, Hal B.
**Director(s)** Walsh, Raoul
**Screenwriter(s)** Macaulay, Richard; Wald, Jerry

**Cast** Robinson, Edward G.; Catlett, Walter; Dietrich, Marlene; Raft, George; Hale, Alan; McHugh, Frank; Brecher, Egon; Bond, Ward; Arden, Eve; Compton, Joyce; Quinn, Anthony

**Song(s)** I'm in No Mood for Music [1]; He Lied and I Listened

**Notes** [1] Instrumental use only.

## 3668 ✦ MAN-PROOF
Metro–Goldwyn–Mayer, 1937

**Musical Score** Waxman, Franz

**Producer(s)** Lighton, Louis D.
**Director(s)** Thorpe, Richard
**Screenwriter(s)** Lawrence, Vincent; Young, Waldemar; Oppenheimer, George
**Source(s)** *The Four Marys* (novel) Lee, Fanny Hesslip

**Cast** Loy, Myrna; Tone, Franchot; Russell, Rosalind; Pidgeon, Walter; Bryant, Nana; Hussey, Ruth; Miljan, John

**Song(s)** On a Sunday Afternoon [1] (C: Brown, Nacio Herb; L: Freed, Arthur)

**Notes** [1] Also in BROADWAY MELODY OF 1936.

## 3669 ✦ MAN'S FAVORITE SPORT
Universal, 1963

**Musical Score** Mancini, Henry

**Producer(s)** Hawks, Howard
**Director(s)** Hawks, Howard
**Screenwriter(s)** Murray, John Fenton; McNeil, Steve
**Source(s)** "The Girl Who Almost Got Away" (story) Frank, Pat

**Cast** Hudson, Rock; Prentiss, Paula; McGiver, John; Karns, Roscoe; Toomey, Regis

**Song(s)** Man's Favorite Sport (C: Mancini, Henry; L: Mercer, Johnny)

## 3670 ✦ MANSLAUGHTER
Paramount, 1930

**Director(s)** Abbott, George
**Screenwriter(s)** Abbott, George

**Cast** March, Fredric; Colbert, Claudette; Dunn, Emma; Moorhead, Natalie; Tucker, Richard

**Song(s)** Heavy, Heavy Mah Por Heart (C: Akst, Harry; L: Clarke, Grant)

## 3671 ✦ A MAN'S MAN
Metro–Goldwyn–Mayer, 1929

**Director(s)** Cruze, James
**Screenwriter(s)** Halsey, Forrest
**Source(s)** *A Man's Man* (play) Kearney, Patrick

**Cast** Haines, William; Dunn, Josephine; Busch, Mae; Hardy, Sam; Gilbert, John

**Song(s)** I'll Never Ask For More [1] (C/L: DeSylva, B.G.; Unknown); My Heart Is Bluer Than Your Eyes, Cherie (C: Bryan, Alfred; L: Wilhite, Monte)

**Notes** [1] ASCAP credits Roy Turk and Fred Ahlert.

## 3672 ✦ MAN TROUBLE
Twentieth Century–Fox, 1930

**Composer(s)** Hanley, James F.
**Lyricist(s)** McCarthy, Joseph

**Director(s)** Viertel, Berthold
**Screenwriter(s)** Watters, George Manker; Burke, Edwin

**Cast** McKenna, Kenneth; Lynn, Sharon; Karns, Roscoe; Apfel, Oscar; Bradbury, James; Harvey, Lew; Clark, Harvey; Chapman, Edythe; Sills, Milton; Mackaill, Dorothy

**Song(s)** You Do Don't You; Pick Yourself Up; Now I Ask You; What's the Use of Living without Love [1]; You Got Nobody to Love

**Notes** Originally titled A PRACTICAL JOKE. [1] Also in Once a Sinner (1931).

## 3673 ✦ THE MAN WHO CAME BACK
Fox, 1931

**Director(s)** Walsh, Raoul
**Screenwriter(s)** Burke, E.J.
**Source(s)** *The Man Who Came Back* (play) Goodman, Jules Eckert; Wilson, J.F.

**Cast** Gaynor, Janet; Farrell, Glenda; MacKenna, Kenneth; Holden, William; Forbes, Mary

**Song(s)** I Have a Thought in My Heart for You [1] [2] (C/L: Hoopii Jr., Sol); Sweet Hawaiian Memories [1] (C/L: Kernell, William); My Dream of Love [3] (C/L: Malotte, Albert Hay)

**Notes** [1] Apparently these are only used in the foreign prints. [2] Also used in THE BLACK CAMEL. [3] Sheet music only.

## 3674 ✦ THE MAN WHO DARED
Fox, 1933

**Director(s)** McFadden, Hamilton
**Screenwriter(s)** Nichols, Dudley; Trotti, Lamar

**Cast** Foster, Preston; Johann, Zita; Marsh, Joan; Hiller, Irene; Jones, Clifford

**Song(s)** Bohemian Drinking Song (C/L: Jason, Will; Burton, Val); Walking with Susie [1] (C/L: Conrad, Con; Gottler, Archie; Mitchell, Sidney D.)

**Notes** [1] Also in FOX MOVIETONE FOLLIES OF 1929. Parody lyrics were written by Will Jason and Val Burton.

## 3675 ✦ THE MAN WHO KNEW TOO MUCH
Paramount, 1956

**Musical Score** Herrmann, Bernard
**Composer(s)** Livingston, Jay; Evans, Ray
**Lyricist(s)** Livingston, Jay; Evans, Ray

**Producer(s)** Hitchcock, Alfred
**Director(s)** Hitchcock, Alfred
**Screenwriter(s)** McPhail, Angus; Hayes, John Michael

**Cast** Stewart, James; Day, Doris; Miles, Bernard; De Banzie, Brenda; Truman, Ralph; Gelin, Daniel; Mowbray, Alan

**Song(s)** Whatever Will Be, Will Be (Que Sera, Sera) [2]; We'll Love Again; Holy Cow [1]

**Notes** [1] Not used. Also titled HOLY GEE. [2] Oscar winner.

## 3676 ✦ THE MAN WHO LAUGHS
Universal, 1927

**Director(s)** Leni, Paul
**Screenwriter(s)** Anthony, Walter
**Source(s)** *L'Homme qui Rit* (novel) Hugo, Victor

**Cast** Veidt, Conrad; Philbin, Mary; Baclanova, Olga; Crowell, Josephine; Siegmann, George; Hurst, Brandon

**Song(s)** When Love Comes Stealing (C/L: Rapee, Erno; Hirsch, Walter; Pollack, Lew)

**Notes** No cue sheet available.

## 3677 ✦ THE MAN WHO LOVED WOMEN
Columbia, 1983

**Musical Score** Mancini, Henry

**Producer(s)** Edwards, Blake; Adams, Tony
**Director(s)** Edwards, Blake
**Screenwriter(s)** Edwards, Blake; Edwards, Geoffrey; Wexler, Milton

**Cast** Reynolds, Burt; Andrews, Julie; Basinger, Kim; Henner, Marilu; Sikes, Cynthia; Edwards, Jennifer

**Song(s)** Little Boys (C: Mancini, Henry; L: Bergman, Alan; Bergman, Marilyn)

## 3678 ✦ THE MAN WHO SHOT LIBERTY VALANCE
Paramount, 1961

**Musical Score** Mockridge, Cyril J.

**Producer(s)** Goldbeck, Willis
**Director(s)** Ford, John
**Screenwriter(s)** Bellah, James Warner; Goldbeck, Willis

**Cast** Wayne, John; Stewart, James; Miles, Vera; Marvin, Lee; O'Brien, Edmond; Devine, Andy; Murray, Ken; Carradine, John; Nolan, Jeanette; Strode, Woody;

Pyle, Denver; Martin, Strother; Van Cleef, Lee; Whitehead, O.Z.

**Song(s)** The Man Who Shot Liberty Valance [1] (C: Bacharach, Burt; L: David, Hal)

**Notes** [1] Written for exploitation only.

### 3679 ✦ THE MAN WHO UNDERSTOOD WOMEN
Twentieth Century–Fox, 1959

**Musical Score** Dolan, Robert Emmett

**Producer(s)** Johnson, Nunnally
**Director(s)** Johnson, Nunnally
**Screenwriter(s)** Johnson, Nunnally
**Source(s)** *The Colors of the Day* (novel) Gary, Romain

**Cast** Caron, Leslie; Fonda, Henry; Danova, Cesare; McCormick, Myron; Nagel, Conrad; Cady, Frank

**Song(s)** A Paris Valentine (C: Dolan, Robert Emmett; L: Webster, Paul Francis)

### 3680 ✦ MAN WHO WALKED ALONE
PRC, 1945

**Musical Score** Hajos, Karl

**Producer(s)** Fromkess, Leon
**Director(s)** Cabanne, Christy
**Screenwriter(s)** Johnson, Robert Lee

**Cast** O'Brien, Dave; Aldridge, Kay; Catlett, Walter; Williams, Guinn "Big Boy"; Randolph, Isabel; Ballew, Smith; Oakland, Vivian

**Song(s)** Say It with Love (C/L: Livingston, Jay; Evans, Ray; Bellin, Lewis)

### 3681 ✦ THE MAN WITH A CLOAK
Metro–Goldwyn–Mayer, 1951

**Musical Score** Raksin, David

**Producer(s)** Ames, Stephen
**Director(s)** Markle, Fletcher
**Screenwriter(s)** Fenton, Frank

**Cast** Cotten, Joseph; Stanwyck, Barbara; Calhern, Louis; Caron, Leslie; DeSantis, Joe; Backus, Jim; Wycherly, Margaret

**Song(s)** Another Yesterday (C/L: Brent, Earl)

**Notes** There is also a vocal of "Katy Darling" by Bellini and Greenham.

### 3682 ✦ THE MAN WITH BOGART'S FACE
Twentieth Century–Fox, 1980

**Musical Score** Duning, George

**Producer(s)** Fenady, Andrew J.
**Director(s)** Day, Robert

**Screenwriter(s)** Fenady, Andrew J.
**Source(s)** *The Man with Bogart's Face* (novel) Fenady, Andrew J.

**Cast** Sacchi, Robert; Nero, Franco; Phillips, Michelle; Hussey, Olivia; Rowe, Misty; Buono, Victor; Lom, Herbert; Danning, Sybil; Raft, George; De Carlo, Yvonne; Mazurki, Mike; Wilcoxon, Henry; Theismann, Joe

**Song(s)** Looking At You (C: Duning, George; L: Fenady, Andrew J.); The Man with Bogart's Face (C: Duning, George; L: Fenady, Andrew J.)

**Notes** No cue sheet available.

### 3683 ✦ MAN WITH 100 FACES
Gainsborough, 1938

**Producer(s)** Black, Edward
**Director(s)** De Courville, Albert
**Screenwriter(s)** Rawlinson, A.R.; Pertwee, Michael; Mason, Basil
**Source(s)** (novel) Ferguson, W.B.

**Cast** Walls, Tom; Palmer, Lilli; Madison, Noel; Linn, Leon M.

**Song(s)** Stick 'Em Up (C/L: Pola, Eddie)

**Notes** Titled CRACKERJACK in Great Britain. Distributed by Twentieth Century–Fox.

### 3684 ✦ MAN WITHOUT A STAR
Universal, 1955

**Producer(s)** Rosenberg, Aaron
**Director(s)** Vidor, King
**Screenwriter(s)** Chase, Borden; Beauchamp, D.D.
**Source(s)** *Man Without a Star* (novel) Linford, Dee

**Cast** Douglas, Kirk; Campbell, William; Crain, Jeanne; Trevor, Claire; Flippen, Jay C.; Boone, Richard; Corday, Mara

**Song(s)** Man Without a Star (C: Hughes, Arnold; L: Herbert, Frederick); And the Moon Grew Brighter and Brighter (C/L: Singer, Lou; Kennedy, Jimmy)

**Notes** Remade as A MAN CALLED GANNON (1969).

### 3685 ✦ THE MAN WITH THE GOLDEN GUN
United Artists, 1974

**Musical Score** Barry, John

**Producer(s)** Broccoli, Albert R.; Saltzman, Harry
**Director(s)** Hamilton, Guy
**Screenwriter(s)** Maibaum, Richard; Mankiewicz, Tom
**Source(s)** *The Man with the Golden Gun* (novel) Fleming, Ian

**Cast** Moore, Roger; Lee, Christopher; Ekland, Britt; Adams, Maud; Villechaize, Herve; Lee, Bernard; Llewelyn, Desmond; Maxwell, Lois

**Song(s)** The Man with the Golden Gun (C: Barry, John; L: Black, Don)

### 3686 ✦ MAN, WOMAN AND CHILD
Paramount, 1983

**Musical Score** Delerue, Georges

**Producer(s)** Williams, Elmo; Kastner, Elliott
**Director(s)** Richards, Dick
**Screenwriter(s)** Segal, Erich; Goodman, David Zelig
**Source(s)** *Man, Woman and Child* (novel) Segal, Erich

**Cast** Sheen, Martin; Danner, Blythe; Nelson, Craig T.; Anderman, Maureen; Nell, Nathalie; Francois, Jacques; Hemmings, David

**Song(s)** Never Gone (C: Delerue, Georges; L: Pomeranz, David; Kaye, Buddy)

### 3687 ✦ MAN, WOMAN AND WIFE
Universal, 1928

**Director(s)** Laemmle, Edward
**Screenwriter(s)** Anthony, Walter
**Source(s)** "Fallen Angels" (story) Roche, Arthur Somers

**Cast** Kerry, Norman; Starke, Pauline; Nixon, Marion; Douglas, Byron; Harlan, Kenneth; Kent, Crauford

**Song(s)** Love Can Never Die (C: Ruby, Herman; L: Cherniavsky, Joseph)

**Notes** No cue sheet available. Also titled FALLEN ANGELS.

### 3688 ✦ THE MANY ADVENTURES OF WINNIE THE POOH
Disney, 1967

**Musical Score** Baker, Buddy
**Composer(s)** Sherman, Richard M.; Sherman, Robert B.
**Lyricist(s)** Sherman, Richard M.; Sherman, Robert B.

**Producer(s)** Reitherman, Wolfgang
**Director(s)** Reitherman, Wolfgang; Lounsbery, John
**Screenwriter(s)** Clemmons, Larry; Gerry, Vance; Anderson, Ken; Berman, Ted; Wright, Ralph; Atencio, Xavier; Svendsen, Julius; Cleworth, Eric
**Source(s)** Pooh stories (stories) Milne, A.A.
**Voices** Cabot, Sebastian; Matthews, Junius; Morris, Howard; Wright, Ralph; Howard, Clint; Luddy, Barbara; Fiedler, John; Reitherman, Bruce; Whitaker, Dori; Holloway, Sterling; Winchell, Paul

**Song(s)** Heffalumps and Woozles [1]; Hip Hip Pooh-Ray [1]; Little Black Rain Cloud; Mind Over Matter; The Rain, Rain, Rain Came Down, Down, Down [1]; A Rather Blustery Day [1]; Rumbly in My Tumbly [2]; Up, Down and Touch the Ground; Winnie the Pooh; The Wonderful Thing About Tiggers [1] [2]

**Notes** Animated feature. [1] Also in WINNIE THE POOH AND THE BLUSTERY DAY. [2] Also in WINNIE THE POOH AND TIGGER TOO.

### 3689 ✦ MANY HAPPY RETURNS
Paramount, 1934

**Director(s)** McLeod, Norman Z.
**Screenwriter(s)** McEvoy, J.P.; Binyon, Claude
**Source(s)** *Mr. Dayton Darling* (novel) Cameron, Lady Mary

**Cast** Burns, George; Allen, Gracie; Guy Lombardo and His Orchestra

**Song(s)** The Boogie Man [5] (C/L: Coslow, Sam); Yolanda (inst.) [5] (C: Johnston, Arthur); Do I Love You [1] (C: Rainger, Ralph; L: Robin, Leo); The Sweetest Music This Side of Heaven (C: Lombardo, Carmen; L: Friend, Cliff); I Don't Wanna Play [2] (C: Johnston, Arthur; L: Coslow, Sam); The Lights Are Low the Music Is Sweet [2] (C: Lombardo, Carmen; L: Friend, Cliff); The Morning After [2] [3] (C: Johnston, Arthur; L: Coslow, Sam); Fare thee Well [4] [5] (C/L: Coslow, Sam)

**Notes** [1] Used in SHOOT THE WORKS. [2] Not used. [3] Recorded for but not used in HANDS ACROSS THE TABLE but without Johnston credit. See note below. [4] Sheet music only. [5] According to a memo: There is some controversy concerning whether or not he (Johnston) has written the music for "Fare Thee Well" and "The Boogie Man." By the same token—Sam's name should not appear on "Yolanda."

### 3690 ✦ MANY RIVERS TO CROSS
Metro–Goldwyn–Mayer, 1955

**Musical Score** Mockridge, Cyril J.

**Producer(s)** Cummings, Jack
**Director(s)** Rowland, Roy
**Screenwriter(s)** Brown, Harry; Trosper, Guy

**Cast** Taylor, Robert; Parker, Eleanor; McLaglen, Victor; Richards, Jeff; Tamblyn, Russ; Arness, James; Hale Jr., Alan; Hudson, John; Williams, Rhys; Hutchinson, Josephine; Rumann, Sig; De Camp, Rosemary; Johnson, Russell

**Song(s)** Weavily Wheat (C/L: Chaplin, Saul; Mockridge, Cyril J.); The Berry Tree (C/L: Chaplin, Saul)

### 3691 ✦ MARACAIBO
Paramount, 1958

**Producer(s)** Wilde, Cornel
**Director(s)** Wilde, Cornel

**Screenwriter(s)**   Sherdeman, Ted
**Source(s)**   *Maracaibo* (novel) Silliphant, Stirling

**Cast**   Wilde, Cornel; Landon, Michael; Lane, Abbe; Wallace, Jean; Lederer, Francis

**Song(s)**   Maracaibo (Maracaibo Moon) (I Am Yours) (C: Almeida, Laurindo; L: Pascal, Jefferson [1])

**Notes**   [1] Pseudonym for Cornel Wilde.

## 3692 ◆ MARCHING ALONG

See STARS AND STRIPES FOREVER.

## 3693 ◆ MARCH OF THE WOODEN SOLDIERS

See BABES IN TOYLAND (1934).

## 3694 ◆ MARCH OF TIME (1930)
### RKO, 1930

**Song(s)**   Here Comes the Sun (C: Woods, Harry; L: Freed, Arthur)

**Notes**   No other information available.

## 3695 ◆ MARCH OF TIME (1933)

See BROADWAY TO HOLLYWOOD.

## 3696 ◆ MARCO THE MAGNIFICENT
### Metro–Goldwyn–Mayer, 1965

**Musical Score**   Garvarentz, Georges

**Producer(s)**   Manley, Walter
**Director(s)**   de la Patelliere, Denys
**Screenwriter(s)**   de la Patelliere, Denys; Levv, Raoul J.

**Cast**   Buchholz, Horst; Aslan, Gregoire; Hossein, Robert; Martinelli, Elsa; Tamiroff, Akim; Sharif, Omar; Welles, Orson; Quinn, Anthony

**Song(s)**   Somewhere [1] (C: Garvarentz, Georges; L: Aznavour, Charles)

**Notes**   No cue sheet available. The film was released as FABULEUSES AVENTURE DE MARCO POLO in its initial European release. [1] Probably written for exploitation only.

## 3697 ◆ MARDI GRAS (1943)
### Paramount, 1943

**Cast**   Rhodes, Betty Jane; Johnston, Johnnie

**Song(s)**   At the Mardi Gras (C/L: Lee, Lester; Seelen, Jerry); All the Way (C: Styne, Jule; L: Gannon, Kim)

**Notes**   Short subject.

## 3698 ◆ MARDI GRAS (1958)
### Twentieth Century–Fox, 1958

**Musical Score**   Newman, Lionel
**Composer(s)**   Fain, Sammy
**Lyricist(s)**   Webster, Paul Francis
**Choreographer(s)**   Foster, Bill

**Producer(s)**   Wald, Jerry
**Director(s)**   Goulding, Edmund
**Screenwriter(s)**   Miller, Winston; Kanter, Hal

**Cast**   Boone, Pat; Carere, Christine [1]; Sands, Tommy; North, Sheree [1]; Crosby, Gary; Clark, Fred; Chase, Barrie

**Song(s)**   The Mardi Gras March; Bourbon Street Blues; Stonewall Jackson; A Fiddle, A Rifle, An Axe and a Bible; I'll Remember Tonight; Bigger Than Texas; That Man Could Sell Me the Brooklyn Bridge; Loyalty

**Notes**   [1] Dubbed by Eileen Wilson.

## 3699 ◆ MARGIE
### Universal, 1940

**Composer(s)**   Previn, Charles
**Lyricist(s)**   Smith, Paul Gerard

**Producer(s)**   Sandford, Joseph G.
**Director(s)**   Garrett, Otis
**Screenwriter(s)**   Lazarus, Erna; Darling, W. Scott; Smith, Paul Gerard

**Cast**   Brown, Tom; Grey, Nan; Quillan, Eddie; Vernon, Wally

**Song(s)**   Rub a Dub, Dub (C: Schwarzwald, Milton); When Banana Blossoms Bloom [1] (L: Lerner, Sam); Oh, Fly with Me

**Notes**   There is also a vocal of "Margie" by Benny Davis, Con Conrad and J.R. Robinson. [1] Also in GOOD MORNING, JUDGE.

## 3700 ◆ MARIANNE
### Metro–Goldwyn–Mayer, 1929

**Musical Score**   Maxwell, Charles
**Composer(s)**   Ahlert, Fred E.
**Lyricist(s)**   Turk, Roy

**Director(s)**   Leonard, Robert Z.
**Screenwriter(s)**   Stallings, Laurence; Unger, Gladys

**Cast**   Davies, Marion; Gray, Lawrence; Rubin, Benny; Edwards, Cliff; Baxter, George

**Song(s)**   Marianne; Hinky Dinky (C: Traditional L: Dubin, Al); When I See My Sugar; Blondy (C: Brown, Nacio Herb; L: Freed, Arthur); Just You, Just Me [2] (C: Greer, Jesse; L: Klages, Raymond); Hang on to Me [1] (C: Greer, Jesse; L: Klages, Raymond); Oh Frenchy (C/L: Conrad, Con); The Girl from Noofchateau;

Oo-La-La (Joli Fifi); Wait Till You See Ma Cherie [3] (C: Whiting, Richard A.; L: Robin, Leo); Where Do We Go from Here (C: Wenrich, Percy; L: Unknown)

**Notes**   This was also made in a silent version with Oscar Shaw and Robert Ames. [1] Also in STARLIT DAYS AT THE LIDO. [2] Also in THE WOMAN RACKET. [3] Also in INNOCENTS OF PARIS.

## 3701 ✦ MARIA'S LOVERS
Cannon, 1985

**Musical Score**   Remal, Gary S.

**Producer(s)**   Djordjevic, Bosko; Taylor-Mortoroff, Lawrence
**Director(s)**   Konchalovsky, Andrei
**Screenwriter(s)**   Brach, Gerard; Konchalovsky, Andrei; Zindel, Paul; David, Marjorie

**Cast**   Kinski, Nastassia; Savage, John; Mitchum, Robert; Carradine, Keith; Morris, Anita; Cort, Bud; Young, Karen; Nelson, Tracy; Goodman, John; Stone, Danton; Spano, Vincent; Ivey, Lela

**Song(s)**   Maria's Eyes (C: Konchalovsky, Andrei; L: Carradine, Keith)

**Notes**   No cue sheet available.

## 3702 ✦ MARIE ANTOINETTE
Metro–Goldwyn–Mayer, 1938

**Musical Score**   Stothart, Herbert
**Choreographer(s)**   Rasch, Albertina

**Producer(s)**   Stromberg, Hunt
**Director(s)**   Van Dyke II, W.S.
**Screenwriter(s)**   West, Claudine; Stewart, Donald Ogden; Vajda, Ernest
**Source(s)**   *Marie Antoinette* (book) Zweig, Stefan

**Cast**   Shearer, Norma; Power, Tyrone; Barrymore, John; Morley, Robert; Louise, Anita; Schildkraut, Joseph; George, Gladys; Stephenson, Henry; Witherspoon, Cora; Gardiner, Reginald

**Song(s)**   Amour Eternal Amour [1] (C: Stothart, Herbert; L: Wright, Bob; Forrest, Chet)

**Notes**   Sidney Franklin was replaced by Van Dyke shortly before filming began. [1] Used instrumentally only.

## 3703 ✦ MARIE GALANTE
Fox, 1934

**Composer(s)**   Gorney, Jay
**Lyricist(s)**   Hartman, Don

**Producer(s)**   Sheehan, Winfield
**Director(s)**   King, Henry
**Screenwriter(s)**   Berkeley, Reginald
**Source(s)**   *Marie Galante* (novel) Deval, Jacques

**Cast**   Tracy, Spencer; Gallian, Ketti; Morgan, Helen

**Song(s)**   Celles de Chez Nous (C: Lange, Arthur; L: Silver, Abner); Elle Est Belle (C/L: Naish); Song of a Dreamer; Serves Me Right for Treating Him Wrong (C/L: Sigler, Maurice; Goodhart, Al; Hoffman, Al); It's Home (L: Yellen, Jack); Shim Shammy (C/L: Fetchit, Stepin); Let's Have Another [1] (L: Yellen, Jack); Girl of All Nations [2] (C: Akst, Harry; L: Grossman, Bernie); Je T'Adore [2] [3] (C: Akst, Harry; L: Grossman, Bernie); Enclosed Please Find [4] (C: Whiting, Richard A.; L: Robin, Leo); Un Peu Beaucoup [5] (C: Lange, Arthur; Silver, Marcel); Ting A Ling A Ling [2]

**Notes**   As an example of the unreliability of credits, note that this film is based on the novel "That Girl," which is an English translation of the French novel credited above. Also, though Reginald Berkeley is credited with the screenplay, Seymour Stern contributed to the treatment; Dudley Nichols, William Drake, Courtenay Terrett, Sonya Levien and Sam Hoffenstein contributed in the screenplay construction; Seton I. Miller helped out on the dialogue and Henry King, Robert Low, Jack Yellen and Marcel Silver aided on special sequences. [1] Not used. Cut after a preview in Jersey City. [2] Not used. [3] Used in UNDER THE PAMPAS MOON. [4] Not used. Also not used in HANDLE WITH CARE. [5] Sheet music only.

## 3704 ✦ MARIE-OCTOBRE

See SECRET MEETING.

## 3705 ✦ MARINES, LET'S GO
Twentieth Century–Fox, 1961

**Musical Score**   Gertz, Irving

**Producer(s)**   Walsh, Raoul
**Director(s)**   Walsh, Raoul
**Screenwriter(s)**   Twist, John

**Cast**   Tryon, Tom; Hedison, David; Reese, Tom

**Song(s)**   Marines, Let's Go (C/L: Phillips, Mike; Watson, George)

## 3706 ✦ MARJORIE MORNINGSTAR
Warner Brothers, 1958

**Musical Score**   Steiner, Max

**Producer(s)**   Sperling, Milton
**Director(s)**   Rapper, Irving
**Screenwriter(s)**   Freeman, Everett
**Source(s)**   *Marjorie Morningstar* (novel) Wouk, Herman

**Cast**   Kelly, Gene; Wood, Natalie; Trevor, Claire; Sloane, Everett; Milner, Martin; Jones, Carolyn; Tobias, George; Balsam, Martin; White, Jesse; Byrnes, Edward; Picerni, Paul; Reed, Alan; Lee, Ruta; Wynn, Ed

**Song(s)** A Very Precious Love [1] (C: Fain, Sammy; L: Webster, Paul Francis); O Tamarack (C/L: Adelson, Lenny); Rock Cucaracha (C: Heindorf, Ray; L: Murray, Lyn)

**Notes** [1] Also in HEARTBREAK RIDGE.

### 3707 ✦ MARKED FOR MURDER
PRC, 1945

**Musical Score** Zahler, Lee; Grigor, Nico

**Producer(s)** Alexander, Arthur
**Director(s)** Clifton, Elmer
**Screenwriter(s)** Clifton, Elmer

**Cast** Ritter, Tex; O'Brien, Dave; Wilkerson, Guy; McConnell, Marilyn; Hall, Henry; King, Charles; The Milo Twins; Maynard, Kermit

**Song(s)** Tears of Regret (C/L: Weston, Don); Long Time (C/L: Ritter, Tex; Frank, Lt.)

**Notes** There are also vocals of "Froggy Went a Courtin'" and "Great Grand Dad."

### 3708 ✦ MARKED WOMAN
Warner Brothers, 1937

**Producer(s)** Wallis, Hal B.
**Director(s)** Bacon, Lloyd
**Screenwriter(s)** Rossen, Robert; Finkel, Abem

**Cast** Davis, Bette; Bogart, Humphrey; Lane, Lola; Jewell, Isabel; Ciannelli, Eduardo; Bryan, Jane; Marquis, Rosalind; Methot, Mayo; Jenkins, Allen; Litel, John; Welden, Ben

**Song(s)** My Silver Dollar Man (C: Warren, Harry; L: Dubin, Al); Mr. and Mrs. Dokes (C: Jerome, M.K.; L: Scholl, Jack)

### 3709 ✦ THE MARK OF THE HAWK
Universal, 1958

**Musical Score** Seiber, Matyas

**Producer(s)** Young, Lloyd
**Director(s)** Audley, Michael
**Screenwriter(s)** Carmichael, H. Kenn

**Cast** Kitt, Eartha; Poitier, Sidney; Hernandez, Juano; McIntire, John

**Song(s)** This Man Is Mine (C: Darby, Ken; L: Quinn, Don)

### 3710 ✦ MARLOWE
Metro–Goldwyn–Mayer, 1969

**Musical Score** Matz, Peter

**Producer(s)** Katzka, Gabriel; Beckerman, Sidney
**Director(s)** Bogart, Paul

**Screenwriter(s)** Silliphant, Stirling
**Source(s)** *The Little Sister* (novel) Chandler, Raymond

**Cast** Daniels, William; Farrell, Sharon; Moreno, Rita; O'Connor, Carroll; Hunnicutt, Gayle; Garner, James

**Song(s)** Little Sister (C: Matz, Peter; L: Gimbel, Norman)

**Notes** Originally titled THE LITTLE SISTER.

### 3711 ✦ MARRIAGE BY CONTRACT
Tiffany–Stahl, 1928

**Musical Score** Baer, Manny

**Producer(s)** Stahl, John M.
**Director(s)** Flood, James
**Screenwriter(s)** Perez, Paul

**Cast** Miller, Patsy Ruth; Gray, Lawrence; Edeson, Robert; Emerson, Ralph; Palmer, Shirley

**Song(s)** When the Right One Comes Along (C: Wayne, Mabel; L: Gilbert, L. Wolfe); Come Back to Me (C/L: Goldberg, Dave; Joffe, A.E.)

**Notes** No cue sheet available.

### 3712 ✦ THE MARRIAGE-GO-ROUND
Twentieth Century–Fox, 1961

**Musical Score** Frontiere, Dominic

**Producer(s)** Stevens, Leslie
**Director(s)** Lang, Walter
**Screenwriter(s)** Stevens, Leslie

**Cast** Hayward, Susan; Mason, James; Newmar, Julie

**Song(s)** Marriage-Go-Round (C: Spence, Lew; L: Bergman, Alan; Keith, Marilyn)

**Notes** Note the use of Marilyn Bergman's maiden name.

### 3713 ✦ MARRIAGE OF A YOUNG STOCKBROKER
Twentieth Century–Fox, 1971

**Musical Score** Karlin, Fred

**Producer(s)** Turman, Lawrence
**Director(s)** Turman, Lawrence
**Screenwriter(s)** Semple Jr., Lorenzo
**Source(s)** (novel) Webb, Charles

**Cast** Benjamin, Richard; Shimkus, Joanna; Ashley, Elizabeth; West, Adam; Barry, Patricia; Bolling, Tiffany; Prentiss, Ed; Forrest, William

**Song(s)** Can It Be True (C: Karlin, Fred; L: Kymry, Tylwyth)

**Notes** Originally titled THOUGHTS OF A YOUNG STOCK BROKER.

## 3714 ✦ MARRIAGE ON THE ROCKS
Warner Brothers, 1965

**Musical Score** Riddle, Nelson

**Producer(s)** Daniels, William H.
**Director(s)** Donohue, Jack
**Screenwriter(s)** Howard, Cy
**Source(s)** "Community Property" (story) Howard, Cy

**Cast** Sinatra, Frank; Kerr, Deborah; Martin, Dean; Romero, Cesar; Baddeley, Hermione; Bill, Tony; McGiver, John; Sinatra, Nancy; Lopez, Trini; Freeman, Kathleen; Petit, Michael

**Song(s)** There Was a Sinner Man (C/L: Lopez, Trini; Weinstein, Bobby; Hart, Bobby; Barberis, Billy; Randazzo, Teddy)

## 3715 ✦ MARRIED BEFORE BREAKFAST
Metro–Goldwyn–Mayer, 1937

**Musical Score** Snell, Dave

**Producer(s)** Zimbalist, Sam
**Director(s)** Marin, Edwin L.
**Screenwriter(s)** Freeman, Everett; Oppenheimer, George

**Cast** Young, Robert; Rice, Florence; Clayworth, June; Parker, Barnett; Hymer, Warren; Flint, Helen; Franklin, Irene

**Song(s)** Fit As a Fiddle [1] (C: Hoffman, Al; Goodhart, Al; L: Freed, Arthur)

**Notes** [1] Also in SINGIN' IN THE RAIN.

## 3716 ✦ MARRIED IN HOLLYWOOD
Fox, 1929

**Composer(s)** Stamper, Dave
**Lyricist(s)** Thompson, Harlan
**Choreographer(s)** Royce, Edward

**Producer(s)** Fox, William
**Director(s)** Silver, Marcel
**Screenwriter(s)** Thompson, Harlan

**Cast** Murray, J. Harold; Terris, Norma; Catlett, Walter; Patricola, Tom; Palatsy, Irene; Pawle, Lennox

**Song(s)** Opening Number (C/L: Stamper, Dave); Dance Away the Night; Deep in Love (C: Straus, Oscar); Peasant Love Song; Once Upon a Time; A Man—A Maid (C: Straus, Oscar); Bridal Chorus (C: Kay, Arthur); Hungarian Festivities (C/L: Kay, Arthur); Folk Song (C/L: Kay, Arthur); Ship's Ballet (Inst.)

## 3717 ✦ MARSHAL OF GUNSMOKE
Universal, 1944

**Producer(s)** Drake, Oliver
**Director(s)** Keays, Vernon
**Screenwriter(s)** Lively, William

**Cast** Ritter, Tex; Hayden, Russell; Knight, Fuzzy; Holt, Jennifer; Woods, Harry; Rawlinson, Herbert; Bond, Johnny; Whitaker, Slim

**Song(s)** My Saddle Serenade (C/L: Bond, Johnny); Sundown Trail (C/L: Marvin, Johnny)

**Notes** No cue sheet available.

## 3718 ✦ THE MARSHAL'S DAUGHTER
United Artists, 1953

**Musical Score** Calker, Darrell

**Producer(s)** Murray, Ken
**Director(s)** Berke, William
**Screenwriter(s)** Duncan, Bob

**Cast** Anders, Laurie; Gibson, Hoot; Murray, Ken; Lauter, Harry; Bray, Bob; Duncan, Bob

**Song(s)** The Marshal's Daughter (C/L: Jones, Stan); My Heart Has Plenty of Room (C/L: Thrasher, Marjorie); If You Would Only Be Mine (C/L: Rivers, Jack)

## 3719 ✦ MARSHMALLOW MOON

See AARON SLICK FROM PUNKIN CRICK.

## 3720 ✦ MARTY
Paramount, 1955

**Producer(s)** Hecht, Harold
**Director(s)** Mann, Delbert
**Screenwriter(s)** Chayefsky, Paddy
**Source(s)** *Marty* (teleplay) Chayefsky, Paddy

**Cast** Borgnine, Ernest; Blair, Betsy; Minciotti, Esther; Ciolli, Augusta; Steele, Karen; Paris, Jerry

**Song(s)** Hey, Marty (C: Warren, Harry; L: Chayefsky, Paddy)

**Notes** No cue sheet available.

## 3721 ✦ MARX BROTHERS AT THE CIRCUS

See AT THE CIRCUS.

## 3722 ✦ MARYLAND
Twentieth Century–Fox, 1940

**Producer(s)** Markey, Gene
**Director(s)** King, Henry
**Screenwriter(s)** Hill, Ethel; Andrews, Jack

**Cast** Brennan, Walter; Bainter, Fay; Joyce, Brenda; Payne, John; Ruggles, Charles; McDaniel, Hattie; Weaver, Marjorie; Blackmer, Sidney

**Song(s)** Amen! (C/L: Crawford, Joseph)

### 3723 ✦ MARY LOU
Columbia, 1948

**Director(s)**  Dreifuss, Arthur
**Screenwriter(s)**  Webster, M. Coates

**Cast**  Frankie Carle and His Orchestra; Lowery, Robert; Barton, Joan; Farrell, Glenda; Adams, Abigail; Jenks, Frank; Watkin, Pierre

**Song(s)**  Don't Mind My Troubles [1] (C/L: Lee, Lester; Roberts, Allan); I'm Sorry I Didn't Say I'm Sorry [2] (C/L: Lee, Lester; Roberts, Allan); That's Good Enough for Me [3] (C/L: Roberts, Allan; Fisher, Doris); Wasn't It Swell Last Night? (C/L: Roberts, Allan; Fisher, Doris); Carle's Boogie Woogie (Inst.) (C/L: Carle, Frankie); Learning to Speak English (C: Rivero, Facundo; L: Blossner, Ben); Mary Lou (C/L: Lyman, Abe; Waggner, George; Robinson, J. Russel)

**Notes**  No cue sheet available. [1] Considered for SLIGHTLY FRENCH but not used. [2] Also in WHEN A GIRL'S BEAUTIFUL. [3] Also in LITTLE MISS BROADWAY (1947).

### 3724 ✦ MARY POPPINS
Disney, 1964

**Composer(s)**  Sherman, Richard M.; Sherman, Robert B.
**Lyricist(s)**  Sherman, Richard M.; Sherman, Robert B.
**Choreographer(s)**  Breaux, Marc; Wood, Dee Dee

**Producer(s)**  Walsh, Bill
**Director(s)**  Stevenson, Robert
**Screenwriter(s)**  Walsh, Bill; DaGradi, Don
**Source(s)**  Mary Poppins books (novels) Travers, P.L.

**Cast**  Andrews, Julie; Van Dyke, Dick; Tomlinson, David; Johns, Glynis; Baddeley, Hermione; Dotrice, Karen; Garber, Matthew; Lanchester, Elsa; Treacher, Arthur; Owen, Reginald; Wynn, Ed; Shaw, Reta; Darwell, Jane

**Song(s)**  Chim Chim Cher-ee; Feed the Birds (Tuppence a Bag); Fidelity Fiduciary Bank; I Love to Laugh; Jolly Holiday; Let's Go Fly a Kite; The Life I Lead; The Perfect Nanny; Sister Suffragette; A Spoonful of Sugar; Stay Awake; Step in Time; Supercalifragilisticexpialidocious; The Chimpanzoo [1]; You Think—You Blink [1]; The Eyes of Love [1]; Land and Sand [1] [2]

**Notes**  [1] Not used. [2] Music later used for "Trust in Me" from JUNGLE BOOK.

### 3725 ✦ MARY QUEEN OF SCOTS
Universal, 1971

**Musical Score**  Barry, John
**Composer(s)**  Barry, John
**Lyricist(s)**  Black, Don

**Producer(s)**  Wallis, Hal B.
**Director(s)**  Jarrott, Charles
**Screenwriter(s)**  Hale, John

**Cast**  Redgrave, Vanessa; Harris, Beth; Jackson, Glenda; McGoohan, Patrick; Dalton, Timothy; Davenport, Nigel; Howard, Trevor; Massey, Daniel; Holm, Ian

**Song(s)**  Farewell - Farewell (C: Delerue, Georges; L: Hale, John); Mary's Song (L: Mary Queen of Scots); This Way Mary [1]; Wish Now Was Then [1]

**Notes**  [1] Sheet music only.

### 3726 ✦ M*A*S*H
Twentieth Century–Fox, 1969

**Musical Score**  Mandel, Johnny

**Producer(s)**  Preminger, Inge
**Director(s)**  Altman, Robert
**Screenwriter(s)**  Lardner Jr., Ring
**Source(s)**  M*A*S*H (novel) Hooker, Richard

**Cast**  Sutherland, Donald; Gould, Elliott; Skerritt, Tom; Kellerman, Sally; Duvall, Robert; Pflug, Jo Ann; Auberjonois, Rene; Brown, Roger; Burghoff, Gary; Williamson, Fred

**Song(s)**  Suicide Is Painless (C: Mandel, Johnny; L: Altman, Mike)

### 3727 ✦ MASK
Universal, 1985

**Producer(s)**  Starger, Martin
**Director(s)**  Bogdanovich, Peter
**Screenwriter(s)**  Phelan, Anna Hamilton

**Cast**  Cher; Elliott, Sam; Stoltz, Eric; Getty, Estelle; Dern, Laura; Dysart, Richard; Mercurio, Micole; Carey Jr., Harry; Piazza, Ben

**Song(s)**  Where Did the Naughty Little Girl Go (C/L: Guida, Frank; Matthews, P.); Magic Carpet Ride [1] (C/L: Moreve, Rushton; Kay, John); Quarter to Three (C/L: Guida, Frank; Barge, G.; Royster, J.; Anderson, G.); Dirty Work (C/L: Fagen, Donald; Becker, Walter); Do It Again (C/L: Fagen, Donald; Becker, Walter); Not Me (C/L: Guida, Frank; Anderson, G.); Havin' So Much Fun (C/L: Guida, Frank; Barge, G.; Anderson, G.); Because She Wants To (C/L: Dudek, Les); Dear Lady Twist (C/L: Guida, Frank); Roll Me Away (C/L: Seger, Bob)

**Notes**  Some of these songs may not have been written for this picture. [1] Also in LEGAL EAGLES.

### 3728 ✦ THE MASKED RIDER
Universal, 1941

**Producer(s)**  Cowan, Will
**Director(s)**  Taylor, Ray
**Screenwriter(s)**  Lowe, Sherman; McLeod, Victor

**Cast**  Brown, Johnny Mack; Knight, Fuzzy

**Song(s)** Carmencita [1] (C: Rosen, Milton; L: Carter, Everett)

**Notes** [1] Also in BAD MEN OF THE BORDER.

## 3729 ✦ MASK OF DIIJON
PRC, 1946

**Musical Score** Hajos, Karl

**Producer(s)** Alexander, Max; Stern, Alfred
**Director(s)** Landers, Lew
**Screenwriter(s)** St. Claire, Arthur; Jay, Griffin

**Cast** von Stroheim, Erich; Bates, Jeanne

**Song(s)** White Roses (C: Zahler, Lee; L: Cooper, Carroll); Disillusion (C: Zahler, Lee; L: Austin, Billy)

**Notes** Cue sheet doesn't differentiate between vocals and instrumentals.

## 3730 ✦ THE MASKS OF THE DEVIL
Metro–Goldwyn–Mayer, 1928

**Musical Score** Axt, William

**Director(s)** Seastrom, Victor
**Screenwriter(s)** Rubens, Alma
**Source(s)** *The Masks of Erwin Reiner* (novel) Wasserman, Jacob

**Cast** Gilbert, John; Rubens, Alma; Roberts, Theodore; Reicher, Frank; Forbes, Ralph; Von Berne, Eva; Young, Polly Ann

**Song(s)** Live and Love (C: Axt, William; L: Mendoza, David)

## 3731 ✦ MASQUERADE (1929)
Fox, 1929

**Director(s)** Hare, Lumsden; Birdwell, Russell J.
**Screenwriter(s)** Brennan, Frederick Hazlitt; Boylan, Malcolm Stuart
**Source(s)** *The Brass Bowl* (novel) Vance, Louis Joseph

**Cast** Hyams, Leila; Birmingham, Alan; MacDonald, J. Farrell; Hare, Lumsden

**Song(s)** Anything to Hold Your Baby (C/L: Conrad, Con; Gottler, Archie; Mitchell, Sidney D.)

## 3732 ✦ MASQUERADE (1965)
United Artists, 1965

**Musical Score** Green, Philip

**Producer(s)** Relph, Michael; Dearden, Basil
**Director(s)** Dearden, Basil
**Screenwriter(s)** Relph, Michael; Goldman, William
**Source(s)** *Castle Minerva* (novel) Canning, Victor

**Cast** Robertson, Cliff; Hawkins, Jack; Witty, Christopher; Mell, Marisa; Fraser, Bill

**Song(s)** Masquerade (C: Green, Philip; L: Newell, Norman)

## 3733 ✦ MASQUERADE IN MEXICO
Paramount, 1945

**Producer(s)** Tunberg, Karl
**Director(s)** Leisen, Mitchell
**Screenwriter(s)** Tunberg, Karl

**Cast** Lamour, Dorothy; de Cordova, Arturo; Dvorak, Ann; Knowles, Patric; Rigaud, George; Daniels, Billy

**Song(s)** Adios and Farewell, My Lover [1] (C: Jimenez, Marcos A.; L: Jimenez, Marcos A.; Raleigh, Ben); La Petenera (C/L: Galindo, Pedro); Noche de Ronda [5] (C/L: Lara, Maria Teresa); That's Love [2] [3] (C: Lara, Augustin; L: Lara, Augustin; Raleigh, Ben; Wayne, Bernie); Buscandote [3] [7] (C/L: Lara, Augustin); Perfidia [8] (C/L: Dominguez, Alberto); A Night to Remember [4] (C: Ruiz, Gabriel; L: Ruiz, Gabriel; Raleigh, Ben; Wayne, Bernie); Where Is Our Song? [4] (C: Dominguez, Alberto; L: Dominguez, Alberto; Raleigh, Ben; Wayne, Bernie); I'll Search for You [4] (C: Lara, Augustin; L: Raleigh, Ben); Masquerade in Mexico [6] (C: Wayne, Bernie; L: Raleigh, Ben); Forever Mine [9] (C: Lara, Maria Teresa; L: Lisbona, Eddie; Musel, Robert)

**Notes** [1] English lyrics by Raleigh. The songs's Spanish title is "Adios Mariquita Linda." [2] English lyrics by Raleigh and Wayne. The song's Spanish title is "Buscandote." [3] Same song. [4] Not used. [5] Titled "And So I Dream" with English lyrics by Wanda Wood. However, these were probably not used in the picture. Also (sometimes with English lyrics) in SOMBRERO (MGM); Spanish language version of THE BIG BROADCAST OF 1938 (Paramount); HAVANA ROSE (Republic) and RIDE CLEAR OF DIABLO (Universal). [6] Not in film. Written for exploitation only. [7] Also in STALLION ROAD (Warner Brothers). [8] Also in STARDUST ON THE SAGE (Republic) with additional English lyrics and in FATHER TAKES A WIFE (RKO). [9] Sheet music only.

## 3734 ✦ MASSACRE
Twentieth Century–Fox, 1956

**Musical Score** Curiel, Gonzalo

**Producer(s)** Lippert Jr., Robert L.
**Director(s)** King, Louis
**Screenwriter(s)** Beauchamp, D.D.

**Cast** Clark, Dane; Craig, James; Roth, Marta; Fernandez, Jaime; Ferrusquilla; Torruco, Miguel

**Song(s)** El Jinete (C/L: Jimeniz, Jose Alfredo)

## 3735 ✦ MASTER OF THE WORLD
American International, 1961

**Musical Score** Baxter, Les

**Producer(s)** Nicholson, James H.
**Director(s)** Witney, William
**Screenwriter(s)** Matheson, Richard
**Source(s)** *Master of the World* (novel) Verne, Jules

**Cast** Price, Vincent; Bronson, Charles; Hull, Henry; Webster, Mary; Franklham, David

**Song(s)** Master of the World (C: Baxter, Les; L: Adelson, Lenny); Come Dance My Love (C/L: Baxter, Les)

**Notes** No cue sheet available.

### 3736 ◆ THE MATCH KING
Warner Brothers, 1932

**Producer(s)** Wallis, Hal B.
**Director(s)** Bretherton, Howard
**Screenwriter(s)** Branch, Houston
**Source(s)** (novel) Thorvaldson, Elinar

**Cast** William, Warren; Damita, Lily; Farrell, Glenda; Huber, Harold; Charters, Spencer; Hale, Alan

**Song(s)** On the Beach at Waikiki (C/L: Cunha, Sonny)

### 3737 ◆ THE MATCHMAKER
Paramount, 1958

**Musical Score** Deutsch, Adolph

**Producer(s)** Hartman, Don
**Director(s)** Anthony, Joseph
**Screenwriter(s)** Hayes, John Michael
**Source(s)** *The Matchmaker* (play) Wilder, Thornton

**Cast** Booth, Shirley; Perkins, Anthony; MacLaine, Shirley; Ford, Paul

**Song(s)** Love, Lovely Love [1] (C/L: Deutsch, Adolph)

**Notes** [1] Not used. Also not used in HELLER IN PINK TIGHTS.

### 3738 ◆ MATING CALL
Paramount, 1928

**Producer(s)** Hughes, Howard
**Director(s)** Cruze, James
**Screenwriter(s)** Mankiewicz, Herman J.
**Source(s)** *The Mating Call* (novel) Beach, Rex

**Cast** Meighan, Thomas; Brent, Evelyn; Adoree, Renee; Foster, Helen; Roscoe, Alan

**Song(s)** The Mating Call [1] (C/L: Broones, Martin; Ring, Frances)

**Notes** No cue sheet available. [1] The *AFI Catalog* says William Axt and David Mendoza wrote the song. Sheet music indicates otherwise.

### 3739 ◆ THE MATING GAME
Metro–Goldwyn–Mayer, 1959

**Musical Score** Alexander, Jeff

**Producer(s)** Barry Jr., Philip
**Director(s)** Marshall, George
**Screenwriter(s)** Roberts, William
**Source(s)** *The Darling Buds of May* (novel) Bates, H.S.

**Cast** Reynolds, Debbie; Randall, Tony; Douglas, Paul; Clark, Fred; Merkel, Una; Ober, Philip; Coolidge, Philip; Lane, Charles

**Song(s)** The Mating Game (C: Strouse, Charles; L: Adams, Lee)

**Notes** There is also a vocal of "I've Got You Under My Skin" by Cole Porter.

### 3740 ◆ THE MATING SEASON
Paramount, 1951

**Musical Score** Lilley, Joseph J.

**Producer(s)** Brackett, Charles
**Director(s)** Leisen, Mitchell
**Screenwriter(s)** Brackett, Charles; Reisch, Walter; Breen, Richard L.

**Cast** Tierney, Gene; Lund, John; Hopkins, Miriam; Ritter, Thelma; Sterling, Jan; Keating, Larry

**Song(s)** The Mating Season (C/L: Livingston, Jay; Evans, Ray); Je N'en Connais Pas La Fin [1] (C: Monnot, Marguerite; L: Asso, Raymond); My Lost Melody [2] (C: Monnot, Marguerite; L: Rome, Harold)

**Notes** Called A RELATIVE STRANGER before release. [1] Also in SINGAPORE (Universal). Same music as "My Lost Melody." [2] Lyric written for exploitation to the tune of "Je N'en Connais Pas La Fin."

### 3741 ◆ THE MATRIMONIAL BED
Warner Brothers, 1930

**Director(s)** Curtiz, Michael
**Screenwriter(s)** Thew, Harvey; Hicks, Seymour
**Source(s)** *The Matrimonial Bed* (play) Mirande, Yves; Mouezy-Eon, Andre

**Cast** Fay, Frank; Tashman, Lilyan; Gleason, James; Mercer, Beryl; Oakland, Vivian

**Song(s)** Fleur d'Amour (C: Meyer, George W.; Gottler, Archie; L: Mitchell, Sidney D.)

**Notes** No cue sheet available.

### 3742 ◆ A MATTER OF INNOCENCE
Universal, 1967

**Musical Score** Legrand, Michel
**Composer(s)** Legrand, Michel
**Lyricist(s)** Black, Don

**Producer(s)** Granat, George
**Director(s)** Green, Guy
**Screenwriter(s)** Hall, Willis; Waterhouse, Keith

**Cast** Mills, Hayley; Howard, Trevor; Kapoor, Shashi; de Banzie, Brenda; Routledge, Patricia

**Song(s)** Oh La De Dah; Pretty Polly

**Notes** Originally titled PRETTY POLLY.

## 3743 ✦ A MATTER OF TIME
American International, 1976

**Musical Score**   Oliviero, Nino

**Producer(s)**   Skirball, Jack H.; Grainger, Edmund
**Director(s)**   Minnelli, Vincente
**Screenwriter(s)**   Gay, John

**Cast**   Minnelli, Liza; Bergman, Ingrid; Boyer, Charles; Andros, Spiros

**Song(s)**   A Matter of Time (C: Ebb, Fred; L: Kander, John); The Me I Haven't Met Yet (C: Ebb, Fred; L: Kander, John)

**Notes**   No cue sheet available. A remake of the film THE FILM OF MEMORY by Maurice Druon. There is also a vocal of "Do It Again" by George Gershwin and B.G. DeSylva.

## 3744 ✦ A MATTER OF WHO
Metro–Goldwyn–Mayer, 1962

**Musical Score**   Astley, Edwin

**Producer(s)**   Shenson, Walter; Holmes, Milton
**Director(s)**   Chaffey, Don
**Screenwriter(s)**   Holmes, Milton

**Cast**   Terry-Thomas; Ziemann, Sonja; Nicol, Alex; Blackman, Honor

**Song(s)**   A Matter of Who (C/L: Russell, Bob)

## 3745 ✦ THE MAVERICK QUEEN
Republic, 1956

**Musical Score**   Young, Victor

**Producer(s)**   Kane, Joseph
**Director(s)**   Kane, Joseph
**Screenwriter(s)**   Gamet, Kenneth; Scott, DeVallon
**Source(s)**   *The Maverick Queen* (novel) Grey, Zane

**Cast**   Stanwyck, Barbara; Sullivan, Barry; Brady, Scott; Ford, Wallace; Murphy, Mary

**Song(s)**   The Maverick Queen (C: Young, Victor; L: Washington, Ned)

**Notes**   There is also a vocal of "My Lulu."

## 3746 ✦ MAXIMUM OVERDRIVE
De Laurentiis Entertainment, 1986

**Musical Score**   AC/DC

**Producer(s)**   Schumacher, Martha
**Director(s)**   King, Stephen
**Screenwriter(s)**   King, Stephen
**Source(s)**   "Trucks" (story) King, Stephen

**Cast**   Estevez, Emilio; Hingle, Pat; Harrington, Laura; Smith, Yeardley; Short, John; Quinn, J.C.; Faison, Frankie; Esposito, Giancarlo

**Song(s)**   Who Made Who (C/L: Young, Angus; Young, Malcolm; Johnson, Brian)

**Notes**   No cue sheet available.

## 3747 ✦ MAYBE DARWIN WAS RIGHT
Warner Brothers, 1942

**Song(s)**   Rosenbloom That's Me (C: Jerome, M.K.; L: Scholl, Jack)

**Notes**   Short subject.

## 3748 ✦ MAYBE IT'S LOVE
Warner Brothers, 1930

**Composer(s)**   Gottler, Archie; Meyer, George W.
**Lyricist(s)**   Mitchell, Sidney D.

**Director(s)**   Wellman, William A.
**Screenwriter(s)**   Jackson, Joseph; Canfield, Mark [1]
**Source(s)**   "College Widows" (story) Ade, George

**Cast**   Bennett, Joan; Brown, Joe E.; Hall, James; Lee, Laura; Randolf, Anders; Getchell, Sumner; Irving, George; Bickel, George; Jones, Howard

**Song(s)**   Parsons; Maybe It's Love; The All American; Keep It Up for Upton; I Love to Do It [2]

**Notes**   [1] Pseudonym for Darryl Zanuck. [2] Not used.

## 3749 ✦ THE MAYOR OF 44TH STREET
RKO, 1942

**Musical Score**   Webb, Roy
**Composer(s)**   Revel, Harry
**Lyricist(s)**   Greene, Mort

**Producer(s)**   Reid, Cliff
**Director(s)**   Green, Alfred E.
**Screenwriter(s)**   Foster, Lewis R.; Ryan, Frank
**Source(s)**   (article) Davis, Luther; Cleveland, John

**Cast**   Murphy, George; Shirley, Anne; Gargan, William; Barthelmess, Richard; Merrill, Joan; Freddy Martin and His Orchestra; Wickes, Mary

**Song(s)**   You're Bad for Me [3]; When There's a Breeze on Lake Louise; A Millon Miles from Manhattan; Your Face Looks Familiar [1]; Heavenly, Isn't It [2]

**Notes**   [1] Used instrumentally only. [2] Used instrumentally only. Later sung in RADIO STARS ON PARADE. [3] Also in FALLEN SPARROW.

## 3750 ✦ MAYTIME
Metro–Goldwyn–Mayer, 1937

**Musical Score**   Stothart, Herbert; Ward, Edward
**Composer(s)**   Romberg, Sigmund
**Lyricist(s)**   Young, Rida Johnson
**Choreographer(s)**   Raset, Val

**Producer(s)**   Stromberg, Hunt
**Director(s)**   Leonard, Robert Z.

**Screenwriter(s)** Langley, Noel
**Source(s)** *Maytime* (musical) Romberg, Sigmund; Young, Rida Johnson

**Cast** MacDonald, Jeanette; Eddy, Nelson; Barrymore, John; Brown, Tom; Bing, Herman; The Don Cossack Chorus; Judels, Charles; Rumann, Sig; Porcasi, Paul

**Song(s)** May Pole (C/L: Ward, Edward); Will You Remember; Students' Drinking Song (1); Vive L'Opera (C: Stothart, Herbert; L: Forrest, Chet; Wright, Bob); Students' Drinking Song (2) (C/L: Stothart, Herbert); Street Singer (C/L: Stothart, Herbert); La Tzarine [1] (C: Tchaikovsky, Peter I.; L: Wright, Bob; Forrest, Chet)

**Notes** There are also vocals of "Les Filles de Cadiz" by Delibes; "Le Regiment de Sambre et Meuse" by Planquette; "La Marseillaise" by de Lisle; "Caro Nome" and "La Donna e Mobile" from RIGOLETTO; "Anvil Chorus" from IL TROVATORE by Verdi; "Largo al Factotum" from BARBER OF SEVILLE by Rossini; "O Du, Mein Holder Abendstern" from TANNHAUSER by Wagner; "Soldiers' Chorus" from FAUST by Gounod; "Sextette" from LUCIA DI LAMMERMOOR by Donizetti; Overture from WILLIAM TELL by Rossini; "Carry Me Back to Old Virginny" by James A. Bland and "Les Huguenots" by Meyerbeer. [1] Based on the music of the 5th Symphony. French lyrics by Gilles Guilbert.

## 3751 ✦ MCCABE AND MRS. MILLER
### Warner Brothers, 1971

**Composer(s)** Cohen, Leonard
**Lyricist(s)** Cohen, Leonard

**Producer(s)** Foster, David; Brower, Mitchell
**Director(s)** Altman, Robert
**Screenwriter(s)** Altman, Robert; McKay, Brian
**Source(s)** *McCabe* (novel) Naughton, Edmund

**Cast** Beatty, Warren; Christie, Julie; Auberjonois, Rene; Millais, Hugh; Schuck, John; Duvall, Shelley; Fischer, Corey; Murphy, Michael; Carradine, Keith; Devane, William; Holland, Anthony

**Song(s)** The Stranger Song; Winter Lady

## 3752 ✦ MCLINTOCK
### United Artists, 1963

**Musical Score** De Vol, Frank
**Composer(s)** Dunham, "By"
**Lyricist(s)** Dunham, "By"

**Producer(s)** Wayne, Michael
**Director(s)** McLaglen, Andrew V.
**Screenwriter(s)** Grant, James Edward

**Cast** Wayne, John; O'Hara, Maureen; Powers, Stefanie; Wayne, Patrick; de Carlo, Yvonne; Buchanan, Edgar; Cabot, Bruce; Lopez, Perry; Pate, Michael; Wills, Chill; Krueschen, Jack; Blanchard, Mari

**Song(s)** Love in the Country (C: De Vol, Frank); Just Right for Me; Katie with the Light Red Hair

## 3753 ✦ ME AND MY GAL
### Fox, 1932

**Director(s)** Walsh, Raoul
**Screenwriter(s)** Kober, Arthur

**Cast** Tracy, Spencer; Bennett, Joan; Burns, Marion; Walsh, George

**Song(s)** Oleo the Gigolo [1] (C: Hanley, James F.; L: Burton, Val)

**Notes** Previously titled PIER 13. [1] Also in SAILOR'S LUCK.

## 3754 ✦ THE MEANING OF LIFE

See MONTY PYTHON'S THE MEANING OF LIFE.

## 3755 ✦ MEAN STREETS
### Warner Brothers, 1973

**Producer(s)** Taplin, Jonathan T.
**Director(s)** Scorsese, Martin
**Screenwriter(s)** Scorsese, Martin; Martin, Mardik

**Cast** Keitel, Harvey; De Niro, Robert; Robinson, Amy; Danova, Cesare

**Song(s)** Be My Baby (C/L: Barry, Jeff; Spector, Phil; Greenwich, Ellie); Tell Me (You're Coming Back) (C/L: Jagger, Mick; Richards, Keith); I Looked Away (C/L: Whitlock, B.; Clapton, Eric); The Jumping Jack Flash (C/L: Jagger, Mick; Richards, Keith); Those Oldies but Goodies (Remind Me of You) (C/L: Politi, Paul; Curinga, Nick); Desiree (C/L: Cooper, Leslie; Johnson, Clarence); Canta Pe Me (C/L: De Curtis, Ernesto; Bovio, Libero); I Met Him on a Sunday (C/L: Owens, Shirley; Harris, Addie; Coley, Doris; Lee, Beverly); Florence (C/L: Winley, Paul; McMichaels, Julius); Please Mr. Postman (C/L: Garrett, W.; Dobbins, G.; Gorman, F.; Gert, B.); Malafemmena (C/L: Toto); Maruzzella (C/L: Carosone, Renato; Bonagura, Enzo); Addio Sogni di Gloria (C/L: Innocenzi, Carlo; Rivi, Marcella); You (C: Goddard, Dave; Vannata, Larry); Munasteria e Santa Chiarra (C/L: Barberis, Alberto; Galdieri, Michel); Shoop Shoop Song (It's in His Kiss) (C/L: Clark, Rudy); I Love You So (C/L: Norton, Sonny; Levy, Morris); Rubbe

**Notes** Some of these songs were not written for the film. They are all background vocals.

## 3756 ✦ MEATBALLS
### Paramount, 1979

**Composer(s)** Bernstein, Elmer
**Lyricist(s)** Gimbel, Norman

**Producer(s)** Goldberg, Dan
**Director(s)** Ramis, Harold
**Screenwriter(s)** Goldberg, Dan; Blum, Len; Allen, Janis; Ramis, Harold

**Cast** Murray, Bill; Atkin, Harvey; Lynch, Kate; Banham, Russ; De Bell, Kristine; Torbov, Sarah; Makepeace, Chris

**Song(s)** Are You Ready for the Summer; Meatballs; Good Friend; Moondust; Makin' It (C/L: Fekaris, Dino; Perren, Freddie); Let's Walla Walla Down By the Mango Tree [1] (C/L: Blum, Len; Ley, Bruce)

**Notes** [1] Not on cue sheet.

## 3757 ✦ MEATBALLS PART II
### Tri-Star, 1984

**Musical Score** Harrison, Ken

**Producer(s)** Bishop, Tony; Poe, Stephen
**Director(s)** Wiederhorn, Ken
**Screenwriter(s)** Singer, Bruce

**Cast** Reubens, Paul; Hahn, Archie; Ryan, Nick; Rowe, Misty; Boosler, Elayne; Camp, Hamilton; Larroquette, John

**Song(s)** We've Been Waiting for the Summer (C: Harrison, Ken; L: Hilton, Hermine)

**Notes** No cue sheet available.

## 3758 ✦ MEDALS

See SEVEN DAYS LEAVE.

## 3759 ✦ MEDICINE BALL CARAVAN
### Warner Brothers, 1971

**Producer(s)** Reichenbach, Francois; Donahue, Tom
**Director(s)** Reichenbach, Francois

**Cast** Donahue, Tom; Melvin, Milin; Lochman, Chan; Gravey, Wavey; Nourton, Willie; Titcomb, Maurine; Peel, David; King, B.B.; Cooper, Alice; Kershaw, Doug; Valentino, Sal; Stoneground

**Song(s)** Hippie from Olema (C/L: Levinger, Lowell); How Blue Can You Get (C/L: Feather, Leonard; Feather, Jane); (All I Want) Is Just a Little Love (C/L: King, B.B.); America (C/L: Smith, S.; Musicus, T.); Act Naturally (C/L: Russell, Johnny; Morrison, Vonie); Louisiana Man (C/L: Kershaw, Doug); Battle of New Orleans (C/L: Driftwood, Jimmy); Dreambo (C/L: Valentino, Sal); Black Juju (C/L: Dunaway, Dennis); Freakout (C/L: Stoneground); It Takes a Lot to Laugh, It Takes a Train to Cry (C/L: Dylan, Bob); Up Against the Wall Motherfucker (C/L: Peel, David); Free the People (C/L: Keith, Barbara)

**Notes** Released in Great Britain as WE HAVE COME FOR YOUR DAUGHTERS. A documentary.

## 3760 ✦ MEET DANNY WILSON
### Universal, 1951

**Choreographer(s)** Belfer, Hal

**Producer(s)** Goldstein, Leonard
**Director(s)** Pevney, Joseph
**Screenwriter(s)** McGuire, Don

**Cast** Sinatra, Frank; Burr, Raymond; Nicol, Alex; Winters, Shelley

**Song(s)** You're a Sweetheart [1] (C: McHugh, Jimmy; L: Adamson, Harold); Lonesome Man Blues (C/L: Oliver, Sy); All of Me (C/L: Simons, Seymour; Marks, Gerald)

**Notes** There are also vocals of "She's Funny That Way" by Richard Whiting and Neil Moret; "A Good Man Is Hard to Find" by Eddie Green; "That Old Black Magic" by Johnny Mercer and Harold Arlen; "When You're Smiling" by Mark Fisher, Joe Goodwin and Larry Shay; "I've Got a Crush on You" by George and Ira Gershwin and "How Deep Is the Ocean" by Irving Berlin. It is not known if any of these songs were written for this picture. [1] Also in HOW'S ABOUT IT and YOU'RE A SWEETHEART.

## 3761 ✦ MEET ME AFTER THE SHOW
### Twentieth Century–Fox, 1951

**Musical Score** Darby, Ken
**Composer(s)** Styne, Jule
**Lyricist(s)** Robin, Leo
**Choreographer(s)** Cole, Jack

**Producer(s)** Jessel, Raymond
**Director(s)** Sale, Richard
**Screenwriter(s)** Loos, Mary; Sale, Richard

**Cast** Grable, Betty; Carey, Macdonald; Calhoun, Rory; Albert, Eddie; Clark, Fred; Andrews, Lois; Ryan, Irene; Condos, Steve; Brandow, Jerry; Verdon, Gwen

**Song(s)** (Ev'ry Day Is Like) A Day in Maytime; Behind the Footlights (C/L: Darby, Ken); Meet Me After the Show; Betting on a Man; It's a Hot Night in Alaska; No Talent Joe; I Feel Like Dancing; Night Music (Inst.) (C: Schaefer, Hal); Let Go of My Heart [1]; Li'l Ol' You and Li'l Ol' Me [1]

**Notes** There is also a vocal of "Miami" by Ralph Rainger and Leo Robin. [1] Not used.

## 3762 ✦ MEET ME AT DAWN
### Twentieth Century–Fox, 1947

**Musical Score** Spoliansky, Mischa

**Producer(s)** Hellman, Marcel
**Director(s)** Freeland, Thornton
**Screenwriter(s)** Storm, Lesley; Seymour, James

3763 ♦ MEET ME AT THE FAIR

**Cast** Eythe, William; Holloway, Stanley; Campbell, Beatrice; Thorpe, George; Browne, Irene; Court, Haze; Sydney, Basil; Rutherford, Margaret; Reeve, Ada; Hyde-White, Wilfrid

**Song(s)** I Guess I'm not the Type (C: Spoliansky, Mischa; L: Musel, Robert)


## 3763 ♦ MEET ME AT THE FAIR
### Universal, 1953

**Musical Score** Rosen, Milton
**Choreographer(s)** Williams, Kenny

**Producer(s)** Cohen, Albert J.
**Director(s)** Sirk, Douglas
**Screenwriter(s)** Wallace, Irving
**Source(s)** *The Great Companions* (novel) Markey, Gene

**Cast** Dailey, Dan; Mathews, Carole [1]; Crothers, Benjamin "Scatman"; Allen, Chet; Lynn, Diana; O'Brian, Hugh; Williams, Rhys; Chandler, George

**Song(s)** I Was There (C/L: Crothers, Benjamin "Scatman"; Miller, F.E.); Remember the Time (C/L: Williams, Kenny; Wright, Marvin); Meet Me at the Fair [2] (C: Rosen, Milton; L: Herbert, Frederick); I Got the Shiniest Mouth in Town (C/L: Freberg, Stan)

**Notes** There are also vocals of "All God's Chillun Got Wings," "Oh Susanna," "Ave Maria" and "Bill Bailey, Won't You Please Come Home?" by Hughie Cannon and "Sweet Genevieve" by George Cooper and Henry Tucker. [1] Dubbed by Jo Ann Greer. [2] Also in MAN OF A THOUSAND FACES.


## 3764 ♦ MEET ME IN LAS VEGAS
### Metro–Goldwyn–Mayer, 1956

**Composer(s)** Brodszky, Nicholas
**Lyricist(s)** Cahn, Sammy
**Choreographer(s)** Loring, Eugene; Pan, Hermes

**Producer(s)** Pasternak, Joe
**Director(s)** Rowland, Roy
**Screenwriter(s)** Lennart, Isobel

**Cast** Dailey, Dan; Charisse, Cyd; Moorehead, Agnes; Darvas, Lili; Backus, Jim; Karlweis, Oscar; Montevecchi, Liliane; Williams, Cara; Kerris, George; Lynn, Betty; Rugolo, Pete; Colonna, Jerry; Henreid, Paul; Horne, Lena; Laine, Frankie; Sawamura, Mitsuko

**Song(s)** Meet Me in Las Vegas; If You Can Dream; The Gal with the Yaller Shoes; I Refuse to Rock 'N' Roll; My Lucky Charm; Hell Hath No Fury; Frankie and Johnny (C: Traditional); You Got Looks [1]; It's Fun to Be in Love [2]

**Notes** Sammy Davis Jr. sang "Frankie and Johnny" offscreen. Released internationally as VIVA LAS VEGAS. [1] Used instrumentally only. [2] Recorded but not used.


## 3765 ♦ MEET ME IN ST. LOUIS
### Metro–Goldwyn–Mayer, 1944

**Musical Score** Edens, Roger
**Composer(s)** Martin, Hugh; Blane, Ralph
**Lyricist(s)** Martin, Hugh; Blane, Ralph
**Choreographer(s)** Walters, Charles

**Producer(s)** Freed, Arthur
**Director(s)** Minnelli, Vincente
**Screenwriter(s)** Brecher, Irving; Finklehoffe, Fred F.
**Source(s)** *5135 Kensington* (novel) Benson, Sally

**Cast** Garland, Judy; O'Brien, Margaret; Astor, Mary [4]; Ames, Leon [1]; Main, Marjorie; Bremer, Lucille; Drake, Tom; Davenport, Harry; Lockhart, June; Wills, Chill; Daniels Jr., Henry H.

**Song(s)** The Boy Next Door; Skip to My Lou [5] (C/L: Traditional; Martin, Hugh; Blane, Ralph); The Trolley Song; You and I (C: Brown, Nacio Herb; L: Freed, Arthur); Have Yourself a Merry Little Christmas; Boys and Girls Like You and Me [2] (C: Rodgers, Richard; L: Hammerstein II, Oscar); Know Where You're Goin' and You'll Get There [3]

**Notes** There are also vocals of "Meet Me in St. Louis, Louis" by Kerry Mills and Andrew B. Sterling; "Under the Bamboo Tree" by Bob Cole and J. Rosamond Johnson; and "Over the Bannister." [1] Dubbed by Arthur Freed. [2] Deleted from final print and also deleted from TAKE ME OUT TO THE BALL GAME. Originally written for stage version of SOUTH PACIFIC. [3] Not used. [4] Dubbed by D. Markas. [5] Martin and Blane's arrangement of this folk favorite was originally recorded in 1941 by The Martins (Hugh Martin, Jo Jean Rogers, Phyllis Rogers and Ralph Blane) on Columbia 36480.


## 3766 ♦ MEET ME ON BROADWAY
### Columbia, 1946

**Composer(s)** Chaplin, Saul
**Lyricist(s)** DeLange, Eddie
**Choreographer(s)** Cole, Jack

**Producer(s)** Kelly, Burt
**Director(s)** Jason, Leigh
**Screenwriter(s)** Bricker, George; Henley, Jack

**Cast** Reynolds, Marjorie [3]; Byington, Spring [4]; Brady, Fred; Falkenburg, Jinx; Tindall, Loren; Lockhart, Gene; Jenkins, Allen; Forrest, William; Rice, Jack

**Song(s)** Fifth Avenue; Only for Me; I Never Had a Chance; Is It Worth It; She Was a Good Girl (C/L: Roberts, Allan; Fisher, Doris); No One Seems to Care; Daffodils and Red Red Robins [1]; Christmas Came in May [2]

**Notes** Previously titled SONG OF BROADWAY. Hirschhorn says Billy Daniels did the choreography. This isn't listed in Cole's biography. [1] Used as instrumental only, though recorded by Martha Mears. [2] Cut. [3] Dubbed by Martha Mears. [4] Dubbed by Elva Kellogg.

## 3767 ✦ MEET MISS BOBBY SOCKS
### Columbia, 1944

**Composer(s)**  Kent, Walter
**Lyricist(s)**  Gannon, Kim

**Producer(s)**  Richmond, Ted
**Director(s)**  Tryon, Glenn
**Screenwriter(s)**  Bolton, Muriel Roy

**Cast**  Merrick, Lynn; Freeman, Howard; Parrish, Pat; Bliss, Sally; Louis Jordan and his Tympany Five; Crosby, Bob; The Kim Loo Sisters [2]

**Song(s)**  I'm Not Afraid; Come Rain Come Shine

**Notes**  There are also vocals of "Fellow on a Furlough" by Bobby Worth; "Two Heavens" by Don George and Ted Grouya; "Come with Me Honey" by Mack David, Joan Whitney and Alex Kramer; "Deacon Jones" by Johnny Lange, Hy Heath, and Richard Loring and "Take It Easy" by Irving Taylor, Vic Mizzy, and Albert DeBru (also in YELLOW ROSE OF TEXAS and BABES ON SWING STREET). [1] Not written for film. [2] Consisted of Alice, Margaret and Patricia Louie.

## 3768 ✦ MEET THE BARON
### Metro–Goldwyn–Mayer, 1933

**Composer(s)**  McHugh, Jimmy
**Lyricist(s)**  Fields, Dorothy

**Producer(s)**  Selznick, David O.
**Director(s)**  Lang, Walter
**Screenwriter(s)**  Rivkin, Allen; Wolfson, P.J.; Kober, Arthur; Wells, William K.

**Cast**  Pearl, Jack; Durante, Jimmy; Pitts, ZaSu; Ted Healy and His Stooges [1]; Oliver, Edna May; The Metro–Goldwyn–Mayer Girls; Bard, Ben

**Song(s)**  Hail to the Baron Munchausen; Musical Opening; Bus Ride Sequence; Minnie the Moocher (C/L: Calloway, Cab; Mills, Irving); Clean As a Whistle; Drumming Out; Don't Blame Me [2]; Yes Me [2] (C/L: Rodgers, Richard; Durante, Jimmy; Hart, Lorenz)

**Notes**  [1] The Stooges were Moe Howard, Larry Howard and Larry Fine. [2] Not used.

## 3769 ✦ MEET THE BOY FRIEND
### Republic, 1937

**Composer(s)**  Ingraham, Roy
**Lyricist(s)**  Tobias, Harry

**Producer(s)**  Clark, Colbert
**Director(s)**  Staub, Ralph
**Screenwriter(s)**  Ropes, Bradford

**Cast**  Carlyle, David; Hughes, Carol; Hymer, Warren; Kelton, Pert; Tombes, Andrew; Andre, Gwili; Oscar and Elmer; Burnette, Smiley; Kinsky, Leonid; Beverly Hill Billies

**Song(s)**  Sweet Lips (Kiss My Blues Away); You Are My Rosebud (C/L: Colombo, Alberto); Singing My Hill-Billy Songs (C/L: Burnette, Smiley); This Business of Love; The Sandman Is Waiting (C/L: Colombo, Alberto); To Know You Care

## 3770 ✦ MEET THE PEOPLE
### Metro–Goldwyn–Mayer, 1944

**Musical Score**  Hayton, Lennie
**Composer(s)**  Fain, Sammy
**Lyricist(s)**  Harburg, E.Y.
**Choreographer(s)**  Lee, Sammy; Walters, Charles; Donohue, Jack

**Producer(s)**  Harburg, E.Y.
**Director(s)**  Riesner, Charles F.
**Screenwriter(s)**  Herzig, Sig [2]; Saidy, Fred
**Source(s)**  *Meet the People* (musical) Myers, Henry; Eliscu, Edward; Gorney, Jay

**Cast**  Ball, Lucille; Powell, Dick; O'Brien, Virginia; Lahr, Bert; Ragland, Rags; Allyson, June; Vaughn Monroe and His Orchestra; Spike Jones and His City Slickers

**Song(s)**  I Can't Dance (C/L: Williams; Gaines); In Times Like These; Meet the People [1] (C: Gorney, Jay; L: Meyers, Henry); Shicklegruber; Heave Ho! . . . Let the Wind Blow (C: Arlen, Harold); I Like to Recognize the Tune (C: Rodgers, Richard; L: Hart, Lorenz); Say That We're Sweethearts Again (C/L: Brent, Earl); It's Smart to Be People (C: Lane, Burton)

**Notes**  Dick Powell's last musical. [1] From Broadway revue. [2] Billed as S.M. Herzig.

## 3771 ✦ MEET THE WILDCAT
### Universal, 1940

**Producer(s)**  Sandford, Joseph G.
**Director(s)**  Lubin, Arthur
**Screenwriter(s)**  Gottlieb, Alex

**Cast**  Bellamy, Ralph; Lindsay, Margaret; Schildkraut, Joseph; Jenkins, Allen

**Song(s)**  Heart of Mine [1] (C: Skinner, Frank; L: Freed, Ralph)

**Notes**  [1] Used instrumentally only

## 3772 ✦ MEET WHIPLASH WILLIE

See THE FORTUNE COOKIE.

## 3773 ✦ MEGAFORCE
### Twentieth Century–Fox, 1982

**Musical Score**  Immel, Jerrold

**Producer(s)**  Ruddy, Albert S.
**Director(s)**  Needham, Hal

**Screenwriter(s)**  Whittaker, James; Ruddy, Albert S.; Needham, Hal; Morgan, Andre

**Cast**  Bostwick, Barry; Khambatta, Persis; Beck, Michael; Mulhare, Edward; Furth, George; Silva, Henry

**Song(s)**  Mega Force (C/L: Howarth, Tod; Russell, Kevin; McClarty, J.; Cain, Jonathan)

## 3774 ✦ MELINDA
Metro–Goldwyn–Mayer, 1972

**Musical Score**  Butler, Jerry; Peters, Jerry
**Composer(s)**  Butler, Jerry; Peters, Jerry
**Lyricist(s)**  Butler, Jerry; Peters, Jerry

**Producer(s)**  Atkins, Perry
**Director(s)**  Robertson, Hugh A.
**Screenwriter(s)**  Elder III, Lonne

**Cast**  Lockhart, Calvin; Cash, Rosalind; McGee, Vonetta; Stevens, Paul; Tarkington, Rockne; Hagen, Ross; Elder, Lonne

**Song(s)**  Frankie's Car; It's Frankie J; Love Is; Baby Please Don't Go

## 3775 ✦ MELODY
Disney, 1953

**Musical Score**  Dubin, Joseph S.
**Composer(s)**  Burke, Sonny
**Lyricist(s)**  Webster, Paul Francis

**Song(s)**  The Bird and the Cricket and the Willow Tree; Roll-Call Song (C: Dubin, Joseph S.; L: Huemer, Dick); Melody; Lemon Drop Moon; The Old Iron Horse; Motherhood; We Sing About the Moon [1] (C: Burke, Sonny; L: Webster, Paul Francis; Huemer, Dick)

**Notes**  Cartoon. No credit sheet available. [1] BMI list only.

## 3776 ✦ MELODY AND MOONLIGHT
Republic, 1940

**Composer(s)**  Styne, Jule
**Lyricist(s)**  Brown, George; Meyer, Sol
**Choreographer(s)**  Broadbent, Aida

**Producer(s)**  North, Robert
**Director(s)**  Santley, Joseph
**Screenwriter(s)**  Ropes, Bradford

**Cast**  Downs, Johnny; Allen, Barbara Jo [1]; Colonna, Jerry; Frazee, Jane; Lee, Mary; Jenks, Frank; Hale, Jonathan; The Kidoodlers

**Song(s)**  Tahiti Honey [3]; Top of the Mornin'; Rooftop Serenade; I Close My Eyes [2]; Colonna and Vague Specialty; Melody and Moonlight

**Notes**  [1] Also known as Vera Vague. She is billed here as Barbara Allen. [2] Also in MOUNTAIN MOONLIGHT. [3] Also in TAHITI HONEY.

## 3777 ✦ MELODY CRUISE
RKO, 1933

**Composer(s)**  Burton, Val; Jason, Will
**Lyricist(s)**  Burton, Val; Jason, Will
**Choreographer(s)**  Gould, Dave

**Producer(s)**  Brock, Lou
**Screenwriter(s)**  Holmes, Ben; Sandrich, Mark

**Cast**  Ruggles, Charles; Harris, Phil; Mack, Helen; Nissen, Greta; Chandler, Chick; Brewster, June; Gateson, Marjorie

**Song(s)**  Isn't This a Night for Love; Ticket Office; This Is the Hour (C: Jason, Will; Burton, Val; Steiner, Max); I Met Her at a Party [1] (C: Jason, Will; Burton, Val; Webb, Roy); He's Not the Marrying Kind

**Notes**  Cue sheet doesn't differentiate between vocals and instrumentals. [1] Used instrumentally only.

## 3778 ✦ MELODY FOR TWO
Warner Brothers, 1937

**Composer(s)**  Jerome, M.K.
**Lyricist(s)**  Scholl, Jack
**Choreographer(s)**  Connolly, Bobby; Vreeland, Richard

**Producer(s)**  Foy, Bryan
**Director(s)**  King, Louis
**Screenwriter(s)**  Bricker, George; Ward, Luci; Watson, Joseph K.
**Source(s)**  "Special Arrangements" (story) Macaulay, Richard

**Cast**  Melton, James; Ellis, Patricia; Wilson, Marie; Keating, Fred; Purcell, Dick; Shaw, Winifred; Reynolds, Craig; Foy, Charles; Anderson, Eddie "Rochester"; O'Connor, Jack; O'Connor, Donald

**Song(s)**  A Flat in Manhattan; Melody for Two (C: Warren, Harry; L: Dubin, Al); Dangerous Rhythm; Excuse for Dancing; September in the Rain [1] (C: Warren, Harry; L: Dubin, Al); Jose O'Neill (The Cuban Heel)

**Notes**  There is also a vocal of "Macushla" by MacMurrough. [1] Briefly used in STARS OVER BROADWAY.

## 3779 ✦ MELODY GARDEN
Universal, 1944

**Composer(s)**  Rosen, Milton
**Lyricist(s)**  Carter, Everett

**Song(s)**  Slightly Sentimental [2]; I Like to Be Loved [1]

**Notes**  There are other vocals in this short subject. [1] Also in THE MYSTERY OF THE RIVER BOAT and WEEK-END PASS. [2] Also in HAT CHECK HONEY.

## 3780 ✦ MELODY GIRL

See SING, DANCE, PLENTY HOT.

## 3781 ✦ MELODY INN

See RIDING HIGH.

## 3782 ✦ MELODY IN SPRING
### Paramount, 1934

**Composer(s)** Gensler, Lewis E.
**Lyricist(s)** Thompson, Harlan

**Director(s)** McLeod, Norman Z.
**Screenwriter(s)** Levy, Benn W.

**Cast** Ross, Lanny; Ruggles, Charles; Sothern, Ann; Boland, Mary; Meeker, George

**Song(s)** Melody in Spring; Ending with a Kiss; Goodbye My Sweetheart (L: Gensler, Lewis E.); Yodel [1] (L: Gensler, Lewis E.); The Open Road; It's Psychological [2]

**Notes** [1] There were no actual lyrics—this was yodeled. [2] Not used but published.

## 3783 ✦ MELODY LANE (1929)
### Universal, 1929

**Composer(s)** Leonard, Eddie; Stern, Jack; Stern, Grace [1]
**Lyricist(s)** Leonard, Eddie; Stern, Jack; Stern, Grace [1]

**Director(s)** Hill, Robert F.
**Screenwriter(s)** Hill, Robert F.; Hawks, J.G.
**Source(s)** *The Understander* (play) Swerling, Jo

**Cast** Leonard, Eddie; Dunn, Josephine; La Verne, Jane; Gordon, Huntley; Coe, Rose; Stone, George E.

**Song(s)** Here I Am; Beautiful; There's Sugar Cane Round My Door; The Boogey Man Is Here (C/L: Leonard, Eddie; Stern, Jack); Roly Boly Eyes (C/L: Leonard, Eddie); Song of the Islands [2] (C/L: King, Charles E.); Aloha (C/L: Liliuokalani, Queen)

**Notes** Universal's first all-talkie musical. There is also a vocal of Eddie Leonard's 1903 song, "Ida! Sweet As Apple Cider." [1] The Sterns are not mentioned on the cue sheet. Jack Stern is credited in the *Variety* review. Sheet music credits are reflected above. Jack and Grace are credited in the *AFI Catalog*. [2] Also in SONG OF THE ISLANDS (20th) and FLIRTATION WALK (Warner).

## 3784 ✦ MELODY LANE (1942)
### Universal, 1942

**Composer(s)** Berens, Norman
**Lyricist(s)** Brooks, Jack

**Producer(s)** Goldsmith, Ken
**Director(s)** Lamont, Charles
**Screenwriter(s)** Wedlock Jr., Hugh; Snyder, Howard; Grant, Morton

**Cast** The Merry Macs; Errol, Leon; Gwynne, Anne; Paige, Robert; Lenhart, Billy

**Song(s)** Peaceful Ends the Day; Cherokee Charlee; Changeable Heart; Since the Farmer in the Dell Learned to Swing; Swing-A-Bye My Baby [1]; If It's a Dream; Let's Go to Caliacabu

**Notes** [1] Also used in YOU'RE A LUCKY FELLOW, MR. SMITH.

## 3785 ✦ THE MELODY MAN
### Columbia, 1930

**Director(s)** Neill, Roy William
**Screenwriter(s)** Green, Howard J.
**Source(s)** *The Melody Man* (musical) Fields, Herbert; Rodgers, Richard; Hart, Lorenz

**Cast** Collier Jr., William; Day, Alice; St. Polis, John; Walker, Johnny; Conti, Albert

**Song(s)** Broken Dreams (C: Johnston, Arthur; L: Dreyer, Dave; Macdonald, Ballard)

## 3786 ✦ MELODY OF YOUTH

See THEY SHALL HAVE MUSIC.

## 3787 ✦ MELODY PARADE
### Monogram, 1943

**Composer(s)** Kay, Edward J.
**Lyricist(s)** Cherkose, Eddie
**Choreographer(s)** Boyle, Jack

**Producer(s)** Parsons, Lindsley
**Director(s)** Dreifuss, Arthur
**Screenwriter(s)** Ryan, Tim; Marion, Charles R.

**Cast** Hughes, Mary Beth; Quillan, Eddie; Ryan, Tim; Ryan, Irene; Moreland, Mantan; Cooper, Jerry; Armida; Charlot, Andre; Harlan, Kenneth; Ros, Ramon; Loumell Morgan Trio; Anson Weeks and His Orchestra; Ted Fiorito and His Orchestra; Dandridge, Ruby

**Song(s)** The Woman Behind the Man Behind the Gun; I Don't Know; Whatever Posessed Me?; Don't Fall in Love; Speechless; Amigo; Mr. and Mrs. Commando

**Notes** No cue sheet available. Armida also contributed songs.

## 3788 ✦ MELODY RANCH
### Republic, 1940

**Composer(s)** Styne, Jule
**Lyricist(s)** Cherkose, Eddie

**Producer(s)**  Siegel, Sol C.
**Director(s)**  Santley, Joseph
**Screenwriter(s)**  Moffitt, Jack; Herbert, F. Hugh

**Cast**  Autry, Gene; Durante, Jimmy; Miller, Ann; MacLane, Barton; Allen, Barbara Jo [1]; Hayes, George "Gabby"; Cowan, Jerome; Lee, Mary; Sawyer, Joe; MacMahon, Horace; Wilson, Clarence; Benedict, William

**Song(s)**  Torpedo Joe; What Are Cowboys Made Of [3]; Rodeo Rose [4] (Stake Your Dreams on) Melody Ranch; Jim Corny Well Dressed Man; Never Dream the Same Dream Twice (C/L: Autry, Gene; Rose, Fred); Back in the Saddle Again [2] (C/L: Whiting, Ray)

**Notes**  [1] Also known as Vera Vague. She is billed here as Barbara Jo Allen. [2] Also in BACK IN THE SADDLE, ROVIN' TUMBLEWEEDS and BORDER G-MEN (RKO). Autry is usually credited with coauthoring this song but he probably never wrote any songs. Since he was the music publisher he added his name to songs he didn't write. [3] Also in THE DAKOTA KID. [4] Cue sheet indicates Gene Autry wrote this song but sheet music credits Styne and Cherkose.

### 3789 ◆ MELODY TIME
Disney, 1948

**Producer(s)**  Sharpsteen, Ben
**Director(s)**  Geronimi, Clyde; Jackson, Wilfred; Luske, Hamilton; Kinney, Jack
**Screenwriter(s)**  Hibler, Winston; Reeves, Harry; Anderson, Ken; Penner, Erdman; Brightman, Homer; Sears, Ted; Rinaldi, Joe; Gramatky, Hardie
**Voices**  Rogers, Roy; Day, Dennis; The Andrews Sisters; Fred Waring and His Pennsylvanians; Martin, Freddy; Smith, Ethel; Langford, Frances; Clark, Buddy; Nolan, Bob; Sons of the Pioneers; The Dinning Sisters; Driscoll, Bobby; Patten, Luana

**Directing Animator(s)**  Larson, Eric; Kimball, Ward; Kahl, Milt; Johnston, Ollie; Lounsberry, John; Clark, Les

**Song(s)**  Melody Time (C/L: Benjamin, Ben; Weiss, George David); Sing About Something [1] (C: DePaul, Gene; L: Raye, Don)

**Notes**  This is a cartoon compilation consisting of the following cartoons: ONCE UPON A WINTERTIME, BUMBLE BOOGIE, JOHNNY APPLESEED, LITTLE TOOT, TREES, BLAME IT ON THE SAMBA and PECOS BILL. See the individual titles for their songs. However, all credits are listed here since they are not differentiated elsewhere. [1] Not used.

### 3790 ◆ MELODY TRAIL
Republic, 1935

**Composer(s)**  Autry, Gene; Burnette, Smiley
**Lyricist(s)**  Autry, Gene; Burnette, Smiley

**Producer(s)**  Levine, Nat
**Director(s)**  Kane, Joseph
**Screenwriter(s)**  Lowe, Sherman

**Cast**  Autry, Gene; Burnette, Smiley; Rutherford, Ann; Boteler, Wade; Bridge, Al; Castello, Willy; Quillan, Marie; Emmett, Fern

**Song(s)**  Hold on Little Dogies Hold On [1]; Melody Trail (C/L: Burnette, Smiley); Where Will the Wedding Supper Be; My Neighbor Hates Music (C/L: Burnette, Smiley); Western Lullaby; A Long Cowboy on a Lone Prairie; Way Down on the Bottom (C/L: Burnette, Smiley)

**Notes**  [1] Autry alone credited on sheet music.

### 3791 ◆ MELVIN AND HOWARD
Universal, 1980

**Musical Score**  Langhorne, Bruce

**Producer(s)**  Linson, Art; Phillips, Don
**Director(s)**  Demme, Jonathan
**Screenwriter(s)**  Goldman, Bo

**Cast**  Robards Jr., Jason; Le Mat, Paul; Cheshire, Elizabeth; Steenburgen, Mary; Taylor, Chip; Dummar, Melvin E.; Pollard, Michael J.; Grahame, Gloria; Faye, Herbie; Coleman, Dabney; Glover, John; Sullivan, Kathleen; Lenz, Rick

**Song(s)**  Souped-Up Santa's Sleigh (C/L: Dummar, Melvin; Dummar, Bonnie)

**Notes**  There are other songs on the soundtrack but this appears to be the only original.

### 3792 ◆ MEMORY FOR TWO

See I LOVE A BANDLEADER.

### 3793 ◆ MEN ARE NOT GODS
Twentieth Century–Fox, 1936

**Producer(s)**  Korda, Alexander
**Director(s)**  Reisch, Walter
**Screenwriter(s)**  Stern, G.B.; Wright, Iris

**Cast**  Lawrence, Gertrude; Shaw, Sebastian; Harrison, Rex; Matthews, A.E.; Gielgud, Val; Grossmith, Lawrence

**Song(s)**  Two People in Love (C/L: Ellis, Vivian)

### 3794 ◆ MEN ARE SUCH FOOLS
RKO, 1933

**Musical Score**  Bakaleinikoff, Constantin
**Composer(s)**  Harling, W. Franke
**Lyricist(s)**  Brennan, J. Keirn

**Director(s)**  Nigh, William
**Screenwriter(s)**  Jewell, Edward C.

**Cast**  Carrillo, Leo; Osborne, Vivienne; Merkel, Una; Cawthorn, Joseph; Hurst, Paul; Nugent, Eddie; Conti, Albert

**Song(s)**  Rhapsody of Life; Dream Song; No No Monsieur (L: Robin, Leo); March

**Notes**  It is believed the songwriters were W. Franke Harling and J. Kiern Brennan with an additional lyric by Leo Robin but existing records are unclear.

### 3795 ◆ ME, NATALIE
National General, 1969

**Musical Score**  Mancini, Henry
**Composer(s)**  Mancini, Henry
**Lyricist(s)**  McKuen, Rod

**Producer(s)**  Shapiro, Stanley
**Director(s)**  Coe, Fred
**Screenwriter(s)**  Zweiback, A. Martin

**Cast**  Duke, Patty; Farentino, James; Balsam, Martin; Lanchester, Elsa; Jens, Salome; Marchand, Nancy; Balaban, Bob; Pacino, Al

**Song(s)**  Natalie; We

**Notes**  No cue sheet available.

### 3796 ◆ MEN IN HER DIARY
Universal, 1945

**Composer(s)**  Rosen, Milton
**Lyricist(s)**  Carter, Everett
**Choreographer(s)**  Romero, Carlos

**Producer(s)**  Welsch, Howard
**Director(s)**  Barton, Charles
**Screenwriter(s)**  Herbert, F. Hugh; Ullman, Elwood; Davis, Stanley

**Cast**  Ryan, Peggy; Hall, Jon; Allbritton, Louise; Grey, Virginia

**Song(s)**  Keep Your Chin Up; We're Makin' a Million [1]

**Notes**  [1] Also in SEE MY LAWYER.

### 3797 ◆ MEN OF STEEL
Metro–Goldwyn–Mayer, 1938

**Musical Score**  Snell, Dave
**Composer(s)**  Wright, Bob; Forrest, Chet
**Lyricist(s)**  Wright, Bob; Forrest, Chet

**Director(s)**  Lee, Sammy
**Screenwriter(s)**  Rauh, Stanley

**Cast**  Stevens, Kenneth; Weston, Doris; Tombes, Andrew

**Song(s)**  Men of Steel; The Play's the Thing; It Dawned on Me; Four Little Maids (C/L: Brent, Earl)

**Notes**  Short subject.

### 3798 ◆ MEN OF THE SKY
Warner Brothers–First National, 1931

**Composer(s)**  Kern, Jerome
**Lyricist(s)**  Harbach, Otto

**Director(s)**  Green, Alfred E.
**Screenwriter(s)**  Kern, Jerome; Harbach, Otto

**Cast**  Delroy, Irene; Whiting, Jack; Fletcher, Bramwell; St. Polis, John; McHugh, Frank; Maxwell, Edwin; Matiesen, Otto; Loder, Lotti; Kaliz, Armand

**Song(s)**  Cottage of Content [1]; Man in the Sky [1]; Ev'ry Little While [1]; All's Well with the World [1]; Stolen Dreams (Who Steals All My Dreams) [1]; You've Got to Meet Marguerite [1]; What's Become of Spring [1]; Canzonetta (I'll Share Them All With You) [1]; Chamber Music and Boy's March [1]; Choir [1]; Flying Field [1]; Suzette [1]

**Notes**  Originally titled STOLEN DREAMS and MEN IN THE SKY. [1] This film was released without songs.

### 3799 ◆ THE MEN'S CLUB
Atlantic, 1986

**Musical Score**  Holdridge, Lee

**Producer(s)**  Gottfried, Howard
**Director(s)**  Medak, Peter
**Screenwriter(s)**  Michaels, Leonard
**Source(s)**  (book) Michaels, Leonard

**Cast**  Kudes, David; Jordan, Richard; Keitel, Harvey; Langella, Frank; Scheider, Roy; Wasson, Craig; Williams, Treat; Channing, Stockard; Dusenberry, Ann; Wedgeworth, Ann

**Song(s)**  A Fool for Love (C: Holdridge, Lee; L: Bettis, John); Shake Me Up (C/L: Wright, Gary); Taking a Stand (C/L: Beckett, Peter)

**Notes**  No cue sheet available.

### 3800 ◆ MEN WITH WINGS
Paramount, 1938

**Musical Score**  Harling, W. Franke

**Producer(s)**  Wellman, William A.
**Director(s)**  Wellman, William A.
**Screenwriter(s)**  Carson, Robert

**Cast**  MacMurray, Fred; Milland, Ray; Campbell, Louise; Devine, Andy; Abel, Walter; Overman, Lynne; Hall, Porter; O'Connor, Donald; Cook, Billy; Weidler, Virginia

**Song(s)**  Men with Wings [1] (C: Carmichael, Hoagy; L: Loesser, Frank)

**Notes**  [1] Used instrumentally only though recorded.

## 3801 ◆ MERELY MARY ANN
Fox, 1931

**Director(s)**   King, Henry
**Screenwriter(s)**   Furthman, Jules

**Cast**   Gaynor, Janet; Farrell, Charles; Mercer, Beryl; Kerrigan, J.M.

**Song(s)**   Kiss Me Goodnight (Not Goodbye) [2] (C: Hanley, James F.; L: Furthman, Jules); Mary Ann [1] (C: Fall, Leo; Kernell, William)

**Notes**   [1] From "Song of Spring." [2] Also in PEPPER with new lyrics by Sidney Clare.

## 3802 ◆ MERRY ANDREW
Metro–Goldwyn–Mayer, 1958

**Musical Score**   Riddle, Nelson
**Composer(s)**   Chaplin, Saul
**Lyricist(s)**   Mercer, Johnny
**Choreographer(s)**   Kidd, Michael

**Producer(s)**   Siegel, Sol C.
**Director(s)**   Kidd, Michael
**Screenwriter(s)**   Lennart, Isobel; Diamond, I.A.L.
**Source(s)**   "The Romance of Henry Menafee" (story) Gallico, Paul

**Cast**   Kaye, Danny; Angeli, Pier [1]; Baccaloni, Salvatore; Purcell, Noel; Coote, Robert; Rall, Tommy; Cutts, Patricia; Evans, Rex

**Song(s)**   The Pipes of Pan; Chin Up—Stout Fellow; Everything Is Tickety-Boo; Buona Fortuna; The Square of the Hypotenuse; You Can't Always Have What You Want

**Notes**   [1] Dubbed by Betty Wand.

## 3803 ◆ MERRY-GO-ROUND OF 1938
Universal, 1938

**Composer(s)**   McHugh, Jimmy
**Lyricist(s)**   Adamson, Harold

**Producer(s)**   Rogers, Charles R.
**Director(s)**   Cummings, Irving
**Screenwriter(s)**   Brice, Monte; Otvos, A. Dorian

**Cast**   Lahr, Bert; Savo, Jimmy; Auer, Mischa; House, Billy; Brady, Alice; Hodges, Joy; Fazenda, Louise; Dave Apollon and His Orchestra

**Song(s)**   Six of One and Half a Dozen of the Other; I'm in My Glory; More Power to You; Song of the Woodman (C: Arlen, Harold; L: Harburg, E.Y.); You're My Dish; A Masher Is a Bad, Bad Boy [1]

**Notes**   There are also vocals of "Sleep, Baby, Sleep" by John Handley; "I Wonder What's Become of Sally" by Jack Yellen and Milton Ager; "Take Me Back to My Boots and Saddles" by Samuels, Whitcup and Powell and

"River Stay Away from My Door" by Harry Woods. [1] Not used.

## 3804 ◆ THE MERRY MONAHANS
Universal, 1944

**Composer(s)**   George, Don
**Lyricist(s)**   Bibo, Irving
**Choreographer(s)**   Da Pron, Louis

**Producer(s)**   Fessier, Michael; Pagano, Ernest
**Director(s)**   Lamont, Charles
**Screenwriter(s)**   Fessier, Michael; Pagano, Ernest

**Cast**   O'Connor, Donald; Ryan, Peggy; Oakie, Jack; Blyth, Ann

**Song(s)**   Lovely; Impersonations; We're Havin' a Wonderful Time; Beautiful to Look At; Stop Foolin' [1]

**Notes**   There are also vocals of "Some of These Days" by Shelton Brooks; "Rock-A-Bye Your Baby with a Dixie Melody" by Sam M. Lewis, Joe Young and Jean Schwartz; "Missouri Waltz" by Frederick Knight Logan and J.R. Shannon; "Carry Me Back to Old Virginny" by James A. Bland; "I Love You California" by F.B. Silverwood and A.F. Frankenstein; "When You Wore a Tulip" by Jack Mahoney and Percy Wenrich; "What Do You Want to Make Those Eyes at Me For?" by Joseph McCarthy, Howard Johnson and James V. Monaco; "In My Merry Oldsmobile" by Vincent Bryan and Gus Edwards; "Isle D'Amour" by Earl Carroll and Leo Edwards; "I Hate to Lose You" by Grant Clarke and Archie Gottler; "Rose Room" by Harry Williams and Art Hickman and "I'm Always Chasing Rainbows" by Joseph McCarthy and Harry Carroll. [1] Used instrumentally only.

## 3805 ◆ THE MERRY WIDOW (1934)
Metro–Goldwyn–Mayer, 1934

**Composer(s)**   Lehar, Franz
**Lyricist(s)**   Hart, Lorenz; Kahn, Gus
**Choreographer(s)**   Rasch, Albertina

**Director(s)**   Lubitsch, Ernst
**Screenwriter(s)**   Vajda, Ernest; Raphaelson, Samson
**Source(s)**   *The Merry Widow* (operetta) Lehar, Franz

**Cast**   Chevalier, Maurice; MacDonald, Jeanette; Horton, Edward Everett; Merkel, Una; Barbier, George; Gombell, Minna; Bing, Herman; Meek, Donald

**Song(s)**   Vilia (L: Hart, Lorenz); Maxim's (L: Hart, Lorenz); Girls, Girls, Girls! (L: Hart, Lorenz); The Merry Widow Waltz (L: Hart, Lorenz); Melody of Laughter; If Widows Are Rich (L: Hart, Lorenz); It Must Be Love [1] (C: Unknown); A Widow Is a Lady [1] (C: Unknown); Dolores [1] (C: Unknown); Muchacha (Little Dolores) [1] (C: Unknown)

**Notes**   No cue sheet available. Additional music is by Richard Rodgers and Herbert Stothart. Hart was the primary lyricist, translating Victor Leon and Leo Stein's originals. It is not known which of these songs Hart wrote (except where indicated) with or without Kahn, nor if all the music was based on Lehar's score. "Unknown" indicates it couldn't be ascertained whether Lehar, Rodgers or Stothart wrote the music. [1] Not used.

## 3806 ✦ THE MERRY WIDOW (1952)
Metro–Goldwyn–Mayer, 1952

**Musical Score**   Blackton, Jay
**Composer(s)**   Lehar, Franz
**Lyricist(s)**   Webster, Paul Francis
**Choreographer(s)**   Cole, Jack

**Producer(s)**   Pasternak, Joe
**Director(s)**   Bernhardt, Curtis
**Screenwriter(s)**   Levien, Sonya; Ludwig, William
**Source(s)**   *The Merry Widow* (operetta) Lehar, Franz; Leon, Victor; Stein, Leo

**Cast**   Turner, Lana [1]; Lamas, Fernando; Merkel, Una; Haydn, Richard; Gomez, Thomas; Abbott, John; Dalio, Marcel; Donovan, King; Coote, Robert; Sujata

**Song(s)**   Merry Widow Waltz; Girls, Girls, Girls; Opening Chorus Act 2; Vilia; Gypsy; Night; Maxim's; Can Can (inst.)

**Notes**   [1] Dubbed by Trudy Erwin.

## 3807 ✦ METAMORPHOSES
Sanrio Film, 1978

**Musical Score**   Studer, Jim; Young, Michael J.; Goldenberg, Billy
**Composer(s)**   Young, Michael J.
**Lyricist(s)**   Young, Michael J.

**Producer(s)**   Takashi; Ogisu, Terry; Tsugawa, Hiro
**Director(s)**   Takashi
**Screenwriter(s)**   Takashi
**Source(s)**   *Metamorphoses* (poetry) Ovid

**Song(s)**   Changes; Lookout; Will of the Wind; Skatin' on Air (C/L: Studer, Jim); Just Another Old Hag; Reaching Forever (C/L: Young, Michael J.; Randles, Bob); Criss Cross Man (C/L: Rolling Stones, The)

**Notes**   An animated feature.

## 3808 ✦ METROPOLITAN (1935)
Twentieth Century–Fox, 1935

**Producer(s)**   Zanuck, Darryl F.
**Director(s)**   Boleslawski, Richard
**Screenwriter(s)**   Meredyth, Bess; Marion Jr., George

**Cast**   Bruce, Virginia; Romero, Cesar; Alberni, Luis; Hall, Thurston; Marion, George F.; Donnelly, Ruth

**Song(s)**   Last Night When We Were Young [1] (C: Arlen, Harold; L: Harburg, E.Y.)

**Notes**   No cue sheet available. There were no original songs in this score. Vocals include "De Glory Road" by Clement Wood and J. Russell Bodley; "On the Road to Mandalay" by Rudyard Kipling and Oley Speaks; excerpts from Gounod's FAUST and Rossini's THE BARBER OF SEVILLE; the prologue to Leoncavallo's PAGLIACCI and "The Toreador Song" and "The Gypsy Song" from Bizet's CARMEN. [1] Used instrumentally only.

## 3809 ✦ MEXICALI ROSE
Republic, 1939

**Producer(s)**   Grey, Harry
**Director(s)**   Sherman, George
**Screenwriter(s)**   Geraghty, Gerald

**Cast**   Autry, Gene; Burnette, Smiley; Beery, Noah; Walters, Luana; Farnum, Walter; Royle, William; Barcroft, Roy

**Song(s)**   Mexicali Rose [1] (C: Tenney, Jack; L: Stone, Helen); You're the Only Star in My Blue Heaven [2] (C/L: Autry, Gene); My Orchestra's Driving Me Crazy (C/L: Burnette, Smiley); Alla en el Rancho Grande [3] (C: Ramos, Silvano; L: Costello, Bartley); With My Concertina (C: Ward, Edward; L: Wright, Bob; Forrest, Chet; Ruffino, Carlos); Robin Hood (C/L: Samuels, Walter G.)

**Notes**   No cue sheet available. [1] Also in ROOTIN' TOOTIN' RHYTHM and BARBED WIRE (Columbia) (without Stone credit). Also in the 1929 Columbia film MEXICALI ROSE which starred Barbara Stanwyck. [2] Also in RIM OF THE CANYON (Columbia), THE OLD BARN DANCE and SPRINGTIME IN THE ROCKIES (1937). [3] Also in MEXICANA with Spanish lyrics.

## 3810 ✦ MEXICALI SMOES
Warner Brothers, 1959

**Musical Score**   Franklyn, Milton J.
**Composer(s)**   Stalling, Carl
**Lyricist(s)**   Stalling, Carl

**Director(s)**   Freling, Friz

**Cast**   Gonzales, Speedy

**Song(s)**   Mexicali Smoes; In Guadalajara

**Notes**   Looney Tune.

## 3811 ✦ MEXICANA (1929)
Metro–Goldwyn–Mayer, 1929

**Composer(s)**   Edwards, Gus
**Lyricist(s)**   Brockman, James

**Cast**   Murray, Mae; Armida; Williams; Golden, Ruth; Lola; Triana

**Song(s)** Mexicana [1]; Tia Juana; Terrible Toreador; Spanish Eyes [1]; (Wrap Me Up in a) Spanish Shawl

**Notes** Short subject. There are also vocals of "Estrellita" by Ponce; "El Capotin;" "Toreador" from Bizet's CARMEN and "Cielito Lindo" by Fernandez. [1] Used instrumentally only.

## 3812 ✦ MEXICANA (1945)
### Republic, 1945

**Composer(s)** Ruiz, Gabriel
**Lyricist(s)** Washington, Ned
**Choreographer(s)** Castle, Nick

**Producer(s)** Santell, Alfred
**Director(s)** Santell, Alfred
**Screenwriter(s)** Gill, Frank, Jr.

**Cast** Guizar, Tito; Moore, Constance; Carrillo, Leo; Freeman, Howard; Geray, Steven; Stevens, Jean; St. Luke's Choirsters; Peter Meremblum Junior Orchestra; Rodriguez, Estelita

**Song(s)** Corazon a Corazon [1]; Guadalajara [2] (C/L: Guizar, Pepe); Alla en el Rancho Grande [3] (C: Ramos, Silvano; L: Del Moral, J.D.); Little Sir Echo (C/L: Marsala, Joe; Girard, Adele); See Mexico; Somewhere There's a Rainbow (C: Scharf, Walter); Lupita; Heartless; Time Out for Dreaming; Children's Song; Mexicana

**Notes** Reissued as BEYOND THE RIO GRANDE. [1] Also in FEDERAL AGENT AT LARGE. [2] Also in WEEKEND AT THE WALDORF (MGM), FUN IN ACAPULCO (Paramount) and PAN AMERICANA (RKO). [3] Also in MEXICALI ROSE with English lyrics.

## 3813 ✦ MEXICAN HAYRIDE
### Universal, 1948

**Musical Score** Scharf, Walter

**Producer(s)** Arthur, Robert
**Director(s)** Barton, Charles T.
**Screenwriter(s)** Brodney, Oscar; Grant, John
**Source(s)** *Mexican Hayride* (musical) Porter, Cole; Fields, Herbert; Fields, Joseph

**Cast** Abbott, Bud; Costello, Lou; Malina, Luba; Hubbard, John; de Cordoba, Pedro; Feld, Fritz

**Song(s)** Is It Yes or Is It No? (C: Scharf, Walter; L: Brooks, Jack)

## 3814 ✦ MEXICAN SPITFIRE
### RKO, 1940

**Musical Score** Dreyer, Dave; Sawtell, Paul

**Producer(s)** Reid, Cliff
**Director(s)** Goodwins, Leslie
**Screenwriter(s)** Fields, Joseph; Roberts, Charles E.

**Cast** Velez, Lupe; Errol, Leon; Woods, Donald; Hayes, Linda; Risdon, Elizabeth; Kellaway, Cecil

**Song(s)** Negrita No Me Dejes [1] (C/L: Gonzales, Aaron); My Vaquero (C/L: Whitley, Ray; Rose, Fred)

**Notes** [1] Also in FALCON IN MEXICO and WITHOUT RESERVATIONS.

## 3815 ✦ MEXICAN SPITFIRE AT SEA
### RKO, 1941

**Musical Score** Webb, Roy

**Producer(s)** Reid, Cliff
**Director(s)** Goodwins, Leslie
**Screenwriter(s)** Cady, Jerry; Roberts, Charles E.

**Cast** Velez, Lupe; Errol, Leon; Rogers, Charles "Buddy"; Pitts, ZaSu; Risdon, Elizabeth; Bates, Florence

**Song(s)** Take the World Off Your Shoulders [1] (C: Fain, Sammy; L: Brown, Lew)

**Notes** [1] Also in CONSPIRACY.

## 3816 ✦ MGM BIG PARADE OF COMEDY
### Metro–Goldwyn–Mayer, 1967

**Musical Score** Green, Bernie
**Composer(s)** Green, Bernie
**Lyricist(s)** Youngson, Robert

**Producer(s)** Youngson, Robert
**Screenwriter(s)** Youngson, Robert
**Narrator(s)** Tremayne, Les

**Song(s)** The Big Parade of Comedy; Marie; Jean, Oh Jean; Bob Benchley

**Notes** This is a compilation of comedy scenes from past movies.

## 3817 ✦ MICHIGAN KID
### Universal, 1947

**Musical Score** Salter, Hans J.

**Producer(s)** Welsch, Howard
**Director(s)** Taylor, Ray
**Screenwriter(s)** Chanslor, Roy

**Cast** Hall, Jon; McLaglen, Victor; Johnson, Rita; Devine, Andy; Stone, Milburn

**Song(s)** Whoops My Dear (C: Salter, Hans J.; L: Brooks, Jack)

## 3818 ✦ MICKEY AND THE BEANSTALK
### Disney, 1947

**Musical Score** Daniel, Eliot; Wallace, Oliver; Smith, Paul J.
**Composer(s)** Noble, Ray

**Director(s)**   Roberts, Bill
**Screenwriter(s)**   Brightman, Homer; Reeves, Harry; Sears, Ted; Dedini, Eldon
**Source(s)**   "Jack and the Beanstalk" (story) Traditional

**Cast**   Bergen, Edgar; McCarthy, Charlie; Snerd, Mortimer; Mouse, Mickey; Duck, Donald

**Song(s)**   My What a Happy Day (L: Walsh, William; Gilbert, Ray); Fe-Fi-Fo-Fum (C: Smith, Paul J.; L: Quenzer, Arthur); My Favorite Dream (L: Walsh, William); Close Your Eyes [1] (C/L: Wallace, Oliver); Everything's Just Right [1] (C/L: Wallace, Oliver); Follow the Leader [1] (C: Smith, Paul J.; L: Quenzer, Arthur); Hello There—Goodbye Now [1] (C: Smith, Paul J.; L: Quenzer, Arthur); If I Play the Harp, and You Lay the Eggs [1] (C: Smith, Paul J.; L: Quenzer, Arthur); Laff-Happy Valley [1] (C: Smith, Paul J.; L: Quenzer, Arthur); Poor Brother Knute—The Flute Song [1] (C: Smith, Paul J.; L: Quenzer, Arthur)

**Notes**   Animated cartoon. This is a part of FUN AND FANCY FREE. Quenzer also added lyrics to "Funiculi Funicula." [1] Not used.

## 3819   ✦   MICKEY MOUSE DISCO
### Disney, 1979

**Composer(s)**   Charouhas, George Thomas; Furman, Steven
**Lyricist(s)**   Charouhas, George Thomas; Furman, Steven

**Producer(s)**   Brandt, Frank; King, Bob; Klawitter, John
**Director(s)**   Thompson, Riley; Hand, David D.; Nichols, Charles; King, Jack; Kinney, Jack; Sharpsteen, Ben; Ferguson, Norman

**Cast**   Mouse, Mickey; Duck, Donald; Goofy

**Song(s)**   Disco Mickey Mouse (C/L: Worrall, Tom); Macho Duck (C/L: Worrall, Tom); Mouse Trap (C/L: Magon, Jymn); Watch Out for Goofy; Welcome to Rio

**Notes**   Cartoon short.

## 3820   ✦   MICKEY'S CHRISTMAS CAROL
### Disney, 1982

**Musical Score**   Kostal, Irwin

**Producer(s)**   Mattinson, Burny
**Director(s)**   Mattinson, Burny
**Screenwriter(s)**   Mattinson, Burny; Marion, Tony L.; Gombert, Ed; Griffith, Don; Young, Alan; Dinehart, Alan
**Source(s)**   "A Christmas Carol" (story) Dickens, Charles
**Voices**   Young, Alan; Allwine, Wayne; Smith, Hal; Ryan, Will; Carroll, Eddy; Parris, Patricia; Billingsley, Dick; Nash, Clarence

**Song(s)**   Oh, What a Merry Christmas Day (C/L: Kostal, Irwin; Searles, Frederick); Merry Christmas One and All (C/L: Kostal, Irwin)

**Notes**   Animated feature.

## 3821   ✦   MICKEY'S FOLLIES
### Disney

**Cast**   Mouse, Mickey; Mouse, Minnie

**Song(s)**   Minnie's Yoo Hoo (C: Stalling, Carl; L: Disney, Walter E.; Stalling, Carl)

**Notes**   Cartoon short.

## 3822   ✦   MICKEY'S GALA PREMIERE
### Disney

**Musical Score**   Churchill, Frank E.
**Composer(s)**   Churchill, Frank E.
**Lyricist(s)**   Churchill, Frank E.

**Cast**   Mouse, Mickey

**Song(s)**   Here Come the Movie Stars; Hello, Everybody, Howdy Do

**Notes**   Animated cartoon. No credit sheet available.

## 3823   ✦   MICKI AND MAUDE
### Columbia, 1984

**Musical Score**   Holdridge, Lee

**Producer(s)**   Adams, Tony
**Director(s)**   Edwards, Blake
**Screenwriter(s)**   Reynolds, Jonathan

**Cast**   Moore, Dudley; Irving, Amy; Reinking, Ann; Mulligan, Richard; Gaynes, George; Shawn, Wallace; Pleshette, John; Leonard, Lu; Pointer, Priscilla

**Song(s)**   Something New in My Life (C: Legrand, Michel; L: Bergman, Marilyn; Bergman, Alan)

## 3824   ✦   MIDAS RUN
### Cinerama Releasing, 1969

**Musical Score**   Bernstein, Elmer

**Producer(s)**   Stross, Raymond
**Director(s)**   Kjellin, Alf
**Screenwriter(s)**   Buchanan, James David; Austin, Ronald

**Cast**   Crenna, Richard; Heywood, Anne; Astaire, Fred; McDowall, Roddy; Richardson, Sir Ralph; Romero, Cesar; Celi, Adolfo; Astaire Jr., Fred

**Song(s)**   Midas Run (C: Bernstein, Elmer; L: Black, Don)

**Notes**   No cue sheet available.

## 3825   ✦   MIDDLE AGE CRAZY
### Twentieth Century–Fox, 1980

**Musical Score**   McCauley, Matthew

**Producer(s)**   Cooper, Robert; Cohen, Ronald M.
**Director(s)**   Trent, John
**Screenwriter(s)**   Kleinschmitt, Carl
**Source(s)**   (song) Throckmorton, Sonny

**Cast** Dern, Bruce; Ann-Margaret; Jarvis, Graham; Christmas, Eric; Wakeham, Deborah

**Song(s)** Where Did the Time Go (C: Bacharach, Burt; L: Sager, Carole Bayer); You Make It All So Easy (C/L: Meissner, Stan); Middle Age Crazy (C/L: Throckmorton, Sonny); Just Friends (C: Bacharach, Burt; L: Sager, Carole Bayer); Now That I Know (C/L: McCauley, Matthew)

## 3826 ✦ MIDNIGHT
### Paramount, 1939

**Choreographer(s)** Prinz, LeRoy

**Producer(s)** Hornblow Jr., Arthur
**Director(s)** Leisen, Mitchell
**Screenwriter(s)** Brackett, Charles; Wilder, Billy

**Cast** Colbert, Claudette; Barrymore, John; Lederer, Francis; Astor, Mary; Hopper, Hedda; Ameche, Don; O'Malley, Rex; Woolley, Monty; Kaliz, Armand; Barrie, Elaine

**Song(s)** Midnight (C: Hollander, Frederick; L: Freed, Ralph)

## 3827 ✦ MIDNIGHT CLUB
### Paramount, 1933

**Director(s)** Hall, Alexander; Somnes, George
**Screenwriter(s)** Miller, Seton I.; Charteris, Leslie
**Source(s)** (story) Oppenheim, E. Phillips

**Cast** Brook, Clive; Raft, George; Vinson, Helen; Skipworth, Alison; Standing, Sir Guy; Mowbray, Alan; Gottschalk, Ferdinand; Griffies, Ethel; Bevan, Billy

**Song(s)** In a Midnight Club [1] (C: Rainger, Ralph; L: Robin, Leo)

**Notes** [1] Not used.

## 3828 ✦ MIDNIGHT COWBOY
### United Artists, 1969

**Musical Score** Barry, John

**Producer(s)** Hellman, Jerome
**Director(s)** Schlesinger, John
**Screenwriter(s)** Salt, Waldo

**Cast** Hoffman, Dustin; Voight, Jon; Miles, Sylvia; McGiver, John; Vaccaro, Brenda; Hughes, Barnard; White, Ruth; Owens, Gary

**Song(s)** Everybody's Talkin' at Me (C/L: Neil, Fred); A Famous Myth (C/L: Comanor, Jeffrey); Tears of Joy (C/L: Comanor, Jeffrey); He Quit Me (C/L: Zevon, Warren); Jungle Jim at the Zoo (C/L: Bronstein, Stanley; Frank, Richard); Old Man Willow (C/L: Sussman, R.; Bronstein, Stanley; Yules, M.; Shapiro, M.)

**Notes** No cue sheet available.

## 3829 ✦ MIDNIGHT CROSSING
### Vestron, 1988

**Producer(s)** Hayden, Mathew
**Director(s)** Holzberg, Roger
**Screenwriter(s)** Holzberg, Roger; Weiser, Doug

**Cast** Dunaway, Faye; Travanti, Daniel J.; Cattrall, Kim; Laughlin, John; Beatty, Ned; de Pool, Pedro

**Song(s)** Love Thing (C/L: Tyrell, Steve; Hall, Ashley; Tyrell, Stephanie); After Midnight (C/L: Rogers, Mark); Erik A (C/L: Mann, Bob); Alone (C/L: Brown, Peter; Saulsberg, Rodney); Eao, Eao, Ahh (C/L: Hall, Ashley; Buckmaster, Paul); Barbados (C/L: Coffing, Barry; Settle, Phillip); Lost In You (C/L: Coffing, Barry; Sotoodeh; Ginsburg, Robert)

**Notes** No cue sheet available.

## 3830 ✦ MIDNIGHT LACE
### Universal, 1960

**Musical Score** Skinner, Frank

**Producer(s)** Hunter, Ross; Melcher, Martin
**Director(s)** Miller, David
**Screenwriter(s)** Goff, Ivan; Roberts, Ben
**Source(s)** *Matilda Shouted Fire* (novel) Green, Janet

**Cast** Day, Doris; Harrison, Rex; Gavin, John; Loy, Myrna; McDowall, Roddy; Marshall, Herbert; Parry, Natasha; Baddeley, Hermione; Williams, Rhys

**Song(s)** Midnight Lace (C/L: Lubin, Joe; Howard, Jerome); What Does a Woman Do? (C: Wrubel, Allie; L: Anderson, Maxwell)

**Notes** No cue sheet available.

## 3831 ✦ MIDNIGHT MADNESS
### Disney, 1980

**Musical Score** Wechter, Julius
**Composer(s)** Wechter, David; Wechter, Julius
**Lyricist(s)** Wechter, David

**Producer(s)** Miller, Ron
**Director(s)** Wechter, David; Nankin, Michael
**Screenwriter(s)** Wechter, David; Nankin, Michael

**Cast** Naughton, David; Clinger, Debra; Deezen, Eddie; Wilkin, Brad; Rosewell, Maggie; Furst, Stephen; Tedrow, Irene; Fox, Michael J.; Blocker, Dirk; Tennant, Andy

**Song(s)** Midnight Madness; Someone New; Don't Know Why I Came (C: Wechter, David); Dreams (C/L: Jackman, Bob)

## 3832 ✦ MIDNIGHT MADONNA
### Paramount, 1937

**Producer(s)** Cohen, Emanuel
**Director(s)** Flood, James
**Screenwriter(s)** Malloy, Doris; Lehman, Gladys

Cast    William, Warren; Carroll, Mady; Clancy, Kitty; Hale, Jonathan; Crehan, Joseph; Franklin, Irene

Song(s)    Love Didn't Know Any Better (C: Johnston, Arthur; L: Burke, Johnny); The Plain Old Blues (C: Johnston, Arthur; L: Burke, Johnny)

## 3833 ◆ MIDNIGHT MAN
### Universal, 1974

Musical Score    Grusin, Dave

Director(s)    Kibbee, Roland; Lancaster, Burt
Screenwriter(s)    Kibbee, Roland; Lancaster, Burt
Source(s)    *The Midnight Lady and the Mourning Man* (novel) Anthony, David

Cast    Lancaster, Burt; Yulin, Harris; Winterstein, Richard; Tyner, Charles; Woodward, Morgan; Lauter, Ed; Watson, Mills; Clark, Susan; Mitchell, Cameron

Song(s)    Come On Back Where You Belong (C: Grusin, Dave; L: Ames, Morgan)

## 3834 ◆ MIDSTREAM
### Tiffany–Stahl, 1929

Musical Score    Riesenfeld, Hugo

Director(s)    Flood, James
Screenwriter(s)    Hatton, Frederic; Hatton, Fanny

Cast    Cortez, Ricardo; Windsor, Claire; Love, Montagu; Kent, Larry; Eddy, Helen Jerome; Brigham, Leslie; Alvarez, Luis; Schrader, Genevieve; Foyer, Florence

Song(s)    Midstream (C: Baer, Abel; L: Gilbert, L. Wolfe)

Notes    No cue sheet available.

## 3835 ◆ THE MIKADO
### Warner Brothers, 1967

Producer(s)    Havelock-Allan, Anthony; Brabourne, John
Director(s)    Burge, Stuart
Screenwriter(s)    Gilbert, W.S.; Sullivan, Arthur; Besch, Anthony
Source(s)    *The Mikado* (operetta) Gilbert, W.S.; Sullivan, Arthur

Cast    Adams, Donald; Jones, Peggy-Ann; Lawlor, Thomas; Masterson, Valerie; Palmer, Christene; Potter, Philip; Reed, John; Sandford, Kenneth; Wales, Pauline; Cook, George

Notes    No cue sheets available. The music is that of THE MIKADO as performed by members of the D'Oyly Carte Opera Company.

## 3836 ◆ MIKE'S MURDER
### Warner Brothers, 1984

Musical Score    Barry, John
Composer(s)    Jackson, Joe
Lyricist(s)    Jackson, Joe

Producer(s)    Kurumada, Kim
Director(s)    Bridges, James
Screenwriter(s)    Bridges, James

Cast    Winger, Debra; Keyloun, Mark; Winfield, Paul; Larson, Darrell; Alderson, Brooke; Crosson, Robert

Song(s)    Memphis; Zemio; L.A.C.A. (C/L: Adams, Doug; Sherman, Wilson); Cosmopolitan; Out of the Business (C/L: Anderson; Cotten; Prince; Steen; Welnick; Waybill; Spooner); 1-2-3 Go; Moonlight; It's a Beautiful World (C/L: Mothersbaugh, Mark; Casals; General Boy); Get Down on It (C/L: Bell; Taylor; Kool & the Gang); Laundromat Monday; Rebels Rule (C/L: Setzer, Brian); Breakdown; Big Bird (C/L: B-52s); Without You (C/L: Jankel; Weymouth, Tina)

Notes    It is not known which, if any, of these songs were written for the picture.

## 3837 ◆ MIKEY AND NICKY
### Paramount, 1976

Composer(s)    Strauss, John
Lyricist(s)    Strauss, John

Producer(s)    Hausman, Michael
Director(s)    May, Elaine
Screenwriter(s)    May, Elaine

Cast    Falk, Peter; Cassavetes, John; Beatty, Ned; Van Patten, Joyce

Song(s)    Good Times, Bad Times; Peanut Spread

## 3838 ◆ MILAGRO BEANFIELD WAR
### Universal, 1988

Musical Score    Grusin, Dave

Producer(s)    Redford, Robert; Esparza, Moctesuma
Director(s)    Redford, Robert
Screenwriter(s)    Ward, David S.; Nichols, John
Source(s)    *The Milagro Beanfield War* (novel) Nichols, John

Cast    Blades, Ruben; Bradford, Richard; Braga, Sonia; Carmen, Julie; Gammon, James; Griffith, Melanie; Heard, John; Riquelme, Carlos; Stern, Daniel; Vennera, Chick; Walken, Christopher; Walsh, M. Emmet

Song(s)    Parranda Larga (C/L: Reyes, Judith)

Notes    Only songs of over a minute listed.

## 3839 ◆ THE MILKMAN
### Universal, 1950

Musical Score    Rosen, Milton
Composer(s)    Fain, Sammy
Lyricist(s)    Barnett, Jackie
Choreographer(s)    Belfer, Hal

**Producer(s)**   Richmond, Ted
**Director(s)**   Barton, Charles T.
**Screenwriter(s)**   Beich, Albert; O'Hanlon, James; Ragaway, Martin A.; Stern, Leonard

**Cast**   O'Connor, Donald; Durante, Jimmy; Holden, Joyce; Conrad, William; Laurie, Piper; O'Neill, Henry; Risdon, Elizabeth

**Song(s)**   Nobody Wants My Money (C: Durante, Jimmy); The Early Morning Song; It's Bigger Than Both of Us; That's My Boy

## 3840 ✦ THE MILKY WAY (1936)
Paramount, 1936

**Producer(s)**   Sheldon, E. Lloyd
**Director(s)**   McCarey, Leo
**Screenwriter(s)**   Jones, Grover; Butler, Frank; Cornell, Richard
**Source(s)**   *The Milky Way* (play) Root, Lynn; Clork, Harry

**Cast**   Lloyd, Harold; Menjou, Adolphe; Teasdale, Verree; Mack, Helen; Gargan, William; Stander, Lionel; Gateson, Marjorie

**Song(s)**   The Slumber Boat [1] (C: Gaynor, Jessie L.; L: Riley, Alice C.D.); Tannenbaum's Skin Balm [2] (C/L: McCarey, Leo); The Milky Way [3] (C: Lawnhurst, Vee; L: Seymour, Tot)

**Notes**   [1] Not used. Used in TORCH SINGER. [2] Used instrumentally only. [3] Not used. Written for exploitation only.

## 3841 ✦ THE MILKY WAY (1940)
Metro–Goldwyn–Mayer, 1940

**Musical Score**   Bradley, Scott

**Song(s)**   The Milky Way (C: Bradley, Scott; L: Ising, Rudolf)

**Notes**   Animated cartoon.

## 3842 ✦ A MILLIONAIRE FOR CHRISTY
Twentieth Century–Fox, 1951

**Musical Score**   Young, Victor
**Composer(s)**   Young, Victor

**Producer(s)**   Friedlob, Bert
**Director(s)**   Marshall, George
**Screenwriter(s)**   Englund, Ken

**Cast**   MacMurray, Fred; Parker, Eleanor; Carlson, Richard; Merkel, Una; Buckley, Kay; Dumbrille, Douglass; Greenleaf, Raymond; Paiva, Nestor

**Song(s)**   Repello Wine (L: Young, Victor); I Don't Stand a Ghost of a Chance with You [1] (L: Crosby, Bing; Washington, Ned)

**Notes**   [1] Also in FOLIES BERGERE (United Artists).

## 3843 ✦ MILLION DOLLAR BABY
Warner Brothers–First National, 1941

**Producer(s)**   Warner, Jack L.; Wallis, Hal B.
**Director(s)**   Bernhardt, Curtis
**Screenwriter(s)**   Robinson, Casey; Macaulay, Richard; Wald, Jerry
**Source(s)**   "Miss Wheelwright Discovers America" (story) Spigelgass, Leonard

**Cast**   Lane, Priscilla; Lynn, Jeffrey; Reagan, Ronald; Robson, May; Patrick, Lee; Westley, Helen; Barbier, George; Wynn, Nan; Qualen, John; Catlett, Walter; Carle, Richard

**Song(s)**   I Found a Million Dollar Baby (In a Five and Ten Cent Store) [1] (C: Warren, Harry; L: Rose, Billy; Dixon, Mort); Who Is In Your Dreams Tonight (C/L: Hollander, Frederick)

**Notes**   [1] Later featured in FUNNY LADY.

## 3844 ✦ MILLION DOLLAR LEGS
Paramount, 1932

**Director(s)**   Cline, Edward F.
**Screenwriter(s)**   Mankiewicz, Joseph L.

**Cast**   Fields, W.C.; Oakie, Jack; Roberti, Lyda; Clyde, Andy; Turpin, Ben; Herbert, Hugh; Barbier, George; Gilbert, Billy; Hart, Teddy; Fleming, Susan; Moore, Dickie

**Song(s)**   It's Terrific (C/L: Rainger, Ralph); One Hour with You [1] (C: Whiting, Richard A.; L: Robin, Leo); Tonight (C/L: Johnston, Arthur)

**Notes**   Originally titled ON YOUR MARK. [1] Also used in ONE HOUR WITH YOU.

## 3845 ✦ MILLION DOLLAR MERMAID
Metro–Goldwyn–Mayer, 1952

**Choreographer(s)**   Berkeley, Busby

**Producer(s)**   Hornblow Jr., Arthur
**Director(s)**   LeRoy, Mervyn
**Screenwriter(s)**   Freeman, Everett

**Cast**   Williams, Esther; Mature, Victor; Pidgeon, Walter; Brian, David; Corcoran, Donna; White, Jesse; Tallchief, Maria

**Notes**   No cue sheet available. Titled ONE PIECE BATHING SUIT overseas. This film has no songs but it does have production numbers.

## 3846 ✦ MILLION DOLLAR MYSTERY
De Laurentiis Entertainment, 1987

**Musical Score**   Gorgoni, Al

**Producer(s)**   Kesten, Stephen F.
**Director(s)**   Fleischer, Richard

**Screenwriter(s)**  Metcalfe, Tim; Tejada-Flores, Miguel; De Luca, Rudy

**Cast**  Deezen, Eddie; Sherman, Wendy; Overton, Rick; Lyden, Mona; Emerson, Douglas; Bosley, Tom; De Luca, Rudy

**Song(s)**  Million $ Mystery (C/L: Mann, Barry; Parker, John Lewis); E Z Money (C/L: Parker, John Lewis); Maybe Tonight (C/L: Mann, Barry; Parker, John Lewis)

**Notes**  No cue sheet available.

### 3847 ✦ MILLION DOLLAR PURSUIT
Republic, 1951

**Producer(s)**  Auer, Stephen
**Director(s)**  Springsteen, R.G.
**Screenwriter(s)**  Foote, Bradbury; De Mond, Albert

**Cast**  Edwards, Penny; Withers, Grant; Budd, Norman; Flagg, Steve

**Song(s)**  What Am I Doing [2] (C: Revel, Harry; L: Greene, Mort); Sentimental [1] (C: Kent, Walter; L: Gannon, Kim)

**Notes**  [1] Also in HITCH HIKE TO HAPPINESS. [2] Also in MOONLIGHT MASQUERADE.

### 3848 ✦ MILLION DOLLAR WEEKEND
Eagle Lion, 1948

**Musical Score**  Ohman, Phil

**Producer(s)**  Kemp, Matty
**Director(s)**  Raymond, Gene
**Screenwriter(s)**  Belden, Charles

**Cast**  Raymond, Gene; Paull, Stephanie; Lederer, Francis; Warwick, Robert; Shay, Patricia; Craven, James

**Song(s)**  My Destiny (C/L: Daniels, Dorothy; Roberts, Dorothy); Where Have You Been? (C/L: Daniels, Dorothy; Roberts, Dorothy)

### 3849 ✦ MILLIONS IN THE AIR
Paramount, 1935

**Composer(s)**  Rainger, Ralph
**Lyricist(s)**  Robin, Leo

**Producer(s)**  Hurley, Harold
**Director(s)**  McCarey, Ray
**Screenwriter(s)**  Herzig, Sig; Storm, Jane

**Cast**  Barrie, Wendy [2]; Howard, John [3]; Howard, Willie; Whitney, Eleanore; Cummings, Robert; Courtney, Inez; Chasen, Dave; Bacon, Irving; Baker, Benny; Barbier, George; Hobbes, Halliwell

**Song(s)**  Laughin' at the Weather Man [4]; Love Is Just Around the Corner [7] (C: Gensler, Lewis E.); A Penny in My Pocket [8]; Crooner's Lullaby [4] (C: Johnston, Arthur; L: Coslow, Sam); You Tell Her, I Stutter [6]

(C/L: Friend, Cliff; Rose, Billy); Crazy People [1] [5] (C: Monaco, James V.; L: Leslie, Edgar); Tap Happy [1]; Heat It Up [1]; Do Your Stuff [1]

**Notes**  Also contains versions of "Donna e Mobile" by Verdi. [1] Not used. [2] Dubbed by Miss Lane. [3] Dubbed by Mr. Cotton. [4] Written for THE BIG BROADCAST OF 1936. [5] This was not written for the film. It was recorded but Halliwell Hobbs couldn't get the hang of it and the number was dropped. [6] Not written for the film. [7] Not used in HER MASTER'S VOICE, but also used in MILLIONS IN THE AIR. [8] Also used in FOUR HOURS TO KILL.

### 3850 ✦ MINSTREL DAYS
Warner Brothers, 1941

**Composer(s)**  Jerome, M.K.
**Lyricist(s)**  Scholl, Jack

**Song(s)**  A Song Is the Thing; Minstrel Days [1]

**Notes**  There are also turn-of-the-century songs featured in this short subject. [1] Also in HORSE AND BUGGY DAYS and MY WILD IRISH ROSE.

### 3851 ✦ MINSTREL MAN
PRC, 1944

**Composer(s)**  Revel, Harry
**Lyricist(s)**  Webster, Paul Francis

**Producer(s)**  Fromkess, Leon
**Director(s)**  Lewis, Joseph H.
**Screenwriter(s)**  Franklin, Irwin; Gendron, Pierre

**Cast**  Fields, Benny; George, Gladys; Dinehart, Alan; Karns, Roscoe; Clark, Judy; Raitt, John; Lamont, Molly

**Song(s)**  Remember Me to Carolina; I Don't Care If the World Knows It; Cindy; Shakin' Hands with the Sun; My Bamboo Cane

**Notes**  No cue sheet available. There is also a vocal of "Melancholy Baby" by Ernie Burnett and George A. Norton.

### 3852 ✦ THE MINUTE MAN

See SIX CYLINDER LOVE (1931).

### 3853 ✦ MIRACLE IN SOHO
United Artists, 1957

**Musical Score**  Easdale, Brian

**Producer(s)**  Rank, J. Arthur
**Director(s)**  Pressburger, Emeric
**Screenwriter(s)**  Amyes, Julian

**Cast**  Gregson, John; Lee, Belinda; Cusack, Cyril; Illing, Peter; Bannen, Ian

**Song(s)** The Miracle (C: Easdale, Brian; L: Fishman, Jack)

## 3854 ✦ MIRACLE IN THE RAIN
### Warner Brothers–First National, 1956

**Musical Score** Waxman, Franz

**Producer(s)** Rosenberg, Frank P.
**Director(s)** Mate, Rudolph
**Screenwriter(s)** Hecht, Ben

**Cast** Wyman, Jane; Johnson, Van; Castle, Peggie; Clark, Fred; Heckart, Eileen; Hutchinson, Josephine; Gargan, William; Dalio, Marcel; Givot, George; Nichols, Barbara; Hobbes, Halliwell; King, Alan; Johnson, Arte

**Song(s)** Miracle in the Rain [1] (I'll Always Believe in You) (C: Heindorf, Ray; Jerome, M.K.; L: Washington, Ned)

**Notes** [1] The title song is used as a background vocal. "With Plenty of Money and You" by Harry Warren and Al Dubin is used as a visual vocal.

## 3855 ✦ THE MIRACLE OF MORGAN'S CREEK
### Paramount, 1944

**Producer(s)** Sturges, Preston
**Director(s)** Sturges, Preston
**Screenwriter(s)** Sturges, Preston

**Cast** Hutton, Betty; Bracken, Eddie; Demarest, William; Lynn, Diana; Hall, Porter; Donlevy, Brian; Tamiroff, Akim; Howard, Esther

**Song(s)** The Bell in the Bay (C/L: Sturges, Preston); One Dozen Roses [2] (C: Jergens, Dick; Donovan, Walter; L: Lewis, Roger; Washburn, Country; Sleepy Summer Days [1] (C: Snyder, Ted; L: Sturges, Preston)

**Notes** [1] Not used. [2] Not written for this production.

## 3856 ✦ MIRACLE OF THE BELLS
### RKO, 1946

**Musical Score** Harline, Leigh

**Producer(s)** Lasky, Jesse L.; MacEwen, Walter
**Director(s)** Pichel, Irving
**Screenwriter(s)** Hecht, Ben; Reynolds, Quentin
**Source(s)** *The Miracle of the Bells* (novel) Janney, Russell

**Cast** MacMurray, Fred; Valli, Alida; Cobb, Lee J.; Sinatra, Frank; Vermilyea, Harold; Meredith, Charles; Nolan, Jim; Ahn, Philip

**Song(s)** Powrot (C: Lubomirski; L: Lurie, I.); Ever Homeward [1] (C: Styne, Jule; L: Cahn, Sammy); Miracle of the Bells [2] (C: Norman, Pierre; L: Janney, Russell)

**Notes** [1] Music based on a traditional Polish tune. [2] Sheet music only.

## 3857 ✦ MIRACLE OF THE HILLS
### Twentieth Century–Fox, 1959

**Musical Score** Sawtell, Paul; Shefter, Bert; Jackson

**Producer(s)** Lyons, Richard E.
**Director(s)** Landres, Paul
**Screenwriter(s)** Hoffman, Charles

**Cast** Reason, Rex; Leslie, Nan; Gerson, Betty Lou; North, Jay

**Song(s)** Frankie Don't Bother Me (C/L: Sawtell, Paul; Shefter, Bert; Jackson)

## 3858 ✦ MIRACLE OF THE WHITE STALLIONS
### Disney, 1963

**Musical Score** Smith, Paul J.

**Producer(s)** Herald, Peter V.
**Director(s)** Hiller, Arthur
**Screenwriter(s)** Carothers, A.J.
**Source(s)** *The Dancing White Horses of Vienna* (book) Podhajsky, Alois

**Cast** Taylor, Robert; Palmer, Lilli; Jurgens, Curt; Albert, Eddie; Franciscus, James

**Song(s)** Just Say, "Auf Wiedersehen" (C/L: Sherman, Richard M.; Sherman, Robert B.)

## 3859 ✦ THE MISADVENTURES OF MERLIN JONES
### Disney, 1964

**Musical Score** Baker, Buddy

**Producer(s)** Miller, Ron
**Director(s)** Stevenson, Robert
**Screenwriter(s)** August, Tom; August, Helen

**Cast** Kirk, Tommy; Funicello, Annette; Ames, Leon; Erwin, Stuart; Hewitt, Alan; Gilchrist, Connie; McKennon, Dallas; Grabowski, Norman

**Song(s)** Merlin Jones (C/L: Sherman, Richard M.; Sherman, Robert B.)

## 3860 ✦ MIS DOS AMORES
### Paramount, 1938

**Cast** Guizar, Tito; DeCastejon, Blanca

**Song(s)** Vuelveme A Besar (Kiss Me Again) (C/L: Gonzales, Aaron); Rosas y Mujeres (Roses and Women) (C/L: Gonzales, Aaron); Primer Amor (First Love) (C/L: Guizar, Tito); Jalando (Hauling) (C/L: Guizar, Tito); Madre (Mother) (C/L: Guizar, Tito; Gama, Rafael); Que Hubo (H'ya Toots) [1] (C/L: Guizar, Tito)

**Notes** [1] Sheet music titles song "Quiubo Quiubo" and also credits Nanette Noriega.

## 3861 ✦ MISSING
### Universal, 1982

**Musical Score** Vangelis

**Producer(s)** Lewis, Edward; Lewis, Mildred
**Director(s)** Costa-Gavras
**Source(s)** *The Execution of Charles Horman* (book) Hauser, Thomas

**Cast** Lemmon, Jack; Spacek, Sissy; Mayron, Melanie; Shea, John; Cioffi, Charles; Clennon, David; Venture, Richard; Hardin, Jerry; Costello, Ward

**Song(s)** My Whole World Is Falling Down (C/L: Crutchfield, Jerry; Anderson, Bill)

**Notes** It is uncertain if the above was written for this film.

## 3862 ✦ MISSISSIPPI
### Paramount, 1935

**Composer(s)** Rodgers, Richard
**Lyricist(s)** Hart, Lorenz

**Producer(s)** Hornblow Jr., Arthur
**Director(s)** Sutherland, Edward
**Screenwriter(s)** Martin, Francis; Cunningham, Jack
**Source(s)** *Magnolia* (play) Tarkington, Booth

**Cast** Crosby, Bing; Fields, W.C.; Bennett, Joan; Smith, Queenie; Patrick, Gail; Gillingwater, Claude

**Song(s)** It's Easy to Remember; Soon; Down By the River; Roll, Mississippi; Mississippi Opening (No Bottom) (The Leadsman's Song); The Steely Glint in My Eye [1]; Pablo, You Are My Heart [1] [3]; The Notorious Colonel Blake [1]; I Keep on Singing [1]; You Are So Lovely and I'm So Lonely [1] [2]

**Notes** Ann Sheridan had a bit part. [1] Not used. [2] Later used in the Broadway play SOMETHING GAY (1935). [3] Music later reworked and new lyric added to make "Johnny One-Note" in Broadway musical BABES IN ARMS (1937).

## 3863 ✦ MISSISSIPPI BELLE
### Warner Brothers, 1943 (unproduced)

**Composer(s)** Porter, Cole
**Lyricist(s)** Porter, Cole

**Song(s)** Amo Amas [1]; Hip, Hip, Hooray for Andy Jackson; I Like Pretty Things; I'm Not Myself; In the Green Hills of County Mayo [2]; Kathleen; Loading Song (C: Traditional); Mamie Magdalin (C: Traditional); Mississippi Belle; My Broth of a Boy [3]; School, School, Heaven-Blessed School; So Long [4]; When a Woman's in Love [5]; When McKinley Marches On (C:

Traditional); When You and I Were Strangers; Who'll Bid? [6]

**Notes** [1] Adapted from 18th-century drinking song "Amo Amas." [2] Melody adapted from Dobbins' "Flowery Vale." [3] Lyrics adapted from traditional Irish song "Lullaby." [4] A revision of "So Long, San Antonio" used in the stage musical SOMETHING FOR THE BOYS. [5] Lyrics from poem "Oh, Say No Woman's Love Is Bought." [6] Adapted from the American folk song "The Female Auctioneer."

## 3864 ✦ THE MISSISSIPPI GAMBLER (1929)
### Universal, 1929

**Director(s)** Barker, Reginald
**Screenwriter(s)** Reeve, Winifred; Van Loan, H.H.

**Cast** Schildkraut, Joseph; Bennett, Joan; Geraghty, Carmelita; Francis, Alec B.; Harlan, Otis; Welsh, William

**Song(s)** Father Mississippi (C: Akst, Harry; L: Gilbert, L. Wolfe)

**Notes** No cue sheet available.

## 3865 ✦ MISSISSIPPI GAMBLER (1942)
### Universal, 1942

**Composer(s)** Rosen, Milton
**Lyricist(s)** Carter, Everett
**Choreographer(s)** Verdon, Gwen [4]

**Producer(s)** Malvern, Paul
**Director(s)** Rawlins, John
**Screenwriter(s)** Chanslor, Roy; Martin, Al

**Cast** Taylor, Kent; Litel, John; Langford, Frances

**Song(s)** There Goes My Romance [3]; Got Love [1]; I'm Hittin' the Hot Spots [2] (C: McHugh, Jimmy; L: Adamson, Harold)

**Notes** [1] Also in GET GOING, I'M NOBODY'S SWEETHEART NOW and SWING IT SOLDIER. [2] Also in WHEN LOVE IS YOUNG and BREEZING HOME. [3] Also in I'M NOBODY'S SWEETHEART NOW. [4] Billed as Gwyneth Verdon.

## 3866 ✦ THE MISSISSIPPI GAMBLER (1953)
### Universal, 1953

**Musical Score** Skinner, Frank

**Producer(s)** Richmond, Ted
**Director(s)** Mate, Rudolph
**Screenwriter(s)** Miller, Seton I.

**Cast** Power, Tyrone; Laurie, Piper; Randell, Ron; Adams, Julia; Cavanagh, Paul; McIntire, John; Dumke, Ralph; Warwick, Robert; Reynolds, William; Williams, Guy

**Song(s)** De Lawd's Plan (C: Mancini, Henry; Skinner, Frank; L: Herbert, Frederick); Haitian Devil Song (C/L: Antoine, Le Roi)

## 3867 ✦ MISSISSIPPI RHYTHM
Monogram, 1949

**Composer(s)** Davis, Jimmie
**Lyricist(s)** Davis, Jimmie

**Producer(s)** Parsons, Lindsley
**Director(s)** Abrahams, Derwin
**Screenwriter(s)** Darling, Gretchen

**Cast** Davis, Jimmie; White, Lee "Lasses"; Borg, Veda Ann; England, Sue; Flavin, James; Talbot, Lyle; Maxey, Paul; Bryer, Paul; The Sunshine Boys

**Song(s)** You Are My Sunshine; I Can't Say Good Bye; No One Will Ever Know; It Makes No Difference Now

**Notes** No cue sheet available. There are 12 songs in this film.

## 3868 ✦ THE MISSOURI TRAVELER
Disney, 1957

**Musical Score** Marshall, Jack
**Composer(s)** Marshall, Jack
**Lyricist(s)** Curtis, Ken

**Producer(s)** Ford, Patrick
**Director(s)** Hopper, Jerry
**Screenwriter(s)** Hall, Norman S.
**Source(s)** *The Missouri Traveler* (novel) Burress, John

**Cast** de Wilde, Brandon; Marvin, Lee; Merrill, Gary; Ford, Paul; Horsford, Mary; Curtis, Ken; Tinny, Cal; Cady, Frank; Freeman, Kathleen; Wright, Will

**Song(s)** Finas Daugherty; In Missouri (L: Raskin, Milton); Old Fashioned Sweetheart; The Piney Woods (Biarn's Song) (L: Mercer, Johnny)

## 3869 ✦ MISS SADIE THOMPSON
Columbia, 1953

**Musical Score** Duning, George
**Composer(s)** Lee, Lester
**Lyricist(s)** Washington, Ned
**Choreographer(s)** Scott, Lee

**Producer(s)** Wald, Jerry
**Director(s)** Bernhardt, Curtis
**Screenwriter(s)** Kleiner, Harry
**Source(s)** "Miss Thompson" (story) Maugham, W. Somerset

**Cast** Hayworth, Rita [1]; Ferrer, Jose; Ray, Aldo; Bellaver, Harry; Collins, Russell; Converse, Peggy; Costello, Diosa

**Song(s)** A Marine, A Marine, A Marine (L: Roberts, Allan); Hear No Evil; The Heat Is On; Blue Pacific Blues; Sadie Thompson's Song [2]

**Notes** Filmed in 3-D. [1] Dubbed by Jo Ann Greer. [2] Sheet music only.

## 3870 ✦ MISS SUSIE SLAGLE'S
Paramount, 1945

**Musical Score** Amfitheatrof, Daniele

**Producer(s)** Houseman, John
**Director(s)** Berry, John
**Screenwriter(s)** Froelick, Anne; Butler, Hugo
**Source(s)** *Miss Susie Slagle's* (novel) Tucker, Augustus

**Cast** Gish, Lillian; Lake, Veronica; Tufts, Sonny; Caulfield, Joan; De Wolfe, Billy; Bridges, Lloyd; Collins, Ray; Carnovsky, Morris

**Song(s)** Little Eliza (C: Wayne, Bernie; L: Raleigh, Ben)

**Notes** Also includes "Let Me Call You Sweetheart" by Beth Whitson and Leo Friedman; "In the Evening by the Moonlight" by James H. Bland and "When You Wore a Tulip" by Percy Wenrich and Mahoney.

## 3871 ✦ MR. ACE
United Artists, 1946

**Musical Score** Roemheld, Heinz

**Producer(s)** Bogeaus, Benedict
**Director(s)** Marin, Edwin L.
**Screenwriter(s)** Finklehoffe, Fred F.

**Cast** Raft, George; Sidney, Sylvia; Ridges, Stanley; Haden, Sara; Cowan, Jerome; Silvers, Sid

**Song(s)** Now and Then (C/L: Silvers, Sid; Finklehoffe, Fred F.)

## 3872 ✦ MR. BELVEDERE GOES TO COLLEGE
Twentieth Century–Fox, 1949

**Producer(s)** Engel, Samuel G.
**Director(s)** Nugent, Elliott
**Screenwriter(s)** Sale, Richard; Loos, Mary; McCall Jr., Mary C.
**Source(s)** (Character) Davenport, Gwen

**Cast** Webb, Clifton; Temple, Shirley; Drake, Tom; Young, Alan; Landis, Jessie Royce; Hughes, Kathleen; Holmes, Taylor; Chandler, Jeff

**Song(s)** Dear Old Clemens (C: Newman, Alfred; L: Darby, Ken)

**Notes** There are also vocals of "We Belong to Alma" by Val Burton and Will Jason; "Fare-thee-Well Dear Alma Mater" by Josef Myrow and Mack Gordon and "Collegiate" by Nat Bonx and Moe Jaffe.

## 3873 ✦ MISTER BIG
### Universal, 1943

**Composer(s)**  Pepper, Buddy; James, Inez
**Lyricist(s)**  Pepper, Buddy; James, Inez
**Choreographer(s)**  Da Pron, Louis

**Producer(s)**  Goldsmith, Ken
**Director(s)**  Lamont, Charles
**Screenwriter(s)**  Pollexfen, Jack; Bennett, Dorothy

**Cast**  Jean, Gloria; O'Connor, Donald; Ryan, Peggy; Paige, Robert; Knox, Elyse

**Song(s)**  Serenade (C: Schubert, Franz); Soliloquy; This Must Be a Dream; All the Things I Wanta Say; Rude, Crude and Unattractive; We're Not Obvious; Thee and Me; Hi Character; The Spirit Is In Me; Boogie Woogie Sandman [1]; Kittens with their Mittens Laced [1]

**Notes**  There are also vocals of "Moonlight and Roses" by Edwin H. Lemare, Ben Black and Neil Moret; "Come Along My Mandy" by Tom Mellor, Alfred J. Lawrence, Nora Bayes and Jack Norworth; the spiritual "Little David Play on Yo' Harp" and "We'll Meet Again" by Ross Parker and Hughie Charles. [1] Sheet music only.

## 3874 ✦ MISTER BUDDWING
### Metro–Goldwyn–Mayer, 1966

**Musical Score**  Hopkins, Kenyon

**Producer(s)**  Mann, Delbert; Laurence, Douglas
**Director(s)**  Mann, Delbert
**Screenwriter(s)**  Wasserman, Dale
**Source(s)**  *Buddwing* (novel) Hunter, Evan

**Cast**  Garner, James; Simmons, Jean; Pleshette, Suzanne; Ross, Katharine; Lansbury, Angela; Voskovec, George; Gilford, Jack; Mantell, Joe; St. Jacques, Raymond; Lynch, Ken; Vincent, Romo; Addy, Wesley

**Song(s)**  Talkin' Law [1] (C: Hopkins, Kenyon; L: Wasserman, Dale)

**Notes**  Titled FACE WITHOUT A NAME outside U.S. [1] Also in DOCTOR, YOU'VE GOT TO BE KIDDING!

## 3875 ✦ MR. BUG GOES TO TOWN
### Paramount, 1941

**Musical Score**  Harline, Leigh
**Composer(s)**  Carmichael, Hoagy
**Lyricist(s)**  Loesser, Frank

**Producer(s)**  Fleischer, Max
**Director(s)**  Fleischer, Dave
**Screenwriter(s)**  Gordon, Dan; Pierce, Ted; Sparber, Isadore; Turner, William; Meyer, Carl; Place, Graham; Wickersham, Bob; Howard, Cal

**Song(s)**  I'll Dance at Your Wedding (Honey Dear); Katy Did—Katy Didn't; Be My Little Baby Bumble Bee [1] (C: Marshall, Henry; L: Murphy, Stanley); We're the Couple in the Castle; Boy, Oh Boy! (C: Timberg, Sammy)

**Notes**  Animated feature. [1] Not written for this picture. Also known as HOPPITY GOES TO TOWN.

## 3876 ✦ MR. CHUMP
### Warner Brothers, 1938

**Musical Score**  Jackson, Howard
**Composer(s)**  Hanighen, Bernie

**Producer(s)**  Foy, Bryan
**Director(s)**  Clemens, William
**Screenwriter(s)**  Bricker, George

**Cast**  Davis, Johnnie; Lane, Lola; Singleton, Penny; Briggs, Donald; Clute, Chester; Orth, Frank; Bates, Granville; Charters, Spencer; Bevans, Clem

**Song(s)**  It's Against the Law in Arkansas (L: Henderson, Charles); As Long As You Live You'll Be Dead When You Die (L: Mercer, Johnny)

## 3877 ✦ MR. DODD TAKES THE AIR
### Warner Brothers, 1937

**Musical Score**  Deutsch, Adolph
**Composer(s)**  Warren, Harry
**Lyricist(s)**  Dubin, Al

**Producer(s)**  LeRoy, Mervyn
**Director(s)**  Green, Alfred E.
**Screenwriter(s)**  Wister, William; Ryan, Haines; Ryan, Elaine
**Source(s)**  "The Great Crooner" (story) Kelland, Clarence Budington

**Cast**  Baker, Kenny; Wyman, Jane; Michael, Gertrude; Brady, Alice; McHugh, Frank; Alberni, Luis; O'Neill, Henry; Soubier, Cliff; Harris, Sybil; Taylor, Ferris

**Song(s)**  If I Were a Lily; Here Comes the Sandman; Am I in Love? [1]; The Girl You Used to Be; Remember Me? [2]

**Notes**  Tony Thomas doesn't list "If I Were the Lily" in his Harry Warren biography but it is on the cue sheet. [1] Later in SHE'S WORKING HER WAY THROUGH COLLEGE. [2] Also in NEVER SAY GOODBYE.

## 3878 ✦ MR. DOODLE KICKS OFF
### RKO, 1936

**Musical Score**  Webb, Roy
**Composer(s)**  Webb, Roy
**Lyricist(s)**  Raynor, Hal

**Producer(s)**  Sisk, Robert
**Director(s)**  Goodwins, Leslie
**Screenwriter(s)**  Granet, Bert

**Cast**  Travis, June; Lane, Richard; Alexander, Ben; Gilbert, Billy; Carson, Jack; Bruce, Alan

**Song(s)** My All American Band; It's a Mystery to Me

**Notes** Raynor alone is credited with songs in credits.

### 3879 ✦ MR. HOBBS TAKES A VACATION
Twentieth Century–Fox, 1962

**Musical Score** Mancini, Henry

**Producer(s)** Wald, Jerry
**Director(s)** Koster, Henry
**Screenwriter(s)** Johnson, Nunnally
**Source(s)** *Mr. Hobbs' Holiday* (novel) Streeter, Edward

**Cast** Stewart, James; O'Hara, Maureen; Fabian; Saxon, John; Wilson, Marie; Gardiner, Reginald; Peters, Lauri; McGiver, John; Urecal, Minerva

**Song(s)** Creampuff (C: Mancini, Henry; L: Mercer, Johnny)

### 3880 ✦ MR. IMPERIUM
Metro–Goldwyn–Mayer, 1951

**Musical Score** Kaper, Bronislau
**Composer(s)** Arlen, Harold
**Lyricist(s)** Fields, Dorothy

**Producer(s)** Knopf, Edwin H.
**Director(s)** Hartman, Don
**Screenwriter(s)** Knopf, Edwin H.; Hartman, Don
**Source(s)** (play) Knopf, Edwin H.

**Cast** Turner, Lana [1]; Pinza, Ezio; Main, Marjorie; Sullivan, Barry; Reynolds, Debbie; Hardwicke, Sir Cedric

**Song(s)** Sing Yippi Ki Yi [2] (C: Rosen, Milton; L: Carter, Everett); My Love and My Mule; Let Me Look at You; Andiamo; Solamente Una Vez [3] (You Belong to My Heart) (C: Lara, Augustin; L: Gilbert, Ray)

**Notes** Released internationally as YOU BELONG TO MY HEART. [1] Dubbed by Trudy Erwin. [2] Also in SON OF ROARING SAM (Universal). [3] Also in THE THREE CABALLEROS (Disney), THE GAY RANCHERO (Republic) and THE BIG SOMBRERO (Columbia).

### 3881 ✦ MR. LEMON OF ORANGE
Fox, 1931

**Director(s)** Blystone, John
**Screenwriter(s)** Cantor, Eddie; Burke, Edwin

**Cast** Brendel, El; D'Orsay, Fifi; Collier Jr., William; Warren, Ruth; Pendleton, Nat

**Song(s)** My Racket Is You (C/L: Hanley, James F.); Hinky Dee (Wishing Song) (Inst.) (C: Brendel, El)

### 3882 ✦ MR. MOTO TAKES A VACATION
Twentieth Century–Fox, 1939

**Producer(s)** Wurtzel, Sol M.
**Director(s)** Foster, Norman

**Screenwriter(s)** MacDonald, Philip; Foster, Norman
**Source(s)** characters by Marquand, J.P.

**Cast** Lorre, Peter; Schildkraut, Joseph; Atwill, Lionel; Field, Virginia; King, John

**Song(s)** The Emperor Drinks in the Garden (C/L: Suey, Chan)

### 3883 ✦ MR. MUSIC
Paramount, 1950

**Composer(s)** Van Heusen, James
**Lyricist(s)** Burke, Johnny
**Choreographer(s)** Champion, Gower

**Producer(s)** Welch, Robert L.
**Director(s)** Haydn, Richard
**Screenwriter(s)** Sheekman, Arthur
**Source(s)** *Accent on Youth* (play) Raphaelson, Samson

**Cast** The Merry Macs; Lee, Peggy; Crosby, Bing; Champion, Marge; Champion, Gower; Kirsten, Dorothy; Larsen, Norma; Bouley, Frank; Marx, Groucho; Olson, Nancy; Coburn, Charles; Hussey, Ruth; Stack, Robert; Ewell, Tom

**Song(s)** Wasn't I There?; Wouldn't It Be Funny?; Accidents Will Happen; (If I Linger with) Milady; Life Is So Peculiar; Once More the Blue and White; High on the List; And You'll Be Home; Mr. Music; I'll Never Let My Heart Get Out of Hand [1]

**Notes** [1] Not used.

### 3884 ✦ MR. PEABODY AND THE MERMAID
Universal, 1948

**Musical Score** Dolan, Robert Emmett

**Producer(s)** Johnson, Nunnally
**Director(s)** Pichel, Irving
**Screenwriter(s)** Johnson, Nunnally
**Source(s)** *Peabody's Mermaid* (novel) Jones, Guy; Jones, Constance

**Cast** Powell, William; Smith, Art; Blyth, Ann; Hervey, Irene; Sundberg, Clinton; French, Hugh; Hare, Lumsden; Clark, Fred; King, Andrea

**Song(s)** The Caribees (C: Dolan, Robert Emmett; L: Mercer, Johnny)

### 3885 ✦ MR. QUILP

See QUILP.

### 3886 ✦ MR. ROCK AND ROLL
Paramount, 1957

**Producer(s)** Serpe, Ralph; Kreitsek, Howard B.
**Director(s)** Dubin, Charles S.
**Screenwriter(s)** Blumgarten, James

**Cast** Freed, Alan; Graziano, Rocky; O'Brien, Lois

**Song(s)** Mister Rock and Roll (C/L: Otis, Clyde; Jennings, Joe; Colacrai, Cirino; Randazzo, Teddy); Kiddio (C/L: Benton, Brook; Otis, Clyde); Your Love Alone (C/L: Benton, Brook; Myles, Billy); Sing Song Siren (C/L: Otis, Clyde; Hendricks, B.); Confess It to Your Heart (C/L: Corso, Vincent; Otis, Clyde); You'll Be There (C/L: Leiber, Jerry; Stoller, Mike; Relf, Bobby); It's Simply Heavenly (C/L: Otis, Clyde; Randazzo, Teddy); Love Put Me Out of My Head (C/L: Sherman, Joe; Sherman, Noel); Get Acquainted Waltz (C/L: Edwards, Sherman); Barcelona Rock (C/L: Twomey, Kay; Fields, Irving); This Moment of Love (C/L: Fiocca, Gene ); Baby Doll (C/L: Berry, Chuck); If Only I Had Known (C/L: Benton, Brook; Otis, Clyde); Next Stop Paradise (C/L: Dreyer, Dave; Owens, Cliff; Diamond, Oramay); I Was the Last One to Know (C/L: Randazzo, Teddy; Otis, Clyde; Colacrai, Cirino); Unhappy Blues (C/L: Benton, Brook; Otis, Clyde; Randazzo, Teddy); Lucille (C/L: Little Richard); Hello Folks (C/L: Hampton, Lionel; Hampton, Gladys; Hampton, Locksley); Hey, Poppa Rock (C/L: Hampton, Lionel; Duval, Reggie; Hampton, Gladys); Humpty Dumpty Heart (C/L: Boye, Henry); Make Me Live Again (C/L: Morton, Jerry; Bland, Tommy; Husky, Ferlin); Rock and Cry (C/L: Heath, Joyce); Star Rocket (C/L: Hampton, Lionel); Love Me Right (In the Morning) (C/L: Kirshner, Don; Darin, Bobby); Pathway to Sin (C/L: Russ, Al); Fortunate Fella (C/L: Abrams, Vic; Reid, Irving); I'll Stop Anything I'm Doing (C/L: Benton, Brook; Otis, Clyde)

**Notes** It is not known which of these songs were written for the film.

### 3887 ✦ MR. TOPAZE
Twentieth Century–Fox, 1961

**Musical Score** Van Parys, Georges

**Producer(s)** Rouve, Pierre; de Grunwald, Dimitri
**Director(s)** Sellers, Peter
**Screenwriter(s)** Rouve, Pierre
**Source(s)** *Topaze* (play) Pagnol, Marcel

**Cast** Sellers, Peter; Sims, Joan; Le Mesurier, John; Gray, Nadia; Lom, Herbert; McKern, Leo; Hunt, Martita; Neville, John; Whitelaw, Billie; Gough, Michael

**Song(s)** I Like Money [1] (C: Martin, George; L: Kretzmer, Herbert)

**Notes** Released also as I LIKE MONEY. [1] Sheet music credits music to Graham Fisher. Perhaps it is a pseudonym for Martin.

### 3888 ✦ MODERN DIXIE
Twentieth Century–Fox, 1937

**Song(s)** Pickin' Cotton (C/L: O'Keefe, Lester; Wellesley, Grant); Ole South (C: Zamecnik, J.S.; L: Bryan, Alfred)

**Notes** This is a Lowell Thomas Magic Carpet of Movietone travelogue.

### 3889 ✦ MODERN PROBLEMS
Twentieth Century–Fox, 1981

**Musical Score** Frontiere, Dominic
**Composer(s)** Frontiere, Dominic
**Lyricist(s)** Anderson, Adrienne

**Producer(s)** Greisman, Alan; Shamberg, Michael
**Director(s)** Shapiro, Ken
**Screenwriter(s)** Shapiro, Ken; Sherohman, Tom; Sellers, Arthur

**Cast** Chase, Chevy; D'Arbanville, Patti; Place, Mary Kay; Carter, Nell; Doyle-Murray, Brian; Coleman, Dabney

**Song(s)** Gonna Get It Next Time; She Takes All of Me

### 3890 ✦ THE MODERNS
Alive, 1988

**Musical Score** Isham, Mark
**Composer(s)** Couture, Charlelie
**Lyricist(s)** Couture, Charlelie

**Producer(s)** Pfeiffer, Carolyn; Blocker, David
**Director(s)** Rudolph, Alan
**Screenwriter(s)** Rudolph, Alan; Bradshaw, Jon

**Cast** Carradine, Keith; Fiorentino, Linda; Bujold, Genevieve; Chaplin, Geraldine; Shawn, Wallace; O'Connor, Kevin; Lone, John; Raven, Elsa; Couture, Charlelie

**Song(s)** Paris La Nuitsalavy; I Swear I Do; Dad Je Suis

**Notes** No cue sheet available.

### 3891 ✦ MODESTY BLAISE
Twentieth Century–Fox, 1966

**Musical Score** Dankworth, John
**Composer(s)** Dankworth, John
**Lyricist(s)** Green, Benny

**Producer(s)** Janni, Joseph
**Director(s)** Losey, Joseph
**Screenwriter(s)** Jones, Evan
**Source(s)** *Modesty Blaise* (comic strip) O'Donnell, Peter

**Cast** Vitti, Monica; Stamp, Terence; Bogarde, Dirk; Andrews, Harry; Knox, Alexander; Revill, Clive

**Song(s)** Song on Vesuvius; We Should've Had (L: Green, Benny; Jones, Evan); Modesty

### 3892 ✦ MOHAWK
Twentieth Century–Fox, 1956

**Musical Score** Alperson Jr., Edward L.
**Composer(s)** Alperson Jr., Edward L.
**Lyricist(s)** Herrick, Paul

**Producer(s)** Alperson, Edward L.
**Director(s)** Neumann, Kurt
**Screenwriter(s)** Geraghty, Maurice; Krims, Milton

**Cast** Brady, Scott; Gam, Rita; Brand, Neville; Nelson, Lori; Vague, Vera; Williams, Rhys

**Song(s)** Mohawk; Love Plays the Strings of My Banjo

### 3893 ✦ THE MOLE PEOPLE
Universal–International, 1956

**Producer(s)** Alland, William
**Director(s)** Vogel, Virgil
**Screenwriter(s)** Gorog, Laszlo

**Cast** Agar, John; Patrick, Cynthia; Beaumont, Hugh; Napier, Alan

**Song(s)** Love Theme from The Mole People (C/L: Livingston, Jay; Evans, Ray)

**Notes** No cue sheet available.

### 3894 ✦ MOLLY AND ME (1929)
Tiffany–Stahl, 1929

**Musical Score** Riesenfeld, Hugo

**Director(s)** Ray, Albert
**Screenwriter(s)** Hatton, Frederic; Hatton, Fanny

**Cast** Bennett, Belle; Brown, Joe E.; Vaughn, Alberta; Byer, Charles

**Song(s)** In the Land of Make Believe (C: Baer, Abel; L: Gilbert, L. Wolfe)

**Notes** No cue sheet available.

### 3895 ✦ MOLLY AND ME (1945)
Twentieth Century–Fox, 1945

**Producer(s)** Bassler, Robert
**Director(s)** Seiler, Lewis
**Screenwriter(s)** Praskins, Leonard
**Source(s)** *Molly, Bless Her* (novel) Marion, Frances

**Cast** Fields, Gracie; Woolley, Monty; McDowall, Roddy; Gardiner, Reginald; Schafer, Natalie; Barrett, Edith; Leonard, Queenie

**Song(s)** The Wickedness of Men (C/L: Haines, Will E.); I Passed By Your Window (C/L: Breahe, May H.); Let's All Sing Like the Birdies Sing (C/L: Evans, Tolchard); Christopher Robin Is Saying His Prayers (C/L: Fraser-Simson, Harold)

**Notes** It is not known if any of these were written for this picture.

### 3896 ✦ THE MOLLY MAGUIRES
Paramount, 1970

**Musical Score** Mancini, Henry

**Producer(s)** Ritt, Martin; Bernstein, Walter
**Director(s)** Ritt, Martin
**Screenwriter(s)** Bernstein, Walter

**Cast** Harris, Richard; Connery, Sean; Eggar, Samantha; Finlay, Frank; Zerbe, Anthony; Lund, Art; Leslie, Bethel; Costello, Anthony

**Song(s)** The Hills of Yesterday [1] (C: Mancini, Henry; L: Webster, Paul Francis); The Song of the Molly Maguires [2] (C: Strouse, Charles; L: Adams, Lee); Oh, I Want to Go Home [2] (C: Strouse, Charles; L: Adams, Lee)

**Notes** [1] The lyrics were for exploitation use only. [2] Not used. Charles Strouse wrote an entire score which was not accepted.

### 3897 ✦ MOMENT BY MOMENT
Universal, 1978

**Musical Score** Holdridge, Lee

**Producer(s)** Stigwood, Robert
**Director(s)** Wagner, Jane
**Screenwriter(s)** Wagner, Jane

**Cast** Tomlin, Lily; Travolta, John; Akers, Andra; Kramer, Bert; Bonus, Shelley R.

**Song(s)** Moment By Moment (C: Holdridge, Lee; L: Leikin, Molly-Ann); Hollywood Boulevard (C/L: Parker Jr., Ray)

**Notes** No cue sheet available.

### 3898 ✦ MOMENT TO MOMENT
Universal, 1965

**Musical Score** Mancini, Henry

**Producer(s)** LeRoy, Mervyn
**Director(s)** LeRoy, Mervyn
**Screenwriter(s)** Mahin, John Lee; Coppel, Alec
**Source(s)** "Laughs with a Stranger" (story) Coppel, Alec

**Cast** Seberg, Jean; Garrison, Sean; Hill, Arthur; Blackman, Honor; Aslan, Gregoire; Woods, Donald

**Song(s)** Moment to Moment (C: Mancini, Henry; L: Mercer, Johnny)

### 3899 ✦ MOMMIE DEAREST
Paramount, 1981

**Producer(s)** Yablans, Frank
**Director(s)** Perry, Frank
**Screenwriter(s)** Yablans, Frank; Perry, Frank; Hotchner, Tracy; Getchell, Robert
**Source(s)** *Mommie Dearest* (memoir) Crawford, Christina

**Cast** Dunaway, Faye; Scarwid, Diana; Hobel, Mara; Forrest, Steve; Alda, Rutanya; Da Silva, Howard

**Song(s)** Bittersweet [1] (C: Mancini, Henry; L: Kusik, Larry)

**Notes** [1] Lyric for exploitation use only.

## 3900 ✦ MONA LISA
### Island, 1986

**Musical Score**   Kamen, Michael

**Producer(s)**   Woolley, Stephen; Cassavetti, Patrick
**Director(s)**   Jordan, Neil
**Screenwriter(s)**   Jordan, Neil; Leland, David

**Cast**   Hoskins, Bob; Tyson, Cathy; Caine, Michael; Coltrane, Robbie; Hardie, Kate; Peters, Clarke; Davies, Sammi

**Song(s)**   In Too Deep (C/L: Genesis)

**Notes**   No cue sheet available.

## 3901 ✦ MONDO TEENO
### Trans-American, 1967

**Musical Score**   Curb, Mike

**Producer(s)**   Herman, Norman
**Director(s)**   Herman, Norman
**Screenwriter(s)**   Herman, Norman
**Narrator(s)**   Topper, Burt

**Song(s)**   Teenage Rebellion (C: Curb, Mike; L: Hatcher, Harley)

**Notes**   Also known as TEENAGE REBELLION. A documentary with foreign footage directed by John Donner (Sweden), Eriprando Visconti (Italy), Jean Herman (France) and Walt Sheldon (Japan).

## 3902 ✦ MONEY FROM HOME
### Paramount, 1953

**Musical Score**   Harline, Leigh
**Composer(s)**   Lilley, Joseph J.
**Lyricist(s)**   Brooks, Jack

**Producer(s)**   Wallis, Hal B.
**Director(s)**   Marshall, George
**Screenwriter(s)**   Kanter, Hal
**Source(s)**   "Money from Home" (story) Runyon, Damon

**Cast**   Martin, Dean; Lewis, Jerry; Millar, Marjie; Crowley, Pat; Haydn, Richard; Leonard, Sheldon; Kruschen, Jack

**Song(s)**   Be Careful Song; Love Is the Same (All Over the World)

**Notes**   Jerry Lewis staged some of the "special material in score." There is also a vocal of "Moments Like This" by Burton Lane and Frank Loesser (also in COLLEGE SWING, LAS VEGAS NIGHTS and recorded but not used in TRUE TO LIFE) and one of "I Only Have Eyes for You" by Harry Warren and Al Dubin, which was written for the Warner Brothers picture DAMES.

## 3903 ✦ THE MONEY PIT
### Universal, 1986

**Musical Score**   Colombier, Michel
**Composer(s)**   Colombier, Michel
**Lyricist(s)**   Wakefield, Kathleen

**Producer(s)**   Marshall, Frank; Kennedy, Kathleen; Levinson, Art
**Director(s)**   Benjamin, Richard
**Screenwriter(s)**   Giler, David

**Cast**   Hanks, Tom; Long, Shelley; Godunov, Alexander; Stapleton, Maureen; Mantegna, Joe; Bosco, Philip; Mostel, Josh; Smirnoff, Yakov; Dillon, Mia; Browning, Susan; Faison, Frankie; Wilson, Mary Louise

**Song(s)**   The Heart Is So Willing; Web of Desire (C/L: Tramp, Mike; Bratta, Vito); Sittin' on a Dream; Skin Tight

## 3904 ✦ THE MONEY TRAP
### Metro–Goldwyn–Mayer, 1965

**Musical Score**   Schaefer, Hal

**Producer(s)**   Youngstein, Max E.; Karr, David
**Director(s)**   Kennedy, Burt
**Screenwriter(s)**   Bernstein, Walter
**Source(s)**   *The Money Trap* (novel) White, Lionel

**Cast**   Ford, Glenn; Sommer, Elke; Hayworth, Rita; Montalban, Ricardo; Cotten, Joseph

**Song(s)**   The Money Trap [1] (C: Schaefer, Hal; L: Schaefer, Milton)

**Notes**   [1] Used instrumentally only.

## 3905 ✦ MONEY, WOMEN AND GUNS
### Universal, 1958

**Musical Score**   Stein, Herman

**Producer(s)**   Howritz, Howie
**Director(s)**   Bartlett, Richard
**Screenwriter(s)**   Pittman, Montgomery

**Cast**   Hovey, Tim; Campbell, William; Meredith, Judi; Gleason, James; Stone, Jeffrey; Mahoney, Jock; Hunter, Kim; Chaney Jr., Lon; Drake, Tom

**Song(s)**   Lonely Is the Hunter (C/L: Wakely, Jimmy; Horwitz, Howie)

## 3906 ✦ THE MONITORS
### Commonwealth United, 1969

**Musical Score**   Kaz, Fred
**Composer(s)**   Kaz, Fred
**Lyricist(s)**   Kaz, Fred

**Producer(s)**   Sahlins, Bernard
**Director(s)**   Shea, Jack
**Screenwriter(s)**   Gold, Myron J.
**Source(s)**   (novel) Laumer, Keith

**Cast**   Arkin, Alan; Stockwell, Guy; Oliver, Susan; Shreiber, Avery; Jackson, Sherry; Strudwick, Shepperd; Wynn, Keenan; Begley, Ed; Arkin, Adam; Cugat, Xavier; Dana, Barbara; Dirkson, Senator Everett; Kaye, Stubby; Kaz, Fred; Lipton, Lynn; Vernon, Jackie

**Song(s)**   Voice of the Flowers; Monitor's Jingle; Swamp Draining Song

## 3907 ✦ MONKEY BUSINESS
Paramount, 1931

**Director(s)** McLeod, Norman Z.
**Screenwriter(s)** Sheekman, Arthur

**Cast** Marx, Groucho; Marx, Chico; Marx, Harpo; Marx, Zeppo; Todd, Thelma; Fellowes, Rockliffe; Woods, Harry

**Song(s)** I'm Daffy Over You [1] (C: Marx, Chico; L: Violinsky, Sol)

**Notes** The movie also featured brief renditions of "O Sole Mio" and "You Brought a New Kind of Love to Me" by Sammy Fain, Pierre Norman and Irving Kahal and "Sweet Adeline" by Henry Gerard and Henry Armstrong. [1] Performed instrumentally only. It was also performed instrumentally in HORSE FEATHERS. Later with additional lyrics by Benny Davis the song became known as "Lucky Little Penny."

## 3908 ✦ MONKEYS, GO HOME!
Disney, 1966

**Musical Score** Brunner, Robert F.

**Producer(s)** Miller, Ron
**Director(s)** McLaglen, Andrew V.
**Screenwriter(s)** Tombragel, Maurice
**Source(s)** *The Monkeys* (novel) Wilkinson, G.K.

**Cast** Chevalier, Maurice; Jones, Dean; Mimieux, Yvette; Woringer, Bernard; Harari, Clement; Constant, Yvonne; Hillaire, Marcel; Munshin, Jules; Carney, Alan; Carr, Darleen

**Song(s)** Ce Soir (This Night) (C: Brunner, Robert F.; L: Jackman, Bob); Joie De Vivre (C/L: Sherman, Richard M.; Sherman, Robert B.)

## 3909 ✦ THE MONKEY'S UNCLE
Disney, 1964

**Musical Score** Baker, Buddy

**Producer(s)** Miller, Ron
**Director(s)** Stevenson, Robert
**Screenwriter(s)** August, Tom; August, Helen

**Cast** Kirk, Tommy; Funicello, Annette; Ames, Leon; Faylen, Frank; O'Connell, Arthur; Tyler, Leon; Hewitt, Alan; Miller, Cheryl

**Song(s)** The Monkey's Uncle (C/L: Sherman, Richard M.; Sherman, Robert B.); I Can Fly (C: Baker, Buddy; L: August, Tom); Flying High (C: Baker, Buddy; L: Jackman, Bob)

## 3910 ✦ MONSIEUR BEAUCAIRE
Paramount, 1946

**Musical Score** Dolan, Robert Emmett
**Composer(s)** Livingston, Jay; Evans, Ray
**Lyricist(s)** Livingston, Jay; Evans, Ray
**Choreographer(s)** Daniels, Billy; Earl, Josephine

**Producer(s)** Jones, Paul
**Director(s)** Marshall, George [2]
**Screenwriter(s)** Frank, Melvin; Panama, Norman

**Cast** Caulfield, Joan [1]; Hope, Bob; Schildkraut, Joseph; Knowles, Patric; Reynolds, Marjorie; Kellaway, Cecil; Owen, Reginald; Collier, Constance; Dumbrille, Douglass; Kinskey, Leonid

**Song(s)** A Coach and Four; We'll Drink Every Drop in the Shop; Warm As Wine

**Notes** [1] It is possible she was dubbed by a Miss Finch. [2] Frank Tashlin directed the dueling sequence after principal photography was completed.

## 3911 ✦ MONSIGNOR
Twentieth Century–Fox, 1982

**Musical Score** Williams, John

**Producer(s)** Yablans, Frank; Niven Jr., David
**Director(s)** Perry, Frank
**Screenwriter(s)** Polonsky, Abraham; Mayes, Wendell
**Source(s)** (novel) Leger, Jack Alain

**Cast** Reeve, Christopher; Bujold, Genevieve; Rey, Fernando; Miller, Jason; Cortese, Joe; Cimino, Leonard; Prosky, Robert

**Song(s)** Song (C: Williams, John; L: McCarthy, John)

## 3912 ✦ THE MONSTER SQUAD
Tri-Star, 1987

**Musical Score** Broughton, Bruce

**Producer(s)** Zimbert, Jonathan
**Director(s)** Dekker, Fred
**Screenwriter(s)** Black, Shane; Dekker, Fred

**Cast** Gower, Andre; Kiger, Robby; Nacht, Stephen; Regehr, Duncan; Noonan, Tommy; Gwillim, Jack

**Song(s)** Rock Until You Drop (C/L: Sembello, Michael; Rudolph, Dick; Sembello, Danny); The Monster Squad (C/L: Sembello, Michael; Rudolph, Dick)

**Notes** No cue sheet available.

## 3913 ✦ MONTANA
Warner Brothers–First National, 1950

**Musical Score** Buttolph, David

**Producer(s)** Jacobs, William
**Director(s)** Enright, Ray
**Screenwriter(s)** Webb, James R.; Chase, Borden; O'Neal, Charles

**Cast** Flynn, Errol; Smith, Alexis; Sakall, S.Z.; Kennedy, Douglas; Brown, James; MacDonald, Ian; Irwin, Charles; Burns, Paul E.; Blue, Monte

**Song(s)** Reckon I'm in Love (C/L: David, Mack; Hoffman, Al; Livingston, Jerry)

**3914 ✦ MONTANA BELLE**
RKO, 1949

**Musical Score**   Scott, Nathan

**Producer(s)**   Welsch, Howard
**Director(s)**   Dwan, Allan
**Screenwriter(s)**   McCoy, Horace; Hall, Norman S.

**Cast**   Russell, Jane; Brent, George; Brady, Scott; Tucker, Forrest; Devine, Andy; Litel, John

**Song(s)**   The Gilded Lily (C/L: Nelson, Portia; Martinez, Margaret)

**Notes**   There is also a vocal of "My Sweetheart's the Man in the Moon" by James Thornton and Frank Harding.

**3915 ✦ MONTANA MOON**
Metro–Goldwyn–Mayer, 1930

**Composer(s)**   Brown, Nacio Herb
**Lyricist(s)**   Freed, Arthur

**Director(s)**   St. Clair, Malcolm
**Screenwriter(s)**   Farnham, Joe

**Cast**   Crawford, Joan; Brown, Johnny Mack; Sebastian, Dorothy; Cortez, Ricardo; Rubin, Benny; Edwards, Cliff; Dane, Karl; Ingraham, Lloyd

**Song(s)**   Montana Call (C: Stothart, Herbert; L: Grey, Clifford); The Moon Is Low; Happy Cowboy; Snap Your Fingers at the Blues (C: Ahlert, Fred E.; L: Turk, Roy); Trailin' in Old Montana (C: Stothart, Herbert; L: Grey, Clifford); Sing a Song of Old Montana; Let Me Give You Love [1] (C: Stothart, Herbert; L: Grey, Clifford)

**Notes**   [1] Not on cue sheet.

**3916 ✦ MONTE CARLO**
Paramount, 1930

**Composer(s)**   Whiting, Richard A.; Harling, W. Franke
**Lyricist(s)**   Robin, Leo

**Director(s)**   Lubitsch, Ernst
**Screenwriter(s)**   Vajda, Ernest; Lawrence, Vincent
**Source(s)**   *Blue Coast* (play) Mueller, Hans

**Cast**   MacDonald, Jeanette; Buchanan, Jack; Pitts, ZaSu; Allister, Claud; Conti, Albert; Novis, Donald

**Song(s)**   Day of Days; Beyond the Blue Horizon; Give Me a Moment Please (C: Whiting, Richard A.); Trimmin' the Women; What Ever It Is It's Grand; She'll Love Me and Like It; Always in All Ways (C: Whiting, Richard A.); Opera Sequence; A Job with a Future [1]; Play It Slow and Easy—I'll Dance All Night [1] [3]; [2] I'm a Simple Hearted Man

**Notes**   First titled THE BLUE COAST. [1] Not used. [2] Not on cue sheets. Listed in AFI catalog. [3] A song of the same title was considered for the unproduced BUDDY ROGERS MUSICAL but was listed under different songwriters.

**3917 ✦ MONTE CARLO OR BUST**

See THOSE DARING YOUNG MEN IN THEIR JAUNTY JALOPIES.

**3918 ✦ MONTY PYTHON'S THE MEANING OF LIFE**
Universal, 1983

**Musical Score**   DuPrez, John

**Producer(s)**   Goldstone, John
**Director(s)**   Jones, Terry
**Screenwriter(s)**   Chapman, Graham; Cleese, John; Gilliam, Terry; Idle, Eric; Jones, Terry; Palin, Michael

**Cast**   Chapman, Graham; Cleveland, Carol; Cleese, John; Loe, Judy; Gilliam, Terry; Jones, Simon; Idle, Eric; MacLachlan, Andrew; Jones, Terry; Whittington, Valerie; Palin, Michael

**Song(s)**   The Accountancy Shanty (C/L: Idle, Eric; DuPrez, John); The Meaning of Life (C: Idle, Eric; DuPrez, John; L: Idle, Eric); Every Sperm Is Sacred (C: Jacquemin, Andre; Howman, Dave; L: Palin, Michael; Jones, Terry); Oh Lord Please Don't Burn Us (C: Idle, Eric; DuPrez, John; L: Cleese, John; Chapman, Graham); Galaxy Song (C: Idle, Eric; DuPrez, John; L: Idle, Eric); Penis Song (C/L: Idle, Eric); Christmas in Heaven (C: Idle, Eric; L: Jones, Terry)

**3919 ✦ THE MOONBEAM RIDER**

See FAST CHARLIE . . . THE MOONBEAM RIDER.

**3920 ✦ THE MOON IS BLUE**
United Artists, 1953

**Musical Score**   Gilbert, Herschel Burke

**Producer(s)**   Preminger, Otto
**Director(s)**   Preminger, Otto
**Screenwriter(s)**   Herbert, F. Hugh
**Source(s)**   *The Moon Is Blue* (play) Herbert, F. Hugh

**Cast**   Niven, David; Holden, William; McNamara, Maggie

**Song(s)**   The Moon Is Blue [1] (C: Gilbert, Herschel Burke; L: Fine, Sylvia); Chloro-Foam Beer Song (C/L: Gilbert, Herschel Burke)

**Notes**   [1] Instrumental use only.

**3921 ✦ MOONLIGHT AND CACTUS**
Universal, 1943

**Choreographer(s)**   O'Curran, Charles

**Producer(s)**   Gross, Frank
**Director(s)**   Cline, Edward F.
**Screenwriter(s)**   Conrad, Eugene; Smith, Paul Gerard

**Cast**   The Andrews Sisters; Seidel, Tom; Knox, Elyse; Mitchell Ayres and His Orchestra; Carrillo, Leo;

*THE COMPLETE MUSICAL COMPANION*

Howard, Shemp; Quillan, Eddie; Alper, Murray; Kennedy, Tom; Urecal, Minerva

**Song(s)** Heave Ho! My Lads, Heave Ho! (C/L: Lawrence, Jack); Wah Hoo! [1] (C/L: Friend, Cliff); Down in the Valley (C/L: Luther, Frank); C'Mere Baby (C/L: Jordan, Roy; Grey, Lanny); Send Me a Man, Amen (C/L: Miller, Sidney; Gilbert, Ray); Home (C/L: Van Steeden, Peter; Clarkson, Harry; Clarkson, Jeff); Sing (It's Good for Ya) (C/L: Mooney, Hal; Prince, Hughie); Chiapanecas (C: Uranza, M.; L: Curtis, Mann)

**Notes** [1] Also in ROCKIN' IN THE ROCKIES (Columbia).

## 3922 ♦ MOONLIGHT AND MELODY

See MOONLIGHT AND PRETZELS.

## 3923 ♦ MOONLIGHT AND PRETZELS
### Universal, 1933

**Composer(s)** Gorney, Jay
**Lyricist(s)** Harburg, E.Y.

**Director(s)** Freund, Karl
**Screenwriter(s)** Brice, Monte; Herzig, Sig

**Cast** Pryor, Roger; Brian, Mary; Carrillo, Leo; Miles, Lillian; Watson, Bobby; Frawley, William; Jack Denny and His Orchestra; Claire, Bernice; Gray, Alexander; Keene, Richard; Lang, Mary

**Song(s)** Are You Makin' Any Money Baby? (C/L: Hupfeld, Herman); Ah But Is It Love?; Moonlight and Pretzels; Dusty Shoes; Let's Make Love Like the Crocodiles; There's a Little Bit of You in Every Love Song (C: Fain, Sammy); Gotta Get Up and Go to Work (C/L: Hupfeld, Herman)

**Notes** No cue sheet available. Titled MOONLIGHT AND MELODY internationally.

## 3924 ♦ MOONLIGHT IN HAVANA
### Universal, 1942

**Composer(s)** Franklin, Dave
**Lyricist(s)** Franklin, Dave
**Choreographer(s)** Prinz, Eddie

**Producer(s)** Burton, Bernard W.
**Director(s)** Mann, Anthony
**Screenwriter(s)** Brodney, Oscar

**Cast** Jones, Allan; Grace and Nico; Frawley, William; Frazee, Jane; The Jivin' Jacks and Jills

**Song(s)** Moonlight in Havana; I Don't Need Money; Only You; Got Music; Rhythm of the Tropics; Isn't It Lovely

**Notes** There are also vocals of "I Wonder Who's Kissing Her Now" by Will M. Hough, Frank R. Adams and Joseph E. Howard and "When Irish Eyes Are Smiling" by Chauncey Olcott, George Graff Jr. and Ernest R. Ball.

## 3925 ♦ MOONLIGHT IN HAWAII
### Universal, 1941

**Composer(s)** de Paul, Gene
**Lyricist(s)** Raye, Don
**Choreographer(s)** Ceballos, Larry

**Producer(s)** Goldsmith, Ken
**Director(s)** Lamont, Charles
**Screenwriter(s)** Grant, Morton; Gow, James; Lazarus, Erna

**Cast** The Merry Macs; Frazee, Jane; Errol, Leon; Auer, Mischa; Downs, Johnny; O'Dea, Sunnie; Montez, Maria

**Song(s)** Moonlight in Hawaii; All for One; It's People Like You; We'll Have a Lot of Fun; Poi; Aloha Lowdown

**Notes** There are also vocals of "Hawaiian War Chant" by Johnny Noble and Queen Liluokalani and "Lovely Hula Hands" by Alex Anderson.

## 3926 ♦ MOONLIGHT IN VERMONT
### Universal, 1943

**Composer(s)** Miller, Sidney; James, Inez
**Lyricist(s)** Miller, Sidney; James, Inez
**Choreographer(s)** Da Pron, Louis

**Producer(s)** Burton, Bernard W.
**Director(s)** Lilley, Edward
**Screenwriter(s)** Conrad, Eugene

**Cast** Jean, Gloria; Malone, Ray; Dolenz, George; Helm, Fay

**Song(s)** They Got Me in the Middle of Things; Be a Good, Good Girl; Dobbin and a Wagon of Hay; Pickin' the Beets; Something Tells Me [1]; After the Beat [1]

**Notes** There is also a vocal of "Lover" by Lorenz Hart and Richard Rodgers. [1] Not used.

## 3927 ♦ MOONLIGHT MASQUERADE
### Republic, 1942

**Composer(s)** Revel, Harry
**Lyricist(s)** Greene, Mort

**Producer(s)** Auer, John H.
**Director(s)** Auer, John H.
**Screenwriter(s)** Kimble, Lawrence

**Cast** O'Keefe, Dennis; Frazee, Jane; Kean, Betty; Foy Jr., Eddie; Verebes, Erno; Pangborn, Franklin; Harvey, Paul; Prouty, Jed; Adrian, Iris; The Three Chocolateers

**Song(s)** What Am I Doing (Here in Your Arms) [2]; But Are We Worried Yes!; Liver Lipped Louie [1]

**Notes** [1] Used instrumentally only. [2] Also in MILLION DOLLAR PURSUIT.

## 3928 ✦ MOONLIGHT ON THE PRAIRIE
Warner Brothers, 1935

**Producer(s)** Foy, Bryan
**Director(s)** Lederman, D. Ross
**Screenwriter(s)** Jacobs, William

**Cast** Foran, Dick; Mannors, Sheila; Stone, George E.; Sawyer, Joe; King, Joseph; Barrat, Robert; Jones, Dickie; Heywood, Herbert; Brown, Raymond; Carle, Richard

**Song(s)** Covered Wagon Days (C: Jerome, M.K.; L: Jasmyn, Joan); Moonlight on the Prairie (C/L: Nelson, Bob; Spencer, Tim)

## 3929 ✦ MOON OVER BURMA
Paramount, 1940

**Producer(s)** Veiller, Anthony
**Director(s)** King, Louis
**Screenwriter(s)** Wead, Frank; Lipscomb, W.P.; Clork, Harry

**Cast** Lamour, Dorothy; Preston, Robert; Foster, Preston; Nolan, Doris

**Song(s)** Moon Over Burma (C: Hollander, Frederick; L: Loesser, Frank); Mexican Magic (C: Revel, Harry; L: Loesser, Frank)

## 3930 ✦ MOON OVER HER SHOULDER
Twentieth Century–Fox, 1941

**Producer(s)** Morosco, Walter
**Director(s)** Werker, Alfred
**Screenwriter(s)** Bullock, Walter

**Cast** Bari, Lynn; Sutton, John; Dailey, Dan [1]; Mowbray, Alan; Carey, Leonard; Bacon, Irving; Compton, Joyce

**Song(s)** The Girl with the Sugar Brown Hair (C: Newman, Alfred; L: Bullock, Walter)

**Notes** [1] Billed as Dan Dailey Jr.

## 3931 ✦ MOON OVER LAS VEGAS
Universal, 1944

**Composer(s)** Rosen, Milton
**Lyricist(s)** Carter, Everett

**Producer(s)** Yarbrough, Jean
**Director(s)** Yarbrough, Jean
**Screenwriter(s)** Jeske, George; Bruckman, Clyde

**Cast** Vague, Vera; Gwynne, Anne; Bruce, David

**Song(s)** Faithful Flo; Oklahoma Is Oke with Me (C/L: Dodd, Jimmy); You, Marvelous You (C/L: Austin, Gene); Moon Over Las Vegas; Touch of Texas [2] (C: McHugh, Jimmy; L: Loesser, Frank); A Dream Ago [1]

**Notes** There is also a vocal of "My Blue Heaven" by Walter Donaldson and George Whiting. [1] Also in HAT CHECK HONEY, HI 'YA, SAILOR and STARS AND VIOLINS. [2] Also in the RKO pictures GILDERSLEEVE ON BROADWAY and SEVEN DAYS LEAVE.

## 3932 ✦ MOON OVER MIAMI
Twentieth Century–Fox, 1941

**Composer(s)** Rainger, Ralph
**Lyricist(s)** Robin, Leo
**Choreographer(s)** Pan, Hermes

**Producer(s)** Brown, Harry Joe
**Director(s)** Lang, Walter
**Screenwriter(s)** Lawrence, Vincent; Holmes, Brown

**Cast** Grable, Betty; Ameche, Don; Cummings, Robert; Greenwood, Charlotte; Haley, Jack; Landis, Carole; Wright Jr., Cobina; Lessey, George; The Condos Brothers; Watson, Minor; Charters, Stephen; Roberts, Lynne

**Song(s)** Hooray for Today; I've Got You All to Myself [1]; Miami; You Started Something [2]; Is That Good?; Loveliness and Love; The Kindergarten Conga (Ring Around the Rosie); Seminole Legend (Solitary Seminole)

**Notes** [1] Also in DRESSED TO KILL. [2] Also in CADET GIRL.

## 3933 ✦ MOON OVER PARADOR
Universal, 1989

**Musical Score** Jarre, Maurice

**Producer(s)** Mazursky, Paul
**Director(s)** Mazursky, Paul
**Screenwriter(s)** Capetanos, Leon; Mazursky, Paul

**Cast** Dreyfuss, Richard; Julia, Raul; Braga, Sonia; Winters, Jonathan; Rey, Fernando; Davis Jr., Sammy; Greene, Michael; Holliday, Polly; Goncalves, Milton; Sagebrecht, Marianne; Ramos, Richard Russell; Cavett, Dick; Pappas, Ike; Asner, Edward

**Song(s)** Parador [1] (C: Traditional; L: Mazursky, Paul)

**Notes** [1] Music based on "O Tannenbaum."

## 3934 ✦ MOON PILOT
Disney, 1961

**Musical Score** Smith, Paul J.
**Composer(s)** Sherman, Richard M.; Sherman, Robert B.
**Lyricist(s)** Sherman, Richard M.; Sherman, Robert B.

**Producer(s)** Anderson, Bill
**Director(s)** Neilson, James
**Screenwriter(s)** Tombragel, Maurice

**Cast** Keith, Brian; Tryon, Tom; O'Brien, Edmond; Saval, Dany; Sweeney, Bob; Smith, Kent; Kirk, Tommy

**Song(s)** Moon Pilot Song (Seven Moons of Beta-Lyrae); True Love Is an Apricot; The Void

## 3935 ✦ MOONRAKER
United Artists, 1978

**Musical Score**  Barry, John

**Producer(s)**  Broccoli, Albert R.
**Director(s)**  Gilbert, Lewis
**Screenwriter(s)**  Wood, Christopher
**Source(s)**  *Moonraker* (novel) Fleming, Ian

**Cast**  Moore, Roger; Chiles, Lois; Lonsdale, Michael; Kiel, Richard; Revalec, Blanche; Lee, Bernard; Llewelyn, Desmond

**Song(s)**  Moonraker (C: Barry, John; L: David, Hal)

## 3936 ✦ MOONRISE
Republic, 1948

**Musical Score**  Lava, William

**Producer(s)**  Haas, Charles
**Director(s)**  Borzage, Frank
**Screenwriter(s)**  Haas, Charles

**Cast**  Clark, Dane; Russell, Gail; Barrymore, Ethel; Joslyn, Allyn; Ingram, Rex; Morgan, Henry; Street, David; Royle, Selena; Carey Jr., Harry; Bacon, Irving; Bridges, Lloyd

**Song(s)**  The Moonrise Song (C: Lava, William; L: Tobias, Harry); Lonesome (C: Lava, William; L: Strauss, Theodore)

## 3937 ✦ MOONRUNNERS
United Artists, 1974

**Musical Score**  Jennings, Waylon; Mooney, R.

**Producer(s)**  Clark, Robert B.
**Director(s)**  Waldron, Gy
**Screenwriter(s)**  Waldron, Gy

**Cast**  Mitchum, James; Martin, Kiel; Hunnicutt, Arthur; Forbes, Chris; Ellis, George; Jennings, Waylon; McFarland, George "Spanky"

**Song(s)**  Slow Rolling Low (C/L: Shaver, Billy Joe)

**Notes**  Vocals and instrumentals are not differentiated on the cue sheets.

## 3938 ✦ THE MOONSHINE WAR
Metro–Goldwyn–Mayer, 1970

**Musical Score**  Karger, Fred

**Producer(s)**  Ransohoff, Martin
**Director(s)**  Quine, Richard
**Screenwriter(s)**  Leonard, Elmore
**Source(s)**  *The Moonshine War* (novel) Leonard, Elmore

**Cast**  McGoohan, Patrick; Widmark, Richard; Alda, Alan; Zenor, Susanne; Hazlewood, Lee; Johnson, Melodie; Geer, Will; Williams, Joe; Showalter, Max

**Song(s)**  Ballad of the Moonshine (C/L: Curb, Mike); Moonshine (C/L: Emmerson, Les); It Takes All Kinds of People (C/L: Orbison, Roy; Curb, Mike)

## 3939 ✦ THE MOON'S OUR HOME
Paramount, 1936

**Producer(s)**  Wanger, Walter
**Director(s)**  Seiter, William A.
**Screenwriter(s)**  Dawn, Isabel; DeGaw, Boyce; Parker, Dorothy; Campbell, Alan
**Source(s)**  *The Moon's Our Home* (novel) Baldwin, Faith

**Cast**  Sullavan, Margaret; Fonda, Henry; Bondi, Beulah; Butterworth, Charles; Hamilton, Margaret; Brennan, Walter

**Song(s)**  The Moon's Our Home [1] (C: Hollander, Frederick; L: Coslow, Sam)

**Notes**  [1] Only used instrumentally.

## 3940 ✦ THE MOON-SPINNERS
Disney, 1964

**Musical Score**  Grainer, Ron

**Producer(s)**  Anderson, Bill
**Director(s)**  Neilson, James
**Screenwriter(s)**  Dyne, Michael
**Source(s)**  *The Moon-Spinners* (novel) Stewart, Mary

**Cast**  Mills, Hayley; Wallach, Eli; McEnery, Peter; Greenwood, Joan; Papas, Irene; Le Mesurier, John; Stassino, Paul; Hancock, Sheila; Davis, Michael; Negri, Pola

**Song(s)**  The Moon-Spinners Song (C/L: Gilkyson, Terry)

## 3941 ✦ MOON ZERO TWO
Warner Brothers, 1970

**Musical Score**  Ellis, Don

**Producer(s)**  Carreras, Michael
**Director(s)**  Baker, Roy Ward
**Screenwriter(s)**  Carreras, Michael

**Cast**  Olson, James; Von Schell, Catherina; Mitchell, Warren; Corri, Adrienne; Levy, Ori; Foster, Dudley

**Song(s)**  Moon Zero Two (C: Ellis, Don; L: Davison, Martin)

## 3942 ✦ MORE DEAD THAN ALIVE
United Artists, 1969

**Musical Score**  Springer, Phil

**Producer(s)**  Klein, Hal
**Director(s)**  Sparr, Robert
**Screenwriter(s)**  Schenck, George

Cast   Walker, Clint; Price, Vincent; Hampton, Paul; Henry, Mike

Song(s)   The Messenger (C: Springer, Phil; L: Levine, Irwin)

## 3943 ✦ THE MORE THE MERRIER
Columbia, 1943

Musical Score   Harline, Leigh

Producer(s)   Stevens, George
Director(s)   Stevens, George
Screenwriter(s)   Russell, Robert Wallace; Ross, Frank; Flournoy, Richard; Foster, Lewis R.

Cast   Arthur, Jean; McCrea, Joel; Coburn, Charles; Bennett, Bruce; Sully, Frank; Doran, Ann

Song(s)   Damn the Torpedoes (C: Gorney, Jay; L: Myers, Henry; Eliscu, Edward)

## 3944 ✦ MORMON TRAILS
Twentieth Century–Fox, 1943

Song(s)   Echoes of the Trail (C/L: Allan, Fleming; Autry, Gene); Headin for the Trail (C: Stryker, Fred; L: Lange, J.)

Notes   This is a Lowell Thomas Magic Carpet of Movieland short.

## 3945 ✦ MORNING GLORY
RKO, 1933

Musical Score   Steiner, Max

Producer(s)   Berman, Pandro S.
Director(s)   Sherman, Lowell
Screenwriter(s)   Green, Howard J.
Source(s)   Morning Glory (play) Akins, Zoe

Cast   Hepburn, Katharine; Fairbanks Jr., Douglas; Menjou, Adolphe; Smith, C. Aubrey

Song(s)   Morning Glory [1] (C: Steiner, Max; L: Young, Joe)

Notes   [1] Lyric written for exploitation only.

## 3946 ✦ MOROCCO
Paramount, 1930

Composer(s)   Hajos, Karl
Lyricist(s)   Robin, Leo

Director(s)   von Sternberg, Josef
Screenwriter(s)   Furthman, Jules
Source(s)   Amy Jolly (play) Vigny, Benno

Cast   Dietrich, Marlene; Cooper, Gary; Menjou, Adolphe; Compton, Juliette; Haupt, Ullrich

Song(s)   What Am I Bid for My Apple; Give Me the Man Who Does Things

Notes   There is also a rendition of "Love's Last Word" by Octave Cremieux.

## 3947 ✦ MORONS FROM OUTER SPACE
Universal, 1985

Musical Score   Brewis, Peter

Producer(s)   Hanson, Barry
Director(s)   Hodges, Mike
Screenwriter(s)   Rhys Jones, Griff; Smith, Mel

Cast   Smith, Mel; Rhys Jones, Griff; Sikking, James B.; Landen, Dinsdale; Nail, Jimmy; Pearce, Joanne

Song(s)   Morons from Outer Space (C/L: Smith, Mel; Brewis, Peter)

Notes   No cue sheet available.

## 3948 ✦ LA MORTADELLA
Warner Brothers, 1972

Composer(s)   Nilsson, Harry
Lyricist(s)   Nilsson, Harry

Producer(s)   Ponti, Carlo
Director(s)   Monicelli, Mario
Screenwriter(s)   D'Amico, Suso Cecchi; Monicelli, Mario; Lardner Jr., Ring

Cast   Loren, Sophia; Proietti, Luigi; Devane, William; Carroll, Beeson

Song(s)   (I Guess) the Lord Must Be in New York City; Parson and His Son (C/L: Parham, W.); The Puppy Song; That's the Way I've Always Heard It Should Be (C/L: Brackman, Jacob; Simon, Carly); Story of Maddalena (C/L: Dalla, L.; Cellamare, R.; Bardotti, Sergio; Baldazzi, G.)

Notes   It is not known which, if any, of these songs were written for the film.

## 3949 ✦ THE MORTAL STORM
Metro–Goldwyn–Mayer, 1940

Musical Score   Kaper, Bronislau
Lyricist(s)   Brent, Earl

Producer(s)   Franklin, Sidney
Director(s)   Borzage, Frank
Screenwriter(s)   West, Claudine; Ellis, Anderssen; Froeschel, George
Source(s)   The Mortal Storm (novel) Bottome, Phyllis

Cast   Sullavan, Margaret; Stewart, James; Morgan, Frank; Young, Robert; Stack, Robert; Rich, Irene; Granville, Bonita; Orr, William T.; Reynolds, Gene; Ouspenskaya, Maria

Song(s)   Ergo Bibamus (C: Eberwein); Close Up the Ranks [1] (C: Kaper, Bronislau); Ha, Ha, Ha, Ha, Ho, Ho, Ho, Ho (C: Traditional)

**Notes** [1] Also in REUNION IN FRANCE but with music credited to Edward Kane.

## 3950 ◆ MOSCOW ON THE HUDSON
Columbia, 1984

**Musical Score** McHugh, David

**Producer(s)** Mazursky, Paul
**Director(s)** Mazursky, Paul
**Screenwriter(s)** Mazursky, Paul; Capetanos, Leon

**Cast** Williams, Robin; Alonso, Maria Conchita; Derricks, Cleavant; Rey, Alejandro; Kramarov, Savely; Haynes, Tiger; Rudnik, Oleg

**Song(s)** People Up in Texas (C/L: Jennings, Waylon); Suenos (Freedom) [1] (C/L: McHugh, David)

**Notes** [1] Spanish adaptation by Maria Conchita Alonso.

## 3951 ◆ A MOST IMMORAL LADY
Warner Brothers–First National, 1929

**Composer(s)** Jerome, M.K.
**Lyricist(s)** Ruby, Herman

**Director(s)** Wray, John Griffith
**Screenwriter(s)** Halsey, Forrest
**Source(s)** *A Most Immoral Lady* (play) Martin, Townsend

**Cast** Joy, Leatrice; Pidgeon, Walter; Blackmer, Sidney; Love, Montagu; Dunn, Josephine; Edeson, Robert; Reed, Donald

**Song(s)** Toujours; That's How Much I Need You

**Notes** No cue sheet available.

## 3952 ◆ MOTEL HELL
United Artists, 1980

**Musical Score** Rubin, Lance

**Producer(s)** Jaffe, Robert; Jaffe, Steven-Charles
**Director(s)** Connor, Kevin
**Screenwriter(s)** Jaffe, Robert; Jaffe, Steven-Charles

**Cast** Calhoun, Rory; Parsons, Nancy; Linke, Paul; Axelrod, Nina; Jack, Wolfman; Joyce, Elaine

**Song(s)** Eating Out My Heart and Soul (C/L: Rubin, Lance)

## 3953 ◆ MOTHER CAREY'S CHICKENS
RKO, 1938

**Musical Score** Tours, Frank

**Producer(s)** Berman, Pandro S.
**Director(s)** Lee, Rowland V.
**Screenwriter(s)** Lauren, S.K.; Purcell, Gertrude

**Source(s)** *Mother Carey's Chickens* (play) Wiggin, Kate Douglas; Crothers, Rachel; *Mother Carey's Chickens* (novel) Wiggin, Kate Douglas

**Cast** Shirley, Anne; Keeler, Ruby; Ellison, James; Bainter, Fay; Brennan, Walter; Dunagen, Donnie; Albertson, Frank; Kruger, Alma; Moran, Jackie; Hamilton, Margaret; Weidler, Virginia; Morgan, Ralph

**Song(s)** Long Live the Carey's (C/L: Tours, Frank)

## 3954 ◆ MOTHER, JUGS AND SPEED
Twentieth Century–Fox, 1976

**Producer(s)** Yates, Peter; Mankiewicz, Tom
**Director(s)** Yates, Peter
**Screenwriter(s)** Mankiewicz, Tom

**Cast** Cosby, Bill; Welch, Raquel; Keitel, Harvey; Garfield, Allen; Butkus, Dick; Davison, Bruce; Hagman, Larry; Kamen, Milt

**Song(s)** Dance (C/L: Jabara, Paul); Star in My Life (C: Marriott, Steve; L: Wallace, Ian); Show Me the Way (C/L: Frampton, Peter); My Soul Is a Witness (C/L: Preston, Billy; Green, Joe); California Girls (C/L: Wilson, Brian); No Love Today (C: Nichols, Roger; L: Jennings, Will); Get the Funk Out Ma Face (C/L: Jones, Quincy; Johnson, George; Johnson, Louis)

**Notes** It is not known which, if any, were written for this picture.

## 3955 ◆ MOTHER KNOWS BEST
Fox, 1928

**Musical Score** Rapee, Erno; Rothafel, S.L.

**Director(s)** Blystone, John
**Screenwriter(s)** Walter, Eugene
**Source(s)** "Mother Knows Best" (story) Ferber, Edna

**Cast** Norton, Barry; Bellamy, Madge; Dresser, Louise; Littlefield, Lucien; Gran, Albert

**Song(s)** Sally of My Dreams [1] (C/L: Kernell, William)

**Notes** [1] Sheet music titled "Sally of Our Dreams."

## 3956 ◆ MOTHER'S BOY
Pathe, 1929

**Composer(s)** Stept, Sam H.
**Lyricist(s)** Green, Bud

**Producer(s)** Kane, Robert T.
**Director(s)** Barker, Bradley
**Screenwriter(s)** Markey, Gene

**Cast** Downey, Morton; Mercer, Beryl; Doyle, John T.; Donlevy, Brian; Chandler, Helen; Perkins, Osgood

**Song(s)** There'll Be You and I; I'll Always Be Mother's Boy; The World Is Yours and Mine (C: Stept, Sam H.; Hanley, James F.); There's a Place in the Sun for You (C: Fain, Sammy); (When Nobody Wants You and

Nobody Cares) Come to Me (C/L: Stept, Sam H.;
Collins, W.; Green, Bud)

**Notes**   No cue sheet available.


## 3957   ✦   MOTHER WORE TIGHTS
### Twentieth Century–Fox, 1947

**Composer(s)**   Myrow, Josef
**Lyricist(s)**   Gordon, Mack
**Choreographer(s)**   Felix, Seymour; Williams, Kenny

**Producer(s)**   Trotti, Lamar
**Director(s)**   Lang, Walter
**Screenwriter(s)**   Trotti, Lamar
**Source(s)**   (book) Young, Miriam

**Cast**   Grable, Betty; Dailey, Dan; Freeman, Mona [1];
Marshall, Connie; Brown, Vanessa; Frawley, William;
Nelson, Ruth; Cleveland, George; Borg, Veda Ann;
Patrick, Lee; Wences, Senor; Bryant, Nana

**Song(s)**   You Do; This Is My Favorite City; Broadway
Prologue to Kokomo, Indiana; Kokomo, Indiana; The
Mountain (C/L: Wences, Senor); Tra-La-La-La (C:
Warren, Harry); Swingin' Down the Lane (C: Jones,
Isham; L: Kahn, Gus); Prologue to Vaudeville Act;
There's Nothing Like a Song; Fare-Thee-Well, Dear
Alma Mater; (Rolling Down Bowling Green) On a Little
Two-Seat Tandem

**Notes**   There are also vocals of "M-O-T-H-E-R (A
Word that Means the World to Me)" by Theodore
Morse and Howard Johnson; "Daddy, You've Been a
Mother to Me" by Fred Fisher; "Burlington Bertie from
Bow" by William Hargreaves; "Paddlin' Madelin'
Home" by Harry Woods; "A Little Bit of Heaven (Sure
They Call It Ireland)" by Ernest R. Ball and J. Kiern
Brennan; "Bedelia" by Jean Schwartz and William
Jerome; "In the Evening by the Moonlight" by James A.
Bland; "Put Your Arms Around Me Honey" by Albert
Von Tilzer and Junie McCree; "Ida, Sweet as Apple
Cider" by Eddie Leonard; "Lily of the Valley" by L.
Wolfe Gilbert and Anatol Friedland and "Stumbling" by
Zez Confrey. [1] Dubbed by Imogene Lynch.


## 3958   ✦   MOULIN ROUGE
### United Artists, 1934

**Composer(s)**   Warren, Harry
**Lyricist(s)**   Dubin, Al

**Producer(s)**   Zanuck, Darryl F.
**Director(s)**   Lanfield, Sidney
**Screenwriter(s)**   Johnson, Nunnally; Lehrman,
Henry

**Cast**   Bennett, Constance; Tone, Franchot; Carminati,
Tullio; Westley, Helen; Tombes, Andrew; Brown, Russ;
Cavanaugh, Hobart; Lebedeff, Ivan; Columbo, Russ;
The Boswell Sisters

**Song(s)**   Boulevard of Broken Dreams; Song of
Surrender; Coffee in the Morning and Kisses at Night;
Putting It On (C/L: Boswell Sisters, The)

**Notes**   No cue sheet available. This was produced by
Zanuck for his 20th Century pictures before the merging
with Fox.


## 3959   ✦   THE MOUNTAIN
### Paramount, 1956

**Producer(s)**   Dmytryk, Edward
**Director(s)**   Dmytryk, Edward
**Screenwriter(s)**   MacDougall, Ranald
**Source(s)**   *The Mountain* (novel) Troyat, Henri

**Cast**   Tracy, Spencer; Wagner, Robert; Trevor, Claire

**Song(s)**   The Mountain (C: Amfitheatrof, Daniele; L:
David, Mack)


## 3960   ✦   MOUNTAIN FAMILY ROBINSON
### Pacific International, 1979

**Musical Score**   Ragland, Robert O.
**Composer(s)**   Ragland, Robert O.
**Lyricist(s)**   Connors, Carol

**Producer(s)**   Dubs, Arthur R.
**Director(s)**   Cotter, John
**Screenwriter(s)**   Dubs, Arthur R.

**Cast**   Logan, Robert; Damante Shaw, Susan; Rattray,
Heather

**Song(s)**   Come Share My Dream; Being Loved Is Being
Free; Life Is So Wonderful; Planting and Harvesting
Songs (L: Ramer, Jack)

**Notes**   No cue sheet available.


## 3961   ✦   MOUNTAIN MOONLIGHT
### Republic, 1941

**Composer(s)**   Styne, Jule
**Lyricist(s)**   Brown, George; Meyer, Sol

**Producer(s)**   Schaefer, Armand
**Director(s)**   Grinde, Nick
**Screenwriter(s)**   Krafft, John; Grashin, Mauri;
McGowan, Dorrell; McGowan, Stuart

**Cast**   Weaver, Leon; Weaver, June; Weaver, Frank;
Elviry; Rhodes, Betty Jane; Archer, John; Richmond,
Kane; Sully, Frank; Arthur, Johnny; Weaver, Loretta;
Chandler, George; Ates, Roscoe

**Song(s)**   From You [1]; Drinking Song (L: Meyer, Sol);
Gee, But It's Great to Meet a Friend from Your Home
Town (C/L: Tracey, William; McGavisk, James); I Close
My Eyes [2]

**Notes**   Originally titled THUNDER OVER THE
OZARKS. [1] Also in TRAGEDY AT MIDNIGHT. [2]
Also in MELODY AND MOONLIGHT.

## 3962 ◆ MOUNTAIN MUSIC
Paramount, 1937

**Composer(s)** Coslow, Sam
**Lyricist(s)** Coslow, Sam

**Producer(s)** Glazer, Benjamin
**Director(s)** Florey, Robert
**Screenwriter(s)** Moffitt, John C.; Atteberry, Duke; Crouse, Russel; Lederer, Charles

**Cast** Raye, Martha; Burns, Bob; Howard, John; Walker, Terry; Hayes, George "Gabby"; Duggan, Ian; Knight, Fuzzy; Davis, Rufe; Howland, Olin

**Song(s)** Mama Don't Allow It [3] (C/L: Davenport, Charles [4]); If I Put My Heart in My Song (C: Siegel, Al); Good Mornin'; Finale (C: Siegel, Al); Can't You Hear that Mountain Music [1] [2]; Lobelia's Wedding Day [1] (C: Alter, Louis; L: Webster, Paul Francis); One Night My Paw Went Hunting with Me Down in Arkansas [1] (C/L: Burns, Bob); Down in Arkansas [1] (C/L: Burns, Bob; Coslow, Sam; Atteberry, Duke; Kisco, Charley); There's Rhythm in Them Thar Hills [1] (C: Kisco, Charley; L: Freed, Ralph); Thar She Comes (Hill Billy Wedding Song)

**Notes** Sylvia Jones sang for someone, although exactly who is unclear in existing records. She may also have been in the picture and not just a dubber. [1] Not used but recorded. [2] Published although not used. [3] Also in BARNYARD FOLLIES (Republic) credited as above; and the Warner Brothers picture BANDS ACROSS THE SEA and BOB WILLS AND HIS TEXAS PLAYBOYS with Sammy Cahn credited for lyrics. [4] Billed as Charles "Cow Cow" Davenport.

## 3963 ◆ MOUNTAIN RHYTHM (1939)
Republic, 1939

**Composer(s)** Autry, Gene; Rose, Fred; Marvin, Johnny
**Lyricist(s)** Autry, Gene; Rose, Fred; Marvin, Johnny

**Producer(s)** Grey, Harry
**Director(s)** Eason, B. Reeves
**Screenwriter(s)** Geraghty, Gerald

**Cast** Autry, Gene; Burnette, Smiley; Storey, June; Eburne, Maude; Taylor, Ferris; Fenner, Walter

**Song(s)** Highways Are Happy Ways [2] (C/L: Shay, Larry; Malie, Tommie; Harris, Harry); It Makes No Difference Now [1] (C/L: Davis, Jimmie; Tillman, Floyd); It Was Only a Hobo's Dream; Gold Mine in Your Heart; Knights of the Open Road

**Notes** [1] Also in RIDERS IN THE SKY (Columbia). [2] Malie and Harris not on cue sheet.

## 3964 ◆ MOUNTAIN RHYTHM (1942)
Republic, 1942

**Producer(s)** Schaefer, Armand
**Director(s)** McDonald, Frank
**Screenwriter(s)** McGowan, Dorrell; McGowan, Stuart

**Cast** Weaver, Lyon; Weaver, Frank; Weaver, June; Merrick, Lynn; Thomas, Frank M.; Payne, Sally; Jones, Dickie; Allen Jr., Joseph

**Song(s)** Welcome to Tudor [1] (C/L: Henderson, Charles); Pull the Trigger (C: Revel, Harry; L: Greene, Mort); Hillbilly Bond Song (C/L: Henderson, Charles)

**Notes** [1] Also in SING, NEIGHBOR, SING with additional writing credits.

## 3965 ◆ THE MOUSE AND HIS CHILD
Sanrio Film, 1978

**Musical Score** Kellaway, Roger
**Composer(s)** Kellaway, Roger
**Lyricist(s)** Lees, Gene

**Producer(s)** deFaria, Walt
**Director(s)** Wolf, Fred; Swenson, Charles
**Screenwriter(s)** Mon Pere, Carol
**Source(s)** (novel) Hoban, Russell

**Song(s)** Tell Me My Name; Skat Rat; Much in Little

**Notes** Animated feature. No cue sheet available.

## 3966 ◆ MOVE
Twentieth Century–Fox, 1970

**Musical Score** Hamlisch, Marvin

**Producer(s)** Berman, Pandro S.
**Director(s)** Rosenberg, Stuart
**Screenwriter(s)** Lieber, Joel; Hart, Stanley
**Source(s)** (novel) Lieber, Joel

**Cast** Gould, Elliott; Prentiss, Paula; Waite, Genevieve; Larch, John; Silver, Joe; Jarvis, Graham; O'Neal, Ron; Burns, David; Bull, Richard; Questel, Mae; Bond, Rudy

**Song(s)** Move (C: Hamlisch, Marvin; L: Bergman, Alan; Bergman, Marilyn)

## 3967 ◆ MOVE OVER DARLING
Twentieth Century–Fox, 1963

**Musical Score** Newman, Lionel; Lubin, Joe

**Producer(s)** Rosenberg, Aaron; Melcher, Martin
**Director(s)** Gordon, Michael
**Screenwriter(s)** Kanter, Hal; Sher, Jack

**Cast** Day, Doris; Garner, James; Bergen, Polly; Connors, Chuck; Ritter, Thelma; Clark, Fred; Knotts, Don; Reid, Elliott; Buchanan, Edgar; Astin, John; Harrington Jr., Pat; Quillan, Eddie

**Song(s)** Move Over Darling (C: Lubin, Joe; L: Kanter, Hal; Melcher, Terry); Twinkle Lullaby [1] (C/L: Lubin, Joe)

**Notes** This is a remake of MY FAVORITE WIFE. [1] Sheet music only.

### 3968 ✦ MOVERS AND SHAKERS
United Artists, 1985

**Musical Score**   Welch, Ken; Welch, Mitzi

**Producer(s)**   Asher, William; Grodin, Charles
**Director(s)**   Asher, William
**Screenwriter(s)**   Grodin, Charles

**Cast**   Matthau, Walter; Grodin, Charles; Gardenia, Vincent; Daly, Tyne; Macy, Bill; Radner, Gilda; Martin, Steve; Marshall, Penny

**Song(s)**   Got to Have You Baby (C/L: Nepus, Ira); Can't We Go Home Again? (C/L: Welch, Ken; Welch, Mitzi)

### 3969 ✦ MOVIELAND MAGIC
Warner Brothers, 1946

**Composer(s)**   Jerome, M.K.
**Lyricist(s)**   Scholl, Jack

**Song(s)**   Movieland Magic; So You Want to Be in Movies; Springtime in Vienna; Jitterbug Dance; You're Lovely As You Are; Two Hearts in the Moonlight [2]; The Soubrette on the Police Gazette [1]; Headin' for the Rodeo; The Good Old American Way

**Notes**   Short subject. [1] Also in THE BIG TREES. [2] Also in MUSICAL MOVIELAND.

### 3970 ✦ MOVIE, MOVIE
Warner Brothers, 1978

**Musical Score**   Burns, Ralph
**Composer(s)**   Burns, Ralph; Davis, Buster
**Lyricist(s)**   Gelbart, Larry; Keller, Sheldon
**Choreographer(s)**   Kidd, Michael

**Producer(s)**   Donen, Stanley
**Director(s)**   Donen, Stanley
**Screenwriter(s)**   Gelbart, Larry; Keller, Sheldon

**Cast**   York, Rebecca; Scott, George C.; Harris, Barbara; Van Devere, Trish; Buttons, Red; Wallach, Eli

**Song(s)**   Torchin' for Bill (C/L: Burns, Ralph); Air Force Anthem (C: Burns, Ralph; L: Gelbart, Larry); I Just Need the Girl; Just Shows to Go Ya; Your Lucky Day Is Here

**Notes**   The first half of this picture, which approximates a double feature, is DYNAMITE HANDS, a send up of boxing films. Harry Hamlin, Kathleen Beller, Eli Wallach, George C. Scott, Trish Van Devere, Michael Kidd, Jocelyn Brando, Ann Reinking, Art Carney and Barry Bostwick are featured. After a preview for an imaginary war picture titled ZERO HOUR, the second half was BAXTER'S BEAUTIES OF 1933 which is a satire on Busby Berkeley musicals. The credits above are for that effort.

### 3971 ✦ MOVIETONE FOLLIES OF 1929

See FOX MOVIETONE FOLLIES OF 1929.

### 3972 ✦ MOVIETONE FOLLIES OF 1930
Fox, 1930

**Composer(s)**   Conrad, Con
**Lyricist(s)**   Meskill, Jack
**Choreographer(s)**   Dare, Danny; Kusell, Maurice L.; Scheck, Max

**Producer(s)**   Rockett, Al
**Director(s)**   Stoloff, Benjamin
**Screenwriter(s)**   Wells, William K.

**Cast**   Brendel, El; White, Marjorie; Richardson, Frank; Francis, Noel; Collier Jr., William; Seegar, Miriam

**Song(s)**   Movietonia (Talking Picture Queen) (C: Hanley, James F.; Brockman, James; L: McCarthy, Joseph); I Feel That Certain Feeling Coming On (C: Monaco, James V.; L: Friend, Cliff); Here Comes Emily Brown; Bashful (C: Monaco, James V.; L: Friend, Cliff); You'll Give In (C: Hanley, James F.; L: McCarthy, Joseph); Doing the Derby; Cheer Up and Smile

### 3973 ✦ MOVING
Warner Brothers, 1988

**Musical Score**   Shore, Howard

**Producer(s)**   Cornfeld, Stuart
**Director(s)**   Metter, Alan
**Screenwriter(s)**   Breckman, Andy

**Cast**   Pryor, Richard; Todd, Beverly; Dash, Stacey; Harris, Raphael; Harris, Ishmael; Quaid, Randy; Lin, Traci; Jump, Gordon; Osterwald, Bibi; Allen, Rae

**Song(s)**   Moving (C/L: Brown, Ollie E.)

**Notes**   No cue sheet available.

### 3974 ✦ MOVING VIOLATION (1976)
Twentieth Century–Fox, 1976

**Musical Score**   Peake, Don

**Producer(s)**   Corman, Julie
**Director(s)**   Dubin, Charles S.
**Screenwriter(s)**   Osterhout, David R.; Norton, William

**Cast**   McHattie, Stephen; Lenz, Kay; Albert, Eddie; Chapman, Lonny; Geer, Will

**Song(s)**   I Got You (I Feel Good) (C/L: Brown, James)

### 3975 ✦ MOVING VIOLATIONS (1985)
Twentieth Century–Fox, 1985

**Musical Score**   Burns, Ralph

**Producer(s)**   Roth, Joe; Ufland, Harry
**Director(s)**   Israel, Neal
**Screenwriter(s)**   Israel, Neal; Proft, Pat

**Cast**   Murray, John; Tilly, Jennifer; Keach, James; Backer, Brian; Eisenberg, Ned; Peller, Clara; Sperber, Wendie Jo; Willard, Fred

**Song(s)**   Moving Violations (C/L: Roberts, Bruce)

**Notes**   No cue sheet available.

## 3976 ✦ MOZAMBIQUE
### Seven Arts, 1965

**Musical Score**   Douglas, Johnny

**Producer(s)**   Unger, Oliver A.
**Director(s)**   Lynn, Robert
**Screenwriter(s)**   Yeldham, Peter

**Cast**   Cochran, Steve; Neff, Hildegarde; Hubschmid, Paul; Bach, Vivi

**Song(s)**   Das Geht Beim Ersten Mal Vorbei (C/L: Niessen, Charly); Hey You (C/L: Backus, Gus)

**Notes**   No cue sheet available.

## 3977 ✦ MRS. BROWN, YOU'VE GOT A LOVELY DAUGHTER
### Metro–Goldwyn–Mayer, 1969

**Musical Score**   Goodwin, Ron
**Composer(s)**   Gouldman, Graham
**Lyricist(s)**   Gouldman, Graham

**Producer(s)**   Klein, Allen
**Director(s)**   Swimmer, Saul
**Screenwriter(s)**   Vane, Norman Thaddeus

**Cast**   Noone, Peter [1]; Hopwood, Keith [1]; Leckenby, Derek [1]; Green, Karl [1]; Whitwam, Barry [1]; Holloway, Stanley; Rhodes, Marjorie; Percival, Lance; Washbourne, Mona; White, Sheila; Caldwell, Sarah

**Song(s)**   It's Nice to Be Out in the Morning; Holiday Inn (C/L: Stevens, Jeffrey; Carter, John); Don't Poop the Group (C/L: Percival, Lance); Oh, She's Done It Again; There's a Kind of a Hush (All Over the World) (C/L: Read; Stevens, Jeffrey); My Old Man's a Dustman (C/L: Donnegan, Lonny; Buckham, Peter; Thorn, Beverly); Lemon and Lime; All Day, All Night, I'm Not a Tramp (C/L: Percival, Lance); The Most Beautiful Thing in My Life (C/L: Young, Kenny); The World Is For the Young; Mrs. Brown, You've Got a Lovely Daughter (C: Goodwin, Ron; L: Peacock, Trevor)

**Notes**   It is not known if the above were written for this film. There is also a vocal of "Any Old Iron" by Charles Collins, E.A. Shepherd and Fred Terry. [1] Members of Herman's Hermits.

## 3978 ✦ MRS. LADYBUG
### Metro–Goldwyn–Mayer, 1940

**Musical Score**   Bradley, Scott

**Song(s)**   Mrs. Ladybug (C/L: Bradley, Scott)

**Notes**   Animated cartoon.

## 3979 ✦ MRS. LORING'S SECRET

See IMPERFECT LADY.

## 3980 ✦ MRS. MIKE
### United Artists, 1949

**Musical Score**   Steiner, Max

**Producer(s)**   Bischoff, Sam; Gross, Edward
**Director(s)**   King, Louis
**Screenwriter(s)**   Levitt, Alfred Lewis; Bodeen, DeWitt
**Source(s)**   Mrs. Mike (novel) Freedman, Benedict; Freedman, Nancy

**Cast**   Powell, Dick; Keyes, Evelyn; Kerrigan, J.M.; Clarke, Angela; Miljan, John; Wright, Will; Boardman, Nan

**Song(s)**   Kathy (C: Steiner, Max; L: Washington, Ned)

**Notes**   There is also a vocal of "Rose of Tralee."

## 3981 ✦ MRS. MINIVER
### Metro–Goldwyn–Mayer, 1942

**Musical Score**   Stothart, Herbert

**Producer(s)**   Franklin, Sidney
**Director(s)**   Wyler, William
**Screenwriter(s)**   Wimperis, Arthur; Froeschel, George; Hilton, James; West, Claudine
**Source(s)**   Mrs. Miniver (novel) Struther, Jan

**Cast**   Garson, Greer; Pidgeon, Walter; Wright, Teresa; Whitty, Dame May; Owen, Reginald; Travers, Henry; Ney, Richard; Wilcoxon, Henry

**Song(s)**   Midsummer's Day (C/L: Lockhart, Gene)

## 3982 ✦ MRS. O'MALLEY AND MR. MALLONE
### Metro–Goldwyn–Mayer, 1950

**Musical Score**   Deutsch, Adolph

**Producer(s)**   Wright, William H.
**Director(s)**   Taurog, Norman
**Screenwriter(s)**   Bowers, William

**Cast**   Main, Marjorie; Whitmore, James; Dvorak, Ann; Kirk, Phyllis; Clark, Fred; Malone, Dorothy; Sundberg, Clinton; Fowley, Douglas; Waterman, Willard; Porter, Don

**Song(s)**   Missus O'Malley and Mister Malone (C: Deutsch, Adolph; L: Webster, Paul Francis)

## 3983 ✦ MULE TRAIN
### Columbia, 1949

**Producer(s)**   Schaefer, Armand
**Director(s)**   English, John
**Screenwriter(s)**   Geraghty, Gerald

**Cast** Autry, Gene; Champion; Ryan, Sheila; Livingston, Robert; Barnett, Vince; Saylor, Syd; Sanders, Sandy; Buttram, Pat

**Song(s)** Mule Train [1] (C/L: Lange, Johnny; Heath, Hy; Glickman, Fred)

**Notes** There are also vocal renditions of "Roomful of Roses" by Tim Spencer and "The Old Chisholm Trail." [1] Also in SINGING GUNS (Columbia).

## 3984 ✦ THE MUMMY'S CURSE
### Universal, 1944

**Musical Score** Sawtell, Paul

**Producer(s)** Drake, Oliver
**Director(s)** Goodwins, Leslie
**Screenwriter(s)** Schubert, Bernard

**Cast** Chaney Jr., Lon; Christine, Virginia; Coe, Peter; Harding, Kay; Moore, Dennis; Richards, Addison; Farnum, William

**Song(s)** Hey You (C/L: Orth, Frank; Drake, Oliver)

## 3985 ✦ THE MUPPET MOVIE
### AFD, 1979

**Musical Score** Williams, Paul; Ascher, Kenny
**Composer(s)** Williams, Paul; Ascher, Kenny
**Lyricist(s)** Williams, Paul; Ascher, Kenny

**Producer(s)** Henson, Jim
**Director(s)** Frawley, James
**Screenwriter(s)** Juhl, Jerry; Burns, Jack

**Cast** Henson, Jim; Oz, Frank; Nelson, Jerry; Hunt, Richard; Goelz, Dave; Durning, Charles; Pendleton, Austin; Bergen, Edgar; Berle, Milton; Brooks, Mel; Coburn, James; DeLuise, Dom; Gould, Elliott; Hope, Bob; Kahn, Madeline; Kane, Carol; Leachman, Cloris; Martin, Steve; Pryor, Richard; Savalas, Telly; Welles, Orson; Williams, Paul

**Song(s)** Rainbow Connection; Movin' Right Along; Never Before Never Again; I Hope That Somethin Better Comes Along; Can You Picture That; I'm Going to Back there Someday

**Notes** No cue sheet available.

## 3986 ✦ THE MUPPETS TAKE MANHATTAN
### Tri-Star, 1984

**Composer(s)** Moss, Jeff
**Lyricist(s)** Moss, Jeff
**Choreographer(s)** Chadman, Chris

**Producer(s)** Lazer, David
**Director(s)** Oz, Frank
**Screenwriter(s)** Oz, Frank; Patchett, Tom; Tarses, Jay

**Cast** Henson, Jim; Oz, Frank; Whitmore, Steve; Goelz, Dave; Nelson, Jerry; Hunt, Richard; Price, Lonny;

Zorich, Louis; Carney, Art; Coco, James; Coleman, Dabney; Hines, Gregory; Lavin, Linda; Minnelli, Liza; Rivers, Joan; Gould, Elliott; Shields, Brooke; Bergen, Frances; Koch, Edward I.; Sardi, Vincent; Landis, John

**Song(s)** Together Again; You Can't Take No for an Answer; Saying Goodbye; Rat Scat; I'm Gonna Always Love You; Right Where I Belong

**Notes** No cue sheet available.

## 3987 ✦ MURDER AT THE VANITIES
### Paramount, 1934

**Composer(s)** Johnston, Arthur
**Lyricist(s)** Coslow, Sam

**Producer(s)** Sheldon, E. Lloyd
**Director(s)** Leisen, Mitchell
**Screenwriter(s)** Wilson, Carey; Hellman, Sam; Gollomb, Joseph
**Source(s)** *Murder at the Vanities* (musical) Carroll, Earl; King, Rufus

**Cast** Michael, Gertrude; McLaglen, Victor; Carlisle, Kitty; Oakie, Jack; Stickney, Dorothy; Middleton, Charles; Ralph, Jessie; Patrick, Gail; Meek, Donald; Sheridan, Ann [5]; Duke Ellington and His Orchestra

**Song(s)** Cocktails for Two; Murder at the Vanities; Where Do They Come From [3]; Lovely One; Live and Love Tonight [8] [6]; Marahuana (Lotus Blossom) [7]; Ebony Rhapsody [2]; Fare Thee Well [4]; Finale; Bachelor of the Art [1]

**Notes** [1] Instrumental only. [2] Music based on Liszt's "Hungarian Rhapsody #2." [3] "Idea for this composition suggested by Esther Muir." [4] See note under MANY HAPPY RETURNS. [5] Billed as Clara Lou Sheridan. [6] Not used in DANCERS IN THE DARK and WE'RE NOT DRESSING. [7] Not used in BELLE OF THE NINETIES. [8] Coslow, Con Conrad and Al Dubin credited by ASCAP.

## 3988 ✦ MURDERER'S ROW
### Columbia, 1966

**Musical Score** Schifrin, Lalo

**Producer(s)** Allen, Irving
**Director(s)** Levin, Henry
**Screenwriter(s)** Baker, Herbert
**Source(s)** *Murderer's Row* (novel) Hamilton, Donald

**Cast** Martin, Dean; Ann-Margaret; Malden, Karl; Sparv, Camilla; Gregory, James; Adams, Beverly; Eastham, Richard

**Song(s)** I'm Not the Marrying Kind (C: Schifrin, Lalo; L: Greenfield, Howard); If You're Thinkin' What I'm Thinkin' [1] (C/L: Boyce, Tommy; Hart, Bobby)

**Notes** [1] Sheet music only.

## 3989 ✦ MURDER, HE SAYS
Paramount, 1945

**Producer(s)**   Leshin, E.D.
**Director(s)**   Marshall, George
**Screenwriter(s)**   Breslow, Lou

**Cast**   MacMurray, Fred; Walker, Helen; Main, Marjorie; Hall, Porter; Heather, Jean; Pepper, Barbara

**Song(s)**   My Life Is No Bed of Roses (C/L: Tableporter, F.J.; Porter, Lew)

**Notes**   No cue sheet available.

## 3990 ✦ MURDER, INC.
Twentieth Century–Fox, 1960

**Musical Score**   De Vol, Frank
**Composer(s)**   Weiss, George David
**Lyricist(s)**   Unknown

**Producer(s)**   Balaban, Burt
**Director(s)**   Balaban, Burt; Rosenberg, Stuart
**Screenwriter(s)**   Tunick, Irv; Barr, Mel
**Source(s)**   *Murder, Inc.* (book) Turkus, Burton; Feder, Sid

**Cast**   Whitman, Stuart; Britt, May; Morgan, Henry; Falk, Peter; Stewart, David J.; Oakland, Simon; Amsterdam, Morey; Gardenia, Vincent; Mintz, Eli; Vaughan, Sarah

**Song(s)**   The Awakening; Hey Mister; Fan My Brow

## 3991 ✦ MURDER IN THE BLUE ROOM
Universal, 1944

**Producer(s)**   Gross, Frank
**Director(s)**   Goodwins, Leslie
**Screenwriter(s)**   Diamond, I.A.L.; Davis, Stanley

**Cast**   Gwynne, Anne; Cook, Donald; Litel, John; McDonald, Grace; Kean, Betty; Preisser, June; Toomey, Regis; Walker, Nella; Tombes, Andrew

**Song(s)**   One Starry Night (C/L: Franklin, Dave; George, Don); A-Doo-Dee-Doo-Doo [2] (C/L: Tableporter, F.J.; Erdody, Leo; Porter, Lew); The Boogie Woogie Man [1] (C: Rosen, Milton; L: Carter, Everett)

**Notes**   A remake of SECRET OF THE BLUE ROOM (1933) and THE MISSING GUEST (1938). [1] Also in the short IN THE GROOVE and in SING ANOTHER CHORUS. [2] Also in JIVE JUNCTION (PRC) but with additional credit to June Stillman.

## 3992 ✦ MURDER IN THE MUSIC HALL
Republic, 1946

**Producer(s)**   Millakowsky, Herman
**Director(s)**   English, John
**Screenwriter(s)**   Gorog, Laszlo; Hyland, Frances

**Cast**   Ralston, Vera Hruba; Marshall, William; Walker, Helen; Kelly, Nancy; Gargan, William; Rutherford, Ann; Cowan, Jerome; Bishop, Julie

**Song(s)**   If You Are There [1] (C: Ohman, Phil; L: Washington, Ned); Mess Me Up [2] (C: Kent, Walter; L: Gannon, Kim); Susie (C/L: Scharf, Walter); My Pushover Heart [3] (C: Kent, Walter; L: Gannon, Kim)

**Notes**   There is also a vocal of "Wonderful One" by Paul Whiteman, Ferde Grofe and Dorothy Terris. [1] Also in SLEEPY LAGOON. [2] Also in CASANOVA IN BURLESQUE. [3] Also in HITCH HIKE TO HAPPINESS and RENDEZVOUS WITH ANNIE.

## 3993 ✦ MURDER ON THE ORIENT EXPRESS
Paramount, 1974

**Musical Score**   Bennett, Richard Rodney

**Producer(s)**   Brabourne, John; Goodwin, Richard
**Director(s)**   Lumet, Sidney
**Screenwriter(s)**   Dehn, Paul
**Source(s)**   *Murder on the Orient Express* (novel) Christie, Agatha

**Cast**   Finney, Albert; Bacall, Lauren; Balsam, Martin; Bergman, Ingrid; Bisset, Jacqueline; Cassel, Jean-Pierre; Connery, Sean; Gielgud, John; Hiller, Wendy; Perkins, Anthony; Redgrave, Vanessa; Roberts, Rachel; Widmark, Richard; York, Michael

**Song(s)**   Silky [1] (C: Bennett, Richard Rodney; L: Kusik, Larry)

**Notes**   [1] Lyric for exploitation use only.

## 3994 ✦ MURDER ON THE WATERFRONT
Warner Brothers, 1943

**Musical Score**   Jackson, Howard

**Producer(s)**   Jacobs, William
**Director(s)**   Eason, B. Reeves
**Screenwriter(s)**   Kent, Robert E.
**Source(s)**   *Without Warning* (play) Zink, Ralph Spencer

**Cast**   Douglas, Warren; Winfield, Joan; Loder, John; Ford, Ruth; Crago, Bill; Kennedy, Bill; Davidson, William B.; Costello, John; Flavin, James; Edward, Bill; Hopper, DeWolf

**Song(s)**   I'd Love to Take Orders From You (C: Warren, Harry; L: Dubin, Al)

**Notes**   Formerly titled THE NAVY GETS ROUGH.

## 3995 ✦ MURDER ON THE YUKON
Monogram, 1941

**Composer(s)**   Lange, Johnny; Knight, Vick
**Lyricist(s)**   Porter, Lew; Knight, Vick

**Producer(s)**   Krasne, Philip N.
**Director(s)**   Gasnier, Louis

**Screenwriter(s)**   Halson, Milton
**Source(s)**   "Renfrew of the Royal Mounted" (stories) Erskine, Laurie York

**Cast**   Newill, James; Young, Polly Ann; O'Brien, Dave; St. John, Al; Royle, William; Pollard, Snub

**Song(s)**   Mounted Men [1] (C/L: Laidlow, Betty; Lively, Robert); Riding Down the Yukon Trail; Ah! Here's Romance

**Notes**   [1] Also in CRASHING THRU, DANGER AHEAD, FIGHTING MAN, RENFREW AND THE GREAT WHITE TRAIL, SKY BANDITS and YUKON FLIGHT.

## 3996 ✦ MURIETA
Warner Brothers, 1965

**Musical Score**   Olea, Antonio Perez

**Producer(s)**   Sainz de Vicuna, Jose
**Director(s)**   Sherman, George
**Screenwriter(s)**   O'Hanlon, James

**Cast**   Hunter, Jeffrey; Kennedy, Arthur; Lorys, Diana

**Song(s)**   Rosita (C/L: Michel, Paco); Corrido of Joaquin Murieta (C/L: Michel, Paco)

**Notes**   No cue sheet available.

## 3997 ✦ MURPHY'S LAW
Cannon, 1986

**Producer(s)**   Kohner, Pancho
**Director(s)**   Thompson, J. Lee
**Screenwriter(s)**   Hickman, Gail Morgan

**Cast**   Bronson, Charles; Wilhoite, Kathleen; Snodgress, Carrie; Lyons, Robert F.; Romanus, Richard; Luisi, James; McCallum, Paul

**Song(s)**   Murphy's Law (C/L: McCallum, Paul; Wilhote, Kathleen; Bisharat, John)

**Notes**   No cue sheet available.

## 3998 ✦ MURPHY'S ROMANCE
Columbia, 1986

**Musical Score**   King, Carole
**Composer(s)**   King, Carole
**Lyricist(s)**   King, Carole

**Producer(s)**   Ziskin, Laura
**Director(s)**   Ritt, Martin
**Screenwriter(s)**   Frank Jr., Harriet; Ravetch, Irving
**Source(s)**   *Murphy's Romance* (novel) Schott, Max

**Cast**   Field, Sally; Garner, James; Kerwin, Brian; Haim, Corey; Burkley, Dennis; Duckworth, Dortha; Sharkey, Billy Ray

**Song(s)**   Running Lonely; Hungry Howling at the Moon; Love for the Last Time; I Love You Only

**Notes**   All background vocals.

## 3999 ✦ MUSCLE BEACH PARTY
American International, 1964

**Musical Score**   Baxter, Les
**Composer(s)**   Christian, Roger; Usher, Gary
**Lyricist(s)**   Christian, Roger; Usher, Gary

**Producer(s)**   Nicholson, James H.; Dillon, Robert
**Director(s)**   Asher, William
**Screenwriter(s)**   Dillon, Robert

**Cast**   Avalon, Frankie; Funicello, Annette; Paluzzi, Luciana; Ashley, John; Rickles, Don; McCrea, Jody; Wonder, Little Stevie; Amsterdam, Morey; Hackett, Buddy

**Song(s)**   Muscle Beach Party; Runnin' Wild; Muscle Bustle; My First Love; Surfin' Woodie; Surfer's Holiday; Happy Street (C/L: Hemric, Guy; Styner, Jerry); A Girl Needs a Boy (C/L: Hemric, Guy; Styner, Jerry)

**Notes**   No cue sheet available.

## 4000 ✦ MUSICAL DOCTOR
Paramount, 1932

**Cast**   Vallee, Rudy

**Song(s)**   Keep a Little Song Handy (C: Timberg, Sammy; L: Lerner, Sam)

**Notes**   Short subject. No cue sheet available.

## 4001 ✦ MUSICAL JUSTICE
Paramount, 1934

**Song(s)**   Don't Take My Boop-oop-a-doop Away (C: Timberg, Sammy; L: Lerner, Sam)

**Notes**   Animated short. No cue sheet available. A Betty Boop cartoon.

## 4002 ✦ MUSICAL MEMORIES
Warner Brothers, 1951

**Song(s)**   Memories from Melody Lane [1] (C: Jerome, M.K.; L: Scholl, Jack); Turn Back the Days (C/L: Scholl, Jack)

**Notes**   Short subject. [1] Also in IN OLD NEW YORK.

## 4003 ✦ MUSICAL MOVIELAND
Warner Brothers, 1944

**Composer(s)**   Jerome, M.K.
**Lyricist(s)**   Scholl, Jack

**Song(s)**   Musical Movieland; Queen of the Border Cantina; My Journey's End [4] (C: Fain, Sammy; L: Kahal, Irving); Song of the Mounted Police [2]; Zuyder Zee (C: Alter, Louis); Girl on the Little Blue Plate (C: Alter, Louis); Changing of the Guard; King's Serenade [1] (C/L: King, Charles E.); Whistle Song; Two Hearts in the Moonlight [3]

**Notes** Short subject. [1] Also in FLIRTATION WALK. [2] Also in HEART OF THE NORTH. [3] Also in MOVIELAND MAGIC. [4] Written in 1934.

## 4004 ◆ MUSIC FOR MADAME
### RKO, 1937

**Composer(s)** Friml, Rudolf
**Lyricist(s)** Kahn, Gus

**Producer(s)** Lasky, Jesse L.
**Director(s)** Blystone, John
**Screenwriter(s)** Purcell, Gertrude; Harari, Robert

**Cast** Martini, Nino; Fontaine, Joan; Mowbray, Alan; Gilbert, Billy; Hale, Alan; Mitchell, Grant; Rhodes, Erik; Patrick, Lee; Vincent, Romo

**Song(s)** My Sweet Bambina; King of the Road (C: Shilkret, Nathaniel; L: Cherkose, Eddie); Music for Madame (C: Wrubel, Allie; L: Magidson, Herb); I Want the World to Know

**Notes** There are also a couple of operatic arias.

## 4005 ◆ MUSIC FOR MILLIONS
### Metro–Goldwyn–Mayer, 1944

**Musical Score** Michelet, Michel
**Choreographer(s)** Donohue, Jack

**Producer(s)** Pasternak, Joe
**Director(s)** Koster, Henry
**Screenwriter(s)** Connolly, Myles

**Cast** O'Brien, Margaret; Iturbi, Jose; Allyson, June; Durante, Jimmy; Hunt, Marsha; Herbert, Hugh; Davenport, Harry; Wilson, Marie; Adler, Larry; Iturbi, Jose; Griffies, Ethel; Gilchrist, Connie; Lessy, Ben

**Song(s)** Toscanini, Stokowski and Me (C/L: Durante, Jimmy; Bullock, Walter; Spina, Harold); Umbriago (C/L: Durante, Jimmy; Caesar, Irving); At Sundown (C/L: Donaldson, Walter)

## 4006 ◆ THE MUSIC GOES ROUND
### Columbia, 1936

**Composer(s)** Akst, Harry
**Lyricist(s)** Brown, Lew

**Director(s)** Schertzinger, Victor
**Screenwriter(s)** Buchman, Sidney; Swerling, Jo

**Cast** Richman, Harry; Hudson, Rochelle; Connolly, Walter; Dumbrille, Douglass; Mollison, Henry; Birch, Wyrley; Killian, Victor; Morgan, Gene; Anderson, Eddie "Rochester"; Stander, Lionel

**Song(s)** Rolling Along; Suzannah [1]; Life Begins When You're In Love (C: Schertzinger, Victor); Let's Go (C: Schertzinger, Victor; L: Richman, Harry); There'll Be No South [1] (C: Schertzinger, Victor)

**Notes** A remake of MATINEE IDOL (1928). Originally titled HELLO BIG BOY. There is also a vocal of "The Music Goes Round and Round" by Edward Farley, Michael Riley and Red Hodgson. Also used in the Republic picture TROCADERO and the Fox picture SING BABY SING. [1] Credits on sheet music are for Brown, Akst and Harry Richman. Richman probably had his name put on music since he was the star. Note that cue sheet for "There'll Be No South" credits Schertzinger.

## 4007 ◆ MUSIC IN MANHATTAN
### RKO, 1944

**Musical Score** Harline, Leigh
**Composer(s)** Pollack, Lew
**Lyricist(s)** Magidson, Herb
**Choreographer(s)** O'Curran, Charles

**Producer(s)** Auer, John H.
**Director(s)** Auer, John H.
**Screenwriter(s)** Kimble, Lawrence

**Cast** Shirley, Anne; Day, Dennis; Terry, Phillip; Walburn, Raymond; Darwell, Jane; Brill, Patti; Charles Barnet and His Orchestra; Nilo Menendez and His Rhumba Band

**Song(s)** One Night In Acapulco; I Can See You Now; Did You Happen to Find a Heart; I Like a Man Who Makes Music; When Romance Comes Along

## 4008 ◆ MUSIC IN MY HEART
### Columbia, 1940

**Composer(s)** Forrest, Chet; Wright, Bob
**Lyricist(s)** Forrest, Chet; Wright, Bob

**Producer(s)** Starr, Irving
**Director(s)** Santley, Joseph
**Screenwriter(s)** Grant, James Edward

**Cast** Martin, Tony; Hayworth, Rita; Fellows, Edith; Mowbray, Alan; Blore, Eric; Tobias, George; Crehan, Joseph

**Song(s)** It's a Blue World [2]; Punchinello; Hearts in the Sky; No Other Love [1]; Oh What a Lovely Dream; Music in My Heart; Prelude to Love [3]

**Notes** [1] Based on "Romance" by A. Rubenstein. Also in SHE'S A SWEETHEART. [2] Also in MAKE BELIEVE BALLROOM and SING WHILE YOU DANCE. [3] Sheet music only.

## 4009 ◆ MUSIC IN THE AIR
### Fox, 1934

**Composer(s)** Kern, Jerome
**Lyricist(s)** Hammerstein II, Oscar
**Choreographer(s)** Donohue, Jack

**Producer(s)** Pommer, Erich
**Director(s)** May, Joe
**Screenwriter(s)** Young, Howard I.; Wilder, Billy

**Source(s)** *Music in the Air* (musical) Kern, Jerome; Hammerstein II, Oscar

**Cast** Swanson, Gloria; Boles, John; Montgomery, Douglass [2]; Lang, June [3]; Owen, Reginald; Shean, Al; Cawthorn, Joseph; Bosworth, Hobart; Haden, Sara; Prouty, Jed; Knight, Fuzzy

**Song(s)** Schoolroom Prayer; I've Told Every Little Star; Melodies of May [1]; There's a Hill Beyond a Hill; Egern on the Tegern Sea [2]; I Am So Eager; Letter Song; Adrietta; One More Dance [4]; Night Flies By [4]; I Am Alone

**Notes** [1] Music based on Beethoven's "Piano Sonata No. 3, opus 2." [2] Dubbed by James O'Brien. [3] Dubbed by Betty Hiestand. [4] Same music.

## 4010 ✦ MUSIC IS MAGIC
### Twentieth Century–Fox, 1935

**Composer(s)** Levant, Oscar
**Lyricist(s)** Clare, Sidney
**Choreographer(s)** Donohue, Jack

**Producer(s)** Stone, John
**Director(s)** Marshall, George
**Screenwriter(s)** Eliscu, Edward; Breslow, Lou
**Source(s)** *Private Beach* (play) Lasky Jr., Jesse; Unger, Gladys

**Cast** Faye, Alice; Walker, Ray; Daniels, Bebe; Mitchell, Frank; Durant, Jack; McDaniel, Hattie; Tombes, Andrew

**Song(s)** Love Is Smiling At Me; La Locumba [1] (C: Roulien, Raul); Honey Chile; Music Is Magic (C: Johnston, Arthur)

**Notes** [1] Also in TE QUIERO CON LOCURA with Roulien's lyrics.

## 4011 ✦ MUSIC MAN (1948)
### Monogram, 1948

**Producer(s)** Jason, Will
**Director(s)** Jason, Will
**Screenwriter(s)** Mintz, Sam

**Cast** Stewart, Freddie; Preisser, June; Brito, Phil; Jimmy Dorsey and His Orchestra; Neill, Noel; Hale Jr., Alan; Narisco, Grazia; Chandler, Chick; Astor, Gertrude

**Song(s)** I Could Swear It Was You (C/L: Brito, Phil; Stock, Larry; Flynn, Allan)

**Notes** No cue sheet available.

## 4012 ✦ THE MUSIC MAN (1962)
### Warner Brothers, 1962

**Composer(s)** Willson, Meredith
**Lyricist(s)** Willson, Meredith
**Choreographer(s)** White, Onna [1]

**Producer(s)** DaCosta, Morton
**Director(s)** DaCosta, Morton [1]

**Screenwriter(s)** Hargrove, Marion
**Source(s)** *The Music Man* (musical) Willson, Meredith; Lacey, Franklin

**Cast** Preston, Robert [1]; Jones, Shirley; Hackett, Buddy; Gingold, Hermione; Ford, Paul; Kelton, Pert [1]; The Buffalo Bills [1]; Everett, Timmy; Luckey, Susan; Howard, Ron [5]; Hickox, Harry; Lane, Charles; Wickes, Mary

**Song(s)** Rock Island; Iowa Stubborn; Ya Got Trouble; If You Don't Mind My Saying So; Goodnight My Someone [3]; Sincere; 76 Trombones [3]; Pick-a-Little, Talk-a-Little; [6]; The Sadder but Wiser Girl; Marian the Librarian; Gary Indiana; Wells Fargo; Lida Rose; Will I Ever Tell You?; Shipoopi; It's You; Wah-Tan-Ee; Being in Love [2]; Till There Was You [4]; Fireworks [7]

**Notes** [1] Repeating Broadway assignment. [2] Written for film. [3] These two songs share the same melody line. [4] Originally a popular song "Till I Met You." [5] Billed as Ronny Howard. [6] The reprise seems to have been filmed but not used. [7] Not used.

## 4013 ✦ MUSTANG COUNTRY
### Universal, 1976

**Musical Score** Holdridge, Lee

**Producer(s)** Champion, John
**Director(s)** Champion, John
**Screenwriter(s)** Champion, John

**Cast** McCrea, Joel; Fuller, Robert; Wayne, Patrick; Mina, Nika

**Song(s)** Follow Your Restless Dreams (C: Holdridge, Lee; L: Henry, Joe)

## 4014 ✦ MUTINY ON THE BLACKHAWK
### Universal, 1939

**Producer(s)** Pivar, Ben
**Director(s)** Cabanne, Christy
**Screenwriter(s)** Simmons, Michael L.

**Cast** Arlen, Richard; Devine, Andy; Moore, Constance; Williams, Guinn "Big Boy"

**Song(s)** Xa Mele O Kuu Puu Wai (C/L: Hoopii Jr., Sol)

## 4015 ✦ MUTINY ON THE BOUNTY (1935)
### Metro–Goldwyn–Mayer, 1935

**Musical Score** Stothart, Herbert

**Producer(s)** Lewin, Albert
**Director(s)** Lloyd, Frank
**Screenwriter(s)** Jennings, Talbot; Furthman, Jules; Wilson, Carey
**Source(s)** *Mutiny on the Bounty* (novel) Nordhoff, Charles; Hall, James Norman

**Cast** Laughton, Charles; Gable, Clark; Tone, Franchot; Mundin, Herbert; Digges, Dudley; Quillan, Eddie; Crisp, Donald

**Song(s)** Love Song of Tahiti (C: Kaper, Bronislau; Jurmann, Walter; L: Kahn, Gus)

### 4016 ◆ MUTINY ON THE BOUNTY (1963)
Metro–Goldwyn–Mayer, 1963

**Musical Score** Kaper, Bronislau

**Producer(s)** Rosenberg, Aaron
**Director(s)** Milestone, Lewis
**Screenwriter(s)** Lederer, Charles
**Source(s)** *Mutiny on the Bounty* (novel) Nordhoff, Charles; Hall, James Norman

**Cast** Brando, Marlon; Howard, Trevor; Harris, Richard; Griffith, Hugh; Haydn, Richard; Tarita; Herbert, Percy; Lamont, Duncan; Jackson, Gordon; Rafferty, Chips; Purcell, Noel

**Song(s)** Maeve, Maeve (C/L: Moenau, Riri; Graham, Steve); Ori E Ori E (C/L: Graham, Steve); Te Manu Pukarua (C/L: Lund, Eddie); Follow Me (C: Kaper, Bronislau; L: Webster, Paul Francis); Tahitian Farewell Song: Maururu a Vau (C/L: Lund, Eddie)

**Notes** Carol Reed was replaced by Milestone during filming.

### 4017 ◆ MY BEST FRIEND IS A VAMPIRE
Kings Road, 1988

**Musical Score** Dorff, Stephen H.

**Producer(s)** Murphy, Dennis
**Director(s)** Huston, Jimmy
**Screenwriter(s)** Murphy, Tab

**Cast** Leonard, Sean; Pollak, Cheryl; Auberjonois, Rene; Mirand, Evan; Willson, Paul; Kimmins, Ken; Flagg, Fannie; Warner, David; Bates, Kathy O.

**Song(s)** When It Comes to Me and You (C/L: Dorff, Stephen H.; Brown, Milton); Coming Back for More (C/L: Dorff, Stephen H.; Chemay, Joe; Hobbs, John)

**Notes** No cue sheet available.

### 4018 ◆ MY BEST GAL
Republic, 1952

**Composer(s)** Kent, Walter
**Lyricist(s)** Gannon, Kim

**Producer(s)** Grey, Harry
**Director(s)** Mann, Anthony
**Screenwriter(s)** Cooper, Olive; Felton, Earl

**Cast** Withers, Jane; Lydon, Jimmy; Craven, Frank; Pangborn, Franklin; Bonanova, Fortunio; Cleveland, George; Newton, Mary

**Song(s)** I've Got the Flyinist Feelin'; Where There's Love; Ida (C/L: Leonard, Eddie); Upsy Downsy

### 4019 ◆ MY BLOODY VALENTINE
Paramount, 1981

**Musical Score** Zaza, Paul
**Composer(s)** Zaza, Paul
**Lyricist(s)** Zaza, Paul

**Producer(s)** Dunning, John; Link, Andre; Miller, Stephen
**Director(s)** Mihalka, George
**Screenwriter(s)** Beaird, John

**Cast** Kelman, Paul; Hallier, Lori; Affleck, Neil; Knight, Keith; Francks, Don; Cowper, Peter

**Song(s)** Ballad of Valentine; Gateway to Hell; Part Time Lover Full Time Fool; Let the Good Times Roll; Sitting Here Thinking of You; Just a Guitar Man [1]; Wheels Run My Life; Come Back Home; Can't Believe I Lost You; Home Along the Highway (C/L: Bach, Lee); The Star (C/L: Bach, Lee); Party Music (Let the Good Times Roll); Wheels Run My Life [2]; Come Back Home [2]

**Notes** Some of these may not be songs but rather instrumentals with humming or vocal effects. [1] Also used in BULLIES (Universal) but with Bill Cuff credited with lyrics. [2] Listed in the *Academy Guide* but not on cue sheets.

### 4020 ◆ MY BLUE HEAVEN
Twentieth Century–Fox, 1950

**Composer(s)** Arlen, Harold
**Lyricist(s)** Blane, Ralph; Arlen, Harold

**Producer(s)** Siegel, Sol C.
**Director(s)** Koster, Henry
**Screenwriter(s)** Trotti, Lamar; Binyon, Claude

**Cast** Grable, Betty; Dailey, Dan; Wayne, David; Wyatt, Jane; Gaynor, Mitzi [2]; Merkel, Una; Beavers, Louise

**Song(s)** It's Deductible; What a Man; Cosmo Cosmetics; Halloween; I Love a New Yorker; Live Hard, Work Hard, Love Hard; The Friendly Islands [3]; Don't Rock the Boat, Dear; Says So Here [1] (C: Myrow, Josef; L: Gordon, Mack); Happy Little Verse and Chorus [1] [4]

**Notes** "My Blue Heaven" by Walter Donaldson and George Whiting and "Was that the Human Thing to Do" by Sammy Fain and Joe Young are also give a vocal rendition. [1] Not used. [2] During production she was still referred to as Mitzi Gerber. [3] Also in DOWN AMONG THE SHELTERING PALMS. [4] Was considered for CALL ME MISTER but not used.

### 4021 ◆ MY BUDDY
Republic, 1944

**Producer(s)** White, Eddy
**Director(s)** Sekely, Steven
**Screenwriter(s)** Manoff, Arnold

**Cast**  Barry, Donald; Roberts, Lynne; Terry, Ruth; Dunn, Emma; Litel, John; Granach, Alexander

**Song(s)**  Whodunit (C/L: Elliott, Jack)

**Notes**  There are also vocals of "Irish Washerwoman" and "My Buddy" by Walter Donaldson and Gus Kahn and "Waitin' for the Evenin' Mail" by Billy Baskette.

---

## 4022 ◆ MY DREAM IS YOURS
### Warner Brothers, 1949

**Composer(s)**  Warren, Harry
**Lyricist(s)**  Blane, Ralph
**Choreographer(s)**  Prinz, LeRoy

**Producer(s)**  Curtiz, Michael
**Director(s)**  Curtiz, Michael
**Screenwriter(s)**  Kurnitz, Harry; Lussier, Dane
**Source(s)**  "Hot Air" (story) Wald, Jerry; Moss, Paul Finder

**Cast**  Day, Doris; Carson, Jack; Bowman, Lee; Menjou, Adolphe; Arden, Eve; Sakall, S.Z.; Royle, Selena; Kennedy, Edgar; Leonard, Sheldon; Pangborn, Franklin; Berkes, John; Leonard, Ada; Carle, Frankie; Bunny, Bugs

**Song(s)**  Love Finds a Way; Canadian Capers (C/L: Chandler, Gus; White, Bert; Cohen, Henry; Burtnett, Earle); My Dream Is Yours; Tick, Tick, Tick; Someone Like You [1]; Freddie, Get Ready

**Notes**  A remake of TWENTY MILLION SWEETHEARTS (1934). Some of these numbers are in medleys. There are also vocals of the following songs with music by Harry Warren: "With Plenty of Money and You" and "I'll String Along with You," both with lyrics by Al Dubin; "Nagasaki" with lyrics by Mort Dixon and "You Must Have Been a Beautiful Baby" with lyrics by Johnny Mercer (also in DEEP ADVENTURE, HARD TO GET, MILDRED PIERCE, THE HARD WAY and THE EDDIE CANTOR STORY). [1] From the unproduced film TAKE ME OUT TO THE BALL GAME (MGM).

---

## 4023 ◆ MY FAIR LADY
### Warner Brothers, 1964

**Composer(s)**  Loewe, Frederick
**Lyricist(s)**  Lerner, Alan Jay
**Choreographer(s)**  Pan, Hermes

**Producer(s)**  Warner, Jack L.
**Director(s)**  Cukor, George
**Screenwriter(s)**  Lerner, Alan Jay
**Source(s)**  *My Fair Lady* (musical) Lerner, Alan Jay; Loewe, Frederick

**Cast**  Hepburn, Audrey [2]; Harrison, Rex [1]; Holloway, Stanley [1]; Hyde-White, Wilfrid; Cooper, Gladys; Brett, Jeremy [3]; Bikel, Theodore; Washbourne, Mona; Elsom, Isobel; Holland, John

**Song(s)**  Why Can't the English; Wouldn't It Be Loverly; I'm an Ordinary Man; With a Little Bit of Luck; Just You Wait; The Servants' Chorus; The Rain in Spain; I Could Have Danced All Night; Ascot Gavotte; On the Street Where You Live; You Did It; Show Me; Get Me to the Church on Time; A Hymn to Him; Without You; I've Grown Accustomed to Her Face

**Notes**  All songs are from the Broadway musical. [1] Appeared in original Broadway production. [2] Dubbed by Marni Nixon. [3] Dubbed by Bill Shirley.

---

## 4024 ◆ MY FAVORITE BRUNETTE
### Paramount, 1947

**Musical Score**  Dolan, Robert Emmett
**Composer(s)**  Livingston, Jay; Evans, Ray
**Lyricist(s)**  Livingston, Jay; Evans, Ray

**Producer(s)**  Dare, Danny [2]
**Director(s)**  Nugent, Elliott
**Screenwriter(s)**  Rose, Jack; Beloin, Edmund

**Cast**  Hope, Bob; Ladd, Alan; Lamour, Dorothy; Lorre, Peter; Chaney Jr., Lon; Dingle, Charles; Denny, Reginald; LaRue, Jack

**Song(s)**  Beside You; My Favorite Brunette [1]

**Notes**  [1] Not used but published. [2] Billed as Daniel Dare.

---

## 4025 ◆ MY FAVORITE SPY (1942)
### RKO, 1942

**Musical Score**  Webb, Roy
**Composer(s)**  Van Heusen, James
**Lyricist(s)**  Burke, Johnny

**Producer(s)**  Lloyd, Harold
**Director(s)**  Garnett, Tay
**Screenwriter(s)**  Herzig, Sig; Bowers, William

**Cast**  Kay Kyser and His Band; Babbitt, Harry; Kabibble, Ish; Mason, Sully; Irwin, Trudy; Dunn, Dorothy; Drew, Ellen; Wyman, Jane; Armstrong, Robert; Westley, Helen; Demarest, William; O'Connor, Una

**Song(s)**  Just Plain Lonesome; Got the Moon in My Pocket

---

## 4026 ◆ MY FAVORITE SPY (1951)
### Paramount, 1951

**Producer(s)**  Jones, Paul
**Director(s)**  McLeod, Norman Z.
**Screenwriter(s)**  Hartmann, Edmund L.; Shor, Jack; Kanter, Hal

**Cast**  Hope, Bob; Lamarr, Hedy

**Song(s)**  Just a Moment More (C/L: Livingston, Jay; Evans, Ray); I Wind Up - Taking a Fall (C: Dolan, Robert Emmett; L: Mercer, Johnny)

## 4027 ✦ MY FOOLISH HEART
### RKO, 1949

**Musical Score**   Young, Victor

**Producer(s)**   Goldwyn, Samuel
**Director(s)**   Robson, Mark
**Screenwriter(s)**   Epstein, Julius J.; Epstein, Philip G.
**Source(s)**   "Uncle Wiggily in Connecticut" (story) Salinger, J.D.

**Cast**   Andrews, Dana; Hayward, Susan; Keith, Robert; Smith, Kent; Wheeler, Lois; Landis, Jessie Royce; Perreau, Gigi; Booth, Karin; Mears, Martha

**Song(s)**   My Foolish Heart (C: Young, Victor; L: Washington, Ned)

## 4028 ✦ MY FORBIDDEN PAST
### RKO, 1950

**Musical Score**   Hollander, Frederick
**Composer(s)**   Bennett, Norman; Parsonnet, Marion
**Lyricist(s)**   Parsonnet, Marion; Bennett, Norman

**Producer(s)**   Banks, Polan
**Director(s)**   Stevenson, Robert
**Screenwriter(s)**   Parsonnet, Marion
**Source(s)**   *Carriage Entrance* (novel) Banks, Polan

**Cast**   Mitchum, Robert; Gardner, Ava; Douglas, Melvyn; Watson, Lucile; Carter, Janis; Ruysdael, Basil; Muse, Clarence; Wright, Will

**Song(s)**   The Spirits Creep; Juber Juberee (C: Webb, Roy; L: Parsonnet, Marion); Buy a Candle

## 4029 ✦ MY FRIEND IRMA
### Paramount, 1949

**Musical Score**   Webb, Roy
**Composer(s)**   Livingston, Jay; Evans, Ray
**Lyricist(s)**   Livingston, Jay; Evans, Ray

**Producer(s)**   Wallis, Hal B.
**Director(s)**   Marshall, George
**Screenwriter(s)**   Levy, Parke; Howard, Cy
**Source(s)**   "My Friend Irma" (radio program) Howard, Cy

**Cast**   Lewis, Jerry; Martin, Dean; Wilson, Marie; Lund, John; Lynn, Diana; DeFore, Don; Conried, Hans

**Song(s)**   Here's to Love; My Friend Irma [1]; Just for Fun; My One, My Only, My All

**Notes**   [1] Not used but published.

## 4030 ✦ MY FRIEND IRMA GOES WEST
### Paramount, 1950

**Musical Score**   Harline, Leigh
**Composer(s)**   Livingston, Jay; Evans, Ray
**Lyricist(s)**   Livingston, Jay; Evans, Ray

**Producer(s)**   Wallis, Hal B.
**Director(s)**   Walker, Hal
**Screenwriter(s)**   Howard, Cy; Levy, Parke
**Source(s)**   "My Friend Irma" (radio program) Howard, Cy

**Cast**   Wilson, Marie; Lund, John; Calvet, Corinne; Lynn, Diana; Martin, Dean; Lewis, Jerry

**Song(s)**   Baby, Obey Me!; I'll Always Love You (Querida Mia) [1]; The Fiddle and Gittar Band

**Notes**   There is also a vocal of "Singing a Vagabond Song" (also in SING BABY SING) by Harry Richman, Val Burton and Sam Messenheimer. [1] Also in TROPIC ZONE.

## 4031 ✦ MY GAL LOVES MUSIC
### Universal, 1944

**Composer(s)**   Rosen, Milton
**Lyricist(s)**   Carter, Everett

**Producer(s)**   Lilley, Edward
**Director(s)**   Lilley, Edward
**Screenwriter(s)**   Conrad, Eugene

**Cast**   Catlett, Walter; McDonald, Grace; Mowbray, Alan; Crosby, Bob; Kean, Betty

**Song(s)**   Give Out [1]; Sing a Jingle [3] (C/L: James, Inez; Miller, Sidney); Over and Over and Over; Vitamin U (C/L: Gaskill, Clarence); Rhumba Matumba [2] (C/L: Callazo, Bobby); Somebody's Rockin' My Rainbow; Pepita; Bogo Jo [4] (C/L: Calendar, George)

**Notes**   [1] Also in JUKE BOX JENNY. [2] Also in HOLLYWOOD BOND CARAVAN (Paramount) and CUBAN PETE. [3] Also in SING A JINGLE. [4] Sheet music only.

## 4032 ✦ MY GAL SAL
### Twentieth Century–Fox, 1942

**Composer(s)**   Rainger, Ralph
**Lyricist(s)**   Robin, Leo
**Choreographer(s)**   Pan, Hermes; Raset, Val

**Producer(s)**   Bessler, Robert
**Director(s)**   Cummings, Irving
**Screenwriter(s)**   Miller, Seton I.; Ware, Darrell; Tunberg, Karl
**Source(s)**   *My Brother Paul* (novel) Dreiser, Theodore

**Cast**   Hayworth, Rita [1]; Mature, Victor; Sutton, John; Landis, Carole; Gleason, James; Silvers, Phil; Catlett, Walter; Maris, Mona; Orth, Frank; Andrews, Stanley; Kelly, John; Pan, Hermes

**Song(s)**   On the Gay White Way; Oh the Pity of It All; Here You Are; Me and My Fella and a Big Umbrella; Midnight at the Masquerade

**Notes**   No cue sheet available. There are also vocals of the following songs by Paul Dresser: "Come Tell Me What's Your Answer (Yes or No?);" "The Convict and the Bird," "Mr. Volunteer," "I'se Your Honey," "If You Want Me," "Liza Jane," "On the Banks of the Wabash" and "My Gal Sal." "Two Little Girls in Blue" by Charles Graham and "Daisy Bell" by Harry Dacre were also used. [1] Dubbed by Nan Wynn.

## 4033 ◆ MY GEISHA
Paramount, 1962

**Musical Score**   Waxman, Franz

**Producer(s)**   Parker, Steve
**Director(s)**   Cardiff, Jack
**Screenwriter(s)**   Krasna, Norman

**Cast**   MacLaine, Shirley; Montand, Yves; Robinson, Edward G.; Cummings, Robert; Tani, Yoko

**Song(s)**   'Sall Right, 'Sall Right, 'Sall Right [2] (C/L: Lilley, Joseph J.); My Geisha (You Are Sympathy to Me) [1] (C: Waxman, Franz; L: David, Hal)

**Notes**   There are also some renditions from Puccini's MADAME BUTTERLFY. [1] Lyric added for exploitation only. [2] This song is on screen for exactly 11 seconds.

## 4034 ◆ MY GIRL TISA
Warner Brothers, 1948

**Musical Score**   Steiner, Max

**Producer(s)**   Sperling, Milton
**Director(s)**   Nugent, Elliott
**Screenwriter(s)**   Boretz, Allen
**Source(s)**   *Ever the Beginning* (play) Smith, Sara B.; Prumbs, Lucille S.

**Cast**   Palmer, Lilli; Wanamaker, Sam; Tamiroff, Akim; Hale, Alan; Haas, Hugo; Robbins, Gale; Adler, Stella; Baker, Benny; Feld, Fritz

**Song(s)**   At the Candlelight Cafe [1] (C/L: David, Mack)

**Notes**   [1] Also in ROPE.

## 4035 ◆ MY LADY'S PAST
Tiffany–Stahl, 1929

**Musical Score**   Riesenfeld, Hugo

**Director(s)**   Ray, Albert
**Screenwriter(s)**   Hatton, Frederic; Hatton, Fanny

**Cast**   Bennett, Belle; Brown, Joe E.; Bennett, Alma; Simpson, Russell; Standing, Joan; Bennett, Billie

**Song(s)**   A Kiss to Remember (C: Goering, Al; Pettis, Jack; L: Bryan, Alfred)

**Notes**   No cue sheet available.

## 4036 ◆ MY LIPS BETRAY
Fox, 1933

**Composer(s)**   Kernell, William
**Lyricist(s)**   Kernell, William

**Director(s)**   Blystone, John
**Screenwriter(s)**   Behrman, S.N.
**Source(s)**   *Der Komet* (play) Orbok, Attila

**Cast**   Harvey, Lilian; Boles, John; Brendel, El; Browne, Irene; Eburne, Maude

**Song(s)**   To Romance; His Majesty's Car; I'll Build a Nest [1]; Why Am I Happy?; The Band Is Gayly Playing

**Notes**   [1] Also in IT'S GREAT TO BE ALIVE.

## 4037 ◆ MY LITTLE CHICKADEE
Universal, 1940

**Musical Score**   Freed, Ralph; Skinner, Frank

**Producer(s)**   Cowan, Lester
**Director(s)**   Cline, Edward F.
**Screenwriter(s)**   Fields, W.C.; West, Mae

**Cast**   West, Mae; Fields, W.C.; Calleia, Joseph; Foran, Dick; Donnelly, Ruth; Hamilton, Margaret; Meek, Donald; Knight, Fuzzy; Robertson, Willard

**Song(s)**   Willie of the Valley (C: Oakland, Ben; L: Drake, Milton)

## 4038 ◆ MY LITTLE DUCKAROO
Warner Brothers, 1954

**Musical Score**   Franklyn, Milton J.

**Director(s)**   Jones, Chuck
**Screenwriter(s)**   Maltese, Michael

**Cast**   Duck, Daffy; Pig, Porky

**Song(s)**   Lazy Will (C/L: Maltese, Michael)

**Notes**   Merrie Melodie.

## 4039 ◆ MY LITTLE GIRL
Hemdale, 1987

**Musical Score**   Robbins, Richard

**Producer(s)**   Merchant, Ismail
**Director(s)**   Kaiserman, Connie
**Screenwriter(s)**   Kaiserman, Connie; Mason, Nan

**Cast**   Jones, James Earl; Page, Geraldine; Masterson, Mary Stuart; Meara, Anne; Payton-Wright, Pamela; Goetz, Peter Michael; Gallagher, Peter

**Song(s)**   Let's Get Fresh (C: Carter, Juliet; Kahn, Walter; L: Carter, Juliet; Kahn, Walter; Kaiserman, Connie); Baby Boy (C/L: Moses, Kala); Alice's Song (C/L: Lin, Traci; Robbins, Richard)

**Notes**   No cue sheet available.

## 4040 ✦ MY LOVER, MY SON
### Metro–Goldwyn–Mayer, 1970

**Musical Score**   Paramor, Norrie; Vickers, Mike
**Composer(s)**   Paramor, Norrie; Vickers, Mike
**Lyricist(s)**   Paramor, Norrie; Vickers, Mike; Vickers, Sue

**Producer(s)**   Stark, Wilbur
**Director(s)**   Newland, John
**Screenwriter(s)**   Marchant, William; Hall, Jenni
**Source(s)**   *Reputation for a Song* (novel) Grierson, Edward

**Cast**   Schneider, Romy; Waterman, Dennis; Brake, Patricia; Houston, Donald; Bastedo, Alexandra

**Song(s)**   What's On Your Mind?; Summer's Here; I Want the Good Things (C: Vickers, Sue; Paramor, Norrie; Vickers, Mike; L: Vickers, Sue; White, Billy)

## 4041 ✦ MY LUCKY STAR
### Twentieth Century–Fox, 1938

**Composer(s)**   Revel, Harry
**Lyricist(s)**   Gordon, Mack
**Choreographer(s)**   Castle, Nick; Sawyer, Geneva

**Producer(s)**   Zanuck, Darryl F.
**Director(s)**   Del Ruth, Roy
**Screenwriter(s)**   Tugend, Harry; Yellen, Jack

**Cast**   Henie, Sonja; Greene, Richard; Davis, Joan; Romero, Cesar; Ebsen, Buddy; Treacher, Arthur; Barbier, George; Hovick, Louise [2]; Gilbert, Billy; Wilder, Patricia; Cook Jr., Elisha

**Song(s)**   Marching Along (Plymouth Welcome Song); This May Be the Night; Plymouth Rock; Classy Clothes Chris; By a Wishing Well; Could You Pass in Love; Plymouth Farewell Song (Alma Mater); I've Got a Date with a Dream; Where in the World [1]; The All-American Swing [3]; Bo-Peep Theme [3]

**Notes**   [1] Used instrumentally only. [2] Gypsy Rose Lee. [3] Not used.

## 4042 ✦ MY MAN
### Warner Brothers, 1928

**Director(s)**   Mayo, Archie
**Screenwriter(s)**   Lord, Robert; Jackson, Joseph

**Cast**   Brice, Fanny; Williams, Guinn "Big Boy"; Murphy, Edna; Tucker, Richard; de Segurola, Andres; Seay, Billy; Selwynne, Clarissa

**Song(s)**   I'd Rather Be Blue [2] (C: Fisher, Fred; L: Rose, Billy); My Man [1] [2] (C: Yvain, Maurice; L: Pollock, Channing); Second Hand Rose [1] [2] (C: Hanley, James F.; L: Clarke, Grant); If You Want the Rainbow, You Must Have the Rain (C: Levant, Oscar; L: Dixon, Mort; Rose, Billy); I'm an Indian (C: Edwards, Leo; L: Merrill, Blanche); I Was a Florodora Baby (C: Carroll, Harry; L: Macdonald, Ballard)

**Notes**   No cue sheet available. It is not known if any of these songs were written for this film. [1] From stage show ZIEGFELD FOLLIES OF 1921. [2] Later in FUNNY GIRL (Columbia).

## 4043 ✦ MY MAN GODFREY
### Universal, 1957

**Musical Score**   Skinner, Frank

**Producer(s)**   Hunter, Ross
**Director(s)**   Koster, Henry
**Screenwriter(s)**   Freeman, Everett; Bermeis, Peter; Bowers, William
**Source(s)**   *My Man Godfrey* (novel) Hatch, Eric

**Cast**   Allyson, June; Niven, David; Landis, Jessie Royce; Keith, Robert; Gabor, Eva; Donnell, Jeff; Hyer, Martha; Anderson, Herbert

**Song(s)**   Lovely (C/L: Gershenson, Joseph); My Man Godfrey [1] (C: Burke, Sonny; L: Lee, Peggy)

**Notes**   A remake of MY MAN GODFREY (1936). [1] Not used.

## 4044 ✦ MY MAN JASPER
### Paramount, 1945

**Musical Score**   Wheeler, Clarence

**Producer(s)**   Pal, George
**Director(s)**   Pal, George

**Song(s)**   Courtroom Boogie (C/L: Wheeler, Clarence)

**Notes**   This was a Puppetoon short. "Blue Hawaii" by Ralph Rainger and Leo Robin was also heard briefly in a vocal.

## 4045 ✦ MY MARRIAGE
### Twentieth Century–Fox, 1935

**Producer(s)**   Wurtzel, Sol M.
**Director(s)**   Archainbaud, George
**Screenwriter(s)**   Hyland, Frances

**Cast**   Trevor, Claire; Taylor, Kent; Frederick, Pauline; Kelly, Paul; Wood, Helen; Beck, Thomas; Mercer, Beryl; Kolker, Henry

**Song(s)**   According to the Moonlight (C: Meyer, Joseph; L: Magidson, Herb; Yellen, Jack)

## 4046 ✦ MY OWN TRUE LOVE
### Paramount, 1948

**Producer(s)**   Lewton, Val
**Director(s)**   Bennett, Compton
**Screenwriter(s)**   Strauss, Theodore; Mischel, Josef

**Source(s)**   *Make You a Fine Wife* (novel) Foldes, Yolanda

**Cast**   Douglas, Melvyn; Calvert, Phyllis; Hendrix, Wanda

**Song(s)**   My Own True Love [1] (C/L: Livingston, Jay; Evans, Ray)

**Notes**   [1] Not used.

## 4047 ✦ MY PAL TRIGGER
Republic, 1946

**Producer(s)**   Schaefer, Armand
**Director(s)**   MacDonald, Frank
**Screenwriter(s)**   Townley, Jack; Butler, John K.

**Cast**   Rogers, Roy; Trigger; Hayes, George "Gabby"; Evans, Dale; Holt, Jack; Mason, LeRoy; Barcroft, Roy; Sons of the Pioneers; Briggs, Harlan; Haade, William; Reicher, Frank

**Song(s)**   Livin' Western Style (C/L: Hershey, June; Swander, Don); Harriet (C: Baer, Abel; L: Cunningham, Paul); Alla en el Rancho Grande [1] (C: Ramos, Silvano; L: del Moral, J.D.); Ole Faithful (C/L: Kennedy, Hamilton; Carr, Michael)

**Notes**   It is unlikely that any of these were written for this film. [1] English lyric by Bartley Costello.

## 4048 ✦ MYRA BRECKINRIDGE
Twentieth Century–Fox, 1970

**Producer(s)**   Fryer, Robert
**Director(s)**   Sarne, Michael
**Screenwriter(s)**   Sarne, Michael; Giler, David
**Source(s)**   *Breckinridge, Myra* (novel) Vidal, Gore

**Cast**   West, Mae; Huston, John; Welch, Raquel; Reed, Rex; Fawcett, Farrah; Carmel, Roger C.; Furth, George; Lockhart, Calvin; Backus, Jim; Carradine, John; Devine, Andy; Herren, Roger

**Song(s)**   Secret Place (C/L: Phillips, John); You Gotta Taste All the Fruit (C: Fain, Sammy; L: Bergman, Marilyn; Bergman, Alan)

**Notes**   There are also vocals of "May I Tempt You with a Big Red Rosy Apple" by Joseph Myrow and Mack Gordon; "America, I Love You" by Archie Gottler and Edgar Leslie; "You Gotta S-M-I-L-E" by Mack Gordon and Harry Revel; "The Man's in the Navy" by Frederick Hollander and Frank Loesser; "Hard to Handle" by Otis Redding, Allen Jones and Alvertis Isabell and other songs with shorter uses.

## 4049 ✦ MY REPUTATION
Warner Brothers–First National, 1946

**Musical Score**   Steiner, Max

**Producer(s)**   Blanke, Henry
**Director(s)**   Bernhardt, Curtis

**Screenwriter(s)**   Turney, Catherine
**Source(s)**   "Instruct My Sorrows" (story) Jaynes, Clare

**Cast**   Stanwyck, Barbara; Brent, George; Watson, Lucile; Arden, Eve; Anderson, Warner; Ridgely, John; Cowan, Jerome; Dale, Esther; Beckett, Scotty; Todd, Ann

**Song(s)**   While You're Away (C: Steiner, Max; L: Adams, Stanley)

## 4050 ✦ MYRT AND MARGE
Universal, 1934

**Composer(s)**   Jerome, M.K.
**Lyricist(s)**   Jasmyn, Joan

**Director(s)**   Boasberg, Al
**Screenwriter(s)**   Banyard, Beatrice
**Source(s)**   "Myrt and Marge" (radio program)

**Cast**   Vail, Myrtle; Dammerel, Donna; Foy Jr., Eddie; Healy, Ted; Jackson, Thomas; Friganza, Trixie; MacDonald, J. Farrell; The Three Stooges

**Song(s)**   Draggin' My Heels Around; Isle of Blues; What Is Sweeter?

**Notes**   No cue sheet available. Released as LAUGHTER IN THE AIR in Great Britain.

## 4051 ✦ MY SCIENCE PROJECT
Touchstone, 1985

**Musical Score**   Bernstein, Peter

**Producer(s)**   Taplin, Jonathan T.
**Director(s)**   Betuel, Jonathan R.
**Screenwriter(s)**   Betuel, Jonathan R.

**Cast**   Hopper, Dennis; Wedgeworth, Ann; Corbin, Barry; Masur, Richard; Sbarge, Raphael; Stevens, Fisher; Von Zerneck, Danielle; Stockwell, John

**Song(s)**   Hard to Believe (C/L: Held, Bob; Heller, Bill; Hill, Matthew); Hit and Run (C/L: Gordon, Jeff; Held, Bob; Heller, Bill); My Mind's Made Up (C/L: Held, Bob; Hiller, Bill); My Science Project (C/L: Held, Bob; Heller, Bill; Colina, Michael)

## 4052 ✦ MY SECOND WIFE
Fox, 1934

**Song(s)**   Que Sabes Tu (C/L: Grever, Maria)

**Notes**   No other information available. There is also a vocal rendition of "A Guy What Takes His Time" by Ralph Rainger.

## 4053 ✦ MY SIDE OF THE MOUNTAIN
Paramount, 1969

**Musical Score**   Bikel, Theodore; Josephs, Wilfred

**Producer(s)**   Radnitz, Robert B.
**Director(s)**   Clark, James B.

**Screenwriter(s)** Sherdeman, Ted; Clove, Jane; Crawford, Joanna
**Source(s)** *My Side of the Mountain* (novel) George, Jean

**Cast** Eccles, Ted; Bikel, Theodore

**Song(s)** My Side of the Mountain (C/L: Bikel, Theodore); A World Like Mine [1] (C: Josephs, Wilfred; L: Kusik, Larry; Snyder, Eddie)

**Notes** [1] Lyrics added for exploitation use only.

## 4054 ✦ MY SISTER EILEEN
### Columbia, 1955

**Musical Score** Duning, George
**Composer(s)** Styne, Jule
**Lyricist(s)** Robin, Leo
**Choreographer(s)** Fosse, Bob

**Producer(s)** Kohlmar, Fred
**Director(s)** Quine, Richard
**Screenwriter(s)** Edwards, Blake; Quine, Richard
**Source(s)** Eileen stories [2] (stories) McKenney, Ruth

**Cast** Garrett, Betty; Leigh, Janet; Lemmon, Jack; Marlow, Lucy; York, Richard; Kasnar, Kurt; Fosse, Bob; Rall, Tommy

**Song(s)** Atmosphere; As Soon As They See Eileen; I'm Great; Got No Room for Mr. Gloom [1]; There's Nothin' Like Love; Tonight [1]; It's Bigger Than You and Me; Give Me a Band and My Baby; What Happened to the Conga; Competition Dance (inst.)

**Notes** [1] Used instrumentally only. [2] Also based on the play MY SISTER EILEEN by Joseph Fields and Jerome Chodorov.

## 4055 ✦ MY SIX LOVES
### Paramount, 1963

**Producer(s)** Gaither, Gant
**Director(s)** Champion, Gower
**Screenwriter(s)** Fante, John; Calvelli, Joseph; Wood, William

**Cast** Reynolds, Debbie; Robertson, Cliff; Janssen, David; Heckart, Eileen; Backus, Jim; Conried, Hans

**Song(s)** It's a Darn Good Thing (C: Van Heusen, James; L: Cahn, Sammy); My Six Loves [1] (C: Van Heusen, James; L: Cahn, Sammy)

**Notes** [1] Instrumental use only.

## 4056 ✦ MY SON JOHN
### Paramount, 1952

**Musical Score** Dolan, Robert Emmett

**Producer(s)** McCarey, Leo
**Director(s)** McCarey, Leo
**Screenwriter(s)** Connolly, Myles; McCarey, Leo

**Cast** Hayes, Helen; Heflin, Van; Walker, Robert; Jagger, Dean

**Song(s)** Alma Mater (C: Dolan, Robert Emmett; McCarey, Leo; L: McCarey, Leo); Girls School Alma Mater [1] (C: Waxman, Franz; Loesser, Frank; L: Loesser, Frank)

**Notes** [1] Not used.

## 4057 ✦ MY SON, MY SON!
### United Artists, 1940

**Producer(s)** Small, Edward
**Director(s)** Vidor, Charles
**Screenwriter(s)** Coffee, Lenore
**Source(s)** *My Son, My Son* (novel) Spring, Howard

**Cast** Aherne, Brian; Beckett, Scotty; Hayward, Louis; Day, Laraine; Hull, Henry; Carroll, Madeleine; Hutchinson, Josephine; Logan, Stanley

**Song(s)** My Son, My Son (C: Pollack, Lew; L: Gilbert, L. Wolfe)

**Notes** No cue sheet available.

## 4058 ✦ MYSTERIOUS CROSSING
### Universal, 1937

**Producer(s)** Paul, Val
**Director(s)** Lubin, Arthur
**Screenwriter(s)** Parker, Jefferson; Grey, John

**Cast** Dunn, James; Rogers, Jean; Devine, Andy

**Song(s)** The Railroad That Ran Through Our Land (C: Actman, Irving; L: Loesser, Frank)

## 4059 ✦ MYSTERIOUS MR. MOTO
### Twentieth Century–Fox, 1938

**Producer(s)** Wurtzel, Sol M.
**Director(s)** Foster, Norman
**Screenwriter(s)** MacDonald, Philip; Foster, Norman
**Source(s)** Mr. Moto novels characters Marquand, J.P.

**Cast** Lorre, Peter; Maguire, Mary; Wilcoxon, Henry; Rhodes, Erik; Huber, Harold; Ames, Leon; Harvey, Forrester

**Song(s)** Black Black Sheep [1] (C: DeFrancesco, Louis E.; L: Tuttle, Frank)

**Notes** [1] Also in SPRINGTIME FOR HENRY.

## 4060 ✦ MYSTERY IN MEXICO
### RKO, 1948

**Musical Score** Sawtell, Paul; Webb, Roy

**Producer(s)** Rogell, Sid
**Director(s)** Wise, Robert
**Screenwriter(s)** Kimble, Lawrence

Cast    Lundigan, William; White, Jacqueline; Cortez, Ricardo; Barrett, Tony; Dalya, Jacqueline; Reed, Walter

Song(s)    Ven Aqui (C: Harline, Leigh; L: Greene, Mort)

## 4061 ◆ MYSTERY MAN
### United Artists, 1944

Producer(s)    Sherman, Harry
Director(s)    Archainbaud, George
Screenwriter(s)    Cheney, J. Benton
Source(s)    characters by Mulford, Clarence E.

Cast    Boyd, William; Clyde, Andy; Rogers, Jimmy; Tucker, Forrest

Song(s)    Tie a Saddle String Around Your Troubles [1] (C: Waters, Vernon "Ozie"; L: Johnson, Forrest "Trees")

Notes    [1] Not written for picture.

## 4062 ◆ MYSTERY OF MARIE ROGET
### Universal, 1942

Producer(s)    Malvern, Paul
Director(s)    Rosen, Phil
Screenwriter(s)    Jacoby, Michel
Source(s)    "Mystery of Marie Roget" (story) Poe, Edgar Allen

Cast    Knowles, Patric; Montez, Maria; Ouspenskaya, Maria; Litel, John; Norris, Edward; Corrigan, Lloyd; O'Day, Nell; Reicher, Frank; Fillmore, Clyde; Middleton, Charles

Song(s)    Mama-Dit-Moi, Do the Oo-La-La (C/L: Carter, Everett; Rosen, Milton)

Notes    No cue sheet available.

## 4063 ◆ THE MYSTERY OF MR. X
### Metro–Goldwyn–Mayer, 1934

Musical Score    Axt, William

Producer(s)    Weingarten, Lawrence
Director(s)    Selwyn, Edgar
Screenwriter(s)    Rogers, Howard Emmett; Hoffe, Monckton
Source(s)    Mystery of the Dead Police (novel) MacDonald, Philip

Cast    Allan, Elizabeth; Montgomery, Robert; Stone, Lewis; Forbes, Ralph; Stephenson, Henry

Song(s)    This Is the Night (C: Brown, Nacio Herb; L: Freed, Arthur)

## 4064 ◆ THE MYSTERY OF THE RIVER BOAT
### Universal, 1944

Composer(s)    Rosen, Milton
Lyricist(s)    Carter, Everett

Director(s)    Taylor, Ray; Collins, Lewis D.

Cast    Lowery, Robert; Quillan, Eddie; Martin, Marion; Clements, Marjorie; Talbot, Lyle; Moreland, Mantan; Novello, Jay; McDonald, Francis

Song(s)    Loo-Loo-Louisiana [1] [8]; I Am, Are You? [1] [5]; Rhythm Rhapsody [1] (C/L: Dodd, Jimmy); I Like to Be Loved [2] [7]; Dancin' on Air [3] [4]; I Get Mellow in the Yellow of the Moon [3] [6] (C/L: Dodd, Jimmy)

Notes    This is a serial in 13 chapters. [1] In chapter one. [2] In chapter two. [3] In chapter three. [4] Also in SING ANOTHER CHORUS and STRICTLY IN THE GROOVE. [5] Also in WEEK-END PASS. [6] Also in TWILIGHT ON THE PRAIRIE. [7] Also in MELODY GARDEN and WEEK-END PASS. [8] Also in SENORITA FROM THE WEST.

## 4065 ◆ MYSTERY RANCH
### Fox, 1932

Director(s)    Howard, David
Screenwriter(s)    Cohn, Alfred A.
Source(s)    The Killer (novel) White, Stewart Edward

Cast    O'Brien, George; Parker, Cecilia; Middleton, Charles; Stevens, Charles; Harvey, Forrester

Song(s)    Cowboy Dan (C/L: Friend, Cliff)

## 4066 ◆ MYSTIC PIZZA
### Samuel Goldwyn, 1988

Musical Score    McHugh, David

Producer(s)    Levinson, Mark; Rosenfelt, Scott
Director(s)    Petrie, Donald
Screenwriter(s)    Jones, Amy; Howze, Perry; Howze, Randy; Uhry, Alfred

Cast    Gish, Annabeth; Roberts, Julia; Taylor, Lili; D'Onofrio, Vincent Phillip; Moses, William R.; Storke, Adam; Ferrell, Conchata; Merlin, Joanna; Cunningham, John; Turenne, Louis

Song(s)    These Are the Times to Remember (C: Previte, Franke; Fiedel, Brad; L: Previte, Franke)

Notes    No cue sheet available.

## 4067 ◆ MY TUTOR
### Crown International, 1983

Musical Score    Lewis, Webster
Composer(s)    Lewis, Webster
Lyricist(s)    Hamilton, Arthur

Producer(s)    Tenser, Marilyn J.
Director(s)    Bowers, George
Screenwriter(s)    Roberts, Joe

Cast    Kaye, Caren; Lattanzi, Matt; McCarthy, Kevin; Brandon, Clark; Golonka, Arlene; Glover, Crispin

**Song(s)** The First Time We Make Love; Now You Must Pay; You're My Tutor

**Notes** No cue sheet available.

## 4068 ✦ MY WEAKNESS
Fox, 1933

**Composer(s)** Whiting, Richard A.
**Lyricist(s)** Robin, Leo; DeSylva, B.G.

**Producer(s)** DeSylva, B.G.
**Director(s)** Butler, David
**Screenwriter(s)** DeSylva, B.G.; Ryan, Ben; Hanlon, Bert

**Cast** Harvey, Lilian; Brendel, El; Bentley, Irene; Ayres, Lew; Butterworth, Charles; Langdon, Harry; Silvers, Sid

**Song(s)** Musical Scene #1 - Opening; Musical Scene #2 - Examination of Loo Loo; You Can Be Had - Be Careful; How Do I Look; Gather Lip Rouge While You May

## 4069 ✦ MY WIFE'S RELATIVES
Republic, 1939

**Producer(s)** Siegel, Sol C.
**Director(s)** Meins, Gus
**Screenwriter(s)** Townley, Jack

**Cast** Gleason, James; Gleason, Lucille; Gleason, Russell; Davenport, Harry; Hart, Mary; Pratt, Purnell; Eburne, Maude; Gateson, Marjorie

**Song(s)** Daddy Dear We Love You (C: Kraushaar, Raoul; Lava, William; L: Cherkose, Eddie); Over the Hill to the Poorhouse (C: Lava, William; L: Cherkose, Eddie)

## 4070 ✦ MY WILD IRISH ROSE
Warner Brothers, 1947

**Musical Score** Steiner, Max
**Composer(s)** Jerome, M.K.
**Lyricist(s)** Koehler, Ted

**Producer(s)** Jacobs, William
**Director(s)** Butler, David
**Screenwriter(s)** Milne, Peter
**Source(s)** "Song In His Heart" (story) Olcott, Rita

**Cast** Morgan, Dennis; Dahl, Arlene; King, Andrea; Hale, Alan; Tobias, George; O'Brien, George; Blue, Ben; Allgood, Sara; Frawley, William; McGuire, Don; Cleveland, George; Sutton, Grady

**Song(s)** The Natchez and the Robert E. Lee; Miss Lindy Lou; Let Me Dream Some More; The Mirror Song (Inst.); Hush-A-Bye Wee Rose of Killarney; Sing an Irish Song (L: Scholl, Jack); Show Me the Way to the Kerry Fair; There's Room in My Heart for Them All; Minstrel Days [1] (L: Scholl, Jack)

**Notes** This is a film biography of Chauncey Olcott. Renditions of the following songs are also undertaken, some in medleys: My "Wild Irish Rose" by Chauncey Olcott; "When Irish Eyes Are Smiling" by Ernest R. Ball, Chauncey Olcott and George Graff Jr.; "Mother Machree" by Ernest R. Ball, Chauncey Olcott and Rida Johnson Young; the traditional songs "Dear Old Donegal," "Polly Wolly Doodle," and "Gyp Gyp My Little Horse;" "One Little Sweet Little Girl" by Dan Sullivan; "A Little Bit of Heaven (Sure They Call It Ireland)" by Ernest R. Ball and J. Kiern Brennan; "I Love the Name of Mary" by Ernest R. Ball, Chauncey Olcott and George Graff Jr.; "Sweet Inniscarra" by Chauncey Olcott; "'Twas Only an Irishman's Dream" by John J. O'Brien, Al Dubin and Rennie McCormack; "In the Evening by the Moonlight" by James A. Bland; "Come Down Ma Evening Star" by John Stromberg and Robert B. Smith; "My Nell's Blue Eyes" by William J. Scanlan; "You Tell Me Your Dream I'll Tell You Mine" by Charles Daniels, Seymour Rice and Albert Brown; "Wait Till the Sun Shines Nellie" by Harry Von Tilzer and Andrew B. Sterling; "Will You Love Me in December As You Do in May" by Ernest R. Ball and James J. Walker and "By the Light of the Silvery Moon" by Gus Edwards and Edward Madden. [1] Also in HORSE AND BUGGY DAYS and MINSTREL DAYS.

# N

### 4071 ✦ NADA MAS QUE UNA MUJER
Fox, 1934

**Producer(s)**  Stone, John
**Director(s)**  Lachman, Harry

**Cast**  Singerman, Berta; del Diestro, Alfredo

**Song(s)**  Carnival Song (Czardas) [1] (C: Vecsei, Armand; L: Gilbert, L. Wolfe)

**Notes**  The Brazilian folk song "Tu Tu Maramba" is also given a vocal treatment. [1] Also in EL REY DE LOS GITANOS and RASCALS with lyrics credited to Harry Akst and Sidney Clare.

### 4072 ✦ NAKED ALIBI
Universal, 1954

**Musical Score**  Stein, Herman
**Choreographer(s)**  Williams, Kenny

**Producer(s)**  Hunter, Ross
**Director(s)**  Hopper, Jerry
**Screenwriter(s)**  Roman, Lawrence
**Source(s)**  "Cry Copper" (story) Bren, J. Robert; Atwater, Gladys

**Cast**  Hayden, Sterling; Barry, Gene; Grahame, Gloria; Connors, Chuck

**Song(s)**  Ace in the Hole (C/L: Mitchell, George; Dempsey, James)

### 4073 ✦ THE NAKED APE
Universal, 1973

**Musical Score**  Webb, Jimmy
**Composer(s)**  Webb, Jimmy
**Lyricist(s)**  Webb, Jimmy

**Producer(s)**  Bufman, Zev; Lang, Jennings
**Director(s)**  Driver, Donald
**Screenwriter(s)**  Driver, Donald
**Source(s)**  *The Naked Ape* (book) Morris, Desmond

**Cast**  Crawford, Johnny; Principal, Victoria; Olivieri, Dennis

**Song(s)**  Saturday Suit; Finger Paint Me; Survival Rag

### 4074 ✦ THE NAKED DAWN
Universal, 1955

**Musical Score**  Gilbert, Herschel Burke

**Producer(s)**  Radford, James Q.
**Director(s)**  Ulmer, Edgar G.
**Screenwriter(s)**  Schneider, Nina; Schneider, Herman

**Cast**  Kennedy, Arthur; St. John, Betta; Iglesias, Eugene; Charlita

**Song(s)**  Ai Hombre (C: Gilbert, Herschel Burke; L: Copeland, Bill); I Love a Stranger [1] (C: Gilbert, Herschel Burke; L: Heyman, Edward)

**Notes**  [1] Sheet music only.

### 4075 ✦ THE NAKED EARTH
Twentieth Century–Fox, 1958

**Musical Score**  Benjamin, Arthur

**Producer(s)**  Worker, Adrian
**Director(s)**  Sherman, Vincent
**Screenwriter(s)**  Helmes, Milton

**Cast**  Todd, Richard; Greco, Juliette; Kitzmiller, John; Currie, Finlay; Naismith, Laurence

**Song(s)**  Demain Il Fera Jour [1] (C/L: Patterson, Henri)

**Notes**  [1] Sheet music title - "Tomorrow My Love." Lyrics by Carey Starr.

### 4076 ✦ THE NAKED HILLS
Allied Artists, 1956

**Musical Score**  Gilbert, Herschel Burke

**Producer(s)**  Shaftel, Josef
**Director(s)**  Shaftel, Josef
**Screenwriter(s)**  Shaftel, Josef

**Cast**  Wayne, David; Wynn, Keenan; Barton, James; Henderson, Marcia; Backus, Jim; Pyle, Denver; Dell, Myrna

**Song(s)** The Four Seasons (C: Gilbert, Herschel Burke; L: Russell, Bob)

**Notes** No cue sheet available.

## 4077 ◆ THE NAKED JUNGLE
Paramount, 1954

**Producer(s)** Pal, George
**Director(s)** Haskin, Byron
**Screenwriter(s)** MacDougall, Ranald; Yordan, Philip
**Source(s)** "Leiningen Versus the Ants" (story) Stephenson, Carl

**Cast** Heston, Charlton; Parker, Eleanor

**Song(s)** Survey of the Plantation (C: Amfitheatrof, Daniele; L: Singh, Reginald Lai); Song of Longing for the Jungle [1] (C: Sanders, Troy; L: Singh, Reginald Lai); An Aboriginal Love Song [1] (C/L: Singh, Reginald Lai)

**Notes** [1] Not used.

## 4078 ◆ THE NAKED MAJA
United Artists, 1959

**Musical Score** Lavagnino, Angelo Francesco
**Composer(s)** Lavagnino, Angelo Francesco
**Lyricist(s)** Simoni, Sylvana

**Producer(s)** Lombardo, Goffredo
**Director(s)** Koster, Henry
**Screenwriter(s)** Prosperi, Giorgio; Corwin, Norman; Lewin, Albert; Saul, Oscar

**Cast** Franciosa, Anthony; Gardner, Ava; Padrovani, Lea; Cervi, Gino

**Song(s)** Embrujado; Church Choir; Carnival

## 4079 ◆ THE NAKED STREET
United Artists, 1955

**Producer(s)** Small, Edward
**Director(s)** Shane, Maxwell
**Screenwriter(s)** Shane, Maxwell; Katcher, Leo

**Cast** Quinn, Anthony; Granger, Farley; Bancroft, Anne; Graves, Peter

**Song(s)** Wrong Guy (C: Newman, Emil; L: Pober, Leon)

## 4080 ◆ NAMU THE KILLER WHALE
United Artists, 1966

**Musical Score** Van Eps, Robert

**Producer(s)** Benedek, Laslo
**Director(s)** Benedek, Laslo
**Screenwriter(s)** Weiss, Arthur

**Cast** Lansing, Robert; Anderson, John; Mattson, Robin; Erdman, Richard; Meriwether, Lee

**Song(s)** Namu the Killer Whale (C/L: Glazer, Tom)

## 4081 ◆ NANA
United Artists, 1934

**Producer(s)** Goldwyn, Samuel
**Director(s)** Arzner, Dorothy
**Screenwriter(s)** Mack, Willard; Gribble, H.W.
**Source(s)** *Nana* (novel) Zola, Emile

**Cast** Sten, Anna; Bennett, Richard; Atwill, Lionel; Holmes, Phillips; Clarke, Mae; Kirkland, Muriel; Owen, Reginald; Ralph, Jessie; Grant, Lawrence

**Song(s)** That's Love (C: Rodgers, Richard; L: Hart, Lorenz)

**Notes** No cue sheet available.

## 4082 ◆ NANCY FROM NAPLES

See OH! SAILOR, BEHAVE!

## 4083 ◆ NANCY GOES TO RIO
Metro–Goldwyn–Mayer, 1950

**Musical Score** Stoll, George
**Choreographer(s)** Castle, Nick

**Producer(s)** Pasternak, Joe
**Director(s)** Leonard, Robert Z.
**Screenwriter(s)** Sheldon, Sidney

**Cast** Sothern, Ann; Calhern, Louis; Powell, Jane; Miranda, Carmen; Sullivan, Barry [3]; Beckett, Scotty; Bonanova, Fortunio; Walker, Nella; Conried, Hans

**Song(s)** Time and Time Again (C: Spielman, Fred; L: Brent, Earl K.); Magic Is the Moonlight (C: Grever, Maria; L: Pasquale, Charles); Nancy's Goin' to Rio (C: Stoll, George; L: Brent, Earl); Cae Cae [4] (C: Martins, Roberto; L: Latouche, John); Yipsee-I-O (C/L: Gilbert, Ray); Ca-Room' Pa Pa [1] (C: Gonzaga; Teixeira; Gilbert, Ray; L: Gilbert, Ray); Love Is Like This [2] (C: Vianna, A.; Gilbert, Ray; L: Gilbert, Ray)

**Notes** A remake of the Universal film IT'S A DATE. There are also vocals of "Shine on Harvest Moon" by Nora Bayes and Jack Norworth; "Musetta's Aria" from LA BOHEME by Puccini; and "Embraceable You" by George and Ira Gershwin. [1] Gilbert based his melody on "Baiao." [2] Gilbert based his melody on "Carinhosa" by DeBarro and Vianna. [3] Dubbed by Danny Scholl. [4] Also in THAT NIGHT IN RIO (with the original Martins lyrics).

## 4084 ◆ NAPOLEON AND SAMANTHA
Disney, 1972

**Musical Score** Baker, Buddy
**Composer(s)** Baker, Buddy
**Lyricist(s)** Adair, Tom

**Producer(s)** Hibler, Winston
**Director(s)** McEveety, Bernard
**Screenwriter(s)** Raffill, Stewart

**Cast** Douglas, Michael; Geer, Will; Johnson, Arch; Whitaker, Johnny; Foster, Jodie; Jones, Henry; Major

**Song(s)** Napoleon and Samantha [1]; Last Voyage Home [1]

**Notes** [1] Lyric written for exploitation only.

## 4085 ✦ NASHVILLE
Paramount, 1975

**Composer(s)** Baskin, Richard

**Producer(s)** Altman, Robert
**Director(s)** Altman, Robert
**Screenwriter(s)** Tewkesbury, Joan

**Cast** Blakley, Ronee; Tomlin, Lily; Carradine, Keith; Gibson, Henry; Baxley, Barbara; Harris, Barbara; Wynn, Keenan; Duvall, Shelley; Garfield, Allen; Chaplin, Geraldine

**Song(s)** 200 Years (L: Gibson, Henry); Yes, I Do (L: Tomlin, Lily); I Never Get Enough (L: Raleigh, Ben); It Don't Worry Me (C/L: Carradine, Keith); The Day I Looked Jesus in the Eye (L: Altman, Robert); Old Man Mississippi (C/L: Grizzle, Juan); Down to the River (C/L: Blakley, Ronee); Let Me Be the One (C/L: Baskin, Richard); Rose's Cafe (C/L: Nicholls, Allan); Sing (Sing a Song) (C/L: Raposo, Joseph); Bluebird [2] (C/L: Blakley, Ronee); For the Sake of the Children (L: Reicheg, Richard); Keep a' Goin' (L: Gibson, Henry); Memphis (C/L: Black, Karen); I Don't Know If I Found It in You (C/L: Black, Karen); Rolling Stone (C/L: Black, Karen); Honey (C/L: Carradine, Keith); I'm Easy [1] (C/L: Carradine, Keith); Tapedeck in His Tractor (C/L: Blakley, Ronee); Dues [2] (C/L: Blakley, Ronee); My Baby's Cookin, in Another Man's Pan (C/L: Barnett, Jonnie); Since You've Gone (C/L: Busey, Gary); One, I Love You (L: Baskin, Richard); (There's) Trouble in the U.S.A. (C/L: Barnett, Arleigh); Idaho Home (C/L:

**Notes** [1] Oscar winner. [2] Also in WELCOME HOME SOLDIER BOYS.

## 4086 ✦ NATIONAL BARN DANCE
Paramount, 1944

**Producer(s)** Pine, William; Thomas, William
**Director(s)** Bennett, Hugh
**Screenwriter(s)** Loeb, Lee; Fimberg, Hal

**Cast** Heather, Jean; Quigley, Charles; Benchley, Robert

**Song(s)** Angels Never Leave Heaven (C/L: Pelosi, Don; Noel, Art; Ilda, Lewis); The Barn Dance Polka (C:

Lee, Lester; L: Seelen, Jerry); Livin' in My Own Sweet Way [1] (C: Revel, Harry; L: Webster, Paul Francis); It's a Small World [2] (C: Revel, Harry; L: Webster, Paul Francis)

**Notes** There are also vocals of "When Paw Was Courtin' Ma" by Leonard Joy and Jack Manus (Jack Frost); "This Is the Chorus" by Brooke Johns and Ray Perkins; "Goin' to Have a Big Time Tonight" by Carson J. Robison (also in the Universal film BADLANDS OF DAKOTA); "I Did It and I'm Glad" by Pinky Tomlin, Harry Tobias and Harry Pease; "Bringing in the Sheaves" by C.A. Minor; "Swing, Little Indians, Swing" by Gracie Worth; "Which Comes First, the Egg or the Chicken" by Jack Frost and "From the Indies to the Andes in His Undies" by Ernie Burnett. [1] Not used but recorded. [2] Not used.

## 4087 ✦ NATIONAL LAMPOON GOES TO THE MOVIES
United Artists, 1982

**Musical Score** Stein, Andy

**Producer(s)** Simmons, Matty
**Director(s)** Giraldi, Bob; Jaglom, Henry
**Screenwriter(s)** Carroll, Tod; Flenniken, Shary; Mephitis, Pat; Sussman, Gerald; Weiner, Ellis; O'Rourke, P.J.

**Cast** Clark, Candy; Dusenberry, Ann; Culp, Robert; Benson, Robby; Widmark, Richard

**Song(s)** Going to the Movies (C/L: Stein, Andy)

**Notes** Also known as NATIONAL LAMPOON'S MOVIE MADNESS. There are three films in this feature. The first is GROWING YOUR SELF; the second, SUCCESS WANTERS and the last, MUNICIPALIANS. It is not known which of the screenwriters' names are pseudonyms. P.J. O'Rourke had his name taken off the credits.

## 4088 ✦ NATIONAL LAMPOON'S ANIMAL HOUSE
Universal, 1978

**Producer(s)** Simmons, Matty; Reitman, Ivan
**Director(s)** Landis, John
**Screenwriter(s)** Ramis, Harold; Kenney, Douglas; Miller, Chris

**Cast** Belushi, John; Matheson, Tim; Hulce, Tom; Furst, Stephen; Vernon, John; Metcalf, Mark; Weller, Mary Louise; Smith, Martha; McGill, Bruce; Bacon, Kevin; Allen, Karen; Sutherland, Donald

**Song(s)** Dream Girl (C/L: Bishop, Stephen); The Way of the Wand'rer (C: Williams, John; L: Gladstone, Jerry); Shama-Lama Ding, Dong (C/L: Davis, Mark); Animal House (C/L: Bishop, Stephen)

## 4089 ✦ NATIONAL LAMPOON'S CLASS REUNION
### Twentieth Century–Fox, 1982

**Musical Score** Bernstein, Peter; Goldenberg, Mark
**Composer(s)** Berry, Chuck
**Lyricist(s)** Berry, Chuck

**Producer(s)** Simmons, Matty
**Director(s)** Miller, Michael
**Screenwriter(s)** Hughes, John

**Cast** Graham, Gerrit; Lerner, Michael; Furst, Stephen; Ramsey, Anne; McCarren, Fred; Buzby, Zane; Small, Marya; Flynn, Miriam

**Song(s)** Class Renunion (C/L: Bernstein, Peter; Goldenberg, Mark); It Wasn't Me; My Ding-A-Ling; Festival

## 4090 ✦ NATIONAL LAMPOON'S EUROPEAN VACATION
### Warner Brothers, 1985

**Musical Score** Fox, Charles

**Producer(s)** Simmons, Matty
**Director(s)** Heckerling, Amy
**Screenwriter(s)** Hughes, John; Klane, Robert

**Cast** Chase, Chevy; D'Angelo, Beverly; Hill, Dana; Lively, Jason

**Song(s)** Baby It's You, Yes I Am (C/L: Chiate, Lloyd; Nelson, John); New Looks [1] (C: Fox, Charles; L: Bettis, John); Back in America [1] (C/L: Brock, Terry; Odom, Jim)

**Notes** It is not known which of these was written for the movie. [1] Background vocal use only.

## 4091 ✦ NATIONAL LAMPOON'S MOVIE MADNESS

See NATIONAL LAMPOON GOES TO THE MOVIES.

## 4092 ✦ NATIONAL LAMPOON'S VACATION
### Warner Brothers, 1983

**Musical Score** Burns, Ralph

**Producer(s)** Simmons, Matty
**Director(s)** Ramis, Harold
**Screenwriter(s)** Hughes, John

**Cast** Chase, Chevy; D'Angelo, Beverly; Hall, Anthony Michael; Coca, Imogene; Quaid, Randy; Barron, Dana; Candy, John; Bracken, Eddie; Brinkley, Christie

**Song(s)** Holiday Road (C/L: Buckingham, Lindsey); Mr. Blue (C/L: Blackwell, DeWayne); Little Boy Sweet [1] (C/L: Golde, Franne; Ivers, Peter); Dancin' Across the U.S.A. (C/L: Buckingham, Lindsey)

**Notes** All background vocal uses. It is not known which were written for this production. [1] Also in SEVEN MINUTES IN HEAVEN.

## 4093 ✦ NATIONAL VELVET
### Metro–Goldwyn–Mayer, 1944

**Musical Score** Stothart, Herbert

**Producer(s)** Berman, Pandro S.
**Director(s)** Brown, Clarence
**Screenwriter(s)** Reeves, Theodore; Deutsch, Helen
**Source(s)** *National Velvet* (novel) Bagnold, Enid

**Cast** Rooney, Mickey; Crisp, Donald; Taylor, Elizabeth; Revere, Anne; Lansbury, Angela; Jenkins, Jackie "Butch"; Treacher, Arthur; Owen, Reginald

**Song(s)** Summer Holidays (C: Stothart, Herbert; L: Deutsch, Helen)

## 4094 ✦ NATIVE SON
### Cinecom, 1986

**Musical Score** Mtume, James

**Producer(s)** Silver, Diane
**Director(s)** Freedman, Jerrold
**Screenwriter(s)** Wesley, Richard
**Source(s)** *Native Son* (novel) Wright, Richard

**Cast** Baker, Carroll; Busia, Akosua; Dillon, Matt; Evans, Art; McGovern, Elizabeth; Love, Victor; McMartin, John; Page, Geraldine; Pugh, Willard; Winfrey, Oprah; Rhames, Ving; Wesley, Richard [1]

**Song(s)** Jones Comes Down (Call Me, Call Me, Call Me) (C: Mtume, James; L: Mtume, James; Silver, Diane)

**Notes** No cue sheet available. [1] Played the Bartender.

## 4095 ✦ NAUGHTY BUT NICE
### Warner Brothers, 1939

**Composer(s)** Warren, Harry
**Lyricist(s)** Mercer, Johnny

**Producer(s)** Bischoff, Sam
**Director(s)** Enright, Ray
**Screenwriter(s)** Wald, Jerry; Macualay, Richard
**Source(s)** "Always Leave Them Laughing" (story) Wald, Jerry; Macaulay, Richard

**Cast** Sheridan, Ann; Powell, Dick; Page, Gale; Broderick, Helen; Reagan, Ronald; Jenkins, Allen; Pitts, ZaSu; Rosenbloom, Maxie; Colonna, Jerry; Alberni, Luis; Lewis, Vera

**Song(s)** I Dreamt That I Dwelt in Marble Halls (C: Balfe, M.W.); Remember Dad [1] (C: Beethoven, Ludwig von); Hooray for Spinach; I'm Happy About the Whole Thing; In a Moment of Weakness; Corn Pickin'; I Don't Believe in Signs

**Notes** [1] Based on the "5th Symphony."

## 4096 ✦ NAUGHTY MARIETTA
### Metro–Goldwyn–Mayer, 1935

**Musical Score**   Stothart, Herbert
**Composer(s)**   Herbert, Victor
**Lyricist(s)**   Kahn, Gus

**Producer(s)**   Stromberg, Hunt
**Director(s)**   Van Dyke, W.S.
**Screenwriter(s)**   Mahin, John Lee; Goodrich, Frances; Hackett, Albert
**Source(s)**   *Naughty Marietta* (musical) Young, Rida Johnson; Herbert, Victor

**Cast**   MacDonald, Jeanette; Eddy, Nelson; Morgan, Frank; Lanchester, Elsa; Dumbrille, Douglass; Cawthorn, Joseph; Parker, Cecilia; Kingsford, Walter; Tamiroff, Akim

**Song(s)**   Italian Street Song (L: Young, Rida Johnson); Punchinello; Students' Song (C: Stothart, Herbert); Finale - First Act Naughty Marietta; Loves of New Orleans; Dance of the Marionettes; Opening - First Act Naughty Marietta; Yesterthoughts; Ah, Sweet Mystery of Life (L: Young, Rida Johnson); Tramp, Tramp, Tramp [1]; If I Were Anybody Else But Me; 'Neath the Southern Moon (L: Young, Rida Johnson; Kahn, Gus); I'm Falling in Love with Someone (L: Young, Rida Johnson)

**Notes**   There is also a vocal of "Au Clair de la Lune." [1] Although Rida Johnson Young wrote the Broadway lyrics, Gus Kahn is credited on the cue sheet.

## 4097 ✦ NAUGHTY NANETTE
### Paramount, 1946

**Composer(s)**   Wayne, Bernie
**Lyricist(s)**   Raleigh, Ben

**Producer(s)**   Templeton, George
**Director(s)**   Templeton, George
**Screenwriter(s)**   Pratt, Carolyn; Rosenwald, Franz

**Cast**   Graham, Bob; Franklin, Miriam; Porter, Dorothy; Myrtil, Odette

**Song(s)**   Apple Bee Polka (C: Boutelje, Phil); You're Lovely, Madame [1] (C: Rainger, Ralph; L: Robin, Leo); Baby Sister; Song of the Mounties

**Notes**   Short subject. "Darling Je Vous Aime Beaucoup" by Anna Sosenko was also used vocally. [1] Also in ARTISTS AND MODELS ABROAD.

## 4098 ✦ THE NAUGHTY NINETIES
### Universal, 1945

**Composer(s)**   Fairchild, Edgar
**Lyricist(s)**   Brooks, Jack
**Choreographer(s)**   Boyle, Johnny

**Producer(s)**   Hartmann, Edmund L.
**Director(s)**   Yarbrough, Jean
**Screenwriter(s)**   Hartmann, Edmund L.; Grant, John; Joseph, Edmund; Fimberg, Hal

**Cast**   Abbott, Bud; Costello, Lou; Curtis, Alan; Johnson, Rita; Travers, Henry; Collier, Lois

**Song(s)**   I Can't Get You Out of My Mind [1]; Rollin' Down the River; Uncle Tom's Cabin

**Notes**   There are also short vocals of several turn of the century songs. [1] Also in IDEA GIRL.

## 4099 ✦ NAVY BLUE AND GOLD
### Metro–Goldwyn–Mayer, 1937

**Musical Score**   Ward, Edward

**Producer(s)**   Zimbalist, Sam
**Director(s)**   Wood, Sam
**Screenwriter(s)**   Bruce, George
**Source(s)**   (novel) Bruce, George

**Cast**   Young, Robert; Stewart, James; Rice, Florence; Burke, Billie; Barrymore, Lionel; Brown, Tom; Hinds, Samuel S.; Kelly, Paul

**Song(s)**   Navy Victory March (C/L: Sima; Collins; Martin);

## 4100 ✦ NAVY BLUES (1929)
### Metro–Goldwyn–Mayer, 1929

**Director(s)**   Brown, Clarence
**Screenwriter(s)**   Nugent, J.C.; Nugent, Elliott; River, W.L.

**Cast**   Haines, William; Page, Anita; Dane, Karl; Nugent, J.C.

**Song(s)**   Navy Blues (C: Ahlert, Fred E.; L: Turk, Roy)

## 4101 ✦ NAVY BLUES (1941)
### Warner Brothers–First National, 1941

**Composer(s)**   Schwartz, Arthur
**Lyricist(s)**   Mercer, Johnny
**Choreographer(s)**   Felix, Seymour

**Producer(s)**   Wallis, Hal B.
**Director(s)**   Bacon, Lloyd
**Screenwriter(s)**   Wald, Jerry; Macaulay, Richard; Horman, Arthur T.; Perrin, Sam

**Cast**   Sheridan, Ann; Oakie, Jack; Raye, Martha; Haley, Jack; Anderson, Herbert; Carson, Jack; Gleason, Jackie; Lane, Richard; Orr, William T.; Ridgely, John; Wilcox, Frank; Justice, William; Cooke, Ray; Jackson, Selmer

**Song(s)**   Navy Blues; When Are We Gonna Land Abroad; Hawaiian Party; In Waikiki; You're a Natural [1]; Old Honolulu (Inst.)

**Notes** [1] Listed on cue sheets as background vocal only.

## 4102 ✦ THE NAVY GETS ROUGH
### Warner Brothers, 1943

**Musical Score** Jackson, Howard

**Song(s)** I'd Love to Take Orders from You (C: Warren, Harry; L: Dubin, Al)

**Notes** No other information is available.

## 4103 ✦ NAVY WIFE (1935)
### Twentieth Century–Fox, 1935

**Producer(s)** Wurtzel, Sol M.
**Director(s)** Dwan, Allan
**Screenwriter(s)** Levien, Sonya

**Cast** Trevor, Claire; Bellamy, Ralph; Darwell, Jane; Hymer, Warren; Lyon, Ben; Burke, Kathleen; Irving, George; Howard, Anne

**Song(s)** The Luau (C: Buttolph, David; L: Hoopii Jr., Sol); Ai Kakou (C/L: Hoopii Jr., Sol)

## 4104 ✦ NAVY WIFE (1956)
### Allied Artists, 1956

**Musical Score** Salter, Hans J.

**Producer(s)** Wanger, Walter
**Director(s)** Bernds, Edward
**Screenwriter(s)** Lenard, Kay
**Source(s)** *Mother Sir* (novel) Blain, Tats

**Cast** Bennett, Joan; Merrill, Gary; Nugent, Judy; Manson, Maurice; Shimada, Teru

**Song(s)** Mother Sir (C: Salter, Hans J.; L: Brooks, Jack)

**Notes** No cue sheet available.

## 4105 ✦ NEAR THE RAINBOW'S END
### Tiffany, 1930

**Producer(s)** Carr, Trem
**Director(s)** McGowan, J.P.
**Screenwriter(s)** Post, Charles A.

**Cast** Steele, Bob; Lorraine, Louise; McKee, Lafe; Ferguson, Al; Hewston, Alfred

**Song(s)** Ro-Ro-Rolling Along (C: Mencher, Murray; L: Moll, Billy; Richman, Harry)

**Notes** No cue sheet available.

## 4106 ✦ NELLIE BLY
### Studio Unknown, 1956 unproduced

**Song(s)** Stay Out of My Dream (C: Arlen, Harold; L: Harburg, E.Y.)

**Notes** No other information available.

## 4107 ✦ NELLY'S FOLLY
### Warner Brothers, 1961

**Musical Score** Franklyn, Milton J.

**Director(s)** Jones, Chuck

**Song(s)** The Gal from the Wild Prairie (C/L: Franklyn, Milton J.; Maltese, Michael); The Lonesomest Gal (C/L: Franklyn, Milton J.; Jones, Chuck; Detiege, Dave)

**Notes** Merrie Melodie.

## 4108 ✦ NEPTUNE'S DAUGHTER
### Metro–Goldwyn–Mayer, 1949

**Composer(s)** Loesser, Frank
**Lyricist(s)** Loesser, Frank
**Choreographer(s)** Donohue, Jack

**Producer(s)** Cummings, Jack
**Director(s)** Buzzell, Edward
**Screenwriter(s)** Kingsley, Dorothy; Singer, Ray; Chevillat, Dick

**Cast** Williams, Esther; Skelton, Red; Montalban, Ricardo; Garrett, Betty; Wynn, Keenan; Xavier Cugat and His Orchestra; Mazurki, Mike; De Corsia, Ted

**Song(s)** I Love Those Men; My Heart Beats Faster; Baby, It's Cold Outside; Jungle Rhumba (C/L: Beaulieu)

## 4109 ✦ NEVADA
### RKO, 1944

**Musical Score** Sawtell, Paul; Dreyer, Dave

**Producer(s)** Schlom, Herman
**Director(s)** Killy, Edward
**Screenwriter(s)** Houston, Norman
**Source(s)** *Nevada* (novel) Grey, Zane

**Cast** Mitchum, Robert [1]; Jeffreys, Anne; Williams, Guinn "Big Boy"; Gates, Nancy; Martin, Richard; Reynolds, Craig; Woods, Harry

**Song(s)** Remember the Girl You Left Behind [2] (C: Revel, Harry; L: Greene, Mort)

**Notes** [1] Billed as Bob Mitchum. [2] Also in THE HALF-BREED.

## 4110 ✦ NEVADA CITY
### Republic, 1941

**Composer(s)** Styne, Jule
**Lyricist(s)** Cherkose, Eddie; Meyer, Sol

**Producer(s)** Kane, Joseph
**Director(s)** Kane, Joseph
**Screenwriter(s)** Webb, James R.

Cast   Rogers, Roy; Hayes, George "Gabby"; Payne, Sally; Lee, Billy; Cleveland, George; Crehan, Joseph; Kohler Jr., Fred

Song(s)   Lonely Hills; Prairie Serenade; Stars Over the Prairie [1] (C/L: Tinturin, Peter)

Notes   [1] Also in CITADEL OF CRIME.

## 4111 ✦ NEVADA SMITH
### Paramount, 1966

Producer(s)   Hathaway, Henry
Director(s)   Hathaway, Henry
Screenwriter(s)   Hayes, John Michael

Cast   McQueen, Steve; Malden, Karl; Pleshette, Suzanne; Keith, Brian; Kennedy, Arthur; Vallone, Raf; Hingle, Pat; Da Silva, Howard; Landau, Martin

Song(s)   Nevada Smith [1] (C: Newman, Alfred; L: David, Hal)

Notes   [1] Lyric for exploitation use only.

## 4112 ✦ NEVER A DULL MOMENT (1943)
### Universal, 1943

Composer(s)   Rose, David
Lyricist(s)   Cherkose, Eddie

Producer(s)   Benedict, Howard
Director(s)   Lilley, Edward
Screenwriter(s)   Ronson, Mel; Roberts, Stanley

Cast   The Ritz Brothers; Hughes, Mary Beth; Langford, Frances; Crawford, Stuart; Risdon, Elizabeth

Song(s)   Hello; Yakimboomba; Mr. Five by Five (C: de Paul, Gene; L: Raye, Don); He's My Guy [1] (C: de Paul, Gene; L: Raye, Don)

Notes   There are also vocals of "My Blue Heaven" by George Whiting and Walter Donaldson and "Sleepy Time Gal" by Joseph E. Alden, Ange Lorenzo, Richard Whiting and Raymond B. Egan. [1] Sheet music only.

## 4113 ✦ NEVER A DULL MOMENT (1950)
### RKO, 1950

Musical Score   Hollander, Frederick
Composer(s)   Swift, Kay
Lyricist(s)   Swift, Kay

Producer(s)   Parsons, Harriet
Director(s)   Marshall, George
Screenwriter(s)   Breslow, Lou; Anderson, Doris
Source(s)   Who Could Ask for Anything More? (novel) Swift, Kay

Cast   Dunne, Irene; MacMurray, Fred; Demarest, William; Devine, Andy; Perreau, Gigi; Wood, Natalie; Ober, Philip; Kirkwood, Jack; Doran, Ann

Song(s)   Once You Find Your Guy; The Man with the Big Felt Hat; Sagebrush Lullaby

## 4114 ✦ THE NEVERENDING STORY
### Warner Brothers, 1984

Musical Score   Doldinger, Klaus

Producer(s)   Eichinger, Bernd; Geissier, Dieter
Director(s)   Petersen, Wolfgang
Screenwriter(s)   Petersen, Wolfgang; Weigel, Herman
Source(s)   The Neverending Story (novel) Ende, Michael

Cast   Oliver, Barret; McRaney, Gerald; Hill, Thomas; Gunn, Moses; Hayes, Patricia; Oppenheimer, Alan

Song(s)   Neverending Story Song (C: Moroder, Giorgio; L: Forsey, Keith)

Notes   Background vocal only.

## 4115 ✦ NEVER GIVE A SUCKER AN EVEN BREAK
### Universal, 1941

Director(s)   Cline, Edward F.
Screenwriter(s)   Neville, John Thomas; Chaplin, Prescott

Cast   Fields, W.C.; Dumont, Margaret; Miller, Susan; Jean, Gloria; Errol, Leon; Butch and Buddy; Pangborn, Franklin; Barrie, Mona; Lang, Charles; Nagel, Anne; O'Day, Nell

Song(s)   Hot Cha Cha (C/L: Previn, Charles); Voices of Spring (C: Strauss, Johann; L: Previn, Charles); Chickens Lay Eggs in Kansas (C/L: Fields, W.C.)

Notes   Released as WHAT A MAN in Great Britain. There are also vocals of "Estrellita" by Manuel Ponce; "Comin' Through the Rye" by Robert Burns and "Otchi Tchorniya."

## 4116 ✦ NEVER LET GO
### Continental Dist., 1963

Musical Score   Barry, John

Producer(s)   de Sarigny, Peter
Director(s)   Guillermin, John
Screenwriter(s)   Guillermin, John

Cast   Todd, Richard; Sellers, Peter; Sellars, Elizabeth; Faith, Adam

Song(s)   Never Let Go (C: Barry, John; L: Bart, Lionel)

Notes   No cue sheet available.

## 4117 ✦ NEVER LOVE A STRANGER
### Allied Artists, 1958

Musical Score   Scott, Raymond
Composer(s)   Scott, Raymond
Lyricist(s)   Elow, Lawrence

Producer(s)   Robbins, Harold; Day, Richard
Director(s)   Stevens, Robert
Screenwriter(s)   Robbins, Harold; Day, Richard

**Source(s)** *Never Love a Stranger* (novel) Robbins, Harold

**Cast** Barrymore, John Drew; Milan, Lita; Bray, Robert; McQueen, Steve; Armstrong, R.G.

**Song(s)** Never Love a Stranger; Oh Baby

## 4118 ✦ NEVER ON SUNDAY
United Artists, 1960

**Musical Score** Hadjidakis, Manos
**Composer(s)** Hadjidakis, Manos

**Producer(s)** Dassin, Jules
**Director(s)** Dassin, Jules
**Screenwriter(s)** Dassin, Jules

**Cast** Mercouri, Melina; Dassin, Jules; Foundas, Georges; Vandis, Titos; Liguisos, Mitsos; Diamantidou, Despo

**Song(s)** Never on Sunday [1] (L: Towne, Billy); Athens By Night [2] (L: Mandel, Mel; Sachs, Norman)

**Notes** [1] Lyrics added for exploitation only. [2] Sheet music only.

## 4119 ✦ NEVER PUT IT IN WRITING
Allied Artists, 1964

**Musical Score** Cordell, Frank

**Producer(s)** Stone, Andrew L.
**Director(s)** Stone, Andrew L.
**Screenwriter(s)** Stone, Andrew L.

**Cast** Boone, Pat; O'Shea, Milo; Murphy, Fidelma; Beckwith, Reginald; Blakely, Colin

**Song(s)** Never Put It in Writing (C/L: Boone, Pat)

**Notes** No cue sheet available.

## 4120 ✦ NEVER SAY DIE
Paramount, 1939

**Choreographer(s)** Prinz, LeRoy

**Producer(s)** Jones, Paul
**Director(s)** Nugent, Elliott
**Screenwriter(s)** Sturges, Preston; Hartman, Don; Butler, Frank

**Cast** Raye, Martha [2]; Hope, Bob; Sondergaard, Gale; Mowbray, Alan; Devine, Andy; Rumann, Sig; Cossart, Ernest; Arms, Frances; Woolley, Monty

**Song(s)** The Tra La La and the Oom Pah Pah [1] (C: Rainger, Ralph; L: Robin, Leo)

**Notes** [1] The song was filmed in two ways: One with Raye and Bob Hope leading a group of Swiss dancers into a big production number and another with Raye singing just one chorus. [2] Georgia Stark did the whistling for Martha Raye.

## 4121 ✦ NEVER SAY GOODBYE (1946)
Warner Brothers, 1946

**Musical Score** Hollander, Frederick

**Producer(s)** Jacobs, William
**Director(s)** Kern, James V.
**Screenwriter(s)** Diamond, I.A.L.; Kern, James V.
**Source(s)** "Don't Ever Leave Me" (story) Barzman, Norma; Barzman, Ben

**Cast** Flynn, Errol; Parker, Eleanor; Watson, Lucile; Sakall, S.Z.; Brady, Patti; Tucker, Forrest; Woods, Donald; Knudsen, Peggy; D'Andrea, Tom; McDaniel, Hattie

**Song(s)** Remember Me? [1] (C: Warren, Harry; L: Dubin, Al)

**Notes** [1] Also in "Mr. Dodd Takes the Air."

## 4122 ✦ NEVER SAY GOODBYE (1955)
Universal, 1955

**Musical Score** Skinner, Frank

**Producer(s)** Cohen, Albert J.
**Director(s)** Hopper, Jerry
**Screenwriter(s)** Hoffman, Charles
**Source(s)** *Come Prima Meglio de Prima* (play) Pirandello, Luigi

**Cast** Hudson, Rock; Borchers, Cornell; Sanders, George; Fabares, Shelley; Collins, Ray; Janssen, David; Greenleaf, Raymond; Wilcox, Frank

**Song(s)** For the First Time (C: McHugh, Jimmy; L: Adamson, Harold)

**Notes** A remake of THIS LOVE OF OURS (1945).

## 4123 ✦ NEVER SAY NEVER AGAIN
Warner Brothers, 1983

**Musical Score** Legrand, Michel
**Composer(s)** Legrand, Michel

**Producer(s)** Schwartzman, Jack
**Director(s)** Kershner, Irvin
**Screenwriter(s)** Semple Jr., Lorenzo
**Source(s)** *Thunderball* (novel) Fleming, Ian

**Cast** Connery, Sean; Brandauer, Klaus Maria; Von Sydow, Max; Carrera, Barbara; Basinger, Kim; Casey, Bernie; McCowen, Alec; Fox, Edward

**Song(s)** Never Say Never Again (L: Bergman, Marilyn; Bergman, Alan); Sauna (L: Della, Sophie; Drejac, Jean)

## 4124 ✦ NEVER STEAL ANYTHING SMALL
Universal, 1959

**Musical Score** Mancini, Henry
**Composer(s)** Wrubel, Allie
**Lyricist(s)** Anderson, Maxwell
**Choreographer(s)** Pan, Hermes

**Producer(s)**   Rosenberg, Aaron
**Director(s)**   Lederer, Charles
**Screenwriter(s)**   Lederer, Charles
**Source(s)**   *The Devil's Hornpipe* (musical) Anderson, Maxwell; Mamoulian, Rouben

**Cast**   Cagney, James; Jones, Shirley; Smith, Roger; Williams, Cara; Persoff, Nehemiah; Caruso, Anthony; Dano, Royal; Albertson, Jack

**Song(s)**   Never Steal Anything Small; I Haven't Got a Thing to Wear; I'm Sorry, I Want a Ferrari (L: Wrubel, Allie); It Takes Love to Build a Home [2]; I Look Across the Table [1]; Helping Our Neighbors [1] [3]; Now Is the Only Time Ever [1]; I'm Looking for an Honest Face [4]; Innocent Appearance [4]; Now Is the Only Time Ever [4]; Starting Out to Live Alone Again [4]; What Does a Woman Do? [4]; Old Fashioned Political Rally (Invitation) [4] (L: Lederer, Charles)

**Notes**   [1] Used instrumentally only. [2] Published as "It Takes Love to Make a Home." [3] Published as "Helping Our Friends." [4] Not used.

## 4125 ✦ NEVER THE TWAIN SHALL MEET
### Metro–Goldwyn–Mayer, 1931

**Director(s)**   Van Dyke, W.S.
**Screenwriter(s)**   Mayer, Edwin Justus; Cummings, Ruth; Lynch, John
**Source(s)**   "Never the Twain Shall Meet" (story) Kyne, Peter B.

**Cast**   Howard, Leslie; Montenegro, Conchita; Smith, C. Aubrey

**Song(s)**   Islands of Love (C/L: Freed, Arthur)

**Notes**   A remake of a 1925 film.

## 4126 ✦ NEVER TOO LATE
### Warner Brothers–First National, 1965

**Musical Score**   Rose, David

**Producer(s)**   Lear, Norman
**Director(s)**   Yorkin, Bud
**Screenwriter(s)**   Long, Sumner Arthur
**Source(s)**   *Never Too Late* (play) Long, Sumner Arthur

**Cast**   Ford, Paul; Stevens, Connie; O'Sullivan, Maureen; Hutton, Jim; Wyatt, Jane; Jones, Henry; Nolan, Lloyd

**Song(s)**   Never Too Late (C: Rose, David; L: Livingston, Jay; Evans, Ray)

## 4127 ✦ NEVER WAVE AT A WAC
### RKO, 1953

**Producer(s)**   Brisson, Frederick
**Director(s)**   McLeod, Norman Z.
**Screenwriter(s)**   Englund, Ken

**Cast**   Ching, William; Douglas, Paul; Whelan, Arleen; Erickson, Leif; Brooke, Hillary; Toomey, Regis; Inescort, Frieda; Beavers, Louise

**Song(s)**   WAC Song (C/L: Douglass, Jane; Frank, Camilla Mays)

**Notes**   No cue sheet available. Also known as THE PRIVATE WORE SKIRTS.

## 4128 ✦ THE NEW ADVENTURES OF GET RICH QUICK WALLINGFORD
### Metro–Goldwyn–Mayer, 1931

**Director(s)**   Wood, Sam
**Screenwriter(s)**   MacArthur, Charles
**Source(s)**   stories by Chester, George Randolph

**Cast**   Haines, William; Durante, Jimmy; Torrence, Ernest; Hyams, Leila; Kibbee, Guy; Hamilton, Hale; Blandick, Clara

**Song(s)**   Did You Ever Have the Feeling that You Wanted to Go (C/L: Durante, Jimmy)

## 4129 ✦ THE NEW ADVENTURES OF PIPPI LONGSTOCKING
### Columbia, 1988

**Musical Score**   Segal, Misha
**Composer(s)**   Segal, Misha
**Lyricist(s)**   Schock, Harriet

**Producer(s)**   Mehlman, Gary; Moshay, Walter
**Director(s)**   Annakin, Ken
**Screenwriter(s)**   Annakin, Ken
**Source(s)**   Pippi Longstocking series (novels) Lindren, Astrid

**Cast**   Erin, Tami; Brennan, Eileen; Dugan, Dennis; Hull, Dianne; De Cenzo, George; Van Patten, Dick; Schuck, John

**Song(s)**   Pippi Longstocking (Is Coming Into Your Town); We Live on the Seas; Scrubbing Day; Runnin' Away; Sticky Situation; Merry Christmas Tree

## 4130 ✦ THE NEW CENTURIONS
### Columbia, 1972

**Musical Score**   Jones, Quincy

**Producer(s)**   Winkler, Irwin; Chartoff, Robert
**Director(s)**   Fleischer, Richard
**Screenwriter(s)**   Silliphant, Stirling
**Source(s)**   *The New Centurions* (novel) Wambaugh, Joseph

**Cast**   Scott, George C.; Keach, Stacy; Alexander, Jane; Wilson, Scott; Cash, Rosalind; Estrada, Erik

**Song(s)**   How Long Has It Been Since You've Had Your Back Cracked (C: Jones, Quincy; L: Adams, Arthur)

## 4131 ✦ THE NEW DIVORCE
Paramount, 1936 unproduced

**Song(s)**   Love or Infatuation (C: Hollander, Frederick; L: Coslow, Sam); I Let My Heart Command Me (C: Hollander, Frederick; L: Coslow, Sam)

## 4132 ✦ NEW FACES (1937)
RKO, 1937

**Composer(s)**   Fain, Sammy
**Lyricist(s)**   Brown, Lew
**Choreographer(s)**   Lee, Sammy

**Producer(s)**   Small, Edward
**Director(s)**   Jason, Leigh
**Screenwriter(s)**   Perrin, Nat; Epstein, Philip G.; Brecher, Irving; Freedman, David

**Cast**   Cowan, Jerome; Berle, Milton; Penner, Joe; Parkyakarkus [1]; Hilliard, Harriet; Brady, William; Leeds, Thelma; Mack, Tommy; Gordon, Bert; Krueger, Lorraine; The Four Playboys; The Rio Brothers; The Loria Brothers; The Brian Sisters; The Three Chocolateers; Miller, Ann; Robinson, Dewey

**Song(s)**   Widow in Lace (C: Spina, Harold; L: Bullock, Walter); Our Penthouse on Third Avenue [2]; Speak Only Speak (C/L: Dorsley); It Goes to Your Feet; If I Didn't Have You; Love Is Never Out of Season; New Faces (C/L: Henderson, Charles); Where the Berry Blossoms Bloom (C/L: Penner, Joe; Raynor, Hal); Peckin' (C/L: James, Harry; Pollack, Ben)

**Notes**   [1] Real name: Harry Einstein. [2] Also in STAGE DOOR for 17 seconds.

## 4133 ✦ NEW FACES (1954)
Twentieth Century–Fox, 1954

**Musical Score**   Kraushaar, Raoul
**Composer(s)**   Siegel, Arthur
**Lyricist(s)**   Carroll, June

**Producer(s)**   Alperson, Edward L.
**Director(s)**   Horner, Harry
**Screenwriter(s)**   Graham, Ronny; Brooks, Mel; Lynde, Paul; Davis, Luther; Cleveland, John
**Source(s)**   *New Faces of 1952* (musical) Siegel, Arthur; Carroll, June; Graham, Ronny; Brooks, Mel; Lynde, Paul; Davis, Luther; Cleveland, John

**Cast**   Graham, Ronny [1]; Kitt, Eartha [1]; Clary, Robert [1]; Ghostley, Alice [1]; Carroll, June [1]; DeLuce, Virginia [1]; Lynde, Paul [1]; O'Reilly, Rosemary [1]; Lawrence, Carol

**Song(s)**   Opening [1] (C/L: Graham, Ronny); C'est Si Bon (C: Betti, Henri; L: Seelen, Jerry; Hornez, Andre); He Takes Me Off His Income Tax [1]; Lucky Pierre [1] (C/L: Graham, Ronny); Penny Candy [1]; Boston Beguine [1] (C/L: Harnick, Sheldon); Love Is a Simple

Thing [1]; Time for Tea [1]; Santa Baby (C: Springer, Phil; L: Javits, Joan); Waltzing in Venice [1] (C/L: Graham, Ronny); Take Off the Mask [1] [2] (C/L: Graham, Ronny); Monotonous [1]; Nanty Puts Her Hair Up [2] (L: Farjeon, Herbert); I'm in Love with Miss Logan [1] (C/L: Graham, Ronny); Raining Memories [1] [2] (C/L: Graham, Ronny); Uskadara (C/L: Traditional); Lizzie Bordon [1] (C/L: Brown, Michael); Bal Petit Bal [1] (C/L: Lemarque, Francis)

**Notes**   [1] From original show. [2] Used instrumentally only.

## 4134 ✦ THE NEW FRONTIER
Republic, 1935

**Musical Score**   Strange, Glenn

**Producer(s)**   Berke, William
**Director(s)**   Sherman, George
**Screenwriter(s)**   Ward, Luci; Burbridge, Betty

**Cast**   Wayne, John; Corrigan, Ray; Hatton, Raymond; Isley, Phyllis; Waller, Eddy; McKim, Sammy; Mason, LeRoy

**Song(s)**   The New Frontier (C/L: Strange, Glenn); Outlaw Range (C/L: Strange, Glenn)

## 4135 ✦ THE NEW INTERNS
Columbia, 1964

**Musical Score**   Hagen, Earle

**Producer(s)**   Cohn, Robert
**Director(s)**   Rich, John
**Screenwriter(s)**   Schiller, Wilton

**Cast**   Callan, Michael; Eden, Barbara; Jones, Dean; Powers, Stefanie; Stevens, Inger; Segal, George; Stevens, Kay; Savalas, Telly; Furth, George; Wood, Ellie

**Song(s)**   (Come On) Let Yourself Go (C/L: Berry, Jan; Kornfield, Dean); Wolfsbane Watusi (C/L: Hagen, Earle)

## 4136 ✦ THE NEW KIDS
Columbia, 1985

**Musical Score**   Schifrin, Lalo

**Producer(s)**   Cunningham, Sean S.; Fogelson, Andrew
**Director(s)**   Cunningham, Sean S.
**Screenwriter(s)**   Gyllenhaal, Stephen

**Cast**   Presby, Shannon; Loughlin, Lori; Spader, James; Philbin, John; Jones, Eddie

**Song(s)**   Send Up (C/L: Wray, Bill; Medica, Leon); Making a Move (C/L: Archerd, Evan; Nelson, Steve); Over & Over & Over Again (C/L: Rubini, Michael; Cutler, Miriam); Edge of Survival (C/L: Rubini, Michael; Harnell, Jess)

**4137 ✦ A NEW KIND OF LOVE**
Paramount, 1963

**Producer(s)**   Shavelson, Melville
**Director(s)**   Shavelson, Melville
**Screenwriter(s)**   Shavelson, Melville

**Cast**   Newman, Paul; Woodward, Joanne; Chevalier, Maurice; Ritter, Thelma; Gabor, Eva; Tobias, George

**Song(s)**   All Yours [1] (C: Garner, Erroll; L: Heyman, Edward)

**Notes**   Maurice Chevalier rerecorded his hits "Mimi," "Louise," "You Brought a New Kind of Love to Me" (published as "A New Kind of Love") and "In the Park in Paree" for this movie. [1] Lyrics for exploitation use only.

**4138 ✦ NEW MOON (1930)**
Metro–Goldwyn–Mayer, 1930

**Musical Score**   Stothart, Herbert
**Composer(s)**   Romberg, Sigmund
**Lyricist(s)**   Hammerstein II, Oscar

**Director(s)**   Conway, Jack
**Screenwriter(s)**   Hume, Cyril; Thalberg, Sylvia; Butler, Frank
**Source(s)**   *New Moon* (musical) Hammerstein II, Oscar; Mandel, Frank; Schwab, Laurence; Romberg, Sigmund

**Cast**   Moore, Grace; Tibbett, Lawrence; Menjou, Adolphe; Young, Roland

**Song(s)**   (Once There Was a) Farmer's Daughter [3] (C: Stothart, Herbert; L: Grey, Clifford; Johnson, Howard); Wanting You; Lover Come Back to Me; One Kiss; What Is Your Price, Madam? [3] (C: Stothart, Herbert; L: Grey, Clifford; Johnson, Howard); Balcony Episode [3] (C: Stothart, Herbert; L: Grey, Clifford; Johnson, Howard); Stout Hearted Men; Softly, As in a Morning Sunrise [2]

**Notes**   There is also a vocal of the Russian folk song "Barinia." [1] From original Broadway production. [2] Listed in the *Rogers and Hammerstein Fact Book* but not on cue sheet. [3] The Stothart lyrics are credited to Clifford Grey and Howard Johnson. It is not known if the lyricists worked together and should be credited together or if each wrote separately.

**4139 ✦ NEW MOON (1940)**
Metro–Goldwyn–Mayer, 1940

**Composer(s)**   Romberg, Sigmund
**Lyricist(s)**   Hammerstein II, Oscar
**Choreographer(s)**   Raset, Val

**Producer(s)**   Leonard, Robert Z.
**Director(s)**   Leonard, Robert Z.
**Screenwriter(s)**   Deval, Jacques; Arthur, Robert

**Source(s)**   *New Moon* (musical) Romberg, Sigmund; Hammerstein II, Oscar; Mandel, Frank; Schwab, Laurence

**Cast**   MacDonald, Jeanette; Eddy, Nelson; Boland, Mary; Warner, H.B.; Zucco, George; Mitchell, Grant

**Song(s)**   Wanting You; Lover Come Back to Me; Funny Little Sailor Men; Tavern Scene; Gorgeous Alexander; Softly, As in a Morning Sunrise; One Kiss; Stouthearted Men; Marianne

**Notes**   There is also a vocal of "Soon I Will Be Done." All songs are from the Broadway original. Different sources list different songs. The above list is from the cue sheet.

**4140 ✦ NEW ORLEANS (1929)**
Tiffany–Stahl, 1929

**Musical Score**   Talbot, Irvin

**Director(s)**   Barker, Reginald
**Screenwriter(s)**   Hatton, Frederic; Hatton, Fanny

**Cast**   Cortez, Ricardo; Collier Jr., William; Bennett, Alma

**Song(s)**   Pals Forever (C: Riesenfeld, Hugo; Shapiro, Ted; L: Adam, Ben)

**Notes**   No cue sheet available.

**4141 ✦ NEW ORLEANS (1947)**
United Artists, 1947

**Composer(s)**   Alter, Louis
**Lyricist(s)**   DeLange, Eddie

**Producer(s)**   Levey, Jules
**Director(s)**   Lubin, Arthur
**Screenwriter(s)**   Paul, Elliot; Hyland, Dick Irving

**Cast**   Armstrong, Louis; Holiday, Billie; Lewis, Meade Lux; Bigard, Barney; Ory, Kid; Beal, Charlie; Woody Herman and His Orchestra; Patrick, Dorothy [1]; de Cordova, Arturo; Hageman, Richard; Rich, Irene; Lord, Marjorie; Winters, Shelley

**Song(s)**   Do You Know What It Means to Miss New Orleans?; Blues Are Brewin'; Endie; Where the Blues Are Born in New Orleans (C/L: Carleton, Bob; Dixon, Cliff); Farewell to Storyville (C/L: Williams, Spencer); West End Blues (C: Oliver, Joe; L: Williams, Clarence)

**Notes**   No cue sheet available. [1] Dubbed by Theodora Lynch.

**4142 ✦ NEW SHOES**
Metro–Goldwyn–Mayer, 1936

**Musical Score**   Ward, Edward

**Director(s)**   Lee, Sammy
**Screenwriter(s)**   Lee, Sammy

**Song(s)**   O Bless My Soul (C/L: Wright, Bob; Forrest, Chet); I Stumbled Over Love (C/L: Wright, Bob; Forrest, Chet)

**Notes**   Short subject.

## 4143 ✦ THE NEW SPIRIT
### Disney, 1942

**Cast**   Edwards, Cliff

**Song(s)**   The Yankee Doodle Spirit (C: Wallace, Oliver; L: Edwards, Cliff)

**Notes**   No cue sheet available. Animated cartoon.

## 4144 ✦ NEW YEAR'S EVE
### Fox, 1929

**Musical Score**   Rothafel, S.L. [1]

**Producer(s)**   Hawks, Kenneth
**Director(s)**   Lehrman, Henry
**Screenwriter(s)**   Cummings, Dwight; Kernell, William
**Source(s)**   "$100.00" (story) Connell, Richard

**Cast**   Astor, Mary; Morton, Charles; Stone, Arthur; Ware, Helen; Foxe, Earle; Lake, Florence; Erwin, Stuart

**Song(s)**   Waiting (C/L: Conrad, Con; Gottler, Archie)

**Notes**   The cue sheet does not identify vocals. [1] S.L. Rothafel is better known under his nickname "Roxy."

## 4145 ✦ NEW YORK, NEW YORK
### United Artists, 1977

**Musical Score**   Burns, Ralph
**Composer(s)**   Kander, John
**Lyricist(s)**   Ebb, Fred
**Choreographer(s)**   Field, Ron

**Producer(s)**   Winkler, Irwin; Chartoff, Robert
**Director(s)**   Scorsese, Martin
**Screenwriter(s)**   Mac Rauch, Earl; Martin, Mardik

**Cast**   De Niro, Robert [2]; Minnelli, Liza; Stander, Lionel; Primus, Barry

**Song(s)**   There Goes the Ballgame; But the World Goes 'Round; New York, New York; Happy Endings [1]

**Notes**   There are also vocals of "You Are My Lucky Star" by Nacio Herb Brown and Arthur Freed; "You Brought a New Kind of Love to Me" by Pierre Norman, Sammy Fain and Irving Kahal; "Once in a While" by Bud Green and Michael Edwards; "The Man I Love" by George and Ira Gershwin; "Taking a Chance on Love" by Vernon Duke, John Latouche and Ted Fetter; "Just You, Just Me" by Jesse Greer and Raymond Klages; "Do Nothin' Till You Hear from Me" by Duke Ellington and Bob Russell; "Blue Moon" by Richard Rodgers and Lorenz Hart and "Honeysuckle Rose" by Thomas "Fats"

Waller and Andy Razaf. [1] Not used. Put back in when reissued. [2] Sax playing dubbed by Georgie Auld.

## 4146 ✦ NEW YORK NIGHTS
### United Artists, 1929

**Producer(s)**   Schenck, Joseph M.
**Director(s)**   Milestone, Lewis
**Screenwriter(s)**   Furthman, Jules
**Source(s)**   *Tin Pan Alley* (play) Stange, Stanislaus

**Cast**   Talmadge, Norma; Roland, Gilbert; Wray, John; Tashman, Lilyan; Doran, Mary; Karns, Roscoe

**Song(s)**   A Year from Today (C: Dreyer, Dave; L: Macdonald, Ballard; Jolson, Al)

**Notes**   No cue sheet available.

## 4147 ✦ NEW YORK STORIES
### Touchstone, 1989

**Notes**   This film consists of three short films: LIFE LESSONS, LIFE WITHOUT ZOE and OEDIPUS WRECKS. See LIFE WITHOUT ZOE for its songs.

## 4148 ✦ NEW YORK TOWN
### Paramount, 1941

**Producer(s)**   Veiller, Anthony
**Director(s)**   Vidor, Charles
**Screenwriter(s)**   Swerling, Jo; Meltzer, Lewis

**Cast**   MacMurray, Fred; Martin, Mary; Tamiroff, Akim; Kellaway, Cecil; Overman, Lynne; Blore, Eric; Adrian, Iris; Knight, Fuzzy; Hayes, Margaret; Blue, Monte; Preston, Robert

**Song(s)**   Tropical Serenade (Inst.) (C: Boutelje, Phil); Love in Bloom [1] (C: Rainger, Ralph; L: Robin, Leo)

**Notes**   There is also a vocal of "Yip-I-Addy-I-Ay!" by Will D. Cobb and J.H. Flynn. [1] Also used in THE BIG BROADCAST OF 1938, $1,000 A TOUCHDOWN and SHE LOVES ME NOT. Not used in KISS AND MAKE UP.

## 4149 ✦ THE NEXT MAN
### Allied Artists, 1976

**Musical Score**   Kamen, Michael
**Composer(s)**   Kamen, Michael
**Lyricist(s)**   Kamen, Michael

**Producer(s)**   Bregman, Martin
**Director(s)**   Sarafian, Richard C.
**Screenwriter(s)**   Fine, Mort; Trustman, Lana; Wolf, David; Sarafian, Richard C.

**Cast**   Connery, Sean; Sharpe, Cornelia; Paulsen, Albert; Celi, Adolfo; St. John, Marco; Beniades, Ted

**Song(s)**   Stay with Me; Nicole's Theme (L: Mercer, Rosco); Sweet, Sweet Baby Girl

**Notes**   No cue sheet available.

## 4150 ✦ NEXT YEAR IF ALL GOES WELL
### New World, 1983

**Musical Score**   Cosma, Vladimir

**Producer(s)**   Laski, Serge; Fleury, Jean-Claude
**Director(s)**   Hubert, Jean-Loup
**Screenwriter(s)**   Hubert, Jean-Loup

**Cast**   Adjani, Isabelle; Lhermitte, Thierry; Chazel, Mari-Anne

**Song(s)**   Next Year If All Goes Well (C: Cosma, Vladimir; L: Kremen, Sofie)

**Notes**   No cue sheet available.

## 4151 ✦ NIAGARA
### Twentieth Century–Fox, 1953

**Musical Score**   Kaplan, Sol

**Producer(s)**   Brackett, Charles
**Director(s)**   Hathaway, Henry
**Screenwriter(s)**   Brackett, Charles; Reisch, Walter; Breen, Richard L.

**Cast**   Monroe, Marilyn; Cotten, Joseph; Peters, Jean; Adams, Casey; Wilson, Don; Tuttle, Lurene; Wright, Will

**Song(s)**   Kiss [1] (C: Newman, Lionel; L: Gillespie, Haven); Marilyn [2] (C/L: Drake, Ervin; Shirl, Jimmy)

**Notes**   [1] Also in LA LUNA. [2] Song written for exploitation only.

## 4152 ✦ NICE DREAMS
### Columbia, 1981

**Musical Score**   Betts, Harry R.

**Producer(s)**   Brown, Howard
**Director(s)**   Chong, Thomas
**Screenwriter(s)**   Chong, Thomas; Marin, Richard "Cheech"

**Cast**   Marin, Richard "Cheech"; Chong, Thomas; Keach, Stacy; Leary, Dr. Timothy; Guerrero, Evelyn; Reubens, Paul; Winslow, Michael

**Song(s)**   Theme from Nice Dreams (C/L: Guevara, Ruben); Save the Whales (C/L: Marin, Richard "Cheech"; Chong, Thomas)

## 4153 ✦ NICE GIRL?
### Universal, 1941

**Producer(s)**   Pasternak, Joe
**Director(s)**   Seiter, William A.
**Screenwriter(s)**   Connell, Richard; Lehman, Gladys

**Cast**   Durbin, Deanna; Tone, Franchot; Stack, Robert; Brennan, Walter; Benchley, Robert; Gillis, Ann; Broderick, Helen; Gwynne, Anne; Risdon, Elizabeth; Bryant, Nana

**Song(s)**   Perhaps (C: Franchetti, Aldo; L: De Segurola, Andres); Beneath the Lights of Home (C: Jurmann, Walter; L: Grossman, Bernie); Love at Last (C: Press, Jacques; L: Cherkose, Eddie); Thank You America (C: Jurmann, Walter; L: Grossman, Bernie)

**Notes**   There is also a vocal of "There'll Always Be an England" by Ross Parker and Hughie Charles.

## 4154 ✦ NICKEL RIDE
### Twentieth Century–Fox, 1975

**Musical Score**   Grusin, Dave

**Producer(s)**   Mulligan, Robert
**Director(s)**   Mulligan, Robert
**Screenwriter(s)**   Roth, Eric

**Cast**   Miller, Jason; Haynes, Linda; French, Victor; Hillerman, John; Hopkins, Bo; Evans, Richard

**Song(s)**   Anytime There's Music, You're My Song (C/L: Chain, Michael)

## 4155 ✦ NIGHT AMBUSH
### United Artists, 1957

**Musical Score**   Theodorakis, Mikis

**Producer(s)**   Powell, Michael; Pressburger, Emeric
**Director(s)**   Powell, Michael; Pressburger, Emeric
**Screenwriter(s)**   Powell, Michael; Pressburger, Emeric
**Source(s)**   *Ill Met By Moonlight* (novel) Moss, W. Stanley

**Cast**   Bogarde, Dirk; Goring, Marius; Oxley, David; Cusack, Cyril; Gough, Michael

**Song(s)**   Philidem (C/L: Theodorakis, Mikis)

**Notes**   Originally titled ILL MET BY MOONLIGHT.

## 4156 ✦ NIGHT AND DAY
### Warner Brothers–First National, 1946

**Composer(s)**   Porter, Cole
**Choreographer(s)**   Prinz, LeRoy

**Producer(s)**   Schwartz, Arthur
**Director(s)**   Curtiz, Michael
**Screenwriter(s)**   Hoffman, Charles; Townsend, Leo; Bowers, William

**Cast**   Grant, Cary; Smith, Alexis; Woolley, Monty; Simms, Ginny; Wyman, Jane; Arden, Eve; Ramirez, Carlos; Woods, Donald; Martin, Mary; Francen, Victor; Hale, Alan; Malone, Dorothy; D'Andrea, Tom; Royle, Selena; Stephenson, Henry; Rumann, Sig

**Notes**   This is a biography of Cole Porter. None of these songs were written for the picture. Many of these are included in medleys. "Sons of Eli" by Henry Beston and Stanleigh Friedman, "I Wonder What's Become of Sally" by Milton Ager and Jack Yellen, "I Am in Love Again," "Bull-Dog," "In the Still of the Night," "Old Fashioned Garden," "You've Got That Thing," "Let's Do It (Let's Fall in Love)," "You Do Something to Me," "Begin the Beguine," "Night and Day" (also in ROSALIE and THE GAY DIVORCEE), "I'm Unlucky at Gambling," "Miss Otis Regrets," "What Is This Thing Called Love," "I've Got You Under My Skin," "Rosalie," "Just One of Those Things," "You're the Top," "I Get a Kick Out of You," "Easy to Love," "My Heart Belongs to Daddy" and "Do I Love You" by Cole Porter.

### 4157 ◆ NIGHT AND THE CITY
Twentieth Century–Fox, 1950

**Musical Score**  Waxman, Franz

**Producer(s)**  Engel, Samuel G.
**Director(s)**  Dassin, Jules
**Screenwriter(s)**  Elsinger, Jo
**Source(s)**  *Night and the City* (novel) Kersh, Gerald

**Cast**  Widmark, Richard; Tierney, Gene; Withers, Googie; Marlowe, Hugh; Sullivan, Francis L.; Lom, Herbert; Farrell, Charles; Mazurki, Mike

**Song(s)**  Here's to Champagne (C/L: Gay, Noel)

### 4158 ◆ NIGHT AT EARL CARROLL'S
Paramount, 1940

**Lyricist(s)**  Loesser, Frank

**Producer(s)**  Carroll, Earl
**Director(s)**  Neumann, Kurt
**Screenwriter(s)**  Starling, Lynn

**Cast**  Murray, Ken; Hobart, Rose; Naish, J. Carrol; Allman, Elvia; Carroll, Earl; Hicks, Russell; Wallace, Beryl; Ash, Sam

**Song(s)**  I Wanna Make with the Happy Times [2] (C: Niesen, Gertrude); Cali-Conga [4] (C: Menendez, Nilo; L: Cochran, Dorcas; Carroll, Earl); One Look At You (C: Young, Victor; L: Carroll, Earl; Washington, Ned); Li'l Boy Love (C: Hollander, Frederick); I've Walked Through Wonderland [1] (C: Hollander, Frederick); My Beautiful [1] (C: Young, Victor); There Goes My Dream [1] [3] (C: Hollander, Frederick)

**Notes**  [1] Not used. [2] A 24 second background vocal. [3] Used in TORNADO. [4] Marylan Cook recorded the "Cali-Conga."

### 4159 ◆ A NIGHT AT THE OPERA
Metro–Goldwyn–Mayer, 1935

**Musical Score**  Stothart, Herbert
**Choreographer(s)**  Hale, Chester

**Director(s)**  Wood, Sam
**Screenwriter(s)**  Kaufman, George S.; Ryskind, Morrie

**Cast**  Marx, Groucho; Marx, Chico; Marx, Harpo; Carlisle, Kitty; Jones, Allan; King, Walter Woolf; Dumont, Margaret; Rumann, Sig [2]; O'Connor, Robert Emmett

**Song(s)**  Alone (C: Brown, Nacio Herb; L: Freed, Arthur); Cosi Cosa [3] (C: Kaper, Bronislau; Jurmann, Walter; L: Washington, Ned); A Kiss to Build a Dream On [1] (C: Ruby, Harry; L: Kalmar, Bert; Hammerstein II, Oscar)

**Notes**  There are vocals of "Quartet," "Chorus of Gypsys," "Di Quella Pira," "Introduction Act III," "Miserere," "Mal Reggendo," "Stride la Vampa" and "Questa O Quella" from RIGOLETTO by Verdi. [1] Not used. Based on a previous Kalmar Ruby song titled "Moonlight on the Meadow." Used in THE STRIP (1951). [2] Billed as Siegfried Rumann. [3] Also in EVERYBODY SING and A DAY AT THE RACES.

### 4160 ◆ NIGHT AT THE SHOOTING GALLERY
Metro–Goldwyn–Mayer, 1930

**Musical Score**  Tiomkin, Dimitri
**Choreographer(s)**  Rasch, Albertina

**Song(s)**  Sax Appeal (C: Tiomkin, Dimitri; L: Unknown)

**Notes**  Short subject.

### 4161 ◆ NIGHT CLUB
Paramount, 1929

**Director(s)**  Florey, Robert
**Screenwriter(s)**  Thompson, Keene
**Source(s)**  (novel) Brush, Katherine

**Cast**  Stewart, Donald Ogden; Brice, Fanny; Pennington, Ann; Geva, Tamara; Arnst, Bobbe; Dupree, Minnie; Pat Rooney and Son; Carr, Jimmie

**Notes**  Short subject. This was to have been a feature but ended up as a 28 minute revue. The cue sheet lists only titles without songwriter credits and without differentiating between songs and background instrumentals. The titles are "Valse Pathetic," "Mysterioso," "La Bella Cubano" and "Booster." All are credited to Lake.

### 4162 ◆ NIGHT CLUB GIRL
Universal, 1944

**Producer(s)**  Gross, Frank
**Director(s)**  Cline, Edward F.
**Screenwriter(s)**  Blankfort, Henry; Hyland, Dick Irving

**Cast**  Austin, Vivian; Dunn, Billy; Norris, Edward; Rosenbloom, Maxie

**Song(s)**  Vingo Jingo (C: de Paul, Gene; L: Raye, Don); I Need Love (C: Fairchild, Edgar; L: Pascal, Milton); It's a Wonderful Day (C: Sherman, Al; L: Tobias, Harry)

**Notes** There are also vocals of "One O'Clock Jump" by Count Basie; "The Peanut Song" by Nate Wexler, Red Maddock and Al Trace and "Wo-Ho" by Jimmy Nolan and Jimmy Kennedy.

## 4163 ◆ NIGHT CLUB HOSTESS

See UNMARRIED.

## 4164 ◆ NIGHT CLUB SCANDAL
### Paramount, 1937

**Director(s)** Murphy, Ralph
**Screenwriter(s)** Hayward, Lillie
**Source(s)** *Riddle Me This* (play) Eubin, Daniel N.

**Cast** Barrymore, John; Overman, Lynne; Campbell, Louise; Bickford, Charles; Brent, Evelyn; Patterson, Elizabeth; Naish, J. Carrol

**Song(s)** No More Tears [1] (C: Lane, Burton; L: Freed, Ralph)

**Notes** Originally titled CITY HALL SCANDAL. [1] Also in HER HUSBAND LIES.

## 4165 ◆ NIGHT FLIGHT
### Metro–Goldwyn–Mayer, 1933

**Musical Score** Stothart, Herbert

**Producer(s)** Selznick, David O.
**Director(s)** Brown, Clarence
**Screenwriter(s)** Garrett, Oliver H.P.
**Source(s)** (novel) de Saint-Exupery, Antoine

**Cast** Barrymore, John; Hayes, Helen; Gable, Clark; Barrymore, Lionel; Montgomery, Robert; Loy, Myrna

**Song(s)** Gaucho Lament (C: Stothart, Herbert; L: Unknown)

## 4166 ◆ NIGHT HAS A THOUSAND EYES
### Paramount, 1948

**Musical Score** Young, Victor

**Producer(s)** Bohem, Endre
**Director(s)** Farrow, John
**Screenwriter(s)** Lyndon, Barre; Latimer, Jonathan

**Cast** Robinson, Edward G.; Russell, Gail; Lund, John

**Song(s)** The Night Has a Thousand Eyes [1] (C: Brainin, Jerome; L: Bernier, Buddy)

**Notes** [1] Written for exploitation only.

## 4167 ◆ THE NIGHT HAWK
### Republic, 1938

**Producer(s)** Schlom, Herman
**Director(s)** Salkow, Sidney
**Screenwriter(s)** Felton, Earl

**Cast** Livingston, Robert; Travis, June; Armstrong, Robert; Welden, Ben; Littlefield, Lucien; Downing, Joseph

**Song(s)** Never a Dream Goes By (C: Kent, Walter; L: Kurtz, Manny; Sherman, Al)

## 4168 ◆ NIGHTHAWKS (1979)
### Nu–Image, 1979

**Musical Score** Ellis, David Graham

**Producer(s)** Peck, Ron; Hallam, Paul
**Director(s)** Peck, Ron
**Screenwriter(s)** Peck, Ron; Hallam, Paul

**Cast** Robertson, Ken; Nicholas, Rachel; Stuart, James

**Song(s)** So Long (C: Steed, Pinky; L: Turton, Stuart Craig)

**Notes** No cue sheet available.

## 4169 ◆ NIGHTHAWKS (1981)
### Universal, 1981

**Musical Score** Emerson, Keith

**Producer(s)** Poll, Martin
**Director(s)** Malmuth, Bruce
**Screenwriter(s)** Shaber, David

**Cast** Stallone, Sylvester; Williams, Billy Dee; Wagner, Lindsay; Khambatta, Persis; Davenport, Nigel; Hauer, Rutger

**Song(s)** Chic-Charni Disco (C: Emerson, Keith; L: Hall, Ken)

## 4170 ◆ THE NIGHT HOLDS TERROR
### Columbia, 1955

**Producer(s)** Stone, Andrew L.
**Director(s)** Stone, Andrew L.
**Screenwriter(s)** Stone, Andrew L.

**Cast** Kelly, Jack; Parks, Hildy; Edwards, Vince; Cassavetes, John; Kruschen, Jack; Cross, David

**Song(s)** Perfume (C/L: Baldwin, Mary; Baxter, Eddie); Every Now and Then (C/L: Stone, Virginia)

**Notes** No cue sheet available.

## 4171 ◆ NIGHT IN NEW ORLEANS
### Paramount, 1942

**Producer(s)** Siegel, Sol C.
**Director(s)** Clemens, William
**Screenwriter(s)** Latimer, Jonathan

**Cast** Foster, Preston; Morison, Patricia; Dekker, Albert; Butterworth, Charles; Wilson, Dooley; Phillips, Jean [1]

**Song(s)** Small Fry [2] (C: Carmichael, Hoagy; L: Loesser, Frank)

**Notes**   Film originally titled THE MORNING AFTER. [1] Martha Tilton dubbed her voice. [2] Also in SING YOU SINNERS.

## 4172 ◆ NIGHT IN PARADISE
Universal, 1946

**Musical Score**   Skinner, Frank

**Producer(s)**   Wanger, Walter
**Director(s)**   Lubin, Arthur
**Screenwriter(s)**   Pascal, Ernest
**Source(s)**   *Peacock's Feather* (novel) Lavery, Emmet

**Cast**   Oberon, Merle; Gomez, Thomas; Bey, Turhan; Sondergaard, Gale; Collins, Ray; Dolenz, George; Litel, John; Truex, Ernest; Cowan, Jerome

**Song(s)**   Night in Paradise (C: Skinner, Frank; L: Brooks, Jack)

## 4173 ◆ THE NIGHT IS YOUNG
Metro–Goldwyn–Mayer, 1935

**Composer(s)**   Romberg, Sigmund
**Lyricist(s)**   Hammerstein II, Oscar
**Choreographer(s)**   Hale, Chester

**Producer(s)**   Rapf, Harry
**Director(s)**   Murphy, Dudley
**Screenwriter(s)**   Woolf, Edgar Allan; Schulz, Franz

**Cast**   Novarro, Ramon; Laye, Evelyn; Butterworth, Charles; Merkel, Una; Horton, Edward Everett; Cook, Donald; Stephenson, Henry; Russell, Rosalind; Bing, Herman; Mitzi

**Song(s)**   My Old Mare; When I Grow Too Old To Dream; The Noble Duchess; Lift Your Glass; There's a Riot in Havana; The Night Is Young; Lena, I Love You [1]; Vienna Will Sing [1]; Wiener Schnitzel [1]

**Notes**   Ramon Novarro's last MGM film. [1] Not on cue sheet. Listed in the *Rodgers and Hammerstein Fact Book*.

## 4174 ◆ NIGHT LIFE OF THE GODS
Universal, 1936

**Musical Score**   Morton, Arthur

**Producer(s)**   Sherman, Lowell
**Director(s)**   Sherman, Lowell
**Screenwriter(s)**   Trivers, Barry
**Source(s)**   *Night Life of the Gods* (novel) Smith, Thorne

**Cast**   Mowbray, Alan; McKinney, Florine; Shannon, Peggy

**Song(s)**   Gladiator Papa (C/L: Morton, Arthur)

## 4175 ◆ NIGHTMARE
United Artists, 1956

**Musical Score**   Gilbert, Herschel Burke
**Composer(s)**   Gilbert, Herschel Burke
**Lyricist(s)**   Houck, Doris

**Producer(s)**   Pine, Howard; Thomas, William
**Director(s)**   Shane, Maxwell
**Screenwriter(s)**   Shane, Maxwell
**Source(s)**   (novel) Woolrich, Cornell

**Cast**   McCarthy, Kevin; Robinson, Edward G.; Russell, Connie; Christine, Virginia; Clarke, Gage; Williams, Rhys; Lewis, Meade Lux; Billy May and His Orchestra

**Song(s)**   Nightmare [1]; The Last I Ever Saw of My Man; Closet Full of Men's Clothes (L: Shane, Maxwell); What's Your Sad Story (C/L: Sherman, Dick)

**Notes**   A remake of FOUR IN THE NIGHT (1947). [1] Used instrumentally only.

## 4176 ◆ A NIGHTMARE ON ELM STREET
New Line Cinema, 1984

**Musical Score**   Bernstein, Charles

**Producer(s)**   Shaye, Robert
**Director(s)**   Craven, Wes
**Screenwriter(s)**   Craven, Wes

**Cast**   Saxon, John; Blakley, Ronee; Langenkamp, Heather; Wyss, Amanda; Depp, Johnny; Fleischer, Charles; Englund, Robert

**Song(s)**   Nightmare (C/L: Kent, Martin; Karshner, Steve; Schurig, Michael)

**Notes**   No cue sheet available.

## 4177 ◆ A NIGHTMARE ON ELM STREET 4: THE DREAM MASTER
New Line, 1988

**Musical Score**   Safan, Craig

**Producer(s)**   Talalay, Rachel; Shaye, Robert
**Director(s)**   Harlin, Renny
**Screenwriter(s)**   Helgeland, Brian; Scott, Pierce

**Cast**   Englund, Robert; Eastman, Rodney; Hassel, Danny; Jones, Andras; Knight, Tuesday; Sagoes, Ken; Wilcox, Lisa

**Song(s)**   Nightmare (C/L: Egizi, Michael; Knight, Tuesday); Are You Ready for Freddy (C/L: Wells, Matthew; Anderson, Mike; Thomas, Giovanni K.; Klein, Patrick)

**Notes**   No cue sheet available.

## 4178 ◆ NIGHTMARES
Universal, 1983

**Musical Score**   Safan, Craig

**Producer(s)**   Crowe, Christopher
**Director(s)**   Sargent, Joseph
**Screenwriter(s)**   Crowe, Christopher; Bloom, Jeffrey

**Cast**   Raines, Cristina; Lambie, Joe; Estevez, Emilio; Zappa, Moon; Cartwright, Veronica; Hague, Albert

**Song(s)** I Don't Care About You (C/L: Ving, Lee); Mercenaries (C: Gray, Craig; L: Shatter, Will); Let's Have a War [1] (C/L: Ving, Lee); I Got Power (C: Gray, Craig; L: Rik, Rik L.)

**Notes** [1] Also in REPO MAN with additional credit of Philo Cramer.

## 4179 ✦ NIGHT OF THE FOLLOWING DAY
Universal, 1968

**Musical Score** Myers, Stanley

**Producer(s)** Cornfield, Hubert
**Director(s)** Cornfield, Hubert
**Screenwriter(s)** Cornfield, Hubert
**Source(s)** *The Snatchers* (novel) White, Lionel

**Cast** Brando, Marlon; Boone, Richard; Moreno, Rita; Hahn, Jess; Franklin, Pamela

**Song(s)** Theme Song (C: Myers, Stanley; L: Hendricks, Jon)

## 4180 ✦ NIGHT OF THE GENERALS
Columbia, 1967

**Musical Score** Jarre, Maurice

**Producer(s)** Speigel, Sam
**Director(s)** Litvak, Anatole
**Screenwriter(s)** Dehn, Paul; Kessel, Joseph
**Source(s)** *The Night of the Generals* (novel) Kirst, Hans Hellmut

**Cast** O'Toole, Peter; Sharif, Omar; Courtenay, Tom; Pleasence, Donald; Gray, Charles; Pettet, Joanna; Noiret, Philippe; Plummer, Christopher; Browne, Coral; Andrews, Harry

**Song(s)** Au Coin D'Une Rue (C/L: Jarre, Maurice); The World Will Smile Again [1] (C: Jarre, Maurice; L: Greenfield, Howard)

**Notes** [1] Sheet music only.

## 4181 ✦ THE NIGHT OF THE GRIZZLY
Paramount, 1966

**Producer(s)** Dunne, Burt
**Director(s)** Pevney, Joseph
**Screenwriter(s)** Douglas, Warren

**Cast** Walker, Clint; Wynn, Keenan; Elam, Jack; Culp, Nancy; Brodie, Kevin; Corby, Ellen; Ely, Ron

**Song(s)** Angela (C/L: Livingston, Jay; Evans, Ray)

## 4182 ✦ NIGHT OF THE HUNTER
United Artists, 1955

**Musical Score** Schumann, Walter
**Composer(s)** Schumann, Walter
**Lyricist(s)** Grubb, Davis

**Producer(s)** Gregory, Paul
**Director(s)** Laughton, Charles
**Screenwriter(s)** Agee, James
**Source(s)** *Night of the Hunter* (novel) Grubb, Davis

**Cast** Mitchum, Robert; Winters, Shelley; Gish, Lillian; Chapin, Billy; Bruce, Sally Jane

**Song(s)** Night of the Hunter; Hing, Hang, Hung; Cresap's Landing; Pretty Fly; Lullaby

## 4183 ✦ THE NIGHT OF THE IGUANA
Metro–Goldwyn–Mayer, 1965

**Musical Score** Frankel, Benjamin

**Producer(s)** Stark, Ray
**Director(s)** Huston, John
**Screenwriter(s)** Veiller, Anthony; Huston, John
**Source(s)** *The Night of the Iguana* (play) Williams, Tennessee

**Cast** Burton, Richard; Gardner, Ava; Kerr, Deborah; Lyon, Sue; Ward, James; Boylan, Mary

**Song(s)** La Negra (C/L: Fuentes, Ruben; Vargas, Silvestre)

## 4184 ✦ NIGHT OF THE QUARTER MOON
Metro–Goldwyn–Mayer, 1959

**Musical Score** Glasser, Albert

**Producer(s)** Zugsmith, Albert
**Director(s)** Haas, Hugo
**Screenwriter(s)** Davis, Frank; Coen, Franklin

**Cast** London, Julie; Barrymore, John Drew; Kashfi, Anna; Moorehead, Agnes; Cole, Nat "King"; Anthony, Ray; Coogan, Jackie; Chaplin Jr., Charles; Daniels, Billy; Crosby, Cathy

**Song(s)** Night of the Quarter Moon (C: Van Heusen, James; L: Cahn, Sammy); To Whom It May Concern [1] (C: Cole, Nat "King"; L: Hawkins, Charlotte)

**Notes** There is also a vocal of "Blue Moon" by Richard Rodgers and Lorenz Hart. [1] Also in THE BEAT GENERATION.

## 4185 ✦ NIGHT PASSAGE
Universal, 1957

**Musical Score** Tiomkin, Dimitri
**Composer(s)** Tiomkin, Dimitri
**Lyricist(s)** Washington, Ned

**Producer(s)** Rosenberg, Aaron
**Director(s)** Neilson, James
**Screenwriter(s)** Chase, Borden

**Cast** Stewart, James; Murphy, Audie; Duryea, Dan; Foster, Dianne; Stewart, Elaine; Flippen, Jay C.; de Wilde, Brandon; Anderson, Herbert; Wilke, Robert J.; Beaumont, Hugh; Elam, Jack

**Song(s)**   Follow the River; You Can't Get Far Without a Railroad

## 4186 ✦ NIGHT SHIFT
Ladd Company–Warner Brothers, 1982

**Musical Score**   Bacharach, Burt

**Producer(s)**   Grazer, Brian
**Director(s)**   Howard, Ron
**Screenwriter(s)**   Ganz, Lowell; Mandel, Babaloo

**Cast**   Winkler, Henry; Keaton, Michael; Long, Shelley; Hecht, Gina; Corley, Pat; CiCicco, Bobby; Talbot, Nita; Howard, Clint; Spinell, Joe

**Song(s)**   Night Shift (C/L: Bacharach, Burt; Sager, Carole Bayer; Ross, Marv); Girls Know How (C/L: Bacharach, Burt; Sager, Carole Bayer; Foster, David); The Love Too Good to Last (C/L: Bacharach, Burt; Sager, Carole Bayer; Allen, Peter); That's What Friends Are For (C: Bacharach, Burt; L: Sager, Carole Bayer); Street Talk [1] (C: Bacharach, Burt; L: Sager, Carole Bayer)

**Notes**   All background vocals. [1] Not used.

## 4187 ✦ NIGHT SONG
RKO, 1947

**Musical Score**   Stevens, Leith

**Producer(s)**   Parsons, Harriet
**Director(s)**   Cromwell, John
**Screenwriter(s)**   Fenton, Frank; Hyland, Dick Irving

**Cast**   Andrews, Dana; Oberon, Merle; Barrymore, Ethel; Carmichael, Hoagy; White, Jacqueline; Curtis, Donald; Reed, Walter

**Song(s)**   Who Killed 'Er (C/L: Spielman, Fred; Torre, Janice; Carmichael, Hoagy); Piano Concerto (Inst.) (C: Stevens, Leith)

## 4188 ✦ NIGHT SPOT
RKO, 1938

**Producer(s)**   Sisk, Robert
**Director(s)**   Cabanne, Christy
**Screenwriter(s)**   Houser, Lionel

**Cast**   Parkyakarkus; Lane, Allan; Jones, Gordon; Woodbury, Joan; Kellaway, Cecil; Carson, Jack; Patrick, Lee

**Song(s)**   There's Only One Way to Say I Love You (C: Stept, Sam H.; L: Ruby, Herman)

## 4189 ✦ NIGHT STAGE TO GALVESTON
Columbia, 1952

**Producer(s)**   Schaefer, Armand
**Director(s)**   Archainbaud, George
**Screenwriter(s)**   Hall, Norman S.

**Cast**   Autry, Gene; Buttram, Pat; Huston, Virginia; Hall, Thurston; Nugent, Judy; Moore, Clayton; Lauter, Harry

**Song(s)**   Down in Slumberland (C/L: Burnette, Smiley); I've Got a Heart As Big as Texas (C/L: Haldeman, Oakley; Feyne, Buddy)

## 4190 ✦ THE NIGHT THE LIGHTS WENT OUT IN GEORGIA
Avco Embassy, 1981

**Musical Score**   Shire, David
**Composer(s)**   Quaid, Dennis
**Lyricist(s)**   Quaid, Dennis

**Producer(s)**   Geisinger, Elliot; Kuperman, Howard; Saland, Ronald; Smith, Howard
**Director(s)**   Maxwell, Ronald
**Screenwriter(s)**   Bonney, Bob
**Source(s)**   "The Night the Lights Went Out in Georgia" (song) Russell, Bobby

**Cast**   McNichol, Kristy; Quaid, Dennis; Hamill, Mark; Johnson, Sunny; Stroud, Don

**Song(s)**   I Love My Truck (C/L: Campbell, Glen); Freeborn Man (C/L: Allison, Keith; Lindsay, Mark); Amanda; Hound Dog (C/L: Quaid, Dennis; Allison, Keith); Baby Bye Bye (C/L: Allison, Keith); Rodeo Girl (C/L: Tucker, Tanya); It's So Easy (C/L: Syreeta; Preston, Billy); Hangin' Up the Gun (C/L: Allison, Keith; Wakefield, Kathy); If You Don't Know By Now; I Need You to Be Strong for Me (C/L: Shire, David; Connors, Carol)

**Notes**   No cue sheet available.

## 4191 ✦ THE NIGHT THEY INVENTED STRIPTEASE

See THE NIGHT THEY RAIDED MINSKY'S.

## 4192 ✦ THE NIGHT THEY RAIDED MINSKY'S
United Artists, 1968

**Musical Score**   Strouse, Charles
**Composer(s)**   Strouse, Charles
**Lyricist(s)**   Adams, Lee

**Producer(s)**   Lear, Norman
**Director(s)**   Friedkin, William
**Screenwriter(s)**   Schulman, Arnold; Michaels, Sidney; Lear, Norman
**Source(s)**   *The Night They Raided Minksy's* (novel) Barber, Rowland

**Cast**   Robards Jr., Jason; Tucker, Forrest; Ekland, Britt; Wisdom, Norman; Gould, Elliott

**Song(s)**   Take Ten Terrific Girls (But Only 9 Costumes); Powder My Back; Perfect Gentleman; You Rat You [2]; How I Loved Her [1]; Wait for Me [1]; The Night They Raided Minsky's [3]

**Notes** Titled THE NIGHT THEY INVENTED STRIPTEASE for the international market. [1] Used instrumentally only. [2] Music used later for Broadway musical ANNIE as song "Something Was Missing." [3] Recorded but not used.

### 4193 ✦ NIGHTTIME IN NEVADA
Republic, 1948

**Producer(s)** White, Eddy
**Director(s)** Witney, William
**Screenwriter(s)** Nibley, Sloan

**Cast** Rogers, Roy; Trigger; Mara, Adele; Devine, Andy; Bob Nolan and the Sons of the Pioneers

**Song(s)** Over Nevada (C/L: Spencer, Tim); When It's Night Time in Nevada [1] (C: Dulmage, Will; Clint, H.; L: Pascoe, Richard); Sweet Laredo Lou (C/L: Nolan, Bob; Morrissey, Ed)

**Notes** There is also a vocal of "The Big Rock Candy Mountain." [1] Spanish lyrics by Aaron Gonzalez.

### 4194 ✦ NIGHT TRAIN
Twentieth Century–Fox, 1940

**Composer(s)** Woods
**Lyricist(s)** Unknown

**Producer(s)** Osterer, Maurice
**Director(s)** Reed, Carol
**Screenwriter(s)** Gilliat, Sidney; Launder, Frank

**Cast** Lockwood, Margaret; Harrison, Rex; Henreid, Paul [1]; Radford, Basil

**Song(s)** Only Love Can Lead the Way; It's True

**Notes** Originally titled GESTAPO. [1] Billed as Paul von Henreid.

### 4195 ✦ NIGHT TRAIN TO MEMPHIS
Republic, 1946

**Producer(s)** McGowan, Stuart; McGowan, Dorrell
**Director(s)** Selander, Lesley
**Screenwriter(s)** McGowan, Dorrell; McGowan, Stuart

**Cast** Acuff, Roy; Lane, Allan; Mara, Adele; Bacon, Irving; Crehan, Joseph; Dunn, Emma; Stewart, Nicodemus; McKinney, Nina Mae; Mason, LeRoy

**Song(s)** Night Train to Memphis [1] (C/L: Smith, Beasley; Hughes, Marvin; Bradley, Owen); That Glory Bound Train (C/L: Acuff, Roy; McLeod, Odell); No One Will Ever Know (C/L: Foree, Mel; Rose, Fred)

**Notes** [1] Also in COWBOY CANTEEN (Columbia).

### 4196 ✦ NIGHT TRAIN TO PARIS
Twentieth Century–Fox, 1964

**Musical Score** Graham, Kenny
**Composer(s)** Potter, Brian; Dee, Graham
**Lyricist(s)** Potter, Brian; Dee, Graham

**Producer(s)** Lippert, Robert L.; Parsons, Jack
**Director(s)** Douglas, Robert
**Screenwriter(s)** Cross, Henry

**Cast** Nielsen, Leslie; Gur, Alizia; Stevens, Dorinda; Oates, Simon

**Song(s)** Night Train to Paris; Chit Chat; Look After My Baby; Hey There Girl

**Notes** No cue sheet available.

### 4197 ✦ NIGHTWING
Columbia, 1979

**Musical Score** Mancini, Henry

**Producer(s)** Ransohoff, Martin
**Director(s)** Hiller, Arthur
**Screenwriter(s)** Shaken, Steve; Shrake, Bud; Smith, Martin Cruz
**Source(s)** *Nightwing* (novel) Shrake, Bud

**Cast** Mancuso, Nick; Warner, David; Harrold, Kathryn; Macht, Stephen; Martin, Strother; Clutesi, George; Piazza, Ben; Hotton, Donald

**Song(s)** Bat Song (C: Mancini, Henry; L: Mancini, Chris)

### 4198 ✦ NIGHT WITHOUT SLEEP
Twentieth Century–Fox, 1952

**Musical Score** Newman, Alfred
**Composer(s)** Newman, Alfred

**Producer(s)** Bassler, Robert
**Director(s)** Baker, Roy
**Screenwriter(s)** Partos, Frank; Moll, Elick

**Cast** Darnell, Linda; Merrill, Gary; Neff, Hildegarde; MacKenzie, Joyce; Beaumont, Hugh; Lynn, Mauri; Marsh, Mae

**Song(s)** Look at Me [1] (L: Darby, Ken); Too Late for Spring (L: Gillespie, Haven)

**Notes** [1] Assigned under the title "Lucy Lee."

### 4199 ✦ NIGHT WITHOUT STARS
RKO, 1953

**Producer(s)** Stewart, Hugh
**Director(s)** Pellissier, Anthony
**Screenwriter(s)** Graham, Winston
**Source(s)** *Night Without Stars* (novel) Graham, Winston

**Cast** Farrar, David; Gray, Nadia; Teynac, Maurice; Clyde, June; Landry, Gerald; Morton, Clive

**Song(s)** If You Go (C: Emer, Michael; L: Parsons, Geoffrey); Lingering Down the Lane [1] (C: Clerc, C. Borel; L: Lawrence, Jack)

**Notes** No cue sheet available. A General Film Distributors production. Produced by Rank in England in 1947. [1] English sheet music only.

### 4200 ✦ NIGHT WORK
Pathe, 1930

**Producer(s)** Derr, E.B.
**Director(s)** Mack, Russell
**Screenwriter(s)** De Leon, Walter

**Cast** Quillan, Eddie; Starr, Sally; Upton, Frances; Murray, John T.; Duryea, George; McWade, Robert; Caine, Georgia; Scott, Douglas

**Song(s)** Deep in Your Heart (C: Snyder, Ted; L: Harris, Mort); I'm Gettin' Tired of My Tired Man (C: Snyder, Ted; L: Harris, Mort)

**Notes** No cue sheet available.

### 4201 ✦ NIGHT WORLD
Universal, 1932

**Musical Score** Newman, Alfred
**Choreographer(s)** Berkeley, Busby

**Director(s)** Henley, Hobart
**Screenwriter(s)** Schayer, Richard

**Cast** Ayres, Lew; Clarke, Mae; Revier, Dorothy; Hopton, Russell; Karloff, Boris; Raft, George; Muse, Clarence; Roach, Bert; Lake, Florence; Hopper, Hedda; Beavers, Louise

**Notes** There are no original songs in this movie. The two that are used are "Who's Your Little Who-Zis" by Ben Bernie, Al Goering and Walter Hirsch and "Prisoner of Love" by Russ Columbo and Leo Robin.

### 4202 ✦ NIJINSKY
Paramount, 1980

**Producer(s)** Kaye, Nora; O'Toole, Stanley
**Director(s)** Ross, Herbert
**Screenwriter(s)** Wheeler, Hugh

**Cast** de la Pena, George; Bates, Alan; Browne, Leslie; Irons, Jeremy; Blakely, Colin; Dolin, Anton

**Song(s)** Serenata de la Notte [1] (C: Lanchbery, John; L: Sciarrilli, Rick)

**Notes** [1] Not used.

### 4203 ✦ THE NINE LIVES OF ELFEGO BACA
Disney, 1959

**Musical Score** Baker, Buddy; Marks, Franklyn

**Producer(s)** Pratt, James
**Director(s)** Foster, Norman
**Screenwriter(s)** Foster, Norman

**Cast** Loggia, Robert; Simon, Robert F.; Montell, Lisa; Paiva, Nestor

**Song(s)** The Nine Lives of Elfego Baca (C/L: Dehr, Richard; Miller, Frank); Anita the Bonita (C: Lava, William; L: Foster, Norman); Lolita (C: Baker, Buddy; L: Jackman, Bob)

### 4204 ✦ NINETEEN EIGHTY-FOUR
Atlantic, 1984

**Musical Score** Eurythmics, The; Muldowney, Dominic
**Composer(s)** Muldowney, Dominic
**Lyricist(s)** Gems, Jonathan; Orwell, George

**Producer(s)** Perry, Simon
**Director(s)** Radford, Michael
**Screenwriter(s)** Radford, Michael
**Source(s)** *Nineteen Eighty-Four* (novel) Orwell, George

**Cast** Hurt, John; Burton, Richard; Hamilton, Suzanna; Cusack, Cyril; Fisher, Gregory

**Song(s)** Oceania 'Tis for Thee; The Hiking Song (L: Gems, Jonathan); The Washerwoman's Song

**Notes** No cue sheet available.

### 4205 ✦ NINE TO FIVE
Twentieth Century–Fox, 1980

**Musical Score** Fox, Charles

**Producer(s)** Gilbert, Bruce
**Director(s)** Higgins, Colin
**Screenwriter(s)** Higgins, Colin; Resnick, Patricia

**Cast** Fonda, Jane; Tomlin, Lily; Parton, Dolly; Coleman, Dabney; Hayden, Sterling; Wilson, Elizabeth; Mercer, Marian; Woods, Ren

**Song(s)** Nine to Five Song (C/L: Parton, Dolly); House of the Rising Sun [1] (C/L: Parton, Dolly; Post, Mike)

**Notes** [1] Sheet music only.

### 4206 ✦ 99 AND 44/100% DEAD
Twentieth Century–Fox, 1974

**Musical Score** Mancini, Henry

**Producer(s)** Wizan, Joe
**Director(s)** Frankenheimer, John
**Screenwriter(s)** Dillon, Robert

**Cast** Harris, Richard; O'Brien, Edmond; Dillman, Bradford; Turkel, Ann; Ford, Constance

**Song(s)** Easy Baby (C: Mancini, Henry; L: Bergman, Marilyn; Bergman, Alan)

### 4207 ✦ NINJA III: THE DOMINATION
Cannon, 1984

**Musical Score** Harpaz, Udi; Segal, Misha; Kempel, Arthur
**Composer(s)** Powell, Dave
**Lyricist(s)** Powell, Dave

**Producer(s)**   Golan, Menahem; Globus, Yoram
**Director(s)**   Firstenberg, Sam
**Screenwriter(s)**   Silke, James R.

**Cast**   Kosugi, Sho; Dickey, Lucinda; Bennett, Jordan; Chung, David; Ishimoto, Dale; Hong, James; Padilla, Roy

**Song(s)**   Body Shop; Starting Out Right; Love Bites (C/L: Powell, Dave; Harris, Margaret; Zapulla, Sally); Obsession; What Kind of Boy Is This; Welcome to the Party

**Notes**   No cue sheet available.

## 4208 ✦ THE NINTH CONFIGURATION

See TWINKLE TWINKLE "KILLER" KANE.

## 4209 ✦ THE NITWITS
RKO, 1935

**Producer(s)**   Marcus, Lee
**Director(s)**   Stevens, George
**Screenwriter(s)**   Guiol, Fred; Boasberg, Al

**Cast**   Wheeler, Bert; Woolsey, Robert; Keating, Fred; Grable, Betty; Brent, Evelyn; Rhodes, Erik; Hamilton, Hale; Wilson, Charles; Aylesworth, Arthur

**Song(s)**   You Opened My Eyes (C: Bernard, Felix; L: Gilbert, L. Wolfe); Music in My Heart (C: McHugh, Jimmy; L: Fields, Dorothy)

## 4210 ✦ NIX ON DAMES
Fox, 1929

**Composer(s)**   Baer, Abel
**Lyricist(s)**   Gilbert, L. Wolfe

**Producer(s)**   Middleton, George
**Director(s)**   Gallagher, Donald
**Screenwriter(s)**   Fulton, Maude; Gay, Frank

**Cast**   Clarke, Mae; Ames, Robert; Harrigan, William; Fulton, Maude; MacFarlane, George; Beavers, Louise; Rovelle, Camille

**Song(s)**   Two Pals; Song of My Heart; Walkin' with Susie (C/L: Conrad, Con; Gottler, Archie; Mitchell, Sidney D.); Say the Word; Oh, Lord, Pour Down Your Waters and Baptize Me [1]; Fading Away [2]; One Sweetheart [2]; I'm Wingin' Home [2]

**Notes**   [1] Not on cue sheets. [2] Not on cue sheets but in *Variety* review.

## 4211 ✦ NOAH'S ARK (1929)
Warner Brothers, 1929

**Musical Score**   Silvers, Louis

**Director(s)**   Curtiz, Michael
**Screenwriter(s)**   Coldeway, Anthony; Anthony, B. Leon

**Cast**   Costello, Dolores; O'Brien, George; Beery, Noah; Fazenda, Louise; Williams, Guinn "Big Boy"; McAllister, Paul; Randolf, Anders; De Brulier, Nigel; Kaliz, Armand; Loy, Myrna

**Song(s)**   Heart o' Mine (C: Silvers, Louis; L: Rose, Billy); Old Timer (C: Silvers, Louis; L: Rose, Billy)

**Notes**   No cue sheet available.

## 4212 ✦ NOAH'S ARK (1959)
Disney, 1959

**Musical Score**   Bruns, George
**Composer(s)**   Leven, Mel
**Lyricist(s)**   Leven, Mel

**Director(s)**   Justice, Bill
**Screenwriter(s)**   Hee, T.
**Voices**   Courtland, Jerome; Gayle, Jeanne; MacDonald, James; Frees, Paul

**Song(s)**   The Building of the Ark; Love One Another; The Maiden Cruise; Don't Mention His Name to Me

**Notes**   Cartoon.

## 4213 ✦ NOB HILL
Twentieth Century–Fox, 1945

**Musical Score**   Buttolph, David
**Composer(s)**   McHugh, Jimmy
**Lyricist(s)**   Adamson, Harold
**Choreographer(s)**   Castle, Nick

**Producer(s)**   Daven, Andre
**Director(s)**   Hathaway, Henry
**Screenwriter(s)**   Tuchock, Wanda; Raine, Norman Reilly

**Cast**   Raft, George; Bennett, Joan; Blaine, Vivian; Garner, Peggy Ann; Reed, Alan; Pully, B.S.; Coleman, Emil; Barrier, Edgar; Smith, Joe; Dale, Charles; The Three Swifts

**Song(s)**   I Don't Care Who Knows It; I Walked In (With My Eyes Wide Open); Touring San Francisco; What Do You Want to Make Those Eyes at Me For (C: Monaco, James V.; L: Johnson, Howard; McCarthy, Joseph)

**Notes**   Vocals also include: "On San Francisco Bay" by Gertrude Hoffman and Vincent Bryan; "Hello Frisco! (I Called Up to Say Hello)" by Louis A. Hirsch and Gene Buck; "When You Wore a Tulip and I Wore a Big Red Rose" by Percy Wenrich and Jack Mahoney; "Hello, Ma Baby" by Joseph E. Howard and Ida Emerson; "San Francisco, the Paris of the U.S.A." by Hirshel Hendler; "San Francisco" by Bronislau Kaper and Walter Jurmann; "When Irish Eyes Are Smiling" by Chauncey Olcott, George Graff Jr. and Ernest R. Ball and "(Too-Ra-Loo-Ra-Loo-Ral) That's An Irish Lullaby" by J.R. Shannon (James Royce) from musical show SHAMEEN DHU.

## 4214 ✦ NO BLADE OF GRASS
Metro–Goldwyn–Mayer, 1971

**Musical Score**   Nelius, Louis; Carroll, Charles

**Producer(s)**   Wilde, Cornel
**Director(s)**   Wilde, Cornel
**Screenwriter(s)**   Forestal, Sean; Pascal, Jefferson
**Source(s)**   (novel) Christopher, John

**Cast**   Davenport, Nigel; Wallace, Jean; May, Anthony; Richard, Wendy; Hamill, John; Frederick, Lynne; Coulouris, George

**Song(s)**   No Blade of Grass (C/L: Nelius, Louis; Carroll, Charles)

## 4215 ✦ NOBODY LIVES FOREVER
Warner Brothers–First National, 1946

**Musical Score**   Deutsch, Adolph

**Producer(s)**   Buckner, Robert
**Director(s)**   Negulesco, Jean
**Screenwriter(s)**   Burnett, W.R.
**Source(s)**   "I Wasn't Born Yesterday" (story) Burnett, W.R.

**Cast**   Garfield, John; Fitzgerald, Geraldine; Brennan, Walter; Emerson, Faye; Coulouris, George; Tobias, George; Shayne, Robert; Gaines, Richard; Sutton, Grady

**Song(s)**   You Again [1] (C: Jerome, M.K.; L: Scholl, Jack)

**Notes**   [1] Also in THE PLAYGIRLS (1941).

## 4216 ✦ NOBODY'S BABY
Metro–Goldwyn–Mayer, 1937

**Composer(s)**   Hatley, Marvin
**Lyricist(s)**   Bullock, Walter
**Choreographer(s)**   Randolph, Roy

**Producer(s)**   Roach, Hal
**Director(s)**   Meins, Gus
**Screenwriter(s)**   Law, Harold; Yates, Hal; Flick, Pat C.

**Cast**   Kelly, Patsy; Roberti, Lyda; Overman, Lynne; Armstrong, Robert; Alvarado, Don; Lawrence, Rosina; Jimmy Grier's Orchestra; The Rhythm Rascals; The Avalon Boys

**Song(s)**   Quien Sabe; I've Dreamed About This; I'm All Dressed Up in Rhythm; Nobody's Baby; The West Ain't Wild and Wooly Anymore

**Notes**   No cue sheet available.

## 4217 ✦ NOBODY'S DARLING
Republic, 1943

**Producer(s)**   Grey, Harry
**Director(s)**   Mann, Anthony
**Screenwriter(s)**   Cooper, Olive

**Cast**   Lee, Mary; George, Gladys; Calhern, Louis; Moran, Jackie; Patrick, Lee; Bartlett, Bennie; Jones, Marcia Mae; Corrigan, Lloyd

**Notes**   No cue sheet available. There are no original songs in this film. Vocals include "It Had to Be You" by Isham Jones and Gus Kahn; "Blow, Gabriel Blow" by Cole Porter; "I'm Always Chasing Rainbows" by Joseph McCarthy and Harry Carroll; "On the Sunny Side of the Street" by Dorothy Fields and Jimmy McHugh and "Row, Row, Row Your Boat."

## 4218 ✦ NOCTURNE
RKO, 1946

**Musical Score**   Harline, Leigh

**Producer(s)**   Harrison, Joan
**Director(s)**   Marin, Edwin L.
**Screenwriter(s)**   Latimer, Jonathan

**Cast**   Raft, George; Bari, Lynn [1]; Huston, Virginia; Pevney, Joseph; Dell, Myrna; Ashley, George; Smith, Queenie

**Song(s)**   Nocturne (C: Harline, Leigh; L: Greene, Mort); Why Pretend (C/L: Rudolph, Eleanor); A Little Bit Is Better Than None (C/L: Rudolph, Eleanor)

**Notes**   [1] Dubbed by Martha Mears.

## 4219 ✦ NO DOWN PAYMENT
Twentieth Century–Fox, 1957

**Producer(s)**   Wald, Jerry
**Director(s)**   Ritt, Martin
**Screenwriter(s)**   Yordan, Philip
**Source(s)**   *No Down Payment* (novel) McPartland, John

**Cast**   Woodward, Joanne; North, Sheree; Randall, Tony; Hunter, Jeffrey; Mitchell, Cameron; Owen, Patricia; Rush, Barbara; Harris, Robert

**Song(s)**   The Drive-In Rock (C: Newman, Lionel; L: Coates, Carroll); No Down Payment [1] (C/L: Mure, Bill; Discant, N.)

**Notes**   [1] Written for exploitation only.

## 4220 ✦ NO LEAVE, NO LOVE
Metro–Goldwyn–Mayer, 1946

**Musical Score**   Stoll, George; Jackson, Calvin
**Composer(s)**   Fain, Sammy
**Lyricist(s)**   Freed, Ralph

**Producer(s)**   Pasternak, Joe
**Director(s)**   Martin, Charles
**Screenwriter(s)**   Martin, Charles; Kardos, Leslie

**Cast**   Johnson, Van; Wynn, Keenan; Kirkwood, Pat; Guy Lombardo and His Orchestra; Arnold, Edward; Wilson, Marie; Robinson, Frank "Sugarchile"; Ames, Leon; Royle, Selena; Xavier Cugat and His Orchestra; The Garcias

**Song(s)** It'll Be Great to Get Back Home (C: Martin, Charles; L: Martin, Charles; Stoll, George; Freed, Ralph); Love on a Greyhound Bus (C: Stoll, George; L: Blane, Ralph; Thompson, Kay); Oye Negra (C/L: Morales, Noro; Camacho, John A.); All the Time; Caldonia (C/L: Moore, Fleecie); Chto Mnie Gore (C/L: Pokrass, Sam); Isn't It Wonderful (C/L: Thompson, Kay); When It's Love (C: Kharito, Nicholas; L: De Lange, Eddie); Walter Winchell Rumba [1] (C: Morales, Noro; L: Sigman, Carl); I'd Love to Go On Dreaming [2]; It's Fun to Take a Bubble Bath [2]; Love Is a Penny Postcard [2]; On a Slow Boat to China; Spring Will Miss You and So Will I [2]

**Notes** [1] Sheet music only. Also not used in HOLIDAY IN MEXICO (MGM). [2] Not used.

## 4221 ✦ NOMADS
### Atlantic, 1986

**Musical Score** Conti, Bill
**Composer(s)** Conti, Bill; Nugent, Ted
**Lyricist(s)** Conti, Bill; Nugent, Ted

**Producer(s)** Pappas, George; Elwes, Cassian
**Director(s)** McTiernan, John
**Screenwriter(s)** McTiernan, John

**Cast** Brosnan, Pierce; Down, Lesley-Anne; Monticelli, Anna-Maria; Elias, Jeannie; Ant, Adam; Woronov, Mary; Foch, Nina

**Song(s)** Strangers; Nomads; Dancing Mary

**Notes** No cue sheet available.

## 4222 ✦ NO MAN IS AN ISLAND
### Universal, 1962

**Musical Score** Umali, Restie

**Producer(s)** Monks Jr., John; Goldstone, Richard
**Director(s)** Monks Jr., John; Goldstone, Richard
**Screenwriter(s)** Monks Jr., John; Goldstone, Richard

**Cast** Hunter, Jeffrey; Thompson, Marshall; Perez, Barbara

**Song(s)** Maulik Trabajo (C/L: Umali, Restie)

**Notes** No cue sheet available.

## 4223 ✦ NO MORE WOMEN
### Paramount, 1934

**Producer(s)** Rogers, Charles R.
**Director(s)** Rogell, Albert S.
**Screenwriter(s)** Daves, Delmer; Breslow, Lou

**Cast** Lowe, Edmund; McLaglen, Victor; Blane, Sally

**Song(s)** No More Women [1] (C: Revel, Harry; L: Gordon, Mack)

**Notes** [1] The song was not used in the film.

## 4224 ✦ NO, NO, NANETTE (1930)
### Warner Brothers–First National, 1930

**Composer(s)** Ward, Edward
**Lyricist(s)** Bryan, Alfred
**Choreographer(s)** Ceballos, Larry

**Director(s)** Badger, Clarence
**Screenwriter(s)** Rogers, Howard Emmett; Van, Beatrice
**Source(s)** *No, No, Nonette* (musical) Youmans, Vincent; Caesar, Irving; Mandel, Frank; Harbach, Otto

**Cast** Claire, Bernice; Gray, Alexander; Tashman, Lilyan; Roach, Bert; Pitts, ZaSu; Fazenda, Louise; Littlefield, Lucien

**Song(s)** Dance of the Wooden Shoes (C: Cleary, Michael; L: Magidson, Herb; Washington, Ned); As Long As I'm with You (C: Akst, Harry; L: Clarke, Grant); King of the Air; No, No, Nanette; Dancing to Heaven; Tea for Two [1] (C: Youmans, Vincent; L: Caesar, Irving); I Want to Be Happy [1] (C: Youmans, Vincent; L: Caesar, Irving); Dancing on Mars (C: Cleary, Michael; L: Washington, Ned; Magidson, Herb); Were You Just Pretending (C: Jerome, M.K.; L: Ruby, Herman)

**Notes** No cue sheet available. [1] From original Broadway musical.

## 4225 ✦ NO NO NANETTE (1940)
### RKO, 1940

**Composer(s)** Youmans, Vincent
**Lyricist(s)** Caesar, Irving

**Producer(s)** Wilcox, Herbert
**Director(s)** Wilcox, Herbert
**Screenwriter(s)** Englund, Ken
**Source(s)** *No No Nanette* (musical) Youmans, Vincent; Caesar, Irving; Mandel, Frank

**Cast** Neagle, Anna; Young, Roland; Broderick, Helen; Pitts, ZaSu; Arden, Eve; Gilbert, Billy; Carlson, Richard; Mature, Victor; Tamara; Robertson, Stuart; Hicks, Russell

**Song(s)** No, No, Nanette (L: Harbach, Otto); I Want to Be Happy; Tea for Two

## 4226 ✦ NO PARKING HARE
### Warner Brothers, 1954

**Musical Score** Stalling, Carl

**Director(s)** McKimson, Robert
**Screenwriter(s)** Marcus, Sid

**Cast** Bunny, Bugs

**Song(s)** Hole in the Ground (C/L: Marcus, Sid; McKimson, Robert)

**Notes** Looney Tune.

## 4227 ✦ NO PLACE LIKE ROME
### Metro–Goldwyn–Mayer, 1936

**Composer(s)** Burton, Val; Jason, Will
**Lyricist(s)** Burton, Val; Jason, Will

**Director(s)** LeBorg, Reginald
**Screenwriter(s)** Burton, Val; Jason, Will; Rauh, Stanley

**Cast** Kaaren, Suzanne; Albertson, Frank

**Song(s)** Opening Sequence; Song of Flavius; Here's a Spot to Sing a Song of Love; Tableaux

**Notes** Short subject.

## 4228 ✦ NO QUESTIONS ASKED
### Metro–Goldwyn–Mayer, 1951

**Musical Score** Stevens, Leith

**Producer(s)** Nayfack, Nicholas
**Director(s)** Kress, Harold F.
**Screenwriter(s)** Sheldon, Sidney

**Cast** Sullivan, Barry; Dahl, Arlene; Murphy, George; Hagen, Jean; Anderson, Richard; Olsen, Moroni; Dayton, Dan

**Song(s)** The Royal Order of Civic Boosters (C: Colombo, Alberto; L: Colombo, Alberto; Sheldon, Sidney)

**Notes** There is also a vocal of "I've Got You Under My Skin."

## 4229 ✦ NORA PRENTISS
### Warner Brothers, 1947

**Musical Score** Waxman, Franz
**Composer(s)** Jerome, M.K.
**Lyricist(s)** Scholl, Jack

**Producer(s)** Jacobs, William
**Director(s)** Sherman, Vincent
**Screenwriter(s)** Nash, N. Richard
**Source(s)** "The Man Who Died Twice" (story) Webster, Paul; Sobell, Jack

**Cast** Sheridan, Ann; Smith, Kent; Bennett, Bruce; Alda, Robert; De Camp, Rosemary; Arthur, Robert; Hendrix, Wanda

**Song(s)** Prologue (C/L: Jerome, M.K.; Scholl, Jack; Cherkose, Eddie); Would You Like a Souvenir (C/L: Jerome, M.K.; Scholl, Jack; Cherkose, Eddie); Who Cares What People Say

## 4230 ✦ "NORMAN . . . IS THAT YOU?"
### Metro–Goldwyn–Mayer, 1976

**Lyricist(s)** Miller, Ron

**Producer(s)** Schlatter, George
**Director(s)** Schlatter, George

**Screenwriter(s)** Schlatter, George; Clark, Ron; Bobrick, Sam
**Source(s)** *Norman . . . Is That You?* (play) Clark, Ron; Bobrick, Sam

**Cast** Foxx, Redd; Bailey, Pearl; Warren, Michael; Dobson, Tamara; Dugan, Dennis

**Song(s)** An Old Fashioned Man (C: Goldstein, William); Milly's on the Methadone Blues (C/L: Barer, Marshall); For Once in My Life (C/L: Murden, Orlando); Touch Me in the Morning (C: Masser, Michael); One Out of Every Six (C: Goldstein, William; L: Miller, Ron; Schlatter, George)

**Notes** Only original songs listed.

## 4231 ✦ NORMAN NORMAL
### Warner Brothers, 1968

**Musical Score** Lava, William

**Director(s)** Lovy, Alex

**Cast** Normal, Norman

**Song(s)** Norman Normal (C/L: Stookey, Paul)

**Notes** Animated short.

## 4232 ✦ NORMA RAE
### Twentieth Century–Fox, 1979

**Musical Score** Shire, David

**Producer(s)** Assayev, Tamara; Rose, Alex
**Director(s)** Ritt, Martin
**Screenwriter(s)** Ravetch, Irving; Frank Jr., Harriet

**Cast** Field, Sally; Bridges, Beau; Leibman, Ron; Hingle, Pat; Baxley, Barbara; Strickland, Gail

**Song(s)** It Goes Like It Goes (C: Shire, David; L: Gimbel, Norman); It's All Wrong but It's All Right (C/L: Parton, Dolly); Cindy I Love You (C/L: Cash, Johnny)

**Notes** It is not known if the Parton and Cash songs were written for the picture.

## 4233 ✦ NO ROOM AT THE INN
### Republic, 1948

**Producer(s)** Foxwell, Ivan
**Director(s)** Birt, Dan
**Screenwriter(s)** Foxwell, Ivan; Thomas, Dylan
**Source(s)** *No Room at the Inn* (play) Temple, Joan

**Cast** Jackson, Freda; Shelton, Joy; Baddeley, Hermione; Dowling, Joan; Bryan, Dora

**Song(s)** Run Rabbit Run (C: Gay, Noel; L: Gay, Noel; Butler, Ralph)

**Notes** A British National film.

## 4234 ✦ THE NORTH AVENUE IRREGULARS
Disney, 1978

**Musical Score**   Brunner, Robert F.; Bowden, Richard
**Composer(s)**   Kasha, Al; Hirschhorn, Joel
**Lyricist(s)**   Kasha, Al; Hirschhorn, Joel

**Producer(s)**   Miller, Ron
**Director(s)**   Bilson, Bruce
**Screenwriter(s)**   Tait, Don
**Source(s)**   (book) Hill, The Rev. Albert Fay

**Cast**   Herrmann, Edward; Harris, Barbara; Clark, Susan; Valentine, Karen; Constantine, Michael; Leachman, Cloris; Kelly, Patsy; Fowley, Douglas; Capers, Virginia; Hale, Alan

**Song(s)**   Mississippi Magic; Pass a Little Love Around; Been Nice to Know You, Reverend Hill [1]

**Notes**   [1] Not used.

## 4235 ✦ NOR THE MOON BY NIGHT

See ELEPHANT GUN.

## 4236 ✦ NORTHERN LIGHTS
New Front, 1979

**Musical Score**   Ahlers, David Ozzie
**Composer(s)**   Ahlers, David Ozzie
**Lyricist(s)**   Ahlers, David Ozzie

**Producer(s)**   Hanson, John; Nilsson, Rob
**Director(s)**   Nilsson, Rob; Hanson, John
**Screenwriter(s)**   Nilsson, Rob; Hanson, John

**Cast**   Behling, Bob; Lynch, Susan; Spano, Joe; Astrom-De Fina, Marianne

**Song(s)**   Northern Lights (C/L: Nilsson, Rob); Romance Theme; Elation; Dance in the Fields; Monster Game; Frustration; Henry's Theme; Driving Theme; Lullaby

**Notes**   No cue sheet available.

## 4237 ✦ NORTH FROM THE LONE STAR
Columbia, 1941

**Composer(s)**   Drake, Milton
**Lyricist(s)**   Drake, Milton

**Producer(s)**   Barsha, Leon
**Director(s)**   Hillyer, Lambert
**Screenwriter(s)**   Royal, Charles Francis

**Cast**   Elliott, Bill; Fiske, Richard; Fay, Dorothy; Taylor, Dub; Loft, Arthur; Roper, Jack; Morrison, Chuck; Rochelle, Claire

**Song(s)**   Of Course It's Your Horse; Saturday Night in San Antone

## 4238 ✦ NORTH OF THE GREAT DIVIDE
Republic, 1950

**Composer(s)**   Elliott, Jack
**Lyricist(s)**   Elliott, Jack

**Producer(s)**   White, Edward J.
**Director(s)**   Witney, William
**Screenwriter(s)**   Taylor, Eric

**Cast**   Rogers, Roy; Trigger; Edwards, Penny; Jones, Gordon; Barcroft, Roy; Lambert, Jack; Foy Willing and the Riders of the Purple Sage

**Song(s)**   Just Keep a Movin' [1]; By the Laughing Spring; North of the Great Divide

**Notes**   [1] Spanish lyrics by Aaron Gonzalez.

## 4239 ✦ NORTH SHORE
Universal, 1987

**Musical Score**   Stone, Richard

**Producer(s)**   Finnegan, William
**Director(s)**   Phelps, William
**Screenwriter(s)**   McCanlies, Tim; Phelps, William

**Cast**   Adler, Matt; Harrison, Gregory; Peeples, Nia; Philbin, John; Lopez, Gerry

**Song(s)**   Living in a Dream (C/L: Chanham, Brian); Be My Lover (C/L: Ballard, Glen; Magness, Clif); Sounds of Then (C/L: Callaghan, Mark); Blue Hotel (C/L: Isaak, Chris); M-Style (C/L: Bator, Stiv; James, Brian; Tregunna, Dave); Party Next Door (C/L: Rose, Michael); Body and the Beat (C/L: Taylor, Robert; Hunter, Mark); Shine (C/L: Dorman, Greg; Woodhead, Greg; Carne, Scott; Harnath, Craig; Curnow, Bruce); He Manao He Aloha (Ipo Lei Manu) (C/L: Kalapana, John); Am I the One (C/L: Wright, Gary; Ferris, Steve); Pearly Shells (C/L: Kalapana, John; Pober, Leon); Papalina Lahilahi (C/L: Noble, Johnny; Johnson, Alice); Feel the Spirit (C/L: Matthews, Winston; McDonald, Lloyd); Chessboards (C/L: Killing Joke); Nature of the Beast (C/L: Neeson, Doc; Paris, Jeff); Listening (C/L: Canham, Brian; Lugton, Tony); Stonewall (C/L: Brewster, Rick; Eccles, Brent; Brewster, John); Happy to Give (C/L: Perry, Steve; Cain, Johnathan); Funkytown (C/L: Greenberg, Steven); North Shore Roar (C/L: Delph, Paul; Parnell, Rebecca; Parnell, Rick)

**Notes**   It is not known if all these songs were written for this film.

## 4240 ✦ THE NORTH STAR
RKO, 1943

**Musical Score**   Copland, Aaron
**Composer(s)**   Copland, Aaron
**Lyricist(s)**   Gershwin, Ira

**Producer(s)**   Goldwyn, Samuel
**Director(s)**   Milestone, Lewis
**Screenwriter(s)**   Hellman, Lillian

**Cast**   Baxter, Anne; Andrews, Dana; Huston, Walter; Brennan, Walter; Harding, Ann; Withers, Jane; Granger, Farley; von Stroheim, Erich; Jagger, Dean

**Song(s)**   The Younger Generation; No Village Like Mine [1]; Song of the Guerrillas; Can I Help It?; Loading Song (From the Baltic to the Atlantic); Loading Time at Last Is Over; Wagon Song; Workers of All Nations [2]

**Notes**   Later released as ARMORED ATTACK. [1] Based on "All Thru Out the Universe I Wandered." [2] Not used.

### 4241 ✦ NORTH TO ALASKA
Twentieth Century–Fox, 1960

**Producer(s)**   Hathaway, Henry
**Director(s)**   Hathaway, Henry
**Screenwriter(s)**   Mahin, John Lee; Rackin, Martin; Binyon, Claude
**Source(s)**   *Birthday Gift* (play) Fodor, Laszlo

**Cast**   Wayne, John; Granger, Stewart; Kovacs, Ernie; Fabian; Capucine; Shaughnessy, Mickey; Swenson, Karl; Sawyer, Joe; Freeman, Kathleen; Adams, Stanley

**Song(s)**   North to Alaska (C/L: Phillips, Mike); If You Knew (C: Faith, Russell; L: Marcucci, Robert; DeAngelis, Peter)

**Notes**   There is also a vocal of "I Love You, I Love You, I Love You, Sweetheart" by Art Fitch, Kay Fitch and Bert Lowe.

### 4242 ✦ NORTHWEST MOUNTED POLICE
Paramount, 1940

**Musical Score**   Young, Victor

**Producer(s)**   De Mille, Cecil B.
**Director(s)**   De Mille, Cecil B.
**Screenwriter(s)**   LeMay, Alan; Lasky Jr., Jesse; Sullivan, C. Gardner

**Cast**   Cooper, Gary; Carroll, Madeleine; Goddard, Paulette; Foster, Preston; Preston, Robert; Bancroft, George; Overman, Lynne; Tamiroff, Akim; Hampden, Walter; Chaney Jr., Lon; Love, Montagu; McDonald, Francis

**Song(s)**   Does the Moon Shine Through the Tall Pine? [1] (C: Young, Victor; L: Loesser, Frank)

**Notes**   [1] Not used in picture. Lyric may have been added for exploitation.

### 4243 ✦ NORTHWEST OUTPOST
Republic, 1947

**Composer(s)**   Friml, Rudolf
**Lyricist(s)**   Heyman, Edward

**Producer(s)**   Dwan, Allan
**Director(s)**   Dwan, Allan
**Screenwriter(s)**   Meehan, Elizabeth; Sale, Richard

**Cast**   Eddy, Nelson; Massey, Ilona; Schildkraut, Joseph; Lanchester, Elsa; Haas, Hugo; Ulric, Lenore; Shayne, Tamara; Vallin, Rick

**Song(s)**   Weary; Tell Me with Your Eyes; One More Mile to Go; Raindrops on a Drum; Nearer and Dearer; Love Is the Time

### 4244 ✦ NORTHWEST RANGERS
Metro–Goldwyn–Mayer, 1942

**Producer(s)**   Marx, Samuel
**Director(s)**   Newman, Joseph
**Screenwriter(s)**   Lang, David; Kahn, Gordon

**Cast**   Craig, James; Lundigan, William; Holt, Jack; Dane, Patricia; Carradine, John; Wynn, Keenan; Withers, Grant; Hickman, Darryl

**Song(s)**   That Good for Nothin' Man of Mine (C: Brent, Earl; L: Freed, Ralph)

**Notes**   A remake of MANHATTAN MELODRAMA.

### 4245 ✦ NORWOOD
Paramount, 1970

**Musical Score**   De Lory, Al
**Composer(s)**   Davis, Mac
**Lyricist(s)**   Davis, Mac

**Producer(s)**   Wallis, Hal B.
**Director(s)**   Haley Jr., Jack
**Screenwriter(s)**   Roberts, Marguerite
**Source(s)**   (novel) Portis, Charles

**Cast**   Campbell, Glen; Darby, Kim; Namath, Joe; Lynley, Carol; Hingle, Pat; Sterling, Tisha; DeLuise, Dom; MacRae, Meredith; Haley, Jack; Lamb, Gil; Daley, Cass; Oakie, Joe; Capers, Virginia

**Song(s)**   Ol' Norwood's Comin' Home (C/L: Torok, Mitchell; Redd, Ramona); Anywhere (C/L: De Lory, Al); Norwood (Me and My Guitar); The Repo Man; Marie (C/L: Torok, Mitchell; Redd, Ramona); I'll Paint You a Song; Down Home; Settlin' Down (C/L: Torok, Mitchell; Redd, Ramona); Everything a Man Could Ever Need

### 4246 ✦ NO SAD SONGS FOR ME
Columbia, 1950

**Musical Score**   Duning, George

**Producer(s)**   Adler, Buddy
**Director(s)**   Mate, Rudolph
**Screenwriter(s)**   Koch, Howard W.

**Source(s)** "No Sad Songs for Me" (story) Southard, Ruth

**Cast** Corey, Wendell; Sullavan, Margaret; Lindfors, Viveca; McIntire, John; Wood, Natalie; Nolan, Jeanette; Leonardos, Urylee; Quine, Richard; Doran, Ann

**Song(s)** No Sad Songs for Me [1] (C/L: Fisher, Doris; Roberts, Allan)

**Notes** [1] Not in picture. Written for exploitation only.

## 4247 ✦ NO SMALL AFFAIR
### Columbia, 1984

**Musical Score** Holmes, Rupert
**Composer(s)** Holmes, Rupert
**Lyricist(s)** Holmes, Rupert

**Producer(s)** Sackheim, William
**Director(s)** Schatzberg, Jerry
**Screenwriter(s)** Bolt, Charles; Mulcahy, Terence

**Cast** Cryer, Jon; Moore, Demi; Wendt, George; Frechette, Peter; Daily, Elizabeth; Wedgeworth, Ann; Tambor, Jeffrey; Robbins, Tim; Camp, Hamilton; Getlin, Scott; Tilly, Jennifer

**Song(s)** Only One Thing (C/L: Delph, Paul); Hot Headed; Double Barrels; Itchin' for a Fight; No Small Affair; Love Makes You Blind (C/L: Marchello, Peppi); Otherwise Fine

## 4248 ✦ NOT AS A STRANGER
### United Artists, 1955

**Musical Score** Antheil, George

**Producer(s)** Kramer, Stanley
**Director(s)** Kramer, Stanley
**Screenwriter(s)** Anhalt, Edna; Anhalt, Edward
**Source(s)** *Not As a Stranger* (novel) Thompson, Morton

**Cast** Mitchum, Robert; de Havilland, Olivia; Bickford, Charles; Grahame, Gloria; Sinatra, Frank; Crawford, Broderick; McCormick, Myron; Chaney Jr., Lon; White, Jesse; Morgan, Harry; Marvin, Lee; Christine, Virginia; Bissell, Whit; Clarke, Mae

**Song(s)** Not As a Stranger [1] (C: Van Heusen, James; L: Kaye, Buddy)

**Notes** [1] Used instrumentally only.

## 4249 ✦ NOT DAMAGED
### Fox, 1930

**Composer(s)** Monaco, James V.
**Lyricist(s)** Friend, Cliff
**Choreographer(s)** Dare, Danny

**Director(s)** Sprague, Chandler; Burke, Melville
**Screenwriter(s)** Atteridge, Harold
**Source(s)** "The Solid Gold Article" (story) Connell, Richard

**Cast** Moran, Lois; Byron, Walter; Ames, Robert; Courtney, Inez

**Song(s)** Nothing's Going to Hold Us Down; Whisper You Love Me; Business Is Business with Me [1]

**Notes** Copyright registrations for both these songs list them as having been written for a Fox film called THE SOLID GOLD ARTICLE but a reference to that title could not be found. [1] Not used.

## 4250 ✦ NOT FOR PUBLICATON
### Goldwyn, 1984

**Musical Score** Meyer, John

**Producer(s)** Kimmel, Anne
**Director(s)** Bartel, Paul
**Screenwriter(s)** Bartel, Paul; Meyer, John

**Cast** Allen, Nancy; Naughton, David; Luckinbill, Laurence; Ghostley, Alice

**Song(s)** You Bring Out the Beast in Me (C/L: Meyer, John)

**Notes** No cue sheet available.

## 4251 ✦ NOTHING BUT THE BEST
### Columbia, 1964

**Musical Score** Grainer, Ron

**Producer(s)** Deutsch, David
**Director(s)** Donner, Clive
**Screenwriter(s)** Raphael, Frederic
**Source(s)** "The Best of Everything" (story) Ellin, Stanley

**Cast** Bates, Alan; Andrews, Harry; Elliott, Denholm; Martin, Millicent

**Song(s)** Nothing But the Best (C: Grainer, Ron; L: Raphael, Frederic)

## 4252 ✦ NOTHING BUT THE TRUTH
### Paramount, 1929

**Director(s)** Schertzinger, Victor; Collier Sr., William
**Screenwriter(s)** McGowan, Jack
**Source(s)** *Nothing But the Truth* (play) Montgomery, James H.

**Cast** Dix, Richard; Gibson, Wynne; Churchill, Berton; Sparks, Ned; Kane, Helen; Bartels, Louis John; Hall, Dorothy

**Song(s)** Do Something [1] (C/L: Stept, Sam H.; Green, Bud)

**Notes** [1] Also in THE BIG POND.

## 4253 ✦ NOTHING IN COMMON
### Tri-Star, 1986

**Musical Score** Leonard, Patrick

**Producer(s)** Rose, Alexandra
**Director(s)** Marshall, Garry
**Screenwriter(s)** Podell, Rick; Preminger, Michael

**Cast** Hanks, Tom; Gleason, Jackie; Saint, Eva Marie; Elizondo, Hector; Corbin, Barry; Armstrong, Bess; Ward, Sela

**Song(s)** Loving Strangers (C/L: Leonard, Patrick; Cross, Christopher; Bettis, John); Nothing in Common (C/L: Bialey, Tom; Currie, Alannah)

**Notes** No cue sheet available.

## 4254 ✦ NOTHING PERSONAL
### American International, 1980

**Producer(s)** Perlmutter, David M.
**Director(s)** Bloomfield, George
**Screenwriter(s)** Kaufman, Robert

**Cast** Sutherland, Donald; Somers, Suzanne; Dane, Lawrence; Browne, Roscoe Lee; Coleman, Dabney; Steinberg, David; O'Hara, Catherine

**Song(s)** Nothing Personal (C/L: Mann, Peter)

**Notes** No cue sheet available.

## 4255 ✦ NO TIME FOR TEARS

See PURPLE HEART DIARY.

## 4256 ✦ NOT WITH MY WIFE, YOU DON'T
### Warner Brothers, 1967

**Musical Score** Williams, John
**Composer(s)** Williams, John
**Lyricist(s)** Mercer, Johnny

**Producer(s)** Panama, Norman
**Director(s)** Panama, Norman
**Screenwriter(s)** Panama, Norman; Gelbart, Larry; Barnes, Peter
**Source(s)** "The Big Brass" (story) Panama, Norman; Frank, Melvin

**Cast** Curtis, Tony; Lisi, Virna; Scott, George C.; O'Connor, Carroll; Eastham, Richard; Ryder, Eddie; Tyne, George

**Song(s)** A Big Beautiful Ball; My Inamorata; Not with My Wife, You Don't

**Notes** All background vocals.

## 4257 ✦ NO WAY OUT
### Orion, 1987

**Musical Score** Jarre, Maurice

**Producer(s)** Ziskin, Laura; Garland, Robert
**Director(s)** Donaldson, Roger
**Screenwriter(s)** Garland, Robert
**Source(s)** *The Big Clock* (novel) Fearing, Kenneth

**Cast** Costner, Kevin; Hackman, Gene; Young, Sean; Patton, Will; Duff, Howard; Dzundza, George; Bernard, Jason

**Song(s)** No Way Out (C/L: Anka, Paul; McDonald, Michael); Say It (C/L: Anka, Paul; Marx, Richard)

**Notes** No cue sheet available.

## 4258 ✦ NO WAY TO TREAT A LADY
### Paramount, 1968

**Producer(s)** Siegel, Sol C.
**Director(s)** Smight, Jack
**Screenwriter(s)** Gay, John
**Source(s)** *No Way to Treat a Lady* (novel) Goldman, William

**Cast** Steiger, Rod; Segal, George; Remick, Lee; Heckart, Eileen; Dunn, Michael; Hamilton, Murray; Baxley, Barbara; White, Ruth

**Song(s)** A Quiet Place (C: Myers, Stanley; L: Belling, Andrew)

## 4259 ✦ NOW HARE THIS
### Warner Brothers, 1958

**Musical Score** Franklyn, Milton J.

**Director(s)** McKimson, Robert

**Cast** Bunny, Bugs

**Song(s)** Carrot Song (C: Franklyn, Milton J.; L: Maltese, Michael)

**Notes** Looney Tune.

## 4260 ✦ NOW I'LL TELL
### Fox, 1934

**Composer(s)** Akst, Harry
**Lyricist(s)** Brown, Lew

**Producer(s)** Sheehan, Winfield
**Director(s)** Burke, Edwin
**Screenwriter(s)** Burke, Edwin
**Source(s)** (novel) Rothstein, Mrs. Arnold

**Cast**  Tracy, Spencer; Twelvetrees, Helen; Faye, Alice; Temple, Shirley

**Song(s)**  Foolin' with the Other Woman's Man; Harlem vs. Jungle [1]

**Notes**  Titled WHILE NEW YORK SLEEPS in Great Britain. [1] Used instrumentally only.

## 4261 ✦ NOW, VOYAGER
### Warner Brothers, 1942

**Musical Score**  Steiner, Max

**Producer(s)**  Wallis, Hal B.
**Director(s)**  Rapper, Irving
**Screenwriter(s)**  Robinson, Casey
**Source(s)**  *Now, Voyager* (novel) Prouty, Olive Higgens

**Cast**  Davis, Bette; Henreid, Paul; Rains, Claude; Cooper, Gladys; Granville, Bonita; Loder, John; Chase, Ilka; Patrick, Ilka; Rennie, James; Drake, Charles; Wickes, Mary; Pangborn, Franklin

**Song(s)**  It Can't Be Wrong (C: Steiner, Max; L: Gannon, Kim)

**Notes**  No cue sheet available.

## 4262 ✦ THE NUDE BOMB
### Universal, 1980

**Musical Score**  Schifrin, Lalo

**Producer(s)**  Lang, Jennings
**Director(s)**  Donner, Clive
**Screenwriter(s)**  Sultan, Arne; Dana, Bill; Stern, Leonard
**Source(s)**  "Get Smart" (TV series) Brooks, Mel; Henry, Buck

**Cast**  Adams, Don [1]; Platt, Edward [1]; Feldon, Barbara [1]; Kristel, Sylvia; Fleming, Rhonda; Elcar, Dana; Dana, Bill

**Song(s)**  You're Always There When I Need You (C: Schifrin, Lalo; L: Black, Don)

**Notes**  [1] From TV series cast.

## 4263 ✦ NUDE ODYSSEY
### Davis–Royal, 1962

**Musical Score**  Lavagnino, Angelo Francesco
**Composer(s)**  Roche, Yves
**Lyricist(s)**  Roche, Yves

**Producer(s)**  Colonna, Golfiero; Ercoli, Luciano; Pugliese, Alberto
**Director(s)**  Rossi, Franco
**Screenwriter(s)**  De Concini, Ennio; Rossi, Franco; Alessi, Ottavio

**Cast**  Salerno, Enrico Maria; Venantini, Venantino; Donlon, Patricia Dolores; Logue, Elisabeth

**Song(s)**  Bon Voyage (C/L: Small, Danny); Roi Mata; The Legend of Hinano

**Notes**  No cue sheet available.

## 4264 ✦ NUMBER ONE WITH A BULLET
### Cannon, 1987

**Musical Score**  Clauson, Alf

**Producer(s)**  Golan, Menahem; Globus, Yoram
**Director(s)**  Smight, Jack
**Screenwriter(s)**  Hickman, Gail Morgan; Kurtzman, Andrew; Riley, Rob; Belushi, James

**Cast**  Carradine, Robert; Williams, Billy Dee; Bertinelli, Valerie; Graves, Peter; Roberts, Doris

**Song(s)**  Canyon Blues (C/L: Bram, Martin)

**Notes**  No cue sheet available.

## 4265 ✦ NUNZIO
### Universal, 1978

**Musical Score**  Schifrin, Lalo

**Producer(s)**  Lang, Jennings
**Director(s)**  Williams, Pauli
**Screenwriter(s)**  Andronica, James

**Cast**  Proval, David; Andronica, James; King, Morgana; Spinell, Joe; Feldshuh, Tovah; Smith-Caffey, Maria

**Song(s)**  Goodnight, My Little One (C/L: Andronica, Vincent)

**Notes**  No cue sheet available.

## 4266 ✦ NURSE FROM BROOKLYN
### Universal, 1938

**Producer(s)**  Grainger, Edmund
**Director(s)**  Simon, S. Sylvan
**Screenwriter(s)**  Chanslor, Roy

**Cast**  Eilers, Sally; Kelly, Paul; Murphy, Maurice; Blake, Larry; Conway, Morgan; Gleason, Lucille

**Song(s)**  Once You're in Love [1] (C: McHugh, Jimmy; L: Adamson, Harold)

**Notes**  [1] Also in BEHIND THE MIKE.

## 4267 ✦ NUTS
### Warner Brothers, 1988

**Musical Score**  Streisand, Barbra

**Producer(s)**  Streisand, Barbra
**Director(s)**  Ritt, Martin
**Screenwriter(s)**  Topor, Tom; Ponicsan, Darryl; Sargent, Alvin
**Source(s)**  *Nuts* (play) Topor, Tom

**Cast** Streisand, Barbra; Dreyfuss, Richard; Stapleton, Maureen; Malden, Karl; Wallach, Eli; Webber, Robert; Whitmore, James; Nielsen, Leslie

**Song(s)** Here We Are At Last (C/L: Streisand, Barbra; Baskin, Richard)

### 4268 ✦ THE NUTTY PROFESSOR
Paramount, 1963

**Producer(s)** Lewis, Jerry; Glucksman, Ernest D.
**Director(s)** Lewis, Jerry
**Screenwriter(s)** Lewis, Jerry; Richmond, Bill

**Cast** Lewis, Jerry; Stevens, Stella; Moore, Del; Freeman, Kathleen; Morris, Howard

**Song(s)** We've Got a World that Swings (C/L: Mattis, Lil; Brown, Louis Yule); Love, Love, Love (C/L: Scharf, Walter)

### 4269 ✦ NYMPH ERRANT
Twentieth Century–Fox, 1935 unproduced

**Composer(s)** Porter, Cole
**Lyricist(s)** Porter, Cole

**Producer(s)** DeSylva, B.G.
**Source(s)** *Nymph Errant* (musical) Porter, Cole

**Notes** Lew Pollack and Paul Francis Webster wrote four songs for this unproduced film.

# O

## 4270 ✦ OASIS
Twentieth Century–Fox, 1955

**Musical Score**  Misraki, Paul

**Producer(s)**  Waldleitner, Luggi; Oswald, Gerd
**Director(s)**  Allegret, Yves
**Screenwriter(s)**  Barzman, Ben

**Cast**  Morgan, Michele; Brasseur, Pierre

**Song(s)**  Soir Espangnol (C/L: Misraki, Paul); Ma Gal Lia (C/L: Attoun, Maurice; Bouchaid, Hocine)

## 4271 ✦ O.C. AND STIGGS
Metro–Goldwyn–Mayer, 1987

**Composer(s)**  Ade, King Sunny
**Lyricist(s)**  Ade, King Sunny

**Producer(s)**  Altman, Robert; Newman, Peter
**Director(s)**  Altman, Robert
**Screenwriter(s)**  Cantrell, Donald; Mann, Ted

**Cast**  Jenkins, Daniel H.; Barry, Neill; Curtin, Jane; Dooley, Paul; Cryer, Jon; Urstein, Laura; Ho, Victor; Hopper, Dennis; Nye, Louis; Mull, Martin

**Song(s)**  Schwab Insurance (C/L: Nicholls, Allan); Mo Ti Mo; Ire; No Pity in the City; Penkele; O.C. and Stiggs

## 4272 ✦ OCEAN'S ELEVEN
Warner Brothers, 1960

**Musical Score**  Riddle, Nelson
**Composer(s)**  Van Heusen, James
**Lyricist(s)**  Cahn, Sammy

**Producer(s)**  Milestone, Lewis
**Director(s)**  Milestone, Lewis
**Screenwriter(s)**  Brown, Harry; Lederer, Charles

**Cast**  Sinatra, Frank; Martin, Dean; Davis Jr., Sammy; Lawford, Peter; Dickinson, Angie; Conte, Richard; Romero, Cesar; Wymore, Patrice; Bishop, Joey; Tamiroff, Akim; Silva, Henry; Chase, Ilka; Skelton, Red; Raft, George; Lester, Buddy; Henry, Hank; Fell, Norman; MacLaine, Shirley; Gibson, Hoot

**Song(s)**  Eee-O Eleven; Ain't that a Kick in the Head; A Man Could Be a Wonderful Thing (C: Carr, Leon; L:

Corday, Leo); I'm Gonna Live 'Till I Die [1] (C: Kent, Walter; L: Hoffman, Al; Curtis, Mann)

**Notes**  [1] Also in THIS COULD BE THE NIGHT (MGM). Sometimes known as "I'm Gonna Live, Live, Live Until I Die."

## 4273 ✦ OCTOPUSSY
United Artists, 1983

**Musical Score**  Barry, John

**Producer(s)**  Broccoli, Albert R.
**Director(s)**  Glen, John
**Screenwriter(s)**  Fraser, George MacDonald; Maibaum, Richard; Wilson, Michael G.
**Source(s)**  *Octopussy* (novel) Fleming, Ian

**Cast**  Moore, Roger; Adams, Maud; Jourdan, Louis; Wayborn, Kristina; Bedi, Kabir; Berkoff, Steven; Brown, Robert; Llewelyn, Desmond; Maxwell, Lois

**Song(s)**  All Time High (C: Barry, John; L: Rice, Tim)

## 4274 ✦ THE ODD COUPLE
Paramount, 1968

**Musical Score**  Hefti, Neal
**Composer(s)**  Hefti, Neal
**Lyricist(s)**  Cahn, Sammy

**Producer(s)**  Koch, Howard W.
**Director(s)**  Saks, Gene
**Screenwriter(s)**  Simon, Neil
**Source(s)**  *The Odd Couple* (play) Simon, Neil

**Cast**  Matthau, Walter; Lemmon, Jack; Fiedler, John; Edelman, Herb; Evans, Monica; Shelley, Carole; Adrian, Iris

**Song(s)**  The Odd Couple [1]; Tomatoes [2]

**Notes**  [1] Lyrics for exploitation only. [2] Not used.

## 4275 ✦ ODE TO BILLY JOE
Warner Brothers, 1976

**Composer(s)**  Legrand, Michel
**Lyricist(s)**  Bergman, Marilyn; Bergman, Alan

**Producer(s)**  Baer, Max; Camras, Roger
**Director(s)**  Baer, Max

**Screenwriter(s)** Raucher, Herman
**Source(s)** "Ode to Billy Joe" (song) Gentry, Bobbie

**Cast** Benson, Robby; O'Connor, Glynnis; Hotchkis, Joan; McPeak, Sandy; Best, James; Goodman, Terence

**Song(s)** Ode to Billy Joe (C/L: Gentry, Bobbie); Memphis Thelma (C/L: Parks, Sherrill; Evans, John; Dickenson, Jim); By the Pond Again [1]; With Benjamin [1]; There'll Be Time

**Notes** [1] Presented as background instrumentals. The title tune was not written for the picture, and is presented as a background vocal only. It is not known if "Memphis Thelma" was written for the picture.

### 4276 ◆ ODE TO VICTORY
Metro–Goldwyn–Mayer, 1943

**Musical Score** Shilkret, Nathaniel

**Director(s)** Cahn, Edward L.
**Screenwriter(s)** James, Polly

**Song(s)** Ode to Victory (C: Shilkret, Nathaniel; L: Johnston, Arthur)

**Notes** Short subject.

### 4277 ◆ THE OFFICE GIRL
RKO, 1932

**Composer(s)** Abraham, Paul
**Lyricist(s)** Carter, Desmond; Eyton, Frank

**Director(s)** Saville, Victor
**Screenwriter(s)** Stevenson, Robert

**Cast** Mueller, Renate [1]; Nares, Owen; Hulbert, Jack; Harvey, Morris

**Song(s)** Today I Feel So Happy; Just Because I Lost My Heart to You; I'll Get There in the End; I Have My Aunt Eliza

**Notes** No cue sheet available. Released in Great Britain as SUNSHINE SUSIE. A remake of DIE PRIVATSEKRETAERIN. [1] From German original.

### 4278 ◆ AN OFFICER AND A GENTLEMAN
Paramount, 1982

**Producer(s)** Elfand, Martin
**Director(s)** Hackford, Taylor
**Screenwriter(s)** Stewart, Douglas Day

**Cast** Gere, Richard; Eyestone, Gerald; Lynn, Shannon; Haar, Keith; Keith, David; Gossett, Lou [3]; Winger, Debra; Loggia, Robert; Blount, Lisa; Eilbacher, Lisa

**Song(s)** Up Where We Belong (C: Nitzsche, Jack; Sainte-Marie, Buffy; L: Jennings, Will); Treat Me Right [1] (C/L: Benatar, Pat; Lubahn, Doug); Tie a Yellow Ribbon 'Round the Old Oak Tree [1] (C/L: Levine, Irwin; L: Brown, L. Russell); Hungry for Your Love [1]

(C/L: Morrison, Van); Be Real [1] (C: Sahm, Doug); Tush [1] (C/L: Gibbons, Billy; Hill, Dusty; Beard, Frank); Tunnel of Love [1] (C/L: Knopfler, Mark)

**Notes** [1] Not written for film.

### 4279 ◆ OFF LIMITS
Paramount, 1953

**Composer(s)** Livingston, Jay; Evans, Ray
**Lyricist(s)** Livingston, Jay; Evans, Ray

**Producer(s)** Tugend, Harry
**Director(s)** Marshall, George
**Screenwriter(s)** Kanter, Hal; Sher, Jack

**Cast** Hope, Bob; Rooney, Mickey; Maxwell, Marilyn; Mayehoff, Eddie; Dempsey, Jack

**Song(s)** The Military Policeman; Right or Wrong [1]; All About Love

**Notes** Released as MILITARY POLICEMEN outside the U.S. [1] Used instrumentally only.

### 4280 ◆ OFF THE BEATEN TRACK

See BEHIND THE EIGHT BALL.

### 4281 ◆ OFF TO THE RACES
Twentieth Century–Fox, 1937

**Producer(s)** Golden, Max H.
**Director(s)** Strayer, Frank R.
**Screenwriter(s)** Ellis, Robert; Logan, Helen

**Cast** Summerville, Slim; Prouty, Jed; Deane, Shirley; Byington, Spring; Gleason, Russell; Chandler, Chick

**Song(s)** Meet the Family [1] (C/L: Bernard, Felix)

**Notes** This is one of the Jones Family series. [1] Not written for this production.

### 4282 ◆ OF LOVE AND DESIRE
Twentieth Century–Fox, 1963

**Musical Score** Stein, Ronald

**Producer(s)** Stoloff, Victor
**Director(s)** Rush, Richard
**Screenwriter(s)** Gorog, Laszlo; Rush, Richard

**Cast** Oberon, Merle; Cochran, Steve; Jurgens, Curt; Agar, John; Brodie, Steve; Noriega, Eduardo

**Song(s)** Katharine's Theme (C/L: Stein, Ronald)

**Notes** Originally titled THE FORESAKEN GARDEN.

### 4283 ◆ OF MEN AND MUSIC
Twentieth Century–Fox, 1951

**Producer(s)** Polk, Rudolph; Luber, Bernard
**Director(s)** Reis, Irving; Hammid, Alex

**Screenwriter(s)** O'Brien, Liam; Kurnitz, Harry; Paxton, John; Epstein, David

**Cast** Rubinstein, Arthur; Peerce, Jan; Connor, Nadine; Heifitz, Jascha; Mitriopoulis, Dimitri; Taylor, Deems; The Philharmonic Symphony Orchestra

**Notes** No cue sheet available. There are no original songs in this film. Vocals and instrumentals include Mendelssohn's "Spinning Song;" Liszt's "Liebestraum;" "Waltz in C Sharp Minor" and "Polonaise in A Major" by Chopin; "Pop Goes the Weasel" and "O Paridos" from Meyerbeer's L'AFRICAINE; "Matinata" by Leoncavallo; an aria from DON PASQUALE by Donizetti; a duet from Donizetti's LUCIA DI LAMMERMOOR; "Partita Prelude" by Bach; "The Girl with the Flaxen Hair" by Debussy; "Scherzo Tarantelle" by Wieniewski; Paganini's "Caprice No. 24" and the third movement of Liszt's "Faust Symphony."

## 4284 ✦ OF RICE AND HEN
Warner Brothers, 1953

**Musical Score** Stalling, Carl

**Director(s)** McKimson, Robert
**Screenwriter(s)** Foster, Warren

**Cast** Leghorn, Foghorn J.; Miss Prissy

**Song(s)** Old Hound Dog (C/L: Foster, Warren)

**Notes** Looney Tune.

## 4285 ✦ OH DAD, POOR DAD, MAMMA'S HUNG YOU IN THE CLOSET AND I'M FEELIN' SO SAD
Paramount, 1967

**Musical Score** Hefti, Neal
**Composer(s)** Hefti, Neal
**Lyricist(s)** Hefti, Neal

**Producer(s)** Stark, Ray; Rubin, Stanley
**Director(s)** Quine, Richard
**Screenwriter(s)** Bernard, Ian
**Source(s)** *Oh Dad, Poor Dad, Mamma's Hung You in the Closet and I'm Feelin' So Sad* (play) Kopit, Arthur L.

**Cast** Russell, Rosalind; Morse, Robert; Harris, Barbara; Griffith, Hugh; Winters, Jonathan

**Song(s)** Like Heaven; Oh Dad, Poor Dad, Mamma's Hung You in the Closet and I'm Feelin' So Sad; One Little Girl at a Time [1] (L: David, Hal)

**Notes** [1] Lyrics for exploitation use only.

## 4286 ✦ OH, FOR A MAN!
Fox, 1930

**Composer(s)** Kernell, William
**Lyricist(s)** Kernell, William

**Director(s)** MacFadden, Hamilton
**Screenwriter(s)** Klein, Philip; Starling, Lynn
**Source(s)** "Stolen Thunder" (story) Watkins, Mary T.

**Cast** MacDonald, Jeanette; Denny, Reginald; White, Marjorie; Hymer, Warren; Lugosi, Bela; Skipworth, Alison

**Song(s)** On a Summer Night; I'm Just Nuts About You

**Notes** There are also vocals of "Liebestod" from TRISTAN AND ISOLDE by Wagner; "Believe Me If All Those Endearing Young Charms" with lyrics by Thomas Moore to a traditional German art song.

## 4287 ✦ OH GOD! BOOK II
Warner Brothers, 1980

**Musical Score** Fox, Charles

**Producer(s)** Cates, Gilbert
**Director(s)** Cates, Gilbert
**Screenwriter(s)** Greenfeld, Josh; Goldman, Hal; Fox, Fred S.; Jacobs, Seaman; Miller, Melissa

**Cast** Burns, George; Pleshette, Suzanne; Birney, David; Louanne; Louis, John; Janis, Conrad; Holland, Anthony; Downs, Hugh; Brothers, Dr. Joyce

**Song(s)** Doctor Are You Sure It's Morning? (C/L: Fox, Charles)

## 4288 ✦ OH GOD! YOU DEVIL
Warner Brothers, 1984

**Musical Score** Shire, David
**Composer(s)** Bettis, John; Post, Mike
**Lyricist(s)** Bettis, John; Post, Mike

**Producer(s)** Sherman, Robert M.
**Director(s)** Bogart, Paul
**Screenwriter(s)** Bergman, Andrew

**Cast** Burns, George; Wass, Ted; Hart, Roxanne; Roche, Eugene; Silver, Ron

**Song(s)** Oh God! You Devil (C/L: Shire, David); If It Was Only Up to Me; Dangerous Eyes

## 4289 ✦ OH HEAVENLY DOG
Twentieth Century–Fox, 1980

**Producer(s)** Camp, Joe
**Director(s)** Camp, Joe
**Screenwriter(s)** Browning, Rod

**Cast** Chase, Chevy; Benji; Seymour, Jane; Sharif, Omar; Morley, Robert; Sues, Alan; Music, Lorenzo

**Song(s)** Arrow Through Me (C/L: McCartney, Paul); Return to Paradise (C/L: John, Elton)

**Notes** It is not known if these were written for this film.

**4290** ✦ **OH JOHNNY, HOW YOU CAN LOVE**
Universal, 1940

**Composer(s)** Skinner, Frank
**Lyricist(s)** Smith, Paul Gerard

**Producer(s)** Goldsmith, Ken
**Director(s)** Lamont, Charles
**Screenwriter(s)** Rutt, Edwin

**Cast** Brown, Tom; Moran, Peggy; Rhodes, Betty Jane; Jenkins, Allen; Meek, Donald; Quigley, Juanita; Jewell, Isabel

**Song(s)** Swing, Chariot, Swing; Maybe I Like What You Like; Thistle Bottom's Theme Song (C/L: Schwarzwald, Milton)

**Notes** There are also vocals of "Believe Me If All Those Endearing Young Charms" by Thomas Moore; "Drink to Me Only with Thine Eyes" by Ben Jonson; "Oh! Susanna" by Stephen Foster; "The Curse of an Aching Heart" by Henry Fink and Al Piantadosi; "Home on the Range" and "Oh Johnny, Oh Johnny, Oh!" by Abe Olman and Ed Rose

**4291** ✦ **OH! SAILOR, BEHAVE!**
Warner Brothers, 1930

**Composer(s)** Burke, Joe
**Lyricist(s)** Dubin, Al

**Director(s)** Mayo, Archie
**Screenwriter(s)** Jackson, Joseph; Silvers, Sid
**Source(s)** *See Naples and Die* (play) Rice, Elmer

**Cast** Delroy, Irene; King, Charles; Loder, Lotti; Sherman, Lowell; Oakland, Vivian; Olsen, Ole; Johnson, Chic; Bartlett, Elsie; Judels, Charles

**Song(s)** When Love Comes in the Moonlight; Leave a Little Smile; Tell Us Which One Do You Love; Highway to Heaven; The Laughing Song (C/L: Olsen, Ole; Johnson, Chic); Too Bad I Can't Be Good [1]

**Notes** Originally titled NANCY FROM NAPLES. Titled OH, SAILOR BEWARE! in some sources. [1] Not used. Written for NANCY FROM NAPLES.

**4292** ✦ **OH SUSANNA! (1936)**
Republic, 1936

**Musical Score** Butts, Dale

**Producer(s)** Schaefer, Armand
**Director(s)** Kane, Joseph
**Screenwriter(s)** Drake, Oliver

**Cast** Autry, Gene; Burnette, Smiley; Grant, Frances; Hodgins, Earl; Kirke, Donald; Howard, Boothe; The Light Crust Doughboys; Young, Clara Kimball

**Song(s)** Is Someone Lonely? (C/L: Elliott, Jack); Dear Old Western Skies (C/L: Autry, Gene); By a Waterwheel (C/L: Unknown); Ti Yi Tippi I O (C/L: Unknown); Old Susanna (C/L: Unknown); Hold that Tiger (C/L: Unknown); Don't Trust a Bicycle Racer (C/L: Unknown); Ride On Vaquero [1] (C: Baer, Abel; L: Gilbert, L. Wolfe); I'll Go Ridin' Down that Old Texas Trail (C/L: Autry, Gene; Burnette, Smiley)

**Notes** No cue sheet available. [1] Also in the Fox pictures ROMANCE OF THE RIO GRANDE (1929) and (1940) and IN OLD CALIENTE.

**4293** ✦ **OH! SUSANNA (1951)**
Republic, 1951

**Producer(s)** Kane, Joseph
**Director(s)** Kane, Joseph
**Screenwriter(s)** Warren, Charles Marquis

**Cast** Cameron, Rod; Booth, Adrian; Tucker, Forrest; Wills, Chill; Ching, William; Davis, Jim; Lydon, James; Haade, William

**Song(s)** Is Someone Lonely? (C/L: Elliott, Jack)

**Notes** There are also vocals of "Oh, Susanna" by Stephen Foster and "The Regular Army, Oh" by Edward Harrigan.

**4294** ✦ **OH! WHAT A LOVELY WAR**
Paramount, 1969

**Producer(s)** Attenborough, Richard; Duffy, Brian
**Director(s)** Attenborough, Richard
**Screenwriter(s)** Deighton, Len
**Source(s)** *Oh! What a Lovely War* (musical) Littlewood, Joan; Chilton, Charles

**Cast** Richardson, Ralph; Gielgud, John; Olivier, Laurence; Mills, John; Bogarde, Dirk; Redgrave, Michael; Redgrave, Vanessa; Hawkins, Jack; Smith, Maggie; More, Kenneth; York, Susannah; Clements, John; Calvert, Phyllis; Cassel, Jean-Pierre; Daneman, Paul

**Notes** There were no original songs written for this movie. Among the early twentieth century songs used were "Oh! It's a Lovely War" by J.P. Long and Maurice Scott; "I Do Like to Be Beside the Seaside" by John Glover-Kind with a parody lyric by P. Tilley; "Belgium Put the 'Kibosh' on the Kaiser" by Alf Ellerton; "Are We Downhearted - No!" by Worton David and Lawrence Wright; "It's a Long Way to Tipperary" by Jack Judge and Harry Williams; "Your King and Country Want You" by Paul A. Rubens; "I'll Make a Man of You" by Arthur Wimperis and Herman Finck; "The Old Brigade" by F.E. Weatherly and Odoardo Barri; "Pack Up Your Troubles in Your Old Kit Bag" by George Asaf and Felix Powell; "Silent Night" by Franz Gruber; "Christmas Day in the Cookhouse" with music and new lyrics by Charles Chilton; "Good-Bye-Ee" by R.P. Weston and Bert Lee;

"Gassed Last Night" with new words and music by Charles Chilton; "Comrades" by Felix McGlennon; "Hush Here Comes a Whizbang," a parody of "Hush! Here Comes the Dream Man" by R.P. Weston, F.J. Barnes and Maurice Scott; "There's a Long, Long Trail" by Stoddard King and Zo Elliott; "Rule Britannia" by Thomas Arne; "I Don't Want to Be a Soldier," a parody of "I'll Make a Man of You" by Arthur Wimperis and Herman Finck; "Mademoiselle from Armentierres" by Harry Carlton and J.A. Tunbridge; "The Moon Shines Bright on Charlie Chaplin," a parody to the music of "Red Wing" by Kerry Mills and Thurland Chattaway; "C'est a Craonne (Adieu la Vie)," lyric sung to music of "Bonsoir M'Amour" by A. Sablon and R. Le Peltier; "They Were Only Playing Leapfrog," parody lyric to the music of "Battle Hymn of the Republic" by William Steffe and Julia Ward Howe; "Joe Soap's Army," a parody lyric of "Onward Christian Soldiers" with new lyrics and arrangements by Charles Chilton; "Fred Karno's Army," parody lyric to music of "The Church's One Foundation" by Samuel J. Stone and Samuel Wesley; "When This Lousy War Is Over," parody lyric to music of "What a Friend We Have in Jesus" by C.C. Converse and Joseph Scriven; "Wash Me in the Water," a parody lyric to the music of the traditional tune "Whiter Than the Snow;" "I Want to Go Home" by an unknown writer or writers; "The Bells of Hell," a parody lyric to the music of "Ting-A-Ling" by Harry Dacre; "Old Soldiers Never Die" by Jack Foley; "Never Mind" by Harry Dent and Tom Goldburn; "Far Far From Wipers," a parody lyric to music of "Sing Me to Sleep" by Edwin Greene and Clifton Bingham; "The Old Barbed Wire," a parody lyric to music of "Alley Alley Oh," a traditional song; "Keep the Home Fires Burning" by Ivor Novello and Lena Guilbert Ford; "Over There" by George M. Cohan and "And When They Ask Us," a parody lyric to "They Didn't Believe Me" by Jerome Kern and M.E. Rourke.

## 4295 ✦ OH YEAH!
Pathe, 1929

**Director(s)** Garnett, Tay
**Screenwriter(s)** Garnett, Tay; Gleason, James
**Source(s)** "No Brakes" (story) Somerville, Andrew W.

**Cast** Armstrong, Robert; Gleason, James; Caron, Patricia; Pitts, ZaSu; Fine, Bud; Tyler, Bud

**Song(s)** Love Found Me When I Found You [1] (C: Waggner, George; L: Green, George; Garnett, Tay)

**Notes** No cue sheet available. [1] *Variety* review does not list Garnett.

## 4296 ✦ OH YOU BEAUTIFUL DOLL
Twentieth Century–Fox, 1949

**Producer(s)** Jessel, George
**Director(s)** Stahl, John M.
**Screenwriter(s)** Lewis, Albert; Lewis, Arthur

**Cast** Haver, June [2]; Stevens, Mark [1]; Sakall, S.Z.; Greenwood, Charlotte; Robbins, Gale; Flippen, Jay C.; Tombes, Andrew

**Notes** There are no original songs in this film. The Tin Pan Alley songs that are featured vocally include: "Oh You Beautiful Doll" by Nat D. Ayer and A. Seymour Brown; "Come Josephine in My Flying Machine (Up She Goes!)," "Who Paid the Rent for Mrs. Rip Van Winkle?" and "Peg O' My Heart" by Fred Fisher and Alfred Bryan; "Down Among the Sheltering Palms" by Abe Olman and James Brockman; "I Want You to Want Me (To Want You)" by Fred Fisher, Bob Schafer and Alfred Bryan; "Dardanella" by Felix Bernard, Fred Fisher and Johnny S. Black; "Chicago" and "Daddy You've Been a Mother to Me" by Fred Fisher; "When I Get You Alone Tonight" by Fred Fisher, Joseph McCarthy and Joe Goodwin and "There's a Broken Heart for Every Light on Broadway" by Fred Fisher and Howard Johnson. [1] Dubbed by Bill Shirley. [2] Dubbed by Bonnie Lou Williams.

## 4297 ✦ OKAY AMERICA
Universal, 1932

**Musical Score** Newman, Alfred

**Director(s)** Garnett, Tay
**Screenwriter(s)** McGuire, William Anthony

**Cast** Arnold, Edward; O'Sullivan, Maureen; Lindsay, Margaret; Calhern, Louis; Dinehart, Alan; Lloyd, Rollo; O'Neil, Nance; Gateson, Marjorie

**Song(s)** Bananas (C/L: Samuels, G.; Whitcup, Leonard); If It Ain't Love (C/L: Razaf, Andy; Redman, Don; Waller, Thomas "Fats"); Get Cannibal (C/L: Nichols; Weems)

## 4298 ✦ O.K. CONNERY

See OPERATION KID BROTHER.

## 4299 ✦ OKLAHOMA!
Magna Theater Corp., 1955

**Composer(s)** Rodgers, Richard
**Lyricist(s)** Hammerstein II, Oscar
**Choreographer(s)** de Mille, Agnes

**Producer(s)** Hornblow Jr., Arthur
**Director(s)** Zinnemann, Fred
**Screenwriter(s)** Levien, Sonya; Ludwig, William
**Source(s)** *Oklahoma!* (musical) Rodgers, Richard; Hammerstein II, Oscar

**Cast** MacRae, Gordon [1]; Grahame, Gloria; Jones, Shirley [2]; Greenwood, Charlotte; Albert, Eddie; Nelson, Gene; Whitmore, James; Steiger, Rod; Flippen, Jay C.; Lawrence, Barbara; Barcroft, Roy; Platt, Marc; Mitchell, James; Lynn, Bambi

**Song(s)** Oh, What a Beautiful Mornin'; The Surry with the Fringe on Top; Kansas City; I Cain't Say No; Many a New Day; People Will Say We're in Love; Pore Jud Is Daid; Out of My Dreams; The Farmer and the Cowman; All er Nothin'; Oklahoma!

**Notes** All songs from Broadway original. [1] Danced by James Mitchell in ballet. [2] Danced by Bambi Lynn in ballet.

## 4300 ♦ OKLAHOMA ANNIE
### Republic, 1952

**Musical Score** Scott, Nathan

**Producer(s)** Picker, Sidney
**Director(s)** Springsteen, R.G.
**Screenwriter(s)** Townley, Jack

**Cast** Canova, Judy; Russell, John; Withers, Grant; Barcroft, Roy; Lynn, Emmett; Urecal, Minerva; Sessions, Almira

**Song(s)** Blow the Whistle [1] (C/L: McClintock, Harry; Sherwin, Sterling); Never Never Never (C: Burke, Sonny; L: Elliott, Jack)

**Notes** [1] Also in THRILL OF A LIFETIME (Paramount).

## 4301 ♦ OKLAHOMA CRUDE
### Columbia, 1973

**Musical Score** Mancini, Henry

**Producer(s)** Kramer, Stanley
**Director(s)** Kramer, Stanley
**Screenwriter(s)** Norman, Marc

**Cast** Scott, George C.; Dunaway, Faye; Mills, John; Palance, Jack

**Song(s)** Send a Little Love My Way (C: Mancini, Henry; L: David, Hal)

## 4302 ♦ OKLAHOMA FRONTIER
### Universal, 1939

**Producer(s)** Ray, Albert
**Director(s)** Beebe, Ford
**Screenwriter(s)** Beebe, Ford

**Cast** Brown, Johnny Mack; Knight, Fuzzy; Gwynne, Anne

**Song(s)** In Old Oklahoma (C/L: Tomlin, Pinky); Cincinnati Ohio (C/L: Knight, Fuzzy)

## 4303 ♦ OKLAHOMA RAIDERS
### Universal, 1943

**Producer(s)** Drake, Oliver
**Director(s)** Collins, Lewis D.
**Screenwriter(s)** Burridge, Betty

**Cast** Ritter, Tex; Knight, Fuzzy

**Song(s)** Out on the Open Range (C/L: Bond, Johnny); Starlight on the Prairie (C/L: Bond, Johnny)

## 4304 ♦ OKLAHOMA RENEGADES
### Republic, 1940

**Producer(s)** Grey, Harry
**Director(s)** Watt, Nate
**Screenwriter(s)** Snell, Earle; Schroeder, Doris

**Cast** Livingston, Bob; Hatton, Raymond; Renaldo, Duncan; White, Lee "Lasses"; McKinney, Florine; Dean, Eddie; Lescoulie, Jack

**Song(s)** Minstrel Overture (C/L: White, Lee "Lasses"); Way Down in Texas (C/L: White, Lee "Lasses")

## 4305 ♦ THE OLD BARN DANCE
### Republic, 1938

**Producer(s)** Siegel, Sol C.
**Director(s)** Kane, Joseph
**Screenwriter(s)** McConville, Bernard; Royal, Charles Francis

**Cast** Autry, Gene; Burnette, Smiley; Valkis, Helen; McKim, Sammy; The Colorado Hillbillies; Hatchley, Hooper

**Song(s)** You're the Only Star in My Blue Heaven [1] (C/L: Autry, Gene); The Old Mill (C/L: Marvin, Johnny); Ten Little Miles (C: Tinturin, Peter; L: Lawrence, Jack); At the Old Barn Dance (C: Tinturin, Peter; L: Lawrence, Jack); Old Nell (C/L: Marvin, Frankie); Rocky Mountain Rose (C/L: Jerome, M.K.); The Railroad Track (C/L: Shrum, Walt); Roamin' Around the Range (C/L: Burnette, Smiley); Eating Wax (C/L: Colorado Hillbillies; Wilder, Abner); Mississippi Sawyer (C/L: Colorado Hillbillies); The Tree in the Woods (C/L: Colombo, Alberto); Smiling (C/L: Burnette, Smiley)

**Notes** No cue sheet available. [1] Also in RIM OF THE CANYON (Columbia), MEXICALI ROSE and SPRINGTIME IN THE ROCKIES (1937).

## 4306 ♦ THE OLD CORRAL
### Republic, 1936

**Producer(s)** Schaefer, Armand
**Director(s)** Kane, Joseph
**Screenwriter(s)** Poland, Joseph; Lowe, Sherman

**Cast** Autry, Gene; Burnette, Smiley; Manning, Hope; Sons of the Pioneers; Champion; Chaney Jr., Lon; Keefe, Cornelius; Oscar and Elmer

**Song(s)** Old Corral (C/L: Higdon, Walter); So Long Old Pinto (C/L: Drake, Oliver); Come Along the Sleepy Rio Grande [1] (C/L: Spencer, Tim); He's Come Up the Trail (C/L: Spencer, Tim); In the Heart of the West

[2] (C/L: Autry, Gene; Miller); Money Ain't No Use Anyway (C/L: Autry, Gene); Silent Trails (C/L: Spencer, Tim); One Man Band (C/L: Burnette, Smiley)

**Notes** There is also a vocal of "With All My Heart" by J. Strauss. [1] There is a song published under this film's name titled "Down Along the Sleepy Rio Grande" by Roy Rogers. [2] Sheet music credits Gene Autry and Fleming Allen.

## 4307 ✦ THE OLD CURIOSITY SHOP

See QUILP.

## 4308 ✦ AN OLD-FASHIONED GIRL
### Eagle Lion, 1948

**Director(s)** Dreifuss, Arthur
**Screenwriter(s)** Dreifuss, Arthur
**Source(s)** "An Old-Fashioned Girl" (story) Alcott, Louisa May

**Cast** Jean, Gloria; Lydon, Jimmy; Hubbard, John; Rafferty, Frances; Ryan, Irene; Wood, Douglas; Donahue, Mary Eleanor

**Song(s)** When Life Is Good to You (C: Previn, Charles; L: Moore, McElbert); Kitchen Serenade (C/L: Worth, Bobby; Sendrey, Al; Moore, McElbert)

**Notes** There are also vocals of "God Rest Ye Merry Gentlemen;" "Wiere" by Franz Schubert and "At the Opera" from Mozart's THE MAGIC FLUTE.

## 4309 ✦ THE OLD FASHIONED WAY
### Paramount, 1934

**Composer(s)** Revel, Harry
**Lyricist(s)** Gordon, Mack

**Producer(s)** LeBaron, William
**Director(s)** Beaudine, William
**Screenwriter(s)** Bogle, Charles [1]

**Cast** Fields, W.C.; LeRoy, Baby; Allen, Judith; Morrison, Joe; Duggan, Jan; Henderson, Del; Wilson, Clarence; Carle, Richard; Harlan, Otis

**Song(s)** (We're Just Poor Folks) Rolling in Love; A Little Bit of Heaven Known As Mother; Guess Again [2]; Hail Happy Pair (C/L: Bell, Galt); Gathering Shells from the Sea Shore [3] (C/L: Thompson, Will)

**Notes** [1] Pseudonym for W.C. Fields. [2] Written for COLLEGIATE but not used. Used also in READY FOR LOVE. [3] Sheet music only.

## 4310 ✦ THE OLD HOMESTEAD
### Republic, 1942

**Producer(s)** Schaefer, Armand
**Director(s)** McDonald, Frank
**Screenwriter(s)** McGowan, Stuart; McGowan, Dorrell

**Cast** Weaver, Leon; Weaver, Frank; Weaver, June; Purcell, Dick; Prouty, Jed; Jeffreys, Anne; Nixon, Marie

**Song(s)** Bell Commercial (C: Kraushaar, Raoul; L: Meyer, Sol); Ferris Wheel (C/L: Stryker, Fred); Dig Dig Dig for Victory (C: Styne, Jule; L: Meyer, Sol)

**Notes** There is also a vocal of "In the Town Where I Was Born" by Al Harriman, Dick Howard and Billy Tracey. Although Dick Howard was the pseudonym for Howard Dietz, it is not known if this is Dietz.

## 4311 ✦ OLD LOS ANGELES
### Republic, 1948

**Producer(s)** Kane, Joseph
**Director(s)** Kane, Joseph
**Screenwriter(s)** Adams, Gerald Drayson; Ripley, Clements

**Cast** Elliott, William; Carroll, John; McLeod, Catherine; Schildkraut, Joseph; Devine, Andy; Rodriguez, Estelita; Brissac, Virginia; Renaldo, Tito; Barcroft, Roy

**Song(s)** Eres Tan Fina (C: Scott, Nathan; L: Gonzales, Aaron); On the Boulevard (Jesusita en Chihuahua) (C: Mendoza Y Cortes, Quirino F.; L: Elliott, Jack); Jarabe Tapatio (C: Traditional; L: Elliott, Jack; Gonzales, Aaron); Ever Faithful [1] (C: Traditional; L: Elliott, Jack)

**Notes** [1] Spanish lyrics by Aaron Gonzales.

## 4312 ✦ THE OLD MAN AND THE SEA
### Warner Brothers, 1958

**Musical Score** Tiomkin, Dimitri
**Composer(s)** Tiomkin, Dimitri
**Lyricist(s)** Amaral, Nestor

**Producer(s)** Hayward, Leland
**Director(s)** Sturges, John
**Screenwriter(s)** Viertel, Peter
**Source(s)** *The Old Man and the Sea* (novel) Hemingway, Ernest

**Cast** Tracy, Spencer; Pazos, Felipe; Bellaver, Harry

**Song(s)** Cancion De Pescador; I Am Your Dream [1] (L: Webster, Paul Francis); Cubana; Mar Bravio

**Notes** [1] Used as background instrumental only.

## 4313 ✦ OLD MAN RHYTHM
### RKO, 1935

**Composer(s)** Gensler, Lewis E.
**Lyricist(s)** Mercer, Johnny
**Choreographer(s)** Pan, Hermes [2]; White, Sam [3]

**Producer(s)** Myers, Zion
**Director(s)** Ludwig, Edward
**Screenwriter(s)** Herzig, Sig; Pagano, Ernest; Hanemann, H.W.

**Cast** Rogers, Charles "Buddy"; Barbier, George; Kent, Barbara; Bradley, Grace; Grable, Betty; Blore, Eric; Rhodes, Erik; Arledge, John; Mercer, Johnny; Meek, Donald; Poe, Evelyn

**Song(s)** There's Nothing Like a College Education; Boys Will Be Boys; Comes the Revolution Baby; I Never Saw a Better Night [1]; Old Man Rhythm; When You Are in My Arms [4]

**Notes** One of Johnny Mercer's few screen appearances. [1] Also in CHINA PASSAGE. [2] Dances staged by. [3] Songs staged by. [4] Sheet music only.

### 4314 ◆ THE OLD MILL POND
Metro–Goldwyn–Mayer, 1936

**Musical Score** Bradley, Scott

**Song(s)** Preacher Song (C: Bradley, Scott; L: Hanna, William); Jungle Rhythm (C/L: Hanna, William); Mistah Sippy (C/L: Keyes, Baron)

**Notes** Animated cartoon. There are also vocals of "I Heard" by Don Redman and "Kickin' the Gong Around" by Ted Koehler and Harold Arlen.

### 4315 ◆ OLD MOTHER RILEY, DETECTIVE
Republic, 1943

**Musical Score** Russell, Kennedy

**Producer(s)** Baxter, John
**Director(s)** Comfort, Lance
**Screenwriter(s)** Melford, Austin; Orme, Geoffrey; Emary, Barbara K.; Lucan, Arthur

**Cast** Lucan, Arthur; McShane, Kitty; Brandt, Ivan; Reynolds, Owen

**Song(s)** Let the Wheels Go Round (C: Russell, Kennedy; L: O'Connor, Desmond); If You Have the Sun in Your Heart (C/L: Klein, A.)

**Notes** A British National picture.

### 4316 ◆ OLD MOTHER RILEY IN BUSINESS
Republic, 1940

**Musical Score** Russell, Kennedy

**Producer(s)** Corfield, John
**Director(s)** Baxter, John
**Screenwriter(s)** Orme, Geoffrey; West, Con

**Cast** Lucan, Arthur; McShane, Kitty; Chamberlain, Cyril

**Song(s)** Alabama Jubilee [1] (C: Cobb, George L.; L: Yellen, Jack); I'll Be Waiting (C/L: Russell, Kennedy)

**Notes** Arthur Lucan played Old Mother Riley in this series. [1] Written in 1915.

### 4317 ◆ OLD MOTHER RILEY IN SOCIETY
Republic, 1940

**Musical Score** Russell, Kennedy

**Producer(s)** Corfield, John
**Director(s)** Baxter, John
**Screenwriter(s)** Melford, Austin; Emary, Barbara K.; Borer, Mary Cathcart

**Cast** Lucan, Arthur; McShane, Kitty; Stuart, John; Wyndham, Dennis

**Song(s)** No Matter Where You Are (C/L: Bernard, Peter); It's Not the Clothes that Make the Girl (C/L: Munro, Ronnie)

**Notes** A British National picture.

### 4318 ◆ OLD MOTHER RILEY JOINS UP
Republic, 1939

**Musical Score** Munro, Ronnie

**Producer(s)** Corfield, John
**Director(s)** Rogers, Maclean
**Screenwriter(s)** Butler, Kathleen; Sharman, Maisie

**Cast** Lucan, Arthur; McShane, Kitty; Seton, Bruce; Hunt, Martita

**Song(s)** Women of England (C: Munro, Ronnie; L: Sonin, Ray)

**Notes** A British National picture.

### 4319 ◆ OLD MOTHER RILEY OVERSEAS
Republic, 1943

**Musical Score** Mackey, Percival

**Producer(s)** Mitchell, Oswald
**Director(s)** Mitchell, Oswald
**Screenwriter(s)** Mear, H. Fowler; Lucan, Arthur

**Cast** Lucan, Arthur; McShane, Kitty; Marvey, Morris; Kitchen Jr., Fred; Rosarito & Paula

**Song(s)** There's No Place Like the Old Home (C/L: Warner, W.; O'Keefe, D.); Moonlight in Lisbon (C/L: O'Keefe, D.)

**Notes** A British National picture.

### 4320 ◆ OLD MOTHER RILEY'S CIRCUS
Republic, 1941

**Musical Score** Russell, Kennedy

**Producer(s)** Orton, Wallace
**Director(s)** Bentley, Thomas
**Screenwriter(s)** West, Con; Orme, Geoffrey; Emary, Barbara K.; Lucan, Arthur

**Cast** Lucan, Arthur; McShane, Kitty; Longden, John; Emerton, Roy; The Hindustans; The Balstons; The Carsons; Reading & Grant; Medlock & Marlow; Speedy;

Isabel & Emma; Barnyard, Eve & Joan; Koady, Harry; Black, Jean

**Song(s)**   A Smile, a Tear, a Sigh (C/L: McShane, Kitty); Hand in Hand (C: Russell, Kennedy; L: O'Connor, Desmond)

**Notes**   A British National picture.

## 4321 ✦ OLD OVERLAND TRAIL
### Republic, 1952

**Producer(s)**   White, Edward J.
**Director(s)**   Witney, William
**Screenwriter(s)**   Raison, Milton

**Cast**   Allen, Rex; Koko; Pickens, Slim; Barcroft, Roy; Hall, Virginia; Nimoy, Leonard; The Republic Rhythm Riders

**Song(s)**   Cowboy's Dream of Heaven [1] (C/L: Elliott, Jack); Work for the Night Is Coming (C/L: Mason, L.; Coghill, A.; Rice, Darol)

**Notes**   [1] Also in BELLS OF SAN ANGELO.

## 4322 ✦ THE OLD PLANTATION
### Metro–Goldwyn–Mayer, 1935

**Musical Score**   Bradley, Scott

**Song(s)**   Pickin' Cotton (C: Bradley, Scott; L: Hanna, William)

**Notes**   Animated cartoon. There were also some Stephen Foster songs on the soundtrack.

## 4323 ✦ THE OLD SOAK

See THE GOOD OLD SOAK.

## 4324 ✦ THE OLD TEXAS TRAIL
### Universal, 1944

**Producer(s)**   Drake, Oliver
**Director(s)**   Collins, Lewis D.
**Screenwriter(s)**   Lively, William

**Cast**   Cameron, Rod; Dew, Eddie; Knight, Fuzzy

**Song(s)**   Ridin' Down that Old Texas Trail (C/L: Allan, Fleming); Little Joe, the Wrangler [1] (C: Hollander, Frederick; L: Loesser, Frank); Trail Dust (C/L: Nale, W.S.; deSavis, Ferdinand; Scrogin, Morris)

**Notes**   [1] Also in DESTRY RIDES AGAIN (1939), LITTLE JOE, THE WRANGLER and MAN FROM MONTANA.

## 4325 ✦ THE OLD WEST
### Columbia, 1951

**Director(s)**   Archainbaud, George
**Screenwriter(s)**   Geraghty, Gerald

**Cast**   Autry, Gene; Champion; Jones, Dick; Davis, Gail; Buttram, Pat; Talbot, Lyle

**Song(s)**   Somebody Bigger Than You and I (C/L: Lange, Johnny; Heath, Hy; Burke, Sonny); Music By the Angels (C/L: Altman, Arthur; Symes, Marty)

## 4326 ✦ OLD YELLER
### Disney, 1957

**Musical Score**   Wallace, Oliver

**Director(s)**   Stevenson, Robert
**Screenwriter(s)**   Gipson, Fred; Tunberg, William
**Source(s)**   *Old Yeller* (novel) Gipson, Fred

**Cast**   McGuire, Dorothy; Parker, Fess; Kirk, Tommy; Corcoran, Kevin; York, Jeff; Washburn, Beverly; Connors, Chuck

**Song(s)**   Old Yeller (C: Wallace, Oliver; L: George, Gil)

## 4327 ✦ OLE REX
### Universal, 1961

**Musical Score**   Bagley, Donald; Hinshaw, William

**Producer(s)**   Hinkle, Robert
**Director(s)**   Hinkle, Robert
**Screenwriter(s)**   Hinkle, Robert

**Cast**   Rex; Hughes, Billy; Foster, William; Hinkle, Robert; Hughes, Whitey

**Song(s)**   Ole Rex (C/L: Sargent, Don)

**Notes**   No cue sheet available.

## 4328 ✦ OLIVER!
### Columbia, 1968

**Musical Score**   Green, Johnny
**Composer(s)**   Bart, Lionel
**Lyricist(s)**   Bart, Lionel
**Choreographer(s)**   White, Onna

**Producer(s)**   Woolf, John
**Director(s)**   Reed, Carol
**Screenwriter(s)**   Harris, Vernon
**Source(s)**   *Oliver!* (musical) Bart, Lionel

**Cast**   Lester, Mark; Moody, Ron [1]; Secombe, Harry; Wallis, Shani; Reed, Oliver; Wild, Jack; Griffith, Hugh; Rossiter, Leonard

**Song(s)**   Food Glorious Food; Where Is Love; Boy for Sale; Consider Yourself; You've Got to Pick a Pocket; It's a Fine Life; I'd Do Anything; Be Back Soon; Who Will Buy; As Long As He Needs Me; Reviewing the Situation; Oom-Pah-Pah; Oliver

**Notes**   All songs from Broadway musical version. [1] From Broadway musical.

## 4329 ✦ OLIVER AND COMPANY
### Disney, 1988

**Musical Score**  Redford, J.A.C.

**Director(s)**  Scribner, George
**Screenwriter(s)**  Gerry, Vance; Gabriel, Mike; Ranft, Joe; Mitchell, Jim; Bailey, Chris; Wise, Kirk; Michener, David; Allers, Roger; Trousdale, Gary; Lima, Kevin; Cedeno, Michael; Young, Pete; Joosen, Leon
**Source(s)**  *Oliver Twist* (novel) Dickens, Charles
**Voices**  Lawrence, Joey; Joel, Billy; Marin, Richard "Cheech"; Mulligan, Richard; Browne, Roscoe Lee; Ralph, Sheryl Lee; DeLuise, Dom; Blacque, Taurean; Weintraub, Carl; Loggia, Robert; Gregory, Natalie; Glover, William; Midler, Bette

**Song(s)**  Why Should I Worry (C/L: Hartman, Don; Midnight, Charlie); Once Upon a Time in New York City (C: Mann, Barry; L: Ashman, Howard); Streets of Gold (C: Snow, Tom; L: Pitchford, Dean); Good Company (C/L: Rocha, Ron; Minkoff, Robert); Perfect Isn't Easy (C: Manilow, Barry; L: Sussman, Bruce; Feldman, Jack); Fast Lane (Oliver's Rap) (C/L: St. James, Jon; Pedilla, Fidel "Rocky"; Eckart, Michael)

**Notes**  Animated feature.

## 4330 ✦ OLIVER'S STORY
### Paramount, 1978

**Musical Score**  Holdridge, Lee

**Producer(s)**  Picker, David V.
**Director(s)**  Korty, John
**Screenwriter(s)**  Segal, Erich; Korty, John
**Source(s)**  *Oliver's Story* (novel) Segal, Erich

**Cast**  O'Neal, Ryan; Bergen, Candice; Pagett, Nicola; Milland, Ray

**Song(s)**  The Music's Too Sweet not to Dance (Oliver's Story Theme) [1] (C: Lai, Francis; L: Korty, John)

**Notes**  [1] Lyric for exploitation use only.

## 4331 ✦ OLSEN'S BIG MOMENT
### Fox, 1933

**Director(s)**  St. Clair, Malcolm
**Screenwriter(s)**  Johnson, Henry; Tynan, James

**Cast**  Brendel, El; Catlett, Walter; Fleming, Susan; Weeks, Barbara

**Song(s)**  Oh the Wedding of the Spider and the Fly [1] (C/L: Catlett, Walter)

**Notes**  Originally titled OLSEN'S NIGHT OUT. [1] This song only lasts three bars.

## 4332 ✦ OLSEN'S NIGHT OUT

See OLSEN'S BIG MOMENT.

## 4333 ✦ OLYMPIA

See A BREATH OF SCANDAL.

## 4334 ✦ THE OMAHA TRAIL
### Metro–Goldwyn–Mayer, 1942

**Musical Score**  Snell, Dave

**Director(s)**  Buzzell, Edward
**Screenwriter(s)**  Lasky Jr., Jesse; Butler, Hugo

**Cast**  Craig, James; Blake, Pamela; Jagger, Dean; Ellis, Edward; Meek, Donald; Wills, Chill

**Song(s)**  'Taters and Corn (C/L: Buzzell, Eddie); Bang, Bang, Bang, Bang (C: Brent, Earl; Buzzell, Eddie)

**Notes**  There are also two vocals of "If Indeed You Earnest Be" and "Eat When You're Hungry."

## 4335 ✦ OMAR KHAYYAM
### Paramount, 1957

**Musical Score**  Young, Victor
**Composer(s)**  Livingston, Jay; Evans, Ray
**Lyricist(s)**  Livingston, Jay; Evans, Ray

**Producer(s)**  Freeman Jr., Frank
**Director(s)**  Dieterle, William
**Screenwriter(s)**  Lyndon, Barre

**Cast**  Wilde, Cornel; Paget, Debra; Rennie, Michael; Derek, John; Massey, Raymond; Hayes, Margaret; Sumac, Yma; Taylor, Joan

**Song(s)**  The Loves of Omar Khayyam [1]; Take My Heart (C: Young, Victor; L: David, Mack); Tell My Love [2] (C: Young, Victor; Livingston, Jay; Evans, Ray)

**Notes**  "Lament" by Moises Vivanco was used but not written for the picture. [1] Originally titled "The Song of Omar Khayyam." [2] Used instrumentally only.

## 4336 ✦ O, MY DARLING CLEMENTINE
### Republic, 1955

**Producer(s)**  Schaefer, Armand
**Director(s)**  McDonald, Frank
**Screenwriter(s)**  McGowan, Stuart; McGowan, Dorrell

**Cast**  Acuff, Roy; Randolph, Isabel; Albertson, Frank; Gray, Lorna; The Smoky Mountain Boys and Girls; The Radio Rogues; Cheshire, Perry; Ryan, Irene; Kennedy, Tom

**Song(s)**  Barrel House Bessie from Basin Street [1] (C: Styne, Jule; L: Magidson, Herb); Fire Ball Mail (C/L: Jenkins, Floyd); Low and Lonely (C/L: Jenkins, Floyd); The Show (C/L: Henderson, Charles); Smoke on the Water (C/L: Clemons, Zeke; Nunn, Earl); Diggin' the Doe See Doe (C/L: Gilbert, Ray; Miller, Sidney)

**Notes**  There is also a vocal of "Clementine" by Percy Montrose. [1] Also in THAT NIGHT IN RIO.

## 4337 ◆ ON A CLEAR DAY YOU CAN SEE FOREVER
### Paramount, 1970

**Composer(s)**  Lane, Burton
**Lyricist(s)**  Lerner, Alan Jay
**Choreographer(s)**  Jeffrey, Howard

**Producer(s)**  Koch, Howard W.
**Director(s)**  Minnelli, Vincente
**Screenwriter(s)**  Lerner, Alan Jay
**Source(s)**  *On a Clear Day You Can See Forever* (musical) Lane, Burton; Lerner, Alan Jay

**Cast**  Streisand, Barbra; Montand, Yves; Newhart, Bob; Blyden, Larry; Oakland, Simon; Nicholson, Jack; Brown, Pamela; Handl, Irene; Kinnear, Roy; Richardson, John

**Song(s)**  Hurry! It's Lovely Up Here [1]; On a Clear Day [1]; Love with All the Trimmings; Melinda [1]; Go to Sleep; He Isn't You [1] [2]; What Did I Have that I Don't Have? [1]; Come Back to Me [1]; Thank God for People Like Me [3]; Who Is There Among Us Who Knows? [3]; Wait Till We're Sixty Five [1] [3]; On the S.S. Bernard Cohn [1] [4]

**Notes**  Early in 1968 Paddy Chayefsky was hired to work on the screenplay. Some other Broadway songs were heard as background. [1] From Broadway score. [2] Also recorded (but not used) under its Broadway title "She Wasn't You." [3] Not used but recorded. [4] Lyric consisted of improvised humming.

## 4338 ◆ ON AGAIN—OFF AGAIN
### RKO, 1937

**Composer(s)**  Dreyer, Dave
**Lyricist(s)**  Ruby, Herman

**Producer(s)**  Marcus, Lee
**Director(s)**  Cline, Edward F.
**Screenwriter(s)**  Perrin, Nat; Rubin, Benny

**Cast**  Wheeler, Bert; Woolsey, Robert; Lord, Marjorie; Wilder, Patricia; Muir, Esther; Harvey, Paul; Hicks, Russell

**Song(s)**  One Happy Family; Thanks to You

## 4339 ◆ ON AN ISLAND WITH YOU
### Metro–Goldwyn–Mayer, 1949

**Musical Score**  Stoll, George; Sendrey, Al
**Composer(s)**  Brown, Nacio Herb
**Lyricist(s)**  Heyman, Edward
**Choreographer(s)**  Donohue, Jack

**Producer(s)**  Pasternak, Joe
**Director(s)**  Thorpe, Richard
**Screenwriter(s)**  Kingsley, Dorothy; Cooper, Dorothy; Martin, Charles; Wilhelm, Hans

**Cast**  Williams, Esther; Lawford, Peter; Montalban, Ricardo [1]; Durante, Jimmy; Charisse, Cyd; Xavier Cugat and His Orchestra; Simmons, Dick

**Song(s)**  On an Island with You; The Dog Song; Charisse (L: Katz, William); I Can Do Without Broadway (C/L: Durante, Jimmy); Takin' Miss Mary to the Ball; The Beauty Hula [2] (C/L: Almeida, Laurindo; Noble, Ray); Anapau (C/L: Kamana); Maile Lan Liilii (C/L: Kinney; Burrows); The Pagan Mask (C/L: Previn, Andre); I'll Do the Strutaway (in My Cutaway) (C/L: Donnelly, Harry; Caesar, Irving; Durante, Jimmy); If I Were You; You Gotta Start Off Each Day with a Song (C/L: Durante, Jimmy; Donnelly, Harry); All Aboard (C/L: Previn, Andre); La Cumbanchero (C/L: Hernandez)

**Notes**  [1] Dubbed by Bill Lee. [2] Also in HONOLULU but without Almeida credit.

## 4340 ◆ ONCE A SINNER
### Fox, 1931

**Director(s)**  McClintic, Guthrie
**Screenwriter(s)**  Middleton, George

**Cast**  Mackaill, Dorothy; McCrea, Joel; Halliday, John; Chase, Ilka; Brent, George

**Song(s)**  What's the Use of Living Without Love [1] (C: Hanley, James F.; L: McCarthy, Joseph)

**Notes**  [1] Originally in MAN TROUBLE.

## 4341 ◆ ONCE IS NOT ENOUGH
### Paramount, 1975

**Musical Score**  Mancini, Henry

**Producer(s)**  Koch, Howard W.
**Director(s)**  Green, Guy
**Screenwriter(s)**  Epstein, Julius J.
**Source(s)**  *Once Is Not Enough* (novel) Susann, Jacqueline

**Cast**  Douglas, Kirk; Smith, Alexis; Janssen, David; Hamilton, George; Mercouri, Melina; Vaccaro, Brenda; Raffin, Deborah

**Song(s)**  Once Is Not Enough (C: Mancini, Henry; L: Kusik, Larry); There's a Feeling in the Air [1] (L: Link, Peter)

**Notes**  [1] Lyric written for exploitation only. Based on cue "Something for Alexis."

## 4342 ◆ ONCE OVER LIGHTLY
### Metro–Goldwyn–Mayer, 1939

**Musical Score**  Snell, Dave
**Composer(s)**  Jason, Will; Greene, Mort
**Lyricist(s)**  Jason, Will; Greene, Mort

**Director(s)**  Jason, Will
**Screenwriter(s)**  Green, Mort; Hochfelder, Julian; Gilbert, Billy

**Cast**  Dunbar, Dixie; Melton, Frank; Gilbert, Billy; Downs, Johnny

**Song(s)** Fight Clifton Fight; Let's Live Happily Ever After; We're Here to Cheer

**Notes** Short subject.

## 4343 ◆ ONCE UPON A HORSE
### Universal, 1958

**Musical Score** Skinner, Frank

**Producer(s)** Kanter, Hal
**Director(s)** Kanter, Hal
**Screenwriter(s)** Kanter, Hal

**Cast** Rowen, Dan; Martin, Dick; Hyer, Martha; Talbot, Nita; Gleason, James; McGiver, John; Burns, David

**Song(s)** Once Upon a Horse (C/L: Livingston, Jay; Evans, Ray)

## 4344 ◆ ONCE UPON A WINTERTIME
### Disney, 1948

**Song(s)** Once Upon a Wintertime (C: Worth, Bobby; L: Gilbert, Ray)

**Notes** This cartoon is part of MELODY TIME.

## 4345 ◆ ONCE YOU KISS A STRANGER
### Warner Brothers, 1969

**Musical Score** Fagas, Jimmie

**Producer(s)** Goldstein, Harold A.
**Director(s)** Sparr, Robert
**Screenwriter(s)** Tarloff, Frank; Katkov, Norman
**Source(s)** "Strangers on a Train" (story) Highsmith, Patricia

**Cast** Burke, Paul; Lynley, Carol; Hyer, Martha; Hayes, Peter Lind; Carey, Philip; McNally, Stephen; Bissell, Whit; Devry, Elaine

**Song(s)** Once You Kiss a Stranger (C: Fagas, Jimmie; L: Darby, Ken)

## 4346 ◆ ON DANGEROUS GROUND
### Warner Brothers, 1986

**Musical Score** Levay, Sylvester

**Song(s)** Bargain with the Devil (C/L: Wayn, Sit; Micalizzi, F.)

**Notes** No other information available.

## 4347 ◆ THE ONE AND ONLY
### Paramount, 1978

**Producer(s)** Picker, David V.
**Director(s)** Reiner, Carl
**Screenwriter(s)** Gordon, Steve

**Cast** Winkler, Henry; Darby, Kim; Villechaize, Herve; Saks, Gene; Daniels, William; Gould, Harold; Holliday, Polly; Begley Jr., Ed; Flippen, Lucy Lee

**Song(s)** The One and Only (C: Williams, Patrick; L: Bergman, Marilyn; Bergman, Alan)

## 4348 ◆ THE ONE AND ONLY, GENUINE, ORIGINAL FAMILY BAND
### Disney, 1968

**Musical Score** Elliott, Jack
**Composer(s)** Sherman, Richard M.; Sherman, Robert B.
**Lyricist(s)** Sherman, Richard M.; Sherman, Robert B.
**Choreographer(s)** Lambert, Hugh

**Producer(s)** Anderson, Bill
**Director(s)** O'Herlihy, Michael
**Screenwriter(s)** Hawley, Lowell S.
**Source(s)** (book) Van Nuys, Laura Bower

**Cast** Brennan, Walter; Ebsen, Buddy; Warren, Lesley Ann; Davidson, John; Blair, Janet; Russell, Kurt; Cox, Wally; Deacon, Richard

**Song(s)** 'Bout Time; Dakota; Drummin' Drummin' Drummin'; The Happiest Girl Alive; Let's Put It Over with Grover; Oh, Benjamin Harrison; The One and Only, Genuine, Original Family Band; Ten Feet Off the Ground; West o' the Wide Missouri; Westerin' [1]

**Notes** The film was originally set to star Bing Crosby. [1] Not used.

## 4349 ◆ ONE CRAZY SUMMER
### Warner Brothers, 1986

**Musical Score** Lerios, Cory; DiPasquale, James

**Producer(s)** Jaffe, Michael
**Director(s)** Holland, "Savage" Steve
**Screenwriter(s)** Holland, "Savage" Steve

**Cast** Cusack, John; Moore, Demi; Armstrong, Curtis; Hickey, William; Flaherty, Joe; Villard, Tom; Matuszak, John; Metcalf, Mark; Waterbury, Laura; Little Richard; Goldthwait, Bobcat

**Song(s)** Don't Look Back (C/L: Wolinski, Hawk); Take a Bow (C/L: Leonard, Patrick; Carter, Keithen)

**Notes** No cue sheet available.

## 4350 ◆ ONE EXCITING WEEK
### Republic, 1946

**Producer(s)** Brown, Donald H.
**Director(s)** Beaudine, William
**Screenwriter(s)** Townley, Jack; Butler, John K.
**Source(s)** "Welcome Home Dan" (story) Murray, Dennis

**Cast** Pearce, Al; Cowan, Jerome; Lee, Pinky; Howard, Shemp; Treen, Mary; Harris, Arlene; The Teen Agers [1]

**Song(s)** Bounce Me Brother with a Solid Four [2] (C/L: Raye, Don; Prince, Hughie); Heave Ho! My Lads, Heave Ho! (C/L: Lawrence, Jack)

**Notes** "Ciribiribin" by A. Pestalozza was also given a vocal in the American release only. [1] From the HOAGY CARMICHAEL RADIO SHOW. [2] Also in BUCK PRIVATES (1941) and WILLIE AND JOE IN BACK AT THE FRONT.

## 4351 ✦ ONE-EYED JACKS
Paramount, 1961

**Producer(s)** Rosenberg, Frank P.
**Director(s)** Brando, Marlon
**Screenwriter(s)** Trosper, Guy; Willingham, Calder
**Source(s)** *The Authentic Death of Hendry Jones* (novel) Neider, Charles

**Cast** Brando, Marlon; Malden, Karl; Pellicer, Pina; Jurado, Katy; Johnson, Ben; Pickens, Slim; Cook Jr., Elisha

**Song(s)** The Ballad of One-Eyed Jacks [1] (C: Morgan, McKayla)

**Notes** [1] Not used.

## 4352 ✦ ONE FOR THE BOOK
Studio Unknown

**Composer(s)** Chaplin, Saul
**Lyricist(s)** Cahn, Sammy

**Cast** Hutton, Betty

**Notes** No cue sheet available. Short subject.

## 4353 ✦ ONE FROGGY EVENING
Warner Brothers, 1955

**Musical Score** Franklyn, Milton J.

**Director(s)** Jones, Chuck
**Screenwriter(s)** Maltese, Michael

**Song(s)** Michigan Rag (C/L: Maltese, Michael)

**Notes** Merrie Melodie. There are also vocals of turn-of-the-century songs.

## 4354 ✦ ONE FROM THE HEART
Columbia, 1982

**Musical Score** Waits, Tom
**Composer(s)** Waits, Tom
**Lyricist(s)** Waits, Tom

**Producer(s)** Frederickson, Gray; Roos, Fred
**Director(s)** Coppola, Francis Ford
**Screenwriter(s)** Bernstein, Armyan; Coppola, Francis Ford

**Cast** Forrest, Frederic; Garr, Teri; Julia, Raul; Kinski, Nastassia; Kazan, Lainie; Stanton, Harry Dean; Anders, Luana; Coppola, Carmine; de Mornay, Rebecca

**Song(s)** Once Upon a Town; Wages of Love; Is There Any Way Out of This Dream?; Picking Up After You; I Beg Your Pardon; Ray's Song; Little Boy Blue; You Can't Unring a Bell; This One's From the Heart; Take Me Home

## 4355 ✦ ONE GIANT LEAP
Warner Brothers, 1971

**Musical Score** Adlam, Basil
**Composer(s)** Adlam, Basil
**Lyricist(s)** Hendricks, William L.

**Song(s)** Come Fly with Me; One Giant Leap; O'er Roman Roads; A Bright New World; Frontiers; We'll Saddle a Rocket and Ride [1]; Look to the Stars [1]; Age of Space; Spacecraft Home; Space Age Wonders; That's Us in the U.S.A. [1]; Beyond the Mystic Veil

**Notes** Short subject. All background vocals. [1] Also in THAT'S US IN THE U.S.A.

## 4356 ✦ ONE HEAVENLY NIGHT
United Artists, 1931

**Composer(s)** Brown, Nacio Herb
**Lyricist(s)** Eliscu, Edward

**Producer(s)** Goldwyn, Samuel
**Director(s)** Fitzmaurice, George
**Screenwriter(s)** Bromfield, Louis; Howard, Sidney

**Cast** Laye, Evelyn; Boles, John; Tashman, Lilyan; Errol, Leon; Cameron, Hugh; Lord, Marion; Alberni, Luis; Belmore, Lionel

**Song(s)** Heavenly Night; Along the Road of Dreams (C: Granichstaedten, Bruno; L: Grey, Clifford); Anybody But You [1]; Goodnight Serenade [1]; I Belong to Everybody [1]; My Cymbalum [1] (L: Grey, Clifford)

**Notes** No cue sheet available. [1] Not used.

## 4357 ✦ ONE HOUR LATE
Paramount, 1935

**Producer(s)** Lewis, Albert
**Director(s)** Murphy, Ralph
**Screenwriter(s)** Scola, Kathryn; Smith, Paul Gerard

**Cast** Twelvetrees, Helen; Morrison, Joe; Nagel, Conrad; Judge, Arline; Walker, Ray

**Song(s)** Me Without You [2] (C: Gensler, Lewis E.; L: Robin, Leo); A Little Angel Told Me So (C/L: Coslow, Sam); The Last Round-Up [1] (C/L: Hill, Billy); With My Eyes Wide Open I'm Dreaming [4] (C: Revel, Harry; L: Gordon, Mack); Penthouse Serenade [3] (C/L: Burton, Val; Jason, Will)

**Notes** [1] Also in the Republic pictures DON'T FENCE ME IN, SINGING HILL, STAND UP AND CHEER (Fox) and THE LAST ROUNDUP (Columbia). [2] Written for HERE IS MY HEART. [3]

Also in STRANGE LOVE OF MOLLY LOUVAIN (Warner) and BEAU JAMES (Paramount). The song is sometimes referred to as "When We're Alone." [4] Also in COLLEGIATE, SHOOT THE WORKS and STOLEN HARMONY.

**4358 ◆ ONE HOUR WITH YOU**
Paramount, 1932

**Musical Score**   Straus, Oscar
**Composer(s)**   Whiting, Richard A.
**Lyricist(s)**   Robin, Leo

**Producer(s)**   Lubitsch, Ernst
**Director(s)**   Lubitsch, Ernst
**Screenwriter(s)**   Raphaelson, Samson
**Source(s)**   *Only a Dream* (play) Schmidt, Lothar

**Cast**   Chevalier, Maurice; MacDonald, Jeanette; Tobin, Genevieve

**Song(s)**   One Hour with You [2]; We Will Always Be Sweethearts (C: Straus, Oscar); It Was Only a Dream Kiss [1] (C: Straus, Oscar); What Would You Do?; Oh That Mitzi (C: Straus, Oscar); Three Times a Day; What a Little Thing Like a Wedding Can Do (C: Straus, Oscar); Police Number [3] (C: Straus, Oscar); Blessed Event [4] (L: DeSylva, B.G.); Enclosed Please Find [4]; I Couldn't Be r 1128Annoyed [4]; If I'm Blue to You [4] (L: DeSylva, B.G.); I'll Be Seeing You [4] (C: Whiting, Richard A.; Brown, Nacio Herb; L: Egan, Raymond B.); I've Got Nothin', You've Got Nothin', We've Got Nothin' to Lose [4] (L: DeSylva, B.G.); An Old Friend Is Sweet in September [4] (L: Egan, Raymond B.); Song of the Red-Headed Woman [4] (L: Egan, Raymond B.); Tonight's the Night [4] (L: Egan, Raymond B.); You'll Do [4] (L: DeSylva, B.G.)

**Notes**   George Cukor was originally the director but Lubitsch soon took over and reshot much of Cukor's footage. [1] Also called I JUST HAD A DREAM. [2] Also used in MILLION DOLLAR LEGS (1932). Eddie Cantor added new lyrics when he used the song for his radio show. [3] Lyrics only used. [4] Not used.

**4359 ◆ ONE HUNDRED AND ONE DALMATIANS**
Disney, 1960

**Musical Score**   Bruns, Mel
**Composer(s)**   Leven, Mel
**Lyricist(s)**   Leven, Mel

**Director(s)**   Reitherman, Wolfgang; Luske, Hamilton; Geronimi, Clyde
**Screenwriter(s)**   Peet, Bill
**Source(s)**   *The One Hundred and One Dalmatians* (novel) Smith, Dodie
**Voices**   Taylor, Rod; O'Malley, J. Pat; Gerson, Betty Lou; Wentworth, Martha; Wright, Ben; Bauer, Cate; Frankham, Dave; Worlock, Frederick; Leonard, Queenie; Ravenscroft, Thurl; Wickes, Mary; Luddy, Barbara

**Directing Animator(s)**   Kahl, Milt; Davis, Marc; Johnston, Ollie; Thomas, Franklin; Lounsbery, John; Larson, Eric

**Song(s)**   Cruella De Ville; Kanine Krunchies Kommercial; Dalmatian Plantation; Playful Melody (C: Bruns, George; L: Dunham, "By"); Remember When [1] (C: Marks, Franklyn; L: Jackman, Bob); Cherio, Good-Bye, Toodle-oo, Hip Hip! [2]; Don't Buy a Parrot from a Sailor [2]; March of the One Hundred and One [2] (C: Baker, Buddy; L: Adair, Tom); 101 Dalmatians [3] (C/L: Sherman, Richard M.; Sherman, Robert B.)

**Notes**   Animated feature. [1] Used instrumentally only. [2] Not used. [3] Written for exploitation only.

**4360 ◆ ONE HUNDRED MEN AND A GIRL**
Universal, 1937

**Producer(s)**   Pasternak, Joe; Rogers, Charles R.
**Director(s)**   Koster, Henry
**Screenwriter(s)**   Manning, Bruce; Kenyon, Charles; Kraly, Hans; Mulhauser, James

**Cast**   Durbin, Deanna; Stokowski, Leopold; Menjou, Adolphe; Pallette, Eugene; Auer, Mischa; Brady, Alice

**Song(s)**   It's Raining Sunbeams (C: Hollander, Frederick; L: Coslow, Sam); Music in My Dreams [1] (C: Hollander, Frederick; L: Coslow, Sam)

**Notes**   There are also vocals of "A Heart that's Free" by Railey and Robyn; "The Drinking Song" from LA TRAVIATA by Verdi and "Alleluja" by Mozart. [1] Sheet music only.

**4361 ◆ ONE IN A MILLION**
Twentieth Century–Fox, 1936

**Composer(s)**   Pollack, Lew
**Lyricist(s)**   Mitchell, Sidney D.
**Choreographer(s)**   Haskell, Jack

**Producer(s)**   Zanuck, Darryl F.
**Director(s)**   Lanfield, Sidney
**Screenwriter(s)**   Praskins, Leonard; Kelly, Mark

**Cast**   Henie, Sonja; Menjou, Adolphe; Ameche, Don; Sparks, Ned; Hersholt, Jean; The Ritz Brothers; Judge, Arline; Minnevitch, Borrah; Dunbar, Dixie; Love, Montagu; Tannen, Julius

**Song(s)**   The Moonlit Waltz [4]; We're Back in Circulation Again; Who's Afraid of Love [2]; One in a Million; We're the Horror Boys of Hollywood [1] (C/L: Lee, Lester; Pokrass, Sam); Lovely Lady in White [3]

**Notes**   There are brief uses of other songs in the Ritz Brothers and Borrah Minnevitch routines. One of the Ritz Brothers routines is titled "Train Song" and consists entirely of old songs. [1] Pokrass may just have arranged the number. [2] Also in ONE MILE FROM HEAVEN. [3] Sheet music only. [4] Used Instrumentally only.

## 4362 ✦ ONE IS A LONELY NUMBER
Metro–Goldwyn–Mayer, 1972

**Musical Score**  Legrand, Michel

**Producer(s)**  Wolper, David L.
**Director(s)**  Margulies, Stan
**Screenwriter(s)**  Seltzer, David
**Source(s)**  (story) Morris, Rebecca

**Cast**  Van Devere, Trish; Markham, Monte; Leigh, Janet; Douglas, Melvyn; Elliott, Jane

**Song(s)**  Le Soleil, la Mer et les Bateaux (C: Legrand, Michel; L: Drejac, Jean)

## 4363 ✦ ONE LITTLE INDIAN
Disney, 1973

**Musical Score**  Goldsmith, Jerry

**Producer(s)**  Hibler, Winston
**Director(s)**  McEveety, Bernard
**Screenwriter(s)**  Spalding, Harry

**Cast**  Garner, James; Miles, Vera; Hingle, Pat; Woodward, Morgan; Doucette, John; O'Brien, Clay; Pine, Robert; Swofford, Ken; Silverheels, Jay; Prine, Andrew; Glover, Bruce

**Song(s)**  It Only Takes Time [1] (C: Goldsmith, Jerry; L: Goldsmith, Carol)

**Notes**  [1] Used instrumentally only.

## 4364 ✦ ONE MAD KISS
Fox, 1930

**Composer(s)**  Kernell, William
**Lyricist(s)**  Kernell, William
**Choreographer(s)**  Duval, Juan

**Director(s)**  Silver, Marcel; Tinling, James; Merlin, Frank
**Screenwriter(s)**  Nichols, Dudley

**Cast**  Mojica, Jose [3]; Maria, Mona; Moreno, Antonio; Patricola, Tom

**Song(s)**  Oh Where Are You [4] (C: Sanders, Troy; L: Mojica, Jose); Market Scene (C/L: Sanders, Troy); Only One (C: Stamper, Dave; L: Kummer, Clare); Look Behind the Mask (C: Hanley, James F.; L: McCarthy, Joseph); Drinking Song (C: Stamper, Dave; L: Kummer, Clare); In My Arms; One Mad Kiss (C: Sanders, Troy; L: Mojica, Jose); Paco Theme #2; Once in a While (C: Stamper, Dave; Arnold, Cecil; L: Kummer, Clare); I Am Free; Monkey on a String [1] (C: Hanley, James F.; L: McCarthy, Joseph); Oh! Have I a Way with the Girls! [1] (C/L: Hanley, James F.; L: McCarthy, Joseph); The Gay Heart [1] (C: Stamper, Dave; L: Kummer, Clare); Lament [1] (C/L: Mojica, Jose; Nichols, Dudley); Gitana [2] (C/L: Sanders, Troy; Mojica, Jose; Del Moral, Jarge); Florero Espanol [2] (C/L: Sanders, Troy; Mojica, Jose; Del Moral, Jarge); Fiesta [2] (C/L: Sanders, Troy; Mojica, Jose; Del Moral, Jarge)

**Notes**  Originally released briefly by RKO. [1] Not on cue sheets. [2] Used in Spanish language version only. Not on cue sheets. [3] Billed as Don Jose Mojica. [4] Also in LAS FRONTERAS DEL AMOR.

## 4365 ✦ ONE MEAT BRAWL
Warner Brothers, 1947

**Musical Score**  Stalling, Carl

**Director(s)**  McKimson, Robert
**Screenwriter(s)**  Foster, Warren

**Cast**  Pig, Porky; Groundhog, Grover; Mandrake

**Song(s)**  Ground Hog Song (A Groundhog and His Shadow Just Doesn't Mean a Thing) (C: Stalling, Carl; L: Foster, Warren)

**Notes**  Merrie Melodie.

## 4366 ✦ ONE MILE FROM HEAVEN
Twentieth Century–Fox, 1937

**Producer(s)**  Wurtzel, Sol M.
**Director(s)**  Dwan, Allan
**Screenwriter(s)**  Breslow, Lou; Patrick, John
**Source(s)**  "Little Colored White Child" (stories) Lindsey, Judge Ben B.

**Cast**  Trevor, Claire; Blane, Sally; Fowley, Douglas; Washington, Fredi; Carol, Joan; McVey, Paul; Anderson, Eddie "Rochester"; Robinson, Bill

**Song(s)**  Who's Afraid of Love [1] (C: Pollack, Lew; L: Mitchell, Sidney D.)

**Notes**  [1] Also in ONE IN A MILLION.

## 4367 ✦ ONE MORE SATURDAY NIGHT
Columbia, 1986

**Musical Score**  McHugh, David

**Producer(s)**  Laiter, Tova; Kosberg, Robert; Bernstein, Jonathan
**Director(s)**  Klein, Dennis
**Screenwriter(s)**  Franken, Al; Davis, Tom

**Cast**  Davis, Tom; Franken, Al; Harris, Moira; Howard, Frank

**Song(s)**  One More Saturday Night (C/L: Sandstrom, Bobby; Price, Michael)

## 4368 ✦ ONE MORE SPRING
Fox, 1935

**Producer(s)**  Sheehan, Winfield
**Director(s)**  King, Henry
**Screenwriter(s)**  Burke, Edwin
**Source(s)**  *One More Spring* (novel) Nathan, Robert

**Cast**  Gaynor, Janet; Baxter, Warner

**Song(s)**  Misunderstanding Moon (C/L: Fetchit, Stepin)

**Notes**   There is also a vocal of the Pinky Tomlin song "The Object of My Affection."

## 4369 ✦ ONE MORE TIME
### United Artists, 1970

**Musical Score**   Reed, Les

**Producer(s)**   Ebbins, Milton
**Director(s)**   Lewis, Jerry
**Screenwriter(s)**   Pertwee, Michael

**Cast**   Lawford, Peter; Davis Jr., Sammy; Anderson, Esther; Wright, Maggie; Sands, Leslie

**Song(s)**   One More Time; Where Do I Go From Here; When the Feeling Hits You (C/L: Doyle, Bobby)

**Notes**   A sequel to SALT AND PEPPER.

## 4370 ✦ ONE MORE TOMORROW
### Warner Brothers, 1946

**Musical Score**   Steiner, Max

**Producer(s)**   Blanke, Henry
**Director(s)**   Godfrey, Peter
**Screenwriter(s)**   Hoffman, Charles; Turney, Catherine; Epstein, Julius J.; Epstein, Philip G.
**Source(s)**   *The Animal Kingdom* (play) Barry, Philip

**Cast**   Sheridan, Ann; Morgan, Dennis; Carson, Jack; Smith, Alexis; Wyman, Jane; Gardiner, Reginald; Loder, John; Gateson, Marjorie; Hall, Thurston; Abbott, John

**Song(s)**   One More Tomorrow (C: Lecuona, Ernesto; L: DeLange, Eddie; Myrow, Josef)

## 4371 ✦ ONE MORE TRAIN TO ROB
### Universal, 1970

**Musical Score**   Shire, David

**Producer(s)**   Arthur, Robert
**Director(s)**   McLaglen, Andrew V.
**Screenwriter(s)**   Tait, Don; Nelson, Dick

**Cast**   Peppard, George; Vernon, John; Muldaur, Diana; Nuyen, France; Sandor, Steve

**Song(s)**   Havin' Myself a Fine Time (C: Shire, David; L: Maltby Jr., Richard)

## 4372 ✦ ONE NIGHT IN THE TROPICS
### Universal, 1940

**Composer(s)**   Kern, Jerome
**Lyricist(s)**   Fields, Dorothy

**Producer(s)**   Spigelgass, Leonard
**Director(s)**   Sutherland, Edward
**Screenwriter(s)**   Purcell, Gertrude; Grayson, Charles
**Source(s)**   *Love Insurance* (novel) Biggers, Earl Derr

**Cast**   Abbott, Bud; Costello, Lou; Purcell, Gertrude; Jones, Allan; Kelly, Nancy [2]; Frawley, William; Boland, Mary; Moran, Peggy; Carrillo, Leo

**Song(s)**   Remind Me; You and Your Kiss; Back in My Shell; Your Dream [1] (L: Hammerstein II, Oscar; Harbach, Otto); Farandola

**Notes**   [1] Originally in stage show GENTLEMEN UNAFRAID (1938). [2] Dubbed.

## 4373 ✦ ONE NIGHT OF LOVE
### Columbia, 1934

**Producer(s)**   Cohn, Harry
**Director(s)**   Schertzinger, Victor
**Screenwriter(s)**   Lauren, S.K.; Gow, James; North, Edmund
**Source(s)**   *Don't Fall in Love* (play) Beahan, Charles; Speare, Dorothy

**Cast**   Moore, Grace; Carminati, Tullio; Westman, Nydia; Ralph, Jessie; Talbot, Lyle; Barrie, Mona

**Song(s)**   One Night of Love (C: Schertzinger, Victor; L: Kahn, Gus)

**Notes**   All other songs are classical.

## 4374 ✦ ONE ON ONE
### Warner Brothers, 1977

**Musical Score**   Fox, Charles
**Composer(s)**   Fox, Charles
**Lyricist(s)**   Williams, Paul

**Producer(s)**   Horstein, Martin
**Director(s)**   Johnson, Lamont
**Screenwriter(s)**   Benson, Robby; Segal, Jerry

**Cast**   Benson, Robby; O'Toole, Annette; Spradlin, G.D.; Strickland, Gail; Griffith, Melanie; Richardson, James G.

**Song(s)**   This Day Belongs to Me; My Fair Share; Hustle [1]; John Wayne; Love Conquers All

**Notes**   [1] Used instrumentally only.

## 4375 ✦ ONE PIECE BATHING SUIT

See MILLION DOLLAR MERMAID.

## 4376 ✦ ONE SINGS, THE OTHER DOESN'T
### Cinema 5, 1977

**Musical Score**   Wertheimer, Francois
**Composer(s)**   Wertheimer, Francois
**Lyricist(s)**   Varda, Agnes

**Producer(s)**   Varda, Agnes
**Director(s)**   Varda, Agnes
**Screenwriter(s)**   Varda, Agnes

**Cast** Papineau, Micou; Mairesse, Valerie; Liotard, Thereses; Raffi, Ali

**Song(s)** Bubble Bubble Gum Rock (C: Mercier, Jacques; L: Wertheimer, Francois); Mon Corps est a Midi; Je Voiu Salue les Marie (C: Papineau, Micou); Mi Cocotte (C: Greffier, Doudou; Papineau, Joelle); Amsterdam; Theme des Amies

**Notes** No cue sheet available.

## 4377 ✦ ONE STOLEN NIGHT
### Warner Brothers, 1929

**Director(s)** Dunlap, Scott R.
**Screenwriter(s)** Lowe Jr., Edward T.

**Cast** Bronson, Betty; Collier Jr., William; Lewis, Mitchell; Quartero, Nena

**Song(s)** My Cairo Love (C: Zamecnik, J.S.; L: Kerr, Harry D.)

## 4378 ✦ ONE SUNDAY AFTERNOON (1933)
### Paramount, 1933

**Producer(s)** Lighton, Louis D.
**Director(s)** Roberts, Stephen
**Screenwriter(s)** Jones, Grover; McNutt, William Slavens
**Source(s)** *One Sunday Afternoon* (play) Hagan, James

**Cast** Cooper, Gary; Fuller, Frances; Wray, Fay; Hamilton, Neil; Karns, Roscoe; Darwell, Jane; Blandick, Clara; Hardy, Sam

**Song(s)** One Sunday Afternoon [1] (C: Johnston, Arthur; L: Coslow, Sam)

**Notes** [1] Not used. There were however, short renditions of "Bill Bailey Won't You Please Come Home" and "In the Good Old Summer Time" by Ren Shields and George "Honeyboy" Evans; "Goodbye Dolly Gray" by Will Cobb and Paul Barnes and "Goodbye Little Girl Goodbye" by Cobb and Evans.

## 4379 ✦ ONE SUNDAY AFTERNOON (1949)
### Warner Brothers, 1948

**Musical Score** Buttolph, David
**Composer(s)** Blane, Ralph
**Lyricist(s)** Blane, Ralph
**Choreographer(s)** Prinz, LeRoy

**Producer(s)** Wald, Jerry
**Director(s)** Walsh, Raoul
**Screenwriter(s)** Richards, Robert L.
**Source(s)** *One Sunday Afternoon* (play) Hagan, James

**Cast** Morgan, Dennis; Malone, Dorothy [1]; DeFore, Don; Paige, Janis; Blue, Ben; O'Shea, Oscar; Hale Jr., Alan; Neise, George

**Song(s)** One Sunday Afternoon; West Virginia [2]; Someday; Johnny and Lucille; Sweet Corner Girl; Girls Were Made to Take Care of Boys

**Notes** "Daisy Bell" by Harry Dacre and "Mary You're a Bit Old-Fashioned" by Marion Sunshine and Henry Marshall are also used in the picture. [1] Dubbed by Marion Morgan. [2] Also in CATTLE TOWN.

## 4380 ✦ 1001 ARABIAN NIGHTS
### Columbia, 1959

**Musical Score** Duning, George
**Composer(s)** Duning, George
**Lyricist(s)** Washington, Ned

**Producer(s)** Bosustow, Stephen
**Director(s)** Kinney, Jack
**Screenwriter(s)** Ormonde, Czenzi
**Voices** Backus, Jim; Bernardi, Herschel; Butler, Daws; Clark, Peggy; Friley, Jean; Terry, Ann; Conried, Hans; Hickman, Dwayne; Reed, Alan; Grant, Katharyn

**Song(s)** Magoo's Blues; You Are My Dream

**Notes** Animated feature. Also called MAGOO'S ARABIAN NIGHTS.

## 4381 ✦ $1,000 A TOUCHDOWN
### Paramount, 1939

**Producer(s)** Thomas, William
**Director(s)** Hogan, James
**Screenwriter(s)** Daves, Delmer

**Cast** Brown, Joe E.; Raye, Martha; Hayward, Susan; Blore, Eric; Dugan, Tom; Robinson, Dewey

**Song(s)** Love with a Capital "You" [1] (C: Rainger, Ralph; L: Robin, Leo); Fight on for Madison (C: Young, Victor; L: Loesser, Frank); Love in Bloom [2] (C: Rainger, Ralph; L: Robin, Leo)

**Notes** [1] Considered for THE BIG BROADCAST OF 1938, COLLEGE SWING and MAN ABOUT TOWN but not used. Sometimes spelled "Love with a Capital 'U'," but not on sheet music. [2] Also used in THE BIG BROADCAST OF 1938, NEW YORK TOWN and SHE LOVES ME NOT. Not used for KISS AND MAKE UP.

## 4382 ✦ ONE TOUCH OF VENUS
### Universal, 1948

**Musical Score** Ronell, Ann
**Composer(s)** Weill, Kurt
**Lyricist(s)** Nash, Ogden
**Choreographer(s)** Daniels, Billy

**Producer(s)** Cowan, Lester
**Director(s)** Seiter, William A.
**Screenwriter(s)** Kurnitz, Harry; Tashlin, Frank
**Source(s)** *One Touch of Venus* (musical) Weill, Kurt; Nash, Ogden; Perelman, S.J.

**Cast** Gardner, Ava [3]; Walker, Robert; Haymes, Dick; Arden, Eve; San Juan, Olga; Conway, Tom; Flavin, James; Allgood, Sara

**Song(s)** Speak Low [1]; That's Him [1]; Don't Look Now But My Heart Is Showing (L: Ronell, Ann); My Week [2] (L: Ronell, Ann)

**Notes** Some of the other songs from the Broadway original are used as underscoring. [1] From original Broadway show but with "Additional music and routine" by Ann Ronell added for the movie. [2] Used instrumentally only. [3] Dubbed by Eileen Wilson.

### 4383 ✦ ONE-TRICK PONY
Warner Brothers, 1980

**Composer(s)** Simon, Paul
**Lyricist(s)** Simon, Paul

**Producer(s)** Tannen, Michael
**Director(s)** Young, Robert M.
**Screenwriter(s)** Simon, Paul

**Cast** Simon, Paul; Brown, Blair; Torn, Rip; Hackett, Joan; Goorwitz, Allen; Winningham, Mare; Reed, Lou

**Song(s)** Late in the Evening; One Trick Pony; Rock Lobster (C/L: Schneider; Wilson); How the Heart Approaches What It Yearns; God Bless the Absentee; Nobody; Ace in the Hole; Long, Long Day; Jonah; Oh, Marion; Soul Man [2] (C/L: Porter, David; Hayes, Isaac); Do You Believe in Magic (C/L: Sebastian, John); Soft Parachutes; Take Me to the Mardi Gras [1]; Bathtub Guitar [1]; I Do It for Love [1]; That's Why God Made the Movies [1]

**Notes** It is not known which of the songs not written by Simon were for this film. [1] Background Instrumental only. [2] Also in LICENSE TO DRIVE.

### 4384 ✦ ON GOLDEN POND
Universal, 1981

**Musical Score** Grusin, Dave

**Producer(s)** Gilbert, Bruce
**Director(s)** Rydell, Mark
**Screenwriter(s)** Thompson, Ernest
**Source(s)** *On Golden Pond* (play) Thompson, Ernest

**Cast** Hepburn, Katharine; Fonda, Henry; Fonda, Jane; Coleman, Dabney; McKeon, Doug

**Song(s)** We're the Girls (C/L: Thompson, Ernest)

### 4385 ✦ ON HER MAJESTY'S SECRET SERVICE
United Artists, 1969

**Musical Score** Barry, John
**Composer(s)** Barry, John
**Lyricist(s)** David, Hal

**Producer(s)** Saltzman, Harry; Broccoli, Albert R.
**Director(s)** Hunt, Peter
**Screenwriter(s)** Maibaum, Richard
**Source(s)** *On Her Majesty's Secret Service* (novel) Fleming, Ian

**Cast** Lazenby, George; Rigg, Diana; Savalas, Telly; Ferzetti, Gabriele; Lee, Bernard

**Song(s)** On Her Majesty's Secret Service; Do You Know How Christmas Trees Are Grown [1]; We Have All the Time in the World

**Notes** [1] Sheet music only.

### 4386 ✦ ONLY ONCE IN A LIFETIME
Ellman Film Enterprises, 1978

**Musical Score** Ragland, Robert O.

**Producer(s)** Exparza, Moctesuma; Grattan, Alejandro
**Director(s)** Grattan, Alejandro
**Screenwriter(s)** Grattan, Alejandro

**Cast** Robelo, Miguel; Lopez, Estrellita Lenore; Carricart, Robert; North, Sheree

**Song(s)** Only Once in a Lifetime (C: Ragland, Robert O.; L: Wayne, Sid)

**Notes** No cue sheet available.

### 4387 ✦ ONLY SAPS WORK
Paramount, 1930

**Composer(s)** Dreyer, Dave
**Lyricist(s)** Macdonald, Ballard

**Director(s)** Gardner, Cyril; Knopf, Edwin H.
**Screenwriter(s)** Mintz, Sam; Heath, Percy; Mankiewicz, Joseph L.
**Source(s)** *Easy Come Easy Go* (play) Davis, Owen

**Cast** Errol, Leon; Arlen, Richard; Brian, Mary; Erwin, Stuart; Lawler, Anderson; Grapewin, Charley; Chandler, George

**Song(s)** The Money I've Got to Get [1]; Find the Girl; Jappalappa

**Notes** Originally titled EASY COME EASY GO and SOCIAL ERRORS. There were also vocals of "Come Back to Erin" by C.C. Barnard; "Merrily We Roll Along," "London Bridge" and "Volga Boat Song." [1] Originally written for the unproduced movie GIVE 'EM THE AXE.

### 4388 ✦ ONLY THE VALIANT
Warner Brothers, 1951

**Musical Score** Waxman, Franz

**Producer(s)** Cagney, William
**Director(s)** Douglas, Gordon M.
**Screenwriter(s)** North, Edmund; Brown, Harry

**Source(s)** *Only the Valiant* (novel) Warren, Charles Marquis

**Cast** Peck, Gregory; Payton, Barbara; Bond, Ward; Young, Gig; Chaney, Lon; Brand, Neville; Corey, Jeff; Anderson, Warner; Brodie, Steve; Ansara, Michael

**Song(s)** Dear Barney (C: Heindorf, Ray; L: Miller, Sy)

## 4389 ✦ ON MOONLIGHT BAY
Warner Brothers, 1951

**Musical Score** Steiner, Max
**Choreographer(s)** Prinz, LeRoy

**Producer(s)** Jacobs, William
**Director(s)** Del Ruth, Roy
**Screenwriter(s)** Rose, Jack; Shavelson, Melville
**Source(s)** "Penrod"; "Penrod and Sam" (stories) Tarkington, Booth

**Cast** Day, Doris; MacRae, Gordon; Smith, Jack; Ames, Leon; De Camp, Rosemary; Wickes, Mary; Corby, Ellen; Gray, Billy; East, Henry; Stevens, Jeffrey; Marr, Eddie

**Song(s)** Tell Me (Tell Me Why) (C: Kortlander, Max; L: Callahan, J. Will); Love Ya (C/L: Tobias, Charles; De Rose, Peter); Christmas Story (C/L: Walsh, Pauline)

**Notes** It is not known if there are any original songs in this score. Vocals included "Moonlight Bay" by Percy Wenrich and Edward Madden; "Cuddle Up a Little Closer, Lovey Mine" by Karl Hoschna and Otto Harbach; "I'm Forever Blowing Bubbles" by Jaan Kenbrovin and John William Kellette; "Pack Up your Troubles in Your Old Kit Bag" by Felix Powell and George Asaf; "Every Little Movement" by Karl Hoschna and Otto Harbach and "Till We Meet Again" by Richard A. Whiting and Raymond B. Egan.

## 4390 ✦ ON STAGE EVERYBODY
Universal, 1945

**Composer(s)** James, Inez; Miller, Sidney
**Lyricist(s)** James, Inez; Miller, Sidney
**Choreographer(s)** Da Pron, Louis

**Producer(s)** Wilson, Warren
**Director(s)** Yarbrough, Jean
**Screenwriter(s)** Wilson, Warren; Brodney, Oscar

**Cast** Oakie, Jack; Ryan, Peggy; The King Sisters; Coy, Johnny; London, Julie

**Song(s)** Put - Put - Put (Your Arms Around Me) (C/L: Hoffman, Al; Curtis, Mann; Livingston, Jerry); It Was the Sullivans; Dance with a Dolly (C/L: Shand, Terry; Eaton, Jimmy; Leader, Mickey); For Him, No Love; Stuff Like That There (C/L: Livingston, Jay; Evans, Ray); It'll All Come Out in the Wash; What Do I Have to Do to Be a Star [1] (C: Kroll, Bobby; L: Carter, Everett)

**Notes** It is not known if all the above songs were written for the film. Other vocals included "On the Sunny Side of the Street" by Dorothy Fields and Jimmy McHugh; "Take Me in Your Arms" by Mitchell Parish and Fred Markush; "Hark, Hark the Lark" by Franz Schubert; "Old Folks at Home" by Stephen Foster and "The One I Love" by Gus Kahn and Isham Jones. [1] Carter not credited on cue sheet.

## 4391 ✦ ON THE AVENUE
Twentieth Century–Fox, 1936

**Composer(s)** Berlin, Irving
**Lyricist(s)** Berlin, Irving
**Choreographer(s)** Felix, Seymour

**Producer(s)** Zanuck, Darryl F.
**Director(s)** Del Ruth, Roy
**Screenwriter(s)** Markey, Gene; Conselman, William

**Cast** Powell, Dick; Carroll, Madeleine; Faye, Alice; The Ritz Brothers; Barbier, George; Mowbray, Alan; Witherspoon, Cora; Catlett, Walter; Fowley, Douglas; Fetchit, Stepin; Davis, Joan; Rumann, Sig; Gilbert, Billy; Gerrits, Paul; Wood, Douglas

**Song(s)** He Ain't Got Rhythm; Girl on the Police Gazette; Slumming on Park Avenue; You're Laughing at Me; This Year's Kisses; I've Got My Love to Keep Me Warm; On the Avenue [1]; Swing Sister [1]; On the Steps of Grant's Tomb [1]

**Notes** There is also a vocal of "Sonya" by Fred Fisher. [1] Recorded but not used.

## 4392 ✦ ON THE DOUBLE
Paramount, 1961

**Composer(s)** Fine, Sylvia
**Lyricist(s)** Fine, Sylvia

**Producer(s)** Rose, Jack
**Director(s)** Shavelson, Melville
**Screenwriter(s)** Shavelson, Melville; Rose, Jack

**Cast** Kaye, Danny; Wynter, Dana; Dors, Diana; Rutherford, Margaret; White, Wilfred Hyde; Cuthbertson, Allan; White, Jesse

**Song(s)** The Mackenzie Hielanders [1] [2]; Darlin' Meggie [1]

**Notes** [1] Same music. [2] First titled ON THE DOUBLE.

## 4393 ✦ ON THE GREAT WHITE TRAIL
Grand National, 1938

**Composer(s)** Porter, Lew; Taylor, Bob; Laidlow, Betty; Lively, Robert
**Lyricist(s)** Porter, Lew; Taylor, Bob; Laidlow, Betty; Lively, Robert

**Producer(s)**   Herman, Al
**Director(s)**   Herman, Al
**Screenwriter(s)**   Logue, Charles; Poland, Joseph F.

**Cast**   Newill, James; Walker, Terry; Fraser, Robert; Alexander, Richard; King, Charles

**Notes**   No cue sheet available.

## 4394 ✦ ON THE LEVEL
### Fox, 1930

**Producer(s)**   McGuinness, James Kevin
**Director(s)**   Cummings, Irving
**Screenwriter(s)**   Wells, William K.; Bennison, Andrew

**Cast**   McLaglen, Victor; D'Orsay, Fifi; Tashman, Lilyan; Harrigan, William; Stone, Arthur

**Song(s)**   Good Intentions (C: Monaco, James V.; L: Friend, Cliff); Good for Nothing but Love [1] (C/L: Kernell, William)

**Notes**   [1] Not listed on cue sheet. Also in THE BIG PARTY and SONG OF KENTUCKY.

## 4395 ✦ ON THE NICKEL
### Ralph Waite, 1980

**Musical Score**   Myrow, Fred

**Producer(s)**   Waite, Ralph
**Director(s)**   Waite, Ralph
**Screenwriter(s)**   Waite, Ralph

**Cast**   Waite, Ralph; Moffat, Donald; Williams, Hal; Allen, Penelope; Kehoe, Jack

**Song(s)**   On the Nickel (C/L: Waits, Tom); Roll Along (C: Myrow, Fred; L: Fleischer, Mark)

**Notes**   No cue sheet available.

## 4396 ✦ ON THE OLD SPANISH TRAIL
### Republic, 1947

**Producer(s)**   White, Eddy
**Director(s)**   Witney, William
**Screenwriter(s)**   Nibley, Sloan

**Cast**   Rogers, Roy; Trigger; Guizar, Tito; Frazee, Jane; Devine, Andy; Rodriguez, Estelita; McGraw, Charles; Graham, Fred; Bob Nolan and the Sons of the Pioneers

**Song(s)**   On the Old Spanish Trail (C/L: Kennedy, Jimmy; Smith, Ken L.); Here Is My Helping Hand (C/L: Nolan, Bob; Carson, Ken); I'll Never Love Again (C: Esperon, Ignacio Fernandez; L: Stewart, Al); My Adobe Hacienda [1] (C/L: Massey, Louise; Penny, Lee)

**Notes**   There are also vocals of "Guadalajara" by Pepe Guizar and "Una Furtiva Lagrima" by Donizetti. [1] Also in THE BIG SOMBRERO (Columbia) and BOB WILLS AND HIS TEXAS PLAYBOYS (Warner).

## 4397 ✦ ON THE RIGHT TRACK
### Twentieth Century–Fox, 1981

**Musical Score**   Rubinstein, Arthur B.

**Producer(s)**   Jacobs, Ronald
**Director(s)**   Philips, Lee
**Screenwriter(s)**   Pine, Tina; Buddy, Avery; Moses, Richard

**Cast**   Coleman, Gary; Lembeck, Michael; Eilbacher, Lisa; Stapleton, Maureen; Fell, Norman; Edelman, Herb

**Song(s)**   Take It Like a Woman (C/L: Sullett, Norman)

## 4398 ✦ ON THE RIVIERA
### Twentieth Century–Fox, 1951

**Composer(s)**   Fine, Sylvia
**Lyricist(s)**   Fine, Sylvia
**Choreographer(s)**   Cole, Jack

**Producer(s)**   Siegel, Sol C.
**Director(s)**   Lang, Walter
**Screenwriter(s)**   Davies, Valentine; Ephron, Phoebe; Ephron, Henry
**Source(s)**   (play) Lothar, Rudolph; Adler, Hans

**Cast**   Kaye, Danny; Tierney, Gene; Calvet, Corinne [3]; Dalio, Marcel; Letondal, Henri; Sundberg, Clinton; Rumann, Sig

**Song(s)**   On the Riviera; Scotch Number; Sur La Riviera (C: Newman, Alfred; L: Surmagne, Jacques); Viendras Ce Soir [2] (C: Newman, Alfred; L: Surmagne, Jacques); Rhythm of a New Romance; La Seine [1] (C: LaFarge, Guy; L: Monod, Flavien; LaFarge, Guy); Ballin' the Jack (C: Smith, Chris; L: Burris, Jim); Popo the Puppet; Happy Ending

**Notes**   This is a remake of FOLIES BERGERE (1935) as was THAT NIGHT IN RIO (1945). [1] Not written for this picture. [2] Also in UNDER MY SKIN. [3] Dubbed by Paula Dehelly.

## 4399 ✦ ON THE SUNNY SIDE OF THE STREET
### Columbia, 1951

**Choreographer(s)**   Brier, Audrene

**Producer(s)**   Taps, Jonie
**Director(s)**   Quine, Richard
**Screenwriter(s)**   Loeb, Lee

**Cast**   Laine, Frankie; Arden, Toni; Daniels, Billy; Courtland, Jerome; Bari, Lynn; Hale, Jonathan; Moore, Terry; Waterman, Willard

**Song(s)**   Munchee Commercial [1] (L: Loeb, Lee); Bockman's Beer [2] (L: Loeb, Lee)

**Notes**   There are no original songs in this movie. Songs given vocal treatment are: "On the Sunny Side of the Street" by Dorothy Fields and Jimmy McHugh; "Torna a Surriento" by E. De Curtis (also in Paramount's SEPTEMBER AFFAIR); "Pennies from Heaven" by

Arthur Johnston and Johnny Burke; "Let's Fall in Love" by Harold Arlen and Ted Koehler; "Too Marvelous for Words" by Johnny Mercer and Richard A. Whiting; "I Hadn't Anyone Till You" by Ray Noble; "I'm Gonna Live Till I Die" by Al Hoffman, Walter Kent and Manny Kurtz; "I May Be Wrong But I Think You're Wonderful" by Harry Ruskin and Henry Sullivan; "I Get a Kick Out of You" by Cole Porter; "The Love of a Gypsy" by Morris Stoloff and Fred Karger. [1] Based on "Oh Susanna." [2] Based on "Sing a Song of Sixpence."

## 4400 ✦ ON THE TOWN
### Metro–Goldwyn–Mayer, 1949

**Composer(s)** Bernstein, Leonard
**Lyricist(s)** Comden, Betty; Green, Adolph
**Choreographer(s)** Kelly, Gene; Donen, Stanley

**Producer(s)** Freed, Arthur
**Director(s)** Kelly, Gene; Donen, Stanley
**Screenwriter(s)** Green, Adolph; Comden, Betty
**Source(s)** *On the Town* (musical) Comden, Betty; Green, Adolph; Bernstein, Leonard

**Cast** Kelly, Gene; Sinatra, Frank; Garrett, Betty; Miller, Ann; Munshin, Jules; Vera-Ellen [2]; Bates, Florence; Pearce, Alice [1]; Meader, George

**Song(s)** New York, New York [1]; Miss Turnstiles Ballet (Inst.) [1]; Prehistoric Man (C: Edens, Roger); I Can Cook Too (Taxi Number) [1]; Main Street (C: Edens, Roger); You're Awful (C: Edens, Roger); On the Town (C: Edens, Roger); That's All There Is Folks (C: Edens, Roger); Count on Me (C: Edens, Roger); On the Town Ballet (Inst.); Pearl of the Persian Sea (C: Edens, Roger)

**Notes** An agreement between Bernstein and MGM listed several titles that were purchased along with the stage score. These were all written and deleted from the Broadway show. They are: "The Nicest Time of the Year," "Ain't Got No Tears Left" (this was cut from the musical and the music became a theme in the AGE OF ANXIETY symphony. Some of the music also appeared in Kelly's ballet in the film.), "Lonely Me," "Sleep in Your Lady's Arms," "Carnegie Hall Pavanne," "Say When," "I'm Afraid It's Love," "The Intermission's Great," "Got to Be Bad to Be Good" and "Dream with Me." [1] From Broadway musical. [2] Dubbed.

## 4401 ✦ ON THE WATERFRONT
### Columbia, 1954

**Musical Score** Bernstein, Leonard

**Producer(s)** Spiegel, Sam
**Director(s)** Kazan, Elia
**Screenwriter(s)** Schulberg, Budd

**Cast** Brando, Marlon; Malden, Karl; Cobb, Lee J.; Steiger, Rod; Henning, Pat; Saint, Eva Marie; Erickson, Leif; Westerfield, James; Galento, Tony; Gwynne, Fred; Balsam, Martin [2]

**Song(s)** On the Waterfront [1] (C: Bernstein, Leonard; L: Latouche, John)

**Notes** Schulberg's story is based on stories by Malcolm Johnson. [1] Lyric written for exploitation use only. [2] Billed as Marty Balsam.

## 4402 ✦ ON TOP OF OLD SMOKY
### Columbia, 1953

**Producer(s)** Schaefer, Armand
**Director(s)** Archainbaud, George

**Cast** Autry, Gene; Burnette, Smiley; Davis, Gail; Rhodes, Grandon; Ryan, Sheila; Champion; O'Malley, Pat

**Song(s)** I Saw Her First (C/L: Unknown); Hang My Head and Cry (C/L: Unknown); If It Wasn't for the Rain (C/L: Autry, Gene; Rose, Fred); Down the Trail to Mexico (C/L: Unknown)

**Notes** No cue sheet available. There is also a vocal of "On Top of Old Smokey."

## 4403 ✦ ON WINGS OF SONG

See LOVE ME FOREVER.

## 4404 ✦ ON WITH THE SHOW
### Warner Brothers, 1929

**Composer(s)** Akst, Harry
**Lyricist(s)** Clarke, Grant
**Choreographer(s)** Ceballos, Larry

**Director(s)** Crosland, Alan
**Screenwriter(s)** Lord, Robert
**Source(s)** *Shoestring* (play) Pearson, Humphrey

**Cast** Compson, Betty; Fazenda, Louise; O'Neil, Sally; Brown, Joe E.; Pratt, Purnell; Bakewell, William; The Fairbanks Twins; Hardy, Sam; Lake, Arthur; Waters, Ethel; The Harmony Four Quartette; The Four Covans; Fink, Henry [1]

**Song(s)** In the Land of Let's Pretend; Let Me Have My Dreams [3]; Welcome Home; Don't It Mean a Thing to You?; Lift the Juleps to Your Two Lips; On with the Show; Birmingham Bertha; Am I Blue? [2]

**Notes** No cue sheet available. [1] Fink, who sang "Lift the Juleps to Your Two Lips," was, according to *Variety*, "reputed one of the busiest ghost singers in Hollywood." [2] Also in SO LONG, LETTY and in FUNNY LADY. [3] Also in SO LONG, LETTY.

## 4405 ✦ ON YOUR BACK
### Fox, 1930

**Producer(s)** Middleton, George
**Director(s)** McClintic, Guthrie
**Screenwriter(s)** Green, Howard J.
**Source(s)** "On Your Back" (story) Weiman, Rita

**Cast** Rich, Irene; Hackett, Raymond; Warner, H.B.; Chase, Ilka; Shilling, Marion

**Song(s)** Bluer Than Blue Over You [1] (C: Kernell, William; L: Thompson, Harlan)

**Notes** [1] From THE BIG PARTY.

## 4406 ◆ ON YOUR TOES
### Warner Brothers–First National, 1939

**Musical Score** Roemheld, Heinz
**Choreographer(s)** Balanchine, George

**Producer(s)** Lord, Robert
**Director(s)** Enright, Ray
**Screenwriter(s)** Wald, Jerry; Macaulay, Richard
**Source(s)** *On Your Toes* (musical) Rodgers, Richard; Hart, Lorenz; Abbott, George

**Cast** Zorina, Vera; Albert, Eddie; Gleason, James; Hale, Alan; McHugh, Frank; Kinskey, Leonid; Dickson, Gloria; Smith, Queenie; Rhodes, Erik; Churchill, Berton; Wooten, Sarita; O'Connor, Donald

**Song(s)** La Princesse Zenobia (Inst.) (C: Rodgers, Richard); Slaughter on Tenth Avenue (Inst.) (C: Rodgers, Richard)

**Notes** No songs were retained from the Broadway score although "On Your Toes," "Quiet Night" and "There's a Small Hotel" are heard instrumentally as background music. The above ballets were from the Broadway musical and were choreographed by Balanchine for stage and screen.

## 4407 ◆ OPENING NIGHT
### Faces, 1977

**Musical Score** Harwood, Bo

**Producer(s)** Ruban, Al
**Director(s)** Cassavetes, John
**Screenwriter(s)** Cassavetes, John

**Cast** Rowlands, Gena; Cassavetes, John; Blondell, Joan; Stewart, Paul; Gazzara, Ben; Lampert, Zohra

**Song(s)** Comin' Home Again (C: Harwood, Bo; L: Cassavetes, John)

**Notes** No cue sheet available.

## 4408 ◆ OPERATION EICHMANN
### Allied Artists, 1961

**Musical Score** Alexander, Alex

**Producer(s)** Bischoff, Sam
**Director(s)** Springsteen, R.G.
**Screenwriter(s)** Coppley, Lewis

**Cast** Klemperer, Werner; Lee, Ruta; Buka, Donald; Turner, Barbara; Banner, John

**Song(s)** Es Muss Nur der Richtige Kommen (C: Steininger, Franz; L: Heimo, Gustav)

**Notes** No cue sheet available.

## 4409 ◆ OPERATION KID BROTHER
### United Artists, 1967

**Musical Score** Morricone, Ennio; Nicolai, Bruno

**Producer(s)** Sabatello, Dario
**Director(s)** De Martino, Alberto
**Screenwriter(s)** Levi, Paul; Walker, Frank

**Cast** Connery, Neil; Bianchi, Daniela; Celi, Adolfo; Flori, Agata; Lee, Bernard; Maxwell, Lois; Dawson, Anthony

**Song(s)** The Man for Me (C: Morricone, Ennio; Nicolai, Bruno; L: Nohra, Audrey)

**Notes** Also known as O.K. CONNERY.

## 4410 ◆ OPERATION PACIFIC
### Warner Brothers, 1951

**Musical Score** Steiner, Max

**Producer(s)** Edelman, Louis F.
**Director(s)** Waggner, George
**Screenwriter(s)** Waggner, George

**Cast** Wayne, John; Neal, Patricia; Bond, Ward; Forbes, Scott; Carey, Philip; Milner, Martin

**Song(s)** Round Ripe and Ruby Red (C: Heindorf, Ray; L: Waggner, George)

## 4411 ◆ OPERATION PETTICOAT
### Universal, 1959

**Musical Score** Rose, David

**Producer(s)** Arthur, Robert
**Director(s)** Edwards, Blake
**Screenwriter(s)** Shapiro, Stanley; Richlin, Maurice

**Cast** Grant, Cary; Curtis, Tony; O'Brien, Joan; Merrill, Dina; Evans, Gene; O'Connell, Arthur; Darro, Frankie; Sargent, Richard

**Song(s)** You Can't Win (C/L: Lampert, Diane; Loring, Richard)

## 4412 ◆ OPERATOR 13
### Metro–Goldwyn–Mayer, 1934

**Composer(s)** Donaldson, Walter
**Lyricist(s)** Kahn, Gus

**Producer(s)** Hubbard, Lucien
**Director(s)** Boleslawski, Richard
**Screenwriter(s)** Thew, Harvey; Sears, Zelda; Greene, Eve
**Source(s)** stories by Chambers, Robert W.

**Cast** Parker, Jean; Alexander, Katherine; Healy, Ted; The Four Mills Brothers; Davies, Marion; Cooper, Gary; Gateson, Marjorie

**Song(s)** Colonel, Major and Captain; Sleepy Head; Jungle Fever (L: Dietz, Howard); There's Someone Dreaming Tonight; Once in a Lifetime; Little Liza Lee [1]; My Heart Will Sing [1]

**Notes** [1] Used instrumentally only.

## 4413 ✦ THE OPPOSITE SEX
Metro–Goldwyn–Mayer, 1956

**Musical Score** Stoll, George
**Composer(s)** Brodszky, Nicholas
**Lyricist(s)** Cahn, Sammy
**Choreographer(s)** Sidney, Robert

**Producer(s)** Pasternak, Joe
**Director(s)** Miller, David
**Screenwriter(s)** Kanin, Michael; Kanin, Fay
**Source(s)** *The Women* (play) Boothe, Clare [3]

**Cast** Allyson, June [2]; Collins, Joan; Gray, Dolores; Sheridan, Ann; Miller, Ann; Nielsen, Leslie; Richards, Jeff; Moorehead, Agnes; Greenwood, Charlotte; Blondell, Joan; Levene, Sam; James, Harry; Shawn, Dick; Backus, Jim; Mooney, Art; Pearce, Alice; Jones, Carolyn

**Song(s)** The Opposite Sex; Dere's Yellow Gold on De Trees; The Young Man with a Horn [4] (C: Stoll, George; L: Freed, Ralph); A Perfect Love; Now! Baby! Now!; The Rock and Roll Tumbleweed; Jungle Red [1]

**Notes** [1] Used instrumentally only. [2] Dubbed by Jo Ann Greer for "A Perfect Love" but not for "The Young Man with a Horn" and "Now! Baby! Now!" [3] Known later as Clare Boothe Luce. [4] Same vocal recording (but abridged) used in TWO GIRLS AND A SAILOR.

## 4414 ✦ THE OPTIMISTS
Paramount, 1973

**Composer(s)** Bart, Lionel
**Lyricist(s)** Bart, Lionel

**Producer(s)** Gaye, Adrian; Lyndon, Victor
**Director(s)** Simmons, Anthony
**Screenwriter(s)** Gates, Tudor; Simmons, Anthony
**Source(s)** *The Optimists of Nine Elms* (novel) Simmons, Anthony

**Cast** Sellers, Peter; Yates, Marjorie; Mullane, Donna

**Song(s)** Sometimes; High and Dry; Something Special [1]

**Notes** The song "Mr. Bass Drum Man" by Alan Bernard and Don Crown was used but not written for the picture. [1] Written for but not used in the Broadway musical LA STRADA.

## 4415 ✦ ORCA
Paramount, 1977

**Musical Score** Morricone, Ennio

**Producer(s)** Vincenzoni, Luciano
**Director(s)** Anderson, Michael
**Screenwriter(s)** Vincenzoni, Luciano; Donati, Sergio

**Cast** Harris, Richard; Rampling, Charlotte; Wynn, Keenan; Derek, Bo; Sampson, Will; Carradine, Robert

**Song(s)** My Love, We Are One (C: Morricone, Ennio; L: Connors, Carol)

**Notes** Sometimes titled ORCA, THE KILLER WHALE.

## 4416 ✦ ORCHESTRA WIVES
Twentieth Century–Fox, 1942

**Composer(s)** Warren, Harry
**Lyricist(s)** Gordon, Mack
**Choreographer(s)** Castle, Nick

**Producer(s)** LeBaron, William
**Director(s)** Mayo, Archie
**Screenwriter(s)** Tunberg, Karl

**Cast** Montgomery, George [3]; Rutherford, Ann; Romero, Cesar [4]; Gleason, Jackie [5]; Glenn Miller and His Band; Bari, Lynn [1]; Landis, Carole; Gilmore, Virginia; Hughes, Mary Beth; The Nicholas Brothers; Geva, Tamara; Orth, Frank; Mitchell, Grant; Morgan, Henry; Eberle, Ray; Hutton, Marion; The Modernaires

**Song(s)** People Like You and Me; At Last [2]; Serenade in Blue; I've Got a Gal in Kalamazoo; Boom Shot (Inst.) (C: Miller, Glenn; May, Billy); Bugle Call Rag (Inst.) [6] (C: Pettis, Jack; Meyers, Billy; Schoebel, Elmer); That's Sabotage

**Notes** [1] Dubbed by Pat Friday. [2] Also used in SUN VALLEY SERENADE. [3] Trumpet playing dubbed by Steve Lipkin. [4] Piano playing dubbed by Chummy McGregor. [5] Bass dubbed by Doc Goldberg. [6] Written in 1923. Irving Mills, not Meyers is credited on cue sheet.

## 4417 ✦ THE OREGON TRAIL
Twentieth Century–Fox, 1959

**Musical Score** Dunlap, Paul

**Producer(s)** Einfeld, Richard
**Director(s)** Fowler Jr., Gene
**Screenwriter(s)** Vittes, Louis; Fowler Jr., Gene

**Cast** MacMurray, Fred; Bishop, William; Shipman, Nina; Talbot, Gloria; Hull, Henry; Carradine, John; Fowler, Gene N.

**Song(s)** Ballad of Oregon Trail (C: Dunlap, Paul; L: Devlan, Charles)

## 4418 ◆ ORGASMO

See PARANOIA.

## 4419 ◆ ORIENT EXPRESS
Fox, 1934

**Producer(s)** Wurtzel, Sol M.
**Director(s)** Martin, Paul
**Screenwriter(s)** Martin, Paul; Hovey, Carl; Levant, Oscar
**Source(s)** (novel) Greene, Graham

**Cast** Foster, Norman; Angel, Heather

**Song(s)** The Kitten Song (C: Tresselt, Frank; L: Tresselt, Frank; O'Keefe; Friedhofer, Hugo; Field); Impressions Rhapsodique Hongroise (C: De Francesco, Louis E.; L: Gyory)

## 4420 ◆ ORPHANS OF THE STREET
Republic, 1938

**Producer(s)** Schlom, Herman
**Director(s)** Auer, John H.
**Screenwriter(s)** Cooper, Olive; Townley, Jack; Taylor, Eric

**Cast** Ryan, Tommy; Livingston, Robert; Storey, June; Morgan, Ralph; Davenport, Harry; Blackmer, Sidney; Burke, James; Killian, Victor; Cavanaugh, Hobart

**Song(s)** Yo Ho Ho (C: Lava, William; L: Cherkose, Eddie)

## 4421 ◆ THE OSCAR
Paramount, 1966

**Musical Score** Faith, Percy
**Composer(s)** Faith, Percy
**Lyricist(s)** Livingston, Jay; Evans, Ray

**Producer(s)** Green, Clarence
**Director(s)** Rouse, Russell
**Screenwriter(s)** Ellison, Harlan; Rouse, Russell; Greene, Clarence
**Source(s)** *The Oscar* (novel) Sale, Richard

**Cast** Boyd, Stephen; Sommer, Elke; Berle, Milton; Parker, Eleanor; Cotten, Joseph; St. John, Jill; Bennett, Tony; Adams, Edie; Borgnine, Ernest

**Song(s)** The Glass Mountain; Maybe September [1]

**Notes** [1] Used instrumentally only.

## 4422 ◆ O'SHAUGHNESSY'S BOY
Metro–Goldwyn–Mayer, 1935

**Musical Score** Axt, William

**Producer(s)** Goldstone, Philip
**Director(s)** Boleslawski, Richard
**Screenwriter(s)** Praskins, Leonard; Garrett, Otis

**Cast** Cooper, Jackie; McFarland, George "Spanky"; Beery, Wallace; Robertson, Willard; Muse, Clarence; Maricle, Leona; Stephenson, Henry; Haden, Sara

**Song(s)** The Tattooed Lady [2] (C/L: O'Keefe, Walter); I Heard a Blind Man Singing (in the Street) [1] (C/L: Muse, Clarence)

**Notes** [1] Also in AFTER THE DANCE (Columbia). [2] Also in CALM YOURSELF and ELMER AND ELSIE (Paramount).

## 4423 ◆ THE OTHER LOVE
United Artists, 1947

**Musical Score** Rozsa, Miklos

**Producer(s)** Lewis, David
**Director(s)** de Toth, Andre
**Screenwriter(s)** Fodor, Ladislas; Brown, Harry
**Source(s)** "Beyond" (story) Remarque, Erich Maria

**Cast** Stanwyck, Barbara; Niven, David; Palmer, Maria; Lorring, Joan; Conte, Richard; Shafer, Natalie

**Song(s)** I Suppose It's Love (C: Rozsa, Miklos; L: Lorraine, Bobbie)

## 4424 ◆ THE OTHER SIDE OF THE MOUNTAIN
Universal, 1975

**Musical Score** Fox, Charles

**Producer(s)** Feldman, Edward S.
**Director(s)** Peerce, Larry
**Screenwriter(s)** Seltzer, David
**Source(s)** *A Long Way Up* (book) Valens, E.G.

**Cast** Hassett, Marilyn; Bridges, Beau; Montgomery, Belinda J.; Martin, Nan; Bryant, William; Coleman, Dabney; Vint, Bill

**Song(s)** Richard's Window (C: Fox, Charles; L: Gimbel, Norman)

**Notes** Titled A WINDOW IN THE SKY outside the U.S.

## 4425 ◆ THE OTHER SIDE OF THE MOUNTAIN PART 2
Universal, 1978

**Musical Score** Holdridge, Lee

**Producer(s)** Feldman, Edward S.
**Director(s)** Peerce, Larry
**Screenwriter(s)** Stewart, Douglas Day

**Cast** Hassett, Marilyn; Bottoms, Timothy; Martin, Nan; Montgomery, Belinda J.

**Song(s)** It's Time to Say I Love You (C: Holdridge, Lee; L: Leikin, Molly-Ann)

**4426 ✦ OTLEY**
Columbia, 1968

**Musical Score**    Myers, Stanley

**Producer(s)**    Curtis, Bruce Cohn
**Director(s)**    Clement, Dick
**Screenwriter(s)**    Clement, Dick; La Frenais, Ian

**Cast**    Courtenay, Tom; Schneider, Romy; Badel, Alan; Villiers, James; Rossiter, Leonard; Jones, Freddie

**Song(s)**    Homeless Bones (C: Myers, Stanley; L: Partridge, Don); Tell Her You Love Her [1] (C: Myers, Stanley; L: Sharper, Hal)

**Notes**    [1] Sheet music only.

**4427 ✦ OUR DANCING DAUGHTERS**
Metro–Goldwyn–Mayer, 1928

**Producer(s)**    Stromberg, Hunt
**Director(s)**    Beaumont, Harry
**Screenwriter(s)**    Ainslee, Marian; Cummings, Ruth
**Source(s)**    (serialized novel) Lovett, Josephine

**Cast**    Crawford, Joan; Brown, Johnny Mack; Asther, Nils; Sebastian, Dorothy; Page, Anita

**Song(s)**    I Loved You Then As I Love You Now [1] (C: Axt, William; L: Mendoza, David; Macdonald, Ballard); Low Down (C: De Rose, Peter; L: Unknown); Me and the Boy Friend [2] (C: Monaco, James V.; L: Clare, Sidney)

**Notes**    [1] Macdonald not listed in all sources. [2] Written in 1923.

**4428 ✦ OUR HEARTS WERE GROWING UP**
Paramount, 1946

**Producer(s)**    Dare, Danny [2]
**Director(s)**    Russell, William D.
**Screenwriter(s)**    Panama, Norman; Frank, Melvin
**Source(s)**    *Our Hearts Were Growing Up* (book) Skinner, Cornelia Otis; Kimbrough, Emily

**Cast**    Russell, Gail; Lynn, Diana; Donlevy, Brian; De Wolfe, Billy; Demarest, William; Faylen, Frank

**Song(s)**    Going Back to Nassau Hall [1] (C/L: Clark, Kenneth S.); Your Heart Just Can't Go Wrong [1] [3] (C: Whiting, Richard A.; L: Robin, Leo)

**Notes**    [1] Not written for production. [2] Billed as Daniel Dare. [3] Written in 1930.

**4429 ✦ OUR HEARTS WERE YOUNG AND GAY**
Paramount, 1944

**Producer(s)**    Gibney, Sheridan
**Director(s)**    Allen, Lewis

**Screenwriter(s)**    Gibney, Sheridan
**Source(s)**    *Our Hearts Were Young and Gay* (book) Skinner, Cornelia Otis; Kimbrough, Emily

**Cast**    Russell, Gail; Lynn, Diana; Ruggles, Charles; Gish, Dorothy; Brown, James; Edwards, Bill; Heather, Jean; Kruger, Alma

**Song(s)**    When Our Hearts Were Young and Gay [1] (C: Grouya, Ted; L: Goell, Kermit)

**Notes**    [1] Not used in picture. Written for exploitation.

**4430 ✦ OUR LITTLE GIRL**
Fox, 1935

**Producer(s)**    Butcher, Edward
**Director(s)**    Robertson, John
**Screenwriter(s)**    Avery, Stephen Morehouse; Rivkin, Allen; Yellen, Jack; Beckhard, Arthur
**Source(s)**    "Heaven's Gate" (story) Pfalzgraf, Florence Leighton

**Cast**    Temple, Shirley; Ames, Rosemary; McCrea, Joel

**Song(s)**    Our Little Girl (C: Pollack, Lew; L: Webster, Paul Francis)

**Notes**    Originally titled HEAVEN'S GATE.

**4431 ✦ OUR MAN FLINT**
Twentieth Century–Fox, 1965

**Musical Score**    Goldsmith, Jerry

**Producer(s)**    David, Saul
**Director(s)**    Mann, Daniel
**Screenwriter(s)**    Fimberg, Hal; Starr, Ben

**Cast**    Coburn, James; Cobb, Lee J.; Golan, Gila; Mulhare, Edward; Fong, Benson; Grant, Shelby; St. Clair, Michael; Williams, Rhys

**Song(s)**    Our Man Flint [1] (C: Goldsmith, Jerry; L: Wayne, Bernie)

**Notes**    [1] Used instrumentally only.

**4432 ✦ OUR TIME**
Warner Brothers, 1974

**Musical Score**    Legrand, Michel

**Producer(s)**    Roth, Richard A.
**Director(s)**    Hyams, Peter
**Screenwriter(s)**    Stanton, Jane C.

**Cast**    Slade, Betty; Martin, Pamela Sue; Stevenson, Parker; O'Hanlon Jr., George; Walden, Robert; Balkin, Karen

**Song(s)**    All Things Bright and Beautiful (C: Legrand, Michel; Alexander, Cecil F.)

## 4433 ✦ OUT CALIFORNIA WAY
### Republic, 1946

**Producer(s)** Gray, Louis
**Director(s)** Springsteen, R.G.
**Screenwriter(s)** Burbridge, Betty

**Cast** Hale, Monte; Booth, Adrian; Blake, Bobby; Dehner, John; Graham, Fred; Leary, Nolan; St. Luke's Choirsters; Foy Willing and the Riders of the Purple Sage

**Song(s)** Out California Way [1] (C/L: Carling, Foster; Meskin, Jack); Little Bronc of Mine (C/L: Carlson, Tex); Hello Monte (C/L: Willing, Foy); Detour (C/L: Westmoreland, Paul); Rose of Santa Fe (C/L: Willing, Foy); Ridin' Down the Sunset Trail [2] (C/L: Elliott, Jack); Boogie Woogie Cowboy (C/L: Dean, Eddie; Blair, Hal; Statham, Jack; Snow, Gus)

**Notes** [1] Also in HIT PARADE OF 1947. [2] Also in RAINBOW OVER TEXAS.

## 4434 ✦ OUTCAST OF BLACK MESA
### Columbia, 1950

**Composer(s)** Burnette, Smiley
**Lyricist(s)** Burnette, Smiley

**Director(s)** Nazarro, Ray
**Screenwriter(s)** Shipman, Barry

**Cast** Starrett, Charles; Burnette, Smiley; Hyer, Martha; Andrews, Stanley

**Song(s)** Nobody Fire the Boss; Just Sittin' Round in Jail [1] (L: Clark, Frances); Donkey Engine

**Notes** [1] Based on "Shoo Fly."

## 4435 ✦ OUTCASTS OF THE TRAIL
### Republic, 1949

**Producer(s)** Tucker, Melville
**Director(s)** Ford, Philip
**Screenwriter(s)** Cooper, Olive

**Cast** Hale, Monte; Hurst, Paul; Barcroft, Roy; Donnell, Jeff

**Song(s)** I Wish I Was a Kid Again (C/L: Elliott, Jack)

## 4436 ✦ OUTLAW BLUES
### Warner Brothers, 1977

**Producer(s)** Tisch, Steve
**Director(s)** Heffron, Richard T.
**Screenwriter(s)** Norton, B.W.L.

**Cast** Fonda, Peter; Callahan, James; Saint James, Susan; Crawford, John; Lerner, Michael; Clar, Matt

**Song(s)** Outlaw Blues (C/L: Oates, John); Jailbirds Can't Fly (C/L: O'Leary, Richard C.; Sanders, Harlan); Beyond These Walls (C/L: Axton, Hoyt); Whisper in a Velvet Night (C/L: Clayton, Lee); I Dream of Highways (C/L: Axton, Hoyt); Water for My Horses (C/L: Axton, Hoyt)

## 4437 ✦ OUTLAW EXPRESS
### Universal, 1938

**Composer(s)** Allan, Fleming
**Lyricist(s)** Allan, Fleming

**Producer(s)** Carr, Trem
**Director(s)** Waggner, George
**Screenwriter(s)** Parker, Norton S.

**Cast** Baker, Bob; Callejo, Cecilia

**Song(s)** Down the Trail with the Pony Express; Out to California; Amigo Mio; Then You'll Be My Loretta; La Cucaracha (C/L: Savino, Domenico; Washington, Ned)

## 4438 ✦ OUTLAWS OF SONORA
### Republic, 1938

**Producer(s)** Berke, William
**Director(s)** Sherman, George
**Screenwriter(s)** Burbridge, Betty; Kelso, Edmund

**Cast** Livingston, Robert; Terhune, Max; Corrigan, Ray; Mulhall, Jack; Harlan, Otis; Joyce, Jean; Peluffo, Stelita; London, Tom

**Song(s)** Camioneros (C/L: Durant, Eddie)

## 4439 ✦ OUTLAWS OF THE DESERT
### Paramount, 1941

**Producer(s)** Sherman, Harry
**Director(s)** Bretherton, Howard
**Screenwriter(s)** De Mond, Albert

**Cast** Boyd, William; King, Brad; Deste, Luli; Clyde, Andy

**Song(s)** Riding for a Fall (C/L: Schertzinger, Victor)

## 4440 ✦ OUT OF BOUNDS
### Columbia, 1986

**Musical Score** Copeland, Stewart

**Producer(s)** Fries, Charles; Rosenfeld, Mike
**Director(s)** Tuggle, Richard
**Screenwriter(s)** Kayden, Tony

**Cast** Hall, Anthony Michael; Wright, Jenny; Kober, Jeff; Turman, Glynn; Barry, Raymond J.; Serna, Pepe; Meat Loaf

**Song(s)** Little By Little (C/L: Daigle, Robert J.); Wild If I Want To (C/L: Alves, Joseph; Haze, Leonard E.; Kemmore, Phillip M.); Run Away (C/L: Berry, Robert); Out of Bounds (C: Copeland, Stewart; L: Ant, Adam); Run Now (C/L: Keene, Tommy)

**4441 ✦ OUT OF IT**
United Artists, 1969

**Musical Score**   Small, W.

**Director(s)**   Oury, Gerard
**Screenwriter(s)**   Oury, Gerard; Thompson, Daniele

**Cast**   Richard, Pierre; Lanoux, Victor; Bussieres, Raymond; Darras, Jean-Pierre; Godeau, Yvonne

**Song(s)**   Electric Days (C: Small, W.; L: Benedikt, M.); You Surprise Me (C: Small, W.; L: Benedikt, M.)

**4442 ✦ OUT OF SIGHT**
Universal, 1966

**Musical Score**   Darian, Fred; De Lory, Al [1]

**Producer(s)**   Weinrib, Lennie; Patton, Bart
**Director(s)**   Weinrib, Lennie
**Screenwriter(s)**   Hovis, Larry

**Cast**   Gary Lewis and the Playboys; Freddie and the Dreamers; The Turtles; The Astronauts; The Knickerbockers; Lawrence, John; Daly, Jonathan; Jensen, Karen; Pine, Carole; Shelyn, Carole

**Song(s)**   Malibu Run (C/L: Karstein, Jim; Russell, Leon; Lewis, Gary; Lesslie, Thomas); It's Not Unusual (C/L: Mills, Gordon; Reed, Les); Baby Please Don't Go (C/L: Williams, Joe); She'll Come Back (C: Garfield, Nita; L: Kaylan, Howard); Funny Over You (C/L: Garrity, Freddie); A Love Like You (C/L: Quinn, Derek; James, Alan)

**Notes**   [1] Billed as Alfred V. De Lory.

**4443 ✦ OUT OF THE BLUE**
Eagle Lion, 1947

**Musical Score**   Dragon, Carmen
**Composer(s)**   Nemo, Henry
**Lyricist(s)**   Jason, Will

**Producer(s)**   Foy, Bryan
**Director(s)**   Jason, Leigh
**Screenwriter(s)**   Bullock, Walter; Caspary, Vera; Eliscu, Edward

**Cast**   Mayo, Virginia; Brent, George; Bey, Turhan; Dvorak, Ann; Landis, Carole; Brooks, Hedda; Smith, Charlie; Patterson, Elizabeth; Dean, Julia

**Song(s)**   Out of the Blue [1]; Piano Blues

**Notes**   [1] Also in IN THIS CORNER.

**4444 ✦ OUT OF THE PAST**
RKO, 1947

**Musical Score**   Webb, Roy

**Producer(s)**   Duff, Warren
**Director(s)**   Tourneur, Jacques
**Screenwriter(s)**   Homes, Geoffrey

**Source(s)**   *Build My Gallows High* (novel) Homes, Geoffrey

**Cast**   Mitchum, Robert; Greer, Jane; Douglas, Kirk; Fleming, Rhonda; Webb, Richard; Brodie, Steve; Huston, Virginia; Valentine, Paul; Moore, Dickie; Niles, Ken

**Song(s)**   The First Time I Saw You [1] (C: Shilkret, Nathaniel; L: Wrubel, Allie)

**Notes**   [1] Also in THE FALCON TAKES OVER, LAW OF THE UNDERWORLD and TOAST OF NEW YORK.

**4445 ✦ OUT OF THIS WORLD**
Paramount, 1945

**Choreographer(s)**   Lee, Sammy

**Producer(s)**   Coslow, Sam
**Director(s)**   Walker, Hal
**Screenwriter(s)**   De Leon, Walter; Phillip, Arthur

**Cast**   Bracken, Eddie [5]; Lynn, Diana; Lake, Veronica; Bates, Florence; Paige, Mabel; Parkyakarkus; Daley, Cass; MacBride, Donald; San Juan, Olga; Noble, Ray; Cavallaro, Carmen; Fiorito, Ted

**Song(s)**   Out of This World (C: Arlen, Harold; L: Mercer, Johnny); June Comes Around Every Year (C: Arlen, Harold; L: Mercer, Johnny); The Ghost of Mr. Chopin (C: Wayne, Bernie; L: Raleigh, Ben); Rednow Lipstick [1] (L: Coslow, Sam); I'd Rather Be Me [3] (C: Bernard, Felix; L: Coslow, Sam; Cherkose, Eddie); It Takes a Little Bit More (C/L: Coslow, Sam); All I Do Is Beat This Gol-Durn Drum (C: Wayne, Bernie; L: Raleigh, Ben; Coslow, Sam); When My Man Comes Home [2] (C: Wayne, Bernie; L: Raleigh, Ben); Please Don't Ration the Boogie Woogie [2] [7] (C: Wayne, Bernie; L: Raleigh, Ben); A Sailor with an Eight Hour Pass [2] (C: Wayne, Bernie; L: Raleigh, Ben); Double Bubble Bath Salts [2] (C: Wayne, Bernie; L: Raleigh, Ben); I Owe It All to You [2] (C: Arlen, Harold; L: Mercer, Johnny); Let's Take the Long Way Home [2] [6] (C: Arlen, Harold; L: Mercer, Johnny)

**Notes**   Movie first titled DIVIDED BY FIVE. [1] Music based on "Frere Jacques." [2] Not used. [3] Coslow revised the lyrics. [5] Dubbed by Bing Crosby. Which is a joke in the movie, not a secret. [6] Used in HERE COME THE WAVES. [7] Also in BOOGIE WOOGIE.

**4446 ✦ THE OUT-OF-TOWNERS**
Paramount, 1970

**Musical Score**   Jones, Quincy

**Producer(s)**   Nathan, Paul
**Director(s)**   Hiller, Arthur
**Screenwriter(s)**   Simon, Neil

**Cast**   Dennis, Sandy; Lemmon, Jack; Meara, Anne; Montalban, Carlos; Williams, Billy Dee

**Song(s)** The Out-of-Towners [1] (C: Jones, Quincy; L: Gimbel, Norman)

**Notes** [1] Not used.

### 4447 ◆ OUTRAGEOUS FORTUNE
Disney, 1987

**Musical Score** Silvestri, Alan

**Producer(s)** Field, Ted; Cort, Robert W.
**Director(s)** Hiller, Arthur
**Screenwriter(s)** Dixon, Leslie

**Cast** Long, Shelley; Midler, Bette; Coyote, Peter; Prosky, Robert; Schuck, John; Carlin, George; Heald, Anthony; Zaks, Jerry

**Song(s)** Something Special (C/L: Rice, Howie; Rich, Allan Dennis)

**Notes** No cue sheet available.

### 4448 ◆ OUTSIDE OF PARADISE
Republic, 1938

**Composer(s)** Tinturin, Peter
**Lyricist(s)** Lawrence, Jack

**Producer(s)** Sauber, Harry
**Director(s)** Auer, John H.
**Screenwriter(s)** Sauber, Harry

**Cast** Regan, Phil; Singleton, Penny; Gordon, Bert; Kinskey, Leonid; Coleman, Ruth; Pape, Lionel; Nazarro, Cliff; Lind Hayes, Peter

**Song(s)** A Sweet Irish Sweetheart of Mine; I Was the Power Behind the Throne; All for One and One for All; Outside of Paradise; Shenanigans; A Little Bit of Everything

### 4449 ◆ THE OUTSIDER
Paramount, 1980

**Director(s)** Luraschi, Tony
**Screenwriter(s)** Luraschi, Tony
**Source(s)** *The Heritage of Michael Flaherty* (novel) Leinster, Colin

**Cast** Wasson, Craig; Hayden, Sterling; Quinn, Patricia; Toibin, Niall; McKenna, T.P.; Grimes, Frank; MacAnally, Ray; Dowling, Joe

**Song(s)** Finbar's Song (C/L: Hogan, Bosco)

### 4450 ◆ THE OUTSIDERS
Warner Brothers, 1983

**Musical Score** Coppola, Carmine

**Producer(s)** Roos, Fred; Frederickson, Gray
**Director(s)** Coppola, Francis Ford
**Screenwriter(s)** Rowell, Kathleen Knutson
**Source(s)** *The Outsiders* (novel) Hinton, S.E.

**Cast** Dillon, Matt; Macchio, Ralph; Howell, C. Thomas; Swayze, Patrick; Lowe, Rob; Estevez, Emilio; Cruise, Tom; Withrow, Glenn; Lane, Diane; Garrett, Leif; Waits, Tom

**Song(s)** So Gold (C: Coppola, Carmine; L: Wonder, Stevie); The Loveless Motel (C/L: Sanders, Harlan; Bannon, Royal C.); Jack Daniels If You Please (C/L: Coe, David Allan); Outside In [1] (C: Coppola, Carmine; L: Pennino, Italia; Seeman, Roxanne)

**Notes** Van Morrison's "Gloria" is also heard on the soundtrack. These are all background vocals. [1] Sheet music only.

### 4451 ◆ OUTSIDE THE LAW
Universal, 1930

**Musical Score** Perry, Sam A.

**Director(s)** Browning, Tod
**Screenwriter(s)** Browning, Tod; Fort, Garrett

**Cast** Robinson, Edward G.; Nolan, Mary; Moore, Owen; Sturgis, Edwin

**Song(s)** That's How I Need You (C/L: Piantadosi, Al)

**Notes** A remake of a 1921 version also directed by Browning.

### 4452 ◆ OVERBOARD
Metro–Goldwyn–Mayer, 1987

**Musical Score** Silvestri, Alan

**Producer(s)** Rose, Alexandra; Sylbert, Anthea
**Director(s)** Marshall, Garry
**Screenwriter(s)** Dixon, Leslie

**Cast** Hawn, Goldie; Russell, Kurt; Herrmann, Edward; Helmond, Katherine; Hagerty, Michael; McDowall, Roddy; Rushton, Jared

**Song(s)** Jim Dandy (C/L: Chase, Lincoln); Show Down in Hot Blood (C/L: Hellard, Ron; Jones, Bucky; Shapiro, Tom); Legs (C/L: Gibbons, Billy; Hill, Dusty; Beard, Frank); Something Special About Our Love (C/L: Newman, Randy)

**Notes** It is not known which of the above were written for this film.

### 4453 ◆ OVER THE GOAL
Warner Brothers–First National, 1937

**Musical Score** Roemheld, Heinz
**Composer(s)** Jerome, M.K.
**Lyricist(s)** Scholl, Jack

**Producer(s)** Foy, Bryan
**Director(s)** Smith, Noel
**Screenwriter(s)** Jacobs, William; Coldeway, Anthony
**Source(s)** "Block That Kick" (story) Jacobs, William

**Cast** Hopper, William; Travis, June; Davis, Johnnie; Harrigan, William; Hatton, Raymond; Rawlinson,

Herbert; Todd, Mabel; Oliver, Gordon; Parker, Willard; Anderson, Eddie "Rochester"; McDaniel, Hattie

**Song(s)** Carlton Victory March; As Easy As Rolling Off a Log; Scattin' with Mister Bear; Girl of My College Days [1]

**Notes** [1] Heard instrumentally only.

## 4454 ✦ OVER THE HILL
Fox, 1931

**Director(s)** King, Henry
**Screenwriter(s)** Barry, Tom; Furthman, Jules
**Source(s)** "Over the Hill to the Poorhouse" (poems) Carleton, Will

**Cast** Marsh, Mae; Kirkwood, James; Dunn, James; Eilers, Sally; Howland, Olin

**Song(s)** Contented (C/L: Hanley, James F.)

## 4455 ✦ OVER THE TOP
Warner Brothers, 1987

**Musical Score** Moroder, Giorgio
**Composer(s)** Moroder, Giorgio
**Lyricist(s)** Whitlock, Tom

**Producer(s)** Golan, Menahem; Globus, Yoram
**Director(s)** Golan, Menahem
**Screenwriter(s)** Silliphant, Stirling; Stallone, Sylvester

**Cast** Stallone, Sylvester; Loggia, Robert; Blakely, Susan; Zumwalt, Rick; Mendenhall, David

**Song(s)** In This Country; Bad Night (C/L: Stallone, Frank; Schless, Peter H.); Gypsy Soul; All I Need Is You; I Will Be Strong; Meet Me Halfway; Mind Over Matter; Winner Takes All; Take It Higher

**Notes** Some of these are background vocals.

## 4456 ✦ OVER THE WALL
Warner Brothers, 1938

**Composer(s)** Jerome, M.K.
**Lyricist(s)** Scholl, Jack

**Producer(s)** Foy, Bryan
**Director(s)** McDonald, Frank
**Screenwriter(s)** Wilbur, Crane; Bricker, George
**Source(s)** "One More Tomorrow" (story) Lawes, Lewis E.

**Cast** Foran, Dick; Travis, June; Litel, John; Purcell, Dick; Borg, Veda Ann; Stone, George E.; Bond, Ward; Hamilton, John

**Song(s)** Have You Met Lulu; The Little White House on the Hill; One More Tomorrow

**Notes** Originally titled EVIDENCE.

## 4457 ✦ THE OWL AND THE PUSSYCAT
Columbia, 1970

**Musical Score** Halligan, Richard
**Composer(s)** Halligan, Richard
**Lyricist(s)** Fielder, Jim

**Producer(s)** Stark, Ray
**Director(s)** Ross, Herbert
**Screenwriter(s)** Henry, Buck; Bernard, Ian; Friedman, Bruce Jay
**Source(s)** *The Owl and the Pussycat* (play) Manhoff, Bill

**Cast** Streisand, Barbra; Segal, George

**Song(s)** Jackson Highway; What Are You Doin'; Celebration

**Notes** All the songs are background vocals.

## 4458 ✦ THE OX-BOW INCIDENT
Twentieth Century–Fox, 1943

**Musical Score** Mockridge, Cyril J.

**Producer(s)** Trotti, Lamar
**Director(s)** Wellman, William A.
**Screenwriter(s)** Trotti, Lamar
**Source(s)** *The Ox-Bow Incident* (novel) Clark, Walter Van Tilberg

**Cast** Fonda, Henry; Andrews, Dana; Hughes, Mary Beth; Quinn, Anthony; Eythe, William; Morgan, Henry; Darwell, Jane; Briggs, Matt; Davenport, Harry; Lawrence, Marc; Killian, Victor; Martin, Chris-Pin; Hamilton, Margaret; Meeker, George

**Song(s)** You Got to Go Through the Lonesome Valley (C/L: Whipper, Leigh)

## 4459 ✦ OXFORD BLUES
MGM/UA, 1984

**Musical Score** Duprez, Jean

**Producer(s)** Elwes, Cassian; Kastner, Elliott
**Director(s)** Boris, Robert
**Screenwriter(s)** Boris, Robert

**Cast** Lowe, Rob; Sheedy, Ally; Pays, Amanda; Sands, Julian; Firth, Julian; Elwes, Cary; Gough, Michael; Howard, Alan

**Song(s)** I've Got What You Want (C/L: Jabara, Paul; Wheeler, Harold); Find the Girl (C/L: Thornally, Phil); Risking It All on Love (C/L: Chesky, Norman; Brandt, Galen; Gray, Jody; Chesky, David); Stowaway (C/L: Ryder, Mark)

**Notes** It is not known which of these were written for this picture.

# P

## 4460 ✦ PACIFIC BLACKOUT
### Paramount, 1941

**Producer(s)**  Siegel, Sol C.
**Director(s)**  Murphy, Ralph
**Screenwriter(s)**  Cole, Lester; Lipscomb, W.P.

**Cast**  Gabor, Eva [1]; Preston, Robert; O'Driscoll, Martha

**Song(s)**  I Met Him in Paris [2] (C: Carmichael, Hoagy; L: Meinardi, Helen)

**Notes**  First called MIDNIGHT ANGEL and also AIR RAID ANGEL. [1] Dubbed by Martha Mears. [2] See note under I MET HIM IN PARIS.

## 4461 ✦ PACIFIC HIGH
### Roy E. Disney, 1980

**Musical Score**  Brunner, Robert F.

**Producer(s)**  Disney, Roy Edward
**Director(s)**  Ahnemann, Michael

**Cast**  Disney, Roy Edward; Pasquini, Bill; Livingston, Monte; Boettcher, Buzz; Kristov, Kris

**Song(s)**  Sometimes (C: Brunner, Robert F.; L: Disney, Roy Edward)

**Notes**  No cue sheet available.

## 4462 ✦ PACIFIC LINER
### RKO, 1938

**Musical Score**  Bennett, Russell

**Producer(s)**  Sisk, Robert
**Director(s)**  Landers, Lew
**Screenwriter(s)**  Twist, John

**Cast**  McLaglen, Victor; Morris, Chester; Barrie, Wendy; Hale, Alan; Fitzgerald, Barry; Lane, Allan; Hobbes, Halliwell

**Song(s)**  Tonight Lover Tonight [1] (C/L: Stern, Jack; Tobias, Harry); Voodoo Chant (C/L: Bennett, Robert Russell)

**Notes**  [1] Also in CRIMINAL LAWYER.

## 4463 ✦ PACIFIC PARADISE
### Metro–Goldwyn–Mayer, 1937

**Composer(s)**  Owens, Harry
**Lyricist(s)**  Owens, Harry

**Producer(s)**  Lewyn, Louis
**Director(s)**  Sidney, George

**Cast**  Edwards, Cliff; The Royal Hawaiian Hula Girls; Harger and Maye; Harry Owens Royal Hawaiian Orchestra

**Song(s)**  Hawaiian Paradise; O-K-Le-Ma-Lu-Na; If Your Aloha Means I Love You; Oni Oni; To You Sweetheart Aloha

**Notes**  Short subject.

## 4464 ✦ PACK TRAIN
### Columbia, 1953

**Producer(s)**  Schaefer, Armand
**Director(s)**  Archainbaud, George
**Screenwriter(s)**  Hall, Norman S.

**Cast**  Autry, Gene; Burnette, Smiley; Davis, Gail; Duncan, Kenne; Ryan, Sheila; Maynard, Kermit; Champion

**Song(s)**  Hominy Grits (C/L: Unknown); Wagon Trail (C/L: Unknown); God's Little Candles (C/L: Unknown)

**Notes**  No cue sheet available.

## 4465 ✦ PACK UP YOUR TROUBLES
### Twentieth Century–Fox, 1939

**Producer(s)**  Wurtzel, Sol M.
**Director(s)**  Humberstone, H. Bruce
**Screenwriter(s)**  Breslow, Lou; Francis, Owen

**Cast**  Withers, Jane; The Ritz Brothers; Bari, Lynn; Schildkraut, Joseph; Fields, Stanley; Leiber, Fritz; Royce, Lionel; Ames, Leon

**Song(s)**  Who'll Buy My Flowers (C: Styne, Jule; L: Clare, Sidney); Forever (C/L: Kaylin, Samuel)

**4466 ✦ THE PAD (AND HOW TO USE IT)**
Universal, 1966

**Producer(s)**   Hunter, Ross
**Director(s)**   Hutton, Brian G.
**Screenwriter(s)**   Ryan, Thomas C.; Starr, Ben
**Source(s)**   *The Private Ear* (play) Shaffer, Peter

**Cast**   Bedford, Brian; Farentino, James; Sommers, Julie; Williams, Edy; Navarro, Nick; Shear, Pearl; London, Barbara

**Song(s)**   The Pad (And How to Use It) (C/L: Allen, Robert)

**4467 ✦ PADDY O'DAY**
Twentieth Century–Fox, 1935

**Composer(s)**   Akst, Harry
**Lyricist(s)**   Clare, Sidney; Eliscu, Edward
**Producer(s)**   Wurtzel, Sol M.
**Director(s)**   Seiler, Lewis
**Screenwriter(s)**   Breslow, Lou; Eliscu, Edward

**Cast**   Withers, Jane; Tomlin, Pinky; Cansino, Rita [1]; Darwell, Jane; Givot, George; Ford, Francis; Lewis, Vera

**Song(s)**   Keep That Twinkle in Your Eye; Changing My Ambitions (C/L: Tomlin, Pinky; Poe, Coy); I Like a Balalaika; Which Is Which (C: Sanders, Troy; L: Clare, Sidney)

**Notes**   [1] Rita Hayworth.

**4468 ✦ THE PAGAN**
Metro–Goldwyn–Mayer, 1929

**Director(s)**   Van Dyke, W.S.
**Screenwriter(s)**   Farnum, Dorothy

**Cast**   Novarro, Ramon; Adoree, Renee; Crisp, Donald; Janis, Dorothy [1]

**Song(s)**   The Pagan Love Song [2] (C: Brown, Nacio Herb; L: Freed, Arthur)

**Notes**   [1] Dubbed. [2] Also in PAGAN LOVE SONG.

**4469 ✦ PAGAN LOVE SONG**
Metro–Goldwyn–Mayer, 1950

**Composer(s)**   Warren, Harry
**Lyricist(s)**   Freed, Arthur
**Choreographer(s)**   Alton, Robert
**Producer(s)**   Freed, Arthur
**Director(s)**   Alton, Robert
**Screenwriter(s)**   Nathan, Robert; Davis, Jerry
**Source(s)**   *Tahiti Landfall* (novel) Stone, William S.

**Cast**   Williams, Esther; Keel, Howard; Gombell, Minna; Mauu, Charles; Moreno, Rita

**Song(s)**   Pagan Love Song [1] (C: Brown, Nacio Herb); The House of Singing Bamboo [4]; Singing in the Sun; Etiquette; Why Is Love So Crazy?; The Sea of the Moon; Tahiti [2]; Here in Tahiti We Make Love [3]; Music on the Water [3]

**Notes**   [1] Originally in THE PAGAN. [2] Used instrumentally only. [3] Filmed but not used. [4] Music the same as "Hayride" deleted in THE HARVEY GIRLS (1946).

**4470 ✦ PAGE MISS GLORY**
Warner Brothers, 1935

**Producer(s)**   Lord, Robert
**Director(s)**   LeRoy, Mervyn
**Screenwriter(s)**   Daves, Delmer; Lord, Robert
**Source(s)**   (play) Dunning, Philip; Schrank, Joseph

**Cast**   Davies, Marion; O'Brien, Pat; Powell, Dick; Astor, Mary; McHugh, Frank; Talbot, Lyle; Kelly, Patsy; Jenkins, Allen; MacLane, Barton; Cavanaugh, Hobart; Cawthorn, Joseph; Shean, Al; Churchill, Berton; Lowell, Helen; Stander, Lionel

**Song(s)**   Page Miss Glory (C: Warren, Harry; L: Dubin, Al)

**4471 ✦ PAID IN FULL**
Paramount, 1950

**Producer(s)**   Wallis, Hal B.
**Director(s)**   Dieterle, William
**Screenwriter(s)**   Blees, Robert; Schnee, Charles

**Cast**   Scott, Lizabeth; Lynn, Diana; Cummings, Robert; Arden, Eve; Collins, Ray; Ridges, Stanley; Bromfield, John; McHugh, Frank; Elliot, Laura

**Song(s)**   You're Wonderful (C: Young, Victor; L: Livingston, Jay; Evans, Ray)

**Notes**   Movie was originally to be titled BITTER VICTORY.

**4472 ✦ THE PAINTED ANGEL**
Warner Brothers–First National, 1929

**Composer(s)**   Jerome, M.K.
**Lyricist(s)**   Ruby, Herman
**Director(s)**   Webb, Millard
**Screenwriter(s)**   Halsey, Forrest
**Source(s)**   "Give The Little Girl a Hand" (story) Hurst, Fannie

**Cast**   Dove, Billie; Lowe, Edmund; McFarlane, George; Fitzgerald, Cissy; MacDonald, J. Farrell; Selby, Norman; Baker, Betty Bly

**Song(s)**   Help Yourself to Love; A Bride Without a Groom; Only the Girl [1]; Everybody's Darling; That Thing

**Notes** No cue sheet available. [1] According to some sources this is in BROADWAY HOSTESS.

## 4473 ✦ PAINTED DESERT
RKO, 1938

**Producer(s)** Gilroy, Bert
**Director(s)** Howard, David
**Screenwriter(s)** Rathmell, John; Drake, Oliver

**Cast** O'Brien, George; Johnson, Laraine; Whitley, Ray; Allen, Maude; Fields, Stanley; Kohler, Fred

**Song(s)** Moonlight on the Painted Desert (C/L: Drake, Oliver); Painted Desert (C/L: Whitley, Ray)

## 4474 ✦ PAINTED FACES
Tiffany–Stahl, 1929

**Director(s)** Rogell, Albert S.
**Screenwriter(s)** Hatton, Frederic; Hatton, Fanny

**Cast** Brown, Joe E.; Foster, Helen; Tucker, Richard; Davidson, William B.; Hepburn, Barton; Gulliver, Dorothy; Cole, Lester; Sojin

**Song(s)** Somebody Just Like You (C/L: Silver, Abner)

**Notes** No cue sheet available.

## 4475 ✦ THE PAINTED STALLION
Republic, 1937

**Producer(s)** Wickland, J. Lawrence
**Director(s)** Taylor, Rex; Witney, William; James, Alan
**Screenwriter(s)** Shipman, Barry; Miller, Winston

**Cast** Corrigan, Ray; Gibson, Hoot; Mason, LeRoy; Renaldo, Duncan; McKim, Sammy; Taliaferro, Hal; Cesar and Elmer; Canutt, Yakima; Thayer, Julia; Perrin, Jack

**Song(s)** Wagon Train [1] (C/L: Burnette, Smiley; Gibson, Hoot)

**Notes** A serial. [1] There is a song titled "Wagon Train" in the 1935 picture THE SINGING VAGABOND credited to Smiley Burnette and Gene Autry.

## 4476 ✦ PAINTED WOMAN
Fox, 1932

**Director(s)** Blystone, John
**Screenwriter(s)** Gordon, Leon
**Source(s)** After the Rain Kennedy, A.C.

**Cast** Tracy, Spencer; Shannon, Peggy; Boyd, William; Pichel, Irving

**Song(s)** Say You'll Be Good to Me (C/L: Hanley, James F.); Beside the Coral Sea [1] (C: Hanley, James F.; L: Gilbert, L. Wolfe)

**Notes** [1] Not used.

## 4477 ✦ PAINTING THE CLOUDS WITH SUNSHINE
Warner Brothers, 1951

**Composer(s)** Burke, Joe
**Lyricist(s)** Dubin, Al
**Choreographer(s)** Prinz, LeRoy

**Producer(s)** Jacobs, William
**Director(s)** Butler, David
**Screenwriter(s)** Clork, Harry; Kibbee, Roland; Milne, Peter
**Source(s)** The Gold Diggers (play) Hopwood, Avery

**Cast** Morgan, Dennis; Mayo, Virginia [1]; Nelson, Gene; Norman, Lucille; Sakall, S.Z.; Gibson, Virginia; Conway, Tom; Ford, Wallace; Dugan, Tom

**Song(s)** Painting the Clouds with Sunshine [2]; Man Is a Necessary Evil (C: Burke, Sonny; L: Elliott, Jack); Tip Toe Thru the Tulips with Me [3]; Vienna Dreams (C: Sieczynski, Rudolf; L: Caesar, Irving); The Mambo Man (C: Burke, Sonny; L: Elliott, Jack)

**Notes** It is not known which of these were original to this film. Vocals also include "We're in the Money" by Harry Warren and Al Dubin; "When Irish Eyes Are Smiling" by Ernest R. Ball, Chauncey Olcott and George Graff Jr.; "With a Song in My Heart" by Richard Rodgers and Lorenz Hart; "The Birth of the Blues" by Ray Henderson, B.G. DeSylva and Lew Brown; "You're My Everything" by Harry Warren, Mort Dixon and Joe Young; "Jalousie" by Jacob Gade and Vera Bloom and "I Like Mountain Music" by Frank Weldon and James Cavanaugh. [1] Dubbed by Bonnie Lou Williams. [2] Also in GOLD DIGGERS OF BROADWAY and LITTLE JOHNNY JONES. [3] Also in THE GOLD DIGGERS on Broadway.

## 4478 ✦ PAINT YOUR WAGON
Paramount, 1969

**Musical Score** Riddle, Nelson
**Composer(s)** Loewe, Frederick
**Lyricist(s)** Lerner, Alan Jay
**Choreographer(s)** Baker, Jack

**Producer(s)** Lerner, Alan Jay
**Director(s)** Logan, Joshua
**Screenwriter(s)** Lerner, Alan Jay
**Source(s)** Paint Your Wagon (musical) Lerner, Alan Jay; Loewe, Frederick

**Cast** Marvin, Lee; Eastwood, Clint; Seberg, Jean [2]; Walston, Ray; Presnell, Harve; Ligon, Tom

**Song(s)** I'm On My Way [1]; I Still See Elisa [1]; The First Thing You Know (C: Previn, Andre); Hand Me Down that Can o' Beans [1]; They Call the Wind Maria [1]; Yankee Doodle (C: Traditional); Oh Susanna (C: Traditional); Here We Go Round the Mulberry Bush (C: Traditional); A Million Miles Away Behind the Door (C: Previn, Andre); I Talk to the Trees [1]; There's a Coach

Comin' In [1]; The Gospel of No Name City (C: Previn, Andre); Best Things (C: Previn, Andre); Wand'rin' Star [1]; Rumson Town [1]; Gold Fever (C: Previn, Andre); Whoop-Ti-Ay! [1]; Another Autumn [1] [3]

**Notes** Screenplay adaptation by Paddy Chayefsky. [1] From original production. [2] Dubbed by Anita Gordon. Listed as Anita Conroy in Andre Previn's Biography. [3] Recorded but not used.

## 4479 ◆ THE PAJAMA GAME
Warner Brothers, 1957

**Composer(s)** Adler, Richard [1]; Ross, Jerry [1]
**Lyricist(s)** Adler, Richard [1]; Ross, Jerry [1]
**Choreographer(s)** Fosse, Bob [1]

**Producer(s)** Donen, Stanley; Abbott, George
**Director(s)** Abbott, George [1]; Donen, Stanley
**Screenwriter(s)** Abbott, George [1]; Bissell, Richard [1]
**Source(s)** *The Pajama Game* (musical) Bissell, Richard; Abbott, George; Adler, Richard; Ross, Jerry

**Cast** Day, Doris; Raitt, John [1]; Haney, Carol [1]; Foy Jr., Eddie [1]; Shaw, Reta [1]; Nichols, Barbara; Pelish, Thelma [1]; Straw, Jack; Dunn, Ralph; Martin, Owen; Kelk, Jackie; Chambers, Ralph [1]; Stanton, Mary [1]; Miller, Buzz [1]; LeRoy, Kenneth

**Song(s)** The Pajama Game; Racing with the Clock; I'm Not At All in Love; I'll Never Be Jealous Again; Hey There; Once a Year Day; Small Talk; There Once Was a Man; Steam Heat; Hernando's Hideaway; Seven and a Half Cents; The Man Who Invented Love [2] (C/L: Adler, Richard)

**Notes** All songs used in film are from the Broadway musical comedy. [1] Repeating their Broadway assignments. [2] Not used. Written for film. Doris Day did a released recording for Columbia.

## 4480 ◆ PAJAMA PARTY
American International, 1964

**Musical Score** Baxter, Les
**Composer(s)** Hemric, Guy; Styner, Jerry
**Lyricist(s)** Hemric, Guy; Styner, Jerry

**Producer(s)** Nicholson, James H.; Arkoff, Samuel Z.
**Director(s)** Weis, Don
**Screenwriter(s)** Heyward, Louis M.

**Cast** Kirk, Tommy; Funicello, Annette; Lanchester, Elsa; Lembeck, Harvey; White, Jesse; McCrea, Jody; Lessy, Ben; Keaton, Buster; Lamour, Dorothy; The Nooney Rickett Four

**Song(s)** It's That Kind of Day; There Has to Be a Reason; Where Did I Go Wrong?; Pajama Party; Beach Ball; Among the Young; Stuffed Animal

**Notes** No cue sheet available.

## 4481 ◆ THE PALEFACE
Paramount, 1948

**Musical Score** Young, Victor
**Composer(s)** Livingston, Jay; Evans, Ray
**Lyricist(s)** Livingston, Jay; Evans, Ray
**Choreographer(s)** Daniels, Billy

**Producer(s)** Welch, Robert L.
**Director(s)** McLeod, Norman Z.
**Screenwriter(s)** Hartmann, Edmund L.; Tashlin, Frank

**Cast** Hope, Bob; Russell, Jane; Armstrong, Robert; Adrian, Iris; Watson, Bobby; Searl, Jackie; Vitale, Joseph; Bevans, Clem; Trowbridge, Charles; Andrews, Stanley

**Song(s)** Buttons and Bows [2]; Meetcha 'Round the Corner; Get a Man (C/L: Lilley, Joseph J.); It's a Dirty Shame [1]

**Notes** [1] Not used. [2] Oscar winner. Later with additional lyrics in SON OF PALEFACE.

## 4482 ◆ PAL JOEY
Columbia, 1957

**Composer(s)** Rodgers, Richard
**Lyricist(s)** Hart, Lorenz
**Choreographer(s)** Pan, Hermes

**Producer(s)** Kohlmar, Fred
**Director(s)** Sidney, George
**Screenwriter(s)** Kingsley, Dorothy
**Source(s)** *Pal Joey* (musical) O'Hara, John; Rodgers, Richard; Hart, Lorenz

**Cast** Hayworth, Rita [2]; Sinatra, Frank; Novak, Kim [3]; Nichols, Barbara; Sherwood, Bobby; Henry, Hank; Patterson, Elizabeth; Morse, Robin; Wilcox, Frank; Watkin, Pierre; Bernard, Berry; Kent, Ellie

**Song(s)** Zip [1]; Great Big Town (Chicago) [1]; That Terrific Rainbow [1]; Pal Joey [1]; Bewitched, Bothered and Bewildered [1]; I Didn't Know What Time It Was [3]; There's a Small Hotel [2]; My Funny Valentine [4]; The Lady Is a Tramp [4]

**Notes** Sammy Cahn may have worked on the lyrics. [1] From original production. [2] Dubbed by Jo Ann Greer. [3] Dubbed by Trudy Erwin. [3] From Broadway musical ON YOUR TOES. [3] From Broadway musical and subsequent film TOO MANY GIRLS. [4] From Broadway musical BABES IN ARMS.

## 4483 ◆ PALM SPRINGS
Paramount, 1936

**Composer(s)** Rainger, Ralph
**Lyricist(s)** Robin, Leo

**Producer(s)** Wanger, Walter
**Director(s)** Scotto, Aubrey
**Screenwriter(s)** Fields, Joseph
**Source(s)** *Lady Smith* (novel) Connolly, Myles

*THE COMPLETE MUSICAL COMPANION*

**Cast** Langford, Frances; Ballew, Smith; Standing, Sir Guy

**Song(s)** Will I Ever Know [5] (C: Revel, Harry; L: Gordon, Mack); I Don't Want to Make History (I Just Want to Make Love) [4]; Hills of Old Wyoming [3]; Doin' All Right [1]; Dreaming Out Loud [1] [2]; In Old Palm Springs [1]

**Notes** Released as PALM SPRINGS AFFAIR in Great Britain. [1] Not used. [2] Published and also not used in WE'RE NOT DRESSING. [3] Also used in HILLS OF OLD WYOMING. [4] Also in BIG BROADCAST OF 1936. [5] Not used in COLLEGIATE.

## 4484 ◆ PALM SPRINGS AFFAIR

See PALM SPRINGS.

## 4485 ◆ PALM SPRINGS WEEKEND
### Warner Brothers, 1963

**Musical Score** Perkins, Frank
**Composer(s)** Perkins, Frank
**Lyricist(s)** Perkins, Frank

**Producer(s)** Hoey, Michael A.
**Director(s)** Taurog, Norman
**Screenwriter(s)** Hammer, Earl, Jr.

**Cast** Donahue, Troy; Stevens, Connie; Hardin, Ty; Powers, Stefanie; Conrad, Robert; Duggan, Andrew; Weston, Jack; Cook, Carole; Van Dyke, Jerry; Mumy, Billy; Dempsey, Mark

**Song(s)** Live Young (C: Evans, Paul; L: Kusik, Larry); Go Go Devil; Hurricane Twist; Roll with the Punch Bowl Rock; I Was Born in East Virginia (C/L: Deacon, Paul; Thompson, Fred; Sean, Sonny; Casteaux, Bob)

**Notes** It is not known if all of these were written for the movie.

## 4486 ◆ PALMY DAYS
### United Artists, 1931

**Composer(s)** Conrad, Con
**Lyricist(s)** Macdonald, Ballard
**Choreographer(s)** Berkeley, Busby

**Producer(s)** Goldwyn, Samuel
**Director(s)** Sutherland, Edward
**Screenwriter(s)** Cantor, Eddie; Ryskind, Morrie; Freeman, David

**Cast** Cantor, Eddie; Raft, George; Greenwood, Charlotte; Charters, Spencer; Weeks, Barbara; Middleton, Charles; Page, Paul; Woods, Henry

**Song(s)** Bend Down Sister (L: Macdonald, Ballard; Silverstein, Dave); My Baby Said Yes, Yes (C/L: Friend, Cliff); There's Nothing Too Good for My Baby [1]

(C/L: Cantor, Eddie; Davis, Benny; Akst, Harry); Goose Pimples; Dunk, Dunk, Dunk

**Notes** No cue sheet available. [1] Canto not credited by ASCAP.

## 4487 ◆ PALOOKA
### United Artists, 1934

**Producer(s)** Small, Edward
**Director(s)** Stoloff, Benjamin
**Screenwriter(s)** Purcell, Gertrude; Jevne, Jack; Kober, Arthur; Ryan, Ben; Roth, Murray
**Source(s)** *Joe Palooka* (comic strip) Fisher, Ham

**Cast** Erwin, Stuart; Durante, Jimmy; Velez, Lupe; Cagney, William; Rambeau, Marjorie; Carlisle, Mary; Todd, Thelma; Williams, Guinn "Big Boy"; Ardell, Franklyn

**Song(s)** Like Me a Little Bit Less (Love Me a Little Bit More) (C: Lane, Burton; L: Adamson, Harold); Palooka (C: Burke, Johnny; L: Ronell, Ann); It's a Grand Old Name (C: Burke, Joe; L: Ronell, Ann); Count Your Blessings (C: Grofe, Ferde; L: Caesar, Irving); Inka Dinka Doo (C/L: Ryan, Ben; Durante, Jimmy; Donnelly, Harry)

**Notes** No cue sheet available. Also known as JOE PALOOKA. Released internationally as THE GREAT SCHNOZZLE.

## 4488 ◆ PALS OF THE GOLDEN WEST
### Republic, 1951

**Musical Score** Wilson, Stanley
**Composer(s)** Elliott, Jack
**Lyricist(s)** Elliott, Jack

**Producer(s)** White, Edward J.
**Director(s)** Witney, William
**Screenwriter(s)** Taylor, Eric; De Mond, Albert

**Cast** Rogers, Roy; Evans, Dale; Lee, Pinky; Rodriguez, Estelita; Border Patrol Riders

**Song(s)** You Never Know When Love May Come Along; Pals of the Golden West; Slumber Trail (C/L: Elliott, Jack; Gonzales, Aaron); Beyond the Great Divide (C/L: Smith, Jordan)

## 4489 ◆ PANAMA HATTIE
### Metro–Goldwyn–Mayer, 1942

**Composer(s)** Porter, Cole
**Lyricist(s)** Porter, Cole
**Choreographer(s)** Dare, Danny; Lee, Sammy

**Producer(s)** Freed, Arthur
**Director(s)** McLeod, Norman Z.
**Screenwriter(s)** McGowan, Jack; Mahoney, Wilkie
**Source(s)** *Panama Hattie* (musical) Porter, Cole; Fields, Herbert; DeSylva, B.G.

**Cast**    Sothern, Ann; Skelton, Red; Blue, Ben; Ragland, Rags; The Berry Brothers; Horne, Lena; Hunt, Marsha; Dailey, Dan; Horner, Jackie; Mowbray, Alan; O'Brien, Virginia; Esmond, Carl

**Song(s)**    Hattie from Panama (C/L: Edens, Roger); I've Still Got My Health; Just One of Those Things [3]; Fresh As a Daisy; Serenata (C/L: Nacho); Good Neigbors (C/L: Edens, Roger); Let's Be Buddies; Did I Get Stinkin' at the Club Savoy (C/L: Donaldson, Walter); The Sping (C: Moore, Phil; L: Le Gon, J.; Moore, Alfred; Moore, Phil); The Son of a Gun Who Picks on Uncle Sam (C: Lane, Burton; L: Harburg, E.Y.); Fiesta en Sevilla (C/L: Matos, Manuel; Sabicas; Amaya); Fiesta por Bolerias (C/L: Matos, Manuel; Sabicas; Amaya); Salome [1] [5] (C/L: Edens, Roger); Stop Off in Panama [1] (C/L: Edens, Roger); Cookin' with Gas [1] [2] (C: Hayton, Lennie; L: Edens, Roger); Make It Another Old Fashioned Please [4]; I'd Do Anything for You [4] (C/L: Edens, Roger)

**Notes**    Vincente Minnelli might have also contributed to the choreography. [1] Deleted from final prints. [2] Used in MAISIE GETS HER MAN (1942). [3] Also in AT LONG LAST LOVE (20th) and CAN-CAN (20th). [4] Recorded but not used. [5] Recorded twice for this film: once by Ann Southern and once by Virginia O'Brien. The O'Brien version was used in DUBARRY WAS A LADY.

## 4490 ◆ PANAMA LADY
RKO, 1939

**Musical Score**    Webb, Roy

**Producer(s)**    Reid, Cliff
**Director(s)**    Hively, Jack
**Screenwriter(s)**    Kanin, Michael

**Cast**    Ball, Lucille; Lane, Allan; Duna, Steffi; Briggs, Donald; Hayes, Bernadene

**Song(s)**    La Chaparrita (C/L: Esperon, Ignacio Fernandez; Luban, Francia)

## 4491 ◆ PANAMA SAL
Republic, 1957

**Musical Score**    Hooven, Joe
**Composer(s)**    Hooven, Joe
**Lyricist(s)**    Hooven, Marilyn
**Choreographer(s)**    Dupree, Roland

**Producer(s)**    White, Edward J.
**Director(s)**    Witney, William
**Screenwriter(s)**    Belgard, Arnold

**Cast**    Verdugo, Elena; Kemmer, Edward; Rivas, Carlos; The Ukonu Calypsonians

**Song(s)**    I've Got My Fingers Crossed (C/L: Ukina); Beat of a Bongo; Panama Sal

## 4492 ◆ PAN AMERICANA
RKO, 1945

**Choreographer(s)**    O'Curran, Charles

**Producer(s)**    Auer, John H.
**Director(s)**    Auer, John H.
**Screenwriter(s)**    Kimble, Lawrence

**Cast**    Terry, Phillip; Long, Audrey; Benchley, Robert; Arden, Eve; Truex, Ernest; Cramer, Marc; Isabelita; Rosario and Antonio; Valdes, Miguelito; Harold and Lola; Burnett, Louise; Marin, Chinita; Castillon, Chuy; The Padilla Sisters; Chuy Reyes and His Orchestra; Nestor Amaral and His Samba Band

**Song(s)**    Rumba Matumba [4] (C/L: Collazo, Bobby); Guadalajara [1] (C/L: Guizar, Pepe); Mar (C: Ruiz, Gabriel; L: Greene, Mort); La Morena de Mi Copla [2] (C/L: Castellanos, C.); Babalu (C/L: Lecuona, Margarita); Negra Leono [3] (C/L: Fernandez, Antonio); Baramba (C: Lecuona, Margarita; L: Greene, Mort); No Taboleiro da Bahiana (C: Barroso, Ary; L: Greene, Mort); Stars in Your Eyes [5] (C: Ruiz, Gabriel; L: Greene, Mort)

**Notes**    [1] Also in WEEKEND AT THE WALDORF (MGM); FUN IN ACAPULCO (Paramount) and MEXICANA (Republic). [2] Also in MAKE MINE LAUGHS. [3] Also in THE HEAT'S ON (Columbia), SLIGHTLY SCANDALOUS (Universal) credited to Fernandez and also in GAY SENORITA (Columbia) credited to Don George and Serge Walter. [4] Also in ALLERGIC TO LOVE. [5] Sheet music only.

## 4493 ◆ PAN AMERICAN SHOWTIME
Republic

**Cast**    Robbins, Gale; Sevilla, Ninon; Armar, Lenor; Lou & Nellie; Barbar, Nesha; Pons, Maria Antonieta; Savage, Bob; Aguilar, Amelia; Lamarque, Liberad; Vargas, Pedro

**Song(s)**    Pan American Showtime [1] (C/L: Owens, Jack); Everywhere Is You [2] [9] (C/L: Sherman, Richard M.; Sherman, Robert B.); Runnin' Around in Circles [3] (C/L: Warren, Don; Dunne, Jeanne); Possession [4] [6] [12] (C: Stewart, Al; L: Carpenter, Imogene); I'll Love You Always [4] [13] (C: Owens, Jack; L: Pacino, Frank); Old Rusty Trunk [5] (C: Sherman, Al; L: Ingham, Nelson); When I Break the News to My Heart [5] (C/L: Stewart, Al); A Little Less Talk [6] (C/L: Liblick, Marvin); Boogie Samba [6] (C/L: Marcotte, Don; Rose, Irvin); I'm Just a No One (C/L: Sherman, Richard M.; Sherman, Robert B.); You Promised Me the Moon [7] (C/L: Prichard, Henry); Havin' a Time (C/L: Sherman, Al); Dream Souvenirs [8] [10] (C/L: Sherman, Al); Passion [8] (C/L: Savage, Robert); When Will It Be [9] (C: Owens, Jack; L: Pacino, Frank); Livin' High [10] (C/L: Savage, Robert); Here Am I [11] [12] [13] (C/L: Dunn, Jeanne; Warren, Don); Security [11] (C/L: Sherman, Richard M.;

Sherman, Robert B.); Lonely As Me [12] (C/L: Kim, Robert); The Lord's Been Good to Me [13] (C/L: Dunne, Jeanne)

**Notes**  A series of mini-musicals in 13 shows. Not all members of the cast appear in all 13 episodes. It is not clear which songs were written for these films as there were not vocal or instrumental designations on the cue sheets. Each show was designated with a different Latin American city. [1] In all episodes. [2] In Show # 12—Havana, Cuba. [3] In Show # 10 —Asuncion, Paraguay. [4] In Show # 9—Quito, Ecuador. [5] In Show # 8—Bogota, Columbia. [6] In Show # 7—La Paz, Bolivia. [7] In Show # 6—Lima, Peru. [8] In Show # 6—Montevideo, Uruguay. [9] In Show # 5—Panama. [10] In Show # 3—Buenos Aires. [11] In Show # 2—Mexico City. [12] In Show # 1—Rio de Janeiro. [13] In Show # 13—Acapulco.

## 4494 ◆ PANDORA AND THE FLYING DUTCHMAN
### Metro–Goldwyn–Mayer, 1951

**Musical Score**  Rawsthorne, Alan

**Producer(s)**  Lewin, Albert; Kaufman, Joseph
**Director(s)**  Lewin, Albert
**Screenwriter(s)**  Lewin, Albert
**Source(s)**  The Flying Dutchman (legend)

**Cast**  Mason, James; Gardner, Ava; Patrick, Nigel; Sim, Sheila; Warrender, Harold; Cabre, Mario; Laurie, John; Kellino, Pamela; Raine, Patricia; d'Alvarez, Marguerite

**Song(s)**  Pandora [1] (C: Green, Johnny; L: Lewin, Albert)

**Notes**  [1] Not used in picture.

## 4495 ◆ PANIC IN THE STREETS
### Twentieth Century–Fox, 1950

**Producer(s)**  Siegel, Sol C.
**Director(s)**  Kazan, Elia
**Screenwriter(s)**  Murphy, Richard

**Cast**  Widmark, Richard; Douglas, Paul; Bel Geddes, Barbara; Palance, Jack; Mostel, Zero; Tsiang, H.T.

**Song(s)**  The Old Master Painter (C: Smith, Beasley; L: Gillespie, Haven); No Good Man (C: Carter, Benny; L: Vandervoort II, Paul); Fine and Mellow (C/L: Holiday, Billie)

## 4496 ◆ PAPA GETS THE BIRD
### Metro–Goldwyn–Mayer, 1940

**Musical Score**  Bradley, Scott

**Song(s)**  Canary and the Bear (C: Bradley, Scott; L: Harmon, Hugh)

**Notes**  Animated cartoon.

## 4497 ◆ PAPA'S DELICATE CONDITION (1952)
### Paramount, 1952 unproduced

**Composer(s)**  Lane, Burton
**Lyricist(s)**  Robin, Leo

**Song(s)**  The Greatest Papa in the World; The Way We Are [1]; Hooray for Ghio [2]; Ambolyn [2]; Hoby Tyler Campaign Song; Yes, Mister Cosgrove; Off to Wonderland; It's Love—Love—Lovely You; Ki Yi Yippee Yi Yo What a Night!

**Notes**  Burton Lane wrote a letter to Paramount in 1956 asking for the songs back. He wrote "I want to take this opportunity to thank you, not only for your prompt response to my letters, but for your friendly attitude. Without exception, this is the first time getting something back from a studio was accomplished in a most happy way." Lane was a bit premature, he finally got the songs back in 1966. Lane wanted the songs returned because he planned to use them for a musical. "My main concern is how to protect whoever my new collaborator may be. I have absolutely no intention of using Leo Robin's lyrics. As you know, I didn't like them before, and certainly would not use them now." [1] The music was written for the musical FLAHOOLEY for which E.Y. Harburg supplied the lyric "The World Is Your Balloon." Lane dropped out of the project and used the song for this ill-fated movie. [2] Same music.

## 4498 ◆ PAPA'S DELICATE CONDITION (1963)
### Paramount, 1963

**Musical Score**  Lilley, Joseph J.
**Composer(s)**  Van Heusen, James
**Lyricist(s)**  Cahn, Sammy

**Producer(s)**  Rose, Jack
**Director(s)**  Marshall, George
**Screenwriter(s)**  Rose, Jack
**Source(s)**  (novel) Griffith, Corinne

**Cast**  Gleason, Jackie; Johns, Glynis; Ruggles, Charles; Goodwin, Laurel; Bruhl, Linda

**Song(s)**  Call Me Irresponsible; Some Sweet Day [1]; Wouldn't It Be Nice? [1]; Walking Happy [1] [2]; I Left the Door Wide Open [1]

**Notes**  [1] Not used in film. [2] Later used in Broadway musical WALKING HAPPY. All these songs were written seven years earlier for an abandoned version of the Griffith novel. The star was to be Fred Astaire, the producer was Robert Emmett Dolan and the script was by Henry and Phoebe Ephron.

## 4499 ◆ PAPA SOLTERO
### Paramount, 1939

**Composer(s)**  Guizar, Tito
**Lyricist(s)**  Noriega, Nenette

**Producer(s)**   Faralla, Dario
**Director(s)**   Harlan, Richard
**Screenwriter(s)**   Wilma, Dana; Vernon, Arthur

**Song(s)**   Yo Ya Me Voy; Chichen-Itza; Pecesitos; Es un Pecado Querer; Cancion de Cuba (Starland) [1] (C: Hollander, Frederick; L: Freed, Ralph; Tana); El Amor Que Florece; Perdi me Amor (C/L: Tana); Pardonnez Mois Madame [1] (C: Templeton, Alec; L: Fleeson, Neville; Tana)

**Notes**   This is a Spanish language feature. [1] Tana supplied the Spanish lyrics to these songs which were written for this film.

## 4500 ✦ PAPA WAS A PREACHER
La Rose, 1986

**Musical Score**   Sutherland, Ken

**Producer(s)**   Jurow, Martin
**Director(s)**   Feke, Steve
**Screenwriter(s)**   Feke, Steve
**Source(s)**   (book) Porter, Alyene

**Cast**   Pine, Robert; Engel, Georgia; Stockwell, Dean; Coca, Imogene; Benton, Dallas; Wilder, Scott

**Song(s)**   The Door Is Open the Light Is On (C/L: Sutherland, Ken); Back in Line Again (C/L: Sutherland, Ken)

**Notes**   No cue sheet available.

## 4501 ✦ PAPER BULLETS
PRC, 1941

**Producer(s)**   Kazinsky, Maurice
**Director(s)**   Kazinsky, Franklin
**Screenwriter(s)**   Mooney, Martin

**Cast**   Woodbury, Joan; LaRue, Jack; Ware, Linda; Archer, John; Barnett, Vince; Ladd, Alan; Pembroke, George

**Song(s)**   I Know I Know (C/L: Knight, Vick; Lange, Johnny; Porter, Lew); Blue Is the Day (C/L: Kazinsky, Maurice; Lange, Johnny; Porter, Lew)

**Notes**   No cue sheet available.

## 4502 ✦ PARACHUTE BATTALION
RKO, 1941

**Musical Score**   Webb, Roy

**Producer(s)**   Benedict, Howard
**Director(s)**   Goodwins, Leslie
**Screenwriter(s)**   Twist, John; Fite, Major Hugh

**Cast**   Preston, Robert; Kelly, Nancy; O'Brien, Edmond; Carey, Harry; Ebsen, Buddy; Kelly, Paul; Cromwell, Richard; Barrat, Robert

**Song(s)**   Parachute Battalion (C: Webb, Roy; L: Ruby, Herman)

## 4503 ✦ PARADISE
Embassy, 1982

**Musical Score**   Hoffert, Paul

**Producer(s)**   Lantos, Robert; Roth, Stephen J.
**Director(s)**   Gillard, Stuart
**Screenwriter(s)**   Gillard, Stuart

**Cast**   Aames, Willie; Cates, Phoebe; Curnock, Richard; Tavi, Tuvia

**Song(s)**   Paradise (C/L: Diamond, Joel; Brown, L. Russell)

**Notes**   No cue sheet available.

## 4504 ✦ PARADISE ALLEY
Universal, 1978

**Musical Score**   Conti, Bill

**Producer(s)**   Roach, John F.
**Director(s)**   Stallone, Sylvester
**Screenwriter(s)**   Stallone, Sylvester

**Cast**   Stallone, Sylvester; Canalito, Lee; Assante, Armand; Conway, Kevin; Rae, Frank; Archer, Anne; Ingalls, Joyce; Eccles, Aimee

**Song(s)**   Too Close to Paradise (C: Conti, Bill; L: Roberts, Bruce; Sager, Carole Bayer)

## 4505 ✦ PARADISE FOR TWO

See THE GAIETY GIRLS.

## 4506 ✦ PARADISE, HAWAIIAN STYLE
Paramount, 1966

**Composer(s)**   Giant, Bill; Baum, Bernie; Kaye, Florence
**Lyricist(s)**   Giant, Bill; Baum, Bernie; Kaye, Florence
**Choreographer(s)**   Regas, Jack

**Producer(s)**   Wallis, Hal B.
**Director(s)**   Murphy, Michael
**Screenwriter(s)**   Weiss, Allan; Lawrence, Anthony

**Cast**   Presley, Elvis; Leigh, Suzanna; Shigeta, James; Hill, Marianna; Ahn, Philip; Doucette, John; Treen, Mary; Sutton, Grady

**Song(s)**   Paradise, Hawaiian Style; Queenie Wahine's Papaya; Scratch My Back; Pupu A O Ewa (C/L: Perry, Alfred Kealoha); Drums of the Islands (C: Traditional; L: Tepper, Sid; Bennett, Roy C.); A Dog's Life (C: Weisman, Ben; L: Wayne, Sid); Datin' (C/L: Wise, Fred; Starr, Randy); House of Sand; Stop, Where You Are; This Is My Heaven; Sand Castles [1] (C/L: Hess, David; Goldberg, Herb); Hawaii U.S.A. [1]

**Notes**   Formerly titled HAWAII, U.S.A., HAWAIIAN PARADISE and POLYNESIAN PARADISE. [1] Not used.

## 4507 ◆ PARADISE ISLAND
Tiffany, 1930

**Composer(s)**   Jason, Will; Burton, Val
**Lyricist(s)**   Jason, Will; Burton, Val

**Director(s)**   Glennon, Bert
**Screenwriter(s)**   Katterjohn, Monte

**Cast**   Harlan, Kenneth; Day, Marceline; James, Gladden; Santechi, Tom; Boyd, Betty; Hurst, Paul; Potel, Victor; Stanton, Will

**Song(s)**   I've Got a Girl in Every Port; Drinking Song; Lazy Breezes; Just Another Dream

**Notes**   No cue sheet available.

## 4508 ◆ PARAMOUNT ON PARADE
Paramount, 1930

**Choreographer(s)**   Bennett, David

**Producer(s)**   Kaufman, Albert
**Director(s)**   Arzner, Dorothy; Brower, Otto; Goulding, Edmund; Heerman, Victor; Knopf, Edwin H.; Lee, Rowland V.; Lubitsch, Ernst; Mendes, Lothar; Schertzinger, Victor; Sutherland, Edward; Tuttle, Frank

**Song(s)**   Paramount on Parade (C: King, Jack; L: Janis, Elsie); (We're the) Masters of Ceremony (C: Dreyer, Dave; L: Macdonald, Ballard); Anytime's the Time to Fall in Love (C: King, Jack; L: Janis, Elsie); Carmen (C: Bizet, Georges; L: Silvers, Sid); My Marine (C: Whiting, Richard A.; L: Egan, Raymond B.); All I Want Is Just One Girl (C: Whiting, Richard A.; L: Robin, Leo); What Did Cleopatra Say? (Helen Kane's Schoolroom) (C: King, Jack; L: Janis, Elsie); Nichavo! [4] (C: Mana-Zucca, Mme.; L: Jerome, Helen); (Let Us) Drink to the Girl of My Dreams (C: Baer, Abel; L: Gilbert, L. Wolfe); I'm True to the Navy Now [5] (C: King, Jack; L: Janis, Elsie); Sweeping the Clouds Away (C/L: Coslow, Sam); Dancing to Save Your Sole (C: Baer, Abel; L: Gilbert, L. Wolfe); It's Tough to Be a Prima Donna [1] (C/L: Rose, Billy); Music in the Moonlight [2] [6] (C: Coslow, Sam; L: Chase, Newell); (I'm Afraid to Try It) I Might Like It [3] (C: Cleary, Michael H. L: Magidson, Herb; Washington, Ned); Come Back to Sorrento (Torna a Sorrento) (C: de Curtis, Ernesto; L: Robin, Leo); I'm in Training for You (C: Baer, Abel; L: Gilbert, L. Wolfe); I'm Isadore, the Toreador (C/L: Franklin, Dave)

**Notes**   Supervision by Elsie Janis. [1] Recorded but not used. The song contains snatches of the following selections: "Vidor Theme," "That's My Weakness Now," and "Spring Song" by Mendelssohn; "The Flowers That Bloom in the Spring," "Some of These Days," "Music in the Moonlight" and "Cadenza" by Max Terr (A Paramount arranger). [2] Recorded but not used. Both these songs were recorded by Jeanette MacDonald. [3] Not used. This was written originally for the Warner Brothers musical LITTLE JOHNNY JONES but was not used there. Helen Kane, meant to sing it in PARAMOUNT ON PARADE, spoiled her chances by singing the number at the Palace Theatre on November 5th, 1929. Paramount then figured the song was old hat. [4] Written in 1921. [5] Also in UNFAITHFUL. [6] Jimmy Grier also credited on Coslow's ASCAP records.

## 4509 ◆ PARAMOUNT PRESENTS HOAGY CARMICHAEL
Paramount, 1939

**Cast**   Carmichael, Hoagy

**Song(s)**   That's Right - I'm Wrong (C: Carmichael, Hoagy; L: Adams, Stanley)

**Notes**   Short subject.

## 4510 ◆ PARANOIA
Commonwealth United, 1969

**Musical Score**   Umiliani, Pietro

**Director(s)**   Lenzi, Umberto; Moretti, Ugo
**Screenwriter(s)**   Lenzi, Umberto

**Cast**   Baker, Carroll; Castel, Lou; Carraro, Tino

**Song(s)**   Fate Had Planned It So (C: Umiliani, Pietro; L: MacDonald)

**Notes**   An Italian film, whose title, in Italian is ORGASMO.

## 4511 ◆ PARDNERS
Paramount, 1956

**Composer(s)**   Van Heusen, James
**Lyricist(s)**   Cahn, Sammy
**Choreographer(s)**   Castle, Nick

**Producer(s)**   Jones, Paul
**Director(s)**   Taurog, Norman
**Screenwriter(s)**   Sheldon, Sidney

**Cast**   Martin, Dean; Lewis, Jerry; Moorehead, Agnes; Chaney Jr., Lon; Nelson, Lori; Van Cleef, Lee; Elam, Jack

**Song(s)**   Pardners; The Wind! the Wind!; Me 'n' You 'n' the Moon; Buckskin Beauty; The Test of Time [2]; Carry Me Back to Laramie [1]

**Notes**   [1] Not used. [2] Used instrumentally only.

## 4512 ◆ PARDON MY GUN
Pathe, 1930

**Producer(s)**   Derr, E.B.
**Director(s)**   De Lacy, Robert
**Screenwriter(s)**   Cummings, Hugh

**Cast**   Starr, Sally; Duryea, George; Ray, Mona; Moran, Lee; Edeson, Robert; MacFarlane, Frank; MacFarlane, Tom; Woods, Harry; Abe Lyman and His Band

Song(s)   Deep Down South (C: Green, George; L: Collins, Monte)

Notes   No cue sheet available.

## 4513 ✦ PARDON MY RHYTHM
### Universal, 1944

**Producer(s)**   Burton, Bernard W.
**Director(s)**   Feist, Felix E.
**Screenwriter(s)**   Burton, Val; Conrad, Eugene
**Source(s)**   story by Barrett, Hurd

**Cast**   Torme, Mel; Jean, Gloria; Weaver, Marjorie; Crosby, Bob; Knowles, Patric

**Song(s)**   Shame on Me (C/L: Crago, Bill; Shannon, Grace); Munchies (C/L: Bibo, Irving; Torme, Mel); Do You Believe in Dreams (C/L: Bibo, Irving; George, Don; Piantadosi, Al); You've Got to Hand It to the Band (C/L: James, Inez; Miller, Sidney); Spell of the Moon (C: Rosen, Milton; L: Carter, Everett); Drummer Boy (C/L: Torme, Mel)

**Notes**   There is also a vocal of "I'll See You in My Dreams" by Gus Kahn and Isham Jones.

## 4514 ✦ PARDON MY SARONG
### Universal, 1942

**Composer(s)**   de Paul, Gene
**Lyricist(s)**   Raye, Don
**Choreographer(s)**   Dunham, Katherine

**Producer(s)**   Gottlieb, Alex
**Director(s)**   Kenton, Erle C.
**Screenwriter(s)**   Boardman, True; Perrin, Nat; Grant, John

**Cast**   Abbott, Bud; Costello, Lou; Atwill, Lionel; The Ink Spots; Paige, Robert; Bruce, Virginia; Demarest, William; Erickson, Leif; Hinds, Samuel S.; Wynn, Nan; The Sarango Girls; LaRue, Jack; Tip, Tap and Toe; Katherine Dunham and Her Troupe

**Song(s)**   Do I Worry? (C/L: Cowan, Stanley; Worth, Bobby); Shout, Brother, Shout (C/L: Fairbanks, Herman; Watson, Ivory); Lovely Luana; Malayan Funeral Procession (C: Previn, Charles; L: Waggner, George); Vingo; Vingo Jingo; The Island of the Moon; Java Jive [1] (C: Oakland, Ben; L: Drake, Milton); Come Back Again Ya Hear [1]

**Notes**   [1] Not used.

## 4515 ✦ PARENTHOOD
### Universal, 1989

**Musical Score**   Newman, Randy

**Producer(s)**   Grazer, Brian
**Director(s)**   Howard, Ron
**Screenwriter(s)**   Ganz, Lowell; Mandel, Babaloo

**Cast**   Martin, Steve; Steenburgen, Mary; Wiest, Dianne; Robards Jr., Jason; Moranis, Rick; Hulce, Tom; Plimpton, Martha; Reeves, Keanu; Kozak, Harley; Dugan, Dennis; Phoenix, Leaf; Ganz, Lowell; Howard, Clint

**Song(s)**   I Love to See You Smile (C/L: Newman, Randy)

## 4516 ✦ THE PARENT TRAP
### Disney, 1961

**Musical Score**   Smith, Paul J.
**Composer(s)**   Sherman, Richard M.; Sherman, Robert B.
**Lyricist(s)**   Sherman, Richard M.; Sherman, Robert B.

**Director(s)**   Swift, David
**Screenwriter(s)**   Swift, David
**Source(s)**   *Das Doppelte Lottchen* (novel) Kastner, Erich

**Cast**   Mills, Hayley; O'Hara, Maureen; Keith, Brian; Ruggles, Charles; Merkel, Una; Carroll, Leo G.; Barnes, Joanna; Nesbitt, Cathleen; McDevitt, Ruth; Kulp, Nancy; De Vol, Frank

**Song(s)**   For Now For Always (Maggie's Theme); The Parent Trap; Let's Get Together; Petticoats and Blue Jeans (Whistling at the Boys) [1]; Susan and I [2]

**Notes**   [1] Used instrumentally only. [2] Not used.

## 4517 ✦ PARIS
### Warner Brothers, 1929

**Composer(s)**   Ward, Edward
**Lyricist(s)**   Bryan, Alfred
**Choreographer(s)**   Ceballos, Larry

**Director(s)**   Badger, Clarence
**Screenwriter(s)**   Loring, Hope
**Source(s)**   *Paris* (musical) Porter, Cole; Goetz, E. Ray; Brown, Martin

**Cast**   Bordoni, Irene [1]; Buchanan, Jack; Hale, Louise Closser; Robards, Jason; Fielding, Margaret; Pitts, ZaSu

**Song(s)**   Paris; I Wonder What Is Really On His Mind; I'm a Little Negative; Somebody Mighty Like You; My Lover; Crystal Girl; Miss Wonderful Land of Going to Be (C/L: Kollo, Walter; Goetz, E. Ray); Don't Look at Me That Way [1] (C/L: Porter, Cole)

**Notes**   No cue sheet available. There is also a vocal of "Among My Souveniers" by Horatio Nicholls and Edgar Leslie. [1] From original Broadway production.

## 4518 ✦ PARIS AFTER DARK
### Twentieth Century–Fox, 1943

**Producer(s)**   Daven, Andre
**Director(s)**   Moguy, Leonide
**Screenwriter(s)**   Buchman, Harold

*THE COMPLETE MUSICAL COMPANION*

**Cast**   Sanders, George; Dorn, Philip; Marshall, Brenda; Lewis, Robert; Bois, Curt

**Song(s)**   The Sun Will Shine Again [1] (C: Fragey, Margot; L: Fragey, Margot; Henderson, Charles)

**Notes**   [1] Special lyrics by Henderson.

## 4519 ✦ PARIS FOLLIES OF 1956
Allied Artists, 1955

**Composer(s)**   Sherrell, Pony; Moody, Phil
**Lyricist(s)**   Sherrell, Pony; Moody, Phil
**Choreographer(s)**   Arden, Donn

**Producer(s)**   Tabakin, Bernard
**Director(s)**   Goodwins, Leslie
**Screenwriter(s)**   Lazarus, Milton

**Cast**   Tucker, Forrest; Corrigan, Lloyd; Whiting, Margaret; Wesson, Dick; Hyer, Martha; Cassell, Wally; Parker, Frank; The Sportsmen

**Song(s)**   Can This Be Love?; I Love a Circus; Have You Ever Been in Paris?; I'm All Aglow Again; I'm in a Mood Tonight; The Hum Song (C/L: Kuller, Sid); Lonely Town

**Notes**   No cue sheet availablle.

## 4520 ✦ PARIS HOLIDAY
United Artists, 1958

**Musical Score**   Lilley, Joseph J.
**Composer(s)**   Van Heusen, James
**Lyricist(s)**   Cahn, Sammy

**Producer(s)**   Hope, Bob
**Director(s)**   Oswald, Gerd
**Screenwriter(s)**   Beloin, Edmund; Riesner, Dean

**Cast**   Hope, Bob; Fernandel; Ekberg, Anita; Hyer, Martha; Morell, Andre; Murat, Jean

**Song(s)**   Nothing in Common; Paris Holiday

**Notes**   All titles not given on cue sheet.

## 4521 ✦ PARIS HONEYMOON
Paramount, 1939

**Composer(s)**   Rainger, Ralph
**Lyricist(s)**   Robin, Leo

**Producer(s)**   Thompson, Harlan
**Director(s)**   Tuttle, Frank
**Screenwriter(s)**   Butler, Frank; Hartman, Don

**Cast**   Crosby, Bing; Ross, Shirley; Gaal, Francisca; Horton, Edward Everett; Tamiroff, Akim; Blue, Ben; Gaye, Gregory; Hatton, Raymond

**Song(s)**   The Funny Old Hills [4]; Work While You May (Bulgarian Rose Song); I Have Eyes [5]; You're a Sweet Little Headache; Joobalai; Maiden By the Brook [1]; So Tired of It All [2]; A Rendezvous in Rose Time [2]; Beyond the Moon [2]; Bobotchka [2]; Bluebirds in the Moonlight [3]; Sunbeams in the Moonlight [2]

**Notes**   [1] Not used but recorded. [2] Not used. [3] Not used but used in GULLIVER'S TRAVELS after not being used for CAFE SOCIETY and MAN ABOUT TOWN. [4] Also in TWILIGHT ON THE TRAIL. [5] Not used in ARTISTS AND MODELS (1937) and WAIKIKI WEDDING.

## 4522 ✦ PARIS IN SPRING (1935)
Paramount, 1935

**Composer(s)**   Revel, Harry
**Lyricist(s)**   Gordon, Mack

**Producer(s)**   Glazer, Benjamin
**Director(s)**   Milestone, Lewis
**Screenwriter(s)**   Hoffenstein, Samuel; Schulz, Franz
**Source(s)**   *Two on a Tower* (play) Taylor, Dwight

**Cast**   Ellis, Mary; Carminati, Tullio; Lupino, Ida

**Song(s)**   Paris in the Spring; Jealousy; Hail the Groom; Bonjour Mam'selle; Why Do They Call It Gay Paree [1] [3]; Printemps [1]; Suicide Part II [2]; Rhythm of the Rain [4]

**Notes**   Originally titled TWO ON A TOWER. Released in Great Britian as PARIS LOVE SONG. [1] Used only instrumentally. [2] Based on "Paris in the Spring." [3] Recorded as a vocal with Mary Ellis and Tulio Carminatti. Also published. [4] Not used.

## 4523 ✦ PARIS IN THE SPRING (1947)
Paramount, 1947

**Producer(s)**   Grey, Harry
**Director(s)**   Epstein, Mel

**Cast**   Dann, Roger; Rawlinson, Sally; Allen, Dorothy

**Song(s)**   At the Carnival (C/L: Livingston, Jay; Evans, Ray)

**Notes**   Short subject? There are also renditions of "Pigalle" by Georges Ulmer, George Kober and Charles Newman and "Paris in the Spring" by Mack Gordon and Harry Revel.

## 4524 ✦ PARIS LOVE SONG

See PARIS IN SPRING.

## 4525 ✦ PARIS WHEN IT SIZZLES
Paramount, 1964

**Producer(s)**   Axelrod, George
**Director(s)**   Quine, Richard
**Screenwriter(s)**   Axelrod, George

**Cast** Hepburn, Audrey; Holden, William; Coward, Noel; Aslan, Gregoire; Busieres, Raymond; Dietrich, Marlene; Curtis, Tony

**Song(s)** The Girl Who Stole the Eiffel Tower (C: Riddle, Nelson; L: Quine, Richard); That Face (C: Spence, Lew; L: Bergman, Alan)

## 4526 ✦ PARRISH
### Warner Brothers, 1961

**Musical Score** Steiner, Max

**Producer(s)** Daves, Delmer
**Director(s)** Daves, Delmer
**Screenwriter(s)** Daves, Delmer

**Cast** Donahue, Troy; Colbert, Claudette; Malden, Karl; Jagger, Dean; Stevens, Connie; McBain, Diane; Hugueny, Sharon; Miles, Sylvia; Osterwald, Bibi; Sherwood, Madeleine; Rorke, Hayden; O'Connor, Carroll

**Song(s)** Puttin' Tobacco in the Ground (C/L: Barracuda, John); Birthday Song (C/L: Daves, Delmer); High Spirits (C: Meyer, Joseph; L: Curtis, Mann)

**Notes** It is not known if any of these were written for the film.

## 4527 ✦ THE PARSON OF PANAMINT
### Paramount, 1941

**Producer(s)** Rachmil, Lewis J.; Sherman, Harry
**Director(s)** McGann, William
**Screenwriter(s)** Shumate, Harold; Scott, Adrian
**Source(s)** *The Parson of Panamint* (novel) Kyne, Peter B.

**Cast** Drew, Ellen [1]; Ruggles, Charles

**Song(s)** Merry Go Round [2] (C/L: Ronell, Ann); No Ring on Her Finger [3] (C: Sherwin, Manning; L: Loesser, Frank); It's in the Cards (C: Rainger, Ralph; L: Coslow, Sam)

**Notes** The production also features "My Sweetheart's the Man in the Moon" by James Thornton and "Rock of Ages." [1] Dubbed by Martha Mears. [2] Also in CHAMPAGNE WALTZ. See note under CHAMPAGNE WALTZ. [3] Also in BLOSSOMS ON BROADWAY and FLAMING FEATHER.

## 4528 ✦ PARTNERS OF THE PLAINS
### Paramount, 1937

**Producer(s)** Sherman, Harry
**Director(s)** Selander, Lesley
**Screenwriter(s)** Jacobs, Harrison
**Source(s)** Man from Bar-20 by Mulford, Clarence E.

**Cast** Boyd, William; Hayden, Russell

**Song(s)** Moonlight on the Sunset Trail (C: Lane, Burton; L: Freed, Ralph)

**Notes** Picture first titled MOONLIGHT ON THE SUNSET TRAIL.

## 4529 ✦ THE PARTY
### United Artists, 1968

**Musical Score** Mancini, Henry
**Composer(s)** Mancini, Henry
**Lyricist(s)** Black, Don

**Producer(s)** Edwards, Blake
**Director(s)** Edwards, Blake
**Screenwriter(s)** Edwards, Blake; Waldman, Tom; Waldman, Frank

**Cast** Sellers, Peter; MacLeod, Gavin; McKinley, J. Edward; Longet, Claudine; Champion, Marge; Franken, Steve

**Song(s)** The Party; Nothing to Lose; Oh, You Gypsy Song (C/L: Mashe, Wladimir; Stewart, Leon)

## 4530 ✦ PARTY GIRL (1930)
### Tiffany, 1930

**Composer(s)** Stoddard, Harry
**Lyricist(s)** Klauber, Marcy

**Producer(s)** Halperin, Victor
**Director(s)** Halperin, Edward
**Screenwriter(s)** Katterjohn, Monte; Draney, George; Halperin, Victor
**Source(s)** *Dangerous Business* (novel) Belmer, Edwin

**Cast** Fairbanks Jr., Douglas; Loff, Jeanette; Barrie, Judith; Prevost, Marie; St. Polis, John

**Song(s)** Farewell; Oh, How I Adore You

**Notes** No cue sheet available.

## 4531 ✦ PARTY GIRL (1958)
### Metro–Goldwyn–Mayer, 1958

**Musical Score** Alexander, Jeff
**Choreographer(s)** Sidney, Robert

**Producer(s)** Pasternak, Joe
**Director(s)** Ray, Nicholas
**Screenwriter(s)** Wells, George

**Cast** Taylor, Robert; Charisse, Cyd; Cobb, Lee J.; Smith, Kent; Allen, Corey; Kelly, Claire; Charles, Lewis; Opatoshu, David; McVey, Patrick; Lang, Barbara; Hansen, Myrna; Utey, Betty

**Song(s)** Party Girl (C: Brodszky, Nicholas; L: Cahn, Sammy)

## 4532 ✦ A PASSAGE TO INDIA
### Columbia, 1984

**Musical Score** Jarre, Maurice

**Producer(s)** Brabourne, John; Goodwin, Richard
**Director(s)** Lean, David

**Screenwriter(s)**   Lean, David
**Source(s)**   *A Passage to India* (novel) Forster, E.M.; *A Passage to India* (play) Rau, Santha Rama

**Cast**   Davis, Judy; Banerjee, Victor; Ashcroft, Peggy; Fox, James; Guinness, Alec; Havers, Nigel; Wilson, Richard; Jaffrey, Saeed

**Song(s)**   Freely Maisie (C/L: Dalby, John)

**Notes**   No cue sheet available.

## 4533 ✦ PASSAGE TO MARSEILLE
### Warner Brothers, 1944

**Musical Score**   Steiner, Max

**Producer(s)**   Wallis, Hal B.
**Director(s)**   Curtiz, Michael
**Screenwriter(s)**   Robinson, Casey; Moffitt, Jack
**Source(s)**   "Sans Patrie" (story) Nordhoff, Charles; Hall, James Norman

**Cast**   Bogart, Humphrey; Rains, Claude; Morgan, Michele; Dorn, Philip; Greenstreet, Sydney; Dantine, Helmut; Lorre, Peter; Tobias, George; Loder, John; Francen, Victor; Sokoloff, Vladimir; Ciannelli, Eduardo; Blue, Monte; Conried, Hans; Roy, Billy

**Song(s)**   Someday I'll Meet You Again (C: Steiner, Max; L: Washington, Ned)

## 4534 ✦ PAST PERFUMANCE
### Warner Brothers, 1955

**Musical Score**   Franklyn, Milton J.

**Director(s)**   Jones, Chuck
**Screenwriter(s)**   Maltese, Michael

**Cast**   Le Pew, Pepe

**Song(s)**   We Had No Place to Go (C/L: Maltese, Michael)

**Notes**   Merrie Melodie.

## 4535 ✦ PATERNITY
### Paramount, 1981

**Composer(s)**   Shire, David

**Producer(s)**   Gordon, Lawrence; Moonjean, Hank
**Director(s)**   Steinberg, David
**Screenwriter(s)**   Peters, Charlie

**Cast**   Reynolds, Burt; D'Angelo, Beverly; Ashley, Elizabeth; Hutton, Lauren; Moore, Juanita; Fell, Norman; Dooley, Paul

**Song(s)**   Baby Talk (L: Frishberg, David); It's His Birthday [1] (C/L: Dunne, Murphy); Love's Gonna Find You [1] (L: Shire, David)

**Notes**   [1] Not used.

## 4536 ✦ PAT GARRETT AND BILLY THE KID
### Metro–Goldwyn–Mayer, 1973

**Musical Score**   Dylan, Bob
**Composer(s)**   Dylan, Bob
**Lyricist(s)**   Dylan, Bob

**Producer(s)**   Carroll, Gordon
**Director(s)**   Peckinpah, Sam
**Screenwriter(s)**   Wurlitzer, Rudolph

**Cast**   Coburn, James; Kristofferson, Kris; Dylan, Bob; Jaeckel, Richard; Jurado, Katy; Wills, Chill; Robards Jr., Jason

**Song(s)**   Billy Surrenders; Billy's Song

## 4537 ✦ PATRICK THE GREAT
### Universal, 1944

**Composer(s)**   James, Inez; Miller, Sidney
**Lyricist(s)**   James, Inez; Miller, Sidney
**Choreographer(s)**   Da Pron, Louis

**Producer(s)**   Benedict, Howard
**Director(s)**   Ryan, Frank
**Screenwriter(s)**   Millhauser, Bertram; Bennett, Dorothy

**Cast**   O'Connor, Donald; Ryan, Peggy; Arden, Eve; Dee, Frances; Cook, Donald; Gomez, Thomas; Tombes, Andrew; Bacon, Irving

**Song(s)**   Song of Love (C/L: Previn, Charles); When You Bump Into Someone You Know; Madam Zam; For the First Time (C: Kapp, David; L: Tobias, Charles); Let Me See (C: Skinner, Frank; L: Cherkose, Eddie); Don't Move; The Cubacha

## 4538 ✦ THE PATSY
### Paramount, 1964

**Musical Score**   Raksin, David

**Producer(s)**   Glucksman, Ernest D.
**Director(s)**   Lewis, Jerry
**Screenwriter(s)**   Lewis, Jerry; Richmond, Bill

**Cast**   Lewis, Jerry; Balin, Ina; Lorre, Peter; Sloane, Everett; Harris, Phil; Wynn, Keenan; Carradine, John; Conried, Hans; Deacon, Richard; Hamilton, Neil; Fleming, Rhonda; Foster, Phil; Hopper, Hedda; Raft, George; The Step Brothers; Torme, Mel; Wynn, Ed

**Song(s)**   I Lost My Heart in a Drive-In Movie (C: Raksin, David; L: Brooks, Jack)

## 4539 ✦ PAUL AND MICHELLE
### Paramount, 1974

**Composer(s)**   Colombier, Michel
**Lyricist(s)**   Black, Don

**Producer(s)**   Gilbert, Lewis
**Director(s)**   Gilbert, Lewis
**Screenwriter(s)**   Harris, Vernon; Huth, Angela

**Cast**  Dullea, Keir; Alvina, Anicee; Bury, Sean

**Song(s)**  Paul and Michelle; Good; Queen of the Nasties (C/L: Gilbert, Steve)


## 4540 ◆ PAUL BUNYAN
Disney, 1957

**Musical Score**  Bruns, George

**Director(s)**  Clark, Les
**Screenwriter(s)**  Nolley, Lance; Berman, Ted
**Voices**  The Mello Men

**Song(s)**  Paul Bunyan (C: Bruns, George; L: Adair, Tom); A Little Bit More [1] (C/L: Brooks, Jack)

**Notes**  Cartoon. [1] Not used.


## 4541 ◆ PAYMENT IN BLOOD
Columbia, 1968

**Musical Score**  De Masi, Francesco

**Producer(s)**  Orefici, F.
**Director(s)**  Rowland, E.G.
**Screenwriter(s)**  Carpi, Tito; Rowland, E.G.

**Cast**  Byrnes, Edward; Girolami, Enio; Barrett, Louise; Boyd, Rik

**Song(s)**  Seven Men (C: De Masi, Francesco; L: Nohra, Audrey; Alessandroni)

**Notes**  No cue sheet available.


## 4542 ◆ PAYROLL
Allied Artists, 1962

**Musical Score**  Owen, Reg

**Producer(s)**  Priggen, Norman
**Director(s)**  Hayes, Sidney
**Screenwriter(s)**  Baxt, George

**Cast**  Craig, Michael; Prevost, Francoise; Whitelaw, Billie; Lucas, William

**Song(s)**  It Happens Every Day (C: Osborne, Tony; L: Newell, Norman)

**Notes**  No cue sheet available.


## 4543 ◆ THE PEACEMAKER
United Artists, 1956

**Musical Score**  Greeley, George

**Producer(s)**  Makelim, Hal R.
**Director(s)**  Post, Ted
**Screenwriter(s)**  Richards, Hal; Ingram, Jay

**Cast**  Mitchell, James; Bowe, Rosemarie; Merlin, Jan; Barker, Jess; Sanders, Hugh; Holmes, Taylor; Tonge, Philip; Patrick, Dorothy

**Song(s)**  The Peacemaker (C: Greeley, George; L: Richards, Hal); Church Scene (C: Greeley, George; L: Unknown)


## 4544 ◆ PEACH O'RENO
RKO, 1931

**Producer(s)**  LeBaron, William
**Director(s)**  Seiter, William A.
**Screenwriter(s)**  Spence, Ralph; Whelan, Tim; Welch, Eddie

**Cast**  Wheeler, Bert; Woolsey, Robert; Lee, Dorothy; O'Neal, Zelma; Cawthorn, Joseph; Witherspoon, Cora; Hardy, Sam

**Song(s)**  From Niagara Falls to Reno (C/L: Akst, Harry; Clarke, Grant; Whiting, Richard A.)


## 4545 ◆ PECOS BILL
Disney, 1948

**Composer(s)**  Daniel, Eliot
**Lyricist(s)**  Lange, Johnny

**Director(s)**  Geronimi, Clyde
**Screenwriter(s)**  Penner, Erdman; Rinaldi, Joe

**Cast**  Rogers, Roy; Trigger; Sons of the Pioneers

**Song(s)**  Blue Shadows on the Trail; Pecos Bill; Slue Foot Sue (C: Nolan, Bob; Spencer, Tim; L: Penner, Erdman; Hibler, Winston); Rancho in the Sky [1]; You Rounded Up My Heart (In Love's Corral) [1] (C: Heath, Hy)

**Notes**  This cartoon is a part of MELODY TIME. [1] Not used.


## 4546 ◆ PEG O' MY HEART
Metro–Goldwyn–Mayer, 1933

**Musical Score**  Stothart, Herbert
**Composer(s)**  Stothart, Herbert; Brown, Nacio Herb
**Lyricist(s)**  Kahn, Gus; Freed, Arthur

**Director(s)**  Leonard, Robert Z.
**Screenwriter(s)**  Adams, Frank R.
**Source(s)**  *Peg O' My Heart* (play) Manners, J. Hartley

**Cast**  Davies, Marion; Stevens, Onslow; MacDonald, J. Farrell; Compton, Juliette

**Song(s)**  Sweetheart Darlin' (C: Stothart, Herbert; L: Kahn, Gus); Irish Serenade; I'll Remember Only You (C: Brown, Nacio Herb; L: Freed, Arthur); Hold Me [2] (C/L: Little, Little Jack; Oppenheim, Dave; Schuster, Ira); Boots and Saddles (C: Stothart, Herbert; L: Kahn, Gus); Trophy Room Episode (C/L: Stothart, Herbert); Birthday Party; When You're Falling in Love with the Irish [1] (C: Rodgers, Richard; L: Hart, Lorenz)

**Notes**  [1] Not used. [2] Also in THREE FACES OF EVE (20th).

## 4547 ✦ PENDULUM
Columbia, 1969

**Musical Score**   Scharf, Walter

**Producer(s)**   Niss, Stanley
**Director(s)**   Schaefer, George
**Screenwriter(s)**   Niss, Stanley

**Cast**   Peppard, George; Seberg, Jean; Kiley, Richard; McGraw, Charles; Sherwood, Madeleine; Lyons, Robert F.

**Song(s)**   The Pendulum Swings Both Ways (C: Scharf, Walter; L: David, Mack)

**Notes**   No cue sheet available.

## 4548 ✦ PENELOPE
Metro–Goldwyn–Mayer, 1966

**Musical Score**   Williams, John

**Producer(s)**   Loew Jr., Arthur M.
**Director(s)**   Hiller, Arthur
**Screenwriter(s)**   Wells, George
**Source(s)**   *Penelope* (novel) Cunningham, E.V.

**Cast**   Wood, Natalie; Bannen, Ian; Shawn, Dick; Falk, Peter; Kedrova, Lila; Jacobi, Lou; Winters, Jonathan; Crane, Norma; Cowan, Jerome; Golonka, Arlene; Wolfington, Iggie; Ballantine, Carl

**Song(s)**   Penelope (C: Williams, John; L: Bricusse, Leslie); The Sun Is Gray (C/L: Garnett, Gale)

## 4549 ✦ PENNIES FROM HEAVEN (1936)
Columbia, 1936

**Composer(s)**   Johnston, Arthur
**Lyricist(s)**   Burke, Johnny

**Director(s)**   McLeod, Norman Z.
**Screenwriter(s)**   Swerling, Jo
**Source(s)**   *The Peacock Feather* (novel) Moore, Katherine Leslie

**Cast**   Crosby, Bing; Evans, Madge; Fellows, Edith; Armstrong, Louis; Gallaudet, John; Bryant, Nana; Meek, Donald; Dugan, Tom; Westman, Nydia; Hampton, Lionel

**Song(s)**   So Do I; Pennies From Heaven; The Skeleton in the Closet; Let's Call a Heart a Heart; One Two Button Your Shoe; Now I've Got Some Dreaming to Do [1]; What This Country Needs [1]

**Notes**   [1] Not used.

## 4550 ✦ PENNIES FROM HEAVEN (1981)
Metro–Goldwyn–Mayer, 1981

**Choreographer(s)**   Daniels, Danny

**Producer(s)**   Kaye, Nora; Ross, Herbert
**Director(s)**   Ross, Herbert

**Screenwriter(s)**   Potter, Dennis
**Source(s)**   "Pennies from Heaven" (TV series) Potter, Dennis

**Cast**   Martin, Steve; Peters, Bernadette; Harper, Jessica; Bagneris, Vernel; McMartin, John; Karlen, John; Garner, Jay; Fitch, Robert; Rall, Tommy; Krupka, Elisha; Walken, Christopher

**Notes**   There are no original songs in this film. The vocals (all background from original sources and lip-synching by the stars) include: "The Clouds Will Soon Roll By" by Harry Woods and George Brown; "I'll Never Have to Dream Again" by Charles Newman and Isham Jones; "Yes, Yes" by Con Conrad and Cliff Friend; "Did You Ever See a Dream Walking" by Harry Revel and Mack Gordon; "Pennies From Heaven" by Arthur Johnson and Johnny Burke; "It's The Girl" by Abel Baer and Dave Oppenheim; "Love Is Good for Anything that Ails You" by Matty Malneck and Cliff Friend; "Let's Put Out the Lights" by Herman Hupfeld; "Painting the Clouds with Sunshine" by Joe Burke and Al Dubin; "It's a Sin to Tell a Lie" by Billy Mayhew; "I Want to Be Bad" by B.G. DeSylva, Lew Brown and Ray Henderson; "Let's Misbehave" by Cole Porter; "Life Is Just a Bowl of Cherries" by Ray Henderson and Lew Brown; "Let's Face the Music and Dance" by Irving Berlin; "I Get a Kick Out of You" by Cole Porter and "The Glory of Love" by Billy Hill.

## 4551 ✦ PENTHOUSE (1933)
Metro–Goldwyn–Mayer, 1933

**Musical Score**   Axt, William

**Director(s)**   Van Dyke, W.S.
**Screenwriter(s)**   Goodrich, Frances; Hackett, Albert

**Cast**   Loy, Myrna; Baxter, Warner; Butterworth, Charles; Clarke, Mae; Holmes, Phillips; Gordon, C. Henry

**Song(s)**   Stay on the Right Side of the Road (C: Bloom, Rube; L: Koehler, Ted)

**Notes**   Remade in 1939 as SOCIETY LAWYER.

## 4552 ✦ THE PENTHOUSE (1967)
Paramount, 1967

**Producer(s)**   Fine, Harry
**Director(s)**   Collinson, Peter
**Screenwriter(s)**   Collinson, Peter
**Source(s)**   *The Meter Man* (play) Forbes, C. Scott

**Cast**   Morgan, Terence; Kendall, Suzy; Beckley, Tony; Rodway, Norman; Beswick, Martine

**Song(s)**   One of Those Things (C/L: Hawksworth, John); The World Is Full of Lonely Men (C: Hawksworth, John; L: Shaper, Hal); The Penthouse [1] (C/L: Anka, Paul; Pinz, Shelley)

**Notes**   [1] Written for exploitation only. Not used in film.

## 4553 ✦ PENTHOUSE RHYTHM
### Universal, 1945

**Composer(s)**  Berens, Norman
**Lyricist(s)**  Brooks, Jack

**Producer(s)**  Gross, Frank
**Director(s)**  Cline, Edward F.
**Screenwriter(s)**  Roberts, Stanley; Dimsdale, Howard

**Cast**  Dodd, Jimmy; Worth, Bobby; Da Pron, Louis; Clark, Judy; Velasco and Lence

**Song(s)**  Peter Had a Wife and Couldn't Keep Her; Society Behavior (C/L: James, Inez; Miller, Sidney); Up Comes Love; When I Think of Heaven; Let's Go Americana

## 4554 ✦ PEOPLE ARE FUNNY
### Paramount, 1946

**Producer(s)**  White, Sam
**Director(s)**  White, Sam
**Screenwriter(s)**  Lang, David; Shane, Maxwell

**Cast**  Haley, Jack; Reed, Philip; Vallee, Rudy; Walker, Helen; Langford, Frances; Nelson, Ozzie; Linkletter, Art; Blandick, Clara

**Song(s)**  I'm in the Mood for Love [3] (C: McHugh, Jimmy; L: Fields, Dorothy); Every Hour on the Hour (C: Ellington, Duke; L: George, Don); Cielito Lindo (C/L: Fernandez, C.); Hey, Jose (Que Sera) [1] (C: Guizar, Pepe; Guizar, Tito; L: Guizar, Pepe; Guizar, Tito; Livingston, Jay; Evans, Ray); Angelina (C/L: Roberts, Allan; Fisher, Doris); Chuck-A-Luckin' (C/L: Gottler, Archie; Milton, Jay; Samuels, Walter G. G.); The Old Square Dance Is Back Again (C/L: Reid, Don; Tobias, Henry); Alouette [2] (C/L: Traditional)

**Notes**  None of these numbers appear to have been written for this film. [1] English lyrics by Jay Livingston and Ray Evans. [2] Musical version and English translation by Rudy Vallee. [3] Also in ABOUT MRS. LESLIE, EVERY NIGHT AT EIGHT and THAT'S MY BOY.

## 4555 ✦ PEPE
### Columbia, 1960

**Musical Score**  Green, Johnny
**Composer(s)**  Previn, Andre
**Lyricist(s)**  Langdon, Dory

**Producer(s)**  Sidney, George
**Director(s)**  Sidney, George
**Screenwriter(s)**  Kingsley, Dorothy; Binyon, Claude; Spigelgass, Leonard; Levien, Sonya
**Source(s)**  *Broadway Zauber* (play) Bush-Feket, Laci

**Cast**  Cantinflas; Dailey, Dan; Jones, Shirley; Chevalier, Maurice; Davis Jr., Sammy; Gabor, Zsa Zsa; Kovacs, Ernie; Curtis, Tony; Lemmon, Jack; North, Jay [3]; Novak, Kim; Previn, Andre; Reed, Donna; Reynolds, Debbie; Burke, Billie; Davis, Ann B. "Schultzy"; Coburn, Charles; Robinson, Edward G.; Mattox, Matt;

Crosby, Bing; Conte, Richard; Durante, Jimmy; Hopper, Hedda; Lawford, Peter; Martin, Dean; Demarest, William; Romero, Cesar; Garson, Greer; Darin, Bobby; Callan, Michael; Sinatra, Frank

**Song(s)**  Pepe [2] (C: Wittstatt, Hans); That's How It Went All Right; Far Away Part of Town; Lovely Day [1] (C: Lara, Augustin; Lara, Maria Teresa); Suzie [4] (C: Green, Johnny)

**Notes**  Judy Garland was heard on the soundtrack but not seen. There are also vocals of "Hooray for Hollywood" by Richard A. Whiting and Johnny Mercer; "Mimi" by Richard Rodgers and Lorenz Hart (from LOVE ME TONIGHT) and "September Song" by Kurt Weill and Maxwell Anderson (also in KNICKERBOCKER HOLIDAY and SEPTEMBER SONG). Dory Langdon is the maiden name of Dory Previn. [1] Special lyric by Dory Langdon to Spanish song "Concha Nacar." [2] Originally titled "Andalusian Girl" before the Langdon lyric was added. [3] Billed as Jay "Dennis the Menace" North. [4] Sheet music only.

## 4556 ✦ PEPPER
### Twentieth Century–Fox, 1936

**Lyricist(s)**  Clare, Sidney

**Producer(s)**  Stone, John
**Director(s)**  Tinling, James
**Screenwriter(s)**  Trotti, Lamar

**Cast**  Withers, Jane; Cobb, Irvin S.; Summerville, Slim; Jagger, Dean; Roberts, Muriel; Lebedeff, Ivan

**Song(s)**  Take Me Back to My Boots and Saddle [1] (C: Samuels, Walter G.; Whitcup, Leonard; Powell, Teddy); Song of the Coyotes (C: Akst, Harry; Rose, Gene); Kiss Me Goodnight (Not Goodbye) [2] (C: Hanley, James F.)

**Notes**  [1] Assigned as SONG OF THE COYOTES. Also in the Republic pictures BOOTS AND SADDLES (as "Take Me Back to My Boots and Saddles") and CALL OF THE CANYON. [2] Sidney Clare added new lyrics to the 1931 tune which originally had lyrics by Jules Furthman.

## 4557 ✦ PEPPERMINT SODA
### Gaumont–New Yorker, 1979

**Musical Score**  Simon, Yves
**Composer(s)**  Simon, Yves
**Lyricist(s)**  Simon, Yves

**Director(s)**  Kurys, Diane
**Screenwriter(s)**  Kurys, Diane

**Cast**  Klarwein, Eleanore; Michel, Odile; Clement, Coralie; Maurin, Marie Veronique

**Song(s)**  Theme de Anne; Frederique en Auto Stop; Anne et les Collants; Vacances de Paques; Diabolo Menthe

**Notes**  No cue sheet available.

## 4558 ✦ PERFECT
Columbia, 1985

**Musical Score**   Burns, Ralph

**Producer(s)**   Bridges, James
**Director(s)**   Bridges, James
**Screenwriter(s)**   Latham, Aaron
**Source(s)**   "Looking for Mr. Goodbody" (*Rolling Stone* magazine article) Latham, Aaron

**Cast**   Travolta, John; Curtis, Jamie Lee; De Salvo, Anne; Newman, Laraine; Henner, Marilu; Reed, Mathew; Gierasch, Stefan; Wenner, Jann

**Song(s)**   (Closest Thing to) Perfect (C/L: Omartian, Michael; Sudano, Bruce; Jackson, Jermaine); Hot Hips (C/L: Reed, Lou); Shock Me (C/L: Roberts, Bruce; Goldmark, Andy); Nightmares Come True (C/L: Coppock, Van); Watcha Gonna Do (C/L: Newborn, Brant); Wear Out the Grooves (C/L: Goldmark, Andy; Roberts, Bruce); Alone in the Dark (C/L: Sherba, Glenn); When the Lights Go Down (C/L: Lawrence, Karen; Hostetler, Fred); Talking to the Wall (C/L: Hartman, Don; Midnight, Charlie)

## 4559 ✦ A PERFECT COUPLE
Twentieth Century–Fox, 1979

**Producer(s)**   Altman, Robert
**Director(s)**   Altman, Robert
**Screenwriter(s)**   Altman, Robert; Nicholls, Allan

**Cast**   Dooley, Paul; Heflin, Marta; Vandis, Titos; Nicholls, Belita; Gibson, Henry; Arliss, Dimitra; Nicholls, Allan; Franz, Dennis; Neeley, Ted; MacRae, Heather

**Song(s)**   Don't Take Forever (C/L: Gibson, B.G.; Berg, Tony; Nicholls, Allan); Fantasy (C/L: Nicholls, Allan); Goodbye Friends (C/L: Nicholls, Allan); Hurricane (C/L: Berg, Tony; Neeley, Ted; Nicholls, Allan); Let the Music Play (C/L: Nicholls, Allan; Stephens, Oatis); Lonely Millionaire (C/L: De Young, Cliff; Berg, Tony); Love Is All There Is (C/L: Berg, Tony; Neeley, Ted; Nicholls, Allan); Somp'ins Got a Hold on Me (C/L: Berg, Tony; Neeley, Ted); Weekend Holiday (C/L: Berg, Tony; Gibson, B.G.; Nicholls, Allan); Won't Somebody Care (C/L: Berg, Tony; Nicholls, Allan); Searchin' for the Light (C/L: Bradley, Tomi-Lee; Berg, Tony; Nicholls, Allan; Neeley, Ted)

**Notes**   No cue sheet available.

## 4560 ✦ THE PERFECT GENTLEMAN
Metro–Goldwyn–Mayer, 1935

**Composer(s)**   Kaper, Bronislau; Jurmann, Walter
**Lyricist(s)**   Washington, Ned

**Director(s)**   Whelan, Tim
**Screenwriter(s)**   Carpenter, Edward Childs
**Source(s)**   "The Prodigal Father" (story) Hamilton, Cosmo

**Cast**   Morgan, Frank; Courteneidge, Cicely; Angel, Heather; Mundin, Herbert; O'Connor, Una

**Song(s)**   There's Something in a Big Parade; It's Only Human [1] (C: Lane, Burton; L: Adamson, Harold); Tillie the Tight Rope Walker [1]

**Notes**   Titled THE IMPERFECT GENTLEMAN overseas. There is also a vocal of "Pack Up Your Troubles" by George Asaf and Felix Powell. [1] Not used.

## 4561 ✦ THE PERFECT SPECIMEN
Warner Brothers, 1937

**Producer(s)**   Wallis, Hal B.
**Director(s)**   Curtiz, Michael
**Screenwriter(s)**   Raine, Norman Reilly; Riley, Lawrence; Morse, Brewster; Falkenstein, Fritz

**Cast**   Flynn, Errol; Blondell, Joan; Herbert, Hugh; Horton, Edward Everett; Foran, Dick; Roberts, Beverly; Robson, May; Jenkins, Allen; Moore, Dennie; Bates, Granville; Davenport, Harry

**Song(s)**   As Sure As You're in Love [1] (C: Jerome, M.K.; Scholl, Jack)

**Notes**   [1] Used instrumentally only. Also used instrumentally in BROADWAY MUSKETEERS.

## 4562 ✦ PERFORMANCE
Warner Brothers, 1970

**Musical Score**   Nitzsche, Jack

**Producer(s)**   Lieberson, Sandy
**Director(s)**   Cammell, Donald; Roeg, Nicolas
**Screenwriter(s)**   Cammell, Donald

**Cast**   Fox, James; Jagger, Mick; Pallenberg, Anita; Breton, Michele; Sidney, Ann; Bindon, John; Meadows, Stanley

**Song(s)**   Gone Dead Train (C: Nitzsche, Jack; L: Titleman, Russ); Wake Up Niggers (C/L: Pudim, Alafia); Jagger's Blues (C/L: Jagger, Mick); Poor White Hound Dog (C/L: Nitzsche, Jack)

**Notes**   Hirschhorn also lists the songs "Performance" and "Memo from T. Turner's Murder" but they do not appear on the cue sheet.

## 4563 ✦ A PERILOUS JOURNEY
Republic, 1953

**Musical Score**   Young, Victor
**Composer(s)**   Young, Victor
**Lyricist(s)**   Heyman, Edward

**Producer(s)**   O'Sullivan, William J.
**Director(s)**   Springsteen, R.G.
**Screenwriter(s)**   Wormser, Richard E.
**Source(s)**   *The Golden Tide* (novel) Roe, Vingle E.

**Cast**    Ralston, Vera Hruba; Brian, David; Brady, Scott; Winninger, Charles; Emerson, Hope

**Song(s)**    Bon Soir; On the Rue de la Paix; California

## 4564 ✦ THE PERILS OF PAULINE (1947)
### Paramount, 1947

**Musical Score**    Dolan, Robert Emmett
**Composer(s)**    Loesser, Frank
**Lyricist(s)**    Loesser, Frank
**Choreographer(s)**    Daniels, Billy

**Producer(s)**    Siegel, Sol C.
**Director(s)**    Marshall, George
**Screenwriter(s)**    Wolfson, P.J.; Butler, Frank

**Cast**    Hutton, Betty; Lund, John; Conklin, Chester; Farnum, William; Pollard, Snub; Finlayson, James; Hale, Creighton; Mann, Hank; Conklin, Heinie; Roach, Bert; McDonald, Francis; Panzer, Paul; Demarest, William; Collier, Constance; De Wolfe, Billy; Faylen, Frank

**Song(s)**    The Sewing Machine; Rumble, Rumble, Rumble; I Wish I Didn't Love You So; Poppa Don't Preach to Me; The French [1]

**Notes**    There is also a quote from the song "Poor Pauline" by composer Raymond Walker and lyricist Charles McCarron which was written in 1914 commemorating the original PERILS OF PAULINE serial with Pearl White. Robert Emmett Dolan wrote a hymn, "The Angels Sing," based on D. Bortniansky's Vesper Hymn. [1] Not used. May be "We French Get So Excited" which was not used in VARIETY GIRL.

## 4565 ✦ THE PERILS OF PAULINE (1967)
### Universal, 1967

**Musical Score**    Mizzy, Vic

**Producer(s)**    Leonard, Herbert B.
**Director(s)**    Leonard, Herbert B.; Shelley, Joshua
**Screenwriter(s)**    Beich, Albert

**Cast**    Austin, Pamela; Boone, Pat; Horton, Edward Everett; Terry-Thomas; Camp, Hamilton; Packer, Doris; Kasznar, Kurt; Scotti, Vito

**Song(s)**    My Pretty Pauline (C/L: Mizzy, Vic)

## 4566 ✦ A PERIOD OF ADJUSTMENT
### Metro–Goldwyn–Mayer, 1962

**Musical Score**    Murray, Lyn

**Producer(s)**    Weingarten, Lawrence
**Director(s)**    Hill, George Roy
**Screenwriter(s)**    Lennart, Isobel
**Source(s)**    *A Period of Adjustment* (play) Williams, Tennessee

**Cast**    Franciosa, Anthony; Fonda, Jane; Hutton, Jim; Nettleton, Lois; McGiver, John; Albertson, Mabel; Albertson, Jack

**Song(s)**    A Few Tender Words [1] (C: Murray, Lyn; L: David, Mack); As Big As Texas [1] (C: Murray, Lyn; L: David, Mack)

**Notes**    [1] Used instrumentally only.

## 4567 ✦ PERMANENT RECORD
### Paramount, 1988

**Musical Score**    Strummer, Joe
**Composer(s)**    Strummer, Joe
**Lyricist(s)**    Strummer, Joe

**Producer(s)**    Mancuso Jr., Frank
**Director(s)**    Silver, Marisa
**Screenwriter(s)**    Fees, Jarre; Liddle, Alice; Ketron, Larry

**Cast**    Reeves, Keanu; Boyce, Alan; Meyrink, Michelle; Corbin, Barry; Rubin, Jennifer

**Song(s)**    Wishing on Another Lucky Star (C/L: Sother, J.D.); Something Happened (C/L: Reed, Lou); Waiting on Love (C/L: Neumann, Kurt; Llanas, Sam); Nothin' 'Bout Nothin'; Trash City; Nefertiti Rock

## 4568 ✦ PERRI
### Disney, 1957

**Musical Score**    Smith, Paul J.
**Composer(s)**    Bruns, George
**Lyricist(s)**    Hibler, Winston; Wright, Ralph

**Producer(s)**    Hibler, Winston
**Director(s)**    Kenworthy Jr., N. Paul; Wright, Ralph
**Screenwriter(s)**    Wright, Ralph; Hibler, Winston
**Source(s)**    *Perri* (novel) Salten, Felix

**Cast**    Hibler, Winston

**Song(s)**    Together Time (C: Smith, Paul J.; George, Gil); Break of Day [1] (L: Hibler, Winston); Now to Sleep; Perri [2] (C: Smith, Paul J.; L: George, Gil)

**Notes**    [1] Written for SLEEPING BEAUTY. [2] Written for exploitation only.

## 4569 ✦ PETE KELLY'S BLUES
### Warner Brothers, 1955

**Musical Score**    Buttolph, David

**Director(s)**    Webb, Jack
**Screenwriter(s)**    Breen, Richard L.

**Cast**    Webb, Jack [3]; Leigh, Janet; O'Brien, Jack; Lee, Peggy; Devine, Andy; Marvin, Lee; Fitzgerald, Ella; Milner, Martin; Wyenn, Than; Ellis, Herb; Dennis, John; Mansfield, Jayne; Marshall, Mort; The Tuxedo Band [1]; Pete Kelly and His Big Seven [2]

**Song(s)**    He Needs Me (C/L: Hamilton, Arthur); Sing a Rainbow (C/L: Hamilton, Arthur); Pete Kelly's Blues (C: Heindorf, Ray; L: Cahn, Sammy); Ella Hums the Blues (C/L: Fitzgerald, Ella)

**Notes**    It is not known which of these were written for the picture. There are also renditions of "Just a Closer

Walk with Thee" and "I'm Gonna Meet My Sweetie Now" by Benny Davis and Jesse Greer; "Bye Bye Blackbird" by Ray Henderson and Mort Dixon; "Hard Hearted Hannah (The Vamp of Savannah)" by Milton Ager, Jack Yellen, Bob Bigelow and Charles Bates; "Sugar (That Sugar Baby of Mine)" by Maceo Pinkard, Sidney Mitchell and Edna Alexander and "Somebody Loves Me" by George Gershwin, B.G. DeSylva and Ballard Macdonald. [1] Featuring Joe Venuti, Harper Goff and Perry Bodkin. [2] Featuring Dick Cathcart, Matty Matlock, "Moe" Schneider, Eddie Miller, George Van Eps, Nick Fatool, Ray Sherman and Jud De Naut. [3] Trumpet playing dubbed by Dick Cathcart.

## 4570 ✦ PETER PAN
Disney, 1952

**Musical Score** Wallace, Oliver
**Composer(s)** Fain, Sammy
**Lyricist(s)** Cahn, Sammy

**Director(s)** Luske, Hamilton; Geronimi, Clyde; Jackson, Wilfred
**Screenwriter(s)** Sears, Ted; Penner, Erdman; Peet, Bill; Hibler, Winston; Rinaldi, Joe; Banta, Milt; Wright, Ralph; Cottrell, William
**Source(s)** *Peter Pan* (play) Barrie, James M.

**Directing Animator(s)** Kahl, Milt; Thomas, Franklin; Reitherman, Wolfang; Kimball, Ward; Johnston, Ollie; Davis, Marc; Larson, Eric; Lounsbery, John; Clark, Les; Ferguson, Norm
**Cast** Driscoll, Bobby; Beaumont, Kathryn; Conried, Hans; Thompson, Bill; Angel, Heather; Collins, Paul; Luske, Tommy; Candido, Candy; Conway, Tom; Dupree, Roland; Barclay, Don

**Song(s)** The Second Star to the Right [2]; You Can Fly! You Can Fly! You Can Fly!; Your Mother and Mine; What Made the Red Man Red?; The Elegant Captain Hook; A Pirate's Life (C: Wallace, Oliver; L: Penner, Erdman); Following the Leader (Tee-Dum, Tee-Dum) (C: Wallace, Oliver; L: Hibler, Winston; Sears, Ted); Never Smile at a Crocodile [4] (C: Churchill, Frank E.; L: Lawrence, Jack); Ho-Hum [1] (C: Wolcott, Charles; L: Penner, Erdman); Peter Pan [3] (C: Wallace, Oliver; Young, Victor; L: Lawrence, Jack)

**Notes** Animated feature. [1] Not used. [2] The music was written for ALICE IN WONDERLAND as "Beyond the Laughing Sky" but not used there. [3] Wallace's music is used in the film. The additional music by Victor Young and the lyrics by Jack Lawrence were added for exploitation only. [4] Used instrumentally only.

## 4571 ✦ THE PETER TCHAIKOVSKY STORY
Disney, 1959

**Musical Score** Bruns, George

**Producer(s)** Geronimi, Clyde
**Director(s)** Barton, Joe
**Screenwriter(s)** Englander, Otto; Rinaldi, Joe

**Cast** Ulanova, Galina; Bolshoi Ballet

**Song(s)** Open Your Eyes [1] (C: Tchaikovsky, Peter; L: Sykes, Sam; George, Gil)

**Notes** [1] Based on the waltz of the "Serenade for String." This might have been cut from SLEEPING BEAUTY.

## 4572 ✦ PETE'S DRAGON
Disney, 1977

**Musical Score** Kostal, Irwin
**Composer(s)** Kasha, Al; Hirschhorn, Joel
**Lyricist(s)** Kasha, Al; Hirschhorn, Joel
**Choreographer(s)** White, Onna

**Producer(s)** Miller, Ron; Courtland, Jerome
**Director(s)** Chaffey, Don
**Screenwriter(s)** Marmorstein, Malcolm

**Cast** Reddy, Helen; Dale, Jim; Rooney, Mickey; Buttons, Red; Winters, Shelley; Marshall, Sean; Kean, Jane; Backus, Jim; Tyner, Charles; Morgan, Gary; Conaway, Jeff; Bartlett, Cal; Callas, Charlie

**Song(s)** Bill of Sale; Boo Bop Bopbop Bop (I Love You, Too); Brazzle Dazzle Day; Candle on the Water; Every Little Piece; The Happiest Home in These Hills; I Saw a Dragon; It's Not Easy; Passamashloddy; There's Room for Everyone

## 4573 ✦ THE PETTY GIRL
Columbia, 1950

**Composer(s)** Arlen, Harold
**Lyricist(s)** Mercer, Johnny

**Producer(s)** Perrin, Nat
**Director(s)** Levin, Henry
**Screenwriter(s)** Perrin, Nat

**Cast** Cummings, Robert; Caulfield, Joan; Lanchester, Elsa; Long, Audrey; Wickes, Mary; Cooper, Melville; Orth, Frank

**Song(s)** Fancy Free; Calypso Song; Ah Loves Ya; The Petty Girl

**Notes** TItled GIRL OF THE YEAR overseas.

## 4574 ✦ PEYTON PLACE
Twentieth Century–Fox, 1957

**Musical Score** Waxman, Franz

**Producer(s)** Wald, Jerry
**Director(s)** Robson, Mark
**Screenwriter(s)** Hayes, John Michael
**Source(s)** *Peyton Place* (novel) Metalious, Grace

**Cast** Turner, Lana; Lange, Hope; Philips, Lee; Nolan, Lloyd; Varsi, Diane; Kennedy, Arthur; Tamblyn, Russ; Moore, Terry; Nelson, David; Field, Betty; Dunnock, Mildred; Ames, Leon

**Song(s)** The Wonderful Season of Love [1] (C: Waxman, Franz; L: Webster, Paul Francis)

**Notes** [1] Also in RETURN TO PEYTON PLACE.

## 4575 ◆ PHANTASM
### Avco Embassy, 1979

**Musical Score** Myrow, Fred; Seagrave, Malcolm

**Producer(s)** Coscarelli, D.A.; Pepperman, Paul
**Director(s)** Coscarelli, Don
**Screenwriter(s)** Coscarelli, Don

**Cast** Baldwin, Michael; Thornbury, Bill; Bannister, Reggie; Lester, Kathy

**Song(s)** Sittin' Here at Midnight (C/L: Thornbury, Bill)

**Notes** No cue sheet available.

## 4576 ◆ THE PHANTOM EMPIRE
### Mascot, 1935

**Musical Score** Zahler, Lee
**Composer(s)** Autry, Gene; Burnette, Smiley
**Lyricist(s)** Autry, Gene; Burnette, Smiley

**Producer(s)** Levine, Nat
**Director(s)** Brower, Otto; Eason, B. Reeves
**Screenwriter(s)** Schaefer, Armand; Rathmell, John

**Cast** Autry, Gene; Darro, Frankie; Ross, Betsy King; Christie, Dorothy; Burnette, Smiley

**Song(s)** Uncle Noah's Ark [1] [4] [7] [8]; In My Vine Covered Cottage [1]; I'm Oscar, I'm Pete [2]; No Need to Worry [3] [5]; Uncle Henry's Vacation [3]; She's Done and Gone Away [6]; I'm Getting a Moon's Eye View of the World [6]; Just Come On Back [7]; My Cross-Eyed Gal [9] (C/L: Autry, Gene; Long, Jimmy); That Silver Haired Daddy of Mine [9] (C/L: Autry, Gene; Long, Jimmy)

**Notes** A serial in 12 episodes. Just as an example I thought I'd list the chapter titles of this serial: THE SINGING COWBOY, THE THUNDER RIDERS, THE LIGHTNING CHAMBER, PHANTOM BROADCAST, BENEATH THE EARTH, DISASTER FROM THE SKIES, FROM DEATH TO LIFE, JAWS OF JEOPARDY, PRISONERS OF THE RAY, THE REBELLION, A QUEEN IN CHAINS and THE END OF MURANIA. [1] In episode # 1. [2] In episode # 2. [3] In episode # 4. [4] In episode # 5. [5] In episode # 6. [6] In episode # 8. [7] In episode # 12. [8] Also in ROUND-UP TIME IN TEXAS. [9] Sheet music only.

## 4577 ◆ THE PHANTOM IN THE HOUSE
### Continental Talking Pictures, 1929

**Director(s)** Rosen, Phil
**Screenwriter(s)** Hoerl, Arthur
**Source(s)** The Phantom in the House Soutar, Andrew

**Cast** Cortez, Ricardo; Welford, Nancy; Walthall, Henry B.; Valentine, Grace; Curran, Thomas A.; Curtis, Jack; Elliott, John

**Song(s)** You'll Never Be Forgotten (C/L: Silver, Abner; Pinkard, Maceo)

**Notes** No cue sheet available.

## 4578 ◆ PHANTOM LADY
### Universal, 1944

**Choreographer(s)** Horton, Lester

**Producer(s)** Harrison, Joan
**Director(s)** Siodmak, Robert
**Screenwriter(s)** Schoenfeld, Bernard C.

**Cast** Raines, Ella; Tone, Franchot; Curtis, Alan; Gomez, Thomas; Helm, Fay; Novello, Jay; Tombes, Andrew; Cook Jr., Elisha; Toomey, Regis; Crehan, Joseph

**Song(s)** Chick-Ee-Chick (C/L: Cherkose, Eddie; Press, Jacques)

**Notes** No cue sheet available.

## 4579 ◆ PHANTOM OF THE OPERA
### Universal, 1943

**Musical Score** Ward, Edward

**Producer(s)** Waggner, George
**Director(s)** Lubin, Arthur
**Screenwriter(s)** Taylor, Eric; Hoffenstein, Samuel
**Source(s)** *The Phantom of the Opera* (novel) Leroux, Gaston

**Cast** Eddy, Nelson; Foster, Susanna; Rains, Claude; Mander, Miles; Barrier, Edgar; Farrar, Jane; Everest, Barbara; Cronyn, Hume; Leiber, Fritz

**Song(s)** Lullaby of the Bells (C: Ward, Edward; L: Waggner, George); French Opera Sequence [1] (C: Chopin, Frederic; L: Waggner, George)

**Notes** There are also some opera excerpts including MARTHA by Frederich Von Flowtow with French lyrics by William Wymetal, adapted by Edward Ward; and a Russian opera sequence based on Tschaikowsky's "Symphony #4." [1] Lyrics translated into French by William Wymetal.

## 4580 ◆ PHANTOM OF THE PARADISE
### Twentieth Century–Fox, 1974

**Musical Score** Tipton, George Aliceson
**Composer(s)** Williams, Paul
**Lyricist(s)** Williams, Paul
**Choreographer(s)** Oblong, Harold; Shepherd, William

**Producer(s)** Pressman, Edward R.
**Director(s)** De Palma, Brian
**Screenwriter(s)** De Palma, Brian

**Cast** Williams, Paul; Finley, William; Harper, Jessica; Memmoli, George; Graham, Gerrit; Comanor, Jeffrey

**Song(s)** Goodbye Eddie, Goodbye; Faust; Have to Be Seen (C/L: Tipton, George Aliceson); Upholstery; Special to Me; Phantom's Theme; Life at Last; Someone Super Like You; Old Souls; Audition Sequence

### 4581 ✦ THE PHANTOM PRESIDENT
Paramount, 1932

**Composer(s)** Rodgers, Richard
**Lyricist(s)** Hart, Lorenz

**Director(s)** Taurog, Norman
**Screenwriter(s)** De Leon, Walter; Thompson, Harlan
**Source(s)** (novel) Worts, George F.

**Cast** Cohan, George M.; Colbert, Claudette; Durante, Jimmy; Barbier, George; Toler, Sidney; Mowbray, Alan; Middleton, Charles

**Song(s)** The Country Needs a Man; Phantom President Prelude; Somebody Ought to Wave the Flag; The Medicine Show [1]; Robinson Crusoe (C: Johnston, Arthur; L: Durante, Jimmy); Schnozzola [2] (C: Johnston, Arthur; Durante, Jimmy; L: Hart, Lorenz); Sick [2] (C/L: Durante, Jimmy; Hart, Lorenz); Give Her a Kiss; The Convention; There He Is - Theodore K. Blair [3]; We Need a Man [4] (C/L: Cohan, George M.)

**Notes** [1] Sequence contains reprise of "Somebody Ought to Wave the Flag;" new lyrics to Eddie Leonard's "Roly Boly Eyes," "A Schnozzola" and "Sick." [2] Part of "The Medicine Show" sequence. [3] Not used. [4] Sheet music only.

### 4582 ✦ THE PHANTOM SPEAKS
Republic, 1945

**Producer(s)** Brown, Donald H.
**Director(s)** English, John
**Screenwriter(s)** Butler, John K.

**Cast** Arlen, Richard; Ridges, Stanley; Roberts, Lynne; Powers, Tom

**Song(s)** Who Took Me Home Last Night [1] (C: Styne, Jule; L: Adamson, Harold)

**Notes** [1] Also in CASANOVA IN BURLESQUE, CHANGE OF HEART, HIT PARADE OF 1943 and THUMBS UP.

### 4583 ✦ THE PHANTOM STAGE
Universal, 1939

**Composer(s)** Allan, Fleming
**Lyricist(s)** Allan, Fleming

**Producer(s)** Carr, Trem
**Director(s)** Eberson, Drew
**Screenwriter(s)** West, Joseph

**Cast** Jones, Buck; Reynolds, Marjorie; Cleveland, George; Taylor, Forrest; Howes, Reed; Strange, Glenn; Kirk, Jack

**Song(s)** Give Me the Life of a Cowboy; Road to Santa Fe; We're Brandin' Today; Ridin' Down the Utah Trails

### 4584 ✦ PHANTOM STALLION
Republic, 1954

**Musical Score** Butts, Dale

**Producer(s)** Ralston, Rudy
**Director(s)** Keller, Harry
**Screenwriter(s)** Geraghty, Gerald

**Cast** Allen, Rex [2]; Koko [1]; Pickens, Slim; Balenda, Carla; Shannon, Harry; Haggerty, Don

**Song(s)** Born to the Saddle [3] (C/L: Cherkose, Eddie)

**Notes** [1] The Miracle Horse of the Movies. [2] The Arizona Cowboy. [3] Also in BILLY THE KID RETURNS and UNDER MEXICALI STARS.

### 4585 ✦ THE PHANTOM TOLLBOOTH
Metro–Goldwyn–Mayer, 1970

**Musical Score** Elliott, Dean
**Composer(s)** Pockriss, Lee
**Lyricist(s)** Gimbel, Norman

**Producer(s)** Levitow, Abe; Goldman, Les
**Director(s)** Jones, Chuck; Levitow, Abe; Monahan, Dave [1]
**Screenwriter(s)** Jones, Chuck; Rosen, Sam
**Source(s)** *The Phantom Tollbooth* (novel) Juster, Norton
**Voices** Blanc, Mel; Butler, Daws; Candido, Candy; Conried, Hans; Foray, June; Gilbert, Patti; Menken, Shep; Norton, Cliff; Thor, Larry; Tremayne, Les

**Cast** Patrick, Butch

**Song(s)** Milo's Song; Don't Say There's Nothing to Do in the Doldrums (L: Vance, Paul); Time Is a Gift; Noise, Beautiful Noise (L: Vance, Paul); Word Market (Words in a Word); Numbers Are the Only Thing That Count; Rhyme and Reason Reign

**Notes** [1] Live action directed by Monahan. He is billed as David Monahan.

### 4586 ✦ PHILBERT
Warner Brothers, 1963

**Musical Score** Jackson, Howard

**Song(s)** Philbert (C: Fain, Sammy; L: Miller, Sy)

**Notes** Short subject.

### 4587 ✦ THE PHYNX
Warner Brothers, 1970

**Musical Score** Stoller, Mike; Haskell, Jimmie
**Composer(s)** Stoller, Mike
**Lyricist(s)** Leiber, Jerry

**Producer(s)**  Foster, George
**Director(s)**  Katzin, Lee H.
**Screenwriter(s)**  Cornyn, Stan

**Cast**  Blondell, Joan; Cugat, Xavier; Devine, Andy; Feld, Fritz; Gorcey, Leo; Hayward, Louis; Jessel, George; Keeler, Ruby; Kelly, Patsy; Lamour, Dorothy; Lombardo, Guy; Louis, Joe; Maxwell, Marilyn; McQueen, Butterfly; O'Brien, Pat; O'Sullivan, Maureen; Vallee, Rudy; Weissmuller, Johnny; Antonio, Lou; Kellin, Mike; Ansara, Michael; Tobias, George

**Song(s)**  What Is Your Sign?; I've Got Them Feelin' Too Good Today Blues; Hello; You Know the Feeling; Trip with Me; They Say that You're Mad; It Nearly Blew My Mind; The Boys in the Band

---

**4588 ✦ PICCADILLY JIM**
Metro–Goldwyn–Mayer, 1936

**Musical Score**  Axt, William

**Producer(s)**  Rapf, Harry
**Director(s)**  Leonard, Robert Z.
**Screenwriter(s)**  Brackett, Charles; Knopf, Edwin H.
**Source(s)**  *Piccadilly Jim* (novel) Wodehouse, P.G.

**Cast**  Montgomery, Robert; Morgan, Frank; Evans, Madge; Blore, Eric; Burke, Billie; Benchley, Robert; O'Keefe, Dennis; Pringle, Aileen; Bevan, Billy

**Song(s)**  Night of Nights (C: Donaldson, Walter; L: Adamson, Harold); In the Shadow of the Old Oak Tree [1] (C/L: Wright, Bob; Forrest, Chet)

**Notes**  [1] Sheet music only.

---

**4589 ✦ PICK A STAR**
Metro–Goldwyn–Mayer, 1937

**Producer(s)**  Roach, Hal
**Director(s)**  Sedgwick, Edward
**Screenwriter(s)**  Flournoy, Richard; Jones, A.V.; Dugan, Tom

**Cast**  Kelly, Patsy; Auer, Mischa; Lawrence, Rosina; Halton, Charles; Haley, Jack; Roberti, Lyda; Finlayson, James; Laurel, Stan; Hardy, Oliver

**Song(s)**  Without Your Love (C: Stryker, Fred; L: Lange, Johnny)

**Notes**  No cue sheet available.

---

**4590 ✦ PICKUP ALLEY**
Columbia, 1957

**Producer(s)**  Allen, Irving; Broccoli, Albert R.
**Director(s)**  Gilling, John
**Screenwriter(s)**  Paxton, John

**Cast**  Mature, Victor; Ekberg, Anita; Howard, Trevor; Colleano, Bonar; Morell, Andre

**Song(s)**  Anyone for Love (C: Lee, Lester; L: Washington, Ned)

**Notes**  No cue sheet available.

---

**4591 ✦ THE PICK-UP ARTIST**
Twentieth Century–Fox, 1987

**Musical Score**  Delerue, Georges

**Producer(s)**  MacLeod, David L.
**Director(s)**  Toback, James
**Screenwriter(s)**  Toback, James

**Cast**  Ringwald, Molly; Downey Jr., Robert; Hopper, Dennis; Aiello, Danny; Dunnock, Mildred; Jackson, Victoria; Koehler, Frederick; Gunton, Bob; Keitel, Harvey; Bruno, Tamara; Baranski, Christine; Williams, Vanessa; Towne, Robert; Santoni, Reni

**Song(s)**  The Pickup Artist (C/L: Wonder, Stevie); Da Doo Ron Ron (C/L: Spector, Phil; Barry, Jeff; Greenwich, Ellie); Don't Hang Up (C/L: Mann, Kal; Appell, Dave); Susie Darlin' (C/L: Luke, Robin); Lonely Boy (C/L: Anka, Paul); (The Best Part of) Breakin' Up (C/L: Spector, Phil; Poncia, Vincent; Andreoli, Pete); Under the Boardwalk (C/L: Resnick, Arthur; Young, Kenny); She's Crafty (C/L: Beastie Boys, The; Rubin, Rick); Blue Suede Shoes (C/L: Perkins, Carl); Casanova [1] (C/L: Calloway, Reggie)

**Notes**  Some of these obviously were not written for this film. It is not known which were. [1] Also in FATAL BEAUTY (UA).

---

**4592 ✦ PICKUP ON SOUTH STREET**
Twentieth Century–Fox, 1953

**Musical Score**  Harline, Leigh

**Producer(s)**  Schermer, Jules
**Director(s)**  Fuller, Samuel
**Screenwriter(s)**  Fuller, Samuel

**Cast**  Widmark, Richard; Peters, Jean; Ritter, Thelma; Vye, Murvyn; Kiley, Richard; Stone, Milburn

**Song(s)**  Mam'Selle [1] (C: Goulding, Edmund; L: Gordon, Mack)

**Notes**  [1] From THE RAZOR'S EDGE.

---

**4593 ✦ PICNIC**
Columbia, 1955

**Musical Score**  Duning, George

**Producer(s)**  Kohlmar, Fred
**Director(s)**  Logan, Joshua
**Screenwriter(s)**  Taradash, Daniel
**Source(s)**  *Picnic* (play) Inge, William

**Cast**  Holden, William; Russell, Rosalind; Novak, Kim; Field, Betty; Strasberg, Susan; Robertson, Cliff;

---

O'Connell, Arthur; Felton, Verna; Shaw, Reta; Adams, Nick; Bailey, Raymond

**Song(s)**  Theme from Picnic [1] (C: Duning, George; L: Allen, Steve)

**Notes**  [1] Lyric added for exploitation use only.

## 4594 ♦ A PIECE OF THE ACTION
### Warner Brothers, 1977

**Musical Score**  Askey, Gil; Mayfield, Curtis
**Composer(s)**  Mayfield, Curtis
**Lyricist(s)**  Mayfield, Curtis

**Producer(s)**  Tucker, Melville
**Director(s)**  Poitier, Sidney
**Screenwriter(s)**  Blackwell, Charles

**Cast**  Poitier, Sidney; Cosby, Bill; Jones, James Earl; Nicholas, Denise; Clarke, Hope; Vandis, Titos; Foster, Frances; Reed, Tracy

**Song(s)**  A Piece of the Action; Orientation

## 4595 ♦ PIECES OF DREAMS
### United Artists, 1970

**Musical Score**  Legrand, Michel

**Producer(s)**  Blumofe, Robert F.
**Director(s)**  Haller, Daniel
**Screenwriter(s)**  Hirson, Roger O.
**Source(s)**  *The Wine and the Music* (novel) Barrett, William E.

**Cast**  Forster, Robert; Hutton, Lauren; Geer, Will; Francis, Ivor

**Song(s)**  Pieces of Dreams (C: Legrand, Michel; L: Bergman, Alan; Bergman, Marilyn)

## 4596 ♦ THE PIED PIPER (1942)
### Twentieth Century–Fox, 1942

**Producer(s)**  Johnson, Nunnally
**Director(s)**  Pichel, Irving
**Screenwriter(s)**  Johnson, Nunnally
**Source(s)**  *Pied Piper* (novel) Shute, Nevil

**Cast**  Woolley, Monty; McDowall, Roddy; Baxter, Anne; Preminger, Otto; Naish, J. Carrol; Garner, Peggy Ann

**Song(s)**  Ma Grand'-Tante (C: Arnaud, Leo; L: Johnson, Nunnally)

## 4597 ♦ THE PIED PIPER (1972)
### Paramount, 1972

**Composer(s)**  Donovan
**Lyricist(s)**  Donovan

**Producer(s)**  Puttnam, David; Lieberson, Sandy
**Director(s)**  Demy, Jacques

**Screenwriter(s)**  Demy, Jacques; Birkin, Andrew; Peplow, Mark

**Cast**  Donovan; Pleasence, Donald; Kinnear, Roy; Dors, Diana; Wild, Jack; Hurt, John; Hordern, Michael; Harrison, Cathryn

**Song(s)**  Sailing Homeward; People Call Me the Pied Piper; Bring Down—Send Up

## 4598 ♦ PIERNAS DE SEDA (FREE AND EASY)
### Twentieth Century–Fox, 1935

**Composer(s)**  Kernell, William
**Lyricist(s)**  Roulien, Raul

**Song(s)**  You've Got Me That Way; Penitentiary Blues; Stocking Show Opening; Pantalette; Rhythmic Dialog; Modern Girl; Futuristic Lady; Cubanita [1]

**Notes**  No other information available. [1] Not on cue sheet.

## 4599 ♦ PIERRE OF THE PLAINS
### Metro–Goldwyn–Mayer, 1942

**Musical Score**  Hayton, Lennie

**Director(s)**  Seitz, George B.
**Screenwriter(s)**  Kimble, Lawrence; Millhauser, Bertram
**Source(s)**  *Pierre of the Plains* (play) Selwyn, Edgar

**Cast**  Carroll, John; Hussey, Ruth; Cabot, Bruce; Owen, Reginald; Brown, Phil; Travers, Henry; Ankers, Evelyn; Leonard, Sheldon

**Song(s)**  Saskatchewan (C: Stothart, Herbert; L: Freed, Ralph)

**Notes**  This was the third filming of this story. It was first filmed in 1918 as HEART OF THE WILD by Artcraft and in 1922 by Paramount as OVER THE BORDER.

## 4600 ♦ PIGSKIN PARADE
### Twentieth Century–Fox, 1936

**Composer(s)**  Pollack, Lew
**Lyricist(s)**  Mitchell, Sidney D.

**Producer(s)**  Rogers, Bogart
**Director(s)**  Butler, David
**Screenwriter(s)**  Tugend, Harry; Yellen, Jack; Conselman, William

**Cast**  Erwin, Stuart; Kelly, Patsy; Haley, Jack; The Yacht Club Boys [1]; Downs, Johnny; Grable, Betty; Judge, Arline; Dunbar, Dixie; Garland, Judy; Kohler Jr., Fred; Sutton, Grady; Cook Jr., Elisha; Nugent, Eddie; Tannen, Julius

**Song(s)**  TSU (Alma Mater); You're Slightly Terrific; Woo! Woo! (C/L: The Yacht Club Boys); You Do the Darndest Things Baby; We'd Rather Be in College (C/L: The Yacht Club Boys); Down with Everything

(C/L: The Yacht Club Boys); The Balboa; Texas Tornado; It's Love I'm After; Football Song (C/L: The Yacht Club Boys)

**Notes** [1] Consisted of Charles Adler, James V. Kern, William B. Mann and George Kelly.

## 4601 ✦ PILLOW TALK
### Universal, 1959

**Musical Score** De Vol, Frank
**Composer(s)** Lubin, Joe; Roth, I.J.
**Lyricist(s)** Lubin, Joe; Roth, I.J.

**Producer(s)** Hunter, Ross
**Director(s)** Gordon, Michael
**Screenwriter(s)** Shapiro, Stanley; Richlin, Maurice

**Cast** Day, Doris; Hudson, Rock; Randall, Tony; Ritter, Thelma; Adams, Nick; McCarty, Mary; Gerry, Alex; Dalio, Marcel; Patrick, Lee

**Song(s)** Pillow Talk (C/L: James, Inez; Pepper, Buddy); Inspiration; Roly Poly (C/L: Doran, Elsa; Lake, Sol); I Need No Atmosphere; Possess Me; You Lied [1]; Convince Me [1]; The Careless Years [1]

**Notes** [1] BMI list only.

## 4602 ✦ PILLOW TO POST
### Warner Brothers, 1945

**Musical Score** Hollander, Frederick

**Producer(s)** Gottlieb, Alex
**Director(s)** Sherman, Vincent
**Screenwriter(s)** Hoffman, Charles
**Source(s)** *Pillar to Post* (play) Kohn, Rose Simon

**Cast** Lupino, Ida; Greenstreet, Sydney; Prince, William; Erwin, Stuart; Mitchell, Johnny; Donnelly, Ruth; Brown, Barbara; Orth, Frank; Louis Armstrong and His Orchestra; Harvey, Paul; McGuire, Don; Compton, Joyce

**Song(s)** Watcha Say (C: Lane, Burton; L: Koehler, Ted)

## 4603 ✦ PINK FLOYD THE WALL
### Metro–Goldwyn–Mayer, 1982

**Musical Score** Waters, Roger; Gilmour, David
**Composer(s)** Waters, Roger
**Lyricist(s)** Waters, Roger

**Producer(s)** Marshal, Alan
**Director(s)** Parker, Alan
**Screenwriter(s)** Waters, Roger

**Cast** Geldof, Bob; Hargreaves, Christine; Laurenson, James; David, Eleanor; McKeon, Kevin; Hoskins, Bob; Bingham, David; Wright, Jenny

**Song(s)** The Little Boy that Santa Claus Forgot (C/L: Connor; Leach; Carr); When the Tigers Broke Free; In the Flesh; The Thin Ice; Another Brick in the Wall;

Goodbye Blue Sky; The Happiest Days of Our Lives; Mother; Empty Spaces; Young Lust (C/L: Waters, Roger; Gilmour, David); One of My Turns; Don't Leave Me Now; Goodbye Cruel World; Is There Anybody Out There; Nobody Home; Vera; Bring the Boys Back Home; Comfortably Numb (C/L: Waters, Roger; Gilmour, David); In the Flesh; Run Like Hell; Waiting for the Worms; Bob Geldorf's Ad Lib Vocal in Toilet; The Trial (C/L: Waters, Roger; Ezrin, Bob); Outside the Wall

## 4604 ✦ THE PINK PANTHER
### United Artists, 1963

**Musical Score** Mancini, Henry

**Director(s)** Edwards, Blake
**Screenwriter(s)** Edwards, Blake; Richlin, Maurice

**Cast** Sellers, Peter; Niven, Robert; Wagner, Robert; Capucine; Cardinale, Claudia

**Song(s)** It Had Better Be Tonight [1] (C: Mancini, Henry; L: Mercer, Johnny)

**Notes** [1] Foreign language lyrics by F. Migliacci.

## 4605 ✦ THE PINK PANTHER STRIKES AGAIN
### United Artists, 1976

**Musical Score** Mancini, Henry
**Composer(s)** Mancini, Henry
**Lyricist(s)** Black, Don

**Producer(s)** Edwards, Blake
**Director(s)** Edwards, Blake
**Screenwriter(s)** Edwards, Blake; Waldman, Frank

**Cast** Sellers, Peter; Lom, Herbert; Blakely, Colin; Down, Lesley-Anne; Rossiter, Leonard

**Song(s)** Until You Love Me; Come to Me

## 4606 ✦ PINK TIGHTS
### Twentieth Century–Fox

**Composer(s)** Styne, Jule

**Song(s)** Pink Tights

**Notes** No other information available.

## 4607 ✦ PINKY
### Twentieth Century–Fox, 1949

**Musical Score** Newman, Alfred

**Producer(s)** Zanuck, Darryl F.
**Director(s)** Kazan, Elia
**Screenwriter(s)** Dunne, Philip; Nichols, Dudley
**Source(s)** *Quality* (novel) Sumner, Cid Ricketts

**Cast** Crain, Jeanne; Barrymore, Ethel; Waters, Ethel; Lundigan, William; Ruysdael, Basil; Washington, Kenny; McKinney, Nina Mae; O'Neal, Frederick; Barnett, Griff; Varden, Evelyn; Hunnicutt, Arthur

**Song(s)** Blue (with You or Without You) [1] (C: Newman, Alfred; L: Ruby, Harry)

**Notes** [1] Not on cue sheet. Lyrics were written for exploitation only.

## 4608 ✦ PINOCCHIO
### Disney, 1940

**Musical Score** Smith, Paul J.
**Composer(s)** Harline, Leigh
**Lyricist(s)** Washington, Ned

**Director(s)** Sharpsteen, Ben; Luske, Hamilton
**Screenwriter(s)** Sears, Ted; Smith, Webb; Sabo, Joseph; Englander, Otto; Cottrell, William; Penner, Erdman; Battaglia, Aurelius
**Source(s)** "Pinocchio" (story) Collodi
**Voices** Jones, Dickie; Rub, Christian; Edwards, Cliff; Venable, Evelyn; Catlett, Walter; Judels, Charles; Darro, Frankie

**Directing Animator(s)** Moore, Fred; Kahl, Milton; Kimball, Ward; Larson, Eric; Thomas, Franklin; Tytla, Vladimir; Babbitt, Arthur; Reitherman, Woolie
**Sequence Director(s)** Roberts, Bill; Kinney, Jack; Ferguson, Norman; Jackson, Wilfred; Hee, T.

**Song(s)** When You Wish Upon a Star; Little Wooden Head [4]; Give a Little Whistle; Turn on the Old Music Box (Inst.); Hi-Diddle-Dee-Dee (An Actor's Life for Me); I've Got No Strings; Three Cheers for Anything [1]; Monstro the Whale [2]; Jiminy Cricket Is the Name [2]; Honest John [2]; Figaro and Cleo [2]; I'm a Happy-Go-Lucky Fellow [3]

**Notes** Animated feature. [1] Not used. [2] Written for exploitation only. [3] Not used. This number was prerecorded by Cliff Edwards and finally turned up in BONGO, part of FUN AND FANCY FREE. [4] Used instrumentally only.

## 4609 ✦ PINOCCHIO AND THE EMPEROR OF THE NIGHT
### New World, 1987

**Musical Score** Marinelli, Anthony; Banks, Brian

**Producer(s)** Scheimer, Lou
**Director(s)** Sutherland, Hal
**Screenwriter(s)** London, Robby; O'Brien, Barry; O'Flaherty, Dennis
**Voices** Grimes, Scott; Asner, Edward; Bosley, Tom; Beeson, Lana; Gary, Linda; Harris, Jonathan; Jones, James Earl; Jones, Rickie Lee; Knotts, Don; Welker, Frank; Windom, William

**Song(s)** Love Is the Light Inside Your Heart (C: Mann, Barry; L: Jennings, Will); You're a Star (C/L: Jennings, Will); Do What Makes You Happy (C: Tyrell, Steve; L: Jennings, Will)

**Notes** No cue sheet available. Animated cartoon.

## 4610 ✦ PIN-UP GIRL
### Twentieth Century–Fox, 1944

**Composer(s)** Monaco, James V.
**Lyricist(s)** Gordon, Mack
**Choreographer(s)** Pan, Hermes [3]; Sullivan, Alice [3]; Fanchon; Foster, Gay [2]

**Producer(s)** LeBaron, William
**Director(s)** Humberstone, H. Bruce
**Screenwriter(s)** Ellis, Robert; Logan, Helen; Baldwin, Earl

**Cast** Grable, Betty; Harvey, John; Raye, Martha; Brown, Joe E.; Pallette, Eugene; Skating Vanities; Kent, Dorothea; The Condos Brothers; Charlie Spivak and His Orchestra; Willcock, Dave

**Song(s)** You're My Little Pin-Up Girl; Time Alone Will Tell; Red Robins, Bob Whites and Bluebirds; Don't Carry Tales Out of School; Yankee Doodle Hayride; Once Too Often; The Story of the Very Merry Widow; This Is It [1]

**Notes** [1] Not used. [2] Choreographed military number. [3] Choreographed roller skating. He is also Betty Grable's dancing partner in "Once Too Often."

## 4611 ✦ THE PIRATE
### Metro–Goldwyn–Mayer, 1948

**Composer(s)** Porter, Cole
**Lyricist(s)** Porter, Cole
**Choreographer(s)** Alton, Robert; Kelly, Gene

**Producer(s)** Freed, Arthur
**Director(s)** Minnelli, Vincente
**Screenwriter(s)** Hackett, Albert; Goodrich, Frances
**Source(s)** *The Pirate* (play) Behrman, S.N.

**Cast** Garland, Judy; Kelly, Gene; Slezak, Walter; Cooper, Gladys; Owen, Reginald; The Nicholas Brothers

**Song(s)** Mack the Black; Nina; Sweet Ices, Papayas, Berry Man (C/L: Edens, Roger); You Can Do No Wrong; Be a Clown; Love of My Life; Voodoo [1]; Manuela [2]

**Notes** [1] Deleted from final print. [2] Not used.

## 4612 ✦ PIRATE MOVIE
### Twentieth Century–Fox, 1982

**Producer(s)** Joseph, David
**Director(s)** Annakin, Ken
**Screenwriter(s)** Farrant, Trevor
**Source(s)** *Pirates of Penzance* (operetta) Gilbert, W.S.; Sullivan, Arthur

**Cast** McNichol, Kristy; Atkins, Christopher; Hamilton, Ted; Kerr, Bill; McDonald, Garry; Kirkpatrick, Maggie

**Song(s)** Victory Song (C/L: Britten, Terry); Rocky Mountain (C/L: Unknown); First Love (C/L: Hain, Kit); Pumping and Blowing (C/L: Britten, Terry;

Robertson, B.A.); How Can I Live Without Her (C/L: Britten, Terry; Shifrin, Sue); Hold On (C/L: Britten, Terry; Shifrin, Sue); We Are the Pirates (C/L: Hain, Kit); Happy Ending (C/L: Britten, Terry; Robertson, B.A.)

**Notes** There are also six Gilbert and Sullivan songs retained.

## 4613 ✦ THE PIRATES
Metro–Goldwyn–Mayer, 1930

**Composer(s)** Messenheimer, Sam
**Lyricist(s)** Messenheimer, Sam

**Director(s)** Brooks, Marty

**Cast** Rubin, Benny; The Connor Sisters; Randall, Jack

**Song(s)** Pirate Song (L: Johnson, Howard); I Am a Pirate Bold (L: Murray, John T.); Hitting the Deck (L: Johnson, Howard); Pirates of Love (C: Edwards, Gus; L: Bryan, Vincent); Wooden Leg Parade

**Notes** Short subject.

## 4614 ✦ PIRATES OF MONTEREY
Universal, 1947

**Musical Score** Rosen, Milton

**Producer(s)** Malvern, Paul
**Director(s)** Werker, Alfred
**Screenwriter(s)** Hellman, Sam; Wilder, Margaret Buell

**Cast** Cameron, Rod; Montez, Maria; Rasumny, Mikhail; Roland, Gilbert; Sondergaard, Gale

**Song(s)** Song of the Ladies Man (C/L: Brooks, Jack)

## 4615 ✦ THE PIRATES OF PENZANCE
Universal, 1983

**Musical Score** Elliott, William

**Producer(s)** Papp, Joseph
**Director(s)** Leach, Wilford
**Screenwriter(s)** Leach, Wilford
**Source(s)** *The Pirates of Penzance* (operetta) Gilbert, W.S.; Sullivan, Arthur

**Cast** Kline, Kevin; Lansbury, Angela; Ronstadt, Linda; Rose, George; Smith, Rex; Azito, Tony; Hatton, David [1]; Arundell, Anthony; Gold, Louise [2]; Codling, Teresa [3]

**Notes** No cue sheet available. No original songs. [1] Dubbed by Stephen Hanan. [2] Dubbed by Alexandra Kerey. [3] Dubbed by Marcia Shaw.

## 4616 ✦ PIRATES OF THE PRAIRIE
RKO, 1942

**Composer(s)** Rose, Fred; Whitley, Ray
**Lyricist(s)** Rose, Fred; Whitley, Ray

**Producer(s)** Gilroy, Bert
**Director(s)** Bretherton, Howard
**Screenwriter(s)** Schroeder, Doris; Cheney, J. Benton

**Cast** Holt, Tim; Edwards, Cliff; O'Day, Nell; Elliott, John; Barcroft, Roy

**Song(s)** Grandpop; Where the Mountains Meet the Sunset

**Notes** No cue sheet available.

## 4617 ✦ PISTOL PACKIN' MAMA
Republic, 1943

**Composer(s)** Styne, Jule
**Lyricist(s)** Cahn, Sammy

**Producer(s)** White, Eddy
**Director(s)** Woodruff, Frank
**Screenwriter(s)** Dein, Edward; Schiller, Fred

**Cast** Terry, Ruth; Livingston, Robert; Vernon, Wally; LaRue, Jack; Alyn, Kirk; Parker, Edwin

**Song(s)** Pistol Packin' Mama [3] (C/L: Dexter, Al); Love Is a Corny Thing [2]; I've Heard That Song Before [1]; You Could Hear a Pin Drop [4] (C: Newman, Charles; L: Pollack, Lew); I'm an Errand Boy for Rhythm, Send Me (C: Miller, Johnny; L: Cole, Nadine)

**Notes** [1] Also in SHANTYTOWN and YOUTH ON PARADE. [2] Also in THUMBS UP. [3] Also in BEAUTIFUL BUT BROKE (Columbia). [4] Also in TAHITI HONEY.

## 4618 ✦ P.J.
Universal, 1967

**Musical Score** Hefti, Neal

**Producer(s)** Montagne, Edward J.
**Director(s)** Guillermin, John
**Screenwriter(s)** Reisman Jr., Philip

**Cast** Peppard, George; Burr, Raymond; Hunnicutt, Gayle; Peters, Brock; Hyde-White, Wilfrid; Saint James, Susan; Darden, Severn

**Song(s)** Welcome to St. Crispin (C: Faith, Percy; L: Reisman Jr., Philip); When Will It End [1] (C: Hefti, Neal; Cahn, Sammy)

**Notes** [1] Sheet music only.

## 4619 ✦ A PLACE FOR LOVERS
Metro–Goldwyn–Mayer, 1969

**Musical Score** de Sica, Manuel

**Producer(s)** Ponti, Carlo
**Director(s)** De Sica, Vittorio
**Screenwriter(s)** Halevy, Julian; Baldwin, Peter; De Concini, Ennio; Guerra, Tonino; Zavattini, Cesare

**Cast** Mastroianni, Marcello; Dunaway, Faye; Mortimer, Caroline; Engh, Karin

**Song(s)**    A Place for Lovers (C: de Sica, Manuel; L: Gimbel, Norman)

### 4620    ◆    A PLACE IN THE SUN
Paramount, 1951

**Producer(s)**    Stevens, George
**Director(s)**    Stevens, George
**Screenwriter(s)**    Wilson, Michael; Brown, Harry
**Source(s)**    *An American Tragedy* (novel) Dreiser, Theodore

**Cast**    Clift, Montgomery; Taylor, Elizabeth; Winters, Shelley; Revere, Anne; Brasselle, Keefe; Clark, Fred

**Song(s)**    A Place in the Sun [1] (C: Waxman, Franz; L: Livingston, Jay; Evans, Ray)

**Notes**    "The Girls School Alma Mater" by Franz Waxman and Frank Loesser is also used. [1] Not used in film. Later a new lyric was added titled "Tonight, My Love."

### 4621    ◆    PLANE NUTS
Metro–Goldwyn–Mayer

**Song(s)**    Noontime Is Luncheon (C: Healy, Ted; L: Unknown); We'll Dance Until the Dawn [2] (C: McHugh, Jimmy; L: Fields, Dorothy); I'll Make a Happy Landing [1] (C: McHugh, Jimmy; L: Fields, Dorothy)

**Notes**    Short subject. There is also a vocal of "Dinah" by Harry Akst. [1] Also in FLYING HIGH. [2] Also in RED-HEADED WOMAN and FLYING HIGH.

### 4622    ◆    PLANES, TRAINS AND AUTOMOBILES
Paramount, 1987

**Musical Score**    Newborn, Ira

**Producer(s)**    Hughes, John
**Director(s)**    Hughes, John
**Screenwriter(s)**    Hughes, John

**Cast**    Martin, Steve; Candy, John; Robins, Laila; McKean, Michael

**Song(s)**    I Can Take Anything (C/L: Steele, David; Cox, Andy; Hughes, John); Everytime You Go Away (C/L: Hall, Daryl)

### 4623    ◆    PLANET OF THE APES
Twentieth Century–Fox, 1968

**Musical Score**    Goldsmith, Jerry

**Producer(s)**    Jacobs, Arthur P.
**Director(s)**    Schaffner, Franklin J.
**Screenwriter(s)**    Wilson, Michael; Serling, Rod
**Source(s)**    *Planet of the Apes* (novel) Boulle, Pierre

**Cast**    Heston, Charlton; McDowall, Roddy; Hunter, Kim; Evans, Maurice; Whitmore, James; Daly, James; Gunner, Robert

**Song(s)**    Planet of the Apes [1] (C/L: Knight, Gary; Levine, Irwin)

**Notes**    [1] Written for exploitation only.

### 4624    ◆    PLATINUM HIGH SCHOOL
Metro–Goldwyn–Mayer, 1960

**Musical Score**    Alexander, Van

**Producer(s)**    Doff, Red
**Director(s)**    Haas, Charles
**Screenwriter(s)**    Smith, Robert

**Cast**    Rooney, Mickey; Moore, Terry; Duryea, Dan; Twitty, Conway; Berlinger, Warren; Mimieux, Yvette; Boyd, Jimmy; Jaeckel, Richard; Cook Jr., Elisha; Lloyd Jr., Harold

**Song(s)**    Platinum High School (C/L: Twitty, Conway)

**Notes**    Titled RICH, YOUNG AND DEADLY internationally.

### 4625    ◆    PLAYBOY OF PARIS
Paramount, 1930

**Composer(s)**    Whiting, Richard A.; Chase, Newell
**Lyricist(s)**    Robin, Leo

**Director(s)**    Berger, Ludwig
**Screenwriter(s)**    Lawrence, Vincent
**Source(s)**    *Le Petit Cafe* (play) Bernard, Tristan

**Cast**    Chevalier, Maurice; Dee, Frances; Heggie, O.P.; Erwin, Stuart; Pallette, Eugene; Christy, Dorothy; Cunningham, Cecil; Brooke, Tyler

**Song(s)**    In the Heart of Old Paree; It's a Great Life (If You Don't Weaken); My Ideal; Dites Moi [2] (C: Yvain, Maurice; L: Willemetz, Albert); Yvonne's Song; Why Am I So Sensitive to You [1]; For Honor [1]; Good Spirits [1]

**Notes**    Originally titled THE LITTLE CAFE. [1] Not used. [2] Not written for picture. Also in INNOCENTS OF PARIS.

### 4626    ◆    PLAY DIRTY
United Artists, 1969

**Musical Score**    Legrand, Michel
**Composer(s)**    Legrand, Michel
**Lyricist(s)**    Nicolas, Jean

**Producer(s)**    Saltzman, Harry
**Director(s)**    de Toth, Andre
**Screenwriter(s)**    Colin, Lotte; Bragg, Melvyn

**Cast**    Caine, Michael; Davenport, Nigel; Green, Nigel; Andrews, Harry; Ben Ayed, Aly; Archard, Bernard

**Song(s)**    Unknown [1]; Domani e Primavera (L: Testa, Alberto); Unknown [2]

**Notes**    [1] Cue sheet is barely readable. Title is "Alles Geht V. . . ." [2] Cue sheet is barely readable. Title is "Mann wir Mar.chieren."

## 4627 ✦ PLAYERS
Paramount, 1979

**Producer(s)**   Evans, Robert
**Director(s)**   Harvey, Anthony
**Screenwriter(s)**   Schulman, Arnold

**Cast**   Martin, Dean Paul; MacGraw, Ali; Schell, Maximilian

**Song(s)**   Meant to Be [1] (C: Goldsmith, Jerry; L: Heather, Carol)

**Notes**   [1] Not used.


## 4628 ✦ PLAYGIRL (1932)
Warner Brothers, 1932

**Director(s)**   Enright, Ray
**Screenwriter(s)**   Watkins, Maurine
**Source(s)**   "God's Gift to Women" (story) Brennan, Frederick Hazlitt

**Cast**   Young, Loretta; Lightner, Winnie; Foster, Norman; Kibbee, Guy; Madison, Noel; Walters, Polly; Burgess, Dorothy; Madison, Mae; Carlisle, Eileen; Whitney, Renee; Ellison, James; Pendleton, Nat

**Song(s)**   This Is My Love Song [1] (C: Burke, Joe; L: Dubin, Al)

**Notes**   [1] Performed instrumentally only.


## 4629 ✦ PLAYGIRL (1954)
Universal, 1954

**Producer(s)**   Cohen, Albert J.
**Director(s)**   Pevney, Joseph
**Screenwriter(s)**   Blees, Robert

**Cast**   Miller, Colleen; Winters, Shelley; Sullivan, Barry; Palmer, Gregg

**Song(s)**   Lie to Me (C/L: Gilbert, Ray)

**Notes**   There is also a vocal of "There'll Be Some Changes Made" by Billy Higgins, W. Benton Overstreet and Herbert Reynolds.


## 4630 ✦ THE PLAYGIRLS
Warner Brothers, 1941

**Song(s)**   You Again [1] (C: Jerome, M.K.; L: Scholl, Jack)

**Notes**   Short subject. [1] Also in NOBODY LIVES FOREVER.


## 4631 ✦ PLAYING AROUND
Warner Brothers–First National, 1930

**Composer(s)**   Stept, Sam H.
**Lyricist(s)**   Green, Bud

**Director(s)**   LeRoy, Mervyn
**Screenwriter(s)**   Comandini, Adele; Nordstrom, Frances; Pearson, Humphrey
**Source(s)**   "Sheba" (story) Delmar, Vina

**Cast**   White, Alice; Morris, Chester; Bakewell, William; Carlyle, Richard; Byron, Marion; Black, Maurice; Belmore, Lionel; Camp, Shep; Brody, Ann; Nichols, Nellie V.

**Song(s)**   That's the Lowdown on the Lowdown; You Learn About Love Every Day; You're My Captain Kidd; Playing Around

**Notes**   No cue sheet available.


## 4632 ✦ PLAYING THE GAME

See TOUCHDOWN.


## 4633 ✦ PLAY IT AGAIN, SAM
Paramount, 1972

**Musical Score**   Goldenberg, Billy
**Composer(s)**   Goldenberg, Billy
**Lyricist(s)**   Kronsberg, Graeme

**Producer(s)**   Jacobs, Arthur P.
**Director(s)**   Ross, Herbert
**Screenwriter(s)**   Allen, Woody
**Source(s)**   *Play It Again, Sam* (play) Allen, Woody

**Cast**   Allen, Woody; Keaton, Diane; Roberts, Tony; Lacy, Jerry; Anspach, Susan; Salt, Jennifer; Viva

**Song(s)**   Easy Lovin'; Theme from Play It Again Sam [1] (C/L: Goldenberg, Billy); It's the Same Sad Story All Over Again [2]

**Notes**   [1] Not used in picture. Written for exploitation. [2] Not used in film.


## 4634 ✦ PLAYMATES
RKO, 1941

**Musical Score**   Webb, Roy
**Composer(s)**   Van Heusen, James
**Lyricist(s)**   Burke, Johnny
**Choreographer(s)**   Crosby, Jack

**Producer(s)**   Butler, David
**Director(s)**   Butler, David
**Screenwriter(s)**   Kern, James V.; Phillips, Arthur

**Cast**   Kay Kyser and His Band; Babbitt, Harry; Kabibble, Ish; Mason, Sully; Barrymore, John; Velez, Lupe; Simms, Ginny; Robson, May; Kelly, Patsy; Hayes, Peter Lind

**Song(s)**   Thank Your Lucky Stars and Stripes; How Long Did I Dream; Que Chica [2]; Humpty Dumpty Heart [1]; Romeo Smith and Juliet Jones

**Notes**   [1] Later in GANGWAY FOR TOMORROW. [2] Also in ZOMBIES ON BROADWAY.

## 4635 ✦ PLEASE DON'T EAT THE DAISIES
### Metro–Goldwyn–Mayer, 1960

**Musical Score**   Rose, David

**Producer(s)**   Pasternak, Joe
**Director(s)**   Walters, Charles
**Screenwriter(s)**   Lennart, Isobel
**Source(s)**   *Please Don't Eat the Daisies* (book) Kerr, Jean

**Cast**   Day, Doris; Niven, David; Paige, Janis; Byington, Spring; Haydn, Richard; Kelly, Patsy; Weston, Jack; Herbert, Charles; Livingston, Stanley; Mark, Flip; Gellert, Baby

**Song(s)**   Please Don't Eat the Daisies (C/L: Lubin, Joe); Any Way the Wind Blows (C: Hooven, Marilyn; Hooven, Joe; L: Dunham, "By")

**Notes**   There is also a vocal of "Whatever Will Be, Will Be (Que Sera, Sera)" by Jay Livingston and Ray Evans.

## 4636 ✦ PLEASURE CRAZED
### Fox, 1929

**Producer(s)**   Klein, Philip
**Director(s)**   Klein, Charles
**Screenwriter(s)**   Kummer, Clare
**Source(s)**   *The Scent of Sweet Almonds* (play) Hoffe, Monckton

**Cast**   Churchill, Marguerite; MacKenna, Kenneth; Bell, Rex; Burgess, Dorothy

**Song(s)**   I Only Knew It Was You (C/L: Kummer, Clare)

## 4637 ✦ PLEASURE CRUISE
### Fox, 1933

**Director(s)**   Tuttle, Frank
**Screenwriter(s)**   Bolton, Guy
**Source(s)**   (play) Allen, Aumen

**Cast**   Tobin, Genevieve; Young, Roland; Forbes, Ralph; O'Connor, Una; Mundin, Herbert; Gombell, Minna

**Song(s)**   Is This a Sovenir? (C/L: Jason, Will; Burton, Val)

**Notes**   [1] Lange not credited on sheet music. [2] Sheet music only.

## 4638 ✦ THE PLEASURE OF HIS COMPANY
### Paramount, 1961

**Producer(s)**   Perlberg, William
**Director(s)**   Seaton, George
**Screenwriter(s)**   Taylor, Samuel
**Source(s)**   *The Pleasure of His Company* (play) Skinner, Cornelia Otis; Taylor, Samuel

**Cast**   Astaire, Fred; Reynolds, Debbie; Palmer, Lilli; Merrill, Gary; Hunter, Tab; Ruggles, Charles

**Song(s)**   The Pleasure of His Company [1] (C: Newman, Alfred; L: Cahn, Sammy)

**Notes**   [1] Used instrumentally only.

## 4639 ✦ THE PLEASURE SEEKERS
### Twentieth Century–Fox, 1964

**Musical Score**   Courage, Alexander
**Composer(s)**   Van Heusen, James
**Lyricist(s)**   Cahn, Sammy

**Producer(s)**   Weisbart, David
**Director(s)**   Negulesco, Jean
**Screenwriter(s)**   Sommer, Edith
**Source(s)**   *Three Coins in the Fountain* (book) Secondari, John H.

**Cast**   Ann-Margret; Franciosa, Anthony; Lynley, Carol; McKay, Gardner; Tiffin, Pamela; Tierney, Gene; Keith, Brian; Scotti, Vito; Elsom, Isobel

**Song(s)**   The Pleasure Seekers; Something to Think About; Next Time; Everything Makes Music When You're in Love [1]; Costa Del Sol [1]; The Pleasure Seekers Bossa Nova [1]

**Notes**   [1] Not used.

## 4640 ✦ THE PLOT THICKENS

See HERE COMES COOKIE.

## 4641 ✦ THE PLUNDERERS
### Republic, 1948

**Musical Score**   Butts, Dale

**Producer(s)**   Kane, Joseph
**Director(s)**   Kane, Joseph
**Screenwriter(s)**   Geraghty, Gerald; Adams, Gerald Drayson

**Cast**   Cameron, Rod; Massey, Ilona; Booth, Adrian; Tucker, Forrest; Cleveland, George; Withers, Grant; Holmes, Taylor; Fix, Paul

**Song(s)**   Walking Down Broadway (C: Lingard, William; L: Pratt, Charles E.); I'll Sing a Love Song [1] (C/L: Elliott, Jack)

**Notes**   [1] Spanish lyrics by Aaron Gonzalez. Also in SOUTH PACIFIC TRAIL.

## 4642 ✦ PLUNDER OF THE SUN
### Warner Brothers, 1953

**Musical Score**   Conde, Antonio

**Producer(s)**   Fellows, Robert
**Director(s)**   Farrow, John
**Screenwriter(s)**   Latimer, Jonathan
**Source(s)**   *Plunder of the Sun* (novel) Dodge, David

Cast Ford, Glenn; Lynn, Diana; Medina, Patricia; Sullivan, Francis L.; McClory, Sean; Noriega, Eduardo; Villareal, Julio; Dumbrille, Douglass

Song(s) Sin Ella (C/L: Marroquin, Jose)

## 4643 ✦ POCKETFUL OF MIRACLES
United Artists, 1961

Musical Score Scharf, Walter

Producer(s) Capra, Frank
Director(s) Capra, Frank
Screenwriter(s) Kanter, Hal; Tugend, Harry
Source(s) "Madam La Gimp" (story) Runyon, Damon

Cast Ford, Glenn; Davis, Bette; Ann-Margaret; Falk, Peter; O'Connell, Arthur; Lange, Hope; Brian, David; Cowan, Jerome; Mitchell, Thomas; Horton, Edward Everett; Leonard, Sheldon; MacLane, Barton; Feld, Fritz; Elam, Jack; Rubin, Benny; Pollard, Snub

Song(s) Pocketful of Miracles (C: Van Heusen, James; L: Cahn, Sammy); Polly Wolly Doodle (C: Traditional; L: Capra, Frank)

Notes A remake of LADY FOR A DAY (1933).

## 4644 ✦ POETIC GEMS
Studio Unknown, 1935

Composer(s) Herscher, Louis
Lyricist(s) Loesser, Frank

Song(s) Ev'rybody's Ship Comes In (But Mine) [1]; A Symphony in Green [2]; Take Me Home to the Mountains [3]; Indian Moon [4]; Little Miss Mischief [5]; Down the Lane to Yesterday [6]; By a Silvery Stream [7]; The Snowflakes [8]; Don't Grow Any Older (My Little Boy Blue) [9]; Here's to the Builder [10]; Get Under the Sun [11]; A Real True Pal [12]; Back Seat Drivers [13]

Notes Short subjects. All lyrics based on poems by Edgar A. Guest. [1] Based on poem "Sea Dreams." [2] Based on poem "Early in the Mornin'." [3] Based on poem "The Old Prospector." [4] Based on poems "Poetic Gems." [5] Based on poem "Worn Out." [6] Based on poem "Boyhood." [7] Based on poem "Bill and I Went Fishing." [8] Based on poems "Call of the Woods" and "Silence of the Snow." [9] Based on poem "Couldn't Live Without You." [10] Based on poem "Song of the Builder." [11] Based on poems "After the Storm" and "When We Were Kids." [12] From "Poetic Gems." [13] From poem "Ma and the Auto."

## 4645 ✦ POINT BLANK
Metro–Goldwyn–Mayer, 1967

Musical Score Mandel, Johnny

Producer(s) Bernard, Judd; Chartoff, Robert
Director(s) Boorman, John

Screenwriter(s) Jacobs, Alexander; Newhouse, Rafe; Newhouse, David
Source(s) The Hunter (novel) Stark, Richard

Cast Dickinson, Angie; Marvin, Lee; O'Connor, Carroll; Wynn, Keenan; Bochner, Lloyd; Strong, Michael; Vernon, John; Acker, Sharon

Song(s) Mighty Good Times (C/L: Gardner, Stu)

## 4646 ✦ POINTED HEELS
Paramount, 1929

Composer(s) Whiting, Richard A.
Lyricist(s) Robin, Leo

Director(s) Sutherland, Edward
Screenwriter(s) Ryerson, Florence; Weaver, John V.A.
Source(s) "Pointed Heels" (story) Brackett, Charles [4]

Cast Powell, William; Wray, Fay; Holmes, Phillips; Gallagher, Skeets [5]; Kane, Helen; Holmes, Phillips; Dore, Adrienne; Pallette, Eugene

Song(s) Aintcha? (C: Rich, Max; L: Gordon, Mack); I Have to Have You; Reach for a Sweetie [3] (L: Marion Jr., George); Wuzza Matter Baby [1] [2] (C: Rich, Max; L: Gordon, Mack; Rule, Bert); He's Perfect for Me [1] (C/L: Unknown); Pointed Heels Ballet (inst.) (C: Tiomkin, Dimitri)

Notes A letter from Irene Scott to Evelyn Winters, both of the Paramount music department: "Thank you very much for the two rotten titles ("Wuzza Matter Baby" and "Aintcha") for POINTED HEELS. If Helen Kane sings these in her inimitable childish manner, God help the people who have to listen to her, or probably most of the radio loud speakers will just burst with glee." [1] Not used. [2] Recorded. [3] Written for SWEETIE but not used. [4] Billed as Charles William Brackett. [5] Billed as Richard "Skeets" Gallagher.

## 4647 ✦ POLICE ACADEMY
Ladd Company–Warner Brothers, 1984

Musical Score Folk, Robert

Producer(s) Maslansky, Paul
Director(s) Wilson, Hugh
Screenwriter(s) Israel, Neal; Proft, Pat; Wilson, Hugh

Cast Guttenberg, Steve; Cattrall, Kim; Bailey, G.W.; Smith, Bubba; Scott, Donovan; Gaynes, George; Rubin, Andrew; Easterbrook, Leslie

Song(s) Relax (C/L: Gill; Johnson; O'Toole); True Lovin' Woman (C/L: Gronenthal, Max); She's in My Corner (C/L: Gronenthal, Max; Kastner, Andrew); Will You Love Me Tomorrow (C/L: Goffin, Gerry; King, Carole); I'm Gonna Be Somebody (C/L: Gronenthal, Max; Kastner, Andrew)

**Notes** It is not known if any of these were written for the film.

## 4648 ◆ POLICE ACADEMY 2 THEIR FIRST ASSIGNMENT
Ladd Company–Warner Brothers, 1985

**Musical Score** Folk, Robert

**Producer(s)** Maslansky, Paul
**Director(s)** Paris, Jerry
**Screenwriter(s)** Blaustein, Barry; Sheffield, David

**Cast** Guttenberg, Steve; Smith, Bubba; Graf, David; Winslow, Michael; Mahler, Bruce; Ramsey, Marion; Camp, Colleen; Hesseman, Howard; Gaynes, George

**Song(s)** Dirty Work (C/L: Goetzman, Gary; Piccirillo, Mike); Johnny Get the Handcuffs (C/L: Martin, John Moon); Temporary Insanity (C/L: White, Linsey; Rochelle, Michael; Berry, Steve)

**Notes** It is not known if any of these were written for the picture.

## 4649 ◆ POLICE ACADEMY 3 BACK IN TRAINING
Warner Brothers, 1986

**Musical Score** Folk, Robert

**Producer(s)** Maslansky, Paul
**Director(s)** Paris, Jerry
**Screenwriter(s)** Quintano, Gene

**Cast** Guttenberg, Steve; Smith, Bubba; Draf, David; Winslow, Michael; Ramsey, Marion; Easterbrook, Leslie; Kazurinsky, Tim; Goldthwait, Bobcat; Gaynes, George

**Song(s)** Team Thing (C/L: Clark, Tena; Warren, Tony); This Is What Love's About (C/L: Clark, Tena; Pryor, Lorenzo)

## 4650 ◆ POLICE ACADEMY IV CITIZENS ON PATROL
Warner Brothers, 1987

**Musical Score** Folk, Robert

**Producer(s)** Maslansky, Paul
**Director(s)** Drake, Jim
**Screenwriter(s)** Quintano, Gene

**Cast** Guttenberg, Steve; Smith, Bubba; Winslow, Michael; Graf, David; Kazurinsky, Tim; Stone, Sharon; Easterbrook, Leslie; Ramsey, Marion; Kinsey, Lance; Bailey, G.W.

**Song(s)** Citizens on Patrol [1] (C/L: Stuart, Mike; Funaro, Arthur); Shoot for the Top [2] (C/L: Howell, Kurt; Maslin, Harry); Mope Mope Mope [1] (C/L: Winslow, Michael); Winning Streak (C/L: Glenn, Garry); Rescue Me (C/L: Pardee, Rudy; Perison, Michael; Brooks, Victor); It's Time to Move (C/L: Boston, Rick; Lowen, Eric; Navarro, Dan); Dancin' Up a

Storm (C/L: Sherman, Sandy; Liebhart, Janice); Zed's Tune [1] (C/L: Folk, Robert)

**Notes** It is not known how many of these were written for the picture. [1] Vocal visual use. [2] Also in DOIN' TIME.

## 4651 ◆ POLICE ACADEMY V ASSIGNMENT MIAMI BEACH
Warner Brothers, 1988

**Musical Score** Folk, Robert

**Producer(s)** Maslansky, Paul
**Director(s)** Myerson, Alan
**Screenwriter(s)** Curwick, Stephen J.

**Cast** Smith, Bubba; Graf, David; Winslow, Michael; Easterbrook, Leslie; Ramsey, Marion; Jones, Janet; Kinsey, Lance; McCoy, Matt; Bailey, G.W.; Gaynes, George; Auberjonois, Rene

**Song(s)** How Low Can You Go (C/L: Coffing, Barry)

## 4652 ◆ POLLYANNA
Disney, 1960

**Musical Score** Smith, Paul J.
**Composer(s)** Smith, Paul J.

**Producer(s)** Golitzin, George
**Director(s)** Swift, David
**Screenwriter(s)** Swift, David

**Cast** Wyman, Jane; Egan, Richard; Malden, Karl; Olson, Nancy; Menjou, Adolphe; Crisp, Donald; Moorehead, Agnes; Corcoran, Kevin; Mills, Hayley; Drury, James; Shaw, Reta; Seymour, Anne; Platt, Edward

**Song(s)** Pollyanna's Song [1] [3] (L: Swift, David; George, Gil); Jimmy Bean [1] (L: George, Gil); Pollyanna (The Glad Game) [2] [3] (L: George, Gil)

**Notes** [1] Used instrumentally only. [2] Written for exploitation only. [3] Same music.

## 4653 ◆ POLTERGEIST III
Metro–Goldwyn–Mayer, 1988

**Musical Score** Renzutti, Joe

**Producer(s)** Bernardi, Barry
**Director(s)** Sherman, Gary
**Screenwriter(s)** Sherman, Gary; Taggert, Brian

**Cast** Skerritt, Tom; O'Rourke, Heather; Allen, Nancy; Rubinstein, Zelda

**Song(s)** Jungle Music (C/L: Stokes, Simon; Cioffi, Billy); Night Rider (C/L: Forte, Michael; Weeden, Bruce)

**Notes** It is not known if the songs were written for this film.

## 4654 ✦ POLYESTER
### New Line, 1981

**Musical Score**   Stein, Chris; Kamen, Michael
**Composer(s)**   Stein, Chris
**Lyricist(s)**   Harry, Deborah

**Producer(s)**   Waters, John
**Director(s)**   Waters, John
**Screenwriter(s)**   Waters, John

**Cast**   Divine; Hunter, Tab; Massey, Edith; Mink Stole; Samson, David

**Song(s)**   Polyester; Daddy Daddy; Love Theme

**Notes**   No cue sheet available.

## 4655 ✦ PONY EXPRESS RIDER
### Warner Brothers, 1936

**Musical Score**   Jackson, Howard
**Composer(s)**   Jerome, M.K.
**Lyricist(s)**   Scholl, Jack

**Song(s)**   Ridin' the Mail [1]; Love Begins at Evening [1]

**Notes**   No other information available. [1] Used in THE CALIFORNIA MAIL.

## 4656 ✦ POOR LITTLE ME
### Metro–Goldwyn–Mayer, 1935

**Musical Score**   Bradley, Scott

**Song(s)**   I've Got a Cold In My Nose (C: Bradley, Scott; L: Hanna, Joseph)

**Notes**   Animated cartoon.

## 4657 ✦ POOR LITTLE RICH GIRL
### Twentieth Century–Fox, 1936

**Composer(s)**   Revel, Harry
**Lyricist(s)**   Gordon, Mack
**Choreographer(s)**   Haskell, Jack; Cooper, Ralph

**Producer(s)**   Zanuck, Darryl F.
**Director(s)**   Cummings, Irving
**Screenwriter(s)**   Hellman, Sam; Lehman, Gladys; Tugend, Harry
**Source(s)**   "Poor Little Rich Girl" (story) Gates, Eleanor

**Cast**   Temple, Shirley; Faye, Alice; Stuart, Gloria; Haley, Jack; Whalen, Michael; Haden, Sara; Darwell, Jane; Gillingwater, Claude; Stanton, Paul; Armetta, Henry; Martin, Tony

**Song(s)**   Oh My Goodness; Lookie Lookie Lookie Here Comes Cookie; Buy a Bar of Barry's; When I'm with You; But Definitely; Peck's Theme Song; You Gotta Eat Your Spinach, Baby [1]; Military Man

**Notes**   There are also brief renditions of "The Kitten Song" by Frank Tresselt; the traditional song "Ride a Cock Horse" and "Dinah" by Harry Akst, Sam Lewis

and Joe Young; "Where the Blue of the Night" by Roy Turk, Bing Crosby and Fred E. Ahlert; "On the Good Ship Lollypop" by Richard Whiting and Sidney Clare. [1] Not used for SITTING PRETTY (Paramount).

## 4658 ✦ POOR WHITE TRASH

See BAYOU.

## 4659 ✦ POPEYE
### Paramount/Disney, 1980

**Composer(s)**   Nilsson, Harry
**Lyricist(s)**   Nilsson, Harry
**Choreographer(s)**   Kinney, Sharon; Burgess, Hovey; Wills, Lou

**Producer(s)**   Evans, Robert
**Director(s)**   Altman, Robert
**Screenwriter(s)**   Feiffer, Jules

**Cast**   Williams, Robin; Duvall, Shelley; Walston, Ray; Dooley, Paul; Smith, Paul L.; Libertini, Richard; Moffat, Donald; Dixon, MacIntyre; Maxwell, Roberta; Scott, Donovan; Nicholls, Allan; Irwin, Bill; Hurt, Wesley Ivan; Hunt, Linda; Parks, Van Dyke

**Song(s)**   Sweethaven; Blow Me Down; Everything Is Food; He's Large; I'm Mean; Sailin'; I Yam What I Yam; He Needs Me; Swee'pea's Lullaby; It's Not Easy Being Me; Kids

## 4660 ✦ POPEYE CARTOONS
### Paramount

**Composer(s)**   Lawnhurst, Vee
**Lyricist(s)**   Seymour, Tot

**Song(s)**   I'm Popeye the Sailor Man (C/L: Lerner, Sam); Sing a Song of Popeye; Moving Man (C: Timberg, Sammy; L: Rothberg, Bob); I'm One of the Jones Boys; Pooey to You from Me; I Wanna Be a Life Guard (C: Timberg, Sammy; L: Rothberg, Bob); I'm King of the Mardi Gras (C: Timberg, Sammy; L: Rothberg, Bob); I'll Be Seein' Ya in the Movies; Brotherly Love (C: Timberg, Sammy; L: Rothberg, Bob); I Want a Clean Shaven Man (C: Timberg, Sammy; L: Fleischer, Dave); Hamburger Mine (C: Timberg, Sammy; L: Rothberg, Bob); The Looney Goon; Won't You Come and Climb the Mountain with Me (C: Timberg, Sammy; L: Rothberg, Bob); Popeye on Parade; Olive Oyl's Family Reunion; I Spy a Spy; I Wants What I Wants When I Wants It; Let's Build a Bridge Today (C: Timberg, Sammy; L: Rothberg, Bob); Strike Me Pink Do I See Red; I'm Sinbad the Sailor (C: Timberg, Sammy; L: Rothberg, Bob); Ain'tcha Got No Ettyket?; Popeye's Eye Popped Out of His Head; The Land of Popeye; Jump Jeep I Give You Orchids; I'm Popeye's Poop Deck Pappy (C: Timberg, Sammy; L: Neiburg, Al J.)

**Notes** These songs appear in a variety of Popeye cartoons produced by the Fleischer Studios.

## 4661 ✦ POPI
United Artists, 1969

**Musical Score** Frontiere, Dominic

**Producer(s)** Leonard, Herbert B.
**Director(s)** Hiller, Arthur
**Screenwriter(s)** Pine, Lester; Pine, Tina

**Cast** Arkin, Alan; Moreno, Rita; Alejandro, Miguel; Figueroa, Ruben

**Song(s)** Cuando Estoy Contigo [1] (C: Holmes, Leroy; L: Rodriquez, Tito); Popi [2] (C: Frontiere, Dominic; L: Gimbel, Norman)

**Notes** [1] Used instrumentally only. [2] Sheet music only.

## 4662 ✦ POPPY
Paramount, 1936

**Producer(s)** LeBaron, William
**Director(s)** Sutherland, Edward
**Screenwriter(s)** Van Upp, Virginia; Young, Waldemar
**Source(s)** *Poppy* (musical) Jones, Stephen; Samuels, Arthur; Donnelly, Dorothy

**Cast** Fields, W.C.; Hudson, Rochelle; Cromwell, Richard; Coucet, Catherine; Overman, Lynne; Eburne, Maude

**Song(s)** Poppy (C: Hollander, Frederick; L: Coslow, Sam); A Rendezvous with a Dream [1] (C: Rainger, Ralph; L: Robin, Leo)

**Notes** [1] Not used in STICK TO YOUR GUNS and also used in ALONG CAME LOVE.

## 4663 ✦ PORGY AND BESS
Columbia, 1959

**Composer(s)** Gershwin, George
**Lyricist(s)** Gershwin, Ira; Heyward, DuBose
**Choreographer(s)** Pan, Hermes

**Producer(s)** Goldwyn, Samuel
**Director(s)** Preminger, Otto
**Screenwriter(s)** Nash, N. Richard
**Source(s)** *Porgy and Bess* (musical) Gershwin, George; Gershwin, Ira; Heyward, DuBose

**Cast** Poitier, Sidney [1]; Dandridge, Dorothy [2]; Davis Jr., Sammy; Bailey, Pearl; Peters, Brock; Scott, Leslie; Carroll, Diahann [3]; Attaway, Ruth; Muse, Clarence; Wilson, Everdinne; Jackson, Earl; Thigpen, Helen; Atkins, Claude

**Song(s)** Summertime (L: Heyward, DuBose); I Been Sweatin' All Day (L: Unknown); A Woman Is a Sometime Thing (L: Heyward, DuBose); The Honeyman (L: Unknown); They Pass By Singin' (L: Heyward, DuBose); Yo' Mammy's Gone (L: Unknown); Crown Cockeyed Drunk (L: Unknown); Oh Little Stars (L: Unknown); (He's A-)Gone, Gone, Gone (L: Heyward, DuBose); Fill Up de Saucer (L: Unknown); My Man's Gone Now (L: Heyward, DuBose); Train Is at the Station (L: Unknown); I Got Plenty o' Nuttin'; Lawyer Frazier (L: Unknown); Bess, You Is My Woman Now; Oh, I Can't Sit Down (L: Gershwin, Ira); I Ain't Got No Shame; It Ain't Necessarily So (L: Gershwin, Ira); It's Like Dis, Crown (L: Unknown); What You Want Wid Bess? (L: Heyward, DuBose); It Takes a Long Pull (L: Heyward, DuBose); The P'liceman (L: Unknown); Serena's Prayer (L: Unknown); Strawberries (L: Heyward, DuBose); Devil Crabs (L: Heyward, DuBose); I Loves You, Porgy; Oh De Lawd Shake De Heavens (L: Heyward, DuBose); Oh, Dere's Somebody Knockin' at De Do' (L: Unknown); If Gawd Want to Kill Me (L: Unknown); A Redheaded Woman (L: Gershwin, Ira); Clara, Clara (L: Heyward, DuBose); There's a Boat That's Leavin' (L: Gershwin, Ira); Good Mornin' Sistuh (L: Heyward, DuBose); Oh, Bess, Where's My Bess (L: Gershwin, Ira); Oh Lawd, I'm on My Way (L: Heyward, DuBose)

**Notes** [1] Dubbed by Robert McFerrin. [2] Dubbed by Adele Addison. [3] Dubbed by Loulie Jean Price.

## 4664 ✦ PORT AFRIQUE
Columbia, 1956

**Producer(s)** Rose, David E.
**Director(s)** Mate, Rudolph
**Screenwriter(s)** Partos, Frank; Cresswell, John

**Cast** Angeli, Pier; Carey, Philip; Price, Dennis; Newley, Anthony; Lee, Christopher

**Song(s)** Melody from Heaven (C: Arique, Luis; L: Fishman, Jack)

**Notes** No cue sheet available.

## 4665 ✦ PORTRAITS IN DIAMONDS

See ADVENTURES IN DIAMONDS.

## 4666 ✦ THE POSEIDON ADVENTURE
Twentieth Century–Fox, 1972

**Musical Score** Williams, John

**Producer(s)** Allen, Irwin
**Director(s)** Neame, Ronald
**Screenwriter(s)** Silliphant, Stirling; Mayes, Wendell
**Source(s)** (novel) Gallico, Paul

**Cast** Hackman, Gene; Borgnine, Ernest; Buttons, Red; Lynley, Carol; McDowall, Roddy; Stevens, Stella; Winters, Shelley; Albertson, Jack; Martin, Pamela Sue; O'Connell, Arthur

**Song(s)** The Morning After (C: Kasha, Al; L: Hirschhorn, Joel)

## 4667 ✦ POSSE
### Paramount, 1975

**Musical Score** Jarre, Maurice

**Producer(s)** Douglas, Kirk
**Director(s)** Douglas, Kirk
**Screenwriter(s)** Knopf, Christopher; Roberts, William

**Cast** Douglas, Kirk; Dern, Bruce; Hopkins, Bo; Stacy, James; Arau, Alfonso

**Song(s)** Once to Each Man [1] (C: Jarre, Maurice; L: Webster, Paul Francis)

**Notes** [1] Lyrics written for exploitation only.

## 4668 ✦ POSSESSED
### Metro–Goldwyn–Mayer, 1931

**Director(s)** Brown, Clarence
**Screenwriter(s)** Coffee, Lenore
**Source(s)** *The Mirage* (play) Selwyn, Edgar

**Cast** Crawford, Joan; Gable, Clark; Ford, Wallace; Gallagher, Skeets; Miljan, John

**Song(s)** How Long Will It Last (C: Meyer, Joseph; L: Leif, Max)

## 4669 ✦ POSTAL INSPECTOR
### Universal, 1936

**Composer(s)** Actman, Irving
**Lyricist(s)** Loesser, Frank

**Producer(s)** Presnell, Robert
**Director(s)** Friedlander, Louis
**Screenwriter(s)** McCoy, Horace

**Cast** Lugosi, Bela; Ellis, Patricia; Cortez, Ricardo; Loring, Michael

**Song(s)** Let's Have Bluebirds; Hot Towel; Don't Let Me Love You [1]

**Notes** [1] Used instrumentally only.

## 4670 ✦ POSTMAN'S KNOCK
### Metro–Goldwyn–Mayer, 1965

**Musical Score** Goodwin, Ron

**Producer(s)** Kinnoch, Ronald
**Director(s)** Lynn, Robert
**Screenwriter(s)** Briley, John; Story, Jack Trevor; Milligan, Spike; Barclay, George

**Cast** Lawson, Wilfred; Milligan, Spike; Shelley, Barbara; Woods, John

**Song(s)** Postman's Knock (C: Goodwin, Ron; L: Kretzmer, Herbert)

**Notes** Not released in the U.S.

## 4671 ✦ POT O' GOLD
### United Artists, 1941

**Composer(s)** Forbes, Louis
**Lyricist(s)** Russell, Henry
**Choreographer(s)** Ceballos, Larry

**Producer(s)** Roosevelt, James
**Director(s)** Marshall, George
**Screenwriter(s)** De Leon, Walter

**Cast** Horace Heidt and His Musical Knights; Winninger, Charles; Stewart, James; Goddard, Paulette; Gordon, Mary; Melton, Frank; Prouty, Jed; Hogan, Dick; Burke, James

**Song(s)** Do You Believe in Fairy Tales? (C: Lawnhurst, Vee; L: David, Mack); When Johnny Toots His Horn (C/L: Heath, Hy; Rose, Fred); A Knife, A Fork and a Spoon (C/L: Franklin, Dave); Broadway Caballero (C/L: Russell, Henry); Pete the Piper (C/L: Russell, Henry); Hi, Cy, What's Cookin'?; Slap Happy Band

**Notes** No cue sheet available. Released as THE GOLDEN HORN overseas.

## 4672 ✦ POUND PUPPIES AND THE LEGEND OF BIG PAW
### Tri-Star, 1988

**Musical Score** Kosinski, Richard; Winans, Sam; Reichenbach, Bill; Hall, Ashley; Mann, Bob
**Composer(s)** Hall, Ashley; Tyrell, Steve
**Lyricist(s)** Tyrell, Stephanie

**Producer(s)** Kushner, Donald; Locke, Peter
**Director(s)** Decelles, Pierre
**Screenwriter(s)** Carlson, Jim; McDonnell, Terrence
**Voices** Berg, Greg; Cartwright, Nancy; Cavadini, Cathy; Davis, Ryan; Deidio, Joe; Hall, Ashley; Kushner, Jasper; Rose, George

**Song(s)** Now That You're Here (C: Hall, Ashley); The King of Everything; All in Your Mind; Puppy Power's Back

**Notes** No cue sheet available. Animated cartoon.

## 4673 ✦ THE POWERS GIRL
### United Artists, 1943

**Composer(s)** Styne, Jule
**Lyricist(s)** Gannon, Kim

**Producer(s)** Rogers, Charles R.
**Director(s)** McLeod, Norman Z.
**Screenwriter(s)** Moran, E. Edwin; Segall, Harry

**Cast**  Shirley, Anne; Landis, Carole; Murphy, George; Mowbray, Alan; Treen, Mary; Ames, Jean; Storm, Rafael; Day, Dennis; Benny Goodman and His Orchestra

**Song(s)**  Three Dreams; Out of This World; The Lady Who Didn't Believe in Love; Partners [1]; We're Looking for the Big Bad Wolf [1]; Roll 'Em (C/L: Styne, Jule; Williams, Mary Lou)

**Notes**  Released overseas as HELLO BEAUTIFUL. [1] Used instrumentally only.

### 4674 ✦ PRACTICALLY YOURS
Paramount, 1944

**Producer(s)**  Leisen, Mitchell
**Director(s)**  Leisen, Mitchell
**Screenwriter(s)**  Krasna, Norman

**Cast**  Colbert, Claudette; MacMurray, Fred; Kellaway, Cecil; Benchley, Robert; Lamb, Gil; Frazee, Jane; De Camp, Rosemary; Powers, Tom

**Song(s)**  I Knew It Would Be This Way (C/L: Coslow, Sam)

### 4675 ✦ PRAIRIE JUSTICE
Universal, 1938

**Composer(s)**  Allan, Fleming
**Lyricist(s)**  Allan, Fleming

**Producer(s)**  Carr, Trem
**Director(s)**  Waggner, George
**Screenwriter(s)**  West, Joseph

**Cast**  Baker, Bob; Fay, Dorothy; Taliaferro, Hal; Rockwell, Jack; Taylor, Forrest; Kirk, Jack; Strange, Glenn

**Song(s)**  Dry and Dusty; Hi' Falutin' Cowboy; Starlight on the Prairie; Rocky Mountain Trail

### 4676 ✦ PRAIRIE LAW
RKO, 1940

**Musical Score**  Dreyer, Dave; Sawtell, Paul

**Producer(s)**  Gilroy, Bert
**Director(s)**  Howard, David
**Screenwriter(s)**  Schroeder, Doris; Jones, Arthur V.

**Cast**  O'Brien, George; Vale, Virginia; Hogan, Dick; MacDonald, J. Farrell; Whitaker, Slim; Kendall, Cyrus W.

**Song(s)**  Rocky Canyon Road (C/L: Whitley, Ray; Rose, Fred)

### 4677 ✦ PRAIRIE MOON
Republic, 1938

**Composer(s)**  Kent, Walter
**Lyricist(s)**  Cherkose, Eddie

**Producer(s)**  Grey, Harry
**Director(s)**  Staub, Ralph
**Screenwriter(s)**  Roberts, Stanley; Burbridge, Betty

**Cast**  Autry, Gene; Burnette, Smiley; Deane, Shirley; Ryan, Tommy; Tetley, Walter; Andrews, Stanley

**Song(s)**  The Girl in the Middle of My Heart; Welcome Strangers; The Story of Trigger Joe; In the Jailhouse Now (C/L: Rodgers, Jimmie); The West, a Nest and You (C/L: Yoell, Larry; Hill, Billy); Rhythm of the Hoofbeats [1] (C/L: Marvin, Johnny; Rose, Fred)

**Notes**  No cue sheet available. [1] Gene Autry also credited on sheet music.

### 4678 ✦ PRAIRIE OUTLAWS
Eagle Lion, 1948

**Producer(s)**  Tansey, Robert Emmett
**Director(s)**  Tansey, Robert Emmett
**Screenwriter(s)**  Kavanaugh, Frances

**Cast**  Dean, Eddie; Ates, Roscoe; Padden, Sarah; LaRue, AL "Lash"

**Song(s)**  Ride on the Tide of a Song [1] (C/L: Cochran, Dorcas; Rosoff, Charles); Journey's End [1] (C/L: Cochran, Dorcas; Rosoff, Charles)

**Notes**  [1] Also in WILD WEST (PRC).

### 4679 ✦ PRAIRIE PIONEERS
Republic, 1941

**Producer(s)**  Gray, Louis
**Director(s)**  Orlebeck, Lester
**Screenwriter(s)**  Shipman, Barry
**Source(s)**  characters by MacDonald, William Colt

**Cast**  Livingston, Robert; Steele, Bob; Davis, Rufe; Estrella, Esther; Kellard, Robert; Ingraham, Jack; Canutt, Yakima

**Song(s)**  La Cucaracha (C: Traditional; L: Cherkose, Eddie)

### 4680 ✦ PRAIRIE RUSTLERS
Eagle Lion, 1945

**Musical Score**  Zahler, Lee; Grigor, Nico

**Producer(s)**  Neufeld, Sigmund
**Director(s)**  Newfield, Sam
**Screenwriter(s)**  Myton, Fred

**Cast**  Crabbe, Buster; St. John, Al; Finlay, Evelyn; Hackett, Karl; Osborne, Bud; Maynard, Kermit; Vernon, Dorothy

**Song(s)**  It's Over So Goodbye (C/L: Porter, Lew)

## 4681 ✦ PRAIRIE STRANGER
Columbia, 1941

**Composer(s)**   Preston, Lou
**Lyricist(s)**   Preston, Lou

**Producer(s)**   Berke, William
**Director(s)**   Hillyer, Lambert
**Screenwriter(s)**   Miller, Winston
**Source(s)**   *The Medico Rides the Trail* (novel) Rubel, James L.

**Cast**   Starrett, Charles; Edwards, Cliff; McCarthy, Patti; Murray, Forbes

**Song(s)**   I'm Just a Small Town Scallywag; I'll Be a Cowboy 'Till I Die (C/L: Willingham, Lopez); Ride Cowboy Ride; Doing It Right

## 4682 ✦ PRAIRIE THUNDER
Warner Brothers–First National, 1937

**Musical Score**   Jackson, Howard
**Composer(s)**   Jerome, M.K.
**Lyricist(s)**   Scholl, Jack

**Producer(s)**   Foy, Bryan
**Director(s)**   Eason, B. Reeves
**Screenwriter(s)**   Repp, Ed Earl

**Cast**   Foran, Dick; Clancy, Ellen; Smith, Al; Canutt, Yakima; Orth, Frank; Ellis, Frank; Whitaker, Slim; Wallace, Fred

**Song(s)**   Over the Trail Again; Sunset on the Rio Grande; Song of the Plains; The Prairie Is My Home [2]; My Home in Texas [1]; In a Little Prairie Town [1]; It's God's Country [1]

**Notes**   [1] Background instrumental use only. [2] Also in EMPTY HOLSTER, THE LAND BEYOND THE LAW and GUNS OF THE PECOS.

## 4683 ✦ PRESENTING LILY MARS
Metro–Goldwyn–Mayer, 1943

**Composer(s)**   Jurmann, Walter
**Lyricist(s)**   Webster, Paul Francis
**Choreographer(s)**   Matray, Ernst

**Producer(s)**   Pasternak, Joe
**Director(s)**   Taurog, Norman
**Screenwriter(s)**   Connell, Richard; Lehman, Gladys
**Source(s)**   (novel) Tarkington, Booth

**Cast**   Garland, Judy; Heflin, Van; Bainter, Fay; Byington, Spring; Gilchrist, Connie; Carlson, Richard; Eggerth, Marta; Kinsky, Leonid; Bob Crosby and His Orchestra; Tommy Dorsey and His Orchestra

**Song(s)**   Presenting Lily Mars (C/L: Edens, Roger); Is It Really Love; Tom Tom the Piper's Son (C: Lane, Burton; L: Harburg, E.Y.); Tovaritch (C/L: Edens, Roger); When I Look at You; Russian Rhapsody;

Kulebiaka; Where There's Music (C/L: Edens, Roger); Paging Mr. Greenback [1] (C/L: Fain, Sammy; Edens, Roger; Harburg, E.Y.; Brown, Lew)

**Notes**   There are also vocals of "Every Little Movement" by Karl Hoschna and Otto Harbach; "Three O'Clock in the Morning" by Dorothy Terris (Theodora Morse) and Julian Robledo; "Broadway Rhythm" by Arthur Freed and Nacio Herb Brown (also in BABES IN ARMS, BROADWAY MELODY OF 1936, SINGIN' IN THE RAIN and BROADWAY MELODY OF 1938) and "Think of Me" by Swander and Tenney. The following songs were cut from the finale: "St. Louis Blues," "It's a Long Way to Tipperary," "In the Shade of the Old Apple Tree" and "Don't Sit Under the Apple Tree." [1] Not used.

## 4684 ✦ THE PRESIDENT'S ANALYST
Paramount, 1967

**Producer(s)**   Rubin, Stanley
**Director(s)**   Flicker, Theodore J.
**Screenwriter(s)**   Flicker, Theodore J.

**Cast**   Coburn, James; Cambridge, Godfrey; Darden, Severn; Delaney, Joan; Geer, Will; Franz, Eduard; Harrington Jr., Pat

**Song(s)**   Hey Me (C: Schifrin, Lalo; L: Flicker, Theodore J.); Inner Manipulations (C/L: McGuire, Barry; Potash, Paul); She's Ready to Be Free (C/L: Clear Light); The Warmth of Her [1] (C: Schifrin, Lalo; L: Robison, C. Robbie); She's My Destiny [1] (C: Schifrin, Lalo; L: Robison, C. Robbie)

**Notes**   [1] Not used.

## 4685 ✦ PRESTIGE
RKO, 1932

**Producer(s)**   Brown, Harry Joe
**Director(s)**   Garnett, Tay
**Screenwriter(s)**   Faragoh, Francis Edwards

**Cast**   Harding, Ann; Douglas, Melvyn; Menjou, Adolphe; MacLaren, Ian; Post, Guy Bates; Geraghty, Carmelita; Hale, Creighton; Muse, Clarence; Lloyd, Rollo

**Song(s)**   I Don't Know What You Do to Me (C/L: Lewis, Harold; Grossman, Bernie)

## 4686 ✦ PRETTY IN PINK
Paramount, 1986

**Musical Score**   Gore, Michael

**Producer(s)**   Shuler, Lauren
**Director(s)**   Deutch, Howard
**Screenwriter(s)**   Hughes, John

**Cast** Cryer, Jon; Potts, Annie; Spader, James; McCarthy, Andrew; Stanton, Harry Dean; Ringwald, Molly

**Song(s)** Left of Center (C/L: Vega, Suzanne; Addabbo, Steve); Get to Know Ya (C/L: Johnson, Jesse); If You Leave (C/L: Humphreys, Paul David; McCluskey, Andy); Pretty in Pink [1] (C/L: Butler, T.; Butler, R.; Ely, V.; Ashton, J.; Kilburn, D.; Morris, R.)

**Notes** [1] Sheet music only.

### 4687 ✦ PRETTY MAIDS ALL IN A ROW
Metro–Goldwyn–Mayer, 1971

**Musical Score** Schifrin, Lalo

**Producer(s)** Roddenberry, Gene
**Director(s)** Vadim, Roger
**Screenwriter(s)** Roddenberry, Gene
**Source(s)** (novel) Pollini, Francis

**Cast** Hudson, Rock; Dickinson, Angie; Savalas, Telly; McDowell, Roddy; Wynn, Keenan; Carson, John David

**Song(s)** Chilly Winds (C: Schifrin, Lalo; L: Curb, Mike); Ocean Front School Song [1] (C: Traditional; L: Roddenberry, Gene)

**Notes** [1] Music based on "Annie Lisle."

### 4688 ✦ PRETTY POLLY

See A MATTER OF INNOCENCE.

### 4689 ✦ PRETTY SMART
New World, 1987

**Musical Score** Levy, Jay; Arkin, Eddie
**Composer(s)** Levy, Jay; Arkin, Eddie
**Lyricist(s)** Levy, Jay; Arkin, Eddie

**Producer(s)** Solomon, Ken; Begun, Jeff
**Director(s)** Logothetis, Dimitri
**Screenwriter(s)** Begun, Jeff; Alschuler, Melanie J.

**Cast** Fisher, Tricia Leigh; Zutaut, Brad; Lorient, Lisa

**Song(s)** Pretty Smart; Breakdown; Where Is the Man; Good Love Turn to Bad; Keep on Following Your Heart; Born to Rock [1]

**Notes** No cue sheet available. [1] Also in THUNDER RUN though credited to Jay Levy and Terry Shaddick.

### 4690 ✦ PREVIEW MURDER MYSTERY
Paramount, 1936

**Producer(s)** Hurley, Harold
**Director(s)** Florey, Robert
**Screenwriter(s)** Marlow, Brian; Yost, Robert

**Cast** Denny, Reginald; Patrick, Gail; Drake, Frances; La Rocque, Rod

**Song(s)** Promise with a Kiss (C: Kisco, Charley; L: Robin, Leo)

### 4691 ✦ THE PRIDE AND THE PASSION
United Artists, 1957

**Musical Score** Antheil, George
**Composer(s)** Antheil, George
**Lyricist(s)** Bergman, Alan

**Producer(s)** Kramer, Stanley
**Director(s)** Kramer, Stanley
**Screenwriter(s)** Anhalt, Edna; Anhalt, Edward
**Source(s)** *The Gun* (novel) Forester, C.S.

**Cast** Grant, Cary; Loren, Sophia; Sinatra, Frank; Bikel, Theodore; Wengraf, John; Novello, Jay; Nieto, Jose; Van Zandt, Philip

**Song(s)** Procession (L: Perry, Alfred); I Never Said I Love You [1]; Dawn at Avila [1]

**Notes** [1] Used instrumentally only.

### 4692 ✦ PRIDE OF THE PLAINS
Republic, 1943

**Producer(s)** Gray, Louis
**Director(s)** Fox, Wallace W.
**Screenwriter(s)** Butler, John K.; Williams, Bob

**Cast** Livingston, Robert; Burnette, Smiley; Gay, Nancy; Barclay, Stephen; Miller, Charles; Duncan, Kenne; Kirk, Jack; Canutt, Yakima

**Song(s)** Dr. Millhouse (C/L: Burnette, Smiley)

### 4693 ✦ PRIDE OF THE WEST
Paramount, 1938

**Producer(s)** Sherman, Harry
**Director(s)** Selander, Lesley
**Screenwriter(s)** Watt, Nate

**Cast** Boyd, William; Hayden, Russell; Hayes, George "Gabby"

**Song(s)** Wide Open Spaces (C: Stern, Jack; L: Tobias, Harry)

### 4694 ✦ PRIEST OF LOVE
Filmways, 1981

**Musical Score** James, Joseph

**Producer(s)** Miles, Christopher; Donally, Andrew
**Director(s)** Miles, Christopher
**Screenwriter(s)** Plater, Alan
**Source(s)** "The Priest of Love: A Life of D.H. Lawrence" (biography) Moore, H.T.

**Cast** Gifford, Mary; Gielgud, John; Hudson, John; McKellen, Ian; Suzman, Janet; Keith, Penelope; Gardner, Ava

**Song(s)**   The Way We Get It Together (C: James, Joseph; L: Cone, Christopher)

**Notes**   No cue sheet available.

## 4695 ✦ THE PRIEST'S WIFE
### Warner Brothers, 1971

**Musical Score**   Travaioli, Armando

**Producer(s)**   Ponti, Carlo
**Director(s)**   Risi, Dino
**Screenwriter(s)**   Maccari, Ruggero; Risi, Dino; Zapponi, Bernardino

**Cast**   Loren, Sophia; Mastroianni, Marcello; Venantini, Venantino; Stany, Jacques; Starnazza, Pippo; Mastrantoni, Augusto

**Song(s)**   Anyone (C: Travaioli, Armando; L: Bergman, Boris); (I Think I'm) Goin' Out of My Head (C/L: Randazzo, Teddy; Weinstein, Bobby); La Prima Cosa Bella (C/L: Mogol; Di Bari, Nicola); Twenty-Five Miles (C/L: Bristol, Johnny; Fuqua, Harvey; Starr, Edwin; Wexler, Jerry; Berns, Bert); It Can Happen to You (C/L: Renzetti, Joe); Io Mi Fermo Qui (C/L: Riccardi, E.; Albertelli, L.); Terribilis Est-Mot-Teto (C/L: Travaioli, Armando)

**Notes**   It is not known if any of these were written for the film.

## 4696 ✦ THE PRIME OF MISS JEAN BRODIE
### Twentieth Century–Fox, 1968

**Musical Score**   McKuen, Rod
**Composer(s)**   McKuen, Rod
**Lyricist(s)**   McKuen, Rod

**Producer(s)**   Fryer, Robert
**Director(s)**   Neame, Ronald
**Screenwriter(s)**   Allen, Jay Presson
**Source(s)**   *The Prime of Miss Jean Brodie* (novel) Spark, Muriel

**Cast**   Smith, Maggie; Stephens, Robert; Franklin, Pamela; Jackson, Gordon; Johnson, Celia; Carr, Jane; Grayson, Diane

**Song(s)**   Jean; Bend Down and Touch Me [1]; Somebody's Crying; The Ivy That Clings to the Wall [1]; A Red, Red Rose

**Notes**   Allen had also written a play of the same name. [1] Used instrumentally only although heard with lyrics on the soundtrack.

## 4697 ✦ THE PRINCE AND THE PAUPER
### Warner Brothers, 1937

**Musical Score**   Korngold, Erich Wolfgang

**Producer(s)**   Wallis, Hal B.
**Director(s)**   Keighley, William

**Screenwriter(s)**   Doyle, Laird
**Source(s)**   *The Prince and the Pauper* (novel) Twain, Mark

**Cast**   Mauch, Billy; Mauch, Bobby; Flynn, Errol; Rains, Claude; Stephenson, Henry; MacLane, Barton; Hale, Alan; Portman, Eric; Pape, Lionel; Willey, Leonard; Kinnell, Murray; Hobbes, Halliwell; Love, Montagu

**Song(s)**   The Roost Song (C/L: Korngold, Erich Wolfgang; Jerome, M.K.)

## 4698 ✦ THE PRINCE AND THE SHOWGIRL
### Warner Brothers, 1957

**Musical Score**   Addinsell, Richard
**Choreographer(s)**   Chappell, William

**Producer(s)**   Olivier, Laurence
**Director(s)**   Olivier, Laurence
**Screenwriter(s)**   Rattigan, Terence
**Source(s)**   *The Sleeping Prince* (play) Rattigan, Terence

**Cast**   Monroe, Marilyn; Olivier, Laurence; Thorndike, Sybil; Wattis, Richard; Spenser, Jeremy; Knight, Esmond; Hardwick, Paul; Greenwood, Rosamund

**Song(s)**   I Found a Dream (C: Addinsell, Richard; L: Hassall, Christopher)

## 4699 ✦ PRINCE OF DARKNESS
### Universal, 1987

**Musical Score**   Carpenter, John; Howarth, Alan

**Producer(s)**   Franco, Larry J.
**Director(s)**   Carpenter, John
**Screenwriter(s)**   Quartermass, Martin

**Cast**   Pleasence, Donald; Parker, Jameson; Wong, Victor; Blount, Lisa; Dun, Dennis; Cooper, Alice; Bray, Thom

**Song(s)**   Prince of Darkness (C/L: Cooper, Alice; Roberts, Kane)

## 4700 ✦ PRINCE OF FOXES
### Twentieth Century–Fox, 1949

**Musical Score**   Newman, Alfred

**Producer(s)**   Siegel, Sol C.
**Director(s)**   King, Henry
**Screenwriter(s)**   Krims, Milton
**Source(s)**   *Prince of Foxes* (novel) Shellabarger, Samuel

**Cast**   Power, Tyrone; Welles, Orson; Hendrix, Wanda; Berti, Marina; Sloane, Everett

**Song(s)**   Notturno (Nocturne) (C: Newman, Alfred; L: Coccaro, Aristide); Festival Scene (C: Newman, Alfred; L: Coccaro, Aristide)

## 4701 ◆ THE PRINCESS AND THE PIRATE
RKO, 1944

**Musical Score** Rose, David

**Producer(s)** Goldwyn, Samuel
**Director(s)** Butler, David
**Screenwriter(s)** Hartman, Don; Shavelson, Melville; Freeman, Everett

**Cast** Hope, Bob; McLaglen, Victor; Mayo, Virginia; Slezak, Walter; Brennan, Walter; Haas, Hugo; Lawrence, Marc; Eburne, Maude; Kennedy, Tom; Andrews, Stanley

**Song(s)** (How Would You Like to) Kiss Me in the Moonlight (C: McHugh, Jimmy; L: Adamson, Harold)

## 4702 ◆ THE PRINCESS BRIDE
Twentieth Century–Fox, 1987

**Musical Score** Knopfler, Mark

**Producer(s)** Scheinman, Andrew; Reiner, Rob
**Director(s)** Reiner, Rob
**Screenwriter(s)** Goldman, William
**Source(s)** *The Princess Bride* (novel) Goldman, William

**Cast** Elwes, Cary; Pantinkin, Mandy; Sarandon, Chris; Guest, Christopher; Shawn, Wallace; Andre the Giant; Savage, Fred; Wright, Robin; Falk, Peter; Cook, Peter; Kane, Carol; Smith, Mel; Crystal, Billy

**Song(s)** Storybook Love (C: Knopfler, Mark; L: DeVille, Willy)

## 4703 ◆ THE PRINCESS COMES ACROSS
Paramount, 1936

**Producer(s)** Hornblow Jr., Arthur
**Director(s)** Howard, William K.
**Screenwriter(s)** De Leon, Walter; Martin, Francis; Butler, Frank; Hartman, Don; Binyon, Claude; Priestley, J.B.

**Cast** Lombard, Carole; MacMurray, Fred; Dumbrille, Douglass; Skipworth, Alison; Frawley, William; Rumann, Sig; Auer, Mischa; Hall, Porter; Barbier, George

**Song(s)** My Concertina (C: Boutelje, Phil; L: Scholl, Jack)

**Notes** There is also a brief rendition of "Awake in a Dream" by Leo Robin and Frederick Hollander.

## 4704 ◆ PRINCESS O'HARA
Universal, 1935

**Musical Score** Morton, Arthur

**Director(s)** Burton, David
**Screenwriter(s)** Malloy, Doris; Clork, Harry
**Source(s)** "Princess O'Hara" (story) Runyon, Damon

**Cast** Morris, Chester; Parker, Jean; Errol, Leon

**Song(s)** Dancing in the Street (C: Morton, Arthur; L: Trivers, Barry)

**Notes** Remade as IT AIN'T HAY (1943) for Abbott and Costello and again as MONEY FROM HOME (1954) for Martin and Lewis.

## 4705 ◆ PRINCESS O'ROURKE
Warner Brothers, 1943

**Musical Score** Hollander, Frederick

**Producer(s)** Wallis, Hal B.
**Director(s)** Krasna, Norman
**Screenwriter(s)** Krasna, Norman

**Cast** de Havilland, Olivia; Cummings, Robert; Coburn, Charles; Carson, Jack; Wyman, Jane; Davenport, Harry; Cooper, Gladys; Watson, Minor; Wynn, Nan; Bois, Curt; Walker, Ray; Ford, Ruth; Bishop, Julie; Puglia, Frank

**Song(s)** Honorable Moon (C: Schwartz, Arthur; L: Gershwin, Ira; Harburg, E.Y.)

## 4706 ◆ THE PRINCIPAL
Tri-Star, 1987

**Musical Score** Gruska, Jay

**Producer(s)** Brodek, Thomas H.
**Director(s)** Cain, Christopher
**Screenwriter(s)** Deese, Frank

**Cast** Belushi, James; Gossett, Lou [1]; Chong, Rae Dawn; Wright, Michael

**Song(s)** Livin' in the Line of Fire (C/L: Gruska, Jay; Roberts, Bruce; Goldmark, Andy); Straight Into the Fire (C/L: Gruska, Jay; Lind, Jon); Our Own Eyes (C/L: Gruska, Jay; Gordon, Paul)

**Notes** No cue sheet available. [1] Billed as Louis Gossett Jr.

## 4707 ◆ PRIORITIES ON PARADE
Paramount, 1942

**Composer(s)** Styne, Jule
**Lyricist(s)** Loesser, Frank

**Producer(s)** Siegel, Sol C.
**Director(s)** Rogell, Albert S.
**Screenwriter(s)** Loesser, Frank; Arthur, Art

**Cast** Miller, Ann; Colonna, Jerry; Johnston, Johnnie; Rhodes, Betty Jane; Allen, Barbara Jo [1]; Cameron, Rod; Quillan, Eddie; Barris, Harry

**Song(s)** I'd Love to Know You Better (L: Magidson, Herb); Johnny's Patter (C: Sanders, Troy; L: Loesser, Frank; Arthur, Art); Here Comes Katrinka; Conchita Marquita Lolita Pepita Rosita Juanita Lopez (L: Magidson, Herb); The Jitterbug (inst); Anywhere On

Earth Is Heaven (C: Young, Victor; L: Washington, Ned); I Said "No" [2]; You're In Love with Someone Else (but I'm in Love with You); Cooperate with Your Air Raid Warden (L: Magidson, Herb); Pay Day

**Notes** The movie was originally titled PRIORITIES OF 1942. There is also a brief (48 seconds) rendition of Frank Loesser and Victor Schertzinger's "Kiss the Boys Goodbye." [1] Known also as Vera Vague. [2] Also used in SWEATER GIRL.

### 4708 ✦ PRISONER OF WAR
Metro–Goldwyn–Mayer, 1954

**Producer(s)** Berman, Henry
**Director(s)** Marton, Andrew
**Screenwriter(s)** Rivkin, Allen

**Cast** Reagan, Ronald; Forrest, Steve; Martin, Dewey; Homolka, Oscar; Horton, Robert; Stewart, Paul; Morgan, Henry; Bekassy, Stephen

**Song(s)** Uncle Sam and Uncle Joe (C: Traditional; L: Alexander, Jeff)

### 4709 ✦ PRIVATE AFFAIRS OF BEL AMI
United Artists, 1947

**Musical Score** Milhaud, Darius

**Producer(s)** Lewin, Albert; Loew, David L.
**Director(s)** Lewin, Albert
**Screenwriter(s)** Lewin, Albert
**Source(s)** *Bel Ami* (novel) de Maupassant, Guy

**Cast** Sanders, George; Lansbury, Angela; Dvorak, Ann; Dee, Frances; Carradine, John; Haas, Hugo

**Song(s)** My Bel Ami (C: Drutman, Irving; L: Lawrence, Jack); The Lark (C/L: Lewin, Albert)

### 4710 ✦ PRIVATE BENJAMIN
Warner Brothers, 1980

**Musical Score** Conti, Bill

**Producer(s)** Meyers, Nancy
**Director(s)** Zieff, Howard
**Screenwriter(s)** Meyers, Nancy

**Cast** Hawn, Goldie; Brennan, Eileen; Assante, Armand; Webber, Robert; Wanamaker, Sam; Barrie, Barbara; Place, Mary Kay; Stanton, Harry Dean; Brooks, Albert

**Song(s)** Thornbird Hymn (C/L: Meyers, Nancy; Miller, Harvey; Shyer, Charles)

### 4711 ✦ PRIVATE BUCKAROO
Universal, 1942

**Choreographer(s)** Mattison, John

**Producer(s)** Goldsmith, Ken
**Director(s)** Cline, Edward F.
**Screenwriter(s)** Kelso, Edmund; James, Edward

**Cast** The Andrews Sisters; Harry James and His Music Makers; Foran, Dick; Lewis, Joe E.; Howard, Shemp; Davies, Richard; Wickes, Mary; O'Connor, Donald; Ryan, Peggy; Hall, Huntz; The Jivin' Jacks and Jills

**Song(s)** Three Little Sisters (C: Mizzy, Vic; L: Taylor, Irving); You Made Me Love You (C: Monaco, James V.; L: McCarthy, Joseph); Private Buckaroo (C: Wrubel, Allie; L: Newman, Charles); The Good Old South (C/L: Lee, Lester; Shapiro, Dan; Seelen, Jerry); Ma, I Miss Your Apple Pie (C/L: Lombardo, Carmen; Loeb, John Jacob); Six Jerks in a Jeep (C/L: Robin, Sid); That's the Moon, My Son (C/L: Kassel, Art; Gallop, Sammy; Litman, Norman); Don't Sit Under the Apple Tree (C: Stept, Sam H.; L: Brown, Lew; Tobias, Charles); We've Got a Job to Do (C/L: Knight, Vick); Johnny Get Your Gun Again (C: de Paul, Gene; L: Raye, Don)

**Notes** There is also a vocal of "Nobody Knows the Trouble I've Seen."

### 4712 ✦ PRIVATE LIVES
Metro–Goldwyn–Mayer, 1931

**Director(s)** Franklin, Sidney
**Screenwriter(s)** Kraly, Hans; Schayer, Richard
**Source(s)** *Private Lives* (play) Coward, Noel

**Cast** Shearer, Norma; Montgomery, Robert; Denny, Reginald; Hersholt, Jean; Merkel, Una; Hersholt, Jean

**Song(s)** Someday I'll Find You [1] (C/L: Coward, Noel)

**Notes** A performance from the Broadway production was filmed for Shearer, Montgomery and others to see. It would be interesting to see if the film still exists. [1] From stage production.

### 4713 ✦ THE PRIVATE LIVES OF ADAM AND EVE
Universal, 1960

**Musical Score** Alexander, Van

**Producer(s)** Doff, Red
**Director(s)** Rooney, Mickey; Zugsmith, Albert
**Screenwriter(s)** Hill, Robert

**Cast** Rooney, Mickey; Van Doren, Mamie; Milner, Martin; Spain, Fay; Torme, Mel; Kellaway, Cecil; Weld, Tuesday; Anka, Paul

**Song(s)** The Private Lives of Adam and Eve (C/L: Anka, Paul); Slapping the Vine (C: Alexander, Van; L: Hill, Robert)

### 4714 ✦ THE PRIVATE LIVES OF ELIZABETH AND ESSEX
Warner Brothers, 1939

**Musical Score** Korngold, Erich Wolfgang

**Producer(s)** Wallis, Hal B.
**Director(s)** Curtiz, Michael

**Screenwriter(s)**    Raine, Norman Reilly; MacKenzie, Aeneas
**Source(s)**    *Elizabeth the Queen* (play) Anderson, Maxwell

**Cast**    Davis, Bette; Flynn, Errol; de Havilland, Olivia; Crisp, Donald; Hale, Alan; Price, Vincent; Stephenson, Henry; Stephenson, James; Daniell, Henry; Fabares, Nanette [1]; Forbes, Ralph; Warwick, Robert; Carroll, Leo G.

**Song(s)**    The Passionate Shepherd to His Love (C: Korngold, Erich Wolfgang; L: Raleigh, Sir Walter)

**Notes**    [1] Nanette Fabray.

## 4715 ◆ A PRIVATE'S AFFAIR
### Twentieth Century–Fox, 1959

**Musical Score**    Mockridge, Cyril J.
**Composer(s)**    McHugh, Jimmy; Livingston, Jay; Evans, Ray
**Lyricist(s)**    McHugh, Jimmy; Livingston, Jay; Evans, Ray

**Producer(s)**    Weisbart, David
**Director(s)**    Walsh, Raoul
**Screenwriter(s)**    Miller, Winston

**Cast**    Mineo, Sal; Carere, Christine; Coe, Barry; Eden, Barbara; Crosby, Gary; Moore, Terry; Backus, Jim; Landis, Jessie Royce

**Song(s)**    The Same Old Army; 36-24-36; Warm and Willing; A Private Affair [1]

**Notes**    [1] Not used.

## 4716 ◆ PRIVATE SCHOOL
### Universal, 1983

**Composer(s)**    Wray, Bill; Goldstein, Steve
**Lyricist(s)**    Wray, Bill; Goldstein, Steve

**Producer(s)**    Enfraim, R. Ben; Enright, Don
**Director(s)**    Black, Noel
**Screenwriter(s)**    Greenburg, Dan; O'Malley, Suzanne

**Cast**    Cates, Phoebe; Russell, Betsy; Modine, Matthew; Zorek, Michael; Ryan, Fran; Wilhoite, Kathleen; Walston, Ray; Aletter, Frank; Stahl, Richard; Kristel, Sylvia

**Song(s)**    You're Breaking My Heart (C/L: Nilsson, Harry); Rock This Town (C/L: Setzer, Brian); She Said No (C/L: Wray, Bill; Medica, Leon); Just One Touch; American Girl (C/L: Springfield); How Do I Let You Know; She Said No (C/L: Wray, Bill; Medica, Leon); Nasty Girl (C/L: Vanity); I Want Candy (C/L: Feldman, Robert; Goldstein, Jerry; Gotterher, Richard); Lil Red Riding Hood (C/L: Blackwell, Ronald); Just One Touch; Best Years of Our Lives (C/L: Jaymes, David); Da Da Da (C/L: Remmier, Stephan; Kralle)

**Notes**    It is not known which of these were written for this film.

## 4717 ◆ PRIVATES ON PARADE
### Orion, 1984

**Musical Score**    King, Dennis

**Producer(s)**    Relph, Simon
**Director(s)**    Blakemore, Michael
**Screenwriter(s)**    Nichols, Peter
**Source(s)**    *Privates on Parade* (play) Nichols, Peter

**Cast**    Cleese, John; Quilley, Denis; Elphick, Michael; Pagett, Nicola; Payne, Bruce; Jones, Simon; Sands, Julian; Melia, Joe; Bamber, David; Pearson, Patrick

**Song(s)**    Privates on Parade (C: King, Dennis; L: Nichols, Peter); Sadusea (C: King, Dennis; L: Nichols, Peter)

**Notes**    No cue sheet available.

## 4718 ◆ PRIVILEGE
### Universal, 1967

**Musical Score**    Leander, Mike
**Composer(s)**    Leander, Mike
**Lyricist(s)**    Leander, Mike

**Producer(s)**    Heyman, John
**Director(s)**    Watkins, Peter
**Screenwriter(s)**    Bogner, Norman; Watkins, Peter

**Cast**    Jones, Paul; Shrimpton, Jean; London, Mark; Job, William; Bacon, Max; Child, Jeremy; Cossins, James; George Bean Group

**Song(s)**    Free Me [1] (L: London, Mark); I've Been a Bad Bad Boy [2]; Privilege [2]

**Notes**    A Rank Organisation film. [1] London not credited on sheet music. [2] Sheet music only.

## 4719 ◆ THE PRIZE FIGHTER
### New World, 1980

**Musical Score**    Matz, Peter

**Producer(s)**    Elliott, Lang; Dell, Wanda
**Director(s)**    Preece, Michael
**Screenwriter(s)**    Conway, Tim; Myhers, John

**Cast**    Conway, Tim; Knotts, Don; Wayne, David; Clarke, Robin; Cameron, Cissie; O'Neill, Mary Ellen

**Song(s)**    'Til the End (C/L: Matz, Peter)

**Notes**    No cue sheet available.

## 4720 ◆ THE PRIZE FIGHTER AND THE LADY
### Metro–Goldwyn–Mayer, 1933

**Producer(s)**    Stromberg, Hunt
**Director(s)**    Van Dyke, W.S.
**Screenwriter(s)**    Mahin, John Lee; Meehan, John

**Cast**    Loy, Myrna; Baer, Max; Carnera, Primo; Dempsey, Jack; Huston, Walter; Kruger, Otto

**Song(s)** 'Cause I'm Just a Downstream Drifter (C: Snell, Dave; L: Egan, Raymond B.; Kahn, Gus); Lucky Fella (C: McHugh, Jimmy; L: Fields, Dorothy); You've Got Everything [1] (C: Donaldson, Walter; L: Kahn, Gus)

**Notes** Titled EVERYWOMAN'S MAN overseas. Vaudeville sketch by Seymour Felix. [1] Used instrumentally only.

## 4721 ✦ A PRIZE OF GOLD
### Columbia, 1955

**Producer(s)** Allen, Irving; Broccoli, Albert R.
**Director(s)** Robson, Mark
**Screenwriter(s)** Buckner, Robert; Paxton, John

**Cast** Widmark, Richard; Zetterling, Mai; Patrick, Nigel; Cole, George; Wolfit, Donald; Tomelty, Joseph; Ray, Andrew

**Song(s)** In Love, In Love (C: Bronner, Gerhardt; L: O'Connor, Tommie); A Prize of Gold (C: Lee, Lester; L: Washington, Ned)

**Notes** No cue sheet available.

## 4722 ✦ THE PRODIGAL (1931)
### Metro–Goldwyn–Mayer, 1931

**Director(s)** Pollard, Harry
**Screenwriter(s)** Meredyth, Bess; Root, Wells

**Cast** Tibbett, Lawrence; Ralston, Esther; Young, Roland; Edwards, Cliff; Pratt, Purnell; Hopper, Hedda; Fetchit, Stepin

**Song(s)** Life Is a Dream (C: Straus, Oscar; L: Freed, Arthur); Chidlins (C: Stothart, Herbert; L: Johnson, Howard); Without a Song [1] (C: Youmans, Vincent; L: Rose, William; Eliscu, Edward)

**Notes** No cue sheet available. [1] Not written for this film.

## 4723 ✦ THE PRODIGAL (1985)
### World Wide, 1984

**Musical Score** Broughton, Bruce

**Producer(s)** Wales, Ken
**Director(s)** Collier, James F.
**Screenwriter(s)** Collier, James F.

**Cast** Hammand, John; Lange, Hope; Cullum, John; Brittany, Morgan; Smart, Jean; Duckworth, Dortha

**Song(s)** I Have Today (C: Broughton, Bruce; L: Spiegel, Dennis)

**Notes** No cue sheet available.

## 4724 ✦ THE PRODIGAL RETURNS
### Paramount, 1939

**Composer(s)** Guizar, Tito
**Lyricist(s)** Noriega, Nenette

**Song(s)** Vagabundo [2]; Matarili-ri-li-ron; Tal Vez [2]; Caprice Gitane [1] (C/L: Tana); El Dia Que Yo Pueda (C/L: Flores, Celedonio E.; Canaro, Francisco); Castilian Moonlight (C: Longas, Frederico; L: Rose, Ed; Schipa, Tito)

**Notes** Tana was the professional name of Cielo Alba de Ganez. The Spanish title was EL OTRO SOY YO. [1] Also in EL TROVADOR DE LA RADIO with composer credit going to Tito Guizar. [2] Not used in EL TROVADOR DE LA RADIO.

## 4725 ✦ THE PRODUCERS
### Embassy, 1967

**Musical Score** Morris, John
**Composer(s)** Brooks, Mel
**Lyricist(s)** Brooks, Mel
**Choreographer(s)** Johnson, Alan

**Producer(s)** Glazier, Sidney
**Director(s)** Brooks, Mel
**Screenwriter(s)** Brooks, Mel

**Cast** Mostel, Zero; Wilder, Gene; Shawn, Dick; Mars, Kenneth; Winwood, Estelle; Hewitt, Christopher; Voutsinas, Andreas; Meredith, Lee; Taylor, Renee; Martin, Barney; Hickey, William

**Song(s)** Prisoners of Love; Springtime for Hitler

**Notes** No cue sheet available.

## 4726 ✦ PROFESSIONAL SOLDIER
### Twentieth Century–Fox, 1935

**Producer(s)** Zanuck, Darryl F.
**Director(s)** Garnett, Tay
**Screenwriter(s)** Fowler, Gene; Smith, Howard Ellis
**Source(s)** "Gentlemen, The King!" (story) Runyon, Damon

**Cast** McLaglen, Victor; Bartholomew, Freddie; Stuart, Gloria; Collier, Constance; Whalen, Michael; de Cordoba, Pedro; Hare, Lumsden; Dunbar, Dixie

**Song(s)** Joan of Arkansaw (C: Green, Johnny; L: Heyman, Edward)

## 4727 ✦ PROFESSIONAL SWEETHEART
### RKO, 1933

**Musical Score** Steiner, Max

**Director(s)** Seiter, William A.
**Screenwriter(s)** Watkins, Maurine

**Cast** Rogers, Ginger; Foster, Norman; Pitts, ZaSu; McHugh, Frank; Jenkins, Allen; Ratoff, Gregory; Pangborn, Franklin; Kennedy, Edgar; Holloway, Sterling

**Song(s)** My Imaginary Sweetheart (C: Akst, Harry; L: Eliscu, Edward)

## 4728 ✦ THE PROMISE
### Universal, 1978

**Musical Score**   Shire, David

**Producer(s)**   Weintraub, Fred; Heller, Paul
**Director(s)**   Cates, Gilbert
**Screenwriter(s)**   White, Garry Michael

**Cast**   Quinlan, Kathleen; Straight, Beatrice; Collins, Stephen; Luckinbill, Laurence; Besch, Bibi

**Song(s)**   I'll Never Say Goodbye (The Promise) (C: Shire, David; L: Bergman, Marilyn; Bergman, Alan)

## 4729 ✦ PROMISE HER ANYTHING
### Paramount, 1966

**Producer(s)**   Rubin, Stanley
**Director(s)**   Hiller, Arthur
**Screenwriter(s)**   Blatty, William Peter

**Cast**   Beatty, Warren; Caron, Leslie; Cummings, Robert; Gingold, Hermione; Stander, Lionel; Wynn, Keenan; Nesbitt, Cathleen

**Song(s)**   Something's Comin' Off Tonight (C/L: Grainer, Ron); Promise Her Anything (C: Bacharach, Burt; L: David, Hal)

## 4730 ✦ PROPHECY
### Paramount, 1979

**Producer(s)**   Rosen, Robert L.
**Director(s)**   Frankenheimer, John
**Screenwriter(s)**   Seltzer, David

**Cast**   Shire, Talia; Foxworth, Robert; Assante, Armand; Racimo, Victoria

**Song(s)**   Just a Little Bit of Funk (C/L: Job, Lionel; Gillman, Delwin); No, No, No, My Friend (C/L: Thalheimer, Norman; Crittendon, Will); Sweet Ride (C/L: Job, Lionel; Gillman, Delwin)

## 4731 ✦ THE PROTECTOR
### Warner Brothers, 1985

**Musical Score**   Thorne, Ken

**Producer(s)**   Chan, David
**Director(s)**   Glickenhaus, James
**Screenwriter(s)**   Glickenhaus, James

**Cast**   Chan, Jackie; Aiello, Danny; Arnold, Victor

**Song(s)**   One Up for the Good Guys (C/L: Taylor, Chip)

**Notes**   It is not known if this was written for the film.

## 4732 ✦ THE PROUD AND THE PROFANE
### Paramount, 1956

**Producer(s)**   Perlberg, William
**Director(s)**   Seaton, George
**Screenwriter(s)**   Seaton, George

**Source(s)**   *The Magnificent Bastards* (novel) Crockett, Lucy Herndon

**Cast**   Holden, William; Kerr, Deborah; Ritter, Thelma; Martin, Dewey; Redfield, William; Ross, Marion; Bagdasarian, Ross

**Song(s)**   The Proud and the Profane (The Ballad of Colin Black) [1] (C/L: Bagdasarian, Ross); (I Only Live) To Love You (C: Young, Victor; L: Gordon, Mack)

**Notes**   [1] Not used.

## 4733 ✦ PSYCHIC KILLER
### Avco Embassy, 1976

**Musical Score**   Kraft, William

**Producer(s)**   Rustam, Mardi
**Director(s)**   Danton, Raymond
**Screenwriter(s)**   Clark, Greydon; Angel, Mike; Danton, Raymond

**Cast**   Hutton, Jim; Adams, Julie; Burke, Paul; Persoff, Nehemiah; Ray, Aldo; Brand, Neville; Reese, Della; Cameron, Rod; Bissell, Whit

**Song(s)**   You Perfect Stranger (C/L: Corda, Mike)

**Notes**   No cue sheet avaiable.

## 4734 ✦ PSYCHO
### Universal, 1960

**Producer(s)**   Hitchcock, Alfred
**Director(s)**   Hitchcock, Alfred
**Screenwriter(s)**   Stefano, Joseph
**Source(s)**   *Psycho* (novel) Bloch, Robert

**Cast**   Perkins, Anthony; Leigh, Janet; Balsam, Martin; Gavin, John; Miles, Vera; McIntire, John; Albertson, Frank; Oakland, Simon; Hitchcock, Patricia; Taylor, Vaughn; Tuttle, Lurene

**Song(s)**   Psycho [1] (C: Herrmann, Bernard; L: unknown)

**Notes**   [1] Not used in picture.

## 4735 ✦ PSYCHO III
### Universal, 1986

**Musical Score**   Burwell, Carter
**Composer(s)**   Burwell, Carter; Bray, Steve

**Producer(s)**   Green, Hilton
**Director(s)**   Perkins, Anthony
**Screenwriter(s)**   Pogue, Charles Edward

**Cast**   Perkins, Anthony; Scarwid, Diana; Fahey, Jeff; Maxwell, Roberta; Gillin, Hugh

**Song(s)**   Dirty Street (L: Bray, Steve; Stanton-Miranda, D.); Cathrine Mary (L: Stanton-Miranda, D.)

## 4736 ✦ PUBERTY BLUES
### Universal/Twentieth Century–Fox, 1983

**Musical Score**   Gock, Les
**Composer(s)**   Finn, Tim
**Lyricist(s)**   Finn, Tim

**Producer(s)**   Long, Joan; Kelly, Margaret
**Director(s)**   Beresford, Bruce
**Screenwriter(s)**   Kelly, Margaret
**Source(s)**   *Puberty Blues* (novel) Lette, Kathy; Carey, Gabrielle

**Cast**   Schofield, Nell; Capelja, Jad; Rhoe, Geoff; Hughes, Tony

**Song(s)**   Stars In Her Eyes (C/L: Manzies, Jim; Wirth, Jarryl); Lipstick and Leather (C/L: Manzies, Jim; Owley, Kim); I Hope I Never; Nobody Takes Me Seriously; Puberty Blues; On the Roof (C/L: Gock, Les)

**Notes**   An Australian film.

## 4737 ✦ PUBLIC COWBOY NUMBER ONE
### Republic, 1937

**Producer(s)**   Siegel, Sol C.
**Director(s)**   Kane, Joseph
**Screenwriter(s)**   Drake, Oliver

**Cast**   Autry, Gene; Burnette, Smiley; Rutherford, Ann; Farnum, William; Loft, Arthur

**Song(s)**   Hike Yaa Move Along [1] (C/L: Burnette, Smiley); Wanderers of the Wasteland (C/L: Unknown); The West Ain't What It Used to Be (C/L: Allan, Fleming); Old Buckaroo [2] (C/L: Autry, Gene; Allan, Fleming); I Picked Out a Trail to Your Heart (C/L: Unknown); Defective Detective from Brooklyn (C/L: Unknown); I Picked Up the Trail When I Found You (C/L: Allan, Fleming)

**Notes**   No cue sheet available. [1] Also in GOLD MINE IN THE SKY. [2] Also in BARBED WIRE (Columbia).

## 4738 ✦ THE PUBLIC EYE
### Universal, 1972

**Musical Score**   Barry, John

**Producer(s)**   Wallis, Hal B.
**Director(s)**   Reed, Carol
**Screenwriter(s)**   Shaffer, Peter
**Source(s)**   *The Public Eye* (play) Shaffer, Peter

**Cast**   Jayston, Michael; Farrow, Mia; Topol; Rawlings, Margaret; Crosbie, Annette; Foster, Dudley

**Song(s)**   Follow, Follow (C: Barry, John; L: Black, Don)

**Notes**   Released overseas as FOLLOW ME.

## 4739 ✦ PUBLIC PIGEON NO. 1
### RKO, 1956

**Musical Score**   Rose, David
**Composer(s)**   Malneck, Matty

**Lyricist(s)**   Marley, Eve
**Choreographer(s)**   Nelson, Miriam

**Producer(s)**   Tugend, Harry
**Director(s)**   McLeod, Norman Z.
**Screenwriter(s)**   Tugend, Harry
**Source(s)**   (teleplay) Freeman, Devery

**Cast**   Skelton, Red; Blaine, Vivian; Blair, Janet; Joslyn, Allyn; Baker, Benny; Frome, Milton; Abbott, John; The Seven Ashtons

**Song(s)**   Don't Be Chicken Chicken; Pardon Me! Gotta Go Mambo

## 4740 ✦ PUBLIC WEDDING
### Warner Brothers, 1937

**Musical Score**   Jackson, Howard

**Producer(s)**   Foy, Bryan
**Director(s)**   Grinde, Nick
**Screenwriter(s)**   Chanslor, Roy; Branch, Houston
**Source(s)**   "The Inside" (story) Branch, Houston

**Cast**   Wyman, Jane; Hopper, William; Purcell, Dick; Wilson, Marie; Churchill, Berton; Robbins, James; Hatton, Raymond; Borg, Veda Ann

**Song(s)**   Public Wedding (C: Jerome, M.K.; L: Scholl, Jack)

## 4741 ✦ PUDDIN' HEAD
### Republic, 1941

**Musical Score**   Scharf, Walter
**Composer(s)**   Styne, Jule
**Lyricist(s)**   Cherkose, Eddie

**Producer(s)**   Cohen, Albert J.
**Director(s)**   Santley, Joseph
**Screenwriter(s)**   Townley, Jack; Gross, Milt

**Cast**   Canova, Judy; Lederer, Francis; Walburn, Raymond; Summerville, Slim; Allwyn, Astrid; Foy Jr., Eddie; Kruger, Alma; O'Connell, Hugh; Chandler, Chick

**Song(s)**   Minnie Hotcha; Puddin' Head (C: Meyer, Sol; Styne, Jule); Hey Junior; You're Tellin' I; Manhattan Holiday; Ghost Routine; Sky's the Limit [1]

**Notes**   Titled JUDY GOES TO TOWN internationally. [1] Sheet music only.

## 4742 ✦ PUDDY TAT TROUBLES
### Warner Brothers, 1951

**Musical Score**   Stalling, Carl

**Director(s)**   Freling, Friz

**Cast**   Tweety; Sylvester

**Song(s)**   Tweety (C/L: Stalling, Carl)

**Notes**   Looney Tune.

## 4743 ✦ PUFNSTUF
Universal, 1970

**Composer(s)** Fox, Charles
**Lyricist(s)** Gimbel, Norman

**Producer(s)** Rose, Si
**Director(s)** Morse, Hollingsworth
**Screenwriter(s)** Rose, Si; Murray, John Fenton

**Cast** Elliott, "Mama" Cass; Raye, Martha; Wild, Jack; Hayes, Billie; Camonet, Roberto; Baird, Sharon

**Song(s)** If I Could; A Friend in You; Living Island; Pufnstuf; Different; Zap the World

## 4744 ✦ PUMPING IRON II THE WOMEN
Cincom, 1985

**Musical Score** McHugh, David

**Producer(s)** Butler, George
**Director(s)** Butler, George
**Screenwriter(s)** Gaines, Charles; Butler, George
**Source(s)** *Pumping Iron II: The Unprecedented Woman* (book) Gaines, Charles; Butler, George

**Cast** Bowen, Lori; Dunlap, Carla; Francis, Bev; McLish, Rachel; Alexander, Kris; Cheng, Lydia

**Song(s)** Future Sex (C: Montes, Michael; L: Roderick, Kyle)

**Notes** No cue sheet available. Documentary.

## 4745 ✦ PUNCHLINE
Columbia, 1988

**Musical Score** Gross, Charles

**Producer(s)** Melnick, Daniel; Rachmil, Michael
**Director(s)** Seltzer, David
**Screenwriter(s)** Seltzer, David

**Cast** Field, Sally; Hanks, Tom; Rydell, Mark; Goodman, John; Mazursky, Paul; Greist, Kim; Wayans, Damon

**Song(s)** Remember Tonight and Smile (C/L: Pollock, Michael)

**Notes** No cue sheet available.

## 4746 ✦ THE PURPLE GANG
Allied Artists, 1960

**Musical Score** Dunlap, Paul

**Producer(s)** Parsons, Lindsley
**Director(s)** McDonald, Frank
**Screenwriter(s)** DeWitt, Jack

**Cast** Sullivan, Barry; Blake, Robert; Edwards, Elaine; Cavell, Marc; Lawrence, Jody; Paiva, Nestor

**Song(s)** Runnin' Wild (C/L: Gray, Joe; Wood, Leo; Gibbs, A. Harrington)

**Notes** No cue sheet available.

## 4747 ✦ PURPLE HEART DIARY
Columbia, 1951

**Composer(s)** Romano, Tony; Hayden, Barbara; Bradford, Johnny
**Lyricist(s)** Romano, Tony; Hayden, Barbara; Bradford, Johnny

**Producer(s)** Katzman, Sam
**Director(s)** Quine, Richard
**Screenwriter(s)** Sackheim, William

**Cast** Langford, Frances; Lessy, Ben; Romano, Tony; Guardino, Harry; Talbot, Lyle

**Song(s)** Hold Me in Your Arms; Hi, Fellow Tourists; Bread and Butter Woman [2] (C/L: Roberts, Allan; Lee, Lester); Anywhere [1] (C: Styne, Jule; L: Cahn, Sammy); Tattletale Eyes (C/L: Romano, Tony; Bradford, Johnny); Where Are You From

**Notes** Released in Great Britain as NO TIME FOR TEARS. Based on a column in the Hearst papers by Frances Langford. [1] From TONIGHT AND EVERY NIGHT. [2] Also in ARKANSAS SWING and SLIGHTLY FRENCH.

## 4748 ✦ PURPLE RAIN
Warner Brothers, 1984

**Musical Score** Colombier, Michel
**Composer(s)** Prince
**Lyricist(s)** Prince

**Producer(s)** Cavallo, Robert; Ruffalo, Joseph; Fargnoli, Steven
**Director(s)** Magnoli, Albert
**Screenwriter(s)** Magnoli, Albert; Blinn, William

**Cast** Prince; Kotero, Apollonia; Day, Morris; Karlatos, Olga; Williams III, Clarence; Benton, Jerome; Sparks, Billy

**Song(s)** Let's Go Crazy; Jungle Love (C/L: Day, Morris; Starr, Jamie); Take Me with U; Modernaire (C/L: Dickerson, Dez); The Beautiful Ones; When Doves Cry; Computer Blue (C/L: Prince; Melvoin, Wendy; Coleman, Lisa; Nelson, John L.); Darling Nikki; Sex Shooter (C/L: Starr, Jamie); The Bird (C/L: Starr, Jamie; Day, Morris); Purple Rain; Baby I'm a Star; I Would Die 4 U [1]

**Notes** [1] Sheet music only.

## 4749 ✦ PURSUED (1934)
Fox, 1934

**Producer(s)** Wurtzel, Sol M.
**Director(s)** King, Louis
**Screenwriter(s)** Cole, Lester; Anthony, Stuart
**Source(s)** "The Painted Lady" (story) Evans, Larry

**Cast** Ames, Rosemary; Jory, Victor; Hardie, Russell

**Song(s)** Wanted—Someone (C: Akst, Harry; L: Clare, Sidney); Polynesian Whoopee [1] (C: Friedhofer, Hugo)

**Notes** [1] There are not lyrics just meaningless syllables.

## 4750 ✦ PURSUED (1947)
### Warner Brothers, 1947

**Musical Score** Steiner, Max
**Choreographer(s)** Prinz, LeRoy

**Producer(s)** Sperling, Milton
**Director(s)** Walsh, Raoul
**Screenwriter(s)** Busch, Niven

**Cast** Wright, Teresa; Mitchum, Robert; Anderson, Judith; Jagger, Dean; Hale, Alan; Carey Jr., Harry

**Song(s)** My Gentle Harp (C/L: Moore, T.)

**Notes** There is also a vocal of "The Cowboy's Lament."

## 4751 ✦ THE PURSUIT OF D.B. COOPER
### Universal, 1981

**Musical Score** Horner, James
**Composer(s)** Smotherman, Michael
**Lyricist(s)** Smotherman, Michael

**Producer(s)** Wigutow, Daniel; Taylor, Michael
**Director(s)** Spottiswoode, Roger
**Screenwriter(s)** Fiskin, Jeffrey Alan
**Source(s)** *Free Fall* (novel) Reed, J.D.; Kramm, Mark

**Cast** Duvall, Robert; Williams, Treat; Harrold, Kathryn; Flanders, Ed; Gleason, Paul; Armstrong, R.G.; Fielding, Dorothy; Coster, Nicolas; Smith, Howard K.

**Song(s)** You Were Never There; Silk Dresses; Bittersweet Love Affair (C/L: Levine, Enid); Maybe He Knows About You (C/L: Levine, Enid)

## 4752 ✦ PURSUIT OF THE GRAF SPEE
### United Artists, 1956

**Musical Score** Easdale, Brian

**Producer(s)** Powell, Michael; Pressburger, Emeric
**Director(s)** Powell, Michael; Pressburger, Emeric
**Screenwriter(s)** Powell, Michael; Pressburger, Emeric

**Cast** Gregson, John; Quayle, Anthony; Finch, Peter; Hunter, Ian; Gwillim, Jack; Lee, Bernard; Dove, Patrick; Newley, Anthony

**Song(s)** Guaracha (C: Easdale, Brian; L: Salinger, Manuel)

## 4753 ✦ PURSUIT TO ALGIERS
### Universal, 1945

**Composer(s)** Rosen, Milton

**Director(s)** Neill, Roy William
**Screenwriter(s)** Lee, Leonard
**Source(s)** characters by Doyle, Arthur Conan

**Cast** Rathbone, Basil; Bruce, Nigel; Vincent, Leslie; Kosleck, Martin; Riordan, Marjorie; Ivan, Rosalind

**Song(s)** There Isn't Any Harm in That (L: Brooks, Jack); Cross My Heart (L: Carter, Everett)

**Notes** There are also vocals of "Flow Gently, Sweet Afton" by Robert Burns and J.E. Spilman and "Loch Lomand."

## 4754 ✦ PUSSYCAT, PUSSYCAT, I LOVE YOU
### United Artists, 1970

**Musical Score** Schifrin, Lalo
**Composer(s)** Schifrin, Lalo
**Lyricist(s)** Lees, Gene

**Producer(s)** Bresler, Jerry
**Director(s)** Amateau, Rod
**Screenwriter(s)** Amateau, Rod

**Cast** McShane, Ian; Calder-Marshall, Anna; Loncar, Beba; Smith, Madeline; Carlson, Veronica; Gavin, John; Mase, Marion; Darden, Severn

**Song(s)** Groove Into It; Le Accetiamo; Happily Ever After

## 4755 ✦ PUTTIN' ON THE RITZ
### United Artists, 1930

**Composer(s)** Berlin, Irving
**Lyricist(s)** Berlin, Irving
**Choreographer(s)** Kusell, Maurice L.

**Producer(s)** Considine Jr., John W.
**Director(s)** Sloman, Edward
**Screenwriter(s)** Considine Jr., John W.; Wells, William K.

**Cast** Richman, Harry; Bennett, Joan; Gleason, James; Tashman, Lilyan; Pringle, Aileen; Pratt, Purnell; Tucker, Richard

**Song(s)** Puttin' on the Ritz; With You; Alice in Wonderland; There's Danger in Your Eyes, Cherie (C/L: Richman, Harry; Meskill, Jack; Wendling, Pete)

# Q

## 4756 ◆ QUADROPHENIA
World Northal, 1979

**Producer(s)**   Baird, Roy; Curbishley, Bill
**Director(s)**   Roddam, Franc
**Screenwriter(s)**   Humphries, Dave; Stellman, Martin; Roddam, Franc

**Cast**   Daniels, Phil; Wingett, Mark; Davis, Philip; Ash, Leslie; Cooper, Garry; Wilcox, Toyah; Sting; Laird, Trevor; Barrie, Amanda

**Song(s)**   Get Out and Stay Out (C/L: Townsend, Pete); Love Reign Over Me (C/L: Townsend, Pete)

**Notes**   No cue sheet available.

## 4757 ◆ QUANTEZ
Universal, 1957

**Musical Score**   Stein, Herman

**Producer(s)**   Kay, Gordon
**Director(s)**   Keller, Harry
**Screenwriter(s)**   Campbell, R. Wright

**Cast**   MacMurray, Fred; Malone, Dorothy; Barton, James; Chaplin, Sydney; Gavin, John; Larch, John; Ansara, Michael

**Song(s)**   True Love (C: Hughes, Arnold; L: Herbert, Frederick)

## 4758 ◆ THE QUARTERBACK
Paramount, 1940

**Producer(s)**   Veiller, Anthony
**Director(s)**   Humberstone, H. Bruce
**Screenwriter(s)**   Pirosh, Robert

**Cast**   Morris, Wayne; Dale, Virginia; Frawley, William

**Song(s)**   (There I Go Again) Sentimental Me [1] (C: Mann, Paul; Weiss, Stephan; L: Lawrence, Jack); Out with Your Chest and Up with Your Chin (C: Malneck, Matty; L: Loesser, Frank)

**Notes**   Originally titled TOUCHDOWN. [1] Ned Washington wrote one chorus about getting an urge again and being a victim of that thing called love so he should beware but he doesn't care.

## 4759 ◆ QUARTET
New World, 1982

**Musical Score**   Robbins, Richard

**Producer(s)**   Merchant, Ismail; Mahot de la Querantonnais, J.P.
**Director(s)**   Ivory, James
**Screenwriter(s)**   Jhabvala, Ruth Prawer
**Source(s)**   *Quartet* (novel) Rhys, Jean

**Cast**   Bates, Alan; Smith, Maggie; Adjani, Isabelle; Higgins, Anthony; McQueen, Armelia; Chatto, Daniel; Clement, Pierre

**Song(s)**   9:05 (C/L: Robbins, Richard); Full Time Lover (C/L: Robbins, Richard)

**Notes**   No cue sheet available.

## 4760 ◆ QUEEN HIGH
Paramount, 1930

**Producer(s)**   Mandel, Frank; Schwab, Laurence
**Director(s)**   Newmeyer, Fred
**Screenwriter(s)**   Mandel, Frank
**Source(s)**   *Queen High!* (musical) Gensler, Lewis E.; DeSylva, B.G.; Schwab, Laurence

**Cast**   Ruggles, Charles; Morgan, Frank; Smith, Stanley; Rogers, Ginger; Carrington, Helen

**Song(s)**   It Seems to Me (C: Rainger, Ralph; L: Howard, Dick [1]); Brother, Just Laugh It Off [3] (C: Schwartz, Arthur; Rainger, Ralph; L: Harburg, E.Y.); I'm Afraid of You [4] (C: Schwartz, Arthur; L: Eliscu, Edward); I Love the Girls in My Own Peculiar Way (C: Souvaine, Henry; L: Harburg, E.Y.); Everything Will Happen for the Best [2] (C: Gensler, Lewis E.; L: Rose, Billy)

**Notes**   These credits, which differ from sheets which credit Schwartz and Rainger for all compositions, are per a letter from Rainger to Paramount on July 8, 1930. [1] Dick Howard is a pseudonym for Howard Dietz. [2] Not on cue sheet. [3] Also in FOLLOW THE LEADER, on which cue sheet Rainger is not listed. [4] Rainger credited on sheet music though not on cue sheet. See explanation above.

## 4761 ✦ QUEEN OF SPIES

See JOAN OF OZARK.

## 4762 ✦ QUEEN OF THE NIGHT CLUBS
### Warner Brothers, 1929

**Director(s)**   Foy, Bryan
**Screenwriter(s)**   Burkhart, Addison; Roth, Murray

**Cast**   Guinan, Texas; Davidson, William B.; Foy Jr., Eddie; Lee, Lila; Norworth, Jack; Davidson, John; Miljan, John; Housman, Arthur; Merriam, Charlotte; Raft, George

**Song(s)**   It's Tough to Be a Hostess on Broadway (C/L: Unknown)

**Notes**   No cue sheet available.

## 4763 ✦ THE QUEEN'S AFFAIR

See THE RUNAWAY QUEEN.

## 4764 ✦ QUICK MILLIONS
### Fox, 1931

**Director(s)**   Brown, Rowland
**Screenwriter(s)**   Terrell, Courtney; Brown, Rowland; Wray, John

**Cast**   Tracy, Spencer; Churchill, Marguerite; Eilers, Sally; Wray, John; Raft, George

**Song(s)**   Up the River Blues (C/L: Burns, Robert)

## 4765 ✦ QUICKSILVER
### Columbia, 1986

**Musical Score**   Banks, Tony

**Producer(s)**   Rachmil, Michael; Melnick, Daniel
**Director(s)**   Donnelly, Tom
**Screenwriter(s)**   Donnelly, Tom

**Cast**   Bacon, Kevin; Gertz, Jami; Rodriguez, Paul; Ramos, Rudy; Smith, Andrew; Anderson, Louis

**Song(s)**   Nothing at All (C/L: Frampton, Peter); Casual Thing (C/L: Willis, Allee; Melnick, Peter R.; Mathieson, Greg); One Sunny Day (C/L: Pitchford, Dean; Wolfer, Bill); Quicksilver Lighting (C: Moroder, Giorgio; L: Pitchford, Dean); Through the Night (Love Theme from Quicksilver) (C/L: Parr, John; Lyth, Geoff)

## 4766 ✦ QUIET COOL
### New Line, 1986

**Musical Score**   Ferguson, Jay

**Producer(s)**   Shaye, Robert; Olson, Gerald T.
**Director(s)**   Borris, Clay
**Screenwriter(s)**   Borris, Clay; Vercellino, Susan

**Cast**   Remar, James; Coleman-Howard, Adam; Ashbrook, Daphne; Cassavetes, Nick

**Song(s)**   California Dreaming (C/L: Phillips, John; Gilliam, Michelle); Quiet Cool (C: Ferguson, Jay; L: Lamont, Joe)

**Notes**   No cue sheet available.

## 4767 ✦ THE QUILLER MEMORANDUM
### Twentieth Century–Fox, 1966

**Musical Score**   Barry, John

**Producer(s)**   Foxwell, Ivan
**Director(s)**   Anderson, Michael
**Screenwriter(s)**   Pinter, Harold
**Source(s)**   *The Berlin Memorandum* (novel) Hall, Adam

**Cast**   Segal, George; Guinness, Alec; Von Sydow, Max; Berger, Senta; Sanders, George; Helpmann, Robert

**Song(s)**   Wednesday's Child (C: Barry, John; L: David, Mack)

## 4768 ✦ QUILP
### Reader's Digest, 1975

**Composer(s)**   Newley, Anthony
**Lyricist(s)**   Newley, Anthony
**Choreographer(s)**   Lynne, Gillian

**Producer(s)**   Strauss, Helen M.
**Director(s)**   Tuchner, Michael
**Screenwriter(s)**   Kamp, Irene; Kamp, Louis
**Source(s)**   *The Old Curiousity Shop* (novel) Dickens, Charles

**Cast**   Newley, Anthony; Hemmings, David; Warner, David; Hordern, Michael; Rogers, Paul; Bennett, Jill; Washbourne, Mona; Varley, Sara Jane; Webb, Sarah

**Song(s)**   Quilp; Somewhere; Happiness Pie; The Sport of Kings; Every Dog Has Its Day; When a Felon Needs a Friend; Love Has the Longest Memory; Unsong

**Notes**   Also titled MR. QUILP and THE OLD CURIOUSITY SHOP.

# R

### 4769 ✦ RABBIT RUN
Warner Brothers, 1970

**Producer(s)**   Kreitsek, Howard B.
**Director(s)**   Smight, Jack
**Screenwriter(s)**   Kreitsek, Howard B.
**Source(s)**   *Rabbit Run* (novel) Updike, John

**Cast**   Caan, James; Comer, Anjanette; Albertson, Jack; Snodgress, Carrie; Hill, Arthur; Johnson, Melodie; James, Henry; Matthews, Carmen; Vincent, Virginia; Kercheval, Ken

**Song(s)**   Hey Man (C/L: Burton, R.; King, B.; Gregory, M.K.); For Your Love (C/L: Townsend, Ed); You're Gonna Love Me (C/L: Burton, R.; Michael, G.K.)

**Notes**   All background vocals.

### 4770 ✦ RACE FOR YOUR LIFE, CHARLIE BROWN
Paramount, 1977

**Producer(s)**   Melendez, Bill; Mendelson, Lee
**Director(s)**   Melendez, Bill
**Screenwriter(s)**   Schulz, Charles M.
**Source(s)**   *Peanuts* (comic strip) Schulz, Charles M.

**Song(s)**   The Greatest Leader (C: Bogas, Ed; L: Mendelson, Lee); Race for Your Life, Charlie Brown (C/L: Bogas, Ed)

**Notes**   Animated feature.

### 4771 ✦ THE RACERS
Twentieth Century–Fox, 1955

**Musical Score**   North, Alex

**Producer(s)**   Blaustein, Julian
**Director(s)**   Hathaway, Henry
**Screenwriter(s)**   Kaufman, Charles
**Source(s)**   *The Racer* (novel) Ruesch, Hans

**Cast**   Douglas, Kirk; Darvi, Bella; Roland, Gilbert; Romero, Cesar; Cobb, Lee J.; Jurado, Katy; Goldner, Charles

**Song(s)**   I Belong to You (C: North, Alex; L: Brooks, Jack)

### 4772 ✦ RACE STREET
RKO, 1948

**Musical Score**   Webb, Roy
**Choreographer(s)**   O'Curran, Charles

**Producer(s)**   Holt, Nat
**Director(s)**   Marin, Edwin L.
**Screenwriter(s)**   Rackin, Martin

**Cast**   Raft, George; Bendix, William; Maxwell, Marilyn; Faylen, Frank; Morgan, Henry; Robbins, Gale; Richards, Tully; Hicks, Russell

**Song(s)**   I Saw You First [1] (C: McHugh, Jimmy; L: Adamson, Harold); I'm in a Jam with Baby [2] (C: Heindorf, Ray; Jerome, M.K.; L: Koehler, Ted); Love That Boy (C: de Paul, Gene; L: Raye, Don)

**Notes**   [1] Also in DING DONG WILLIAMS and HIGHER AND HIGHER. [2] Also in LOVE AND LEARN (Warner).

### 4773 ✦ RACE WITH THE DEVIL
Twentieth Century–Fox, 1975

**Musical Score**   Rosenman, Leonard

**Producer(s)**   Bishop, Wes
**Director(s)**   Starrett, Jack
**Screenwriter(s)**   Bishop, Wes; Frost, Lee

**Cast**   Fonda, Peter; Oates, Warren; Swit, Loretta; Parker, Lara; Armstrong, R.G.; Blodgett, Carol

**Song(s)**   Never on Credit (Living on Credit) (C/L: Rabin, Buzz; Johnson, J.H.)

### 4774 ✦ RACHEL AND THE STRANGER
RKO, 1954

**Musical Score**   Webb, Roy
**Composer(s)**   Webb, Roy
**Lyricist(s)**   Salt, Waldo

**Producer(s)**   Berger, Richard H.
**Director(s)**   Foster, Norman
**Screenwriter(s)**   Salt, Waldo
**Source(s)**   "Rachel" (story) Fast, Howard

**Cast**   Young, Loretta; Holden, William; Mitchum, Robert; Gray, Gary; Tully, Tom

**Song(s)** Just Like Me; Oh He Oh Hi Oh·Ho; Summer Song; Along Came a Tall Dark Stranger; Foolish Pride; Rachel [1]

**Notes** [1] Used instrumentally only.

## 4775 ✦ RACHEL, RACHEL
### Warner Brothers, 1968

**Musical Score** Moross, Jerome
**Composer(s)** Moross, Jerome
**Lyricist(s)** Stern, Stewart

**Producer(s)** Newman, Paul
**Director(s)** Newman, Paul
**Screenwriter(s)** Stern, Stewart
**Source(s)** *A Jest of God* (novel) Laurence, Margaret

**Cast** Woodward, James; Olson, James; Harrington, Kate; Parsons, Estelle; Moffat, Donald; Kiser, Terry; Corsaro, Frank; Barrow, Bernard; Fitzgerald, Geraldine; Potts, Nell; Singer, Izzy

**Song(s)** Lazy Mary Will You Get Up? (C: Traditional); Rachel's Song [1] ; Love and Kisses; Make Me Care; Tabernacle Hymn [1]

**Notes** [1] Visual vocals.

## 4776 ✦ RACING BLOOD
### Twentieth Century–Fox, 1954

**Musical Score** Kay, Edward J.
**Composer(s)** Rose, Earl
**Lyricist(s)** Russell, Hilda; Schneider, Dave

**Producer(s)** Barry, Wesley
**Director(s)** Barry, Wesley
**Screenwriter(s)** Rocca, Sam

**Cast** Williams, Bill; Porter, Jean; Boyd, Jimmy; Cleveland, George; Eldredge, John; Flint, Sam

**Song(s)** Fa-La Link-A-Di-Do (Three String Guitar) (L: Russell, Hilda); Pardners

## 4777 ✦ THE RACKET
### RKO, 1951

**Musical Score** Sawtell, Paul; Webb, Roy

**Producer(s)** Grainger, Edmund
**Director(s)** Milestone, Lewis
**Screenwriter(s)** Haines, William Wister; Burnett, W.R.
**Source(s)** *The Racket* (play) Cormack, Bartlett

**Cast** Mitchum, Robert; Ryan, Robert; Scott, Lizabeth; Talman, William; Collins, Ray; MacKenzie, Joyce; Hutton, Robert; Huston, Virginia; Conrad, William; Porter, Don; Tremayne, Les

**Song(s)** A Lovely Way to Spend an Evening [1] (C: McHugh, Jimmy; L: Adamson, Harold)

**Notes** [1] Originally in HIGHER AND HIGHER.

## 4778 ✦ RACKETEERS OF THE RANGE
### RKO, 1939

**Musical Score** Webb, Roy

**Producer(s)** Marcus, Lee
**Director(s)** Lederman, D. Ross
**Screenwriter(s)** Drake, Oliver

**Cast** O'Brien, George; Wills, Chill; Reynolds, Marjorie; Seabrook, Gay; Fiskie, Robert; Dilson, John; Montague, Monte; Whitley, Ray; Marvin, Frankie

**Song(s)** The Guy That Shook Hands with Buffalo Bill (C/L: Wills, Chill); Sleepy Wrangler (C/L: Whitley, Ray); Caboose on the Red Ball Train (C/L: Whitley, Ray)

## 4779 ✦ RACKETY RAX
### Fox, 1932

**Composer(s)** Hanley, James F.
**Lyricist(s)** Gilbert, L. Wolfe

**Director(s)** Werker, Alfred
**Screenwriter(s)** Markson, Ben; Breslow, Lou

**Cast** McLaglen, Victor; Nissen, Greta; O'Day, Nell; Dinehart, Alan

**Song(s)** Old Soldiers Never Die [1] (C/L: Conrad, Con; Gottler, Archie; Mitchell, Sidney D.); The Puce and the Green; Rackety Rax

**Notes** [1] Also in WHY LEAVE HOME? See note under that film.

## 4780 ✦ RADIO CITY REVELS
### RKO, 1938

**Composer(s)** Magidson, Herb
**Lyricist(s)** Wrubel, Allie
**Choreographer(s)** Pan, Hermes

**Producer(s)** Kaufman, Edward
**Director(s)** Stoloff, Benjamin
**Screenwriter(s)** Davis, Eddie; Brooks, Matt; Veiller, Anthony; Offner, Mortimer

**Cast** Burns, Bob; Oakie, Jack; Baker, Kenny; Miller, Ann; Moore, Victor; Berle, Milton; Broderick, Helen; Froman, Jane; West, Buster; Mason, Melissa; Hal Kemp and His Orchestra

**Song(s)** Take a Tip from the Tulip; I'm Taking a Shine to You; There's a New Moon Over the Old Mill; Speak Your Heart; You're the Apple of My Eye; Swingin' in the Corn; Morning Glories in the Moonlight; Goodnight Angel; Love Honor and Oh Baby; Why Must I Love You; The Miller's Four Daughters (C/L: Vass; Dreyer, Dave)

**Notes** The musical production numbers were directed by Joseph Santley.

## 4781  ◆  RADIO STARS ON PARADE
RKO, 1945

**Musical Score**  Webb, Roy
**Composer(s)**  McHugh, Jimmy
**Lyricist(s)**  Adamson, Harold

**Producer(s)**  Stoloff, Ben
**Director(s)**  Goodwins, Leslie
**Screenwriter(s)**  Kent, Robert E.; Brice, Monte

**Cast**  Brown, Wally; Carney, Alan; Langford, Frances; Edwards, Ralph; Skinnay Ennis and His Band; Wilson, Don; Romano, Tony; The Town Criers; The Cappy Barra Boys; Davis, Rufe; Clarke, Robert; Leonard, Sheldon; Wagner, Max; Peters, Ralph

**Song(s)**  Can't Get Out of This Mood [2] (L: Loesser, Frank); Don't Believe Everything You Dream [1]; I Couldn't Sleep a Wink Last Night [4]; My Shining Hour [7] (C: Arlen, Harold; L: Mercer, Johnny); I'm the Sound Effects Man [5] (C: "Jock" [6]; L: Gray, George); Heavenly, Isn't It [3] (C: Revel, Harry; L: Greene, Mort); That Old Black Magic [8] (C: Arlen, Harold; L: Mercer, Johnny)

**Notes**  [1] Also in AROUND THE WORLD. [2] Also in SEVEN DAYS LEAVE. [3] Written for THE MAYOR OF 44TH STREET but only used instrumentally. [4] Also in BEAT THE BAND and HIGHER AND HIGHER. [5] Also in THIS WAY PLEASE (Paramount). [6] Pseudonym for Jack Rock. [7] Also in THE SKY'S THE LIMIT. [8] Also in the Paramount films HERE COME THE WAVES and STAR-SPANGLED RHYTHM and SENIOR PROM (Columbia).

## 4782  ◆  RAGE TO LIVE
United Artists, 1965

**Musical Score**  Riddle, Nelson

**Producer(s)**  Rachmil, Lewis J.
**Director(s)**  Grauman, Walter
**Screenwriter(s)**  Kelley, John T.

**Cast**  Pleshette, Suzanne; Dillman, Bradford; Gazzara, Ben; Graves, Peter; Leslie, Bethel; Gregory, James

**Song(s)**  Rage to Live (C: Ferrante and Teicher; L: Sherman, Noel)

## 4783  ◆  RAGGEDY ANN AND RAGGEDY ANDY
Paramount, 1941

**Composer(s)**  Timberg, Sammy
**Lyricist(s)**  Neiburg, Al J.; Fleischer, Dave

**Producer(s)**  Fleischer, Max

**Song(s)**  You're a Nobody Without a Name; You're a Calico Millionaire; Raggedy Ann (I Love You); No Speak 'Merican

**Notes**  Short. No cue sheet available. Sheet music only.

## 4784  ◆  RAGS TO RICHES
Republic, 1941

**Musical Score**  Glickman, Mort
**Composer(s)**  Styne, Jule
**Lyricist(s)**  Meyer, Sol

**Producer(s)**  Kane, Joseph
**Director(s)**  Kane, Joseph
**Screenwriter(s)**  Webb, James R.

**Cast**  Baxter, Alan; Carlisle, Mary; Cowan, Jerome; Morris, Michael; Harolde, Ralf; Acuff, Eddie

**Song(s)**  Never Never Never; Magnolias in the Moonlight [1] (C: Schertzinger, Victor; L: Bullock, Walter); Call of Love

**Notes**  [1] Also in FOLLOW YOUR HEART.

## 4785  ◆  RAGTIME
Paramount, 1981

**Musical Score**  Newman, Randy

**Producer(s)**  De Laurentiis, Dino
**Director(s)**  Forman, Milos
**Screenwriter(s)**  Weller, Michael
**Source(s)**  *Ragtime* (novel) Doctorow, E.L.

**Cast**  Cagney, James; Dourif, Brad; Gunn, Moses; McGovern, Elizabeth; McMillan, Kenneth; O'Brien, Pat; O'Connor, Donald; Olson, James; Patinkin, Mandy; Rollins Jr., Howard E.; Steenburgen, Mary; Allen, Debbie; DeMunn, Jeffrey; Joy, Robert; Mailer, Norman; Daniels, Jeff; Drescher, Fran; Faison, Frankie; Jeter, Michael; Levels, Calvin; Norman, Zack; Ross, Ted; Wright, Dorsey

**Song(s)**  One More Hour (C/L: Newman, Randy); Change Your Ways (C/L: Newman, Randy)

**Notes**  No cue sheet available.

## 4786  ◆  RAH! RAH! RAH!
Publix, 1929

**Song(s)**  More Than Anybody (I Love You) (C/L: Porter, Del)

**Notes**  No cue sheet available. Sheet music only.

## 4787  ◆  RAIDERS OF SAN JOAQUIN
Universal, 1942

**Producer(s)**  Drake, Oliver
**Director(s)**  Collins, Lewis D.
**Screenwriter(s)**  Cox, Morgan B.; Clifton, Elmer

**Cast**  Brown, Johnny Mack; Ritter, Tex; Knight, Fuzzy

**Song(s)**  I'd Rather Be Footloose and Fancy Free [1] (C/L: Drake, Oliver); A Carefree Cowboy (C: Rosen,

Milton; L: Drake, Oliver; Wakely, Jimmy); The Hatches and the Morgans (C/L: Drake, Oliver)

**Notes** [1] The RKO film ARIZONA LEGION has an Oliver Drake song titled "I'd Rather Be Footloose than Free." Could it be the same song?

### 4788 ✦ RAIDERS OF SUNSET PASS
Republic, 1943

**Producer(s)** Gray, Louis
**Director(s)** English, John
**Screenwriter(s)** Butler, John K.

**Cast** Revere, John Paul [1]; Burnette, Smiley; Holt, Jennifer; Mason, LeRoy; Barcroft, Roy; Doyle, Maxine; Kirk, Jack; Duncan, Kenneth

**Song(s)** Who'd a Thunk It? (C/L: Burnette, Smiley)

**Notes** [1] Eddie Dew.

### 4789 ✦ RAIDERS OF THE RANGE
Republic, 1942

**Producer(s)** Gray, Louis
**Director(s)** English, John
**Screenwriter(s)** Shipman, Barry

**Cast** Tyler, Tom; Steele, Bob; Davis, Rufe; Phipps, Charles

**Song(s)** Whistle of the Five Twenty-Seven (C: Kraushaar, Raoul; L: Meyer, Sol)

### 4790 ✦ RAIDERS OF TOMAHAWK CREEK
Columbia, 1950

**Composer(s)** Burnette, Smiley
**Lyricist(s)** Burnette, Smiley

**Producer(s)** Clark, Colbert
**Director(s)** Sears, Fred F.
**Screenwriter(s)** Shipman, Barry

**Cast** Starrett, Charles; Burnette, Smiley; Dearing, Edgar; Buckley, Kay; McGuire, Paul

**Song(s)** I'm Too Smart for That; The Grasshopper Polka

### 4791 ✦ RAILROADED (1947)
Eagle Lion, 1947

**Musical Score** Levin, Alvin

**Producer(s)** Riesner, Charles F.
**Director(s)** Mann, Anthony
**Screenwriter(s)** Higgins, John C.

**Cast** Ireland, John; Ryan, Sheila; Beaumont, Hugh; Kelly, Ed; Randolph, Jane; Brasselle, Keefe

**Song(s)** Tell Me (C: Kernell, William; L: Ferris, Don)

### 4792 ✦ RAILS INTO LARAMIE
Universal, 1954

**Musical Score** Stein, Herman

**Producer(s)** Richmond, Ted
**Director(s)** Hibbs, Jesse
**Screenwriter(s)** Beauchamp, D.D.; Hoffman, Joseph

**Cast** Payne, John; Duryea, Dan; Blanchard, Mari; Van Cleef, Lee; MacLane, Barton; MacKenzie, Joyce

**Song(s)** Laramie [1] (C: Hughes, Arnold; L: Herbert, Frederick)

**Notes** Frankie Lee also credited on sheet music.

### 4793 ✦ THE RAINBOW (1930)
Tiffany, 1930

**Cast** Sebastian, Dorothy; Gray, Lawrence

**Song(s)** The Song of Gold (C: Monaco, James V.; L: Leslie, Edgar)

**Notes** No cue sheet available.

### 4794 ✦ RAINBOW BRITE AND THE STAR STEALER
Warner Brothers, 1985

**Producer(s)** Chalopin, Jean; Heyward, Andy; Katayama, Tetsuo
**Director(s)** Deyries, Bernard; Yabuki, Kimio
**Screenwriter(s)** Cohen, Howard
**Voices** Bettina; Fraley, Patrick; Cullen, Peter; Lee, Robbie; Stojka, Andre; Aldrich, Rhonda; Tremayne, Les; Mendenhall, David

**Song(s)** "Opening Song" (C/L: Saban, Haim; Levy, Shuki; Cohen, Howard); Rainbow Brite and Me (C/L: Saban, Haim; Levy, Shuki; Cohen, Howard)

**Notes** Animated feature.

### 4795 ✦ RAINBOW ISLAND
Paramount, 1944

**Musical Score** Webb, Roy
**Composer(s)** Lane, Burton
**Lyricist(s)** Koehler, Ted
**Choreographer(s)** Dare, Danny

**Producer(s)** Leshin, E.D.
**Director(s)** Murphy, Ralph
**Screenwriter(s)** De Leon, Walter; Phillips, Arthur

**Cast** Lamour, Dorothy; Sullivan, Barry; Bracken, Eddie; Lamb, Gil; Revere, Anne; Lawrence, Marc; San Juan, Olga; De Carlo, Yvonne

**Song(s)** What a Day; Beloved (Aloha - Nui - Ia); Boogie Woogie Boogie Man; Tomorrow; We Have So Little Time [1]; Drum Dance (C: Webb, Roy; L: Stewart, Dan K.); New Moon [2]

**Notes** "The Drum Dance" lyrics are pidgen native noises. There are also some chants by Augie Goupil which are not really songs. [1] Presented instrumentally only. [2] Not used.

## 4796 ✦ THE RAINBOW MAN
### Paramount, 1929

**Composer(s)** Hanley, James F.
**Lyricist(s)** Dowling, Eddie

**Producer(s)** Weeks, George W.
**Director(s)** Newmeyer, Fred
**Screenwriter(s)** Crone, George J.

**Cast** Dowling, Eddie; Nixon, Marian; Darro, Frankie; Hardy, Sam; Ingraham, Lloyd; Hayes, George "Gabby"

**Song(s)** Rainbow Man; Sleepy Valley (L: Sterling, Andrew B.); Little Pal; Tambourine Tune [1]

**Notes** *Variety* lists this as a Sono-Art picture. [1] Sheet music only.

## 4797 ✦ RAINBOW ON THE RIVER
### RKO, 1936

**Producer(s)** Lesser, Sol
**Director(s)** Neumann, Kurt
**Screenwriter(s)** Hurlbut, William; Chandlee, Harry
**Source(s)** *Toinette's Philip* (novel) Jamison, C.V.

**Cast** Breen, Bobby; Robson, May; Butterworth, Charles; Beavers, Louise; Mowbray, Alan; Hume, Benita; O'Neill, Henry; Beard, Stymie; Anderson, Eddie "Rochester"; The Hall Johnson Choir

**Song(s)** Flower Song (C: Riesenfeld, Hugo; L: Hautzik, Selma); Waitin' for the Sun to Rise (C: Hajos, Karl; L: Swanstrom, Arthur); Rainbow on the River (C: Alter, Louis; L: Webster, Paul Francis)

**Notes** There are also vocals of "Camptown Races," "Old Folks at Home" and "Ring Ring de Banjo" by Stephen Foster; "Holy, Holy, Holy;" "Ave Maria" and "Hymn" from STRADELLA by Von Flotow.

## 4798 ✦ RAINBOW OVER TEXAS
### Republic, 1946

**Composer(s)** Elliott, Jack
**Lyricist(s)** Elliott, Jack

**Producer(s)** White, Edward J.
**Director(s)** McDonald, Frank
**Screenwriter(s)** Geraghty, Gerald
**Source(s)** "Senor Coyote" (story) Brand, Max

**Cast** Rogers, Roy; Trigger; Hayes, George "Gabby"; Evans, Dale; Leonard, Sheldon; Keane, Robert Emmett; Duncan, Kenne; Urecal, Minerva

**Song(s)** Lights of Old Santa Fe [1]; Little Senorita; Cowboy Camp Meeting (C/L: Forster, Gordon); Ridin'

Down the Sunset Trail [3]; Rainbow Over Texas [2]; Outlaw; Texas, U.S.A. (C/L: Forster, Gordon)

**Notes** [1] Also in LIGHTS OF OLD SANTA FE. [2] Also in SPOILERS OF THE PLAINS. [3] Also in OUT CALIFORNIA WAY.

## 4799 ✦ RAINBOW OVER THE RANGE
### Monogram, 1940

**Musical Score** Wilcox, Art

**Producer(s)** Finney, Edward
**Director(s)** Herman, Al
**Screenwriter(s)** Lynch, Rolland; Emmett, Robert; Morton, Roger

**Cast** Ritter, Tex; Richmond, Warner; Pierce, Jim; Ray, Dorothy; Morrison, Chuck; Moore, Dennis; Andrews, Lloyd "Slim"; Lorber, Steve

**Song(s)** Rainbow Over the Range (C/L: Allan, Fleming); Poor Slim (C: Lange, Johnny; L: Porter, Lew)

**Notes** No cue sheet available.

## 4800 ✦ RAINBOW 'ROUND MY SHOULDER
### Columbia, 1952

**Choreographer(s)** Scott, Lee

**Producer(s)** Taps, Jonie
**Director(s)** Quine, Richard
**Screenwriter(s)** Edwards, Blake; Quine, Richard

**Cast** Laine, Frankie; Daniels, Billy; Austin, Charlotte [2]; Franz, Arthur; Moore, Ida; Corrigan, Lloyd

**Song(s)** Wonderful Wasn't It (C: Rodney, Don; L: David, Hal); Girl in the Wood (C/L: Stuart, Neal; Gilkyson, Terry); Bubble, Bubble, Bubble [3] (C/L: Wright, Robert; Forrest, George)

**Notes** There are also vocals of "Ain't Misbehavin'" by Thomas "Fats" Waller, Harry Brooks and Andy Razaf; "She's Funny That Way" by Richard A. Whiting and Neil Moret; "Bye Bye Blackbird" by Ray Henderson and Mort Dixon and "Rainbow 'Round My Shoulder" by Dave Dreyer, Al Jolson and Billy Rose. [2] Dubbed by Jo Ann Greer. [3] Sheet music only.

## 4801 ✦ RAINBOW TRAIL
### Fox, 1932

**Director(s)** Howard, David
**Screenwriter(s)** Connors, Barry; Klein, Philip
**Source(s)** "Rainbow Trail" (story) Grey, Zane

**Cast** O'Brien, George; Parker, Cecilia; Gombell, Minna; Ates, Roscoe; Kerrigan, J.M.; Kirkwood, James

**Song(s)** My Wife Does Fancy Work [1] (C: Friedhofer, Hugo; Tresselt, Frank; L: Connors, Barry; Hanley, James F.)

**Notes** [1] The lyrics for the first rendition are credited to Barry Connors, the second time through the cue sheet credits James F. Hanley.

## 4802 ✦ THE RAINMAKER
### Paramount, 1956

**Musical Score** North, Alex

**Producer(s)** Wallis, Hal B.
**Director(s)** Anthony, Joseph [1]
**Screenwriter(s)** Nash, N. Richard
**Source(s)** *The Rainmaker* (play) Nash, N. Richard

**Cast** Lancaster, Burt; Hepburn, Katharine; Corey, Wendell; Bridges, Lloyd; Holliman, Earl; Prud'homme, Cameron; Ford, Wallace

**Song(s)** The Rainmaker [2] (C: North, Alex; L: David, Hal)

**Notes** [1] Director of original play and also subsequent Broadway musical 110 IN THE SHADE. [2] Used instrumentally only.

## 4803 ✦ THE RAINMAKERS
### RKO, 1935

**Musical Score** Webb, Roy

**Producer(s)** Marcus, Lee
**Director(s)** Guiol, Fred
**Screenwriter(s)** Garrett, Grant; Goodwins, Leslie

**Cast** Wheeler, Bert; Woolsey, Robert; Lee, Dorothy; Churchill, Berton; Meeker, George

**Song(s)** Isn't Love the Grandest Thing (C: Alter, Louis; L: Scholl, Jack)

## 4804 ✦ RAIN MAN
### United Artists, 1988

**Musical Score** Zimmer, Hans

**Producer(s)** Johnson, Mark
**Director(s)** Levinson, Barry
**Screenwriter(s)** Bass, Ronald; Morrow, Barry

**Cast** Hoffman, Dustin; Cruise, Tom; Golino, Valeria; Molen, Jerry; Murdock, Jack; Levinson, Barry

**Song(s)** I Like to Sing (C/L: Mattingly, Matt); Please Love Me Forever (C/L: Malone, Johnny; Blanchard, Ollie); Lonely Avenue (C/L: Pomus, Doc); Wishful Thinking (C/L: Marcellino, Jocko; Handley, Randy); Lonely Women Make Good Lovers (C/L: Weller, Freddy; Olkham, Spooner); Lovin' Ain't So Hard to Find (C/L: Marcellino, Jocko); Nathan Jones (C/L: Caston, Leonard; Wakefield, Kathy)

**Notes** It is not known if any of the above were written for this film.

## 4805 ✦ RAIN OR SHINE
### Columbia, 1930

**Director(s)** Capra, Frank
**Screenwriter(s)** Howell, Dorothy; Swerling, Jo
**Source(s)** *Rain or Shine* (musical) Gleason, James; Marks, Maurice

**Cast** Cook, Joe; Chasen, Dave; Howard, Tom; Fazenda, Louise; Muse, Clarence; Martindel, Edward

**Song(s)** Rain or Shine [1] (C: Ager, Milton; L: Yellen, Jack); Happy Days Are Here Again [1] [2] (C: Ager, Milton; L: Yellen, Jack)

**Notes** There are also vocals of "It Ain't Gonna Rain No More" by W. Woods Hall; "Keep Your Sunnyside Up" by Ray Henderson, Lew Brown and B.G. DeSylva; "Sitting on a Rainbow" by Dan Daugherty and Jack Yellen (sung in CALL OF THE WEST but whistled in this picture). [1] Not on cue sheet. [2] Also in CHASING RAINBOWS (MGM).

## 4806 ✦ THE RAINS CAME
### Twentieth Century–Fox, 1939

**Musical Score** Newman, Alfred
**Composer(s)** Mehra, Lal Chand
**Lyricist(s)** Mehra, Lal Chand

**Producer(s)** Brown, Harry Joe
**Director(s)** Brown, Clarence
**Screenwriter(s)** Dunne, Philip; Josephson, Julien
**Source(s)** *The Rains Came [2]* (novel) Bromfield, Louis

**Cast** Loy, Myrna; Power, Tyrone; Brent, George; Joyce, Brenda; Bruce, Nigel; Ouspenskaya, Maria; Schildkraut, Joseph; Nash, Mary; Darwell, Jane; Rambeau, Marjorie; Travers, Henry; Warner, H.B.; Crews, Laura Hope

**Song(s)** Students' Song; Hindu Song of Love [1]; Hindu Death Chant; The Rains Came [3] (C/L: Gordon, Mack)

**Notes** [1] Also in THE SECRET GARDEN (MGM). Philip Dunne may have contributed some English lyrics. [2] Originally based on his own story titled "Bitter Lotus." [3] Written for exploitation only.

## 4807 ✦ RAINTREE COUNTY
### Metro–Goldwyn–Mayer, 1958

**Musical Score** Green, Johnny

**Producer(s)** Dmytryk, Edward
**Director(s)** Lewis, David
**Screenwriter(s)** Kaufman, Millard
**Source(s)** *Raintree County* (novel) Lockridge Jr., Ross

**Cast** Clift, Montgomery; Taylor, Elizabeth; Saint, Eva Marie; Patrick, Nigel; Marvin, Lee; Taylor, Rod; Moorehead, Agnes; Abel, Walter; Lewis, Jarma; Drake, Tom; Williams, Rhys; Collins, Russell; Kelley, DeForest

**Song(s)** The Song of Raintree County (C: Green, Johnny; L: Webster, Paul Francis); Never Till Now [1] (C: Green, Johnny; Webster, Paul Francis)

**Notes** [1] Sheet music only.

### 4808 ✦ RAINY DAY FRIENDS
Powderdance, 1985

**Musical Score** Haskell, Jimmie

**Producer(s)** Barrett, Tomi; Boxer, Walter
**Director(s)** Kent, Gary
**Screenwriter(s)** Kent, Gary

**Cast** Morales, Esai; Bail, Chuck; Rule, Janice; Snodgress, Carrie; Goldoni, Lelia; Law, John Phillip

**Song(s)** Compromise (C/L: Hill, Kimberley; Harris, Jed); Ain't Got the Time (C/L: Hill, Kimberley; Harris, Jed); Rainy Day Friends (C/L: Kent, Gary)

**Notes** No cue sheet available.

### 4809 ✦ RAISING ARIZONA
Twentieth Century–Fox, 1986

**Musical Score** Nolan, Bob

**Producer(s)** Coen, Ethan
**Director(s)** Coen, Joel
**Screenwriter(s)** Coen, Ethan; Coen, Joel

**Cast** Cage, Nicolas; Hunter, Holly; Wilson, Trey; Goodman, John; Forsythe, William; McMurray, Sam; McDormand, Frances; Cobb, Randall "Tex"

**Song(s)** Leonard, Meine Kinder (C/L: Burwell, Carter)

### 4810 ✦ RALLY 'ROUND THE FLAG, BOYS!
Twentieth Century–Fox, 1958

**Musical Score** Mockridge, Cyril J.

**Producer(s)** McCarey, Leo
**Director(s)** McCarey, Leo
**Screenwriter(s)** Binyon, Claude; McCarey, Leo
**Source(s)** *Rally 'Round the Flag, Boys!* (novel) Shulman, Max

**Cast** Newman, Paul; Woodward, Joanne; Collins, Joan; Carson, Jack; Hickman, Dwayne; Weld, Tuesday; Gordon, Gale; Gilson, Tom; Whitehead, O.Z.

**Song(s)** You're My Boojum (C: Henderson, Charles; L: McCarey, Leo)

### 4811 ✦ RAMONA (1928)
United Artists, 1928

**Director(s)** Carewe, Edwin
**Screenwriter(s)** Fox, Finis
**Source(s)** *Ramona* (novel) Jackson, Helen Hunt

**Cast** Del Rio, Dolores; Baxter, Warner; Drew, Roland; Lewis, Vera; Visaroff, Michael; Prince, John T.

**Song(s)** Ramona (C: Wayne, Mabel; L: Gilbert, L. Wolfe); Dolores [1] (C/L: Grossman, Edward; Ward, Edward)

**Notes** No cue sheet available. This is a silent film with a theme song. [1] Used in REVENGE (UA) (1928).

### 4812 ✦ RAMONA (1936)
Twentieth Century–Fox, 1936

**Composer(s)** Kernell, William
**Lyricist(s)** Kernell, William

**Producer(s)** Wurtzel, Sol M.
**Director(s)** King, Henry
**Screenwriter(s)** Trotti, Lamar

**Cast** Young, Loretta; Ameche, Don; Taylor, Kent; Frederick, Pauline; Darwell, Jane; de Mille, Katherine; Carradine, John; de Cordoba, Pedro; Naish, J. Carrol; Killian, Victor

**Song(s)** Sunrise Hymn (Blessed Be the Dawning) [2]; Under the Redwood Tree [1]; How the Rabbit Lost His Tail [1]

**Notes** [1] Only a few lines each. [2] Also in SHOW THEM NO MERCY.

### 4813 ✦ RAMPAGE
Warner Brothers, 1963

**Musical Score** Bernstein, Elmer

**Producer(s)** Fadiman, William
**Director(s)** Karlson, Phil
**Screenwriter(s)** Holt, Robert I.; Roberts, Marguerite
**Source(s)** *Rampage* (novel) Caillou, Alan

**Cast** Mitchum, Robert; Martinelli, Elsa; Hawkins, Jack; Sabu; Carrillo, Cely; Genest, Emile; Schnabel, Stefan; Cadiente, David

**Song(s)** Big Cat (C: Bernstein, Elmer; L: David, Mack); Rampage [1] (C: Bernstein, Elmer; L: David, Mack)

**Notes** [1] Written for exploitation only.

### 4814 ✦ RANCHO DELUXE
United Artists, 1975

**Musical Score** Buffett, Jimmy
**Composer(s)** Buffett, Jimmy
**Lyricist(s)** Buffett, Jimmy

**Producer(s)** Kastner, Elliott
**Director(s)** Perry, Frank
**Screenwriter(s)** McGuane, Thomas

**Cast** Bridges, Jeff; Waterston, Sam; Ashley, Elizabeth; Dallas, Charlene; James, Clifton; Pickens, Slim; Stanton, Harry Dean; Bright, Richard

**Song(s)** Rancho Deluxe; Livingston Saturday Night; Las Vegas Glitter

## 4815 ✦ RANCHO NOTORIOUS
### RKO, 1951

**Musical Score** Newman, Emil

**Producer(s)** Welsch, Howard
**Director(s)** Lang, Fritz
**Screenwriter(s)** Taradash, Daniel

**Cast** Dietrich, Marlene; Kennedy, Arthur; Ferrer, Mel; Henry, Gloria; Frawley, William; Ferraday, Lisa; Reeves, George; Seymour, Dan; Raven, John

**Song(s)** The Legend of Chuck-A-Luck (C/L: Darby, Ken); Get Away Young Man (C/L: Darby, Ken); Gypsy Davey (C/L: Darby, Ken)


## 4816 ✦ RANGE BEYOND THE BLUE
### PRC, 1952

**Musical Score** Hajos, Karl

**Producer(s)** Thomas, Jerry
**Director(s)** Taylor, Ray
**Screenwriter(s)** Harper, Patricia

**Cast** Dean, Eddie; Ates, Roscoe; Mowery, Helen; Duncan, Bob; The Sunshine Boys

**Song(s)** West of the Pecos (C/L: Gates, V.W.); The Pony with the Uncombed Hair (C/L: Dean, Eddie; Blair, Hal); Range Beyond the Blue [1] (C/L: Dean, Eddie; Dean, Bob)

**Notes** [1] Used instrumentally only.


## 4817 ✦ THE RANGE BUSTERS
### Monogram, 1940

**Musical Score** Sanucci, Frank

**Producer(s)** Weeks, George W.
**Director(s)** Luby, S. Roy
**Screenwriter(s)** Rathmell, John

**Cast** Corrigan, Ray; King, John; Terhune, Max; Walters, Luana; Hodgins, Earl; Maynard, Kermit; Mason, Leroy; LaRue, Frank

**Song(s)** Get Along Cowboy (C: Lange, Johnny; L: Porter, Lew)


## 4818 ✦ RANGE DEFENDERS
### Republic, 1938

**Musical Score** Hajos, Karl

**Producer(s)** Siegel, Sol C.
**Director(s)** Wright, Mack V.
**Screenwriter(s)** Poland, Joseph
**Source(s)** *Hold That Range* (novel) MacDonald, William Colt

**Cast** Livingston, Robert; Corrigan, Ray; Terhune, Max; Stewart, Eleanor; Woods, Harry; Hodgins, Earl; Canutt, Yakima; Snowflake

**Song(s)** Give Me the Life of a Cowboy (C/L: Allan, Fleming)


## 4819 ✦ THE RANGER AND THE LADY
### Republic, 1940

**Producer(s)** Kane, Joseph
**Director(s)** Kane, Joseph
**Screenwriter(s)** Geraghty, Gerald

**Cast** Rogers, Roy; Hayes, George "Gabby"; Wells, Jacqueline; Canutt, Yakima

**Song(s)** Chiquita [1] (C/L: Tinturin, Peter); As Long As We Are Dancing (C/L: Tinturin, Peter)

**Notes** [1] Also in COMIN' ROUND THE MOUNTAIN (1936).


## 4820 ✦ RAPPIN'
### Cannon, 1985

**Producer(s)** Golan, Menahem; Globus, Yoram
**Director(s)** Silberg, Joel
**Screenwriter(s)** Litz, Robert; Friedman, Adam

**Cast** Van Peebles, Mario; Valenza, Tasia; Floye, Charles; O'Brien, Leo; La Salle, Eriq; Abanes, Richie; Hardison, Kadeem; Jaroslow, Ruth

**Song(s)** Snack Attack (C/L: Smith, Larry; Litz, Robert; Friedman, Adam; Van Peebles, Mario; Kobrin, Robert); Dodge (C/L: Smith, Larry); Golly Gee (C/L: Evans, J. Eric); Colors (C/L: Smith, Larry; Litz, Robert; Friedman, Adam; Van Peebles, Mario; O'Brien, Leo); Lady Alcohol (C/L: Smith, Larry; Van Peebles, Mario); First Love Never Dies (C/L: Sanders, Bonnie; Schwartz, Ellen; Maskelaris, Sue); The Game (C/L: Smith, Larry; Van Peebles, Mario); Fu 12 (C/L: Link, Peter); Courtroom (C/L: Smith, Larry; Litz, Robert; Friedman, Adam; La Salle, Eriq; Van Peebles, Mario); Finale (C/L: Smith, Larry; Litz, Robert; Friedman, Adam; Kobrin, Robert; Van Peebles, Mario)

**Notes** No cue sheet available.


## 4821 ✦ RAPTURE
### United Artists, 1950

**Musical Score** Rosati, Guiseppe

**Producer(s)** Palham, David M.
**Director(s)** Allessandrini, Goffredo
**Screenwriter(s)** Herczeg, Geza; Pelham, David M.; Shepbridge, John C.

**Cast** Langan, Glenn; Albin, Elsy; Miller, Lorraine; Dumbrille, Douglass; Ciannelli, Eduardo

**Song(s)** Eterno Ritornello (C/L: Bidoli, Bruno)

## 4822 ✦ RASCAL
Disney, 1969

**Musical Score** Baker, Buddy

**Producer(s)** Algar, James
**Director(s)** Tokar, Norman
**Screenwriter(s)** Swanton, Harold
**Source(s)** *Rascal* (novel) North, Sterling

**Cast** Forrest, Steve; Mumy, Billy [2]; Toll, Pamela; Lanchester, Elsa; Jones, Henry; Ackerman, Bettye; Daly, Jonathan; Fiedler, John; Carlson, Steve

**Song(s)** Summer Sweet (C/L: Russell, Bobby); Country Boy [1] (C/L: Gilkyson, Terry)

**Notes** [1] Not used. [2] Billed as Bill Mumy.

## 4823 ✦ RASCALS
Twentieth Century–Fox, 1938

**Composer(s)** Akst, Harry
**Lyricist(s)** Clare, Sidney

**Producer(s)** Stone, John
**Director(s)** Humberstone, H. Bruce
**Screenwriter(s)** Ellis, Robert; Logan, Helen

**Cast** Withers, Jane; Hudson, Rochelle; Wilcox, Robert; Borrah Minnevitch and His Gang; Duna, Steffi; Alexander, Katherine

**Song(s)** Carnival Song (Czardas) (What a Gay Occasion) [1] (C: Vecsei, Armand; L: Akst, Harry; Clare, Sidney); Take a Tip from a Gypsy; Blue Is the Evening; Song of the Gypsy Band

**Notes** [1] Also in EL REY DE LOS GITANOS and in NADA MAS QUE UNA MUJER with lyrics credited to L. Wolfe Gilbert.

## 4824 ✦ RATBOY
Warner Brothers, 1987

**Musical Score** Niehaus, Lennie
**Composer(s)** Dorff, Stephen H.; Diamond, Steve
**Lyricist(s)** Dorff, Stephen H.; Diamond, Steve

**Producer(s)** Manes, Fritz
**Director(s)** Locke, Sondra
**Screenwriter(s)** Thompson, Rob

**Cast** Locke, Sondra; Townsend, Robert; Hewitt, Christopher; Hankin, Larry; Anderson, Louie; Baird, S.L.

**Song(s)** Pretty Face (C/L: Dorff, Stephen H.; Bettis, John; Brown, Phil); Out of Control; Gotta Get Rich; Personality (C/L: Logan, Harold; Price, Lloyd); I Get Mental (C/L: Matkosky, Dennis; Sembello, Danny; Batteau, David); Don't Follow Me (C/L: O'Connell, Marc; Saba, Shari); Tangled Up in You (C/L: Dorff, Stephen H.; Bettis, John; Brown, Phil); Looking for Trouble [1] (C/L: Lorber, Sam; Innis, Dave); Throw Down (C/L: Matkosky, Dennis; Wolf, Richard); Hollywood Boulevard Street Rap (C/L: Dorff, Stephen H.; Brown, Milton); In the Name of Love (C/L: Dorff, Stephen H.; Brown, Phil); The Heart I Left Behind Me (C/L: Dorff, Stephen H.; Brown, Milton)

**Notes** It is not known if all of these were written for the picture. [1] Also in INSTANT JUSTICE.

## 4825 ✦ RATON PASS
Warner Brothers, 1951

**Musical Score** Steiner, Max

**Producer(s)** Elkins, Saul
**Director(s)** Marin, Edwin L.
**Screenwriter(s)** Blackburn, Tom; Webb, James R.
**Source(s)** "Whiteface" (story) Blackburn, Tom

**Cast** Morgan, Dennis; Neal, Patricia; Cochran, Steve; Forbes, Scott; Hart, Dorothy; Ruysdael, Basil; Heydt, Louis Jean; Winters, Roland; Burke, James; Curci, Elvira; Conde, Carlos; Crawford, John

**Song(s)** I Don't Wish to Marry (C/L: LaForge, Frank)

**Notes** Released in Great Britain as CANYON PASS.

## 4826 ✦ RAW EDGE
Universal, 1956

**Musical Score** Gertz, Irving

**Producer(s)** Baird, Michael
**Director(s)** Sherwood, John
**Screenwriter(s)** Essex, Harvey; Hill, Robert

**Cast** Calhoun, Rory; De Carlo, Yvonne; Corday, Mara; Rudley, Herbert; Brand, Neville

**Song(s)** Raw Edge (C/L: Gilkyson, Terry)

## 4827 ✦ RAWHIDE
Twentieth Century–Fox, 1951

**Musical Score** Kaplan, Sol

**Producer(s)** Engel, Samuel G.
**Director(s)** Hathaway, Henry
**Screenwriter(s)** Nichols, Dudley

**Cast** Power, Tyrone; Hayward, Susan; Marlowe, Hugh; Jagger, Dean; Buchanan, Edgar; Elam, Jack; Tobias, George; Corey, Jeff; Heydt, Louis Jean

**Song(s)** A Rollin' Stone (C: Newman, Lionel; Russell, Bob)

## 4828 ✦ RAWHIDE RANGERS
Universal, 1941

**Producer(s)** Cowan, Will
**Director(s)** Taylor, Ray
**Screenwriter(s)** Repp, Ed Earl

**Cast** Brown, Johnny Mack; Knight, Fuzzy; Adams, Kathryn

**Song(s)** Then We Go Ridin' (C/L: Cool, Gomer); Huckleberry Pie [2] (C: Rosen, Milton; L: Carter, Everett); A Cowboy Is Happy [1] (C: Rosen, Milton; L: Carter, Everett); It's a Ranger's Life (C/L: Cool, Gomer)

**Notes** [1] Also in COWBOY IN MANHATTAN and GUN TOWN. [2] Also in TRAIL TO VENGEANCE.

## 4829 ✦ THE RAWHIDE YEARS
### Universal, 1956

**Musical Score** Skinner, Frank
**Composer(s)** Hughes, Arnold
**Lyricist(s)** Herbert, Frederick

**Producer(s)** Rubin, Stanley
**Director(s)** Mate, Rudolph
**Screenwriter(s)** Felton, Earl
**Source(s)** *The Rawhide Years* (novel) Fox, Norman A.

**Cast** Curtis, Tony; Miller, Colleen; Kennedy, Arthur; Demarest, William; Gargan, William; Watson, Minor

**Song(s)** The Gypsy with the Fire in His Shoes (C: Almeida, Laurindo; L: Lee, Peggy); Happy Go Lucky; Give Me Your Love

## 4830 ✦ RAW WIND IN EDEN
### Universal, 1958

**Musical Score** Salter, Hans J.

**Producer(s)** Alland, William
**Director(s)** Wilson, Richard
**Screenwriter(s)** Wilson, Richard; Wilson, Elizabeth

**Cast** Williams, Esther; Thompson, Carlos; Chandler, Jeff; Podesta, Rossana; De Filippo, Eduardo

**Song(s)** The Magic Touch (C/L: Livingston, Jay; Evans, Ray)

## 4831 ✦ THE RAZOR'S EDGE
### Twentieth Century–Fox, 1946

**Musical Score** Newman, Alfred
**Composer(s)** Goulding, Edmund
**Lyricist(s)** Surmagne, Jacques
**Choreographer(s)** Pilcer, Harry

**Producer(s)** Zanuck, Darryl F.
**Director(s)** Goulding, Edmund
**Screenwriter(s)** Trotti, Lamar
**Source(s)** *The Razor's Edge* (novel) Maugham, W. Somerset

**Cast** Power, Tyrone; Tierney, Gene; Payne, John; Baxter, Anne; Webb, Clifton; Marshall, Herbert; Watson, Lucile; Lanchester, Elsa; Wright Jr., Cobina; Pilcer, Harry

**Song(s)** Night Was So Dark (L: Koshetz, Nina); The Miner's Song; J'Aime Ta Pomme; Mamselle [1] (L: Gordon, Mack)

**Notes** [1] Sheet music only.

## 4832 ✦ REACHING FOR THE MOON
### United Artists, 1931

**Producer(s)** Schenck, Joseph M.
**Director(s)** Goulding, Edmund
**Screenwriter(s)** Goulding, Edmund

**Cast** Fairbanks, Douglas; Horton, Edward Everett; Daniels, Bebe; Allister, Claud; Mulhall, Jack; MacCloy, June; Walker, Walter; Eddy, Helen Jerome; Crosby, Bing

**Song(s)** Reaching for the Moon (C/L: Berlin, Irving); When the Folks Up High Do the Mean Low-Down (C/L: Berlin, Irving)

**Notes** No cue sheet available.

## 4833 ✦ READY FOR LOVE
### Paramount, 1934

**Producer(s)** Lewis, Albert
**Director(s)** Gering, Marion
**Screenwriter(s)** McEvoy, J.P.; McNutt, William Slavens
**Source(s)** *The Whipping* (play) Spence, Eulalie

**Cast** Rambeau, Marjorie [1]; Arlen, Richard; Lupino, Ida

**Song(s)** Guess Again [2] (C: Revel, Harry; L: Gordon, Mack)

**Notes** The original play is based on a novel of the same name by Roy Flannagan. There is also a vocal of "Some of These Days" by Shelton Brooks (also in HONKY TONK). [1] Dubbed by Mona Lowe. [2] Written for COLLEGIATE but not used. Used also in THE OLD FASHIONED WAY.

## 4834 ✦ READY, WILLING AND ABLE
### Warner Brothers, 1937

**Musical Score** Roemheld, Heinz
**Composer(s)** Whiting, Richard A.
**Lyricist(s)** Mercer, Johnny
**Choreographer(s)** Connolly, Bobby

**Producer(s)** Bischoff, Sam
**Director(s)** Enright, Ray
**Screenwriter(s)** Wald, Jerry; Herzig, Sig; Duff, Warren

**Cast** Keeler, Ruby; Dixon, Lee; Jenkins, Allen; Fazenda, Louise; Hughes, Carl; Alexander, Ross [1]; Shaw, Winifred; Hart, Teddy; O'Connell, Hugh; Richards, Addison; Shaw and Lee; Boley, May; Clive, E.E.; Wyman, Jane; Halton, Charles; Kemble-Cooper, Lillian

**Song(s)** The World Is My Apple; The Little House on the Hill; Handy with Your Feet; Too Marvelous for

Words [2]; Just a Quiet Evening; Sentimental and Melancholy; Fair Lady (Inst.)

**Notes**  Hirschhorn lists the songs "Ready, Willing and Able" and "Gasoline Gypsies" but they are not on cue sheet. [1] Dubbed by James Newill. [2] Also in DECEPTION and YOUNG MAN WITH A HORN.

### 4835  ◆  REAP THE WILD WIND
Paramount, 1942

**Musical Score**  Young, Victor

**Producer(s)**  De Mille, Cecil B.
**Director(s)**  De Mille, Cecil B.
**Screenwriter(s)**  LeMay, Alan; Bennett, Charles; Lasky Jr., Jesse
**Source(s)**  "Reap the Wild Wind" (story) Strabel, Thelma

**Cast**  Massey, Raymond; Goddard, Paulette; Wayne, John; Milland, Ray; Hayward, Susan; Preston, Robert; Bickford, Charles; Overman, Lynne; Beavers, Louise; Hampden, Walter; Risdon, Elizabeth; Hopper, Hedda; Melford, George

**Song(s)**  Sea Chanty (C: Young, Victor; L: Loesser, Frank); Bye and Bye (C/L: Sanders, Troy); 'Tis but a Little Faded Flower [1] (C: Sanders, Troy; Thomas, J.R.; L: Thomas, J.R.); When I'm Gone Away (C/L: Sanders, Troy); Reap the Wild Wind [2] (C: Pollack, Lew; L: Washington, Ned)

**Notes**  [1] Troy Sanders arranged the old tune and wrote a new middle strain. [2] Not used in picture. Written for exploitation use only.

### 4836  ◆  REAR WINDOW
Paramount, 1954

**Producer(s)**  Hitchcock, Alfred
**Director(s)**  Hitchcock, Alfred
**Screenwriter(s)**  Hayes, Michael

**Cast**  Stewart, James; Kelly, Grace; Ritter, Thelma; Corey, Wendell; Burr, Raymond; Evelyn, Judith

**Song(s)**  Lisa (C: Waxman, Franz; L: Rome, Harold)

### 4837  ◆  REBECCA OF SUNNYBROOK FARM
Twentieth Century–Fox, 1938

**Composer(s)**  Revel, Harry
**Lyricist(s)**  Gordon, Mack
**Choreographer(s)**  Castle, Nick; Sawyer, Geneva

**Producer(s)**  Zanuck, Darryl F.
**Director(s)**  Dwan, Allan
**Screenwriter(s)**  Tunberg, Karl; Ettlinger, Don
**Source(s)**  Rebecca of Sunnybrook Farm (novel) Wiggin, Kate Douglas

**Cast**  Temple, Shirley; Scott, Randolph; Haley, Jack; Stuart, Gloria; Brooks, Phyllis; Westley, Helen; Summerville, Slim; Robinson, Bill; Bromberg, J.

Edward; Dinehart, Alan; The Raymond Scott Quintet; Dunbar, Dixie; Hurst, Paul

**Song(s)**  Happy Ending (C: Pollack, Lew; L: Mitchell, Sidney D.); You Gotta Eat Your Spinach, Baby; An Old Straw Hat; Crackly Grain Flakes (C: Pollack, Lew; L: Mitchell, Sidney D.); Alone with You (C: Pollack, Lew; L: Mitchell, Sidney D.); Come and Get Your Happiness (C: Pokrass, Sam; L: Yellen, Jack); The Toy Trumpet (C: Scott, Raymond; L: Mitchell, Sidney D.; Pollack, Lew); Broadcasting Medley [1]

**Notes**  [1] Consists of many songs with brief transitions.

### 4838  ◆  REBEL IN TOWN
United Artists, 1956

**Musical Score**  Baxter, Les

**Producer(s)**  Koch, Howard W.
**Director(s)**  Werker, Alfred
**Screenwriter(s)**  Arnold, Danny

**Cast**  Payne, John; Roman, Ruth; Naish, J. Carrol; Cooper, Ben; Smith, John

**Song(s)**  Rebel in Town (C: Baxter, Les; L: Adelson, Lenny)

### 4839  ◆  RECKLESS (1935)
Metro–Goldwyn–Mayer, 1935

**Choreographer(s)**  Randall, Carl; Hale, Chester

**Producer(s)**  Selznick, David O.
**Director(s)**  Fleming, Victor
**Screenwriter(s)**  Wolfson, P.J.

**Cast**  Harlow, Jean [2]; Powell, William; Tone, Franchot; Healy, Ted; Robson, May; Pendleton, Nat; Russell, Rosalind; Rooney, Mickey; Stephenson, Henry; Dean, Man Mountain; Light, Robert; Randall, Carl; Jones, Allan; Waycoff, Leon; McKinney, Nina Mae; Ellison, James

**Song(s)**  Reckless (C: Kern, Jerome; L: Hammerstein II, Oscar); Asi Se Besa (Inst.) (C: Kern, Jerome); Everything's Been Done Before (C: King, Jack; L: Adamson, Harold; Knopf, Edwin H.); Hear What My Heart Is Saying (C: Lane, Burton; L: Adamson, Harold); Hi-Diddle-Dee-Dum [1] (C: Conrad, Con; L: Magidson, Herb)

**Notes**  [1] Used instrumentally only. [2] Dubbed for both singing (by Virginia Verrill) and dancing. [3] Name changed later to Leon Ames.

### 4840  ◆  RECKLESS (1984)
MGM/UA, 1984

**Musical Score**  Newman, Thomas

**Producer(s)**  Scherick, Edgar J.; Rudin, Scott
**Director(s)**  Foley, James
**Screenwriter(s)**  Columbus, Chris

**Cast**    Quinn, Aidan; Hannah, Daryl; McMillan, Kenneth; De Young, Cliff; Smith, Lois; Baldwin, Adam; Hedaya, Dan; Jacoby, Billy; Kalem, Toni; Grey, Jennifer; Morris, Haviland; Springsteen, Pamela

**Song(s)**    The One Thing (C/L: Farriss, Andrew; Hutchence, Michael); One in a Million You (C/L: Dees, Sam); Never Say Never (C/L: Iyall, D.; Carter, L.; Bossi, B.; Zincavage, F.; Woods, P.); Soul Mistake (C/L: Farriss, Andrew; Hutchence, Michael); Kids in America (C/L: Wilde, Ricky; Wilde, Marty); To Look At You (C/L: Farriss, Andrew); Roll Me Away (C/L: Seger, Bob)

**Notes**    It is not known if all these were written for this picture.

## 4841 ✦ RECKLESS AGE
### Universal, 1944

**Musical Score**    Skinner, Frank

**Producer(s)**    Feist, Felix E.
**Director(s)**    Feist, Felix E.
**Screenwriter(s)**    Purcell, Gertrude; Blankfort, Henry

**Cast**    Jean, Gloria; The Delta Rhythm Boys; Darwell, Jane; Pangborn, Franklin

**Song(s)**    Get on Board, Little Children (C: de Paul, Gene; L: Raye, Don); Very Often on My Face (C/L: Crago, Bill; Shannon, Grace); We'll Come Through (C/L: Horwitt, Arnold; Herron, Joel); Cradle Song (C: Brahms, Johannes; L: Bibo, Irving)

**Notes**    There are also vocals of "Il Bacio" by Arditi; "Mama Yo Quiero (I Want My Mama)" by George Negrette and Jaraca and Vincente Paiva and "Santa Lucia."

## 4842 ✦ RECKLESS LIVING
### Universal, 1938

**Composer(s)**    McHugh, Jimmy
**Lyricist(s)**    Adamson, Harold

**Producer(s)**    Paul, Val
**Director(s)**    McDonald, Frank
**Screenwriter(s)**    Grayson, Charles

**Cast**    Wilcox, Robert; Grey, Nan

**Song(s)**    When the Stars Go to Sleep; Heigh-Ho the Merry-O [1]; For the First Time [1]

**Notes**    [1] Not used.

## 4843 ✦ RED BALL EXPRESS
### Universal, 1952

**Producer(s)**    Rosenberg, Aaron
**Director(s)**    Boetticher, Budd
**Screenwriter(s)**    Hayes, Michael

**Cast**    Chandler, Jeff; Nicol, Alex; Poitier, Sidney; Braun, Judith; Duval, Jacqueline; O'Brian, Hugh; Kelly, Jack

**Song(s)**    Lift and Load (C/L: Rosen, Milton)

## 4844 ✦ THE RED BARON

See VON RICHTOFEN AND BROWN.

## 4845 ✦ THE RED DANCE
### Fox, 1928

**Musical Score**    Rothafel, S.L.; Rapee, Erno

**Director(s)**    Walsh, Raoul
**Screenwriter(s)**    Creelman, James Ashmore
**Source(s)**    *The Red Dancer of Moscow* (novel) Gates, Henry Layford

**Cast**    Del Rio, Dolores; Farrell, Charles; Linow, Ivan; Charsky, Boris; de Segurola, Andres; Alexis, Demetrius

**Song(s)**    Someday, Somewhere We'll Meet Again (C: Rapee, Erno; L: Pollack, Lew)

**Notes**    No cue sheet available.

## 4846 ✦ RED GARTERS
### Paramount, 1954

**Composer(s)**    Livingston, Jay; Evans, Ray
**Lyricist(s)**    Livingston, Jay; Evans, Ray
**Choreographer(s)**    Castle, Nick

**Producer(s)**    Duggan, Pat
**Director(s)**    Marshall, George
**Screenwriter(s)**    Fessier, Michael

**Cast**    Clooney, Rosemary; Carson, Jack; Mitchell, Guy; Crowley, Pat; Barry, Gene; Daley, Cass; Gilbert, Joanne; Faylen, Frank; Owen, Reginald; Ebsen, Buddy; Hale, Richard

**Song(s)**    Red Garters; A Dime and a Dollar; The Robin Randall Song; Man and Woman; Lady Killer; Good Intentions; Vaquero!; Bad News; Brave Man [2]; Meet a Happy Guy; This Is Greater Than I Thought; I'm a Strange Little Girl Today [1]; Let Me Love You (Que Te Amo!) [3]; Big Doin's [3]; And I Love You [3]; Here You Are [3]; Too Happy to Fall in Love [3]; It's a Woman's World [3]; The Code of the West [3]

**Notes**    [1] Not used but recorded. [2] Originally titled "Goodbye Jane, Goodbye Joe." [3] Not used.

## 4847 ✦ RED-HEADED WOMAN
### Metro–Goldwyn–Mayer, 1932

**Director(s)**    Conway, Jack
**Screenwriter(s)**    Loos, Anita
**Source(s)**    *Red-Headed Woman* (novel) Brush, Katherine

**Cast**    Harlow, Jean; Morris, Chester; Stone, Lewis; Hyams, Leila; Merkel, Una; Robson, May; Boyer, Charles

**Song(s)** The Red Headed Woman (C: Whiting, Richard A.; L: Egan, Raymond B.); We'll Dance Until the Dawn [1] (C: McHugh, Jimmy; L: Fields, Dorothy)

**Notes** [1] Also in FLYING HIGH and PLANE NUTS.

## 4848 ✦ REDHEAD FROM MANHATTAN
### Columbia, 1943

**Composer(s)** Chaplin, Saul
**Lyricist(s)** Samuels, Walter G.

**Producer(s)** MacDonald, Wallace
**Director(s)** Landers, Lew
**Screenwriter(s)** Hoffman, Joseph

**Cast** Duane, Michael; Wilson, Lewis; Leavitt, Douglas; Drake, Douglas; Velez, Lupe; Ryan, Tim

**Song(s)** Ounce of Bounce; The Fiestigo; I'm Undecided (I Can't Make Up My Mind); Why Be Downhearted (Keep 'Em Happy); Let's Fall in Line

## 4849 ✦ REDHEADS ON PARADE
### Fox, 1935

**Composer(s)** Gorney, Jay
**Lyricist(s)** Hartman, Don

**Producer(s)** Lasky, Jesse L.
**Director(s)** McLeod, Norman Z.
**Screenwriter(s)** James, Rian; Hartman, Don

**Cast** Boles, John; Lee, Dixie; Haley, Jack

**Song(s)** Redheads on Parade (1) [1]; I Found a Dream; I've Got Your Future All Planned; Redheads on Parade (2) (L: Stahlberg, Herbert); Redheads on Parade (3) [2] [3]; Good Night Kiss [3]; Beautiful Thing [3]

**Notes** [1] This version of the song used music Gorney originally used in STAND UP AND CHEER titled "The Doll Dance" (danced by Janet Gaynor). [2] This rejected version was the first written and is a march. [3] Not used.

## 4850 ✦ RED, HOT AND BLUE
### Paramount, 1949

**Composer(s)** Loesser, Frank
**Lyricist(s)** Loesser, Frank

**Producer(s)** Fellows, Robert
**Director(s)** Farrow, John
**Screenwriter(s)** Farrow, John; Wilde, Hagar

**Cast** Hutton, Betty; Mature, Victor; Demarest, William; Havoc, June; Walburn, Raymond; Stevens, Onslow; Vitale, Joseph; Nigh, Jane; Talman, William; Smith, Art; Loesser, Frank

**Song(s)** I Wake Up in the Morning Feeling Fine; That's Loyalty; Hamlet; (Where Are You) Now That I Need You

**Notes** Originally titled BROADWAY STORY. Loesser refused to sign certificates of originality on the original

manuscript of the songs from this picture. Frank Loesser is seen and heard playing the piano in one scene and appears in other scenes.

## 4851 ✦ RED HOT RHYTHM
### Pathe, 1930

**Composer(s)** Dolan, Robert Emmett [1]
**Lyricist(s)** O'Keefe, Walter

**Director(s)** McCarey, Leo
**Screenwriter(s)** Conselman, William; McCarey, Leo

**Cast** Dunn, Josephine; O'Keefe, Walter; Garvin, Anita; Chase, Ilka

**Song(s)** Red Hot Rhythm; At Last I'm In Love; The Night Elmer Died

**Notes** [1] Billed as Bobby Dolan.

## 4852 ✦ RED LINE 7000
### Paramount, 1965

**Composer(s)** Cason, Buzz
**Lyricist(s)** Connors, Carol

**Producer(s)** Hawks, Howard
**Director(s)** Hawks, Howard
**Screenwriter(s)** Kirgo, George

**Cast** Caan, James; Alden, Norman; Takei, George

**Song(s)** Wildcat Jones; Let Me Find Someone New (C: Riddle, Nelson)

## 4853 ✦ RED MORNING
### RKO, 1934

**Musical Score** Steiner, Max

**Producer(s)** Reid, Cliff
**Director(s)** Fox, Wallace W.
**Screenwriter(s)** Twist, John; Fox, Wallace W.

**Cast** Duna, Steffi; Toomey, Regis; Hatton, Raymond; Lewis, Mitchell; Middleton, Charles; Lewis, George; McDonald, Francis

**Song(s)** Out of the Blue [1] (C: Steiner, Max; L: Eliscu, Edward); Mau Wai Ke Manao-Ka Wahine E (C: Steiner, Max; L: Hoopii Jr., Sol)

**Notes** Cue sheet does not differentiate between vocals and instrumentals. [1] May be used vocally in BIRD OF PARADISE (1932).

## 4854 ✦ RED NICHOLS AND HIS FIVE PENNIES
### Universal, 1950

**Cast** Red Nichols and His Five Pennies

**Song(s)** I Got Tookin' (C: Spina, Harold; L: Elliott, Jack); Vaudeville Is Back (C/L: Brent, Earl)

**Notes**   Short subject. These are the only original vocals in this short.

## 4855 ✦ RED RHUMBA
Warner Brothers, 1936

**Song(s)**   Tell Me Your Troubles (C: Henderson, Ray; L: Dixon, Mort)

**Notes**   No other information available. I found this reference on an ASCAP sheet.

## 4856 ✦ RED RIVER ROBIN HOOD
RKO, 1943

**Musical Score**   Sawtell, Paul; Dreyer, Dave

**Producer(s)**   Gilroy, Bert
**Director(s)**   Selander, Lesley
**Screenwriter(s)**   Cohen, Bennett R.

**Cast**   Holt, Tim; Edwards, Cliff; Moffett, Barbara; Dew, Eddie; Hoffman, Otto; Wade, Russell

**Song(s)**   Twilight on the Prairie [1] (C/L: Rose, Fred; Whitley, Ray)

**Notes**   [1] Also in THE FARGO KID and, without the Rose credit, in TRIGGER TRAIL (Universal).

## 4857 ✦ RED RIVER VALLEY (1936)
Republic, 1936

**Composer(s)**   Burnette, Smiley
**Lyricist(s)**   Burnette, Smiley

**Producer(s)**   Schaefer, Armand
**Director(s)**   Eason, B. Reeves
**Screenwriter(s)**   McGowan, Dorrell; McGowan, Stuart

**Cast**   Autry, Gene; Burnette, Smiley; Grant, Frances; Howard, Boothe; Chesebro, George; King, Charles; Flint, Sam; Kennedy, Jack; Champion

**Song(s)**   Red River Sweetheart; Keen Goin' Little Pony; Yodelling Cowboy (C/L: Autry, Gene); Fetch Me Down My Trusty 45 [1] (C/L: Burnette, Smiley); Construction Song (C/L: Stept, Sam H.); Red River Valley (C/L: Manoloff, Nick); Where a Waterwheel Keeps Turning On (C/L: Drake, Oliver; Stept, Sam H.)

**Notes**   No cue sheet available. I believe the TV version was titled MAN OF THE FRONTIER. [1] Also in Columbia's WINNING OF THE WEST. Sometimes referred to as "Hand Me Down My Trusty 45."

## 4858 ✦ RED RIVER VALLEY (1941)
Republic, 1941

**Composer(s)**   Spencer, Tim
**Lyricist(s)**   Spencer, Tim

**Producer(s)**   Kane, Joseph
**Director(s)**   Kane, Joseph
**Screenwriter(s)**   Boylan, Malcolm Stuart

**Cast**   Rogers, Roy; Hayes, George "Gabby"; Payne, Sally; Bardette, Trevor; Storm, Gale; Taliaferro, Hal; Sons of the Pioneers

**Song(s)**   Square Dance (C/L: Farr, Hugh); Sunset on the Trail; Lily of Hillbilly Valley [1]; Chant of the Wanderer (C/L: Nolan, Bob); When Pay Day Rolls Around (C/L: Nolan, Bob); Springtime on the Range Today

**Notes**   [1] Also in SONS OF THE PIONEERS.

## 4859 ✦ REDS
Paramount, 1981

**Musical Score**   Sondheim, Stephen

**Producer(s)**   Beatty, Warren
**Director(s)**   Beatty, Warren
**Screenwriter(s)**   Beatty, Warren; Griffiths, Trevor

**Cast**   Beatty, Warren; Stapleton, Maureen; Keaton, Diane; Nicholson, Jack; Herrmann, Edward; Hackman, Gene; Kosinski, Jerzy; Sorvino, Paul; Love, Bessie

**Song(s)**   Goodbye for Now [1] (C/L: Sondheim, Stephen)

**Notes**   [1] Used instrumentally only.

## 4860 ✦ THE RED SHOES
United Artists, 1948

**Musical Score**   Easdale, Brian

**Producer(s)**   Pressburger, Emeric
**Director(s)**   Powell, Michael
**Screenwriter(s)**   Powell, Michael; Pressburger, Emeric; Winter, Keith

**Cast**   Walbrook, Anton; Shearer, Moira; Goring, Marius; Massine, Leonide; Helpmann, Robert; Basserman, Albert; Knight, Esmond; Tcherina, Ludmilla

**Song(s)**   Cupid and Psyche (C: Easdale, Brian; L: Evans, Patrick)

## 4861 ✦ REDSKIN
Paramount, 1929

**Musical Score**   Zamecnik, J.S.

**Director(s)**   Schertzinger, Victor
**Screenwriter(s)**   Pickett, Elizabeth

**Cast**   Dix, Richard; Belmont, Gladys; Novak, Jane; Steers, Larry; Marshall, Tully; Johnson, Noble

**Song(s)**   Redskin (C: Zamecnik, J.S.; L: Kerr, Harry D.)

**Notes**   No cue sheet available.

## 4862 ✦ RED SUNDOWN
Universal, 1955

**Musical Score**  Salter, Hans J.

**Producer(s)**  Zugsmith, Albert
**Director(s)**  Arnold, Jack
**Screenwriter(s)**  Berkeley, Martin
**Source(s)**  "Black Trail" (story) Patten, Lewis B.

**Cast**  Calhoun, Rory; Middleton, Robert; Williams, Grant; Hyer, Martha; Jagger, Dean

**Song(s)**  Red Sundown (C/L: Gilkyson, Terry)

## 4863 ✦ THE RED TENT
Paramount, 1971

**Musical Score**  Morricone, Ennio
**Composer(s)**  Morricone, Ennio
**Lyricist(s)**  Simon, Norman; Mark, Lowell

**Producer(s)**  Cristaldi, Franco
**Director(s)**  Kalatozov, Mickail K.
**Screenwriter(s)**  De Concini, Ennio; Adams, Richard

**Cast**  Connery, Sean; Cardinale, Claudia; Kruger, Hardy; Finch, Peter; Girotti, Massimo; Adorf, Mario

**Song(s)**  In My Thoughts of You [1]; Do Dreams Go On (La Tenda Rossa) [1]

**Notes**  [1] Lyric written for exploitation.

## 4864 ✦ THE REFORMER AND THE REDHEAD
Metro–Goldwyn–Mayer, 1950

**Musical Score**  Raksin, David

**Producer(s)**  Panama, Norman; Frank, Melvin
**Director(s)**  Panama, Norman; Frank, Melvin
**Screenwriter(s)**  Panama, Norman; Frank, Melvin

**Cast**  Allyson, June; Powell, Dick; Wayne, David; Kellaway, Cecil; Collins, Ray; Keith, Robert

**Song(s)**  Orphan Annie (C: Traditional; L: Frank, Melvin; Panama, Norman)

## 4865 ✦ REFORM SCHOOL GIRLS
New World, 1986

**Musical Score**  Gabriel, Tedra

**Producer(s)**  Cummings, Jack
**Director(s)**  DeSimone, Tom
**Screenwriter(s)**  DeSimone, Tom; Wray, Daniel Arthur; Cummings, Jack

**Cast**  Carol, Linda; Williams, Wendy O.; Ast, Pat; Danning, Sybil; McGinnis, Charlotte

**Song(s)**  Reform School Girls (C/L: Paine, Bobby; Paine, Larson); So Young, So Bad, So What (C/L: Paine, Bobby; Paine, Larson)

**Notes**  No cue sheet available.

## 4866 ✦ REGISTERED NURSE
Warner Brothers, 1934

**Producer(s)**  Bischoff, Sam
**Director(s)**  Florey, Robert; Collins, Arthur Greville
**Screenwriter(s)**  Hayward, Lillie; Milne, Peter
**Source(s)**  (play) Johns, Florence; Lackaye Jr., Wilton

**Cast**  Daniels, Bebe; Talbot, Lyle; Halliday, John; Franklin, Irene; Toler, Sidney; Westcott, Gordon; Gombell, Minna; Bondi, Beulah; Barnett, Vince; Reed, Philip; Methot, Mayo; Sale, Virginia

**Song(s)**  Goldfish Song (C: Fain, Sammy; L: Kahal, Irving)

## 4867 ✦ REG'LAR FELLERS
PRC, 1941

**Musical Score**  DeMaggio, Ross
**Composer(s)**  Harmon, Dean; Meglin, Ethel
**Lyricist(s)**  Harmon, Dean; Meglin, Ethel

**Producer(s)**  Eudemiller, Joe
**Director(s)**  Dreifuss, Arthur
**Screenwriter(s)**  Hoerl, Arthur; Dreifuss, Arthur; Kent, William C.

**Cast**  Lee, Billy; Switzer, Carl "Alfalfa"; Dempsey, Janet; Boles, Buddy; Hutton, Malcolm; O'Malley, Pat

**Song(s)**  Reg'lar Fellers; Hooray for Fun

**Notes**  No cue sheet available.

## 4868 ✦ RELENTLESS FOUR
United Artists

**Musical Score**  Giombini, Marcello

**Director(s)**  Zeglio, Primo
**Screenwriter(s)**  de Urritia, Ferderico

**Cast**  West, Adam; Hundar, Robert; Ross, Red; Baards, Pauline

**Song(s)**  Ranger (C: Giombini, Marcello; L: Scoponi)

## 4869 ✦ THE RELUCTANT ASTRONAUT
Universal, 1967

**Musical Score**  Mizzy, Vic

**Producer(s)**  Montagne, Edward J.
**Director(s)**  Montagne, Edward J.
**Screenwriter(s)**  Fritzell, Jim; Greenbaum, Everett

**Cast**  Knotts, Don; O'Connell, Arthur; Nielsen, Leslie; Freeman, Joan; White, Jesse; Nolan, Jeanette; McGrath, Frank

**Song(s)**  The Space Song (C: Gershenson, Joseph; L: Fritzell, Jim; Greenbaum, Everett)

## 4870 ◆ THE RELUCTANT DRAGON
Disney, 1953

**Musical Score**  Churchill, Frank E.

**Director(s)**  Werker, Alfred; Luske, Hamilton
**Screenwriter(s)**  Sears, Ted; Clemmons, Larry; Perkins, Al; Cottrell, William; Benchley, Robert; Clork, Harry
**Source(s)**  "The Reluctant Dragon" (story) Grahame, Kenneth
**Voices**  Gifford, Frances; Bryant, Nana; Parker, Barnett; Pepper, Buddy; Allister, Claud; Lee, Billy; Gill, Florence; Nash, Clarence; Ferguson, Norman; Kimball, Ward; Luske, Jimmy; Ladd, Alan; Woodworth, Truman; MacFadden, Hamilton; Murphy, Maurice

**Cast**  Benchley, Robert

**Song(s)**  I'm the Reluctant Dragon (1) (C: Wolcott, Charles; L: Penner, Erdman; Hee, Thornton); I'm the Reluctant Dragon (2) [1] (C: Wolcott, Charles; L: Penner, Erdman; Hee, Thornton)

**Notes**  Animated cartoon. [1] Not used.

## 4871 ◆ REMAINS TO BE SEEN
Metro–Goldwyn–Mayer, 1953

**Musical Score**  Alexander, Jeff

**Producer(s)**  Hornblow Jr., Arthur
**Director(s)**  Weis, Don
**Screenwriter(s)**  Sheldon, Sidney
**Source(s)**  *Remains to Be Seen* (play) Lindsay, Howard; Crouse, Russel

**Cast**  Allyson, June; Johnson, Van; Calhern, Louis; Lansbury, Angela; Beal, John; Dandrige, Dorothy; Kelley, Barry; White, Sammy; Card, Kathryn; Harvey, Paul

**Notes**  There are no original songs in this film. Vocals include "Toot Toot Tootsie" by Ernie Erdman, Dan Russo and Gus Kahn; "Too Marvelous for Words" by Richard A. Whiting and Johnny Mercer and "Taking a Chance on Love" by Vernon Duke, John Latouche and Ted Fetter.

## 4872 ◆ REMEMBER LAST NIGHT
Universal, 1935

**Producer(s)**  Laemmle Jr., Carl
**Director(s)**  Whale, James
**Screenwriter(s)**  Clork, Harry; Malloy, Doris; Totheroh, Dan
**Source(s)**  "Hangover Murder" (story) Hobhouse, Adam

**Cast**  Stanwyck, Barbara; MacMurray, Fred; Bondi, Beulah; Holloway, Sterling

**Song(s)**  Remember Last Night (C/L: Coslow, Sam)

## 4873 ◆ REMEMBER MY NAME
Mariposa Films, 1978

**Musical Score**  Hunter, Alberta
**Composer(s)**  Hunter, Alberta
**Lyricist(s)**  Hunter, Alberta

**Producer(s)**  Altman, Robert
**Director(s)**  Rudolph, Alan
**Screenwriter(s)**  Rudolph, Alan

**Cast**  Chaplin, Geraldine; Perkins, Anthony; Gunn, Moses; Berenson, Berry; Goldblum, Jeff; Thomerson, Tim; Woodard, Alfre

**Song(s)**  Remember My Name; The Love I Have for You

**Notes**  No cue sheet available.

## 4874 ◆ REMEMBER PEARL HARBOR
Republic, 1942

**Producer(s)**  Cohen, Albert J.
**Director(s)**  Santley, Joseph
**Screenwriter(s)**  Boylan, Malcolm Stuart; Dawn, Isabel

**Cast**  Barry, Donald; Curtis, Alan; McKenzie, Fay; Rumannr 266, Sig; Keith, Ian

**Song(s)**  Hip Cat from Havana (Gangarria) (C: Martel, Gus; L: Meyer, Sol); Because We Are Americans [1] (C/L: Head, Emily Robinson)

**Notes**  [1] Also in SAILORS ON LEAVE.

## 4875 ◆ REMEMBER THE NIGHT
Paramount, 1940

**Producer(s)**  Leisen, Mitchell
**Director(s)**  Leisen, Mitchell
**Screenwriter(s)**  Sturges, Preston

**Cast**  Stanwyck, Barbara; MacMurray, Fred; Bondi, Beulah; Patterson, Elizabeth; Holloway, Sterling

**Song(s)**  Easy Living [1] (C: Rainger, Ralph; L: Robin, Leo); Back Home Again in Indiana [1] (C: Hanley, James F.; L: Macdonald, Ballard)

**Notes**  [1] These songs were not written for the film.

## 4876 ◆ REMOTE CONTROL
Metro–Goldwyn–Mayer, 1930

**Composer(s)**  Meyer, Joseph
**Lyricist(s)**  Johnson, Howard

**Director(s)**  Sedgwick, Edward
**Screenwriter(s)**  Thalberg, Sylvia; Butler, Frank
**Source(s)**  *Remote Control* (play) North, Clyde; Fuller, Albert C.; Nelson, Jack T.

**Cast**  Haines, William; King, Charles; Doran, Mary; Moran, Polly; Miljan, John; Nugent, J.C.

**Song(s)**  Just a Little Closer; Hip Hip Hooray for the Rainbows [1]; Shakin' Like a Leaf [1]

**Notes** A number of directors worked on this film. Malcolm St. Clair and Nick Grinde receive credit in some sources but not on MGM script. [1] Not used.

### 4877 ◆ REMO WILLIAMS: THE ADVENTURE BEGINS
Orion, 1985

**Musical Score** Safan, Craig

**Producer(s)** Spiegel, Larry
**Director(s)** Hamilton, Guy
**Screenwriter(s)** Wood, Christopher
**Source(s)** *The Destroyer* (novel series) Sapir, Richard; Murphy, Warren

**Cast** Ward, Fred; Grey, Joel; Brimley, Wilford; Preston, J.A.; Coe, George; Wilson, Scott; Cioffi, Charles; Mulgrew, Kate; Hickey, William

**Song(s)** Remo's Theme (What If) (C/L: Shaw, Tommy; Cannata, Richie)

**Notes** No cue sheet available.

### 4878 ◆ RENALDO AND CLARA
Lombard Street Films, 1978

**Composer(s)** Dylan, Bob
**Lyricist(s)** Dylan, Bob

**Producer(s)** Howard, Mel
**Director(s)** Dylan, Bob
**Screenwriter(s)** Dylan, Bob; Shepard, Sam

**Cast** Dylan, Bob; McGuinn, Roger; Dylan, Sara; Baez, Joan; Blakley, Ronee; Hawkins, Ronnie; Ginsberg, Allen; Shepard, Sam

**Song(s)** Isis I Want You; It Ain't Me Babe; Knockin' On Heaven's Door; Hurricane; Romance in Durango; One Too Many Mornings; One More Cup of Coffee; Sara; Patty's Gone to Laredo; Just Like a Woman; A Hard Rain's A-Gonna Fall; Sad-Eyed Lady of the Lowlands; When I Paint My Masterpiece; Chestnut Mare (C/L: McGuinn, Roger); Diamonds and Rust (C/L: Baez, Joan); Suzanne (C/L: Cohen, Leonard); Need a New Sun Rising (C/L: Blakley, Ronee); Salt Pork West Virginia (C/L: Elliott, Jack); Kaddish (C/L: Ginsberg, Allen); CuCuRuCuCu Paloma (C/L: Mendez, Tomas); Time of the Preacher (C/L: Nelson, Willie)

**Notes** No cue sheet available. It is not known which of the above were written for this film.

### 4879 ◆ RENDEZVOUS WITH ANNIE
Republic, 1946

**Producer(s)** Dwan, Allan
**Director(s)** Dwan, Allan
**Screenwriter(s)** Sale, Richard; Loos, Mary

**Cast** Albert, Eddie; Marlowe, Faye; Patrick, Gail; Reed, Philip; Smith, Sir C. Aubrey

**Song(s)** Dream Man (C/L: Elliott, Jack); My Pushover Heart [1] (C: Kent, Walter; L: Gannon, Kim)

**Notes** [1] Also in HITCH HIKE TO HAPPINESS and MURDER IN THE MUSIC HALL.

### 4880 ◆ THE RENEGADE RANGER
RKO, 1938

**Musical Score** Webb, Roy

**Producer(s)** Gilroy, Bert
**Director(s)** Howard, David
**Screenwriter(s)** Drake, Oliver

**Cast** O'Brien, George; Hayworth, Rita; Holt, Tim; Whitley, Ray; Villegas, Lucio

**Song(s)** Senorita [1] (C/L: Malotte, Albert Hay); Cielito Lindo (C/L: Fernandez, C.); Move Slow Little Dogies (C/L: Phelps, Willie)

**Notes** [1] Also in WE'RE RICH AGAIN.

### 4881 ◆ RENEGADES (1930)
Fox, 1930

**Director(s)** Fleming, Victor
**Screenwriter(s)** Furthman, Jules
**Source(s)** Le Renegat by Armandy, Andre

**Cast** Baxter, Warner; Loy, Myrna; Beery, Noah; Gaye, Gregory; Lugosi, Bela

**Song(s)** I Got What I Wanted (C: Monaco, James V.; L: Friend, Cliff)

### 4882 ◆ RENEGADES (1989)
Universal, 1989

**Musical Score** Kamen, Michael

**Producer(s)** Madden, David
**Director(s)** Sholder, Jack
**Screenwriter(s)** Rich, David

**Cast** Sutherland, Kiefer; Phillips, Lou Diamond; Gertz, Jami; Knepper, Rob; Smitrovich, Bill

**Song(s)** Before the Bullets Fly (C/L: Haynes, Warren; Williams, Jack; Jaworowicz, John); La Cumbita (C/L: Rivera, Ismael); House Arrest (C/L: Vormawah, Mark; Brown, Colin); Only the Strong Survive (C/L: Adams, Bryan; Vallance, Jim)

**Notes** It is not known which of the songs were written for this film.

### 4883 ◆ RENEGADES OF THE RIO GRANDE
Universal, 1945

**Producer(s)** Drake, Oliver
**Director(s)** Bretherton, Howard
**Screenwriter(s)** Lamb, Ande

**Cast**   Cameron, Rod; Knight, Fuzzy; Dew, Eddie; Holt, Jennifer

**Song(s)**   Down an Old Spanish Trail (C/L: Walker, Buzz; Buntin, Pauline; McCormick, Nora F.); Pedro, the Gay Vaquero (C/L: Allen, Maude; Snyder, Harry; Rein, Zendell); Along the Rio Grande (C/L: Allan, Fleming); I'm the Son of the Son of a Gunman (C/L: Drake, Oliver)

## 4884 ✦ THE RENEGADE TRAIL
### Paramount, 1939

**Composer(s)**   Ohman, Phil
**Lyricist(s)**   Carling, Foster

**Producer(s)**   Sherman, Harry
**Director(s)**   Selander, Lesley
**Screenwriter(s)**   Rothmell, John; Jacobs, Harrison

**Cast**   Boyd, William; Hayden, Russell; de Cordoba, Pedro

**Song(s)**   Lazy Rolls the Rio Grande; Hi Thar, Stranger; Lullaby of the Herd [1]

**Notes**   Originally titled ARIZONA BRACELETS. [1] Not used. Used in THE KANSAN (United Artists).

## 4885 ✦ RENFREW ON THE GREAT WHITE TRAIL
### Monogram, 1938

**Composer(s)**   Porter, Lew
**Lyricist(s)**   Porter, Lew

**Producer(s)**   Goldstone, Philip
**Source(s)**   "Renfrew of the Royal Mounted" (stories) Erskine, Laurie York

**Cast**   Newill, James; Walker, Terry

**Song(s)**   Mounted Men [1] (C/L: Laidlow, Betty; Lively, Bob); Beautiful (C: Taylor, Bob); Blue Eyes Are True Eyes; Je T'Aime

**Notes**   [1] Also in CRASHING THRU, DANGER AHEAD, FIGHTING MAN, MURDER ON THE YUKON, SKY BANDITS and YUKON FLIGHT.

## 4886 ✦ RENO
### Sono-Art, 1930

**Producer(s)**   Weeks, George W.
**Director(s)**   Crone, George J.
**Screenwriter(s)**   Chandlee, Harry; Churchill, Douglas W.
**Source(s)**   Reno; Vanderbilt Jr., Cornelius

**Cast**   Roland, Ruth; Love, Montagu; Thomson, Kenneth; Hardy, Sam; McCormick, Alyce; Hearn, Edward

**Song(s)**   At Last We're Together (C/L: Bard, Ben; Barton, Leslie)

**Notes**   No cue sheet available.

## 4887 ✦ REPEAT PERFORMANCE
### Eagle Lion, 1947

**Musical Score**   Antheil, George
**Composer(s)**   Kent, Walter
**Lyricist(s)**   Gannon, Kim

**Producer(s)**   Schenck, Aubrey
**Director(s)**   Werker, Alfred
**Screenwriter(s)**   Bullock, Walter
**Source(s)**   *Repeat Performance* (novel) O'Farrell, William

**Cast**   Hayward, Louis; Leslie, Joan; Basehart, Richard; Field, Virginia; Conway, Tom; Schafer, Natalie; Venuta, Benay; Gruning, Ilka

**Song(s)**   Never Knew I Could Sing; I'm So in Love; Repeat Performance [1] (C/L: Snyder, Patrece; Weingarten, Ann)

**Notes**   [1] No cue sheet available.

## 4888 ✦ REPO MAN
### Universal, 1984

**Producer(s)**   Wacks, Jonathan; McCarthy, Peter
**Director(s)**   Cox, Alex
**Screenwriter(s)**   Cox, Alex

**Cast**   Stanton, Harry Dean; Estevez, Emilio; Walter, Tracey; Barash, Olivia; Richardson, Sy; Sandoval, Michael

**Song(s)**   Repo Man (C/L: Pop, Iggy); Coup d'Etat (C/L: Morris, Keith; Hetson, Greg); T.V. Party (C/L: Ginn, Greg); El Clavo Y La Cruz (C/L: Larriva, Tito); Happy Animals (C/L: Wool, Dan; Shoemaker, Dodie; Trupin, Paul; Woody, Jim); Pablo Picasso (C/L: Richman, Jonathan); When the Shit Hits the Fan (C/L: Morris, Keith; Hetson, Greg); Milk Cow Blues (C/L: Arnold, Kokomo); Let's Have a War [1] (C/L: Ving, Lee; Cramer, Philo)

**Notes**   It is not known which of these were written for this film. [1] Also in NIGHTMARES but without Cramer credit.

## 4889 ✦ THE RESCUERS
### Disney, 1977

**Musical Score**   Butler, Artie
**Composer(s)**   Connors, Carol
**Lyricist(s)**   Connors, Carol; Robbins, Ayn

**Producer(s)**   Reitherman, Wolfgang
**Director(s)**   Reitherman, Wolfgang; Lounsbery, John; Stevens, Art
**Screenwriter(s)**   Clemmons, Larry; Anderson, Ken; Gerry, Vance; Berman, Ted; Mattinson, Burny; Thomas, Franklin; Michener, David; Lucky, Fred; Sebast, Dick
**Source(s)**   The Rescuers (stories) Miss Bianca
**Voices**   Newhart, Bob; Gabor, Eva; Page, Geraldine; Flynn, Joe; Nolan, Jeanette; Buttram, Pat; Jordan, Jim; McIntire, John; Stacy, Michelle; Fox, Bernard; Clemmons, Larry; MacDonald, James; Lindsey, George; Fiedler, John

**Directing Animator(s)** Johnston, Ollie; Thomas, Franklin; Kahl, Milt; Bluth, Don

**Song(s)** The Journey; R-E-S-C-U-E, Rescue Aid Society (1); Tomorrow Is Another Day; Someone's Waiting for You [2] (C: Fain, Sammy); I Never Had It So Good [1] (C/L: Huddleston, Floyd); Just Might Be Tomorrow [1]; The Need to Be Loved [1] [2] (C: Fain, Sammy; L: Webster, Paul Francis); Peoplitis [1] (C/L: Huddleston, Floyd); Rescue Aid Society (2) [1] (C: Bruns, George; L: Clemmons, Larry); Rescue Aid Society (3) [1] (C: Fain, Sammy; L: Clemmons, Larry)

**Notes** Animated feature. [1] Not used. [2] Same music.

### 4890 ♦ THE RESTLESS BREED
Twentieth Century–Fox, 1957

**Musical Score** Alperson Jr., Edward L.
**Composer(s)** Alperson Jr., Edward L.
**Lyricist(s)** Hughes, Dick; Stapley, Richard

**Producer(s)** Alperson, Edward L.
**Director(s)** Dwan, Allan
**Screenwriter(s)** Fisher, Steve

**Cast** Brady, Scott; Bancroft, Anne; Flippen, Jay C.; Williams, Rhys; King Jr., Dennis

**Song(s)** The Restless Breed; Calliope; Never Alone; Angelita

### 4891 ♦ THE RESTLESS YEARS
Universal, 1958

**Musical Score** Skinner, Frank

**Producer(s)** Hunter, Ross
**Director(s)** Kautner, Helmut
**Screenwriter(s)** Anhalt, Edward
**Source(s)** *Teach Me How to Cry* (play) Joudry, Patricia

**Cast** Dee, Sandra; Saxon, John; Whitmore, James; Wright, Teresa; Lindsay, Margaret; Grey, Virginia; McCrea, Jody; Rorke, Hayden

**Song(s)** The Wonderful Years [1] (C: Fain, Sammy; L: Leigh, Carolyn)

**Notes** [1] Used instrumentally only. The title tune when the picture was called THE WONDERFUL YEARS.

### 4892 ♦ RESURRECTION
Universal, 1980

**Musical Score** Jarre, Maurice

**Producer(s)** Missel, Renee; Rosenman, Howard
**Director(s)** Petrie, Daniel
**Screenwriter(s)** Carlino, Lewis John

**Cast** Burstyn, Ellen; DeMunn, Jeffrey; Blossom, Roberts; Shepard, Sam; Le Gallienne, Eva; Farnsworth, Richard; David, Clifford; Wright, Pamela Payton

**Song(s)** Fill My Life with Love (C/L: Tate, Richard; McDermott, Carol)

### 4893 ♦ RETURN OF A MAN CALLED HORSE
United Artists, 1976

**Musical Score** Kershner, Irvin

**Producer(s)** Morse Jr., Terry
**Director(s)** Kershner, Irvin
**Screenwriter(s)** Dewitt, Jack

**Cast** Harris, Richard; Sondergaard, Gale; Lewis, Geoffrey; Luke, Jorge; Brook, Claudio

**Song(s)** Sanctify (C/L: Cass, Ronnie)

### 4894 ♦ RETURN OF SABATA
United Artists, 1972

**Musical Score** Giombini, Marcello

**Producer(s)** Grimaldi, Alberto
**Director(s)** Kramer, Frank [1]
**Screenwriter(s)** Izzo, Renato; Kramer, Frank [1]

**Cast** Van Cleef, Lee; Schone, Reiner; Incontrera, Annabella; Rizzo, Gianni; Albertini, Gianpiero

**Song(s)** Sabata (C/L: Giombini, Marcello)

**Notes** [1] Pseudonym for Gianfranco Parolini.

### 4895 ♦ RETURN OF THE BADMEN
RKO, 1947

**Musical Score** Sawtell, Paul; Webb, Roy

**Producer(s)** Holt, Nat
**Director(s)** Enright, Ray
**Screenwriter(s)** O'Neal, Charles; Natteford, Jack; Ward, Luci

**Cast** Scott, Randolph; Ryan, Robert; Jeffreys, Anne; Hayes, George "Gabby"; White, Jacqueline; Brodie, Steve; Powers, Richard; Bray, Robert; Barker, Lex; Reed, Walter; Harvey, Michael; Harvey, Lew; Robards, Jason; Tyler, Tom; White, Dean; Armstrong, Robert; Gombell, Minna

**Song(s)** Remember the Girl You Left Behind (C: Revel, Harry; L: Greene, Mort)

### 4896 ♦ RETURN OF THE DURANGO KID
Columbia, 1944

**Director(s)** Abrahams, Derwin
**Screenwriter(s)** Cheney, J. Benton

**Cast** Lincoln, Elmo; Harding, Tex; Calvert, John; Stevens, Jean; Starrett, Charles

**Song(s)** Ole Pinto (C/L: Whitcup, Leonard; Cunningham, Paul); When They Fiddle Out the Polka [2] (C/L: Seiler, Eddie; Marcus, Sol); He Holds the Lantern (While His Mother Chops the Wood) (C/L: Grey, Lanny; Terker, Arthur; Jacobs, Roy); We'll Hang Old Leland Kirby [1] (C/L: Silva, Mario)

**Notes** [1] Only song written for film. [2] Al Neiburg also credited on sheet music.

## 4897 ✦ RETURN OF THE FRONTIERSMAN
Warner Brothers, 1950

**Musical Score** Buttolph, David

**Producer(s)** Elkins, Saul
**Director(s)** Bare, Richard
**Screenwriter(s)** Anhalt, Edward

**Cast** MacRae, Gordon; London, Julie; Calhoun, Rory; Holt, Jack; Clark, Fred; Rand, Edwin; Bond, Raymond; McHugh, Matt

**Song(s)** Underneath a Western Sky [1] (C: Jerome, M.K.; L: Scholl, Jack)

**Notes** [1] Also used in CATTLE TOWN (with Ted Fiorito credit also), COWBOY QUARTERBACK and RETURN OF THE FRONTIERSMAN. Jack Scholl and M.K. Jerome have a song in SONG OF THE SADDLE titled "Underneath the Western Skies." Could it be the same or similar?

## 4898 ✦ RETURN OF THE JEDI
Twentieth Century–Fox, 1983

**Musical Score** Williams, John

**Producer(s)** Kazanjian, Howard
**Director(s)** Marquand, Richard
**Screenwriter(s)** Kasdan, Lawrence; Lucas, George

**Cast** Hamill, Mark; Ford, Harrison; Fisher, Carrie; Williams, Billy Dee; Daniels, Anthony; Mayhew, Peter; Shaw, Sebastian; Oz, Frank; Prowse, David [1]; Guinness, Alec; Baker, Kenny

**Song(s)** Lapti Nek (C: Williams, John; L: Arbogast, Annie); Ewok Celebration (C: Williams, John; L: Williams, Joseph)

**Notes** No cue sheet available. [1] Dubbed by James Earl Jones. The character is Darth Vadar.

## 4899 ✦ THE RETURN OF THE LIVING DEAD
Orion, 1985

**Musical Score** Clifford, Matt

**Producer(s)** Fox, Tom
**Director(s)** O'Bannon, Dan
**Screenwriter(s)** O'Bannon, Dan

**Cast** Gulager, Clu; Karen, James; Calfa, Don; Mathews, Thom; Randolph, Beverly; Philbin, John

**Song(s)** The Trioxin Theme (C/L: Haines, Francis); Tonight (We'll Make Love Until We Die) (C/L: St. James, Jon; Swain, Stacey); Take a Walk (C/L: Lewis, Nigel; Robertson, Mark)

**Notes** No cue sheet available.

## 4900 ✦ RETURN OF THE LIVING DEAD PART II
Lorimar, 1988

**Musical Score** Robinson, J. Peter

**Producer(s)** Fox, Tom
**Director(s)** Wiederhorn, Ken
**Screenwriter(s)** Wiederhorn, Ken

**Cast** Karen, James; Mathews, Thom; Ashbrook, Dana; Dietlein, Marsha; Snyder, Suzanne

**Song(s)** Flesh to Flesh (C/L: Lamont, Joe; Cadd, Brian); Spacehopper (C/L: Cope, Julian); Alone in the Night (C/L: Gayer, Geoffrey; Howe, Carey; Oliveri, Michael; Roberts, Dean; Carmen, Paul); Bad Case of Loving You (C/L: Martin, John Moon); Looking for Clues (C/L: Palmer, Robert)

**Notes** No cue sheet available.

## 4901 ✦ RETURN OF THE PINK PANTHER
United Artists, 1975

**Musical Score** Mancini, Henry

**Producer(s)** Edwards, Blake
**Director(s)** Edwards, Blake
**Screenwriter(s)** Waldeman, Frank; Edwards, Blake

**Cast** Sellers, Peter; Plummer, Christopher; Schell, Catherine; Lom, Herbert; Arne, Peter

**Song(s)** The Greatest Gift (C: Mancini, Henry; L: David, Hal)

## 4902 ✦ RETURN OF THE SECAUCUS 7
Specialty/Libra Films, 1980

**Composer(s)** Le Fevre, Adam
**Lyricist(s)** Le Fevre, Adam

**Producer(s)** Nelson, Jeffrey; Aydelott, William
**Director(s)** Sayles, John
**Screenwriter(s)** Sayles, John

**Cast** Sayles, John; Renzi, Maggie; Clapp, Gordon; Strathairn, David; Trott, Karen; Arnott, Mark; Mac Donald, Bruce; Le Fevre, Adam

**Song(s)** Mean to Me; I Brake for Animals; Free, White and 21

**Notes** No cue sheet available.

## 4903 ✦ RETURN TO HORROR HIGH
New World, 1987

**Musical Score** Widelitz, Stacy

**Producer(s)** Lisson, Mark
**Director(s)** Froehlich, Bill
**Screenwriter(s)** Froehlich, Bill; Lisson, Mark; Escalente, Dana; Sims, Greg H.

**Cast**  Lethin, Lori; Hughes, Brendan; Rocco, Alex; Jacoby, Scott; Romano, Andy; Brestoff, Richard; Martin, Pepper; Edwards, Vince; McKeon, Philip

**Song(s)**  Greet the Teacher (C/L: Weir, Larry); Man for Me (C/L: Widelitz, Stacy; Fraser, Wendy); Scary Movies (C/L: Weir, Larry)

**Notes**  No cue sheet available.

## 4904 ◆ RETURN TO PEYTON PLACE
Twentieth Century–Fox, 1961

**Musical Score**  Waxman, Franz

**Producer(s)**  Wald, Jerry
**Director(s)**  Ferrer, Jose
**Screenwriter(s)**  Alexander, Ronald
**Source(s)**  *Return to Peyton Place* (novel) Metalious, Grace

**Cast**  Lynley, Carol; Chandler, Jeff; Parker, Eleanor; Astor, Mary; Sterling, Robert; Weld, Tuesday; MacDonald, Kenneth; Crane, Bob; Bradley, Bill; Paluzzi, Luciana

**Song(s)**  The Wonderful Season of Love [1] (C: Waxman, Franz; L: Webster, Paul Francis)

**Notes**  [1] Also in PEYTON PLACE.

## 4905 ◆ REUNION IN FRANCE
Metro–Goldwyn–Mayer, 1942

**Musical Score**  Waxman, Franz

**Producer(s)**  Mankiewicz, Joseph L.
**Director(s)**  Dassin, Jules
**Screenwriter(s)**  Lustig, Jan; Borowsky, Marvin; Connelly, Marc

**Cast**  Crawford, Joan; Wayne, John; Dorn, Philip; Owen, Reginald; Basserman, Albert; Carradine, John; Ayars, Ann; Bromberg, J. Edward

**Song(s)**  Close Up the Ranks [1] (C: Kane, Edward; L: Brent, Earl)

**Notes**  Released as MADEMOISELLE FRANCE overseas. There is also a vocal of "I'll Be Glad When You're Dead You Rascal You" by Charles Davenport. [1] Also in THE MORTAL STORM, but with music by Bronislau Kaper.

## 4906 ◆ REUNION IN VIENNA
Metro–Goldwyn–Mayer, 1933

**Musical Score**  Axt, Walter

**Director(s)**  Franklin, Sidney
**Screenwriter(s)**  Vajda, Ernest; West, Claudine
**Source(s)**  *Reunion in Vienna* (play) Sherwood, Robert E.

**Cast**  Barrymore, John; Wynyard, Diana; Morgan, Frank; Travers, Henry; Robson, May; Ciannelli, Eduardo; Merkel, Una; Walker, Nella

**Song(s)**  Vienna in May (C: Axt, Walter; L: Kahn, Gus)

## 4907 ◆ REVEILLE WITH BEVERLY
Columbia, 1943

**Producer(s)**  White, Sam
**Director(s)**  Barton, Charles
**Screenwriter(s)**  Duffy, Albert; Green, Howard J.; Henley, Jack
**Source(s)**  "It's a Date with Reveille with Beverly" (radio show) Ruth, Jean

**Cast**  Miller, Ann; Wright, William; Leavitt, Douglas; Mara, Adele; Parks, Larry; Sinatra, Frank; Pangborn, Franklin; Ryan, Tim; Tombes, Andrew; The Mills Brothers; Bob Crosby and His Orchestra; Freddie Slack and His Orchestra; Duke Ellington and His Orchestra; Count Basie and His Orchestra; The Radio Rogues

**Notes**  Also known as IT'S A DATE AT REVEILLE WITH BEVERLY. There are no original songs in this musical. Numbers include "I-Yi-Yi-Yi (So Wish Me Luck Amigo)" by C. Fernandez with lyrics by John Redmond and Jimmy Cavanaugh and based on Fernandez' songs "Cielito Lindo," "One O'Clock Jump" by Bob Zurke; "Big Noise from Winnetka" by Ray Bauduc and Bob Haggart; "Take the 'A' Train" by Billy Strayhorn; "Night and Day" by Cole Porter; "Cow Cow Boogie" by Don Raye and Gene DePaul; "Sweet Lucy Brown" by Leon and Otis Rene; "Wabash Moon" by Morton Downey, Dave Dreyer and Billy McKenny; "When the Moon Comes Over the Mountain" by Harry Woods and Howard Johnson and "Thumbs Up and 'V'" by Paul Francis Webster and Ted Fiorito.

## 4908 ◆ REVENGE OF THE NERDS
Twentieth Century–Fox, 1984

**Musical Score**  Newman, Thomas

**Producer(s)**  Field, Ted; Samuelson, Peter
**Director(s)**  Kanew, Jeff
**Screenwriter(s)**  Zacharias, Steve; Buhai, Jeff

**Cast**  Carradine, Robert; Edwards, Anthony; Busfield, Tim; Cassese, Andrew; Armstrong, Curtis

**Song(s)**  Revenge of the Nerds (C/L: Paine, Bobby; Helmut, Gerhard); Burning Down the House [1] (C/L: Bryne, David); Breakdown (C/L: Dunbar, Tommy; Judge, C.); One Foot in Front of the Other (C/L: Wilk, Scott; Levinthal, Marc); Don't Talk (C/L: Hart, Lea; Callcut, Ray; Coler, Nick); All Night Party (C/L: Bohem, Les; Kendrick, David); Are You Ready for the Sex Girls (C/L: Bohem, Les; Kendrick, David); Thriller (C/L: Temperton, Rod); Right Time for Love (C/L: Michaels, Stephen; Pomeranz, David); Tricycle Races (C/L: Newman, Thomas); Mr. Touchdown U.S.A.

(C/L: Katz, Bill; Piller, Gene; Roberts, Ruth); Nerds Jam (C/L: Newman, Thomas); We Are the Champions (C/L: Mercury, Freddie); It's So Incredible (C/L: Brown, Ollie E.; Knight, Jerry; Newman, Thomas)

**Notes**   It is not known which of these were written for this film. [1] Also in TURK 182 where credits also included Chris Frantz, Tina Weymouth and Herry Harrison.

## 4909   ✦   REVENGE OF THE NERDS II: NERDS IN PARADISE
### Twentieth Century–Fox, 1987

**Musical Score**   Mothersbaugh, Mark; Casale, Gerald V.

**Producer(s)**   Field, Ted; Cort, Robert W.; Bart, Peter
**Director(s)**   Roth, Joe
**Screenwriter(s)**   Guntzelman, Dan; Marshall, Steve

**Cast**   Carradine, Robert; Armstrong, Curtis; Scott, Larry B.; Busfield, Larry B.; Thorne-Smith, Courtney; Cassese, Andrew; Gibb, Donald; Whitford, Bradley; Lauter, Ed; Sobel, Barry; Lopez, Priscilla

**Song(s)**   No On Fifteen (C: Moore, J.B.; L: Scott, Larry B.; Sobel, Barry; Solomon, Ed); Back to Paradise (C/L: Adams, Bryan; Vallance, Jim; Giraldo, Pat)

**Notes**   No cue sheet available.

## 4910   ✦   REVENGE OF THE PINK PANTHER
### United Artists, 1978

**Musical Score**   Mancini, Henry

**Producer(s)**   Edwards, Blake
**Director(s)**   Edwards, Blake
**Screenwriter(s)**   Waldman, Frank; Clark, Ron; Edwards, Blake

**Cast**   Sellers, Peter; Lom, Herbert; Cannon, Dyan; Webber, Robert

**Song(s)**   Move 'Em Out (C: Mancini, Henry; L: Bricusse, Leslie)

## 4911   ✦   THE REVOLT OF MAMIE STOVER
### Twentieth Century–Fox, 1956

**Musical Score**   Friedhofer, Hugo

**Producer(s)**   Adler, Buddy
**Director(s)**   Walsh, Raoul
**Screenwriter(s)**   Boehm, Sydney
**Source(s)**   *The Revolt of Mamie Stover* (novel) Hule, William Bradford

**Cast**   Russell, Jane; Egan, Richard; Leslie, Joan; Moorehead, Agnes; Pate, Michael; Reed, Alan

**Song(s)**   If You Wanna See Mamie Tonight (C: Fain, Sammy; L: Webster, Paul Francis); Walkin' Home with the Blues [1] (C: Friedhofer, Hugo; L: Washington,

Ned); Keep Your Eyes on the Hands (C/L: Todaro, Tony; Johnston, Mary)

**Notes**   [1] Instrumental use only.

## 4912   ✦   REVOLUTION
### United Artists, 1968

**Producer(s)**   Leder, Robert J.
**Director(s)**   O'Connell, Jack

**Cast**   Malone, Today; Caen, Herb; Davis, Ronnie; Gottlieb, Lou; Hirschhorn, Dr. Kurt; Mother Earth; Ann Halprin's Dancers Workshop Company; Steve Miller Band; Country Joe and the Fish; Quicksilver Messenger Company

**Song(s)**   Revolution (C/L: Martin, Norman; O'Connell, Jack); Grass Is Greener (C/L: Hursh, Diane; Kaufman, Denise; Gannon, Mary Pat; Hunt, Marla); Mercury Blues (C/L: Miller, Steve; Douglas, K.C.)

**Notes**   There are other vocals of popular tunes of the time.

## 4913   ✦   THE REWARD
### Twentieth Century–Fox, 1965

**Musical Score**   Bernstein, Elmer
**Composer(s)**   Bernstein, Elmer
**Lyricist(s)**   Guerrero, Margaret

**Producer(s)**   Rosenberg, Aaron
**Director(s)**   Bourguignon, Serge
**Screenwriter(s)**   Bourguignon, Serge; Millard, Oscar
**Source(s)**   (novel) Barrett, Michael

**Cast**   Von Sydow, Max; Mimieux, Yvette; Zimbalist Jr., Efrem; Roland, Gilbert; Castelnuovo, Nino; Silva, Henry; Acosta, Rodolfo

**Song(s)**   Dame Tu Corazon; Song for the Reward

## 4914   ✦   RHAPSODY IN BLUE
### Warner Brothers, 1945

**Choreographer(s)**   Prinz, LeRoy

**Producer(s)**   Lasky, Jesse L.
**Director(s)**   Rapper, Irving
**Screenwriter(s)**   Koch, Howard W.; Paul, Elliot

**Cast**   Alda, Robert [2]; Leslie, Joan [1]; Smith, Alexis; Coburn, Charles; Levant, Oscar; Whiteman, Paul; White, George; Scott, Hazel; Brown, Anne; Jolson, Al; Bishop, Julie; Basserman, Albert; Carnovsky, Morris; De Camp, Rosemary; Rudley, Herbert; Hughes, John B.; Roth, Mickey; Hickman, Darryl; Halton, Charles; Tombes, Andrew; Downs, Johnny

**Notes**   This is a film biography of George Gershwin. Some of these are background vocals and some are briefly in medleys. None were written for this picture. All have music by George Gershwin and lyrics by Ira Gershwin unless the lyricist appears in quotations:

"Swanee" (Irving Caesar), "'S Wonderful," "Somebody Loves Me" (B.G. DeSylva and Ballard Macdonald), "I'll Build a Stairway to Paradise" (B.G. DeSylva and Arthur Francis, pseudonym for Ira Gershwin), "Oh Lady Be Good," "135th Street Blues" (Irving Caesar), "The Man I Love," "Clap Yo' Hands," "Fascinating Rhythm," "Do It Again," "I Got Rhythm," "Yankee Doodle Blues" (Irving Caesar and B.G. DeSylva), "Bidin' My Time," "Embraceable You," "Mine," "Delishious," "Summertime" (Du Bose Heyward), "I Got Plenty O' Nuttin'" (Du Bose Heyward and Ira Gershwin) and "Love Walked In." [1] Dubbed by Louanne Hogan. [2] Piano playing dubbed by Ray Turner.

## 4915 ◆ RHAPSODY IN WOOD
Paramount, 1947

**Musical Score**  Burns, Ralph

**Producer(s)**  Pal, George
**Director(s)**  Pal, George

**Cast**  Woody Herman and His Orchestra

**Song(s)**  Chop It (C/L: Burns, Ralph)

**Notes**  This is a Puppetoon short.

## 4916 ◆ RHINESTONE
Twentieth Century–Fox, 1984

**Musical Score**  Post, Mike
**Composer(s)**  Parton, Dolly
**Lyricist(s)**  Parton, Dolly

**Producer(s)**  Smith, Howard; Worth, Marvin
**Director(s)**  Clark, Bob
**Screenwriter(s)**  Robinson, Phil Alden; Stallone, Sylvester

**Cast**  Stallone, Sylvester; Parton, Dolly; Farnsworth, Richard; Leibman, Ron; Thomerson, Tim

**Song(s)**  Tennessee Homesick Blues; The Day My Baby Died (C/L: Post, Mike); Too Much Water; Devil with the Blue Dress On (C/L: Long, Frederick; Stevenson, William); Goin' Back to Heaven; Your Cheatin' Heart (C/L: Williams, Hank); One Emotion After Another; Sad, Sad Tale; Drinkin' Stein; Honky Tonkin' (C/L: Williams, Hank); Waltz Me to Heaven; Sweet Lovin' Friends; God Won't Get You; Woke Up in Love; Butterflies; What a Heartache; I Hope You're Never Happy; Stay Out of My Bedroom; Be There

**Notes**  It is not known which of these were written for the film.

## 4917 ◆ RHUBARB
Paramount, 1951

**Composer(s)**  Livingston, Jay; Evans, Ray
**Lyricist(s)**  Livingston, Jay; Evans, Ray

**Producer(s)**  Perlberg, William; Seaton, George
**Director(s)**  Lubin, Arthur

**Screenwriter(s)**  Reid, Dorothy; Cockrell, Francis
**Source(s)**  *Rhubarb* (novel) Smith, H. Allen

**Cast**  Milland, Ray; Sterling, Jan; Lockhart, Gene; Frawley, William; Waterman, Willard; Rhubarb

**Song(s)**  Friendly Finance Company; It's a Priv'lege to Live in Brooklyn

## 4918 ◆ RHUMBA RHYTHM
Metro–Goldwyn–Mayer, 1939

**Song(s)**  Canto De Dolar (C/L: Sanchez, Alfonso); Conga (C/L: Duran, Carlos)

**Notes**  Short subject.

## 4919 ◆ RHYTHM HITS THE ICE
Studio Unknown

**Notes**  A re-issue of ICE-CAPADES REVUE. See ICE CAPADES REVUE.

## 4920 ◆ RHYTHM INN
Monogram, 1951

**Composer(s)**  Kay, Edward J.
**Lyricist(s)**  Kay, Edward J.

**Producer(s)**  Parsons, Lindsley
**Director(s)**  Landres, Paul
**Screenwriter(s)**  Raynor, Bill

**Cast**  Smith, Charles; Collier, Lois; Grant, Kirby; Frazee, Jane; Feld, Fritz; Sanford, Ralph; Armida; Anson Weeks and His Orchestra; Ritchie, Jean; Ames and Arno; Rox, Ramon

**Song(s)**  Chi Chi (C/L: Armida); Love (C/L: Kay, Edward J.; Raynor, Bill); B Flat Blues; Return Trip; What Does It Matter?; With a Twist of the Wrist (C/L: Graham, Irvin)

**Notes**  No cue sheet available. There is also a vocal of "It's a Big Wide Wonderful World" by John Rox.

## 4921 ◆ RHYTHM IN THE CLOUDS
Republic, 1937

**Composer(s)**  Handman, Lou
**Lyricist(s)**  Hirsch, Walter

**Producer(s)**  Levoy, Albert E.
**Director(s)**  Auer, John H.
**Screenwriter(s)**  Cooper, Olive

**Cast**  Ellis, Patricia; Hull, Warren; Newell, William; Carle, Richard; Judels, Charles; Tilbury, Zeffie; Sedan, Rolfe

**Song(s)**  Don't Ever Change; Hawaiian Hospitality [1] (C/L: Owens, Harry); Two Hearts Are Dancing

**Notes**  [1] Ray Kinney also credited on sheet music.

## 4922 ✦ RHYTHM OF THE ISLANDS
Universal, 1943

**Composer(s)** Long, Andy Ione; Herscher, Louis
**Lyricist(s)** Long, Andy Ione; Herscher, Louis

**Producer(s)** Burton, Bernard W.
**Director(s)** Neill, Roy William
**Screenwriter(s)** Brodney, Oscar; Musselman, M.M.

**Cast** Jones, Allan; Devine, Andy; Truex, Ernest; Frazee, Jane; Gateson, Marjorie; Acquanetta; Paiva, Nestor; Maxwell, John; The Step Brothers; The Horton Dancers

**Song(s)** It Happened in Kaloha (Isle of Romance) (C: Skinner, Frank; L: Pepper, Buddy; James, Inez); Blue Mist; Hura Hura; I've Got My Mind on You (C: Mizzy, Vic; L: Taylor, Irving); Drifting in the Moonlight; Savage Serenade (C/L: Franklin, Dave); Chant of the Tom Tom (C/L: Pepper, Buddy; James, Inez); Bonga Bonga [1]

**Notes** [1] Sheet music only.

## 4923 ✦ RHYTHM OF THE SADDLE
Republic, 1938

**Composer(s)** Marvin, Johnny; Rose, Fred
**Lyricist(s)** Marvin, Johnny; Rose, Fred

**Producer(s)** Grey, Harry
**Director(s)** Sherman, George
**Screenwriter(s)** Franklin, Paul

**Cast** Autry, Gene; Burnette, Smiley; Kelton, Pert; Moran, Peggy; Mason, LeRoy; Loft, Arthur; Laidlaw, Ethan; Acuff, Eddie

**Song(s)** The Old Trail (C/L: Autry, Gene; Marvin, Johnny; Rose, Fred); Oh, Ladies!; Merry-Go-Roundup (C/L: Autry, Gene; Marvin, Johnny; Rose, Fred); When Mother Nature Sings Her Lullaby (C/L: Toell, Larry; Brown, Glenn)

**Notes** No cue sheet available.

## 4924 ✦ RHYTHM ON ICE
Warner Brothers, 1945

**Song(s)** Rhythm on Ice (C: Jerome, M.K.; L: Scholl, Jack)

**Notes** Short subject. "The Lullaby of Broadway" by Al Dubin and Harry Warren was also used.

## 4925 ✦ RHYTHM ON THE RANGE
Paramount, 1936

**Producer(s)** Glazer, Benjamin
**Director(s)** Taurog, Norman
**Screenwriter(s)** Moffitt, John C.; Salkow, Sidney; De Leon, Walter; Marion, Frances

**Cast** Farmer, Frances; Sons of the Pioneers [1]; Crosby, Bing; Raye, Martha; Burns, Bob; Gleason, Lucille; Hinds, Samuel S.; Hymer, Warren; Stone, George E.

**Song(s)** Empty Saddles [7] (C: Hill, Billy; L: Brennan, J. Keirn); Roundup Lullaby (C: Ross, Gertrude; L: Clark, Badger); I Can't Escape from You [6] (C: Whiting, Richard A.; L: Robin, Leo); Mr. Paganini (If You Can't Sing It You'll Have to Swing It) [4] (C/L: Coslow, Sam); Drink It Down (C: Rainger, Ralph; L: Robin, Leo); I'm an Old Cowhand [11] (C/L: Mercer, Johnny [5]); Wing Ding (C/L: Sons of the Pioneers [1]); The House Jack Built for Jill [2] [8] (C: Hollander, Frederick; L: Robin, Leo); Rhythm on the Range [3] [8] (C: Whiting, Richard A.; L: Bullock, Walter); Hang Up My Saddle [3] (C: Whiting, Richard A.; L: Bullock, Walter); Low [3] (C: Rainger, Ralph; L: Robin, Leo); The Call of the Prairie [3] (C: Lawnhurst, Vee; L: Seymour, Tot); Rhythm of the Range [3] (C/L: Wolfe; Brennon); Song of the River [3] (C/L: Wolfe; Brennon); Guitars of Love [3] (C/L: Wolfe; Brennon); I Can't Play the Banjo with Susannah on My Knee [3] [10] (C: Boutelje, Phil; L: Scholl, Jack); My Donkey and Me [3] (C: Boutelje, Phil; L: Scholl, Jack)

**Notes** [1] These included Tim Spencer, Hugh Farr, Bob Nolan, Len Slye (two years later to begin a new career as Roy Rogers) and Carl Farr. [2] Not used but recorded. [3] Not used. [4] Originally titled "Mr. Toscanini." [5] The Russioni character's lyrics were written by Sam Coslow. Coslow also wrote a chorus about the cowhand who could make a steer do a hand stand. Mercer wrote the special lyric for Crosby and Raye about how their characters Jeff and Emma sing duets with a cowboy band. [6] Not used in film.

## 4926 ✦ RHYTHM ON THE RIVER
Paramount, 1940

**Composer(s)** Monaco, James V.
**Lyricist(s)** Burke, Johnny

**Producer(s)** LeBaron, William
**Director(s)** Schertzinger, Victor
**Screenwriter(s)** Taylor, Dwight

**Cast** Rathbone, Basil; Crosby, Bing; Martin, Mary; Levant, Oscar; Shaw, Oscar; Grapewin, Charley; Frawley, William; Cornell, Lillian; Cagney, Jeanne; Lane, Charles

**Song(s)** What Would Shakespeare Have Said; That's for Me; Only Forever; When the Moon Comes Over Madison Square (The Love Lament of a Western Gent); Rhythm on the River; Ain't It a Shame About Mame; I Don't Want to Cry Any More (C/L: Schertzinger, Victor); Two Hearts Deep in Love [1] (C/L: Schertzinger, Victor); It's a Good Thing I Don't Care [1]; My Heart Is a Hobo [1] [2]

**Notes** Film originally titled GHOST MUSIC. [1] Not used. [2] This is the same title of a song Johnny Burke wrote with Jimmy Van Heusen for WELCOME STRANGER in 1947. About 80% of the lyric is the same however the lyric has been restructured slightly to fit a new tune.

## 4927 ◆ RHYTHM PARADE
Monogram, 1942

**Choreographer(s)**   Gould, Dave

**Producer(s)**   Williams, Sydney M.
**Director(s)**   Bretherton, Howard; Gould, Dave
**Screenwriter(s)**   Foreman, Carl; Marion, Charles R.

**Cast**   Ted Fiorito and His Orchestra; The Mills Brothers; Candido, Candy; Chandler, Chick; Nazarro, Cliff; Granlund, Nils T.; Storm, Gale; Lowery, Robert; Dumont, Margaret; Milton, Julie; Geise, Sugar

**Song(s)**   Tootin' My Own Horn (C/L: Kay, Edward J.; Cherkose, Eddie); Petticoat Army (C/L: Oppenheim, Dave; Ingraham, Roy); 'Neath the Yellow Moon in Old Tahiti (C/L: Kay, Edward; Cherkose, Eddie); Mimi from Tahiti (C/L: Oppenheim, Dave; Ingraham, Roy); You're Drafted (C/L: Oppenheim, Dave; Ingraham, Roy)

**Notes**   No cue sheet available. There are also vocals of "Wait Till the Sun Shines Nellie" by Andrew B. Sterling and Harry Von Tilzer and "Sweet Sue" by Will J. Harris and Victor Young.

## 4928 ◆ RHYTHM ROUND-UP
Columbia, 1945

**Producer(s)**   Clark, Colbert
**Director(s)**   Keays, Vernon
**Screenwriter(s)**   Marion, Charles R.

**Cast**   Curtis, Ken; Walker, Cheryl; The Hoosier Hotshots [1]; Bob Wills and His Texas Playboys; The Pied Pipers; Williams, Guinn "Big Boy"; Hatton, Raymond

**Song(s)**   That's What I Learned in College (C/L: Andrews, Andy; Davis, Johnny); San Antonio Rose [3] (C/L: Wills, Bob); Empty Saddles [2] (C/L: Hill, Billy); Mysterious Mose (C/L: Weems, Ted; Doyle, Walter); Beautiful Dreamer (C/L: Foster, Stephen); Don't Be Tellin' Me Your Troubles (C/L: Seeley, Ray); Corrine Corrina (C/L: Traditional); Tumbling Tumbleweeds [4] (C/L: Nolan, Bob); Mind If I Love You (C/L: Hopper, Hal; Adair, Tom); The Berrys and the Nutts (C/L: Frost, Jack)

**Notes**   There are no original songs in this picture. [1] Consisted of Kenneth H. Trietsch, Paul F. Trietsch, Charles O. Ward and Gilbert O. Taylor. [2] Also in RHYTHM ON THE RANGE (Paramount) with lyrics credited to J. Kiern Brennan. [3] Also in UNDER COLORADO SKIES (Republic), SAN ANTONIO ROSE (Universal), BOB WILLS AND HIS TEXAS PLAYBOYS (Warner) and HONKYTONK MAN

(Warner). [4] Also in DON'T FENCE ME IN, IN OLD MONTEREY, SILVER SPURS, TUMBLING TUMBLEWEEDS (all by Republic) and HOLLYWOOD CANTEEN (Warner).

## 4929 ◆ THE RICH ARE ALWAYS WITH US
Warner Brothers, 1932

**Producer(s)**   Griffith, Ray
**Director(s)**   Green, Alfred E.
**Screenwriter(s)**   Parker, Austin
**Source(s)**   (novel) Pettit, E.

**Cast**   Chatterton, Ruth; Brent, George; Davis, Bette; Miljan, John; Warwick, Robert; Wray, John; Churchill, Berton; Walker, Walter

**Song(s)**   What a Life (C: Alter, Louis; L: Kent, Charlotte)

## 4930 ◆ RICH KIDS
United Artists, 1979

**Musical Score**   Doerge, Craig
**Composer(s)**   Doerge, Craig
**Lyricist(s)**   Nicholls, Allan

**Producer(s)**   George, George W.; Hausman, Michael
**Director(s)**   Young, Robert M.
**Screenwriter(s)**   Ross, Judith

**Cast**   Alvarado, Trini; Levy, Jeremy; Walker, Kathryn; Lithgow, John; Kiser, Terry; Worth, Irene

**Song(s)**   I Don't Want to Dance; Hot Love in a Minute; You Changed All of That; Reasons; You Knock Me Out; Fast Asleep; Good Bye Yesterday (C/L: Alper, John; Bllink, Alan; Drachman, Ted); Happy Ida and Broken Hearted John (L: Henske, Judy)

**Notes**   Cue sheet does not differentiate between vocals and instrumentals.

## 4931 ◆ RICH, YOUNG AND DEADLY

See PLATINUM HIGH SCHOOL.

## 4932 ◆ RICH, YOUNG AND PRETTY
Metro–Goldwyn–Mayer, 1951

**Musical Score**   Rose, David
**Composer(s)**   Brodszky, Nicholas
**Lyricist(s)**   Cahn, Sammy
**Choreographer(s)**   Castle, Nick

**Producer(s)**   Pasternak, Joe
**Director(s)**   Taurog, Norman
**Screenwriter(s)**   Cooper, Dorothy; Sheldon, Sidney

**Cast**   Powell, Jane; Darrieux, Danielle; Corey, Wendell; Lamas, Fernando; Dalio, Marcel; Merkel, Una; Anderson, Richard; Murat, Jean; deKerekjarto, Duci; Damone, Vic

**Song(s)** Paris; Mlle from Armentiers (C: Traditional; L: Brent, Earl); L'Amour Toujours (Tonight for Sure); Wonder Why [2]; I Can See You; We Never Talk Much; Dark Is the Night (C'est Fini) [1]; How D'Ya Like Your Eggs in the Morning

**Notes** There are also vocals of "Deep in the Heart of Texas" by Don Swander and June Hershey; "There's Danger in Your Eyes, Cherie" by Harry Richman, Jack Meskill and Pete Wendling and "The Old Piano Roll Blues" by Cy Coben. [1] Also in STORY OF THREE LOVES. [2] Also in SMALL TOWN GIRL (1953) and HOLIDAY FOR SINNERS.

## 4933 ✦ RICOCHET ROMANCE
Universal, 1954

**Musical Score** Lava, William

**Producer(s)** Arthur, Robert
**Director(s)** Lamont, Charles
**Screenwriter(s)** Lenard, Kay

**Cast** Main, Marjorie; Wills, Chill; Gonzales-Gonzales, Pedro; Bedoya, Alfonso; Vallee, Rudy; Hampton, Ruth; Venuta, Benay; Ryan, Irene; Hickman, Darryl

**Song(s)** Un Tequila (C/L: Gonzalez-Gonzalez, Arturo); Ricochet Romance (C/L: Coleman, Larry; Darion, Joe; Gimbel, Norman); Para Vigo Me Voy (C/L: Lecuona, Ernesto)

## 4934 ✦ RIDE A WILD PONY
Disney, 1975

**Musical Score** Addison, John

**Producer(s)** Courtland, Jerome
**Director(s)** Chaffey, Don
**Screenwriter(s)** Sisson, Rosemary Anne
**Source(s)** A Sporting Proposition (novel) Aldridge, James

**Cast** Craig, Michael; Meillon, John; Bettles, Robert; Griffith, Eva; Rouse, Graham; Bell, Alfred

**Song(s)** Ride a Wild Pony [1] (C: Addison, John; L: Jackman, Bob)

**Notes** [1] Used instrumentally only.

## 4935 ✦ THE RIDE BACK
United Artists, 1957

**Musical Score** De Vol, Frank

**Producer(s)** Conrad, William
**Director(s)** Miner, Allen H.
**Screenwriter(s)** Ellis, Anthony

**Cast** Quinn, Anthony; Conrad, William; Jilan, Lita; Trevino, George; Monroe, Ellen Hope

**Song(s)** The Ride Back (C/L: De Vol, Frank); It Is Not Far (C: De Vol, Frank; L: Unknown)

## 4936 ✦ RIDE BEYOND VENGEANCE
Columbia, 1966

**Musical Score** Markowitz, Richard

**Producer(s)** Fenady, Andrew J.
**Director(s)** McEveety, Bernard
**Screenwriter(s)** Fenady, Andrew J.
**Source(s)** The Night of the Tiger (novel) Dewlen, Al

**Cast** Connors, Chuck; Rennie, Michael; Hays, Kathryn; Blondell, Joan; Grahame, Gloria; Merrill, Gary; Bixby, Bill; Akins, Claude; Fix, Paul; MacArthur, James; O'Connell, Arthur; Warwick, Ruth; Baer, Buddy; Gorshin, Frank; Lewis, Robert Q.; Farr, Jamie

**Song(s)** You Can't Ever Go Home Again (C: Markowitz, Richard; L: Fenady, Andrew J.)

**Notes** No cue sheet available.

## 4937 ✦ RIDE CLEAR OF DIABLO
Universal, 1953

**Producer(s)** Rogers, John W.
**Director(s)** Hibbs, Jesse
**Screenwriter(s)** Zuckerman, George; Beauchamp, D.D.

**Cast** Murphy, Audie; Duryea, Dan; Johnson, Russell; Birch, Paul; Pullen, William; Pyle, Denver; Cabot, Susan; Lane, Abbe; Elam, Jack

**Song(s)** Wanted (C: Hughes, Arnold; L: Herbert, Frederick); Noche de Ronda [1] (C/L: Lara, Maria Teresa)

**Notes** [1] Also used (sometimes with English lyrics) in SOMBRERO (MGM), Spanish language versions of THE BIG BROADCAST OF 1938 (Paramount), MASQUERADE IN MEXICO (Paramount) and HAVANA ROSE (Republic).

## 4938 ✦ RIDE 'EM COWBOY (1932)
Warner Brothers, 1932

**Director(s)** Allen, Fred
**Screenwriter(s)** Mason, Scott

**Cast** Wayne, John; Hall, Ruth; Harlan, Otis; Walthall, Henry B.; Gribbon, Harry; Hagney, Frank

**Song(s)** Till We Meet Again (C/L: Whiting, Richard A.)

## 4939 ✦ RIDE 'EM COWBOY (1942)
Universal, 1942

**Musical Score** Skinner, Frank
**Composer(s)** de Paul, Gene
**Lyricist(s)** Raye, Don

**Producer(s)** Gottlieb, Alex
**Director(s)** Lubin, Arthur
**Screenwriter(s)** Boardman, True; Grant, John

**Cast** Abbott, Bud; Costello, Lou; Foran, Dick; Gwynne, Anne; The Merry Macs; Fitzgerald, Ella; Brown, Johnny Mack; Hinds, Samuel S.; Dumbrille, Douglass; Lane, Richard; Lane, Charles; The Hi-Hatters; The Buckaroos Band; The Ranger Chorus of Forty

**Song(s)** Give Me My Saddle; Wake Up, Jacob; Beside the Rio Tonto; I'll Remember April [1] (C/L: de Paul, Gene; Raye, Don; Johnston, Pat); Rockin' and Reelin'; Ride 'Em Cowboy

**Notes** There is also a vocal of "A Tisket, A Tasket" by Ella Fitzgerald and Al Feldman. [1] Also in THE GHOST CATCHERS, IDEA GIRL and I'LL REMEMBER APRIL. Not used in STRICTLY IN THE GROOVE.

## 4940 ◆ RIDE 'EM COWGIRL
### Grand National, 1939

**Composer(s)** Drake, Milton
**Lyricist(s)** Drake, Milton

**Producer(s)** Dreifuss, Arthur
**Director(s)** Diege, Samuel
**Screenwriter(s)** Hoerl, Arthur

**Cast** Page, Dorothy; Frome, Milton; Barnett, Vince; Mayberry, Lynn; Girad, Joseph; Reynolds, Harrington

**Song(s)** Campfire; Prairie Moon; You; I Love the Wide Open Spaces

**Notes** No cue sheet available.

## 4941 ◆ RIDE KELLY RIDE
### Twentieth Century–Fox, 1941

**Producer(s)** Wurtzel, Sol M.
**Director(s)** Foster, Norman
**Screenwriter(s)** Conselman Jr., William; Cummings, Irving

**Cast** Pallette, Eugene; Stephens, Marvin; Quigley, Rita; Healy, Mary; Lane, Richard; Brown, Charles D.; Chandler, Chick

**Song(s)** Dancing for Nickels and Dimes [1] (C: Newman, Lionel; L: Loesser, Frank)

**Notes** [1] Also in JOHNNY APOLLO.

## 4942 ◆ RIDE, RANGER, RIDE
### Republic, 1936

**Producer(s)** Schaefer, Armand
**Director(s)** Kane, Joseph
**Screenwriter(s)** McGowan, Dorrell; McGowan, Stuart

**Cast** Autry, Gene; Burnette, Smiley; Hughes, Kay; Blue, Monte; Lewis, George; Terhune, Max; The Tennessee Ramblers

**Song(s)** Ride, Ranger, Ride [1] (C/L: Spencer, Tim); The Bugle Song (C/L: Burnette, Smiley); On the Sunset Trail (C: Stept, Sam H.; L: Mitchell, Sidney D.); Song of the Pioneers (C/L: Spencer, Tim); Goin' Down the Road (C/L: Tennessee Ramblers, The)

**Notes** [1] Also in GANGSTERS OF THE FRONTIER (PRC), KING OF THE COWBOYS, THE BIG SHOW and TEXANS NEVER CRY (Columbia).

## 4943 ◆ RIDER ON A DEAD HORSE
### Allied Artists, 1962

**Musical Score** Hooven, Joseph

**Producer(s)** Altose, Kenneth
**Director(s)** Strock, Herbert L.
**Screenwriter(s)** Longstreet, Stephen

**Cast** Vivyan, John; Gordon, Bruce; Hagen, Kevin

**Song(s)** Rider on a Dead Horse (C: Hooven, Joe; L: Alperson Jr., Edward; Winn, Jerry)

**Notes** No cue sheet available.

## 4944 ◆ RIDERS IN THE SKY
### Columbia, 1949

**Director(s)** English, John
**Screenwriter(s)** Geraghty, Gerald
**Source(s)** "Fool and His Gold" (story) Woodbury, Herbert A.

**Cast** Autry, Gene; Champion; Henry, Gloria; Buttram, Pat; Hale Jr., Alan

**Song(s)** Ghost Riders in the Sky (C/L: Jones, Stan); It Makes No Difference Now [1] (C/L: Davis, Jimmie; Tillman, Floyd)

**Notes** [1] Also in MOUNTAIN RHYTHM (1939) (Republic).

## 4945 ◆ RIDERS OF DEATH VALLEY
### Universal, 1941

**Producer(s)** MacRae, Henry
**Director(s)** Beebe, Ford; Taylor, Ray
**Screenwriter(s)** Lowe, Sherman; Plympton, George; Dickey, Basil; O'Donnell, Jack

**Cast** Foran, Dick; Carrillo, Leo; Jones, Buck; Bickford, Charles; Chaney Jr., Lon; Beery Jr., Noah; Williams, Guinn "Big Boy"; Kelly, Jeanne; Blaine, James; Blue, Monte; Strange, Glenn

**Song(s)** Ride Along (C: Rosen, Milton; L: Carter, Everett)

**Notes** This is a serial in 15 chapters.

## 4946 ◆ RIDERS OF PASCO BASIN
### Universal, 1940

**Composer(s)** Rosen, Milton
**Lyricist(s)** Carter, Everett

**Director(s)**    Taylor, Ray
**Screenwriter(s)**    Beebe, Ford

**Cast**    Brown, Johnny Mack; Knight, Fuzzy; Baker, Bob

**Song(s)**    I'm Tying Up My Bridle to the Door of Your Heart [1]; Song of the Prairie [2]

**Notes**    Originally titled VIGILANTE WAR. [1] Also in GUNMAN'S CODE. [2] Also in BOSS OF HANGTOWN MESA.

## 4947 ✦ RIDERS OF THE NORTHLAND
### Columbia, 1942

**Producer(s)**    Fier, Jack
**Director(s)**    Berke, William
**Screenwriter(s)**    Franklin, Paul

**Cast**    Starrett, Charles; Hayden, Russell; Edwards, Cliff; Sutton, Paul; Bridges, Lloyd; Patterson, Shirley

**Song(s)**    Silver Sage in the Twilight (C/L: Unknown); We'll Carry the Torch for Miss Liberty (C/L: Wakely, Jimmy; Marvin, Johnny; Briggs, Jack)

**Notes**    No cue sheet available.

## 4948 ✦ RIDERS OF THE RIO GRANDE
### Republic, 1943

**Producer(s)**    Geay, Louis
**Director(s)**    Bretherton, Howard
**Screenwriter(s)**    De Mond, Albert
**Source(s)**    characters by MacDonald, William Colt

**Cast**    Steele, Bob; Tyler, Tom; Dodd, Jimmy; Van Sloan, Edward; Vallin, Rick; Barcroft, Roy

**Song(s)**    Wailin' in the Jailhouse Blues (C/L: Dodd, Jimmy)

## 4949 ✦ RIDERS OF THE TIMBERLINE
### Paramount, 1941

**Producer(s)**    Sherman, Harry
**Director(s)**    Selander, Lesley
**Screenwriter(s)**    Cheney, J. Benton
**Source(s)**    characters by Mulford, Clarence E.

**Cast**    Boyd, William; King, Brad; Stewart, Eleanor; Clyde, Andy; Nilsson, Anna Q.

**Song(s)**    The Fightin' Forty (C: Stern, Jack; L: Hamilton, Grace)

**Notes**    Originally titled TIMBER WOLVES.

## 4950 ✦ RIDERS OF THE WHISTLING PINES
### Columbia, 1948

**Composer(s)**    Burnette, Smiley
**Lyricist(s)**    Burnette, Smiley

**Producer(s)**    Schaefer, Armand
**Director(s)**    English, John
**Screenwriter(s)**    Townley, Jack

**Cast**    Autry, Gene; Champion; White, Patricia; Lloyd, Jimmy; 3 Pinafores [1]; Robards, Jason; Moore, Clayton; Dumbrille, Douglass

**Song(s)**    Let's Go Roamin' Around the Range; It's My Lazy Day; Hair of Gold, Sky of Blue [2] (C/L: Skylar, Sunny); Little Big Dry (C/L: Weber, Billy); Toolie Oolie Doolie (C/L: Horton, Vaughn; Buel, Art)

**Notes**    "Everytime I Feel Dr. Spirit" and "Yellow Rose of Texas" are also used vocally. [1] Consisted of Bula, Iona and Eunice Kettle. [2] May be titled "Hair of Gold, Eyes of Blue" which is a similar song title to one in SINGING SPURS.

## 4951 ✦ RIDERS OF VENGEANCE
### Universal, 1952

**Producer(s)**    Alland, William
**Director(s)**    Selander, Lesley
**Screenwriter(s)**    James, Polly; Hayward, Lillie

**Cast**    Conte, Richard; Lindfors, Viveca; Ankrum, Morris; Martin, Richard; Bishop, William; Britton, Barbara; O'Brian, Hugh

**Song(s)**    Farruca (C/L: Villarino, Jeronimo)

**Notes**    Formerly titled THE RAIDERS.

## 4952 ✦ RIDERS TO THE STARS
### United Artists, 1954

**Musical Score**    Sukman, Harry

**Producer(s)**    Tors, Ivan
**Director(s)**    Carlson, Richard
**Screenwriter(s)**    Siodmak, Curt

**Cast**    Lundigan, William; Marshall, Herbert; Carlson, Richard; Hyer, Martha; Addams, Dawn; Karnes, Robert

**Song(s)**    Riders to the Stars (C: Sukman, Harry; L: Pober, Leon)

## 4953 ✦ RIDE THE WILD SURF
### Columbia, 1964

**Musical Score**    Phillips, Stu

**Producer(s)**    Napoleon, Jo; Napoleon, Art
**Director(s)**    Taylor, Don
**Screenwriter(s)**    Napoleon, Jo; Napoleon, Art

**Cast**    Fabian; Hayes, John Anthony; Eden, Barbara; Fabares, Shelley; Mitchum, James; Hunter, Tab

**Song(s)**    Ride the Wild Surf (C/L: Berry, Jan; Wilson, Brian; Christian, Roger)

**Notes**    [1] Background vocal only.

## 4954 ✦ RIDIN' DOWN THE CANYON
### Republic, 1942

**Composer(s)** Spencer, Tim
**Lyricist(s)** Spencer, Tim

**Producer(s)** Grey, Harry
**Director(s)** Kane, Joseph
**Screenwriter(s)** De Mond, Albert

**Cast** Rogers, Roy; Hayes, George "Gabby"; Nolan, Bob; Sons of the Pioneers; Henry, Dee; Richards, Addison; Taliaferro, Hal

**Song(s)** Ridin' Down the Canyon [1] (C/L: Burnette, Smiley); Sagebrush Symphony; Who Am I [2] (C: Styne, Jule; L: Bullock, Walter); Blue Prairie (C/L: Spencer, Tim; Nolan, Bob); Curley Joe

**Notes** There are also vocals of "My Little Buckaroo" by Jack Scholl and M.K. Jerome and "In a Little Spanish Town" by Sam Lewis and Joe Young. [1] Also in SILVER CANYON (Columbia) and TUMBLING TUMBLEWEEDS. Gene Autry and Nick Manoloff also credited on sheet music. [2] Also in HIT PARADE OF 1941 and THE TIGER WOMAN.

## 4955 ✦ RIDING HIGH (1943)
### Paramount, 1943

**Composer(s)** Rainger, Ralph
**Lyricist(s)** Robin, Leo

**Producer(s)** Kohlmar, Fred
**Director(s)** Marshall, George
**Screenwriter(s)** Arthur, Art; De Leon, Walter; Phillips, Arthur
**Source(s)** *Broadway Bill* (movie) Riskin, Robert

**Cast** Lamour, Dorothy; Powell, Dick; Moore, Victor; Daley, Cass; Lamb, Gil; Langan, Glenn; Cameron, Rod; Goodwin, Bill; Britton, Milt

**Song(s)** Whistling in the Light; I'm the Secretary to the Sultan [4] (C: Lilley, Joseph J.); Injun Gal - Heap Hep [3] (C: Rainger, Ralph; Lilley, Joseph J.; L: Lilley, Joseph J.; Robin, Leo); He Loved Me Till the All Clear Came [1] (C: Arlen, Harold; L: Mercer, Johnny); You're the Rainbow; Get Your Man; Willie the Wolf of the West (C: Lilley, Joseph J.); Lucky Cowboy [2]; No Love, No Nothin' [2] [6] (C/L: Robin, Leo); Rhythm in the Rockies [2]; Ooh, What You Could Do! [2]; Music from Paradise [5] (C: McHugh, Jimmy; L: Loesser, Frank)

**Notes** First titled CALGARY STAMPEDE and CANADIAN CAPERS. Titled MELOODY INN internationally. [1] Not written for this production. First appeared in STAR SPANGLED RHYTHM. [2] Not used. [3] The song was originally written by Rainger and Robin. Lilley rewrote the melody and some of the lyrics. The publication credits read: "Music: Ralph Rainger. Lyrics: Joseph J. Lilley and Leo Robin." [4] Lilley did not want to take any official credit for this song and

publication reads: "Words and Music by Leo Robin." [5] This is a lyric originally written to a tune by Manning Sherwin. When that team broke up the song was split and returned to its collaborators. Loesser then matched his lyric to music by Jimmy McHugh. It is used as as an instrumental in this film as well as in BOOGIE WOOGIE and THE STOOGE and was considered for but not used in BUCK BENNY RIDES AGAIN. [6] Same title as song in "The Gang's All Here" (20th), also with Robin lyric but with music by Harry Warren.

## 4956 ✦ RIDING HIGH (1950)
### Paramount, 1950

**Composer(s)** Van Heusen, James
**Lyricist(s)** Burke, Johnny

**Producer(s)** Capra, Frank
**Director(s)** Capra, Frank
**Screenwriter(s)** Shavelson, Melville; Rose, Jack

**Cast** Crosby, Bing; Gray, Coleen; Walburn, Raymond; Dumbrille, Douglass; Muse, Clarence; Harvey, Paul; Bond, Ward; Bickford, Charles; Demarest, William; Gifford, Frances; Gleason, James; Baer, Max; Darro, Frankie; Hamilton, Margaret; Kilbride, Percy; Lockhart, Gene; Lane, Charles; Hardy, Oliver

**Song(s)** Sunshine Cake; (We've Got a) Sure Thing; Someplace on Anywhere Road; The Horse Told Me; I'm Rolling in Rainbows [1]

**Notes** A remake of BROADWAY BILL. This project originated at Columbia as a remake of BROADWAY BILL. Capra took the project to Paramount along with some shot footage. This screenplay is very similar to the original by Riskin. The source of all this is a story by Mark Hellinger. Paramount bought the property and the film used in the Columbia picture. Some old footage was added to the new film, now titled RIDING HIGH. The footage included the sequence with "Miss Ma-Goof" (see below), "Reminiscent" by Louis Silvers and "Mirak March" by Constantine Bakeleinikoff. "The Whiffenpoof Song" by Meade Minnigerode, George S. Pomeroy and Tod B. Galloway was used as was Stephen Foster's "Camptown Races" and "Miss Ma-Goof" by Dave Dreyer and Cliff Friend. [1] Not used.

## 4957 ✦ RIDIN' ON A RAINBOW
### Republic, 1941

**Composer(s)** Styne, Jule
**Lyricist(s)** Meyer, Sol

**Producer(s)** Grey, Harry
**Director(s)** Landers, Lew
**Screenwriter(s)** Malloy, Doris; Ropes, Bradford

**Cast** Autry, Gene; Burnette, Smiley; Lee, Mary; Adams, Carol; Taylor, Ferris; Caine, Georgia; Conlin, Jimmy

**Song(s)** Steamboat Bill (C/L: Shields, Ken; Leighton Brothers, The); Ridin' on a Rainbow (C/L: George, Don; Herbert, Jean; Hall, Teddy); Hunky Dunky Dory (L: Gannon, Kim); Sing a Song of Laughter; What's Your Favorite Holiday; I'm the One Who's Lonely; You Are My Sunshine [2] (C/L: Davis, Jimmie; Mitchell, Charles); Uncle Luke Had a Beard; Carry Me Back to the Lone Prairie (C/L: Robison, Carson J.); Some Dancin' (C/L: Burnette, Smiley); Where the River Meets the Range [1]; Be Honest with Me [2] (C/L: Autry, Gene; Rose, Fred)

**Notes** [1] Also in BACK IN THE SADDLE. [2] Also in COWBOY SERENADE, I'M FROM ARKANSAS (PRC) and STRICTLY IN THE GROOVE (Universal).

## 4958 ✦ RIFF RAFF
### RKO, 1947

**Musical Score** Webb, Roy

**Producer(s)** Holt, Nat
**Director(s)** Tetzlaff, Ted
**Screenwriter(s)** Rackin, Martin

**Cast** O'Brien, Pat; Slezak, Walter; Jeffreys, Anne; Kilbride, Percy; Cowan, Jerome; Givot, George; Robards, Jason; Krah, Marc

**Song(s)** Money Is the Root of All Evil (C/L: Kramer, Alex; Whitney, Joan)

## 4959 ✦ THE RIGHT APPROACH
### Twentieth Century–Fox, 1961

**Producer(s)** Brodney, Oscar
**Director(s)** Butler, David
**Screenwriter(s)** Kanin, Fay; Kanin, Michael
**Source(s)** *The Live Wire* (play) Kanin, Garson

**Cast** Prowse, Juliet; Vaughan, Frankie; Hyer, Martha; Crosby, Gary; McLean, David

**Song(s)** The Right Approach [1] (C: Spence, Lew; L: Bergman, Alan; Keith, Marilyn); Lady Love Me (C/L: Stone, Kirby)

**Notes** There are also vocals of "Let's Make Love" and "A Certain Smile" by Sammy Fain and Paul Francis Webster. [1] Marilyn Keith later became Marilyn Bergman.

## 4960 ✦ RIKKY AND PETE
### United Artists, 1988

**Musical Score** Rayner, Eddie
**Composer(s)** Judd, Phil
**Lyricist(s)** Judd, Phil

**Producer(s)** Tass, Nadia; Parker, David
**Director(s)** Tass, Nadia
**Screenwriter(s)** Parker, David

**Cast** Kearney, Stephen; Landis, Nina; Agbayani, Tetchie

**Song(s)** Fingers Cross; Cold Shoulder; In the Dark; Tears of Joy; Just Like You; Hard to Believe

**Notes** No cue sheet available.

## 4961 ✦ RIM OF THE CANYON
### Columbia, 1949

**Director(s)** English, John
**Screenwriter(s)** Butler, John
**Source(s)** "Phantom 45's Talk Loud" (story) Chadwick, Joseph

**Cast** Autry, Gene; Champion; Sande, Walter; Mahoney, Jock [1]; Bevans, Clem; Hall, Thurston; Hale Jr., Alan

**Song(s)** Rim of the Canyon (C/L: Heath, Hy; Lange, Johnny); You're the Only Star in My Blue Heaven [2] (C/L: Autry, Gene); I'm Dancing Tonight with Lilly (C/L: Mertz, Paul; Schaefer, Armand)

**Notes** [1] Billed as Jacques O'Mahoney. [2] Also in Republic films: MEXICALI ROSE, THE OLD BARN DANCE and SPRINGTIME IN THE ROCKIES (1937).

## 4962 ✦ RING-A-DING RHYTHM!
### Columbia, 1962

**Producer(s)** Sobotsky, Milton
**Director(s)** Lester, Dick
**Screenwriter(s)** Subotsky, Milton

**Cast** Checker, Chubby; Bonds, Gary U.S.; MacDaniels, Gene; Shannon, Del; Shapiro, Helen; Douglas, Craig; Dukes of Dixieland [2]; The Paris Sisters [1]; The Brook Brothers; Vincent, Gene; Acker Bilk and His Paramount Jazz Band; Chris Barber and His Band with Ottilie Patterson; The Temperance Seven Ltd.; Terry Lightfoot and His New Orleans Jazzmen; Kenny Ball and His Jazz Band; Bob Wallis and His Storyville Jazz Men

**Song(s)** Double Trouble (C/L: Brook, Geoff; Brook, Ricky); Dream Away Romance (C/L: McDowell, Paul; Bevan, Clifford); Everybody Loves My Baby (C/L: Palmer, Jack; Williams, Spencer); Bellissima (C/L: Subotsky, Milton); Seven Day Weekend (C/L: Pomus, Doc; Shuman, Mort); What Am I to Do (C/L: Pomus, Doc; Spector, Phil); You Never Talked About Me (C/L: Pomus, Doc; Shuman, Mort); Another Tear Falls (C: Bacharach, Burt; L: David, Hal); Lose Your Inhibition Twist (C/L: Mann, Kal; Appell, Dave); Lonely City (C/L: Goddard, Geoffrey); Rainbows (C/L: Paramor, Norrie; Lewis, Bunny); Let's Talk About Love (C/L: Paramor, Norrie; Lewis, Bunny); Sometime Yesterday (C/L: Westlake, Clive); Beale Street Blues (C/L: Handy, W.C.); Ring-A-Ding (C/L: Paramor, Norrie; Lewis, Bunny); Aunt Flo [3] (C/L: Rainey, H.)

**Notes** It is not known if any are original songs. [1] Consisted of Albeth, Sherrell and Priscilla Paris. [2] Consisted of Frank and Fred Assunto. [3] BMI list only.

## 4963 ✦ RINGING UP THE CURTAIN

See BROADWAY TO HOLLYWOOD.

## 4964 ✦ RINGO AND HIS GOLDEN PISTOL
Metro–Goldwyn–Mayer, 1966

**Musical Score** Savina, Carlo

**Producer(s)** Fryd, Joseph
**Director(s)** Corbucci, Sergio
**Screenwriter(s)** Rossetti, A.; Bolzoni, F.

**Cast** Damon, Mark; Fabrizi, Valeria; Derosa, Franco; Rubini, Giulia; Loddi, Loris; Aueli, Andrea; Starnazza, Pippo; Manni, Ettore

**Song(s)** Johnny Oro (C: Savina, Carlo; L: Corbucci, B.); A Man of Gold (C: Savina, Carlo; L: MacDonald, L.)

## 4965 ✦ RING OF FEAR
Warner Brothers, 1954

**Musical Score** Newman, Emil; Lange, Arthur

**Producer(s)** Fellows, Robert
**Director(s)** Grant, James Edward
**Screenwriter(s)** Fix, Paul; MacDonald, Philip; Grant, James Edward

**Cast** Beatty, Clyde; O'Brien, Pat; Spillane, Mickey; McClory, Sean; Carr, Marian; Bromfield, John; Tobey, Kenneth

**Song(s)** Here Comes the Circus (C: Newman, Emil; L: Darby, Ken)

## 4966 ✦ RING OF FIRE
Metro–Goldwyn–Mayer, 1961

**Producer(s)** Stone, Andrew L.; Stone, Virginia
**Director(s)** Stone, Andrew L.
**Screenwriter(s)** Stone, Andrew L.

**Cast** Janssen, David; Taylor, Joyce; Gorshin, Frank; Marston, Joel; Johnson, James

**Song(s)** Ring of Fire (C/L: Eddy, Duane); Bobbie [1] (C/L: Winn, Jerry; Alperson Jr., Edward L.)

**Notes** [1] Used instrumentally only.

## 4967 ✦ RIO
Universal, 1939

**Composer(s)** Skinner, Frank
**Lyricist(s)** Freed, Ralph

**Director(s)** Brahm, John
**Screenwriter(s)** Kandel, Aben; Mayer, Edwin Justus; Avery, Stephen Morehouse; Partos, Frank

**Cast** Rathbone, Basil; Gurie, Sigrid; Cummings, Robert; McLaglen, Victor; Carrillo, Leo; Gilbert, Billy; Bacon, Irving; Hinds, Samuel S.

**Song(s)** Heart of Mine [1]; Love Opened My Eyes; Pancho Gonzales Etcetra the Gaucho; After the Rain

**Notes** [1] Also in JAILHOUSE BLUES with lyrics credited to Skinner.

## 4968 ✦ RIO BRAVO
Warner Brothers, 1959

**Musical Score** Tiomkin, Dimitri
**Composer(s)** Tiomkin, Dimitri
**Lyricist(s)** Webster, Paul Francis

**Producer(s)** Hawks, Howard
**Director(s)** Hawks, Howard
**Screenwriter(s)** Furthman, Jules; Brackett, Leigh

**Cast** Wayne, John; Martin, Dean; Nelson, Ricky; Dickinson, Angie; Brennan, Walter; Bond, Ward; Russell, John; Gonzales-Gonzales, Pedro; Akins, Claude; Carey Jr., Harry

**Song(s)** Rio Bravo; Blowing Wild [1]; My Rifle, My Pony and Me

**Notes** [1] Background instrumental use.

## 4969 ✦ RIO CONCHOS
Twentieth Century–Fox, 1964

**Musical Score** Goldsmith, Jerry

**Producer(s)** Weisbart, David
**Director(s)** Douglas, Gordon M.
**Screenwriter(s)** Landon, Joseph; Huffaker, Clair
**Source(s)** *Guns of Rio Conchos* (novel) Huffaker, Clair

**Cast** Boone, Richard; Whitman, Stuart; Franciosa, Anthony; Brown, Jim; O'Brien, Edmond; Acosta, Rodolfo

**Song(s)** Rio Conchos [1] (C: Goldsmith, Jerry; L: Wayne, Bernie)

**Notes** [1] Used instrumentally only.

## 4970 ✦ RIO GRANDE
Republic, 1950

**Composer(s)** Jones, Stan
**Lyricist(s)** Jones, Stan

**Producer(s)** Ford, John; Cooper, Merian C.
**Director(s)** Ford, John
**Screenwriter(s)** McGuinness, James Kevin
**Source(s)** "Million with No Record" (story) Bellah, James Warner

**Cast** Wayne, John; O'Hara, Maureen; Johnson, Ben; Jarman Jr., Claude; Carey Jr., Harry; Wills, Chill; Naish, J. Carrol; McLaglen, Victor

**Song(s)** Cattle Call (C/L: Owens, Tex); Aha, San Antone (C/L: Evans, Dale); My Gal Is Purple; Yellow Stripes [1]; Footsore Cavalry

**Notes**   There is also a vocal of "Down By the Glenside" by Peader Kearney and P.J. Ryan. [1] Also in ESCAPE FROM FORT BRAVO (MGM).

### 4971 ✦ RIO GRANDE PATROL
RKO, 1950

**Musical Score**   Sawtell, Paul; Webb, Roy

**Producer(s)**   Schlom, Herman
**Director(s)**   Selander, Lesley
**Screenwriter(s)**   Houston, Norman

**Cast**   Holt, Tim; Nigh, Jane; Fowley, Douglas; Martin, Richard; Moore, Cleo; Mallin, Rick; Tyler, Tom

**Song(s)**   You May Not Remember [1] (C: Oakland, Ben; L: Jessel, George)

**Notes**   There is also a vocal of "Camptown Races" by Stephen Foster. [1] Also in SHOW BUSINESS and TRAIL STREET.

### 4972 ✦ RIO GRANDE RANGER
Columbia, 1936

**Producer(s)**   Darmour, Larry
**Director(s)**   Bennett, Spencer Gordon
**Screenwriter(s)**   Gatzert, Nate

**Cast**   Allen, Bob; Meredith, Iris; Whitaker, Slim

**Song(s)**   In the Glomin' in Wyomin' (C: Zahler, Lee; L: Ormont, David)

### 4973 ✦ RIO RITA (1929)
RKO, 1929

**Musical Score**   Tierney, Harry
**Composer(s)**   Tierney, Harry
**Lyricist(s)**   McCarthy, Joseph
**Choreographer(s)**   Eaton, Pearl

**Producer(s)**   LeBaron, William
**Director(s)**   Reed, Luther
**Screenwriter(s)**   Reed, Luther; Mack, Russell
**Source(s)**   Rio Rita (musical) Bolton, Guy; Thompson, Fred; Tierney, Harry; McCarthy, Joseph

**Cast**   Nelson, Sam; Wheeler, Bert; Woolsey, Robert; Lee, Dorothy; Boles, John; Daniels, Bebe; Renevant, George

**Song(s)**   Jumping Bean; Kinkajou; Sweetheart; River Song; Rio Rita; Opening Mesa Franceisca; Espanola; Are You There?; The Rangers' Song; You're Always in My Arms, But Only in My Dreams [1]; Beneath Your Silken Shawl; When You're in Love You'll Waltz; Over the Boundry Line; Sweetheart We Need Each Other [2]; Spanish Dance; Following the Sun Around

**Notes**   The cue sheet doesn't differentiate between vocals and instrumentals. [1] Only song written for picture. Others from Broadway original. [2] Also in THE VAGABOND LOVER.

### 4974 ✦ RIO RITA (1942)
Metro–Goldwyn–Mayer, 1942

**Musical Score**   Stothart, Herbert
**Composer(s)**   Arlen, Harold
**Lyricist(s)**   Harburg, E.Y.
**Choreographer(s)**   Connolly, Bobby; Minnelli, Vincente; Robel, David

**Producer(s)**   Berman, Pandro S.
**Director(s)**   Simon, S. Sylvan
**Screenwriter(s)**   Connell, Richard; Lehman, Gladys; Grant, John

**Cast**   Abbott, Bud; Costello, Lou; Grayson, Kathryn; Carroll, John; Dane, Patricia; Conway, Tom; Whitney, Peter; Volusia, Eros

**Song(s)**   Long Before You Came Along; Introduction to Rangers' Song (C: Stothart, Herbert; L: Wright, Bob; Forrest, Chet); Rangers' Song [1] (C: Tierney, Harry; L: McCarthy, Joseph); Grampomix (C: Traditional; L: Mannheimer, Albert); Rio Rita [1] (C: Tierney, Harry; L: McCarthy, Joseph); Brazilian Dance (C/L: Barnet, Nilo M.); A Couple of Caballeros [2]; Most Unusual Weather (It's Such Unusual Weather) [2]; Poor Whippoorwill [2]

**Notes**   Only the title and a couple of songs remain from the stage score. There are also vocals of "Oro O Congo" by Lacerda and "The Shadow Song" by Meyerbeer. [1] From original Broadway show. [2] Not used.

### 4975 ✦ RIOT
Paramount, 1969

**Musical Score**   Komeda, Christopher

**Producer(s)**   Castle, William
**Director(s)**   Kulik, Buzz
**Screenwriter(s)**   Poe, James
**Source(s)**   The Riot (novel) Elli, Frank

**Cast**   Brown, Jim; Hackman, Gene; Kellin, Mike; David, Clifford

**Song(s)**   100 Years (C: Komeda, Christopher; L: Wells, Robert); Queen Stripper (C/L: Komeda, Christopher)

### 4976 ✦ RIOT IN CELL BLOCK 11
Allied Artists, 1953

**Musical Score**   Gilbert, Herschel Burke

**Producer(s)**   Wanger, Walter
**Director(s)**   Siegel, Don
**Screenwriter(s)**   Collins, Richard

**Cast**   Brand, Neville; Meyer, Emile; Faylen, Frank; Frees, Paul; Moore, Alvy; Greer, Dabbs; Bissell, Whit; Young, Carleton; Kennedy, Harold J.; Schallert, William; Hale, Jonathan

**Song(s)**   Can't You See the Answer in My Eyes (C: Gilbert, Herschel Burke; L: Kahn, Donald)

## 4977 ✦ RIPTIDE
Metro–Goldwyn–Mayer, 1934

**Musical Score**  Stothart, Herbert

**Director(s)**  Goulding, Edmund
**Screenwriter(s)**  Goulding, Edmund

**Cast**  Campbell, Mrs. Patrick; Marshall, Herbert; Goulding, Edmund; Shearer, Norma; Montgomery, Robert; Gallagher, Skeets; Forbes, Ralph; Tashman, Lilyan; Eddy, Helen Jerome; Hobbes, Halliwell

**Song(s)**  Riptide [1] (C: Donaldson, Walter; L: Kahn, Gus); We're Together Again [2] (C: Brown, Nacio Herb; L: Freed, Arthur)

**Notes**  [1] Used instrumentally only. [2] Not on cue sheets. Listed in Fordin's Arthur Freed book only.

## 4978 ✦ RISE AND SHINE
Twentieth Century–Fox, 1941

**Composer(s)**  Rainger, Ralph
**Lyricist(s)**  Robin, Leo
**Choreographer(s)**  Pan, Hermes

**Producer(s)**  Hellinger, Mark
**Director(s)**  Dwan, Allan
**Screenwriter(s)**  Mankiewicz, Herman J.
**Source(s)**  *My Life and Hard Times* (memoir) Thurber, James

**Cast**  Oakie, Jack; Murphy, George; Darnell, Linda [1]; Brennan, Walter; Berle, Milton; Leonard, Sheldon; Meek, Donald; Donnelly, Ruth; Walburn, Raymond; MacBride, Donald; Dunn, Emma; Waldron, Charles; Gover, Mildred; Haade, William

**Song(s)**  Hail to Bolenciecwcz; Central Two-Two-Oh-Oh; Men of Clayton; I'm Making a Play for You [2]; I Want to Be the Guy; Get Thee Behind Me, Clayton; Dance It Off [3]

**Notes**  [1] Dubbed. [2] Not used in CADET GIRL. [3] Not used.

## 4979 ✦ RITA SUE AND BOB TOO
Orion, 1987

**Musical Score**  Kamen, Michael

**Producer(s)**  Lieberson, Sandy
**Director(s)**  Clarke, Alan
**Screenwriter(s)**  Dunbar, Andrea
**Source(s)**  *The Arbor; Rita Sue and Bob Too* (plays) Dunbar, Andrea

**Cast**  Finneran, Siobhan; Holmes, Michelle; Costigan, George; Sharp, Lesley; Ross, Willie

**Song(s)**  Rita Sue and Bob Too (C/L: Kamen, Michael)

**Notes**  No cue sheet available.

## 4980 ✦ THE RITZ
Warner Brothers, 1976

**Musical Score**  Thorne, Ken
**Composer(s)**  Thorne, Ken
**Lyricist(s)**  Outten, Peter

**Producer(s)**  O'Dell, Denis
**Director(s)**  Lester, Richard
**Screenwriter(s)**  McNally, Terrance
**Source(s)**  *The Ritz* (play) McNally, Terrance

**Cast**  Weston, Jack [1]; Moreno, Rita [1]; Stiller, Jerry; Ballard, Kaye; Abraham, F. Murray; Price, Paul B.; Williams, Treat; Love, Bessie; King, Dave

**Song(s)**  Won't Make No Difference; Liberated Man

**Notes**  Jule Styne and Stephen Sondheim's "Everything's Comin' Up Roses" and "The Three Caballeros" by Manuel Esperon and Ray Gilbert are given vocal visual performances. [1] From Broadway cast.

## 4981 ✦ THE RIVER CHANGES
Warner Brothers, 1956

**Musical Score**  Webb, Roy

**Producer(s)**  Crump, Owen
**Director(s)**  Crump, Owen
**Screenwriter(s)**  Crump, Owen

**Cast**  Rory, Rosanna; Maresch, Harold; Mannhardt, Renate; Fisher, Henry; Oetzen, Jasper V.; Solomatin, Nick; Friebel, Otto; Magron, Rene; Brandt, Bert

**Song(s)**  I Am Home (C: Webb, Roy; L: Crump, Owen)

## 4982 ✦ RIVER LADY
Universal, 1948

**Musical Score**  Sawtell, Paul

**Producer(s)**  Goldstein, Leonard
**Director(s)**  Sherman, George
**Screenwriter(s)**  Beauchamp, D.D.; Bowers, William
**Source(s)**  *River Lady* (novel) Branch, Houston; Waters, Frank

**Cast**  De Carlo, Yvonne; Duryea, Dan; Cameron, Rod; Carter, Helena; Bates, Florence; McIntire, John; Lambert, Jack

**Song(s)**  Louie Sands and Jim McGee (C: Schumann, Walter; L: Brooks, Jack); In the Lake with Blake (C/L: Sawtell, Paul)

## 4983 ✦ THE RIVER NIGER
Cine Artists, 1976

**Musical Score**  Goldstein, Jerry

**Producer(s)**  Beckerman, Sidney; Jones, Isaac L.
**Director(s)**  Shah, Krishna

**Screenwriter(s)** Walker, Joseph A.
**Source(s)** *The River Niger* (play) Walker, Joseph A.

**Cast** Tyson, Cicely; Jones, James Earl; Gossett, Lou; Turman, Glynn; Allen, Jonelle; Mosley, Roger E.; Wilcox, Ralph

**Song(s)** The River Niger (C/L: Goldstein, Jerry)

**Notes** No cue sheet available.

## 4984 ✦ RIVER OF NO RETURN
Twentieth Century–Fox, 1954

**Composer(s)** Newman, Lionel
**Lyricist(s)** Darby, Ken

**Producer(s)** Rubin, Stanley
**Director(s)** Preminger, Otto
**Screenwriter(s)** Fenton, Frank

**Cast** Mitchum, Robert; Monroe, Marilyn; Calhoun, Rory; Rettig, Tommy; Vye, Murvyn; Spencer, Douglas; Beddoe, Don; Wright, Will; Baylor, Hal

**Song(s)** River of No Return; One Silver Dollar; I'm Gonna File My Claim; Down in the Meadow

## 4985 ✦ RIVER OF ROMANCE
Paramount, 1929

**Director(s)** Wallace, Richard
**Screenwriter(s)** Doherty, Ethel
**Source(s)** *Magnolia* (play) Tarkington, Booth

**Cast** Rogers, Charles "Buddy"; Beery, Wallace; Brian, Mary; Collyer, June; Walthall, Henry B.; Kohler, Fred

**Song(s)** Cotton Field Croon (C/L: Elkin, Clay Miller); Stand Still Jordon (C/L: Johnson, J. Rosamond); Who Will Shoe My Pretty Little Feet (C/L: Traditional); My Gambling Man (C/L: Traditional); Oh I'm a Girl (C/L: Traditional); My Lady Love (C: Coslow, Sam; L: Robin, Leo)

**Notes** The picture was first titled MAGNOLIA then A MAN MUST FIGHT.

## 4986 ✦ THE RIVER RAT
Paramount, 1984

**Musical Score** Post, Mike
**Composer(s)** Post, Mike
**Lyricist(s)** Geyer, Stephen

**Producer(s)** Larson, Bob
**Director(s)** Rickman, Tom
**Screenwriter(s)** Rickman, Tom

**Cast** Jones, Tommy Lee; Dennehy, Brian; Plimpton, Martha

**Song(s)** Rock on the Bayou; Take No Prisoners (L: Plunkett, Steve); Maybe Next Time; Halfway Right (L: Allen, Deborah); Wherever You Are; The River's Song

## 4987 ✦ THE RIVER'S EDGE
Twentieth Century–Fox, 1957

**Musical Score** Forbes, Louis

**Producer(s)** Bogeaus, Benedict
**Director(s)** Dwan, Allan
**Screenwriter(s)** Smith, Harold Jacob; Leicester, James
**Source(s)** *The Highest Mountain* (novel) Smith, Harold Jacob

**Cast** Milland, Ray; Quinn, Anthony; Paget, Debra

**Song(s)** The River's Edge (C: Forbes, Louis; L: Troup, Bobby)

## 4988 ✦ ROAD AGENT
Universal, 1941

**Producer(s)** Pivar, Ben
**Director(s)** Lamont, Charles
**Screenwriter(s)** Cox, Morgan B.; Strawn, Arthur; Tombragel, Maurice

**Cast** Foran, Dick; Carrillo, Leo; Devine, Andy

**Song(s)** Ridin' Home [1] (C: McHugh, Jimmy; L: Adamson, Harold)

**Notes** [1] Also in DESPERATE TRAILS (1939), THE ROAD TO RENO, STRICTLY IN THE GROOVE and TENTING TONIGHT ON THE OLD CAMP GROUND.

## 4989 ✦ ROADBLOCK
RKO, 1951

**Musical Score** Sawtell, Paul; Webb, Roy

**Producer(s)** Rachmil, Lewis J.
**Director(s)** Daniels, Harold
**Screenwriter(s)** Fisher, Steve; Bricker, George

**Cast** McGraw, Charles; Dixon, Jean; Gilmore, Lowell; Heydt, Louis Jean; Stone, Milburn

**Song(s)** So Swell of You (C/L: Davidson, Leona)

## 4990 ✦ ROAD HOUSE
Twentieth Century–Fox, 1948

**Composer(s)** Newman, Lionel

**Producer(s)** Chodorov, Edward
**Director(s)** Negulesco, Jean
**Screenwriter(s)** Chodorov, Edward

**Cast** Lupino, Ida; Wilde, Cornel; Holm, Celeste; Widmark, Richard; Whitehead, O.Z.; Karnes, Richard

**Song(s)** Again (L: Cochran, Dorcas); The Right Kind [1] (L: George, Don; Henderson, Charles)

**Notes** There is also a vocal of "One for My Baby" by Harold Arlen and Johnny Mercer. [1] Also in WITH A

SONG IN MY HEART with additional credit for Lionel Newman.

## 4991 ✦ ROADHOUSE NIGHTS
Paramount, 1930

**Director(s)**   Henley, Hobart
**Screenwriter(s)**   Fort, Garrett

**Cast**   Morgan, Helen; Ruggles, Charles; Clayton, Lou; Jackson, Eddie; Durante, Jimmy; Kohler, Fred; Mellish Jr., Fuller; King, Joseph

**Song(s)**   It Can't Go on Like This (C: Gorney, Jay; L: Harburg, E.Y.); Everything Is on the Up and Up (C/L: Durante, Jimmy); Hello Everybody Folks (C/L: Durante, Jimmy); Everybody Wants My Girl [1] (C/L: Durante, Jimmy); Just a Melody for a Memory [2] (C: Garney, Jay; Fain, Sammy; L: Harburg, E.Y.; Kahal, Irving)

**Notes**   The cue sheet does not credit Lou Clayton and Eddie Jackson, only Jimmy Durante. "That's How the Place Got Its Name" is referred to in *Variety* as having been sung with another number by Clayton, Jackson and Durante. I assume it is one of the above Durante numbers. "How Dry I Am" is also used vocally. [1] In AFI catalog only. [2] Not used.

## 4992 ✦ ROADIE
United Artists, 1980

**Musical Score**   Hundley, Craig

**Producer(s)**   Pfeiffer, Carolyn
**Director(s)**   Rudolph, Alan
**Screenwriter(s)**   Ventura, Michael; Medlin, Big Boy

**Cast**   Meat Loaf; Hunter, Kaki; Carney, Alan; Cornelius, Don

**Song(s)**   Everything Works If You Let It (C/L: Nielsen, Rick); Your Precious Love (C/L: Ashford, Nick; Simpson, Valerie); Road Rats (C/L: Cooper, Alice; Wagner, Richard); Outlaw Women (C/L: Williams Jr., Hank); Family Tradition (C/L: Williams Jr., Hank); Brainlock (C/L: Ely, Joe); Can't We Try (C/L: Miller, Ron; Hirsch, Ken); (Hot Damn) I'm a One Woman Band (C/L: Dosco, Michael; Whiting, Edward); You Better Run (C/L: Cavaliere, Felix; Brigati, Edward); Gonna Raise Hell (C/L: Neilsen, Rick); Dance This Mess Around (C/L: Strickland; Wilson; Wilson; Person; Schneider); Foolish Faith (C/L: Simonds, Leslie); Double Yellow Line (C/L: Saad, Sue; Riparetti, Tony; Lance, James; Monday, Jeff); A Man Needs a Woman (C/L: Cropper, Steve; Parker, John Lewis); American Way (C/L: Williams Jr., Hank); Crystal Ball (C/L: Shaw, Tommy); Ring of Fire (C/L: Carter, June; Kilgore, Merle); Texas, Me and You (C/L: Benson, Ray); Only Women Bleed (C/L: Cooper, Alice; Wagner, Dick); Pain (C/L: Cooper, Alice; Johnstone

**Notes**   It is not known which, if any, of these were written for this picture.

## 4993 ✦ ROAD RUNNER A GO-GO
Warner Brothers, 1965

**Musical Score**   Franklyn, Milton J.

**Song(s)**   The Road-Runner Song (C: Franklyn, Milton J.; L: Jones, Chuck)

**Notes**   Merrie Melodie.

## 4994 ✦ ROAD SHOW
United Artists, 1941

**Composer(s)**   Carmichael, Hoagy
**Lyricist(s)**   Carmichael, Hoagy

**Producer(s)**   Roach, Hal
**Director(s)**   Roach, Hal
**Screenwriter(s)**   Belgard, Arnold; Langdon, Harry; Novak, Mickell
**Source(s)**   *Road Show* (novel) Hatch, Earl

**Cast**   Menjou, Adolphe; Hubbard, John; Landis, Carole; Butterworth, Charles; Kelly, Patsy; Stone, George E.; The Charioteers

**Song(s)**   Slav Annie (L: Adams, Stanley); I Should Have Known You Years Ago [1] (L: Robison, Harris; Carmichael, Hoagy); Caliope Jane; Yum! Yum!; Drago and the Colonel

**Notes**   [1] No cue sheet available.

## 4995 ✦ ROAD TO BALI
Paramount, 1952

**Composer(s)**   Van Heusen, James
**Lyricist(s)**   Burke, Johnny
**Choreographer(s)**   O'Curran, Charles

**Producer(s)**   Tugend, Harry
**Director(s)**   Walker, Hal
**Screenwriter(s)**   Butler, Frank; Kanter, Hal; Morrow, William

**Cast**   Crosby, Bing; Hope, Bob; Lamour, Dorothy; Vye, Murvyn; Coe, Peter; Moody, Ralph; Askin, Leon

**Song(s)**   Chicago Style; Moonflowers; Hoot Mon; To See You; The Merry-Go-Runaround; The Road to Bali; Thistles and Thumbs [1]; You've Been Looking through My Dreams [1] [2]; Jungle Honeymoon [1]; The Jungle Wedding March [1]

**Notes**   [1] Not used. [2] Recorded.

## 4996 ✦ THE ROAD TO HONG KONG
United Artists, 1962

**Musical Score**   Farnon, Robert
**Composer(s)**   Van Heusen, James
**Lyricist(s)**   Cahn, Sammy

**Producer(s)**   Frank, Melvin
**Director(s)**   Panama, Norman
**Screenwriter(s)**   Panama, Norman

**Cast** Hope, Bob; Crosby, Bing; Collins, Joan; Lamour, Dorothy; Morley, Robert; Sellers, Peter; Niven, David; Sinatra, Frank; Martin, Dean; Colonna, Jerry

**Song(s)** Team Work; Road to Hong Kong; Let's Not Be Sensible; Warmer Than a Whisper; This Is the Only Way to Travel [1]

**Notes** [1] Not used.

## 4997 ◆ ROAD TO MOROCCO
### Paramount, 1942

**Composer(s)** Van Heusen, James
**Lyricist(s)** Burke, Johnny
**Choreographer(s)** Oscard, Paul

**Producer(s)** Jones, Paul
**Director(s)** Butler, David
**Screenwriter(s)** Hartman, Don; Butler, Frank

**Cast** Hope, Bob; Crosby, Bing; Lamour, Dorothy; Quinn, Anthony; Drake, Dona; Sokoloff, Vladimir; Rasumny, Mikhail; Givot, George; Tombes, Andrew; De Carlo, Yvonne

**Song(s)** The Road to Morocco; Ain't Got a Dime to My Name (Ho Ho Hum); Constantly; Moonlight Becomes You; Aladdin's Daughter [1]; Don't Disappear [1]; Don't You Know; Any Way the Wind Blows [1]

**Notes** [1] Not used.

## 4998 ◆ THE ROAD TO RENO
### Universal, 1939

**Composer(s)** McHugh, Jimmy
**Lyricist(s)** Adamson, Harold

**Producer(s)** Grainger, Edmund
**Director(s)** Simon, S. Sylvan
**Screenwriter(s)** Chanslor, Roy; Comandini, Adele; Marlow, Brian
**Source(s)** "Puritan at Large" (story) Wylie, I.A.R.

**Cast** Hampton, Hope; Scott, Randolph; Marshal, Alan; Farrell, Glenda; Broderick, Helen; Oliver, David; Osborne, Ted

**Song(s)** Ridin' Home [1]; Tonight Is the Night; I Gave Away My Heart

**Notes** There is also a vocal of "Musetta's Street Song" from Puccini's LA BOHEME. [1] Also in DESPERATE TRAILS (1939), ROAD AGENT, STRICTLY IN THE GROOVE and TENTING TONIGHT ON THE OLD CAMP GROUND.

## 4999 ◆ ROAD TO RIO
### Paramount, 1947

**Composer(s)** Van Heusen, James
**Lyricist(s)** Burke, Johnny
**Choreographer(s)** Pearce, Bernard; Daniels, Billy

**Producer(s)** Dare, Danny
**Director(s)** McLeod, Norman Z.
**Screenwriter(s)** Beloin, Edmund; Rose, Jack

**Cast** Hope, Bob; Lamour, Dorothy; Crosby, Bing; Sondergaard, Gale; Faylen, Frank; Vitale, Joseph; Paiva, Nestor; Barrat, Robert; Colonna, Jerry; The Wiere Brothers; The Andrews Sisters

**Song(s)** Apalachicola, F.L.A.; But Beautiful; You Don't Have to Know the Language; Experience; Diz Que Tem (C/L: Cruz, Hannibal; Paiva, Vincente); Batuque Nio Morro [2] (C/L: de Pandeiro, Russo; Roris, Sa); For What [1]; Olha Ella [3] (C/L: Do Pandeiro, Russo; Pan, Peter)

**Notes** [1] Not used. [2] The English doggerel about chicken cacciatore and chopped chicken livers was written by Bing Crosby. [3] Sheet music only.

## 5000 ◆ ROAD TO SINGAPORE (1931)
### Warner Brothers, 1931

**Director(s)** Green, Alfred E.
**Screenwriter(s)** Alexander, J. Grubb
**Source(s)** "Heat Wave" (story) Pertwee, Roland

**Cast** Powell, William; Kenyon, Doris; Skipworth, Alison; Anson, A.E.; Gerrard, Douglas

**Song(s)** African Lament (C: Lecuona, Ernesto; L: Gilbert, L. Wolfe); Hand In Hand (C: Monaco, James V.; L: Leslie, Edgar; Washington, Ned); Yes or No (C: Rich, Max; L: O'Flynn, Charles); Singapore Tango (C/L: Lucas, Clyde); I'm Just a Fool in Love with You (C: Gottler, Archie; Meyer, George W.; L: Mitchell, Sidney D.)

**Notes** No cue sheet available.

## 5001 ◆ ROAD TO SINGAPORE (1940)
### Paramount, 1940

**Composer(s)** Schertzinger, Victor
**Lyricist(s)** Burke, Johnny
**Choreographer(s)** Prinz, LeRoy

**Producer(s)** Thompson, Harlan
**Director(s)** Schertzinger, Victor
**Screenwriter(s)** Hartman, Don; Butler, Frank

**Cast** Crosby, Bing; Lamour, Dorothy; Hope, Bob; Coburn, Charles; Barrett, Judith; Quinn, Anthony; Colonna, Jerry; Watkin, Pierre

**Song(s)** Captain Custard [3]; The Moon and the Willow Tree; The Sweet Potato Piper (C: Monaco, James V.); (I'm) Too Romantic (C: Monaco, James V.); Kaigoon (C: Monaco, James V.); Captain Vanka [1] [3] (C/L: Schertzinger, Victor); White Shadows of the Moon [1] [2] (C: Schertzinger, Victor; L: Loesser, Frank)

**Notes** [1] Not used. [2] Alternate title is "White Mist of the Moon." [3] Mostly the same music.

## 5002 ✦ ROAD TO UTOPIA
### Paramount, 1945

**Composer(s)** Van Heusen, James
**Lyricist(s)** Burke, Johnny
**Choreographer(s)** Dare, Danny

**Producer(s)** Jones, Paul
**Director(s)** Walker, Hal
**Screenwriter(s)** Panama, Norman; Frank, Melvin

**Cast** Lamour, Dorothy; Crosby, Bing; Hope, Bob; Benchley, Robert; Dumbrille, Douglass; Brooke, Hillary; LaRue, Jack; Paiva, Nestor; Barrat, Robert

**Song(s)** Sunday, Monday or Always [1]; Good Time Charlie; It's Anybody's Spring; Personality; Welcome to My Dream; Put It There, Pal; Would You

**Notes** [1] Also in DIXIE and TAKE IT BIG.

## 5003 ✦ THE ROAD TO VICTORY

See THE SHINING FUTURE.

## 5004 ✦ ROAD TO ZANZIBAR
### Paramount, 1941

**Composer(s)** Van Heusen, James
**Lyricist(s)** Burke, Johnny
**Choreographer(s)** Prinz, LeRoy

**Producer(s)** Jones, Paul
**Director(s)** Schertzinger, Victor
**Screenwriter(s)** Hartman, Don; Butler, Frank
**Source(s)** "Find Colonel Fawcett" (story) Hartman, Don; Bartlett, Sy

**Cast** Merkel, Una; Hope, Bob; Crosby, Bing; Lamour, Dorothy; Blore, Eric; Adrian, Iris; Dumbrille, Douglass; Marsh, Joan; Alberni, Luis; Gorcey, Leo; Royce, Lionel; Whipper, Leigh

**Song(s)** You Lucky People, You; Birds of a Feather [1]; A'Frangesa (C/L: Costa, D.); African Etude; You're Dangerous; It's Always You

**Notes** [1] Only used instrumentally.

## 5005 ✦ ROARING TWENTIES
### Warner Brothers, 1939

**Producer(s)** Wallis, Hal B.
**Director(s)** Walsh, Raoul
**Screenwriter(s)** Wald, Jerry; Macaulay, Richard; Rossen, Robert
**Source(s)** "The World Moves On" (story) Hellinger, Mark

**Cast** Bogart, Humphrey; Cagney, James; Lane, Priscilla; George, Gladys; Lynn, Jeffrey; McHugh, Frank;

Kelly, Paul; Risdon, Elizabeth; Sawyer, Joe; Meeker, George; Lewis, Vera

**Notes** There are no songs original to this film. Vocals include "Love Me and the World Is Mine" by Ernest R. Ball and Dave Reed Jr.; "Melancholy Baby" by Ernie Burnett and George A. Norton; "I'm Just Wild About Harry" by Eubie Blake and Noble Sissle; "It Had to Be You" by Isham Jones and Gus Kahn and "In a Shanty in Old Shanty Town" by Joe Young, Little Jack Little and John Siras.

## 5006 ✦ ROAST BEEF AND MOVIES
### Metro–Goldwyn–Mayer, 1934

**Song(s)** Blue Daughter of Heaven (C/L: Tiomkin, Dimitri; Snell, Dave)

**Notes** Short subject.

## 5007 ✦ ROBBERS OF THE RANGE
### RKO, 1941

**Musical Score** Dreyer, Dave; Sawtell, Paul

**Producer(s)** Gilroy, Bert
**Director(s)** Killy, Edward
**Screenwriter(s)** Grant, Morton; Jones, Arthur V.

**Cast** Holt, Tim; Vale, Virginia; Whitley, Ray; Lynn, Emmett; Mason, LeRoy; Hickman, Howard; Adams, Ernie

**Song(s)** The Railroad's Comin' to Town (C/L: Whitley, Ray; Rose, Fred)

## 5008 ✦ ROBBERS' ROOST (1933)
### Fox, 1933

**Composer(s)** Burton, Val; Jason, Will
**Lyricist(s)** Burton, Val; Jason, Will

**Director(s)** King, Louis
**Screenwriter(s)** Nichols, Dudley
**Source(s)** *Robbers' Roost* (novel) Grey, Zane

**Cast** O'Brien, George; O'Sullivan, Maureen; McGrail, Walter; Owen, Reginald

**Song(s)** Cowboy's Heaven; I Adore You; The Gal from Amarillo [1]

**Notes** [1] Sheet music only.

## 5009 ✦ ROBBER'S ROOST (1955)
### United Artists, 1955

**Musical Score** Romano, Tony; Dunlap, Paul
**Composer(s)** Romano, Tony
**Lyricist(s)** Bradford, John

**Producer(s)** Goldstein, Robert
**Director(s)** Salkow, Sidney
**Screenwriter(s)** O'Dea, John; Geraghty, Maurice; Salkow, Sidney
**Source(s)** *Robber's Roost* (novel) Grey, Zane

**Cast** Montgomery, George; Bennett, Bruce; Findley, Sylvia; Boone, Richard; Graves, Peter; Romano, Tony; Stevens, Warren; Hopper, William; Gordon, Leo

**Song(s)** Robber's Roost; I Turned It Down; This Is the Night

## 5010 ✦ THE ROBE
Twentieth Century–Fox, 1953

**Musical Score** Newman, Alfred

**Producer(s)** Ross, Frank
**Director(s)** Koster, Henry
**Screenwriter(s)** Dunne, Philip
**Source(s)** *The Robe* (novel) Douglas, Lloyd C.

**Cast** Burton, Richard; Simmons, Jean; Mature, Victor; Rennie, Michael; Robinson, Jay; Jagger, Dean; Thatcher, Torin; Boone, Richard; Addams, Dawn; St. John, Betta [2]

**Song(s)** The Ressurection [1] (C: Newman, Alfred; L: Dunne, Philip); Hymn for the Dead (C: Newman, Alfred; L: Book of Lamentations)

**Notes** [1] Lyrics adapted from the Scriptures. [2] Dubbed by Carole Richards.

## 5011 ✦ ROBERTA
RKO, 1935

**Composer(s)** Kern, Jerome
**Lyricist(s)** Harbach, Otto
**Choreographer(s)** Pan, Hermes

**Producer(s)** Berman, Pandro S.
**Director(s)** Seiter, William A.
**Screenwriter(s)** Murfin, Jane; Mintz, Sam; Scott, Allan; Tryon, Glenn
**Source(s)** *Roberta* (musical) Kern, Jerome; Harbach, Otto; Gowns By Roberta Miller, Alice Duer

**Cast** Dunne, Irene; Astaire, Fred; Rogers, Ginger; Scott, Randolph; Westley, Helen; Dodd, Claire; Varconi, Victor; Alberni, Luis; Munier, Ferdinand; Meyer, Torben

**Song(s)** Let's Begin; Russian Lullaby (L: Fields, Dorothy); I'll Be Hard to Handle (L: Dougall, Bernard); Oh Frenchy (C/L: Conrad, Con; Ehrlich, Sam); Yesterdays; I Won't Dance [1] (L: Fields, Dorothy; Hammerstein II, Oscar); Smoke Gets in Your Eyes; Fashion Show (L: Fields, Dorothy); Lovely to Look At (L: Fields, Dorothy)

**Notes** Remade by MGM as LOVELY TO LOOK AT. Jimmy McHugh also credited with Fields' lyrics but he didn't contribute. [1] Though Otto Harbach and Jimmy McHugh are also credited they had no part in the writing of this song. Fields revised Hammerstein's original lyric, written for the show THE THREE SISTERS.

## 5012 ✦ ROBIN AND THE 7 HOODS
Warner Brothers, 1964

**Musical Score** Riddle, Nelson
**Composer(s)** Van Heusen, Jimmy
**Lyricist(s)** Cahn, Sammy
**Choreographer(s)** Baker, Jack

**Producer(s)** Sinatra, Frank
**Director(s)** Douglas, Gordon M.
**Screenwriter(s)** Schwartz, David R.

**Cast** Sinatra, Frank; Martin, Dean; Davis Jr., Sammy; Falk, Peter; Rush, Barbara; Buono, Victor; Crosby, Bing; Henry, Hank; Jenkins, Allen; LaRue, Jack; Foulk, Robert; Crosby, Phillip; Robinson, Edward G.

**Song(s)** All for One and One for All; Give Praise! Give Praise! Give Praise!; I Like to Lead When I Dance; Any Man Who Loves His Mother; Bang Bang; Style; Charlotte Couldn't Charleston; Mister Booze; Don't Be a Do-Badder; My Kind of Town; Baby I Love You Up to Here [1]

**Notes** [1] Not used.

## 5013 ✦ ROBIN HOOD
Disney, 1973

**Musical Score** Bruns, George

**Producer(s)** Reitherman, Wolfgang
**Director(s)** Reitherman, Wolfgang
**Screenwriter(s)** Clemmons, Larry
**Voices** Williams, Roger; Ustinov, Peter; Terry-Thomas; Bedford, Brian; Evans, Monica; Harris, Phil; Devine, Andy; Shelley, Carole; Buttram, Pat; Curtis, Ken; Lindsey, George

**Directing Animator(s)** Kahl, Milt; Thomas, Franklin; Johnston, Ollie; Lounsbery, John

**Song(s)** Love (C: Bruns, George; L: Huddleston, Floyd); The Phony King of England (C: Traditional; L: Mercer, Johnny); Not in Nottingham (C/L: Miller, Roger); Oo-De-Lally (C/L: Miller, Roger); Whistle Stop [1] (C/L: Miller, Roger)

**Notes** Animated feature. [1] Not used.

## 5014 ✦ ROBIN HOOD OF EL DORADO
Metro–Goldwyn–Mayer, 1936

**Musical Score** Stothart, Herbert

**Producer(s)** Considine Jr., John W.
**Director(s)** Wellman, William A.
**Screenwriter(s)** Wellman, William A.; Calleia, Joseph; Levy, Melvin
**Source(s)** *The Robin Hood of El Dorado* (book) Burns, Walter Noble

**Cast** Baxter, Warner; Loring, Ann; Cabot, Bruce; Margo; Naish, J. Carrol; Kennedy, Edgar

**Song(s)** Todo-Para-Ti (C: Stothart, Herbert; L: Sturm, Rafael); Baile de Bandidos (C: Stothart, Herbert; L: Sturm, Rafael)

## 5015 ✦ ROBIN HOOD OF TEXAS
### Republic, 1947

**Producer(s)** Picker, Sidney
**Director(s)** Selander, Lesley
**Screenwriter(s)** Butler, John K.; Snell, Earle

**Cast** Autry, Gene; Roberts, Lynne; Holloway, Sterling; Mara, Adele; Cardwell, James; Kellogg, John; The Cass County Boys

**Song(s)** There's Nothing Like a Good Old Fashioned Hoedown (C/L: Autry, Gene)

**Notes** No cue sheet available.

## 5016 ✦ ROBIN HOOD OF THE PECOS
### Republic, 1940

**Producer(s)** Kane, Joseph
**Director(s)** Kane, Joseph
**Screenwriter(s)** Cooper, Olive

**Cast** Rogers, Roy; Hayes, George "Gabby"; Reynolds, Marjorie; Kendall, Cyrus; Whipper, Leigh; Payne, Sally; Acuff, Eddie; Strange, Robert; Novello, Jay; Ates, Roscoe

**Song(s)** A Sad Sad Story (C/L: Tinturin, Peter); A Certain Place I Know (C/L: Cherkose, Eddie)

## 5017 ✦ ROBINSON CRUSOE ON MARS
### Paramount, 1964

**Musical Score** Van Cleave, Nathan

**Producer(s)** Schenck, Aubrey
**Director(s)** Haskin, Byron
**Screenwriter(s)** Melchior, Ib; Higgins, John C.

**Cast** Mantee, Paul; Lundin, Victor; Mona the Woolly Monkey; West, Adam

**Song(s)** Robinson Crusoe on Mars [1] (C: Carr, Leon; L: Shuman, Earl)

**Notes** [1] Written for exploitation only.

## 5018 ✦ ROB ROY—THE HIGHLAND ROGUE
### Disney, 1954

**Musical Score** Davie, Cedric Thorpe

**Producer(s)** Pearce, Perce
**Director(s)** French, Harold
**Screenwriter(s)** Watkin, Lawrence Edward

**Cast** Todd, Richard; Johns, Glynis; Gough, Michael; Justice, James Robertson

**Song(s)** The Ballad of Rob Roy (Bonnie Anne) (C/L: Gordon, Irving)

## 5019 ✦ ROCKABILLY BABY
### Twentieth Century–Fox, 1957

**Musical Score** Dunlap, Paul
**Composer(s)** Dunlap, Paul
**Lyricist(s)** Kallman, Dick

**Producer(s)** Claxton, William F.
**Director(s)** Claxton, William F.
**Screenwriter(s)** George, Will; Driskill, William

**Cast** Field, Virginia; Kennedy, Douglas; Les Brown and His Band of Renown; Ryan, Irene; Corby, Ellen

**Song(s)** We're On Our Way; Why Can't I (L: Dunlap, Paul); Teen-Age Cutie (C: Kallman, Dick); Is It Love? (L: Murchison, Charles); Calypso Baby (My Baby) (L: Dunlap, Paul); I'd Rather Be (L: Murchison, Charles); Checkin' In (Inst.) (C: Hensel, Wes); Leap Frog [1] (C/L: Garland, Joe; Corday, Leo)

**Notes** Originally titled REVOLUTION IN SPRINGVILLE as well as MOTHER WAS A STRIPPER. [1] Performed instrumentally.

## 5020 ✦ ROCKABYE
### RKO, 1932

**Producer(s)** Selznick, David O.
**Director(s)** Cukor, George
**Screenwriter(s)** Murfin, Jane
**Source(s)** (play) Bronder, Lucia

**Cast** McCrea, Joel; Lukas, Paul; Howland, Jobyna; Pidgeon, Walter; Blandick, Clara; Catlett, Walter; Hammond, Virginia; Kerrigan, J.M.

**Song(s)** Sleep, My Sweet (C: Brown, Nacio Herb; L: Borlini, Jeanne); 'Till the Real Thing Comes My Way (C: Akst, Harry; L: Eliscu, Edward)

## 5021 ✦ ROCK-A-BYE BABY
### Paramount, 1958

**Musical Score** Scharf, Walter
**Composer(s)** Warren, Harry
**Lyricist(s)** Cahn, Sammy
**Choreographer(s)** Castle, Nick

**Producer(s)** Lewis, Jerry
**Director(s)** Tashlin, Frank
**Screenwriter(s)** Tashlin, Frank

**Cast** Lewis, Jerry; Maxwell, Marilyn; Baccaloni, Salvatore; Gardiner, Reginald; Conried, Hans; Gleason, James; Stevens, Connie

**Song(s)** Rock-A-Bye Baby; The Land of La-La-La; Love Is a Lonely Thing; Dormi-Dormi-Dormi (Sleep-Sleep-Sleep); Why Can't He Care for Me; The White Virgin of the Nile; Me and My Baby [1]

**Notes** Commercials for "Burperex," "Chickory Coffee," "Gookum Spray" and "Superbos" were written by Vincent Degen. [1] Not used.

## 5022 ✦ ROCK AROUND THE CLOCK
### Columbia, 1956

**Choreographer(s)**   Barton, Earl

**Producer(s)**   Katzman, Sam
**Director(s)**   Sears, Fred F.
**Screenwriter(s)**   Kent, Robert E.; Gordon, James B.

**Cast**   Bill Haley and His Comets; The Platters; Tony Martinez and His Band; Freddie Bell and His Bellboys; Freed, Alan; Johnston, Johnnie; Talton, Alix

**Notes**   There are no original songs in this picture. Those songs sung include "Rock Around the Clock" by Max C. Freedman and Jimmy De Night; "See You Later Alligator" by Robert Charles Gurdy; "Rock a Beatin' Boogie" by Bill Haley; "ABC Boogie" by Max Spickol and Al Russell; "Cuero" by Tony Martinez; "Razzle Dazzle" by Charles Calhoun; "Teach You to Rock" by Fred Ball; "Codfish and Potatoes (Bacalao Con Papa)" by Tony Martinez; "Mambo Rock" by Bix Reichner, Mildred Phillips and Jimmy Ayre; "Giddy Up Ding Dong" by Fred Ball and Pap Latanzi; "The Great Pretender" by Buck Ram; "Happy Baby" by Frank Pingatore and "Only You" by Buck Ram and Anda Rand.

## 5023 ✦ ROCKET GIBRALTAR
### Columbia, 1988

**Musical Score**   Powell, Andrew

**Producer(s)**   Weiss, Jeff
**Director(s)**   Petrie, Daniel
**Screenwriter(s)**   Poe, Amos

**Cast**   Lancaster, Burt; Amis, Suzy; Clarkson, Patricia; Cusack, Sinead; Glover, John; Martin, George; Conroy, Frances

**Song(s)**   So Tired of Being Alone (C/L: Green, Al)

**Notes**   No cue sheet available.

## 5024 ✦ ROCKIN' IN THE ROCKIES
### Columbia, 1945

**Director(s)**   Keays, Vernon
**Screenwriter(s)**   Cheney, J. Benton

**Cast**   The Three Stooges [2]; Hughes, Mary Beth; Ryan, Tim; Blake, Gladys; The Cappy Barra Boys; Cooley, Spade; The Hoosier Hotshots [3]

**Song(s)**   Rockin' in the Rockies (C/L: Tobias, Henry; Newborn, Max); Upstairs, Downstairs (C/L: Curtis, Mann; Mizzy, Vic); Skee Dee Waddle Dee Waddle Doo (C/L: Trietsch, Kenneth H.); Somewhere Along the Trail [4] (C: Chaplin, Saul; L: Cahn, Sammy); Ever So Quiet (C/L: More, Algy); Miss Molly (C/L: Walker, Cindy); Wah Hoo! [1] (C/L: Friend, Cliff)

**Notes**   [1] Also in MOONLIGHT AND CACTUS (Universal). [2] Consisted of Moe Howard, Larry Fine

and Jerry Howard. [3] Consisted of Kenneth and Paul F. Triestsch, Charles O. Ward and Gilbert O. Taylor. [4] Also in GO WEST, YOUNG LADY.

## 5025 ✦ ROCK ISLAND TRAIL
### Republic, 1950

**Musical Score**   Butts, Dale

**Producer(s)**   Malvern, Paul
**Director(s)**   Kane, Joseph
**Screenwriter(s)**   Grant, James
**Source(s)**   *A Yankee Dared* (novel) Nevins, Frank J.

**Cast**   Tucker, Forrest; Mara, Adele; Booth, Adrian; Cabot, Bruce; Wills, Chill; Withers, Grant; Corey, Jeff

**Song(s)**   Rock Island Trail (C/L: Roy, William)

## 5026 ✦ ROCK 'N' ROLL HIGH SCHOOL
### New World, 1979

**Producer(s)**   Finnell, Michael
**Director(s)**   Arkush, Allan
**Screenwriter(s)**   Whitley, Richard; Dvonch, Russ; McBride, Joseph

**Cast**   Soles, P.J.; Van Patten, Vincent; Howard, Clint; Young, Dey; Woronov, Mary; Bartel, Paul; Miller, Dick; Sutton, Grady; Ramone, Joey; Ramone, Johnny; Ramone, Dee Dee; Ramone, Marky

**Song(s)**   Rock 'N' Roll High School (C/L: The Ramones); I Want You Around (C/L: Ramones, The)

**Notes**   No cue sheet available.

## 5027 ✦ ROCK, PRETTY BABY
### Universal, 1956

**Producer(s)**   Chevie, Edmond
**Director(s)**   Bartlett, Richard
**Screenwriter(s)**   Margolis, Herbert; Raynor, William

**Cast**   Saxon, John; Platt, Edward; Wray, Fay; Mineo, Sal; Patten, Luana; Wilder, John; Reed Jr., Alan; Fabares, Shelley; Winslow, George

**Song(s)**   Rock, Pretty Baby (C/L: Burke, Sonny); Can I Steal a Little Love (C/L: Tuminello, Phil); Happy Is a Boy Named Me (C/L: McKuen, Rod); What's It Gonna Be? (C: Mancini, Henry; L: Carey, Bill); Rock-a-bye Lullaby Blues (C/L: Troup, Bobby); Picnic by the Sea (C/L: McKuen, Rod; Troup, Bobby)

## 5028 ✦ ROCKY
### United Artists, 1976

**Musical Score**   Conti, Bill
**Composer(s)**   Conti, Bill
**Lyricist(s)**   Connors, Carol; Robbins, Ayn

**Producer(s)**    Winkler, Irwin; Chartoff, Robert
**Director(s)**    Avildsen, John G.
**Screenwriter(s)**    Stallone, Sylvester

**Cast**    Stallone, Sylvester; Shire, Talia; Young, Burt; Weathers, Carl; Meredith, Burgess; David, Thayer; Spinell, Joe; Gambina, Jimmy

**Song(s)**    Take Me Back (C/L: Stallone Jr., Frank); You Take My Heart Away; Gonna Fly Now

## 5029  ✦  ROCKY II
### United Artists, 1979

**Musical Score**    Conti, Bill
**Composer(s)**    Stallone, Frank
**Lyricist(s)**    Stallone, Frank

**Producer(s)**    Winkler, Irwin; Chartoff, Robert
**Director(s)**    Stallone, Sylvester
**Screenwriter(s)**    Stallone, Sylvester

**Cast**    Stallone, Sylvester; Shire, Talia; Weathers, Carl; Young, Burt; Meredith, Burgess

**Song(s)**    Street Scat; Two Kinds of Love; All of My Life [1] (C: Conti, Bill; L: Conti, Shelby)

**Notes**    There is also a reprise of "Gonna Fly Now" from ROCKY. [1] Sheet music only.

## 5030  ✦  ROCKY III
### United Artists, 1982

**Musical Score**    Conti, Bill

**Producer(s)**    Winkler, Irwin; Chartoff, Robert
**Director(s)**    Stallone, Sylvester
**Screenwriter(s)**    Stallone, Sylvester

**Cast**    Stallone, Sylvester; Shire, Talia; Young, Burt; Weathers, Carl; Mr. T; Meredith, Burgess; Fried, Ian; Hogan, Hulk; Burton, Tony

**Song(s)**    Eye of the Tiger (C/L: Peterik, Jim; Sullivan, Frank); Take You Back (C/L: Stallone, Frank); Pushin' (C: Conti, Bill; L: Stallone, Frank)

**Notes**    There is also a vocal of "Gonna Fly Now" from ROCKY.

## 5031  ✦  ROCKY IV
### United Artists, 1985

**Musical Score**    DiCola, Vince

**Producer(s)**    Winkler, Irwin; Chartoff, Robert
**Director(s)**    Stallone, Sylvester
**Screenwriter(s)**    Stallone, Sylvester

**Cast**    Stallone, Sylvester; Shire, Talia; Young, Burt; Weathers, Carl; Pataki, Michael; Lundgren, Dolph; Burton, Tony; Nielsen, Brigitte

**Song(s)**    One Way Street (C/L: Go West; Drummie, Richard; Cox, Peter); Double or Nothing (C/L: Dorff, Stephen H.; Williams, Paul); Living in America (C/L: Hartman, Don; Midnight, Charlie); No Easy Way Out (C/L: Tepper, Robert); Burning Heart (C/L: Peterik, Jim; Sullivan, Frank); Hearts on Fire (C/L: DeCola, Vince; Fruge, Ed; Esposito, Joseph)

**Notes**    There is a reprise of "Eye of the Tiger" from ROCKY III.

## 5032  ✦  THE ROCKY HORROR PICTURE SHOW
### Twentieth Century–Fox, 1975

**Composer(s)**    O'Brien, Richard
**Lyricist(s)**    O'Brien, Richard

**Producer(s)**    White, Michael; Adler, Lou
**Director(s)**    Sharman, Jim
**Screenwriter(s)**    Sharman, Jim; O'Brien, Richard
**Source(s)**    *The Rocky Horror Show* (musical) O'Brien, Richard

**Cast**    Curry, Tim; Sarandon, Susan; Bostwick, Barry; O'Brien, Richard; Adams, Jonathan; Campbell, Nell; Hinwood, Peter; Meat Loaf; Quinn, Patricia; Gray, Charles

**Song(s)**    Touch Touch Me; I Can Make You a Man; Hot Pattootie; Charles Atlas; Sword of Damocles; Sweet Transvestite; Time Warp; Frankenstein's Place; Dammit Janet; Science Fiction; Eddie's Teddy; Wise Up Janet Weiss; Hot Dog; Floor Show; Don't Dream It, Do It; Wild and Untamed Thing; I'm Going Home; Gunfight Music; Sweet Transexual; Sweet Hero

## 5033  ✦  RODEO KING AND THE SENORITA
### Republic, 1951

**Producer(s)**    Tucker, Melville
**Director(s)**    Ford, Philip
**Screenwriter(s)**    Butler, John K.

**Cast**    Allen, Rex; Kay, Mary Ellen; Ebsen, Buddy; Koko; Barcroft, Roy

**Song(s)**    Toolie Rollum [2] (C/L: Allen, Rex); Strawberry Roan [1] (C/L: Howard, Fred; Vincent, Nat)

**Notes**    There is also a vocal of "Juanita" by C. Norton. [1] Also in THE STRAWBERRY ROAN (Columbia). [2] Also in THE ARIZONA COWBOY; SHADOWS OF TOMBSTONE; UTAH WAGON TRAIN and SILVER CITY BONANZA.

## 5034  ✦  ROGUE OF THE RIO GRANDE
### Sono-Art, 1930

**Composer(s)**    Meyers, Herbert
**Lyricist(s)**    Drake, Oliver

**Producer(s)**  Broughton, Cliff
**Director(s)**  Bennett, Spencer Gordon
**Screenwriter(s)**  Drake, Oliver

**Cast**  Bohr, Jose; Hatton, Raymond; Loy, Myrna; Geraghty, Carmelita; Miller, Walter; Burt, William P.

**Song(s)**  Argentine Moon; Carmita; Corazon; Song of the Bandoleros

**Notes**  No cue sheet available.

### 5035 ◆ ROGUE'S GALLERY
Paramount, 1968

**Musical Score**  Haskell, Jimmie

**Producer(s)**  Lyles, A.C.
**Director(s)**  Horn, Leonard
**Screenwriter(s)**  Fisher, Steve

**Cast**  Smith, Roger; Baldwin, Greta; Morgan, Dennis; Bergen, Edgar; Donlevy, Brian; Granger, Farley; Powers, Mala; Arlen, Richard; Coogan, Jackie; Ray, Johnnie

**Song(s)**  Valerie (C: Haskell, Jimmie; L: Blair, Hal)

### 5036 ◆ THE ROGUE SONG
Metro–Goldwyn–Mayer, 1930

**Musical Score**  Stothart, Herbert
**Composer(s)**  Stothart, Herbert
**Lyricist(s)**  Grey, Clifford
**Choreographer(s)**  Rasch, Albertina

**Director(s)**  Barrymore, Lionel
**Screenwriter(s)**  Marion, Frances; Colton, John
**Source(s)**  *Gypsy Love* (operetta) Lehar, Franz; Willner, A.M.; Bodansky, Robert

**Cast**  Tibbett, Lawrence; Owen, Catherine Dale; O'Neil, Nance; Voselli, Judith; Haupt, Ullrich; Belmore, Lionel; Lake, Florence; Laurel, Stan; Hardy, Oliver

**Song(s)**  The Rogue Song; Love Comes Like a Bird on the Wing (C: Lehar, Franz; Stothart, Herbert); The Narrative; The White Dove [2] (C: Lehar, Franz; Stothart, Herbert); The Shame Cry; Once in the Georgian Hills (C: Lehar, Franz; Stothart, Herbert); Ballet Music (Inst.) (C: Tiomkin, Dimitri); This Little Foot; When I'm Looking at You; The Lash; Song of the Shirt [1]

**Notes**  *Variety*: "Reports from the coast are that Metro was in some doubt about Tibbett and just what to do with him after he'd been signed. Lots of conference, and then 'The Rogue Song' decision as 'suggested' by Wells Root, according to program credit. After that the difficulty of fitting a powerful baritone to a microphone. Studio hints of toning down are said to have been rejected by the opera singer. Result was quite some expermenting until the sound boys finally finished up with the mikes 15 feet back, the orchestra anchored, everybody grabbing hold of something, and Barrymore dictating, 'Fire when ready, Larry.'" [1] Not on cue sheets. [2] Stothart not credited on sheet music.

### 5037 ◆ ROGUE'S REGIMENT
Universal, 1948

**Musical Score**  Amfitheatrof, Daniele
**Composer(s)**  Walter, Serge
**Lyricist(s)**  Brooks, Jack

**Producer(s)**  Buckner, Robert
**Director(s)**  Florey, Robert
**Screenwriter(s)**  Buckner, Robert

**Cast**  Powell, Dick; McNally, Stephen; Toren, Marta; Rowland, Henry; Price, Vincent

**Song(s)**  Just for a While [1]; Who Can Tell

**Notes**  [1] German lyrics by Walter Jurmann.

### 5038 ◆ ROLLER BOOGIE
United Artists, 1979

**Musical Score**  Esty, Bob
**Composer(s)**  Esty, Bob; Aller, Michele
**Lyricist(s)**  Esty, Bob; Aller, Michele

**Producer(s)**  Curtis, Bruce Cohn
**Director(s)**  Lester, Mark
**Screenwriter(s)**  Schneider, Barry

**Cast**  Blair, Linda; Bray, Jim; Garland, Beverly; Perry, Roger; Van Patten, Jimmy; Beck, Kimberly

**Song(s)**  The Roller Boogie; Summer Love (C: Esty, Bob; L: Brooks, Michael); Top Jammer (C/L: Aller, Michele; Esty, Bob; Prudden, S.A.); All for One, One for All; We Got the Power (C: Esty, Bob; L: Brooks, Michael); Electronix; Conga (C/L: Esty, Bob); Takin' My Life in My Own Hands; Rollin' Up a Storm (Eye of the Hurricane) (C: Esty, Bob; L: Brooks, Michael); Evil Man; Love Fire

**Notes**  No cue sheet available.

### 5039 ◆ ROLLING CARAVANS
Columbia, 1938

**Musical Score**  Zahler, Lee
**Composer(s)**  Zahler, Lee

**Director(s)**  Levering, Joseph
**Screenwriter(s)**  Gatzert, Nate

**Cast**  Luden, John; Stewart, Eleanor; Woods, Harry; Whitaker, Slim

**Song(s)**  Range Ridin' Dreams (L: Ormont, David); Goodbye My Lover Goodbye (L: Grigor, Nico [1]); 'Neath Western Skies [2] (L: Wood, John Hickory)

**Notes**  This was an attempt to introduce John Luden as a cowboy star. [1] Nico Grigor was a pseudonym in this instance. Columbia seemed to use the name simply for legal reasons. [2] Sheet music credits Leon Leon with lyrics.

## 5040 ✦ ROLLING HOME TO TEXAS
### Monogram, 1941

**Composer(s)** Blair, Hal; Hoag, Bob
**Lyricist(s)** Blair, Hal; Hoag, Bob

**Producer(s)** Finney, Edward
**Director(s)** Herman, Al
**Screenwriter(s)** Emmett, Robert

**Cast** Ritter, Tex; Blair, Hal; Shrumm, Cal; Andrews, Lloyd "Slim"; Carpenter, Virginia; Dean, Eddie; Rutherford, Jack; Durfee, Minta

**Song(s)** Under Texas Stars; Rolling Home; Desert Moonlight; Wabash Cannonball (C/L: Carter, A.P.); Cowboy Swing (C/L: Fox, Jules I.; Friedman, S.); Give Me a Horse and a Saddle and You (C/L: Nation, Buck); Why Did I Get Married (C/L: Robison, Carson J.); Slimmy Boy (C/L: Smith, Jack)

**Notes** No cue sheet available.

## 5041 ✦ ROLLING THUNDER
### American International, 1977

**Musical Score** De Vorzon, Barry

**Producer(s)** Herman, Norman T.
**Director(s)** Flynn, John
**Screenwriter(s)** Schrader, Paul; Gould, Heywood

**Cast** Devane, William; Jones, Tommy Lee; Haynes, Linda; Best, James; Coleman, Dabney; Richards, Lisa; Askew, Luke

**Song(s)** San Antone (C/L: De Vorzon, Barry)

**Notes** No cue sheet available.

## 5042 ✦ ROLLING VENGEANCE
### Apollo, 1987

**Musical Score** Marshall, Phil
**Composer(s)** Capello, Timmy
**Lyricist(s)** Capello, Timmy

**Producer(s)** Stern, Steven Hillard
**Director(s)** Stern, Steven Hillard
**Screenwriter(s)** Montgomery, Michael

**Cast** Paul, Don Michael; Dane, Lawrence; Beatty, Ned; Howard, Lisa; Duckworth, Todd; Reynolds, Michael J.

**Song(s)** Thinkin' (C/L: Marshall, Phil); Life on the Outside; Dream Lover; Play Rough (C/L: Shandi); Coming Up on You; Walk with Me (C/L: Mersh Brothers, The)

**Notes** No cue sheet available.

## 5043 ✦ ROLL ON TEXAS MOON
### Republic, 1946

**Composer(s)** Elliott, Jack
**Lyricist(s)** Elliott, Jack

**Producer(s)** White, Eddy
**Director(s)** Witney, William
**Screenwriter(s)** Gangelin, Paul; Grashin, Mauri

**Cast** Rogers, Roy; Trigger; Hayes, George "Gabby"; Evans, Dale; Hoey, Dennis; Risdon, Elizabeth; McDonald, Francis

**Song(s)** What's Doin' Tonight in Dreamland; Roll On Texas Moon; Won'tcha' Be a Friend of Mine; The Jumpin' Bean (C/L: Spencer, Tim)

## 5044 ✦ ROMANCE AND DANCE
### Warner Brothers, 1946

**Musical Score** Gama, Rafael; Jackson, Howard
**Composer(s)** Gama, Rafael; Jackson, Howard
**Lyricist(s)** Gama, Rafael; Jackson, Howard

**Song(s)** Corrido de Guanajuato; Posada Music (C/L: Traditional); Xochimilco

**Notes** Short subject.

## 5045 ✦ ROMANCE AND RHYTHM

See HIT PARADE OF 1941 of which this was a re-edition.

## 5046 ✦ ROMANCE IN MANHATTAN
### RKO, 1934

**Musical Score** Steiner, Max

**Producer(s)** Berman, Pandro S.
**Director(s)** Roberts, Stephen
**Screenwriter(s)** Murfin, Jane; Kaurman, Edward

**Cast** Lederer, Francis; Rogers, Ginger; Hohl, Arthur; Butler, Jimmy; MacDonald, J. Farrell; Ware, Helen; Toler, Sidney; Meek, Donald

**Song(s)** Sing to Me [1] (C: Akst, Harry; L: Eliscu, Edward)

**Notes** [1] Also in DIPLOMANIACS.

## 5047 ✦ ROMANCE IN THE DARK
### Paramount, 1938

**Producer(s)** Thompson, Harlan
**Director(s)** Potter, H.C.
**Screenwriter(s)** Chapin, Anne Morrison; Partos, Frank
**Source(s)** *The Yellow Nightingale* (play) Bahr, Hermann

**Cast** Swarthout, Gladys; Boles, John; Barrymore, John; Dodd, Claire; Feld, Fritz

**Song(s)** None but the Lonely Heart [5] (C: Tchaikovsky, Peter; L: Goethe, Johann von; Westbrook, Arthur); Bewitched by the Night (C/L: Gorney, Jay); Tonight We Love [6] (C: Rainger, Ralph; Robin, Leo); Blue Dawn (C: Boutelje, Phil; L: Washington, Ned); Opening Second Act (C: Rainger, Ralph; L: Robin, Leo; Washington, Ned); Romance in the Dark (1) [2] (C: Young, Victor; Boutelje, Phil; L: Washington, Ned); Romance in the Dark (2) [3] (C/L: Swarthout, Gladys; Coslow, Sam); Romance in the Dark (3) [4] (C/L: Coslow, Sam); Hungarian Fantasy [2] (C: Boutelje, Phil; Stone, Gregory; L: Washington, Ned); The World Began with You [1] (C: Young, Victor; Boutelje, Phil; L: Washington, Ned)

**Notes** The film was originally named THE YELLOW NIGHTINGALE. The movie also contains "Berceuse" from JOCELYN by Godard with English lyrics by Nathan Haskell Dole; "Harbanera" from Bizet's CARMEN; "Una Voce Poco Fa" from Rossini's BARBER OF SEVILLE; Mozart's "La Ci Darem La Mano" from DON GIOVANNI; "Chanson Indoue (Song of India)" from SADKO by Rimsky-Korsakoff with English lyrics by Michel Delines and Louis Laloy and the traditional Russian Gypsy folk song "Dark Eyes." [1] Not used. [2] This is a medley of popular Hungarian airs. It was recorded. [3] Published song not used. [4] Not used. The two Coslow lyrics ([3] and [4]) have no relationship. [5] Also might be used vocally in LOVE IN BLOOM. Based on Tschaikowsky's Opus 6 No. 6. [6] Not used in COLLEGE SWING.

## 5048 ✦ ROMANCE IN THE ROUGH
### Paramount, 1937 unproduced
**Source(s)** (musical)

**Song(s)** The Nearness of You [1] (C: Carmichael, Hoagy; L: Washington, Ned); A Penny for Your Dreams [2] (C: Hollander, Frederick; L: Freed, Ralph); Let's Go to Pieces (C: Puck, Harry; L: Hautzik, Selma); Heelin' (C/L: Rubin, Harold; Luber, Robert)

**Notes** This was to be a remake of FOLLOW THRU. [1] Used in ASH WEDNESDAY. Recorded but not used for GIRLS! GIRLS! GIRLS! Not used in ST. LOUIS BLUES (1939). [2] Not used in COLLEGE SWING.

## 5049 ✦ ROMANCE OF ROSY RIDGE
### Metro–Goldwyn–Mayer, 1947

**Musical Score** Bassman, George
**Composer(s)** Robinson, Earl
**Lyricist(s)** Allen, Lewis
**Choreographer(s)** Donohue, Jack

**Producer(s)** Cummings, Jack
**Director(s)** Rowland, Roy
**Screenwriter(s)** Cole, Lester
**Source(s)** (story) Kantor, MacKinlay

**Cast** Johnson, Van; Mitchell, Thomas; Thompson, Marshall; Royle, Selena; Dingle, Charles; Stockwell, Dean; Kibbee, Guy; Leigh, Janet

**Song(s)** I Come from Missouri; Far From My Darling; Pig in the Parlor

**Notes** Originally titled THE NIGHT RAIDERS. Janet Leigh's debut.

## 5050 ✦ ROMANCE OF THE RIO GRANDE (1929)
### Twentieth Century–Fox, 1929

**Composer(s)** Baer, Abel
**Lyricist(s)** Gilbert, L. Wolfe

**Director(s)** Santell, Alfred
**Screenwriter(s)** Orth, Marion
**Source(s)** *Conquistidor* (novel) Gerould, Katherine Fullerton

**Cast** Baxter, Warner; Duncan, Mary; Moreno, Antonio; Maris, Mona; Edeson, Robert

**Song(s)** You'll Find Your Answer in My Eyes; When My Toreador Starts to Snore; Ride On Vaquero [1]

**Notes** [1] Also in ROMANCE OF THE RIO GRANDE (1940) and the Republic pictures IN OLD CALIENTE and OH SUSANNA! (1936).

## 5051 ✦ ROMANCE OF THE RIO GRANDE (1940)
### Twentieth Century–Fox, 1940

**Composer(s)** Baer, Abel
**Lyricist(s)** Gilbert, L. Wolfe

**Producer(s)** Wurtzel, Sol M.
**Director(s)** Leeds, Herbert I.
**Screenwriter(s)** Buchman, Harold; Engel, Samuel G.
**Source(s)** *Conquistador* (novel) Gerould, Katherine Fullerton

**Cast** Romero, Cesar; Morison, Patricia; Roberts, Lynne; Cortez, Ricardo; Martin, Chris-Pin; de Cordoba, Pedro

**Song(s)** You'll Find Your Answer in My Eyes [1]; Ride on Vaquero [1] [2]

**Notes** There are also brief vocals of "La Cucaracha" and "Ma Mue." [1] From 1929 version. [2] Also in 1929 version and the Republic pictures IN OLD CALIENTE and OH SUSANNA! (1936).

## 5052 ✦ ROMANCE OF THE UNDERWORLD
### Fox, 1928

**Director(s)** Cummings, Irving
**Screenwriter(s)** Doty, Douglas; Graham, Garrett
**Source(s)** *A Romance of the Underworld* (play) Armstrong, Paul

**Cast** Astor, Mary; Boles, John; Bard, Ben; Elliott, Robert; Apfel, Oscar; Lynch, Helen

**Song(s)** Judy [1] (C/L: Fain, Sammy; Kahal, Irving; Norman, Pierre)

**Notes** [1] Sheet music credits Jacques Murray and Pierre Norman.

## 5053 ✦ ROMANCE OF THE WEST
### PRC, 1946

**Director(s)** Tansey, Robert Emmett
**Screenwriter(s)** Kavanaugh, Frances

**Cast** Dean, Eddie; Barton, Joan; Lynn, Emmett; Taylor, Forrest; McKenzie, Robert; Price, Stanley

**Song(s)** Love Song of the Waterfall [1] (C/L: Nolan, Bob)

**Notes** [1] Sheet music credits Nolan, Bernard Barnes and Carl Winge.

## 5054 ✦ ROMANCE ON THE HIGH SEAS
### Warner Brothers, 1948

**Musical Score** Hollander, Frederick
**Composer(s)** Styne, Jule
**Lyricist(s)** Cahn, Sammy
**Choreographer(s)** Berkeley, Busby

**Producer(s)** Gottlieb, Alex
**Director(s)** Curtiz, Michael
**Screenwriter(s)** Epstein, Julius J.; Epstein, Philip G.; Diamond, I.A.L.
**Source(s)** "Romance in High C" (story) Rios, Sixto Pondal; Alivari, Carlos A.

**Cast** Carson, Jack; Paige, Janis; DeFore, Don; Day, Doris; Levant, Oscar; Sakall, S.Z.; Bonanova, Fortunio; Blore, Eric; Bakewell, William; Pangborn, Franklin; Long, Avon; The Samba Kings; Brooks, Leslie; The Page Cavanaugh Trio

**Song(s)** I'm in Love; It's You or No One; The Tourist Trade; It's Magic; Put 'Em in a Box; In Trinidad; Run Run Run; Two Lovers Met in the Night [1]

**Notes** Released in Great Britain as IT'S MAGIC. [1] Instrumental use only.

## 5055 ✦ ROMANCE ON THE RANGE
### Republic, 1942

**Producer(s)** Kane, Joseph
**Director(s)** Kane, Joseph
**Screenwriter(s)** Cheney, J. Benton

**Cast** Rogers, Roy; Hayes, George "Gabby"; Hayes, Linda; Payne, Sally; Pawley, Edward; Strange, Glenn; Taliaferro, Hal; Barcroft, Roy; Sons of the Pioneers

**Song(s)** Coyote Serenade (C/L: Nolan, Bob); When Romance Rides the Range (C/L: Spencer, Glenn); Oh

Wonderful World (C/L: Spencer, Tim; Allen, Sam); Rocky Mountain Lullaby (C/L: Spencer, Tim); Sing As You Work (C/L: Nolan, Bob)

**Notes** Originally titled SPRINGTIME IN THE ROCKIES.

## 5056 ✦ ROMANCE ON THE RUN
### Republic, 1938

**Producer(s)** Schlom, Herman
**Director(s)** Meins, Gus
**Screenwriter(s)** Townley, Jack

**Cast** Woods, Donald; Reynolds, Craig; Ellis, Patricia; Brophy, Edward S.; Tombes, Andrew; Bradley, Grace

**Song(s)** Are You a Dreamer (C/L: Tinturin, Peter; Lawrence, Jack)

## 5057 ✦ ROMANCING THE STONE
### Twentieth Century–Fox, 1984

**Musical Score** Silvestri, Alan

**Producer(s)** Douglas, Michael
**Director(s)** Zemeckis, Robert
**Screenwriter(s)** Thomas, Diane

**Cast** Douglas, Michael; Turner, Kathleen; DeVito, Danny; Norman, Zack; Arau, Alfonso; Taylor, Holland; Silver, Ron

**Song(s)** Romancing the Stone (C/L: Grant, Eddy)

**Notes** No cue sheet available.

## 5058 ✦ ROMAN HOLIDAY
### Paramount, 1968 unproduced

**Composer(s)** Sherman, Richard M.; Sherman, Robert B.
**Lyricist(s)** Sherman, Richard M.; Sherman, Robert B.

**Song(s)** So Simpatico; The Bells of Roma; We'll Still Have Rome

**Notes** This was originally to be Alan Jay Lerner's first project following THE LITTLE PRINCE.

## 5059 ✦ ROMAN SCANDALS
### United Artists, 1933

**Composer(s)** Warren, Harry
**Lyricist(s)** Dubin, Al
**Choreographer(s)** Berkeley, Busby

**Producer(s)** Goldwyn, Samuel
**Director(s)** Tuttle, Frank
**Screenwriter(s)** Sheekman, Arthur; McGuire, William Anthony; Oppenheimer, George; Perrin, Nat

**Cast** Cantor, Eddie; Ball, Lucille; Arnold, Edward; Teasdale, Verree; Stuart, Gloria; Manners, David; Mowbray, Alan; Darwell, Jane; Tuttle, Frank

Song(s)   Keep Young and Beautiful; Build a Little Home; No More Love; Rome Wasn't Built in a Day; Put a Tax on Love (L: Gilbert, L. Wolfe); Those Eddie Cantor Eyes [1] (C: Akst, Harry; Gilbert, L. Wolfe)

Notes   No cue sheet available. Lucille Ball is in the chorus. [1] Written for exploitation only.

## 5060 ✦ THE ROMAN SPRING OF MRS. STONE
### Warner Brothers, 1961

Musical Score   Addinsell, Richard

Producer(s)   de Rochemont, Louis
Director(s)   Quintero, Jose
Screenwriter(s)   Lambert, Gavin
Source(s)   "The Roman Spring of Mrs. Stone" (novella) Williams, Tennessee

Cast   Leigh, Vivien; Beatty, Warren; Lenya, Lotte; Browne, Coral; St. John, Jill; Spenser, Jeremy; Bonheur, Stella; Brown, Josephine; Dyneley, Peter; Laine, Cleo; Love, Bessie

Song(s)   Che Noia L'Amor (C: Addinsell, Richard; L: Roberts, Paddy)

## 5061 ✦ ROMANTIC COMEDY
### MGM/UA, 1983

Musical Score   Hamlisch, Marvin

Producer(s)   Mirisch, Walter; Gottlieb, Morton
Director(s)   Hiller, Arthur
Screenwriter(s)   Slade, Bernard
Source(s)   Romantic Comedy (play) Slade, Bernard

Cast   Moore, Dudley; Steenburgen, Mary; Eilber, Janet; Sternhagen, Frances; Leibman, Ron

Song(s)   Maybe (C: Hamlisch, Marvin; Bacharach, Burt; L: Sager, Carole Bayer)

## 5062 ✦ ROME ADVENTURE
### Warner Brothers, 1962

Musical Score   Steiner, Max

Producer(s)   Daves, Delmer
Director(s)   Daves, Delmer
Screenwriter(s)   Daves, Delmer
Source(s)   "Lovers Must Learn" (story) Fineman, Irving

Cast   Donahue, Troy; Dickinson, Angie; Brazzi, Rossano; Pleshette, Suzanne; Ford, Constance; Hirt, Al; Fancher, Hampton; Everett, Chad

Song(s)   Al Di La [1] (C/L: Donida-Mogol, C.); Rome Adventure [2] (C: Steiner, Max; L: Weiss, George David; Peretti, Hugo; Creatore, Luigi)

Notes   Released in Great Britain s LOVERS MUST LEARN. [1] English lyric written for exploitation only by Ervin Drake. [2] Written for exploitation only.

## 5063 ✦ ROMEO AND JULIET
### Paramount, 1968

Musical Score   Rota, Nino
Composer(s)   Rota, Nino
Lyricist(s)   Walter, Eugene

Producer(s)   Havelock-Allan, Anthony; Brabourne, Allan; Brabourne, John
Director(s)   Zeffirelli, Franco
Screenwriter(s)   Brusati, Franco; D'Amico, Masolino
Source(s)   Romeo and Juliet (play) Shakespeare, William

Cast   Hussey, Olivia; Whiting, Leonard; O'Shea, Milo; York, Michael; McEnery, John; Heywood, Pat; Parry, Natasha; Stephens, Robert

Song(s)   What Is a Youth; The Feast at the House of Capulet (L: Traditional); A Time for Us [1] (L: Kusik, Larry; Snyder, Eddie)

Notes   [1] Lyric for exploitation use only.

## 5064 ✦ ROOKIES ON PARADE
### Republic, 1941

Composer(s)   Chaplin, Saul
Lyricist(s)   Cahn, Sammy

Producer(s)   Cohen, Albert J.
Director(s)   Santley, Joseph
Screenwriter(s)   Brown, Karl; Townley, Jack; Gross, Milt

Cast   Crosby, Bob; Terry, Ruth; Niesen, Gertrude; Foy Jr., Eddie; Wilson, Marie; Nazarro, Cliff; Shirley, Bill; Alexander, Jimmy; Blackmer, Sidney; MacMahon, Horace; Da Pron, Louis; Demarest, William

Song(s)   I Love You More; What More Do You Want; Mother Never Told Me Why; Chula Chihauhau (C: Styne, Jule; L: Castle, Nick; Clare, Sidney); My Kinda Music; Rookies on Parade (C: Styne, Jule; L: Cherkose, Eddie); You'll Never Get Rich; Most Gentlemen Don't Prefer a Lady [1]; Coppin' a Plea [1]; My Kinda Love [1]; Oh He Loves Me [1]

Notes   Originally titled YOU'LL NEVER GET RICH. [1] Not used.

## 5065 ✦ ROONEY
### United Artists, 1958

Musical Score   Green, Philip

Producer(s)   Brown, George H.
Director(s)   Pollock, George
Screenwriter(s)   Kirwan, Patrick
Source(s)   Rooney (novel) Cookson, Catherine

Cast   Gregson, John; Pavlow, Muriel; Fitzgerald, Barry; Thorburn, June; Purcell, Noel; Byrne, Eddie

Song(s)   Rooney (C: Green, Philip; L: Connor, Tommie)

Notes   A Rank Organisation picture.

## 5066 ✦ THE ROOSTER

See THE BOYS WILL NEVER BELIEVE IT.

## 5067 ✦ ROOSTER COGBURN
Universal, 1975

**Musical Score** Rosenthal, Laurence

**Producer(s)** Wallis, Hal B.
**Director(s)** Millar, Stuart
**Screenwriter(s)** Julien, Martin

**Cast** Wayne, John; Hepburn, Katharine; Jordan, Richard; Zerbe, Anthony; Lormer, Jon

**Song(s)** I Painted Her [1] (C: Mooney, Hal; L: Riesner, Dean)

**Notes** [1] Also in CHARLEY VARRICK.

## 5068 ✦ ROOTIN' TOOTIN' RHYTHM
Republic, 1937

**Producer(s)** Schaefer, Armand
**Director(s)** Wright, Mack V.
**Screenwriter(s)** Natteford, Jack

**Cast** Autry, Gene; Burnette, Smiley; Armida; Blue, Monte; Al Caluser and His Oklahoma Outlaws; Taliaferro, Hal; Hoffman Jr., Max; King, Charles

**Song(s)** The Old Home Place (C/L: Allan, Fleming; Natteford, Jack); Little Black Bronc (C/L: Clauser, Al; Hoepner, Tex); I Hate to Say Goodbye to the Prairie (C/L: Autry, Gene); Mexicali Rose [1] (C/L: Stone, Helen; Tenney, Jack); Trail of the Mountain Rose (C/L: Clauser, Al; Hoepner, Tex); Dying Cowgirl (C/L: Autry, Gene)

**Notes** [1] Also in BARBED WIRE (Columbia) (without Stone credit) and MEXICALI ROSE.

## 5069 ✦ ROOTS OF HEAVEN
Twentieth Century–Fox, 1958

**Musical Score** Arnold, Malcolm

**Producer(s)** Zanuck, Darryl F.
**Director(s)** Huston, John
**Screenwriter(s)** Gary, Romain; Leigh-Fermor, Patrick
**Source(s)** The Roots of Heaven (novel) Gary, Romain

**Cast** Flynn, Errol; Greco, Juliette; Howard, Trevor; Albert, Eddie; Welles, Orson; Lukas, Paul; Lom, Herbert

**Song(s)** The Roots of Heaven [1] (C: Patterson, Henri; L: Washington, Ned)

**Notes** Erroll Flynn's last film. [1] Used instrumentally only.

## 5070 ✦ ROPE
Warner Brothers, 1948

**Producer(s)** Hitchcock, Alfred
**Director(s)** Hitchcock, Alfred
**Screenwriter(s)** Laurents, Arthur
**Source(s)** Rope's End (play) Hamilton, Patrick

**Cast** Stewart, James; Dall, John; Granger, Farley; Hardwicke, Sir Cedric; Collier, Constance; Chandler, Joan; Dick, Douglas; Evanson, Edith; Hogan, William

**Song(s)** At the Candlelight Cafe [1] (C/L: David, Mack)

**Notes** [1] Also in MY GIRL TISA.

## 5071 ✦ ROSALIE
Metro–Goldwyn–Mayer, 1937

**Composer(s)** Porter, Cole
**Lyricist(s)** Porter, Cole
**Choreographer(s)** Rasch, Albertina

**Producer(s)** McGuire, William Anthony
**Director(s)** Van Dyke II, W.S.
**Screenwriter(s)** McGuire, William Anthony
**Source(s)** Rosalie (musical) McGuire, William Anthony; Bolton, Guy

**Cast** Eddy, Nelson; Powell, Eleanor; Morgan, Frank; Oliver, Edna May; Bolger, Ray; Massey, Ilona; Gilbert, Billy; Owen, Reginald; Colonna, Jerry; Beecher, Janet; Demarest, William; Grey, Virginia

**Song(s)** Who Knows; I've a Strange New Rhythm in My Heart; Night and Day [1]; Rosalie; Why Should I Care; Spring Love in the Air; In the Still of the Night; It's All Over but the Shouting; To Love or Not to Love

**Notes** There are also vocals of "On Brave Old Army Team" by Egner; "Artillery Song" by Gruber; "Dreadnought Song" by Egner and Mayer and "Anchors Aweigh" by Zimmerman. [1] Also in THE GAY DIVORCEE (RKO) and NIGHT AND DAY (Warner).

## 5072 ✦ THE ROSE
Twentieth Century–Fox, 1979

**Choreographer(s)** Basil, Toni

**Producer(s)** Worth, Marvin; Russo, Aaron
**Director(s)** Rydell, Mark
**Screenwriter(s)** Goldman, Bo; Cimino, Michael; Kerby, William

**Cast** Midler, Bette; Bates, Alan; Forrest, Frederic; Primus, Barry; McCabe, Sandra

**Song(s)** Whose Side Are You On (C/L: Hopkins, Kenny; Williams, Charley); Midnight In Memphis (C/L: Johnson, Tony); When a Man Loves a Woman (C/L: Lewis, Calvin; Wright, Andrew); I've Written a Letter to Daddy (If I Had My Life to Live Over) [2] (C/L: Vincent, Larry; Tobias, Henry; Jaffe, Moe); Fire Down Below (C/L: Seger, Bob); Keep On Rockin' (C/L: Hagar, Sammy; Carter, John); Sold My Soul to Rock 'N' Roll (C/L: Pistilli, Gene); Love Her with a Feeling [1] (C: Hendricks, Jon; L: Tampa Red); Stay with Me (C/L: Ragavoy, Jerry; Weiss, George David); The Rose (C/L: McBroom, Amanda)

**Notes** It is not known if any of these were written for this film. [1] Sheet music credits Hudson Whitaker with this song. [2] From WHATEVER HAPPENED TO BABY JANE.

## 5073 ✦ ROSEANNA MCCOY
RKO, 1949

**Musical Score** Friedhofer, Hugo

**Producer(s)** Goldwyn, Samuel
**Director(s)** Reis, Irving
**Screenwriter(s)** Collier, John
**Source(s)** *Roseanna McCoy* (novel) Hannum, Alberta

**Cast** Evans, Joni; Granger, Farley; Basehart, Richard; Massey, Raymond; Bickford, Charles; Perreau, Gigi; MacMahon, Aline; Thompson, Marshall; Gough, Lloyd; Paige, Mabel

**Song(s)** Roseanna (C/L: Loesser, Frank)

## 5074 ✦ ROSE BOWL
Paramount, 1936

**Producer(s)** Botsford, A.M.
**Director(s)** Barton, Charles
**Screenwriter(s)** Roberts, Marguerite
**Source(s)** *O'Reilly of Notre Dame* (novel) Wallace, Francis

**Cast** Brown, Tom; Whitney, Eleanore; Crabbe, Buster; Frawley, William

**Song(s)** Bellport Will Shine Tonight (C: Pasternacki, Stephen; L: Robin, Leo); Sons of Sierra [1] (C: Kisco, Charley; L: Robin, Leo); At the Rose Bowl [1] [2] (C: Mizzy, Vic; L: Taylor, Irving)

**Notes** [1] Not used. [2] Written for exploitation use only.

## 5075 ✦ ROSEBUD
United Artists, 1975

**Musical Score** Petitgirard, Laurent

**Producer(s)** Preminger, Otto
**Director(s)** Preminger, Otto
**Screenwriter(s)** Preminger, Erik Lee
**Source(s)** *Rosebud* (novel) Hemingway, Joan; Bonnecarrere, Paul

**Cast** O'Toole, Peter; Attenborough, Richard; Gorman, Cliff; Lawford, Peter; Vallone, Raf; Huppert, Isabelle

**Song(s)** The Lord Must Be in New York City (C/L: Nilsson, Harry)

## 5076 ✦ ROSE MARIE (1936)
Metro–Goldwyn–Mayer, 1936

**Musical Score** Stothart, Herbert
**Composer(s)** Friml, Rudolf

**Lyricist(s)** Harbach, Otto; Hammerstein II, Oscar
**Choreographer(s)** Hale, Chester

**Producer(s)** Stromberg, Hunt
**Director(s)** Van Dyke, W.S.
**Screenwriter(s)** Goodrich, Frances; Hackett, Albert; Miller, Alice Duer
**Source(s)** *Rose Marie* (musical) Harbach, Otto; Hammerstein II, Oscar; Stothart, Herbert; Friml, Rudolf

**Cast** MacDonald, Jeanette; Eddy, Nelson; Owen, Reginald; Jones, Allan; Stewart, James; Mowbray, Alan; Gray, Gilda; Niven, David; Bing, Herman; O'Connor, Una; Regas, George; Greig, Robert; Littlefield, Lucien; Conlin, Jimmy; Hobbes, Halliwell; Hicks, Russell

**Song(s)** Indian Love Call [1]; Pardon Me Madame [2] (C: Stothart, Herbert; L: Kahn, Gus); The Mounties [1] (C: Friml, Rudolf; Stothart, Herbert); Oh, Rose-Marie [1]; Totem Tom-Tom [1] (C: Friml, Rudolf; Stothart, Herbert); Just for You (C: Friml, Rudolf; Stothart, Herbert; L: Kahn, Gus)

**Notes** There are also vocals from Charles Gounod's ROMEO AND JULIET including "Capulet's Ball," "Recitative," "Scene Numbers 1 and 2," "Juliet's Waltz Song," a montage of the "Finale Act I," "Finale Act III" and "Scene No. 16," and the "Finale Act V;" "Dinah" by Sam M. Lewis and Joe Young; "Some of These Days" by Shelton Brooks; and the "Finale Act III" of Puccini's TOSCA. The opera scenes are staged by William Von Wymetal. [1] From original Broadway musical. [2] French lyrics by David Ormont.

## 5077 ✦ ROSE MARIE (1954)
Metro–Goldwyn–Mayer, 1954

**Musical Score** Stoll, George; Van Eps, Robert
**Composer(s)** Friml, Rudolf
**Lyricist(s)** Harbach, Otto; Hammerstein II, Oscar
**Choreographer(s)** Berkeley, Busby

**Director(s)** LeRoy, Mervyn
**Screenwriter(s)** Millar, Ronald; Froeschel, George
**Source(s)** *Rose Marie* (musical) Harbach, Otto; Hammerstein II, Oscar; Friml, Rudolf; Stothart, Herbert

**Cast** Blyth, Ann; Keel, Howard; Lamas, Fernando; Lahr, Bert; Main, Marjorie; Taylor, Joan; Collins, Ray; Chief Yowlachie

**Song(s)** The Right Place for a Girl (L: Webster, Paul Francis); The Mounties [1] [2] (C: Friml, Rudolf; Stothart, Herbert; L: Webster, Paul Francis; Harbach, Otto; Hammerstein II, Oscar); Free to Be Free (L: Webster, Paul Francis); Rose Marie [1] [2] (L: Webster, Paul Francis; Harbach, Otto; Hammerstein II, Oscar); I'm a Mountie Who Never Got His Man (C: Stoll, George; L: Stoll, George; Baker, Herbert); Indian Love Call [2]; Totem Tom-Tom [2] (C: Friml, Rudolf; Stothart, Herbert); I Have the Love (L: Webster, Paul Francis); Love and Kisses [3] (C: Friml, Rudolf; Stoll, George; L: Webster, Paul Francis)

**Notes** [1] Additional lyrics by Paul Francis Webster. [2] From Broadway original. [3] Not used. Stoll credit per ASCAP.

## 5078 ◆ ROSEMARY'S BABY
### Paramount, 1968

**Producer(s)** Castle, William
**Director(s)** Polanski, Roman
**Screenwriter(s)** Polanski, Roman
**Source(s)** *Rosemary's Baby* (novel) Levin, Ira

**Cast** Farrow, Mia; Cassavetes, John; Gordon, Ruth; Blackmer, Sidney; Evans, Maurice; Bellamy, Ralph

**Song(s)** Moment in Time (C: Komeda, Christopher; L: Blair, Hal); Sleep Safe and Warm [1] (C: Komeda, Christopher; L: Kusik, Larry; Snyder, Eddie)

**Notes** [1] Lyric for exploitation use only.

## 5079 ◆ ROSE OF SANTA ROSA
### Columbia, 1947

**Director(s)** Nazarro, Ray
**Screenwriter(s)** Shipman, Barry

**Cast** Noriega, Eduardo [2]; White, Patricia [3]; The Hoosier Hotshots; Ciannelli, Eduardo; Codee, Ann; Fowley, Douglas; Aaron Gonzales and His Orchestra; The Philharmonica Trio

**Song(s)** Rose of Santa Rosa (C/L: Hoffman, Al; Roberts, Allan; Livingston, Jerry); Ferdinand the Bull (C: Malotte, Albert Hay; L: Morey, Larry); Relax (C/L: Dennis, Matt); Cocachica [1] (C: Chaplin, Saul; L: Samuels, Walter G.); Lady from Twenty-Nine Palms (C/L: Wrubel, Allie); Be My Darlin' (C/L: Reinhart, Dick)

**Notes** [1] Only song written for picture. [2] Dubbed by Ken Harvey. [3] Dubbed by Jewel Eberly.

## 5080 ◆ ROSE OF THE RANCHO
### Paramount, 1936

**Composer(s)** Rainger, Ralph
**Lyricist(s)** Robin, Leo

**Producer(s)** LeBaron, William
**Director(s)** Gering, Marion
**Screenwriter(s)** Partos, Frank; Brackett, Charles; Sheekman, Arthur; Perrin, Nat
**Source(s)** *Rose of the Rancho* (play) Belasco, David

**Cast** Swarthout, Gladys [4]; Boles, John; Howard, Willie; Bickford, Charles; Bradley, Grace; Warner, H.B.; Alvarado, Don; Williams, Herb; Baker, Benny

**Song(s)** Fight for the Right and Without Freedom (C: Korngold, Erich Wolfgang; L: Ormont, David [3]); He Met Her on the Prairie [7]; Vigilante Song; Got A Gal in Californ-I-A; The Padre and the Bride; Where Is My Love; Little Rose of the Rancho; There's Gold in

Monterey; If I Should Lose You; Bury Me Under the Willow [1]; Thunder Over Paradise [2] [5]; Lone Cowboy [1] [6]; My True Lover [2]; Soliloquy [2]; Don Carlos Is Riding Tonight [2]; To Be Near Him [2] (C: Harling, W. Franke; L: Coslow, Sam); Conchita (2) [2] (C: Harling, W. Franke; L: Coslow, Sam); My Rose of the Rancho [2] (C: Harling, W. Franke; L: Coslow, Sam); Hearts in Harmony [2]; Is Love a Beautiful Illusion [2]; Sombrero Dance [2]; May in Monterey [2]; A Moon and Music [2]; More than a Sweet Romance [2]; How Can We Part [2]; You're a Breeze in the Desert [2]; Tonight We Ride [2]; My Heart and I [2] [8]; Trail of the Ashes [2] (C: Harling, W. Franke; L: Akins, Zoe); Conchita (1) [2] (C: Harling, W. Franke; L: Akins, Zoe); Carriage Duet

**Notes** Zoe Akins had written some lyrics to music by W. Franke Harling prior to Robin and Rainger being assigned the project. [1] Used instrumentally only. [2] Not used. [3] A pseudonym for Davis S. Goldberg. [4] Swarthout's whistling was dubbed by Jack Dale. [5] Recorded by Swarthout and published. [6] Recorded by Willie Howard. Also not used in LONE COWBOY. [7] Also used in FLAMING FEATHER. [8] Used in ANYTHING GOES (1936).

## 5081 ◆ ROSE OF THE YUKON
### Republic, 1948

**Producer(s)** Auer, Stephen
**Director(s)** Blair, George
**Screenwriter(s)** Hall, Norman S.

**Cast** Brodie, Steve; Dell, Myrna; Wright, William; Parnell, Emory; Baker, Benny; Hale, Jonathan

**Song(s)** It's Not the First Love [1] (C/L: Maxwell, Eddie; Scott, Nathan)

**Notes** [1] Also in I COVER THE WATERFRONT and THE TRESPASSER.

## 5082 ◆ ROSE OF WASHINGTON SQUARE
### Twentieth Century–Fox, 1939

**Choreographer(s)** Felix, Seymour

**Producer(s)** Zanuck, Darryl F.
**Director(s)** Ratoff, Gregory
**Screenwriter(s)** Johnson, Nunnally

**Cast** Power, Tyrone; Faye, Alice; Jolson, Al; Frawley, William; Compton, Joyce; Cavanaugh, Hobart; Clive, E.E.; Olsen, Moroni; Prima, Louis; Wilson, Charles; MacMahon, Horace

**Song(s)** I Never Knew Heaven Could Speak (C: Revel, Harry; L: Gordon, Mack)

**Notes** There are also many Tin Pan Alley songs given vocal treatment. Those lasting over a minute include: "I'm Sorry I Made You Cry" by N.J. Clesi; "Mother Machree" by Ernest R. Ball and Chauncey Olcott;

"Ja-Da" by Bob Carleton; "The Vamp" by Byron Gay; "Rock-a-bye Your Baby with a Dixie Melody" by Jean Schwartz, Sam Lewis and Joe Young; "Toot Toot Tootsie" by Gus Kahn, Ernie Erdman and Dan Russo (From stage musical BOMBO. Also in I'LL SEE YOU IN MY DREAMS, THE JOLSON STORY, JOLSON SINGS AGAIN and THE JAZZ SINGER); "Shine on Harvest Moon" by Nora Bayes and Jack Norworth; "I'm Just Wild About Harry" by Noble Sissle and Eubie Blake; "California Here I Come" by Al Jolson, B.G. DeSylva and Joseph Meyer; "Yoo Hoo" by Al Jolson and B.G. DeSylva; "Rose of Washington Square" by James F. Hanley and Ballard Macdonald (from ZIEGFELD MIDNIGHT FROLIC stage show); "My Mammy" by Walter Donaldson, Sam Lewis and Joe Young and "My Man" by Maurice Yvain, A. Willemetz, Jacques Charles and Channing Pollock.

## 5083 ◆ THE ROSE TATTOO
### Paramount, 1955

**Musical Score**  North, Alex

**Producer(s)**  Wallis, Hal B.
**Director(s)**  Mann, Daniel
**Screenwriter(s)**  Williams, Tennessee
**Source(s)**  *The Rose Tattoo* (play) Williams, Tennessee

**Cast**  Magnani, Anna; Lancaster, Burt; Pavan, Marisa; Cooper, Ben; Van Fleet, Jo; Grey, Virginia

**Song(s)**  Vino, Vino [1] (C: North, Alex; L: David, Hal); The Rose Tattoo [2] (C: Warren, Harry; L: Brooks, Jack); Come le Rose [2] (C: Genise, Adolfo; L: Lama, Gaetano)

**Notes**  [1] Lyric for exploitation use only. [2] Not used.

## 5084 ◆ ROSIE!
### Universal, 1967

**Musical Score**  Murray, Lyn

**Producer(s)**  Mapes, Jacques
**Director(s)**  Rich, David Lowell
**Screenwriter(s)**  Taylor, Samuel
**Source(s)**  *A Very Rich Woman* (play) Heriat, Philippe

**Cast**  Russell, Rosalind; Dee, Sandra; Aherne, Brian; Farentino, James; Nielsen, Leslie; Owen, Reginald; Hamilton, Margaret; Meadows, Audrey; Brown, Vanessa

**Song(s)**  Rosie (C: Warren, Harry; L: Mercer, Johnny)

## 5085 ◆ ROSIE THE RIVETER
### Republic, 1944

**Choreographer(s)**  Gould, Dave

**Producer(s)**  Schaefer, Armand
**Director(s)**  Santley, Joseph

**Screenwriter(s)**  Leslie, Aleen; Townley, Jack
**Source(s)**  "Room for Two" (story) Handley, Dorothy Curnow

**Cast**  Frazee, Jane; Allen, Barbara Jo; Albertson, Frank; Jenks, Frank; Fenton, Frank; Eburne, Maude; Corrigan, Lloyd; Switzer, Carl "Alfalfa"

**Song(s)**  Why Can't I Sing a Love Song [2] (C: Akst, Harry; L: Meyer, Sol); I Don't Want Anybody At All [1] (C: Styne, Jule; L: Magidson, Herb)

**Notes**  There are also vocals of "Friendly Tavern Polka" by Frank DeVol and J. Browne and "Rosie the Riveter" by Redd Evans and John Jacob Loeb. [1] Also in SLEEPYTIME GAL. [2] Also in CHATTERBOX.

## 5086 ◆ ROUGH NIGHT IN JERICHO
### Universal, 1967

**Musical Score**  Costa, Don

**Producer(s)**  Rackin, Martin
**Director(s)**  Leven, Arnold
**Screenwriter(s)**  Boehm, Sydney; Albert, Marvin H.

**Cast**  Martin, Dean; Peppard, George; Simmons, Jean; McIntire, John; Pickens, Slim; Galloway, Don; Weston, Brad

**Song(s)**  Hold Me (C: Costa, Don; L: Zeller, Phil); Devil Rides in Jericho [1] (C: Costa, Don; L: Zeller, Phil; Rackin, Martin)

**Notes**  [1] Sheet music only.

## 5087 ◆ ROUGH RIDERS ROUND-UP
### Republic, 1939

**Producer(s)**  Kane, Joseph
**Director(s)**  Kane, Joseph
**Screenwriter(s)**  Natteford, Jack

**Cast**  Rogers, Roy; Hart, Mary; Hatton, Raymond; Acuff, Eddie; Pawley, William; Sebastian, Dorothy; Meeker, George; Strange, Glenn; Renaldo, Duncan; Christie, Dorothy; Kirk, Jack; Chesebro, George

**Song(s)**  Ridin' Down the Trail [1] (C: Feuer, Cy; L: Cherkose, Eddie); Here on the Range (C/L: Spencer, Tim)

**Notes**  [1] Also in MAN FROM RAINBOW VALLEY.

## 5088 ◆ ROUGH ROMANCE
### Fox, 1930

**Composer(s)**  Little, George A.
**Lyricist(s)**  Burke, Johnny

**Director(s)**  Erickson, A.F.
**Screenwriter(s)**  Davis, Donald

**Source(s)** "The Girl Who Wasn't Wanted" (novelette) Clarke, Kenneth B.

**Cast** O'Brien, George; Chandler, Helen; Moreno, Antonio; Francis, Noel; Cording, Harry; Hartford, David

**Song(s)** The Song of the Lumberjacks; She's Somebody's Baby; Nobody Knows

## 5089 ◆ THE ROUGH, TOUGH WEST
### Columbia, 1951

**Producer(s)** Clark, Colbert
**Director(s)** Nazarro, Ray
**Screenwriter(s)** Shipman, Barry

**Cast** Starrett, Charles; Mahoney, Jock [1]; Cotton, Carolina; Pee Wee King and His Band; Burnette, Smiley

**Song(s)** 'Cause I'm in Love (C/L: Jones, Stan); You Gotta Get a Guy with a Gun (C/L: Cotton, Carolina); The Fire of '41 (C/L: Burnette, Smiley); You Don't Need My Love Anymore (C: King, Pee Wee; L: Stewart, Redd)

**Notes** [1] Billed as Jack Mahoney.

## 5090 ◆ ROUND MIDNIGHT
### Warner Brothers, 1986

**Musical Score** Hancock, Herbie

**Producer(s)** Winkler, Irwin
**Director(s)** Tavernier, Bertrand
**Screenwriter(s)** Rayfiel, David; Tavernier, Bertrand

**Cast** Gordon, Dexter; Cluzet, Francois; Haker, Gabrielle; Reeves-Phillips, Sandra; McKee, Lonette; Pascal, Christine; Hancock, Herbie; Hutcherson, Bobby; Scorsese, Martin; Noiret, Philippe; Sarde, Alain

**Song(s)** How Long Has This Been Going On (C: Gershwin, George; L: Gershwin, Ira); Fair Weather [1] (C/L: Dorham, Kenny); Put It Right Here (C/L: Smith, Bessie); Watermelon Man [2] (C/L: Hancock, Herbie)

**Notes** No original songs in this film. Songs with less than a minute's time are not listed. [1] Background vocal. [2] Listed in *Academy Index* but not on cue sheet.

## 5091 ◆ THE ROUND-UP
### Paramount, 1941

**Composer(s)** Ohman, Phil
**Lyricist(s)** Carling, Foster

**Producer(s)** Sherman, Harry
**Director(s)** Selander, Lesley
**Screenwriter(s)** Shumate, Harold
**Source(s)** (play) Day, Edmund

**Cast** Dix, Richard; Morison, Patricia; Foster, Preston

**Song(s)** Love Never Grows Old; Ride 'Em Cowboy; Easy-Go-Slim; Dear Evelina [1]; Believe Me [1]

**Notes** [1] Not used.

## 5092 ◆ ROUND-UP TIME IN TEXAS
### Republic, 1937

**Producer(s)** Schaefer, Armand
**Director(s)** Kane, Joseph
**Screenwriter(s)** Drake, Oliver

**Cast** Autry, Gene; Burnette, Smiley; Doyle, Maxine; The Cabin Kids; Champion; Mason, LeRoy; Hodgins, Earl; Wessell, Dick; Williams, Buddy; Fain, Elmer; Cooper, Ken

**Song(s)** When the Bloom Is on the Sage [2] (C/L: Vincent, Nat; Howard, Fred); Sweet Strain (C/L: Allan, Fleming); Uncle Noah's Ark [1] (C/L: Burnette, Smiley); Prairie Rose (C: Stept, Sam H.; L: Mitchell, Sidney D.); Cave Man (C/L: Burnette, Smiley); Indian Song [3] (C/L: Allan, Fleming)

**Notes** There are also vocals of "On Revival Day" by Andy Razaf; "Dinah" by Joe Young, Harry Akst and Sam Lewis; "The Old Chisholm Trail," "Drink Old England Dry" and "Jacob Drink." [1] Also in THE PHANTOM EMPIRE but credited to Gene Autry. [2] Also in LOADED PISTOLS (Columbia). [3] Sheet music only.

## 5093 ◆ ROUSTABOUT
### Paramount, 1964

**Composer(s)** Giant, Bill; Baum, Bernie; Kaye, Florence
**Lyricist(s)** Giant, Bill; Baum, Bernie; Kaye, Florence
**Choreographer(s)** Barton, Earl

**Producer(s)** Wallis, Hal B.
**Director(s)** Rich, John
**Screenwriter(s)** Lawrence, Anthony; Weiss, Allan

**Cast** Presley, Elvis; Stanwyck, Barbara; Freeman, Joan; Erickson, Leif; Langdon, Sue Ane; Greer, Dabbs; Brodie, Steve; Buttram, Pat; Welch, Raquel

**Song(s)** Roustabout (1); Poison Ivy League; Wheels on My Heels (C/L: Tepper, Sid; Bennett, Roy C.); It's a Wonderful World (C/L: Tepper, Sid; Bennett, Roy C.); There's a Brand New Day on the Horizon (C/L: Byers, Joy); It's Carnival Time (C: Weisman, Ben; L: Wayne, Sid); Carny Town (C/L: Wise, Fred; Starr, Randy); One Track Heart; Little Egypt (C/L: Leiber, Jerry; Stoller, Mike); Hard Knocks (C/L: Byers, Joy); Big Love, Big Heartache (C/L: Fuller, Dolores; Morris, Lee; Hendrix, Sonny); Shout It Out [1] [2]; I Never Had It So Good (C/L: Fuller, Dolores; Barkan, Mark; Morris, Lee); Carnival of Dreams [1] (C: Weisman, Ben; L: Wayne, Sid); Roustabout (2) [1] (C/L: Blackwell, Otis; Scott, Winfield)

**Notes**  [1] Not used. [2] Used in FRANKIE AND
JOHNNY.

## 5094 ✦ ROVIN' TUMBLEWEEDS
Republic, 1939

**Producer(s)**  Berke, William
**Director(s)**  Sherman, George
**Screenwriter(s)**  McGowan, Dorrell; McGowan, Stuart;
Burbridge, Betty

**Cast**  Autry, Gene; Burnette, Smiley; Carlisle, Mary;
Dumbrille, Douglass; Farnum, William; White, Lee
"Lasses"

**Song(s)**  Hurray (C/L: Burnette, Smiley; Cherkose,
Eddie); A Girl Like You and a Night Like This (C/L:
Marvin, Johnny; Rose, Fred); Sunny Side of a Cell (C/L:
Autry, Gene; Marvin, Johnny; Rose, Fred); Back in the
Saddle Again [2] (C/L: Whitley, Ray); Rocky Mountain
Express (C: von Tilzer, Albert; L: Tobias, Harry; Tobias,
Charles); Paradise in the Moonlight (C/L: Autry, Gene;
Rose, Fred); Old Peaceful River [1] (C/L: Marvin,
Johnny); Away Out Yonder (C/L: Marvin, Johnny;
Rose, Fred)

**Notes**  No cue sheet available. Originally titled
WASHINGTON COWBOY. [1] It is not known
whether Marvin collaborated on this song or not. [2]
Also in BLUE MONTANA SKIES. [2] Also in BACK
IN THE SADDLE, MELODY RANCH and BORDER
G-MEN (RKO). Gene Autry is often listed as coauthor
of the song.

## 5095 ✦ ROXANNE
Columbia, 1987

**Musical Score**  Smeaton, Bruce

**Producer(s)**  Rachmil, Michael; Melnick, Daniel
**Director(s)**  Schepisi, Fred
**Screenwriter(s)**  Martin, Steve
**Source(s)**  *Cyrano de Bergerac* (play) Rostand,
Edmond

**Cast**  Martin, Steve; Hannah, Daryl; Rossovich, Rick;
Beri, Shandra; Duvall, Shelley; Pollard, Michael J.

**Song(s)**  Soul Star (C/L: Cox, Terry; Kent, Jeff; Pesco,
Paul); Party Tonight (C/L: Baxter, Jeff "Skunk";
Boston, Rick)

**Notes**  Both background vocals.

## 5096 ✦ A ROYAL AFFAIR
Discina International Film, 1950

**Producer(s)**  Safra, Michel; Paulve, Andre

**Cast**  Chevalier, Maurice

**Song(s)**  Bouquet de Paris (C/L: Boutrayre; Chevalier,
Maurice; Vandair); La Barbe (C/L: Freed, Fred;

Chevalier, Maurice; Vandair); C'est Fini (C/L: Freed,
Fred; Chevalier, Maurice); La Cachucha (C/L:
Boutrayre; Chevalier, Maurice; Vandair)

**Notes**  French title: LE ROI.

## 5097 ✦ A ROYAL ROMANCE
Columbia, 1930

**Director(s)**  Kenton, Erle C.
**Screenwriter(s)**  Houston, Norman
**Souree(s)**  "Private Property" (story)

**Cast**  Collier Jr., William; Starke, Pauline; Besserer,
Eugenie; Muse, Clarence; Brody, Ann

**Song(s)**  Original (C/L: Pearce, Ethel); Singing a Song
to the Stars [1] (C: Meyer, Joseph; L: Johnson,
Howard); Black Minnie's Got the Blues [1] (C/L:
Meskill, Jack; Ray, Cyril)

**Notes**  [1] Not on cue sheet.

## 5098 ✦ ROYAL WEDDING
Metro–Goldwyn–Mayer, 1951

**Musical Score**  Green, Johnny; Sendrey, Al
**Composer(s)**  Lane, Burton
**Lyricist(s)**  Lerner, Alan Jay
**Choreographer(s)**  Castle, Nick

**Producer(s)**  Freed, Arthur
**Director(s)**  Donen, Stanley
**Screenwriter(s)**  Lerner, Alan Jay

**Cast**  Astaire, Fred; Powell, Jane; Lawford, Peter;
Wynn, Keenan; Churchill, Sarah; Sharpe, Albert;
Finlayson, James

**Song(s)**  Ev'ry Night at Seven; Open Your Eyes; The
Happiest Day of My Life; How Could You Believe Me
When I Said I Love You When You Know I've Been a
Liar All My Life; Too Late Now; You're All the World to
Me [3]; I Left My Hat in Haiti; What a Lovely Day for a
Wedding; Sunday Jumps [1]; I Got Me a Baby [2]

**Notes**  Titled WEDDING BELLS in Great Britain.
Judy Garland was set to star but was replaced by Powell
during rehearsals. [1] Used instrumentally only. [2] Not
used. [3] Same music as "I Want to Be a Minstrel Man"
from KID MILLIONS.

## 5099 ✦ R.P.M.
Columbia, 1970

**Composer(s)**  Botkin Jr., Perry; De Vorzon, Barry
**Lyricist(s)**  De Vorzon, Barry; Botkin Jr., Perry

**Producer(s)**  Kramer, Stanley
**Director(s)**  Kramer, Stanley
**Screenwriter(s)**  Segal, Erich

**Cast** Quinn, Anthony; Ann-Margaret; Lockwood, Gary; Winfield, Paul; Jarvis, Graham; Hewitt, Alan; Moffat, Donald

**Song(s)** Stop! I Don't Wanna' Hear It Anymore [1]; All Night Long; We Don't Know Where We're Goin'; When I Get Home to You; Hudson II - I Love You

**Notes** [1] M. Sajka also credited on sheet music.

## 5100 ◆ RUBY
United Artists, 1977

**Musical Score** Ellis, Don

**Producer(s)** Krantz, Steve
**Director(s)** Harrington, Curtis
**Screenwriter(s)** Edwards, George; Schneider, Barry

**Cast** Laurie, Piper; Whitman, Stuart; Davis, Roger; Baldwin, Janit; Sinclaire, Crystin; Kent, Paul; Lesser, Len

**Song(s)** Love's So Easy (C: Ellis, Don; L: Stevens, Sally)

## 5101 ◆ RUBY GENTRY
Twentieth Century–Fox, 1952

**Musical Score** Roemheld, Heinz

**Producer(s)** Vidor, King; Bernhard, Joseph
**Director(s)** Vidor, King
**Screenwriter(s)** Richards, Silvia
**Source(s)** story by Fitz-Richard, Arthur

**Cast** Jones, Jennifer; Heston, Charlton; Malden, Karl; Tully, Tom; Phillips, Bernard; Hutchinson, Josephine

**Song(s)** I'd Jump in the Ocean (C: Roemheld, Heinz; L: Vidor, King); Ruby [1] (C: Roemheld, Heinz; L: Parish, Mitchell)

**Notes** [1] Lyric written for exploitation only.

## 5102 ◆ RUMBA
Paramount, 1935

**Composer(s)** Rainger, Ralph
**Lyricist(s)** Rainger, Ralph

**Producer(s)** LeBaron, William
**Director(s)** Gering, Marion
**Screenwriter(s)** Green, Howard J.; Ruskin, Harry; Partos, Frank

**Cast** Lombard, Carole; Raft, George; Overman, Lynne; Owsley, Monroe; Margo; Patrick, Gail; Adrian, Iris; Tamiroff, Akim

**Song(s)** The Rhythm of the Rumba; Your Eyes Have Said; I'm Yours for Tonight; Stay As Sweet As You Are [3] (C: Revel, Harry; L: Gordon, Mack); If I Knew [1]; Birth of Rumba [1]; The Magic of You [2]

**Notes** [1] Not used. [2] Not used but published. [3] Also used in COLLEGE RHYTHM; COLLEGIATE and STOLEN HARMONY.

## 5103 ◆ RUMBLE FISH
Universal, 1983

**Musical Score** Copeland, Stewart

**Producer(s)** Roos, Fred; Claybourne, Doug
**Director(s)** Coppola, Francis Ford
**Screenwriter(s)** Hinton, S.E.; Coppola, Francis Ford
**Source(s)** *Rumble Fish* (novel) Hinton, S.E.

**Cast** Dillon, Matt; Rourke, Mickey; Lane, Diane; Hopper, Dennis; Scarwid, Diana; Spano, Vincent; Cage, Nicolas; Penn, Christopher; Waits, Tom; Hinton, S.E. [1]

**Song(s)** Don't Box Me In (C: Copeland, Stewart; L: Ridgway, Stan)

**Notes** No cue sheet available. [1] Character name: Hooker on Strip.

## 5104 ◆ RUMBLE ON THE DOCKS
Columbia, 1956

**Producer(s)** Katzman, Sam
**Director(s)** Sears, Fred F.
**Screenwriter(s)** Morheim, Lou; Dewitt, Jack
**Source(s)** *Rumble on the Docks* (novel) Paley, Frank

**Cast** Darren, James; Carroll, Laurie; Granger, Michael; Janger, Jerry; Blake, Robert; Barrier, Edgar; Freddie Bell and His Bellboys

**Song(s)** Get the First Train Out of Town (C: Bell, Freddie; L: Latanzi, Pep); Rumble on the Docks (C/L: De Night, Jimmy; Phillips, Mildred)

**Notes** No cue sheet available.

## 5105 ◆ RUMPLESTILTSKIN
Cannon, 1987

**Musical Score** Robert, Max
**Composer(s)** Robert, Max
**Lyricist(s)** Robert, Max

**Producer(s)** Golan, Menahem; Globus, Yoram
**Director(s)** Irving, David
**Screenwriter(s)** Irving, David
**Source(s)** "Rumplestiltskin" (story) The Grimm Brothers

**Cast** Irving, Amy; Barty, Billy; Revill, Clive; Pointer, Priscilla; Symonds, Robert; Brown, John Moulder

**Song(s)** I'm Queen of the Castle; I Need a Miracle; I'm Greedy; Love the Miller's Daughter (L: Irving, Jules); One Little Name; My Name Is Rumplestiltskin (L: Irving, Jules; Robert, Max)

**Notes** No cue sheet available.

## 5106  ◆  RUN, ANGEL, RUN!
### Fanfare, 1969

**Musical Score**    Phillips, Stu

**Producer(s)**    Solomon, Joe
**Director(s)**    Starrett, Jack
**Screenwriter(s)**    Wish, Jerry; Furlong, V.A. [1]

**Cast**    Smith, William; Starrett, Valerie; Shane, Gene

**Song(s)**    Run, Angel, Run! (C: Phillips, Stu; L: Sherrill, Billy)

**Notes**    No cue sheet available. There are other songs by Byron Cole, James East and Stu Phillips. [1] Valerie Starrett.

## 5107  ◆  RUN, APPALOOSA, RUN
### Disney, 1966

**Musical Score**    Shores, Richard

**Producer(s)**    Lansburgh, Larry
**Director(s)**    Lansburgh, Larry
**Screenwriter(s)**    Lansburgh, Janet

**Cast**    Allen, Rex; Palacios, Adele; Plaugher, Wilbur; Gatlin, Jerry; Cloud, Walter

**Song(s)**    The Ballad of the Appaloosa (C/L: Wayne, Bobby)

## 5108  ◆  THE RUNAWAY QUEEN
### United Artists, 1934

**Producer(s)**    Wilcox, Herbert
**Director(s)**    Wilcox, Herbert
**Screenwriter(s)**    Hoffe, Monckton; Raphaelson, Samson
**Source(s)**    *Die Königin* (operetta) Marischka, Ernst; Granichstaedten, Bruno; Straus, Oscar

**Cast**    Neagle, Anna; Graavey, Fernand [1]; McLaughlin, Gibb; Malleson, Miles; Aked, Muriel

**Notes**    No cue sheet available. Original British title: THE QUEEN'S AFFAIR. [1] Later billed as Gravet. Real name: Gravey.

## 5109  ◆  RUN, COUGAR, RUN
### Disney, 1972

**Musical Score**    Baker, Buddy

**Producer(s)**    Algar, James
**Director(s)**    Courtland, Jerome
**Screenwriter(s)**    Pelletier, Louis
**Source(s)**    *The Mountain Lion* (book) Murphy, Robert

**Cast**    Whitman, Stuart; Aletter, Frank; Chapman, Lonny; Fowley, Douglas; Carey Jr., Harry; Arau, Alfonso; Seeta

**Song(s)**    Let Her Alone (C/L: Gilkyson, Terry)

## 5110  ◆  RUN FOR COVER
### Paramount, 1955

**Producer(s)**    Pine, William; Thomas, William
**Director(s)**    Ray, Nicholas
**Screenwriter(s)**    Miller, Winston

**Cast**    Cagney, James; Derek, John; Lindfors, Viveca; Borgnine, Ernest; Hersholt, Jean; Withers, Grant; Lambert, Jack

**Song(s)**    Run for Cover (C: Jackson, Howard; L: Brooks, Jack)

## 5111  ◆  THE RUNNER STUMBLES
### Twentieth Century–Fox, 1979

**Musical Score**    Gold, Ernest

**Producer(s)**    Kramer, Stanley
**Director(s)**    Kramer, Stanley
**Screenwriter(s)**    Stitt, Milan
**Source(s)**    *The Runner Stumbles* (play) Stitt, Milan

**Cast**    Van Dyke, Dick; Quinlan, Kathleen; Stapleton, Maureen; Bolger, Ray; Grimes, Tammy; Bridges, Beau

**Song(s)**    My Rumble Seat Gal (C: Gold, Ernest; L: Keller, Jeanette)

**Notes**    No cue sheet available.

## 5112  ◆  THE RUNNING MAN
### Tri-Star, 1987

**Musical Score**    Faltermeyer, Harold

**Producer(s)**    Zinnemann, Tim; Linder, George
**Director(s)**    Glaser, Paul Michael
**Screenwriter(s)**    de Souza, Steven E.
**Source(s)**    (novel) Bachman, Richard

**Cast**    Schwarzenegger, Arnold; Alonso, Maria Conchita; Kotto, Yaphet; Dawson, Richard; Brown, Jim; Ventura, Jessie

**Song(s)**    Running Away with You (C/L: Faltermeyer, Harold; Parr, John)

**Notes**    No cue sheet available.

## 5113  ◆  RUNNING SCARED
### MGM/UA, 1986

**Musical Score**    Temperton, Rod
**Composer(s)**    Temperton, Rod
**Lyricist(s)**    Temperton, Rod

**Producer(s)**    Foster, David; Turman, Lawrence
**Director(s)**    Hyams, Peter
**Screenwriter(s)**    Devore, Gary; Huston, Jimmy

**Cast**    Hines, Gregory; Crystal, Billy; Bauer, Steven; Smits, Jimmy; Fluegel, Darlanne; Pantoliano, Joe; Hedaya, Dan

**Song(s)** I Know What I Want (C/L: Rice, Howie; Ellison, Bud; Kimble, Artie Ray); Say You Really Want Me (C/L: Sembello, Danny; Rudolph, Dick; Spencer Jr., Donnell); I Just Want to Be Loved; Sweet Freedom; Once in a Lifetime Groove (C/L: Perren, Freddie; Wyatt Jr., Ric; Perren, Chris); Man Size Love; Never Too Late To Start

### 5114 ✦ RUNNING TARGET
United Artists, 1956

**Musical Score** Gold, Ernest

**Producer(s)** Couffer, Jack C.
**Director(s)** Weinstein, Marvin R.
**Screenwriter(s)** Weinstein, Marvin R.; Couffer, Jack C.; Hall, Conrad

**Cast** Franz, Arthur; Dowling, Doris; Reeves, Richard

**Song(s)** Summer Game (C: Gold, Ernest; L: Jordan, Fred)

### 5115 ✦ RUNNING WILD
Universal, 1955

**Producer(s)** Pine, Howard
**Director(s)** Biberman, Abner
**Screenwriter(s)** Townsend, Leo
**Source(s)** (novel) Benson, Ben

**Cast** Campbell, William; Wynn, Keenan; Van Doren, Mamie; Merlin, Jan; Saxon, John

**Song(s)** Razzle Dazzle (C/L: Calhoun, Charles)

### 5116 ✦ RUN OF THE ARROW
RKO, 1957

**Musical Score** Young, Victor

**Producer(s)** Fuller, Samuel
**Director(s)** Fuller, Samuel
**Screenwriter(s)** Fuller, Samuel

**Cast** McCoy, Tim; Steiger, Rod; Montiel, Sarita; Keith, Brian; Meeker, Ralph; Flippen, Jay C.; Bronson, Charles; Carey, Olive; Wynant, H.M.; Morrow, Neyle; De Kova, Frank

**Song(s)** The Purple Hills (1) (C: Young, Victor; L: Washington, Ned); The Purple Hills (2) [1] (C: L: Berle, Milton; Arnold, Bud)

**Notes** [1] Not used.

### 5117 ✦ THE RUSSIANS ARE COMING, THE RUSSIANS ARE COMING
United Artists, 1966

**Musical Score** Mandel, Johnny

**Producer(s)** Jewison, Norman
**Director(s)** Jewison, Norman
**Screenwriter(s)** Rose, William

**Source(s)** *The Russians Are Coming, The Russians Are Coming* (novel) Benchley, Nathaniel

**Cast** Reiner, Carl; Saint, Eva Marie; Arkin, Alan; Keith, Brian; Winters, Jonathan; Bikel, Theodore; Ford, Paul; O'Shea, Tessie; Law, John Phillip; Dromm, Andrea; Blue, Ben

**Song(s)** Sailors Chorus (C: Mandel, Johnny; L: Shur, Bonia)

### 5118 ✦ THE RUSTLERS
RKO, 1948

**Musical Score** Sawtell, Paul; Webb, Roy

**Producer(s)** Schlom, Herman
**Director(s)** Selander, Lesley
**Screenwriter(s)** Natteford, Jack; Ward, Luci

**Cast** Holt, Tim; Martin, Richard; Hyer, Martha; Brodie, Steve; Andrews, Lois; Shannon, Harry; Richards, Addison

**Song(s)** Annabella's Bustle (C/L: Harris, Harry; Pollack, Lew)

### 5119 ✦ RUSTLERS' RHAPSODY
Paramount, 1985

**Composer(s)** Dorff, Stephen H.
**Lyricist(s)** Brown, Milton

**Producer(s)** Giler, David
**Director(s)** Wilson, Hugh
**Screenwriter(s)** Wilson, Hugh

**Cast** Berenger, Tom; Bailey, G.W.; Henner, Marilu; Rey, Fernando; Griffith, Andy

**Song(s)** I Ride Alone; Lasso the Moon; The Last of the Silver Screen Cowboys (L: Brown, Milton; Garrett, Snuff); I Break Horses Not Hearts [1] (L: Brown, Milton; Masters, Nancy)

**Notes** [1] Used instrumentally only.

### 5120 ✦ RUSTLER'S ROUND-UP
Universal, 1946

**Composer(s)** Rosen, Milton
**Lyricist(s)** Carter, Everett

**Producer(s)** Fox, Wallace W.
**Director(s)** Fox, Wallace W.
**Screenwriter(s)** Natteford, Jack

**Cast** Grant, Kirby; Knight, Fuzzy; Adams, Jane; Cobb, Eddie

**Song(s)** The Western Trail [2]; I Don't Like No Cows; Vote for Emily Morgan [1] (C: Rosen, Milton; L: Wakely, Jimmy; Drake, Oliver)

**Notes** [1] Also in THE SILVER BULLET. [2] Also in MAN FROM MONTANA (1941).

## 5121 ✦ RUSTLER'S VALLEY
Paramount, 1937

**Producer(s)**   Sherman, Harry
**Director(s)**   Watt, Nate
**Screenwriter(s)**   Hoyt, Harry O.

**Cast**   Boyd, William; Hayden, Russell; Hayes, George "Gabby"; Cobb, Lee J.

**Song(s)**   Beneath the Western Sky (C: Stern, Jack; L: Tobias, Harry)

## 5122 ✦ RUTHLESS PEOPLE
Disney, 1986

**Musical Score**   Colombier, Michel

**Producer(s)**   Peyser, Michael
**Director(s)**   Abrahams, Jim; Zucker, David; Zucker, Jerry
**Screenwriter(s)**   Launer, Dale

**Cast**   DeVito, Danny; Midler, Bette; Reinhold, Judge; Slater, Helen; Morris, Anita; Pullman, Bill; Schilling, William G.; Evans, Art; Felder, Clarence

**Song(s)**   Ruthless People (C/L: Hall, D.; Jagger, M.; Stewart, D.); Modern Woman (C/L: Joel, Billy); Waiting to See You (C/L: Midnight, Charlie; Hartman, Don); Give Me the Reason (C/L: Vandross, Luther; Adderley Jr., Nat); Dance Champion (C/L: Bell, R.; Talor, J.; Kool & the Gang)

## 5123 ✦ RYAN'S DAUGHTER
Metro–Goldwyn–Mayer, 1970

**Musical Score**   Jarre, Maurice

**Producer(s)**   Havelock-Allan, Anthony
**Director(s)**   Lean, David
**Screenwriter(s)**   Bolt, Robert

**Cast**   Mitchum, Robert; Howard, Trevor; Jones, Christopher; Mills, John; McKern, Leo; Miles, Sarah

**Song(s)**   It Was a Good Time (Rosie's Theme) [1] (C: Jarre, Maurice; L: Curb, Mike; David, Mack); Where Was I When the Parade Went By [2] (C: Jarre, Maurice; L: Curb, Mike; David, Mack)

**Notes**   [1] Lyrics added for exploitation only. [2] Sheet music only.

# S

**5124 ✦ SABOTEUR**
Universal, 1942

**Musical Score**   Skinner, Frank

**Producer(s)**   Lloyd, Frank
**Director(s)**   Hitchcock, Alfred
**Screenwriter(s)**   Viertel, Peter; Harrison, Joan; Parker, Dorothy

**Cast**   Lloyd, Norman; Cummings, Robert; Summers, Virgil; Lane, Priscilla; Kruger, Otto; Kruger, Alma

**Song(s)**   Tonight We Love [1] (C: Austin, Ray; Martin, Freddy; L: Worth, Bobby)

**Notes**   [1] Music adapted from Tschaikowsky's "Piano Concerto in B-Flat Minor."

**5125 ✦ SABRINA**
Paramount, 1954

**Musical Score**   Hollander, Frederick

**Producer(s)**   Wilder, Billy
**Director(s)**   Wilder, Billy
**Screenwriter(s)**   Wilder, Billy; Taylor, Samuel; Lehman, Ernest
**Source(s)**   *Sabrina Fair* (play) Taylor, Samuel

**Cast**   Holden, William; Williams, John; Hepburn, Audrey; Bogart, Humphrey; Hyer, Martha; Hampden, Walter; Bushman, Francis X.; Corby, Ellen

**Song(s)**   Sabrina [1] (C/L: Stone, Wilson)

**Notes**   Released in Great Britain as SABRINA FAIR. There are also vocal renditions of "My Silent Love" by Edward Heyman and Dana Suesse; "Out of Nowhere" by Edward Heyman and John W. Green; "Isn't It Romantic" by Richard Rodgers and Lorenz Hart; "Yes, We Have No Bananas" by Irving Conn and Frank Silver and "La Vie En Rose" by Louiguy, Edith Piaf and Mack David. [1] Not used in film.

**5126 ✦ THE SACRED FLAME**
Warner Brothers, 1929

**Director(s)**   Mayo, Archie
**Screenwriter(s)**   Thew, Harvey

**Source(s)**   *The Sacred Flame* (play) Maugham, W. Somerset

**Cast**   Nagel, Conrad; Lee, Lila; Frederick, Pauline; Courtenay, William; Byron, Walter; Francis, Alec B.; Fuller, Dale

**Song(s)**   The Sacred Flame (C: Akst, Harry; L: Clarke, Grant)

**Notes**   No cue sheet available.

**5127 ✦ SADDLEMATES**
Republic, 1941

**Producer(s)**   Gray, Louis
**Director(s)**   Orlebeck, Lester
**Screenwriter(s)**   Delmas, Herbert; De Mond, Albert
**Source(s)**   characters by MacDonald, William Colt

**Cast**   Livingston, Robert; Steele, Bob; Davis, Rufe; Storm, Gale; Murray, Forbes; Keefe, Cornelius; Lynn, Peter; Strange, Glenn; Cody, Iron Eyes

**Song(s)**   Just Imagine That (C/L: Burnette, Smiley)

**5128 ✦ SADDLE MOUNTAIN ROUNDUP**
Monogram, 1941

**Musical Score**   Sanucci, Frank
**Composer(s)**   George, Jean [1]
**Lyricist(s)**   King, John

**Director(s)**   Luby, S. Roy
**Screenwriter(s)**   Nolte, William L.

**Cast**   King, John; Corrigan, Ray; Terhune, Max; Conway, Lita; Mulhall, Jack; Chesebro, George

**Song(s)**   Doggone Dogie Got Away; That Little Green Valley

**Notes**   [1] Pseudonym for Lucille Nolte.

**5129 ✦ SADDLE PALS**
Republic, 1947

**Producer(s)**   Picker, Sidney
**Director(s)**   Selander, Lesley
**Screenwriter(s)**   Sackheim, Jerry; Williams, Bob

**Cast**  Autry, Gene; Champion Jr.; Roberts, Lynne; Holloway, Sterling; The Cass County Boys

**Song(s)**  You Stole My Heart [3] (C/L: Adams, Stanley; Sosnik, Harry); Which Way'd They Go? (C/L: Allen, Ray; Botkin, Perry); The Covered Wagon Rolled Right Along [1] (C/L: Wood, Britt; Heath, Hy; Gold, Ernest); apola (C/L: Gamse, Albert; LaCalle, Joseph M.); I Wish I'd Never Met Sunshine [2] (C/L: Evans, Dale; Haldeman, Oakley)

**Notes**  No cue sheet available. [1] Also in APACHE COUNTRY (Columbia) but without Ernest Gold's credit. [2] Gene Autry is often listed as a coauthor of this song but he had nothing to do with the writing of it. He published it and put his name on the music also. [3] Also in SIOUX CITY SUE.

### 5130 ✦ SADDLE THE WIND
Metro–Goldwyn–Mayer, 1958

**Musical Score**  Bernstein, Elmer

**Producer(s)**  Deutsch, Armand
**Director(s)**  Parrish, Robert
**Screenwriter(s)**  Serling, Rod

**Cast**  Taylor, Robert; London, Julie; Cassavetes, John; Crisp, Donald; McGraw, Charles; Dano, Royal; Erdman, Richard; Spencer, Douglas; Teal, Ray

**Song(s)**  Saddle the Wind (C/L: Livingston, Jay; Evans, Ray)

### 5131 ✦ THE SAD HORSE
Twentieth Century–Fox, 1959

**Musical Score**  Sawtell, Paul; Shefter, Bert

**Producer(s)**  Lyons, Richard E.
**Director(s)**  Clark, James B.
**Screenwriter(s)**  Hoffman, Charles

**Cast**  Ladd, David; Wills, Chill; Reason, Rex; Wymore, Patrice; Palmer, Gregg

**Song(s)**  The Sad Horse (C/L: Kent, Walter; Walton, Tom)

### 5132 ✦ SADIE MCKEE
Metro–Goldwyn–Mayer, 1934

**Composer(s)**  Brown, Nacio Herb
**Lyricist(s)**  Freed, Arthur

**Producer(s)**  Weingarten, Lawrence
**Director(s)**  Brown, Clarence
**Screenwriter(s)**  Meehan, John

**Cast**  Crawford, Joan; Raymond, Gene; Arnold, Edward; Tone, Franchot; Ralston, Esther; Austin, Gene; Candy and Coco; Dixon, Jean; Carroll, Leo G.; Tamiroff, Akim; Sears, Zelda; Ware, Helen; Oxford, Earl

**Song(s)**  All I Do Is Dream of You [1]; I Looked Into Your Eyes; After You've Gone (C/L: Layton, Turner; Creamer, Henry); Please Make Me Care

**Notes**  [1] Also in SINGIN' IN THE RAIN, BROADWAY MELODY OF 1936 (in French) and THE BOYFRIEND.

### 5133 ✦ THE SAD SACK
Paramount, 1957

**Musical Score**  Scharf, Walter
**Choreographer(s)**  O'Curran, Charles

**Producer(s)**  Wallis, Hal B.
**Director(s)**  Marshall, George
**Screenwriter(s)**  Beloin, Edmund; Monaster, Nate
**Source(s)**  *Sad Sack* (comic strip) Baker, George

**Cast**  Lewis, Jerry; Lorre, Peter; Wayne, David; Kirk, Phyllis; Strudwick, Shepperd; Evans, Gene; Dolenz, George; Montevecchi, Liliane

**Song(s)**  Sad Sack (C: Bacharach, Burt; L: David, Hal); Why You Pay? (C: O'Curran, Charles; Brooks, Dudley; L: Miller, F.E.); Charlie's Rhumba (inst.) (C: O'Curran, Charles; Brooks, Dudley)

### 5134 ✦ SAFETY IN NUMBERS
Paramount, 1930

**Composer(s)**  Whiting, Richard A.
**Lyricist(s)**  Marion Jr., George
**Choreographer(s)**  Bennett, David

**Director(s)**  Schertzinger, Victor
**Screenwriter(s)**  Dix, Marion

**Cast**  Rogers, Charles "Buddy"; Crawford, Kathryn; Dunn, Josephine; Lombard, Carole; Karns, Roscoe; MacDonald, Francis; Bruce, Virginia; Beavers, Louise

**Song(s)**  My Future Just Passed; Business Girl; Do You Play Madame?; I'd Like to Be a Bee in Your Boudoir; You Appeal to Me; The Pick-Up; Pepola [1]; My Sweeter Than Sweet [1] [3]; If She Hums You a Waltz [2]; That's Enough for Tonight! [2]; Too Bad I'm Good! [2]; Get the Man in the Mood [2]

**Notes**  [1] Used instrumentally only. [2] Not used. [3] Used in HONEY and SWEETIE.

### 5135 ✦ SAGA OF DEATH VALLEY
Republic, 1939

**Producer(s)**  Kane, Joseph
**Director(s)**  Kane, Joseph
**Screenwriter(s)**  DeWolf, Karen; Anthony, Stuart

**Cast**  Rogers, Roy; Hayes, George "Gabby"; Barry, Donald; Day, Doris; Thomas, Frank M.; Ingram, Jack; Taliaferro, Hal

**Song(s)**  Song of the Bandit (C/L: Nolan, Bob); Shadows on the Prairie (C/L: Samuels, Walter G.); Ride

(C/L: Samuels, Walter G.); I've Sold My Saddle for an Old Guitar [1] (C/L: Allan, Fleming)

**Notes**    [1] Roy Rogers also credited on sheet music.

## 5136 ◆ THE SAGA OF WINDWAGON SMITH
Disney, 1961

**Musical Score**    Bruns, George

**Director(s)**    Nichols, C. August
**Screenwriter(s)**    Nolley, Lance; Nichols, C. August

**Cast**    Allen, Rex; Sons of the Pioneers

**Song(s)**    The Saga of Windwagon Smith (C: Bruns, George; L: Nichols, C. August)

## 5137 ◆ SAGEBRUSH AND SILVER
Twentieth Century–Fox, 1941

**Song(s)**    In Old Nevada [1] (C: McConnell, George; L: Allvine, Earl F.)

**Notes**    This is a Lowell Thomas Magic Carpet of Movietone travelogue. [1] This was based on McConnell's song "Dream Moon Valley."

## 5138 ◆ SAGEBRUSH LAW
RKO, 1942

**Musical Score**    Sawtell, Paul; Webb, Roy
**Composer(s)**    Whitley, Ray; Rose, Fred
**Lyricist(s)**    Whitley, Ray; Rose, Fred

**Producer(s)**    Gilroy, Bert
**Director(s)**    Nelson, Sam
**Screenwriter(s)**    Cohen, Bennett R.

**Cast**    Holt, Tim; Edwards, Cliff; Barclay, Joan; Elliott, John H.; Barcroft, Roy; Adams, Ernie

**Song(s)**    Crazy Old Trails [1]; Rockin' Down the Cherokee Trail

**Notes**    [1] May be same song as "Crazy Ole Trails Ahead" in THE FARGO KID.

## 5139 ◆ SAGEBRUSH TROUBADOR
Republic, 1935

**Composer(s)**    Autry, Gene
**Lyricist(s)**    Autry, Gene

**Producer(s)**    Levine, Nat
**Director(s)**    Kane, Joseph
**Screenwriter(s)**    Poland, Joseph; Drake, Oliver

**Cast**    Autry, Gene; Burnette, Smiley; Pepper, Barbara; Kelsey, Fred; Atchley, Hooper L.; Glendon, Frank

**Song(s)**    End of the Trail; Lost Chord (C/L: Burnette, Smiley); Way Out West in Texas; On the Prairie (C/L: Burnette, Smiley); My Prayer for Tonight (C/L: Burnette, Smiley); I'd Love a Home in the Mountains (C/L: Autry, Gene; Burnette, Smiley); Mississippi Valley

(C/L: Unknown); Someday in Wyoming (C/L: Unknown); Hurdy Gurdy Man (C/L: Burnette, Smiley); When the Moon Shines (C/L: Autry, Gene; Burnette, Smiley)

**Notes**    No cue sheet available.

## 5140 ◆ SAGINAW TRAIL
Columbia, 1953

**Producer(s)**    Schaefer, Armand
**Director(s)**    Archainbaud, George
**Screenwriter(s)**    Yost, Dorothy; Cummings, Dwight

**Cast**    Autry, Gene; Burnette, Smiley; Marshall, Connie; Borden, Eugene

**Song(s)**    Mam'selle (C/L: Unknown); When It's Prayer-Meetin' Time in the Hollow (C/L: Unknown)

**Notes**    No cue sheet available. There is also a vocal of "Beautiful Dreamer."

## 5141 ◆ SAIGON
Paramount, 1948

**Producer(s)**    Wolfson, P.J.
**Director(s)**    Fenton, Leslie
**Screenwriter(s)**    Sheekman, Arthur; Wolfson, P.J.

**Cast**    Ladd, Alan; Lake, Veronica; Dick, Douglas; Carnovsky, Morris; Adler, Luther

**Song(s)**    To Each His Own (C/L: Livingston, Jay; Evans, Ray); Boatmen's Chant (C: Boutelje, Phil; L: Vincent, Louis); Dolores [1] (C: Alter, Louis; L: Loesser, Frank)

**Notes**    [1] Also in DR. BROADWAY and LAS VEGAS NIGHTS.

## 5142 ◆ SAILING ALONG
Gaumont-British, 1938

**Composer(s)**    Johnston, Arthur
**Lyricist(s)**    Sigler, Maurice

**Director(s)**    Hale, Sonnie
**Screenwriter(s)**    Samuels, Lesser; Hale, Sonnie

**Cast**    Matthews, Jessie; Mackay, Barry; Whiting, Jack; Young, Roland; Madison, Noel; Pettingell, Frank; Sim, Alistair; Sayler, Athene

**Song(s)**    My River; Souvenir of Love; Your Heart Skips a Beat; I'm Trusting My Luck

**Notes**    No cue sheet available.

## 5143 ◆ SAILOR BEWARE (1936)
Paramount, 1936 unproduced

**Lyricist(s)**    Robin, Leo
**Source(s)**    *Sailor Beware* (play) Nicholson, Kenyon; Robinson, Charles

**Song(s)** Hopelessly in Love [1] (C: Hollander, Frederick); I Wished on the Moon [4] (C: Rainger, Ralph; L: Parker, Dorothy); Sailor Beware [1] (C: Rainger, Ralph; Whiting, Richard A.); I Can't Escape from You [3] (C: Whiting, Richard A.); Hate to Talk About Myself [2] (C: Whiting, Richard A.); Little Lady of the Lamp Light (C: Whiting, Richard A.); Panamericana (C: Whiting, Richard A.)

**Notes** [1] Used in the film ANYTHING GOES (1936). [2] Used in FOUR HOURS TO KILL and STOLEN HEAVEN with additional credit for Ralph Rainger. [3] Used in RHYTHM ON THE RANGE and considered for but not used in ANYTHING GOES (1936). [4] Used in THE BIG BROADCAST OF 1936.

## 5144 ✦ SAILOR BEWARE (1951)
### Paramount, 1951

**Composer(s)** Livingston, Jerry
**Lyricist(s)** David, Mack

**Producer(s)** Wallis, Hal B.
**Director(s)** Walker, Hal
**Screenwriter(s)** Allardice, James B.; Rackin, Martin; Grant, John
**Source(s)** *Sailor Beware* (play) Nicholson, Kenyon; Robinson, Charles

**Cast** Lewis, Jerry; Martin, Dean; Calvet, Corinne; Marshall, Marion; Strauss, Robert; Erickson, Leif; Wilson, Don; Edwards, Vince; Homeier, Skip

**Song(s)** Today-Tomorrow-Forever; The Sailors' Polka; Merci Beaucoup; The Old Calliope; Never Before; Motoraa Rahi (C: Knudson, Thurston); The Navy Blue (Make Way for Navy Blue) [1]

**Notes** Originally titled AT SEA WITH THE NAVY. [1] Not used.

## 5145 ✦ SAILOR'S LUCK
### Fox, 1933

**Director(s)** Walsh, Raoul
**Screenwriter(s)** Roberts, Marguerite; Miller, Charlotte; Hanlon, Bert; Ryan, Ben

**Cast** Dunn, James; Eilers, Sally; Morgan, Frank; Cohen, Sammy; Jory, Victor

**Song(s)** A Sailor's Luck (C: Jason, Will; Burton, Val; L: Ryan, Ben); Oleo the Gigolo [1] (C: Hanley, James F.; L: Burton, Val); Down Where the River Meets the Sea [2] (C/L: Burton, Val; Jason, Will)

**Notes** [1] Also in ME AND MY GAL (1932). [2] Not used.

## 5146 ✦ SAILORS ON LEAVE
### Republic, 1941

**Composer(s)** Styne, Jule
**Lyricist(s)** Loesser, Frank

**Producer(s)** Cohen, Albert J.
**Director(s)** Rogell, Albert S.
**Screenwriter(s)** Boylan, Malcolm Stuart; Arthur, Art

**Cast** Lundigan, William; Ross, Shirley; Chandler, Chick; Clarke, Mae; Donnelly, Ruth; Nazarro, Cliff; Kennedy, Tom; Kean, Jane

**Song(s)** When a Sailor Goes Ashore; Sailor Routine; Since You; Sentimental Folks; Because We Are Americans [1] (C/L: Head, Emily Robinson)

**Notes** [1] Also in REMEMBER PEARL HARBOR.

## 5147 ✦ THE SAILOR TAKES A WIFE
### Metro–Goldwyn–Mayer, 1946

**Musical Score** Green, Johnny; Franklin, Robert

**Producer(s)** Knopf, Edwin H.
**Director(s)** Whorf, Richard
**Screenwriter(s)** Erskine, Chester; Chapin, Anne Morrison; Cook, Whitfield
**Source(s)** *For Better or Worse or Happily Ever After* (play) Erskine, Chester

**Cast** Walker, Robert; Allyson, June; Cronyn, Hume; Totter, Audrey; Anderson, Eddie "Rochester"; Owen, Reginald

**Song(s)** Parlez-Moi d'Amour (Speak to Me of Love) [1] (C/L: Lenoir, Jean)

**Notes** [1] Also in AS HUSBANDS GO (Fox).

## 5148 ✦ THE SAILOR WHO FELL FROM GRACE WITH THE SEA
### Avco Embassy, 1976

**Musical Score** Mandel, Johnny

**Producer(s)** Poll, Martin
**Director(s)** Carlino, Lewis John
**Screenwriter(s)** Carlino, Lewis John
**Source(s)** *The Sailor Who Fell from Grace with the Sea* (novel) Mishima, Yukio

**Cast** Miles, Sarah; Kristofferson, Kris; Kahn, Jonathan; Cunningham, Margo

**Song(s)** Seadreams (C/L: Kristofferson, Kris)

**Notes** No cue sheet available.

## 5149 ✦ ST. BENNY THE DIP
### United Artists, 1951

**Producer(s)** Danziger, Edward; Danziger, Harry
**Director(s)** Ulmer, Edgar G.
**Screenwriter(s)** Roeburt, John

**Cast** Haymes, Dick; Young, Roland; Stander, Lionel; Foch, Nina; Bartholomew, Freddie [1]; Karlweis, Oscar; Clark, Dort

**Song(s)** I Believe (C/L: Stringer, Bob)

**Notes** No cue sheet available. Released overseas as ESCAPE ME IF YOU CAN. [1] Last film appearance.

### 5150 ◆ THE SAINTED SISTERS
Paramount, 1948

**Producer(s)** Maibaum, Richard
**Director(s)** Russell, William D.
**Screenwriter(s)** Clork, Harry; Nash, N. Richard
**Source(s)** "The Sainted Sisters of Sandy Creek" (story) Blalk, Elisa

**Cast** Lake, Veronica; Caulfield, Joan; Fitzgerald, Barry

**Song(s)** Please Put Out the Light (C/L: Livingston, Jay; Evans, Ray)

### 5151 ◆ ST. ELMO'S FIRE
Columbia, 1985

**Musical Score** Foster, David
**Composer(s)** Foster, David

**Producer(s)** Shuler, Lauren
**Director(s)** Schumacher, Joel
**Screenwriter(s)** Schumacher, Joel; Kurlander, Carl

**Cast** Estevez, Emilio; Lowe, Rob; McCarthy, Andrew; Moore, Demi; Nelson, Judd; Sheedy, Ally; Winningham, Mare; Balsam, Martin; Van Patten, Joyce

**Song(s)** Man in Motion (St. Elmo's Fire) (L: Parr, John); Into the Fire (C/L: Smallwood, Todd); Shake Down (C/L: Squier, Billy); One Love (L: Rock, Bob); This Time It Was Really Right (L: Anderson, Jon); If I Turn You Away (L: Marx, Richard); Young and Innocent (C/L: Elefante, Dino; Elefante, John)

### 5152 ◆ ST. LOUIS BLUES (1939)
Paramount, 1939

**Composer(s)** Lane, Burton
**Lyricist(s)** Loesser, Frank

**Producer(s)** Lazarus, Jeff
**Director(s)** Walsh, Raoul
**Screenwriter(s)** Boylan, Malcolm Stuart; Moffitt, John C.

**Cast** Matty Malneck and His Band; Lamour, Dorothy; Cowan, Jerome; Nolan, Lloyd; Guizar, Tito; The Hall Johnson Choir; Sullivan, Maxine; Ralph, Jessie; Frawley, William; Parker, Mary; Nazarro, Cliff

**Song(s)** How'dja Like to Love Me [7]; Oh, You Mississippi; I Go for That (C: Malneck, Matty); I Want to Live (C: Guizar, Tito; Gama, Rafael; L: Noriega, Nenette); Junior [5]; We're in the Jail House (C/L: Darby, Ken); Let's Dream in the Moonlight (C/L: Malneck, Matty; Walsh, Raoul); Kinda Lonesome (C: Carmichael, Hoagy; L: Coslow, Sam; Robin, Leo); Blue Nightfall; Mi Diablesa [1] (C: Guizar, Tito; Gama, Rafael; L: Noriega, Nenette); The Song in My Heart Is a Rhumba [1] [3] [6]; Valencia [1] (C/L: Lara, Augustin); Hangover Joe [2] (C/L: Darby, Ken); I'm

Afraid of You [2] [9] (C: Hollander, Frederick; L: Freed, Ralph); I Know What Aloha Means [2] [8] (C: Rainger, Ralph; L: Robin, Leo); Don't Cry Little Cloud [2]; She Was Wearing a Big Sombrero [2]; The Nearness of You [2] [4] (C: Carmichael, Hoagy; L: Washington, Ned); It's Grand [2]

**Notes** There are also vocals of "Dark Eyes," "Loch Lomond" and "St. Louis Blues" by W.C. Handy (also used in DANCERS IN THE DARK, BANJO ON MY KNEE and the other ST. LOUIS BLUES). [1] In Latin-American prints only. [2] Not used. [3] Recorded. [4] Written for ROMANCE IN THE ROUGH which was unproduced. Recorded but not used in GIRLS! GIRLS! GIRLS! Finally used in ASH WEDNESDAY. [5] Same music as "Sweet Dreams" written by Lane and Ralph Freed for COLLEGE RHYTHM but not used. "Junior" was also considered for COLLEGE RHYTHM. [6] Same music as "Gay Desperado" written by Lane and Ralph Freed for COLLEGE RHYTHM but not used. It is used instrumentally in DOWN WENT MCGINTY. It was originally titled "The Beat of My Heart Is a Rumba." [7] Also in COLLEGE SWING. [8] Also not used in EBB TIDE. [9] Used in TORNADO.

### 5153 ◆ ST. LOUIS BLUES (1958)
Paramount, 1958

**Composer(s)** Handy, W.C.

**Producer(s)** Smith, Robert
**Director(s)** Reisner, Allen
**Screenwriter(s)** Smith, Robert; Sherdeman, Ted

**Cast** Cole, Nat "King"; Kitt, Eartha; Calloway, Cab; Fitzgerald, Ella; Jackson, Mahalia; Dee, Ruby; Hernandez, Juano; Bailey, Pearl

**Song(s)** Morning Star [2] (L: David, Mack); Sheriff Honest John Baile [1] (L: David, Mack); Careless Love [3] (L: Handy, W.C.; Koenig, Martha; Williams, Spencer); Friendless Blues (L: Gilbert, Mercedes)

**Notes** Only new songs with new lyrics listed. Other songs with music and lyrics by W.C. Handy included in the picture are "Beale Street Blues," "Chantez Les Bas," "Goin' to See My Sarah," "Got No Mo' Home Dan a Dog," "Harlem Blues," "Hist De Window, Noah," "John Henry Blues," "St. Louis Blues" and "They That Sow in Tears." [1] Based on Handy's "Yellow Dog Blues." [2] Based on Handy's "Shine Like a Morning Star." [3] Also in BLUES FOR LOVERS (Fox) with music and lyrics by Handy.

### 5154 ◆ THE ST. VALENTINE'S DAY MASSACRE
Twentieth Century–Fox, 1967

**Musical Score** Steiner, Fred

**Producer(s)** Corman, Roger
**Director(s)** Corman, Roger
**Screenwriter(s)** Browne, Howard

**Cast** Robards Jr., Jason; Segal, George; Meeker, Ralph; Hale, Jean; Richie, Clint; Silvera, Frank; Campanella, Joseph; Bakalyan, Richard; Canary, David; Dern, Bruce; Stone, Harold J.

**Song(s)** Smarty (C: Newman, Lionel; L: Hale, Lee)

## 5155 ✦ SALLY
### Warner Brothers–First National, 1929

**Composer(s)** Burke, Joe
**Lyricist(s)** Dubin, Al
**Choreographer(s)** Ceballos, Larry; Rasch, Albertina

**Director(s)** Dillon, John Francis
**Screenwriter(s)** Young, Waldemar
**Source(s)** *Sally* (musical) Bolton, Guy; Kern, Jerome; Wodehouse, P.G.; Grey, Clifford

**Cast** Miller, Marilyn [1]; Gray, Alexander; Brown, Joe E.; Barnes, T. Roy; Kelton, Pert; Sterling, Ford; Gordon, Maude Turner; Ratcliffe, E.J.; Duffy, Jack; Lane, Nora

**Song(s)** Walking Off Those Balkan Blues; After Business Hours (That Certain Business Begins); All I Want to Do, Do, Do Is Dance; If I'm Dreaming Don't Wake Me Up Too Soon; What Will I Do Without You? [2]; Look for the Silver Lining (C: Kern, Jerome; L: DeSylva, B.G.); Wild Rose [1] (C: Kern, Jerome; L: Grey, Clifford); Sally (1) [1] [3] (C: Kern, Jerome; L: Wodehouse, P.G.; Grey, Clifford); Sally (2) [3]

**Notes** No cue sheet available. [1] From Broadway production. [2] Also used in THE GOLD DIGGERS OF BROADWAY and BIG BOY. [3] It is not known which of these were used in this film.

## 5156 ✦ SALLY, IRENE AND MARY
### Twentieth Century–Fox, 1938

**Composer(s)** Spina, Harold
**Lyricist(s)** Bullock, Walter
**Choreographer(s)** Castle, Nick; Sawyer, Geneva

**Producer(s)** Zanuck, Darryl F.
**Director(s)** Seiter, William S.
**Screenwriter(s)** Tugend, Harry; Yellen, Jack
**Source(s)** (play) Dowling, Eddie; Wood, Cyril

**Cast** Faye, Alice; Martin, Tony; Allen, Fred; Durante, Jimmy; Davis, Joan; Ratoff, Gregory; Weaver, Marjorie; Hovick, Louise [1]; Parker, Barnett; Treen, Mary; Bromberg, J. Edward

**Song(s)** Half Moon on the Hudson; Got My Mind on Music (C: Revel, Harry; L: Gordon, Mack); Sweet As a Song (C: Revel, Harry; L: Gordon, Mack); I Could Use a Dream; This Is Where I Came In; Who Stole the Jam?; Turna (C/L: Durante, Jimmy); Help Wanted—Male; Think Twice [2]; Stop Being So Beautiful [2]

**Notes** Moshier also lists "Minuet in Jazz" by Raymond Scott. He also says the Jimmy Durante number is titled "Hot Potata." [1] Gypsy Rose Lee. [2] Recorded but not used.

## 5157 ✦ SAL OF SINGAPORE
### Pathe, 1929

**Musical Score** Zuro, Josiah

**Director(s)** Higgin, Howard
**Screenwriter(s)** Higgin, Howard; Gendron, Pierre
**Source(s)** *The Sentimentalists* (novel) Collins, Dale

**Cast** Haver, Phyllis; Hale, Alan; Kohler, Fred; Johnson, Noble; Wolheim, Dan; Cowles, Jules; Harmon, Pat; Hill, Harold William

**Song(s)** Singapore Sal (C/L: Coppell, Al; Stone, Billy; Weinberg, Charles); Singapore Sal's Lullaby (C: Grun, Jack; L: Wynn, Charley)

**Notes** No cue sheet available.

## 5158 ✦ SALOME, WHERE SHE DANCED
### Universal, 1945

**Musical Score** Ward, Edward
**Choreographer(s)** Horton, Lester

**Producer(s)** Wanger, Walter
**Director(s)** Kenton, Erle C.
**Screenwriter(s)** Stallings, Laurence

**Cast** De Carlo, Yvonne; Slezak, Walter; Biberman, Abner; Bruce, David; Dekker, Albert; Rambeau, Marjorie; Bromberg, J. Edward; Litel, John

**Song(s)** Blue Danube (C: Strauss, Johann; L: Carter, Everett)

**Notes** Erle C. Kenton replaced Charles Lamont in the midst of shooting.

## 5159 ✦ SALSA
### Cannon, 1988

**Producer(s)** Golan, Menahem; Globus, Yoram
**Director(s)** Davidson, Boaz
**Screenwriter(s)** Davidson, Boaz; Benitez, Tomas; Goldman, Shepard

**Cast** Davidson, Boaz; Tabor, Eli; Alvarado, Magali

**Song(s)** Under My Skin (C/L: Sembello, Michael; Waldman, Randy; Magness, Clif); Salsa Heat (C/L: Sembello, Michael; Bell, Rick); Puerto Rico (C/L: Sembello, Michael; Caldwell, Bobby; Waldman, Randy; Wilkens)

**Notes** No cue sheet available.

## 5160 ✦ SALT AND PEPPER
### United Artists, 1968

**Musical Score** Dankworth, John

**Producer(s)** Ebbins, Milton
**Director(s)** Donner, Richard
**Screenwriter(s)** Pertwee, Michael

**Cast** Davis Jr., Sammy; Lawford, Peter; Bates, Michael; Rodgers, Ilona; Le Mesurier, John

**Song(s)**  Salt & Pepper (C/L: Bricusse, Leslie); I Like the Way You Dance (C/L: Rhodes, George; Davis Jr., Sammy)

**Notes**  No cue sheet available.

## 5161  ◆  SALUDOS AMIGOS
### Disney, 1942

**Musical Score**  Wolcott, Charles; Plumb, Ed; Smith, Paul J.
**Composer(s)**  Wolcott, Charles

**Producer(s)**  Ferguson, Norman
**Director(s)**  Roberts, Bill; Luske, Hamilton; Kinney, Jack; Jackson, Wilfred
**Screenwriter(s)**  Brightman, Homer; Williams, Roy; Heumer, Dick; Wright, Ralph; Reeves, Harry; Grant, Joe

**Cast**  Shields, Fred; Duck, Donald

**Song(s)**  Saludos Amigos (L: Washington, Ned); Caxanga (1) (L: de Barro, Jaco); Aquarela Do Brasil (C/L: Barroso, Ary); Caxanga (2) [1] (C: Wolcott, Charles; L: Sears, Ted); Don't Get Off the Beam [1] (L: Quenzer, Arthur)

**Notes**  A mixture of live action and animation. [1] Not used.

## 5162  ◆  SALUTE FOR THREE
### Paramount, 1943

**Composer(s)**  Styne, Jule
**Lyricist(s)**  Gannon, Kim

**Producer(s)**  MacEwen, Walter
**Director(s)**  Murphy, Ralph
**Screenwriter(s)**  Anderson, Doris; Kenyon, Curtis; Wedlock Jr., Hugh; Snyder, Howard

**Cast**  Rhodes, Betty Jane; Carey, Macdonald

**Song(s)**  Wha' D'Ya Do When It Rains?; I'll Do It For You; My Wife's a W.A.A.C.; Don't Worry; Left - Right (L: Gannon, Kim; Meyer, Sol); Ding Dong, Sing a Song [1]

**Notes**  [1] Not used. Used in HENRY ALDRICH SWINGS IT.

## 5163  ◆  SAMBAMANIA
### Paramount, 1948

**Producer(s)**  Mull, William
**Director(s)**  Daniels, Billy

**Song(s)**  Tacos, Tostadas, Tamales (C/L: Chambers, Tommy; Daniels, Billy); Olivia from Olvera Street (C/L: Livingston, Jay; Evans, Ray); Say Si Si [1] [2] (C/L: Lecuona, Ernesto; Luban, Francia; Stillman, Al); Jack, Jack, Jack [1] (C: Castro, Armando; L: Castro, Armando; Davis, Joe)

**Notes**  Short subject. [1] Al Stillman and Joe Davis wrote the English lyrics. [2] Also in CAROLINA MOON (Republic).

## 5164  ◆  SAME TIME NEXT YEAR
### Universal, 1978

**Musical Score**  Hamlisch, Marvin

**Producer(s)**  Gottlieb, Morton; Mirisch, Walter
**Director(s)**  Mulligan, Robert
**Screenwriter(s)**  Slade, Bernard
**Source(s)**  *Same Time Next Year* (play) Slade, Bernard

**Cast**  Alda, Alan; Burstyn, Ellen; Northcutt, David

**Song(s)**  The Last Time I Felt Like This (C: Hamlisch, Marvin; L: Bergman, Alan; Bergman, Marilyn)

## 5165  ◆  SAMMY GOING SOUTH

See A BOY TEN FEET TALL.

## 5166  ◆  SAMMY STOPS THE WORLD
### See Theater Network, 1979

**Composer(s)**  Bricusse, Leslie; Newley, Anthony
**Lyricist(s)**  Bricusse, Leslie; Newley, Anthony

**Producer(s)**  Travis, Mark; Jack, Del
**Director(s)**  Shapiro, Mel
**Screenwriter(s)**  Bricusse, Leslie; Newley, Anthony
**Source(s)**  *Stop the World - I Want to Get Off* (musical) Bricusse, Leslie; Newley, Anthony

**Cast**  Davis Jr., Sammy; Mercer, Marian; Brown, Marcus B.F.; Burch, Shelly; Daniels, Dennis; Edmead, Wendy

**Notes**  No cue sheet available. This is a filming of the live stage show.

## 5167  ◆  SAMSON AND DELILAH
### Paramount, 1949

**Musical Score**  Young, Victor
**Composer(s)**  Young, Victor
**Lyricist(s)**  Lasky Jr., Jesse
**Choreographer(s)**  Kosloff, Theodore

**Producer(s)**  De Mille, Cecil B.
**Director(s)**  De Mille, Cecil B.
**Screenwriter(s)**  Lasky Jr., Jesse; Frank, Fredric M.

**Cast**  Mature, Victor; Lamarr, Hedy; Sanders, George; Lansbury, Angela; Wilcoxon, Henry; Holden, Fay; Tamblyn, Russ; Faye, Julia; Farnum, William; Deering, Olive; Chandler, Lane

**Song(s)**  For to Win a Bride; The Fat Philistine Merchant; Song of Delilah [1] (L: Livingston, Jay; Evans, Ray)

**Notes**  [1] Not in picture. Written for exploitation only.

## 5168 ✦ SAM WHISKEY
United Artists, 1970

**Musical Score** Gilbert, Herschel Burke

**Producer(s)** Laven, Arnold; Levy, Jules V.; Gardner, Arthur
**Director(s)** Laven, Arnold
**Screenwriter(s)** Norton, William

**Cast** Reynolds, Burt; Dickinson, Angie; Walker, Clint; Davis, Ossie

**Song(s)** Whiskey and Gin (C: Gilbert, Herschel Burke; L: Norton, Bill L.)

## 5169 ✦ SAN ANTONE
Republic, 1953

**Musical Score** Butts, Dale

**Producer(s)** Kane, Joseph
**Director(s)** Kane, Joseph
**Screenwriter(s)** Fisher, Steve
**Source(s)** *The Golden Herd* (novel) Carroll, Curt

**Cast** Cameron, Rod; Whelan, Arleen; Tucker, Forrest; Jurado, Katy; Acosta, Rodolfo; Roberts, Roy; Carey Jr., Harry; Steele, Bob

**Song(s)** South of San Antone [1] (C: Traditional; L: Roberts, Gerald)

**Notes** [1] Based on the traditional song "Wide Missouri."

## 5170 ✦ SAN ANTONIO
Warner Brothers, 1945

**Musical Score** Steiner, Max
**Choreographer(s)** Prinz, LeRoy

**Producer(s)** Buckner, Robert
**Director(s)** Butler, David
**Screenwriter(s)** LeMay, Alan; Burnett, W.R.

**Cast** Flynn, Errol; Smith, Alexis; Sakall, S.Z.; Francen, Victor; Litel, John; Bates, Florence; Kelly, Paul; Shayne, Robert; Blue, Monte; Hanneford, Poodles; Weaver, Doodles

**Song(s)** Put Your Little Foot Right Out (C/L: Spier, Larry); Some Sunday Morning [1] (C: Jerome, M.K.; Heindorf, Ray; L: Koehler, Ted); Somewhere in Monterey (C: Kisco, Charley; L: Scholl, Jack)

**Notes** [1] Also in THE MAN BEHIND THE GUN.

## 5171 ✦ SAN ANTONIO ROSE
Universal, 1941

**Producer(s)** Goldsmith, Ken
**Director(s)** Lamont, Charles
**Screenwriter(s)** Hall, Norman S.

**Cast** Frazee, Jane; Paige, Robert; Arden, Eve; Chaney Jr., Lon

**Song(s)** San Antonio Rose [2] (C/L: Wills, Bob); You're Everything Wonderful (C/L: Russell, Henry); You've Got What It Takes (C: de Paul, Gene; L: Raye, Don); Bugle Woogie Boy (C/L: Russell, Henry); Hi, Neighbor [1] (C/L: Owens, Jack); Water (C/L: de Paul, Gene); Mexican Jumping Beat [3] (C: de Paul, Gene; L: Raye, Don); Once Upon a Summertime (C: Berens, Norman; L: Brooks, Jack)

**Notes** There are also vocals of "The Hut-Sut Song" by Leo V. Killion, Ted McMichaels and Jack Owens; "The Old Oaken Bucket" by S. Woodworth and "Oh! Susanna" by Stephen Foster. [1] Also in HI, NEIGHBOR (Republic). [2] Also in RHYTHM ROUND-UP (Columbia), UNDER COLORADO SKIES (Republic), BOB WILLS AND HIS TEXAS PLAYBOYS (Warner) and HONKYTONK MAN (Warner). [3] Spanish version by Oscar Larrisa and Raquel Rojas.

## 5172 ✦ SANCTUARY
Twentieth Century–Fox, 1961

**Musical Score** North, Alex

**Producer(s)** Zanuck, Richard D.
**Director(s)** Richardson, Tony
**Screenwriter(s)** Poe, James
**Source(s)** *Sanctuary* (novel) Faulkner, William

**Cast** Remick, Lee; Montand, Yves; Dillman, Bradford

**Song(s)** Sanctuary [1] (C: North, Alex; L: Bergman, Alan; Keith, Marilyn)

**Notes** There is also a vocal of "Romance" by Walter Donaldson and Edgar Leslie. [1] Lyric written for exploitation only.

## 5173 ✦ SANDERS OF THE RIVER
United Artists, 1935

**Composer(s)** Spoliansky, Mischa
**Lyricist(s)** Wimperis, Arthur

**Producer(s)** Korda, Alexander
**Director(s)** Korda, Zoltan
**Screenwriter(s)** Biro, Lajos; Wimperis, Arthur; Dell, Jeffrey
**Source(s)** "Sanders of the River" (stories) Wallace, Edgar

**Cast** Robeson, Paul; McKinney, Nina Mae; Banks, Leslie; Cochran, Robert; Walker, Martin; Wane, Tony; Grey, Richard

**Song(s)** Canoe Song; Congo Lullaby; Killing Song

**Notes** No cue sheet available.

## 5174 ✦ THE SAND PEBBLES
Twentieth Century–Fox, 1966

**Musical Score** Goldsmith, Jerry

**Producer(s)** Wise, Robert
**Director(s)** Wise, Robert
**Screenwriter(s)** Anderson, Robert
**Source(s)** *The Sand Pebbles* (novel) McKenna, Richard

**Cast** McQueen, Steve; Attenborough, Richard; Crenna, Richard; Bergen, Candice; Andriane, Marayat; Mako; Oakland, Simon; MacLeod, Gavin

**Song(s)** And We Were Lovers [1] (C: Goldsmith, Jerry; L: Bricusse, Leslie)

**Notes** There are also vocals of "Toot Toot Tootsie" by Gus Kahn, Ernie Erdman and Dan Russo and "Five Foot Two, Eyes of Blue" by Ray Henderson, Sam Lewis and Joe Young. [1] Used instrumentally only.

## 5175 ✦ THE SANDPIPER
Metro–Goldwyn–Mayer, 1966

**Musical Score** Mandel, Johnny

**Producer(s)** Ransohoff, Martin
**Director(s)** Minnelli, Vincente
**Screenwriter(s)** Trumbo, Dalton; Wilson, Michael

**Cast** Taylor, Elizabeth; Burton, Richard; Saint, Eva Marie; Bronson, Charles; Webber, Robert; Thatcher, Torin; Drake, Tom; Edwards, James; Henderson, Doug; Mason, Morgan

**Song(s)** The Shadow of Your Smile (C: Mandel, Johnny; L: Webster, Paul Francis)

## 5176 ✦ SAN FERNANDO VALLEY
Republic, 1944

**Choreographer(s)** Ceballos, Larry

**Producer(s)** White, Eddy
**Director(s)** English, John
**Screenwriter(s)** McGowan, Stuart; McGowan, Dorrell

**Cast** Rogers, Roy; Evans, Dale; Porter, Jean; Nolan, Bob; Tombes, Andrew; Gargan, Edward; Lyden, Pierce; Mason, LeRoy; Sons of the Pioneers

**Song(s)** San Fernando Valley (C/L: Jenkins, Gordon); They Went That a Way (C/L: Spencer, Tim); My Hobby Is Love (C/L: Henderson, Charles); Over the Rainbow Trail We'll Ride [2] (C/L: Carson, Ken); I Drottled a Drit Drit (C: Lava, William; L: Walker, A.); How Could Anyone Be Sweeter Than You [1] (C/L: Henderson, Charles)

**Notes** [1] Used instrumentally only. [2] Also in HOME ON THE RANGE.

## 5177 ✦ SAN FRANCISCO
Metro–Goldwyn–Mayer, 1936

**Composer(s)** Kaper, Bronislau; Jurmann, Walter
**Lyricist(s)** Kahn, Gus
**Choreographer(s)** Raset, Val

**Producer(s)** Emerson, John; Hyman, Bernard H.
**Director(s)** Van Dyke, W.S.
**Screenwriter(s)** Loos, Anita

**Cast** Gable, Clark; MacDonald, Jeanette; Tracy, Spencer; Holt, Jack; Ralph, Jessie; Healy, Ted; Ross, Shirley; Kennedy, Edgar; Shean, Al; Ricciardi, William; Judels, Charles; Roach, Bert; Hymer, Warren

**Song(s)** Happy New Year; San Francisco (1); Philippine Dance (C/L: Carleton, Bob); Would You [1] (C: Brown, Nacio Herb; L: Freed, Arthur); San Francisco (2) [2] (C: Donaldson, Walter; L: Kahn, Gus)

**Notes** There are also vocals of "(There'll Be) A Hot Time in the Old Town (Tonight)" by Joseph Hayden and Theodore M. Metz; "Love Me and the World Is Mine" by Dave Reed and Ernest Ball; "A Heart That's Free" by Alfred G. Robyn; "The Holy City" by Stephen Adams; excerpts from FAUST by Gounod; "Sempre Libera" from TRAVIATA by Verdi; "Nearer My God to Thee" by Sarah Adams and Lowell Mason and the "Battle Hymn of the Republic" by Julia Ward Howe. [1] Also in SINGIN' IN THE RAIN. [2] Sheet music only. Not used.

## 5178 ✦ SANGAREE
Paramount, 1953

**Musical Score** Cailliet, Lucien

**Producer(s)** Pine, William; Thomas, William
**Director(s)** Ludwig, Edward
**Screenwriter(s)** Duncan, David
**Source(s)** *Sangaree* (novel) Slaughter, Frank G.

**Cast** Lamas, Fernando; Dahl, Arlene; Medina, Patricia; Sutton, John; Sullivan, Francis L.; Drake, Tom; Korvin, Charles; Matthews, Lester; Parker, Willard

**Song(s)** Sangaree [1] (C/L: Livingston, Jay; Evans, Ray)

**Notes** [1] Not used.

## 5179 ✦ SAN QUENTIN
Warner Brothers–First National, 1937

**Producer(s)** Bischoff, Sam
**Director(s)** Bacon, Lloyd
**Screenwriter(s)** Milne, Peter; Cobb, Humphrey

**Cast** O'Brien, Pat; Sheridan, Ann; Bogart, Humphrey; MacLane, Barton; Sawyer, Joe; Borg, Veda Ann; Robbins, James; King, Joseph; Oliver, Gordon; Owen, Garry; Lawrence, Marc

**Song(s)** How Could You? (C: Warren, Harry; L: Dubin, Al)

## 5180 ✦ SANTA CLAUS—THE MOVIE
### Tri-Star, 1985

**Musical Score** Mancini, Henry
**Composer(s)** Mancini, Henry
**Lyricist(s)** Bricusse, Leslie

**Producer(s)** Salkind, Ilya; Spengler, Pierre
**Director(s)** Szwarc, Jeannot
**Screenwriter(s)** Newman, David

**Cast** Moore, Dudley; Lithgow, John; Huddleston, David; Meredith, Burgess; Cornwell, Judy; Fitzpatrick, Christian

**Song(s)** It's Christmas All Over the World (C/L: House, Bill; Hobbs, John); Every Christmas Eve; Making Toys; It's Christmas Again; Patch! Natch!; Thank You Santa; Shouldn't Do That (C: Croxford, Stuart; Askew, Steve; Askew, Neal; Beggs, Nick; L: Beggs, Nick)

**Notes** No cue sheet available.

## 5181 ✦ SANTA FE SADDLEMATES
### Republic, 1945

**Producer(s)** Carr, Thomas
**Director(s)** Carr, Thomas
**Screenwriter(s)** Cohen, Bennett R.

**Cast** Carson, Sunset; Stirling, Linda; Howland, Olin; Barcroft, Roy; Geary, Bud; Duncan, Kenne; Chesebro, George

**Song(s)** Oh Mister (C/L: Elliott, Jack)

## 5182 ✦ THE SANTA FE TRAIL (1930)
### Paramount, 1930

**Director(s)** Brower, Otto; Knopf, Edwin H.
**Screenwriter(s)** Paramore Jr., Edward E.; Mintz, Sam

**Cast** Arlen, Richard; Moreno, Rosita; Durkin, Junior; Green, Mitzi

**Song(s)** Now That You Are Here [1] (C: Rainger, Ralph; L: Myers, Henry; Howard, Dick [2])

**Notes** Film first titled WEST OF THE LAW. [1] Song first titled "Now That He Is Gone." [2] Pseudonym of Howard Dietz.

## 5183 ✦ SANTA FE TRAIL (1940)
### Warner Brothers, 1940

**Musical Score** Steiner, Max

**Producer(s)** Warner, Jack L.; Wallis, Hal B.
**Director(s)** Curtiz, Michael
**Screenwriter(s)** Buckner, Robert

**Cast** Flynn, Errol; de Havilland, Olivia; Massey, Raymond; Reagan, Ronald; Hale, Alan; Heflin, Van; Reynolds, Gene; O'Neill, Henry; Williams, Guinn "Big Boy"; Bond, Ward; Middleton, Charles

**Song(s)** Holiday Wagon Song (C: Jerome, M.K.; L: Scholl, Jack); Along the Santa Fe Trail [1] (C: Grosz, Will; L: Coolidge, Edwina; Dubin, Al)

**Notes** [1] Not used but published.

## 5184 ✦ THE SAP FROM SYRACUSE
### Paramount, 1930

**Director(s)** Sutherland, Edward
**Screenwriter(s)** Purcell, Gertrude
**Source(s)** *The Sap from Syracuse* (play) Ray, John; O'Donnell, Jack; Hayden, John

**Cast** Rogers, Ginger; Oakie, Jack; Bates, Granville; Barbier, George; Starbuck, Betty; Teasdale, Verree

**Song(s)** How I Wish I Could Sing a Love Song [1] (C: Green, Johnny; L: Harburg, E.Y.); Capitalize That Thing Called It [2] (C: Duke, Vernon; Green, Johnny; L: Harburg, E.Y.); Aw! What's the Use [2] (C: Green, Johnny; L: Harburg, E.Y.)

**Notes** [1] According to *Variety*, Vernon Duke also collaborated on the song. [2] Listed in *AFI Catalog* but not other sources.

## 5185 ✦ SARATOGA
### Metro–Goldwyn–Mayer, 1937

**Musical Score** Ward, Edward
**Composer(s)** Donaldson, Walter
**Lyricist(s)** Wright, Bob; Forrest, Chet

**Producer(s)** Hyman, Bernard H.
**Director(s)** Conway, Jack
**Screenwriter(s)** Loos, Anita; Hopkins, Robert E.

**Cast** Gable, Clark; Harlow, Jean [1]; Barrymore, Lionel; Morgan, Frank; Pidgeon, Walter; Merkel, Una; Edwards, Cliff; Hale, Jonathan; McDaniel, Hattie; Zucco, George

**Song(s)** Saratoga; The Horse with the Dreamy Eyes

**Notes** [1] Jean Harlow died just before filming was complete. Mary Dees replaced her on long shots and Paul Winslowe dubbed her voice.

## 5186 ✦ SARATOGA TRUNK
### Warner Brothers, 1946

**Musical Score** Steiner, Max

**Producer(s)** Wallis, Hal B.
**Director(s)** Wood, Sam
**Screenwriter(s)** Robinson, Casey
**Source(s)** *Saratoga Trunk* (novel) Ferber, Edna

**Cast** Cooper, Gary; Bergman, Ingrid; Robson, Flora; Austin, Jerry; Warburton, John; Bates, Florence; Bois, Curt; Abbott, John; Griffies, Ethel; Shelton, Marla; Freeman, Helen; Huxley, Sophie; de Wit, Jacqueline

**Song(s)** Listen to the Spasm Band (C/L: Bailey, Edward); Ah Suzette Cherie (C/L: Monroe, Minna); Dansez Codaine (C/L: Monroe, Minna); As Long As I Live [1] (C: Steiner, Max; L: Tobias, Charles); Goin' Home [1] (C/L: Steiner, Max; L: Tobias, Charles)

**Notes** It is not known which of these were written for the picture. [1] Used instrumentally only.

## 5187 ✦ SARGE GOES TO COLLEGE
Monogram, 1947

**Producer(s)** Jason, Will
**Director(s)** Jason, Will
**Screenwriter(s)** Collins, Hal

**Cast** Russ Morgan and His Orchestra; Jack McVea and His Orchestra; Manone, Wingy; Candido, Candy; Lyman, Abe; Paul, Les; Stacy, Jess; Venuti, Joe; Hale Jr., Alan; Stewart, Freddie; Preisser, June; Darro, Frankie; Mills, Warren; Neill, Noel; Walsh, Arthur; Collins, Monte

**Song(s)** Open the Door, Richard (C/L: Fletcher, Dusty; Mason, John; McVea, Jack; Howell, Don); I'll Close My Eyes (C/L: Kaye, Buddy; Reid, Billy); Penthouse Serenade (C/L: Jason, Will; Burton, Val); Somebody Else Is Taking My Place (C/L: Howard, Dick; Ellsworth, Bob; Morgan, Russ); Two Are the Same As One (C/L: Unknown); Blues in B Flat (C/L: Unknown)

**Notes** No cue sheet available.

## 5188 ✦ SARONG GIRL
Monogram, 1943

**Composer(s)** Hercher, Lou; Liona, Andy
**Lyricist(s)** Hercher, Lou; Liona, Andy

**Producer(s)** Krasne, Philip N.
**Director(s)** Dreifuss, Arthur
**Screenwriter(s)** Marion, Charles R.; Hoerl, Arthur; Ryan, Tim

**Cast** Corio, Ann; Ryan, Tim; Ryan, Irene; Moreland, Mantan; Henry, Bill; Davis, Johnnie; Kolker, Henry; Krueger, Lorraine

**Song(s)** I'm Nobody's Child; Tawai; Woogie Hula; Saronga

**Notes** No cue sheet available. There is also a vocal of "Darling Nellie Gray."

## 5189 ✦ SATAN NEVER SLEEPS
Twentieth Century–Fox, 1962

**Musical Score** Bennett, Richard Rodney

**Producer(s)** McCarey, Leo
**Director(s)** McCarey, Leo

**Screenwriter(s)** Binyon, Claude; McCarey, Leo
**Source(s)** (novel) Buck, Pearl S.

**Cast** Holden, William; Webb, Clifton; Nuyen, France; Seyler, Athene; Benson, Martin; Lee, Weaver

**Song(s)** Satan Never Sleeps (C: Warren, Harry; L: McCarey, Leo; Adamson, Harold)

## 5190 ✦ SATISFACTION
Twentieth Century–Fox, 1988

**Musical Score** Colombier, Michel

**Producer(s)** Spelling, Aaron; Greisman, Alan
**Director(s)** Freeman, Joan
**Screenwriter(s)** Purpura, Charles

**Cast** Bateman, Justine; Neeson, Liam; Alvarado, Trini; Coffey, Scott; Roberts, Julia; Harry, Deborah; Phillips, Britta

**Song(s)** Knock on Wood (C/L: Cropper, Steve; Floyd, Eddie); Rock and Roll Rebels (C/L: Kay, John; Wilk, Michael; Ritchotte, Rocket); Iko Iko (C/L: Johnson, Joan; Jones, Joe; Jones, Marilyn; Jones, Sharon; Thomas, Jessie; Hawkins, Barbara; Hawkins, Rose); Loving You Is Like a Suicide Mission (C/L: Bethany, David); Come On Everybody (C/L: Cochran, Eddie; Capehart, Jerry); God Bless the Child (C/L: Holiday, Billie; Herzog Jr., Arthur); Dedicated to the One I Love (C/L: Bass, Ralph; Pauling, Lowman); Talk to Me (C/L: Cropper, Steve); Mr. Big Stuff (C/L: Broussard, Joe; Williams, Ralph; Washington, Carrol); Stimulation (C/L: Gray, Paul); I've Been Down Before (C/L: Armato, Antonina; Knight, Jerry); Just Jump Into My Life (C/L: Gurvitz, Paul); Mystery Dance (C/L: Costello, Elvis); Lies (C/L: Charles, Beau; Randell, Buddy); Satisfaction (C/L: Jagger, Mick; Richards, Keith)

**Notes** It is not known which of these were written for the film.

## 5191 ✦ SATURDAY NIGHT FEVER
Paramount, 1977

**Composer(s)** Gibb, Barry; Gibb, Maurice; Gibb, Robin [3]
**Lyricist(s)** Gibb, Barry; Gibb, Maurice; Gibb, Robin [3]

**Producer(s)** Stigwood, Robert
**Director(s)** Badham, John
**Screenwriter(s)** Wexler, Norman

**Cast** Travolta, John; Gorney, Karen Lynn; Miller, Barry; Cali, Joseph; Pape, Paul; Ornstein, Bruce

**Song(s)** Stayin' Alive [2]; Night Fever; If I Can't Have You; More than a Woman; You Should Be Dancing [1]; How Deep Is Your Love

**Notes** Only original songs listed. [1] Not written for film. [2] Also in STAYIN' ALIVE. [3] Known as the Bee Gees.

## 5192 ✦ SATURDAY'S CHILDREN (1929)
Warner Brothers–First National, 1929

**Producer(s)**   Rowland, Richard A.
**Director(s)**   La Cava, Gregory
**Screenwriter(s)**   Halsey, Forrest
**Source(s)**   *Saturday's Children* (play) Anderson, Maxwell

**Cast**   Griffith, Corinne; Conti, Albert; Tell, Alma; Littlefield, Lucien; Lane, Charles; Schaefer, Anne; Harris, Marcia; Withers, Grant

**Song(s)**   I Still Believe in You (C: Akst, Harry; L: Clarke, Grant; Davis, Benny)

**Notes**   No cue sheet available.

## 5193 ✦ SATURDAY'S CHILDREN (1940)
Warner Brothers, 1940

**Musical Score**   Deutsch, Adolph

**Producer(s)**   Warner, Jack L.; Wallis, Hal B.
**Director(s)**   Sherman, Vincent
**Screenwriter(s)**   Epstein, Julius J.; Epstein, Philip G.
**Source(s)**   *Saturday's Children* (play) Anderson, Maxwell

**Cast**   Garfield, John; Shirley, Anne; Rains, Claude; Patrick, Lee; Tobias, George; Churchill, Berton; Karns, Roscoe; Moore, Dennis

**Song(s)**   Saturday's Children [1] (C: Jerome, M.K.; L: Scholl, Jack)

**Notes**   Remake of the 1929 feature. [1] Instrumental use only.

## 5194 ✦ THE SAVAGE HORDE
Republic, 1949

**Musical Score**   Butts, Dale

**Producer(s)**   Kane, Joseph
**Director(s)**   Kane, Joseph
**Screenwriter(s)**   Gamet, Kenneth

**Cast**   Elliott, William; Booth, Adrian; Withers, Grant; Steele, Bob; Dumbrille, Douglass; Barcroft, Roy; Taliaferro, Hal

**Song(s)**   Ride an Old Paint, Lead an Old Bald (C/L: Hamblen, Stuart); Sheepskin Corn [1] (C/L: Hamblen, Stuart)

**Notes**   [1] BMI list only.

## 5195 ✦ THE SAVAGE INNOCENTS
Paramount, 1960

**Composer(s)**   Lavagnino, Angelo Francesco

**Producer(s)**   Malenotti, Maleno
**Director(s)**   Ray, Nicholas
**Screenwriter(s)**   Ray, Nicholas
**Source(s)**   *Top of the World* (novel) Reusch, Hans

**Cast**   Quinn, Anthony; Tani, Yoko; O'Toole, Peter; Wong, Anna May

**Song(s)**   Inuk and Anawrick Paddling; Iceberg (L: Edwards, John); Sexy Rock (L: Panzeri, Mario)

## 5196 ✦ SAVAGE MESSIAH
Metro–Goldwyn–Mayer, 1972

**Composer(s)**   Garrett, Michael
**Lyricist(s)**   Garrett, Michael

**Producer(s)**   Russell, Ken
**Director(s)**   Russell, Ken
**Screenwriter(s)**   Logue, Christopher
**Source(s)**   (book) Ede, H.S.

**Cast**   Tutin, Dorothy; Antony, Scott; Mirren, Helen; Kemp, Lindsay; Gough, Michael; Richards, Aubrey; Justin, John; Vaughan, Peter; Lang, Robert

**Song(s)**   Two Fleas (C/L: Tutin, Dorothy); Olympia Song; Gosh's Song; Gaudier Song

**Notes**   Based on the life of sculptor Henri Gaudier-Brzeska.

## 5197 ✦ SAVAGE SAM
Disney, 1963

**Musical Score**   Wallace, Oliver

**Producer(s)**   Anderson, Bill
**Director(s)**   Tokar, Norman
**Screenwriter(s)**   Gipson, Fred; Tunberg, William
**Source(s)**   *Savage Sam* (children's novel) Gipson, Fred

**Cast**   Keith, Brian; Kirk, Tommy; Corcoran, Kevin; Martin, Dewey; York, Jeff; Kristen, Marta; Acosta, Rodolfo; Pickens, Slim

**Song(s)**   Savage Sam and Me (The Land of the Wild Countree) (C/L: Gilkyson, Terry)

## 5198 ✦ THE SAVAGE SEVEN
American International, 1968

**Musical Score**   Curb, Mike; Styner, Jerry

**Producer(s)**   Clark, Dick
**Director(s)**   Rush, Richard
**Screenwriter(s)**   Fisher, Michael

**Cast**   Walker, Robert; Roarke, Adam; Frank, Joanna; Marshall, Penny

**Song(s)**   The Savage Seven Theme (C/L: Cream); The Ballad of the Savage Seven (C/L: Johns, Valgean)

**Notes**   No cue sheet available.

## 5199 ✦ SAVANNAH SMILES
Embassy, 1983

**Musical Score**   Sutherland, Ken
**Composer(s)**   Sutherland, Ken
**Lyricist(s)**   Sutherland, Ken

**Producer(s)**  Paylow, Clark L.
**Director(s)**  DeMoro, Pierre
**Screenwriter(s)**  Miller, Mark

**Cast**  Miller, Mark; Scott, Donovan; Andersen, Bridgette; Robinson, Chris; Parks, Michael; Morita, Pat; Fiedler, John; Graves, Peter

**Song(s)**  Another Dusty Road; Out of the Shadows; When Savannah Smiles; Pretty Girl; Love Will Never Be the Same Again

**Notes**  No cue sheet available.

## 5200  ◆  SAY IT IN FRENCH
### Paramount, 1938

**Producer(s)**  Stone, Andrew L.
**Director(s)**  Stone, Andrew L.
**Screenwriter(s)**  Jackson, Frederick
**Source(s)**  *Soubrette* (play) Deval, Jacques

**Cast**  Milland, Ray; Bradna, Olympe; Hervey, Irene; Carlisle, Mary

**Song(s)**  April in My Heart [1] (C: Carmichael, Hoagy; L: Meinardi, Helen)

**Notes**  [1] Not used in COLLEGE SWING and EVERY DAY'S A HOLIDAY (1937).

## 5201  ◆  SAY IT WITH MUSIC
### Metro–Goldwyn–Mayer, 1966 unproduced

**Composer(s)**  Berlin, Irving
**Lyricist(s)**  Berlin, Irving

**Producer(s)**  Freed, Arthur
**Director(s)**  Edwards, Blake
**Screenwriter(s)**  Axelrod, George

**Song(s)**  Always the Same; A Guy on Monday; A Man to Cook For; One Man Woman; Outside of Loving You, I Like You; The P.X.; The Ten Best Undressed Women in the World; Whisper It; Let Me Sing; I Used to Play It by Ear; Who Needs the Birds and the Bees; Long As I Can Take You Home; Wait Until You're Married; I Used to Be Color Blind

**Notes**  There were other attempts at a screenplay by Leonard Gershe (1965); Betty Comden and Adolph Green (1966) and George Wells (1967). Julie Andrews and Fred Astaire were originally to play the leads. The songs were submitted by Berlin between 1963 and 1966. Many, if not all of them, were trunk songs. Rumor is that this is the film that inspired Blake Edwards' SOB.

## 5202  ◆  SAY IT WITH SONGS
### Warner Brothers, 1929

**Composer(s)**  Henderson, Ray
**Lyricist(s)**  DeSylva, B.G.; Brown, Lew; Jolson, Al

**Director(s)**  Bacon, Lloyd
**Screenwriter(s)**  Jackson, Joseph

**Cast**  Jolson, Al; Lee, Davey; Nixon, Marian; Herbert, Holmes; Kohler, Fred; Bowers, John; Thomson, Kenneth

**Song(s)**  Little Pal; Why Can't You; Used to You; I'm in Seventh Heaven; Back in Your Own Back Yard (C: Dreyer, Dave; L: DeSylva, B.G.; Jolson, Al); I'm Ka-razy for You (C: Dreyer, Dave; L: DeSylva, B.G.; Jolson, Al); Memories of One Sweet Kiss (C: Dreyer, Dave; L: Jolson, Al)

**Notes**  No cue sheet available. *Variety* and other sources doubted Jolson's claim to have collaborated on all these songs.

## 5203  ◆  SAYONARA
### Warner Brothers, 1957

**Musical Score**  Waxman, Franz
**Choreographer(s)**  Prinz, LeRoy

**Producer(s)**  Goetz, William
**Director(s)**  Logan, Joshua
**Screenwriter(s)**  Osborn, Paul
**Source(s)**  *Sayonara* (novel) Michener, James A.

**Cast**  Brando, Marlon; Owens, Patricia; Garner, James; Scott, Martha; Umeki, Miyoshi; Taka, Miiko; Buttons, Red; Smith, Kent; Montalban, Ricardo; Watson, Douglas

**Song(s)**  Sayonara (C/L: Berlin, Irving); Sakura Sakura (C/L: Matsumoto, Shiro; Kishimoto, Suifu); Hanayome Ningyo (C/L: Fukiya, Koji; Sugiyama, Haseo); Narukami (C/L: Oka, S.); Shinju Tenno Amijima Hashi Zukushi (C/L: Chikamatsu, Monzaemon; Kai, Bunraku Mitsuwa; Toyosawa, Enjiro); Daichoji Zutsumi (C/L: Chikamatsu, Monzaemon; Kai, Bunraku Mitsuwa; Toyosawa, Enjiro); Mountains Beyond the Moon [1] (C: Waxman, Franz; L: Sigman, Carl)

**Notes**  It is not known if the Japanese songs were written for the picture. Berlin's song was. [1] Lyric written for exploitation only.

## 5204  ◆  SAY ONE FOR ME
### Twentieth Century–Fox, 1959

**Composer(s)**  Van Heusen, James
**Lyricist(s)**  Cahn, Sammy
**Choreographer(s)**  Romero, Alex

**Producer(s)**  Tashlin, Frank
**Director(s)**  Tashlin, Frank
**Screenwriter(s)**  O'Brien, Robert

**Cast**  Crosby, Bing; Reynolds, Debbie; Wagner, Robert; Walston, Ray

**Song(s)**  Say One for Me; You Can't Love 'Em All; The Girl Most Likely to Succeed; I Couldn't Care Less; The Night That Rock and Roll Died (Almost); Chico's Choo-Choo (The Choo-Choo Cha-Cha); The Secret of Christmas; Does Santa Claus Believe in You [1]; He's Starting to Get to Me [1]

**Notes**  [1] Not used.

## 5205 ✦ SCALAWAG
Paramount, 1973

**Producer(s)** Douglas, Anne
**Director(s)** Douglas, Kirk
**Screenwriter(s)** Maltz, Albert; Fleischman, Sid
**Source(s)** *Scalawag* (story) Stevenson, Robert Louis

**Cast** Douglas, Kirk; Lester, Mark; Brand, Neville; Down, Lesley-Anne

**Song(s)** When Your Number's Up You Go (C/L: Cameron, John; Bart, Lionel); The Scalawag Song (C/L: Cameron, John)

## 5206 ✦ SCANDAL INCORPORATED
Republic, 1956

**Musical Score** Sawtell, Paul; Shefter, Bert

**Producer(s)** Purcell, Victor; Daniels, Johnathan
**Director(s)** Mann, Edward
**Screenwriter(s)** Mann, Milton

**Cast** Hutton, Robert; Wright, Patricia; Richards, Paul; Knapp, Robert; Davenport, Harris; Hammond, Reid; Paiva, Nestor

**Song(s)** Welcome to the Blues (C/L: Shrager, Al; Shrager, Sid; Chorney, Al)

## 5207 ✦ SCANDALOUS
Orion, 1984

**Musical Score** Grusin, Dave

**Producer(s)** Sellers, Arlene; Winitsky, Alex
**Director(s)** Cohen, Rob
**Screenwriter(s)** Cohen, Rob; Byrum, John

**Cast** Hays, Robert; Travis, Ron; Walsh, M. Emmet; Gielgud, John; Dolan, Ed; Stephenson, Pamela; Dale, Jim

**Song(s)** It's Scandalous (C: Grusin, Dave; L: Block, Don)

**Notes** No cue sheet available.

## 5208 ✦ SCANDALOUS JOHN
Disney, 1971

**Musical Score** McKuen, Rod
**Composer(s)** Marks, Franklyn
**Lyricist(s)** Walsh, Bill

**Producer(s)** Walsh, Bill
**Director(s)** Butler, Robert
**Screenwriter(s)** Walsh, Bill; DaGradi, Don
**Source(s)** (book) Gardner, Richard

**Cast** Keith, Brian; Arau, Alfonso; Carey, Michele; Lenz, Rick; Morgan, Harry; Oakland, Simon; Ritter, John

**Song(s)** Pastures Green/Pavement Gray (C/L: McKuen, Rod); Go 'Long Now [1]; In Kansas [1] (L: Gardiner, Richard); Long Time Ago [1]

**Notes** [1] Not used.

## 5209 ✦ THE SCAPEGOAT
Metro–Goldwyn–Mayer, 1959

**Musical Score** Kaper, Bronislau

**Producer(s)** Balcon, Michael
**Director(s)** Hamer, Robert
**Screenwriter(s)** Hamer, Robert
**Source(s)** *The Scapegoat* (novel) Du Maurier, Daphne

**Cast** Guinness, Alec; Maurey, Nicole; Worth, Irene; Brown, Pamela; Bull, Peter; Davis, Bette

**Song(s)** Take My Love [1] (C: Kaper, Bronislau; L: Deutsch, Helen)

**Notes** [1] Used instrumentally only.

## 5210 ✦ SCARECROW
Warner Brothers, 1973

**Producer(s)** Sherman, Robert M.
**Director(s)** Schatzberg, Jerry
**Screenwriter(s)** White, Garry Michael

**Cast** Hackman, Gene; Pacino, Al; Tristan, Dorothy; Wedgeworth, Ann; Lynch, Richard; Brennan, Eileen; Allen, Penny

**Song(s)** Love Forever (C/L: Selman, Clarence; Wilkin, Maryjohn); Silver Moon (C/L: Nesmith, Michael); Working in a Coal Mine (C/L: Toussaint, Allen); In the Midnight Hour (C/L: Pickett, Wilson; Cropper, Steve); (You Make Me Feel Like) A Natural Woman (C/L: Goffin, Gerry; King, Carole; Wexler, Jerry); Everything I Do Gonna Be Funky (C/L: Toussaint, Allen); The House that Jack Built (C/L: Lance, Bobby; Robbins, Fran)

**Notes** It is not known if any of these were written for the film.

## 5211 ✦ SCARECROW IN A GARDEN OF CUCUMBERS
Maron Films, 1972

**Musical Score** Blatt, Jerry
**Composer(s)** Blatt, Jerry
**Lyricist(s)** Barer, Marshall

**Producer(s)** Alpert, Henry J.; Kaplan, Robert J.
**Director(s)** Kaplan, Robert J.
**Screenwriter(s)** Scoppettone, Sandra

**Cast** Woodlawn, Holly; Brown Tally; Lerner, Yafa; Margulies, David; Hayes, Sonny Boy

**Song(s)** Dusty Rose Hotel; Get It On; Bethesda; Love at Last; A Lot o' Sound, Nothin' Goin' Down at All;

Strawberry, Strawberry, Lavender and Lime; The Up Number; Bubble Gum Boat [1]

**Notes**    No cue sheet available. [1] Written but not finished.

### 5212 ◆ SCARED STIFF
Paramount, 1953

**Musical Score**    Stevens, Leith
**Composer(s)**    Livingston, Jerry
**Lyricist(s)**    David, Mack
**Choreographer(s)**    Daniels, Billy

**Producer(s)**    Wallis, Hal B.
**Director(s)**    Marshall, George
**Screenwriter(s)**    Baker, Herbert; De Leon, Walter; Simmons, Ed; Lear, Norman
**Source(s)**    (play) Dickey, Paul; Goddard, Charles W.

**Cast**    Martin, Dean; Lewis, Jerry; Scott, Lizabeth; Miranda, Carmen

**Song(s)**    The Enchilada Man; When Someone Wonderful Thinks You're Wonderful; The Bongo Bingo; Got a Feelin' [1]; Spanish of Course [1]; San Domingo [1]; I Don't Care If the Sun Don't Shine (C/L: David, Mack); What Have You Done for Me Lately? [1]; Around the Island [1] (C: Oliveira, Louis; L: Gilbert, Ray); Pic-A-Pau Polka [1] (C: Oliveira, Louis; L: Gilbert, Ray)

**Notes**    This film is a musical remake of the Bob Hope and Paulette Goddard film GHOST BREAKERS. [1] Not used. [2] Used for 12 seconds (8 whistled) in JUMPING JACKS.

### 5213 ◆ SCARFACE
Universal, 1983

**Musical Score**    Moroder, Giorgio
**Composer(s)**    Moroder, Giorgio
**Lyricist(s)**    Moroder, Giorgio; Barrow, Arthur

**Producer(s)**    Bregman, Martin
**Director(s)**    De Palma, Brian
**Screenwriter(s)**    Stone, Oliver

**Cast**    Pacino, Al; Bauer, Steven; Pfeiffer, Michelle; Mastrantonio, Mary Elizabeth; Loggia, Robert; Colon, Miriam; Abraham, F. Murray; Yulin, Harris; Beniades, Ted; Belzer, Richard

**Song(s)**    Vamos a Bailar (L: Conchita, Maria); Shake It Up; Rush, Rush (L: Harry, Deborah); She's on Fire (L: Bellotte, Pete); Turn Out the Light (L: Bellotte, Pete); I'm Hot Tonight; Dance, Dance, Dance; Push It to the Limit (L: Bellotte, Pete)

**Notes**    A remake of the 1932 film.

### 5214 ◆ THE SCARLET BUCCANEER

See THE SWASHBUCKLER.

### 5215 ◆ THE SCARLET CLAW
Universal, 1944

**Producer(s)**    Neill, Roy William
**Director(s)**    Neill, Roy William
**Screenwriter(s)**    Neill, Roy William
**Source(s)**    characters by Doyle, Arthur Conan

**Cast**    Rathbone, Basil; Bruce, Nigel; Clyde, David; Cavanagh, Paul; Mander, Miles

**Song(s)**    Carried Off to Sea (C: Traditional; L: Bibo, Irving)

### 5216 ◆ THE SCARLET HOUR
Paramount, 1956

**Producer(s)**    Curtiz, Michael
**Director(s)**    Curtiz, Michael
**Screenwriter(s)**    Ronkel, Rip Von; Tashlin, Frank; Lucas, John Meredyth

**Cast**    Tryon, Tom; Ohmart, Carol; Gregory, James; Lawrence, Jody; Cole, Nat "King"

**Song(s)**    Never Let Me Go [3] (C/L: Livingston, Jay; Evans, Ray); The Scarlet Hour Mambo [1] (C: Stevens, Leith; L: Blake, Bebe); So Little Time [2] (C/L: Livingston, Jay; Evans, Ray); Too Little Time [2] (C/L: Livingston, Jay; Evans, Ray)

**Notes**    [1] Instrumental only. [2] Not used. [3] Also in GIRLS! GIRLS! GIRLS!

### 5217 ◆ THE SCARLET LADY
Columbia, 1928

**Director(s)**    Crosland, Alan
**Screenwriter(s)**    Meredyth, Bess

**Cast**    de Putti, Lya; Alvarado, Don; Oland, Warner; Matiesen, Otto; Peters, John; Zimina, Valentina

**Song(s)**    My Heart Belongs to You (C/L: Herscher, Louis)

### 5218 ◆ SCATTERBRAIN
Republic, 1940

**Producer(s)**    Meins, Gus
**Director(s)**    Meins, Gus
**Screenwriter(s)**    Conlan, Paul; Burton, Val; Townley, Jack

**Cast**    Canova, Judy; Mowbray, Alan; Donnelly, Ruth; Foy Jr., Eddie; Cawthorn, Joseph; Ford, Wallace; Jewell, Isabel; Alberni, Luis; Gilbert, Billy; Matty Malneck and His Orchestra; Cal Shrum's Gang

**Song(s)**    Benny the Beaver (C/L: Heath, Hy; Lange, Johnny; Porter, Lew); Scatterbrain (C: Bean, Keene; Masters, Frankie; L: Burke, Johnny); Scatterbrain Finale [1] (C/L: Styne, Jule; Brown, George; Meyer, Sol)

**Notes** There are also vocals of "She'll Be Comin' 'Round the Mountain" and "Ciribiribin" by Alberto Pestalozza, Harry James and Jack Lawrence and "I Ain't Got Nobody" by Roger Graham and Spencer Williams. [1] The songwriters signed their work Lucius Featherdew, Alvin Zits Flaish and Foldamer Agong on the music sheets. (The cue sheet credits them correctly. The Republic collection at Brigham Young credits their pseudonyms!)

## 5219 ✦ SCATTERGOOD SWINGS IT

See CINDERELLA SWINGS IT.

## 5220 ✦ SCAVENGER HUNT
### Twentieth Century–Fox, 1979

**Musical Score** Goldenberg, Billy

**Producer(s)** Vail, Steven A.
**Director(s)** Schultz, Michael
**Screenwriter(s)** Vail, Steven A.; Harper, Henry

**Cast** Benjamin, Richard; Coco, James; Crothers, Benjamin "Scatman"; Gordon, Ruth; Leachman, Cloris; Little, Cleavon; McDowall, Roddy; Morley, Robert; Mulligan, Richard; Randall, Tony; Benedict, Dirk; Aames, Willie; Furst, Stephen; Masur, Richard; Meat Loaf; McCormick, Pat; Price, Vincent; Faracy, Stephanie; Schreiber, Avery; Schwarzenegger, Arnold; Torres, Liz; Pankin, Stuart

**Song(s)** There's Enough for Everyone (C: Goldenberg, Billy; L: Connors, Carol); Walkin' Papers (C: Goldenberg, Billy; L: Connors, Carol)

**Notes** No cue sheet available.

## 5221 ✦ SCENE OF THE CRIME
### Metro–Goldwyn–Mayer, 1949

**Musical Score** Previn, Andre
**Composer(s)** Previn, Andre
**Lyricist(s)** Katz, William

**Producer(s)** Rapf, Harry
**Director(s)** Rowland, Roy
**Screenwriter(s)** Schnee, Charles

**Cast** Johnson, Van; De Haven, Gloria; Drake, Tom; Dahl, Arlene; Ames, Leon; McIntire, John; Woods, Donald; Lloyd, Norman; Cowan, Jerome; Powers, Tom

**Song(s)** I'm a Goody-Goody Girl; I Call Myself a Lady

**Notes** Producer Rapf died during pre-production.

## 5222 ✦ SCENT OF MYSTERY
### Michael Todd Jr., 1960

**Musical Score** Nascimbene, Mario

**Producer(s)** Todd Jr., Michael
**Director(s)** Cardiff, Jack
**Screenwriter(s)** Roos, William

**Cast** Elliott, Denholm; Bentley, Beverly; Lorre, Peter; Lukas, Paul; Dors, Diana; Redmond, Liam; McKern, Leo

**Song(s)** Scent of Mystery (C: Nascimbene, Mario; L: Adamson, Harold; Ramin, Jordan); Chase (C: Nascimbene, Mario; L: Adamson, Harold)

**Notes** No cue sheet available.

## 5223 ✦ SCHOOL DAZE
### Columbia, 1988

**Musical Score** Lee, Bill

**Producer(s)** Lee, Spike
**Director(s)** Lee, Spike
**Screenwriter(s)** Lee, Spike

**Cast** Fishburne, Larry; Esposito, Giancarlo; Campbell, Tisha; Kyme; Seneca, Joe; Evans, Art; Davis, Ossie; Marsalis, Branford; Lee, Spike; Thomas, Leonard

**Song(s)** (I Don't Wanna) Be Alone Tonight (C/L: Jones, Raymond); Da Butt (C/L: Miller, Marcus; Stevens, Mark)

**Notes** No cue sheet available.

## 5224 ✦ SCHUBERT'S SERENADE
### Paramount, 1936

**Producer(s)** Moulton, Herbert

**Song(s)** Serenade (C: Schubert, Franz; L: Robin, Leo)

**Notes** Short subject.

## 5225 ✦ SCORPIO
### United Artists, 1973

**Musical Score** Fielding, Jerry

**Producer(s)** Mirisch, Walter
**Director(s)** Winner, Michael
**Screenwriter(s)** Rintels, David W.; Wilson, Gerald

**Cast** Lancaster, Burt; Delon, Alain; Scofield, Paul; Colicos, John; Hunnicutt, Gayle; Cannon, J.D.; Linville, Joanne

**Song(s)** Un Dia de Julio (C: Fielding, Jerry; L: Riera, Carlos)

## 5226 ✦ SCRIPT GIRL
### Studio Unknown, 1937

**Song(s)** Just a Simple Melody (C: Chaplin, Saul; L: Cahn, Sammy)

**Notes** No other information available. Short subject.

## 5227 ✦ SCROOGE
### Cinema Center, 1970

**Composer(s)** Bricusse, Leslie
**Lyricist(s)** Bricusse, Leslie
**Choreographer(s)** Stone, Paddy

**Producer(s)**   Solo, Robert H.
**Director(s)**   Neame, Ronald
**Screenwriter(s)**   Bricusse, Leslie
**Source(s)**   *A Christmas Carol* (novel) Dickens, Charles

**Cast**   Finney, Albert; Guinness, Alec; Evans, Edith; More, Kenneth; Naismith, Laurence; Beaumont, Richard; Collings, David; Cuka, Frances; Rodgers, Anton

**Song(s)**   Christmas Children; I Hate People; Father Chris'mas; See the Phantoms; A Christmas Carol; December the 25th; You . . . You . . . ; Happiness; I Like Life; The Beautiful Day; Thank You Very Much; I'll Begin Again; Good Times

**Notes**   No cue sheet available.

### 5228 ✦ SCROOGED
#### Paramount, 1988

**Musical Score**   Elfman, Danny

**Producer(s)**   Linson, Art; Donner, Richard
**Director(s)**   Donner, Richard
**Screenwriter(s)**   Glazer, Mitch; O'Donoghue, Michael

**Cast**   Murray, Bill; Allen, Karen; Forsythe, John; Glover, John; Goldthwait, Bobcat; Johansen, David; Kane, Carol; Mitchum, Robert; Pollard, Michael J.; Woodard, Alfre

**Song(s)**   A Wonderful Life (C/L: Spence, Judson; Jones, Monroe); Get Up 'N' Dance (C/L: Mallison, LaVaba; Dewese, Moedehandes; Isaacs, Radcliff); The Love You Take (C/L: Hartman, Don)

**Notes**   Only songs written for the picture are listed.

### 5229 ✦ SCROOGE MCDUCK AND MONEY
#### Disney, 1966

**Musical Score**   Marks, Franklyn
**Composer(s)**   Leven, Mel
**Lyricist(s)**   Leven, Mel

**Director(s)**   Luske, Hamilton
**Screenwriter(s)**   Berg, Bill

**Cast**   Thompson, Bill; The Mello Men

**Song(s)**   A Billion Dollars; Bonnie Columns; The Budget; It's Gotta Circulate; The Remarkable Sum (Of a Dollar Ninety-Five); We Need Money

**Notes**   Animated short.

### 5230 ✦ THE SEA BAT
#### Metro–Goldwyn–Mayer, 1930

**Composer(s)**   Ward, Edward
**Lyricist(s)**   Montgomery, Reggie

**Director(s)**   Ruggles, Wesley
**Screenwriter(s)**   Meredyth, Bess; Lawson, John Howard

**Cast**   Bickford, Charles; Torres, Raquel; Marion, George F.; Asther, Nils; Miljan, John; Karloff, Boris; Swain, Mack

**Song(s)**   My Love Has Other Charms; Lo Lo

**Notes**   Sheet music credits Felix Feist, Reggie Montgomery; George Ward and Howard Johnson.

### 5231 ✦ THE SEA GOD (SPANISH VERSION)
#### Paramount, 1930

**Song(s)**   Adela Arrolando (C/L: Picarello); Economy Wave (C/L: Pasternacki, Stephen); Mi Triste Adios (C: Rainger, Ralph; L: Ribalto, J. Carner)

### 5232 ✦ THE SEA HAWK
#### Warner Brothers, 1940

**Musical Score**   Korngold, Erich Wolfgang

**Producer(s)**   Warner, Jack L.; Wallis, Hal B.
**Director(s)**   Curtiz, Michael
**Screenwriter(s)**   Miller, Seton I.; Koch, Howard W.
**Source(s)**   *The Sea Hawk* (novel) Sabatini, Rafael

**Cast**   Flynn, Errol; Marshall, Brenda; Rains, Claude; Crisp, Donald; Robson, Flora; Hale, Alan; Daniell, Henry; O'Connor, Una; Stephenson, James; Roland, Gilbert; Lundigan, William; Mitchell, Julian; Love, Montagu; Kerrigan, J.M.

**Song(s)**   Finale (C: Korngold, Erich Wolfgang; L: Scholl, Jack)

### 5233 ✦ THE SEA HORNET
#### Republic, 1951

**Composer(s)**   Elliott, Jack
**Lyricist(s)**   Elliott, Jack

**Producer(s)**   Kane, Joseph
**Director(s)**   Kane, Joseph
**Screenwriter(s)**   Adams, Gerald Drayson
**Source(s)**   *Sea of Darkness* (novel) Adams, Gerald Drayson

**Cast**   Cameron, Rod; Mara, Adele; Booth, Adrian; Wills, Chill; Davis, Jim; Jaeckel, Richard; Corby, Ellen; Brown, Jim

**Song(s)**   A Dream Or Two Ago; I'm Afraid of You; Someone to Remember (C/L: Elliott, Jack; Scott, Nathan)

### 5234 ✦ SEA LEGS
#### Paramount, 1930

**Lyricist(s)**   Marion Jr., George

**Director(s)**   Heerman, Victor
**Screenwriter(s)**   Dix, Marion

**Cast**   Oakie, Jack; Roth, Lillian; Green, Harry; Pallette, Eugene; Conti, Albert; Del Val, Jean

**Song(s)**   (It's So Nice) This Must Be Illegal [3] (C: Rainger, Ralph; Harling, W. Franke); It Was a Frenchman Who Thought of It First [1] (C: Rainger, Ralph; Harling, W. Franke); A Daisy Told Me [1] (C:

Harling, W. Franke); Ten O'Clock Town [2] (C: Cleary, Michael; L: Swanstrom, Arthur)

**Notes** [1] Not used. [2] Listed in AFI catalog but nowhere else. [3] Harling not credited on cue sheet .

## 5235 ◆ SEA OF LOST SHIPS
### Republic, 1953

**Musical Score** Butts, Dale

**Producer(s)** Kane, Joseph
**Director(s)** Kane, Joseph
**Screenwriter(s)** Fisher, Steve

**Cast** Derek, John; Hendrix, Wanda; Brennan, Walter; Jaeckel, Richard; Tully, Tom; MacLane, Barton; Hickman, Darryl; Powers, Tom; Roberts, Roy; Brodie, Steve

**Song(s)** Just One Kiss (C: Young, Victor; L: Washington, Ned)

## 5236 ◆ SEA RACKETEERS
### Republic, 1937

**Producer(s)** Schaefer, Armand
**Director(s)** MacFadden, Hamilton
**Screenwriter(s)** McGowan, Dorrell; McGowan, Stuart

**Cast** Heyburn, Weldon; Madden, Jeanne; Hymer, Warren; McNulty, Dorothy; Naish, J. Carrol; Compton, Joyce

**Song(s)** Lady Wants to Dance (C/L: Hirsch, Walter; Handman, Lou); Just Between You and Me (C/L: Lava, William; Kraushaar, Raoul); Let's Finish the Dream (C: Stept, Sam H.; L: Washington, Ned)

## 5237 ◆ SEARCH FOR BEAUTY
### Paramount, 1934

**Producer(s)** Sheldon, E. Lloyd
**Director(s)** Kenton, Eric
**Screenwriter(s)** Butler, Frank; Binyon, Claude
**Source(s)** Love Your Body by Grey, Schuyler E.; Milton, Paul R.

**Cast** Crabbe, Buster; Lupino, Ida; Armstrong, Robert; Michael, Gertrude

**Song(s)** Search for Beauty [1] (C: Rainger, Ralph; L: Robin, Leo); I'm a Seeker of Beauty [2] (C: Johnston, Arthur; L: Coslow, Sam)

**Notes** [1] Not used. [2] Sheet music only.

## 5238 ◆ THE SEARCHING WIND
### Paramount, 1946

**Musical Score** Young, Victor

**Producer(s)** Wallis, Hal B.
**Director(s)** Dieterle, William
**Screenwriter(s)** Hellman, Lillian
**Source(s)** *The Searching Wind* (play) Hellman, Lillian

**Cast** Young, Robert; Sidney, Sylvia; Richards, Ann; Digges, Dudley [1]; Dick, Douglas; Basserman, Albert

**Song(s)** Searching Wind [2] (C: Young, Victor; L: Heyman, Edward)

**Notes** [1] In original stage production. [2] Lyric written for exploitation only.

## 5239 ◆ THE SEAS BENEATH
### Fox, 1931

**Composer(s)** Sanders, Troy
**Lyricist(s)** Sanders, Troy

**Director(s)** Ford, John
**Screenwriter(s)** Nichols, Dudley

**Cast** O'Brien, George; Lessing, Marion; Hymer, Warren; Loder, John

**Song(s)** My Loves; Marinero (C/L: Grever, Maria); Mi Pobre Corazon; Estrellita [1] (C/L: Ponce, Manuel); Here's My Hand—You're in My Heart (C: Hanley, James F.; L: McCarthy, Joseph)

**Notes** [1] Not written for this production.

## 5240 ◆ SEATTLE
### Studio Unknown, 1943

**Composer(s)** Fain, Sammy
**Lyricist(s)** Freed, Ralph

**Song(s)** More than Ever; Down By the Ocean; Seattle

**Notes** No other information available.

## 5241 ◆ SEA WIFE
### Twentieth Century–Fox, 1957

**Musical Score** Jones, Kenneth V.

**Producer(s)** Hakim, Andre
**Director(s)** McNaught, Bob
**Screenwriter(s)** Burke, George K.
**Source(s)** *Sea Wyf and Biscuit* (novel) Scott, J.M.

**Cast** Collins, Joan; Burton, Richard; Sydney, Basil; Grant, Cy; Squire, Ronald

**Song(s)** I'll Find You (C: Evans, Tolchard; L: Mullan, Richard)

## 5242 ◆ THE SEA WOLF
### Fox, 1930

**Director(s)** Santell, Alfred
**Screenwriter(s)** Behrman, S.N.
**Source(s)** *The Sea Wolf* (novel) London, Jack

**Cast** Sills, Milton; Hackett, Raymond; Keith, Jane; Pendleton, Nat; Harris, Mitchell

**Song(s)** Boiled Beef and Carrots (C/L: Rogers, John)

## 5243 ✦ THE SEA WOLVES
Paramount, 1982

**Musical Score**  Budd, Roy

**Producer(s)**  Lloyd, Euan
**Director(s)**  McLaglen, Andrew V.
**Screenwriter(s)**  Rose, Reginald
**Source(s)**  *Boarding Party* (novel) Leasor, James

**Cast**  Peck, Gregory; Moore, Roger; Niven, David; Howard, Trevor; Kellermann, Barbara; MacNee, Patrick

**Song(s)**  The Precious Moments (C: Addinsell, Richard; L: Bricusse, Leslie)

**Notes**  No cue sheet available.

## 5244 ✦ SEBASTIAN
Paramount, 1967

**Musical Score**  Goldsmith, Jerry
**Composer(s)**  Goldsmith, Jerry
**Lyricist(s)**  Shaper, Hal

**Producer(s)**  Brodkin, Herbert; Powell, Michael
**Director(s)**  Greene, David
**Screenwriter(s)**  Vaughan-Hughes, Gerald

**Cast**  Bogarde, Dirk; York, Susannah; Palmer, Lilli; Gielgud, John; Munro, Janet; Fraser, Ronald; Johnston, Margaret; Davenport, Nigel

**Song(s)**  Hey There! Who Are You?; Comes the Night

## 5245 ✦ SECOND CHANCE
United Artists, 1978

**Musical Score**  Lai, Francis

**Director(s)**  Lelouch, Claude
**Screenwriter(s)**  Lelouch, Claude

**Cast**  Deneuve, Catherine; Aimee, Anouk; Denner, Charles; Huster, Francis; Arestrup, Niels; Baudot, Colette; Papatakis, Manuella

**Song(s)**  Femme Parmi les Femmes (C: Lai, Francis; L: Barouh, Pierre)

**Notes**  French title is SI C'ETAIT A REFAIRE.

## 5246 ✦ SECOND CHORUS
Paramount, 1940

**Lyricist(s)**  Mercer, Johnny
**Choreographer(s)**  Pan, Hermes

**Producer(s)**  Morros, Boris
**Director(s)**  Potter, H.C.
**Screenwriter(s)**  Ryand, Elaine; Hunter, Ian McLellan; Mercer, Johnny

**Cast**  Astaire, Fred; Goddard, Paulette; Artie Shaw and His Band; Butterworth, Charles; Meredith, Burgess

**Song(s)**  I'm Not Hep to that Step (but I'll Dig It) (C: Borne, Hal); Would You Like to Be the Love of My Life [3] (C: Shaw, Artie); Poor Mr. Chisholm [1] (C: Hanighen, Bernie); Me and the Ghost Upstairs [2] (C: Hanighen, Bernie); Long Time No See [2] (C: Donaldson, Walter)

**Notes**  Hermes Pan plays the Ghost. [1] Also titled "The Blues Sneaked In Every Time." [2] Not used. [3] Russian lyrics by Gregory Stone.

## 5247 ✦ SECOND FIDDLE
Twentieth Century–Fox, 1939

**Composer(s)**  Berlin, Irving
**Lyricist(s)**  Berlin, Irving
**Choreographer(s)**  Losee, Harry

**Producer(s)**  Zanuck, Darryl F.
**Director(s)**  Lanfield, Sidney
**Screenwriter(s)**  Tugend, Harry

**Cast**  Henie, Sonja; Power, Tyrone; Vallee, Rudy; Oliver, Edna May; Healy, Mary; Talbot, Lyle; Dinehart, Alan; Gombell, Minna; Charters, Spencer; Lane, Charles; The Brian Sisters; Chandler, George; Bacon, Irving

**Song(s)**  An Old Fashioned Tune Is Always New; The Song of the Metronome; Back to Back; When Winter Comes; I Poured My Heart Into a Song; I'm Sorry for Myself

## 5248 ✦ THE SECOND GREATEST SEX
Universal, 1955

**Musical Score**  Mancini, Henry
**Composer(s)**  Moody, Phil
**Lyricist(s)**  Sherrell, Pony
**Choreographer(s)**  Scott, Lee

**Producer(s)**  Cohen, Albert J.
**Director(s)**  Marshall, George
**Screenwriter(s)**  Hoffman, Charles

**Cast**  Nadar, George; Crain, Jeanne [2]; Kallen, Kitty; Lahr, Bert; Gilbert, Paul; Andes, Keith; Van Doren, Mamie; Rall, Tommy; The Midwesterners

**Song(s)**  Lysistrata; What Good Is a Woman (Without a Man); I'm a Travelin' Man; My Love Is Yours; The Second Greatest Sex (1) (C/L: Livingston, Jay; Evans, Ray); Gonna Be a Weddin'; How Lonely Can I Get? (C/L: Whitney, Joan; Kramer, Alex); Send Us a Miracle; On Your Wedding Day [1]; The Second Greatest Sex (2) [1]; What Appeals to a Man [1]; Two Girls (With a Single Thought) [1] (C: Sandes, Stephen; L: Barclift, Nelson); A Lot of Faith and a Little Luck [1] (C: Sandes, Stephen; L: Barclift, Nelson); Marrying Time [1] (C: Sandes, Stephen; L: Barclift, Nelson); Miserable Morning [1] (C: Sandes, Stephen; L: Barclift, Nelson)

**Notes**  [1] Not used. [2] Dubbed by Doreen Tryden.

## 5249 ✦ SECRET CEREMONY
Universal, 1968

**Musical Score**   Bennett, Richard Rodney

**Producer(s)**   Heyman, John; Priggen, Norman
**Director(s)**   Losey, Joseph
**Screenwriter(s)**   Tabori, George
**Source(s)**   "Life en Espanol" (story) Denevi, Marco

**Cast**   Taylor, Elizabeth; Farrow, Mia; Mitchum, Robert; Ashcroft, Peggy; Brown, Pamela

**Song(s)**   Lenora's Song (C: Bennett, Richard Rodney; L: Tabori, George)

## 5250 ✦ THE SECRET DOOR
Allied Artists, 1964

**Musical Score**   Osborne, Tony

**Producer(s)**   Baldour, Charles
**Director(s)**   Kay, Gilbert L.
**Screenwriter(s)**   Martin, Charles
**Source(s)**   "Paper Door" (story) Longstreet, Stephen

**Cast**   Hutton, Robert; Dorne, Sandra; Illing, Peter; Pastell, George; Dyrenforth, James

**Song(s)**   Lisboa (C/L: Baldour, Charles)

**Notes**   No cue sheet available.

## 5251 ✦ SECRET ENEMIES
Warner Brothers, 1942

**Musical Score**   Jackson, Howard

**Producer(s)**   Jacobs, William
**Director(s)**   Stoloff, Benjamin
**Screenwriter(s)**   Schrock, Raymond
**Source(s)**   "Mr. Farrell" (story) Miller, Seton I.

**Cast**   Stevens, Craig; Emerson, Faye; Ridgely, John; Lang, Charles; Warwick, Robert; Reicher, Frank; Williams, Rex; Wilcox, Frank; Meeker, George; Drew, Roland; Richards, Addison; Blue, Monte

**Song(s)**   I'll Keep the Love-Light Burning (C: Levey, Harold; L: Tobias, Harry; Kenny, Nick)

## 5252 ✦ THE SECRET GARDEN
Metro–Goldwyn–Mayer, 1949

**Musical Score**   Kaper, Bronislau

**Producer(s)**   Brown, Clarence
**Director(s)**   Wilcox, Fred M.
**Screenwriter(s)**   Ardrey, Robert
**Source(s)**   The Secret Garden (novel) Burnett, Frances Hodgson

**Cast**   O'Brien, Margaret [1]; Marshall, Herbert; Stockwell, Dean; Cooper, Gladys; Lanchester, Elsa; Roper, Brian; Owen, Reginald

**Song(s)**   Hindu Song of Love [2] (C/L: Mehra, Lal Chand)

**Notes**   [1] Dubbed by Marni Nixon. [2] Also in THE RAINS CAME (20th).

## 5253 ✦ THE SECRET LIFE OF PLANTS
Paramount, 1978

**Musical Score**   Wonder, Stevie
**Composer(s)**   Wonder, Stevie
**Lyricist(s)**   Wonder, Stevie

**Producer(s)**   Braun, Michael
**Director(s)**   Green, Walon
**Screenwriter(s)**   Tompkins, Peter; Green, Walon; Braun, Michael
**Source(s)**   (book) Tompkins, Peter; Bird, Christopher
**Narrator(s)**   Tompkins, Peter; Vreeland, Elizabeth; Crystal, Ruby

**Song(s)**   The Same Old Story; Black Orchid (L: Wright, Yvonne); Outside My Window; The Secret Life of Plants; Come Back As a Flower (L: Wright, Syreeta)

**Notes**   Documentary. No cue sheet available.

## 5254 ✦ THE SECRET LIFE OF WALTER MITTY
Goldwyn, 1947

**Musical Score**   Raksin, David

**Producer(s)**   Goldwyn, Samuel
**Director(s)**   McLeod, Norman Z.
**Screenwriter(s)**   Englund, Ken; Freeman, Everett
**Source(s)**   "The Secret Life of Walter Mitty" (story) Thurber, James

**Cast**   Kaye, Danny; Karloff, Boris; Mayo, Virginia; Karloff, Boris; Bainter, Fay; Rutherford, Ann; Hall, Thurston; Bates, Florence; Jones, Gordon; Shayne, Konstantin; Denny, Reginald; Corden, Henry; Feld, Fritz

**Song(s)**   The Symphony (for Unstrung Tongue) (C/L: Fine, Sylvia); Anatole (C/L: Fine, Sylvia)

## 5255 ✦ SECRET MEETING
United Artists, 1959

**Musical Score**   Yatove, Jean

**Director(s)**   Duvivier, Julien
**Screenwriter(s)**   Robert, Jacques; Jeanson, Henri

**Cast**   Darrieux, Danielle; Blier, Bernard; Reggiand, Serge

**Song(s)**   Premiere Rondez-Vous (C: Sylviano, Rene; L: Poterat, Louis); Seul ce Soir (C: Durand, Paul; L: Grosjean, Rene; Casanova, J.); Le Chant des Partisans (C: Marly, Anna; L: de Druon, R.; Kessel, Joseph)

**Notes**   This French film is better known under the title MARIE-OCTOBRE.

## 5256 ◆ SECRET OF MADAME BLANCHE
Metro–Goldwyn–Mayer, 1933

**Musical Score**   Axt, William

**Director(s)**   Brabin, Charles R.
**Screenwriter(s)**   Goodrich, Frances; Hackett, Albert
**Source(s)**   *The Lady* (play) Brown, Martin

**Cast**   Dunne, Irene; Atwill, Lionel; Holmes, Phillips; Merkel, Una; Walton, Douglas; Parker, Jean

**Song(s)**   If Love Were All (C: Axt, William; L: Wells, M.L.); Oo-La-La-Jimmie (C: Stothart, Herbert; L: Unknown)

**Notes**   There is also a vocal of "But Every Lover Must Meet His Fate" by Victor Herbert.

## 5257 ◆ THE SECRET OF MY SUCCESS (1968)
Metro–Goldwyn–Mayer, 1968

**Musical Score**   Shaw, Roland

**Producer(s)**   Stone, Andrew L.; Stone, Virginia
**Director(s)**   Stone, Andrew L.
**Screenwriter(s)**   Stone, Andrew L.

**Cast**   Jones, Shirley; Booth, James; Stevens, Stella; Blackman, Honor; Jeffries, Lionel; Vernon, Richard

**Song(s)**   Mangerico Verdi (C/L: Laurenco, Joao Baptista); Guandurian (C/L: New, Derek; Stone, Virginia); No Secrets [1] (C/L: New, Derek)

**Notes**   [1] Used instrumentally only.

## 5258 ◆ THE SECRET OF MY SUCCESS (1987)
Universal, 1987

**Producer(s)**   Ross, Herbert
**Director(s)**   Ross, Herbert
**Screenwriter(s)**   Carothers, A.J.

**Cast**   Fox, Michael J.; Slater, Helen; Jordan, Richard; Whitton, Margaret; Pankow, John; Murney, Christopher; Gwynne, Fred; Franz, Elizabeth; Durang, Christopher; Robbins, Rex; Dixon, MacIntyre; Ramirez, Ray

**Song(s)**   The Secret of My Success (C/L: Foster, David; Blades, Jack; Keane, Tom; Landau, Michael); Come Get My Love (C/L: Marcial, Robert); Something I Gotta Do (C/L: Foster, David; Peck, Danny; DuBois, Tim); Heaven and the Heartaches (C/L: Cumming, David Bruce; Nead, Jeff); The Price of Love (C/L: Foster, David; Blades, Jack); Oh Yeah (C/L: Blank, Boris; Meier, Dieter); Walking on Sunshine (C/L: Rew, Kimberly); Heaving and the Heartaches (C/L: Cumming, David Bruce; Nead, Jeff); El Munequito (C/L: Cruz, Francisco); El Cayuco (C/L: Puente, Tito); Feliz Cumbe (C/L: Cruz, Francisco); Riskin' a Romance (C/L: Fahey, Siobhan; Marland, Ollie; Waller, Paul); Oh Yeah (C/L: Blank, Boris; Meier, Dieter); Sometime the

Good Guys Finish First (C/L: Knight, Holly; Benatar, Pat; McDaniels, Khris (Christopher))

**Notes**   It is not known which of these were written for this film.

## 5259 ◆ THE SECRET OF NIMH
United Artists, 1982

**Musical Score**   Goldsmith, Jerry

**Producer(s)**   Bluth, Don; Goldman, Gary; Pomeroy, John
**Director(s)**   Bluth, Don
**Screenwriter(s)**   Finn, Will; Bluth, Don; Goldman, Gary; Pomeroy, John
**Source(s)**   *Mrs. Friday and the Rats of NIMH* (novel) O'Brien, Robert
**Voices**   Jacobi, Derek; Hartmann, Elizabeth; Carradine, John; DeLuise, Dom; Strauss, Peter; Baddeley, Hermione

**Song(s)**   Flying Dreams (C: Goldsmith, Jerry; L: Williams, Paul)

**Notes**   Animated feature.

## 5260 ◆ SECRET OF SANTA VITTORIO
United Artists, 1969

**Musical Score**   Gold, Ernest

**Producer(s)**   Kramer, Stanley
**Director(s)**   Kramer, Stanley
**Screenwriter(s)**   Rose, William; Maddow, Ben
**Source(s)**   *The Secret of Santa Vittorio* (novel) Creighton, Robert

**Cast**   Quinn, Anthony; Magnani, Anna; Lisi, Virna; Kruger, Hardy; Franchi, Sergio; Giannini, Giancarlo

**Song(s)**   Stay (C: Gold, Ernest; L: Gimbel, Norman)

## 5261 ◆ SECRET OF THE BLUE ROOM
Universal, 1933

**Director(s)**   Neumann, Kurt
**Screenwriter(s)**   Hurlbut, William

**Cast**   Lukas, Paul; Stevens, Onslow; Janney, William; Stuart, Gloria; Atwill, Lionel; Barrat, Robert

**Song(s)**   Blue Room Theme (C: Letton, Heinz; L: Marks, Clarence)

**Notes**   Remade as THE MISSING GUEST (1938) and MURDER IN THE BLUE ROOM (1944).

## 5262 ◆ SECRET OF THE INCAS
Paramount, 1954

**Musical Score**   Buttolph, David
**Composer(s)**   Vivanco, Moises
**Lyricist(s)**   Vivanco, Moises

**Producer(s)**  Epstein, Mel
**Director(s)**  Hopper, Jerry
**Screenwriter(s)**  MacDougall, Ranald; Boehm, Sydney

**Cast**  Heston, Charlton; Young, Robert; Maurey, Nicole; Mitchell, Thomas; Farrell, Glenda; Sumac, Yma

**Song(s)**  High Andes; Virgin of the Sun God; Earthquake

## 5263 ✦ THE SECRET OF THE SWORD
### Atlantic, 1985

**Musical Score**  Levy, Shuki; Saban, Haim; Lane, Erika

**Producer(s)**  Nadel, Arthur H.
**Director(s)**  Friedman, Ed; Kachivas, Lou; Lamore, Marsh; Reed, Bill; Wetzler, Gwen
**Screenwriter(s)**  Ditillio, Larry; Forward, Bob

**Cast**  Britt, Melendy; Dicenzo, George; Gary, Linda; Scheimer, Erika

**Song(s)**  I Have the Power (C: Sheimer, Erika; Levy, Shuki; Saban, Haim; L: Scheimer, Erika)

**Notes**  No cue sheet available.

## 5264 ✦ THE SECRET PLACE
### United Artists, 1958

**Musical Score**  Martin, Ray; Jupp, Eric

**Producer(s)**  Bryan, John
**Director(s)**  Donner, Clive
**Screenwriter(s)**  Perry, Linette

**Cast**  Lee, Belinda; McCallum, David; Blake, Anne; Lewis, Ronald; Gwynn, Michael; Selway, George

**Song(s)**  But You (C: Powell, Lester; L: Maule, Danny)

**Notes**  A Rank Organisation film.

## 5265 ✦ SECRET PLACES
### Twentieth Century–Fox, 1985

**Musical Score**  Legrand, Michel

**Producer(s)**  Relph, Simon; Skinner, Ann
**Director(s)**  Barron, Zelda
**Screenwriter(s)**  Barron, Zelda
**Source(s)**  *Secret Places* (novel) Elliott, Janice

**Cast**  Relin, Marie-Theres; Auger, Claudine; Gwatkin, Ann-Marie; Hinchley, Pippa; Agutter, Jenny; Martin, Rosemary

**Song(s)**  Secret Place (C: Legrand, Michel; L: Lerner, Alan Jay)

**Notes**  No cue sheet available.

## 5266 ✦ SECRETS OF THE WASTELANDS
### Paramount, 1941

**Producer(s)**  Sherman, Harry
**Director(s)**  Abrahams, Derwin

**Screenwriter(s)**  Geraghty, Gerald
**Source(s)**  (novel) Lomax, Bliss

**Cast**  Boyd, William; King, Brad; Britton, Barbara

**Song(s)**  I Can't Play the Banjo with Susannah On My Knee [2] (C: Boutelje, Phil; L: Scholl, Jack); Blue Moon on the Silver Sage [1] (C: Stept, Sam H.; L: Freed, Ralph)

**Notes**  [1] Not used but published under this picture's name. [2] Also used in THE TEXAS RANGERS. Considered but not used in RHYTHM ON THE RANGE.

## 5267 ✦ THE SEDUCTION
### Avco Embassy, 1982

**Musical Score**  Schifrin, Lalo

**Producer(s)**  Yablans, Irwin; Curtis, Bruce Cohn
**Director(s)**  Schmoeller, David
**Screenwriter(s)**  Schmoeller, David

**Cast**  Fairchild, Morgan; Sarrazin, Michael; Edwards, Vince; Stevens, Andrew; Camp, Colleen; Brophy, Kevin; Kean, Betty

**Song(s)**  Love's Hiding Place (C: Schifrin, Lalo; L: Grisham, Cliff)

**Notes**  No cue sheet available.

## 5268 ✦ SEE HERE PRIVATE HARGROVE
### Metro–Goldwyn–Mayer, 1944

**Musical Score**  Snell, Dave

**Producer(s)**  Haight, George
**Director(s)**  Ruggles, Wesley
**Screenwriter(s)**  Kurnitz, Harry
**Source(s)**  *See Here Private Hargrove* (book) Hargrove, Marion

**Cast**  Walker, Robert; Reed, Donna; Wynn, Keenan; Benchley, Robert; Collins, Ray; Wills, Chill; Crosby, Bob

**Song(s)**  In My Arms (C: Grouya, Ted; L: Loesser, Frank)

## 5269 ✦ SEE HOW THEY RUN
### RKO

**Musical Score**  Bath, John
**Composer(s)**  Bath, John
**Lyricist(s)**  Miller, Roy

**Song(s)**  I Want a Lover; Dancing with a Dream

**Notes**  No other information available.

## 5270 ✦ SEE MY LAWYER
### Universal, 1944

**Composer(s)**  Rosen, Milton
**Lyricist(s)**  Carter, Everett

**Producer(s)** Hartmann, Edmund L.
**Director(s)** Cline, Edward F.
**Screenwriter(s)** Hartmann, Edmund L.; Davis, Stanley
**Source(s)** *See My Lawyer* (play) Maibaum, Richard; Clork, Harry

**Cast** Olsen, Ole; Johnson, Chic; Pangborn, Franklin; McDonald, Grace; Curtis, Alan; Beery Jr., Noah; Brophy, Edward S.; Benedict, Richard; Patrick, Lee; Schilling, Gus; Amaya, Carmen; The King Cole Trio; The Cristianis Troupe; The Rogers Adagio Trio; The Six Willys; The Hudson Wonders; The Four Teens

**Song(s)** It's Circus Time; The Penny Arcade (C/L: Franklin, Dave); Take It Away; Man on the Little White Keys (C/L: Cole, Nat "King"; Green, Joe); Fuzzy Wuzzy (C/L: Bell, Bob; Branker, Roy); We're Makin' a Million [1]

**Notes** There is also a vocal of "I'll Be Seeing You" by Irving Kahal and Sammy Fain. [1] Also in MEN IN HER DIARY.

## 5271 ✦ THE SELLOUT
### Metro–Goldwyn–Mayer, 1951

**Musical Score** Buttolph, David

**Producer(s)** Nayfack, Nicholas
**Director(s)** Mayer, Gerald
**Screenwriter(s)** Palmer, Charles

**Cast** Pidgeon, Walter; Hodiak, John; Totter, Audrey; Raymond, Paula; Gomez, Thomas; Mitchell, Cameron; Malden, Karl; Sloane, Everett

**Song(s)** You Can't Do Wrong Doin' Right [1] (C/L: Rinker, Al; Huddleston, Floyd)

**Notes** [1] Also in THE AFFAIRS OF DOBIE GILLIS and DUCHESS OF IDAHO.

## 5272 ✦ SEMI-TOUGH
### United Artists, 1977

**Producer(s)** Merrick, David
**Director(s)** Ritchie, Michael
**Screenwriter(s)** Bernstein, Walter
**Source(s)** *Semi-Tough* (novel) Jenkins, Dan

**Cast** Reynolds, Burt; Kristofferson, Kris; Clayburgh, Jill; Convy, Bert

**Song(s)** The Rest of Your Life (C: Legrand, Michel; L: Bergman, Alan; Bergman, Marilyn)

## 5273 ✦ SEND ME NO FLOWERS
### Universal, 1964

**Musical Score** De Vol, Frank

**Producer(s)** Melcher, Martin; Keller, Harry
**Director(s)** Jewison, Norman
**Screenwriter(s)** Epstein, Julius J.

**Source(s)** *Send Me No Flowers* (play) Barasch, Norman; Moore, Carroll

**Cast** Hudson, Rock; Day, Doris; Randall, Tony; Andrews, Edward; Walker, Clint; Lynde, Paul; March, Hal; Barry, Patricia

**Song(s)** Send Me No Flowers (C: Bacharach, Burt; L: David, Hal)

## 5274 ✦ SENIOR PROM
### Columbia, 1958

**Composer(s)** Gohman, Don
**Lyricist(s)** Hackady, Hal

**Producer(s)** Romm, Harry
**Director(s)** Rich, David
**Screenwriter(s)** Hackady, Hal

**Cast** Schwartz, Paul; Melis, Jose; Prima, Louis; Smith, Keely; Sam Butera and the Witnesses [2]; Komack, James; Corey, Jill; Walters, Selene; Boswell, Connee; Miller, Mitch; Crosby, Bob; Arden, Toni; Martin, Freddy; Sullivan, Ed; Elgart, Les; Miller, Marvin

**Song(s)** Put the Blame on Mame [1] (C/L: Roberts, Allan; Fisher, Doris); Now Is the Time (C: Mure, Bill); Best Way to Keep a Man; Ivy Walls; You Know When It's Him; My Heart Will Play the Music; Never Before; The Longer I Love You; One Year Older; Senior Prom; Do You Care (C: Quadling, Lew; L: Elliott, Jack); Big Daddy (C: Pockriss, Lee; L: Udell, Peter)

**Notes** There are also vocals of "Love" by Otis Blackwell; "Let's Fall in Love" by Harold Arlen and Ted Koehler (also in JUKE BOX RHYTHM, LET'S FALL IN LOVE, ON THE SUNNY SIDE OF THE STREET and SLIGHTLY FRENCH), "Torna a Surriento" by E. De Curtis and B.G. De Sylva and "That Old Black Magic" by Harold Arlen and Johnny Mercer (also in the Paramount pictures HERE COME THE WAVES and STAR-SPANGLED RHYTHM and RKO's RADIO STARS ON PARADE). [1] Also in BETTY CO-ED and GILDA. [2] Consisted of Robert James Robert, Louis Marcel Scioneaus, Anthony S. Liuzza, William MacCumber and Paul Furrara.

## 5275 ✦ SENIORS
### Cinema Shares, 1978

**Musical Score** Williams, Patrick
**Composer(s)** Williams, Patrick
**Lyricist(s)** Gimbel, Norman

**Producer(s)** Shapiro, Stanley; De Haven, Carter
**Director(s)** Amateau, Rod
**Screenwriter(s)** Shapiro, Stanley

**Cast** Barnes, Priscilla; Byron, Jeffrey; Imhoff, Gary; Quaid, Dennis; Richards, Lou; Reed, Alan

**Song(s)** Love Is; Sail On

**Notes** No cue sheet available.

## 5276 ✦ SENORITA FROM THE WEST
### Universal, 1945

**Producer(s)** Schwarzwald, Milton
**Director(s)** Strayer, Frank R.
**Screenwriter(s)** Dimsdale, Howard; Grashin, Mauri

**Cast** Granville, Bonita; Jones, Allan; Barker, Jess; Cleveland, George

**Song(s)** Am I in Love? (C/L: Gardens, Jack; Levant, Mark); Those Hazy Lazy Old Hills (C/L: Blackburn, John; Huntley, Leo); What a Change in the Weather [2] (C/L: Gannon, Kim; Kent, Walter); Loo-Loo-Louisiana [1] (C: Rosen, Milton; L: Carter, Everett); Lonely Love (C: Sinatra, Raymond; L: Carter, Everett); All the Things I Wanta Say (C/L: Pepper, Buddy; James, Inez)

**Notes** [1] Also in THE MYSTERY OF THE RIVER BOAT. [2] Also in IN SOCIETY.

## 5277 ✦ SENSATION HUNTERS
### Monogram, 1933

**Composer(s)** Grossman, Bernie
**Lyricist(s)** Lewis, Harold

**Producer(s)** Welsh, Robert
**Director(s)** Vidor, Charles
**Screenwriter(s)** Schofield, Fred

**Cast** Judge, Arline; Foster, Preston; Burns, Marion; Hansen, Juanita; Hale, Creighton; Walker, Nella

**Song(s)** Something in the Air; If It Ain't One Man It's Another

**Notes** No cue sheet available.

## 5278 ✦ SENSATIONS OF 1945
### United Artists, 1944

**Composer(s)** Sherman, Al
**Lyricist(s)** Tobias, Harry
**Choreographer(s)** Lichine, David; O'Curran, Charles

**Producer(s)** Stone, Andrew L.
**Director(s)** Stone, Andrew L.
**Screenwriter(s)** Stone, Andrew L.; Bennett, Dorothy

**Cast** Fields, W.C.; Tucker, Sophie; Cab Calloway and His Band; Woody Herman and His Band; Powell, Eleanor; O'Keefe, Dennis; Pallette, Eugene; Talbot, Lyle; Donegan, Dorothy; The Cristianis; Forsythe, Mimi; Smith, C. Aubrey; The Johnson Brothers; Hall, Mel; The Copelands; Lichine, David; The Pallenberg Bears; The Les Paul Trio; Blake, Marie; Roach, Bert

**Song(s)** Mister Hepster's Dictionary; Wake Up Man You're Slippin'; One Love; Kiss Serenade; No, Never; Spin Little Pin Ball

**Notes** No cue sheet available. There is also a vocal of "You Can't Sew a Button on a Heart."

## 5279 ✦ THE SENTINEL
### Universal, 1977

**Musical Score** Melle, Gil

**Producer(s)** Winner, Michael; Konvitz, Jerry
**Director(s)** Winner, Michael
**Screenwriter(s)** Winner, Michael; Konvitz, Jerry

**Cast** Raines, Cristina; Sarandon, Chris; Balsam, Martin; Carradine, John; Ferrer, Jose; Gardner, Ava; Kennedy, Arthur; Meredith, Burgess; Miles, Sylvia

**Song(s)** Do Your Own Kind of Dance (C: De Jesus, Luchi; L: Balkin, Larry)

## 5280 ✦ SEPARATE BEDS

See THE WHEELER DEALERS.

## 5281 ✦ SEPARATE TABLES
### United Artists, 1958

**Musical Score** Raksin, David

**Producer(s)** Hecht, Harold
**Director(s)** Mann, Delbert
**Screenwriter(s)** Gay, John; Rattigan, Terence
**Source(s)** *Separate Tables* (plays) Rattigan, Terence

**Cast** Lancaster, Burt; Hayworth, Rita; Niven, David; Kerr, Deborah; Hiller, Wendy

**Song(s)** Separate Tables (C: Warren, Harry; L: Adamson, Harold)

## 5282 ✦ SEPTEMBER AFFAIR
### Paramount, 1950

**Producer(s)** Wallis, Hal B.
**Director(s)** Dieterle, William
**Screenwriter(s)** Thoeren, Robert

**Cast** Cotten, Joseph; Fontaine, Joan; Rosay, Francoise; Tandy, Jessica; Arthur, Robert; Bonanova, Fortunio; Demetrio, Anna; Lydon, Jimmy

**Notes** No original songs in this picture. Vocals include: " O Paradiso" by Giacomo Meyerbeer and Augustin-Eugene Scribe; "O Mama Mama", "Santa Lucia" and "September Song" by Kurt Weill and Maxwell Anderson (heard on the soundtrack with Walter Huston singing. Originally written for stage musical KNICKERBOCKER HOLIDAY. Sung also in PEPE.) and "Torna a Surriento" by E. De Curtis (also in Columbia's SENIOR PROM).

## 5283 ✦ SEPTEMBER STORM
### Twentieth Century–Fox, 1960

**Musical Score** Kraushaar, Raoul; Alperson Jr., Edward L.

**Producer(s)** Alperson, Edward L.
**Director(s)** Haskin, Byron
**Screenwriter(s)** Stader, Paul

**Cast** Dru, Joanne; Stevens, Mark; Strauss, Robert; Dann, Asher; Lapena, Ernesto

**Song(s)** Be By You (C: Alperson Jr., Edward L.; L: Winn, Jerry); Passing By [1] (C: Alperson Jr., Edward L.; L: Winn, Jerry)

**Notes** [1] Instrumental use only.

## 5284 ◆ SEQUOIA
### Metro–Goldwyn–Mayer, 1934

**Musical Score** Stothart, Herbert

**Producer(s)** Considine Jr., John W.
**Director(s)** Franklin, Chester M.
**Screenwriter(s)** Cunningham, Ann; Armstrong, Sam; Wilson, Carey
**Source(s)** *Malibu* (novel) Hoyt, Mance

**Cast** Parker, Jean; Hardie, Russell; Hinds, Samuel S.

**Song(s)** Sequoia (C: Stothart, Herbert; L: Kahn, Gus)

**Notes** Hugh Fordin's *The World of Entertainment!* says Arthur Freed and Nacio Herb Brown wrote the theme song to this film.

## 5285 ◆ SERENADE (1939)

See BROADWAY SERENADE.

## 5286 ◆ SERENADE (1956)
### Warner Brothers, 1956

**Composer(s)** Brodszky, Nicholas
**Lyricist(s)** Cahn, Sammy

**Producer(s)** Blanke, Henry
**Director(s)** Mann, Anthony
**Screenwriter(s)** Goff, Ivan; Roberts, Ben; Twist, John
**Source(s)** *Serenade* (novel) Cain, James M.

**Cast** Lanza, Mario; Fontaine, Joan; Montiel, Sarita; Price, Vincent; Calleia, Joseph; Bellaver, Harry; Edwards, Vince; Minciotti, Silvio

**Song(s)** My Destiny; Serenade

**Notes** The following operatic arias are sung in the picture "La Danza" by Rossini; "Torna a Surriento" by Ernesto De Curtis; "O Soave Fanciulla" by Puccini; an aria by Richard Strauss; "Amor Ti Vieta" by Giordano; "Di Quella Pira" by Verdi; "Dio Mi Potevi Scagtliar" by Verdi; "Dio Ti Giocondi O Sposo" by Verdi; "Il Mio Tesoro" by Mozart; "Ave Maria" by Schubert; "O Paradiso" by Meyerbeer; "Il Lamento Federico" by Cilea and "Nessun Dorma" by Puccini.

## 5287 ◆ THE SERGEANT
### Warner Brothers, 1968

**Musical Score** Magne, Michel

**Producer(s)** Goldstone, Richard
**Director(s)** Flynn, John

**Screenwriter(s)** Murphy, Dennis
**Source(s)** *The Sergeant* (novel) Murphy, Dennis

**Cast** Steiger, Rod; Law, John Phillip; Mikael, Ludmila; Latimore, Frank

**Song(s)** Since I Fell for You (C/L: Johnson, Buddy)

## 5288 ◆ SERGEANT DEADHEAD
### American International, 1965

**Composer(s)** Hemric, Guy; Styner, Jerry
**Lyricist(s)** Hemric, Guy; Styner, Jerry
**Choreographer(s)** Baker, Jack

**Producer(s)** Nicholson, James H.; Arkoff, Samuel Z.
**Director(s)** Taurog, Norman
**Screenwriter(s)** Heyward, Louis M.

**Cast** Avalon, Frankie; Walley, Deborah; Clark, Fred; Romero, Cesar; Gordon, Gale; Lembeck, Harvey; Keaton, Buster; Buttram, Pat; Arden, Eve; Gardiner, Reginald; Shaw, Bobbi

**Song(s)** Sergeant Deadhead; The Difference in Me Is You; Let's Play Love; Two-Timin' Angel; How Can You Tell; You Should Have Seen the One that Got Away; Hurry Up and Wait

**Notes** No cue sheet available.

## 5289 ◆ SGT. PEPPER'S LONELY HEARTS CLUB BAND
### Universal, 1978

**Choreographer(s)** Birch, Patricia

**Producer(s)** Stigwood, Robert
**Director(s)** Schultz, Michael
**Screenwriter(s)** Edwards, Henry

**Cast** Frampton, Peter; The Bee Gees [1]; Pleasence, Donald; Channing, Carol; Howerd, Frankie; Nicholas, Paul; Steinberg, Dianne; Cooper, Alice; Farina, Sandy; Stargard; Preston, Billy; Earth, Wind and Fire; Burns, George; Allen, Peter; Bishop, Stephen; Carradine, Keith; Donovan; Feliciano, Jose; Noone, Peter; Reddy, Helen; Rivera, Chita; Rivers, Johnny; Sha-Na-Na; Aerosmith; Shannon, Del; Stevens, Connie

**Notes** There are no original songs written for this picture. Songs by John Lennon and Paul McCartney included "Sgt. Pepper's Lonely Hearts Club Band," "With a Little Help from My Friends," "Fixing a Hole," "Getting Better," "Long and Winding Road," "I Want You (She's So Heavy)," "Goodmorning, Goodmorning," "Nowhere Man," "Polythene Pam," "She Came in Through the Bathroom Window," "Mean Mr. Mustard," "She's Leaving Home," "Lucy in the Sky with Diamonds," "Oh! Darling," "Get Back," "Maxwell's Silver Hammer," "Because," "Strawberry Fields Forever," "Being for the Benefit of Mr. Kite," "When I'm Sixty-four," "You Never Give Me Your Money," "Got to Get You Into My Life," "Come Together," "Golden Slumbers," "Carry That Weight,"

"A Day in the Life" and "Here Comes the Sun" by George Harrison. [1] The Bee Gees consist of Robin, Barry and Morris Gibb.

## 5290 ✦ SERGEANT RUTLEDGE
### Warner Brothers, 1960

**Musical Score**   Jackson, Howard

**Producer(s)**   Goldbeck, Willis; Ford, Patrick
**Director(s)**   Ford, John
**Screenwriter(s)**   Bellah, James Warner; Goldbeck, Willis
**Source(s)**   *Captain Buffalo* (novel) Bellah, James Warner

**Cast**   Hunter, Jeffrey; Towers, Constance; Burke, Billie; Strode, Woody; Hernandez, Juano; Bouchey, Willis

**Song(s)**   Captain Buffalo (C: Livingston, Jerry; L: David, Mack)

## 5291 ✦ SERGEANTS 3
### United Artists, 1962

**Musical Score**   May, Billy

**Producer(s)**   Sinatra, Frank
**Director(s)**   Sturges, John
**Screenwriter(s)**   Burnett, W.R.

**Cast**   Sinatra, Frank; Martin, Dean; Davis Jr., Sammy; Lawford, Peter; Bishop, Joey; Silva, Henry; Lee, Ruta; Lester, Buddy; Crosby, Phillip; Crosby, Dennis; Crosby, Lindsay; Blake, Madge

**Song(s)**   And the Night Wind Sang (C: Rotella, Johnny; L: Steininger, Franz)

**Notes**   No cue sheet available.

## 5292 ✦ SERIAL
### Paramount, 1980

**Musical Score**   Schifrin, Lalo
**Composer(s)**   Schifrin, Lalo
**Lyricist(s)**   Gimbel, Norman

**Producer(s)**   Beckerman, Sidney
**Director(s)**   Persky, Bill
**Screenwriter(s)**   Eustis, Rich; Elias, Michael

**Cast**   Mull, Martin; Weld, Tuesday; Kellerman, Sally; Lee, Christopher; Macy, Bill; Bonerz, Peter; Smothers, Tom

**Song(s)**   A Changing World; It's Got to Feel Good; Mr. Magic [1]

**Notes**   [1] Not on cue sheet.

## 5293 ✦ THE SERPENT'S EGG
### Paramount, 1977

**Musical Score**   Wilhelm, Rolf

**Producer(s)**   De Laurentiis, Dino
**Director(s)**   Bergman, Ingmar
**Screenwriter(s)**   Bergman, Ingmar

**Cast**   Ullmann, Liv; Carradine, David; Frobe, Gert; Bennent, Heinz; Berger, Toni; Whitmore, James

**Song(s)**   Sweet Bon Bons (C/L: Wilhelm, Rolf)

**Notes**   No cue sheet available.

## 5294 ✦ SERPICO
### Paramount, 1973

**Musical Score**   Theodorakis, Mikis

**Producer(s)**   Bregman, Martin
**Director(s)**   Lumet, Sidney
**Screenwriter(s)**   Salt, Waldo; Wexler, Norman
**Source(s)**   *Serpico* (book) Maas, Peter

**Cast**   Pacino, Al

**Song(s)**   Beyond Tomorrow [1] (C: Theodorakis, Mikis; L: Kusik, Larry)

**Notes**   [1] Lyric added for exploitation.

## 5295 ✦ THE SERVANT
### Warner Brothers, 1963

**Musical Score**   Dankworth, John

**Producer(s)**   Losey, James
**Director(s)**   Losey, James
**Screenwriter(s)**   Pinter, Harold
**Source(s)**   *The Servant* (novel) Maugham, Robin

**Cast**   Bogarde, Dirk; Miles, Sarah; Craig, Wendy; Fox, James; Vernon, Richard; Pinter, Harold

**Song(s)**   All Gone (C: Dankworth, John; L: Pinter, Harold)

## 5296 ✦ SESAME STREET PRESENTS FOLLOW THAT BIRD
### Warner Brothers, 1985

**Musical Score**   Parks, Van Dyke; Niehaus, Lennie
**Composer(s)**   Penning, Jeff; Harrington, Jeff; Pippin, Steve
**Lyricist(s)**   Penning, Jeff; Harrington, Jeff; Pippin, Steve

**Producer(s)**   Garnett, Tony
**Director(s)**   Kwapis, Ken
**Screenwriter(s)**   Geiss, Tony; Freudberg, Judy

**Puppeteer(s)**   Spinney, Caroll; Henson, Jim; Oz, Frank
**Cast**   Bernhard, Sandra; Candy, John; Chase, Chevy; Flaherty, Joe; Jennings, Waylon; Thomas, Dave

**Song(s)**   Grouch Anthem; Ain't No Road Too Long; One Little Star (C/L: Moss, Jeff); Easy Goin' Day; Upside Down World (C/L: Moss, Jeff); All Together Now (C/L: Newton, Wood; Noble, Michael); Workin' on My Attitude (C/L: Seals, Troy; Setser, Eddie); I'm So Blue (The Bluebird Song) (C/L: Sharp, Randy; Brooks, Karen)

## 5297 ◆ SEVEN BRIDES FOR SEVEN BROTHERS
Metro–Goldwyn–Mayer, 1954

**Musical Score** Deutsch, Adolph
**Composer(s)** de Paul, Gene
**Lyricist(s)** Mercer, Johnny
**Choreographer(s)** Kidd, Michael

**Producer(s)** Cummings, Jack
**Director(s)** Donen, Stanley
**Screenwriter(s)** Hackett, Albert; Goodrich, Frances; Kingsley, Dorothy
**Source(s)** "The Sobbin' Women" (story) Benet, Stephen Vincent

**Cast** Powell, Jane; Keel, Howard; Richards, Jeff; Tamblyn, Russ; Rall, Tommy; Petrie, Howard; Gibson, Virginia; Wolfe, Ian; Platt, Marc; Mattox, Matt [1]; d'Amboise, Jacques; Newmeyer, Julie; Kilgas, Nancy; Carr, Betty; Kilmonis, Ruta; Doggett, Norma

**Song(s)** Bless Your Beautiful Hide; Wonderful Wonderful Day; When You're in Love; Goin' Co'tin'; Lonesome Polecat; Sobbin' Women; June Bride; Spring, Spring, Spring

**Notes** [1] Dubbed by Bill Lee.

## 5298 ◆ SEVEN CITIES OF GOLD
Twentieth Century–Fox, 1955

**Musical Score** Friedhofer, Hugo

**Producer(s)** Webb, Robert D.; McLean, Barbara
**Director(s)** Webb, Robert D.
**Screenwriter(s)** Breen, Richard L.
**Source(s)** *The Nine Days of Father Serra* (novel) Ziegler, Isabelle Gibson

**Cast** Egan, Richard; Quinn, Anthony; Rennie, Michael; Hunter, Jeffrey; Moreno, Rita; Noriega, Eduardo

**Song(s)** Senorita Carmelita (C/L: Darby, Ken)

## 5299 ◆ SEVEN DAYS ASHORE
RKO, 1944

**Composer(s)** Pollack, Lew
**Lyricist(s)** Greene, Mort
**Choreographer(s)** O'Curran, Charles

**Producer(s)** Auer, John H.
**Director(s)** Auer, John H.
**Screenwriter(s)** Verdier, Edward; Phillips, Irving; Kimble, Lawrence

**Cast** Brown, Wally; Carney, Alan; McGuire, Marcy; Wilson, Dooley; Oliver, Gordon; Mayo, Virginia; Ward, Amelita; Shepard, Elaine; Gateson, Marjorie; Dinehart, Alan; Dumont, Margaret; Freddie Slack and His Orchestra; Freddie Fisher and His Band

**Song(s)** Apple Blossoms in the Rain; Ready, Aim, Kiss; Hail and Farewell; Sioux City Sue; Jive Samba [1]; Poor

Little Fly on the Wall [3] (C/L: Fisher, Fred); Improvisation in B Flat [2] (C/L: Fisher, Fred)

**Notes** [1] Based on "Over the Waves" by J. Rosas. [2] Cited in credits but not on cue sheet or in script. [3] Also in MAKE MINE LAUGHS.

## 5300 ◆ SEVEN DAYS LEAVE (1930)
Paramount, 1930

**Composer(s)** Terry, Frank
**Lyricist(s)** Terry, Frank

**Producer(s)** Lighton, Louis D.
**Director(s)** Wallace, Richard
**Screenwriter(s)** Totheroh, Dan; Farrow, John

**Cast** Cooper, Gary; Mercer, Beryl; Belmore, Daisy; Cecil, Nora; Piggott, Tempe

**Song(s)** Mother You're the Greatest of Them All; A Lily; Mrs. McGill Is Very Ill [1] (C: Traditional; L: Farrow, John; Totheroh, Dan); Percy's Going to War [2]; That's What We're Fighting For [2]

**Notes** First titled MEDALS, the title under which it was released in Great Britain. *The Film Daily Yearbook* credits John Cromwell as codirector. [1] To the tune of "Yankee Doodle." [2] Not used.

## 5301 ◆ SEVEN DAYS LEAVE (1942)
RKO, 1942

**Musical Score** Webb, Roy
**Composer(s)** McHugh, Jimmy
**Lyricist(s)** Loesser, Frank

**Producer(s)** Whelan, Tim
**Director(s)** Whelan, Tim
**Screenwriter(s)** Bowers, William; Spence, Ralph; Kenyon, Curtis; Earl, Kenneth

**Cast** Mature, Victor; Ball, Lucille; Peary, Harold; Cortes, Mary; Simms, Ginny; Freddy Martin and His Orchestra; Les Brown and His Orchestra; McGuire, Marcy; Stang, Arnold; Lynn, Royce & Vanya; Edwards, Ralph; Hayes, Peter Lind; Reed, Walter; Clark, Buddy; Ford, Wallace; Richards, Addison

**Song(s)** Please Won't You Leave My Girl Alone [3]; Touch of Texas [4]; I Get the Neck of the Chicken; Can't Get Out of This Mood [2]; Puerto Rico [1]; You Speak My Language; Baby [5]; Soft Hearted [6]

**Notes** [1] Added for foreign prints only. [2] Also in RADIO STARS ON PARADE. [3] Also in HEAVENLY DAYS. [4] Also in GILDERSLEEVE ON BROADWAY and MOON OVER LAS VEGAS (Universal). [5] Not used. [6] Sheet music only.

## 5302 ◆ SEVEN HILLS OF ROME
Metro–Goldwyn–Mayer, 1958

**Musical Score** Stoll, George
**Composer(s)** Rascel, Renato

**Lyricist(s)**   Rascel, Renato
**Choreographer(s)**   Steffen, Paul

**Producer(s)**   Welch, Lester
**Director(s)**   Rowland, Roy
**Screenwriter(s)**   Cohn, Art; Prosperi, Giorgio

**Cast**   Lanza, Mario; Rascel, Renato; Allasio, Marisa; Castle, Peggie; Matania, Cielia; Rizzo, Carlo

**Song(s)**   There's Gonna Be a Party Tonight (C/L: Stoll, George); Come Dance with Me (C: Liebert, Dick; L: Blake, George); Goodbye My Friends Goodbye (Goodbye to Rome) [1] (L: Sigman, Carl; Rascel, Renato); Venticello Di Roma; L'Ostricaro Innamorato (L: Nisa); Vogliamoci Tanto Bene; Sotto Gli Archi del Colosseo (C: Taccani; L: Bertini); Stornellata Sentimentale (C/L: Bissi); Te Voglio Bene Tanto Tanto; Arrevederci, Roma (L: Garinei, Enzo; Giovannini); Lolita (C/L: Buzzi; Peccia); Canzone Pe' Fa' L'Amore; Jezebel (C/L: Shanklin, Wayne); Memories Are Made of This (C/L: Gilkyson, Terry; Dehr, Richard; Miller, Frank); Ay, Ay, Ay (C/L: Freire, Osman Perez); The Loveliest Night of the Year (C: Traditional; L: Webster, Paul Francis); The Seven Hills of Rome (C: Young, Victor; L: Adamson, Harold); Venticello di Roma; When the Saints Go Marching In [2] (C: Stoll, George; L: Nelson, David)

**Notes**   It is not known if all these were written for this film. [1] Sigman's lyrics not used in film. [2] Sheet music only.

## 5303 ✦ SEVEN INTO SNOWY
### West Coast Films, 1978

**Producer(s)**   Williams, Allen; Freeman, Davis
**Director(s)**   Shepherd, Antonio
**Screenwriter(s)**   Shepherd, Antonio

**Cast**   Clayton, Abigail; Parker, Kay; Thomas, Paul; Kushman, Karen; Holiday, Bonnie

**Song(s)**   Once Upon a Time Dream (C/L: Shepherd, Antonio)

**Notes**   No cue sheet available.

## 5304 ✦ THE SEVEN LITTLE FOYS
### Paramount, 1955

**Choreographer(s)**   Castle, Nick

**Producer(s)**   Rose, Jack
**Director(s)**   Shavelson, Melville
**Screenwriter(s)**   Shavelson, Melville; Rose, Jack

**Cast**   Hope, Bob; Cagney, James; Vitale, Milly [1]; Tobias, George; Clarke, Angela; Heyes, Herbert; Foy Jr., Eddie

**Song(s)**   I'm the Greatest Father of Them All (C/L: Jerome, William; Foy, Eddie; Lilley, Joseph J.); You're Here My Love [1] (C: Lilley, Joseph J.; L: Burke, Johnny)

**Notes**   [1] Used instrumentally only. The songs also include "Mary's a Grand Old Name" and "Yankee Doodle Boy" by George M. Cohan; "Row Row Row" by William Jerome and James V. Monaco; "Chinatown My Chinatown" and "I'm Tired" by William Jerome and Jean Schwartz and "Nobody" by Bert Williams and Alex Rogers. There Is also a comedy ballet by Joseph Lilley. [1] Dubbed by Viola Vonn.

## 5305 ✦ SEVEN MEN FROM NOW
### Warner Brothers, 1956

**Musical Score**   Vars, Henry
**Composer(s)**   Vars, Henry
**Lyricist(s)**   Dunham, "By"

**Producer(s)**   McLaglen, Andrew V.; Morrison, Robert E.
**Director(s)**   Boetticher, Budd
**Screenwriter(s)**   Kennedy, Burt

**Cast**   Scott, Randolph; Russell, Gail; Cast, Lee; Reed, Walter; Whitman, Stuart; Larch, John; Barry, Donald

**Song(s)**   Seven Men; Good Love

## 5306 ✦ THE SEVEN MINUTES
### Twentieth Century–Fox, 1971

**Musical Score**   Phillips, Stu
**Composer(s)**   Phillips, Stu
**Lyricist(s)**   Stone, Bob

**Producer(s)**   Meyer, Russ
**Director(s)**   Meyer, Russ
**Screenwriter(s)**   Lewis, Richard Warren
**Source(s)**   (novel) Wallace, Irving

**Cast**   Maunder, Wayne; McAndrew, Marianne; De Carlo, Yvonne; Carey, Philip; Flippen, Jay C.; Williams, Edy; Bettger, Lyle; Gayle, Jackie; Carradine, John; Randell, Ron

**Song(s)**   Love Train; Midnight Tricks; Seven Minutes

## 5307 ✦ SEVEN MINUTES IN HEAVEN
### Warner Brothers, 1986

**Musical Score**   Kraft, Robert
**Composer(s)**   Kraft, Robert
**Lyricist(s)**   Kraft, Robert

**Producer(s)**   Roos, Fred
**Director(s)**   Feferman, Linda
**Screenwriter(s)**   Bernstein, Jane; Feferman, Linda

**Cast**   Connelly, Jennifer; Thames, Byron; Draper, Polly; Corman, Maddie; Boyce, Alan; Zaslow, Michael; Gray, Spalding; Dillon, Denny

**Song(s)**   Little Boy Sweet [1] (C: Ivers, Peter; L: Golde, Franne); Two Friends; Fifteen; Inner Logic (L: Golde, Franne; Midler, Bette); Ready or Not; Dear You

**Notes**  Movie also known as SURPRISES. [1] Also in NATIONAL LAMPOON'S VACATION.

## 5308 ◆ THE SEVEN PER-CENT SOLUTION
### Universal, 1976

**Musical Score**  Addison, John

**Producer(s)**  Ross, Herbert
**Director(s)**  Ross, Herbert
**Screenwriter(s)**  Meyer, Nicholas
**Source(s)**  *The Seven Per-Cent Solution* (novel) Meyer, Nicholas

**Cast**  Williamson, Nicol; Duvall, Robert; Arkin, Alan; Olivier, Laurence; Redgrave, Vanessa; Grey, Joel; Eggar, Samantha; Kemp, Jeremy; Gray, Charles; Brown, Georgia; Quayle, Anna; Townsend, Jill; Bird, John

**Song(s)**  I Never Do Anything Twice (C/L: Sondheim, Stephen)

## 5309 ◆ SEVEN SEAS TO CALAIS
### Metro–Goldwyn–Mayer, 1963

**Musical Score**  Mannino, Franco

**Producer(s)**  Moffa, Paolo
**Director(s)**  Mate, Rudolph
**Screenwriter(s)**  Sanjust, Filippo; St. George, George; Galloway, Lindsay

**Cast**  Taylor, Rod; Michell, Keith; Vessel, Hedy; Girotti, Mario; Dignam, Basil; Worth, Irene

**Song(s)**  Apaga La Luz (C/L: Mannino, Franco)

## 5310 ◆ SEVEN SINNERS
### Universal, 1940

**Musical Score**  Skinner, Frank
**Composer(s)**  Hollander, Frederick
**Lyricist(s)**  Loesser, Frank

**Producer(s)**  Pasternak, Joe
**Director(s)**  Garnett, Tay
**Screenwriter(s)**  Meehan, John; Tugend, Harry

**Cast**  Dietrich, Marlene; Wayne, John; Crawford, Broderick; Auer, Mischa; Dekker, Albert; Gilbert, Billy; Homolka, Oscar; Hinds, Samuel S.; Carle, Richard; Denny, Reginald

**Song(s)**  The Man's in the Navy; Egga Dagga [2] (C/L: Cochrane, Nick C.); I've Been in Love Before; I Fell Overboard [1]

**Notes**  There is also a vocal of "I Can't Give You Anything But Love, Baby" by Dorothy Fields and Jimmy McHugh. [1] Used instrumentally only. [2] Also in MGM's HOLLYWOOD PARTY IN TECHNICOLOR, where it is credited to Jean Bouquet and Dorcas Cochrane, and in Fox's HOLY TERROR and Republic's HERE COMES ELMER, where it is credited as above.

## 5311 ◆ THE SEVEN SWEETHEARTS
### Metro–Goldwyn–Mayer, 1942

**Musical Score**  Waxman, Franz
**Choreographer(s)**  Matray, Ernst

**Producer(s)**  Pasternak, Joe
**Director(s)**  Borzage, Frank
**Screenwriter(s)**  Reisch, Walter; Townsend, Leo

**Cast**  Grayson, Kathryn; Hunt, Marsha; Parker, Cecilia; Morris, Dorothy; Moran, Peggy; Rafferty, Frances; Raeburn, Frances; Heflin, Van; Esmond, Carl; Butler, Michael; Danielson, Cliff; Roberts, William; Warren, James; Simmons, Dick; Sakall, S.Z.; Lewis, Diana; Howard, Lewis; Elsom, Isobel; Meek, Donald; Beavers, Louise

**Song(s)**  Tulip Time (C: Lane, Burton; L: Freed, Ralph); Dreamer's Lullaby (C: Mozart; L: Freed, Ralph); Cradle Song (C: Mozart; L: Freed, Ralph; Brent, Earl); You and the Waltz and I (C: Jurmann, Walter; L: Webster, Paul Francis); Little Tingle Tangle Toes (C: Jurmann, Walter; L: Webster, Paul Francis)

**Notes**  There are also vocals of "Je Suis Titania" from MIGNON by Thomas, Carre and Barbier and "New Prayer of Thanksgiving" by Valerius.

## 5312 ◆ SEVENTEEN
### Paramount, 1940

**Lyricist(s)**  Loesser, Frank

**Producer(s)**  Walker, Stuart
**Director(s)**  King, Louis
**Screenwriter(s)**  Johnston, Agnes Christine; Palmer, Stuart
**Source(s)**  "Seventeen" (story) Tarkington, Booth; *Seventeen* (play) Walker, Stuart; Stange, Stanislaus; Mears, Stannard

**Cast**  Cooper, Jackie; Field, Betty; Kruger, Otto

**Song(s)**  The Lady's In Love with You [1] (C: Lane, Burton); Seventeen (C: Loesser, Frank)

**Notes**  [1] Also in SOME LIKE IT HOT.

## 5313 ◆ 1776
### Columbia, 1972

**Composer(s)**  Edwards, Sherman
**Lyricist(s)**  Edwards, Sherman
**Choreographer(s)**  White, Onna

**Producer(s)**  Warner, Jack L.
**Director(s)**  Hunt, Peter
**Screenwriter(s)**  Stone, Peter
**Source(s)**  *1776* (musical) Edwards, Sherman; Stone, Peter

**Cast**  Daniels, William [1]; Da Silva, Howard [1]; Howard, Ken [1]; Madden, Donald; Danner, Blythe; Cullum, John; Poole, Roy [1]; Ford, David [1]; Vestoff,

Virginia [1]; Nathan, Stephen; Bass, Emory [1]; Middleton, Ray; Leyden, Leo; Hines, Patrick [1]; Rule, Charles [1]; Holgate, Ron [1]; Robbins, Rex

**Song(s)**   Sit Down, John; Piddle, Twiddle and Resolve; Till Then; The Lees of Old Virginia; But, Mister Adams; Yours, Yours, Yours!; He Plays the Violin; Mama, Look Sharp; The Egg; Molasses to Rum; Compliments; Is Anybody There; Cool, Cool, Considerate Men [2]

**Notes**   All songs are from the Broadway musical. [2] Recorded but used instrumentally only. [1] Repeating Broadway role.

### 5314   ✦   70,000 WITNESSES
Paramount, 1932

**Composer(s)**   Lewis, Harold
**Lyricist(s)**   Murphy, Ralph

**Director(s)**   Murphy, Ralph
**Screenwriter(s)**   Fort, Garrett; Wolfson, P.J.; Rivkin, Allen
**Source(s)**   (novel) Fitzsimmons, Cortland

**Cast**   Holmes, Phillips; Jordan, Dorothy; Ruggles, Charles; Brown, Johnny Mack

**Song(s)**   State Song; University Song

### 5315   ✦   SEX AND THE SINGLE GIRL
Warner Brothers, 1964

**Musical Score**   Hefti, Neal

**Producer(s)**   Orr, William T.
**Director(s)**   Quine, Richard
**Screenwriter(s)**   Heller, Joseph; Schwartz, David R.
**Source(s)**   "How to Make Love and Like It" (story) Hoffman, Joseph

**Cast**   Curtis, Tony; Wood, Natalie; Fonda, Henry; Bacall, Lauren; Ferrer, Mel; Jeffries, Fran; Parrish, Leslie; Horton, Edward Everett; Storch, Larry; Kaye, Stubby; St. John, Howard; Kruger Otto; Showalter, Max; Count Basie and His Orchestra

**Song(s)**   Sex and the Single Girl (C/L: Quine, Richard)

**Notes**   "The Anniversary Song" by Al Jolson and Saul Chaplin and "What Is This Thing Called Love" by Cole Porter are also given visual vocal uses.

### 5316   ✦   SEX SHOP
United Artists, 1972

**Musical Score**   Gainsbourg, Serge; Vannier, Jean Claude

**Producer(s)**   Berri, Claude
**Director(s)**   Berri, Claude
**Screenwriter(s)**   Berri, Claude

**Cast**   Berri, Claude; Marielle, Jean-Pierre; Berto, Juliet; Delon, Nathalie

**Song(s)**   La Decadence (C: Gainsbourg, Serge; Vannier, Jean Claude; L: Gainsbourg, Serge)

### 5317   ✦   SHADOW OF A DOUBT (1943)
Universal, 1943

**Musical Score**   Tiomkin, Dimitri

**Producer(s)**   Skirball, Jack H.
**Director(s)**   Hitchcock, Alfred
**Screenwriter(s)**   Wilder, Thornton; Benson, Sally; Reville, Alma

**Cast**   Cotten, Joseph; Wright, Teresa; Carey, Macdonald; Ford, Wallace; Cronyn, Hume; Collinge, Patricia; Travers, Henry; Bacon, Irving; Muse, Clarence

**Song(s)**   Shadow of a Doubt [1] (C: Miller, Harry; L: Reed, Bob)

**Notes**   Remade as STEP DOWN TO TERROR (1959). [1] Used instrumentally only.

### 5318   ✦   SHADOW OF DOUBT (1935)
Metro–Goldwyn–Mayer, 1935

**Musical Score**   Radin, Oscar

**Producer(s)**   Hubbard, Lucien
**Director(s)**   Seitz, George B.
**Screenwriter(s)**   Root, Wells

**Cast**   Cortez, Ricardo; Bruce, Virginia; Collier, Constance; Jewell, Isabel; Byron, Arthur; Furness, Betty; Toomey, Regis

**Song(s)**   Beyond the Shadow of a Doubt (C: Lane, Burton; L: Adamson, Harold)

**Notes**   Originally titled BEYOND THE SHADOW OF A DOUBT.

### 5319   ✦   SHADOW OF GLORY
Paramount, 1936 unproduced

**Composer(s)**   Coslow, Sam
**Lyricist(s)**   Coslow, Sam

**Song(s)**   The Chance of a Life Time; Every Day's a Holiday [1]; My Mistake [2]

**Notes**   [1] Used in EVERY DAY'S A HOLIDAY (1937) with additional lyric credit for Barry Trivers. [2] Not used in THRILL OF A LIFETIME.

### 5320   ✦   SHADOW OF THE THIN MAN
Metro–Goldwyn–Mayer, 1941

**Musical Score**   Snell, Dave

**Producer(s)**   Stromberg, Hunt
**Director(s)**   Van Dyke II, W.S.
**Screenwriter(s)**   Brecher, Irving; Kurnitz, Harry
**Source(s)**   characters by Hammett, Dashiell

Cast   Asta; Powell, William; Loy, Myrna; Nelson, Barry; Levene, Sam; O'Neill, Henry; Adler, Stella; Reed, Donna; Baxter, Alan; Hall, Dickie

Song(s)   The Girl Who's Going Places (C: Snell, Dave; L: Unknown)

Notes   The song only lasts 30 seconds.

## 5321 ◆ SHADOWS
### Lion Int., 1961

Musical Score   Mingus, Charles

Producer(s)   McEndree, Maurice
Director(s)   Cassavetes, John

Cast   Hurd, Hugh; Goldoni, Lelia; Carruthers, Ben; Ray, Anthony

Song(s)   Beautiful (C/L: Ackerman, Jack; Stevens, Hunt; Winters, Eleanor)

Notes   No cue sheet available. Improvised drama.

## 5322 ◆ SHADOWS OF TOMBSTONE
### Republic, 1953

Producer(s)   Ralston, Rudy
Director(s)   Witney, William
Screenwriter(s)   Geraghty, Gerald

Cast   Allen, Rex; Koko; Pickens, Slim; Cooper, Jeanne; Barcroft, Roy; Roman, Ric

Song(s)   Toolie Rollum [1] (C/L: Allen, Rex)

Notes   [1] Also in UTAH WAGON TRAIN, SILVER CITY BONANZA, THE ARIZONA COWBOY and RODEO KING AND THE SENORITA.

## 5323 ◆ SHADOWS ON THE SAGE
### Republic, 1942

Producer(s)   Gray, Louis
Director(s)   Orlebeck, Lester
Screenwriter(s)   Cheney, J. Benton
Source(s)   characters by MacDonald, William Colt

Cast   Steele, Bob; Tyler, Tom; Dodd, Jimmy; Walker, Cheryl; Barnett, Griff; Canutt, Yakima

Song(s)   Cowboy Voice Lesson (C/L: Dodd, Jimmy); Happy Cowboy (C/L: Dodd, Jimmy)

## 5324 ◆ SHADY LADY
### Universal, 1945

Choreographer(s)   Horton, Lester

Producer(s)   Waggner, George
Director(s)   Waggner, George
Screenwriter(s)   Siodmak, Curt; Geraghty, Gerald; Musselman, M.M.; Collins, Monty

Cast   Coburn, Charles; Simms, Ginny; Paige, Robert; Curtis, Alan

Song(s)   In Love with Love (C: Rosen, Milton; L: Waggner, George); Dusty Trail [1] (C/L: Sheely, Betty; Sheely, C. Whitney; List, Bud); Xango (C: Fairchild, Edgar; L: Waggner, George)

Notes   There is also a vocal of "Cuddle Up a Little Closer" by Otto Harbach and Karl Hoschna. [1] Also in BEYOND THE PECOS.

## 5325 ◆ SHAFT
### Metro–Goldwyn–Mayer, 1971

Musical Score   Hayes, Isaac
Composer(s)   Hayes, Isaac
Lyricist(s)   Hayes, Isaac

Producer(s)   Silliphant, Stirling; Lewis, Roger
Director(s)   Parks, Gordon
Screenwriter(s)   Tidyman, Ernest; Black, John D.F.
Source(s)   characters by Tidyman, Ernest

Cast   Roundtree, Richard; Gunn, Moses; Cioffi, Charles; St. John, Christopher; Mitchell, Gwenn; Pressman, Lawrence

Song(s)   Shaft; Soulsville; I Can't Get Over Losin' You; Do Your Thang

## 5326 ◆ SHAFT IN AFRICA
### Metro–Goldwyn–Mayer, 1973

Musical Score   Pate, Johnny

Producer(s)   Lewis, Roger
Director(s)   Guillermin, John
Screenwriter(s)   Silliphant, Stirling
Source(s)   characters by Tidyman, Ernest

Cast   Roundtree, Richard; Finlay, Frank; McGee, Vonetta; Arneric, Neda

Song(s)   Are You Man Enough? (C/L: Lambert, Dennis; Potter, Brian)

## 5327 ◆ SHAFT'S BIG SCORE
### Metro–Goldwyn–Mayer, 1972

Musical Score   Parks, Gordon
Composer(s)   Parks, Gordon
Lyricist(s)   Parks, Gordon

Producer(s)   Lewis, Roger; Tidyman, Ernest
Director(s)   Parks, Gordon
Screenwriter(s)   Tidyman, Ernest
Source(s)   characters by Tidyman, Ernest

Cast   Roundtree, Richard; Gunn, Moses; Mascolo, Joseph; Imrie, Kathy; Taylor, Wally; Harris, Julius W.; Brown, Drew Bundini

Song(s)   Blowin' Your Mind; Ev'ry Night When the Moon Comes Up; Move On In; Don't Misunderstand

Notes   There is also a vocal of "Type Thang" by Isaac Hayes.

## 5328 ✦ THE SHAGGY D.A.
Disney, 1976

**Musical Score** Baker, Buddy
**Composer(s)** Tatum, Shane; McKinley, Richard
**Lyricist(s)** Tatum, Shane; McKinley, Richard

**Producer(s)** Anderson, Bill
**Director(s)** Stevenson, Robert
**Screenwriter(s)** Tait, Don
**Source(s)** *The Hound of Florence* (novel) Salten, Felix

**Cast** Jones, Dean; Conway, Tim; Pleshette, Suzanne; Wynn, Keenan; Worley, Jo Anne; Van Patten, Dick; Tayback, Vic; Myhers, John; Bakalyan, Richard [1]; Berlinger, Warren; Schell, Ronnie; Daly, Jonathan; Fiedler, John; Conried, Hans; Gillette, Ruth; Adrian, Iris

**Song(s)** The Daisy Anthem; The Shaggy D.A.

**Notes** [1] Billed as Dick Bakalyan.

## 5329 ✦ THE SHAGGY DOG
Disney, 1959

**Musical Score** Smith, Paul J.

**Producer(s)** Walsh, Bill
**Director(s)** Barton, Charles
**Screenwriter(s)** Walsh, Bill; Hayward, Lillie
**Source(s)** *The Hound of Florence* (novel) Salten, Felix

**Cast** MacMurray, Fred; Hagen, Jean; Kirk, Tommy; Funicello, Annette; Considine, Tim; Corcoran, Kevin; Kellaway, Cecil; Scourby, Alexander; Shore, Roberta; Martin, Strother; Aubuchon, Jacques

**Song(s)** The Shaggy Dog (C: Smith, Paul J.; L: George, Gil)

## 5330 ✦ SHAKEDOWN
Universal, 1988

**Musical Score** Elias, Jonathan

**Producer(s)** Harman Jr., J. Boyce
**Director(s)** Glickenhaus, James
**Screenwriter(s)** Glickenhaus, James

**Cast** Weller, Peter; Elliott, Sam; Charbonneau, Patricia; Fargas, Antonio; Prince, William; Brooks, Richard; Waits, Tom; Baker, Blanche

**Song(s)** Reggae Reverie (C/L: McKeever, Dow; Soucek, Paul); Bizarre Obsession (C: Elias, Jonathan; L: Bennett, Jerry); Reality Rap (C/L: McKeever, Dow); Looking for Love (C: Elias, Jonathan; L: Waite, John)

## 5331 ✦ THE SHAKIEST GUN IN THE WEST
Universal, 1968

**Musical Score** Mizzy, Vic

**Producer(s)** Montagne, Edward J.
**Director(s)** Rafkin, Alan
**Screenwriter(s)** Fritzell, Jim; Greenbaum, Everett

**Cast** Knotts, Don; Rhoades, Barbara; Coogan, Jackie; Barry, Donald; McGrath, Frank; Ballantine, Carl

**Song(s)** Shakiest Gun in the West (C: Blume, Dave; L: Keller, Jerry)

**Notes** A remake of THE PALEFACE (1948).

## 5332 ✦ SHALL WE DANCE
RKO, 1937

**Composer(s)** Gershwin, George
**Lyricist(s)** Gershwin, Ira
**Choreographer(s)** Pan, Hermes; Losee, Harry [1]

**Producer(s)** Berman, Pandro S.
**Director(s)** Sandrich, Mark
**Screenwriter(s)** Scott, Allan; Pagano, Ernest

**Cast** Astaire, Fred; Rogers, Ginger; Horton, Edward Everett; Blore, Eric; Cowan, Jerome; Gallian, Ketti; Brisbane, William; Hoctor, Harriet

**Song(s)** Slap That Bass; I've Got Beginner's Luck; They All Laughed; Let's Call the Whole Thing Off; They Can't Take That Away from Me; Hoctor's Ballet (Inst.); Shall We Dance; Walking the Dog (Promenade) (inst.); Hi-Ho at Last [2]; Wake Up, Brother, and Dance [2]

**Notes** [1] Losee choreographed the ballet. [2] Not used.

## 5333 ✦ SHAMPOO
Columbia, 1975

**Musical Score** Simon, Paul
**Composer(s)** Goffin, Gerry; King, Carole
**Lyricist(s)** Goffin, Gerry; King, Carole

**Producer(s)** Beatty, Warren
**Director(s)** Ashby, Hal
**Screenwriter(s)** Beatty, Warren; Towne, Robert

**Cast** Beatty, Warren; Christie, Julie; Hawn, Goldie; Grant, Lee; Warden, Jack; Bill, Tony; Fisher, Carrie

**Song(s)** I'm a Believer (C/L: Diamond, Neil); It Might As Well Rain Until September [2]; Hey Girl; Don't Say Nothin' Bad (About My Baby) [1]

**Notes** [1] Also in THE BEST OF TIMES (Universal). [2] Also in STARDUST.

## 5334 ✦ SHAMROCK HILL
Eagle Lion, 1948

**Musical Score** Gilbert, Herschel Burke
**Composer(s)** Bilder, Robert
**Lyricist(s)** Bilder, Robert

**Producer(s)** Levinson, Joseph
**Director(s)** Dreifuss, Arthur
**Screenwriter(s)** Hoerl, Arthur; Moore, McElbert

**Cast** Ryan, Peggy; McDonald, Ray; Marshall, Trudy; Vallin, Rick; Litel, John

**Song(s)** A Fine Fine Day; Do You Believe; Troubles to Bed; Leprechaun Song; Madcap Mood

## 5335 ✦ SHANE
Paramount, 1953

**Musical Score** Young, Victor
**Composer(s)** Young, Victor

**Producer(s)** Stevens, George
**Director(s)** Stevens, George
**Screenwriter(s)** Guthrie Jr., A.B.
**Source(s)** *Shane* (novel) Schaefer, Jack

**Cast** Ladd, Alan; Arthur, Jean; Heflin, Van; Cook Jr., Elisha; Palance, Jack; Johnson, Ben; Buchanan, Edgar; de Wilde, Brandon

**Song(s)** The Call of the Far-Away Hills [1] (L: David, Mack); Eyes of Blue [2] (L: Stone, Wilson)

**Notes** [1] Used instrumentally only. The song was originally called "Alone on the Lonesome Trail" with a lyric by Jack Lawrence. But Lawrence refused Paramount's contract and the lyric was returned to him. There is a copy of the original song at Paramount. [2] Used instrumentally only.

## 5336 ✦ SHANGHAI LADY
Universal, 1929

**Director(s)** Robertson, John
**Screenwriter(s)** Branch, Houston; Reeve, Winifred
**Source(s)** *Drifting* (play) Colton, John; Andrews, Daisy H.

**Cast** Nolan, Mary; Murray, James; Titus, Lydia Yeamans; Oakman, Wheeler

**Song(s)** I Wonder If It's Really Love (C: Sizemore, Arthur; L: Grossman, Bernie)

**Notes** No cue sheet available.

## 5337 ✦ SHANGHAI SURPRISE
MGM/UA, 1986

**Musical Score** Kamen, Michael
**Composer(s)** Harrison, George
**Lyricist(s)** Harrison, George

**Producer(s)** Kohn, John
**Director(s)** Goddard, Jim
**Screenwriter(s)** Kohn, John; Bentley, Robert
**Source(s)** *Faraday's Flowers* (novel) Kenrick, Tony

**Cast** Penn, Sean; Madonna; Freeman, Paul; Griffiths, Richard; Sayer, Philip; Harrison, George

**Song(s)** Shanghai Surprise; Hottest Gong in Town; Boat to China Doll; China Doll; Someplace Else; Zig Zag [1]; Breath Away from Heaven [2]

**Notes** [1] Used instrumentally only. [2] Listed in *Academy Guide* but not on cue sheets.

## 5338 ✦ THE SHANNONS OF BROADWAY
Universal, 1929

**Director(s)** Flynn, Emmett J.
**Screenwriter(s)** Gleason, James
**Source(s)** *The Shannons of Broadway* (play) Gleason, James

**Cast** Gleason, James; Gleason, Lucille [1]; Philbin, Mary; Breeden, John; Santschi, Tom; Tyler, Harry; Crolius, Gladys; Summerville, Slim; Brennan, Walter; Kennedy, Tom; Grapewin, Charley

**Song(s)** Somebody to Love Me (C: Greer, Jesse; L: Klages, Raymond); Get Happy (C: Greer, Jesse; Klages, Raymond)

**Notes** No cue sheet available. [1] Billed as Lucille Webster Gleason.

## 5339 ✦ SHANTYTOWN
Republic, 1943

**Composer(s)** Styne, Jule

**Producer(s)** Grey, Harry
**Director(s)** Santley, Joseph
**Screenwriter(s)** Cooper, Olive
**Source(s)** *To Helen* (play) Moritz, Henry

**Cast** Lee, Mary; Archer, John; Lord, Marjorie; Hamilton, J. Frank; Davenport, Harry; Matty Malneck and His Orchestra; Gilbert, Billy; Switzer, Carl "Alfalfa"; Nazarro, Cliff

**Song(s)** On the Corner of Sunshine and Main (L: Gannon, Kim); I've Heard That Song Before [1] (L: Cahn, Sammy)

**Notes** There are also vocals of "When You're Smiling" by Mark Fisher, Joe Goodwin and Larry Shay and "I'm Sitting on Top of the World" by Ray Hendeson, Sam Lewis and Joe Young. [1] Also in PISTOL PACKIN' MAMA and YOUTH ON PARADE.

## 5340 ✦ SHARK'S TREASURE
United Artists, 1975

**Musical Score** Ragland, Robert O.

**Producer(s)** Wilde, Cornel
**Director(s)** Wilde, Cornel
**Screenwriter(s)** Wilde, Cornel

**Cast** Wilde, Cornel; Kotto, Yaphet; Neilson, John; Osmond, Cliff; Canary, David; Gilliam, David

**Song(s)** Money Calypso [1] (C/L: Pascal, Jefferson)

**Notes** [1] Jefferson Pascal is a pseudonym for Cornel Wilde.

## 5341 ✦ SHARKY'S MACHINE
Orion, 1981

**Producer(s)** Moonjean, Hank
**Director(s)** Reynolds, Burt

**Screenwriter(s)** Di Pego, Gerald
**Source(s)** *Sharky's Machine* (novel) Diehl, William

**Cast** Reynolds, Burt; Gassman, Vittorio; Keith, Brian; Durning, Charles; Holliman, Earl; Casey, Bernie; Silva, Henry; Libertini, Richard; Hickman, Darryl; Ward, Rachel; Mascolo, Joseph; Locatell, Carol; Fiedler, John

**Song(s)** Street Life (C/L: Sample, J.; Jennings, Waylon); Dope Bust (C/L: Capps, Al; Garrett, Snuff); Shootout (C/L: Capps, Al; Garrett, Snuff); Let's Keep Dancing (C/L: Crofford, Cliff; Durrill, John; Troup, Bobby; Garrett, Snuff); Sharky's Love Theme (C/L: Crofford, Cliff; Durrill, John; Troup, Bobby; Garrett, Snuff); After Hours (C/L: Bruce, R.; Feyne, Buddy; Parrish, A.); 8 to 5 I Lose (C/L: Crofford, Cliff; Durrill, John; Troup, Bobby; Garrett, Snuff); Before You (C/L: Crofford, Cliff; Durrill, John; Garrett, Snuff)

**Notes** All background vocal uses.

## 5342 ✦ SHE COULDN'T SAY NO
Warner Brothers, 1930

**Composer(s)** Burke, Joe
**Lyricist(s)** Dubin, Al

**Director(s)** Bacon, Lloyd
**Screenwriter(s)** Caesar, Arthur; Lord, Robert
**Source(s)** (play) Kaye, Benjamin M.

**Cast** Lightner, Winnie; Morris, Chester; Eilers, Sally; Arthur, Johnny; Marshall, Tully; Beavers, Louise

**Song(s)** Darn Fool Woman Like Me; Watching My Dreams Go By; Bouncing the Baby Around

**Notes** No cue sheet available.

## 5343 ✦ SHE DANCES ALONE
Continental–Walter Reade, 1982

**Musical Score** Santaolalla, Gustavo

**Producer(s)** De Laurentiis, Federico; Mack, Earle
**Director(s)** Dornhelm, Robert
**Screenwriter(s)** Davids, Paul

**Cast** Nijinsky, Kyra; Cort, Bud; Dupond, Patrick; Kent, Walter; Von Sydow, Max

**Song(s)** She Dances Alone (C/L: Roberts, Bruce)

**Notes** No cue sheet available.

## 5344 ✦ SHE DONE HIM WRONG
Paramount, 1933

**Composer(s)** Rainger, Ralph
**Lyricist(s)** Rainger, Ralph

**Producer(s)** LeBaron, William
**Director(s)** Sherman, Lowell
**Screenwriter(s)** Thew, Harvey; Bright, John
**Source(s)** *Diamond Lil* (play) West, Mae

**Cast** West, Mae; Grant, Cary; Roland, Gilbert; Beery, Noah; Hudson, Rochelle; Moore, Owen; Beavers, Louise; Knight, Fuzzy

**Song(s)** Easy Rider [1] (C/L: Brooks, Shelton); Mazie; A Guy What Takes His Time; Frankie and Johnnie (C/L: Traditional); Haven't Got No Peace of Mind [2] [4]; He Passed Me By [3]; That Dame from Rio [3]; Corn Beef Hash [4]; Goitie [2]

**Notes** First titled DIAMOND LADY then RUBY RED. [1] Special lyrics by Ralph Rainger. [2] Used instrumentally only. [3] Not used. [4] Recorded vocally.

## 5345 ✦ SHE GOES TO WAR
United Artists, 1929

**Composer(s)** Akst, Harry
**Lyricist(s)** Lewis, Sam M.; Young, Joe

**Producer(s)** Halperin, Victor; Halperin, Edward R.
**Director(s)** King, Henry
**Screenwriter(s)** Saunders, John Monk
**Source(s)** "She Goes to War" (story) Hughes, Rupert

**Cast** Boardman, Eleanor; Holland, John; Burns, Edmund; Rubens, Alma; St. John, Al; Walters, Glen; Seddon, Margaret; D'Avril, Yola; Hall, Evelyn; Borgato, Augustino; Smirnova, Dina

**Song(s)** When All Hope Was Gone I Found You Joan; There Is a Happy Land Far Far Away; Wait for Me

**Notes** No cue sheet available. Originally titled THE WAR SONG.

## 5346 ✦ SHE HAD TO EAT
Twentieth Century–Fox, 1937

**Composer(s)** Akst, Harry
**Lyricist(s)** Clare, Sidney

**Producer(s)** Engel, Samuel G.
**Director(s)** St. Clair, Malcolm
**Screenwriter(s)** Engel, Samuel G.

**Cast** Haley, Jack; Hudson, Rochelle; Treacher, Arthur; Pallette, Eugene; Fowley, Douglas; Pangborn, Franklin

**Song(s)** Living on the Town [1]; When a Gal from Alabama Meets a Boy from Tennessee

**Notes** [1] Also in ISLAND IN THE SKY.

## 5347 ✦ SHE HAS WHAT IT TAKES
Columbia, 1943

**Producer(s)** Clark, Colbert
**Director(s)** Barton, Charles
**Screenwriter(s)** Yawitz, Paul

**Cast** Falkenburg, Jinx; Neal, Tom; Leavitt, Douglas; Worth, Constance; Crehan, Joseph; The Radio Rogues;

The Vagabonds [2]; King, Joseph; Carroll, Alma; Adams, Ernie; Brooke, Tyler

**Song(s)** Honk Honk (Rumble Seat Song) [1] (C: DePaul, Gene; L: Jacobs, Roy); I Bumped My Head on a Star (C/L: Walker, Cindy); Moon On My Pillow (C/L: Tobias, Henry; Tobias, Elliott; Tobias, Charles); Peter Vendor [1] (C: Simons, Moises; L: Gilbert, L. Wolfe); Timber, Timber (C/L: Reed, Don; Tobias, Henry); Let's March Together (C/L: Chaplin, Saul)

**Notes** [1] Not written for picture. [2] Consisted of Pete Peterson, Attilio Risso, Dominic Germano and Albert Torrieri.

### 5348 ◆ THE SHEIK STEPS OUT
Republic, 1937

**Musical Score** Colombo, Alberto

**Producer(s)** Schlom, Herman
**Director(s)** Pichel, Irving
**Screenwriter(s)** Buffington, Adele; Kahn, Gordon

**Cast** Navarro, Ramon; Lane, Lola; Lockhart, Gene; Burke, Kathleen; Fields, Stanley; Bevan, Billy; Coote, Robert; Kinskey, Leonid

**Song(s)** Ride with the Wind (C/L: Bernard, Felix; Tharp, W.); Song of the Sand (C: Colombo, Alberto; L: Janis, Elsie)

### 5349 ◆ SHE LEARNED ABOUT SAILORS
Fox, 1934

**Composer(s)** Whiting, Richard A.
**Lyricist(s)** Clare, Sidney

**Producer(s)** Stone, John
**Director(s)** Marshall, George
**Screenwriter(s)** Conselman, William; Johnson, Henry

**Cast** Faye, Alice; Ayres, Lew; Green, Harry

**Song(s)** She Learned About Sailors [1]; Here's the Key to My Heart

**Notes** [1] Also in 365 NIGHTS IN HOLLYWOOD.

### 5350 ◆ SHE LOVED A FIREMAN
Warner Brothers–First National, 1937

**Composer(s)** Jerome, M.K.
**Lyricist(s)** Scholl, Jack

**Producer(s)** Foy, Bryan
**Director(s)** Farrow, John
**Screenwriter(s)** Grant, Morton; Sand, Carleton
**Source(s)** "Two Platoons" (story) Grant, Morton; Sand, Carleton

**Cast** Foran, Dick; Sheridan, Ann; Armstrong, Robert; O'Connell, Hugh; Borg, Veda Ann; Acuff, Eddie

**Song(s)** He Wants to Be a Fireman; Out of the Corner of My Eye [1]

**Notes** [1] Orchestral use only.

### 5351 ◆ SHE LOVES ME NOT
Paramount, 1934

**Composer(s)** Revel, Harry
**Lyricist(s)** Gordon, Mack

**Producer(s)** Glazer, Benjamin
**Director(s)** Nugent, Elliott
**Screenwriter(s)** Glazer, Benjamin
**Source(s)** *She Loves Me Not* (play) Schwartz, Arthur; Heyman, Edward; Lindsay, Howard

**Cast** Crosby, Bing; Nugent, Edward; Hopkins, Miriam; Stephenson, Henry; Carlisle, Kitty; Overman, Lynne; Allen, Judith; Harolde, Ralf; Barbier, George

**Song(s)** Put a Little Rhythm in Every Little Thing You Do; Straight from the Shoulder; I'm Hummin'; I'm Whistlin' I'm Singin'; Tiger Roar [1] [2]; Love in Bloom [3] (C: Rainger, Ralph; L: Robin, Leo); Were Your Ears Burning Baby? [1] [4]

**Notes** There are also renditions of "Going Back to Nassau Hall" by Kenneth S. Clark; "Hear Dem Bells" by D.S. McCosh; "Old Nassau" by H.P. Peck and Karl Langlotz; "Princeton Cannon Song March" by Hewitt and Osborn. Another motion picture version of SHE LOVES ME NOT was produced in 1942 by Paramount under the name TRUE TO THE ARMY, starring Judy Canova and Allan Jones. [1] Not used. [2] Recorded. [3] Also used in THE BIG BROADCAST OF 1938, NEW YORK TOWN and $1,000 A TOUCHDOWN. Not used in KISS AND MAKE UP. [4] Used in SHOOT THE WORKS. Not used in BELLE OF THE NINETIES.

### 5352 ◆ SHE MADE HER BED
Paramount, 1934

**Director(s)** Murphy, Ralph
**Screenwriter(s)** Robinson, Casey; Adams, Frank R.
**Source(s)** "Baby in the Icebox" (story) Cain, James M.

**Cast** Arlen, Richard; Eilers, Sally; Armstrong, Robert

**Song(s)** This Little Piggy Went to Market [1] (C: Lewis, Harold; L: Coslow, Sam)

**Notes** [1] Also in EIGHT GIRLS IN A BOAT.

### 5353 ◆ SHE MARRIED A COP
Republic, 1939

**Composer(s)** Lane, Burton
**Lyricist(s)** Freed, Ralph

**Producer(s)** Siegel, Sol C.
**Director(s)** Salkow, Sidney
**Screenwriter(s)** Cooper, Olive

**Cast**    Regan, Phil; Parker, Jean; Cowan, Jerome; Kent, Dorothea; Baker, Benny; MacMahon, Horace; Ryan, Peggy

**Song(s)**    I Can't Imagine; I'll Remember; Here's to Love [1]

**Notes**    [1] Used instrumentally only.

### 5354 ◆ SHEPHERD OF THE HILLS
Paramount, 1941

**Producer(s)**    Moss, Jack
**Director(s)**    Hathaway, Henry
**Screenwriter(s)**    Jones, Grover; Anthony, Stuart
**Source(s)**    *The Shepherd of the Hills* (novel) Wright, Harold Bell

**Cast**    Wayne, John; Field, Betty; Barton, James

**Song(s)**    There's a Happy Hunting Ground [2] (C/L: Coslow, Sam); Corn Tassel (C: Sanders, Troy; L: Jones, Grover); Moon's Comin' Up [1] (C: Sanders, Troy; L: Jones, Grover); There Was an Old Lady [1] (C/L: Jones, Grover)

**Notes**    [1] Not used. [2] Not used in SPAWN OF THE NORTH.

### 5355 ◆ SHEPHERD OF THE OZARKS
Republic, 1942

**Musical Score**    Glickman, Mort

**Producer(s)**    Schaefer, Armand
**Director(s)**    McDonald, Frank
**Screenwriter(s)**    McGowan, Dorrell; McGowan, Stuart

**Cast**    Weaver, Leon; Weaver, Frank; Weaver, June; Hare, Marilyn; Albertson, Frank; Hall, Thurston; Arthur, Johnny

**Song(s)**    Well Well [1] (C: Styne, Jule; L: Loesser, Frank); Lonely Hill Billy (C/L: Rodgers, Jesse O.)

**Notes**    [1] Also in SIS HOPKINS.

### 5356 ◆ THE SHERIFF OF FRACTURED JAW
Twentieth Century–Fox, 1959

**Musical Score**    Farnon, Robert
**Composer(s)**    Harris, Harry
**Lyricist(s)**    Harris, Harry
**Choreographer(s)**    Carden, George

**Producer(s)**    Angel, Daniel M.
**Director(s)**    Walsh, Raoul
**Screenwriter(s)**    Dales, Arthur

**Cast**    More, Kenneth; Mansfield, Jayne [1]; Hull, Henry; Cabot, Bruce; Squire, Ronald; James, Sidney; Stewart, Donald; Morley, Robert

**Song(s)**    In the Valley of Love; Strolling Down the Lane with Bill; If the San Francisco Hills Could Only Talk

**Notes**    [1] Dubbed by Connie Francis.

### 5357 ◆ SHERIFF OF TOMBSTONE
Republic, 1941

**Composer(s)**    Styne, Jule
**Lyricist(s)**    Meyer, Sol

**Producer(s)**    Kane, Joseph
**Director(s)**    Kane, Joseph
**Screenwriter(s)**    Cooper, Olive

**Cast**    Rogers, Roy; Hayes, George "Gabby"; Knox, Elyse; Payne, Sally; Tilbury, Zeffie; Morris, Michael; Taliaferro, Hal; Novello, Jay

**Song(s)**    Ridin' on a Rocky Road; Ya Should a Seen Pete; Sky Ball Paint (C/L: Nolan, Bob)

### 5358 ◆ SHE'S A SWEETHEART
Columbia, 1944

**Producer(s)**    Richmond, Ted
**Director(s)**    Lord, Del
**Screenwriter(s)**    Bolton, Muriel Roy

**Cast**    Frazee, Jane; Parks, Larry; Darwell, Jane; Foch, Nina; Hunter, Ross; Lloyd, Jimmy; Warren, Ruth

**Song(s)**    No Other Love [2] (C/L: Forrest, Chet; Wright, Bob); I Can't Remember When (C/L: Scherman, Robert); What the Sergeant Said (C/L: Camp, Jackie); Peggy the Pin Up Girl (C/L: Evans, Redd; Loeb, John Jacob); American Prayer (C/L: Stock, Larry; Rose, Vincent; Stillman, Albert); Mom [1] (C/L: Chaplin, Saul); Who Said Dreams Don't Come True [3] (C: Akst, Harry; L: Davis, Benny; Jolson, Al)

**Notes**    [1] Only song written for the film. [2] Based on "Romance" by A. Rubenstein. Also in MUSIC IN MY HEART. [3] Not used. Used in THE IMPATIENT YEARS.

### 5359 ◆ SHE'S BACK ON BROADWAY
Warner Brothers, 1953

**Musical Score**    Buttolph, David
**Composer(s)**    Sigman, Carl
**Lyricist(s)**    Hilliard, Bob
**Choreographer(s)**    Prinz, LeRoy

**Producer(s)**    Blanke, Henry
**Director(s)**    Douglas, Gordon M.
**Screenwriter(s)**    Jennings, Orin

**Cast**    Mayo, Virginia [1]; Nelson, Gene; Lovejoy, Frank; Cochran, Steve; Wymore, Patrice; Gibson, Virginia; Keating, Larry; Picerni, Paul; Young, Ned; Albertson, Mabel

**Song(s)**    One Step Ahead of Everybody; I'll Take You As You Are; Ties that Bind; Breakfast in Bed; Mardi Gras (C/L: Heindorf, Ray; Henderson, Charles); Voodoo (C/L: Heindorf, Ray; Henderson, Charles); Behind the Mask; Tap Dance (Inst.) (C: Heindorf, Ray; Henderson, Charles)

**Notes**    [1] Dubbed by Bonnie Lou Williams.

### 5360 ◆ SHE'S FOR ME
Universal, 1943

**Producer(s)** Gross, Frank
**Director(s)** LeBorg, Reginald
**Screenwriter(s)** Blankfort, Henry

**Cast** Bruce, David; Collier, Lois; McDonald, Grace; Dolenz, George

**Song(s)** Ain't You Got No Time for Love (C/L: Wells, Maurice; Wells, Lottie); Closer and Closer (C: Woods, Harry; L: Parish, Mitchell); Do I Know What I'm Doing (C/L: Costello, Joanne; Stewart, Freddie)

### 5361 ◆ SHE'S GOT EVERYTHING
RKO, 1937

**Musical Score** Webb, Roy

**Producer(s)** Lewis, Albert
**Director(s)** Santley, Joseph
**Screenwriter(s)** Segall, Harry; Shane, Maxwell

**Cast** Raymond, Gene; Sothern, Ann; Moore, Victor; Broderick, Helen; Parkyakarkus; Gilbert, Billy; Brisbane, William; Ward, Solly

**Song(s)** Sleepy Time in Hawaii (C/L: Rene, Leon; Rene, Otis); Hoohena Keia (C/L: Almaida, Johnny; Noble, Johnny)

### 5362 ◆ SHE'S HAVING A BABY
Paramount, 1988

**Musical Score** Copeland, Stewart; Holland, Nicky

**Producer(s)** Hughes, John
**Director(s)** Hughes, John
**Screenwriter(s)** Hughes, John

**Cast** Bacon, Kevin; McGovern, Elizabeth; Baldwin, Alec; Ray, James; Taylor, Holland; Windom, William; Damon, Cathryn; Erwin, Bill; McClurg, Edie

**Song(s)** Apron Strings (C/L: Watt, Ben; Thorn, Tracey); She's Having a Baby (C/L: Ritchie, Ian; Wakeling, Dave); This Woman's Work (C/L: Bush, Kate)

**Notes** No cue sheet available.

### 5363 ◆ SHE STEPS OUT

See HARMONY AT HOME.

### 5364 ◆ SHE'S WORKING HER WAY THROUGH COLLEGE
Warner Brothers, 1952

**Musical Score** Jackson, Howard
**Composer(s)** Duke, Vernon
**Lyricist(s)** Cahn, Sammy
**Choreographer(s)** Prinz, LeRoy

**Producer(s)** Jacobs, William
**Director(s)** Humberstone, H. Bruce
**Screenwriter(s)** Milne, Peter
**Source(s)** *The Male Animal* (play) Nugent, Elliott; Thurber, James

**Cast** Mayo, Virginia [1]; Reagan, Ronald; Nelson, Gene; DeFore, Don; Thaxter, Phyllis; Wymore, Patrice; Winters, Roland; Greenleaf, Raymond; The Blackburn Twins

**Song(s)** All Hail to Midwest State; I'll Be Loving You; The Stuff that Dreams Are Made Of; Love Is Still for Free; You've Got to Give Them What They Want; Oh Me Oh My Oh Me-O

**Notes** Only the Duke and Cahn songs were original to this picture. There are also vocals of "With Plenty of Money and You" (also in GOLD DIGGERS OF 1937 and MY DREAM IS YOURS) and "Am I in Love" by Harry Warren and Al Dubin; "Baby Face" by Harry Akst and Benny Davis; "Gee But You're Swell" by Abel Baer and Charles Tobias; "We're Working Our Way Through College" (from VARSITY SHOW) by Richard A. Whiting and Johnny Mercer and "As Time Goes By" by Herman Hupfeld. [1] Dubbed by Bonnie Lou Williams.

### 5365 ◆ SHINBONE ALLEY
Allied Artists, 1971

**Composer(s)** Kleinsinger, George
**Lyricist(s)** Darion, Joe

**Producer(s)** Fleet, Preston M.
**Director(s)** Wilson, John David
**Screenwriter(s)** Darion, Joe
**Source(s)** Shinbone Alley (musical) Brooks, Mel; Darion, Joe; archy and mehitabel (stories) Marquis, Don
**Voices** Channing, Carol; Bracken, Eddie; Reed, Alan; Carradine, John

**Notes** No cue sheet available. This piece was first done as a Broadway show with Eartha Kitt and Eddie Bracken. Carol Channing and Bracken then appeared on a Columbia records version. Later there was a live TV special with Bracken and Tammy Grimes.

### 5366 ◆ SHINE ON HARVEST MOON (1938)
Republic, 1938

**Producer(s)** Ford, Charles E.
**Director(s)** Kane, Joseph
**Screenwriter(s)** Natteford, Jack

**Cast** Rogers, Roy; Hart, Mary; Lulu Belle and Scotty; Andrews, Stanley; Farnum, William; Jacquet, Frank

**Song(s)** The Man in the Moon Is a Cowhand [1] (C/L: Rogers, Roy); Loueller (C/L: Lair, John); I'm Dying to Get a Nice Feller (C/L: Lair, John); Let Me Build a Cabin (C/L: Kraushaar, Raoul; Cherkose, Eddie; Natteford, Jack); In the Doghouse Now (C/L:

Wiseman, Scott); Headin' for the Open Plain (C: Kent, Walter; L: Cherkose, Eddie)

**Notes**  There is also a vocal of "Shine on Harvest Moon" by Jack Norworth and Nora Bayes. The song is also in the Warner Brothers pictures ALONG CAME RUTH, SHINE ON HARVEST MOON (1944) and I'LL SEE YOU IN MY DREAMS. [1] Also in MAN FROM RAINBOW VALLEY.


**5367  ✦  SHINE ON HARVEST MOON (1944)**
Warner Brothers, 1944

**Composer(s)**  Jerome, M.K.
**Lyricist(s)**  Gannon, Kim
**Choreographer(s)**  Prinz, LeRoy

**Producer(s)**  Jacobs, William
**Director(s)**  Butler, David
**Screenwriter(s)**  Hellman, Sam; Weil, Richard; Swann, Francis; Kern, James V.

**Cast**  Sheridan, Ann [1]; Morgan, Dennis; Carson, Jack; Manning, Irene; Sakall, S.Z.; Wilson, Marie; Shayne, Robert; Murphy, Bob; The Four Step Brothers; The Ashburns; Davidson, William B.; Stanton, Will; Bush, James; Crehan, Joseph; Bryson, Betty; Kramer, Don; Rogers, George; Johnson, Harry; Pietilla, Walter

**Song(s)**  We're Doing Our Best; Don't Let the Rainy Day Get You; Who's Your Honey Lamb [2] (L: Scholl, Jack); So Dumb but So Beautiful; Thank You for the Dance; I Go for You

**Notes**  This is a film biography of Nora Bayes and Jack Norworth. The following songs are also featured, sometimes in brief medleys: "Be My Little Baby Bumble Bee" by Henry I. Marshall and Stanley Murphy; "My Own United States" by Stanislaus Stange and Julian Edwards; "Time Waits for No One" by Cliff Friend and Charles Tobias; "It Looks Like a Big Night Tonight" by Egbert Van Alstyne and Harry Williams; "How Can They Tell That I'm Irish" by C.W. Murphy, Nora Bayes and Jack Norworth; "Shine On Harvest Moon" by Nora Bayes and Jack Norworth (also in ALONG CAME RUTH, I'LL SEE YOU IN MY DREAMS and the Republic picture SHINE ON HARVEST MOON); "When It's Apple Blossom Time in Normandy" by Tom Mellor, Harry Gifford and Huntley Trevor; "Take Me Out to the Ball Game" by Albert Von Tilzer and Jack Norworth; "I've Got a Garden in Sweden" by C.W. Murphy, Hugh Owen, Dan Lipton, Nora Bayes and Jack Norworth; "Breezing Along with the Breeze" by Richard A. Whiting, Haven Gillespie and Seymour Simons; "Mister Dooley" by Jean Schwartz and William Jerome; "He's Me Pal" by Gus Edwards and Vincent Bryan; "What's the Matter with Father" by Egbert Van Alstyne and Harry Williams; "Every Little Movement" by Karl Hoschna and Otto Harbach; "Oh You Beautiful Doll" by Nat D. Ayer and A. Seymour Brown; "Just Like a Gypsy" by Seymour Simons and Nora Bayes; "Daisy

Bell" by Harry Dacre; "In My Merry Oldsmobile" by Gus Edwards and Vincent Bryan and "San Antonio" by Egbert Van Alstyne and Harry Williams. [1] Dubbed by Lynn Martin. [2] Also in THOSE GOOD OLD DAYS.


**5368  ✦  THE SHINING FUTURE**
Warner Brothers, 1944

**Producer(s)**  Hollingshead, Gordon; Albert, Arnold
**Director(s)**  Prinz, LeRoy
**Screenwriter(s)**  Bloodworth, James

**Cast**  Blakeney, Olive; Carson, Jack; Crosby, Bing; Grant, Cary; Lydon, James; Manning, Irene; Morgan, Dennis; Ruggles, Charles; Sinatra, Frank; Durbin, Deanna; Benny Goodman and His Orchestra; James, Harry; Marshall, Herbert; Peary, Harold

**Song(s)**  The Road to Victory (C/L: Loesser, Frank); Hot Time in the Town of Berlin (C: Bushkin, Joe; L: De Vries, John)

**Notes**  No cue sheet available. There are more songs in this short subject produced for Canada's Sixth Victory Loan. Later, this two-reel short was cut to one reel and titled THE ROAD TO VICTORY. In that incarnation Durbin, Goodman, James, Marshall and Peary's parts were deleted.


**5369  ✦  SHIP AHOY**
Metro–Goldwyn–Mayer, 1942

**Composer(s)**  Lane, Burton
**Lyricist(s)**  Harburg, E.Y.
**Choreographer(s)**  Connolly, Bobby

**Producer(s)**  Cummings, Jack
**Director(s)**  Buzzell, Edward
**Screenwriter(s)**  Clork, Harry

**Cast**  Powell, Eleanor; Skelton, Red; Lahr, Bert; O'Brien, Virginia; Tommy Dorsey and His Orchestra; Sinatra, Frank

**Song(s)**  The Last Call for Love (L: Harburg, E.Y.; Cummings, Margery); I'll Take Tallulah [1]; Poor You; Tampico (Inst.) (C: Ruick, Walter); Cape Dance (Inst.) (C: Ruick, Walter); I'll Take Manila [1] [2]

**Notes**  Originally titled I'LL TAKE MANILA. There is also a vocal of "(On) Moonlight Bay" by Percy Wenrich and Edward Madden. [1] Same music. [2] Not used.


**5370  ✦  SHIP CAFE**
Paramount, 1935

**Composer(s)**  Gensler, Lewis E.
**Lyricist(s)**  Thompson, Harlan

**Producer(s)**  Hurley, Harold
**Director(s)**  Florey, Robert
**Screenwriter(s)**  Thompson, Harlan; Fields, Herbert

**Cast**  Brisson, Carl; Christians, Mady; Judge, Arline

**Song(s)**  Fatal Fascination; I Won't Take No for an Answer; Change Your Mind (C/L: Noble, Ray); My Home Town (C: Oakland, Ben; L: Drake, Milton); Who's Afraid of the Big Bad Wolf [1] [6] (C: Churchill, Frank E.; L: Ronell, Ann); Darn Clever These Chinese [2] [3] (C: Davis, Eddie; L: Ruskin, Harry; Davis, Eddie; Robin, Leo); The Girls I Loved and Lost [2] [3] (C: Davis, Eddie; L: Davis, Eddie; Lippman, Arthur); Should I Be Sweet [1] [2] [3] (C: Youmans, Vincent; L: Brown, Lew; DeSylva, B.G.); She Came Rollin' Down the Mountain [4] (C: Sherwin, Manning; L: Richman, Harry; Lippman, Arthur)

**Notes**  First titled THE BOUNCER. [1] Not written for this picture. [2] Not used. [3] Recorded. [4] This number was not written for this picture and was used instrumentally although it was recorded with lyrics. Also used in BLONDE TROUBLE, though not written for that picture either. [5] Considered for LOVE IN BLOOM but not used. [6] Also in THREE LITTLE PIGS (Disney). See note under THREE LITTLE PIGS.

## 5371 ◆ SHIPMATES FOREVER
### Warner Brothers–First National, 1935

**Composer(s)**  Warren, Harry
**Lyricist(s)**  Dubin, Al
**Choreographer(s)**  Connolly, Bobby

**Producer(s)**  Edelman, Louis F.
**Director(s)**  Borzage, Frank
**Screenwriter(s)**  Daves, Delmer

**Cast**  Powell, Dick; Keeler, Ruby; Stone, Lewis; Alexander, Ross; Acuff, Eddie; Foran, Dick; Arledge, John; Light, Robert; King, Joseph; Burton, Frederick; Kolker, Henry; Crehan, Joseph; Merrill, Martha; Treen, Mary

**Song(s)**  Don't Give Up the Ship; I'd Love to Take Orders from You; Abdul Abul Bul Amir (C/L: Traditional); I'd Rather Listen to Your Eyes; All Aboard the Navy [1]; Do I Love My Teacher [1]

**Notes**  [1] Listed in Hirschhorn and Burton but not in cue sheets.

## 5372 ◆ SHIP OF FOOLS
### Columbia, 1965

**Musical Score**  Gold, Ernest
**Composer(s)**  Gold, Ernest
**Lyricist(s)**  Lloyd, Jack

**Producer(s)**  Kramer, Stanley
**Director(s)**  Kramer, Stanley
**Screenwriter(s)**  Mann, Abby
**Source(s)**  *Ship of Fools* (novel) Porter, Katherine Ann

**Cast**  Leigh, Vivien; Signoret, Simone; Ferrer, Jose; Marvin, Lee; Werner, Oskar; Ashley, Elizabeth; Segal, George; Greco, Jose; Dunn, Michael; Korvin, Charles; Skala, Lilia; Luna, Barbara; Adams, Stanley; Calvin, Henry

**Song(s)**  Heute Abend; Geh'n Wir Bummelin Auf Der Peeperbahn; Irgendwie, Irgendwo, Irgenwanh; Ship of Fools (L: Washington, Ned)

**Notes**  No songs listed on cue sheet.

## 5373 ◆ SHIPYARD SALLY
### Twentieth Century–Fox, 1940

**Producer(s)**  Kane, Robert T.
**Director(s)**  Banks, Monty
**Screenwriter(s)**  Turnberg, Karl; Ettlinger, Don

**Cast**  Fields, Gracie; Howard, Sydney; Selton, Morton; Varden, Norma; Wakefield, Oliver

**Song(s)**  Grandfather's Bagpipes (C: Haines, Will E.; L: Harper, Jimmy); Wish Me Luck (C: Park, Phil; L: Parr-Davies, Harry); I Got the Jitterbugs (C/L: Haines, Will E.; Harper, Jimmy; Grant); In Pernamubco (C/L: Parr-Davies, Harry)

## 5374 ◆ THE SHIRALEE
### Metro–Goldwyn–Mayer, 1957

**Musical Score**  Addison, John

**Producer(s)**  Rix, Jack
**Director(s)**  Norman, Leslie
**Screenwriter(s)**  Paterson, Neil; Norman, Leslie
**Source(s)**  (novel) Niland, D'Arcy

**Cast**  Finch, Peter; Sellars, Elizabeth; Harris, Rosemary; O'Shea, Tessie; Rose, George; James, Sidney; Napier, Russell; MacGinnis, Niall

**Song(s)**  The Shiralee (C/L: Steele, Tommy; Bart, Lionel)

## 5375 ◆ SHIRLEY VALENTINE
### Paramount, 1989

**Musical Score**  Russell, Willy

**Producer(s)**  Gilbert, Lewis
**Director(s)**  Gilbert, Lewis
**Screenwriter(s)**  Russell, Willy
**Source(s)**  *Shirley Valentine* (play) Russell, Willy

**Cast**  Bates, Alan; Collins, Pauline; Steadman, Alison; Syms, Sylvia; Hill, Bernard; Lumley, Joanna; Kearney, Gillian; Duncan, Catherine; Bennett, Tracie; Jefferson, Gareth

**Song(s)**  The Girl Who Used to Be Me (C: Hamlisch, Marvin; L: Bergman, Alan; Bergman, Marilyn)

## 5376 ✦ SHOCKER
Universal, 1989

**Musical Score** Goldstein, William

**Producer(s)** Maddalena, Marianne; Kumar, Barin
**Director(s)** Craven, Wes
**Screenwriter(s)** Craven, Wes

**Cast** Murphy, Michael; Berg, Peter; Cooper, Cami; Pileggi, Mitch

**Song(s)** Shocker (C/L: Child, Desmond; Beauvoir, Jean; Mann-Dude, Guy); Love Transfusion (C/L: Child, Desmond; Cooper, Alice; Matetski, Vladimir); No More Mr. Nice Guy (C/L: Cooper, Alice; Bruce, Michael); Different Breed (C/L: Frazitta, Tony); The Ballad of Horace Pinker (C/L: McMaster, Jason; Child, Desmond; Dangerous Toys); Sword and Stone (C/L: Child, Desmond; Stanley, Paul; Kulick, Bruce)

## 5377 ✦ THE SHOCKING MISS PILGRIM
Twentieth Century–Fox, 1947

**Composer(s)** Gershwin, George
**Lyricist(s)** Gershwin, Ira
**Choreographer(s)** Pan, Hermes

**Producer(s)** Perlberg, William
**Director(s)** Seaton, George
**Screenwriter(s)** Seaton, George

**Cast** Revere, Anne; Grable, Betty; Haymes, Dick; Joslyn, Allyn; Lockhart, Gene; Patterson, Elizabeth; Risdon, Elizabeth; Shields, Arthur; Kemper, Charles; Roberts, Roy

**Song(s)** For You, For Me, Forevermore; Aren't You Kind of Glad We Did; Changing My Tune; The Back Bay Polka (But Not in Boston); One, Two, Three; Sweet Packard; Stand Up and Fight; Tour of the Town [1]; Welcome Song [1]; Ask Me Again [1]; Pay Some Attention to Me [1]; Demon Rum [2]

**Notes** Kay Swift put the late George Gershwin's musical sketches together into songs. She later confided some of the tunes were entirely hers. [1] Used instrumentally only. [2] Not used.

## 5378 ✦ SHOOTING HIGH
Twentieth Century–Fox, 1940

**Musical Score** Kaylin, Samuel

**Producer(s)** Stone, John
**Director(s)** Green, Alfred E.
**Screenwriter(s)** Breslow, Lou; Francis, Owen

**Cast** Withers, Jane; Autry, Gene; Weaver, Marjorie; Lowery, Robert; Aldridge, Katharine; Cavanaugh, Hobart; MacFadden, Hamilton

**Song(s)** Wanderers (C: Bernard, Felix; L: Webster, Paul Francis); Shanty of Dreams (C/L: Marvin, Johnny; Autry, Gene); Only One Love in a Lifetime (C/L: Marvin, Johnny; Autry, Gene; Tobias, Harry); Little Old Band of Gold (C/L: Newman, Charles; Glickman, Fred; Autry, Gene); On the Rancho with My Pancho [1] (C: Akst, Harry; L: Clare, Sidney)

**Notes** [1] Autry's biography lists the song but it doesn't appear on the cue sheets.

## 5379 ✦ SHOOT-OUT AT MEDICINE BEND
Warner Brothers, 1957

**Musical Score** Webb, Roy

**Producer(s)** Whorf, Richard
**Director(s)** Bare, Richard
**Screenwriter(s)** Battle, John Tucker; Beauchamp, D.D.

**Cast** Scott, Randolph; Craig, James; Dickinson, Angie; Garner, James; Crayne, Dani; Jones, Gordon

**Song(s)** Kiss Me Quick (And Leave Me Never) (C: Heindorf, Ray; L: Shanklin, Wayne)

## 5380 ✦ SHOOT THE WORKS
Paramount, 1934

**Composer(s)** Revel, Harry
**Lyricist(s)** Gordon, Mack

**Director(s)** Ruggles, Wesley
**Screenwriter(s)** Green, Howard J.
**Source(s)** *The Great Magoo* (play) Hecht, Ben; Fowler, Gene

**Cast** Oakie, Jack; Bernie, Ben; Dell, Dorothy; Judge, Arline; Skipworth, Alison; Cavanaugh, Paul; Karns, Roscoe; Frawley, William; Cody, Lew

**Song(s)** With My Eyes Wide Open I'm Dreaming [7]; Were Your Ears Burning Baby? [6]; A Bowl of Chop Suey and You-ey (C: Goering, Al; Bernie, Ben; L: Bullock, Walter); Do I Love You? [4] (C: Rainger, Ralph; L: Robin, Leo); In the Good Old Winter Time [1] (L: Adamson, Harold; Gordon, Mack); In the Middle of a Kiss [2] [5] (C/L: Coslow, Sam); Take a Lesson from the Lark [2] [3] (C: Rainger, Ralph; L: Robin, Leo); When Ezra Plays the Fiddle (in the Old Town Hall) [2]

**Notes** First titled THE GREAT MAGOO then called THANK YOUR STARS. It was released in Great Britain as THANK YOUR STARS. [1] Not used but recorded and published. Adamson not credited on cue sheet. [2] Not used. [3] Published. [4] Written for MANY HAPPY RETURNS but not used. [5] Used in COLLEGE SCANDAL. [6] Not used in SHE LOVES ME NOT and BELLE OF THE NINETIES. [7] Also used in COLLEGIATE, ONE HOUR LATE and STOLEN HARMONY.

## 5381 ✦ THE SHOPWORN ANGEL
Paramount, 1928

**Director(s)**   Wallace, Richard
**Screenwriter(s)**   Estabrook, Howard; Le Vino, Albert
Shelby
**Source(s)**   "Private Pettigrew's Girl" (story) Burnet,
Dana

**Cast**   Cooper, Gary; Lukas, Paul; Carroll, Nancy; Karns,
Roscoe

**Song(s)**   A Precious Little Thing Called Love (C: Coots,
J. Fred; L: Davis, Lou)

**Notes**   No cue sheet available.

## 5382 ✦ SHORT CIRCUIT
Tri-Star, 1986

**Musical Score**   Shire, David

**Producer(s)**   Foster, David; Turman, Lawrence
**Director(s)**   Badham, John
**Screenwriter(s)**   Wilson, S.S.; Maddock, Brent

**Cast**   Sheedy, Ally; Guttenberg, Steve; Stevens, Fisher;
Pendleton, Austin; Bailey, G.W.; McNamara, Brian;
Blaney, Tim

**Song(s)**   Come and Follow Me (C/L: Shire, David;
Jennings, Will; Carl, Max); Who's Johnny (C/L: Wolf,
Peter; Wolf, Ina)

**Notes**   No cue sheet available.

## 5383 ✦ SHORT EYES
The Film League, 1977

**Musical Score**   Mayfield, Curtis

**Producer(s)**   Harris, Lewis
**Director(s)**   Young, Robert M.
**Screenwriter(s)**   Pinero, Miguel

**Cast**   Davison, Bruce; Perez, Jose; Carberry, Joseph;
Fender, Freddie

**Song(s)**   Do Do Wap Is Strong in Here (C/L: Mayfield,
Curtis); Back Against the Wall (C/L: Mayfield, Curtis);
Break It Down (C/L: Denenberg, H.P.; Hirsch, Martin)

**Notes**   No cue sheet available.

## 5384 ✦ A SHOT IN THE DARK (1941)
Warner Brothers, 1941

**Musical Score**   Lava, William

**Producer(s)**   Jacobs, William
**Director(s)**   McGann, William
**Screenwriter(s)**   Webster, M. Coates
**Source(s)**   "No Hard Feelings" (story) Nebel, Frederick

**Cast**   Lundigan, William; Wynn, Nan; Cortez, Ricardo;
Toomey, Regis; Wrixon, Maris; Carroll, Lucia

**Song(s)**   For You (C: Burke, Joe; L: Dubin, Al); It Just
Happened (C: McHugh, Jimmy; L: Freed, Ralph)

**Notes**   There is also a vocal of "I'm Just Wild about
Harry" by Eubie Blake and Noble Sissle.

## 5385 ✦ A SHOT IN THE DARK (1964)
United Artists, 1964

**Musical Score**   Mancini, Henry

**Producer(s)**   Edwards, Blake
**Director(s)**   Edwards, Blake
**Screenwriter(s)**   Edwards, Blake; Blatty, William Peter
**Source(s)**   *A Shot in the Dark* (play) Kurnitz, Harry;
Achard, Marcel

**Cast**   Sellers, Peter; Sommer, Elke; Sanders, George;
Lom, Herbert; Reed, Tracy

**Song(s)**   Shadows of Paris [1] (C: Mancini, Henry; L:
Wells, Robert); A Shot in the Dark (C: Mancini, Henry;
L: Wells, Robert)

**Notes**   The play is based on the rench original *L'IDIOT*
BY Marchel Archard. [1] Sheet music only.

## 5386 ✦ SHOULD A GIRL MARRY?
Rayart Pictures, 1928

**Director(s)**   Pembroke, Scott
**Screenwriter(s)**   Turner, Terry

**Cast**   Ben Pollack Park Central Orchestra; Foster,
Helen; Keith, Donald; Mong, William V.; Clyde, Andy;
Vernon, Dorothy

**Song(s)**   Haunting Memories (C/L: Bibo, Irving)

**Notes**   No cue sheet available.

## 5387 ✦ SHOULD LADIES BEHAVE?
Metro–Goldwyn–Mayer, 1933

**Producer(s)**   Weingarten, Lawrence
**Director(s)**   Beaumont, Harry
**Screenwriter(s)**   Spewack, Bella; Spewack, Sam
**Source(s)**   *The Vinegar Tree* (play) Osborn, Paul

**Cast**   Barrymore, Lionel; Brady, Alice; Tearle, Conway;
Alexander, Katherine; Carlisle, Mary

**Song(s)**   Lovely Lady (C: Brown, Nacio Herb; L: Freed,
Arthur)

**Notes**   Originally titled THE VINEGAR TREE.

## 5388 ✦ SHOW BOAT (1929)
Universal, 1929

**Director(s)**   Pollard, Harry
**Screenwriter(s)**   Pollard, Harry; Reed, Tom
**Source(s)**   *Show Boat* (novel) Ferber, Edna

Cast    La Plante, Laura [2]; Schildkraut, Joseph; Harlan, Otis; Fitzroy, Emily; Rubens, Alma; Bartlett, Elsie; McDonald, Jack; La Verne, Jane; Edwards, Neely; Howard, Gertrude; Fetchit, Stepin

Song(s)    Look Down that Lonesome Road (C: Shilkret, Nathaniel; L: Austin, Gene); Here Comes the Show Boat (C: Pinkard, Maceo; L: Rose, Billy); Love Sings a Song in My Heart (C: Cherniavsky, Joseph; L: Marks, Clarence); Ol' Man River [1] (C: Kern, Jerome; L: Hammerstein II, Oscar); Lovin' Dat Man [1] (C: Kern, Jerome; L: Hammerstein II, Oscar); Coon, Coon, Coon (C/L: Jefferson, Gene; Friedman, Leo); Down South [3] (C/L: Spaeth, Sigmund; Myddleton, William H.)

Notes    No cue sheet available. This film, originally made as a silent with songs and dialogue added, contains a brief prologue directed by Arch B. Heath. After an introduction by Universal chief Carl Laemmle and SHOW BOAT's Broadway producer Florenz Ziegfeld, members of the New York company were seen singing their songs. This historic footage (of which I believe only the Tess Gardella sequences survive) includes: Tess Gardella (also known as Aunt Jemima) singing "Hey Feller" and "C'Mon Folks" with the Jubilee Singers; Helen Morgan singing "Can't Help Lovin' Dat Man" and "Bill;" and Jules Bledsoe singing "Ol' Man River." The Universal picture also included vocals of the traditional songs "I've Got Shoes" and "Deep River." [1] From the Broadway musical SHOW BOAT. [2] Dubbed by Eva Olivotti. [3] Also in BIG BOY (Warners) but credited to George Myddleton.

## 5389  ◆  SHOW BOAT (1936)
Universal, 1936

Composer(s)    Kern, Jerome
Lyricist(s)    Hammerstein II, Oscar
Choreographer(s)    Prinz, LeRoy

Producer(s)    Laemmle Jr., Carl
Director(s)    Whale, James
Screenwriter(s)    Hammerstein II, Oscar
Source(s)    Show Boat (musical) Kern, Jerome; Hammerstein II, Oscar

Cast    Westley, Helen; Smith, Queenie; Dunne, Irene [4]; Jones, Allan [6]; Winninger, Charles [3]; Robeson, Paul [5]; Morgan, Helen [3]; Cook, Donald; McDaniel, Hattie; Mahoney, Francis X. [3]; Middleton, Charles; White, Sammy [3]; O'Dea, Sunnie; Fields, Stanley; Clive, E.E.; Prinz, LeRoy; Anderson, Eddie "Rochester"; Mulhall, Jack

Song(s)    I Have the Room Above Her; Ah Still Suits Me; Gallavantin' Around; Cotton Blossom [1]; Where's the Mate for Me? [1]; Make Believe [1]; Ol' Man River [1]; Can't Help Lovin' Dat Man [1]; You Are Love [1]; Bill [1] (L: Hammerstein II, Oscar; Wodehouse, P.G.); Got My Eye on You [2]

Notes    No cue sheet available. There are also vocals of "Goodbye My Lady Love" by Joe Howard; "At a Georgia Camp Meeting" by Kerry Mills and "After the Ball" by Charles K. Harris. "Goodbye My Lady Love" and "After the Ball" were interpolated into the original (and all subsequent) productions of the musical. LeRoy Prinz appeared as the dance director. [1] From original Broadway production. [2] Written for film version but not used. [3] From original Broadway cast. [4] Broadway replacement. [5] In 1932 Broadway revival. [6] In St. Louis Muni Opera production (1934).

## 5390  ◆  SHOW BOAT (1951)
Metro–Goldwyn–Mayer, 1951

Composer(s)    Kern, Jerome
Lyricist(s)    Hammerstein II, Oscar
Choreographer(s)    Alton, Robert

Producer(s)    Freed, Arthur
Director(s)    Sidney, George
Screenwriter(s)    Mahin, John Lee
Source(s)    Show Boat (musical) Kern, Jerome; Hammerstein II, Oscar

Cast    Grayson, Kathryn; Gardner, Ava [1]; Keel, Howard; Brown, Joe E.; Champion, Marge; Champion, Gower; Sterling, Robert; Moorehead, Agnes; Erickson, Leif; Warfield, William; Jergens, Adele; Williams, Frances; Toomey, Regis; Knight, Fuzzy; Nilsson, Anna Q.; Roach, Bert; Parnell, Emory

Song(s)    Cotton Blossom; Captain Andy's Entrance; Where's the Mate for Me?; Make Believe; Can't Help Lovin' Dat Man; I Might Fall Back on You; Ol' Man River; You Are Love; Why Do I Love You?; Bill (L: Hammerstein II, Oscar; Wodehouse, P.G.); Life Upon the Wicked Stage; After the Ball (C/L: Harris, Charles K.)

Notes    All songs from the Broadway production. [1] Dubbed by Annette Warren although Ava Gardner is on the soundtrack album recording.

## 5391  ◆  SHOWBOAT SERENADE
Paramount, 1944

Cast    Johnston, Johnnie; Britton, Barbara

Song(s)    I Don't Miss a Trick (C/L: Seelen, Jerry; Lee, Lester)

Notes    Short subject. Originally titled MISSISSIPPI MAGIC.

## 5392  ◆  SHOW BUSINESS
RKO, 1944

Choreographer(s)    Castle, Nick

Producer(s)    Cantor, Eddie
Director(s)    Marin, Edwin L.

**Screenwriter(s)** Quillan, Joseph; Bennett, Dorothy; Elinson, Irving

**Cast** Cantor, Eddie; Murphy, George; Davis, Joan; Kelly, Nancy; Moore, Constance; Douglas, Don

**Song(s)** Introduction to Dinah (C/L: Duning, George; Keith, Bob); You May Not Remember [1] (C: Oakland, Ben; L: Jessel, George)

**Notes** There are also vocals of "They're Wearin' 'Em Higher in Hawaii" by Halsey K. Mohr and Joe Goodwin; "The Curse of an Aching Heart" by Al Piantadosi and Henry Fink; "It Had to Be You" by Gus Kahn and Isham Jones; "I Want a Girl (Just Like the Girl Who Married Dear Old Dad" by Harry Von Tilzer and Will Dillon; "Sextette" from LUCIA D'LAMMERMOOR by Donezetti; "Alabamy Bound" by B.G. DeSylva, Lew Brown and Ray Henderson; "Dinah" by Sam Lewis, Harry Akst and Joe Young; "I Don't Want to Get Well" by Harry Pease, Harry Jentes and Howard Johnson and "Makin' Whoopee" by Gus Kahn and Walter Donaldson. [1] Also in RIO GRANDE PATROL and TRAIL STREET.

## 5393 ✦ THE SHOWDOWN
### Paramount, 1940

**Musical Score** Leopold, John
**Composer(s)** Ohman, Phil
**Lyricist(s)** Carling, Foster

**Producer(s)** Sherman, Harry
**Director(s)** Bretherton, Howard
**Screenwriter(s)** Kusel, Harold; Kusel, Daniel

**Cast** Boyd, William; Hayden, Russell; Wood, Britt; Ankrum, Morris; Clayton, Jane; Kramer, Wright; Bancroft, Roy; Maynard, Kermit; The King's Men

**Song(s)** My Solo Amor

**Notes** No cue sheet available.

## 5394 ✦ SHOWDOWN AT BOOT HILL
### Twentieth Century–Fox, 1958

**Musical Score** Harris, Albert

**Producer(s)** Knox, Harold E.
**Director(s)** Fowler Jr., Gene
**Screenwriter(s)** Vittes, Louis

**Cast** Bronson, Charles; Hutton, Robert; Carradine, John; Mathews, Carole; Maxey, Paul; Smith, Martin

**Song(s)** Don't Ever Pretend (C/L: Hooven, Marilyn; Hooven, Joe)

## 5395 ✦ SHOW FOLKS
### Pathe, 1928

**Producer(s)** Block, Ralph
**Director(s)** Stein, Paul
**Screenwriter(s)** Jungmeyer, Jack; Dromgold, George

**Cast** Quillan, Eddie; Basquette, Lina; Lombard, Carole; Armstrong, Robert; Barriscale, Bessie

**Song(s)** No One But Me Only Me (C/L: Koppel, Al; Stone, Billy; Weinberg, Charles); Love's First Kiss (C: Porter, Lew; L: Perry, Sam)

**Notes** No cue sheet available.

## 5396 ✦ SHOW GIRL
### Warner Brothers–First National, 1928

**Director(s)** Santell, Alfred
**Screenwriter(s)** O'Donohue, James T.
**Source(s)** *Show Girl* (novel) McEvoy, J.P.

**Cast** White, Alice; Moran, Lee; Reed, Donald; Delaney, Charles; Tucker, Richard; Finlayson, James; Lee, Gwen

**Song(s)** Buy, Buy For Baby (C: Meyer, Joseph; L: Caesar, Irving); Show Girl (C: Ward, Edward; Meyer, Joseph; L: Caesar, Irving); L: Grossman, Bernie)

**Notes** No cue sheet available.

## 5397 ✦ SHOW GIRL IN HOLLYWOOD
### Warner Brothers–First National, 1930

**Composer(s)** Stept, Sam H.
**Lyricist(s)** Green, Bud
**Choreographer(s)** Haskell, Jack

**Producer(s)** Lord, Robert
**Director(s)** LeRoy, Mervyn
**Screenwriter(s)** Thew, Harvey
**Source(s)** "Hollywood Girl" (story) McEvoy, J.P.

**Cast** White, Alice; Mulhall, Jack; Sterling, Ford; Sweet, Blanche; Miljan, John; Sale, Virginia; O'Donnell, Spec; Bing, Herman

**Song(s)** Hang Onto the Rainbow; I've Got My Eye on You; There's a Tear for Every Smile in Hollywood

**Notes** No cue sheet available.

## 5398 ✦ THE SHOW-OFF
### Metro–Goldwyn–Mayer, 1946

**Producer(s)** Lewis, Albert
**Director(s)** Beaumont, Harry
**Screenwriter(s)** Wells, George
**Source(s)** *The Show-Off* (play) Kelly, George

**Cast** Skelton, Red; Maxwell, Marilyn; Main, Marjorie; O'Brien, Virginia; Anderson, Eddie "Rochester"; Cleveland, George; Ames, Leon; Thompson, Marshall

**Song(s)** Opening of Tooth-Pep Show (C: Heglen, Wally; Brent, Earl; L: Brent, Earl)

**Notes** This was the fourth film version of the play. There is also a vocal of "I've Got You Under My Skin."

## 5399 ◆ THE SHOW OF SHOWS
Warner Brothers, 1929

**Choreographer(s)** Haskell, Jack; Ceballos, Larry

**Producer(s)** Zanuck, Darryl F.
**Director(s)** Adolfi, John
**Screenwriter(s)** Fay, Frank; Brennan, J. Keirn

**Cast** White, Alice; Young, Loretta; The Ted Williams Adagio Dancers; Fay, Frank; Courteney, William; Warner, H.B.; Bosworth, Hobart; Nixon, Marian; O'Neil, Sally; Loy, Myrna; Day, Alice; Miller, Patsy Ruth; Turpin, Ben; Conklin, Heinie; Lane, Lupino; Moran, Lee; Roach, Bert; Hamilton, Lloyd; Beery, Noah; Marshall, Tully; Oakman, Wheeler; Montana, Bull; Pasha, Kalla; Randolf, Anders; McCullough, Philo; Matiesen, Otto; Curtis, Jack; Arthur, Johnny; Myers, Carmel; Clifford, Ruth; Eilers, Sally; Dana, Viola; Mason, Shirley; Clair, Ethlyne; Lee, Frances; Johnston, Julanne; Fairbanks Jr., Douglas; Conklin, Chester; Withers, Grant; Collier Jr., William; Mulhall, Jack; Morris, Chester; Bakewell, William; Wilson, Lois; Olmstead, Gertrude; Garon, Pauline; Murphy, Edna; Logan, Jacqueline; Blue, Monte; Gran, Albert; Armida; Barrymore, John; Barthelmess, Richard; Blane, Sally; Bordoni, Irene; Bushell, Anthony; Byron, Marion; Carpentier, George; Clemmons, James; Compson, Betty; Costello, Dolores; Costello, Helene; Day, Marceline; Fazenda, Louise; Gray, Alexander; Lillie, Beatrice; Lightner, Winnie; Lake, Harriet [1]; Lee, Lila; Ted Lewis and His Band; Rin-Tin-Tin; Lucas, Nick; O'Day, Molly; Radcliffe, E.J.; Silvers, Sid; Vendrill, Lola; Vaughn, Alberta

**Song(s)** Singing in the Bathtub (C: Cleary, Michael; L: Magidson, Herb; Washington, Ned); Lady Luck (C/L: Perkins, Ray); Motion Picture Pirates (C/L: Jerome, M.K.); If I Could Learn to Love (C: Jerome, M.K.; L: Ruby, Herman); Pingo-Pongo (C: Burke, Joe; L: Dubin, Al); The Only Song I Know (C: Perkins, Ray; L: Brennan, J. Keirn); Meet My Sister (C: Perkins, Ray; L: Brennan, J. Keirn); Your Mother and Mine [5] (C: Edwards, Gus; L: Goodwin, Joe); You Were Meant for Me [4] (C: Brown, Nacio Herb; L: Freed, Arthur); Just an Hour of Love (C: Ward, Edward; L: Bryan, Alfred); Li-Po-Li (C: Ward, Edward; L: Bryan, Alfred); Rock-A-Bye Your Baby with a Dixie Melody (C: Schwartz, Jean; L: Lewis, Sam M.; Young, Joe); If Your Best Friends Won't Tell You (C: Burke, Joe; L: Dubin, Al); Jumping Jack [2] (C: Bloom, Rube; L: Smolev, Marvin; Seaman, Bernie; Ruby, Herman); Your Love Is All I Crave [3] (C: Johnson, Jimmy; L: Bradford, Perry; Dubin, Al); Military March (C: Ward, Edward; L: Bryan, Alfred); What's Become of the Floradora Boys? (C/L: Perkins, Ray); Dear Little Pup (C: Perkins, Ray; L: Brennan, J. Keirn); Believe Me [6] (C: Ward, Edward; L: Bryan, Alfred)

**Notes** No cue sheet available. The screenplay credit was actually for special material. Beatrice Lillie had a comedy scene with midgets that was cut from the final print. [1]

Ann Sothern. [2] Some sources do not list Smolev and Seaman. [3] Some sources list the songwriters as Al Dubin and Arthur Johnston but the sheet music reads as above. [4] Also in the MGM pictures BROADWAY MELODY, DOUGHBOYS, SINGIN' IN THE RAIN and HOLLYWOOD REVUE OF 1929. [5] Also in HOLLYWOOD REVUE OF 1929. [6] Not used.

## 5400 ◆ SHOW PEOPLE
Metro–Goldwyn–Mayer, 1928

**Director(s)** Vidor, King
**Screenwriter(s)** Johnston, Agnes Christine; Stallings, Laurence

**Cast** Davies, Marion; Haines, William; Henderson, Del; Ralli, Paul; Moran, Polly; Conti, Albert

**Song(s)** Cross Roads [1] (C: Axt, William; L: Mendoza, David)

**Notes** There are also cameos by Charlie Chaplin, Mary Pickford, William S. Hart, Douglas Fairbanks Sr., Norma Talmedge, John Gilbert, Mae Murray, Rod La Rocque, Renee Adoree, Leatrice Joy, George K. Arthur, Karl Dane, Aileen Pringle, Claire Windsor, Estelle Taylor, Louella Parsons, Dorothy Sebastian and Polly Moran. [1] Also in A LADY OF CHANCE.

## 5401 ◆ SHOW THEM NO MERCY
Twentieth Century–Fox, 1935

**Producer(s)** Zanuck, Darryl F.
**Director(s)** Marshall, George
**Screenwriter(s)** Glasmon, Kubec; Lehrman, Henry

**Cast** Hudson, Rochelle; Romero, Cesar; Cabot, Bruce; Norris, Edward; Brophy, Edward S.; Hymer, Warren; Rawlinson, Herbert; McVey, Paul

**Song(s)** Sunrise Hymn (Blessed Be the Dawning) [1](C/L: Kernell, William)

**Notes** There is also a vocal of "Nasty Man" by Ray Henderson, Irving Caesar and Jack Yellen with slightly altered lyrics. [1] Also in RAMONA.

## 5402 ◆ SHY PEOPLE
Cannon, 1987

**Musical Score** Tangerine Dream

**Producer(s)** Golan, Menahem; Globus, Yoram
**Director(s)** Konchalovsky, Andrei
**Screenwriter(s)** Brach, Gerard; Konchalovsky, Andrei; David, Marjorie

**Cast** Hershey, Barbara; Plimpton, Martha; Butrick, Merritt; Philbin, John

**Song(s)** Shy People (C: Tangerine Dream; L: Boustead, Ron); Goin' to Town (C: Tangerine Dream; L: Boustead, Ron)

**Notes** No cue sheet available.

**5403 ✦ SIAM**
Disney, 1954

**Musical Score** Wallace, Oliver

**Producer(s)** Sharpsteen, Ben
**Director(s)** Wright, Ralph
**Screenwriter(s)** Wright, Ralph; Hibler, Winston; Sears, Ted; Maiden, Cecil

**Cast** Hibler, Winston

**Song(s)** Song of Siam [1] (C: Wallace, Oliver; L: Hamilton, Arthur)

**Notes** [1] Lyrics written for exploitation only.

**5404 ✦ SI C'ETAIT A REFAIRE**

See SECOND CHANCE.

**5405 ✦ SIDA SANGRE Y SOL**
Twentieth Century–Fox, 1942

**Composer(s)** Cortazar, Ernesto M.
**Lyricist(s)** Cortazar, Ernesto M.

**Song(s)** Juramento (C: Esperon, Manuel); Primavera; Callate Corazon; Toro Bonito (C: Galindo, Pedro)

**Notes** No other information available.

**5406 ✦ SIDECAR BOYS**

See SIDECAR RACERS.

**5407 ✦ SIDECAR RACERS**
Universal, 1975

**Musical Score** Scott, Thomas W.

**Producer(s)** Irving, Richard
**Director(s)** Bellamy, Earl
**Screenwriter(s)** Cleary, Jon

**Cast** Murphy, Ben; Clayton, John; Hughes, Wendy; Graves, Peter

**Song(s)** Turn on the World Tonight (C: Lyons, Shad F.; L: Aranda, Jack)

**Notes** Also titled SIDECAR BOYS.

**5408 ✦ SIDE SHOW**
Warner Brothers, 1931

**Director(s)** Del Ruth, Roy
**Screenwriter(s)** Wells, William K.; Caesar, Arthur

**Cast** Lightner, Winnie; Butterworth, Charles; Kibbee, Guy; Cook, Donald; Knapp, Evalyn; Morgan, Edward; Alberni, Luis

**Song(s)** Girls We Remember [1] (C: Burke, Joe; L: Dubin, Al); Take a Look at This [2] (C: Hanley, James F.; L: Brown, Lew)

**Notes** [1] Also in HOLD EVERYTHING. [2] Written in 1923.

**5409 ✦ SIEGE AT RED RIVER**
Twentieth Century–Fox, 1954

**Producer(s)** Goldstein, Leonard
**Director(s)** Mate, Rudolph
**Screenwriter(s)** Boehm, Sydney

**Cast** Johnson, Van; Dru, Joanne; Boone, Richard; Stone, Milburn; Morrow, Jeff; Hill, Craig

**Song(s)** Tapioca [1] (C: Newman, Lionel; L: Darby, Ken); Commercial (C: Newman, Lionel; L: Townsend, Leo)

**Notes** [1] Music and lyrics based on a song by James A. Bland.

**5410 ✦ SIERRA**
Universal, 1950

**Musical Score** Scharf, Walter
**Composer(s)** Hughes, Arnold
**Lyricist(s)** Herbert, Frederick

**Producer(s)** Kraike, Michel
**Director(s)** Green, Alfred E.
**Screenwriter(s)** Anhalt, Edna; Gunzburg, Milton
**Source(s)** (novel) Hardy, Stuart

**Cast** Hendrix, Wanda; Murphy, Audie; Jagger, Dean; Ives, Burl

**Song(s)** Hideaway; The End of the Road; Sarah, the Mule (C/L: Ives, Burl); The Whale Song (C/L: Ives, Burl); Black Angus McDougal; Drift Along

**Notes** A remake of FORBIDDEN VALLEY (1937).

**5411 ✦ SIERRA SUE**
Republic, 1941

**Producer(s)** Grey, Harry
**Director(s)** Morgan, William
**Screenwriter(s)** Zimet, Julian; Felton, Earl

**Cast** Autry, Gene; Burnette, Smiley; McKenzie, Fay; Thomas, Frank M.; Homans, Robert; Hodgins, Earl; Lease, Rex; Dean, Eddie; Kirk, Jack

**Song(s)** Be Honest with Me [1] (C/L: Autry, Gene; Rose, Fred); I'll Be True When You're Gone (C/L: Autry, Gene; Rose, Fred); Heebie Jeebie Blues [2] (C: Grey, Harry; L: Drake, Oliver); Sierra Sue [4] (C/L: Carey, Joseph B.); Ridin' the Range [3] (C/L: Autry, Gene; Shawn, Nelson; Styne, Jule; Allan, Fleming)

**Notes** No cue sheet available. [1] Also in FLAMING BULLETS (PRC) and STRICTLY IN THE GROOVE

(Universal). [2] Also in SUNSET IN WYOMING. [3] Also in BOOTS AND SADDLES but without the Styne credit. [4] Also in COUNTRY FAIR.

## 5412 ✦ SIGN OF THE RAM
### Columbia, 1947

**Producer(s)**  Cummings, Irving
**Director(s)**  Sturges, John
**Screenwriter(s)**  Bennett, Charles
**Source(s)**  *Sign of the Ram* (novel) Ferguson, Margaret

**Cast**  Garner, Peggy Ann; Peters, Susan; Knox, Alexander; Randell, Ron; Whitty, Dame May; Thaxter, Phyllis

**Song(s)**  I'll Never Say I Love You (C: Lee, Lester; L: Roberts, Allan)

## 5413 ✦ THE SIGN OF ZORRO
### Disney, 1958

**Musical Score**  Lava, William
**Composer(s)**  Lava, William
**Lyricist(s)**  Jackman, Bob

**Producer(s)**  Anderson, William H.
**Director(s)**  Foster, Norman; Foster, Lewis R.
**Screenwriter(s)**  Foster, Norman; Wehling, Bob; Hawley, Lowell S.; Lucas, John Meredyth
**Source(s)**  Zorro stories (stories) McCulley, Johnston

**Cast**  Williams, Guy

**Song(s)**  Zorro (C: Bruns, George; L: Foster, Norman); Don Diego [1]; Bernardo [1]; Forward March [1]

**Notes**  [1] Used instrumentally only.

## 5414 ✦ THE SILENCERS
### Columbia, 1966

**Musical Score**  Bernstein, Elmer
**Composer(s)**  Bernstein, Elmer
**Lyricist(s)**  David, Mack

**Producer(s)**  Allen, Irving
**Director(s)**  Karlson, Phil
**Screenwriter(s)**  Saul, Oscar
**Source(s)**  Matt Helm series (novels) Hamilton, Donald

**Cast**  Martin, Dean; Stevens, Stella; Lavi, Daliah; Buono, Victor; O'Connell, Arthur; Webber, Robert; Gregory, James; Kovack, Nancy; Carmel, Roger C.; Charisse, Cyd

**Song(s)**  The Silencers; Santiago

**Notes**  Special lyrics for "Empty Saddles," "If You Knew Susie," "The Anniversary Song," "Lord, You Made the Night Too Long," "On the Sunny Side of the Street," "The Last Roundup," "South of the Border," "Red Sails in the Sunset," "Side By Side" and "The Glory of Love" were by Herbie Baker.

## 5415 ✦ THE SILENT ENEMY
### Paramount, 1930

**Musical Score**  Kur-Zhene, Massard

**Producer(s)**  Burdon, W. Douglas; Chanler, William
**Director(s)**  Carver, H.P.
**Screenwriter(s)**  Carver, Richard

**Cast**  Chief Yellow Robe; Chief Long Lance; Chief Akawanush; Spotted Elk; Cheeka

**Song(s)**  The Song of the Waters [1] (C: Chase, Newell; L: Coslow, Sam); Ojibwe Summer—Rain-Flower [1] (C: Kur-Zhene, Massard; L: Robin, Leo); Indian Chant (C/L: Kur-Zhene, Massard); Pau-Cuk—Spirit of Death (C/L: Kur-Zhene, Massard)

**Notes**  Documentary. This was originally titled RED GODS. [1] These are only played instrumentally.

## 5416 ✦ SILENT PARTNER
### Republic, 1944

**Musical Score**  Dubin, Joseph S.

**Producer(s)**  Blair, George
**Director(s)**  Blair, George
**Screenwriter(s)**  Lussier, Dane; Walker, Gertrude

**Cast**  Henry, William; Lloyd, Beverly; Withers, Grant; Vernon, Wally; Blair, Joan; Meeker, George; Knox, Patricia

**Song(s)**  If It's Love [1] (C: Styne, Jule; L: Cahn, Sammy)

**Notes**  [1] Also in YOUTH ON PARADE.

## 5417 ✦ SILENT RAGE
### Columbia, 1982

**Producer(s)**  Unger, Anthony
**Director(s)**  Miller, Michael
**Screenwriter(s)**  Fraley, Joseph

**Cast**  Norris, Chuck; Silver, Ron; Keats, Steven; Kalem, Toni; Finley, William; Furst, Stephen

**Song(s)**  Time for Love (C/L: Stoddard, Morgan)

**Notes**  No cue sheet available.

## 5418 ✦ SILENT RUNNING
### Universal, 1972

**Musical Score**  Schickele, Peter
**Composer(s)**  Schickele, Peter
**Lyricist(s)**  Lampert, Diane

**Producer(s)**  Gruskoff, Michael
**Director(s)**  Trumbull, Douglas
**Screenwriter(s)**  Washburn, Deric; Cimino, Michael; Bocho, Steve

**Cast**   Dern, Bruce; Potts, Cliff; Rifkin, Ron; Vint, Jesse

**Song(s)**   Rejoice in the Sun; Silent Running

## 5419 ✦ SILENT SCREAM
American Cinema, 1980

**Musical Score**   Kellaway, Roger

**Producer(s)**   Wheat, Jim; Wheat, Ken
**Director(s)**   Harris, Denny
**Screenwriter(s)**   Wheat, Ken; Wheat, Jim; Bennett, Wallace C.

**Cast**   Balding, Rebecca; Mitchell, Cameron; Schreiber, Avery; Steele, Barbara; Doubet, Steve; Rearden, Brad; Pelish, Thelma; De Carlo, Yvonne

**Song(s)**   I Love You Baby, Oh Baby I Do (C/L: Kellaway, Roger)

**Notes**   No cue sheet available.

## 5420 ✦ SILK STOCKINGS
Metro–Goldwyn–Mayer, 1957

**Composer(s)**   Porter, Cole
**Lyricist(s)**   Porter, Cole
**Choreographer(s)**   Loring, Eugene; Pan, Hermes [3]

**Producer(s)**   Freed, Arthur
**Director(s)**   Mamoulian, Rouben
**Screenwriter(s)**   Gershe, Leonard; Spigelgass, Leonard
**Source(s)**   *Silk Stockings* (musical) Porter, Cole; Kaufman, George S.; McGrath, Leueen; Burrows, Abe

**Cast**   Astaire, Fred; Charisse, Cyd [4]; Paige, Janis; Lorre, Peter; Tobias, George; Munshin, Jules; Buloff, Joseph; Sonneveld, Wim

**Song(s)**   Too Bad; Paris Loves Lovers; Stereophonic Sound; It's a Chemical Reaction That's All; All of You; Satin and Silk; Without Love; Fated to Be Mated [1]; Josephine; Siberia; Red Blues; The Ritz Roll and Rock [1]; Silk Stockings [2]

**Notes**   The show is based on the film NINOTCHKA which is based on the novel of the same name by Melchoir Lengyel. [1] Written for film. All other songs from Broadway original. [2] Used instrumentally only. [3] Hermes Pan choreographeed Fred Astaire's numbers. [4] Dubbed by Carole Richards.

## 5421 ✦ SILLY BILLIES
RKO, 1936

**Musical Score**   Webb, Roy

**Producer(s)**   Marcus, Fred
**Director(s)**   Guiol, Fred
**Screenwriter(s)**   Boasberg, Al; Townley, Jack

**Cast**   Wheeler, Bert; Woolsey, Robert; Lee, Dorothy; Woods, Harry; Laidlaw, Ethan

**Song(s)**   Tumble on Tumble Weed [1] (C: Dreyer, Dave; L: Scholl, Jack)

**Notes**   [1] Also in THE FIGHTING GRINGO and GUN LAW.

## 5422 ✦ THE SILVER BULLET (1942)
Universal, 1942

**Musical Score**   Rosen, Milton
**Composer(s)**   Rosen, Milton
**Lyricist(s)**   Drake, Oliver; Wakely, Jimmy

**Producer(s)**   Drake, Oliver
**Director(s)**   Lewis, Joseph H.
**Screenwriter(s)**   Beecher, Elizabeth

**Cast**   Brown, Johnny Mack; Knight, Fuzzy

**Song(s)**   Sweetheart of the Rio Grande; My Gal She Works in the Laundry; Vote for Emily Morgan [1]

**Notes**   [1] Also in RUSTLER'S ROUND-UP (1946).

## 5423 ✦ SILVER BULLET (1985)
Paramount, 1985

**Musical Score**   Chattaway, Jay

**Producer(s)**   Schumacher, Martha
**Director(s)**   Attias, Daniel
**Screenwriter(s)**   King, Stephen
**Source(s)**   "Cycle of the Werewolf" (novella) King, Stephen

**Cast**   Busey, Gary; McGill, Everett; Haim, Corey; Follows, Megan; O'Quinn, Terry; Smitrovich, Bill

**Song(s)**   Joyride (C: Chattaway, Jay; L: Mathes, Rob B.)

**Notes**   No cue sheet available.

## 5424 ✦ SILVER CANYON
Columbia, 1951

**Director(s)**   English, John
**Screenwriter(s)**   Geraghty, Gerald

**Cast**   Autry, Gene; Champion; Buttram, Pat; Frost, Terry; Steele, Bob; Clark, Bobby; Andrews, Stanley

**Song(s)**   Ridin' Down the Canyon [1] (C/L: Burnette, Smiley); Fort Worth Jail (C/L: Reinhart, Dick)

**Notes**   [1] Also in RIDIN' DOWN THE CANYON and TUMBLING TUMBLEWEEDS, both from Republic. Gene Autry is listed as the coauthor of the song but he did not contribute to its writing. Burnette, who was brought out to Hollywood by Autry, was the sole writer.

## 5425 ✦ SILVER CITY BONANZA
Republic, 1951

**Producer(s)**   Tucker, Melville
**Director(s)**   Blair, George
**Screenwriter(s)**   Williams, Bob

**Cast**    Allen, Rex; Ebsen, Buddy; Kay, Mary Ellen; Kimbley, Billy; Ebsen, Alix; Kennedy, Bill; Bevans, Clem

**Song(s)**    Toolie Rollum [2] (C/L: Allen, Rex); Lollipop Lane [1] (C/L: Rose, Fred; Marvin, Johnny)

**Notes**    There is also a vocal of "Sweet Evalina." [1] Also in BARNYARD FOLLIES. [2] Also in THE ARIZONA COWBOY, RODEO KING AND THE SENORITA, SHADOWS OF TOMBSTONE and UTAH WAGON TRAIN.

## 5426 ✦ SILVER ON THE SAGE
### Paramount, 1939

**Producer(s)**    Sherman, Harry
**Director(s)**    Selander, Lesley
**Screenwriter(s)**    Geraghty, Maurice

**Cast**    Boyd, William; Hayden, Russell; Hayes, George "Gabby"; Rogers, Ruth

**Song(s)**    Silver on the Sage [1] (C: Rainger, Ralph; L: Robin, Leo)

**Notes**    [1] Also in THE TEXANS.

## 5427 ✦ SILVER SKATES
### Monogram, 1943

**Composer(s)**    Ingraham, Roy
**Lyricist(s)**    Oppenheim, Dave

**Producer(s)**    Parsons, Lindsley
**Director(s)**    Goodwins, Leslie
**Screenwriter(s)**    Cady, Jerry

**Cast**    Baker, Kenny; Morison, Patricia; Belita; Dare, Irene; Frick and Frack; Turner, Eugene; Ted Fiorito and His Orchestra; Shaw, Danny; Compton, Joyce; Faylen, Frank; McVey, Paul; Wadsworth, Henry

**Song(s)**    Love Is a Beautiful Song; Dancing on Top of the World; Lovely Lady; Can't You Hear Me Calling from the Mountain; Cowboy Joe; A Boy Like You and a Girl Like Me; Sing a Song of the Sea (C: Gottler, Archie); Victory Party

**Notes**    No cue sheet available.

## 5428 ✦ SILVER SPURS
### Republic, 1943

**Producer(s)**    Grey, Harry
**Director(s)**    Kane, Joseph
**Screenwriter(s)**    Butler, John K.; Cheney, J. Benton

**Cast**    Rogers, Roy; Brooks, Phyllis; Burnette, Smiley; Carradine, John; Cowan, Jerome; Compton, Joyce; Sons of the Pioneers

**Song(s)**    Jubilation Jamboree (C/L: Spencer, Tim); Horses and Women (C/L: Burnette, Smiley); Tumbling Tumbleweeds [1] (C/L: Nolan, Bob)

**Notes**    There is also a vocal of "Back in Your Own Backyard" by Al Jolson, Billy Rose and Dave Dreyer and one of "When It's Springtime in the Rockies" by Mary Hale Woolsey, Robert Sauer and Milton Taggart. [1] Also in RHYTHM ROUND-UP (Columbia), DON'T FENCE ME IN, IN OLD MONTEREY, SILVER SPURS and HOLLYWOOD CANTEEN (Warner).

## 5429 ✦ SIMON
### Orion, 1980

**Musical Score**    Silverman, Stanley
**Composer(s)**    Silverman, Stanley
**Lyricist(s)**    Silverman, Stanley

**Producer(s)**    Bregman, Martin
**Director(s)**    Brickman, Marshall
**Screenwriter(s)**    Brickman, Marshall

**Cast**    Arkin, Alan; Kahn, Madeline; Pendleton, Austin; Graubart, Judy; Finlay, William; Shawn, Wallace; Wright, Max; Gwynne, Fred; Green, Adolph; Epstein, Pierre; Robbins, Rex; Cooper, Roy

**Song(s)**    Origin of Species; A Walk in the Fields; Media Montage

## 5430 ✦ SINCERELY YOURS
### Warner Brothers, 1955

**Producer(s)**    Blanke, Henry
**Director(s)**    Douglas, Gordon M.
**Screenwriter(s)**    Wallace, Irving
**Source(s)**    *The Man Who Played God* (play) Goodman, Jules Eckert

**Cast**    Liberace; Dru, Joanne; Malone, Dorothy; Nicol, Alex; Demarest, William; Tuttle, Lurene; Eyer, Richard

**Song(s)**    Sincerely Yours (C: Liberace; L: Webster, Paul Francis)

**Notes**    Previously filmed in 1932 as THE MAN WHO PLAYED GOD. "When Irish Eyes Are Smiling" by Ernest Ball and Chauncey Olcott is also used as a vocal.

## 5431 ✦ SINCE YOU WENT AWAY
### United Artists, 1944

**Musical Score**    Steiner, Max; Forbes, Louis

**Producer(s)**    Selznick, David O.
**Director(s)**    Cromwell, John
**Screenwriter(s)**    Selznick, David O.
**Source(s)**    (novel) Wilder, Margaret Buell

**Cast**    McDaniel, Hattie; Corrigan, Lloyd; Moorehead, Agnes; Pringle, Aileen; Bacon, Irving; Colbert, Claudette; Jones, Jennifer; Cotten, Joseph; Temple, Shirley; Woolley, Monty; Barrymore, Lionel; Walker, Robert

**Song(s)**    Since You Went Away (C: Grouya, Ted; L: Goell, Kermit); Together [1] (C: Henderson, Ray; L:

Brown, Lew; DeSylva, B.G.); The Dipsy Doodle (C/L: Clinton, Larry)

**Notes**   No cue sheet available. [1] Written in 1927.

## 5432 ◆ SINFUL DAVEY
### United Artists, 1969

**Musical Score**   Thorne, Ken

**Producer(s)**   Graf, William N.
**Director(s)**   Huston, John
**Screenwriter(s)**   Webb, James R.
**Source(s)**   *The Life of David Haggart* (book) Haggart, David

**Cast**   Hurt, John; Franklin, Pamela; Davenport, Nigel; Fraser, Ronald; Morley, Robert; Flanagan, Fionnuala

**Song(s)**   Sinful Davey (C: Thorne, Ken; L: Black, Don)

## 5433 ◆ SING A JINGLE
### Universal, 1943

**Composer(s)**   Miller, Sidney; James, Inez
**Lyricist(s)**   Miller, Sidney; James, Inez

**Producer(s)**   Lilley, Edward
**Director(s)**   Lilley, Edward
**Screenwriter(s)**   Grey, John; Conrad, Eugene; Sands, Lee; Roth, Fred

**Cast**   Jones, Allan; Vincent, June; Love, Dicky; Kean, Betty; Schilling, Gus

**Song(s)**   Sing a Jingle [1]; We're the Janes that Make the Planes; Madam Mozelle (C/L: Miller, Sidney; James, Inez; Pepper, Buddy)

**Notes**   Previously titled LUCKY DAYS. There are also vocal renditions of "Love, You Are My Music" by Daniel S. Twohig and Gustav Klemm; "Believe Me If All Those Endearing Young Charms" by Thomas Moore; "When You and I Were Young Maggie" by J.A. Butterfield and George W. Johnson; "Dear Old Girl" by Richard H. Buck and Theodore Morse; "Let Me Call You Sweetheart" by Beth Slater Whitson and Leo Friedman; "The Night We Called It a Day" by Tom Adair and Matt Dennis and "Beautiful Love" by Haven Gillespie, Victor Young, Wayne King and Egbert van Alstyne. [1] Also in MY GAL LOVES MUSIC.

## 5434 ◆ SING AND BE HAPPY
### Twentieth Century–Fox, 1937

**Composer(s)**   Akst, Harry
**Lyricist(s)**   Clare, Sidney

**Producer(s)**   Field, Milton
**Director(s)**   Tinling, James
**Screenwriter(s)**   Markson, Ben; Breslow, Lou; Patrick, John

**Cast**   Martin, Tony; Ray, Leah; Davis, Joan; Westley, Helen; Lane, Allan; Dunbar, Dixie; Chandler, Chick;

Alberni, Luis; McGlynn, Frank; Tombes, Andrew; Churchill, Berton

**Song(s)**   Travelin' Light; Pickles; What a Beautiful Beginning; When Did I Hear You Tell Me You Love Me; Sing and Be Happy [1]

**Notes**   There is also a vocal of "The Sweetest Story Ever Told" by R.M. Stults. [1] Sheet music only.

## 5435 ◆ SING AND LIKE IT
### RKO, 1934

**Producer(s)**   Green, Howard J.
**Director(s)**   Seiter, William A.
**Screenwriter(s)**   Dix, Marion; Doyle, Laird
**Source(s)**   "So You Won't Sing, Eh?" (story) Kandel, Aben

**Cast**   Pitts, ZaSu; Kelton, Pert; Horton, Edward Everett; Pendleton, Nat; Sparks, Ned; Carle, Richard; Fields, Stanley

**Song(s)**   Your Mother (C: Dreyer, Dave; L: Turk, Roy); Hi-De-Ho (C/L: Burton, Val; Jason, Will)

## 5436 ◆ SING AND SWING
### Universal, 1964

**Musical Score**   Meek, Joe
**Composer(s)**   Meek, Joe
**Lyricist(s)**   Meek, Joe

**Producer(s)**   Comfort, Lance
**Director(s)**   Comfort, Lance
**Screenwriter(s)**   Fairhurst, Lyn

**Cast**   Hemmings, David; Moss, Jennifer; Pike, John; Burt, Heinz; Kenny Ball and His Jazzmen; Vincent, Gene; The Outlaws; Noble, Patsy Ann; Cavell, James

**Song(s)**   Don't Take You from Me; Live It Up; Sometimes I Wish; Loving Me This Way; Butterbells and Buttercups; Accidents Will Happen (C/L: Paramor, Norrie; Barratt, Bob); Temptation Baby; Live It Up; Don't You Understand

**Notes**   A British picture also known as LIVE IT UP.

## 5437 ◆ SING ANOTHER CHORUS
### Universal, 1941

**Composer(s)**   Rosen, Milton
**Lyricist(s)**   Carter, Everett

**Producer(s)**   Goldsmith, Ken
**Director(s)**   Lamont, Charles
**Screenwriter(s)**   Orth, Marion; Smith, Paul Gerard; Weisberg, Brenda

**Cast**   Rosario and Antonio; Frazee, Jane; Downs, Johnny; Adrian, Iris; The Peters Brothers; O'Dea, Sunnie

**Song(s)**   We Too Can Sing (L: Smith, Paul Gerard; Carter, Everett); Walk with Me; Dancin' on Air [2]; Rug

Cuttin' Romeo [4]; The Boogie Woogie Man [1]; Two Vacations with Pay; Peters Brothers Patter; Rosio, La Gitana (C/L: Masciarelli, Selvio); Mister Yankee Doodle [3]

**Notes**    [1] Also in IN THE GROOVE (short) and MURDER IN THE BLUE ROOM. [2] Also in THE MYSTERY OF THE RIVER BOAT and STRICTLY IN THE GROOVE. [3] Also in HI, BUDDY! [4] Also in IN THE GROOVE, SWING IT SOLDIER and WHERE DID YOU GET THAT GIRL.

**5438  ◆  SINGAPORE**
Universal, 1947

**Musical Score**    Amfitheatrof, Daniele

**Producer(s)**    Bresler, Jerry
**Director(s)**    Brahm, John
**Screenwriter(s)**    Miller, Seton I.; Thoeren, Robert

**Cast**    MacMurray, Fred; Gardner, Ava; Hall, Porter; Byington, Spring; Culver, Roland; Lloyd, George; Haydn, Richard

**Song(s)**    Je N'en Connais Pas La Fin [1] (C/L: Asso, Raymond; Monnot, Marguerite)

**Notes**    Remade as ISTANBUL (1957). [1] Also in THE MATING SEASON (Paramount).

**5439  ◆  SING BABY SING**
Twentieth Century–Fox, 1936

**Producer(s)**    Zanuck, Darryl F.
**Director(s)**    Lanfield, Sidney
**Screenwriter(s)**    Sperling, Milton; Yellen, Jack; Tugend, Harry

**Cast**    Faye, Alice; Menjou, Adolphe; Ratoff, Gregory; Healy, Ted; Kelly, Patsy; Whalen, Michael; The Ritz Brothers; Love, Montagu; Dunbar, Dixie; Fowley, Douglas; Martin, Tony

**Song(s)**    Sing Baby Sing (C: Pollack, Lew; L: Yellen, Jack); You Turned the Tables on Me (C: Alter, Louis; L: Mitchell, Sidney D.); Love Will Tell (C: Pollack, Lew; L: Yellen, Jack); Singing a Vagabond Song [1] (C/L: Richman, Harry; Burton, Val; Messenheimer, Sam); When Did You Leave Heaven? [2] (C: Whiting, Richard A.; L: Bullock, Walter); All of a Sudden [3] (C: Pollack, Lew; L: Yellen, Jack)

**Notes**    There are also vocals of "The Music Goes Round and Round" by Red Hodgson, Edward Farley and Michael Riley (also in the Republic picture TROCADERO and the Columbia picture THE MUSIC GOES ROUND); "Thanks a Million" by Arthur Johnston and Gus Kahn (also in THANKS A MILLION) and "When My Baby Smiles at Me" by Bill Munro, Andrew B. Sterling and Ted Lewis. There are also very brief vocal renditions of "When Irish Eyes Are

Smiling" by Ernest R. Ball, Chauncey Olcott and George Graff Jr. (from the stage show THE ISLE O' DREAMS); "Funiculi Funicula" by Luigi Denza; Rachmaninoff's "Prelude in C Sharp Minor;" "Carry me Back to Old Virginny" by James A. Bland; "I'm Shooting High" by Jimmy McHugh and Ted Koehler and "Is It True What They Say About Dixie" by Sammy Lerner, Gerald Marks and Irving Caesar. [1] Also in MY FRIEND IRMA GOES WEST. [2] Also in WILD AND WOOLLY. [3] Not used.

**5440  ◆  SING BOY SING**
Twentieth Century–Fox, 1957

**Choreographer(s)**    Castle, Nick

**Producer(s)**    Ephron, Henry
**Director(s)**    Ephron, Henry
**Screenwriter(s)**    Binyon, Claude

**Cast**    Sands, Tommy; Gentle, Lili; O'Brien, Edmond; McIntire, John; Leith, Virginia; Adams, Nick; Jergens, Diane; Paris, Jerry; Toomey, Regis

**Song(s)**    I'm Gonna Walk and Talk with My Lord (C/L: Carson, Martha); Who Baby [1] (C/L: Carroll, Jeanne; Olofson, Bill); People in Love (C: Newman, Lionel; L: Leven, Mel); Crazy 'Cause I Love You (C/L: Cooley, Spade); Soda-Pop Pop (C/L: Daret, Betty; Daret, Carla); Just a Little Bit More (C/L: Singleton, Charles; McCoy, Rose Marie); Sing Boy Sing (C/L: Sands, Tommy; McKuen, Rod); That's All I Want from You (C/L: Rotha, M.); Bundle of Dreams [2] (C/L: Strange, Billy; Escamilla, Homer); Your Daddy Wants to Be Right [2] (C/L: Sands, Tommy)

**Notes**    Originally titled SINGING IDOL. [1] Also in BLUE DENIM. [2] Sheet music only.

**5441  ◆  SING, DANCE, PLENTY HOT**
Republic, 1940

**Composer(s)**    Styne, Jule
**Lyricist(s)**    Brown, George; Meyer, Sol
**Choreographer(s)**    Brown, George R.; Ceballos, Larry

**Producer(s)**    North, Robert
**Director(s)**    Landers, Lew
**Screenwriter(s)**    Ropes, Bradford

**Cast**    Terry, Ruth; Downs, Johnny; Allen, Barbara Jo [1]; Gilbert, Billy; Carleton, Claire; Lee, Mary; Risdon, Elizabeth; Matthews, Lester; Carey, Leonard

**Song(s)**    Too Toy; When a Fella's Got a Girl [3]; Whatcha Gonna Do; What Fools These Mortals Be; I'm Just a Weakie; Tequila [2]

**Notes**    Titled MELODY GIRL overseas. [1] Also known as Vera Vague. She is billed here as Barbara Allen. [2] Also in ICE CAPADES. [3] Also in HI, NEIGHBOR.

## 5442 ◆ THE SINGER OF NAPLES
### Warner Brothers–Vitaphone, 1934

**Composer(s)** Conti, A.
**Lyricist(s)** Conti, A.

**Producer(s)** Reachi, Manuel
**Director(s)** Bretherton, Howard
**Screenwriter(s)** Reinhardt, Elizabeth
**Source(s)** (novel) Chelieu, Armon

**Cast** Caruso Jr., Enrico; Maris, Mona; Rio, Carmen; Pedroza, Alfonso; Vidal, Antonio; Leovalli, Emilia; Acosta, Enrique

**Song(s)** Original Tarantella

**Notes** "Italian Salad" by Genee; "Corn'grato" by Cordello and Verdi's "Di Quella Pira" from IL TROVATORE are also given vocal performances. Made in Spanish as EL CANTATE DE NAPOLES.

## 5443 ◆ SING FOR YOUR SUPPER
### Columbia, 1941

**Producer(s)** Barsha, Leon
**Director(s)** Barton, Charles
**Screenwriter(s)** Rebuas, Harry [2]

**Cast** Falkenburg, Jinx; Beddoe, Don; Gordon, Bert; Arden, Eve; Kolker, Henry; Rogers, Charles "Buddy"; Barris, Harry; Porter, Don; Baker, Benny; Robinson, Dewey

**Song(s)** Why Is It So (C: Chaplin, Saul; L: Cahn, Sammy); Boogly Woogly Piggy (C: Jacobs, Roy; Chaplin, Saul; L: Jacobs, Roy; Chaplin, Saul; Cahn, Sammy); Until Tomorrow [1] (C/L: Kaye, Sammy)

**Notes** [1] Not written for picture. [2] Pseudonym of Harry Sauber.

## 5444 ◆ THE SINGING CHARO
### Paramount, 1939

**Composer(s)** Guizar, Tito
**Lyricist(s)** Noriega, Nenette

**Song(s)** El Loco; Rio Grande; Por Tus Ojos; Huapango; Marcia [1]

**Notes** [1] Not used.

## 5445 ◆ SINGING COWBOY
### Republic, 1936

**Producer(s)** Levine, Nat
**Director(s)** Wright, Mack V.
**Screenwriter(s)** McGowan, Dorrell; McGowan, Stuart

**Cast** Autry, Gene; Burnette, Smiley; Wilde, Lois; Chaney Jr., Lon; Champion; Gilles, Ann; Van Pet, John; Snowflake

**Song(s)** Empty Cot in the Bunkhouse (C/L: Unknown); Yahoo (C/L: Unknown); We're on the Air (C/L: Unknown); True Blue Bill (C/L: Unknown); Rainbow Trail (C/L: Drake, Oliver; Burnette, Smiley); Slumberland (C/L: Unknown); Listen to the Mockingbird (C/L: Unknown); Washboard and Room (C/L: Unknown); My Old Saddle Pal (C/L: Autry, Gene; Thompson, Oddie); I'll Be Thinking of You, Little Gal (C/L: Unknown)

**Notes** No cue sheet available.

## 5446 ◆ SINGING COWGIRL
### Coronado, 1940

**Composer(s)** Drake, Milton; Sherman, Al; Kent, Walter
**Lyricist(s)** Drake, Milton; Sherman, Al; Kent, Walter

**Producer(s)** Hirliman, George A.
**Director(s)** Diege, Samuel
**Screenwriter(s)** Hoerl, Arthur

**Cast** Page, Dorothy; O'Brien, Dave; Barnett, Vince; Piel, Ed; Davis, Dix

**Song(s)** Prairie Boy (C: Drake, Milton; L: Sherman, Al); You Gotta Sing; Let's Round Up Our Dreams

**Notes** No cue sheet available.

## 5447 ◆ THE SINGING FOOL
### Warner Brothers, 1928

**Composer(s)** Henderson, Ray
**Lyricist(s)** DeSylva, B.G.; Brown, Lew

**Director(s)** Bacon, Lloyd
**Screenwriter(s)** Jackson, Joseph
**Source(s)** "The Singing Fool" (story) Barrows, Leslie S.

**Cast** Jolson, Al; Bronson, Betty; Dunn, Josephine; Lee, Davey; Housman, Arthur; Howes, Reed; Martindel, Edward

**Song(s)** It All Depends on You; I'm Sitting on Top of the World; The Spaniard That Blighted My Life (C/L: Merson, Billy); There's a Rainbow Round My Shoulder (C/L: Jolson, Al; Rose, Billy; Dreyer, Dave); Golden Gate (C: Jolson, Al; Meyer, Joseph; L: Rose, Billy; Dreyer, Dave); Sonny Boy; Keep Smiling at Trouble [1] (C: Gensler, Lewis E.; L: DeSylva, B.G.; Jolson, Al)

**Notes** [1] From the Broadway musical BIG BOY.

## 5448 ◆ SINGING GUNS (1940)
### Studio Unknown, 1940

**Song(s)** One More Hand on the Range (C/L: Drake, Milton)

**Notes** No other information available.

## 5449 ✦ SINGING GUNS (1950)
### Republic, 1950

**Musical Score**  Scott, Nathan

**Producer(s)**  Tucker, Melville
**Director(s)**  Springsteen, R.G.
**Screenwriter(s)**  McGowan, Dorrell; McGowan, Stuart
**Source(s)**  *Singing Guns* (novel) Brand, Max

**Cast**  Monroe, Vaughn; Raines, Ella; Bond, Ward; Brennan, Walter; Corey, Jeff; Kelley, Barry

**Song(s)**  Singing My Way Back Home (C/L: Moore, Wilton; Vann, Al); Mule Train [1] (C/L: Heath, Hy; Lange, Johnny; Glickman, Fred); Mexicali Trail (C/L: Moore, Wilton; Skylar, Sunny)

**Notes**  [1] Also in MULE TRAIN (Columbia).

## 5450 ✦ SINGING HILLS
### Republic, 1941

**Producer(s)**  Grey, Harry
**Director(s)**  Landers, Lew
**Screenwriter(s)**  Cooper, Olive
**Source(s)**  *Singing Hill* (novel) Bower, Bertha M.

**Cast**  Autry, Gene; Burnette, Smiley; Dalte, Virginia; Lee, Mary; Charters, Spencer; Meeker, George; Cactus Mack; Kirk, Jack

**Song(s)**  Tumble Down Shack in Havana (C: Styne, Jule; L: Meyer, Sol; Cherkose, Eddie); Sail the Seven Seas (C/L: Burnette, Smiley); Good Old-Fashioned Hoe Down (C/L: Autry, Gene); The Last Round-Up [2] (C/L: Hill, Billy); Happiest Birthday Routine (C: Styne, Jule; L: Meyer, Sol); Happy Cowboy [1] (C/L: Styne, Jule); Ain't Life Swell (C/L: Burnette, Smiley); Texas Trail (C/L: Styne, Jule)

**Notes**  No cue sheet available. Burton lists "Ridin' Down the Old Texas Trail" by M. Mabre and D. Massey and "Blueberry Hill" by Al Lewis, Larry Stock and Vincent Rose but they don't show up in the Republic collection at Brigham Young. This doesn't mean they weren't in the movie, however. [1] Also in SUNSET IN WYOMING. [2] Also in ONE HOUR LATE (Paramount), DON'T FENCE ME IN (Republic), STAND UP AND CHEER (Fox) and THE LAST ROUNDUP (Columbia).

## 5451 ✦ SINGING IN THE DARK
### ANO/Budsam, 1956

**Musical Score**  Oysher, Moishe
**Composer(s)**  Oysher, Moishe
**Lyricist(s)**  Oysher, Moishe

**Producer(s)**  Adams, Joey
**Director(s)**  Nosseck, Max
**Screenwriter(s)**  Kandel, Aben; Hood, Ann; Kandel, Stephen

**Cast**  Oysher, Moishe; Adams, Joey; Hill, Phyllis; Tierney, Lawrence; Medford, Kay; Knox, Mickey

**Song(s)**  Somewhere; Serba; Come Sing with Me; Balkan Rhapsody; What Would I Do without You; Hymn from the Bible; Lord Full of Compassion; Kiddush

## 5452 ✦ THE SINGING KID
### Warner Brothers (First National), 1936

**Composer(s)**  Arlen, Harold
**Lyricist(s)**  Harburg, E.Y.
**Choreographer(s)**  Connolly, Bobby

**Producer(s)**  Lord, Robert
**Director(s)**  Keighley, William
**Screenwriter(s)**  Duff, Warren; Flick, Pat C.

**Cast**  Jolson, Al; Jason, Sybil; Horton, Edward Everett; Talbot, Lyle; Jenkins, Allen; Roberts, Beverly; Dodd, Claire; Durant, Jack; Mitchell, Frank; King, Joseph; Davidson, William A.; The Yacht Club Boys; Cab Calloway and His Band; Shaw, Winifred

**Song(s)**  I Love to Singa; Original Foxtrot (Inst.); My How This Country's Changed; Keep That Heigh-De-Ho in Your Soul (C/L: Calloway, Cab [1]); Save Me Sister; Here's Looking at You; You're the Cure for What Ails Me; "Original" (Inst.)

**Notes**  There is also a medley including "My Mammy" by Walter Donaldson; "Swanee" by George Gershwin and Irving Caesar; "Rock-A-Bye Your Baby with a Dixie Melody" by Jean Schwartz, Joseph Young and Sam Lewis; "California Here I Come" by Al Jolson, B.G. DeSylva and Joseph Meyer; "April Showers" by Louis Silvers and B.G. DeSylva; "About a Quarter to Nine" by Harry Warren and Al Dubin and "Sonny Boy" by B.G. DeSylva, Ray Henderson and Lew Brown. [1] Irving Mills is also credited by some sources but not on cue sheets.

## 5453 ✦ SINGING KID FROM PINE RIDGE
### Republic, 1937

**Song(s)**  Sing Me a Song of the Saddle [1] (C/L: Harford, Frank); Hittin' the Trail (C: Lava, William; L: Stanley, Jack); Georgia Rodeo (C/L: Allan, Fleming); When a Circus Comes to Town (C/L: Allan, Fleming); Down in Santa Fe (C/L: Autry, Gene)

**Notes**  No other information available. [1] Also in LAST OF THE PONY RIDERS (Columbia) and SUNSET IN WYOMING with Gene Autry contribution also.

## 5454 ✦ THE SINGING MARINE
### Warner Brothers, 1937

**Composer(s)**  Warren, Harry
**Lyricist(s)**  Dubin, Al
**Choreographer(s)**  Berkeley, Busby

**Producer(s)**  Edelman, Louis F.
**Director(s)**  Enright, Ray
**Screenwriter(s)**  Daves, Delmer

**Cast**  Powell, Dick; Weston, Doris; Dixon, Lee; Herbert, Hugh; Darwell, Jane; Jenkins, Allen; Adler, Larry; Williams, Guinn "Big Boy"; Borg, Veda Ann; Wyman, Jane

**Song(s)**  You Can't Run Away from Love Tonight; Stolen Holiday [1]; 'Cause My Baby Says It's So; The Song of the Marines; The Lady Who Couldn't Be Kissed; I Know Now; Night Over Shanghai (L: Mercer, Johnny)

**Notes**  [1] May also have been used as theme of STOLEN HOLIDAY, a 1937 Warner film with Kay Francis, Ian Hunter and Claude Rains.

### 5455 ✦ THE SINGING NUN
Metro–Goldwyn–Mayer, 1966

**Musical Score**  Sukman, Harry
**Composer(s)**  Sourire, Soeur
**Lyricist(s)**  Sparks, Randy
**Choreographer(s)**  Sidney, Robert

**Producer(s)**  Beck, John
**Director(s)**  Koster, Henry
**Screenwriter(s)**  Benson, Sally; Furia Jr., John

**Cast**  Reynolds, Debbie; Montalban, Ricardo; Moorehead, Agnes; Everett, Chad; Ross, Katharine; Sullivan, Ed; Moore, Juanita; Cordell, Ricky; Pate, Michael; Drake, Tom; Garson, Greer

**Song(s)**  Brother John (C/L: Sparks, Randy); Sister Adele; Dominique [1] (L: Sourire, Soeur; Sparks, Randy); Beyond the Stars (Entre Les Etoile); She's My Baby, Yeah! (C/L: Sukman, Harry); Avec Toi (With You I Shall Walk) (L: Sourire, Soeur); Mets Ton Joli Jupon [2] (L: Sourire, Soeur; Dee, John); Je Voudrais [2] (L: Sourire, Soeur; Dee, John); Raindrops [3] (C/L: Sparks, Randy); Lovely (C/L: Sparks, Randy); It's a Miracle (Une Fleur); A Pied Piper's Song (Petit Pierrot)

**Notes**  Father Haazen also adapted "Kyrie" from MISSA LUBA and "Dibwe Diambula Kabonda," an African chant. [1] English lyrics by Randy Sparks. [2] English lyrics by John Dee. [3] Inspired by "Chante Riviere" by Soeur Sourire.

### 5456 ✦ SINGING OUTLAW
Universal, 1938

**Composer(s)**  Allan, Fleming
**Lyricist(s)**  Allan, Fleming

**Director(s)**  Lewis, Joseph H.
**Screenwriter(s)**  Hoyt, Harry O.

**Cast**  Baker, Bob; Barclay, Joan

**Song(s)**  Branding Days (C/L: Taconis); When the Round-Up Days Are Over; There's a Ring Around the Moon; The Jail Song

### 5457 ✦ THE SINGING SHERIFF
Universal, 1944

**Producer(s)**  Burton, Bernard W.
**Director(s)**  Goodwins, Leslie
**Screenwriter(s)**  Blankfort, Henry; Conrad, Eugene

**Cast**  Crosby, Bob; McKenzie, Fay; Knight, Fuzzy

**Song(s)**  Who's Next? (C/L: Wicks, Virginia; Lava, William); Reach for the Sky (C/L: Miller, Sidney; James, Inez); When a Cowboy Sings (C/L: Franklin, Dave); You Look Good to Me (C/L: Pepper, Buddy; James, Inez; Miller, Sidney); Who Broke the Lock on the Hen House Door? (C/L: Troy, Henry; Williams, Sneeze); Another Night (C/L: Piantadosi, Al; George, Don; Bibo, Irving); Court Room Song (C/L: Miller, Sidney; James, Inez)

### 5458 ✦ SINGING SPURS
Columbia, 1948

**Director(s)**  Nazarro, Ray
**Screenwriter(s)**  Shipman, Barry

**Cast**  The Hoosier Hotshots [2]; Egner, Red; Billy Hill and the Shamrock Cowboys; White, Patricia; Sears, Fred F.; Colby, Marion; Grant, Kirby; Patrick, Lee; Silverheels, Jay

**Song(s)**  Singing Spurs (C: Lee, Lester; L: Roberts, Allan); A Valley in Old Montana (C/L: Beck, E.C.; Buck, Ronald); What Do I Have to Do (C/L: Carson, Jenny Lou); Honeymoon Ranch [4] (C/L: Drake, Milton); A Man Is Brother to a Mule [1] (C/L: Roberts, Allan; Fisher, Doris); Hair of Gold, Eyes of Blue [3] (C/L: Skylar, Sunny)

**Notes**  There is also a vocal of "Red Wing" by Kerry Mills and T. Chattaway. [1] Also in LITTLE MISS BROADWAY (1947) and THRILL OF BRAZIL. [2] Consisted of Hezzie, Ken, Gil and Gabe. [3] May be titled "Hair of Gold, Sky of Blue" which is a similar song title to one in RIDERS OF THE WHISTLING PINES. [4] Also in ACROSS THE SIERRAS.

### 5459 ✦ THE SINGING VAGABOND
Republic, 1935

**Producer(s)**  Schaefer, Armand
**Director(s)**  Pierson, Carl
**Screenwriter(s)**  Drake, Oliver; Burbridge, Betty

**Cast**  Autry, Gene; Burnette, Smiley; Rutherford, Ann; Pepper, Barbara; Richmond, Warner; LaRue, Frank; Welch, Niles; Burns, Bob; King, Charles

**Song(s)** Wagon Train [1] (C/L: Autry, Gene; Burnette, Smiley); Farewell Friends of the Prairie (C/L: Autry, Gene; Burnette, Smiley)

**Notes** No cue sheet available. [1] There is another song titled "Wagon Train" in THE PAINTED STALLION but with credit to Smiley Burnette and Hoot Gibson.

## 5460 ✦ SINGIN' IN THE CORN
### Columbia, 1946

**Producer(s)** Richmond, Ted
**Director(s)** Lord, Del
**Screenwriter(s)** Dawn, Isabel; Rice, Monte

**Cast** Canova, Judy; Jenkins, Allen; Williams, Guinn "Big Boy"; Halton, Charles; Bridge, Alan; Rey, Frances; Thompson, Nick; The Singing Indian Braves

**Song(s)** I'm a Gal of Property (C/L: Fisher, Doris; Roberts, Allan); Pepita Chiquita (C/L: Fisher, Doris; Roberts, Allan)

**Notes** Originally titled GHOST TOWN. Released in Great Britain as GIVE AND TAKE.

## 5461 ✦ SINGIN' IN THE RAIN
### Metro–Goldwyn–Mayer, 1952

**Musical Score** Hayton, Lennie
**Choreographer(s)** Kelly, Gene; Donen, Stanley

**Producer(s)** Freed, Arthur
**Director(s)** Kelly, Gene; Donen, Stanley
**Screenwriter(s)** Comden, Betty; Green, Adolph

**Cast** Kelly, Gene; Reynolds, Debbie [2]; O'Connor, Donald; Hagen, Jean; Mitchell, Millard; Charisse, Cyd; Fowley, Douglas; Moreno, Rita; Blake, Madge

**Song(s)** Make 'Em Laugh [1] (C: Brown, Nacio Herb; L: Freed, Arthur); Moses (C: Edens, Roger; L: Comden, Betty; Green, Adolph)

**Notes** Songs not written for this film but used vocally include: "Fit as a Fiddle" by Al Hoffman, Al Goodhart and Arthur Freed (also in MARRIED BEFORE BREAKFAST); "Singin' in the Rain" (Written for show THE HOLLYWOOD MUSIC BOX REVUE (1927). Also in HOLLYWOOD REVUE, LITTLE NELLIE KELLY, HI, BEAUTIFUL (Universal) and A CLOCKWORK ORANGE); "All I Do Is Dream of You" (also in SADIE MCKEE); "I've Got a Feelin' You're Foolin'" (also in BROADWAY MELODY OF 1936 and WITH A SONG IN MY HEART); "Beautiful Girl" (also in GOING HOLLYWOOD and STAGE MOTHER) (filmed in three different versions: two calendar versions and the used fashion version); "Should I"; "You Were Meant for Me" (also in BROADWAY MELODY,

DOUGHBOYS, THE SHOW OF SHOWS and HOLLYWOOD REVUE OF 1929); "Good Morning" (also in BABES IN ARMS); "Would You" (also in SAN FRANCISCO); "Broadway Melody" (also in BROADWAY MELODY, BROADWAY MELODY OF 1936 and BROADWAY MELODY OF 1938); "Broadway Rhythm" (also in PRESENTING LILY MARS; BROADWAY MELODY OF 1936 and BROADWAY MELODY OF 1938); "Wedding of the Painted Doll" (also in BROADWAY MELODY) and "You Are My Lucky Star" (also in BROADWAY MELODY OF 1936, BABES IN ARMS and BORN TO SING), all by Arthur Freed and Nacio Herb Brown. [1] Very similar music to "Be a Clown" by Cole Porter written for THE PIRATE. [2] During a scene where Debbie Reynolds is seen dubbing for Jean Hagen, it is actually Jean Hagan dubbing for Debbie Reynolds dubbing for Jean Hagen! Clear? Also, Debbie Reynolds' singing was dubbed by Betty Royce for the song "Would You."

## 5462 ✦ SING ME A LOVE SONG
### Warner Brothers–First National, 1937

**Musical Score** Roemheld, Heinz
**Composer(s)** Warren, Harry
**Lyricist(s)** Dubin, Al
**Choreographer(s)** Connolly, Bobby

**Producer(s)** Bischoff, Sam
**Director(s)** Enright, Ray
**Screenwriter(s)** Herzig, Sig; Wald, Jerry
**Source(s)** "Let's Pretend" (story) Sauber, Harry

**Cast** Melton, James; Ellis, Patricia; Herbert, Hugh; Jenkins, Allen; Pitts, ZaSu; Moore, Dennis; Pendleton, Nat; Sheridan, Ann; Caine, Georgia; Catlett, Walter; Cavanaugh, Hobart

**Song(s)** The Least You Can Do for a Lady; "Original" (inst.); The Little House that Love Built; Summer Night [1]

**Notes** Released in Great Britain as COME UP SMILING. There are also vocals of "Carry Me Back to the Lone Prairie" by Carson Robinson and "Your Eyes Have Told Me So" by Gus Kahn and Egbert Van Alstyne. [1] Hummed only in COLLEEN.

## 5463 ✦ SING, NEIGHBOR, SING
### Republic, 1944

**Producer(s)** Brown, Donald H.
**Director(s)** McDonald, Frank
**Screenwriter(s)** McGowan, Stuart; McGowan, Dorrell

**Cast** Terry, Ruth; Taylor, Brad; Acuff, Roy; Zinkan, Joe; Brissac, Virginia; Easterday, Jesse; Riddle, Jimmy

**Song(s)** Sing, Neighbor, Sing (C/L: Rose, Fred); Welcome to Tudor [1] (C/L: Butts, Dale; Henderson,

Charles; Elliott, Jack); Durned If It Ain't in My Soul (C/L: Milo, Edward; Milo, Edwin); Phrenology (C/L: Butts, Dale; Elliott, Jack); Easy Rocking Chair (C/L: Rose, Fred); Have I Told You Lately That I Love You (C/L: Wiseman, Scott); Not a Word from Home (C/L: Acuff, Roy); Down By the Railroad Tracks (C: Crumit, Frank; L: Curtis, Billy); Popcorn Polka (C/L: Marvin, Johnny)

**Notes**  [1] Also in MOUNTAIN RHYTHM (1942) with credit solely to Henderson.

## 5464 ◆ SING WHILE YOU DANCE
### Columbia, 1946

**Producer(s)**  Barsha, Leon
**Director(s)**  Lederman, D. Ross
**Screenwriter(s)**  Brode, Robert Stephen

**Cast**  Drew, Ellen; Griffies, Ethel; Stanton, Robert; Tombes, Andrew; Cooper, Edwin; Stevens, Robert; Lane, Amanda

**Song(s)**  Oh What a Lovely Dream (C: Oakland, Ben; L: Drake, Milton); It's a Blue World [1] (C/L: Wright, Bob; Forrest, Chet); I Don't Know How You Did It (C/L: Fisher, Doris; Roberts, Allan)

**Notes**  No cue sheet available. [1] Also in MAKE BELIEVE BALLROOM and MUSIC IN MY HEART.

## 5465 ◆ SING YOUR WAY HOME
### RKO, 1952

**Musical Score**  Webb, Roy
**Composer(s)**  Wrubel, Allie
**Lyricist(s)**  Magidson, Herb
**Choreographer(s)**  O'Curran, Charles

**Producer(s)**  Granet, Bert
**Director(s)**  Mann, Anthony
**Screenwriter(s)**  Bowers, William

**Cast**  Haley, Jack; McGuire, Marcy; Vernon, Glenn; Jeffreys, Anne; Lee, Donna; Brill, Patti; Gargan, Edward

**Song(s)**  Heaven Is a Place Called Home; Seven O'Clock in the Morning; I'll Buy That Dream; Who Did It

## 5466 ◆ SING YOUR WORRIES AWAY
### RKO, 1942

**Composer(s)**  Revel, Harry
**Lyricist(s)**  Greene, Mort

**Producer(s)**  Reid, Cliff
**Director(s)**  Sutherland, Edward
**Screenwriter(s)**  Brice, Monte

**Cast**  Lahr, Bert; Havoc, June; Ebsen, Buddy; Kelly, Patsy; Lovett, Dorothy; Levene, Sam; Dumont,

Margaret; The King Sisters; Alvino Rey and His Orchestra

**Song(s)**  Sing Your Worries Away; Cindy Lou McWilliams; My Poor Heart Is Full of Scars; My Gal Alice; Sally, My Dear Old Sally; Nothing Can Change My Mind; It Just Happens to Happen [2]; I Haven't a Thing to Wear [1]; How Do You Fall in Love? [3]

**Notes**  [1] Used instrumentally only. [2] Also used in FALCON'S ALIBI. [3] Sheet music only.

## 5467 ◆ SING YOU SINNERS
### Paramount, 1938

**Composer(s)**  Monaco, James V.
**Lyricist(s)**  Burke, Johnny

**Producer(s)**  Ruggles, Wesley
**Director(s)**  Ruggles, Wesley
**Screenwriter(s)**  Binyon, Claude

**Cast**  Crosby, Bing; MacMurray, Fred; O'Connor, Donald; Patterson, Elizabeth; Drew, Ellen; Gallaudet, John; Haade, William; Bacon, Irving

**Song(s)**  I've Got A Pocketful of Dreams; Don't Let that Moon Get Away; Laugh and Call It Love; Where Is Central Park? [1]; Small Fry [2] (C: Carmichael, Hoagy; L: Loesser, Frank)

**Notes**  Originally titled HARMONY FOR THREE. [1] Not used. [2] Also in NIGHT IN NEW ORLEANS.

## 5468 ◆ SINNER TAKE ALL
### Metro–Goldwyn–Mayer, 1936

**Musical Score**  Ward, Edward

**Producer(s)**  Hubbard, Lucien; Marx, Samuel
**Director(s)**  Taggart, Errol
**Screenwriter(s)**  Lee, Leonard; Wise, Walter
**Source(s)**  *Murder for a Wanton* (novel) Chambers, Witman

**Cast**  Cabot, Bruce; Lindsay, Margaret; Calleia, Joseph; Ridges, Stanley; Grapewin, Charley; Adams, Edie; Kilgallen, Dorothy; Hatton, Raymond

**Song(s)**  I'd Be Lost without You (C: Donaldson, Walter; L: Forrest, Chet; Wright, Bob)

## 5469 ◆ SINS OF MAN
### Twentieth Century–Fox, 1936

**Musical Score**  Archangelsky, A.
**Composer(s)**  Archangelsky, A.
**Lyricist(s)**  Engel, Samuel G.

**Producer(s)**  Macgowan, Kenneth
**Director(s)**  Ratoff, Gregory; Brower, Otto
**Screenwriter(s)**  Engel, Samuel G.

**Cast** Ameche, Don; Jenkins, Allen; Bromberg, J. Edward; Shoemaker, Ann; Jennings, DeWitt; Leiber, Fritz; Van Sloan, Edward

**Song(s)** Invocation; Wedding Song

## 5470 ✦ SIN TAKES A HOLIDAY
### RKO, 1930

**Producer(s)** Derr, E.B.
**Director(s)** Stein, Paul
**Screenwriter(s)** Jackson, Horace

**Cast** Bennett, Constance; MacKenna, Kenneth; Rathbone, Basil; La Roy, Rita; Pitts, ZaSu

**Song(s)** It Must Be Love [1] (C: Snyder, Ted; L: Silver, Abner; Gordon, Mack); Coquette Charmante (C/L: Zuro, Josiah; Gromon, Francis); Just Like You (C/L: Zuro, Josiah; Gromon, Francis)

**Notes** Since the early (1930—1934) RKO cue sheets don't differentiate between vocals and instrumentals, it is not known if the above songs were treated vocally. However, "Just Like You" did have special Italian lyrics written by Franchetti, indicating that it at least did have a vocal. "It Must Be Love" is indicated on one cue sheet as being in the final print, but not another. This was a Pathe film that was acquired by RKO when they took over Pathe. It was originally released in 1930 by Pathe. [1] Also in SWING HIGH (Pathe).

## 5471 ✦ SIOUX CITY SUE
### Republic, 1946

**Producer(s)** Schaefer, Armand
**Director(s)** McDonald, Frank
**Screenwriter(s)** Cooper, Olive

**Cast** Autry, Gene; Champion; Roberts, Lynne; Holloway, Sterling; Lane, Richard; The Cass County Boys

**Song(s)** Yours (Quiereme Mucho) (C/L: Sheer, Jack; Riog, Gonzalo); Sioux City Sue [1] (C: Davis, Richard; L: Freedman, Ray); Ridin' Double (C/L: Rox, John); Some Day You'll Want Me to Want You (C/L: Hodges, Jimmie); You Stole My Heart [2] (C/L: Sosnik, Harry; Adams, Stanley)

**Notes** No cue sheet available. There may also be vocals of "Chisholm Trail" and "Great-Grandad." [1] Some sources list writers as Dick Thomas and Ray Freedman. [2] Also in SADDLE PALS.

## 5472 ✦ SIOUX ME
### Warner Brothers, 1939

**Musical Score** Stalling, Carl

**Director(s)** Hardaway, J.B. "Bugs"; Dalton, Cal
**Screenwriter(s)** Miller, Melvin

**Song(s)** We Want Rain (C/L: Stalling, Carl)

**Notes** Merrie Melodie.

## 5473 ✦ SIS HOPKINS
### Republic, 1941

**Composer(s)** Styne, Jule
**Lyricist(s)** Loesser, Frank

**Producer(s)** North, Robert
**Director(s)** Santley, Joseph
**Screenwriter(s)** Eliscu, Edward; Gross, Milt; Townley, Jack

**Cast** Canova, Judy; Crosby, Bob; Butterworth, Charles; Colonna, Jerry; Hayward, Susan; Alexander, Katherine; Allman, Elvia; Merrick, Lynn

**Song(s)** That Ain't Hay; Alma Mater (L: Styne, Jule); Well! Well! [1]; Look at You, Look at Me (C: Styne, Jule; Brown, George); Here We Are Studying History; Cleopatra; If You're in Love; Cracker Barrel County [2]

**Notes** There are also vocals of "Some of These Days" by Shelton Brooks and "Ah Fors a Lui" from Verdi's LA TRAVIATA. Bob Crosby's Orchestra played "Sugar Foot Stomp" by Joe Oliver and Louis Armstrong and "South Rampart Street Parade" by Steve Allen, Ray Bauduc and Bob Haggart. [1] Also in SHEPHERD OF THE OZARKS. [2] Sheet music only.

## 5474 ✦ SIT TIGHT
### Warner Brothers, 1931

**Director(s)** Bacon, Lloyd
**Screenwriter(s)** Taylor, Rex; Wells, William K.

**Cast** Lightner, Winnie; Brown, Joe E.; Dell, Claudia; Gregory, Paul; George, Don; Loder, Lotti; Bosworth, Hobart; Hagney, Frank; Edwards, Snitz

**Song(s)** Face It with a Smile (C: Baer, Abel; L: Gilbert, L. Wolfe)

**Notes** No cue sheet available.

## 5475 ✦ SITTING BULL
### United Artists, 1954

**Musical Score** Kraushaar, Raoul

**Producer(s)** Frank, W.R.
**Director(s)** Salkow, Sidney
**Screenwriter(s)** DeWitt, Jack; Salkow, Sidney

**Cast** Robertson, Dale; Naish, J. Carrol; Murphy, Mary; Cody, Iron Eyes; Litel, John; Hamilton, John; Kennedy, Douglas

**Song(s)** Great Spirit (C/L: Rich, Max)

## 5476 ✦ SITTING DUCKS
### United Film Distribution, 1980

**Musical Score** Romanus, Richard

**Producer(s)** Dor, Meira Attia
**Director(s)** Jaglom, Henry
**Screenwriter(s)** Jaglom, Henry

**Cast** Emil, Michael; Norman, Zack; Townsend, Patrice; Forrest, Irene; Romanus, Richard; Jaglom, Henry

**Song(s)** Theme from Sitting Ducks (C/L: Romanus, Richard)

**Notes** No cue sheet available.

## 5477 ◆ SITTING ON THE MOON
### Republic, 1936

**Composer(s)** Stept, Sam H.
**Lyricist(s)** Mitchell, Sidney D.

**Producer(s)** Levoy, Albert E.
**Director(s)** Staub, Ralph
**Screenwriter(s)** Schrock, Raymond
**Source(s)** "Tempermental Lady" (story) Field, Julian

**Cast** Pryor, Roger; Bradley, Grace; Newell, William; Kelton, Pert; Kolker, Henry; Wadsworth, Henry

**Song(s)** Who Am I; Sitting on the Moon [1]; How'm I Doing with You; Lost in My Dreams

**Notes** [1] Also in LARCENY ON THE AIR.

## 5478 ◆ SITTING PRETTY
### Paramount, 1933

**Composer(s)** Revel, Harry
**Lyricist(s)** Gordon, Mack

**Producer(s)** Rogers, Charles R.
**Director(s)** Brown, Harry Joe
**Screenwriter(s)** McGowan, Jack; Perelman, S.J.; Breslow, Lou

**Cast** Oakie, Jack; Haley, Jack; Rogers, Ginger; Todd, Thelma; Ratoff, Gregory; Cody, Lew; Hamilton, Hale; Tucker, Jerry; Walker, Walter; Gordon, Mack; Revel, Harry

**Song(s)** Did You Ever See a Dream Walking? [7]; Blonde, Blase and Beautiful [1]; Good Morning Glory; Lights, Camera, Action, Love; Four Moon Skits (I Can't Find a Mountain for My Moon) [2]; I Wanna Meander with Miranda; You're Such a Comfort to Me [4]; Many Moons Ago; There's a Bluebird at My Window (and a Landlord at My Door); Ballad of the South [3]; I Lost My Heart in the Subway [1]; In the Still of the Night [1] [5]; You Gotta Eat Your Spinach, Baby [5] [6]; How Could a Girl Like You Do a Thing Like That To a Boy Like Me on a Night Like This—Well, I Like That [5]; She Reminds Me of You [5] [9]; Sit Down and Tell Me How I Stand [5] [10]; Yes, My Dear [5]; He's a Cute Little Brute (A Gentleman and a Scholar) [5] [8]; May I? [5]; We're Only Little Extras Looking for an Opportunity [5]

**Notes** The movie was titled SOME FUN I'LL SAY, WE'RE SITTING PRETTY and SHE'S SITTING PRETTY prior to opening. During the filming Mack Gordon was required to come up with some dummy titles to be shown on the screen during the music publishing scene. These are the titles he made up: "I'm Dreaming While I'm Waltzing," "Prairie Mary," "Waitin' for Love," "Ring A'round a Rosie Days," "A Nook By a Brook in the Moonlight," "I Don't Give a Good Gosh Darn," "So's Your Old Man," "Making Me Blue," "Hotcha Baby" and "Chatanooga Choo Choo." The last later became a song by Gordon in conjunction with Harry Warren. [1] These come under the grouped heading And Then We Wrote. [2] The song is sung by a Kate Smith type, a Billy Hill type, a Ruth Etting type and an Irish Tenor type. It was also recorded by the quartet called the Hill Billies. The singers were Adel Burien, Max Burman and Miss Ainsworth. [3] When Jack Haley sings "Ballad of the South" to Jack Oakie's piano playing it is really Harry Revel playing the piano on the recording. [4] When the Pickens Sisters are singing the chorus standing at a piano it is Walter Ruick playing the piano both on screen and on the recording. The incidental music he plays is an original composition by him titled "Loving You." [5] Not used. [6] Also used in Shirley Temple film POOR LITTLE RICH GIRL. [7] Also in TWO FOR TONIGHT. [8] Used in WHITE WOMAN. [9] Used in WE'RE NOT DRESSING. [10] Also not used in COLLEGE RHYTHM where the title is listed as "Sit Down and Tell Me How I Stand."

## 5479 ◆ SITUATION HOPELESS BUT NOT SERIOUS
### Paramount, 1965

**Musical Score** Byrns, Harold

**Producer(s)** Reinhardt, Gottfried
**Director(s)** Reinhardt, Gottfried
**Screenwriter(s)** Reinhardt, Silvia
**Source(s)** *The Hiding Place* (novel) Shaw, Robert

**Cast** Guinness, Alec; Connors, Michael; Dahlke, Paul; Wolff, Frank; Hoefer, Anita; Redford, Robert

**Song(s)** Situation Hopeless but Not Serious [1] (C: Carr, Leon; L: Shuman, Earl)

**Notes** [1] Written for exploitation only.

## 5480 ◆ SIX BRIDGES TO CROSS
### Universal, 1955

**Producer(s)** Rosenberg, Aaron
**Director(s)** Pevney, Joseph
**Screenwriter(s)** Boehm, Sydney
**Source(s)** *They Stole $2,500,000 and Got Away with It.* (book) Dinnen, Joseph F.

**Cast** Curtis, Tony; Nader, George; Mineo, Sal; Flippen, Jay C.; Merlin, Jan; Castle, Richard

**Song(s)** Six Bridges to Cross (C: Mancini, Henry; L: Chandler, Jeff)

## 5481 ◆ SIX CYLINDER LOVE
### Fox, 1931

**Director(s)**  Freeland, Thornton
**Source(s)**  *Six Cylinder Love* (play) McGuire, William Anthony

**Cast**  Tracy, Spencer; Horton, Edward Everett; Fox, Sidney; Collier Sr., William

**Song(s)**  You're Driving Me Crazy [1] (C/L: Donaldson, Walter)

**Notes**  Also titled THE MINUTE MAN. [1] Not written for this film.

## 5482 ◆ SIX GUN GOLD
### RKO, 1941

**Composer(s)**  Whitley, Ray; Rose, Fred
**Lyricist(s)**  Whitley, Ray; Rose, Fred

**Producer(s)**  Gilroy, Bert
**Director(s)**  Howard, David
**Screenwriter(s)**  Parker, Norton S.

**Cast**  Holt, Tim; Whitley, Ray; Clayton, Jan; White, Lee "Lasses"; Mason, LeRoy; Waller, Eddy; Whitaker, Slim

**Song(s)**  Better Be on Our Way; Six Gun Gold

## 5483 ◆ SIX LESSONS FROM MADAME LA ZONGA
### Universal, 1941

**Composer(s)**  Rosen, Milton
**Lyricist(s)**  Carter, Everett

**Producer(s)**  Sandford, Joseph G.
**Director(s)**  Rawlins, John
**Screenwriter(s)**  Rubin, Stanley; Orth, Marion; Rhine, Larry; Chapman, Ben

**Cast**  Errol, Leon; Velez, Lupe; Lang, Charles; Parrish, Helen

**Song(s)**  Rootin' Tootin' Cowboy (C/L: Wakely, Jimmy); Jitterhumba; Mister Moon [1]; Way Back in Oklahoma [2] (C/L: Bond, Johnny); The Matador's Wife; Six Lessons from Madame La Zonga (C: Monaco, James V.; L: Newman, Charles)

**Notes**  [1] Also in COWBOY IN MANHATTAN. [2] Also in THE TIOGA KID (Pathe) and TUMBLEWEED TRAIL (PRC).

## 5484 ◆ SIX OF A KIND
### Paramount, 1934

**Producer(s)**  McLean, Douglas
**Director(s)**  McCarey, Leo
**Screenwriter(s)**  De Leon, Walter; Ruskin, Harry

**Cast**  Boland, Mary; Ruggles, Charles; Burns, George; Allen, Gracie; Fields, W.C.; Skipworth, Alison

**Song(s)**  Six of a Kind [1] (C: Rainger, Ralph; L: Robin, Leo)

**Notes**  [1] Not used in picture.

## 5485 ◆ SIX PACK
### Twentieth Century–Fox, 1982

**Musical Score**  Fox, Charles

**Producer(s)**  Triklilis, Michael
**Director(s)**  Petrie, Daniel
**Screenwriter(s)**  Marvin, Mike; Matter, Alex

**Cast**  Rogers, Kenny; Lane, Diane; Gray, Erin; Corbin, Barry; Kiser, Terry

**Song(s)**  Love Will Turn You Around (C/L: Rogers, Kenny; Stevens, Even; Malloy, David; Schuyler, Thom); Rainbow Stew (C/L: Haggard, Merle); I Can't Love You Enough (C/L: Seals, Troy; Barnes, Max D.); Rocky Top (C/L: Bryant, Felice; Bryant, Boudleaux); Hello I Love You (C/L: Cook, Roger; Cochran, Charles Lincoln)

**Notes**  It is not known if any or all of these were written for the film.

## 5486 ◆ SIXTEEN CANDLES
### Universal, 1984

**Musical Score**  Newborn, Ira

**Producer(s)**  Green, Hilton
**Director(s)**  Hughes, John
**Screenwriter(s)**  Hughes, John

**Cast**  Ringwald, Molly; Henry, Justin; Schoeffling, Michael; Morris, Haviland; Watanabe, Gedde; Dooley, Paul; Glynn, Carlin; Baker, Blanche; Andrews, Edward; Cook, Carole; Showalter, Max; Cusack, John; Cusack, Joan; Doyle-Murray, Brian; Gertz, Jami; Rubinstein, Zelda; Hall, Anthony Michael

**Song(s)**  Today I Met (The Boy I'm Going to Marry) (C/L: Greenwich, Ellie; Spector, Phil; Powers, T.); Love of the Common People (C/L: Wilkins, Ron; Hurley, John); Happy Birthday (C/L: Anderson, Michael; Grogan, Claire Patrick; McDaid, Anton; McElhone, John); Filene (C/L: Newborn, Ira); True (C/L: Kemp, Gary); When It Started to Begin (C/L: Heyward, Nick); Whistle Down the Wind (C/L: Heyward, Nick); Ring Me Up (C/L: McEntee, M.; Amphlett, C.); Rev Up (C/L: Reynolds, Eugene); Farmer John (C/L: Terry Jr., Dewey; Harris, Don); Hang Up the Phone (C/L: Newborn, Ira; Brooks, Pattie); Doowap for Geek and Carolyn (C/L: Newborn, Ira); If You Were Here (C/L: Bailey, Tom; Leeway, Joseph; Curry, Elannah)

**Notes**  It is not known if all the above were written for the movie. There are also background vocals of "New York, New York" by John Kander and Fred Ebb; "Gloria" by Van Morrison; "Sixteen Candles" by A. Khent and L. Dixon; "Young Guns" by George Michael;

"Rebel Yell" by Billy Idol and Steve Stevens and "Young Americans" by David Bowie.

## 5487 ✦ SKATEBOARD
### Universal, 1977

**Musical Score** Snow, Mark
**Composer(s)** Snow, Mark
**Lyricist(s)** Sarstedt, Richard

**Producer(s)** Blum, Wolf; Blum, Harry N.
**Director(s)** Gage, George
**Screenwriter(s)** Gage, George; Wolf, Richard A.

**Cast** Garfield, Allen; Lloyd, Kathleen; Garrett, Leif; Van Der Wyk, Richard; Alva, Tony; Monahan, Steve; Hyde, David

**Song(s)** Skate Out; Riding High; Gotta Be on Top (L: Connors, Carol; Robbins, Ayn); My Heart Is Just a Retread in that Tire Sale Called Life (C/L: Jaep, Roger); Sweet Rider; Point of No Return (C/L: Alexander, Robin; Leonetti, Eddie); Take Me Higher

## 5488 ✦ SKATETOWN U.S.A.
### Columbia, 1979

**Producer(s)** Levey, William A.; Dreyfuss, Lorin
**Director(s)** Levey, William A.
**Screenwriter(s)** Castle, Nick

**Cast** Baio, Scott; Wilson, Flip; Palillo, Ron; Buzzi, Ruth; Mason, Dave; Bradford, Greg; McCormick, Maureen; Swayze, Patrick; Barty, Billy; Landsberg, David; Ross, Joe E.; Bari, Lenny

**Song(s)** Skatetown (C: Mason, Dave; L: Cooper, Brenda); Skatetown USA (C/L: Beal, John); I Fell in Love (C/L: Mason, Dave)

**Notes** No cue sheet available.

## 5489 ✦ SKIN DEEP
### Warner Brothers, 1929

**Director(s)** Enright, Ray
**Screenwriter(s)** Rigby, Gordon
**Source(s)** "Lucky Damage" (story) Jones, Marc Edmond

**Cast** Lee, Davey; Blue, Monte; Compson, Betty; Day, Alice; Marshall, Tully; Bowers, John

**Song(s)** I Came to You (C: Gottler, Archie; L: Mitchell, Sidney D.; Conrad, Con)

**Notes** No cue sheet available. First made as a silent film in 1922.

## 5490 ✦ SKIPALONG ROSENBLOOM
### Eagle Lion Classics, 1951

**Musical Score** Gertz, Irving
**Composer(s)** Riesner, Dean; Kenny, Jack
**Lyricist(s)** Foreman, Eddie

**Producer(s)** Kline, Wally
**Director(s)** Newfield, Sam
**Screenwriter(s)** Riesner, Dean; Forman, Eddie

**Cast** Rosenbloom, Maxie [1]; Baer, Max; Coogan, Jackie; Knight, Fuzzy; Brooke, Hillary; Robinson, Dewey

**Song(s)** Skipalong, Little Maxie, Skipalong; You've Got Plenty to Learn About Love

**Notes** Also known as THE ADVENTURES OF SKIPALONG ROSENBLOOM and THE SQUARE SHOOTER. [1] Billed as "Slapsie" Maxie Rosenbloom.

## 5491 ✦ SKI PARTY
### American International, 1965

**Musical Score** Usher, Gary

**Producer(s)** Nicholson, James H.; Arkoff, Samuel Z.
**Director(s)** Rafkin, Alan
**Screenwriter(s)** Kaufman, Robert

**Cast** Avalon, Frankie; Hickman, Dwayne; Walley, Deborah; Craig, Yvonne; Lewis, Robert Q.; Shaw, Bobbi; Brown, James; Gore, Lesley

**Song(s)** Sunshine, Lollipops and Rainbows (C: Hamlisch, Marvin; L: Liebling, Howard); I Got You (C/L: Wright, Ted); Ski Party (C/L: Usher, Gary; Christian, Roger); The Gasser (C/L: Usher, Gary; Christian, Roger); Paintin' the Town (C/L: Gaudio, Bob); Lots, Lots More (C: Kusik, Larry; L: Adams, Ritchie); We'll Never Change Them (C/L: Hemric, Guy; Styner, Jerry)

**Notes** No cue sheet available.

## 5492 ✦ SKIPPY
### Paramount, 1931

**Producer(s)** Lighton, Louis D.
**Director(s)** Taurog, Norman
**Screenwriter(s)** Mankiewicz, Joseph L.; Mintz, Sam
**Source(s)** *Skippy* (comic strip) Crosby, Percy

**Cast** Cooper, Jackie; Coogan, Robert; Green, Mitzi; Searl, Jackie; Eddy, Helen Jerome; Robertson, Willard; Bennett, Enid; Oliver, Guy

**Song(s)** It's a Beautiful Day to Be Glad [1] (C: King, Jack; L: Coslow, Sam)

**Notes** [1] Also in SOOKY.

## 5493 ✦ SKIRTS AHOY!
### Metro–Goldwyn–Mayer, 1952

**Musical Score** Stoll, George; Sendrey, Al
**Composer(s)** Warren, Harry
**Lyricist(s)** Blane, Ralph
**Choreographer(s)** Castle, Nick

**Producer(s)** Pasternak, Joe
**Director(s)** Lanfield, Sidney
**Screenwriter(s)** Lennart, Isobel

**Cast** Williams, Esther; Evans, Joan; Blaine, Vivian; Sullivan, Barry; Brasselle, Keefe; Eckstine, Billy; Miller, Dean; Gillmore, Margalo; The De Marco Sisters; Donnell, Jeff; Hall, Thurston; Van, Bobby; Wynn, Keenan; Reynolds, Debbie

**Song(s)** Skirts Ahoy!; Glad to Have You Aboard; What Makes a WAVE; What Good Is a Gal (Without a Guy); Hold Me Close to You; I Get a Funny Feeling; The Navy Waltz

**Notes** There is also a vocal of "Oh By Jingo" by Albert Von Tilzer and Lew Brown.

### 5494 ✦ SKY BANDITS
Monogram, 1941

**Composer(s)** Lange, Johnny
**Lyricist(s)** Porter, Lew

**Producer(s)** Goldstone, Philip
**Director(s)** Staub, Ralph
**Screenwriter(s)** Halperin, Edward
**Source(s)** "Refrew of the Royal Mounted" (stories) Erskine, Laurie York

**Cast** Newill, James; Pauley, Bill; Stanley, Louise; Robinson, Dewey; Stephani, Joseph; Frye, Dwight; O'Brien, Dave

**Song(s)** Mounted Men [1] (C/L: Lively, Robert; Laidlow, Betty); Allez Oop; The Lady in the Clouds

**Notes** [1] Also in CRASHING THRU, DANGER AHEAD, FIGHTING MAN, MURDER ON THE YUKON, RENFREW AND THE GREAT WHITE TRAIL and YUKON FLIGHT.

### 5495 ✦ SKY FULL OF MOON
Metro–Goldwyn–Mayer, 1952

**Musical Score** Sawtell, Paul

**Producer(s)** Franklin Jr., Sidney
**Director(s)** Foster, Norman
**Screenwriter(s)** Foster, Norman

**Cast** Carpenter, Carleton; Sterling, Jan; Wynn, Keenan; Burton, Robert; Stewart, Elaine; Lynn, Emmett; Dumbrille, Douglass

**Song(s)** A Cowboy Had Ought to Be Single (C: Wolcott, Charles; L: Hamilton, Harry); Old Paint (Ride Around Little Dogies) (C: Traditional; L: Campbell, Paul)

### 5496 ✦ THE SKY HAWK
Fox, 1929

**Director(s)** Blystone, John; Gullan, Campbell
**Screenwriter(s)** Hughes, Llewellyn
**Source(s)** "Chap Called Bardell" (story) Hughes, Llewellyn

**Cast** Chandler, Helen; Garrick, John; Every, Gilbert; Pawle, Lennox; Hare, Lumsden; Bevan, Billy; Pollard, Daphne; Compton, Joyce

**Song(s)** Song of Courage (C: Cadman, Charles Wakefield; L: Lynn, Edward)

**Notes** No cue sheet available.

### 5497 ✦ THE SKY'S THE LIMIT
RKO, 1943

**Musical Score** Harline, Leigh
**Composer(s)** Arlen, Harold
**Lyricist(s)** Mercer, Johnny
**Choreographer(s)** Astaire, Fred

**Producer(s)** Hempstead, David
**Director(s)** Griffith, Edward H.
**Screenwriter(s)** Fenton, Frank; Root, Lynn

**Cast** Astaire, Fred; Leslie, Joan; Benchley, Robert; Kolb, Clarence; Ryan, Robert; Davies, Richard; Gateson, Marjorie; Blore, Eric; Lawford, Peter; Freddie Slack and His Orchestra; Morse, Ella Mae

**Song(s)** My Shining Hour [1]; A Lot in Common; One for My Baby; Harvey the Victory Garden Man [2]

**Notes** [1] Later in RADIO STARS ON PARADE. [2] Not used.

### 5498 ✦ SLAMDANCE
Island Alive, 1987

**Musical Score** Froom, Mitchell; Lurie, John

**Producer(s)** Harvey, Rupert; Opper, Barry
**Director(s)** Wang, Wayne
**Screenwriter(s)** Opper, Don

**Cast** Hulce, Tom; Mastrantonio, Mary Elizabeth; Ant, Adam; Barsi, Judith

**Song(s)** Bing Can't Walk (C/L: Ridgway, Stan); Art Life (C/L: Song, Maggie; Dentino, John; Corey, Tom; Berardi, John); High Hopes (C/L: Scott, Tim)

**Notes** No cue sheet available.

### 5499 ✦ SLANDER
Metro–Goldwyn–Mayer, 1957

**Musical Score** Alexander, Jeff

**Producer(s)** Deutsch, Armand
**Director(s)** Rowland, Roy
**Screenwriter(s)** Weidman, Jerome

**Cast** Johnson, Van; Blyth, Ann; Cochran, Steve; Rambeau, Marjorie; Eyer, Richard; Stone, Harold J.; Tuttle, Lurene

**Song(s)** I'll Be Waitin' for You Where the Tumbleweed Is Blue [1] (C/L: Wolcott, Charles)

**Notes** [1] Also in CALLAWAY WENT THATAWAY.

## 5500 ✦ SLAPSTICK OF ANOTHER KIND
International Film Marketing, 1984

**Musical Score** Legrand, Michel

**Producer(s)** Paul, Steven
**Director(s)** Paul, Steven
**Screenwriter(s)** Vonnegut Jr., Kurt
**Source(s)** *Slapstick* (novel) Vonnegut Jr., Kurt

**Cast** Lewis, Jerry; Kahn, Madeline; Feldman, Marty; Abbott, John; Backus, Jim; Fuller, Samuel; Griffin, Merv; Morita, Pat [1]; Graham, Virginia

**Song(s)** Puttin Our Heads Together (C/L: Bishop, Randy); Lonesome No More (C: Legrand, Michel; L: Vonnegut Jr., Kurt)

**Notes** No cue sheet available. [1] Billed as Noriyuki "Pat" Morita.

## 5501 ✦ SLAUGHTER TRAIL
RKO, 1952

**Composer(s)** Murray, Lyn
**Lyricist(s)** Kuller, Sid

**Producer(s)** Allen, Irving
**Director(s)** Allen, Irving
**Screenwriter(s)** Kuller, Sid

**Cast** Donlevy, Brian; Young, Gig; Grey, Virginia; Devine, Andy; Hutton, Robert; Gilkyson, Terry

**Song(s)** Ballad Bandelier; Everyone's Crazy 'Ceptin' Me (C/L: Gilkyson, Terry; Kuller, Sid); Hoofbeat Serenade; I Wish I Wuz; Remember Me? (C/L: Gilkyson, Terry); Jittery Deerfoot Dan (C/L: Gilkyson, Terry); The Girl in the Wood [1] (C/L: Gilkyson, Terry; Stuart, Neal)

**Notes** [1] Not used.

## 5502 ✦ SLAVE OF LOVE
Metro–Goldwyn–Mayer, 1929

**Composer(s)** Stothart, Herbert
**Lyricist(s)** Grey, Clifford
**Choreographer(s)** Rasch, Albertina

**Director(s)** Franklin, Sidney
**Screenwriter(s)** Schayer, Richard; Kraly, Hans; Sears, Zelda

**Cast** Novarro, Ramon; Jordan, Dorothy; Harris, Marion; Miljan, John; Humphrey, William; Davis, George; Bruce, Clifford

**Song(s)** The Shepherd's Serenade; Bon Jour; Louis; March of the Old Guard; Why Waste Your Charms?; The Gang Song; Madame Pompadour; Charming If He Cared

**Notes** No cue sheet available. The ballet boasts music by Dimitri Tiomkin.

## 5503 ✦ SLEEPING BEAUTY
Disney, 1958

**Musical Score** Bruns, George; Tchaikovsky
**Composer(s)** Bruns, George; Tchaikovsky
**Lyricist(s)** Adair, Tom

**Director(s)** Geronimi, Clyde; Larson, Eric; Reitherman, Wolfgang; Clark, Les
**Screenwriter(s)** Penner, Erdman
**Source(s)** "Sleeping Beauty" (story) Perrault, Charles
**Voices** Costa, Mary; Audley, Eleanor; Luddy, Barbara; Holmes, Taylor; Shirley, Bill; Felton, Verna; Allen, Barbara Jo; Thompson, Bill

**Directing Animator(s)** Kahl, Milt; Thomas, Franklin; Davis, Marc; Johnston, Ollie; Lounsbery, John

**Song(s)** Hail to the Princess Aurora [1]; Once Upon a Dream [1] (C: Fain, Sammy; Tchaikovsky, Peter; L: Lawrence, Jack); I Wonder [2] (L: Hibler, Winston; Sears, Ted); Sleeping Beauty Song (1) [2]; Skumps (C: Bruns, George; L: Adair, Tom; Penner, Erdman); Sing a Smiling Song [2] [3]; Dance of the Leaves [2] [3] (L: Jackman, Bob); Break of Day [4] [5] (C: Bruns, George; L: Hibler, Winston); Holiday [4] (C: Fain, Sammy; L: Lawrence, Jack); It Happens I Have a Picture [4] (C: Fain, Sammy; L: Lawrence, Jack); Mirage (Follow Your Heart) [4] (C: Fain, Sammy; L: Lawrence, Jack); My Beloved [2] [3] (L: Gil, George); Sleeping Beauty Song (2) [4] (C: Young, Victor; L: Lawrence, Jack); Sunbeam's (Bestowal of Gifts) [4] (C: Fain, Sammy; L: Lawrence, Jack); Sunbeams in Your Pocket [4] (C: Fain, Sammy; L: Lawrence, Jack); Where in the World [4] (C: Fain, Sammy; L: Lawrence, Jack)

**Notes** Animated feature. [1] Based on a theme from Tchaikovsky's SLEEPING BEAUTY. [2] Based on a theme by Tchaikovsky. [3] Used instrumentally only. Lyrics added for exploitation. [4] Not used. [5] Used in PERRI.

## 5504 ✦ SLEEPY LAGOON
Republic, 1943

**Composer(s)** Ohman, Phil
**Lyricist(s)** Washington, Ned

**Producer(s)** Cohen, Albert J.
**Director(s)** Santley, Joseph
**Screenwriter(s)** Gill, Frank, Jr.; Brown, George Carleton
**Source(s)** *The Miracle of Sleepy Hollow* (novel) Chaplin, Prescott

**Cast** Canova, Judy; Day, Dennis; Donnelly, Ruth; Sawyer, Joe; Truex, Ernest; Fowley, Douglas; Corthell, Herbert; Wright, Will

**Song(s)** If You Are There [2]; You're the Fondest Thing I Am Of; I'm Not Myself Anymore [1]; Political Satire

**Notes** There is also a vocal of "Sleepy Lagoon" by E. Coates and Jack Lawrence. [1] Also in GOODNIGHT SWEETHEART. [2] Also in MURDER IN THE MUSIC HALL.

### 5505 ✦ SLEEPYTIME GAL
Republic, 1942

**Composer(s)** Styne, Jule
**Lyricist(s)** Magidson, Herb

**Producer(s)** Cohen, Albert J.
**Director(s)** Rogell, Albert S.
**Screenwriter(s)** Lief, Max; Duffy, Albert; Arthur, Art

**Cast** Canova, Judy; Brown, Tom; Coles, Mildred; Huber, Harold; Ennis, Skinnay; Terry, Ruth; Lester, Jerry; Gilbert, Billy; Feld, Fritz; Novello, Jay; Cook Jr., Elisha

**Song(s)** I Don't Want Anybody At All [2]; When the Cat's Away; Barrel House Bessie from Basin Street [1]

**Notes** There is also a vocal of "Sleepytime Gal" by Ange Lorenzo, Richard A. Whiting, J.R. Alden and Richard B. Egan. [1] Also in O, MY DARLING CLEMENTINE. [2] Also in ROSIE THE RIVETER.

### 5506 ✦ THE SLENDER THREAD
Paramount, 1966

**Musical Score** Jones, Quincy

**Producer(s)** Alexander, Stephen
**Director(s)** Pollack, Sydney
**Screenwriter(s)** Silliphant, Stirling

**Cast** Poitier, Sidney; Bancroft, Anne; Savalas, Telly; Hill, Steven

**Song(s)** The Slender Thread [1] (C: Jones, Quincy; L: David, Mack)

**Notes** [1] Used instrumentally only.

### 5507 ✦ SLIGHT CASE OF MURDER
Warner Brothers–First National, 1936

**Producer(s)** Wallis, Hal B.
**Director(s)** Bacon, Lloyd
**Screenwriter(s)** Baldwin, Earl; Schrank, Joseph
**Source(s)** (play) Runyon, Damon; Lindsay, Howard

**Cast** Robinson, Edward G.; Bryan, Jane; Jenkins, Allen; Donnelly, Ruth; Parker, Willard; Litel, John; Brophy, Edward S.; Hamilton, Margaret; Hanlon, Bert; Compson, Betty

**Song(s)** How Do You Do Mr. Marco (C: Jerome, M.K.; L: Scholl, Jack)

**Notes** There are also vocal renditions of "It Had to Be You" by Gus Kahn and Isham Jones; "Shine On Harvest Moon" by Jack Norworth and Nora Bayes; "The Merry-Go-Round Broke Down" by Cliff Friend and Dave Franklin; "I'm Dancing with Tears in My Eyes" by Joe Burke and Al Dubin and "Melancholy Baby" by George Norton and Ernie Burnett.

### 5508 ✦ SLIGHTLY FRENCH
Columbia, 1949

**Composer(s)** Lee, Lester
**Lyricist(s)** Roberts, Allan

**Producer(s)** Starr, Irving
**Director(s)** Sirk, Douglas
**Screenwriter(s)** De Wolf, Karen

**Cast** Lamour, Dorothy [3]; Ameche, Don; Carter, Janis; Parker, Willard; Jergens, Adele

**Song(s)** Fifi From the Follies Bergere; I Want to Learn About Love; Night (Sings a Lonely Serenade); Let's Fall in Love [1] (C: Arlen, Harold; L: Koehler, Ted); Bread and Butter Woman [2] [4]; Pierre [2]; I Keep Telling Myself [2]; Don't Mind My Troubles [2]

**Notes** Previously titled LET'S FALL IN LOVE. [1] Also in JUKE BOX RHYTHM, LET'S FALL IN LOVE, ON THE SUNNY SIDE OF THE STREET and SENIOR PROM. [2] Not used. [3] Dubbed by Martha Mears. Lamour did record her songs but post recording dubs were made by Mears. [4] Used in PURPLE HEART DIARY and ARKANSAS SWING.

### 5509 ✦ SLIGHTLY SCANDALOUS
Universal, 1946

**Composer(s)** Brooks, Jack
**Lyricist(s)** Brooks, Jack

**Producer(s)** Rubin, Stanley; Grant, Marshall
**Director(s)** Jason, Will
**Screenwriter(s)** Lazarus, Erna; Matthews, David; Malone, Joel; Warner, Jerry

**Cast** Brady, Fred; Isabelita; The Guadalajara Trio; Moro, Nico; Yaconelli, Frank; Midgely, Dorese; Smith, Georgann; Drew, Paula; Ryan, Sheila; Catlett, Walter; Da Pron, Louis

**Song(s)** Baa Baa Baa to You (C/L: Marshall, Jack); The Same Old Routine; Negra Leono [1] (C/L: Fernandez, Antonio); I Couldn't Love You Anymore; The Mad Hatter (C/L: Marshall, Jack); When I Fall in Love

**Notes** [1] Also in THE HEAT'S ON (Columbia) and PAN AMERICANA (RKO). Also in GAY SENORITA and credited to Serge Walter and Don George.

### 5510 ✦ SLIGHTLY SCARLET
Paramount, 1930

**Director(s)** Gensler, Lewis E.; Knopf, Edwin H.
**Screenwriter(s)** Estabrook, Howard; Mankiewicz, Joseph L.

**Cast**   Brook, Clive; Brent, Evelyn; Lukas, Paul

**Song(s)**   You Still Belong to Me (C: King, Jack; L: Janis, Elsie)

**Notes**   This is a remake of the 1915 film BLACKBIRDS.

## 5511 ♦ SLIGHTLY TERRIFIC
Universal, 1944

**Composer(s)**   Rosen, Milton
**Lyricist(s)**   Carter, Everett

**Producer(s)**   Thurn-Taxis, Alexis
**Director(s)**   Cline, Edward F.
**Screenwriter(s)**   Dein, Edward; Davis, Stanley

**Cast**   Quillan, Eddie; Errol, Leon; Rooney, Anne

**Song(s)**   Rhythm's What You Need; Me and My Whistle; Stars and Violins [2]; Hold That Line [1]; Happy Polka

**Notes**   There are also vocals of "Put Your Arms Around Me, Honey" by Junie McCree and Albert Von Tilzer; "Come Back to Erin" by Claribel and "Blue Danube" by Johann Strauss and Katherine Bellamann. [1] Also in GET GOING. [2] Also in STARS AND VIOLINS.

## 5512 ♦ SLIM CARTER
Universal, 1957

**Musical Score**   Stein, Herman

**Producer(s)**   Horwitz, Howie
**Director(s)**   Bartlett, Richard
**Screenwriter(s)**   Pittman, Montgomery

**Cast**   Mahoney, Jock; Adams, Julie; Hovey, Tim; Hale, Barbara

**Song(s)**   Ride Cowboy, Ride (C/L: Wakely, Jimmy); Gold (C/L: Freed, Ralph; Smith, Beasley); Cowboy (C/L: Wakely, Jimmy; Gershenson, Joseph)

## 5513 ♦ THE SLIPPER AND THE ROSE—THE STORY OF CINDERELLA
Universal, 1977

**Composer(s)**   Sherman, Richard M.; Sherman, Robert B.
**Lyricist(s)**   Sherman, Richard M.; Sherman, Robert B.
**Choreographer(s)**   Breaux, Marc

**Producer(s)**   Lyons, Stuart
**Director(s)**   Forbes, Bryan
**Screenwriter(s)**   Forbes, Bryan; Sherman, Richard M.; Sherman, Robert B.
**Source(s)**   "Cinderella" (fairy tale)

**Cast**   Chamberlain, Richard; Craven, Gemma; Crosbie, Annette; Evans, Edith; Gable, Christopher; Hordern, Michael; Lockwood, Margaret; More, Kenneth; Orchard, Julian; Graves, Peter

**Song(s)**   Why Can't I Be Two People; What Has Love Got to Do with Getting Married; Once I Was Loved; What a Comforting Thing; Protocoligorically Correct; A Bride Finding Ball; Suddenly It Happens; Secret Kingdom; He Danced with Me; Tell Him Anything; I Can't Forget the Melody

## 5514 ♦ SLOW DANCING IN THE BIG CITY
United Artists, 1978

**Musical Score**   Conti, Bill

**Producer(s)**   Levee, Michael; Avildsen, John G.
**Director(s)**   Avildsen, John G.
**Screenwriter(s)**   Grant, Barra

**Cast**   Sorvino, Paul; Ditchburn, Anne; Coster, Nicolas; Danglor, Anita; Mercado, Hector Jaime; Pehghlis, Thaao

**Song(s)**   I Feel the Earth Move (C/L: King, Carole); Dancin' Slow [1] (C: Conti, Bill; L: Edelman, Randy)

**Notes**   [1] Sheet music only.

## 5515 ♦ THE SLUGGER'S WIFE
Columbia, 1985

**Musical Score**   Williams, Patrick

**Producer(s)**   Stark, Ray
**Director(s)**   Ashby, Hal
**Screenwriter(s)**   Simon, Neil

**Cast**   O'Keefe, Michael; de Mornay, Rebecca; Ritt, Martin; Quaid, Randy; Derricks, Cleavant

**Song(s)**   Love (It's Just the Way It Goes) (C/L: Jones, Quincy; Ballard, Glen; Magness, Clif; Sager, Carole Bayer)

## 5516 ♦ THE SMALL ONE
Disney, 1977

**Musical Score**   Brunner, Robert F.
**Composer(s)**   Bluth, Don
**Lyricist(s)**   Bluth, Don

**Producer(s)**   Bluth, Don
**Director(s)**   Bluth, Don
**Screenwriter(s)**   Gerry, Vance; Young, Pete
**Source(s)**   (book) Tazewell, Charles

**Cast**   Marshall, Sean; Woodson, William; Soule, Olan; Smith, Hal; Higgins, Joe; Jump, Gordon

**Song(s)**   Small One; The Merchants; A Friendly Face (C/L: Rich, Richard J.)

## 5517 ♦ SMALL TOWN GIRL (1936)
Metro–Goldwyn–Mayer, 1936

**Choreographer(s)**   Berkeley, Busby

**Producer(s)**   Stromberg, Hunt
**Director(s)**   Wellman, William A.

**Screenwriter(s)** Mahin, John Lee; Goodrich, Frances; Hackett, Albert; Fitzgerald, Edith
**Source(s)** *Small Town Girl* (novel) Williams, Ben Ames

**Cast** Gaynor, Janet; Taylor, Robert; Barnes, Binnie; Devine, Andy; Stone, Lewis; Patterson, Elizabeth; Craven, Frank; Stewart, James; Jewell, Isabel; Kennedy, Edgar; Walker, Nella

**Song(s)** Small Town Girl (C: Stothart, Herbert; Ward, Edward; L: Kahn, Gus)

## 5518 ✦ SMALL TOWN GIRL (1953)
### Metro–Goldwyn–Mayer, 1953

**Musical Score** Previn, Andre
**Composer(s)** Brodszky, Nicholas
**Lyricist(s)** Cahn, Sammy
**Choreographer(s)** Berkeley, Busby

**Producer(s)** Pasternak, Joe
**Director(s)** Kardos, Leslie
**Screenwriter(s)** Cooper, Dorothy; Kingsley, Dorothy

**Cast** Powell, Jane; Granger, Farley; Miller, Ann; Sakall, S.Z.; Keith, Robert; Van, Bobby; Burke, Billie; Wray, Fay; Cole, Nat "King"

**Song(s)** The Lullaby of the Lord; Fine, Fine, Fine; Small Towns Are Smile Towns; Take Me to Broadway; Wonder Why [1]; Farfel's Birthday Song (C: Traditional; L: Schary, Dore); The Fellow I'd Follow; I've Gotta Hear That Beat; My Flaming Heart; My Gaucho

**Notes** A remake of the 1936 original. [1] Also in RICH, YOUNG AND PRETTY and HOLIDAY FOR SINNERS.

## 5519 ✦ SMART BLONDE
### Warner Brothers, 1937

**Musical Score** Roemheld, Heinz

**Producer(s)** Foy, Bryan
**Director(s)** MacDonald, Frank
**Screenwriter(s)** Ryan, Don; Gamet, Kenneth
**Source(s)** "No Hard Feelings" (story) Nebel, Frederick

**Cast** Farrell, Glenda; MacLane, Barton; Shaw, Winifred; Reynolds, Craig; Richards, Addison; Wynters, Charlotte; Wyman, Jane; Kennedy, Tom

**Song(s)** Why Do I Have to Sing a Torch Song (C: Jerome, M.K.; L: Scholl, Jack)

## 5520 ✦ SMARTEST GIRL IN TOWN
### RKO, 1936

**Musical Score** Webb, Roy

**Producer(s)** Kaufman, Edward
**Director(s)** Santley, Joseph
**Screenwriter(s)** Shore, Viola Brothers

**Cast** Raymond, Gene; Sothern, Ann; Broderick, Helen; Blore, Eric; Rhodes, Erik; Jans, Harry

**Song(s)** Will You (C/L: Raymond, Gene)

## 5521 ✦ SMART GIRLS DON'T TALK
### Warner Brothers, 1948

**Musical Score** Buttolph, David

**Producer(s)** Elkins, Saul
**Director(s)** Bare, Richard
**Screenwriter(s)** Sackheim, William
**Source(s)** "Dames Don't Talk" (story) Sackheim, William

**Cast** Mayo, Virginia; Bennett, Bruce; Hutton, Robert; D'Andrea Tom; Rober, Richard; Westcott, Helen; Benedict, Richard

**Song(s)** The Stars Will Remember (C/L: Pelosi, Don; Towers, Leo)

## 5522 ✦ SMART POLITICS

See CAMPUS SLEUTH.

## 5523 ✦ SMASHING TIME
### Paramount, 1967

**Musical Score** Addison, John
**Composer(s)** Addison, John
**Lyricist(s)** Melly, George

**Producer(s)** Ponti, Carlo; Millichip, Roy
**Director(s)** Davis, Desmond
**Screenwriter(s)** Melly, George

**Cast** Tushingham, Rita; Redgrave, Lynn; York, Michael; Quayle, Anna; Handl, Irene; Carmichael, Ian

**Song(s)** Smashing Time; Carnaby Street; Waiting for M' Friend; New Clothes; Trouble; It's Always Your Fault; Going to a Party (C/L: Smith, Victor); While I'm Still Young; Lady Marmaduke (C/L: Smith, Victor); Day Out

**Notes** All songs are background vocals.

## 5524 ✦ SMASH-UP
### Universal, 1947

**Composer(s)** McHugh, Jimmy
**Lyricist(s)** Adamson, Harold

**Producer(s)** Wanger, Walter
**Director(s)** Heisler, Stuart
**Screenwriter(s)** Lawson, John Howard

**Cast** Hayward, Susan [1]; Bowman, Lee; Hunt, Marsha; Albert, Eddie; Esmond, Carl; Young, Carleton

**Song(s)** I Miss That Feeling; When Love Is Young [2]; Lonely Little Ranch-House (C: Fairchild, Edgar; L:

Brooks, Jack); Life Can Be Beautiful; A Cowboy's Never Lonesome (C/L: Brooks, Jack); Hush-A-Bye Island

**Notes**    [1] Dubbed by Peg LaCentra. [2] Also in WHEN LOVE IS YOUNG.

## 5525 ✦ SMILE
United Artists, 1976

**Musical Score**    Orsborn, Dan
**Composer(s)**    Orsborn, Dan
**Lyricist(s)**    Ritchie, Michael

**Producer(s)**    Ritchie, Michael
**Director(s)**    Ritchie, Michael
**Screenwriter(s)**    Belson, Jerry

**Cast**    Dern, Bruce; Feldon, Barbara; Kidd, Michael; Lewis, Geoffrey; Prather, Joan; Camp, Colleen

**Song(s)**    The Runway Song; The Hello Song

## 5526 ✦ SMILEY
Twentieth Century–Fox, 1957

**Musical Score**    Alwyn, William

**Producer(s)**    Kimmins, Anthony
**Director(s)**    Kimmins, Anthony
**Screenwriter(s)**    Raymond, Moore; Kimmins, Anthony

**Cast**    Richardson, Sir Ralph; McCallum, John; Peterson, Colin; Archer, Bruce; Rafferty, Chips

**Song(s)**    Smiley (C: Alwyn, William; L: Kimmins, Anthony; Lovelock, Bill)

## 5527 ✦ SMILEY GETS A GUN
Twentieth Century–Fox, 1959

**Musical Score**    Collins, Clyde; Sampson, Wilbur

**Producer(s)**    Kimmins, Anthony
**Director(s)**    Kimmins, Anthony
**Screenwriter(s)**    Kimmins, Anthony; Rienits, Rex

**Cast**    Thorndike, Sybil; Calvert, Keith; Rafferty, Chips

**Song(s)**    A Little Boy Called Smiley (C/L: Collins, Clyde)

## 5528 ✦ SMILING ALONG
Twentieth Century–Fox, 1939

**Composer(s)**    Parr-Davies, Harry
**Lyricist(s)**    Parr-Davies, Harry

**Producer(s)**    Kane, Robert T.
**Director(s)**    Banks, Monty
**Screenwriter(s)**    Conselman, William

**Cast**    Fields, Gracie; Livesey, Roger; Maguire, Mary; Donohue, Jack; Coke, Peter

**Song(s)**    You've Got to Be Smart in the Army Nowaday (C/L: Elliott, Lesley; Rutherford, Robert); Swing Your Way to Happiness; Giddy Up; I Never Cried So Much in All My Life [1] (C/L: Haines, Will E.; Harper, Jimmy; Castling, Harry); Peace of Mind (C/L: Paul, Gerald); Mrs. Binns' Twins [1] (C/L: Long, J.P.; Haines, Will E.; Harper, Jimmy)

**Notes**    Also known as KEEP SMILING. There are also vocals of "The Holy City" by Fred Weatherley and Stephen Adams and "A May Morning" by L. Denza. [1] The English print includes a song called "Mrs. Binns' Twins" by J.P. Long, Will E. Haines and Jimmy Harper. This replaced "I Never Cried So Much in All My Life."

## 5529 ✦ SMILING IRISH EYES
Warner Brothers–First National, 1929

**Composer(s)**    Ruby, Herman
**Lyricist(s)**    Spencer, Norman
**Choreographer(s)**    Ceballos, Larry; Wills, Walter; McBride, Carl

**Producer(s)**    McCormick, John
**Director(s)**    Seiter, William A.
**Screenwriter(s)**    Geraghty, Tom J.

**Cast**    Moore, Colleen; Hall, James; Gillingwater, Claude; Homans, Robert; Herring, Aggie; Francisco, Betty; Johnston, Julanne; O'Connor, Robert Emmett; Hayes, George "Gabby"; Schaefer, Anne

**Song(s)**    A Wee Bit of Love; Old Killarney Fair; Smiling Irish Eyes (C: Perkins, Ray); Then I'll Ride Home with You

**Notes**    No cue sheets available.

## 5530 ✦ SMILING LIEUTENANT
Paramount, 1931

**Composer(s)**    Straus, Oscar
**Lyricist(s)**    Grey, Clifford

**Director(s)**    Lubitsch, Ernst
**Screenwriter(s)**    Vajda, Ernest; Raphaelson, Samson
**Source(s)**    *A Waltz Dream* (musical) Jacobson, Leopold; Doermann, Felix; Straus, Oscar; Herbert, Joseph W.

**Cast**    MacDonald, Jeanette; Chevalier, Maurice; Hopkins, Miriam; Ruggles, Charles; O'Connell, Hugh; Barbier, George; Patterson, Elizabeth

**Song(s)**    That's the Army; While Hearts Are Singing [4]; Breakfast Table Love [6]; One More Hour of Love [5] [6]; Musical Scene [3]; Jazz Up Your Lingerie; Toujours L'amour in the Army [1] [2]; Live for Today [1]; What Can They Expect of Me [1]

**Notes**    [1] Not used. [2] This is only in the French version replacing "That's the Army." They may have the same melody. [3] This is made up of tunes from operetta A WALTZ DREAM plus an instrumental chorus of "One More Hour of Love." [4] The music is from A WALTZ DREAM. [5] This contains the same music as

"I'll Remember You" written for MGM. [6] These two numbers may share the same music. They were listed together on the cue sheet as one number.

**5531  ✦  SMITH!**
Disney, 1969

**Musical Score**    Brunner, Robert F.

**Producer(s)**    Anderson, Bill
**Director(s)**    O'Herlihy, Michael
**Screenwriter(s)**    Pelletier, Louis
**Source(s)**    *Breaking Smith's Quarter Horse* (novel) St. Pierre, Paul

**Cast**    Ford, Glenn; Olson, Nancy; Jagger, Dean; Wynn, Keenan; Oates, Warren; George, Chief Dan; Silverheels, Jay

**Song(s)**    The Ballad of Smith and Gabriel Jimmy Boy (C/L: Russell, Bob); Gotta Need a Man [1] (C/L: Brunner, Robert F.)

**Notes**    [1] Not used.

**5532  ✦  SMOKEY AND THE BANDIT**
Universal, 1977

**Musical Score**    Justis, Bill

**Producer(s)**    Engelberg, Mort
**Director(s)**    Needham, Hal
**Screenwriter(s)**    Barrett, James Lee; Shyer, Charles; Mandel, Alan

**Cast**    Reynolds, Burt; Field, Sally; Gleason, Jackie; Henry, Mike; Reed, Jerry; Williams, Paul; McCormick, Pat

**Song(s)**    The Legend (C/L: Hubbard, Jerry R.); Westbound and Down [1] (C/L: Hubbard, Jerry R.; Feller, Dick); The Bandit (C/L: Feller, Dick); Eastbound and Down [1] (C/L: Hubbard, Jerry R.; Feller, Dick)

**Notes**    [1] Same song.

**5533  ✦  SMOKEY AND THE BANDIT—II**
Universal, 1980

**Musical Score**    Justis, Bill

**Producer(s)**    Moonjean, Hank
**Director(s)**    Needham, Hal
**Screenwriter(s)**    Belson, Jerry; Yates, Brock

**Cast**    Reynolds, Burt; Field, Sally; Gleason, Jackie; Reed, Jerry; DeLuise, Dom; Williams, Paul; McCormick, Pat; Huddleston, David

**Song(s)**    Texas Bound and Flyin' (C/L: Hubbard, Jerry R.); Here's Lookin' at You (C/L: Pinkard, Sandy; Durrill, John; Atchely, Sam); Again and Again (C/L: Peters, Ben); Ride Concrete Cowboy Ride (C/L: Crofford, Cliff; Durrill, John; Garrett, Snuff); Pecos

Prominade (C/L: Collins, Larry; Pinkard, Sandy; Garrett, Snuff); Charlotte's Web (C/L: Crofford, Cliff; Durrill, John; Garrett, Snuff)

**5534  ✦  SMOKEY AND THE BANDIT—PART 3**
Universal, 1983

**Musical Score**    Cansler, Larry

**Producer(s)**    Engelberg, Mort
**Director(s)**    Lowry, Dick
**Screenwriter(s)**    Birnbaum, Stuart; Dashey, David

**Cast**    Gleason, Jackie; Williams, Paul; Reed, Jerry; McCormick, Pat; Henry, Mike; Camp, Colleen; Minton, Faith; Reynolds, Burt

**Song(s)**    Buford T. Justice (C/L: Feller, Dick; Schlitz, Don); The Legend of the Bandit (C/L: Weedman, Sam); The Girl Next Door (C/L: Johnson, Jim; Kipper, Stan); The Bandit Express (C/L: Feller, Dick; Schlitz, Don); Suzi Plastic [1] (C/L: Summers, Bob; Roberts, S.; Escovedo, P.); It Ain't the Gold (C/L: Stewart, John); A Ticket for the Wind (C/L: Stewart, John)

**Notes**    [1] Also in CRACKERS.

**5535  ✦  SMOKY**
Twentieth Century–Fox, 1966

**Composer(s)**    Axton, Hoyt
**Lyricist(s)**    Axton, Hoyt

**Producer(s)**    Rosenberg, Aaron
**Director(s)**    Sherman, George
**Screenwriter(s)**    Medford, Harold
**Source(s)**    *Smoky* (novel) James, Will

**Cast**    Parker, Fess; Hyland, Diana; Jurado, Katy; Axton, Hoyt; Wilke, Robert J.; Silvestre, Armando

**Song(s)**    Queen of the Rockin' R (C/L: Axton, Hoyt; Ulz, Ivan); Five Dollar Bill; Trouble and Misery; Smoky (C: Stevens, Leith; L: Sheldon, Ernie); Smile As You Go By; Sara [1] (C/L: Moreno, David)

**Notes**    [1] Not used.

**5536  ✦  SMOKY MOUNTAIN MELODY**
Columbia, 1949

**Producer(s)**    Clark, Colbert
**Director(s)**    Nazarro, Ray
**Screenwriter(s)**    Shipman, Harry

**Cast**    Acuff, Roy; Williams, Guinn "Big Boy"; Arms, Russell; Robards, Jason; Sears, Fred F.

**Song(s)**    Tennessee Central #9 (C/L: Smith, D.); Smoky Mountain Moon (C/L: Acuff, Roy); Thank God (C/L: Rose, Fred); Party Time on the Prairie [1] (C/L: Bilder, Robert); Ya Sure, You Betcha (C/L: Oliver, Sandy; Herrick, Paul; Soloman, Sid)

**Notes**    [1] Only song written for picture.

## 5537 ✦ SMOKY RIVER SERENADE
### Columbia, 1947

**Producer(s)** Clark, Colbert
**Director(s)** Abrahams, Derwin
**Screenwriter(s)** Shipman, Barry

**Cast** Campbell, Paul; Terry, Ruth; Williams, Billy; Hunter, Virginia; Burns, Paul E.; Hicks, Russell; The Sunshine Boys; Cotton, Carolina; Clark, Cottonseed; The Boyd Triplets; The Hoosier Hotshots

**Song(s)** Wreck of the Old '97 [1] (C/L: Whittier, Henry; Noell, Charles W.; Lewey, Fred J.); You Can Bet Your Boots and Saddle [1] (C/L: Herscher, Louis; Newell, Roy); What a Break (C/L: The Hoosier Hotshots); The Si Si Song (All I Know Is Si Si) [3] (C/L: Fisher, Doris; Roberts, Allan); I Love to Yodel [1] [2] (C/L: Cotton, Carolina); I Just Saddle My Pinto and Ride [1] (C/L: Lewisohn, Arthur; Shepard, Ann); The Style Song (C/L: The Hoosier Hotshots); I Like This Loving You (C: Chaplin, Saul; L: Cahn, Sammy)

**Notes** [1] Not written for this film. [2] Also in APACHE COUNTRY. [3] Also in TWO BLONDES AND A REDHEAD.

## 5538 ✦ SMOOTH SAILING
### Paramount, 1947

**Cast** Tyrrell, Alice; Thomas, Patty

**Song(s)** My Castle on Riverside Drive (C/L: Livingston, Jay; Evans, Ray); Great Feelin' (C/L: Livingston, Jay; Evans, Ray); Audition Sequence (C/L: McCreery, Bud)

**Notes** Short subject. There are also vocal renditions (sometimes in medleys) of "Waltz Huguette" by Brian Hooker and Rudolf Friml; "Lo Hear the Gentle Lark" by H.R. Bishop and "I Feel a Song Coming On" by Jimmy McHugh, Dorothy Fields and George Oppenhiem.

## 5539 ✦ SMOOTH TALK
### Spectrafilm, 1985

**Musical Score** Payne, Bill; Kunkel, Russell; Massenburg, George

**Producer(s)** Rosen, Martin
**Director(s)** Chopra, Joyce
**Screenwriter(s)** Cole, Tom
**Source(s)** Where Are You Going, Where Have You Been? (C/L: Oates, Joyce Carol)

**Cast** Williams, Treat; Dern, Laura; Place, Mary Kay; Berridge, Elizabeth

**Song(s)** Limousine Driver (C/L: Taylor, James)

**Notes** No cue sheet available.

## 5540 ✦ SMUGGLED CARGO
### Republic, 1939

**Producer(s)** Auer, John H.
**Director(s)** Auer, John H.
**Screenwriter(s)** Felton, Earl; Jacoby, Michel

**Cast** Mackay, Barry; Hudson, Rochelle; Barbier, George; Morgan, Ralph; Wray, John; Edwards, Cliff; Loft, Arthur

**Song(s)** Mr. Robin Hood (C/L: Cherkose, Eddie)

## 5541 ✦ SNAKE RIVER DESPERADOS
### Columbia, 1950

**Producer(s)** Clark, Colbert
**Director(s)** Sears, Fred F.
**Screenwriter(s)** Shipman, Barry

**Cast** Starrett, Charles; Reynolds, Don; Ivo, Tommy; Blue, Monte; Burnette, Smiley

**Song(s)** Brass Band Polka (C/L: Burnette, Smiley)

## 5542 ✦ SNIFFLES TAKES A TRIP
### Warner Brothers, 1940

**Musical Score** Stalling, Carl

**Director(s)** Jones, Chuck
**Screenwriter(s)** Monahan, Dave

**Cast** Sniffles

**Song(s)** Sniffles' Serenade (C/L: McGrew; Mitchell)

**Notes** Merrie Melodie.

## 5543 ✦ SNOW CARNIVAL
### Warner Brothers, 1949

**Musical Score** Jackson, Howard

**Song(s)** Skating on the Old Mill Pond (C: Jerome, M.K.; L: Scholl, Jack); What Happened in Aspen (C/L: Roe, B.; Stumph, T.; Talbot, T.; Stevens, K.; Tebfair, B.)

**Notes** Short subject.

## 5544 ✦ SNOW GETS IN YOUR EYES
### Metro–Goldwyn–Mayer, 1938

**Musical Score** Snell, Dave
**Composer(s)** Wright, Bob; Forrest, Chet
**Lyricist(s)** Wright, Bob; Forrest, Chet

**Director(s)** Jason, Will
**Screenwriter(s)** Jason, Will; Rauh, Stanley

**Cast** Grey, Virginia; Judels, Charles; Converse, Roger; Shotwell, Hudson

**Song(s)** Snowbound; Girl Wanted; Harlem Yodel

**Notes** Short subject.

## 5545 ◆ THE SNOWS OF KILIMANJARO
Twentieth Century–Fox, 1952

**Musical Score**  Herrmann, Bernard

**Producer(s)**  Zanuck, Darryl F.
**Director(s)**  King, Henry
**Screenwriter(s)**  Robinson, Casey
**Source(s)**  "The Snows of Kilimanjaro" (story)
Hemingway, Ernest

**Cast**  Peck, Gregory; Hayward, Susan; Gardner, Ava;
Neff, Hildegarde; Carroll, Leo G.; Thatcher, Torin;
Dalio, Marcel

**Song(s)**  Swahili Hunt Song [1] (C/L: Treatt, C.
Court); Swahili Lament (C/L: Knudson, Thurston)

**Notes**  [1] Based on a traditional Swahili chant. Also in
WHITE HUNTER.

## 5546 ◆ SNOW WHITE AND THE SEVEN DWARFS
Disney, 1937

**Musical Score**  Harline, Leigh; Smith, Paul J.;
Churchill, Frank E.
**Composer(s)**  Churchill, Frank E.
**Lyricist(s)**  Morey, Larry

**Producer(s)**  Disney, Walt
**Director(s)**  Hand, David D.
**Screenwriter(s)**  Sears, Ted; Englander, Otto; Hurd,
Earl; Blank, Dorothy Ann; Creedon, Richard; Rickard,
Dick; De Maris, Merrill; Smith, Webb
**Source(s)**  "Snow White and the Seven Dwarfs" (fairy
tale) The Grimm Brothers

**Supervising Animator(s)**  Luske, Hamilton; Tytla,
Vladimir; Moore, Fred; Ferguson, Norman
**Sequence Director(s)**  Pearce, Perce; Morey, Larry;
Cottrell, William; Jackson, Wilfred; Sharpsteen, Ben

**Song(s)**  Bluddle-Uddle-Um-Dum (Washing Song);
Heigh-Ho; I'm Wishing; One Song; The Silly Song
(Dwarf's Yodel Song); Some Day My Prince Will Come;
Whistle While You Work; With a Smile and a Song;
Music in Your Soup [1]; You're Never Too Old to Be
Young [2]; Snow White [3]

**Notes**  Animated feature. [1] Prerecorded but not used.
[2] Written for exploitation only. [3] Sheet music only.

## 5547 ◆ SNOW WHITE AND THE THREE CLOWNS

See SNOW WHITE AND THE THREE STOOGES.

## 5548 ◆ SNOW WHITE AND THE THREE STOOGES
Twentieth Century–Fox, 1961

**Musical Score**  Murray, Lyn
**Composer(s)**  Harris, Harry

**Lyricist(s)**  Harris, Harry
**Choreographer(s)**  Fletcher, Ron

**Producer(s)**  Wick, Charles
**Director(s)**  Lang, Walter
**Screenwriter(s)**  Langley, Noel; Ullman, Elwood

**Cast**  The Three Stooges; Heiss, Carol; Stroll, Edson;
Medina, Patricia; Rolfe, Guy; David, Michael

**Song(s)**  Lookin' for People, Lookin' for Fun; A Place
Called Happiness; Birthday Part III [1] (C: Murray,
Lyn); Birthday Part IV (C: Lane, Ivan; L: Brent, Earl
K.); A Day Like This (C/L: Brent, Earl); Because I'm in
Love; I Said It Then, I Say It Now

**Notes**  Titled SNOW WHITE AND THE THREE
CLOWNS internationally. [1] Lyrics from script.

## 5549 ◆ S.O.B.
Paramount, 1981

**Musical Score**  Mancini, Henry

**Producer(s)**  Edwards, Blake; Adams, Tony
**Director(s)**  Edwards, Blake
**Screenwriter(s)**  Edwards, Blake

**Cast**  Andrews, Julie; Holden, William; Berenson,
Marisa; Hagman, Larry; Loggia, Robert; Margolin,
Stuart; Mulligan, Richard; Preston, Robert; Stevens,
Craig; Swit, Loretta; Vaughn, Robert; Webber, Robert;
Winters, Shelley; Swofford, Ken; Fong, Benson; Storch,
Larry; Kane, Byron; Arquette, Rosanna; Lawlor, John;
Camp, Hamilton; Gregg, Virginia; Nelson, Gene; Penny,
Joe

**Song(s)**  Hustler (C/L: Colyer, Steve); Tomorrow
Morning (C/L: Colyer, Steve)

**Notes**  No cue sheet available.

## 5550 ◆ SOB SISTER
Twentieth Century–Fox, 1931

**Director(s)**  Santell, Alfred
**Screenwriter(s)**  Burke, Edwin
**Source(s)**  (novel) Gilman, Mildred

**Cast**  Dunn, James; Watkins, Linda; O'Day, Molly;
Gombell, Minna; O'Day, Molly

**Song(s)**  If I Had a Talking Picture of You [1] (C:
Henderson, Ray; L: DeSylva, B.G.; Brown, Lew)

**Notes**  [1] Also in SUNNY SIDE UP.

## 5551 ◆ SOCIAL REGISTER
Columbia, 1934

**Composer(s)**  Conrad, Con
**Lyricist(s)**  Heyman, Edward

**Director(s)**  Neilan, Marshall
**Screenwriter(s)**  Creelman, James Ashmore; Perkins,
Grace

**Cast**    Moore, Colleen; Winninger, Charles; Frederick, Pauline; Kirkland, Alexander; Benchley, Robert; Alexander, Ross; Livingston, Margaret; Ramona; Fray and Bragiotti

**Song(s)**    Why Not, Honey Dear [1] (C: Conrad, Con; Dabney, Ford); I Didn't Want to Love You [1] (L: Washington, Ned)

**Notes**    [1] Sheet music only.

## 5552 ◆ SOCIETY GIRL
Fox, 1932

**Director(s)**    Lanfield, Sidney
**Screenwriter(s)**    Harris, Elmer
**Source(s)**    *Society Girl* (play) Larkin Jr., John

**Cast**    Dunn, James; Shannon, Peggy; Tracy, Spencer; Byron, Walter

**Song(s)**    Love Here Is My Heart [1] (C: Silesu, Leo; L: Unknown)

**Notes**    [1] Not written for picture.

## 5553 ◆ SOCIETY LAWYER
Metro–Goldwyn–Mayer, 1939

**Musical Score**    Ward, Edward

**Producer(s)**    Considine Jr., John W.
**Director(s)**    Marin, Edwin L.
**Screenwriter(s)**    Hackett, Albert; Goodrich, Frances; Gordon, Leon; Butler, Hugo

**Cast**    Pidgeon, Walter; Bruce, Virginia; Ciannelli, Eduardo; Carrillo, Leo; Bowman, Lee; Mercer, Frances

**Song(s)**    I'm in Love with the Honorable Mr. So and So (C/L: Coslow, Sam)

**Notes**    A remake of PENTHOUSE.

## 5554 ◆ SOCKEROO
Warner Brothers, 1940

**Musical Score**    Jackson, Howard

**Cast**    Rosenbloom, Maxie

**Song(s)**    Super Special Genius (C: Jerome, M.K.; L: Scholl, Jack)

**Notes**    Short subject.

## 5555 ◆ SO DEAR TO MY HEART
Disney, 1948

**Musical Score**    Smith, Paul J.
**Composer(s)**    Daniel, Eliot
**Lyricist(s)**    Morey, Larry

**Producer(s)**    Pearce, Perce
**Director(s)**    Luske, Hamilton; Schuster, Harold
**Screenwriter(s)**    Battle, John Tucker

**Voices**    Beal, John; Carson, Ken; Stanton, Bob; Rhythmaires, The

**Cast**    Ives, Burl; Bondi, Beulah; Driscoll, Bobby; Patten, Luana; Carey, Harry; Bond, Raymond; Soderling, Walter; Willis, Matt; Collins, Spelman B.

**Song(s)**    So Dear to My Heart (C: Freeman, Ticker; L: Taylor, Irving); Ole Dan Patch; It's Watcha Do With Watcha Got (C: De Paul, Gene; L: Raye, Don); Lavender Blue (Dilly-Dilly); Stick-To-It-Ivity; The County Fair (C/L: Torme, Mel; Wells, Robert); Bah, Bah Black Sheep (C: Johnston, Arthur; L: Traditional); Granny's Rocking Chair [1] (C: Johnston, Arthur; L: Gilbert, Ray); Heavens to Betsy [1] (C: Johnston, Arthur; L: Klages, Raymond); How So Dear to My Heart [1] (C: Johnston, Arthur; L: Coslow, Sam); I Never Go Anywhere (That I Can't Come Back From) [1] (C: Johnston, Arthur; L: Gilbert, Ray); It's Fair Time [1] (C: Johnston, Arthur; L: Gilbert, Ray); My Fair Lady (1) [1] (C: Johnston, Arthur; L: Gilbert, Ray); My Fair Lady (2) [1] (C: Johnston, Arthur; L: Klages, Raymond); Pretty Mathilda [1] (C/L: Johnston, Arthur); Ridin' on the Ninety-Nine [1] (C: Johnston, Arthur; L: Gilbert, Ray); Twenty Third Psalm [1] (C: Johnston, Arthur; L: Traditional)

**Notes**    Originally titled MIDNIGHT & JEREMIAH. There is also a parody of "Ole Dan Tucker" called "Jerry Kincaid Followed a Bee." [1] Not used.

## 5556 ◆ SO FINE
Warner Brothers, 1981

**Musical Score**    Morricone, Ennio

**Producer(s)**    Lobell, Michael
**Director(s)**    Bergman, Andrew
**Screenwriter(s)**    Bergman, Andrew

**Cast**    O'Neal, Ryan; Warden, Jack; Melato, Mariangela; Kiel, Richard; Rounds, David; Gwynne, Fred; Kellin, Mike; Stedman, Joel; Pietropinto, Angela; Lombard, Michael; James, Jessica; Millholland, Bruce; Goldsmith, Merwin

**Song(s)**    Right Now (C: Morricone, Ennio; L: Gould, Danny); So Fine (C/L: Spangler, David; Dale, Grover); I Fall to Pieces (C/L: Cochran, Hank; Howard, Harlan)

## 5557 ◆ SOLARBABIES
United Artists, 1986

**Musical Score**    Jarre, Maurice

**Producer(s)**    Walzer, Irene; Sanders, Jack Frost
**Director(s)**    Johnson, Alan
**Screenwriter(s)**    Green, Walon; Metrov, Douglas Anthony

**Cast**    Jordan, Richard; Gertz, Jami; Patric, Jason; Haas, Lukas; Durning, Charles

**Song(s)**    Love Will Set You Free (C/L: Robinson, William "Smokey"; Stone, Ivory)

## 5558 ✦ THE SOLDIER
Embassy, 1982

**Musical Score**  Tangerine Dream

**Producer(s)**  Glickenhaus, James
**Director(s)**  Glickenhaus, James
**Screenwriter(s)**  Glickenhaus, James

**Cast**  Wahl, Ken; Watson, Alberta; Prince, William; Sullivan, Jeremiah; Kinski, Klaus; Strait, George

**Song(s)**  Fool Hearted Memory (C/L: Hill, Byron; Mevis, Blake)

**Notes**  No cue sheet available.

## 5559 ✦ A SOLDIER'S PLAYTHING
Warner Brothers, 1931

**Composer(s)**  Unknown
**Lyricist(s)**  Unknown

**Director(s)**  Curtiz, Michael
**Screenwriter(s)**  Bekroff, Percy
**Source(s)**  "Come Easy" (story) Delmar, Vina

**Cast**  Lyon, Ben; Langdon, Harry; Loder, Lotti; Kohler, Fred; Beery, Noah; Hersholt, Jean; Matiesen, Otto; Moran, Lee; Campeau, Frank

**Song(s)**  Forever; Oui, Oui; Honey Boy; Ja, Ja, Ja!; Side By Side

**Notes**  No cue sheet available.

## 5560 ✦ A SOLDIER'S STORY
Columbia, 1984

**Musical Score**  Hancock, Herbie
**Composer(s)**  Riley, Larry
**Lyricist(s)**  Riley, Larry

**Producer(s)**  Jewison, Norman; Schwary, Ronald L.; Palmer, Patrick
**Director(s)**  Jewison, Norman
**Screenwriter(s)**  Fuller, Charles
**Source(s)**  A Soldier's Play (play) Fuller, Charles

**Cast**  Rollins Jr., Howard E.; Caesar, Adolph; Evans, Art; Grier, David Alan; Harris, David; Lipscomb, Dennis; Riley, Larry; Townsend, Robert; Washington, Denzel; Young, William Allen; LaBelle, Patti; Hauser, Wings

**Song(s)**  Pourin' Whiskey Blues (C/L: LaBelle, Patti; Ellison, James; Edward, Armistead); Bright Red Zoot Suit; Low Down Dirty Shame; Colored Troops Will Do for You (C/L: Fuller, Charles)

## 5561 ✦ SOLDIERS THREE
Metro–Goldwyn–Mayer, 1951

**Musical Score**  Deutsch, Adolph

**Producer(s)**  Berman, Pandro S.
**Director(s)**  Garnett, Tay

**Screenwriter(s)**  Roberts, Marguerite; Reed, Tom; Boylan, Malcolm Stuart
**Source(s)**  "Soldiers Three" (stories) Kipling, Rudyard

**Cast**  Granger, Stewart; Pidgeon, Walter; Niven, David; Newton, Robert; Cusack, Cyril; Gynt, Greta; Coote, Robert

**Song(s)**  'Old Your Nose and Drink It Down (C: Traditional; L: Brent, Earl); The Colonel Smelled a Skunk (C: Hyde, Alexander; L: Jones, Grover; Lawrence, Vincent)

## 5562 ✦ THE SOLID GOLD ARTICLE
Fox, 1930

**Composer(s)**  Monaco, James V.
**Lyricist(s)**  Friend, Cliff

**Song(s)**  Business Is Business with Me; Nothing's Gonna Hold Us Down [1]; Whisper You Love Me and Make My Dreams Come True [1]

**Notes**  No other information available. [1] In NOT DAMAGED.

## 5563 ✦ SO LONG, LETTY
Warner Brothers, 1929

**Composer(s)**  Akst, Harry
**Lyricist(s)**  Clarke, Grant

**Director(s)**  Bacon, Lloyd
**Screenwriter(s)**  Caesar, Arthur; Lord, Robert
**Source(s)**  So Long Letty (musical) Harris, Elmer; Morosco, Oliver; Carroll, Earl

**Cast**  Greenwood, Charlotte [1]; Withers, Grant; Miller, Patsy Ruth; Byron, Marion; Foster, Helen; Gillingwater, Claude; Roach, Bert

**Song(s)**  One Sweet Little Yes; Clowning; Beauty Shop; Am I Blue? [2]; Let Me Have My Dreams [3]; My Strongest Weakness Is You; So Long Letty [1] (C/L: Carroll, Earl); Down Among the Sugar Cane (C: Tobias, Charles)

**Notes**  No cue sheet available. [1] From Broadway production. [2] Also in FUNNY LADY and ON WITH THE SHOW. [3] Also in ON WITH THE SHOW.

## 5564 ✦ SOMBRAS DE GLORIA
Sono-Art, 1930

**Composer(s)**  Hanley, James F.
**Lyricist(s)**  Tamayo, Fernando C.; Bohr, Jose; Barros, Jose C.; Tobias, Charles

**Producer(s)**  Goebel, O.E.
**Director(s)**  Stone, Andrew L.
**Screenwriter(s)**  Tamayo, Fernando C.
**Source(s)**  "The Long Shot" (story) Boyd, Thomas Alexander

**Cast** Bohr, Jose; Rico, Mona; Maran, Francisco; Vanoni, Cesar; Cayol, Ricardo; Alexis, Demetrius; Torena, Juan; Acosta, Enrique

**Song(s)** Bienvenidos; Arullo; Militar; Oh Paris; Si la Vida te Sonrie; Canoe-dle-oodle Along; Roja Rosa de Amor

**Notes** No cue sheet available. This is a Spanish version of BLAZE O' GLORY. It is not known which of these lyricists wrote which songs.

## 5565 ✦ SOMBRERO
Metro–Goldwyn–Mayer, 1952

**Musical Score** Arnaud, Leo
**Choreographer(s)** Pan, Hermes

**Producer(s)** Cummings, Jack
**Director(s)** Foster, Norman
**Screenwriter(s)** Foster, Norman; Niggli, Josefina
**Source(s)** *Mexican Village* (novel) Niggli, Josefina

**Cast** Gassman, Vittorio; Foch, Nina; De Carlo, Yvonne; Montalban, Ricardo; Charisse, Cyd; Hampden, Walter; Kasznar, Kurt; Jason, Rick; Gomez, Thomas; Greco, Jose

**Song(s)** El Arbolito (C/L: Martinez, Chucho); Cartas a Ufemia (C/L: Chaplin, Saul; Fuentes, Ruben; Mendez, Ricardo Lopez); Mi Viejo Amor (C/L: Oteo, A.E.; Bustamente, A.F.); Noche de Ronda [1] (C/L: Lara, Maria Teresa); La Burrita (C/L: Romero, Ventura)

**Notes** [1] Also in Spanish language versions of THE BIG BROADCAST OF 1938 (Paramount), MASQUERADE IN MEXICO (Paramount), HAVANA ROSE (Republic) and RIDE CLEAR OF DIABLO (Universal).

## 5566 ✦ SOMEBODY LOVES ME
Paramount, 1952

**Composer(s)** Evans, Ray; Livingston, Jay
**Lyricist(s)** Evans, Ray; Livingston, Jay
**Choreographer(s)** O'Curran, Charles

**Producer(s)** Seaton, George; Perlberg, William
**Director(s)** Brecher, Irving
**Screenwriter(s)** Brecher, Irving

**Cast** Hutton, Betty; Meeker, Ralph [1]; Jergens, Adele [5]; Keith, Robert; Slate, Henry [3]; Tomack, Sid [4]; Bird, Billie; Benny, Jack; Legon, Jeni [2]; Allen, Bea [5]; Mason, Virginia

**Song(s)** Love Him; Thanks to You; Honey, Oh, My Honey; On Stage Interlude; Vo-Do-Do-Dee-Oh (C/L: Brooks, Dudley; Clark, Les; O'Curran, Charles)

**Notes** This is a film biography of Blossom Seeley and Benny Fields. Songs with visual vocals include "That Teasing Rag" by Joe Jordan; "Toddling the Todalo" and "June" by A. Baldwin Sloane and E. Ray Goetz; "Smiles" by J. Will Callahan and Lee S. Roberts; "A

Dollar and Thirty Cents" by unknown writers; "I Cried for You" by Gus Arnheim, Arthur Freed and Abe Lyman; "Rose Room" by Harry Williams and Art Hickman; "Way Down Yonder in New Orleans" by Henry Creamer and Turner Layton; "Wang Wang Blues" by Gus Mueller, Buster Johnson and Henry Busse; "Somebody Loves Me" by B.G. De Sylva and George Gershwin; "Jealous" by Jack Little, Tommy Malie and Dick Finch; "Dixie Dreams" by Arthur Johnston, George W. Meyer, Grant Clarke and Roy Turk; "I'm Sorry I Made You Cry" by N.J. Clesi and Theodore Morse; "On San Francisco Bay" by Vincent Bryan and Gertrude Hoffman; and "I Can't Tell You Why I Love You" by Will J. Cobb and Gus Edwards. [1] Dubbed by Pat Morgan. [2] Dubbed by Pearl White. [3] Dubbed by Jack Baker. [4] Dubbed by Les Clark. [5] Both actresses dubbed by Barbara Ames.

## 5567 ✦ SOMEBODY UP THERE LIKES ME
Metro–Goldwyn–Mayer, 1956

**Musical Score** Kaper, Bronislau

**Producer(s)** Schnee, Charles
**Director(s)** Wise, Robert
**Screenwriter(s)** Lehman, Ernest
**Source(s)** *Somebody Up There Likes Me* (autobiography) Graziano, Rocky; Barber, Rowland

**Cast** Newman, Paul; Angeli, Pier; Sloane, Everett; Heckart, Eileen; Mineo, Sal; Stone, Harold J.; Buloff, Joseph; White, Sammy

**Song(s)** Somebody Up There Likes Me (C: Kaper, Bronislau; L: Cahn, Sammy)

## 5568 ✦ SOME CAME RUNNING
Metro–Goldwyn–Mayer, 1958

**Musical Score** Bernstein, Elmer

**Producer(s)** Siegel, Sol C.
**Director(s)** Minnelli, Vincente
**Screenwriter(s)** Patrick, John; Sheekman, Arthur
**Source(s)** *Some Came Running* (novel) Jones, James

**Cast** Sinatra, Frank; Martin, Dean; MacLaine, Shirley; Hyer, Martha; Kennedy, Arthur; Gates, Nancy; Dana, Leora

**Song(s)** To Love and Be Loved (C: Van Heusen, James; L: Cahn, Sammy)

**Notes** There are also vocals of "After You've Gone" by Henry Creamer and Turner Layton and "Don't Blame Me" by Jimmy McHugh and Dorothy Fields.

## 5569 ✦ SOME GIRLS DO
United Artists, 1969

**Musical Score** Blackwell, Charles

**Producer(s)** Box, Betty E.
**Director(s)** Thomas, Ralph
**Screenwriter(s)** Osborn, David; Charles-Williams, Liz

**Cast**   Johnson, Richard; Lavi, Daliah; Loncar, Beba; Villiers, James; Howard, Vanessa; Morley, Robert; Rome, Sydne; North, Virginia

**Song(s)**   Some Girls Do Satisfy You (C: Blackwell, Charles; L: Black, Don)

**Notes**   A sequel to DEADLIER THAN THE MALE.

## 5570  ✦  SOME KIND OF HERO
### Paramount, 1982

**Musical Score**   Williams, Patrick

**Producer(s)**   Koch, Howard W.
**Director(s)**   Pressman, Michael
**Screenwriter(s)**   Kirkwood, James; Boris, Robert
**Source(s)**   *Some Kind of Hero* (novel) Kirkwood, James

**Cast**   Pryor, Richard; Kidder, Margot; Sharkey, Ray; Cox, Ronny; Moody, Lynne; Cole, Olivia

**Song(s)**   Some Kind of Hero [1] (C: Williams, Patrick; L: Jennings, Will)

**Notes**   [1] Background vocal only.

## 5571  ✦  SOME KIND OF WONDERFUL
### Paramount, 1987

**Musical Score**   Hague, Stephen; Musser, John

**Producer(s)**   Hughes, John
**Director(s)**   Deutch, Howard
**Screenwriter(s)**   Hughes, John

**Cast**   Stoltz, Eric; Masterson, Mary Stuart; Sheffer, Craig; Ashton, John; Thompson, Lea; Koteas, Elias; Corman, Maddie

**Song(s)**   I Go Crazy (C/L: Mitchell, James; Mills, Kevin; Marsh, Nick; Barker, Rocco); Do Anything (C/L: Shelley, Pete); Turn to the Sky (C/L: Elliott, Loz; Ashton, Tom; Murray, Cleo); The Shyest Time (C/L: Walsh, Peter Milton); Cry Like This (C/L: Joyner, David; Cook, Tony; Hague, Stephen)

**Notes**   All songs are background vocals. List includes only those songs which appear to be written for the film.

## 5572  ✦  SOME LIKE IT HOT
### Paramount, 1939

**Producer(s)**   Thomas, William
**Director(s)**   Archainbaud, George
**Screenwriter(s)**   Foster, Lewis R.; Mahoney, Wilkie
**Source(s)**   *The Great Magoo* (play) Hecht, Ben; Fowler, Gene

**Cast**   Hope, Bob; Ross, Shirley; Krupa, Gene; Merkel, Una

**Song(s)**   The Lady's in Love with You [2] (C: Lane, Burton; L: Loesser, Frank); Some Like It Hot (C: Krupa, Gene; Biondi, Remo; L: Loesser, Frank); Whodunit [1]

(C: Carmichael, Hoagy; L: Loesser, Frank); Wire Brush Stomp (inst.) (C: Krupa, Gene; Biondi, Remo)

**Notes**   Another Paramount picture based on THE GREAT MAGOO is SHOOT THE WORKS. [1] Not used. Used in TORNADO. [2] Also in SEVENTEEN.

## 5573  ✦  SOMETHING FOR THE BOYS
### Twentieth Century–Fox, 1944

**Composer(s)**   McHugh, Jimmy
**Lyricist(s)**   Adamson, Harold
**Choreographer(s)**   Castle, Nick

**Producer(s)**   Starr, Irving
**Director(s)**   Seiler, Lewis
**Screenwriter(s)**   Ellis, Robert; Logan, Helen; Gabrielson, Frank
**Source(s)**   *Something for the Boys* (musical) Fields, Herbert; Fields, Dorothy; Porter, Cole

**Cast**   Miranda, Carmen; O'Shea, Michael; Blaine, Vivian; Silvers, Phil; Ryan, Sheila; Como, Perry; Williams, Cara; Hall, Thurston; Tombes, Andrew

**Song(s)**   Something for the Boys [1] (C/L: Porter, Cole); Wouldn't It Be Nice?; I Wish We Didn't Have to Say Goodnight; Eighty Miles Outside of Atlanta; Batuca Nega (C/L: Barroso, Ary); In the Middle of Nowhere [2]; Southland (C/L: Silvers, Phil; McHugh, Jimmy; Adamson, Harold); Climbin' Up Dem Golden Stairs; Samba-Boogie

**Notes**   [1] From original show. [2] Also in SOMEWHERE IN THE NIGHT.

## 5574  ✦  SOMETHING IN THE WIND
### Universal, 1947

**Musical Score**   Green, Johnny
**Composer(s)**   Green, Johnny
**Lyricist(s)**   Robin, Leo

**Producer(s)**   Sistrom, Joseph
**Director(s)**   Pichel, Irving
**Screenwriter(s)**   Kurnitz, Harry; Bowers, William

**Cast**   Durbin, Deanna; O'Connor, Donald; Dall, John; Winninger, Charles; Wycherly, Margaret; Carter, Helena; The Williams Brothers; Peerce, Jan

**Song(s)**   The Turntable Song; Deduco Commercial; I'm Happy-Go-Lucky and Free; I Love a Mystery; You Wanna Keep Your Baby Lookin' Right; Something in the Wind; It's Only Love; Il Trovatore (C: Verdi, Giuseppe)

## 5575  ✦  SOMETHING TO LIVE FOR
### Paramount, 1952

**Producer(s)**   Stevens, George
**Director(s)**   Stevens, George
**Screenwriter(s)**   Taylor, Dwight

**Cast**   Milland, Ray; Fontaine, Joan; Wright, Teresa; Dick, Douglas; Derr, Richard

**Song(s)**   Alone at Last [1] [2] (C: Young, Victor; L: Hilliard, Bob); You Can't Turn Back the Clock [2] [3] (C: Young, Victor; L: Hilliard, Bob)

**Notes**   [1] Used instrumentally only. [2] Same music. [3] Not used.

### 5576 ◆ SOMETHING TO SHOUT ABOUT
Columbia, 1943

**Composer(s)**   Porter, Cole
**Lyricist(s)**   Porter, Cole
**Choreographer(s)**   Lichine, David

**Producer(s)**   Ratoff, Gregory
**Director(s)**   Ratoff, Gregory
**Screenwriter(s)**   Breslow, Lou; Eliscu, Edward

**Cast**   Ameche, Don; Wright Jr., Cobina; Oakie, Jack; Blair, Janet; Borg, Veda Ann; Gaxton, William; Scott, Hazel; Green, Harry; The Bricklayers; Teddy Wilson and His Band; Lichine, David

**Song(s)**   You'd Be So Nice to Come Home To; Through Thick and Thin; I Always Knew; Something to Shout About; Lotus Bloom [2]; Hasta Luego; It Might Have Been [1]; I Can Do Without Tea in My Teapot [1]; Couldn't Be [3]; Take It Easy [3]; Let Doctor Schmett Vet Your Pet [3]

**Notes**   [1] Used instrumentally only. [2] Danced by David Lichine and Lily Norwood (Cyd Charisse). [3] Not used.

### 5577 ◆ SOMETHING TO SING ABOUT
Grand National, 1937

**Composer(s)**   Schertzinger, Victor
**Lyricist(s)**   Schertzinger, Victor
**Choreographer(s)**   Dixon, Harland

**Producer(s)**   Myers, Zion
**Director(s)**   Schertzinger, Victor
**Screenwriter(s)**   Parker, Austin

**Cast**   Cagney, James; Thaw, Evelyn; Frawley, William; Lockhart, Kathleen; Newill, James; Barris, Harry

**Song(s)**   Right or Wrong; Any Old Love; Something to Sing About; Loving You (L: Schertzinger, Victor; Alderman, Myrl); Out of the Blue

**Notes**   No cue sheet available.

### 5578 ◆ SOMETHING WICKED THIS WAY COMES
Disney, 1983

**Musical Score**   Horner, James

**Producer(s)**   Douglas, Peter Vincent
**Director(s)**   Clayton, Jack

**Screenwriter(s)**   Bradbury, Ray
**Source(s)**   *Something Wicked This Way Comes* (novel) Bradbury, Ray

**Cast**   Robards Jr., Jason; Pryce, Jonathan; Ladd, Diane; Dano, Royal; Peterson, Vidal; Carson, Shawn

**Song(s)**   Now, When the Dusky Shades of Night (C: James, Sidney; L: Traditional)

### 5579 ◆ SOMETIMES A GREAT NOTION
Universal, 1971

**Musical Score**   Mancini, Henry

**Producer(s)**   Foreman, John
**Director(s)**   Newman, Paul
**Screenwriter(s)**   Gay, John
**Source(s)**   *Sometimes a Great Notion* (novel) Kesey, Ken

**Cast**   Newman, Paul; Fonda, Henry; Sarrazin, Michael; Jaeckel, Richard; Remick, Lee

**Song(s)**   All His Children (C: Mancini, Henry; L: Bergman, Marilyn; Bergman, Alan)

### 5580 ◆ SOME TIME SOON
Metro–Goldwyn–Mayer, 1937

**Musical Score**   Snell, Dave
**Composer(s)**   Burton, Val; Jason, Will
**Lyricist(s)**   Burton, Val; Jason, Will

**Director(s)**   Lee, Sammy
**Screenwriter(s)**   Rauh, Stanley; Goldstone, Richard

**Cast**   Chatburn, Jean; Courtney, Inez; Gaye, Gregory; Auerbach, Arthur

**Song(s)**   Some Day Soon; Play Tzigane

**Notes**   Short subject.

### 5581 ◆ SOMEWHAT SECRET
Metro–Goldwyn–Mayer, 1939

**Musical Score**   Snell, Dave; Brent, Earl

**Director(s)**   Lee, Sammy
**Screenwriter(s)**   Hochfelder, Julian; Greene, Mort

**Cast**   Howard, Mary; Collins, Tom; Rubin, Benny; Bovard, Mary

**Song(s)**   Fair Dimsdale (C: Brent, Earl; L: Greene, Mort); You and I (C: Chopin, Frederic; L: Greene, Mort)

**Notes**   Short subject.

### 5582 ◆ SOMEWHERE IN THE NIGHT
Twentieth Century–Fox, 1946

**Composer(s)**   McHugh, Jimmy
**Lyricist(s)**   Adamson, Harold

**Producer(s)**   Lawler, Anderson
**Director(s)**   Mankiewicz, Joseph L.

**Screenwriter(s)** Dimsdale, Howard; Mankiewicz, Joseph L.

**Cast** Hodiak, John; Guild, Nancy [2]; Nolan, Lloyd; Conte, Richard; Hutchinson, Josephine; Kortner, Fritz; Leonard, Sheldon; Benedict, Richard

**Song(s)** In the Middle of Nowhere [2]

**Notes** [1] Dubbed by Joan Barton. [2] Also in SOMETHING FOR THE BOYS.

## 5583 ◆ THE SON-DAUGHTER
Metro–Goldwyn–Mayer, 1932

**Musical Score** Stothart, Herbert
**Composer(s)** Stothart, Herbert; Goetzl, Anselm
**Lyricist(s)** Stothart, Herbert; Goetzl, Anselm

**Director(s)** Brown, Clarence
**Screenwriter(s)** Goodrich, John; West, Claudine; Gordon, Leon
**Source(s)** *The Son-Daughter* (play) Scarborough, George M.; Belasco, David

**Cast** Hayes, Helen; Novarro, Ramon; Stone, Lewis; Oland, Warner; Hale, Louise Closser; Warner, H.B.; Morgan, Ralph

**Song(s)** Love Theme; Lien Wha Theme

## 5584 ◆ SONG AND DANCE MAN
Twentieth Century–Fox, 1936

**Composer(s)** Clare, Sidney
**Lyricist(s)** Clare, Sidney

**Producer(s)** Wurtzel, Sol M.
**Director(s)** Dwan, Allan
**Screenwriter(s)** Fulton, Maude
**Source(s)** *Song and Dance Man* (play) Cohan, George M.

**Cast** Trevor, Claire; Kelly, Paul; Whalen, Michael; Donnelly, Ruth; Burke, James; Dumont, Margaret; Roy, Gloria; Bevan, Billy

**Song(s)** You Took Me From the Gutter [2] (C: Jarnigin, Jerry); Dancing in the Open; You're My Favorite One (C: Pollack, Lew); (On a Holiday) In My Playroom; Join the Party; Let's Get Going Baby [1]; Ain't He Good Lookin' [3]

**Notes** [1] Used instrumentally only. [2] Not written for this film. Only four lines used. [3] Not used. Used in WHILE NEW YORK SLEEPS.

## 5585 ◆ A SONG FOR MISS JULIE
Republic, 1945

**Composer(s)** Herscher, Louis
**Lyricist(s)** Shelton, Marla
**Choreographer(s)** Ceballos, Larry

**Producer(s)** Rowland, William; Harriman, Curley
**Director(s)** Rowland, William
**Screenwriter(s)** Leigh, Rowland

**Cast** Hepburn, Barton; Clark, Roger; Ross, Shirley; Walker, Cheryl; Risdon, Elizabeth; Farrar, Jane; Markova, Alicia; Dolin, Anton

**Song(s)** It All Could Have Happened Before; That's What I Like About You; The Country Ain't the Country Anymore; I Love to Remember; Sweet Sunday

**Notes** No cue sheet available.

## 5586 ◆ A SONG IS BORN (1938)
Paramount, 1938

**Cast** Larry Clinton and his Orchestra; Wain, Bea

**Song(s)** I Fell Up to Heaven [1] (C: Rainger, Ralph; L: Robin, Leo); Heart and Soul (C: Carmichael, Hoagy; L: Loesser, Frank); Silly Little Sally [2] (C: Hollander, Frederick; L: Freed, Ralph); Love Doesn't Grow on Trees [3] (C: Lane, Burton; L: Freed, Ralph); The Devil with the Devil (C/L: Clinton, Larry)

**Notes** Short subject. [1] Written for but not used in COLLEGE SWING. [2] Not used. [3] Not used in STOLEN HEAVEN.

## 5587 ◆ A SONG IS BORN (1948)
Goldwyn/RKO, 1948

**Musical Score** Friedhofer, Hugo
**Composer(s)** de Paul, Gene
**Lyricist(s)** Raye, Don

**Producer(s)** Goldwyn, Samuel
**Director(s)** Hawks, Howard
**Source(s)** "From A to Z" (story) Wilder, Billy; Monroe, Thomas

**Cast** Kaye, Danny; Goodman, Benny; Dorsey, Tommy; Armstrong, Louis; Hampton, Lionel; Barnet, Charlie; Powell, Mel; Buck and Bubbles; The Page Cavanaugh Trio; The Golden Gate Quartette; Russo and the Samba Kings; Mayo, Virginia [1]; Herbert, Hugh; Cochran, Steve; Bromberg, J. Edward; Bressart, Felix; Stossel, Ludwig; Whitehead, O.Z.; Dale, Esther; Field, Mary; Chamberlin, Howland; Langton, Paul; Blackmer, Sidney; Welden, Ben; Chasen, Ben

**Song(s)** A Song Was Born; Nonu A—Toni E (C/L: Kuaana, Danny); Goldwyn Stomp (inst.) (C: Hampton, Lionel); Daddy-O; Hawk's Nest (inst.) (C: Hampton, Lionel); Redskin Rhumba (inst.) (C: Bennett, Dale)

**Notes** A musicalization of BALL OF FIRE. There is also an instrumental of "Stealin' Apples" by Andy Razaf and Fats Waller and one of "Flying Home" by Benny Goodman and Lionel Hampton. [1] Dubbed by Jeri Southern.

## 5588 ◆ SONG OF ARIZONA
Republic, 1946

**Composer(s)** Elliott, Jack
**Lyricist(s)** Elliott, Jack
**Choreographer(s)** Fanchon

**Producer(s)** White, Edward J.
**Director(s)** McDonald, Frank
**Screenwriter(s)** Webster, M. Coates

**Cast** Rogers, Roy; Trigger; Hayes, George "Gabby";
Evans, Dale; Bob Nolan and the Sons of the Pioneers

**Song(s)** Song of Arizona; Way Out There (C/L:
Nolan, Bob); Half a Chance Ranch; Round and Round;
Michael O'Leary O'Brian O'Toole (C/L: Forster,
Gordon); Mr. Spook Steps Out

**Notes** There are also vocals of "Will Ya Be My Darlin'"
by Mary Ann Owens and "Did You Ever Get That
Feeling in the Moonlight" by Ira Schuster, Larry Stock
and James Cavanaugh.

## 5589 ◆ SONG OF IDAHO
Columbia, 1949

**Producer(s)** Clark, Colbert
**Director(s)** Nazarro, Ray
**Screenwriter(s)** Shipman, Harry

**Cast** Grant, Kirby; Vincent, June; The Sunshine Girls;
The Starlighters; The Hoosier Hotshots; Parnell, Emory;
Acuff, Eddie

**Song(s)** Driftin' (C/L: Unknown); Nobody Else But
You (C/L: Unknown); Idaho [1] (C/L: Unknown)

**Notes** No cue sheet available. [1] May have been the
song "Idaho" by Jesse Stone that was used in the
Republic picture IDAHO.

## 5590 ◆ SONG OF KENTUCKY
Fox, 1929

**Producer(s)** Sprague, Chandler
**Director(s)** Seiler, Lewis; Merlin, Frank
**Screenwriter(s)** Brennan, Frederick Hazlitt

**Cast** Moran, Lois; Wagstaff, Joseph; Burgess, Dorothy;
Hopper, Hedda; Bing, Herman

**Song(s)** Sitting By the Window (C/L: Conrad, Con;
Gottler, Archie; Mitchell, Sidney D.); Remember the
Rose (C: Simons, Seymour B.; L: Mitchell, Sidney D.);
I'm On a Diet of Love [2] (C: Baer, Abel; L: Gilbert, L.
Wolfe); Good for Nothing but Love [1] (C/L: Kernell,
William); A Night of Happiness (C/L: Conrad, Con;
Gottler, Archie; Mitchell, Sidney D.)

**Notes** [1] From THE BIG PARTY and also in ON
THE LEVEL. [2] From HAPPY DAYS.

## 5591 ◆ THE SONG OF LOVE
Columbia, 1929

**Composer(s)** Rich, Max
**Lyricist(s)** Gordon, Mack

**Producer(s)** Small, Edward
**Director(s)** Kenton, Erle C.
**Screenwriter(s)** Howell, Dorothy; Houston, Norman

**Cast** Baker, Belle [2]; Graves, Ralph; Durand, David;
Quedens, Eunice [3]

**Song(s)** I'm Walking with the Moonbeams (Talking to
the Stars) [5]; I'm Somebody's Baby Now; Take
Everything But You (C/L: Abrahams, Maurice; Colby,
Elmer [1]); Italian Chiropractor Song (C/L: Bennett,
George J.; Carlton, S.); Atlas Is Itless (C: Henderson,
Ray; L: Brown, Lew; DeSylva, B.G.); Ireland Must Be
Heaven (C/L: Fisher, Fred; McCarthy, Joseph); I'll Still
Go On Wanting You [4] (C/L: Sizemore, Arthur;
Grossman, Bernie; Abrahams, Maurice); White Way
Blues (C: Wiest, George D.; Rich, Max; L: Gordon,
Mack)

**Notes** [1] Pseudonym for B.G. De Sylva, Lew Brown
and Ray Henderson. [2] Maurice Abrahams' wife. [3]
Eve Arden. [4] Sheet music credits M. Kippel not
Maurice Abrahams. [5] ASCAP credits music to Rich
and Maurice Abrahams.

## 5592 ◆ SONG OF MEXICO
Republic, 1946

**Producer(s)** FitzPatrick, James A.
**Director(s)** FitzPatrick, James A.

**Cast** Mara, Adele; Barrier, Edgar; Lewis, George;
Pulido, Jose; Dalya, Jacqueline; De Alva Raquel; The
Tipica Orchestra

**Song(s)** Xochimilco (C/L: Esperon, Manuel); Acapulco
(C/L: de Borbon, Alfredo Nunez); Midnight Serenade
(C/L: Galindo, Pedro); Cuernavaca (C/L: Lopez, Anita)

## 5593 ◆ SONG OF NEVADA
Republic, 1944

**Producer(s)** Grey, Harry
**Director(s)** Kane, Joseph
**Screenwriter(s)** Cooper, Olive; Kahn, Gordon

**Cast** Rogers, Roy; Lee, Mary; Evans, Dale; Hall,
Thurston; Eldredge, John; Corrigan, Lloyd; Nolan, Bob;
Farr, Hugh; Farr, Karl; Spencer, Tim; Carson, Ken;
Mason, LeRoy; Duncan, Kenne

**Song(s)** There's a New Moon Over Nevada (C/L:
Carson, Ken); Little Joe, the Wrangler (C: Traditional;
L: Thorp, N. Howard); Harum Scarum Baron of the
Harmonium (C/L: Henderson, Charles); Cowboy Has
to Yodel (C/L: Carson, Ken); Home on the Range (C:
Traditional; L: Burnette, Smiley); What Are We Gonna

Do About This Rainy Day (C/L: Henderson, Charles); The Wigwam Song (C/L: Spencer, Glenn); Nevada (C/L: Henderson, Charles)

**Notes** There are also vocals of "It's Love, Love, Love" by Hal David, Joan Whitney and Alex Kramer; "And Her Golden Hair was Hanging Down Her Back" by Felix McGlennon and Monroe H. Rosenfeld and several traditional songs.

## 5594 ✦ SONG OF NORWAY
### ABC, 1970

**Composer(s)** Wright, Robert; Forrest, George; Grieg, Edvard [1]
**Lyricist(s)** Wright, Robert; Forrest, George
**Choreographer(s)** Theodore, Lee

**Producer(s)** Stone, Andrew L.; Stone, Virginia
**Director(s)** Stone, Andrew L.
**Screenwriter(s)** Stone, Andrew L.
**Source(s)** *Song of Norway* (musical) Lazarus, Milton; Wright, Robert; Forrest, George; Grieg, Edvard

**Cast** Maustad, Toralv; Henderson, Florence; Schollin, Christina; Porretta, Frank; Secombe, Harry; Morley, Robert; Robinson, Edward G.; Larner, Elizabeth; Homolka, Oscar; Jaeger, Frederick; Wordsworth, Richard

**Song(s)** Solveig's Song; Piano Concerto in A Minor; Life of a Wife of a Sailor; Freddy and His Fiddle; A Rhyme and a Reason; Strange Music; Song of Norway; Ribbons and Wrappings; The Little House; When We Wed at Christmastime; In the Hall of the Mountain King; Wrong to Dream; Hill of Dreams; Hymn of Betrothal; Be a Boy Again; Hand in Hand; Three there Were; The Solitary Wanderer; I Love You

**Notes** No cue sheet available. [1] Music based on themes by Edvard Grieg.

## 5595 ✦ SONG OF OLD WYOMING
### PRC, 1945

**Director(s)** Tansey, Robert Emmett
**Screenwriter(s)** Kavanaugh, Frances

**Cast** Dean, Eddie; Holt, Jennifer; Padden, Sarah; LaRue, Al "Lash"

**Song(s)** My Wild Prairie Rose (C: Hoefle, Carl; L: Dean, Eddie); Ma at Midnight (C/L: Mayfield, James); My Herdin' Song (C: Mabie, Milt; L: Dean, Eddie)

**Notes** There is also a vocal of "Hills of Old Wyoming" by Leo Robin and Ralph Rainger.

## 5596 ✦ SONG OF RUSSIA
### Metro–Goldwyn–Mayer, 1944

**Musical Score** Stothart, Herbert
**Choreographer(s)** Lichine, David

**Producer(s)** Pasternak, Joe
**Director(s)** Ratoff, Gregory
**Screenwriter(s)** Jarrico, Paul; Collins, Richard

**Cast** Taylor, Robert; Peters, Susan; Hodiak, John; Benchley, Robert; Bressart, Felix; Hickman, Darryl

**Song(s)** When a Man Is Free (C: Stothart, Herbert; L: Freed, Ralph); And Russia Is Her Name (C: Kern, Jerome; L: Harburg, E.Y.); The Guerillas' Song [1] (C: Jurmann, Walter; L: Webster, Paul Francis)

**Notes** Russian Lyrics by V. Dmitrenko. [1] Not used.

## 5597 ✦ SONG OF SCHEHERAZADE
### Universal, 1947

**Composer(s)** Rimsky-Korsakov, Nicholas
**Lyricist(s)** Brooks, Jack
**Choreographer(s)** Losch, Tilly

**Producer(s)** Kaufman, Edward
**Director(s)** Reisch, Walter
**Screenwriter(s)** Reisch, Walter

**Cast** De Carlo, Yvonne; Arden, Eve; Donlevy, Brian; Reed, Philip; Qualen, John; Lane, Richard; Kilburn, Terry; Dolenz, George

**Song(s)** Legendary Tale [1]; Gypsy Song [2]; Fandango [3]; Hymn to the Sun; Capriccio Espanol [4]; Coz D'Or [4]; Dance of the Tumblers [4]; Scheherazade [4]; A Song of India [4]

**Notes** The score was arranged by Miklos Rozsa. [1] Adapted by Miklos Rozsa from "Song of India." [2] Adapted by Miklos Rozsa from "Antar." [3] Adapted by Miklos Rozsa from "Capriccio Espagnol." [4] Not used.

## 5598 ✦ SONG OF SONGS
### Paramount, 1933

**Composer(s)** Hollander, Frederick
**Lyricist(s)** Heyman, Edward

**Director(s)** Mamoulian, Rouben
**Screenwriter(s)** Birinski, Leo; Hoffenstein, Samuel
**Source(s)** (novel) Sudermann, Hermann; (play) Sheldon, Edward

**Cast** Dietrich, Marlene; Aherne, Brian; Atwill, Lionel; Skipworth, Alison; Albright, Hardie; Freeman, Helen

**Song(s)** Jonny; You Are My Song of Songs (C: Myers, Richard)

## 5599 ✦ SONG OF SURRENDER
### Paramount, 1949

**Producer(s)** Maibaum, Richard
**Director(s)** Leisen, Mitchell
**Screenwriter(s)** Maibaum, Richard

**Cast**   Hendrix, Wanda; Rains, Claude; Carey, Macdonald

**Song(s)**   Song of Surrender (C: Young, Victor; L: Livingston, Jay; Evans, Ray); Now and Forever [1] (C: Young, Victor; L: Livingston, Jay; Evans, Ray)

**Notes**   Formerly titled NOW AND FOREVER and THE SIN OF ABBY HUNT. [1] Used instrumentally only.

## 5600 ✦ SONG OF TEXAS
### Republic, 1955

**Producer(s)**   Grey, Harry
**Director(s)**   Kane, Joseph
**Screenwriter(s)**   Miller, Winston

**Cast**   Rogers, Roy; Ryan, Sheila; MacLane, Barton; Haade, William; Shannon, Harry; Judge, Arline; Sons of the Pioneers

**Song(s)**   Rainbow Over the Range (C/L: Spencer, Tim); I Love the Prairie Cowboy [1] (C/L: Spencer, Tim)

**Notes**   This may be an incomplete cue sheet. Other vocals included "Moonlight and Roses" by Edwin H. Lemare, Ben Black and Neil Moret, and "Mexicali Rose" by Jack B. Tenny and Helen Stone. [1] Used instrumentally.

## 5601 ✦ SONG OF THE BUCKAROO
### Monogram, 1939

**Producer(s)**   Finney, Edward
**Director(s)**   Herman, Al
**Screenwriter(s)**   Rathmell, John

**Cast**   Ritter, Tex; Falkenburg, Jinx; London, Tom; LaRue, Frank; King, Charles; Chesebro, George; Pollard, Snub; Adams, Ernie

**Song(s)**   I Promise You (C/L: Harford, Frank; Ritter, Tex); Texas Dan (C/L: Robison, Carson J.); Little Tenderfoot (C/L: Lange, Johnny)

**Notes**   No cue sheet available. Fred Stryker is also credited with songs in *Film Daily*.

## 5602 ✦ SONG OF THE CITY
### Metro–Goldwyn–Mayer, 1937

**Musical Score**   Axt, William

**Producer(s)**   Hubbard, Lucien; Fessier, Michael
**Director(s)**   Taggart, Errol
**Screenwriter(s)**   Fessier, Michael

**Cast**   Lindsay, Margaret; Dean, Jeffrey [1]; Naish, J. Carrol; Pendleton, Nat; Judels, Charles

**Song(s)**   Tonight Will Never Come Again (C: Axt, William; L: Kahn, Gus)

**Notes**   [1] Pseudonym for Dean Jagger.

## 5603 ✦ SONG OF THE EAGLE
### Paramount, 1933

**Producer(s)**   Rogers, Charles R.
**Director(s)**   Murphy, Ralph
**Screenwriter(s)**   Robinson, Casey; Mack, Willard

**Cast**   Arlen, Richard; Brian, Mary; Dresser, Louise; Bickford, Charles

**Song(s)**   Hey! Hey! We're Gonna Be Free (C: Lewis, Harold; L: Grossman, Bernie)

**Notes**   No cue sheet available.

## 5604 ✦ SONG OF THE FLAME
### Warner Brothers–First National, 1930

**Composer(s)**   Akst, Harry
**Lyricist(s)**   Clarke, Grant
**Choreographer(s)**   Haskell, Jack

**Director(s)**   Crosland, Alan
**Screenwriter(s)**   Rigby, Gordon
**Source(s)**   *Song of the Flame* (musical) Hammerstein II, Oscar; Harbach, Otto; Stothart, Herbert; Gershwin, George

**Cast**   Gray, Alexander; Claire, Bernice; Gentle, Alice; Beery, Noah; Roach, Bert; Courtney, Inez; Camp, Shep; Linow, Ivan; Gray, Bernice; Smolinska, Janina

**Song(s)**   Cossack Love Song [1] (C: Gershwin, George; Stothart, Herbert; L: Harbach, Otto; Hammerstein II, Oscar); One Little Drink; Song of the Flame [1] (C: Gershwin, George; Stothart, Herbert; L: Harbach, Otto; Hammerstein II, Oscar); Petrograd; Liberty Song; The Goose Hangs High; Passing Fancy; When Love Calls (C: Ward, Edward)

**Notes**   No cue sheet available. Some sources also credit Ward with collaborating with Akst on the music to the Akst/Clarke songs. [1] From Broadway score.

## 5605 ✦ SONG OF THE ISLANDS
### Twentieth Century–Fox, 1942

**Composer(s)**   Gordon, Mack; Owens, Harry
**Lyricist(s)**   Gordon, Mack; Owens, Harry
**Choreographer(s)**   Pan, Hermes

**Producer(s)**   LeBaron, William
**Director(s)**   Lang, Walter
**Screenwriter(s)**   Schrank, Joseph; Pirosh, Robert; Ellis, Robert; Logan, Helen

**Cast**   Grable, Betty; Mature, Victor [3]; Oakie, Jack; Mitchell, Thomas; Barbier, George; Gilbert, Billy; Harry Owens and His Royal Hawaiians,

**Song(s)**   Song of the Islands [4] (C/L: King, Charles E.); Sing Me a Song of the Islands; Down on Ami Ami Oni Oni Island; Hu'i Mai (C/L: Hoopii Jr., Sol); Maluna, Malalo, Mawaena (Hawaiian Drinking Song);

Cannibal Chant [1] (C/L: Puailoa, Satini); What's Buzzin' Cousin?; Blue Shadows and White Gardenias [2]; The Cockeyed Mayor of Kaunakaki (C: Anderson, R. Alex; L: Anderson, R. Alex; Silverman, Al); O'Brien Has Gone Hawaiian

**Notes** [1] Words are unintelligible on the soundtrack. [2] Recorded but used as instrumental only. [3] Dubbed by Ben Gage. [4] Also in MELODY LANE (Universal) and FLIRTATION WALK (Warner).

## 5606 ✦ SONG OF THE OPEN ROAD
### United Artists, 1944

**Composer(s)** Kent, Walter
**Lyricist(s)** Gannon, Kim

**Producer(s)** Rogers, Charles R.
**Director(s)** Simon, S. Sylvan
**Screenwriter(s)** Mannheimer, Albert

**Cast** Powell, Jane [1]; Fields, W.C.; The Condos Brothers; Bergen, Edgar; McCarthy, Charlie; Granville, Bonita; Moran, Jackie; O'Neill, Peggy; Christy, Bill; Denny, Reginald; Toomey, Regis; Hobart, Rose; Arno, Sig

**Song(s)** Rollin' Down the Road; Delightfully Dangerous; Too Much in Love; Here It Is Monday; Fun in the Sun

**Notes** There is also a vocal of "Carmena" by Lane Wilson and Ellis Walton. [1] Screen debut.

## 5607 ✦ SONG OF THE SADDLE
### Warner Brothers–First National, 1936

**Composer(s)** Jerome, M.K.
**Lyricist(s)** Scholl, Jack

**Producer(s)** Foy, Bryan
**Director(s)** King, Louis
**Screenwriter(s)** Jacobs, William

**Cast** Foran, Dick; Lloyd, Alma; Middleton, Charles; Richards, Addison; Shubert, Eddie; Montague, Monte; Potel, Victor; Harlan, Kenneth; Stedman, Myrtle; Ernest, George; West, Pat; Farley, James; Granville, Bonita; Desmond, William

**Song(s)** Underneath a Western Sky (C: Fiorito, Ted; Jerome, M.K.) [1]; Vengeance

**Notes** Ted Fiorito credited with songs also but not in cue sheets. [1] Also in CATTLE TOWN, COWBOY QUARTERBACK and RETURN OF THE FRONTIERSMAN.

## 5608 ✦ SONG OF THE SARONG
### Universal, 1945

**Composer(s)** Brooks, Jack
**Lyricist(s)** Brooks, Jack

**Producer(s)** Lewis, Gene
**Director(s)** Young, Harold
**Screenwriter(s)** Lewis, Gene

**Cast** Gargan, William; Kelly, Nancy; Quillan, Eddie

**Song(s)** The Island of the Moon (C: de Paul, Gene; L: Raye, Don); Ridin' on the Crest of a Cloud; Pied Pipers from Swingtown U.S.A.; Lovely Luana (C: de Paul, Gene; L: Raye, Don)

## 5609 ✦ SONG OF THE SOUTH
### Disney, 1946

**Musical Score** Amfitheatrof, Daniele; Smith, Paul J.

**Producer(s)** Pearce, Perce
**Director(s)** Jackson, Wilfred; Foster, Harve
**Screenwriter(s)** Reymond, Dalton; Grant, Morton; Rapf, Maurice; Peed, William; Wright, Ralph; Stallings, George
**Source(s)** *Tales of Uncle Remus* (novel) Harris, Joel Chandler

**Directing Animator(s)** Kahl, Milt; Larson, Eric; Johnston, Ollie; Clark, Les; Davis, Marc; Lounsbery, John
**Cast** Warrick, Ruth; Driscoll, Bobby; Baskett, James; Patten, Luana; Watson, Lucile; McDaniel, Hattie; Rolf, Erik; Leedy, Glenn; Field, Mary; Brown, Anita; Nokes, George; Holland, Gene; Stewart, Nicodemus; Lee, Johnny

**Song(s)** Song of the South (C: Johnston, Arthur; L: Coslow, Sam); Uncle Remus Said (C/L: Lange, Johnny; Heath, Hy; Daniel, Eliot); Zip-A-Dee-Doo-Dah (C: Wrubel, Allie; L: Gilbert, Ray); Who Wants to Live Like That? (C: Darby, Ken; L: Carling, Foster); Let the Rain Pour Down [2] (C/L: Darby, Ken; Carling, Foster); How Do You Do (C/L: MacGimsey, Robert); Sooner or Later (C: Wolcott, Charles; L: Gilbert, Ray); Ev'rybody Has a Laughing Place (C: Wrubel, Allie; L: Gilbert, Ray); De Briar Patch [1] (C: Churchill, Frank E.; L: Kelley, Ray); De Lawd Looks After All His Chillun' [1] (C: Harline, Leigh; L: Washington, Ned); De Wuller De Wust [1] (C: Churchill, Frank E.; L: Kelley, Ray); I Ain't Nobody's Fool [1] (C: Harline, Leigh; L: Washington, Ned); I'll Take Mah Troubles Down to the River [1] (C: Harline, Leigh; L: Washington, Ned); Ingle-Go-Jang-Go-Jay [1] (C: Harline, Leigh; L: Washington, Ned); Livin' in a Heavenly Dream [1] (C: Churchill, Frank E.; L: Morey, Larry); Look at That Sun [1] (C/L: Lange, Johnny; Heath, Hy; Daniel, Eliot); My Ridin' Hoss [1] (C: Churchill, Frank E.; L: Kelley, Ray); Ridin' Hoss Spiritual [1] (C: Churchill, Frank E.; L: Kelley, Ray); Walkin' [1] (C: Churchill, Frank E.; L: Morey, Larry)

**Notes** Animated and live action feature. [1] Not used. [2] Music based on the public domain song "Midnight Special."

## 5610 ✦ SONG OF THE THIN MAN
Metro–Goldwyn–Mayer, 1947

**Musical Score**    Snell, Dave

**Producer(s)**    Perrin, Nat
**Director(s)**    Buzzell, Edward
**Screenwriter(s)**    Fisher, Steve; Perrin, Nat; O'Hanlon, James; Crane, Harry
**Source(s)**    characters by Hammett, Dashiell

**Cast**    Powell, William; Loy, Myrna; Wynn, Keenan; Stockwell, Dean; Reed, Philip; Morison, Patricia; Grahame, Gloria; Meadows, Jayne; Taylor, Don; Ames, Leon; Morgan, Ralph

**Song(s)**    You're Not So Easy to Forget (C: Oakland, Ben; L: Magidson, Herb)

## 5611 ✦ SONG OF THE WEST
Warner Brothers, 1930

**Composer(s)**    Youmans, Vincent
**Lyricist(s)**    Hammerstein II, Oscar

**Director(s)**    Enright, Ray
**Screenwriter(s)**    Thew, Harvey
**Source(s)**    *Rainbow* (musical) Hammerstein II, Oscar; Stallings, Laurence; Youmans, Vincent

**Cast**    Boles, John; Segal, Vivienne; Brown, Joe E.; Martindel, Edward; Gribbon, Harry; Wells, Marie; Hardy, Sam; Byron, Marion; Cameron, Rudolph

**Song(s)**    Come Back to Me (C: Akst, Harry; L: Clarke, Grant); The Bride Was Dressed in White! [1]; Hay Straw! [1]; The One Girl [1]; I Like You As You Are [1]; Let Me Give All My Love to Thee [1]; West Wind (L: Robinson, J. Russel); My Mother Told Me Not to Trust a Sailor [1] [2]

**Notes**    No cue sheet available. [1] From Broadway production. [2] Broadway title "My Mother Told Me Not to Trust a Soldier."

## 5612 ✦ SONG O' MY HEART
Fox, 1930

**Director(s)**    Borzage, Frank
**Screenwriter(s)**    Barry, Tom

**Cast**    O'Sullivan, Maureen; Garrick, John; Kerrigan, J.M.; Clifford, Tommy; Joyce, Alice; McCormack, John; Martindel, Edward; de Segurola, Andreas; Fitzroy, Emily

**Song(s)**    I Feel You Near Me (C: Hanley, James F.; L: McCarthy, Joseph); A Pair of Blue Eyes (C/L: Kernell, William); How Dear Is the Hour (inst.) (C: McCormack, John); By the Short Cut to the Roses [1] (C: Traditional; L: Hopper, Nora); Mary Dear [1] (C: Traditional; L: McCormack, John); Song O' My Heart [2] (C/L: Hanley, James F.; McCarthy, Joseph; Kernell, William)

**Notes**    The following songs are also given vocal interpretations: "In the Place Where They Make the Gas," "Mrs. McLeod's Reel," "Then You'll Remember Me" by Balfe from THE BOHEMIAN GIRL, "A Fairy Story by the Fire" by Oscar Merikanto and Angela Campbell McInnes, "Just for Today" by Blanche Ebert Seaver and Sybil Partridge, "Kitty My Love," "Rose of Tralee" by Charles W. Glover and C. Mordaunt Spencer, "Ireland Mother Ireland" by Raymond Loughborough and P.J. O'Reilly, "Little Boy Blue" by Ethelbert Nevin and Eugene Field, "I Hear You Calling Me" by Charles Marshal and Harold Harford, "Loughi Sereni E Cari" by S. Donaudy, "Plaisir D'Amour" by Pader G. Martini, "Minnelied," "Londonderry Air," "Off to Philadelphia" and "Magpie's Nest." "Believe Me If All Those Endearing Young Charms" by Thomas Moore and "Bantry Bay" by Malloy were recorded but not used. [1] Not used but recorded. [2] Not listed in cue sheets but in some sources.

## 5613 ✦ SONG PARADE

See HIT PARADE OF 1951.

## 5614 ✦ SONG SERVICE
Paramount, 1930

**Cast**    Morse, Lee

**Song(s)**    Just Another Dream Gone Wrong (C: De Rose, Peter; L: Harburg, E.Y.)

**Notes**    Short subject. No cue sheet available. Sheet music only.

## 5615 ✦ SONGS OF ALL NATIONS
Warner Brothers, 1951

**Song(s)**    The Song Is the Thing (C: Jerome, M.K.; L: Scholl, Jack)

**Notes**    Short subject. There are also vocals of several foreign songs.

## 5616 ✦ SONGS OF THE RANGE
Warner Brothers, 1944

**Composer(s)**    Jerome, M.K.
**Lyricist(s)**    Scholl, Jack

**Song(s)**    Song of the Circle Bar; West of the Great Divide [1]; I Gotta Get Back to My Gal [2]; Bunk-House Boys [1]; Sons of the Plains; My Little Buckaroo [3]; Along the Santa Fe Trail (C/L: Grosz, Will; Dubin, Al; Coolidge, Edwina); My Texas Home [4]

**Notes**    Short subject. [1] Also in WEST OF THE ROCKIES. [2] Also in EMPTY HOLSTERS, GOLD IS WHERE YOU FIND IT and WEST OF THE ROCKIES. [3] Also in DON'T FENCE ME IN

(Republic), BROTHER ORCHID, THE CHEROKEE STRIP and WEST OF THE ROCKIES. [4] Also used in DEVIL'S SADDLE LEGION and WEST OF THE ROCKIES.

## 5617 ✦ SONGS OF THE ROSES
Metro–Goldwyn–Mayer, 1928

**Composer(s)**   Edwards, Gus

**Producer(s)**   Edwards, Gus

**Song(s)**   For You a Rose [1] (L: Cobb, Will D.); Scandal of the Flowers [2] (L: Macdonald, Ballard); Rosey Posey [3] (L: Smith, Harry B.)

**Notes**   Short subject. There are also vocals and instrumentals of "Rose of Washington Square" by James F. Hanley and Ballard Macdonald (also in ROSE OF WASHINGTON SQUARE); "Irish Washerwoman" and "My Man" by Channing Pollock and Maurice Yvain, "My Wild Irish Rose" by Chauncey Olcott and "Valse des Apaches." [1] Written in 1917. [2] Written in 1912. [3] Written in 1910.

## 5618 ✦ THE SONG WRITERS' REVUE
Metro–Goldwyn–Mayer, 1929

**Director(s)**   Lee, Sammy

**Cast**   Benny, Jack; Edwards, Gus; Dreyer, Dave; Ahlert, Fred E.; Turk, Roy; Heindorf, Ray; Brown, Nacio Herb; Freed, Arthur; Egan, Ray; Fisher, Fred; Snell, Dave; Click, Babe

**Song(s)**   The Birth of a Popular Song (C/L: Dreyer, Dave)

**Notes**   Short subject. There are also vocals of "Japanese Sandman" by Richard A. Whiting and Raymond B. Egan; "Me and My Shadow" by Billy Rose, Al Jolson and Dave Dreyer; "School Days" by Gus Edwards; "Mean to Me" by Roy Turk and Fred E. Ahlert and "The Wedding of the Painted Doll" by Arthur Freed and Nacio Herb Brown. There is also an instrumental of "Dardanella" by Felix Bernard, Johnny S. Black and Fred Fisher.

## 5619 ✦ SON OF FLUBBER
Disney, 1962

**Musical Score**   Bruns, George

**Producer(s)**   Walsh, Bill
**Director(s)**   Stevenson, Robert
**Screenwriter(s)**   Walsh, Bill; DaGradi, Don
**Source(s)**   Danny Dunn books (novels) Taylor, Samuel W.

**Cast**   MacMurray, Fred; Olson, Nancy; Wynn, Keenan; Kirk, Tommy; Wynn, Ed; Ames, Leon; Demarest, William; Reid, Elliott; Ruggles, Charles; Murray, Ken;

Lynde, Paul; Moore, Joanna; Sweeney, Bob; Andrews, Edward; Albertson, Jack; Erwin, Stuart

**Song(s)**   Nineteen Twenty-Five (C: Bruns, George; L: Adair, Tom)

**Notes**   There is also a vocal of "April Showers" by Louis Silvers and B.G. DeSylva.

## 5620 ✦ SON OF FURY
Twentieth Century–Fox, 1941

**Musical Score**   Newman, Alfred

**Producer(s)**   Perlberg, William
**Director(s)**   Cromwell, John
**Screenwriter(s)**   Dunne, Philip
**Source(s)**   (novel) Marshall, Edison

**Cast**   Power, Tyrone; Tierney, Gene; Sanders, George; Farmer, Frances; Lanchester, Elsa; Johnson, Kay; Carradine, John; Davenport, Harry; Digges, Dudley; McDowall, Roddy; de Cordoba, Pedro

**Song(s)**   Maraamu E (The Wind of Terror) (C/L: Goupil, Augie); Farewell Song (C: Newman, Alfred; L: Goupil, Augie); Blue Tahitian Moon [1] (C: Newman, Alfred; L: Gordon, Mack)

**Notes**   [1] This was written for exploitation only. The music may be the same as "Farewell Song" which was also labeled "Theme from Son of Fury."

## 5621 ✦ SON OF INDIA
Metro–Goldwyn–Mayer, 1931

**Director(s)**   Feyder, Jacques
**Screenwriter(s)**   Vajda, Ernest; Meehan, John; West, Claudine
**Source(s)**   *Mr. Isaacs* (novel) Crawford, F. Marion

**Cast**   Novarro, Ramon; Nagel, Conrad; Evans, Madge; Rambeau, Marjorie; Smith, C. Aubrey; Miljan, John

**Song(s)**   Just a Kiss to Treasure (C/L: Ward, Edward)

## 5622 ✦ SON OF PALEFACE
Paramount, 1952

**Composer(s)**   Livingston, Jay; Evans, Ray
**Lyricist(s)**   Livingston, Jay; Evans, Ray
**Choreographer(s)**   Earl, Josephine

**Producer(s)**   Welch, Robert L.
**Director(s)**   Tashlin, Frank
**Screenwriter(s)**   Quillan, Joseph; Tashlin, Frank; Welch, Robert L.

**Cast**   Hope, Bob; Russell, Jane; Rogers, Roy; Williams, Bill; Corrigan, Lloyd; Burns, Paul E.; Dumbrille, Douglass; Von Zell, Harry; Cody, Iron Eyes

**Song(s)**   A Four-Legged Friend (C/L: Brooks, Jack); Wing-Ding Tonight; What a Dirty Shame [2]; California

Rose; Am I in Love? (C/L: Brooks, Jack); Buttons and Bows [1]; There's a Cloud in My Valley of Sunshine (C/L: Hope, Jack; Moraine, Lyle)

**Notes** [1] Originally in THE PALEFACE. Lyrics rewritten for this sequel. [2] Written for, but not used in, THE PALEFACE under the title "It's a Dirty Shame."

## 5623 ✦ SON OF ROARING DAN
Universal, 1940

**Composer(s)** Rosen, Milton
**Lyricist(s)** Carter, Everett

**Director(s)** Beebe, Ford
**Screenwriter(s)** Young, Clarence Upson

**Cast** Brown, Johnny Mack; Knight, Fuzzy; O'Day, Nell

**Song(s)** Sing Yippi Ki Yi [2]; And then I Got Married [1]; Let 'Er Buck, Powder River (C/L: Cool, Gomer)

**Notes** [1] Also in BAD MEN OF THE BORDER. [2] Also in MR. IMPERIUM.

## 5624 ✦ SON OF ROBIN HOOD
Twentieth Century–Fox, 1959

**Musical Score** Lucas, Leighton

**Producer(s)** Sherman, George
**Director(s)** Sherman, George
**Screenwriter(s)** George, George W.; Slavin, George F.

**Cast** Hedison, Al; Laverick, June; Farrar, David; Goring, Marius

**Song(s)** Son of Robin Hood [1] (C/L: Tepper, Sid; Bennett, Roy C.)

**Notes** [1] Song written for exploitation only.

## 5625 ✦ SON OF THE GODS
Warner Brothers, 1930

**Director(s)** Lloyd, Frank
**Screenwriter(s)** King, Bradley
**Source(s)** *Son of the Gods* (novel) Beach, Rex

**Cast** Barthelmess, Richard; Bennett, Constance; Matthews, Dorothy; Leonard, Barbara; Eagles, Jimmy; Albertson, Frank; Van Dorn, Mildred; Moore, Dickie

**Song(s)** Pretty Little You (C: Violinsky, Sol; L: Ryan, Ben); Allana (C/L: Forbstein, Leo; Satterfield, Tom; Murray, John)

**Notes** No cue sheet available.

## 5626 ✦ THE SONS OF KATIE ELDER
Paramount, 1965

**Musical Score** Bernstein, Elmer

**Producer(s)** Wallis, Hal B.
**Director(s)** Hathaway, Henry

**Screenwriter(s)** Wright, William H.; Weiss, Allan; Essex, Harry

**Cast** Wayne, John; Martin, Dean; Hyer, Martha; Anderson Jr., Michael; Holliman, Earl; Slate, Jeremy; Gregory, James; Fix, Paul; Kennedy, George; Hopper, Dennis

**Song(s)** The Sons of Katie Elder [1] (C: Bernstein, Elmer; L: Sheldon, Ernie)

**Notes** [1] Lyric written for exploitation only.

## 5627 ✦ SONS OF NEW MEXICO
Columbia, 1949

**Producer(s)** Schaefer, Armand
**Director(s)** English, John
**Screenwriter(s)** Gangelin, Paul

**Cast** Autry, Gene; Champion; Davis, Gail; Armstrong, Robert; Jones, Dick; Darro, Frankie; Bacon, Irving; Arms, Russell; Blake, Marie; Moore, Clayton; Sanders, Sandy

**Song(s)** Can't Shake the Sands of Texas [1] (C/L: Autry, Gene; Johnston, Diane; Pitts, Kenneth); Sons of New Mexico (C/L: Hunt, Capt. F.E.); There's a Rainbow on the Rio Colorado [2] (C/L: Autry, Gene; Rose, Fred); Honey, I'm in Love with You (C/L: Massey, Curt; Gibbon, Abbie); New Mexico Military Institute March (C: Hunt, Capt. F.E.; L: Mertz, Paul)

**Notes** [1] Also in THE STRAWBERRY ROAN. [2] Also in COWBOY IN THE CLOUDS.

## 5628 ✦ SONS OF SASSOUN
Transcontinental Intermedia, 1976

**Musical Score** Mendoza-Nava, Jaime
**Composer(s)** Mouradian, Sarky
**Lyricist(s)** Mouradian, Sarky

**Producer(s)** Aklan, Paul Z.
**Director(s)** Mouradian, Sarky
**Screenwriter(s)** Mouradian, Sarky

**Cast** Wood, Lana; Lorre Jr., Peter; Izay, Victor

**Song(s)** And We Were in Love (L: Webster, Paul Francis); She's Very Pretty; Two Hearts; Hasmig; Sons of Sassoun; I Am Happy

**Notes** No cue sheet available.

## 5629 ✦ SONS OF THE LEGION
Paramount, 1938

**Producer(s)** Walker, Stuart
**Director(s)** Hogan, James
**Screenwriter(s)** Hayward, Lillie; Foster, Lewis R.; McGowan, Robert F.

**Cast** Overman, Lynne; Keyes, Evelyn; O'Connor, Donald

**Song(s)** Sons of the Legion [1] (C: Hollander, Frederick; L: Freed, Ralph)

**Notes** [1] Not used but published.

## 5630 ✦ SONS OF THE PIONEERS
Republic, 1942

**Producer(s)** Kane, Joseph
**Director(s)** Kane, Joseph
**Screenwriter(s)** Webster, M. Coates; Grashin, Mauri; Shannon, Robert T.

**Cast** Rogers, Roy; Hayes, George "Gabby"; Wrixon, Maris; Page, Bradley; Nolan, Bob; Brady, Pat; Farr, Hugh; Farr, Karl; Spencer, Tim; Taliaferro, Hal

**Song(s)** Come and Get It (C/L: Spencer, Tim); The West Is in My Soul (C/L: Nolan, Bob); Lily of Hillbilly Valley [3] (C/L: Spencer, Tim); Things Are Never What They Seem (C/L: Nolan, Bob); Trail Herdin' Cowboy (C/L: Nolan, Bob); He's Gone Up the Trail [1] (C/L: Spencer, Tim [2])

**Notes** [1] Also in GANGSTERS OF THE FRONTIER (PRC). [2] Credited under real name of Vern Spencer. [3] Also in RED RIVER VALLEY (1941).

## 5631 ✦ SONS OF THE SADDLE
Universal, 1930

**Director(s)** Brown, Harry Joe
**Screenwriter(s)** Mason, Leslie

**Cast** Maynard, Ken; Hill, Doris; Girard, Joseph; Nye, Carroll; Ford, Francis; Todd, Harry; Tarzan [1]

**Song(s)** Down the Home Trail with You (C: Handman, Lou; L: Grossman, Bernie)

**Notes** No cue sheet available. [1] Tarzan is Ken Maynard's horse.

## 5632 ✦ SONS O' GUNS
Warner Brothers, 1936

**Producer(s)** Brown, Harry Joe
**Director(s)** Bacon, Lloyd
**Screenwriter(s)** Wald, Jerry; Epstein, Julius J.
**Source(s)** *Sons O' Guns* (musical) Connolly, Bobby; Swanstrom, Arthur; Davis, Benny; Thompson, Fred; Donohue, Jack; Coots, J. Fred

**Cast** Brown, Joe E.; Blondell, Joan; Blore, Eric; Shaw, Winifred; Barrat, Robert; Roberts, Beverly; Reynolds, Craig; King, Joseph; Huntley Jr., G.P.; Roach, Bert; Auer, Mischa

**Song(s)** Over Here [1] (C: Coots, J. Fred; L: Swanstrom, Arthur; Davis, Benny); For a Buck and a Quarter a Day (C: Warren, Harry; L: Dubin, Al); In the Arms of an Army Man [2] (C: Warren, Harry; L: Dubin, Al)

**Notes** There is also a rendition of "There's a Long Long Trail" by Stoddard King and Zo Elliott. [1] From Broadway production. [2] Used as a 14 second instrumental.

## 5633 ✦ SOOKY
Paramount, 1931

**Producer(s)** Lighton, Louis D.
**Director(s)** Taurog, Norman
**Screenwriter(s)** McLeod, Norman Z.; Mankiewicz, Joseph L.
**Source(s)** "Dear Sooky" (story) Crosby, Percy

**Cast** Cooper, Jackie; Coogan, Robert; Searl, Jackie

**Song(s)** It's a Beautiful Day to Be Glad [1] (C: King, Jack; L: Coslow, Sam)

**Notes** [1] Also in SKIPPY.

## 5634 ✦ THE SOPHOMORE
Pathe, 1929

**Producer(s)** Conselman, William
**Director(s)** McCarey, Leo; Brown, Anthony
**Screenwriter(s)** De Leon, Walter; Baldwin, Earl

**Cast** Quillan, Eddie; O'Neil, Sally; Smith, Stanley; Loff, Jeanette; Gleason, Russell; Padden, Sarah; Benedict, Brooks; O'Keefe, Walter

**Song(s)** Little By Little (C: Dolan, Robert Emmett [1]; L: O'Keefe, Walter)

**Notes** No cue sheet available. [1] Billed as Bobby Dolan.

## 5635 ✦ SO PROUDLY WE HAIL
Paramount, 1943

**Producer(s)** Sandrich, Mark
**Director(s)** Sandrich, Mark
**Screenwriter(s)** Scott, Allan

**Cast** Colbert, Claudette; Goddard, Paulette; Lake, Veronica; Reeves, George; Britton, Barbara; Abel, Walter; Tufts, Sonny

**Song(s)** Loved One (C: Rozsa, Miklos; L: Heyman, Edward)

## 5636 ✦ THE SORCERER
Universal, 1977

**Musical Score** Jarrett, Keith

**Producer(s)** Friedkin, William
**Director(s)** Friedkin, William
**Screenwriter(s)** Green, Walon
**Source(s)** *The Wages of Fear* (novel) Arnaud, Georges

**Cast** Scheider, Roy; Cremer, Bruno; Rabal-Amidou, Francisco; Bieri, Ramon

**Song(s)** El Refran de las Mujeres (C/L: Mejia–Gandulito, Dionisio); Buscame Mi Popa (C/L: Vargas, Ramon Emilio)

**Notes** Only original songs listed.

## 5637 ✦ SO RED THE ROSE
### Paramount, 1935

**Producer(s)** MacLean, Douglas
**Director(s)** Vidor, King
**Screenwriter(s)** Stallings, Laurence; Anderson, Maxwell; Mayer, Edwin Justus
**Source(s)** *So Red the Rose* (novel) Young, Stark

**Cast** Sullavan, Margaret; Scott, Randolph; Connolly, Walter; Cummings, Robert; Beecher, Janet; Patterson, Elizabeth; Moore, Dickie; Starrett, Charles; Downs, Johnny

**Song(s)** So Red the Rose [1] (C/L: Lawrence, Jack; Altman, Arthur)

**Notes** [1] Song written for exploitation only.

## 5638 ✦ SORORITY HOUSE
### RKO, 1939

**Musical Score** Webb, Roy

**Producer(s)** Sisk, Robert
**Director(s)** Farrow, John
**Screenwriter(s)** Trumbo, Dalton
**Source(s)** "Chi House" (story) Chase, Mary

**Cast** Shirley, Anne; Ellison, James; Read, Barbara; Pearce, Adele; Kerrigan, J.M.; Wills, Chill

**Song(s)** I Must See Annie Tonight (C/L: Friend, Cliff; Franklin, Dave)

## 5639 ✦ SORROWFUL JONES
### Paramount, 1949

**Musical Score** Dolan, Robert Emmett
**Composer(s)** Livingston, Jay; Evans, Ray
**Lyricist(s)** Livingston, Jay; Evans, Ray

**Producer(s)** Welch, Robert L.
**Director(s)** Lanfield, Sidney
**Screenwriter(s)** Rose, Jack; Hartmann, Edmund L.; Shavelson, Melville

**Cast** Ball, Lucille [2]; Hope, Bob; Demarest, William; Gomez, Thomas; Cabot, Bruce; Saunders, Mary Jane; Stevenson, Houseley; Welden, Ben; Pedi, Tom

**Song(s)** Havin' a Wonderful Wish (Time You Were Here); Rock-a-bye Bangtail [1] (C: Canning, Effie I.; L: Livingston, Jay; Evans, Ray)

**Notes** [1] Based on the song "Rock-a-bye Baby" by Effie I. Canning. [2] Dubbed by Annette Warren.

## 5640 ✦ SO'S YOUR UNCLE
### Universal, 1943

**Producer(s)** Previn, Charles
**Director(s)** Yarbrough, Jean
**Screenwriter(s)** Leo, Maurice; Bruckman, Clyde

**Cast** Woods, Donald; Knox, Elyse; Burke, Billie

**Song(s)** That's the Way It Goes (C: Rosen, Milton; L: Carter, Everett)

**Notes** There are also vocals of "Liza" by George and Ira Gershwin; "Don't Get Around Much Anymore" by Bob Russell and Duke Ellington and "St. Louis Blues" by W.C. Handy.

## 5641 ✦ SO THIS IS COLLEGE
### Metro–Goldwyn–Mayer, 1929

**Composer(s)** Broones, Martin

**Director(s)** Wood, Sam
**Screenwriter(s)** Farnham, Joe; Boasberg, Al

**Cast** Nugent, Elliott; Montgomery, Robert; Edwards, Cliff; Starr, Sally; Crane, Phyllis; Moran, Polly; Shumway, Lee

**Song(s)** College Days (L: Boasberg, Al); Until the End (L: Fisher, Fred; Boasberg, Al); I Don't Want Your Kisses If I Can't Have Your Love [1] (L: Fisher, Fred); Campus Capers (L: Greenwood, Charlotte); The Sophomore Prom (C: Greer, Jesse; L: Klages, Raymond); Fight On (C/L: Grant, Glen)

**Notes** [1] Also in THE GIRL SAID NO.

## 5642 ✦ SO THIS IS LONDON
### Fox, 1930

**Composer(s)** Hanley, James F.
**Lyricist(s)** McCarthy, Joseph

**Director(s)** Blystone, John
**Screenwriter(s)** Davis, Owen
**Source(s)** *So This Is London* (novel) Goodrich, Arthur Frederick

**Cast** Rogers, Will; Rich, Irene; O'Sullivan, Maureen; Albertson, Frank; Hare, Lumsden; Forbes, Mary; Fletcher, Bramwell

**Notes** Reference to songs in this film listed in the AFI catalog only. The *Variety* review does not mention songs.

## 5643 ✦ SO THIS IS LOVE
### Warner Brothers, 1953

**Choreographer(s)** Prinz, LeRoy

**Producer(s)** Blanke, Henry
**Director(s)** Douglas, Gordon M.
**Screenwriter(s)** Monks Jr., John

**Source(s)** "You're Only Human Once" (story) Moore, Grace

**Cast** Grayson, Kathryn; Griffin, Merv; Weldon, Joan; Abel, Walter; De Camp, Rosemary; Donnell, Jeff; Dick, Douglas; Doran, Ann; Field, Margaret; Albertson, Mabel; Bonanova, Fortunio; Windsor, Marie; Corcoran, Noreen

**Song(s)** I Want to Dance (C/L: Henderson, Charles; Heindorf, Ray); Something Old Something New (C/L: Henderson, Charles; Heindorf, Ray); So This Is Love (C/L: Goetz, E. Ray)

**Notes** Released in Great Britain as THE GRACE MOORE STORY. There are also renditions of "So This Is Love" by E. Ray Goetz; "Je Vieux Vivre" by Charles Gounod; "Memories" by Egbert Van Alstyne and Gus Kahn; "Ciribiribin" by A. Pestalozza; "Pack Up Your Troubles in Your Old Kit Bag" by George Asaf and Felix Powell; "Ev'rybody Ought to Know How to Do the Tickle Toe" by Louis A. Hirsch and Otto Harbach; "I'm Just Wild About Harry" by Noble Sissle and Eubie Blake; "The Kiss Waltz" by Al Dubin and Joe Burke; "I Kiss Your Hand Madame" by Ralph Erwin, Frita Rotter, Sam Lewis and Joe Young; "Voi Che Sapete" by Mozart; "Oh Me, Oh My" by Vincent Youmans and Arthur Francis (Ira Gershwin); "Time on My Hands" by Vincent Youmans, Harold Adamson and Mack Gordon; "Remember" by Irving Berlin; "Jewel Song" by Charles Gounod; "Rudolfo's Aria" and "Mimi's Aria" by Puccini.

## 5644 ◆ SO THIS IS PARIS
Universal, 1954

**Musical Score** Mancini, Henry
**Composer(s)** Moody, Phil
**Lyricist(s)** Sherrell, Pony
**Choreographer(s)** Nelson, Gene; Scott, Lee

**Producer(s)** Cohen, Albert J.
**Director(s)** Quine, Richard
**Screenwriter(s)** Hoffman, Charles

**Cast** Curtis, Tony; De Haven, Gloria; Nelson, Gene; Calvet, Corinne; Gilbert, Paul; Corday, Mara; Hayes, Allison; Martel, Christiane; Hansen, Myrna; Deschner, Sandy

**Song(s)** So This Is Paris; Wait Till Paris Sees Us; Looking for Someone to Love; It's Really Up to You; A Dame's a Dame; If You Were There; The Two of Us; Three Bon Vivants; I Can't Do a Single (But I'll Try)

**Notes** There is also a vocal of "I Can't Give You Anything But Love, Baby" by Dorothy Fields and Jimmy McHugh as translated by Tanis Chandler.

## 5645 ◆ SOUL HUSTLER
American Films, 1977

**Producer(s)** Topper, Burt
**Director(s)** Topper, Burt
**Screenwriter(s)** Topper, Burt

**Cast** Forte, Fabian; Bonet, Nai; Russel, Tony; Bishop, Larry; Kasem, Casey

**Song(s)** Lovin' Man (C: Hatcher, Harley; L: Topper, Burt); Send Me a Friend (C: Beram, Eddie; L: Arakelian, Mel); Listen and Believe (C: Hatcher, Harley; L: Topper, Burt)

**Notes** No cue sheet available.

## 5646 ◆ THE SOUL KISS

See A LADY'S MORALS.

## 5647 ◆ SOUL OF NIGGER CHARLEY
Paramount, 1973

**Musical Score** Costa, Don
**Composer(s)** Costa, Don
**Lyricist(s)** Hemric, Guy

**Producer(s)** Spangler, Larry G.
**Director(s)** Spangler, Larry G.
**Screenwriter(s)** Stone, Harold J.

**Cast** Williamson, Fred; Martin, D'Urville; Nicholas, Denise; Armendariz Jr., Pedro; Calloway, Kirk; Allen, George

**Song(s)** Sometime Day [2]; Lord, It's a Long Time Comin' [2]; Morning Comes Round [2]; The Lonely Summer [1] (L: Caldwell, Gayle)

**Notes** [1] Lyric for exploitation only. [2] Background vocals only.

## 5648 ◆ SOULS AT SEA
Paramount, 1937

**Composer(s)** Rainger, Ralph
**Lyricist(s)** Robin, Leo

**Producer(s)** Hathaway, Henry
**Director(s)** Hathaway, Henry
**Screenwriter(s)** Jones, Grover; Van Every, Dale

**Cast** Cooper, Gary; Raft, George; Dee, Frances; Wilcoxon, Henry; Carey, Harry; Cummings, Robert; Hall, Porter; Schildkraut, Joseph; Weidler, Virginia; Holden, Fay; Blue, Monte; Marshall, Tully

**Song(s)** Hymn; (Dear) Susie Sapple; Polka Tina; Tippety Witchet [1]; This Night [1] [2]

**Notes** [1] Not used. [2] Used in THE TRUMPET BLOWS.

## 5649 ◆ THE SOUND AND THE FURY
Twentieth Century–Fox, 1959

**Musical Score** North, Alex

**Producer(s)** Wald, Jerry
**Director(s)** Ritt, Martin
**Screenwriter(s)** Ravetch, Irving; Frank Jr., Harriet

**Source(s)** *The Sound and the Fury* (novel) Faulkner, William

**Cast** Brynner, Yul; Woodward, Joanne; Leighton, Margaret; Whitman, Stuart; Waters, Ethel; Warden, Jack; Rosay, Francoise; Beal, John; Dekker, Albert

**Song(s)** The Sound and the Fury [1] (C: North, Alex; L: Cahn, Sammy)

**Notes** [1] Used instrumentally only. Based on "Quentin's Theme."

## 5650 ◆ SOUNDER
Twentieth Century–Fox, 1973

**Musical Score** Taj Mahal
**Composer(s)** Taj Mahal
**Lyricist(s)** Taj Mahal

**Producer(s)** Radnitz, Robert B.
**Director(s)** Ritt, Martin
**Screenwriter(s)** Elder III, Lonne
**Source(s)** *Sounder* (novel) Armstrong, William H.

**Cast** Tyson, Cicely; Winfield, Paul; Hooks, Kevin; Matthews, Carmen; Taj Mahal; Best, James; Hooks, Eric; Williams, Sylvia Kuumba

**Song(s)** Back Home; Speedball; Goin' to the Country; Critters Better Hide Tonight; I'd Rather Be Fishin'

## 5651 ◆ SOUND-OFF
Columbia, 1952

**Composer(s)** Lee, Lester
**Lyricist(s)** Russell, Bob
**Choreographer(s)** Castle, Nick; White, Al

**Producer(s)** Taps, Jonie
**Director(s)** Quine, Richard
**Screenwriter(s)** Edwards, Blake; Quine, Richard

**Cast** Rooney, Mickey; Cassell, Wally; White, Sammy; James, Anne

**Song(s)** My Lady Love; It's the Beast in Me; Home Sweet Home in the Army (C: Rinker, Al; L: Adair, Tom); Bugle Blues; Blow Your Own Horn (C/L: Rooney, Mickey); Sound Off [1] (C/L: Duckworth, Willie Lee)

**Notes** [1] Not written for picture.

## 5652 ◆ THE SOUND OF MUSIC
Twentieth Century–Fox, 1965

**Composer(s)** Rodgers, Richard
**Lyricist(s)** Hammerstein II, Oscar
**Choreographer(s)** Breaux, Marc; Wood, Dee Dee

**Producer(s)** Wise, Robert
**Director(s)** Wise, Robert
**Screenwriter(s)** Lehman, Ernest

**Source(s)** *The Sound of Music* (musical) Hammerstein II, Oscar; Rodgers, Richard; Lindsay, Howard; Crouse, Russel

**Cast** Andrews, Julie; Plummer, Christopher [3]; Parker, Eleanor; Haydn, Richard; Wood, Peggy [4]; Lee, Anna [2]; Nelson, Portia; Wright, Ben; Truhitte, Daniel; Varden, Norma; Nixon, Marni; Stuart, Gil; Baker, Evadne; Lloyd, Doris; Carr, Charmian; Hammond, Nicholas; Menzies, Heather; Chase, Duane; Cartwright, Angela; Turner, Debbie; Karath, Kym; Bil Baird's Marionettes [1]

**Song(s)** The Sound of Music [1]; Morning Hymn [1] (L: Traditional); Alleluia [1] (L: Traditional); Maria [1]; I Have Confidence in Me (L: Rodgers, Richard); Sixteen Going on Seventeen [1]; My Favorite Things [1]; Do-Re-Mi [1]; The Lonely Goatherd [1]; Edelweiss [1]; So Long, Farewell [1]; Climb Every Mountain [1]; Something Good (L: Rodgers, Richard)

**Notes** Some of the children's voices were dubbed by Darlene Farnon, Randy Perkins, Diane Burt and Sue McBain. [1] From original Broadway production. [2] Dubbed by Marie Greene. [3] Dubbed by Bill Lee. [4] Dubbed by Margery McKay.

## 5653 ◆ SOUP FOR ONE
Warner Brothers, 1982

**Musical Score** Edwards, Bernard; Rodgers, Nile
**Composer(s)** Edwards, Bernard; Rodgers, Nile
**Lyricist(s)** Edwards, Bernard; Rodgers, Nile

**Producer(s)** Worth, Marvin
**Director(s)** Kaufer, Jonathan
**Screenwriter(s)** Kaufer, Jonathan

**Cast** Rubinek, Saul; Strassman, Marcia; Graham, Gerrit; Pendergrass, Teddy; Libertini, Richard; Martin, Andrea; Lawner, Mordecai; Stadlen, Lewis J.; Merlin, Joanna

**Song(s)** I Work for a Living; Dream Girl [1]; I Want Your Love; Let's Go on Vacation; Jump Jump (C/L: Harry, Deborah; Stein, Chris); Riding

**Notes** [1] Visual vocal. All others are background vocals.

## 5654 ◆ SOUP TO NUTS
Fox, 1930

**Director(s)** Stoloff, Benjamin
**Screenwriter(s)** Goldberg, Rube

**Cast** Ted Healy and His Band; McCoy, Frances; Smith, Stanley; Brown, Lucille; Winninger, Charles; Goldberg, Rube; Barty, Billy; Swain, Mack; Howard, Moe; Fine, Larry; Howard, Shemp

**Song(s)** Tears [1] (C/L: Howard, Moe; Howard, Shemp; Fine, Larry; Sanborn); You Can Only Wear One

Pair of Pants at a Time (C: Monaco, James V.; L: Friend, Cliff); Nellie (C/L: Healy, Ted)

**Notes** [1] Written by members of Ted Healy's Band. Howard, Howard and Fine are members of The Three Stooges.

## 5655 ✦ SOUTH AMERICAN SWAY
### Warner Brothers, 1944

**Song(s)** Gotta Have My Rhythm (C: Jerome, M.K.; L: Scholl, Jack); Negra Baila La Conga (C/L: Gama, Rafael)

**Notes** Short subject.

## 5656 ✦ SOUTHERN AMERICAN RHYTHM
### Studio Unknown, 1940

**Lyricist(s)** Drake, Milton

**Song(s)** Beautiful Sky; The Dove

**Notes** No other information available.

## 5657 ✦ SOUTH OF CALIENTE
### Republic, 1951

**Composer(s)** Elliott, Jack
**Lyricist(s)** Elliott, Jack

**Producer(s)** White, Edward J.
**Director(s)** Witney, William
**Screenwriter(s)** Taylor, Eric

**Cast** Rogers, Roy; Evans, Dale; Lee, Pinky; Fowley, Douglas; Roman, Ric; Best, Willie; Penn, Leonard

**Song(s)** My Home Is Over Yonder; Gypsy Trail [1]; Yasha the Gypsy (C/L: Wainer, Lee); Won'tcha Be a Friend of Mine

**Notes** [1] Special lyrics by Gari Galian.

## 5658 ✦ SOUTH OF DIXIE
### Universal, 1944

**Composer(s)** Rosen, Milton
**Lyricist(s)** Carter, Everett

**Producer(s)** Yarbrough, Jean
**Director(s)** Yarbrough, Jean
**Screenwriter(s)** Bruckman, Clyde

**Cast** Bruce, David; Gwynne, Anne; Morse, Ella Mae; Hinds, Samuel S.

**Song(s)** Weep No More, My Lady (C/L: Whitney, Joan; Kramer, Alex); I'm a-Fixin' for to Be A-Headin' South [1]; Loo-Loo-Louisiana; When It's Darkness on the Delta (C/L: Symes, Marty; Neiburg, Al J.); Cross My Heart; Shoo Shoo Baby [2] (C/L: Moore, Phil); Never Again

**Notes** [1] Also in JIVE BUSTERS. [2] Also in BEAUTIFUL BUT BROKE (Columbia), BIG CITY (1948) and TROCADERO (Republic).

## 5659 ✦ SOUTH OF PAGO PAGO
### United Artists, 1940

**Choreographer(s)** Crosby, Jack

**Producer(s)** Small, Edward
**Director(s)** Green, Alfred E.
**Screenwriter(s)** Bruce, George

**Cast** McLaglen, Victor; Hall, Jon; Farmer, Frances; Bradna, Olympe; Lockhart, Gene; Dumbrille, Douglass; Ford, Francis; de Cordoba, Pedro; Robles, Rudy

**Song(s)** South of Pago Pago (C: Pollack, Lew; L: Forrest, Chet; Wright, Bob

**Notes** No cue sheet available.

## 5660 ✦ SOUTH OF ST. LOUIS
### Warner Brothers, 1949

**Musical Score** Steiner, Max

**Producer(s)** Sperling, Milton
**Director(s)** Enright, Ray
**Screenwriter(s)** Gold, Zachary; Webb, James R.

**Cast** McCrea, Joel; Smith, Alexis; Scott, Zachary; Malone, Dorothy; Kennedy, Douglas; Hale, Alan; Jory, Victor; Smith, Art; Blue, Monte

**Song(s)** Too Much Love (C: Heindorf, Ray; L: Blane, Ralph); As the Brass Band Played [1] (C: Heindorf, Ray; L: Scholl, Jack)

**Notes** [1] Also used in TALL MAN RIDING.

## 5661 ✦ SOUTH OF SANTA FE
### Republic, 1942

**Composer(s)** Nolan, Bob
**Lyricist(s)** Nolan, Bob

**Producer(s)** Kane, Joseph
**Director(s)** Kane, Joseph
**Screenwriter(s)** Webb, James R.

**Cast** Rogers, Roy; Hayes, George "Gabby"; Hayes, Linda; Sons of the Pioneers; Fix, Paul; Beers, Bobby; Clark, Judy; Kirk, Jack

**Song(s)** Headin' for the Home Corral (C/L: Spencer, Tim); Song of the Vaquero; Down the Trail; Yodel Your Troubles Away (C/L: Spencer, Tim); Open Range Ahead

## 5662 ✦ SOUTH OF TAHITI
### Universal, 1941

**Producer(s)** Waggner, George
**Director(s)** Waggner, George
**Screenwriter(s)** Geraghty, Gerald

**Cast** Donlevy, Brian; Crawford, Broderick; Devine, Andy; Wilcoxon, Henry; Montez, Maria [1]; Warner, H.B.

**Song(s)** Melahi (C: Skinner, Frank; L: Waggner, George)

**Notes** [1] Dubbed by Martha Tilton.

## 5663 ✦ SOUTH OF THE BORDER
### Republic, 1939

**Producer(s)** Berke, William
**Director(s)** Sherman, George
**Screenwriter(s)** Burbridge, Betty; Geraghty, Gerald

**Cast** Autry, Gene; Burnette, Smiley; Tovar, Lupita; Storey, June; Lee, Mary; Reicher, Frank; Renaldo, Duncan; Edwards, Alan

**Song(s)** Come to the Fiesta (C/L: Wenzel, Art); The Horse Op'ry (C/L: Nelson, Edward G.; Rose, Fred); Moon Over Manana (C/L: Autry, Gene; Marvin, Johnny); I'll Be with You When the Cactus Blooms Again (C/L: Autry, Gene; Marvin, Johnny); The Fat Caballero (C/L: Burnette, Smiley); South of the Border [1] (C/L: Kennedy, Jimmy; Carr, Michael); Girl of My Dreams (C/L: Clapp, Sunny); Goodbye Little Darlin' Goodbye (C/L: Marvin, Johnny; Autry, Gene)

**Notes** No cue sheet available. [1] Also in DOWN MEXICO WAY.

## 5664 ✦ SOUTH PACIFIC
### Twentieth Century–Fox, 1958

**Composer(s)** Rodgers, Richard
**Lyricist(s)** Hammerstein II, Oscar
**Choreographer(s)** Prinz, LeRoy

**Producer(s)** Adler, Buddy
**Director(s)** Logan, Joshua
**Screenwriter(s)** Osborn, Paul
**Source(s)** *South Pacific* (musical) Rodgers, Richard; Hammerstein II, Oscar; Logan, Joshua

**Cast** Brazzi, Rossano [1]; Gaynor, Mitzi; Kerr, John [4]; Walston, Ray [9]; Hall, Juanita [5]; Nuyen, France; Brown, Russ; Mullaney, Jack [9]; Clark, Ken [3]; Simmons, Floyd; Lee, Candace [6]; Hsieh, Warren [7]; Laughlin, Tom

**Song(s)** Bali Ha'i; Bloody Mary; There Is Nothin' Like a Dame; A Cockeyed Optimist; Twin Soliloquies; Some Enchanted Evening; Dites Moi; I'm Gonna Wash That Man Right Outa My Hair; I'm In Love with a Wonderful Guy; Boar's Tooth Ceremony [8] (C: Darby, Ken; L: Traditional); Younger Than Springtime; This Is How It Feels; Happy Talk; Honey Bun; My Girl Back Home [8]; Carefully Taught; This Nearly Was Mine; Lonliness of Evening [2]

**Notes** All songs but "Boar's Tooth Ceremony," "Loneliness of Evening" and "My Girl Back Home" were from the original production. [1] Dubbed by Giorgio Tozzi except on "Lonliness of Evening." [2] Not used. [3] Dubbed by Thurl Ravensroft. [4] Dubbed by Bill Lee. [5] Dubbed by Muriel Smith. [6] Dubbed by Marie Greene. [7] Dubbed by Betty Wand. [8] Written for film version. [9] The parts of "There is Nothing Like a Dame" sung by Billis (Ray Walston), Stewpot (Ken Clark) and Professor (Jack Mullaney) were dubbed by Thurl Ravenscroft, Rad Robinson and Ernest Newton, but not necessarily in that order.

## 5665 ✦ SOUTH PACIFIC TRAIL
### Republic, 1952

**Producer(s)** White, Edward J.
**Director(s)** Witney, William
**Screenwriter(s)** Orloff, Arthur

**Cast** Allen, Rex; Koko; Rodriguez, Estelita; Paiva, Nestor; The Republic Rhythm Riders; Barcroft, Roy

**Song(s)** Hide Away Your Troubles (C/L: Allen, Rex); I'll Sing a Love Song [1] (C/L: Elliott, Jack)

**Notes** [1] Spanish lyrics by Aaron Gonzalez. Also in THE PLUNDERERS.

## 5666 ✦ SOUTH SEA ROSE
### Fox, 1929

**Composer(s)** Baer, Abel
**Lyricist(s)** Gilbert, L. Wolfe
**Director(s)** Dwan, Allan
**Screenwriter(s)** Lester, Elliott
**Source(s)** *La Gringo* (play) Cushing, Tom

**Cast** Ulric, Lenore; Bickford, Charles; MacKenna, Kenneth; MacDonald, J. Farrell; Patterson, Elizabeth; Patricola, Tom; Chase, Ilka; MacFarlane, George; Hall, Ben; Pollard, Daphne

**Song(s)** South Sea Rose; Palolo (C/L: King, Charles E.); Gag Song; If You Believe in Me [1]; Do What You Like with Me [2]

**Notes** "Down Went McGinty" by George Flynn also receives a vocal treatment. George McFarlane also sings the following traditional songs: "Riley and I" and "We'll All Be Angels." [1] Not on cue sheet. Listed in *AFI Catalog* only. Also in LOVE, LIVE AND LAUGH. [2] Not used.

## 5667 ✦ SOUTH SEA SINNER
### Universal, 1950

**Producer(s)** Kraike, Michel
**Director(s)** Humberstone, H. Bruce
**Screenwriter(s)** Malone, Jeff; Brodney, Oscar

**Cast** Winters, Shelley; Carey, Macdonald; Lovejoy, Frank; Adler, Luther; Carter, Helena; Smith, Art; Liberace

**Song(s)** Blue Lagoon (C: Hughes, Arnold; L: Herbert, Frederick); One Man Woman [1] (C: Schwarzwald, Milton; L: Brooks, Jack)

**Notes** There are also vocals of "It Had to Be You" by Gus Kahn and Isham Jones and "I'm the Lonesomest Gal in Town" by Albert Von Tilzer and Lew Brown (also in the Columbia picture MAKE BELIEVE BALLROOM). [1] Also in THE VIGILANTES RETURN.

## 5668 ✦ SOUTHWARD HO!
Republic, 1939

**Producer(s)** Kane, Joseph
**Director(s)** Kane, Joseph
**Screenwriter(s)** Natteford, Jack; Geraghty, Gerald

**Cast** Rogers, Roy; Hart, Mary; Hayes, George "Gabby"; Boteler, Wade; Chandler, Lane

**Song(s)** Headin' for Texas (C/L: Samuels, Walter G.); I Hope I'm Not Dreaming Again (C/L: Rose, Fred); She's All Wet Now (C/L: Rogers, Roy); Walk the Other Way (C/L: Samuels, Walter G.)

## 5669 ✦ SPACEBALLS
Metro–Goldwyn–Mayer, 1987

**Musical Score** Morris, John

**Producer(s)** Brooks, Mel
**Director(s)** Brooks, Mel
**Screenwriter(s)** Brooks, Mel; Meehan, Thomas; Graham, Ronny

**Cast** Olfson, Ken; Brooks, Mel; Candy, John; Moranis, Rick; Van Patten, Dick; Yarnell, Lorene; Winslow, Michael; Rivers, Joan; Wyner, George; Pullman, Bill; Zuniga, Daphne

**Song(s)** Raise Your Hands (C/L: Bon Jovi, Jon; Sambori, R.); Heart Strings (C/L: Crawford, John; Nunn, Terri; Brill, Rob; Reid, Matt); Spaceballs (C/L: Brooks, Mel; Pescetto, Jeff; Lieberman, Clyde); Good Enough (C/L: Van Halen, Edward; Van Halen, Alex; Hagar, Sammy; Anthony, Michael)

**Notes** It is not known if the rock songs were written for this film.

## 5670 ✦ SPANISH AFFAIR
Paramount, 1957

**Musical Score** Amfitheatrof, Daniele

**Producer(s)** Odlum, Bruce
**Director(s)** Siegel, Don
**Screenwriter(s)** Collins, Richard

**Cast** Sevilla, Carmen; Kiley, Richard; Guardiola, Jose

**Song(s)** The Flaming Rose (C: Amfitheatrof, Daniele; L: David, Mack)

## 5671 ✦ SPANISH MAIN
RKO, 1945

**Musical Score** Eisler, Hanns

**Producer(s)** Ames, Stephen
**Director(s)** Borzage, Frank
**Screenwriter(s)** Yates, George Worthing; Mankiewicz, Herman J.

**Cast** Henreid, Paul; Slezak, Walter; O'Hara, Maureen; Barnes, Binnie; Emery, John; MacLane, Barton; Kerrigan, J.M.; Leiber, Fritz; Gates, Nancy; Mazurki, Mike; Bois, Curt

**Song(s)** Pirate Song (C: Eisler, Hanns; L: Wray, Ardel)

## 5672 ✦ SPARKLE
Warner Brothers, 1976

**Musical Score** Mayfield, Curtis
**Composer(s)** Mayfield, Curtis
**Lyricist(s)** Mayfield, Curtis

**Producer(s)** Rosenman, Howard
**Director(s)** O'Steen, Sam
**Screenwriter(s)** Schumacher, Joel; Rosenman, Howard

**Cast** Cara, Irene; McKee, Lonette; Smith, Dwan; Alice, Mary; Winde, Beatrice; Thomas, Philip Michael; Harewood, Dorian; Lambert, Paul

**Song(s)** Hooked on Your Love; Something He Can Feel; Baby I Love You; Look Into Your Heart; Jump; Loving You Baby

**Notes** I think only the Curtis Mayfield songs are original to this film. Among the other songs which are featured on camera or as background vocals are "Twilight Time" by Buck Ram, Morty Nevins, Al Nevins and Artie Dunn; "Yakety Yak;" "Love Potion Number Nine" and "Lucky Lips" by Jerry Leiber and Mike Stoller; "Jim Dandy" by Lincoln Chase; "Sincerely" by Alan Freed and Harvey Fuqua; "Dedicated to the One I Love" by Lowman Pauling and Ralph Bass; "Giving Up" by Van McCoy and "Take My Hand Precious Lord" by Thomas A. Dorsey.

## 5673 ✦ SPAWN OF THE NORTH
Paramount, 1938

**Composer(s)** Lane, Burton
**Lyricist(s)** Loesser, Frank

**Producer(s)** Lewin, Albert
**Director(s)** Hathaway, Henry
**Screenwriter(s)** Furthman, Jules; Jennings, Talbot

**Cast** Fonda, Henry; Lamour, Dorothy; Raft, George; Barrymore, John; Tamiroff, Akim; Platt, Louise; Overman, Lynne; Renaldo, Duncan; Sokoloff, Vladimir; Knight, Fuzzy; Wray, John

**Song(s)** I Wish I Was the Willow [3]; I Like Humped-Back Salmon [2]; Two Silhouettes (in the Setting Sun) [1] (C/L: Coslow, Sam); There's a Happy Hunting Ground [1] [4] (C/L: Coslow, Sam); Under the Midnight Sun [1] (L: Coslow, Sam)

**Notes** This movie was formerly titled SHOW BOAT. That's what the Paramount records indicate unless they were planning a film version of the stage hit before Universal did it. "I Wish I Was the Willow" is notated as written for SHOW BOAT. [1] Not used. [2] Music is a slightly changed version of "I Like Mountain Music." Also the title and most of the lyrics come from an Alaskan fisherman folk song. [3] Also in ALASKA SEAS. [4] Used in SHEPHERD OF THE HILLS.

## 5674 ✦ SPEAK EASILY
### Metro–Goldwyn–Mayer, 1932

**Director(s)** Sedgwick, Edward
**Screenwriter(s)** Spence, Ralph; Johnson, Laurence E.
**Source(s)** "Speak Easily" (story) Kelland, Clarence Budington

**Cast** Keaton, Buster; Durante, Jimmy; Selwyn, Ruth; Todd, Thelma; Hopper, Hedda; Toler, Sidney

**Song(s)** Good Times Are Here Again (C: Snell, Dave; L: Maxwell); Can Broadway Do Without Me [1] (C/L: Durante, Jimmy); What Is the Psychology of That (C/L: Durante, Jimmy)

**Notes** There are also vocals of "Singin' in the Rain" by Arthur Freed and Nacio Herb Brown and "Oh Susanna" by Stephen Foster. [1] Also in the short HOLLYWOOD PREMIER.

## 5675 ✦ SPEAKEASY
### Fox, 1929

**Director(s)** Stoloff, Benjamin
**Screenwriter(s)** Burke, Edwin

**Cast** Erwin, Stuart; Lynn, Sharon; Lane, Lola; Page, Paul

**Song(s)** Don't Be Like That (C: Gottler, Archie; L: Tobias); Come On Baby (C: Gottler, Archie; L: Clare, Sidney); Song of Broadway [1] (C/L: Denell, Pal; Eckels, Eddy)

**Notes** [1] Sheet music only.

## 5676 ✦ SPECTER OF THE ROSE
### Republic, 1952

**Musical Score** Antheil, George

**Producer(s)** Garmes, Lee
**Director(s)** Hecht, Ben
**Screenwriter(s)** Hecht, Ben
**Source(s)** "Specter of the Rose" (story) Hecht, Ben

**Cast** Anderson, Judith; Chekhov, Michael; Kirov, Ivan; Essen, Viola; Stander, Lionel; Gray, Billy; Pollina, Ferdinand

**Song(s)** Gay Wedding Song (Sugar Bowl) (C: Antheil, George; L: Hecht, Ben)

## 5677 ✦ SPEEDTRAP
### First Artists, 1978

**Musical Score** Harris, Anthony
**Composer(s)** Harris, Anthony
**Lyricist(s)** Harris, Anthony

**Producer(s)** Pine, Howard
**Director(s)** Bellamy, Earl
**Screenwriter(s)** Spear, Walter M.; Segal, Stuart A.

**Cast** Baker, Joe Don; Daly, Tyne; Jaeckel, Richard; Loggia, Robert; Woodward, Morgan; Wood, Lana

**Song(s)** Speedtrap; An American Saint; Psychic Emanations

**Notes** No cue sheet available.

## 5678 ✦ SPEEDWAY
### Metro–Goldwyn–Mayer, 1968

**Musical Score** Alexander, Jeff

**Producer(s)** Laurence, Douglas
**Director(s)** Taurog, Norman
**Screenwriter(s)** Shuken, Phillip

**Cast** Presley, Elvis; Sinatra, Nancy; Bixby, Bill; Gordon, Gale; Meyerink, Victoria; Hagen, Ross; Ballantine, Carl; Ponce, Poncie; Petty, Richard; Baker, Buddy; Yarborough, Cale; Hutcherson, Dick; Lund, Tiny

**Song(s)** Speedway (C/L: Glazer, Mel; Schlaks, Stephen); Let Yourself Go (C/L: Byers, Joy); Your Groovy Self (C/L: Hazlewood, Lee); Your Time Hasn't Come Yet, Baby (C/L: Kasha, Al; Hirschhorn, Joel); He's Your Uncle, Not Your Dad (C/L: Weisman, Ben; Wayne, Sid); Who Are You (C/L: Weisman, Ben; Wayne, Sid); There Ain't Nothing Like a Song (C/L: Byers, Joy; Johnston, Bob)

## 5679 ✦ SPEEDY
### Paramount, 1928

**Director(s)** Wilde, Ted
**Screenwriter(s)** Grey, John; Neal, Lex; Rogers, Howard Emmett; Howe, Jay

**Cast** Lloyd, Harold; Christy, Ann; Woodruff, Bert; Benedict, Brooks; King Tut; Wolheim, Dan; Ruth, Babe; Knight, Hank

**Song(s)** Speedy Boy (C: Greer, Jesse; L: Klages, Raymond)

**Notes** This is a silent film with a theme song.

## 5680 ✦ SPELLBINDER
Metro–Goldwyn–Mayer, 1988

**Musical Score**   Poledouris, Basil

**Producer(s)**   Wizan, Joe; Russell, Brian
**Director(s)**   Greek, Janet
**Screenwriter(s)**   Torme, Tracy

**Cast**   Daly, Timothy; Preston, Kelly; Rossovich, Rick; Lindley, Audra; Crivello, Anthony

**Song(s)**   Blind Alley (C/L: Wright, Gary); If My Love Is Blind (C/L: Herron, Maggie)

## 5681 ✦ SPIES LIKE US
Warner Brothers, 1985

**Musical Score**   Bernstein, Elmer

**Producer(s)**   Grazer, Brian; Folsey Jr., George
**Director(s)**   Landis, John
**Screenwriter(s)**   Aykroyd, Dan; Ganz, Lowell; Mandel, Babaloo

**Cast**   Chase, Chevy; Aykroyd, Dan; Forrest, Steve; Dixon, Donna; Davison, Bruce; Casey, Bernie; Prince, William; Oz, Frank; Gilliam, Terry; Costa-Gavras; Harryhausen, Ray; Lambert, Douglas; Frewer, Matt; Hope, Bob; Raimi, Sam; Apted, Michael; King, B.B.; Cohen, Larry; Brest, Martin; Newman, Edwin

**Song(s)**   Spies Like Us (C/L: McCartney, Paul)

## 5682 ✦ SPIN A DARK WEB
Columbia, 1956

**Musical Score**   Taylor, Richard

**Producer(s)**   Frankovich, M.J.; Maynard, George
**Director(s)**   Sewell, Vernon
**Screenwriter(s)**   Black, Ian Stuart
**Source(s)**   *Wide Boys Never Work* (novel) Westerby, Robert

**Cast**   Domergue, Faith; Patterson, Lee; Anderson, Rona; Benson, Martin

**Song(s)**   Love Me, Love Me Now (C/L: Roberts, Paddy; Paul, Mark)

**Notes**   No cue sheet available.

## 5683 ✦ SPINOUT
Metro–Goldwyn–Mayer, 1966

**Musical Score**   Stoll, George; Van Eps, Robert
**Composer(s)**   Tepper, Sid; Bennett, Roy C.
**Lyricist(s)**   Tepper, Sid; Bennett, Roy C.
**Choreographer(s)**   Baker, Jack

**Producer(s)**   Pasternak, Joe
**Director(s)**   Taurog, Norman
**Screenwriter(s)**   Flicker, Theodore J.; Kirgo, George

**Cast**   Presley, Elvis; Fabares, Shelley; McBain, Diane; Marshall, Dodie; Walley, Deborah; Mullaney, Jack; Hutchins, Will; Berlinger, Warren; Hawkins, Jimmy; Betz, Carl; The Ranleys; Kellaway, Cecil; Merkel, Una; Worlock, Frederick

**Song(s)**   Spinout (C/L: Wayne, Sid; Weisman, Ben; Fuller, Darryl); Stop, Look, Listen (C/L: Byers, Joy); Adam and Evil (C/L: Wise, Fred; Starr, Randy); All That I Am; Am I Ready; Beach Snack (C/L: Giant, Bill; Kaye, Florence; Baum, Bernie); Smorgasbord; I'll Be Back (C: Weisman, Ben; L: Wayne, Sid)

**Notes**   Titled CALIFORNIA HOLIDAY internationally.

## 5684 ✦ THE SPINSTER

See TWO LOVES.

## 5685 ✦ SPIRIT OF CULVER
Universal, 1939

**Producer(s)**   Kelly, Burt
**Director(s)**   Santley, Joseph
**Screenwriter(s)**   Bolton, Whitney; West, Nathanael
**Source(s)**   "Tom Brown of Culver" (story) Green, George; Buckingham, Tom; Marks, Clarence

**Cast**   Cooper, Jackie; Hull, Henry; Bartholomew, Freddie; Devine, Andy; Moran, Jackie; Holt, Tim; Reynolds, Gene; Kane, Kathryn; Tetley, Walter; Stone, Milburn

**Song(s)**   You Are the Words to a Song (C: Skinner, Frank; L: Henderson, Charles)

**Notes**   A remake of TOM BROWN OF CULVER (1932).

## 5686 ✦ SPIRIT OF THE WIND
Raven Pictures, 1979

**Musical Score**   Sainte-Marie, Buffy
**Composer(s)**   Sainte-Marie, Buffy
**Lyricist(s)**   Sainte-Marie, Buffy

**Producer(s)**   Liddle, Ralph R.
**Director(s)**   Liddle, Ralph R.
**Screenwriter(s)**   Liddle, Ralph R.; Logue, John

**Cast**   Savage, Pius; Clutesi, George; Chief Dan George; Pickens, Slim

**Song(s)**   Spirit of the Wind; Sweet Grass Melody; You Always Come Through for Me Sweetheart; Yukon River Valley Blues

**Notes**   No cue sheet available.

## 5687 ✦ SPLASH
Disney, 1984

**Musical Score**   Holdridge, Lee

**Producer(s)**   Grazer, Brian
**Director(s)**   Howard, Ron

**Screenwriter(s)** Ganz, Lowell; Mandel, Babaloo; Friedman, Bruce Jay

**Cast** Hanks, Tom; Hannah, Daryl; Levy, Eugene; Candy, John; Goodman, Dody; Greene, Shecky; Shull, Richard B.; Di Cicco, Bobby; Morris, Howard; Di Benedetto, Tony

**Song(s)** Love Came for Me (C: Holdridge, Lee; L: Jennings, Will)

### 5688 ◆ SPLINTERS
British and Dominion Co., 1930

**Producer(s)** Wilcox, Herbert
**Director(s)** Raymond, Jack
**Screenwriter(s)** Lipscomb, W.P.; Ross, Archie

**Cast** Jones, Hal; Stone, Reg; Lake, Lew; Keys, Nelson; Howard, Sydney

**Notes** No cue sheet available. The songs are popular tunes of World War One. They include "I'll Be on My Way," "Encore" and "Lanky Carrie fra' Lancasheer."

### 5689 ◆ THE SPLIT
Metro–Goldwyn–Mayer, 1968

**Musical Score** Jones, Quincy
**Composer(s)** Jones, Quincy
**Lyricist(s)** Shelby, Ernie

**Producer(s)** Winkler, Irwin; Chartoff, Robert
**Director(s)** Flemyng, Gordon
**Screenwriter(s)** Sabaroff, Robert
**Source(s)** *The Seventh* (novel) Stark, Richard

**Cast** Brown, Jim; Carroll, Diahann; Harris, Julie; Hackman, Gene; Klugman, Jack; Oates, Warren; Whitmore, James; Sutherland, Donald; Borgnine, Ernest

**Song(s)** The Split; A Good Woman's Love (L: Wooley, Sheb); It's Just a Game, Love

### 5690 ◆ SPLIT IMAGE
Orion, 1982

**Musical Score** Conti, Bill

**Producer(s)** Kotcheff, Ted
**Director(s)** Kotcheff, Ted
**Screenwriter(s)** Spencer, Scott; Kaufman, Robert; Kamen, Robert Mark

**Cast** O'Keefe, Michael; Allen, Karen; Fonda, Peter; Woods, James; Ashley, Elizabeth; Dennehy, Brian; Rush, Deborah; Horton, Peter

**Song(s)** The Dark Along the Way (C: Conti, Bill; L: Jennings, Will)

**Notes** No cue sheet available.

### 5691 ◆ SPOILERS OF THE PLAINS
Republic, 1950

**Composer(s)** Elliott, Jack
**Lyricist(s)** Elliott, Jack

**Producer(s)** White, Edward W.
**Director(s)** Witney, William
**Screenwriter(s)** Nibley, Sloan

**Cast** Rogers, Roy; Trigger; Edwards, Penny; Jones, Gordon; Withers, Grant; Haggerty, Don; Foy Willing and the Riders of the Purple Sage

**Song(s)** Rainbow Over Texas [2]; It's a Lead Pipe Cinch; It's an Old Custom [1]; Happy Trails (C/L: Willing, Foy)

**Notes** [1] Spanish lyrics by Aaron Gonzalez. [2] Also in RAINBOW OVER TEXAS.

### 5692 ◆ SPOT

See DOGPOUND SHUFLE.

### 5693 ◆ SPOTLIGHT SCANDALS
Monogram, 1943

**Choreographer(s)** Boyle, Jack

**Producer(s)** Katzman, Sam; Dietz, Jack
**Director(s)** Beaudine, William
**Screenwriter(s)** Crowley, William X.; Sachs, Beryl

**Cast** Gilbert, Billy; Fay, Frank; Baker, Bonnie; Butch and Buddy [1]; The Radio Rogues [2]; Langdon, Harry; Adrian, Iris; Dell, Claudia; Chaplin, Sydney; Blythe, Betty; Hope, Jim; Boyle, Jack; Henry King and His Orchestra; Herb Miller and His Orchestra; Parks, Eddie; Bartell, Eddie

**Song(s)** The Restless Age (C/L: Rose, Ed; Olman, Abe); Goodnight Now (C/L: Unknown); The Lilac Tree (C/L: Unknown); Oh Johnny (C/L: Unknown); Tempo of the Trail (C/L: Unknown)

**Notes** No cue sheet available. [1] Billy Lenhart and Kenneth Brown. [2] Jimmy Hollywood, Eddie Bartell and Syd Charlton.

### 5694 ◆ SPREADIN' THE JAM
Metro–Goldwyn–Mayer, 1945

**Producer(s)** Baerwitz, Sam
**Director(s)** Walters, Charles
**Screenwriter(s)** Kuller, Sid

**Cast** Clayton, Jan; Lessy, Ben; Boise, Helen

**Song(s)** Spreadin' the Jam (C/L: Blane, Ralph; Walters, Charles; Brent, Earl)

**Notes** Short subject.

## 5695 ✦ SPRING BREAK
Columbia, 1983

**Musical Score**   Manfredini, Harry

**Producer(s)**   Cunningham, Sean S.
**Director(s)**   Cunningham, Sean S.
**Screenwriter(s)**   Smilow, David

**Cast**   Knell, David; Lang, Perry; Land, Paul; Bassett, Steve; Cozzens, Mimi; James, Jessica; Shull, Richard B.; Modean, Jayne

**Song(s)**   Friends (C/L: Max, Marilyn); That Lovin' Woman (C/L: Gronenthal, Max); Spring Break (C/L: Neilsen, Rick)

## 5696 ✦ SPRING IS HERE
Warner Brothers–First National, 1930

**Composer(s)**   Rodgers, Richard
**Lyricist(s)**   Hart, Lorenz

**Director(s)**   Dillon, John Francis
**Screenwriter(s)**   Starr, James A.
**Source(s)**   *Spring Is Here* (musical) Davis, Owen; Rodgers, Richard; Hart, Lorenz

**Cast**   Gray, Lawrence; Gray, Alexander; Claire, Bernice; Courtney, Inez; Moorhead, Natalie; Albertson, Frank; Fazenda, Louise; Sterling, Ford; Thomas, Gretchen

**Song(s)**   Spring Is Here [1]; Yours Sincerely [1]; Rich Man, Poor Man [1]; Baby's Awake Now [1]; With a Song in My Heart [1] [2]; Crying for the Carolines (C: Warren, Harry; L: Lewis, Sam M.; Young, Joe); Have a Little Faith in Me (C: Warren, Harry; L: Lewis, Sam M.; Young, Joe); Bad Baby (C: Warren, Harry; L: Lewis, Sam M.; Young, Joe); How Shall I Tell? (C: Warren, Harry; L: Lewis, Sam M.; Young, Joe); What's the Big Idea? (C: Warren, Harry; L: Lewis, Sam M.; Young, Joe); Absence Makes the Heart Grow Fonder (C: Warren, Harry; L: Lewis, Sam M.; Young, Joe)

**Notes**   No cue sheet available. Stanley Green in the *Rodgers and Hammerstein Fact Book* only lists "Spring Is Here," "Yours Sincerely," "With a Song in My Heart," "Crying for the Carolines" and "Have a Little Faith in Me." Tony Thomas' *Harry Warren and the Hollywood Musical* lists all the Warren songs above. Other sources list some or the other. This list is a compilation of all lists. In 1933 a two-reel version of SPRING IS HERE was released. It was titled YOURS SINCERELY. Lanny Ross was the star and Roy Mack directed. [1] From Broadway score. [2] Also in YOUNG MAN WITH A HORN.

## 5697 ✦ SPRING PARADE
Universal, 1940

**Musical Score**   Salter, Hans J.
**Composer(s)**   Stolz, Robert
**Lyricist(s)**   Kahn, Gus
**Choreographer(s)**   Ceballos, Larry

**Producer(s)**   Pasternak, Joe
**Director(s)**   Koster, Henry
**Screenwriter(s)**   Jackson, Felix; Manning, Bruce

**Cast**   Durbin, Deanna; Stephenson, Henry; Cummings, Robert; Sakall, S.Z.; Catlett, Walter; Auer, Mischa; Joslyn, Allyn; Denny, Reginald; Pangborn, Franklin; Butch and Buddy

**Song(s)**   It's Foolish but It's Fun; The Blue Danube Dream (C: Strauss, Johann); Waltzing in the Clouds; When April Sings; In a Spring Parade [1] (C: Previn, Charles)

**Notes**   [1] Used instrumentally only.

## 5698 ✦ SPRING REUNION
United Artists, 1957

**Musical Score**   Hagen, Earle; Spencer, Herbert

**Producer(s)**   Bresler, Jerry
**Director(s)**   Pirosh, Robert
**Screenwriter(s)**   Pirosh, Robert

**Cast**   Hutton, Betty [1]; Andrews, Dana; La Plante, Laura [1]; Simon, Robert F.; Hagen, Jean; Jones, Gordon; Berner, Sara; Gleason, James; Ryan, Irene

**Song(s)**   Spring Reunion (C: Warren, Harry; L: Mercer, Johnny); Carson High (C: Hagen, Earle; Spencer, Herbert; L: Pirosh, Robert)

**Notes**   There is also a vocal of "That Old Feeling" by Lew Brown and Sammy Fain and one of "Three Little Fishies" by Saxie Dowell. [1] Last film appearance.

## 5699 ✦ SPRING SONG
Republic, 1946

**Composer(s)**   May, Hans
**Lyricist(s)**   Stranks, Alan
**Choreographer(s)**   Billings, Jack

**Producer(s)**   Jackson, Louis H.
**Director(s)**   Tully, Montgomery
**Screenwriter(s)**   Tully, Montgomery; Seymour, James

**Cast**   Raye, Carol; Graves, Peter; Lynn, Leni; O'Madden, Lawrence; Currie, Finlay; Carney, George; O'Neill, Maire; Westcott, Netta

**Song(s)**   Jitterbug; All Pull Together; Love Again [1]; I Love the Moon (C/L: Rubens, Paul); I Can't Make Up My Mind; Spring Song; Here's to Music; Give Me a Chance to Dance; My Little Grey Home in the West (C: Lohr, Herman; L: Wilmott, D. Eardley)

**Notes**   A British National picture. [1] Also in COUNTERBLAST.

## 5700 ✦ SPRINGTIME FOR HENRY
Fox, 1934

**Producer(s)**   Lasky, Jesse L.
**Director(s)**   Tuttle, Frank

**Screenwriter(s)** Thompson, Keene; Tuttle, Frank
**Source(s)** *Springtime for Henry* (play) Levy, Benn W.

**Cast** Kruger, Otto; Carroll, Nancy; Angel, Heather

**Song(s)** Forbidden Lips (C: Gorney, Jay; L: Hartman, Don); Black Black Sheep [1] (C: DeFrancesco, Louis E.; L: Tuttle, Frank)

**Notes** [1] Also in MYSTERIOUS MR. MOTO.

## 5701 ✦ SPRINGTIME IN THE ROCKIES (1937)
### Republic, 1937

**Producer(s)** Siegel, Sol C.
**Director(s)** Kane, Joseph
**Screenwriter(s)** Wright, Gilbert; Burbridge, Betty

**Cast** Autry, Gene; Burnette, Smiley; Rowles, Polly; Love, Ula; Bacon, Ruth; Chesebro, George

**Song(s)** Give Me a Pony and an Open Prairie (C/L: Autry, Gene; Harford, Frank); Down in the Land of Zulu (C/L: Autry, Gene; Marvin, Johnny); (There'll Be a) Hayride Weddin' in June (C/L: Marvin, Johnny); Vitamin D (C/L: Burnette, Smiley); When a Cowboy Sings a Song (Sing Your Song Cowboy) (C/L: LeFevre, James; Caruso, Vincent); The Moon Is Ridin' (C/L: Leonardi, Tharpa); Wild and Wooly West (C: Stept, Sam H.; L: Koehler, Ted); You're the Only Star in My Blue Heaven [1] (C/L: Autry, Gene); When It's Springtime in the Rockies (C/L: Woolsey, Mary Hale; Taggart, Milton; Sauer, Robert)

**Notes** No cue sheet available. [1] Also in RIM OF THE CANYON (Columbia), MEXICALI ROSE and THE OLD BARN DANCE.

## 5702 ✦ SPRINGTIME IN THE ROCKIES (1942)
### Twentieth Century–Fox, 1942

**Composer(s)** Warren, Harry
**Lyricist(s)** Gordon, Mack
**Choreographer(s)** Pan, Hermes

**Producer(s)** LeBaron, William
**Director(s)** Cummings, Irving
**Screenwriter(s)** Bullock, Walter; Englund, Ken

**Cast** Grable, Betty; Payne, John; Miranda, Carmen; Romero, Cesar; Greenwood, Charlotte; Horton, Edward Everett; Harry James and His Music Makers; Orth, Frank; Gleason, Jackie; Hayden, Harry

**Song(s)** It Isn't Being Done (C/L: Henderson, Charles); Run, Little Raindrop, Run [3]; I Had the Craziest Dream; Chattanooga Choo Choo [2]; O "Tick Tack" Do Meu Coracao (C/L: Vermelho, Aloyr Pires); Pan American Jubilee; A Poem Set to Music [1]; I Like to Be Loved By You [4]

**Notes** Harry James also plays "You Made Me Love You" by James V. Monaco and "Two O'Clock Jump" by Count Basie and Harry James. [1] Instrumental only. [2] Originally in SUN VALLEY SERENADE. [3] Cut from THE GREAT AMERICAN BROADCAST. [4] Sequence filmed but not used. Put into GREENWICH VILLAGE.

## 5703 ✦ SPRINGTIME IN THE SIERRAS
### Republic, 1947

**Composer(s)** Elliott, Jack
**Lyricist(s)** Elliott, Jack

**Producer(s)** White, Edward J.
**Director(s)** Witney, William
**Screenwriter(s)** Nibley, Sloan

**Cast** Rogers, Roy; Trigger; Frazee, Jane; Devine, Andy; Bachelor, Stephanie; Landon, Hal; Chashire, Harry V.; Barcroft, Roy; Conklin, Chester; Bob Nolan and the Sons of the Pioneers

**Song(s)** Springtime in the Sierras; A Cowboy Has to Sing (C/L: Nolan, Bob); Pedro from Acapulco; Oh, What a Picture; What Are We Gonna Do Then (C/L: Spencer, Tim)

## 5704 ✦ SPRING TONIC
### Fox, 1935

**Producer(s)** Kane, Robert T.
**Director(s)** Bruckman, Clyde
**Screenwriter(s)** McNutt, Patterson; Hanemann, H.W.
**Source(s)** *Man Eating Tiger* (play) Hecht, Ben; Caylor, Rose

**Cast** Ayres, Lew; Trevor, Claire; Haley, Jack

**Song(s)** There's a Spell on the Moon (C/L: Gorney, Jay)

## 5705 ✦ THE SPY WHO LOVED ME
### United Artists, 1977

**Musical Score** Hamlisch, Marvin

**Producer(s)** Broccoli, Albert R.
**Director(s)** Gilbert, Lewis
**Screenwriter(s)** Maibaum, Richard; Wood, Christopher
**Source(s)** *The Spy Who Loved Me* (novel) Fleming, Ian

**Cast** Moore, Roger; Bach, Barbara; Jurgens, Curt; Kiel, Richard; Lee, Bernard; Maxwell, Lois

**Song(s)** Nobody Does It Better (C: Hamlisch, Marvin; L: Sager, Carole Bayer)

## 5706 ✦ THE SQUALL
### Warner Brothers–First National, 1929

**Director(s)** Korda, Alexander
**Screenwriter(s)** King, Bradley
**Source(s)** *The Squall* (play) Bart, Jean

**Cast** Joyce, Alice; Loy, Myrna; Tucker, Richard; Nye, Carroll; Pitts, ZaSu; Young, Loretta; Cording, Harry

**Song(s)** Gypsy Charmer (C: Akst, Harry; L: Clarke, Grant)

**Notes** No cue sheet available.

## 5707 ✦ SQUANDERED SISTERS
### Shavian Films, 1933

**Song(s)** Opium Ballet (Inst.): (C: Margosian, Linda); The Ten Commandments of Love (C/L: Origer, L.A.); The Vestal Vamp (C/L: James, Humphrey)

**Notes** No other information available.

## 5708 ✦ SQUARE DANCE KATY
### Monogram, 1950

**Producer(s)** Parsons, Lindsley
**Director(s)** Yarbrough, Jean
**Screenwriter(s)** Wilson, Warren

**Cast** Vague, Vera; Brito, Phil; Welles, Virginia; Douglas, Warren; Ryan, Sheila; Jimmie Davis and His Sunshine Band

**Song(s)** You Hold the Reins While I Kiss You (C/L: Keith, Raleigh)

**Notes** No cue sheet available.

## 5709 ✦ THE SQUARE PEG
### United Artists, 1958

**Musical Score** Green, Philip

**Producer(s)** Stewart, Hugh
**Director(s)** Carstairs, John Paddy
**Screenwriter(s)** Davies, Jack; Blyth, Henry E.; Wisdom, Norman; Leslie, Eddie

**Cast** Wisdom, Norman; Blackman, Honor; Chapman, Edward; Singer, Campbell; Jacques, Hattie

**Song(s)** The Square Peg (C: Green, Philip; L: Carr, Michael)

**Notes** A Rank Organisation film.

## 5710 ✦ THE SQUARE SHOOTER

See SKIPALONG ROSENBLOOM.

## 5711 ✦ STAGECOACH
### Twentieth Century–Fox, 1965

**Musical Score** Goldsmith, Jerry

**Producer(s)** Rackin, Martin
**Director(s)** Douglas, Gordon M.
**Screenwriter(s)** Landon, Joseph
**Source(s)** *Stagecoach* (screenplay) Nichols, Dudley

**Cast** Ann-Margaret; Buttons, Red; Connors, Michael; Cord, Alex; Crosby, Bing; Cummings, Robert; Heflin, Van; Pickens, Slim; Powers, Stefanie; Wynn, Keenan; Weston, Brad

**Song(s)** Stagecoach to Cheyenne (C: Pockriss, Lee; L: Vance, Paul); I Will Follow [1] (C: Goldsmith, Jerry; L: Batchelor, Ruth)

**Notes** [1] Not used.

## 5712 ✦ STAGECOACH TO DANCERS' ROCK
### Universal, 1964

**Musical Score** Steininger, Franz

**Producer(s)** Bellamy, Earl
**Director(s)** Bellamy, Earl
**Screenwriter(s)** Darling, Kenneth

**Cast** Dan, Judy; Stevens, Warren; Landau, Martin; Lawrence, Jody; Moore, Del; Willbanks, Don

**Song(s)** Ballad of Dancers' Rock (C: Steininger, Franz; L: Ackerman, Jack)

## 5713 ✦ STAGE COACH WAR
### Paramount, 1940

**Composer(s)** Ohman, Phil
**Lyricist(s)** Carling, Foster

**Producer(s)** Sherman, Harry
**Director(s)** Selander, Lesley
**Screenwriter(s)** Houston, Norman; Olmstead, Harry F.

**Cast** Boyd, William; Hayden, Russell; Carter, Julie; Stephens, Harvey; The King's Men

**Song(s)** Westward Ho; Hold Your Horses; Lope-Along-Road

**Notes** The picture was formerly titled HOLD YOUR HORSES.

## 5714 ✦ STAGE DOOR
### RKO, 1937

**Producer(s)** Berman, Pandro S.
**Director(s)** La Cava, Gregory
**Screenwriter(s)** Ryskind, Morrie; Veiller, Anthony
**Source(s)** *Stage Door* (play) Ferber, Edna; Kaufman, George S.

**Cast** Hepburn, Katharine; Rogers, Ginger; Menjou, Adolphe; Patrick, Gail; Collier, Constance; Leeds, Andrea; Hinds, Samuel S.; Ball, Lucille

**Song(s)** Put Your Heart Into Your Feet and Dance [1] (C: Borne, Hal; Greene, Mort); Our Penthouse on Third Avenue [2] (C: Fain, Sammy; L: Brown, Lew); Sailboat in the Moonlight (C/L: Loeb, John Jacob; Lombardo, Carmen)

**Notes** [1] Used instrumentally only. [2] Sung for 17 seconds. Also in NEW FACES (1937).

## 5715 ✦ STAGE DOOR CANTEEN
United Artists, 1943

**Composer(s)** Monaco, James V.
**Lyricist(s)** Dubin, Al

**Producer(s)** Lesser, Sol
**Director(s)** Borzage, Frank
**Screenwriter(s)** Daves, Delmer

**Cast** Anderson, Judith; Bankhead, Tallulah; Basie, Count; Bellamy, Ralph; Bolger, Ray; Cornell, Katherine; Cugat, Xavier; Fields, Gracie; Fontanne, Lynn; Goodman, Benny; Hayes, Helen; Herbert, Hugh; Hersholt, Jean; Jessel, George; Kyser, Kay; Lawrence, Gertrude; Lee, Peggy; Lee, Gypsy Rose; Lombardo, Guy; Lunt, Alfred; Marx, Harpo; Maxwell, Elsa; Merman, Ethel; Menuhin, Yehudi; Muni, Paul; Oberon, Merle; Pangborn, Franklin; Raft, George; Waters, Ethel; Weissmuller, Johnny; Wynn, Ed; Terry, William; Walker, Cheryl; McCallister, Lon; Riordan, Marjorie; Harrison, Michael; Early, Margaret
**Song(s)** We Mustn't Say Goodbye; The Machine Gun Song (C/L: Hoffman, Al; Curtis, Mann; Livingston, Jerry; Corbin, C.); American Boy [2]; Don't Worry Island; Quick Sands; A Rookie and His Rhythm; Sleep Baby Sleep (in Your Jeep); We Meet in the Funniest Places; You're Pretty Terrific Yourself; She's a Bombshell from Brooklyn [1]; The Girl I Love to Leave Behind (C: Rodgers, Richard; L: Hart, Lorenz); Alligator and the Crocodile

**Notes** No cue sheet available. There are also vocals of "Why Don't You Do Right?" by Joe McCoy; "Bugle Call Rag" by Jack Pettis, Billy Meyers and Elmer Schoebel; "Marching Through Berlin" by Bob Reed and Harry Miller and "The Lords's Prayer" by Alfred Hay Malotte. [1] Sol Lesser is also credited with lyrics in some sources but not on copyright records. [2] Also in HEY, ROOKIE.

## 5716 ✦ STAGE FRIGHT
Warner Brothers, 1950

**Musical Score** Lucas, Leighton

**Producer(s)** Hitchcock, Alfred
**Director(s)** Hitchcock, Alfred
**Screenwriter(s)** Cook, Whitfield; Bridie, James
**Source(s)** *Man Running* (novel) Jepson, Selwyn

**Cast** Wyman, Jane; Dietrich, Marlene; Wilding, Michael; Todd, Richard; Walsh, Kay; Thorndike, Sybil; Malleson, Miles; MacGregor, Hector; Grenfell, Joyce; Hitchcock, Patricia; Morell, Andre

**Song(s)** When You Whisper Sweet Nothings to Me (C/L: Spoliansky, M.); Laziest Gal in Town (C/L: Porter, Cole); In Grandma's Day They Never Did the Fox Trot [1] (C: Stamper, Dave; L: Buck, Gene); La Vie en Rose [1] (C/L: Louiguy; Piaf, Edith)

**Notes** All songs were interpolated. None were written for this film. [1] Background vocals.

## 5717 ✦ STAGE MOTHER
Metro–Goldwyn–Mayer, 1933

**Composer(s)** Brown, Nacio Herb
**Lyricist(s)** Freed, Arthur
**Choreographer(s)** Rasch, Albertina

**Producer(s)** Stromberg, Hunt
**Director(s)** Brabin, Charles R.
**Screenwriter(s)** Meehan, John; Ropes, Bradford
**Source(s)** *Stage Mother* (novel) Ropes, Bradford

**Cast** Brady, Alice; O'Sullivan, Maureen; Tone, Franchot; Holmes, Phillips; Healy, Ted; Hardy, Russell

**Song(s)** Patter Song (C: Snell, Dave; L: Healy, Ted); Beautiful Girl [1]; I'm Dancing on a Rainbow

**Notes** There are also vocals of "Any Little Girl That's a Nice Little Girl" by Fred Fisher and Thomas J. Gray; "When Irish Eyes Are Smiling" by Chauncey Olcott, George Graff Jr. and Ernest R. Ball; "How'm I Doin'" by Don Redman and "My Oh My" by Harry Revel. [1] Also in SINGIN' IN THE RAIN and GOING HOLLYWOOD.

## 5718 ✦ STAGE STRUCK
Warner Brothers–First National, 1936

**Composer(s)** Arlen, Harold
**Lyricist(s)** Harburg, E.Y.
**Choreographer(s)** Berkeley, Busby

**Producer(s)** Lord, Robert
**Director(s)** Berkeley, Busby
**Screenwriter(s)** Buckingham, Tom; Flick, Pat C.

**Cast** Powell, Dick; Blondell, Joan; William, Warren; McHugh, Frank; Madden, Jeanne; Hughes, Carol; Reynolds, Craig; Cavanaugh, Hobart; Arthur, Johnny; Byington, Spring; Pogue, Thomas; Tombes, Andrew; McConnell, Lulu; Gargan, Edward

**Song(s)** Lady in the Moon; The Income Tax Number (C/L: The Yacht Club Boys); Fancy Meeting You; The Body Beautiful (C/L: The Yacht Club Boys); In Your Own Quiet Way; You're Kinda Grandish [1]; The New Parade

**Notes** [1] Performed instrumentally only.

## 5719 ✦ STAGE TO CHINO
RKO, 1940

**Producer(s)** Gilroy, Bert
**Director(s)** Killy, Edward
**Screenwriter(s)** Grant, Morton; Jones, Arthur V.

**Cast** O'Brien, George; Vale, Virginia; Cavanaugh, Hobart; Barcroft, Roy; Haade, William; Stockdale, Carl; Strange, Glenn; Cording, Harry; Garralaga, Martin; Pals of the Golden West

**Song(s)**  Riding on the Stage to Chino (C/L: Allan, Fleming); I Love a Cowboy (C/L: Hess, Paul; Mays, Muriel; Jolls, Della)

## 5720 ✦ STAIRCASE
### Twentieth Century–Fox, 1969

**Musical Score**  Moore, Dudley

**Producer(s)**  Donen, Stanley
**Director(s)**  Donen, Stanley
**Screenwriter(s)**  Dyer, Charles
**Source(s)**  *Staircase* (play) Dyer, Charles

**Cast**  Burton, Richard; Harrison, Rex; Nesbitt, Cathleen; Heywood, Pat; Angers, Avril; Lehmann, Beatrix

**Song(s)**  Staircase (C: Moore, Dudley; L: Donen, Stanley; Moore, Dudley); Father Forgive Them (C: Moore, Dudley; L: Donen, Stanley)

## 5721 ✦ STAKEOUT
### Disney, 1987

**Musical Score**  Rubinstein, Arthur B.

**Producer(s)**  Kouf, Jim; Summers, Cathleen
**Director(s)**  Badham, John
**Screenwriter(s)**  Kouf, Jim

**Cast**  Dreyfuss, Richard; Estevez, Emilio; Quinn, Aidan; Stowe, Madeine; Whitaker, Forest; Lauria, Dan

**Song(s)**  This Night Was Made for One Thing Only (C: Rubinstein, Arthur B.; L: Brayfield, Douglas)

## 5722 ✦ STALLION ROAD
### Warner Brothers–First National, 1947

**Musical Score**  Hollander, Frederick

**Producer(s)**  Gottlieb, Alex
**Director(s)**  Kern, James V.
**Screenwriter(s)**  Longstreet, Stephen
**Source(s)**  *Stallion Road* (novel) Longstreet, Stephen

**Cast**  Reagan, Ronald; Smith, Alexis; Scott, Zachary; Knudsen, Peggy; Brady, Patti; Davenport, Harry; Greene, Angela; Puglia, Frank; Corrigan, Lloyd

**Song(s)**  Buscandote [2] (C/L: Lara, Augustin); Lola Te Quiero [1] (C: Hollander, Frederick; L: Cazares, Luis)

**Notes**  "I Gotta Right to Sing the Blues" by Harold Arlen and Ted Koehler is also featured in a vocal. [1] Performed instrumentally only. [2] Also in MASQUERADE IN MEXICO (Paramount).

## 5723 ✦ STAND AND DELIVER
### Warner Brothers, 1988

**Musical Score**  Safan, Craig
**Composer(s)**  Herron, W.
**Lyricist(s)**  Herron, W.

**Producer(s)**  Musca, Tom
**Director(s)**  Menendez, Ramon
**Screenwriter(s)**  Menendez, Ramon; Musca, Tom

**Cast**  Olmos, Edward James; De Soto, Rosana; Phillips, Lou Diamond; Garcia, Andy; Eliot, Mark

**Song(s)**  El Lay (C/L: Herron, W.; Gronk); I Want You (C/L: Clark, Keith); Pacho Jarocho (C/L: Loya, Marcos); Secret Society (C/L: Herron, W.; Valdez, M.); Wake Up John; Cada Quien por Su Camino (C/L: Perez, Rachel); Yamanos Pal Norte (C/L: Loya, Marcos); Psycho Cha-Cha; Stand and Deliver (C/L: Page, Richard; Lang, John; George, Steve)

**Notes**  All songs are background vocals.

## 5724 ✦ STAND BY FOR ACTION
### Metro–Goldwyn–Mayer, 1942

**Musical Score**  Hayton, Lennie

**Producer(s)**  Leonard, Robert Z.; Dull, Orville O.
**Director(s)**  Leonard, Robert Z.
**Screenwriter(s)**  Bruce, George; Balderston, John L.; Mankiewicz, Herman J.
**Source(s)**  "A Cargo of Innocence" (story) Kirk, Laurence

**Cast**  Taylor, Robert; Donlevy, Brian; Laughton, Charles; Brennan, Walter; Maxwell, Marilyn; O'Neill, Henry; Linden, Marte; Wills, Chill; Dumbrille, Douglass; Quine, Richard

**Song(s)**  The Sailor Man (C/L: Wills, Chill)

**Notes**  Released as CARGO OF INNOCENTS overseas.

## 5725 ✦ STAND UP AND CHEER
### Fox, 1934

**Composer(s)**  Gorney, Jay; Brown, Lew
**Lyricist(s)**  Brown, Lew

**Producer(s)**  Sheehan, Winfield
**Director(s)**  MacFadden, Hamilton
**Screenwriter(s)**  Brown, Lew; Spence, Ralph

**Cast**  Baxter, Warner; Evans, Madge; Dunn, James; Temple, Shirley

**Song(s)**  I'm Laughin'; We Are the Roman Soldiers (C: Brown, Lew); Baby Take a Bow; Broadway's Gone Hill-Billy; The Last Round-Up [2] (C/L: Hill, Billy); She's Way Up Thar (I'm Way Down Yar) (C: Brown, Lew); This Is Our Last Night Together; We're Out of the Red (C: Gorney, Jay); Stand Up and Cheer (C: Akst, Harry); The Doll Dance (Inst.) [1]

**Notes**  Brown was listed as cocomposer on all the songs. [1] Later used in REDHEADS ON PARADE as the title song. [2] Also in ONE HOUR LATE (Paramount), THE LAST ROUNDUP (Columbia) and the Republic films SINGING HILL and DON'T FENCE ME IN.

## 5726 ✦ STAR!
Twentieth Century–Fox, 1968

**Choreographer(s)**  Kidd, Michael

**Producer(s)**  Chaplin, Saul
**Director(s)**  Wise, Robert
**Screenwriter(s)**  Fairchild, William

**Cast**  Andrews, Julie; Crenna, Richard; Craig, Michael; Massey, Daniel; Reed, Robert; Forsyth, Bruce; Reed, Beryl; Livingston, Jock; O'Malley, J. Pat; Fox, Bernard

**Song(s)**  Star! (C: Van Heusen, James; L: Cahn, Sammy); In My Garden of Joy (C/L: Chaplin, Saul)

**Notes**  Originally titled THE STAR. There are also vocal renditions of "Down at the Old Bull and Bush" by Harry Von Tilzer and Andrew B. Sterling; "Piccadilly" by Paul Morande, Walter Williams and Bruce Sievier; "Oh! It's a Lovely War" by J.P. Long and Maurice Scott; "Forbidden Fruit," "Parisian Pierrot," "Has Anybody Seen Our Ship" and "Someday I'll Find You" by Noel Coward; "The Physician" by Cole Porter; "N'Everything" by B.G. DeSylva, Gus Kahn and Al Jolson; "Burlington Bertie from Bow" by William Hargreaves; "Rule, Britannia!" by Thomas Arne and Thompson; "My Ship" and "Jenny" by Kurt Weill and Ira Gershwin; "Do-Do-Do," "Someone to Watch Over Me" and "Dear Little Girl" by George and Ira Gershwin; "After the Ball" by Charles K. Harris and "Limehouse Blues" by Philip Braham and Douglas Furber.

## 5727 ✦ STAR BRIGHT
Paramount, 1945

**Choreographer(s)**  Earl, Josephine

**Producer(s)**  Harris, Lou
**Director(s)**  Bennett, Hugh

**Cast**  Walker, Mary

**Song(s)**  My Daddy Told Me [1] (C: Cherkose, Eddie; L: Press, Jacques); The Waltz Lives On [2] (C: Rainger, Ralph; L: Robin, Leo); Patricia Donahue (C/L: Davis, Benny; Morgan, Russ; Murry, Ted)

**Notes**  Short subject. It is not known if any of these were written for the picture. [1] Not used in TRUE TO LIFE. [2] Also in THE BIG BROADCAST OF 1938.

## 5728 ✦ STAR CHAMBER
Twentieth Century–Fox, 1983

**Musical Score**  Small, Michael

**Producer(s)**  Yablans, Frank
**Director(s)**  Hyams, Peter
**Screenwriter(s)**  Taylor, Roderick; Hyams, Peter

**Cast**  Douglas, Michael; Holbrook, Hal; Kotto, Yaphet; Gless, Sharon; Sikking, James B.

**Song(s)**  Boys in the Brigade (C/L: Stern, Shawn); New Church (C/L: Bator, Stiv; James, Brian)

**Notes**  There is also a background vocal of "You Make Me Feel So Young" by Josef Myrow and Mack Gordon.

## 5729 ✦ STAR DUST (1940)
Twentieth Century–Fox, 1940

**Composer(s)**  Gordon, Mack
**Lyricist(s)**  Gordon, Mack

**Producer(s)**  Zanuck, Darryl F.
**Director(s)**  Lang, Walter
**Screenwriter(s)**  Ellis, Robert; Logan, Helen

**Cast**  Darnell, Linda; Payne, John; Young, Roland; Greenwood, Charlotte; Gargan, William; Hughes, Mary Beth; Healy, Mary; Meek, Donald; Green, Harry; Ralph, Jessie; Montgomery, George

**Song(s)**  Secrets in the Moonlight; Sagebrush Sue (C: Buttolph, David; L: Henderson, Charles); Don't Let It Get You Down

**Notes**  There is also a vocal of "Star Dust" by Hoagy Carmichael and Mitchell Parish.

## 5730 ✦ STARDUST (1975)
Columbia, 1975

**Producer(s)**  Puttnam, David; Lieberson, Sandy
**Director(s)**  Apted, Michael
**Screenwriter(s)**  Apted, Michael; Connolly, Ray; Puttnam, David

**Cast**  Hagman, Larry; Faith, Adam; Essex, David; Moon, Keith

**Song(s)**  Happy Birthday Sweet Sixteen (C/L: Sedaka, Neil; Greenfield, Howard); Up on the Roof (C/L: King, Carole; Goffin, Gerry); Hats Off to Larry (C/L: Shannon, Del); When Will I Be Loved (C/L: Everly, Phil); Need a Shot of Rhythm and Blues (C/L: Thompson, T.); It Might As Well Rain Until September [1] (C/L: King, Carole; Goffin, Gerry); Do You Want to Know a Secret (C/L: Lennon, John; McCartney, Paul); Da Doo Ron Ron (C/L: Spector, Phil; Barry, Jeff; Greenwich, Ellie); Let It Be Me (C/L: Curtis, Mann; Becaud, Gilbert; Delahoe); You Kept Me Waiting (C/L: Naumann, P.); You've Got Your Troubles (C/L: Greenaway, R.; Cook, Roger); Some Other Guy (C/L: Glick, E.; Barratt, R.); Take It Away (C/L: Osborne, G.; Vigrass, P.); Make Me Your Baby (C/L: Atkins, R.; Miller, H.); I'm a Believer (C/L: Diamond, Neil); My Generation (C/L: Townsend, Pete); White Rabbit (C/L: Slick, Grace); Let Me Sing and I'm Happy (C/L: Berlin, Irving); Stardust (C/L: Essex, David)

**Notes**  It is not known if any of these were written for the picture. Songs that had a screen time of under 50 seconds are not listed here. [1] Also in SHAMPOO.

## 5731 ✦ STARDUST ON THE SAGE
Republic, 1942

**Producer(s)** Grey, Harry
**Director(s)** Morgan, William
**Screenwriter(s)** Burbridge, Betty

**Cast** Autry, Gene; Burnette, Smiley; Currie, Louise; Fellows, Edith; Henry, Bill

**Song(s)** Perfidia [1] (C: Dominguez, Alberto; L: Leeds, Milton; Dominguez, Alberto); Good Night Sweetheart (C/L: Campbell, Jimmy; Connelly, Reg; Noble, Ray); You'll Be Sorry (C/L: Autry, Gene; Rose, Fred); Wouldn't You Like to Know (C/L: Burnette, Smiley); I'll Never Let You Go (C/L: Wakely, Jimmy); When the Roses Bloom Again (C: Kent, Walter; L: Burton, Nat)

## 5732 ✦ STAR 80
Warner Brothers, 1983

**Musical Score** Burns, Ralph
**Composer(s)** Burns, Ralph
**Lyricist(s)** Burns, Ralph

**Producer(s)** Glattes, Wolfgang; Utt, Kenneth
**Director(s)** Fosse, Bob
**Screenwriter(s)** Fosse, Bob
**Source(s)** "Death of a Playmate" (story) Carpenter, Teresa

**Cast** Hemingway, Mariel; Roberts, Eric; Robertson, Cliff; Baker, Carroll; Rees, Roger; Clennon, David; Mostel, Josh; Gordon, Lisa; Luisi, James; Patterson, Neva; Wayans, Keenan Ivory; Damon, Stuart

**Song(s)** Overkill; Off Ramp (L: Tronick, Michael); Improvise (L: Tronick, Michael); Funky; Just the Way You Are (C/L: Joel, Billy)

**Notes** No cue sheet available.

## 5733 ✦ STAR FOR A NIGHT
Twentieth Century–Fox, 1936

**Composer(s)** Akst, Harry
**Lyricist(s)** Clare, Sidney

**Producer(s)** Wurtzel, Sol M.
**Director(s)** Seiler, Lewis
**Screenwriter(s)** Hyland, Frances; Elkins, Saul

**Cast** Trevor, Claire; Darwell, Jane; Venable, Evelyn; Judge, Arline; Bromberg, J. Edward; Reicher, Frank; Compton, Joyce; Allwyn, Astrid; Jagger, Dean; Chandler, Chick; McDaniel, Hattie

**Song(s)** You're My Favorite One (C: Pollack, Lew); Down Aroun' Malibu Way; Holy Lie Prod. Routine; Over a Cup of Coffee [1]; At the Beach at Malibu (Hullabaloo at Malibu)

**Notes** [1] Also in WOMAN WISE.

## 5734 ✦ STAR IN THE DUST
Universal, 1956

**Musical Score** Skinner, Frank

**Producer(s)** Zugsmith, Albert
**Director(s)** Haas, Charles
**Screenwriter(s)** Brodney, Oscar
**Source(s)** *Law Man* (novel) Leighton, Lee

**Cast** Boone, Richard; Erickson, Leif; Agar, John; Gray, Coleen; Gleason, James; Gilkyson, Terry; Morgan, Henry; Van Doren, Mamie

**Song(s)** Sam Hall [1] (C/L: Gilkyson, Terry)

**Notes** [1] Revised music and lyrics from the traditional original.

## 5735 ✦ A STAR IS BORN (1954)
Warner Brothers, 1954

**Composer(s)** Arlen, Harold
**Lyricist(s)** Gershwin, Ira
**Choreographer(s)** Barstow, Richard

**Producer(s)** Luft, Sidney
**Director(s)** Cukor, George
**Screenwriter(s)** Hart, Moss

**Cast** Garland, Judy; Mason, James; Carson, Jack; Bickford, Charles; Noonan, Tommy [3]; Marlow, Lucy; Blake, Amanda; Bacon, Irving; Shermet, Hazel; Graff, Wilton; Sutton, Grady; Brown, James; Robb, Lotus

**Song(s)** The Man That Got Away; Born in a Trunk (C/L: Gershe, Leonard); Gotta Have Me Go with You; It's a New World; Someone at Last; Here's What I'm Here For [1]; TV Commercial [1]; Lose That Long Face [1]; I'm Off the Downbeat [2]; Green Light Ahead [2]

**Notes** A remake of A STAR IS BORN. Also used in the "Born in a Trunk" sequence were "Swanee" by George Gershwin and Irving Caesar; "Black Bottom" by B.G. DeSylva, Lew Brown and Ray Henderson; "I'll Get By (As Long As I Have You)" by Roy Turk and Fred E. Ahlert; "You Took Advantage of Me" by Richard Rodgers and Lorenz Hart; "The Peanut Vendor" by Marion Sunshine, L. Wolfe Gilbert and Moises Simons and "My Melancholy Baby" by Ernie Burnett, George A. Norton and Maybelle E. Watson. Cut from the sequence was "When My Sugar Walks Down the Street" by Irving Mills, Gene Austin and Jimmy McHugh. However, it has been returned to the sequence in the recently restored print. [1] Cut after roadshow engagement but in the restored version. [2] Not used. [3] Billed as Tom Noonan.

## 5736 ✦ A STAR IS BORN (1976)
Warner Brothers, 1976

**Composer(s)** Williams, Paul; Ascher, Kenny
**Lyricist(s)** Williams, Paul; Ascher, Kenny
**Choreographer(s)** Winters, David

**Producer(s)**   Peters, Jon
**Director(s)**   Pierson, Frank R.
**Screenwriter(s)**   Dunne, John Gregory; Didion, Joan; Pierson, Frank R.

**Cast**   Streisand, Barbra; Kristofferson, Kris; Mazursky, Paul; Busey, Gary; Clarke, Oliver; Fields, Vanetta; King, Clydie; Linville, Joanne

**Song(s)**   Watch Closely Now; Spanish Lies [1]; Hellacious Acres; Queen Bee (C/L: Holmes, Rupert); Everything (C/L: Holmes, Rupert; Williams, Paul); Connection [1] (C/L: Jagger, Mick; Richards, Keith); Cat Food Commercial (C/L: Kristofferson, Kris); Lost Inside of You (C/L: Streisand, Barbra; Russell, Leon); Woman In the Moon; Evergreen (C/L: Williams, Paul; Streisand, Barbra); I Believe in Love (C: Loggins, Kenny; L: Bergman, Alan; Bergman, Marilyn); Crippled Crow [1] (C/L: Weiss, Donna); Won't Be Where I've Been (C: Kellaway, Roger; L: Lees, Gene); With One More Look at You

**Notes**   A remake of A STAR IS BORN. [1] Background vocal use only.

### 5737 ✦ STARLIFT
Warner Brothers, 1951

**Choreographer(s)**   Prinz, LeRoy

**Producer(s)**   Arthur, Robert
**Director(s)**   Del Ruth, Roy
**Screenwriter(s)**   Klorer, John
**Source(s)**   "Operation Starlift" (story) Klorer, John

**Cast**   Day, Doris; MacRae, Gordon; Mayo, Virginia; Nelson, Gene; Roman, Ruth; Rule, Janice; Wesson, Dick; Haggerthy, Ron; Webb, Richard; Roarke, Hayden; St. John, Howard; Cagney, James; Cooper, Gary; Gibson, Virginia; Harris, Phil; Lovejoy, Frank; Norman, Lucille; Parsons, Louella; Scott, Randolph; Wyman, Jane; Wymore, Patrice

**Song(s)**   Noche Caribe (C/L: Faith, Percy); Look Out Stranger, I'm a Texas Ranger [1] (C/L: Raksin, Ruby)

**Notes**   Visual vocals of "You're Gonna Lose Your Gal" by James Monaco and Joe Young; "'S Wonderful" by George and Ira Gershwin; "You Oughta Be in Pictures" by Dana Suesse and Edward Heyman; "You Do Something to Me" and "What Is This Thing Called Love" by Cole Porter; "Liza (All the Clouds'll Roll Away)" by George Gershwin, Ira Gershwin and Gus Kahn; "When Irish Eyes Are Smiling" by Chauncey Olcott, Ernest R. Ball and George Graff Jr.; "The Good Green Acres of Home" by Sammy Fain and Irving Kahal; "It's Magic" by Sammy Cahn and Jule Styne and "I May Be Wrong (But I Think You're Wonderful)" by Harry Ruskin and Henry Sullivan were used in the picture either singly or part of medleys. It is not known if the Percy Faith and Ruby Raksin songs were written for the picture. [1] Some sources list "Look Out Stranger" as written by Ruby Ralesin and Phil Harris.

### 5738 ✦ STARLIGHT OVER TEXAS
Monogram, 1938

**Producer(s)**   Finney, Edward
**Director(s)**   Herman, Al
**Screenwriter(s)**   Rathmell, John

**Cast**   Ritter, Tex; Damino, Salvatore; LaRoux, Carmen; Turick, Rosa; Pollard, Snub; The Northwesterners

**Song(s)**   Starlight Over Texas (C: Ingraham, Roy; L: Tobias, Harry); A Garden in Granada (C/L: Vasilesau, Ion); Ai! Viva Tequilla! (C/L: Von Tilzer, Albert; Unknown)

**Notes**   No cue sheet available.

### 5739 ✦ STARLIT DAYS AT THE LIDO
Metro–Goldwyn–Mayer, 1935

**Producer(s)**   Lewyn, Louis
**Screenwriter(s)**   Van Dorn, Alexander

**Cast**   The Radio Rogues; Henry Busse and His Orchestra; Randall, Judy; Grayson, Carl; Lake, Arthur; Brown, Anne; Stephanie, Marion; The Fanchonettes

**Song(s)**   I Want a Man (C/L: Tic-Toc Girls, The); Hang on to Me [1] (C: Greer, Jesse; L: Klages, Raymond)

**Notes**   Short subject. There are also vocals of "Love Dropped In for Tea" by Harold Spina and Joe Burke; "The Voice of R.K.O." by Milton Schwarzwald and "Hot Lips" by Henry Busse, Henry Lange and Lou Davis. [1] Also in MARIANNE.

### 5740 ✦ THE STAR MAKER
Paramount, 1939

**Composer(s)**   Monaco, James V.
**Lyricist(s)**   Burke, Johnny
**Choreographer(s)**   Prinz, LeRoy

**Producer(s)**   Rogers, Charles R.
**Director(s)**   Del Ruth, Roy
**Screenwriter(s)**   Caesar, Arthur; Butler, Frank; Hartman, Don

**Cast**   Crosby, Bing; Campbell, Louise; Ware, Linda; Sparks, Ned; Crews, Laura Hope; Hall, Thurston; Gilbert, Billy; Hickman, Darryl; Waldo, Janet; Damrosch, Walter

**Song(s)**   A Man and His Dream; Go Fly a Kite; Valse des Fleurs (C: Tchaikovsky, Peter; L: Loesser, Frank); An Apple for the Teacher [2]; Still the Bluebird Sings; A Minuet for Milady [1]

**Notes**   This is a biopic of Gus Edwards. There are also renditions of "I Wonder Who's Kissing Her Now" by Will M. Hough, Frank R. Adams, Joseph E. Howard and Harold Orlob; "Sunbonnet Sue," "School Days," "If I Was a Millionaire," and "I Can't Tell Why I Love You" by Gus Edwards and Will D. Cobb; "Look Out for

Jimmy Valentine" by Edward Madden and Gus Edwards, "In My Merry Oldsmobile" and "He's My Pal" by Gus Edwards and Vincent P. Bryan, and "Darktown Strutters' Ball" by Shelton Brooks. [1] Not used. [2] Later in THE LAST ROUNDUP (Columbia).

## 5741 ✦ STAR OF MIDNIGHT
### RKO, 1935

**Director(s)** Roberts, Stephen
**Screenwriter(s)** Green, Howard J.; Veiller, Anthony; Kaufman, Edward
**Source(s)** *Star of Midnight* (novel) Roche, Arthur Somers

**Cast** Powell, William; Rogers, Ginger; Kelly, Paul; Lockhart, Gene; Morgan, Ralph; Fenton, Leslie; MacDonald, J. Farrell; Hopton, Russell; Oakland, Vivian; O'Connor, Robert Emmett

**Song(s)** Midnight in Manhattan (C: Steiner, Max; L: Scholl, Jack)

## 5742 ✦ STARS AND BARS
### Columbia, 1988

**Musical Score** Myers, Stanley

**Producer(s)** Lieberson, Sandy
**Director(s)** O'Connor, Pat
**Screenwriter(s)** Boyd, William
**Source(s)** *Stars and Bars* (novel) Boyd, William

**Cast** Day-Lewis, Daniel; Stanton, Harry Dean; Broadhurst, Kent; Chaykin, Maury; Cowles, Matthew; Cusack, Joan; David, Keith; Gray, Spalding; Headly, Glenne; Metcalf, Laurie; Plimpton, Martha; Patton, Will

**Song(s)** Love Turns to Hate (C: Myers, Stanley; L: Prescott, Graham)

## 5743 ✦ STARS AND STRIPES FOREVER
### Twentieth Century–Fox, 1952

**Producer(s)** Trotti, Lamar
**Director(s)** Koster, Henry
**Screenwriter(s)** Trotti, Lamar
**Source(s)** *Marching Along* (book) Sousa, John Philip

**Cast** Webb, Clifton; Paget, Debra; Wagner, Robert; Hussey, Ruth; Currie, Finlay; Roberts, Roy; Prickett, Maudie; Vincent, Romo

**Song(s)** My Love Is a Weeping Willow [1] (C: Sousa, John Philip; L: Darby, Ken); I'm Afraid (C: Newman, Alfred; L: O'Keefe, Lester); Springtime in New York (C: Newman, Alfred; L: Darby, Ken)

**Notes** Titled MARCHING ALONG overseas. This is a biopic of John Philip Sousa. Vocals also include "Oh, Why Should the Spirit of Mortal Be Proud" by Sousa and William Knox; "Sweet Marie" by Raymond Moore and Cy Warman; "El Capitan" by Sousa and Charles Klein; "The Battle Hymn of the Republic" by William Steffe and Julia Ward Howe; "The Bowery" by Percy Gaunt and Charles M. Hoyt and "Father's Got 'Em!" by Harry Wincott. [1] Based on Sousa's march "Semper Fidelis."

## 5744 ✦ STARS AND VIOLINS
### Universal, 1944

**Composer(s)** Rosen, Milton
**Lyricist(s)** Carter, Everett

**Song(s)** Stars and Violins [3]; Let's Love Again [2]; A Dream Ago [1]

**Notes** This is a short subject. There are other vocal songs but not written for this production. [1] Also is HAT CHECK HONEY; HI 'YA, SAILOR and MOON OVER LAS VEGAS. [2] Also in TOO MANY BLONDES and TWILIGHT ON THE PRAIRIE. [3] Also in SLIGHTLY TERRIFIC.

## 5745 ✦ THE STARS ARE SINGING
### Paramount, 1953

**Composer(s)** Livingston, Jay; Evans, Ray
**Lyricist(s)** Livingston, Jay; Evans, Ray
**Choreographer(s)** Baker, Jack

**Producer(s)** Asher, Irving
**Director(s)** Taurog, Norman
**Screenwriter(s)** O'Brien, Liam

**Cast** Alberghetti, Anna Maria; Clooney, Rosemary; Melchior, Lauritz; Morton, Tom; Williams, Bob; Clark, Fred; Corrigan, Lloyd; Wilson, Don

**Song(s)** I Do! I Do! I Do!; My Kind of Day; Haven't Got a Worry; Lovely Weather for Ducks [2]; Come On-A-My-House [1] (C: Bagdasarian, Ross; L: Saroyan, William); My Heart Is Home; Rruff Song [3] (C: Rosas, Juventino; L: Livingston, Jay; Evans, Ray); Reach for the Stars [4]; Gadabout [4]

**Notes** The following classical selections are also featured: "Vesti La Giubba" from Leoncavallo's PAGLIACCI; "Voices of Spring" by Johann Strauss and Italo Celesti; "Una Voce Poco Fa" from Rossini's BARBER OF SEVILLE; "Because" by Edward Teschemacher and Guy d'Hardelot and "Ah! Fors'e Lui Che L'Anima" from G. Verdi and Francesca Maria Piave's LA TRAVIATA. [1] Not written for this picture. [2] Written for HERE COMES THE GROOM but not used in that production. [3] Music is "Over the Waves." [4] Not used.

## 5746 ✦ STARS ON PARADE
### Columbia, 1944

**Producer(s)** MacDonald, Wallace
**Director(s)** Landers, Lew
**Screenwriter(s)** Brice, Monte

**Cast** Parks, Larry; Merrick, Lynn; Donnell, Jeff; Williams, Robert; The Chords [1]; The King Cole Trio; The Ben Carter Choir; O'Neill, Danny

**Song(s)** Jumpin' at the Jubilee (C/L: Carter, Ben; Mayes, Marshall); Two Hearts in the Dark (C/L: Franklin, Dave)

**Notes** The cue sheet did not differentiate between vocals and instrumentals therefore the following list may not be correct. Songs not written for the picture that are used vocally include "Taking Care of You" by Lew Brown and Harry Akst; "When They Asked About You" by Sam H. Stept; "Where Am I Without You" by Don Raye and Gene DePaul from HEY ROOKIE; "My Heart Isn't In It" by Jack Lawrence; "Hit That Jive Jack" by Skeets Tolbert and John Alston; "Juke Box Saturday Night" by Paul McGrane and Al Stillman; "It's Love Love Love" by Mack David, Joan Whitney and Alex Kramer; "Boo Hoo" by Carmen Lombardo and Edward Heyman and Philip Loeb. [1] Consisted of Arnold Archer and Gilbert Miller.

---

## 5747 ✦ STARS OVER BROADWAY
### Warner Brothers, 1935

**Composer(s)** Warren, Harry
**Lyricist(s)** Dubin, Al
**Choreographer(s)** Berkeley, Busby; Connolly, Bobby

**Producer(s)** Bischoff, Sam
**Director(s)** Keighley, William
**Screenwriter(s)** Wald, Jerry; Epstein, Julius J.; Flick, Patsy

**Cast** O'Brien, Pat; Froman, Jane; Melton, James; Muir, Jean; McHugh, Frank; Regan, Phil; Ricciardi, William; Wilson, Marie; Fay, Frank; Clive, E.E.; Conrad, Eddy; Flick, Patsy; Chandler, George

**Song(s)** You Let Me Down; Coney Island [5]; Where Am I; At Your Service Madam; Carry Me Back to the Lone Prairie (C/L: Robison, Carson J.); Broadway Cinderella [1]; September in the Rain [4]; Sweet and Slow [2]; Brownstone Baby [3]

**Notes** "Celeste Aida" by Verdi; "Old Faithful" and "Those Pearly Gates" were also heard vocally. The Busby Berkeley book lists the song "Over Yonder Moon" but not "Coney Island." These might be the same song. [1] Vocal cut from final print though filmed. It was used instrumentally. [2] Vocal for 8 seconds. It was also used briefly in BROADWAY HOSTESS and used instrumentally in BROADWAY GONDOLIER. [3] Vocal for 14 seconds. [4] Used briefly, a proposed Busby Berkeley production number was not filmed. In MELODY FOR TWO. [5] Also in CAIN AND MABEL.

---

## 5748 ✦ STARS OVER TEXAS
### Producers Releasing Corporation, 1946

**Producer(s)** Tansey, Robert Emmett
**Director(s)** Tansey, Robert Emmett
**Screenwriter(s)** Kavanaugh, Frances

**Cast** Dean, Eddie; Ates, Roscoe; Patterson, Shirley; Bennett, Lee; Roberts, Lee; Maynard, Kermit; O'Shea, Jack; The Sunshine Boys

**Song(s)** Stars Over Texas [1] (C/L: Dean, Eddie; Blair, Hal); Sands of the Rio Grande [1] (C/L: Dean, Eddie; Strange, Glenn); 1501 Miles of Heaven (C/L: Dean, Eddie)

**Notes** [1] Also in TUMBLEWEED TRAIL.

---

## 5749 ✦ STAR-SPANGLED GIRL
### Paramount, 1971

**Musical Score** Fox, Charles

**Producer(s)** Koch, Howard W.
**Director(s)** Paris, Jerry
**Screenwriter(s)** Margolin, Arnold; Parker, Jim
**Source(s)** *The Star Spangled Girl* (play) Simon, Neil

**Cast** Duncan, Sandy; Roberts, Tony; Susman, Todd; Allan, Elizabeth

**Song(s)** Girl (C: Fox, Charles; L: Gimbel, Norman)

---

## 5750 ✦ STAR-SPANGLED RHYTHM
### Paramount, 1942

**Musical Score** Dolan, Robert Emmett
**Composer(s)** Arlen, Harold
**Lyricist(s)** Mercer, Johnny
**Choreographer(s)** Balanchine, George [3]; Dare, Danny

**Producer(s)** Sistrom, Joseph
**Director(s)** Marshall, George
**Screenwriter(s)** Tugend, Harry

**Cast** Bracken, Eddie; Moore, Victor; Hutton, Betty; Hope, Bob; Crosby, Bing; Martin, Mary; Milland, Ray; Tone, Franchot; MacMurray, Fred; Powell, Dick; Ladd, Alan; Hayward, Susan; Anderson, Eddie "Rochester"; Colonna, Jerry; Bendix, William; Carey, Macdonald; De Mille, Cecil B.; Sturges, Preston; Murphy, Ralph; Zorina, Vera; Goddard, Paulette; Lamour, Dorothy; Lake, Veronica [2]

**Song(s)** Hit the Road to Dreamland; On the Swing Shift; I'm Doin' It for Defense; A Sweater, a Sarong, and a Peekaboo Bang; That Old Black Magic [4]; Sharp As a Tack; Old Glory; Shore Leave (Let's Go Sailor) [1]

**Notes** The film was formerly titled THUMBS UP. The lyrics (rhythm calls) sung by Betty Jane Rhodes and Dona Drake in the "Swing Shift Square Dance" about sashaying fancy and tripping light, through the reference to the Shorty-George and spinning to boot and steady zoot, are by Danny Dare, Harold Knight and Patti Brilhante. [1] Not used. [2] Dubbed by Martha Mears. [3] Choreographed Zorina's dance number. [4] Also in HERE COME THE WAVES, RADIO STARS ON PARADE (RKO) and SENIOR PROM (Columbia).

## 5751 ✦ START CHEERING
Columbia, 1938

**Composer(s)** Green, Johnny
**Lyricist(s)** Koehler, Ted

**Director(s)** Rogell, Albert S.
**Screenwriter(s)** Solow, Eugene; Wormser, Richard E.; Rapp, Philip; Buckner, Robert; Bell, Tom; Manning, Bruce; Winslow, Thrya S.; Kraft, Hy S.; Murphy, Owen
**Source(s)** "College Hero" (story) Ford, Corey

**Cast** Connolly, Walter; Walburn, Raymond; Starrett, Charles; Green, Johnny; Dale, Virginia; The Three Stooges [2]; Durante, Jimmy; Truex, Ernest; Chase, Chas.; Vincent, Romo; LeRoy, Hal; Crawford, Broderick; Niesen, Gertrude; Wallington, Jimmy; Urecal, Minerva; Louis Prima and His Band

**Song(s)** Gang Song; I'll Do the Strutaway (in My Cutaway) (C/L: Durante, Jimmy; Donnelly, Harry; Caesar, Irving); Hail Sigma Psi; My Heaven on Earth [1] (C/L: Tobias, Charles; Pokrass, Sam; Baker, Phil); Rockin' the Town; Start Cheering (C: Oakland, Ben; L: Drake, Milton); Am I in Another World [3]; Love Takes a Holiday [3]; Naughty Naught [3] (C: Oakland, Ben; L: Drake, Milton); The Paper Says Rain [3] (C: Pokrass, Sam; L: Lief, May; Lief, Nat)

**Notes** [1] Not written for picture. [2] Moe Howard, Larry Fine and Jerry Howard. [3] Sheet music only.

## 5752 ✦ STARTING OVER
Paramount, 1979

**Musical Score** Hamlisch, Marvin
**Composer(s)** Hamlisch, Marvin
**Lyricist(s)** Sager, Carole Bayer

**Producer(s)** Pakula, Alan J.; Brooks, James L.
**Director(s)** Pakula, Alan J.
**Screenwriter(s)** Brooks, James L.
**Source(s)** Starting Over (novel) Wakefield, Dan

**Cast** Reynolds, Burt; Clayburgh, Jill; Bergen, Candice; Durning, Charles; Sternhagen, Frances; Pendleton, Austin; Place, Mary Kay; Dixon, MacIntyre; Sanders, Jay O.

**Song(s)** Easy for You; Better Than Ever; Starting Over; I Was Hoping

## 5753 ✦ STAR TREK IV: THE VOYAGE HOME
Paramount, 1986

**Musical Score** Rosenman, Leonard; Yellowjackets, The

**Producer(s)** Bennett, Harve
**Director(s)** Nimoy, Leonard
**Screenwriter(s)** Meerson, Steve; Krikes, Peter; Bennett, Harve; Meyer, Nicholas
**Source(s)** "Star Trek" (TV series) Roddenberry, Gene

**Cast** Nimoy, Leonard; Shatner, William; Kelley, DeForest; Doohan, James; Takei, George; Koenig, Walter; Nichols, Nichelle; Wyatt, Jane; Ellenstein, Robert; Schuck, John; Peters, Brock

**Song(s)** I Hate You (C/L: Thatcher, Kirk)

**Notes** No cue sheet available.

## 5754 ✦ STAR TREK V: THE FINAL FRONTIER
Paramount, 1989

**Musical Score** Goldsmith, Jerry

**Producer(s)** Bennett, Harve
**Director(s)** Shatner, William
**Screenwriter(s)** Loughery, David
**Source(s)** "Star Trek" (TV show) Roddenberry, Gene

**Cast** Shatner, William; Luckinbill, Laurence; Warner, David; Takei, George; Nichols, Nichelle; Koenig, Walter; Koohan, James; Kelley, DeForest; Nimoy, Leonard

**Song(s)** The Moon's a Window to Heaven (C: Goldsmith, Jerry; L: Bettis, John)

## 5755 ✦ STATE FAIR (1933)
Fox, 1933

**Producer(s)** King, Henry
**Director(s)** King, Henry
**Screenwriter(s)** Green, Paul; Levien, Sonya
**Source(s)** State Fair (novel) Strong, Philip

**Cast** Rogers, Will; Gaynor, Janet; Eilers, Sally; Ayres, Lew; Foster, Norman; Jory, Victor; Melton, Frank

**Song(s)** Shanty or Levee Song (C/L: Rycroft, Fred); Romantic [1] (C: DeFrancesco, Louis E.; L: Burton, Val; Jason, Will); Aunt Dinah Going North [2] (C/L: Rycroft, Fred)

**Notes** [1] Also in I LOVED YOU WEDNESDAY. [2] Not used.

## 5756 ✦ STATE FAIR (1945)
Twentieth Century–Fox, 1945

**Composer(s)** Rodgers, Richard
**Lyricist(s)** Hammerstein II, Oscar

**Producer(s)** Perlberg, William
**Director(s)** Lang, Walter
**Screenwriter(s)** Hammerstein II, Oscar
**Source(s)** State Fair (novel) Strong, Philip

**Cast** Crain, Jeanne [2]; Andrews, Dana; Haymes, Dick; Blaine, Vivian; Winninger, Charles; Bainter, Fay; Meek, Donald; McHugh, Frank; Kilbride, Percy; Morgan, Henry

**Song(s)** All I Owe Ioway; It's a Grand Night for Singing; It Might As Well Be Spring; Our State Fair;

Isn't It Kinda Fun?; We Will Be Together [1]; That's for Me; Kiss Me and Go Your Way [1]

**Notes** [1] Not used. [2] Dubbed by Loanne Hogan.

## 5757 ◆ STATE FAIR (1962)
### Twentieth Century–Fox, 1962

**Composer(s)** Rodgers, Richard
**Lyricist(s)** Hammerstein II, Oscar
**Choreographer(s)** Castle, Nick

**Producer(s)** Brackett, Charles
**Director(s)** Ferrer, Jose
**Screenwriter(s)** Breen, Richard L.

**Cast** Boone, Pat; Darin, Bobby; Tiffin, Pamela [2]; Ann-Margret; Ewell, Tom; Faye, Alice; Cox, Wally; Brandon, David; Harvey, Clem; Foulk, Robert; Henrich, Linda; Canutt, Edward Tap

**Song(s)** Our State Fair; That's for Me; More Than Just a Friend (Sweet Hog of Mine) (L: Rodgers, Richard); Isn't It Kinda Fun?; Never Say No to a Man (L: Rodgers, Richard); It's a Grand Night for Singing; This Isn't Heaven [1] (L: Rodgers, Richard); It's the Little Things in Texas (L: Rodgers, Richard); Willing and Eager (L: Rodgers, Richard); It Might As Well Be Spring

**Notes** A remake of STATE FAIR (1945). All songs with Hammerstein lyrics were written for the first film version. [1] Written for FLOWER DRUM SONG (movie version) but not used there. [2] Dubbed by Anita Gordon.

## 5758 ◆ STATION S.E.X.
### Paramount, 1929 unproduced

**Composer(s)** Rainger, Ralph
**Lyricist(s)** Robin, Leo

**Song(s)** Xylophone [1]; I Can't Go On This Way; Haunting My Heart; Too Coo-Coo Birds

**Notes** Intended as a Clara Bow vehicle. [1] Recorded.

## 5759 ◆ STATION WEST
### RKO, 1948

**Musical Score** Roemheld, Heinz
**Composer(s)** Harline, Leigh
**Lyricist(s)** Greene, Mort

**Producer(s)** Sparks, Robert
**Director(s)** Lanfield, Sidney
**Screenwriter(s)** Fenton, Frank; Miller, Winston
**Source(s)** *Station West* (novel) Short, Luke

**Cast** Powell, Dick; Greer, Jane; Moorehead, Agnes; Ives, Burl; Powers, Tom; Oliver, Gordon; Brodie, Steve; Williams, Guinn "Big Boy"; Burr, Raymond; Toomey, Regis

**Song(s)** The Sun Shining Warm (A Man Can't Grow Old); Sometime Remind Me to Tell You

## 5760 ◆ STAY AWAY, JOE
### Metro–Goldwyn–Mayer, 1968

**Musical Score** Marshall, Jack
**Composer(s)** Weisman, Ben
**Lyricist(s)** Wayne, Sid

**Producer(s)** Laurence, Douglas
**Director(s)** Tewksbury, Peter
**Screenwriter(s)** Hoey, Michael A.
**Source(s)** *Stay Away, Joe* (novel) Cushman, Dan

**Cast** Presley, Elvis; Meredith, Burgess; Jurado, Katy; Blondell, Joan; Gomez, Thomas; Jones, Henry; Dean, Quentin; Jones, I.Q.; Seymour, Anne

**Song(s)** Stay Away (C/L: Tepper, Sid; Bennett, Roy C.); Stay Away Joe; Dominic; All I Needed Was Rain

**Notes** STAY AWAY, JOE was also the basis for the Broadway musical WHOOP-UP.

## 5761 ◆ STAYING ALIVE
### Paramount, 1983

**Composer(s)** Gibb, Barry; Gibb, Maurice; Gibb, Robin [2]
**Lyricist(s)** Gibb, Barry; Gibb, Maurice; Gibb, Robin [2]

**Producer(s)** Stallone, Sylvester; Stigwood, Robert
**Director(s)** Stallone, Sylvester
**Screenwriter(s)** Stallone, Sylvester; Wexler, Norman

**Cast** Travolta, John; Rhodes, Cynthia; Hughes, Finola

**Song(s)** Far From Over [1] (C/L: Stallone, Frank; DiCola, Vince); The Woman in You [1]; Look Out for Number One (C/L: Foster, Bruce Stephen; Marolda, Tom); Breakout [1]; Devils and Seducers [1] (C/L: Wright, Dori; Wright, Gary); I Love You Too Much [1]; Hope We Never Change (C/L: Stallone, Frank; DiCola, Vince; Esposito, Joseph); Waking Up (C/L: Stallone, Frank; DiCola, Vince; Colatrella, Arthur); Life Goes On [1]; Moody Girl [1] (C/L: Stallone, Frank; DiCola, Vince; Esposito, Joseph); Finding Out the Hard Way (C/L: Stallone, Frank; Freeland, Roy); Someone Belonging to Someone [1]; (We Dance) So Close to the Fire [1] (C/L: Bishop, Randy; Faragher, Tommy); I'm Never Gonna Give You Up [1] (C/L: Stallone, Frank; DiCola, Vince; Esposito, Joseph); The Winning End [1] (C/L: Stallone, Frank; DiCola, Vince; Esposito, Joseph); Stayin' Alive [1] [2]

**Notes** [1] Background vocal only. [2] Also in SATURDAY NIGHT FEVER. [3] Known as the Bee Gees.

## 5762 ◆ STEALING HOME
### Warner Brothers, 1988

**Musical Score** Foster, David W.

**Producer(s)** Mount, Thom; Moonjean, Hank
**Director(s)** Kampmann, Steven; Aldis, Will
**Screenwriter(s)** Kampmann, Steven; Aldis, Will

Cast Harmon, Mark; Brown, Blair; Silverman, Jonathan; Ramis, Harold; McNamara, William; Jenkins, Richard; Shea, John; Foster, Jodie; Ross, Ted

**Song(s)** And When She Danced (C/L: Foster, David; Thompson-Jenner, Linda)

**Notes** No cue sheet available.

## 5763 ✦ STEAMBOAT ON THE RIVER
Twentieth Century–Fox, 1944

**Song(s)** Negro Cabin Song (C: DeFrancesco, Louis E.; L: Unknown); Pickin' Cotton [2] (C/L: Wellseley, Grant; O'Keefe, Lester); Cabin Dance [1] (C: Henderson, Ray)

**Notes** This is a Lowell Thomas Magic Carpet of Movietone travelogue. [1] Also in GEORGE WHITE'S SCANDALS OF 1934. The cue sheet indicates there might have been lyrics. [2] Also in MODERN DIXIE.

## 5764 ✦ STEAMBOAT ROUND THE BEND
Fox, 1935

**Musical Score** Kaylin, Samuel

**Producer(s)** Wurtzel, Sol M.
**Director(s)** Ford, John
**Screenwriter(s)** Nichols, Dudley; Trotti, Lamar
**Source(s)** *Steamboat Round the Bend* (novel) Burman, Ben Lucien

**Cast** Rogers, Will; Shirley, Anne; Cobb, Irvin S.

**Song(s)** Steamboat Round the Bend (C: Levant, Oscar; L: Clare, Sidney); Eagle Builds His Nest On High (C/L: Burman, Ben Lucien)); Down with Demon Rum [1] (C: Mockridge, Cyril J.; L: Trotti, Lamar; Nichols, Dudley)

## 5765 ✦ STEAMING
New World, 1986

**Musical Score** Harvey, Richard

**Producer(s)** Mills, Paul
**Director(s)** Losey, Joseph
**Screenwriter(s)** Losey, Patricia
**Source(s)** *Steaming* (play) Dunn, Nell

**Cast** Redgrave, Vanessa; Miles, Sarah; Dors, Diana; Love, Patti; Bruce, Brenda; Dean, Felicity; Sagoe, Sally; Tzelniker, Anna

**Song(s)** Steaming (C: Harvey, Richard; L: Bexter, Robin Ellis)

**Notes** No cue sheet available.

## 5766 ✦ THE STEEL TRAP
Twentieth Century–Fox, 1952

**Musical Score** Tiomkin, Dimitri

**Producer(s)** Friedlob, Bert
**Director(s)** Stone, Andrew L.
**Screenwriter(s)** Stone, Andrew L.

Cast Cotten, Joseph; Wright, Teresa; Marr, Eddie; Towne, Aline; Hale, Jonathan

**Song(s)** You Mean So Much to Me (C: Tiomkin, Dimitri; L: Jones, Stan)

## 5767 ✦ STEELYARD BLUES
Warner Brothers, 1973

**Musical Score** Shire, David
**Composer(s)** Gravenites, Nick; Bloomfield, Michael
**Lyricist(s)** Gravenites, Nick; Bloomfield, Michael

**Producer(s)** Bill, Tony; Phillips, Michael; Phillips, Julia
**Director(s)** Myerson, Alan
**Screenwriter(s)** Ward, David S.

**Cast** Fonda, Jane; Sutherland, Donald; Boyle, Peter; Goodrow, Gordon; Hesseman, Howard; Savage, John; Schaal, Richard

**Song(s)** If You Cared; Being Different; Walkin' Man Blues; Theme from Steelyard Blues; My Bag; Brand New Family; Woman's Love; Lonesome Star Blues (C/L: Muldaur, Maria); Headlines; Common Ground; Swing with It [1]

**Notes** All the others are background vocals. [1] Background instrumental.

## 5768 ✦ THE STEPFATHER
Vista, 1987

**Musical Score** Moraz, Patrick

**Producer(s)** Benson, Jay
**Director(s)** Ruben, Joseph
**Screenwriter(s)** Westlake, Donald E.

**Cast** O'Quinn, Terry; Schoelen, Jill; Hack, Shelly; Lanyer, Charles

**Song(s)** Run Between the Raindrops (C/L: Granbacher, M.; Geraldo, N.); Sleeping Beauty (C/L: Amphlett, C.; McEntee, M.); Overload (C/L: Moraz, Patrick; McBurne, John); I Want You (C: Moraz, Patrick; McBurne, John)

**Notes** No cue sheet available.

## 5769 ✦ STEPHEN KING'S SILVER BULLET

See SILVER BULLET.

## 5770 ✦ STEP LIVELY
RKO, 1944

**Composer(s)** Styne, Jule
**Lyricist(s)** Cahn, Sammy
**Choreographer(s)** Matray, Ernst

**Producer(s)** Fellows, Robert
**Director(s)** Whelan, Tim
**Screenwriter(s)** Duff, Warren; Milne, Peter

**Source(s)**   *Room Service* (play) Murray, John; Boretz, Allen

**Cast**   Sinatra, Frank; Murphy, George; Menjou, Adolphe; De Haven, Gloria; Slezak, Walter; Pallette, Eugene; Brown, Wally; Carney, Alan; Mitchell, Grant; Jeffreys, Anne

**Song(s)**   Where Does Love Begin and Where Does Friendship End; As Long As There's Music; Come Out, Come Out Wherever You Are; Some Other Time; Why Must There Be an Op'ning Song; And Then You Kissed Me; Ask the Madame

**Notes**   Originally titled MANHATTAN SERENADE.

## 5771 ◆ STEP LIVELY JEEVES
Twentieth Century–Fox, 1937

**Producer(s)**   Stone, John
**Director(s)**   Forde, Eugene
**Screenwriter(s)**   Fenton, Frank; Root, Lynn

**Cast**   Treacher, Arthur; Ellis, Patricia; Kent, Robert; Dinehart, Alan; Givot, George; Pangborn, Franklin

**Song(s)**   Hunt Song (C/L: Kernell, William; Mojica, Jose; Sanders, Troy)

## 5772 ◆ STEPPING OUT
Metro–Goldwyn–Mayer, 1931

**Director(s)**   Riesner, Charles F.
**Screenwriter(s)**   Harris, Elmer; Hopkins, Robert E.

**Cast**   Greenwood, Charlotte; Denny, Reginald; Bond, Lillian; Hyams, Leila; Edwards, Cliff

**Song(s)**   Just Like Frankie and Johnnie (C/L: Raskin, Willie; Kahal, Irving; Waggner, George)

**Notes**   The song is attributed to Robinson on cue sheets and credits above in script.

## 5773 ◆ STEPPING SISTERS
Fox, 1932

**Director(s)**   Felix, Seymour; Collier Sr., William
**Screenwriter(s)**   Conselman, William
**Source(s)**   *Stepping Sisters* (play) Comstock, H.W.

**Cast**   Dresser, Louise; Gombell, Minna; Collier Sr., William; Howland, Jobyna

**Song(s)**   Look Here Comes a Rainbow (C/L: Hanley, James F.); My World Begins and Ends with You [1] (C/L: Hanley, James F.)

**Notes**   [1] Sheet music only.

## 5774 ◆ STEPPIN' IN SOCIETY
Republic, 1945

**Producer(s)**   Bercholz, Joseph
**Director(s)**   Esway, Alexander
**Screenwriter(s)**   Ropes, Bradford

**Source(s)**   *Extenuating Circumstances* (novel) Arnac, Marcel

**Cast**   Horton, Edward Everett; George, Gladys; Terry, Ruth; Livingston, Robert; LaRue, Jack; Lane, Lola

**Song(s)**   If You Like Me then I'll Like You (C/L: Elliott, Jack)

## 5775 ◆ THE STERILE CUCKOO
Paramount, 1969

**Musical Score**   Karlin, Fred

**Producer(s)**   Pakula, Alan J.
**Director(s)**   Pakula, Alan J.
**Screenwriter(s)**   Sargent, Alvin
**Source(s)**   *The Sterile Cuckoo* (novel) Nichols, John

**Cast**   Minnelli, Liza; Burton, Wendell; McIntire, Tim

**Song(s)**   Come Saturday Morning [1] (C: Karlin, Fred; L: Previn, Dory)

**Notes**   [1] Background vocal only.

## 5776 ◆ STEWARDESS SCHOOL
Columbia, 1986

**Musical Score**   Folk, Robert

**Producer(s)**   Feldman, Phil
**Director(s)**   Blancato, Ken
**Screenwriter(s)**   Blancato, Ken

**Cast**   Frederick, Vicki; Most, Donald; Cullen, Brett; Pulsen, Rob; Bergman, Sandahl; Cadorette, Mary

**Song(s)**   Stew School (C/L: Folk, Robert; Blancato, Ken); Wine You, Dine You (C/L: Blancato, Ken)

## 5777 ◆ STICK
Universal, 1985

**Musical Score**   De Vorzon, Barry; Conlan, Joseph

**Producer(s)**   Lang, Jennings
**Director(s)**   Reynolds, Burt
**Screenwriter(s)**   Leonard, Elmore; Stinson, Joseph C.
**Source(s)**   *Stick* (novel) Leonard, Elmore

**Cast**   Reynolds, Burt; Bergen, Candice; Segal, George; Durning, Charles; Lawson, Richard; Robinson, Dar; Rocco, Alex

**Song(s)**   You Know What I Like (C/L: Nevil, Robert); I Don't Think I'm Ready for You (C/L: Dorff, Stephen H.; Brown, Milton; Reynolds, Burt; Garrett, Snuff)

## 5778 ◆ STICK TO YOUR GUNS
Paramount, 1941

**Producer(s)**   Sherman, Harry
**Director(s)**   Selander, Lesley
**Screenwriter(s)**   Cheney, J. Benton

**Cast**    Boyd, William; King, Brad; Clyde, Andy; Holt, Jacqueline

**Song(s)**    My Kind of Country (C: McHugh, Jimmy; L: Loesser, Frank); On the Strings of My Guitar (C/L: Burnette, Smiley); Got a Gal in Californ-I-A; Blue Moon on the Silver Sage [2] (C: Stept, Sam H.; L: Freed, Ralph); A Rendezvous with a Dream [1] (C: Rainger, Ralph; L: Robin, Leo)

**Notes**    [1] Not used. Used in POPPY and ALONG CAME LOVE. [2] Sheet music credits Smiley Burnette.

## 5779 ◆ STICKY FINGERS
### Spectrafilm, 1988

**Musical Score**    Chang, Gary

**Producer(s)**    Adams, Catlin; Mayron, Melanie
**Director(s)**    Adams, Catlin
**Screenwriter(s)**    Adams, Catlin; Mayron, Melanie

**Cast**    Slater, Helen; Mayron, Melanie; Shaw, Adam; Vance, Danitra; Stoler, Shirley; Brennan, Eileen; Kane, Carol; Devine, Loretta; Guest, Christopher; McHattie, Stephen

**Song(s)**    Sticky Fingers (C/L: Cornell, Allison)

**Notes**    No cue sheet available.

## 5780 ◆ STILETTO
### Avco Embassy, 1969

**Musical Score**    Ramin, Sid

**Producer(s)**    Rosemont, Norman
**Director(s)**    Kowalski, Bernard L.
**Screenwriter(s)**    Russell, A.J.

**Cast**    Cord, Alex; Ekland, Britt; O'Neal, Patrick; Wiseman, Joseph; McNair, Barbara; Dehner, John; Vandis, Titos; Ciannelli, Eduardo; Scheider, Roy; Tolkan, James

**Song(s)**    Sugar in the Rain (C: Ramin, Sid; L: Bergman, Marilyn; Bergman, Alan)

**Notes**    No cue sheet available.

## 5781 ◆ STINGAREE
### RKO, 1934

**Composer(s)**    Steiner, Max
**Lyricist(s)**    Eliscu, Edward

**Producer(s)**    Stone, John
**Director(s)**    Forde, Eugene
**Screenwriter(s)**    Gardiner, Becky
**Source(s)**    stories by Hornung, E.W.

**Cast**    Dunne, Irene; Dix, Richard; Boland, Mary; Tearle, Conway; Devine, Andy; Stephenson, Henry; O'Connor, Una; Owen, Reginald; Pollard, Snub; Barraud, George

**Song(s)**    Rose of the Stingaree (C: Harling, Franke; L: Kahn, Gus); I Wish I Were a Fisherman [1]; Tonight Is Mine (C: Harling, W. Franke; L: Kahn, Gus); Once You're Mine

**Notes**    [1] Also in BEHIND THE HEADLINES.

## 5782 ◆ STINGRAY

See CORVETTE SUMMER.

## 5783 ◆ STIR CRAZY
### Columbia, 1980

**Musical Score**    Scott, Tom
**Composer(s)**    Masser, Michael
**Lyricist(s)**    Goodrum, Randy

**Producer(s)**    Weinstein, Hannah
**Director(s)**    Poitier, Sidney
**Screenwriter(s)**    Friedman, Bruce Jay

**Cast**    Wilder, Gene; Pryor, Richard; Brown, George Stanford; Williams, Jobeth; Suarez, Miguelangel; Nelson, Craig T.; Corbin, Barry; Coster, Nicolas

**Song(s)**    Crazy; Love; Nothing Can Stop Us Now; Eat Your Heart Out (C: Scott, Tom; L: Preston, Rob); Watch Her Dance (C: Scott, Tom; L: Preston, Rob); The Love of a Cowboy (C: Scott, Tom; L: Preston, Rob)

**Notes**    No cue sheet available.

## 5784 ◆ STOLEN HARMONY
### Paramount, 1935

**Composer(s)**    Revel, Harry
**Lyricist(s)**    Gordon, Mack

**Producer(s)**    Lewis, Albert
**Director(s)**    Werker, Alfred
**Screenwriter(s)**    Gordon, Leon; Ruskin, Harry; Foster, Lewis R.; Binyon, Claude

**Cast**    Raft, George; Ben Bernie and His Band; Bradley, Grace

**Song(s)**    Would There Be Love? [3]; Fagin You'se Is a Viper; Stay As Sweet As You Are [5]; Let's Spill the Beans; With My Eyes Wide Open I'm Dreaming [6]; Bradley's Dance [2]; I Never Had a Man to Cry Over [1]; Stolen Harmony [4] (C/L: Lawrence, Jack; Altman, Arthur; Young, Joe)

**Notes**    There is also a vocal of "Hearts and Flowers" by Mary D. Brine and Theodore Moses Tobani. [1] Not used. [2] Instrumental use only. [3] Originally written for LOVE IN BLOOM but not used. [4] Written for exploitation only. [5] Also used in COLLEGE RHYTHM, COLLEGIATE and RUMBA. [6] Also in COLLEGIATE, ONE HOUR LATE and SHOOT THE WORKS.

## 5785 ✦ STOLEN HEAVEN
Paramount, 1938

**Choreographer(s)**   Prinz, LeRoy

**Producer(s)**   Stone, Andrew L.
**Director(s)**   Stone, Andrew L.
**Screenwriter(s)**   Greene, Eve; Jackson, Frederick

**Cast**   Raymond, Gene; Bradna, Olympe; Stone, Lewis; Farrell, Glenda

**Song(s)**   Boys in the Band (C: Sherwin, Manning; L: Loesser, Frank); Hate to Talk About Myself [3] (C: Rainger, Ralph; Whiting, Richard A.; L: Robin, Leo); Stolen Heaven [1] [2] (C: Hollander, Frederick; L: Freed, Ralph); Love Doesn't Grow on Trees [1] [4] (C: Lane, Burton; L: Freed, Ralph); Woe Is Me [1] (C: Boutelje, Phil; L: Myers, Henry); Born to Swing [1] (C: Lane, Burton; L: Freed, Ralph); Bells Are Ringing [1] (C: Unknown; L: Freed, Ralph)

**Notes**   Formerly titled DREAM OF LOVE and STRANGE FASCINATION. [1] Not used. [2] Published though not used. [3] Written for the unproduced film SAILOR BEWARE (1936) without the Rainger credit, and used in FOUR HOURS TO KILL. [4] Used in A SONG IS BORN.

## 5786 ✦ STOLEN HOURS
United Artists, 1963

**Musical Score**   Lindsey, Mort

**Producer(s)**   Holt, Denis
**Director(s)**   Petrie, Daniel
**Screenwriter(s)**   West, Jessamyn
**Source(s)**   *Dark Victory* (play) Brewer Jr., George Emerson; Block, Bertram

**Cast**   Hayward, Susan; Craig, Michael; Baker, Diane; Judd, Edward

**Song(s)**   Stolen Hours (C: Lindsey, Mort; L: Keith, Marilyn [1]; Bergman, Alan)

**Notes**   No cue sheet available. [1] Later known as Marilyn Bergman.

## 5787 ✦ THE STONE BOY
Twentieth Century–Fox, 1984

**Musical Score**   Horner, James

**Producer(s)**   Roth, Joe; Bloch, Ivan
**Director(s)**   Cain, Christopher
**Screenwriter(s)**   Berriault, Gina

**Cast**   Duvall, Robert; Presson, Jason; Close, Glenn; Cain, Dean; Forrest, Frederic; Fisher, Cindy

**Song(s)**   Baby, You're So Young (C/L: Nutter, Mayf); Jamboree in the Hills (C/L: Nutter, Mayf)

**Notes**   No cue sheet available.

## 5788 ✦ THE STOOGE
Paramount, 1951

**Producer(s)**   Wallis, Hal B.
**Director(s)**   Taurog, Norman
**Screenwriter(s)**   Finklehoffe, Fred F.; Rackin, Martin

**Cast**   Martin, Dean; Lewis, Jerry; Bergen, Polly; Marshall, Marion; Mayehoff, Eddie; Erdman, Richard; Bavier, Frances

**Song(s)**   A Girl Named Mary and a Boy Named Bill (C: Livingston, Jerry; L: David, Mack)

**Notes**   Vocals of "I Feel Like a Feather in the Breeze" and "With My Eyes Wide Open I'm Dreaming" by Harry Revel and Mack Gordon; "Lover" by Richard Rodgers and Lorenz Hart; "I'm Yours" by Johnny Green and E.Y. Harburg; "Who's Your Little Who-Zis" by Walter Hirsch, Ben Bernie and Al Goering; "I Feel a Song Comin' On" by Dorothy Fields, Jimmy McHugh and George Oppenheimer and "Just One More Chance" by Sam Coslow and Arthur Johnston are also in the picture.

## 5789 ✦ STOP! LOOK! AND LAUGH!
Columbia, 1960

**Producer(s)**   Romm, Harry
**Director(s)**   White, Jules
**Screenwriter(s)**   Adler, Felix [1]

**Cast**   Winchell, Paul; Mahoney, Jerry; Smiff, Knucklehead; The Three Stooges; The Marquis Chimps

**Song(s)**   Stop, Look and Laugh (C: Duning, George; L: Styne, Stanley); Busy Busy Me (C/L: Kuller, Sid); Happy Happy (C/L: Kuller, Sid)

**Notes**   This consists of previously released Three Stooges material along with new continuity and narration by Paul Winchell and his dummies, Jerry Mahoney and Knucklehead Smiff. [1] Ten other writers also contributed to the original Stooges' material.

## 5790 ✦ STOP, LOOK AND LOVE
Twentieth Century–Fox, 1939

**Producer(s)**   Wurtzel, Sol M.
**Director(s)**   Brower, Otto
**Screenwriter(s)**   Tarshis, Harold; Cowan, Sada

**Cast**   Rogers, Jean; Frawley, William; Kellard, Robert; Gombell, Minna

**Song(s)**   Let's Start Where We Left Off (C: Styne, Jule; L: Clare, Sidney)

## 5791 ✦ STOPOVER TOKYO
Twentieth Century–Fox, 1957

**Musical Score**   Sawtell, Paul

**Producer(s)**   Reisch, Walter
**Director(s)**   Breen, Richard L.

**Screenwriter(s)** Breen, Richard L.; Reisch, Walter
**Source(s)** *Stopover Tokyo* (novel) Marquand, J.P.

**Cast** Wagner, Robert; Collins, Joan; O'Brien, Edmond; Scott, Ken; Keating, Larry; Oyama, Keiko

**Song(s)** Jyan Ken Pon (C/L: Shindo, Tak)

## 5792 ✦ STOP THE WORLD—I WANT TO GET OFF
Warner Brothers, 1966

**Composer(s)** Bricusse, Leslie; Newley, Anthony
**Lyricist(s)** Bricusse, Leslie; Newley, Anthony

**Producer(s)** Sargent, Bill
**Director(s)** Saville, Philip
**Screenwriter(s)** Bricusse, Leslie; Newley, Anthony
**Source(s)** *Stop the World—I Want to Get Off* (musical) Bricusse, Leslie; Newley, Anthony

**Cast** Tanner, Tony; Martin, Millicent; Croft, Leila; Croft, Valerie; Hawley, Neil; Allan, Georgina; Ashton, Natasha; Barrow, Carlotta

**Song(s)** A.B.C. Song; I Wanna Be Rich; Typically English; Lumbered; Glorious Russian; Meilinki Meilchick; Typically Japanese (L: Bricusse, Leslie; Newley, Anthony; Donabie, David); Family Fugue; Nag, Nag, Nag; All American; Gonna Build a Mountain; Mumbo Jumbo; Once in a Lifetime; Someone Nice Like You; I Believed It All [1] (C: Ham, Al; L: Bergman, Marilyn; Bergman, Alan)

**Notes** All songs but "Typically Japanese" and "I Believed It All" are from the stage musical. [1]1 Also in HARLOW (Carol Lynley version).

## 5793 ✦ STOP, YOU'RE KILLING ME
Warner Brothers, 1952

**Musical Score** Buttolph, David
**Composer(s)** Sigman, Carl
**Lyricist(s)** Hilliard, Bob

**Producer(s)** Edelman, Louis F.
**Director(s)** Del Ruth, Roy
**Screenwriter(s)** O'Hanlon, James
**Source(s)** *A Slight Case of Murder* (play) Runyon, Damon; Lindsay, Howard

**Cast** Crawford, Broderick; Trevor, Claire; Gibson, Virginia; Hayes, Bill; Cantor, Charlie; Leonard, Sheldon; Vitale, Joseph; St. John, Howard; Morgan, Henry; Dumont, Margaret

**Song(s)** Stop, You're Killing Me; My Ever-Lovin'; Do You Think I Came Here for My Health [1]; Don't Make Faces [1]; Making a Play for Love [1]; A Tap on the Shoulder and a Guilty Conscience [1]

**Notes** A remake of A SLIGHT CASE OF MURDER (1938). "Let the Rest of the World Go By" by Ernest R. Ball and J. Keirn Brennan and "Baby Face" by Benny Davis and Harry Akst are also used as vocal visuals. [1] Used instrumentally only.

## 5794 ✦ THE STORK CLUB
Paramount, 1945

**Choreographer(s)** Daniels, Billy

**Producer(s)** DeSylva, B.G.
**Director(s)** Walker, Hal
**Screenwriter(s)** McGowan, Jack; DeSylva, B.G.

**Cast** Hutton, Betty; Fitzgerald, Barry; DeFore, Don; Benchley, Robert; Goodwin, Bill; Adrian, Iris; Rasumny, Mikhail

**Song(s)** Doctor, Lawyer, Indian Chief (C: Carmichael, Hoagy; L: Webster, Paul Francis); I'm a Square in the Social Circle (C/L: Livingston, Jay; Evans, Ray); If I Had a Dozen Hearts (C: Revel, Harry; L: Webster, Paul Francis); Love Me (C: Styne, Jule; L: Cahn, Sammy)

**Notes** Also contains a vocal of Harry Williams and Egbert Van Alstyne's "In the Shade of the Old Apple Tree."

## 5795 ✦ STORM AT DAYBREAK
Metro–Goldwyn–Mayer, 1933

**Musical Score** Axt, William

**Producer(s)** Hubbard, Lucien
**Director(s)** Boleslawski, Richard
**Screenwriter(s)** Millhauser, Bertram
**Source(s)** *Black-Stemmed Cherries* (play) Hunyady, Sandor

**Cast** Francis, Kay; Asther, Nils; Huston, Walter; Holmes, Phillips; Pallette, Eugene; Hale, Louise Closser; Parker, Jean

**Song(s)** I Will Be a Soldier Bride (C: Axt, William; L: Kahn, Gus)

## 5796 ✦ STORM FEAR
United Artists, 1955

**Musical Score** Bernstein, Elmer

**Producer(s)** Wilde, Cornel
**Director(s)** Wilde, Cornel
**Screenwriter(s)** Foote, Horton
**Source(s)** *Storm Fear* (novel) Seeley, Clinton

**Cast** Wallace, Jean; Duryea, Dan; Wilde, Cornel; Stollery, David; Grant, Lee; Hill, Steven; Weaver, Dennis

**Song(s)** Storm Fear [1] (C: Bernstein, Elmer; L: Brooks, Jack)

**Notes** [1] Used instrumentally only.

## 5797 ✦ STORMY WEATHER
Twentieth Century–Fox, 1943

**Choreographer(s)** Robinson, Charles

**Producer(s)** LeBaron, William
**Director(s)** Stone, Andrew L.
**Screenwriter(s)** Koehler, Ted; Jackson, Frederick

**Cast** Horne, Lena; Robinson, Bill; Cab Calloway and His Band; Katherine Dunham and her Troupe; Waller, Thomas "Fats"; The Nicholas Brothers; Brown, Ada; Wilson, Dooley; The Tramp Band; Wallace, Babe; Whitman, Ernest; Singleton, Zutty

**Song(s)** Rang Tang Tang [1] (C: Mockridge, Cyril J.; L: Robinson, Bill); Dah, Dat, Dah [1] (C: Mockridge, Cyril J.; L: Robinson, Bill); My, My, Ain't That Something (C/L: Tomlin, Pinky); There's No Two Ways About Love (C: Johnson, James P.; L: Mills, Irving); Patter [2] (C: Newman, Lionel; L: Koehler, Ted)

**Notes** Vocals include "Linda Brown" by Al Cowans; "That Ain't Right" by Nat "King" Cole and Irving Mills; "Ain't Misbehavin'" by Thomas "Fats" Waller and Harry Brooks; "Diga Diga Do" and "I Can't Give You Anything but Love" by Jimmy McHugh and Dorothy Fields; "African Dance" by Clarence Muse and Connie Bemis; "I Lost My Sugar in Salt Lake City" by Leon Rene; "Geechy Joe" by Cab Calloway, Jack Palmer and Andy Gibson; "Stormy Weather" by Harold Arlen and Ted Koehler; "The Jumpin' Jive" by Cab Calloway, Jack Palmer and Frank Froeba and an instrumental of "Rhythm Cocktail" by Cab Calloway, Illinois Jaquet and Buster Harding. Recorded but not used are "Good for Nothin' Joe" by Rube Bloom and Ted Koehler and "Sunday in Savannah." [1] These "songs" consisted of the words of their titles repeated as Bill Robinson tap danced. Later Mockridge added the music score over the dialogue and dancing. [2] This patter appeared between Calloway and Robinson before Horne sang "There's No Two Ways About Love."

## 5798 ◆ STORY CONFERENCE
### Warner Brothers–Vitaphone Pictures, 1934

**Composer(s)** Hess, Cliff
**Lyricist(s)** Hess, Cliff

**Cast** Roth, Lillian

**Song(s)** Working in the Movies; Alimony Sal; My Man Blues; If I Were a Millionaire; Down the Old Back Road (C/L: Hupfeld, Herman)

**Notes** Short subject. Also titled LILLIAN ROTH IN STORY CONFERENCE.

## 5799 ◆ THE STORY OF ALEXANDER GRAHAM BELL
### Twentieth Century–Fox, 1939

**Producer(s)** Zanuck, Darryl F.
**Director(s)** Cummings, Irving
**Screenwriter(s)** Trotti, Lamar

**Cast** Ameche, Don; Young, Loretta; Fonda, Henry; Coburn, Charles; Lockhart, Gene; Byington, Spring; Blane, Sally; Young, Polly Ann; Davenport, Harry; Hicks, Russell

**Song(s)** Call Me Pet Names [1] (C/L: Harris, H.R.)

**Notes** [1] Not written for this film.

## 5800 ◆ STORY OF A TEENAGER

See JIM, THE WORLD'S GREATEST.

## 5801 ◆ THE STORY OF A WOMAN
### Universal, 1970

**Musical Score** Williams, John

**Producer(s)** Bercovici, Leonardo
**Director(s)** Bercovici, Leonardo
**Screenwriter(s)** Bercovici, Leonardo

**Cast** Andersson, Bibi; Stack, Robert; Farentino, James; Girardot, Annie; Nascimbene, Mario

**Song(s)** Uno Di Qua L'Altra Di La (C: Williams, John; L: Amurri, Antonio); Skyll Inte Ta Mej Efterat Bara (C/L: Wallin, Bengt-Arne; Lindroth, Bjorn)

## 5802 ◆ THE STORY OF G.I. JOE
### United Artists, 1945

**Musical Score** Ronell, Ann; Applebaum, Louis
**Composer(s)** Ronell, Ann
**Lyricist(s)** Ronell, Ann

**Producer(s)** Cowan, Lester
**Director(s)** Wellman, William A.
**Screenwriter(s)** Atlas, Leopold; Endore, Guy; Stevenson, Philip

**Cast** Meredith, Burgess; Mitchum, Robert; Steele, Freddie; Cassell, Wally; Lloyd, Jimmy; Reilly, Jack; Murphy, Bill; Self, William

**Song(s)** Linda (C: L: Lawrence, Jack); I'm Coming Back; Infantry March

**Notes** No cue sheet available.

## 5803 ◆ THE STORY OF RUTH
### Twentieth Century–Fox, 1960

**Musical Score** Waxman, Franz

**Producer(s)** Engel, Samuel G.
**Director(s)** Koster, Henry
**Screenwriter(s)** Corwin, Norman

**Cast** Whitman, Stuart; Tryon, Tom; Wood, Peggy; Lindfors, Viveca; Morrow, Jeff; Eden, Elana

**Song(s)** The Song of Ruth [1] (C: Waxman, Franz; L: Webster, Paul Francis)

## 5804 ◆ STORY OF THREE LOVES
### Metro–Goldwyn–Mayer, 1953

**Musical Score** Rozsa, Miklos
**Choreographer(s)** Ashton, Frederick

**Producer(s)** Franklin, Sidney
**Director(s)** Reinhardt, Gottfried; Minnelli, Vincente; Reinhardt, Gottfried
**Screenwriter(s)** Collier, John; Lustig, Jan; Froeschel, George

**Cast**  Angeli, Pier; Barrymore, Ethel; Caron, Leslie; Douglas, Kirk; Granger, Farley; Mason, James; Shearer, Moira; Moorehead, Agnes; Nelson, Ricky; Gabor, Zsa Zsa; Anderson, Richard

**Song(s)**  Dark Is the Night (C'est Fini) [1] (C: Brodszky, Nicholas; L: Cahn, Sammy)

**Notes**  [1] Also in RICH, YOUNG AND PRETTY.

### 5805 ✦ THE STORY OF VERNON AND IRENE CASTLE
RKO, 1939

**Choreographer(s)**  Pan, Hermes

**Producer(s)**  Haight, George
**Director(s)**  Potter, H.C.
**Screenwriter(s)**  Sherman, Richard
**Source(s)**  "My Husband and My Memories of Vernon Castle" (stories) Castle, Irene

**Cast**  Astaire, Fred; Rogers, Ginger; Oliver, Edna May; Brennan, Walter; Fields, Lew; Girardot, Etienne; Beecher, Janet; Kinskey, Leonid; Sedan, Rolfe

**Song(s)**  Only When You're in My Arms (C: Ruby, Harry; L: Conrad, Con; Kalmar, Bert)

**Notes**  Vocals also included "Oh, You Beautiful Doll" by Nat D. Ayer and A. Seymour Brown; "Glow Worm" by Paul Lincke and Lilla Robinson; "By the Beautiful Sea" by Harry Carroll and Harold Atteridge; "Row Row Row" by James V. Monaco and William Jerome; "The Yama Yama Man" by Karl Hoschna and Collin Davis; "Come Josephine in My Flying Machine" by Fred Fisher and Alfred Bryan; "Cuddle Up a Little Closer" by Karl Hoschna and Otto Harbach; "While They Were Dancing Around" by James V. Monaco and Joseph McCarthy; "Waiting for the Robert E. Lee" by Lewis F. Muir and L. Wolfe Gilbert; "The Darktown Strutters Ball" by Shelton Brooks; "Hello! Hello! Who's Your Lady Friend?" by Harry Fragson and Worton David; "It's a Long Way to Tipperary" by Jack Judge and Harry Williams; "Take Me Back to New York Town" by Harry Von Tilzer and Andrew B. Sterling; "Way Down Yonder in New Orleans" by Henry Cremer and Turner Layton and "Chicago" by Fred Fisher.

### 5806 ✦ STOWAWAY
Twentieth Century–Fox, 1936

**Composer(s)**  Revel, Harry
**Lyricist(s)**  Gordon, Mack

**Producer(s)**  DeSylva, B.G.
**Director(s)**  Seiter, William A.
**Screenwriter(s)**  Conselman, William; Sheekman, Arthur; Perrin, Nat

**Cast**  Temple, Shirley; Young, Robert; Faye, Alice; Pallette, Eugene; Westley, Helen; Treacher, Arthur; Bromberg, J. Edward; Allwyn, Astrid; Lane, Allan; Ahn, Philip

**Song(s)**  Goodnight My Love; You've Gotta S-M-I-L-E to be H-A-Double-P-Y; I Wanna Go to the Zoo; One Never Knows Does One; That's What I Want for Christmas (C: Marks, Gerald; L: Caesar, Irving); A Dreamland Choo-Choo to Lullaby Town [1]

**Notes**  There is also a brief vocal of "Please" by Ralph Rainger and Leo Robin [1] Not used.

### 5807 ✦ STRAIGHT IS THE WAY
Metro–Goldwyn–Mayer, 1934

**Musical Score**  Axt, William

**Producer(s)**  Hubbard, Lucien
**Director(s)**  Sloane, Paul
**Screenwriter(s)**  Schubert, Bernard
**Source(s)**  (play) Burnet, Dana; Abbott, George

**Cast**  Tone, Franchot; Morley, Karen; Robson, May; George, Gladys; LaRue, Jack; Pendleton, Nat

**Song(s)**  A Hundred Years from Today (C: Young, Victor; L: Washington, Ned; Young, Joe)

**Notes**  A remake of FOUR WALLS.

### 5808 ✦ STRAIGHT, PLACE AND SHOW
Twentieth Century–Fox, 1938

**Composer(s)**  Pollack, Lew
**Lyricist(s)**  Brown, Lew
**Choreographer(s)**  Castle, Nick; Sawyer, Geneva

**Producer(s)**  Zanuck, Darryl F.
**Director(s)**  Butler, David
**Screenwriter(s)**  Musselman, M.M.; Rivkin, Allen
**Source(s)**  *Saratoga Chips* (play) Runyon, Damon; Caesar, Irving

**Cast**  The Ritz Brothers; Arlen, Richard; Merman, Ethel; Brooks, Phyllis; Barbier, George; Blackmer, Sidney; Stanton, Will; Gargan, Edward

**Song(s)**  With You on My Mind; International Cowboys (C/L: Styne, Jule; Kuller, Sid; Golden, Ray); Why Not String Along with Me

**Notes**  Titled THEY'RE OFF overseas.

### 5809 ✦ STRAIGHT TIME
Warner Brothers, 1978

**Musical Score**  Shire, David

**Producer(s)**  Beck, Stanley; Zinnemann, Tim
**Director(s)**  Grosbard, Ulu
**Screenwriter(s)**  Sargent, Alvin; Bunker, Edward; Boan, Jeffrey
**Source(s)**  *No Beast So Fierce* (novel) Bunker, Edward

**Cast**  Hoffman, Dustin; Russell, Theresa; Busey, Gary; Stanton, Harry Dean; Walsh, M. Emmet; Taggart, Rita; Bates, Kathy; Baron, Sandy

**Song(s)** Two of Us (C: Shire, David; L: Helms, Norma); Doin' Fine [1] (C: Shire, David; L: Helms, Norma)

**Notes** [1] Not on cue sheet.

## 5810 ✦ STRANDED IN PARIS

See ARTISTS AND MODELS ABROAD.

## 5811 ✦ THE STRANGE AFFAIR
### Paramount, 1968

**Musical Score** Kirchin, Basil; Nathan, Jack

**Producer(s)** Harrison, Howard
**Director(s)** Greene, David
**Screenwriter(s)** Mann, Stanley
**Source(s)** *The Strange Affair* (novel) Mann, Stanley

**Cast** York, Michael; Kemp, Jeremy; George, Susan

**Song(s)** What Would You Do? (C/L: Kirchin, Basil; Nathan, Jack)

## 5812 ✦ STRANGE BEHAVIOR
### World Northal, 1981

**Musical Score** Tangerine Dream

**Producer(s)** Ginnane, Anthony I.; Barnett, John
**Director(s)** Laughlin, Michael
**Screenwriter(s)** Condon, William; Laughlin, Michael

**Cast** Murphy, Michael; Fletcher, Louise; Shor, Dan; Lewis, Fiona; McClure, Marc; Brady, Scott

**Song(s)** Jumping Out a Window (C/L: Pop Mechanix); The Ritz (C/L: Pop Mechanix)

**Notes** No cue sheet available.

## 5813 ✦ STRANGE BREW
### MGM/UA, 1983

**Musical Score** Fox, Charles

**Producer(s)** Silverstein, Louis M.
**Director(s)** Moranis, Rick; Thomas, Dave
**Screenwriter(s)** Moranis, Rick; Thomas, Dave; De Jarnatt, Steven

**Cast** Thomas, Dave; Moranis, Rick; Von Sydow, Max; Dooley, Paul; Griffin, Lynne; MacInnes, Angus; McConnachie, Brian

**Song(s)** Strange Brew (C/L: Thomas, Ian)

## 5814 ✦ STRANGE CARGO
### Metro–Goldwyn–Mayer, 1940

**Musical Score** Waxman, Franz

**Producer(s)** Mankiewicz, Joseph L.
**Director(s)** Borzage, Frank
**Screenwriter(s)** Hazard, Lawrence

**Source(s)** *Not Too Narrow . . . Not Too Deep* (book) Sale, Richard

**Cast** Crawford, Joan; Gable, Clark; Lorre, Peter; Lukas, Paul; Bromberg, J. Edward; Dekker, Albert; Ciannelli, Eduardo

**Song(s)** Star of the Sea (C/L: Wright, Bob; Forrest, Chet)

## 5815 ✦ STRANGE LADY IN TOWN
### Warner Brothers, 1955

**Musical Score** Tiomkin, Dimitri
**Choreographer(s)** Carroll, Peggy

**Producer(s)** LeRoy, Mervyn
**Director(s)** LeRoy, Mervyn
**Screenwriter(s)** Butler, Frank

**Cast** Garson, Greer; Andrews, Dana; Mitchell, Cameron; Smith, Lois; Hampden, Walter; Gonzales-Gonzales, Pedro; Camden, Joan; Numkena, Anthony; Adams, Nick

**Song(s)** Strange Lady in Town [1] (C: Tiomkin, Dimitri; L: Washington, Ned)

**Notes** [1] Used as background vocal only.

## 5816 ✦ THE STRANGE LOVE OF MARTHA IVERS
### Paramount, 1946

**Musical Score** Rozsa, Miklos

**Producer(s)** Wallis, Hal B.
**Director(s)** Milestone, Lewis
**Screenwriter(s)** Rossen, Robert

**Cast** Stanwyck, Barbara; Anderson, Judith; Douglas, Kirk; Heflin, Van; Scott, Lizabeth; Hickman, Darryl

**Song(s)** Strange Love [1] (C: Rozsa, Miklos; L: Heyman, Edward)

**Notes** [1] Lyric added for exploitation only.

## 5817 ✦ STRANGE LOVE OF MOLLY LOUVAIN
### Warner Brothers–First National, 1932

**Producer(s)** Wallis, Hal B.
**Director(s)** Curtiz, Michael
**Screenwriter(s)** Gelsey, Erwin; Holmes, Brown
**Source(s)** *Tinsel Girl* (play) Watkins, Maurine

**Cast** Dvorak, Ann; Tracy, Lee; Cromwell, Richard; Kibbee, Guy; Fenton, Leslie; McHugh, Frank; Middleton, Charles; Doran, Mary; Jackson, Thomas

**Song(s)** Penthouse Serenade [1] (C/L: Jason, Will; Burton, Val)

**Notes** [1] Also in ONE HOUR LATE (Paramount) and BEAU JAMES (Paramount). The song is sometimes referred to as "When We're Alone."

## 5818 ✦ THE STRANGER
Columbia, 1987

**Musical Score** Safan, Craig

**Producer(s)** Lamonica, Hugo
**Director(s)** Aristarian, Adolfo
**Screenwriter(s)** Gurskis, Dan

**Cast** Bedelia, Bonnie; Riegert, Peter; Primus, Barry; Spielberg, David

**Song(s)** Mirrors and Lights (C: Safan, Craig; L: Mueller, Mark)

## 5819 ✦ STRANGERS IN THE CITY
Embassy, 1962

**Musical Score** Prince, Bob

**Producer(s)** Carrier, Rick
**Director(s)** Carrier, Rick
**Screenwriter(s)** Carrier, Rick

**Cast** Gentile, Robert; Delgado, Camilo; De Triana, Rosita

**Song(s)** Strangers [1] (C/L: Carrier, Rick)

**Notes** No cue sheet available. [1] This may be an instrumental.

## 5820 ✦ STRANGERS MAY KISS
Metro–Goldwyn–Mayer, 1931

**Director(s)** Fitzmaurice, George
**Screenwriter(s)** Meehan, John
**Source(s)** *Strangers May Kiss* (novel) Parrott, Ursula

**Cast** Shearer, Norma; Montgomery, Robert; Rambeau, Marjorie; Hamilton, Neil; Rich, Irene; Prouty, Jed

**Song(s)** Go Home and Tell Your Mother [1] (C: McHugh, Jimmy; L: Fields, Dorothy)

**Notes** [1] Also in LOVE IN THE ROUGH.

## 5821 ✦ STRANGE TRIANGLE
Twentieth Century–Fox, 1946

**Producer(s)** Schenck, Aubrey
**Director(s)** McCarey, Ray
**Screenwriter(s)** Braus, Mortimer

**Cast** Hasso, Signe; Foster, Preston; Shaw, Anabel; Shepperd, John; Roberts, Roy; Parnell, Emory

**Song(s)** Your Kiss (C: Newman, Alfred; L: Loesser, Frank)

## 5822 ✦ STRATEGIC AIR COMMAND
Paramount, 1955

**Musical Score** Young, Victor
**Composer(s)** Young, Victor

**Producer(s)** Briskin, Samuel J.
**Director(s)** Mann, Anthony
**Screenwriter(s)** Lay Jr., Beirne; Davies, Valentine

**Cast** Stewart, James; Allyson, June; Sullivan, Barry; Lovejoy, Frank; Bennett, Bruce; Nicol, Alex; Flippen, Jay C.

**Song(s)** The World Is Mine [1] (L: Adams, Stanley); The Air Force Takes Command (L: Washington, Ned; Thomson Jr., Maj. C.E.)

**Notes** [1] Lyric added for exploitation only.

## 5823 ✦ THE STRAWBERRY BLONDE
Warner Brothers, 1941

**Musical Score** Roemheld, Heinz

**Producer(s)** Warner, Jack L.; Wallis, Hal B.
**Director(s)** Walsh, Raoul
**Screenwriter(s)** Epstein, Julius J.; Epstein, Philip G.
**Source(s)** *One Sunday Afternoon* (play) Hogan, James

**Cast** Cagney, James; de Havilland, Olivia; Hayworth, Rita [1]; Hale, Alan; Carson, Jack; Tobias, George; O'Connor, Una; Reeves, George; Fairbanks, Lucille; McNamara, Edward; Lynd, Helen

**Notes** This is a remake of a Paramount film of 1933 that starred Gary Cooper. It was remade in 1948 as ONE SUNDAY AFTERNOON. Vocal renditions of "Bill Bailey" by Hughie Cannon; "Meet Me in St. Louis, Louis" by Andrew B. Sterling and Kerry Mills; "The Band Played On" by Charles B. Ward and John F. Palmer; "Wait Till the Sun Shines Nellie" by Harry Von Tilzer and Andrew B. Sterling; "In the Evening by the Moonlight" by James Bland and "Love Me and the World Is Mine" by Ernest R. Ball and David Reed Jr. are used singly or in medleys. There are no original songs written for this picture. [1] Dubbed by Nan Wynn.

## 5824 ✦ THE STRAWBERRY ROAN
Columbia, 1948

**Producer(s)** Schaefer, Armand
**Director(s)** English, John
**Screenwriter(s)** Cummings, Dwight; Yost, Dorothy

**Cast** Autry, Gene; Henry, Gloria; Holt, Jack; Jones, Dick; Buttram, Pat; Davis, Rufe; Champion

**Song(s)** The Strawberry Roan [2] (C/L: Howard, Fred; Vincent, Nat); When the White Rose Blooms in My Red River Valley (C/L: Herrick, Paul; Wrubel, Allie); Can't Shake the Sands of Texas from My Shoes [1] (C/L: Autry, Gene; Johnston, Diane; Pitts, Kenneth); Texas Sandman [3] (C: Fisher, Doris; L: Roberts, Allan)

**Notes** No cue sheet available. [1] Also in SONS OF NEW MEXICO. [2] Also in RODEO KING AND THE SENORITA (Republic). [3] Also in THE ARKANSAS SWING.

## 5825 ✦ THE STRAWBERRY STATEMENT
Metro–Goldwyn–Mayer, 1970

**Musical Score** Freebairn-Smith, Ian
**Composer(s)** Young, Neil
**Lyricist(s)** Young, Neil

**Producer(s)** Chartoff, Robert; Winkler, Irwin
**Director(s)** Hagmann, Stuart
**Screenwriter(s)** Horovitz, Israel
**Source(s)** *The Strawberry Statement: Notes of a College Revolutionary* (book) Kunen, James

**Cast** Cort, Bud; Goldman, Danny; MacLeod, Murray; Holland, Kristina; Balaban, Bob; Margotta, Michael; Bradshaw, Booker; Berlin, Jeannie; Remsen, Bert; Coco, James

**Song(s)** The Circle Game (C/L: Mitchell, Joni); Down By the River; Give Peace a Chance (C/L: Lennon, John; McCartney, Paul); Helpless; Something in the Air (C/L: Keene, John); Long Time Gone (C/L: Crosby, David); The Loner; Our House (C/L: Nash, Graham); Big Cats and Little Pussies (C/L: MacLeod, Murray)

**Notes** It is not known which, if any, of the songs were written for this picture.

## 5826 ✦ STREAMLINED SWING
Metro–Goldwyn–Mayer, 1938

**Producer(s)** Lewyn, Louis
**Director(s)** Keaton, Buster
**Screenwriter(s)** Mack, Marion; Krafft, John

**Cast** Sing Band

**Song(s)** Pack Your Grip and Take a Little Trip (C/L: Ellison; Rene, Leon); Swing As You Work (C/L: Rene, Leon)

**Notes** Short subject. There is also a vocal of "Organ Grinder's Swing" by Herb Magidson and Will Hudson and "Dinah" by Sam M. Lewis and Joe Young.

## 5827 ✦ THE STREET ANGEL
Fox, 1928

**Director(s)** Borzage, Frank
**Screenwriter(s)** Caldwell, H.H.; Hilliker, Katherine
**Source(s)** Cristilinda Hoffe, Monckton

**Cast** Gaynor, Janet; Farrell, Charles; Kingston, Natalie; Trento, Guido

**Song(s)** Angela Mia (C: Rapee, Erno; L: Pollack, Lew)

## 5828 ✦ STREET GIRL
RKO, 1929

**Composer(s)** Levant, Oscar
**Lyricist(s)** Clare, Sidney
**Choreographer(s)** Eaton, Pearl

**Producer(s)** Reed, Luther; Sarecky, Louis
**Director(s)** Ruggles, Wesley
**Screenwriter(s)** Murfin, Jane
**Source(s)** "The Viennese Charmer" (story) Wonderly, William Carey

**Cast** Harron, John; Sparks, Ned; Oakie, Jack; Compson, Betty; Cawthorn, Joseph; Kane, Eddie; Doris Eaton and the Radio Beauty Chorus; Raymond Maurel and the Cimini Male Chorus; Gus Arnheim and His Ambassador Band; Buccola, Guy

**Song(s)** My Dream Memory; Loveable and Sweet; Broken Up Tune; For He's the Prince of Good Fellows

## 5829 ✦ STREET MUSIC
Specialty Films, 1982

**Composer(s)** Munsen, Judy
**Lyricist(s)** Munsen, Judy

**Producer(s)** Bowen, Richard; Berteau, Lawrence
**Director(s)** Bowen, Jenny
**Screenwriter(s)** Bowen, Jenny

**Cast** Daily, Elizabeth; Breeding, Larry; Romano, John; Morford, Sam; Parr, David

**Song(s)** Light on My Feet (C/L: Bogas, Ed); Jazzman (C/L: Bogas, Ed; Daily, Elizabeth); Close the Show; Delores; Happy Birthday Isle; It's Up to You (C/L: Smith, Stuff)

**Notes** No cue sheet available.

## 5830 ✦ STREET OF MEMORIES
Twentieth Century–Fox, 1940

**Producer(s)** Hubbard, Lucien
**Director(s)** Traube, Shepard
**Screenwriter(s)** Lees, Robert; Rinaldo, Frederic I.

**Cast** Roberts, Lynne; Kibbee, Guy; McGuire, John; Gargan, Edward; Cavanaugh, Hobart; Cowan, Jerome; Waldron, Charles; Holloway, Sterling; Beckett, Scotty

**Song(s)** Tonight Will Live (C: Newman, Alfred; L: Gordon, Mack)

## 5831 ✦ STREET OF MISSING MEN
Republic, 1939

**Producer(s)** Schaefer, Armand
**Director(s)** Salkow, Sidney
**Screenwriter(s)** Lee, Leonard; Dolan, Frank

**Cast** Bickford, Charles; Carey, Harry; Ryan, Tommy; Todd, Mabel; Bryant, Nana; Toomey, Regis; Williams, Guinn "Big Boy"

**Song(s)** I Wanna Sing (C: Lava, William; L: Cherkose, Eddie)

## 5832 ✦ STREET SMART
### Cannon, 1987

**Musical Score**   Irving III, Robert; Davis, Miles

**Producer(s)**   Golan, Menaham; Globus, Yoram
**Director(s)**   Schatzberg, Jerry
**Screenwriter(s)**   Freeman, David

**Cast**   Reeve, Christopher; Baker, Kathy; Rogers, Mimi; Patterson, Jay; Horsford, Anna Maria

**Song(s)**   Romance without Finance (C/L: Irving III, Robert); Street Beat (C/L: Irving III, Robert); Beat Box (C/L: Holzman, Adam)

**Notes**   No cue sheet available.

## 5833 ✦ STREETS OF FIRE
### Universal–RKO, 1984

**Musical Score**   Cooder, Ry; Horner, James

**Producer(s)**   Gordon, Lawrence; Silver, Joel
**Director(s)**   Hill, Walter
**Screenwriter(s)**   Hill, Walter; Gross, Larry

**Cast**   Pare, Michael; Lane, Diane; Moranis, Rick; Madigan, Amy; Dafoe, Willem; Van Valkenburgh, Deborah; Rossovich, Rick; Ving, Lee; Townsend, Robert; Thigpen, Lynne; Begley Jr., Ed

**Song(s)**   Nowhere Fast (C/L: Steinman, Jim); Hold That Snake (C: Cooder, Ry; L: Dickinson, Jim); One Bad Stud (C/L: Leiber, Jerry; Stoller, Mike); Blue Shadows (C/L: Alvin, Dave); Sorcerer (C/L: Nicks, Stevie); Countdown to Love (C/L: Vance, Kenny; Kupersmith, Marty); You Got What You Wanted (C: Cooder, Ry; L: Dickinson, Jim); I Can Dream About You (C/L: Hartman, Don); Tonight Is What It Means to Be Young (C/L: Steinman, Jim); Deeper & Deeper (C/L: Curnin, Cy; West-Oran, Jamie; Woods, Adam; Greenwall, Rupert; Brown, Dan K.)

**Notes**   It is not known if all the above were written for this picture.

## 5834 ✦ STREETS OF LAREDO
### Paramount, 1949

**Producer(s)**   Fellows, Robert
**Director(s)**   Fenton, Leslie
**Screenwriter(s)**   Warren, Charles Marquis

**Cast**   Holden, William; Carey, Macdonald; Freeman, Mona; Bendix, William; Ridges, Stanley; Bevans, Clem; Bell, James; Bedoya, Alfonso

**Song(s)**   Streets of Laredo [1] (C/L: Livingston, Jay; Evans, Ray)

**Notes**   [1] Based on the traditional cowboy song.

## 5835 ✦ THE STREET WITH NO NAME
### Twentieth Century–Fox, 1948

**Producer(s)**   Engel, Samuel G.
**Director(s)**   Keighley, William
**Screenwriter(s)**   Kleiner, Harry

**Cast**   Stevens, Mark; Widmark, Richard; Nolan, Lloyd; Lawrence, Barbara; Begley, Ed; McIntire, John; Donahue, Vincent

**Song(s)**   Beg Your Pardon (C/L: Craig, Francis; Smith, Beasley); All Dressed Up with a Broken Heart [1] (C/L: Patrick, Fred; Reese, Claude; Val, Jack)

**Notes**   [1] Not used.

## 5836 ✦ STRICTLY DYNAMITE
### RKO, 1934

**Choreographer(s)**   Pan, Hermes

**Producer(s)**   Swanson, H.N.
**Director(s)**   Nugent, Elliott
**Screenwriter(s)**   Watkins, Maurine; Spence, Ralph; Harvey, Jack; Raison, Milton

**Cast**   Durante, Jimmy; Velez, Lupe; Foster, Norman; Nixon, Marian; Gargan, William; The Mills Brothers

**Song(s)**   Swing It Sister (C: Lane, Burton; L: Adamson, Harold); Money in My Clothes (C: Fain, Sammy; L: Kahal, Irving); Goodbye Blues (C/L: McHugh, Jimmy; Fields, Dorothy; Johnson, Arnold); I'm Putty in Your Hands (C: Durante, Jimmy; L: Adamson, Harold); You Bunch of Fun (C/L: Grossman, Bernie; Lewis, Harold); Hot Potata (C/L: Durante, Jimmy); Oh Me! Oh My! Oh You! (C: Lane, Burton; L: Adamson, Harold)

**Notes**   There is also a vocal of "Manhattan Madness" by Irving Berlin.

## 5837 ✦ STRICTLY IN THE GROOVE
### Universal, 1942

**Producer(s)**   Sandford, Joseph G.
**Director(s)**   Keays, Vernon
**Screenwriter(s)**   Higgins, Kenneth C.; Wilson, Warren

**Cast**   Davies, Richard; Healy, Mary; Errol, Leon; The Jimmy Wakely Trio; The Dinning Sisters; Ozzie Nelson and His Band

**Song(s)**   I Never Knew [5] (C/L: Pitts, Tom; Egan, Raymond B.; Marsh, Roy); Happy Cowboy [4] (C/L: Nolan, Bob); Miss You (C/L: Tobias, Harry; Tobias, Henry; Tobias, Charles); Ridin' Home [6] (C: McHugh, Jimmy; Adamson, Harold); Sweethearts or Strangers [8] (C/L: Davis, Jimmie); Be Honest with Me [2] (C/L: Autry, Gene; Rose, Fred); Dancin' on Air [3] (C: Rosen, Milton; L: Carter, Everett); Somebody Else is Taking My Place [7] (C/L: Morgan, Russ; Ellsworth, Bob; Howard, Dick [1]); Elmer's Tune (C/L: Albrecht, Elmer; Gallop,

Sammy; Jurgens, Dick); You Are My Sunshine [9] (C/L: Davis, Jimmie; Mitchell, Charles); I'll Remember April [10] (C: de Paul, Gene; L: Raye, Don)

**Notes** Not all the above were written for this picture. Jimmie Davis, who wrote two of the songs above, became Governor of Louisiana in 1944. [1] Dick Howard is a pseudonym for Howard Dietz, but it is not certain that this is him. [2] Also in FLAMING BULLETS and SIERRA SUE. [3] Also in THE MYSTERY OF THE RIVER BOAT and STRICTLY IN THE GROOVE. [4] Also in the Republic picture MAN FROM CHEYENNE. [5] Also in THE CRIMSON CANARY, THE CLOWN (MGM) and THE THREE FACES OF EVE (20th). [6] Also in DESPERATE TRAILS (1939), ROAD AGENT, THE ROAD TO RENO and TENTING TONIGHT ON THE OLD CAMP GROUND. [7] Also in CALL OF THE CANYON (Republic). [8] Also in COWBOY SERENADE (Republic). [9] Also in COWBOY SERENADE (Republic), I'M FROM ARKANSAS (PRC) and RIDIN' ON A RAINBOW (Republic). [10] Not used. Used in GHOST CATCHERS, IDEA GIRL, I'LL REMEMBER APRIL, RIDE 'EM COWBOY (1942).

## 5838 ✦ STRIKE ME PINK
### Goldwyn, 1936

**Composer(s)** Arlen, Harold
**Lyricist(s)** Brown, Lew
**Choreographer(s)** Alton, Robert

**Producer(s)** Goldwyn, Samuel
**Director(s)** Taurog, Norman
**Screenwriter(s)** Butler, Frank; Martin, Francis; Rapp, Philip

**Cast** Cantor, Eddie; Eilers, Sally; Merman, Ethel; Frawley, William; Parkyakarkus [1]; Lovell, Helen; Jones, Gordon; Donlevy, Brian; LaRue, Jack; O'Dea, Sunnie; Rio, Rita [2]; Brophy, Edward S.; The Goldwyn Girls

**Song(s)** The Lady Dances; Calabash Pipe; Shake It Off with Rhythm; First You Have Me High (Then You Have Me Low)

**Notes** No cue sheet available. [1] Pseudonym for Harry Parke. [2] Later named Dona Drake.

## 5839 ✦ STRIKE UP THE BAND
### Metro–Goldwyn–Mayer, 1940

**Composer(s)** Edens, Roger
**Lyricist(s)** Edens, Roger
**Choreographer(s)** Berkeley, Busby

**Producer(s)** Freed, Arthur
**Director(s)** Berkeley, Busby
**Screenwriter(s)** Monks Jr., John; Finklehoffe, Fred F.

**Cast** Rooney, Mickey; Garland, Judy; Paul Whiteman and His Orchestra; Preisser, June; Tracy, William; Nunn, Larry; Shoemaker, Ann; Early, Margaret; Brissac, Virginia; Bennett, Enid; Eddy, Helen Jerome

**Song(s)** Our Love Affair (L: Freed, Arthur); Do the La Conga; Nobody; Nell of New Rochelle; Drummer Boy; Strike Up the Band (C: Gershwin, George; L: Gershwin, Ira; Edens, Roger)

**Notes** There are also vocals of "Heaven Will Protect the Working Girl" by A. Baldwin Sloane and Edgar Smith; "Ta-Ra-Ra-Boom-Der-E" by Henry J. Sayers and "Father Dear Father Come Home with Me Now" by Henry Clay Work.

## 5840 ✦ THE STRIP
### Metro–Goldwyn–Mayer, 1951

**Musical Score** Stoll, George; Rugolo, Pete
**Choreographer(s)** Castle, Nick

**Producer(s)** Pasternak, Joe
**Director(s)** Kardos, Leslie
**Screenwriter(s)** Rivkin, Allen

**Cast** Rooney, Mickey; Forrest, Sally; Demarest, William; Craig, James; Powers, Tom; Brown, Kay; Louis Armstrong and His Orchestra [1]; Damone, Vic; Lewis, Monica; Rettig, Tommy

**Song(s)** Shadrack, Mesach and Abednigo (C/L: MacGimsey, Robert); Basin Street Blues (C/L: Williams, Spencer); A Kiss to Build a Dream On [2] (C: Ruby, Harry; L: Kalmar, Bert; Hammerstein II, Oscar); La Bota (C: Wolcott, Charles; L: Gillespie II, Haven); Don't Blame Me (C: McHugh, Jimmy; L: Fields, Dorothy)

**Notes** It is not known if any of these were written for this film. [1] Including Barney Bigard, Jack Teagarden and Earl "Fatha" Hines. [2] Originally written for, but not used in, A NIGHT AT THE OPERA. The song was originally by Bert Kalmar and Harry Ruby alone and titled "Moonlight on the Meadow."

## 5841 ✦ STRIPPER
### Twentieth Century–Fox, 1985

**Composer(s)** Turner, Joe Lynn; Greenwood, Alan; Burgi, Chuck
**Lyricist(s)** Turner, Joe Lynn; Greenwood, Alan; Burgi, Chuck

**Producer(s)** Gary, Jerome; Buntz, Geof; Estrin, Melvin J.
**Director(s)** Gary, Jerome

**Cast** Boyd, Jannette; Costa, Sara; Holcomb, Kimberly

**Song(s)** Look, but Don't Touch; A Need in Me (C/L: Delia, Joe; Delia, Francis); I Found Love (C/L: Turner, Joe Lynn; Cowden-Hyde); Lady Blue; King of Babylon (C/L: Delia, Joe; Johansen, David); Wild for You Baby (C/L: Snow, Tom; Batteau, David); Body Language (C/L: Mercury, Freddie); Cruel (C/L: Turner, Joe Lynn);

Girls Just Want to Have Fun (C/L: Hazard, Robert); Spook Me Out (C/L: Matthews, Scott; Nagle, Ron); Good Girl Gone Bad; Girl Next Door (C/L: Banks, Brian; Marinelli, Anthony); Savoir Faire (C/L: DeVille, Willy)

**Notes**    It is not known if any of these were written for this film.

## 5842 ✦ STRIPTEASE LADY

See LADY OF BURLESQUE.

## 5843 ✦ STROKER ACE
### Universal, 1983

**Musical Score**    Capps, Al

**Producer(s)**    Moonjean, Hank
**Director(s)**    Needham, Hal
**Screenwriter(s)**    Needham, Hal; Wilson, Hugh
**Source(s)**    (novel) Neely, William; Ottum, Robert K.

**Cast**    Reynolds, Burt; Beatty, Ned; Nabors, Jim; Stevenson, Parker; Anderson, Loni; Byner, John; Hill, Frank O.; Peterson, Cassandra; Smith, Bubba; Yarborough, Cale; Economaki, Chris; Dollar, Bill; Hobbs, David; Squier, Ken; Earnhardt, Dale; Gant, Harry; LaBonte, Terry; Parsons, Benny; Petty, Kyle; Richmond, Tim; Rudd, Ricky; Connell, Bill

**Song(s)**    Stroker's Theme (C/L: Daniels, Charles); I Feel a Heartache Comin' On (C: Capps, Al; L: Malony, Phyllis)

## 5844 ✦ THE STRONGEST MAN IN THE WORLD
### Disney, 1974

**Musical Score**    Brunner, Robert F.

**Producer(s)**    Anderson, Bill
**Director(s)**    McEveety, Vincent
**Screenwriter(s)**    McEveety, Joseph L.; Groves, Herman

**Cast**    Russell, Kurt; Flynn, Joe; Arden, Eve; Romero, Cesar; Silvers, Phil; Van Patten, Dick; Gould, Harold; McGreevey, Michael; Schallert, William; Fong, Benson

**Song(s)**    Ode to Medfield [1] (C/L: Tatum, Shane)

**Notes**    [1] Not used.

## 5845 ✦ STRONGHOLD
### Cannon, 1986

**Musical Score**    Pierre, Alain

**Producer(s)**    Bos, Henk; Visscher, Gerrit; Van Raemdonck, Jan
**Director(s)**    Eerhart, Bobby
**Screenwriter(s)**    Thijsse, Felix
**Source(s)**    Wildschut (novel) Thijsse, Felix

**Cast**    Maas, Hidde; Monkau, Jack; Christians, Annick; De Paw, Josse

**Song(s)**    Tune In for Love (C/L: Van Asten, Peter; De Bois, Richard; Schon, Peter)

**Notes**    No cue sheet available.

## 5846 ✦ STRYKE AND HYDE

See JINXED.

## 5847 ✦ THE STUD
### Trans-American, 1980

**Musical Score**    Biddu
**Composer(s)**    Biddu
**Lyricist(s)**    Cahn, Sammy

**Producer(s)**    Kass, Ronald S.
**Director(s)**    Masters, Quentin
**Screenwriter(s)**    Humphries, Dave; Stagg, Christopher
**Source(s)**    The Stud (novel) Collins, Jackie

**Cast**    Collins, Joan; Tobias, Oliver; Lloyd, Sue; Burns, Mark; Fisher, Doug

**Song(s)**    It's Good; Almost; There's a Fire Down Below (L: Biddu); Let's Go Disco (L: Biddu); You Burn a Hole in My Soul (L: Biddu)

**Notes**    No cue sheet available.

## 5848 ✦ STUDENT BODIES
### Paramount, 1981

**Musical Score**    Hobson, Gene
**Composer(s)**    Jan Rockit Band [1]
**Lyricist(s)**    Jan Rockit Band [1]

**Producer(s)**    Smithee, Allen
**Director(s)**    Rose, Mickey
**Screenwriter(s)**    Rose, Mickey

**Cast**    Riter, Kristen; Goldsby, Matt; Brando, Richard; Flood, Joe

**Song(s)**    I Can't Stop Dancin'; I Can't Get Through to You

**Notes**    [1] Including: Robert Q. Hart, Jan G. Elkins, Gary Peacemaker, Ray Brand, Mike Smoot and Thomas Q. McDavid.

## 5849 ✦ THE STUDENT PRINCE
### Metro–Goldwyn–Mayer, 1954

**Composer(s)**    Romberg, Sigmund
**Lyricist(s)**    Donnelly, Dorothy; Webster, Paul Francis [1]
**Choreographer(s)**    Pan, Hermes

**Producer(s)**    Pasternak, Joe
**Director(s)**    Thorpe, Richard
**Screenwriter(s)**    Levien, Sonya; Ludwig, William
**Source(s)**    The Student Prince (musical) Donnelly, Dorothy; Romberg, Sigmund

**Cast** Blyth, Ann; Purdom, Edmund [2]; Calhern, Louis; Ericson, John; Gwenn, Edmund; Sakall, S.Z.; St. John, Betta; Williams, John; Varden, Evelyn; Hoyt, John; Anderson, Richard

**Song(s)** Yu-Hy-Day, Yu-Hy-Dee (C: Traditional; L: Webster, Paul Francis); Crambambuli (C: Traditional; L: Webster, Paul Francis); To the Inn We're Marching; Beer Here (Bier Hier) (C: Traditional; L: Webster, Paul Francis); Come Boys Let's All Be Gay Boys; Du, Du Liegst Mir Im Herzen (C: Traditional; L: Stoll, George); Summertime in Heidelberg (C: Brodszky, Nicholas; L: Webster, Paul Francis); Old Heidelberg, Old Heidelberg (C: Traditional; L: Alexander, Jeff); Drinking Song; Serenade; The Freshman Fills His Stein (C: Traditional; L: Alexander, Jeff); Ergo Bibamus (C: Eberwein; L: Webster, Paul Francis); Deep in My Heart, Dear; Beloved (C: Brodszky, Nicholas; L: Webster, Paul Francis); I'll Walk with God (C: Brodszky, Nicholas; L: Webster, Paul Francis); Golden Days; Round and Round and Round [3] (C: Traditional; L: Webster, Paul Francis)

**Notes** All Romberg songs from Broadway original. [1] Additional lyrics by Webster. [2] Dubbed by Mario Lanza (credited). Lanza had recorded all the numbers and then was fired from the picture due to tempermental differences. Purdom took over, but Lanza's voice remained. [3] Not used.

## 5850 ✦ STUDENT TOUR
### Metro–Goldwyn–Mayer, 1934

**Composer(s)** Brown, Nacio Herb
**Lyricist(s)** Freed, Arthur
**Choreographer(s)** Hale, Chester

**Producer(s)** Bell, Monta
**Director(s)** Riesner, Charles F.
**Screenwriter(s)** Spence, Ralph; Dunne, Philip

**Cast** Durante, Jimmy; Doyle, Maxine; Butterworth, Charles; Regan, Phil; Eddy, Nelson; Fowley, Douglas; Grable, Betty

**Song(s)** College Hymn; Fight 'Em; A New Moon Is Over My Shoulder; I Say It with Music (C/L: Durante, Jimmy); By the Taj Mahal [2]; The Snake Dance; The Carlo [3]; From Now On [1]

**Notes** [1] Used instrumentally only. [2] Same music as "China Seas" from CHINA SEAS. [3] Based on the instrumental piece "American Bolero."

## 5851 ✦ STUDIO ROMANCE

See TALENT SCOUT.

## 5852 ✦ STUDIO VISIT
### Metro–Goldwyn–Mayer, 1946

**Producer(s)** Smith, Pete

**Cast** Horne, Lena

**Song(s)** Ain't It the Truth [1] (C: Arlen, Harold; L: Harburg, E.Y.)

**Notes** Short subject. A Pete Smith specialty. [1] Song cut from CABIN IN THE SKY. Song was later used in musical JAMAICA.

## 5853 ✦ THE STUNT MAN
### Twentieth Century–Fox, 1980

**Musical Score** Frontiere, Dominic

**Producer(s)** Rush, Richard
**Director(s)** Rush, Richard
**Screenwriter(s)** Marcus, Lawrence B.
**Source(s)** (novel) Brodeur, Paul

**Cast** O'Toole, Peter; Railsback, Steve; Hershey, Barbara; Goorwitz, Allen; Rocco, Alex

**Song(s)** Bits and Pieces (C: Frontiere, Dominic; L: Gimbel, Norman)

## 5854 ✦ THE SUBJECT WAS ROSES
### Metro–Goldwyn–Mayer, 1968

**Musical Score** Pockriss, Lee

**Producer(s)** Lansbury, Edgar [1]
**Director(s)** Grosbard, Ulu [1]
**Screenwriter(s)** Gilroy, Frank D.
**Source(s)** *The Subject Was Roses* (play) Gilroy, Frank D.

**Cast** Neal, Patricia; Albertson, Jack [1]; Sheen, Martin [1]; Saxon, Don; Williams, Elaine

**Song(s)** Who Know Where the Time Goes (C/L: Denny, Sandy); Abatross (C/L: Collins, Judy)

**Notes** There are other brief vocals of Tin Pan Alley songs. [1] From Broadway original.

## 5855 ✦ SUBMARINE
### Columbia, 1928

**Director(s)** Capra, Frank [1]
**Screenwriter(s)** Howell, Dorothy

**Cast** Holt, Jack; Graves, Ralph; Burton, Clarence; Rankin, Arthur; Revier, Dorothy

**Song(s)** Pals, Just Pals (C/L: Ruby, Herman; Dreyer, Dave)

**Notes** [1] Billed as Frank R. Capra.

## 5856 ✦ SUBTERFUGE
### Allied Artists, 1968

**Musical Score** Ornadel, Cyril

**Producer(s)** Wallace, Trevor; Snell, Peter
**Director(s)** Scott, Peter Graham
**Screenwriter(s)** Whittaker, David

**Cast**  Barry, Gene; Collins, Joan; Todd, Richard; Adams, Tom; Rennie, Michael; Goring, Marius

**Song(s)**  No Escape (C: Ornadel, Cyril; L: Callender, Peter)

## 5857 ✦ THE SUBTERRANEANS
Metro–Goldwyn–Mayer, 1960

**Musical Score**  Previn, Andre

**Producer(s)**  Freed, Arthur
**Director(s)**  MacDougall, Ranald
**Screenwriter(s)**  Thom, Robert
**Source(s)**  *The Subterraneans* (novel) Kerouac, Jack

**Cast**  Caron, Leslie; Peppard, George; Rule, Janice; McDowall, Roddy; Seymour, Anne; Hutton, Jim; Johnson, Arte; Marlowe, Scott; Storey, Ruth; Freed, Bert; Mulligan, Gerry; McRae, Carmen; Previn, Andre; Manne, Shelly; Mitchell, Red; Bailey, Dave; Farmer, Art; Clark, Buddy; Freeman, Russ; Pepper, Art; Enevoldsen, Bob; Perkins, William R.; Hamilton, Frank

**Song(s)**  Coffee Time [1] (C: Warren, Harry; L: Freed, Arthur); Why Are We Afraid [2] (C: Previn, Andre; L: Langdon, Dory)

**Notes**  [1] Also in YOLANDA AND THE THIEF with different lyrics. [2] Sheet music only.

## 5858 ✦ SUBWAY IN THE SKY
United Artists, 1959

**Musical Score**  Nascimbene, Mario

**Producer(s)**  Temple-Smith, John; Filmer-Sankey, Patrick
**Director(s)**  Box, Muriel
**Screenwriter(s)**  Andrews, Jack

**Cast**  Johnson, Van; Neff, Hildegarde

**Song(s)**  Love Isn't Love (C: Davis, Jeff; L: Parsons, Geoffrey)

## 5859 ✦ SUCH GOOD FRIENDS
Paramount, 1972

**Musical Score**  Shepard, Thomas Z.
**Composer(s)**  Shepard, Thomas Z.

**Producer(s)**  Preminger, Otto
**Director(s)**  Preminger, Otto
**Screenwriter(s)**  Dale, Esther
**Source(s)**  *Such Good Friends* (novel) Gould, Lois

**Cast**  Cannon, Dyan; Coco, James; O'Neill, Jennifer; Howard, Ken; Foch, Nina; Luckinbill, Laurence; Lasser, Louise; Meredith, Burgess; Levene, Sam; Redfield, William; Beard, James; Gam, Rita; Joyce, Elaine; Roberts, Doris; Sabinson, Lee

**Song(s)**  Suddenly It's All Tomorrow (L: Brittan, Robert); Miranda's Song [1] (L: Shakespeare, William)

**Notes**  [1] Background vocal only.

## 5860 ✦ SUCH MEN ARE DANGEROUS
Fox, 1930

**Choreographer(s)**  Dare, Danny

**Producer(s)**  Rockett, Al
**Director(s)**  Hawks, Kenneth; Burke, Melville
**Screenwriter(s)**  Vajda, Ernest

**Cast**  Baxter, Warner; Owen, Catherine Dale; Hopper, Hedda; Lugosi, Bela; Conti, Albert; Allister, Claud

**Song(s)**  Cinderella By the Fire (C/L: Stamper, Dave); Bridal Hymn [1] (C: Malotte, Albert Hay; L: Gramlich, George)

**Notes**  [1] Sheet music only.

## 5861 ✦ SUCH WOMEN ARE DANGEROUS
Fox, 1934

**Producer(s)**  Rockett, Al
**Director(s)**  Flood, James
**Screenwriter(s)**  Storm, Jane; Sheridan, Oscar; Coffee, Lenore

**Cast**  Baxter, Warner; Ames, Rosemary; Hudson, Rochelle

**Song(s)**  Be Sweet to Me Cherie [1] (C: DeFrancesco, Louis E.; L: Unknown)

**Notes**  [1] This wasn't written for this picture.

## 5862 ✦ SUDAN
Universal, 1945

**Producer(s)**  Malvern, Paul
**Director(s)**  Rawlins, John
**Screenwriter(s)**  Hartmann, Edmund L.

**Cast**  Montez, Maria; Hall, Jon; Bey, Turhan; Devine, Andy; Zucco, George

**Song(s)**  Proud and Free (C: Rosen, Milton; L: Carter, Everett)

## 5863 ✦ SUDDEN FEAR
RKO, 1952

**Musical Score**  Bernstein, Elmer

**Producer(s)**  Kaufman, Joseph
**Director(s)**  Miller, David
**Screenwriter(s)**  Coffee, Lenore; Smith, Robert

**Cast**  Crawford, Joan; Palance, Jack; Grahame, Gloria; Bennett, Bruce; Huston, Virginia; Connors, Michael [1]

**Song(s)**  Afraid (C: Bernstein, Elmer; L: Brooks, Jack); Sudden Fear (C: Altman, Arthur; L: Taylor, Irving)

**Notes**  No cue sheet available. [1] Billed as Touch Connors.

## 5864 ◆ SUDDEN IMPACT
Warner Brothers, 1983

**Musical Score**  Schifrin, Lalo

**Producer(s)**  Eastwood, Clint
**Director(s)**  Eastwood, Clint
**Screenwriter(s)**  Stinson, Joseph C.

**Cast**  Eastwood, Clint; Locke, Sondra; Hingle, Pat; Dillman, Bradford; Drake, Paul; Thibeau, Jack; Currie, Michael

**Song(s)**  This Side of Forever (C: Schifrin, Lalo; L: Blackwell, DeWayne)

**Notes**  Used as background vocal only.

## 5865 ◆ SUGARFOOT
Warner Brothers, 1951

**Musical Score**  Steiner, Max

**Producer(s)**  Elkins, Saul
**Director(s)**  Marin, Edwin L.
**Screenwriter(s)**  Hughes, Russell S.
**Source(s)**  *Sugarfoot* (novel) Kelland, Clarence Budington

**Cast**  Scott, Randolph; Jergens, Adele; Massey, Raymond; Sakall, S.Z.; Warwick, Robert; Hunnicutt, Arthur; Sanders, Hugh

**Song(s)**  Oh! He Looked Like He Might Buy Wine (C: Heindorf, Ray; L: Cahn, Sammy)

**Notes**  Retitled SWIRL OF GLORY for television showings.

## 5866 ◆ SULLIVAN'S TRAVELS
Paramount, 1941

**Producer(s)**  Jones, Paul
**Director(s)**  Sturges, Preston
**Screenwriter(s)**  Sturges, Preston

**Cast**  McCrea, Joel; Lake, Veronica; Demarest, William; Blore, Eric; Hayes, Margaret; Warwick, Robert; Hall, Porter; Howard, Esther; Pangborn, Franklin

**Song(s)**  With the Wind and the Rain in Your Hair [1] (C/L: Lawrence, Jack; Edwards, Clara)

**Notes**  [1] Not written for this picture.

## 5867 ◆ THE SULTAN'S DAUGHTER
Monogram, 1943

**Lyricist(s)**  Greene, Mort
**Choreographer(s)**  Alton, John

**Producer(s)**  Krasne, Philip N.; Burkett, James S.
**Director(s)**  Dreifuss, Arthur
**Screenwriter(s)**  Raison, Milton; Ryan, Tim

**Cast**  Corio, Ann; Ryan, Tim; Ryan, Irene; Butterworth, Charles; Bonanova, Fortunio; Norris, Edward; LaRue, Jack; Martin, Chris-Pin; Freddie Fisher and His Orchestra

**Song(s)**  Clickety-Clack Jack (C: Greene, Mort); I'd Love to Make Love to You; I'm Always the Girl; The Sultan's Daughter

**Notes**  No cue sheet available.

## 5868 ◆ SUMMER HEAT
Atlantic, 1987

**Musical Score**  Stone, Richard

**Producer(s)**  Tennant, William
**Director(s)**  Gleason, Michie
**Screenwriter(s)**  Gleason, Michie
**Source(s)**  *Here to Get My Baby Out of Jail* (novel) Shivers, Louise

**Cast**  Singer, Lori; Edwards, Anthony; Abbott, Bruce; Bates, Kathy; Gulager, Clu

**Song(s)**  The Heart Must Have a Home (C: Mann, Barry; Delerue, Georges; L: Jennings, Will)

**Notes**  No cue sheet available.

## 5869 ◆ SUMMER HOLIDAY
Metro–Goldwyn–Mayer, 1948

**Composer(s)**  Warren, Harry
**Lyricist(s)**  Blane, Ralph
**Choreographer(s)**  Walters, Charles

**Producer(s)**  Freed, Arthur
**Director(s)**  Mamoulian, Rouben
**Screenwriter(s)**  Brecher, Irving; Holloway, Jean
**Source(s)**  *Ah, Wilderness!* (play) O'Neill, Eugene

**Cast**  Rooney, Mickey; De Haven, Gloria; Huston, Walter; Morgan, Frank; Jenkins, Jackie "Butch"; Maxwell, Marilyn; Moorehead, Agnes; Royle, Selena; Francis, Anne

**Song(s)**  Our Home Town; Afraid to Fall in Love; Dan-Dan-Danville High (All Hail to Danville High); The Stanley Steamer; Independence Day; While the Men Are All Drinking; Square Dance (C: Edens, Roger); Weary Blues; You're Next; The Sweetest Kid I Ever Met; Spring Isn't Everything [1]; Wish I Had a Braver Heart [1]; Never Again [1]; Omar and the Princess [1]

**Notes**  [1] Deleted from final print.

## 5870 ◆ SUMMER LOVE
Universal, 1957

**Musical Score**  Mancini, Henry
**Composer(s)**  Mancini, Henry
**Lyricist(s)**  Carey, Bill

**Producer(s)**   Grady, William, Jr.
**Director(s)**   Haas, Charles
**Screenwriter(s)**   Raynor, William; Margolis, Herbert

**Cast**   Saxon, John; Wray, Fay; Platt, Edward; Winslow, George; McKuen, Rod; Wilder, John; Courtney, Bob; Donahue, Troy; Socher, Hylton; Meredith, Judi; St. John, Jill; Fabares, Shelley; Bee, Molly

**Song(s)**   Summer Love; To Know You Is to Love You; Calypso Rock (C/L: McKuen, Rod); Ding-A-Ling; So Good Night [1] (C: Rosen, Milton; L: Carter, Everett); Love Is Something [2] (C/L: Reynolds, Malvina); Beatin' the Bongos [2]

**Notes**   A sequel to ROCK PRETTY BABY (1957). [1] Also in HI 'YA SAILOR. [2] Not used.

---

## 5871 ◆ SUMMER LOVERS
### Filmways, 1982

**Musical Score**   Poledouris, Basil

**Producer(s)**   Moder, Mike
**Director(s)**   Kleiser, Randal
**Screenwriter(s)**   Kleiser, Randal

**Cast**   Gallagher, Peter; Hannah, Daryl; Quennessen, Valerie; Rush, Barbara; Cook, Carole; Van Tongeren, Hans

**Song(s)**   Summer Lovers (C/L: Sembello, Michael; Matkosky, Dennis; Batteau, David); Vive le Jetset (C/L: Karalekas, Rosalie Winkler); If Loves Take You Away (C/L: Bishop, Stephen); On Any Night·(C/L: Karalekas, Rosalie Winkler); Hard to Say I'm Sorry (C/L: Foster, David W.; Cetera, Peter)

**Notes**   No cue sheet available.

---

## 5872 ◆ SUMMER MAGIC
### Disney, 1963

**Musical Score**   Baker, Buddy; Camarata, Salvador
**Composer(s)**   Sherman, Richard M.; Sherman, Robert B.
**Lyricist(s)**   Sherman, Richard M.; Sherman, Robert B.

**Producer(s)**   Miller, Ron
**Director(s)**   Neilson, James
**Screenwriter(s)**   Benson, Sally
**Source(s)**   *Mother Carey's Chickens* (novel) Wiggin, Kate Douglas

**Cast**   Mills, Hayley; Ives, Burl; McGuire, Dorothy [2]; Walley, Deborah; Merkel, Una; Hodges, Eddie; Pollard, Michael J.; Brown, Peter; Whitehead, O.Z.

**Song(s)**   Beautiful Beulah; Femininity; Flitterin'; On the Front Porch; The Pink of Perfection; Summer Magic; Ugly Bug Ball; Lead the Rightous Life [1]

**Notes**   [1] Not used. [2] Dubbed by Marilyn Hooven.

---

## 5873 ◆ SUMMER OF '42
### Warner Brothers, 1971

**Musical Score**   Legrand, Michel

**Producer(s)**   Roth, Richard A.
**Director(s)**   Mulligan, Robert
**Screenwriter(s)**   Raucher, Herman

**Cast**   O'Neill, Jennifer; Grimes, Gary; House, Jerry; Conant, Oliver; Allentuck, Katherine; Norris, Christopher; Frizzell, Lou

**Song(s)**   The Summer Knows [1] (C: Legrand, Michel; L: Bergman, Alan; Bergman, Marilyn)

**Notes**   [1] Lyrics were added later for exploitation.

---

## 5874 ◆ A SUMMER PLACE
### Warner Brothers, 1959

**Musical Score**   Steiner, Max

**Producer(s)**   Daves, Delmer
**Director(s)**   Daves, Delmer
**Screenwriter(s)**   Daves, Delmer
**Source(s)**   *A Summer Place* (novel) Wilson, Sloan

**Cast**   Egan, Richard; McGuire, Dorothy; Dee, Sandra; Kennedy, Arthur; Donahue, Troy; Ford, Constance; Bondi, Beulah; Richardson, Jack

**Song(s)**   Theme from A Summer Place [1] (Inst.) (C: Steiner, Max; L: Discant, Mack)

**Notes**   [1] Lyrics were added for exploitation only.

---

## 5875 ◆ SUMMER RENTAL
### Paramount, 1985

**Musical Score**   Silvestri, Alan

**Producer(s)**   Shapiro, George
**Director(s)**   Reiner, Carl
**Screenwriter(s)**   Stevens, Jeremy; Reisman, Mark

**Cast**   Candy, John; Crenna, Richard; Torn, Rip; Austin, Karen; Green, Kerri; Larroquette, John; Lawrence, Joey

**Song(s)**   Turning Around (C/L: Buffett, Jimmy; Utley, Michael; Jennings, Will)

**Notes**   No cue sheet available.

---

## 5876 ◆ SUMMER SCHOOL
### Paramount, 1987

**Musical Score**   Elfman, Danny

**Producer(s)**   Shapiro, George; West, Howard
**Director(s)**   Reiner, Carl
**Screenwriter(s)**   Franklin, Jeff

**Cast**   Harmon, Mark; Alley, Kirstie; Thomas, Robin

**Song(s)**   Happy (C/L: Elfman, Danny); Get an Education (C/L: Burnette, Billy; Malloy, David);

Second Language (C/L: Pain, Duncan; Curiale, Joe);
Brain Power (C/L: Jay, Michael; Scott, Alan Roy);
Jackie (C/L: Steinberg, Billy; Kelly, Tom); Mind Over
Matter (C/L: Jay, Michael; Palombi, Rick)

### 5877 ✦ SUMMER STOCK
Metro–Goldwyn–Mayer, 1950

**Musical Score**  Chaplin, Saul
**Composer(s)**  Warren, Harry
**Lyricist(s)**  Gordon, Mack
**Choreographer(s)**  Castle, Nick

**Producer(s)**  Pasternak, Joe
**Director(s)**  Walters, Charles
**Screenwriter(s)**  Wells, George; Gomberg, Sy

**Cast**  Garland, Judy; Kelly, Gene; Bracken, Eddie; De
Haven, Gloria; Main, Marjorie; Silvers, Phil; Collins, Ray;
Bieber, Nita; Carpenter, Carleton; Conried, Hans [2]

**Song(s)**  If You Feel Like Singing, Sing; Dig-Dig-Dig
Dig for Your Dinner; Mem'ry Island; You, Wonderful
You (L: Brooks, Jack; Chaplin, Saul); Friendly Star; All
for You (C/L: Chaplin, Saul); Happy Harvest Howdy
Neighbor; Heavenly Music (C/L: Chaplin, Saul); Fall in
Love [1]; The Blue Jean Polka [3]

**Notes**  Released as IF YOU FEEL LIKE SINGING
internationally. There is also a vocal of "Get Happy" by
Harold Arlen and Ted Koehler. The number was filmed
after the rest of the movie was in the can. [1] Used
instrumentally only. [2] Dubbed by Peter Roberts. [3]
Not used.

### 5878 ✦ SUMMER WIVES
Studio Unknown, 1936

**Composer(s)**  Morrison, Sam
**Lyricist(s)**  Singer, Dolph

**Producer(s)**  Linder, Jack; Wolfson, D.S.

**Cast**  Smith and Dale; Charleston, Helen; Douglas,
Milton

**Song(s)**  The Chatterbox; Us on a Bus (C: Lawnhurst,
Vee; L: Seymour, Tot); Play Me an Old Time Two-Step;
My Love Carries On; Mickey; I Wrote a Song for You
(L: Singer, Dolph; Dunham, William)

**Notes**  Sheet music only. This is most likely a
Paramount movie. Maybe the title was changed.

### 5879 ✦ THE SUN ALSO RISES
Twentieth Century–Fox, 1957

**Musical Score**  Friedhofer, Hugo

**Producer(s)**  Zanuck, Darryl F.
**Director(s)**  King, Henry
**Screenwriter(s)**  Viertel, Peter
**Source(s)**  *The Sun Also Rises* (novel) Hemingway, Ernest

**Cast**  Power, Tyrone; Gardner, Ava; Ferrer, Mel; Flynn,
Errol; Albert, Eddie; Ratoff, Gregory; Greco, Juliette;
Dalio, Marcel; Evans, Robert

**Song(s)**  The Lights of Paris [1] (C: Friedhofer, Hugo;
L: Henderson, Charles); Levantate, Pamplonica (C/L:
La Costa, Jenaro Monreal; Ramiraz, Nicasio Tejada)

**Notes**  [1] Used instrumentally only.

### 5880 ✦ SUNBONNET SUE
Monogram, 1945

**Musical Score**  Kay, Edward J.
**Choreographer(s)**  Boyle, Jack

**Director(s)**  Murphy, Ralph
**Screenwriter(s)**  Carroll, Richard A.; Murphy, Ralph

**Cast**  Cleveland, George; Storm, Gale; Gombell,
Minna; Regan, Phil; Holland, Edna M.; Hatton,
Raymond; Mowbray, Alan; Judels, Charles

**Notes**  No cue sheet available. It is not known if there
are any original songs in this film. Vocals include
"School Days" by Gus Edwards; "Sunbonnet Sue" by
Gus Edwards and Will D. Cobb; "The Bowery" by
Charles H. Hoyt; "Yip-I- Addy-I-Ay" by Will D. Cobb
and John H. Flynn; "You Hoo, Ain't You Comin' Out
Tonight" by Carson Robison; "By the Light of the
Silvery Moon" by Edward J. Madden and Gus Edwards;
"If I Had My Way" by Lou Klein and James Kendis;
"While Strolling through the Park One Day" by Ed
Haley; "Donegal," "Roll Dem Bones" and "Look for the
Rainbow" by Ralph Murphy and C. Harold Lewis.

### 5881 ✦ SUNBURN
Paramount, 1979

**Musical Score**  Cameron, John

**Producer(s)**  Daly, John; Green, Gerald
**Director(s)**  Sarafian, Richard C.
**Screenwriter(s)**  Daly, John; Oliver, Stephen; Booth,
James
**Source(s)**  *The Bind* (novel) Ellin, Stanley

**Cast**  Fawcett-Majors, Farrah; Grodin, Charles; Carney,
Art; Collins, Joan; Daniels, William; Hillerman, John;
Parker, Eleanor; Wynn, Keenan; Clarke, Robin;
Kruschen, Jack

**Song(s)**  Sunburn (C/L: Gouldman, Graham)

**Notes**  No cue sheet available.

### 5882 ✦ THE SUN COMES UP
Metro–Goldwyn–Mayer, 1948

**Musical Score**  Previn, Andre
**Composer(s)**  Previn, Andre
**Lyricist(s)**  Katz, William

**Producer(s)**    Sisk, Robert
**Director(s)**    Thorpe, Richard
**Screenwriter(s)**    Ludwig, William; Fitts, Margaret
**Source(s)**    *Mountain Prelude* (novel) Rawlings, Marjorie Kinnan

**Cast**    MacDonald, Jeanette; Nolan, Lloyd; Jarman Jr., Claude; Lassie; Stone, Lewis; Kilbride, Percy; Joy, Nicholas; Hamilton, Margaret

**Song(s)**    Cousin Ebeneezer; If You Were Mine (C: Traditional)

**Notes**    Jeanette MacDonald's last film. There are also vocals of "Tes Yeux" by Rabey; "Un Bel Di Vedremo" by Puccini; and "Songs My Mother Taught Me" by Dvorak.

## 5883 ✦ SUNDAY IN NEW YORK
### Metro–Goldwyn–Mayer, 1964

**Musical Score**    Nero, Peter
**Composer(s)**    Nero, Peter
**Lyricist(s)**    Coates, Carroll

**Producer(s)**    Freeman, Everett
**Director(s)**    Tewksbury, Peter
**Screenwriter(s)**    Krasna, Norman
**Source(s)**    *Sunday in New York* (play) Krasna, Norman

**Cast**    Taylor, Rod; Fonda, Jane; Robertson, Cliff; Culp, Robert; Morrow, Jo; Backus, Jim; Nero, Peter

**Song(s)**    Sunday in New York [1]; New York on Sunday [1]; Hello (L: Everett, Roland); More in Love [1]

**Notes**    [1] Used instrumentally only.

## 5884 ✦ THE SUNDOWN TRAIL
### RKO, 1931

**Producer(s)**    Allen, Fred
**Director(s)**    Hill, Robert F.
**Screenwriter(s)**    Hill, Robert F.

**Cast**    Keene, Tom; Shilling, Marion; Stuart, Nick; Atchley, Hooper L.; Blystone, Stanley; Beavers, Louise

**Song(s)**    I Built a Gal (C: Lange, Arthur; L: Hill, Robert F.)

## 5885 ✦ SUNNY (1930)
### Warner Brothers–First National, 1930

**Composer(s)**    Kern, Jerome
**Lyricist(s)**    Hammerstein II, Oscar; Harbach, Otto
**Choreographer(s)**    Kosloff, Theodore

**Director(s)**    Seiter, William A.
**Screenwriter(s)**    Pearson, Humphrey; McCarthy, Henry
**Source(s)**    *Sunny* (musical) Harbach, Otto; Hammerstein II, Oscar; Kern, Jerome

**Cast**    Miller, Marilyn [1]; Gray, Lawrence; Donahue, Joe; Heggie, O.P.; Courtney, Inez; Bedford, Barbara; Vosselli, Judith; Ward, Mackenzie; Cook, Clyde

**Song(s)**    Sunny [1]; Who [1]; D'Ya Love Me? [1]; Two Little Bluebirds [1]; I Was Alone [2] (L: Hammerstein II, Oscar)

**Notes**    No cue sheet available. [1] From Broadway production. [2] This is the first song Kern and Hammerstein wrote for a film.

## 5886 ✦ SUNNY (1941)
### RKO, 1941

**Composer(s)**    Kern, Jerome
**Lyricist(s)**    Harbach, Otto; Hammerstein II, Oscar

**Producer(s)**    Wilcox, Herbert
**Director(s)**    Wilcox, Herbert
**Screenwriter(s)**    Herzig, Sig
**Source(s)**    *Sunny* (musical) Kern, Jerome; Harbach, Otto; Hammerstein II, Oscar

**Cast**    Neagle, Anna; Carroll, John; Bolger, Ray; Westley, Helen; Horton, Edward Everett; Hartman, Grace; Hartman, Paul; Inescort, Frieda; Rubin, Benny; Davies, Muggins; Lane, Richard; Tilton, Martha

**Song(s)**    Sunny; Who; Two Little Bluebirds; D'Ye Love Me; Sunshine

**Notes**    All songs from Broadway original.

## 5887 ✦ SUNNYSIDE
### American International, 1979

**Musical Score**    Douglas, Alan; Wheeler, Harold
**Composer(s)**    Fiske, Stephen Longfellow
**Lyricist(s)**    Fiske, Stephen Longfellow

**Producer(s)**    Schaffel, Robert
**Director(s)**    Galfas, Timothy
**Screenwriter(s)**    Galfas, Timothy; King, Jeff

**Cast**    Travolta, Joey; Lansing, John; Pickren, Stacey; Rubin, Andrew; Darling, Joan

**Song(s)**    Ride that Wave; New York City Band (C/L: Stahns, Steven); Sunnyside; I Gotta Have Your Body (C/L: Leslie, Michael); Loving You (C/L: Fraser, Andrew); Sometimes

**Notes**    No cue sheet available.

## 5888 ✦ SUNNY SIDE UP
### Fox, 1929

**Composer(s)**    Henderson, Ray
**Lyricist(s)**    DeSylva, B.G.; Brown, Lew
**Choreographer(s)**    Felix, Seymour

**Director(s)**    Butler, David
**Screenwriter(s)**    Butler, David

**Cast**   Gaynor, Janet; Farrell, Charles; Brendel, El; White, Marjorie; Richardson, Frank; Lynn, Sharon; Forbes, Mary; Brown, Joe

**Song(s)**   I'm a Dreamer, Aren't We All; You Find the Time and I'll Find the Place; Sunny Side Up [2]; Turn on the Heat; If I Had a Talking Picture of You [1]; It's Great to Be Necked; You've Got Me Pickin' Petals Off o' Daisies

**Notes**   From a letter to Fox—"Mrs. Anna H. of Hoboken, New Jersey, called claiming she wrote the lyrics for the songs recorded in SUNNYSIDE UP stating DeSylva, Brown and Henderson called to see her when she was working at Macy's and all four wrote the numbers right at Macy's. She stated she had been in the hospital at Secaucus, New Jersey, and in St. Mary's Hospital at Jersey City. The songs were written under the name of Viola Brown. Before being a saleslady at Macy's, she stated she was a chorus girl for experience . . ." [1] Also in SOB SISTER. [2] Also in JUST IMAGINE.

### 5889 ◆ SUNNY SKIES
Tiffany, 1930

**Composer(s)**   Burton, Val; Jason, Will
**Lyricist(s)**   Burton, Val; Jason, Will

**Director(s)**   Taurog, Norman; De Lacy, Ralph
**Screenwriter(s)**   Cleveland, George

**Cast**   Rubin, Benny; Day, Marceline; Lease, Rex; Kane, Marjorie "Babe"; Granstedt, Greta; Barry, Wesley

**Song(s)**   I Must Have You; I Want a Boy (Wanna Find a Boy); Must Be Love; You for Me; Sunny Days; Laugh Song (C/L: Burton, Val; Jason, Will; Rubin, Benny)

**Notes**   No cue sheet available. I could not find a source to verify songwriters' names. The song titles are from a variety of sources.

### 5890 ◆ SUNSET BOULEVARD
Paramount, 1950

**Musical Score**   Waxman, Franz
**Composer(s)**   Livingston, Jay; Evans, Ray
**Lyricist(s)**   Livingston, Jay; Evans, Ray

**Producer(s)**   Brackett, Charles
**Director(s)**   Wilder, Billy
**Screenwriter(s)**   Wilder, Billy; Marshman Jr., D.M.; Brackett, Charles

**Cast**   Holden, William; Swanson, Gloria; De Mille, Cecil B.; Warner, H.B.; Nilsson, Anna Q.; Keaton, Buster; von Stroheim, Erich; Olson, Nancy; Clark, Fred; Webb, Jack; Hopper, Hedda

**Song(s)**   Sunset Boulevard [1]; The Paramount-Don't-Want-Me Blues [2]

**Notes**   [1] Written for exploitation only. [2] Not used but recorded by Livingston and Evans.

### 5891 ◆ SUNSET IN EL DORADO
Republic, 1945

**Choreographer(s)**   Ceballos, Larry

**Producer(s)**   Gray, Louis
**Director(s)**   MacDonald, Frank
**Screenwriter(s)**   Butler, John K.

**Cast**   Rogers, Roy; Trigger; Hayes, George "Gabby"; Evans, Dale; Bob Nolan and the Sons of the Pioneers

**Song(s)**   Go West, Go West Young Man (C/L: Forster, Gordon); The Call of the Prairie (C/L: Carson, Ken); Belle of the El Dorado (C/L: Elliott, Jack); It's No Use (C/L: Carson, Ken); The Lady Who Wouldn't Say Yes (C/L: Elliott, Jack)

**Notes**   There is also a vocal of "I'm Awfully Glad I Met You" by George Meyer and Jack Drislane and one of "Be My Little Baby Bumble Bee" by Stanley Murphy and Henry I. Marshall.

### 5892 ◆ SUNSET IN THE WEST
Republic, 1950

**Producer(s)**   White, Edward J.
**Director(s)**   Witney, William
**Screenwriter(s)**   Geraghty, Gerald

**Cast**   Rogers, Roy; Trigger; Edwards, Penny; Rodriguez, Estelita

**Song(s)**   Sunset in the West (C/L: Willing, Foy); When a Pretty Girl Passes By (C/L: Elliott, Jack); Rollin' Wheels (C/L: Elliott, Jack)

### 5893 ◆ SUNSET IN WYOMING
Republic, 1941

**Producer(s)**   Grey, Harry
**Director(s)**   Morgan, William
**Screenwriter(s)**   Chapin, Anne Morrison; Goff, Ivan

**Cast**   Autry, Gene; Burnette, Smiley; Cleveland, George; Wrixon, Maris; Kent, Robert; Blue, Monte

**Song(s)**   I Was Born in Old Wyoming [1] (C/L: Robison, Carson J.); There's a Home in Wyoming (C/L: Autry, Gene); Wyoming (C/L: Autry, Gene); Heebie Jeebie Blues [3] (C: Grey, Harry; L: Drake, Oliver); Twenty-One Years [1] (C/L: Nolan, Bob); Casey Jones (C: Styne, Jule; L: Meyer, Sol); Sing Me a Song of the Saddle [4] (C/L: Autry, Gene; Harford, Frank); Happy Cowboy [2] (C/L: Styne, Jule); My Faith Looks Up to Thee (C/L: Mason, Lowell); Sign Up for Happy Days (C: Styne, Jule; L: Meyer, Sol); Sweet Patootie Kitty (C: Styne, Jule; L: Meyer, Sol); I'm a Cowpoke Pokin' Along (C/L: Autry, Gene)

**Notes**   No cue sheet available. [1] Credited to Bob Miller in Brigham Young collection of Republic music. [2] Also in SINGING HILL. [3] Also in SIERRA SUE. [4] Also in LAST OF THE PONY RIDERS (Columbia) and SINGING KID FROM PINE RIDGE but without Autry credit.

## 5894   ◆   SUNSET ON THE DESERT
### Republic, 1942

**Producer(s)**   Kane, Joseph
**Director(s)**   Kane, Joseph
**Screenwriter(s)**   Geraghty, Gerald

**Cast**   Rogers, Roy; Hayes, George "Gabby"; Carver, L. Lynne; Thomas, Frank M.; Burns, Fred; Fowley, Douglas; Strange, Glenn; Barcroft, Roy; Sons of the Pioneers

**Song(s)**   Yip Pee Yi Your Troubles Away (C/L: Spencer, Tim); It's a Lie (C/L: Nolan, Bob); Don Juan [1] (C/L: Spencer, Tim); Faithful Pal O' Mine (C/L: Spencer, Tim); Remember Me? (C/L: Nolan, Bob)

**Notes**   [1] Also in IDAHO.

## 5895   ◆   SUNSET PASS
### RKO, 1946

**Musical Score**   Sawtell, Paul
**Composer(s)**   Pollack, Lew
**Lyricist(s)**   Harris, Harry

**Producer(s)**   Schlom, Herman
**Director(s)**   Berke, William
**Screenwriter(s)**   Houston, Norman
**Source(s)**   *Sunset Pass* (novel) Grey, Zane

**Cast**   Warren, James; Leslie, Nan; Laurenz, John; Greer, Jane; Barrat, Robert

**Song(s)**   Walking Arm in Arm with Jim [1]; Anabella's Bustle [1]; Lolita [2] (C: Rodgers, Richard; L: Hart, Lorenz)

**Notes**   [1] Also in GIRL RUSH (1944) and THE HALF-BREED. [2] Also in THEY MET IN ARGENTINA.

## 5896   ◆   SUNSET SERENADE
### Republic, 1942

**Producer(s)**   Kane, Joseph
**Director(s)**   Kane, Joseph
**Screenwriter(s)**   Felton, Earl

**Cast**   Rogers, Roy; Hayes, George "Gabby"; Nolan, Bob; Sons of the Pioneers; Brady, Pat; Parrish, Helen; Barcroft, Roy; Kirk, Jack; Stevens, Onslow

**Song(s)**   Cowboy Rockefeller (C/L: Spencer, Tim); Sandman Lullaby (C/L: Nolan, Bob); Mavourreen O'Shea (C/L: Spencer, Tim); He's a No Good Son of a

Gun (C/L: Nolan, Bob); Song of the San Juaquin (C/L: Spencer, Tim); Home Corral (C/L: Nolan, Bob)

## 5897   ◆   SUNSET TRAIL
### Paramount, 1938

**Producer(s)**   Sherman, Harry
**Director(s)**   Selander, Lesley
**Screenwriter(s)**   Houston, Norman

**Cast**   Boyd, William; Hayden, Russell; Hayes, George "Gabby"; Clayton, Jan

**Song(s)**   A Cowgirl Dreams On (C/L: Cowan, Stanley; Worth, Bobby); New Trail [1] (C: Hollander, Frederick; L: Freed, Ralph)

**Notes**   [1] Not used.

## 5898   ◆   SUNSHINE SUSIE

See THE OFFICE GIRL.

## 5899   ◆   SUN VALLEY SERENADE
### Twentieth Century–Fox, 1941

**Composer(s)**   Warren, Harry
**Lyricist(s)**   Gordon, Mack
**Choreographer(s)**   Pan, Hermes

**Producer(s)**   Sperling, Milton
**Director(s)**   Humberstone, H. Bruce
**Screenwriter(s)**   Ellis, Robert; Logan, Helen

**Cast**   Bari, Lynn [1]; Kelly, Paula; Eberle, Ray; The Modernaires; Tilton, Martha; Henie, Sonja; Payne, John; Miller, Glenn; Berle, Milton; Davis, Joan; The Nicholas Brothers; Davidson, William B.; Dandridge, Dorothy; Murray, Forbes

**Song(s)**   It Happened in Sun Valley; I Know Why (And So-Do-You); The Kiss Polka; At Last [2]; Chattanooga Choo Choo [3]; In the Mood (Inst.) (C: Garland, Joe); The World Is Waiting to Waltz Again [4]

**Notes**   [1] Dubbed by Pat Friday. John Russell Taylor and Arthur Jackson's *The Hollywood Musical* says Bari was dubbed by Lorraine Elliot. [2] Later featured in ORCHESTRA WIVES. [3] Also in SPRINGTIME IN THE ROCKIES. [4] Not used though recorded.

## 5900   ◆   SUPERDAD
### Disney, 1973

**Musical Score**   Baker, Buddy
**Composer(s)**   Tatum, Shane
**Lyricist(s)**   Tatum, Shane

**Producer(s)**   Anderson, Bill
**Director(s)**   McEveety, Vincent
**Screenwriter(s)**   McEveety, Joseph L.

**Cast**   Crane, Bob; Rush, Barbara; Russell, Kurt; Flynn, Joe; Cody, Kathleen; Van Patten, Dick

**Song(s)** Los Angeles; These Are the Best Times; When I'm Near You

**Notes** Originally titled SON-IN-LAW FOR CHARLIE MCCREADY.

## 5901 ✦ SUPERFLY
### Warner Brothers, 1972

**Musical Score** Mayfield, Curtis
**Composer(s)** Mayfield, Curtis
**Lyricist(s)** Mayfield, Curtis

**Producer(s)** Shore, Sig
**Director(s)** Parks Jr., Gordon
**Screenwriter(s)** Fenty, Philip

**Cast** O'Neal, Ron; Lee, Carl; Frazier, Sheila; Harris, Julius W.; McGregor, Charles; Adams, Nate; Niles, Polly

**Song(s)** Little Child Runnin' Wild; Pusherman [1]; No Thing on Me; Give Me Your Love; Superfly; Freddie's Dead [2]

**Notes** [1] Only vocal visual. Remainder background vocals. [2] Sheet music only.

## 5902 ✦ SUPERFLY TNT
### Paramount, 1973

**Musical Score** Osibisa [1]
**Composer(s)** Osibisa [1]
**Lyricist(s)** Osibisa [1]

**Producer(s)** Shore, Sig
**Director(s)** O'Neal, Ron
**Screenwriter(s)** Haley, Alex

**Cast** O'Neal, Ron; Browne, Roscoe Lee; Frazier, Sheila; Guillaume, Robert; Sernas, Jacques

**Song(s)** Superfly Man; Prophets

**Notes** [1] Osibisa consists of T. Osei, S. Amarfio, M. Tontoh, R. Bailey, K. Ayivor and J. Mendengue.

## 5903 ✦ SUPERMAN CARTOONS
### Paramount

**Song(s)** Superman March (C/L: Timberg, Sammy)

**Notes** Animated shorts. No cue sheet available.

## 5904 ✦ SUPERMAN: THE MOVIE
### Warner Brothers, 1978

**Musical Score** Williams, John

**Producer(s)** Salkind, Alexander; Salkind, Ilya; Spengler, Pierre
**Director(s)** Donner, Richard
**Screenwriter(s)** Puzo, Mario; Newman, David; Benton, Robert; Newman, Leslie
**Source(s)** *Superman* (comic strip) Shuster, Joe; Siegel, Jerry

**Cast** Hackman, Gene; Reeve, Christopher; Kidder, Margot; Beatty, Ned; Perrine, Valerie; Ford, Glenn; Thaxter, Phyllis; East, Jeff; Cooper, Jackie; York, Susannah; Howard, Trevor; O'Halloran, Jack; Schell, Maria; Stamp, Terence; Douglas, Sarah; McClure, Marc; Andrews, Harry

**Song(s)** Can You Read My Mind (C: Williams, John; L: Bricusse, Leslie)

## 5905 ✦ SUPERMAN III
### Warner Brothers, 1983

**Musical Score** Thorne, Ken

**Producer(s)** Spengler, Pierre
**Director(s)** Lester, Richard
**Screenwriter(s)** Newman, David; Newman, Leslie

**Cast** Reeve, Christopher; Pryor, Richard; Cooper, Jackie; McClure, Marc; O'Toole, Annette; Ross, Annie; Stephenson, Pamela; Vaughn, Robert; Kidder, Margot

**Song(s)** Love Theme (C: Moroder, Giorgio; L: Forsey, Keith)

**Notes** No cue sheet available.

## 5906 ✦ SUPERNATURAL
### Paramount, 1933

**Director(s)** Halperin, Victor
**Screenwriter(s)** Marlow, Brian; Thew, Harvey

**Cast** Lombard, Carole; Scott, Randolph; Osborne, Vivienne

**Song(s)** Lay Your Head on My Shoulder (C/L: Coslow, Sam; Campbell, Jimmy; Conrad, Con)

## 5907 ✦ SUPER VAN
### Empire Releasing, 1978

**Musical Score** DeMartino, Andy; Gibbons, Mark; Stone, Bob

**Producer(s)** Capra, Sal; Cohen, Sandy
**Director(s)** Card, Lamar
**Screenwriter(s)** Friedenn, Neva; Easter, Robert

**Cast** Schneider, Mark; Saylor, Katie; Woodward, Morgan; Lesser, Len; Riley, Skip

**Song(s)** Ridin' High (C/L: Stone, Bob)

**Notes** No cue sheet available.

## 5908 ✦ SUPPORT YOUR LOCAL SHERIFF
### United Artists, 1968

**Musical Score** Alexander, Jeff

**Producer(s)** Finnegan, Bill
**Director(s)** Kennedy, Burt
**Screenwriter(s)** Grant, James Edward

**Cast** Garner, James; Pleshette, Suzanne; Blondell, Joan; Morgan, Harry; Connors, Chuck

**Song(s)** April Country (C: Alexander, Jeff; L: Orenstein, Larry)

## 5909 ✦ THE SURFER GIRLS
Oakwood Releasing, 1980

**Musical Score** Keyes, Kendall; Gabbert, Michael
**Composer(s)** Gabbert, Michael
**Lyricist(s)** Gabbert, Michael

**Producer(s)** Sillman, Frank; Bell, Christopher
**Director(s)** Sillman, Frank
**Screenwriter(s)** Sillman, Frank

**Cast** Johnson, Sandy; Jones, Debbie; Johnson, Elizabeth; Koko; Carpenter, Mary; Johnston, Pam; Atlas, Steve; Rowen, Michael

**Song(s)** Surfer Girls; Good Place to Be; Sunflower; Sailin' On; Ocean Girls; Love's Fool; Always Will; My Love; Grateful Day Dreams

**Notes** No cue sheet available.

## 5910 ✦ SURF NAZIS MUST DIE
Troma, 1987

**Musical Score** McCallum, Jon

**Producer(s)** Tinnell, Robert
**Director(s)** George, Peter
**Screenwriter(s)** Ayre, Jon

**Cast** Neely, Gail; Brenner, Barry; Wildsmith, Dawn

**Song(s)** Nobody Goes Home (C/L: Spindler, Andrew)

**Notes** No cue sheet available.

## 5911 ✦ SURF PARTY
Twentieth Century–Fox, 1964

**Musical Score** Haskell, Jimmie
**Composer(s)** Haskell, Jimmie
**Lyricist(s)** Dunham, "By"

**Producer(s)** Dexter, Maury
**Director(s)** Dexter, Maury
**Screenwriter(s)** Spaulding, Harry

**Cast** Vinton, Bobby; Morrow, Patricia; De Shannon, Jackie; Miller, Kenny; Crane, Richard

**Song(s)** Surf Party (C: Beverly, Bobby); Never Coming Back; If I Were an Artist (C: Beverly, Bobby); That's What Love Is (C: Beverly, Bobby); Pearly Shells [2] (C/L: Dunham, "By"; Edwards, Webley; Pober, Leon); Glory Wave; Crack Up [1]; Fire Water [1]; Great White Water [1]; Surfing [1]; Sorrow Surf [1]

**Notes** [1] Used instrumentally only. [2] Licensing paper reads Jericho Brown, Lani Kai and "By" Dunham. Dunham not credited on cue sheet.

## 5912 ✦ SURPRISE PACKAGE
Columbia, 1960

**Musical Score** Frankel, Benjamin

**Producer(s)** Donen, Stanley
**Director(s)** Donen, Stanley
**Screenwriter(s)** Kurnitz, Harry

**Cast** Brynner, Yul; Nagy, Bill; Gaynor, Mitzi; Murton, Lionel; Foster, Barry; Pohlmann, Eric; Dean Man Mountain; Coward, Noel; Coulouris, George

**Song(s)** Surprise Package (C: Van Heusen, James; L: Cahn, Sammy)

**Notes** No cue sheet available.

## 5913 ✦ SURPRISES

See SEVEN MINUTES IN HEAVEN.

## 5914 ✦ SURRENDER (1950)
Republic, 1950

**Musical Score** Scott, Nathan

**Producer(s)** Dwan, Allan
**Director(s)** Dwan, Allan
**Screenwriter(s)** Grant, James Edward; Nibley, Sloan

**Cast** Ralston, Vera Hruba; Carroll, John; Brennan, Walter; Lederer, Francis; Ching, William; Darwell, Jane; Fix, Paul; Barcroft, Roy

**Song(s)** Surrender (C/L: Elliott, Jack; Carroll, John)

## 5915 ✦ SURRENDER (1987)
Warner Brothers, 1987

**Musical Score** Colombier, Michel

**Producer(s)** Spelling, Aaron; Greisman, Alan
**Director(s)** Belson, Jerry
**Screenwriter(s)** Belson, Jerry

**Cast** Field, Sally; Caine, Michael; Guttenberg, Steve; Boyle, Peter; Kavner, Julie; Cooper, Jackie

**Song(s)** It's Money That I Love (C/L: Newman, Randy)

## 5916 ✦ SURVIVAL RUN
Film Ventures, 1980

**Musical Score** Friedman, Gary William

**Producer(s)** Hool, Lance
**Director(s)** Spiegel, Larry
**Screenwriter(s)** Spiegel, Larry; Cahill, G.M.; Shore, Fredric

**Cast** Graves, Peter; Armendariz Jr., Pedro; O'Hanlon, Susan Pratt; Milland, Ray; Conrad, Alan; Costa, Cosie; Van Patten, Vincent

**Song(s)** Theme from Spree (C: Friedman, Gary William; L: Holt, Will); It Ain't Gonna Rain No More (C/L: Rafkin, Bob); Dream Lover (C/L: Weaver, Robby)

**Notes** No cue sheet available.

## 5917 ✦ SUSANNA PASS
### Republic, 1949

**Producer(s)** White, Edward J.
**Director(s)** Witney, William
**Screenwriter(s)** Nibley, Sloan; Butler, John K.

**Cast** Rogers, Roy; Trigger; Evans, Dale; Rodriguez, Estelita; Littlefield, Lucien; Fowley, Douglas; Foy Willing and the Riders of the Purple Sage

**Song(s)** Two-Gun Rita (C/L: Elliott, Jack); Susanna Pass [1] (C/L: Elliott, Jack); A Good, Good Mornin' (C/L: Robin, Sid; Willing, Foy)

**Notes** There is also a vocal of "Brush Those Tears from Your Eyes" by Oakley Haldeman, Clem Watts and Jimmy Lee. [1] Spanish lyrics by Aaron Gonzalez.

## 5918 ✦ SUSAN SLEPT HERE
### RKO, 1954

**Musical Score** Harline, Leigh
**Lyricist(s)** Lawrence, Jack
**Choreographer(s)** Sidney, Robert

**Producer(s)** Parsons, Harriet
**Director(s)** Tashlin, Frank
**Screenwriter(s)** Gottlieb, Alex
**Source(s)** (play) Gottlieb, Alex; Fisher, Steve

**Cast** Powell, Dick; Reynolds, Debbie; Farrell, Glenda; Francis, Anne; Moore, Alvy; McMahon, Horace; Vigran, Herb; Tremayne, Les

**Song(s)** Susan Slept Here (C: Lawrence, Jack); Hold My Hand (C: Myers, Richard)

## 5919 ✦ SUSIE STEPS OUT
### United Artists, 1946

**Musical Score** Borne, Hal
**Composer(s)** Borne, Hal
**Lyricist(s)** Borne, Hal

**Producer(s)** Rogers, Charles "Buddy"; Cohn, Ralph
**Director(s)** LeBorg, Reginald
**Screenwriter(s)** Ullman, Elwood; Frieberger, Fred

**Cast** Bruce, David; Caldwell, Cleatus

**Song(s)** When Does the Love Begin; I'm So Lonely; When You're Near; For the Right Guy; Bop, Bop, That Did It (L: Borne, Hal; Cherkose, Eddie)

**Notes** Burton indicates that "Bop, Bop, That Did It" is two songs but the cue sheet reads otherwise.

## 5920 ✦ SUSIE, THE LITTLE BLUE COUPE
### Disney, 1952

**Musical Score** Smith, Paul J.

**Director(s)** Geronimi, Clyde
**Screenwriter(s)** Peet, Bill; DaGradi, Don
**Narrator(s)** Holloway, Sterling

**Song(s)** The Little Blue Coupe [1] (C: Smith, Paul J.; L: George, Gil)

**Notes** Animated short. [1] Lyric added for exploitation.

## 5921 ✦ SUZY
### Metro–Goldwyn–Mayer, 1936

**Musical Score** Axt, William

**Producer(s)** Revnes, Maurice
**Director(s)** Fitzmaurice, George
**Screenwriter(s)** Parker, Dorothy; Campbell, Alan; Jackson, Horace; Coffee, Lenore
**Source(s)** *Suzy* (novel) Gorman, Herbert

**Cast** Harlow, Jean [1]; Tone, Franchot; Grant, Cary; Stone, Lewis; Hume, Benita; Mason, Reginald; Courtney, Inez; O'Connor, Una

**Song(s)** Did I Remember (C: Donaldson, Walter; L: Adamson, Harold)

**Notes** [1] Dubbed by Virginia Verrill.

## 5922 ✦ SWANEE RIVER
### Twentieth Century–Fox, 1939

**Choreographer(s)** Castle, Nick; Sawyer, Geneva

**Producer(s)** Zanuck, Darryl F.
**Director(s)** Lanfield, Sidney
**Screenwriter(s)** Foote, John Taintor; Dunne, Philip

**Cast** Ameche, Don; Leeds, Andrea; Jolson, Al; Bressart, Felix; Chandler, Chick; Hicks, Russell; Reed, George; Clarke, Richard; Meeker, George

**Song(s)** Mule Song (C/L: Johnson, Hall); Merry Minstrel Men (C: Silvers, Louis; L: Bullock, Walter); Curry a Mule (C: Silvers, Louis; L: Lanfield, Sidney)

**Notes** Vocals also include the following Stephen Foster songs "Beautiful Dreamer," "Oh Susanna," "De Camptown Races," "My Old Kentucky Home," "Ring, Ring de Banjo," "Jeannie with the Light Brown Hair," "Old Black Joe" and "Swanee River."

## 5923 ✦ THE SWASHBUCKLER
### Universal, 1976

**Musical Score** Addison, John
**Composer(s)** Clancy, Tom [1]
**Lyricist(s)** Clancy, Tom [1]

**Producer(s)** Lang, Jennings; Kastner, Elliott
**Director(s)** Goldstone, James
**Screenwriter(s)** Bloom, Jeffrey

**Cast** Shaw, Robert; Jones, James Earl; Boyle, Peter; Bujold, Genevieve; Behrens, Barnard; Bridges, Beau; Schreiber, Avery; Holder, Geoffrey; Clancy, Tom

**Song(s)** While Cruising Around Yarmough; Hundred Years Ago; Whiskey Is the Life of Man; Hawl on the Bowline; Johnny's Gone to Hilo; The Wild Goose Chanty

**Notes** Also titled THE SCARLET BUCCANEER. [1] Traditional songs with new words and music by Tom Clancy.

---

### 5924 ✦ SWEATER GIRL
Paramount, 1942

**Composer(s)** Styne, Jule
**Lyricist(s)** Loesser, Frank
**Choreographer(s)** Gould, Dave

**Producer(s)** Siegel, Sol C.
**Director(s)** Clemens, William
**Screenwriter(s)** Greene, Eve; Blees, Robert

**Cast** Bracken, Eddie; Preisser, June; Terry, Phillip; Asther, Nils

**Song(s)** I Said "No"; What Gives Out Now [2]; I Don't Want to Walk Without You; Sweater Girl; The Brooker T. Washington Brigade [1]; Love Is Such an Old Fashioned Thing [1] [3]; Hip Hip Hooray [1]

**Notes** Formerly titled SING A SONG OF HOMICIDE. [1] Not used. [2] Originally titled "What Happens Now." [3] Used in GLAMOUR BOY with Victor Schertzinger music.

---

### 5925 ✦ SWEATER GIRLS
Mirror Releasing, 1978

**Musical Score** Hieronymus, Richard

**Producer(s)** Gibbs, Gary; Rubin, Frank
**Director(s)** Jones, Don
**Screenwriter(s)** Jones, Don; Friedenn, Neva

**Cast** Moses, Harry; King, Meegan; North, Noelle; Sarchet, Kate

**Song(s)** Sweater Girl (C: Hieronymus, Richard; L: Somerville, David; Jensen, Gail)

**Notes** No cue sheet available.

---

### 5926 ✦ SWEET ADELINE
Warner Brothers, 1935

**Composer(s)** Kern, Jerome
**Lyricist(s)** Hammerstein II, Oscar
**Choreographer(s)** Connolly, Bobby

**Producer(s)** Chodorov, Edward
**Director(s)** LeRoy, Mervyn
**Screenwriter(s)** Gelsey, Erwin
**Source(s)** *Sweet Adeline* (musical) Kern, Jerome; Hammerstein II, Oscar

**Cast** Dunne, Irene; Woods, Donald; Herbert, Hugh; Sparks, Ned; Cawthorn, Joseph; Calhern, Louis; Shaw, Winifred; Westman, Nydia; Dare, Dorothy; Regan, Phil; Beery, Noah; Alvarado, Don

**Song(s)** Play Us a Polka Dot; Here Am I; Why Was I Born [3]; Oriental Moon; Molly O'Donohue; Lonely Feet [1]; Twas Not So Long Ago; Pretty Jenny Lee [1]; We Were So Young [1]; Don't Ever Leave Me; I Get That Way [1] [2]

**Notes** "Out of the Blue," which was written for the Broadway show, is listed in some sources but is not on the cue sheets. [1] Written for film. [2] Used instrumentally only. [3] Also in THE MAN I LOVE (1947).

---

### 5927 ✦ SWEET AND LOW-DOWN
Twentieth Century–Fox, 1944

**Composer(s)** Monaco, James V.
**Lyricist(s)** Gordon, Mack

**Producer(s)** LeBaron, William
**Director(s)** Mayro, Archie
**Screenwriter(s)** English, Richard

**Cast** Benny Goodman and His Band; Darnell, Linda; Bari, Lynn; Oakie, Jack; Cardwell, James; Joslyn, Allyn; Moore, Dickie

**Song(s)** I'm Making Believe; Hey Bub! Let's Have a Ball; Ten Days with Baby; Chug Chug, Choo-Choo, Chug; One Chord in Two Flats [1]; Tsk, Tsk, That's Love [1]

**Notes** There are also instrumentals of "Jersey Bounce" by Bobby Plater, Edward Johnson and Tiny Bradshaw; "I've Found a New Baby" by Jack Palmer and Spencer Williams; "The World Is Waiting for the Sunrise" by Ernest Seitz and "Rachel's Dream" by Benny Goodman. [1] Not used.

---

### 5928 ✦ SWEET BIRD OF YOUTH
Metro–Goldwyn–Mayer, 1962

**Producer(s)** Berman, Pandro S.
**Director(s)** Brooks, Richard
**Screenwriter(s)** Brooks, Richard
**Source(s)** *Sweet Bird of Youth* (play) Williams, Tennessee

**Cast** Newman, Paul; Page, Geraldine; Knight, Shirley; Begley, Ed; Torn, Rip; Dunnock, Mildred; Abbott, Philip; Sherwood, Madeleine; Cahill, Barry; Taylor, Dub; Douglas, John

**Song(s)** It's a Big, Wide Wonderful World (C/L: Rox, John)

---

### 5929 ✦ SWEET CHARITY
Universal, 1969

**Composer(s)** Coleman, Cy
**Lyricist(s)** Fields, Dorothy
**Choreographer(s)** Fosse, Bob

**Producer(s)** Arthur, Robert
**Director(s)** Fosse, Bob
**Screenwriter(s)** Stone, Peter
**Source(s)** *Sweet Charity* (musical) Coleman, Cy; Fields, Dorothy; Simon, Neil

**Cast** MacLaine, Shirley; Rivera, Chita; Kelly, Paula; Davis Jr., Sammy; Montalban, Ricardo; Kaye, Stubby; McMartin, John; Bouchet, Barbara; Hewitt, Alan

**Song(s)** Sweet Charity [1]; My Personal Property; Big Spender [2]; Rich Man's Frug [2]; If My Friends Could See Me Now [2]; There's Gotta Be Something Better than This [2]; It's a Nice Face; Rhythm of Life [2]; I'm a Brass Band [2]; I Love to Cry at Weddings [2]; Where Am I Going [2]

**Notes** [1] Different tune from Broadway musical. [2] From original Broadway production.

---

### 5930 ✦ SWEET GENEVIEVE
Columbia, 1947

**Composer(s)** Roberts, Allan; Fisher, Doris
**Lyricist(s)** Roberts, Allan; Fisher, Doris
**Choreographer(s)** Brier, Audrene

**Producer(s)** Katzman, Sam
**Director(s)** Dreifuss, Arthur
**Screenwriter(s)** Brewer, Jameson; Dreifuss, Arthur

**Cast** Hirsch, Ray [1]; Porter, Jean; Lydon, Jimmy; Marlen, Gloria; Hodges, Ralph; Littlefield, Lucien; Al Donahue and His Orchestra

**Song(s)** Five o' the Best [3]; Mama (Come Away from That Juke Box); A Song to Remember [2] (C/L: Traditional; Cahn, Sammy; Stoloff, Morris; Chaplin, Saul)

**Notes** "Sweet Genevieve" was sung also. [1] Dubbed by Arthur Malvin. [2] Not used. Music based on Chopin's "E Major Etude." [3] Also in I SURRENDER DEAR.

---

### 5931 ✦ THE SWEETHEART OF SIGMA CHI (1933)
Monogram, 1933

**Director(s)** Marin, Edwin L.
**Screenwriter(s)** Waggner, George; Reed, Luther; De Mond, Albert

**Cast** Carlisle, Mary; Crabbe, Buster; Starrett, Charles; Lake, Florence; Tamblyn, Eddie; Starr, Sally; Blackford, Mary

**Song(s)** Fraternity Walk (C: Ward, Edward; Fiorito, Ted; L: Waggner, George); It's Spring Again (C: Ward, Edward; Fiorito, Ted; L: Waggner, George)

**Notes** No cue sheet available. There is also a vocal of "The Sweetheart of Sigma Chi" by Byron D. Stokes and F. Dudleigh Vernon.

---

### 5932 ✦ THE SWEETHEART OF SIGMA CHI (1946)
Monogram, 1946

**Producer(s)** Bernard, Jeffrey
**Director(s)** Bernhard, Jack
**Screenwriter(s)** Jacoby, Michel

**Cast** Regan, Phil; Knox, Elyse; Brito, Phil; Hunter, Ross; Harmon, Tom; Guilfoyle, Paul; Gillis, Ann; Brophy, Edward S.; Hale Jr., Alan; Beaudine Jr., William; Slim Gaillard Five; Frankie Carle and His Orchestra

**Song(s)** Five Minutes More (C: Styne, Jule; L: Cahn, Sammy); Penthouse Serenade (C/L: Jason, Will; Burton, Val); It's Not I'm Such a Wolf, It's You're Such a Lamb (C/L: Madden, Marle; Darwin, Lanier); And Then It's Heaven (C/L: Seiler, Eddie; Marcus, Sol; Kaufman, Al); Cement Mixer (C/L: Gaillard, Slim; Ricks, Lee); Yeproc-Heresi (inst.) (C: Gaillard, Slim); Bach Meets Carle (inst.) (C: Carle, Frankie)

**Notes** No cue sheet available. There is a vocal of Sweetheart of Sigma Chi by F. Dudleigh Vernon and Byron D. Stokes.

---

### 5933 ✦ SWEETHEART OF THE CAMPUS
Columbia, 1941

**Composer(s)** Press, Jacques
**Lyricist(s)** Cherkose, Eddie
**Choreographer(s)** Da Pron, Louis

**Director(s)** Dmytryk, Edward
**Screenwriter(s)** Andrews, Robert; Hartmann, Edmund L.

**Cast** Keeler, Ruby; Nelson, Ozzie; Hilliard, Harriet; Beddoe, Don; Howard, Kathleen; Lessey, George; Judels, Charles; Conklin, Chester; Four Spirits of Rhythm [1]

**Song(s)** Beat It Out; When the Glee Club Swings the Alma Mater (C/L: Samuels, Walter G.; Newman, Charles); Where (C/L: Krakeur, Jacques); Tap Happy; Tom Tom (C/L: Samuels, Walter G.); Here We Go Again; Zig Me with a Gentle Zag [2]

**Notes** Titled BROADWAY AHEAD in Great Britain. [1] Teddie Bunn, Douglas Daniels, Wilbur Daniels and Leo Watson. [2] Used instrumentally only. Sung in BETTY CO-ED.

---

### 5934 ✦ SWEETHEART OF THE FLEET
Columbia, 1942

**Producer(s)** Fier, Jack
**Director(s)** Barton, Charles
**Screenwriter(s)** Duffy, Albert; Tombragel, Maurice

**Cast** Stewart, Blanche; Allman, Elvia; Davis, Joan; Falkenburg, Jinx; Woodbury, Joan; Ryan, Tim; Stevens, Robert

**Song(s)** We Did It Before (And We'll Do It Again) (C/L: Friend, Cliff; Tobias, Charles); All Over the Place (C/L: Gay, Noel; Eyton, Frank); I Surrender Dear (C: Barris, Harry; L: Clifford, Gordon)

**Notes** No cue sheet available.

## 5935 ◆ SWEETHEARTS
### Metro–Goldwyn–Mayer, 1939

**Musical Score** Stothart, Herbert
**Composer(s)** Stothart, Herbert
**Lyricist(s)** Wright, Bob; Forrest, Chet
**Choreographer(s)** Rasch, Albertina

**Producer(s)** Stromberg, Hunt
**Director(s)** Van Dyke II, W.S.
**Screenwriter(s)** Parker, Dorothy; Campbell, Alan
**Source(s)** *Sweethearts* (musical) Herbert, Victor; Smith, Robert B.; Smith, Harry B.; de Gresac, Fred

**Cast** MacDonald, Jeanette; Eddy, Nelson; Morgan, Frank; Rice, Florence; Bing, Herman; Bolger, Ray; Auer, Mischa; Gardiner, Reginald; Joslyn, Allyn

**Song(s)** Iron, Iron, Iron (C: Herbert, Victor); Dutch Boy; Fisher Boys; Waiting for the Bride (C: Herbert, Victor); The Call; Wooden Shoes (C: Herbert, Victor); The Escape; Every Lover Must Meet His Fate (C: Herbert, Victor); The Game of Love (C: Herbert, Victor); Happy Day; Sweethearts; Pretty As a Picture (C: Herbert, Victor); Mademoiselle (C: Herbert, Victor); We Greet You (L: Stothart, Herbert); Summer Serenade—Badinage (C: Herbert, Victor); On Parade (C: Herbert, Victor); Angelus (C: Herbert, Victor); In the Convent They Never Taught Me That (C: Herbert, Victor)

**Notes** There are also vocals of "Message of the Violet" by Gustave Luders and Frank Pixley; and "Little Grey Home in the West" by Lehr and Eardley-Wilmot.

## 5936 ◆ SWEETHEART SERENADE
### Warner Brothers, 1958

**Song(s)** When You Were a Smile on Your Mother's Lips and a Twinkle in Your Father's Eye [1] (C: Fain, Sammy; L: Kahal, Irving)

**Notes** Short subject. [1] Also in DAMES.

## 5937 ◆ SWEETHEARTS OF THE U.S.A.
### Monogram, 1944

**Composer(s)** Newman, Charles
**Lyricist(s)** Pollack, Lew

**Producer(s)** Cutler, Lester
**Director(s)** Collins, Lewis D.
**Screenwriter(s)** St. Claire, Arthur; Keith, Jane; Long, Richard

**Cast** Merkel, Una; Parkyakarkus; Novis, Donald; Cornell, Lillian; Gibson, Judith; Friend, Joel; Wright Sr.,

Cobina; Martin, Marion; Barnett, Vince; Sanford, Ralph; Jan Garber and His Orchestra; Henry King and His Orchestra; Phil Ohman and His Orchestra

**Song(s)** Sweethearts of the U.S.A.; All the Latins Know Is Si, Si; You Can't Brush Off a Russian; We're the Ones; Hold On to your Hat; That Reminds Me

**Notes** No cue sheet available. Titled SWEETHEARTS ON PARADE overseas.

## 5938 ◆ SWEETHEARTS ON PARADE (1930)
### Columbia, 1930

**Producer(s)** Christie, Al
**Director(s)** Neilan, Marshall
**Screenwriter(s)** Clements, Colin

**Cast** White, Alice; Hughes, Lloyd; Prevost, Marie; Thompson, Ken; Cooke, Ray; Sterling, Ford

**Song(s)** Dream of Me (C/L: Bibo, Irving; Cohen, Henry); Sweethearts on Parade [1] (C: Lombardo, Carmen; L: Newman, Charles); Yearning Just for You [1] (C: Burke, Joe; L: Davis, Benny); Misstep [1] (C/L: Bibo, Irving)

**Notes** [1] Instrumental only.

## 5939 ◆ SWEETHEARTS ON PARADE (1944)

See SWEETHEARTS OF THE U.S.A.

## 5940 ◆ SWEETHEARTS ON PARADE (1953)
### Republic, 1953

**Musical Score** Armbruster, Robert
**Lyricist(s)** Dwan, Allan
**Choreographer(s)** Castle, Nick

**Producer(s)** Dwan, Allan
**Director(s)** Dwan, Allan
**Screenwriter(s)** Branch, Houston

**Cast** Middleton, Ray; Norman, Lucille; Christy, Eileen; Shirley, Bill; Rodriguez, Estelita; Sundberg, Clinton; Carey Jr., Harry; Bacon, Irving; Corday, Mara

**Song(s)** Mating Time (C: Strauss, Johann); Then You'll Remember Me (C: Balfe, M.W.); A-Rovin' (C: Traditional); Blue Juniata (C: Sullivan, M.D.; L: Armbruster, Robert); Molly Darling (C/L: Hays, Will); Ah So Pure [2] (C: Flotow, Frederick; L: Armbruster, Robert); Flow Gently Sweet Afton (C: Traditional; L: Armbruster, Robert); Young Love (C: von Suppe, Franz; L: Armbruster, Robert); Pleased to Meet You [1] (C: Bland, James); Romance (C: Rubinstein, Arthur; L: Armbruster, Robert); You Naughty, Naughty Men (C: Kennick, I.; Bicknell, G.); Love Is a Pain (C: Traditional); Wanderin' (C: Traditional)

**Notes** There are also vocals of "Cindy"; "Regnava Sil Silencio" from LUCIA DI LAMMERMOOR by Donizetti; "I Wish I Was Single Again" and "Nelly Bly"

by Stephen Foster; "Ah Non Guinge" by Bellini; "Kathleen Mavoureen" by Annie Crawford and Frederick William Nichols Crouch and "Sweet Genevieve" by George Cooper and Henry Tucker. [1] Based on the tune "In the Evening." [2] From music in opera MARTHA.

## 5941 ✦ SWEETIE
### Paramount, 1929

**Composer(s)**   Whiting, Richard A.
**Lyricist(s)**   Marion Jr., George
**Choreographer(s)**   Lindsay, Earl

**Director(s)**   Tuttle, Frank
**Screenwriter(s)**   Marion Jr., George; Corrigan, Lloyd
**Source(s)**   *The Charm School* (play)

**Cast**   Kane, Helen; Carroll, Nancy; Oakie, Jack; Smith, Stanley; Erwin, Stuart; Austin, William; The King's Men [3]

**Song(s)**   Bear Down Pelham; My Sweeter Than Sweet [4]; Cute Peekin' Knees [2]; Alma Mammy; He's So Unusual (C/L: Sherman, Al; Lewis, Al; Silver, Abner); The Prep Step; I Think You'll Like It; Cuddlesome Baby (C/L: Coslow, Sam); Reach for a Sweetie [1]

**Notes**   Originally titled SIS BOOM BARBARA. [1] Not used. [2] Marion had previously written a similar song with the same lyrics and title with Jean Schwartz. However the music was completely different. [3] Consisted of Ken Darby, Rad Robinson, Bud Linn and John Dodson. [4] Also used in HONEY and not used in SAFETY IN NUMBERS.

## 5942 ✦ SWEET JESUS, PREACHER MAN
### Metro–Goldwyn–Mayer, 1973

**Musical Score**   Tapscott, Horace

**Producer(s)**   Cady, Daniel B.
**Director(s)**   Schellerup, Henning
**Screenwriter(s)**   Cerullo, John; Madden, M. Stuart; Leitch, Abbey

**Cast**   Mosley, Roger E.; Smith, William; Pataki, Michael; Tornatore, Joe; Gibbs, Marla; Johnigarn, Tom

**Song(s)**   Sweet Jesus (C: Tapscott, Horace; L: Hill, Linda; Bruno, Jo Ann); Forgotten Man (C/L: McNeal, Larry); Cyrus Holmes - Preacher Man (C: Tapscott, Horace; L: Tapscott, Horace; Hill, Linda)

**Notes**   There are also several spirituals which are given vocal treatment.

## 5943 ✦ SWEET KITTY BELLAIRS
### Warner Brothers, 1930

**Composer(s)**   Dolan, Robert Emmett
**Lyricist(s)**   O'Keefe, Walter

**Director(s)**   Green, Alfred E.
**Screenwriter(s)**   Alexander, J. Grubb
**Source(s)**   *Sweet Kitty Bellairs* (play) Belasco, David

**Cast**   Dell, Claudia; Torrence, Ernest; Pidgeon, Walter; Askam, Perry; Collyer, June; Belmore, Lionel; Finch, Flora

**Song(s)**   Tally Ho; Song of the City of Bath; Drunk Song; Pump Song; Duelling Song; My Love; You—O-O, I Love but You; Petty's Leg; Highwayman's Song; Here Is My Heart [1]

**Notes**   [1] Sheet music only.

## 5944 ✦ SWEET LIBERTY
### Universal, 1986

**Musical Score**   Broughton, Bruce

**Producer(s)**   Bregman, Martin
**Director(s)**   Alda, Alan
**Screenwriter(s)**   Alda, Alan

**Cast**   Alda, Alan; Caine, Michael; Pfeiffer, Michelle; Hoskins, Bob; Hilboldt, Lise; Rubinek, Saul; Gish, Lillian; Chiles, Lois; Thorson, Linda; Alda, Anthony

**Song(s)**   Something Special (Is Gonna Happen Tonight) (C/L: Rice, Howie; Rich, Allan Dennis); Knees Up Mother Brown (C/L: Weston, Harris; Lee, Burt; Taylor, Irving)

## 5945 ✦ SWEET LORRAINE
### Angelika, 1987

**Musical Score**   Robbins, Richard

**Producer(s)**   Gomer, Steve
**Director(s)**   Gomer, Steve
**Screenwriter(s)**   Zettler, Michael; Altman, Shelly

**Cast**   Stapleton, Maureen; Alvarado, Trini; Richardson, Lee; Lloyd, John Bedford; Roman, Freddie; Esposito, Giancarlo; Graff, Todd

**Song(s)**   Sweet Lorraine (C: Burwell, Cliff; L: Parish, Mitchell); Time Is Kind (C/L: Graff, Todd); Twenty-Five Hours a Day (C/L: Graff, Todd); Phil's Aerobics (C: Robbins, Richard; L: Adelman, Sam)

**Notes**   No cue sheet available.

## 5946 ✦ SWEET MOMENTS
### Paramount, 1939

**Composer(s)**   Powell, Teddy; Whitcup, Leonard
**Lyricist(s)**   Whitcup, Leonard; Powell, Teddy

**Cast**   Russ Morgan and His Orchestra

**Song(s)**   Sweet Moments (C/L: Morgan, Russ; Franklin, Dave); Old Heart of Mine; Holiday in Toyland; Am I Proud

**Notes**   Short subject. No cue sheet available. Sheet music only.

## 5947 ◆ SWEET MUSIC
### Warner Brothers, 1935

**Musical Score** Kaun, Bernhard
**Composer(s)** Fain, Sammy
**Lyricist(s)** Kahal, Irving
**Choreographer(s)** Connolly, Bobby

**Producer(s)** Bischoff, Sam
**Director(s)** Green, Alfred E.
**Screenwriter(s)** Wald, Jerry; Erickson, Carl; Duff, Warren

**Cast** Vallee, Rudy; Dvorak, Ann; Sparks, Ned; Morgan, Helen; Armstrong, Robert; Jenkins, Allen; White, Alice; Cawthorn, Joseph; Shean, Al; Reed, Philip; Hicks, Russell; O'Neill, Henry; Rudy Vallee's Connecticut Yankees; Frank and Milt Brittone Orchestra

**Song(s)** Sweet Music (C: Warren, Harry; L: Dubin, Al); Don't Go on a Diet Baby; There's a Diff'rent You in Your Heart; Good Green Acres of Home; Selzer Theme Song; Outside [1] (C/L: Flynn, Frank); The Drunkard Song [1] (C/L: Vallee, Rudy); I See Two Lovers [2] (C: Wrubel, Allie; L: Dixon, Mort); Fare Thee Well Annabelle (C: Wrubel, Allie; L: Dixon, Mort); Ev'ry Day

**Notes** [1] Not written for film. Some sources list "Winter Overnight" but it doesn't appear in cue sheets. [2] See note under FLIRTATION WALK.

## 5948 ◆ SWEET NOVEMBER
### Warner Brothers, 1968

**Musical Score** Legrand, Michel

**Producer(s)** Gershwin, Jerry; Kastner, Elliott
**Director(s)** Miller, Robert Ellis
**Screenwriter(s)** Raucher, Herman

**Cast** Dennis, Sandy; Newley, Anthony; Bikel, Theodore; DeBenning, Burr; Baron, Sandy

**Song(s)** Sweet November (C/L: Bricusse, Leslie; Newley, Anthony)

## 5949 ◆ THE SWEET RIDE
### Twentieth Century–Fox, 1967

**Musical Score** Rugolo, Pete

**Producer(s)** Pasternak, Joe
**Director(s)** Hart, Harvey
**Screenwriter(s)** Mankiewicz, Tom

**Cast** Franciosa, Anthony; Sarrazin, Michael; Bisset, Jacqueline; Denver, Bob

**Song(s)** Sweet Ride (C/L: Hazlewood, Lee); Never Again (C/L: Lewis, Peter; Stevenson, Don); Sock Me Choo Choo [1] (C/L: Hazlewood, Lee)

**Notes** [1] This is used instrumentally only. On the cue sheets the title is followed by "(Sweet Ride)." This

indicates the two Hazlewood numbers may be the same song although listed seperately on the cue sheet. A press release for the soundtrack indicates there are two different songs.

## 5950 ◆ SWEET ROSIE O'GRADY
### Twentieth Century–Fox, 1943

**Composer(s)** Warren, Harry
**Lyricist(s)** Gordon, Mack
**Choreographer(s)** Pan, Hermes

**Producer(s)** Perlberg, William
**Director(s)** Cummings, Irving
**Screenwriter(s)** Englund, Ken

**Cast** Grable, Betty; Young, Robert; Menjou, Adolphe; Gardiner, Reginald; Grey, Virginia; Regan, Phil; Rumann, Sig; Dinehart, Alan; Cavanaugh, Hobart; Orth, Frank; Hale, Jonathan

**Song(s)** Where, Oh Where, Is the Groom; My Heart Tells Me; The Wishing Waltz; Get Your Police Gazette; Sad Parisienne (L: Newman, Lionel); Goin' to the County Fair; My Sam; The Bagpipes of Buckingham [1]

**Notes** There are also vocals of "Sweet Rosie O'Grady" by Maud Nugent; "Throw Him Down McCloskey" by J.W. Kelly and "Two Little Girls in Blue" by Charles Graham. [1] Not used.

## 5951 ◆ SWEET SURRENDER
### Universal, 1935

**Composer(s)** Suesse, Dana
**Lyricist(s)** Hyman, Edward

**Producer(s)** Laemmle, Carl
**Director(s)** Brice, Monte
**Screenwriter(s)** Weaver, John V.A.

**Cast** Parker, Frank; Tamara; Lynd, Helen; Brown, Russ; Pearson, Arthur

**Song(s)** Love Makes the World Go 'Round; Take This Ring; I'm So Happy I Could Cry; The Day You Were Born; Twenty-Four Hours a Day (C: Hanley, James F.; L: Swanstrom, Arthur); Let Us Have Peace (C: Wayne, Mabel; L: Fleeson, Neville); Please Put on Your Wraps and Toddle Home (C: Wayne, Mabel; Fleeson, Neville); Sweet Surrender

**Notes** No cue sheet available.

## 5952 ◆ SWEET SWING
### Universal, 1943

**Song(s)** Just a Step Away from Heaven [1] (C: Rosen, Milton; L: Carter, Everett)

**Notes** Short subject. There are other vocals in this short. [1] Also in HI 'YA, SAILOR.

## 5953 ✦ SWING AND SWAY

See SWING IN THE SADDLE.

## 5954 ✦ THE SWINGER
### Paramount, 1965

**Musical Score**  Paich, Marty
**Choreographer(s)**  Winters, David

**Producer(s)**  Sidney, George
**Director(s)**  Sidney, George
**Screenwriter(s)**  Roman, Lawrence

**Cast**  Ann-Margaret; Franciosa, Anthony; Coote, Robert; Romain, Yvonne; McMahon, Horace; Nichols, Barbara

**Song(s)**  The Swinger (C: Previn, Andre; L: Previn, Dory)

## 5955 ✦ SWING FEVER
### Metro–Goldwyn–Mayer, 1943

**Composer(s)**  Fain, Sammy
**Lyricist(s)**  Brown, Lew; Freed, Ralph
**Choreographer(s)**  Matray, Ernst; Matray, Maria

**Producer(s)**  Starr, Irving
**Director(s)**  Whelan, Tim
**Screenwriter(s)**  Perrin, Nat; Wilson, Warren

**Cast**  Kay Kyser and His Orchestra; Maxwell, Marilyn; Gargan, William; Pendleton, Nat; Horne, Lena; Babbitt, Harry; Kabbible, Ish; Mason, Sully; Conway, Julie; Irwin, Trudy; Rosenbloom, Maxie; The Merriel Abbott Dancers

**Song(s)**  Mississippi Dream Boat; You're So Indiff'rent (L: Parish, Mitchell); I Planted a Rose (In the Garden of Your Heart) (C: Brown, Nacio Herb); One Girl and Two Boys (C: Brown, Nacio Herb); Sh! Don't Make a Sound (C/L: Skylar, Sunny); The Trembling of a Leaf [1] (C: Green, Johnny; L: Lawrence, Jack); Just Loving You [2] (C: Edens, Roger); You'd Make a Wonderful Dream [2] (C: Green, Johnny)

**Notes**  Originally titled RIGHT ABOUT FACE. There is also a vocal of "I Never Knew" by Pitts. [1] Not used but recorded. [2] Not used.

## 5956 ✦ SWING HIGH
### Pathe, 1930

**Composer(s)**  Silver, Abner
**Lyricist(s)**  Gordon, Mack

**Producer(s)**  Derr, E.B.
**Director(s)**  Santley, Joseph
**Screenwriter(s)**  Seymour, James

**Cast**  Twelvetrees, Helen; Scott, Fred; Burgess, Dorothy; Sheehan, John; Pollard, Daphne; Fawcett, George; Fetchit, Stepin; Conklin, Chester; Turpin, Ben; Edeson, Robert

**Song(s)**  Do You Think I Could Grow on You?; It Must Be Love [1]; With My Guitar and You [2] (C: Snyder, Ted; L: Harris, Mort; Heyman, Edward); Shoo the Hoodoo Away (C: Snyder, Ted; L: Harris, Mort); There's Happiness Over the Hill (C: Sullivan, Henry; L: Egan, Raymond B.)

**Notes**  No cue sheet available. [1] Also in SIN TAKES A HOLIDAY (RKO). [2] Also in BORDER LEGION (Republic).

## 5957 ✦ SWING HIGH, SWING LOW
### Paramount, 1937

**Producer(s)**  Hornblow Jr., Arthur
**Director(s)**  Leisen, Mitchell
**Screenwriter(s)**  Hammerstein II, Oscar; Van Upp, Virginia
**Source(s)**  *Burlesque* (play) Watters, George Manker; Hopkins, Arthur

**Cast**  Lombard, Carole; MacMurray, Fred; Butterworth, Charles; Dixon, Jean; Lamour, Dorothy; Stephens, Harvey; Judels, Charles; Cunningham, Cecil; Arnt, Charles; Pangborn, Franklin; Quinn, Anthony

**Song(s)**  Lonely Little Senorita [7] (C: Hajos, Karl; L: Robin, Leo); Panamania (C: Siegel, Al; L: Coslow, Sam); I Hear a Call to Arms (C: Siegel, Al; L: Coslow, Sam); If It Isn't Pain (Then It Isn't Love) [4] (C: Rainger, Ralph; L: Robin, Leo); Swing High, Swing Low [1] (C: Lane, Burton; L: Freed, Ralph); Spring Is in the Air [2] [6] (C: Kisco, Charley; L: Freed, Ralph); A Tall, Dark, Lonesome Gentleman [2] (C/L: Coslow, Sam); Let Down Your Hair [2] [5] (C/L: Coslow, Sam); The Voice of Romance [2] (C/L: Coslow, Sam); Panamama [2] (C: Siegel, Al; L: Coslow, Sam); On the Cuff [3] (C/L: Kisco, Charley)

**Notes**  Film formerly titled MORNING, NOON AND NIGHT. [1] Used instrumentally only. [2] Not used. [3] Not used. Written for THREE CHEERS FOR LOVE. [4] Written for THE DEVIL IS A WOMAN. [5] Also not used in THRILL OF A LIFETIME. [6] Published though not used. [7] Also in CRADLE SONG with co-composer credit given to Ralph Rainger.

## 5958 ✦ SWING HOSTESS
### PRC, 1944

**Composer(s)**  Livingston, Jay; Evans, Ray; Bellin, Lewis
**Lyricist(s)**  Livingston, Jay; Evans, Ray; Bellin, Lewis

**Producer(s)**  Neufeld, Sam
**Director(s)**  Neufeld, Sam
**Screenwriter(s)**  Rousseau, Louise; Davenport, Gail

**Cast**  Tilton, Martha; Adrian, Iris; Nazarro, Cliff; Holman, Harry; Lynne, Emmet; Brodel, Betty; Charles Collins and His Band

**Song(s)**   I'll Eat My Hat; Let's Capture This Moment; Say It with Love; Music to My Ears; Highway Polka; Got an Invitation

**Notes**   No cue sheet available.

## 5959   ✦   SWINGIN' ALONG
Twentieth Century–Fox, 1962

**Producer(s)**   Leewood, Jack
**Director(s)**   Barton, Charles
**Screenwriter(s)**   Brewer, Jameson

**Cast**   Noonan, Tommy; Marshall, Pete; Eden, Barbara; Charles, Ray; Williams, Roger; Vee, Bobby; Gilchrist, Connie; Carney, Alan; Mazurki, Mike

**Song(s)**   Song of the City (C/L: Kent, Walter; Farrar, Walton); Sticks and Stones (C/L: Charles, Ray); What'd I Say [1] (C/L: Charles, Ray); More Than I Can Say (C/L: Curtis, Sonny; Allison, Jerry)

**Notes**   [1] Also in VIVA LAS VEGAS (MGM) and BLUES FOR LOVERS.

## 5960   ✦   SWINGIN' ON A RAINBOW
Republic, 1945

**Composer(s)**   Kent, Walter
**Lyricist(s)**   Gannon, Kim

**Producer(s)**   White, Eddy
**Director(s)**   Beaudine, William
**Screenwriter(s)**   Grey, John; Cooper, Olive

**Cast**   Frazee, Jane; Taylor, Brad; Langdon, Harry; Gombell, Minna; Ward, Amelita; Ryan, Tim; Harvey, Paul; Niles, Wendell; Davies, Richard

**Song(s)**   Wrap Your Troubles in a Rainbow; For You and Me [1]; The Music in My Heart Is You [2] (C/L: Elliott, Jack)

**Notes**   [1] Also in HITCH HIKE TO HAPPINESS and MAN FROM OKLAHOMA. [2] Also in SWINGIN' ON A RAINBOW.

## 5961   ✦   THE SWINGIN' SET

See GET YOURSELF A COLLEGE GIRL.

## 5962   ✦   SWING IN THE SADDLE
Columbia, 1944

**Producer(s)**   Fier, Jack
**Director(s)**   Landers, Lew
**Screenwriter(s)**   Beecher, Elizabeth; Grant, Morton; Ropes, Bradford

**Cast**   Frazee, Jane; Williams, Guinn "Big Boy"; Bliss, Sally; Jimmy Wakely and His Oklahoma Cowboys; Red River Dave; The King Cole Trio; Treen, Mary; Summerville, Slim; Mathews, Carole; Foulger, Byron

**Song(s)**   Dude Cowboy (C/L: Massey, Allen; Massey, Curt; Wellington, Larry); Cowboy's Polka (C/L: Patton, Jack); Hey Mable (C/L: Stryker, Fred); You're the Dream, I'm the Dreamer (C/L: Davis, Benny; Burton, Nat; Murry, Ted); The Singing Hills (C/L: David, Mack; Sanford, Dick; Mysels, Sammy); By the River St. Marie (C: Warren, Harry; L: Leslie, Edgar); When It's Harvest Time in Peaceful Valley (C/L: Martin, Robert); She Broke My Heart in Three Places (C/L: Drake, Milton; Hoffman, Al; Livingston, Jerry); Amor (C/L: Ruiz, Gabriel; Skylar, Sunny); There'll Be a Jubilee (C/L: Moore, Phil)

**Notes**   Titled SWING AND SWAY overseas.

## 5963   ✦   SWING IT BUDDY

See SWING IT PROFESSOR.

## 5964   ✦   SWING IT PROFESSOR
1937, Conn-Ambassador

**Composer(s)**   Heath, Al; Lee, Connie; LeRoux, Buddy
**Lyricist(s)**   Heath, Al; Lee, Connie; LeRoux, Buddy

**Director(s)**   Neilan, Marshall
**Screenwriter(s)**   Barrows, Nicholas T.; St. Clair, Robert

**Cast**   Tomlin, Pinky; Stone, Paula; Kornman, Mary; Stone, Milburn; Gleason, Pat; Elliott, Gordon; The Three Gentle Maniacs; The Four Squires

**Song(s)**   I'm Sorta Kinda Glad I Met You; An Old-Fashioned Melody; I'm Richer than a Millionaire

**Notes**   No cue sheet available. Titled SWING IT BUDDY overseas.

## 5965   ✦   SWING IT SOLDIER
Universal, 1941

**Composer(s)**   Rosen, Milton
**Lyricist(s)**   Carter, Everett

**Producer(s)**   Sandford, Joseph G.
**Director(s)**   Young, Harold
**Screenwriter(s)**   Cochran, Dorcas; Jones, Arthur V.

**Cast**   Murray, Ken; Langford, Frances; Wilson, Don; Stewart, Blanche; Adrian, Iris; Hall, Thurston

**Song(s)**   Got Love [1]; Keep Your Thumbs Up (C: Berens, Norman; L: Brooks, Jack); Rug Cuttin' Romeo [2]; Two Hearts That Pass in the Night (C: Lecuona, Ernesto; L: Brown, Forman); Play Fiddle Play (C: Deutsch, Emery; Altman, Arthur; L: Lawrence, Jack); I'm Gonna Swing My Way Up to Heaven (C: Press, Jacques; L: Cherkose, Eddie)

**Notes**   There are also vocals of "My Melancholy Baby" by G.A. Norton, Maybelle E. Watson and Ernie Burnett; "A Bicycle Built for Two" by Harry Dacre; "Mama Don't Allow It" by Charles "Cow Cow" Davenport and "Annie Laurie" by Lady John Scott. [1] Also in GET

GOING, I'M NOBODY'S SWEETHEART NOW and MISSISSIPPI GAMBLER (1942). [2] Also in IN THE GROOVE, SING ANOTHER CHORUS and WHERE DID YOU GET THAT GIRL.

## 5966 ◆ SWING OUT SISTER
### Universal, 1945

**Composer(s)** Berens, Norman
**Lyricist(s)** Brooks, Jack

**Producer(s)** Burton, Bernard W.
**Director(s)** Dein, Edward
**Screenwriter(s)** Blankfort, Henry

**Cast** Raeburn, Frances; Stone, Milburn; Cameron, Rod; The Leo Diamond Quintet

**Song(s)** Happy-Go-Lucky Lady; Love Is a Bluebird on the Wing (C: Fairchild, Edgar); Only in Dreams [1] (C: Strauss, Johann; L: Lerner, Sam); Swing It, Mister Chumbly; All I Want to Do Is Sing

**Notes** [1] Music adapted by Charles Previn from the "Emperor Waltz."

## 5967 ◆ SWING OUT THE BLUES
### Columbia, 1943

**Producer(s)** White, Sam
**Director(s)** St. Clair, Malcolm
**Screenwriter(s)** Cochran, Dorcas

**Cast** Haymes, Bob; Merrick, Lynn; Carter, Janis; The Vagabonds [2]; Ryan, Tim; Elliott, Dick

**Song(s)** Dark Eyes (L: Vagabonds, The); It Can't Be Wrong [1] (C: Steiner, Max; L: Gannon, Kim); Prelude to Love (C/L: Forrest, Chet; Wright, Bob); That Great American Home [3] (C/L: Sherman, Al; Lewis, Al; Wrubel, Allie); Tahitian Lullaby [1] (C/L: Fowler, Robert W.; Gilbert, L. Wolfe); Emmett's Lullaby (L: Vagabonds, The); Our Career (C: Chaplin, Saul; L: Samuels, Walter G.)

**Notes** Also known as RHAPSODY IN A FLAT. [1] Not written for picture. [2] Pete Peterson, Attilio Risso, Dominic Germano and Albert Torrieri. [3] Written in 1933.

## 5968 ◆ SWING PARADE OF 1946
### Monogram, 1946

**Choreographer(s)** Boyle, Jack

**Producer(s)** Parsons, Lindsley; Romm, Harry
**Director(s)** Karlson, Phil
**Screenwriter(s)** Ryan, Tim

**Cast** Storm, Gale; Regan, Phil; Brophy, Edward S.; Treen, Mary; Eldredge, John; Hicks, Russell; Belasco, Leon; The Three Stooges; Boswell, Connee; Louis Jordan and His Tympany Five; Will Osborne and His Orchestra

**Song(s)** Just a Little Fond Affection (C/L: Box, Elton; Cox, Desmond; Ilda, Lewis); Don't Worry About the Mule (C/L: Davis, William; Groner, Duke; Stewart, Charles); A Tender Word Will Mend It All (C/L: Fisher, Doris; Roberts, Allan); Oh, Brother! (C/L: Malneck, Matty; Wrubel, Allie); After All This Time (C/L: DeFur, Paul; Thompson, Ken)

**Notes** No cue sheet available. There are also vocals of "Stormy Weather" by Harold Arlen and Ted Koehler; "On the Sunny Side of the Street" by Jimmy McHugh and Dorothy Fields and "Caldonia" by Fleecie Moore.

## 5969 ◆ SWING SHIFT
### Warner Brothers, 1984

**Musical Score** Williams, Patrick

**Producer(s)** Bick, Jerry
**Director(s)** Demme, Jonathan
**Screenwriter(s)** Morton, Rob

**Cast** Hawn, Goldie; Russell, Kurt; Lahti, Christine; Ward, Fred; Harris, Ed; Bond, Sudie; Hunter, Holly

**Song(s)** Someone Waits for You (C/L: Allen, Peter; Jennings, Will); I Didn't Think I'd Fall in Love [1] (C/L: Langhorne, Bruce); Big Bucks (C/L: Henderson, Horace; Feather, Lorraine); Swing Shift Blues [1] (C/L: Langhorne, Bruce); Magic of You [1] (C/L: Langhorne, Bruce; Goetzman, Gary); Tank Me Brother [1] (C/L: Langhorne, Bruce; Goetzman, Gary)

**Notes** [1] Visual vocals.

## 5970 ◆ SWING SHIFT MAISIE
### Metro–Goldwyn–Mayer, 1943

**Musical Score** Hayton, Lennie

**Producer(s)** Haight, George
**Director(s)** McLeod, Norman Z.
**Screenwriter(s)** McCall Jr., Mary C.; Halff, Robert
**Source(s)** characters Collison, Wilson

**Cast** Sothern, Ann; Craig, James; Rogers, Jean; Gilchrist, Connie; Qualen, John; Medford, Kay; The Wiere Brothers

**Song(s)** There's a Girl Behind the Boy Behind the Gun (C: Hayton, Lennie; L: McCall Jr., Mary C.)

**Notes** Titled THE GIRL IN OVERALLS overseas.

## 5971 ◆ SWING, SISTER, SWING
### Universal, 1939

**Choreographer(s)** King, Matty

**Producer(s)** Kelly, Burt
**Director(s)** Santley, Joseph
**Screenwriter(s)** Grayson, Charles

**Cast**   Murray, Ken; Downs, Johnny; Kane, Kathryn; Quillan, Eddie; Truex, Ernest; Sedgewick, Edna; Bryant, Nana; Ted Weems and His Orchestra

**Song(s)**   Wasn't It You? [1] (C: Skinner, Frank; L: Henderson, Charles); Heigh-Ho the Merry-O (C: McHugh, Jimmy; L: Adamson, Harold); Baltimore Bubble (C/L: Skinner, Frank)

**Notes**   [1] Also in LOVE, HONOR AND OH BABY!

## 5972 ✦ SWING SOCIAL
### Metro–Goldwyn–Mayer, 1940

**Musical Score**   Bradley, Scott
**Composer(s)**   Ruick, Walter
**Lyricist(s)**   Barbera, Joseph; Hanna, William

**Song(s)**   Swing Social (C: Bradley, Scott); Victims; Voo Doo

**Notes**   Animated cartoon.

## 5973 ✦ SWING, TEACHER, SWING

See COLLEGE SWING.

## 5974 ✦ SWING THAT CHEER
### Universal, 1938

**Producer(s)**   Golden, Max H.
**Director(s)**   Shuster, Harold
**Screenwriter(s)**   Loeb, Lee; Grayson, Charles

**Cast**   Brown, Tom; Wilcox, Robert; Devine, Andy; Moore, Constance; Truex, Ernest; Weaver, Doodles

**Song(s)**   Chasing You Around (C/L: Actman, Irving)

## 5975 ✦ SWING TIME
### RKO, 1936

**Composer(s)**   Kern, Jerome
**Lyricist(s)**   Fields, Dorothy
**Choreographer(s)**   Pan, Hermes

**Producer(s)**   Berman, Pandro S.
**Director(s)**   Stevens, George
**Screenwriter(s)**   Lindsay, Howard; Scott, Allan

**Cast**   Astaire, Fred; Rogers, Ginger; Moore, Victor; Broderick, Helen; Blore, Eric; Furness, Betty; Metaxa, Georges

**Song(s)**   Waltz in Swing Time (inst.); Pick Yourself Up; The Way You Look Tonight; Bojangles of Harlem; A Fine Romance; It's Not in the Cards (inst.); Never Gonna Dance; Swing Low, Swing High [1]

**Notes**   [1] Not used.

## 5976 ✦ SWINGTIME JOHNNY
### Universal, 1943

**Producer(s)**   Wilson, Warren
**Director(s)**   Cline, Edward F.
**Screenwriter(s)**   Bruckman, Clyde

**Cast**   The Andrews Sisters; Hilliard, Harriet; Ryan, Tim; Wills, Matt; Dugan, Tom; Mitchell Ayres and His Orchestra

**Song(s)**   I May Be Wrong but I Think You're Wonderful [2] (C/L: Sullivan, Henry; Ruskin, Harry); Sweet and Low (C: Rosen, Milton; L: Carter, Everett); Boogie Woogie Choo Choo (C/L: Jordan, Roy; Schoen, Vic; Murphy, Johnny); You Better Give Me Lots of Lovin Honey (C/L: Goell, Kermit; Spielman, Fred); Boogie Woogie Bugle Boy [1] (C: Prince, Hughie; L: Raye, Don); Poor Nell (C: Rosen, Milton; L: Carter, Everett)

**Notes**   There is also a vocal of "When You and I Were Young, Maggie" by George Johnson and J.A. Butterfield and a medley of old songs including "Long, Long Ago," "Strolling thru the Park One Day," "The Band Played On" by Ward and Palmer and "Good Night Ladies." [1] Also in BUCK PRIVATES (1941). [2] Also used in WALLFLOWER and YOUNG MAN WITH A HORN (both Warners). Some sources also credit Milton Ager as cowriter.

## 5977 ✦ SWING WHILE YOU'RE ABLE
### Melody Pictures, 1937

**Director(s)**   Neilan, Marshall
**Screenwriter(s)**   Condon, Charles; Lowe, Sherman

**Cast**   Tomlin, Pinky; Wing, Toby; Bradley, Harry C.; Collins, Monte; Roach, Bert; Kaaren, Suzanne; Romanoff, Michael; Newell, Jimmy; The Three Brian Sisters

**Song(s)**   I'm Gonna Swing While I'm Able (C/L: Parks, Paul; Lee, Connie); Swing, Brother, Swing (C/L: Heath, Al; LeRoux, Buddy); Leave It Up to Uncle Jake (C/L: Parks, Paul; Lee, Connie; Heath, Al; LeRoux, Buddy); You're My Strongest Weakness (C/L: Poe, Coy; Heath, Al; LeRoux, Buddy); One Girl in My Amrs (C/L: Tobias, Harry; Ingraham, Roy); I'm Just a Country Boy at Heart (C/L: Tomlin, Pinky; Parks, Paul; Lee, Connie)

**Notes**   No cue sheet available.

## 5978 ✦ SWING YOUR LADY
### Warner Brothers, 1938

**Musical Score**   Deutsch, Adolph
**Composer(s)**   Jerome, M.K.
**Lyricist(s)**   Scholl, Jack
**Choreographer(s)**   Connolly, Bobby

**Producer(s)**   Wallis, Hal B.
**Director(s)**   Enright, Ray
**Screenwriter(s)**   Shranck, Joseph; Leo, Maurice
**Source(s)**   (play) Nicholson, Kenyon; Robinson, Charles

**Cast**   Bogart, Humphrey; McHugh, Frank; Fazenda, Louise; Pendleton, Nat; Singleton, Penny; Jenkins, Allen; The Weaver Brothers; Reagan, Ronald; Bupp, Tommy and Sonny; Howard, Joan; Howland, Olin; White, Sammy; Savage, Daniel Boone; O'Connell, Hugh

**Song(s)**   Dig Me a Grave in Missouri; The Old Apple Tree; Swing Your Lady; Original Interlude; The Mountain Swingaroo; Hillbilly from Tenth Avenue

### 5979 ✦ SWING YOUR PARTNER
Republic, 1943

**Musical Score**   Glickman, Mort

**Producer(s)**   Schaefer, Armand
**Director(s)**   MacDonald, Frank
**Screenwriter(s)**   McGowan, Stuart; McGowan, Dorrell

**Cast**   Lulu Belle and Scotty; Dale, Esther; Evans, Dale; Clark, Roger; Sherman, Ransom; Allen, Barbara Jo; The Tennessee Ramblers

**Song(s)**   Birthday Song [1] (C: Traditional; L: McGowan, Stuart; McGowan, D.); Swing Your Partner (C/L: Henderson, Charles); Shug Shug Yodel (C/L: Fisher, George); Cheese Cake (C/L: Henderson, Charles); In the Cool of the Evening [2] (C: Styne, Jule; L: Bullock, Walter); Cracker Barrel County (C: Styne, Jule; L: Loesser, Frank)

**Notes**   There is also a vocal of "Everybody Kiss Your Partner" by Sanford, Redmond and Weldon. [1] Based on "Reuben, Reuben." [2] Also in HIT PARADE OF 1941.

### 5980 ✦ SWISS FAMILY ROBINSON
Disney, 1961

**Musical Score**   Alwyn, William; Baker, Buddy

**Producer(s)**   Anderson, Bill
**Director(s)**   Annakin, Ken
**Screenwriter(s)**   Hawley, Lowell S.
**Source(s)**   *Swiss Family Robinson* (novel) Wyss, Johann

**Cast**   Mills, John; McGuire, Dorothy; MacArthur, James; Munro, Janet; Hayakawa, Sessue; Corcoran, Kevin; Kirk, Tommy; Parker, Cecil; Ho, Andy; Reid, Milton; Taylor, Larry

**Song(s)**   Swiss Family Theme (My Heart Was an Island) (C/L: Gilkyson, Terry); The Swisskapolka (Animal Race) [1] (C: Baker, Buddy; L: Jackman, Bob)

**Notes**   [1] Used instrumentally only.

### 5981 ✦ SWISS MISS
Metro–Goldwyn–Mayer, 1938

**Composer(s)**   Charig, Phil
**Lyricist(s)**   Quenzer, Arthur

**Producer(s)**   Roach, Hal
**Director(s)**   Blystone, John
**Screenwriter(s)**   Parrott, James; Adler, Felix; Melson, Charles

**Cast**   Laurel, Stan; Hardy, Oliver; Lind, Della; King, Walter Woolf; Blore, Eric

**Song(s)**   The Cricket Song; Could You Say No to Me?; Mine to Love; I Can't Get Over the Alps; Yo Ho Dee O Lay Hee

**Notes**   No cue sheet available.

### 5982 ✦ THE SWORD AND THE ROSE
Disney, 1953

**Choreographer(s)**   Paltenghi, David

**Producer(s)**   Pearce, Perce
**Director(s)**   Annakin, Ken
**Screenwriter(s)**   Watkin, Lawrence Edward
**Source(s)**   *When Knighthood Was in Flower* (novel) Major, Charles

**Cast**   Todd, Richard; Johns, Glynis; Justice, James Robertson; Barrett, Jane

**Song(s)**   The Sword and the Rose [1] (C/L: Spielman, Fred; Brown, George R.)

**Notes**   [1] Written for exploitation only.

### 5983 ✦ THE SWORD IN THE STONE
Disney, 1963

**Musical Score**   Bruns, George
**Composer(s)**   Sherman, Richard M.; Sherman, Robert B.
**Lyricist(s)**   Sherman, Richard M.; Sherman, Robert B.

**Director(s)**   Reitherman, Wolfgang
**Screenwriter(s)**   Peet, Bill
**Source(s)**   *The Once and Future King* (novel) White, T.H.
**Voices**   Cabot, Sebastian; Sorensen, Rickie; Tyler, Ginny; Alden, Norman; Reitherman, Richard; Reitherman, Robert; Napier, Alan; Wentworth, Martha; Matthews, Junius; Swenson, Karl

**Directing Animator(s)**   Thomas, Franklin; Johnston, Ollie; Kahl, Milt; Lounsbery, John

**Song(s)**   Blue Oak Tree; Higitus Figitus (Merlin's Magic Song); The Legend of the Sword in the Stone; Mad Madam Min; A Most Befuddling Thing; That's What Makes the World Go 'Round

**Notes**   Animated feature.

## 5984 ✦ SYLVESTER
### Columbia, 1985

**Musical Score**   Holdridge, Lee

**Producer(s)**   Jurow, Martin
**Director(s)**   Hunter, Tim
**Screenwriter(s)**   Sobieski, Carol

**Cast**   Farnsworth, Robert; Gilbert, Melissa; Schoeffling, Michael; Towers, Constance; Kowanko, Pete

**Song(s)**   It's Okay (C/L: Callins, George)

## 5985 ✦ SYLVIA
### Paramount, 1964

**Musical Score**   Raksin, David

**Producer(s)**   Poll, Martin H.
**Director(s)**   Douglas, Gordon M.
**Screenwriter(s)**   Boehm, Sydney
**Source(s)**   Sylvia by Cunningham, E.V.

**Cast**   Baker, Carroll; Maharis, George; Dru, Joanne; Lawford, Peter; Lindfors, Viveca; O'Brien, Edmond; Ray, Aldo; Sothern, Ann; Bochner, Lloyd; Novello, Jay

**Song(s)**   Sylvia [1] (C: Raksin, David; L: Webster, Paul Francis)

**Notes**   [1] Background vocal use only. "Dissertation on the State of Bliss (Love and Learn)" by Ira Gershwin and Harold Arlen from THE COUNTRY GIRL is given a visual vocal rendition.

## 5986 ✦ SYLVIA SCARLETT
### RKO, 1935

**Musical Score**   Webb, Roy

**Producer(s)**   Berman, Pandro S.
**Director(s)**   Cukor, George
**Screenwriter(s)**   Unger, Gladys; Collier, John; Offner, Mortimer
**Source(s)**   *The Early Life and Adventures of Sylvia Scarlett* (novel) Mackenzie, Compton

**Cast**   Hepburn, Katharine; Aherne, Brian; Grant, Cary; Gwenn, Edmund; Paley, Natalie

**Song(s)**   Who Wants a Kiss from Me? (C/L: Colombo, Alberto); Hello! Hello! (C/L: Colombo, Alberto)

**Notes**   There are also vocals of "Hello! Hello! Who's Your Lady Friend?" by Harry Fragson and Worton David and "I'll Be Your Sweetheart" by Harry Dacre.

## 5987 ✦ SYMPHONY IN SWING
### Universal, 1949

**Cast**   Duke Ellington and His Orchestra

**Song(s)**   Knock Me a Kiss (C/L: Jackson, Mike)

**Notes**   Short subject. There are other vocals in this short subject.

## 5988 ✦ SYMPOSIUM ON POPULAR SONGS
### Disney, 1962

**Composer(s)**   Sherman, Richard M.; Sherman, Robert B.
**Lyricist(s)**   Sherman, Richard M.; Sherman, Robert B.

**Director(s)**   Justice, Bill
**Screenwriter(s)**   Atencio, Xavier
**Voices**   Frees, Paul; Wood, Gloria; Strom, Gilly; Farrell, Skip

**Song(s)**   I'm Ludwig Von Drake; Charleston Charlie; Boo Boo Boo; Puppy Love Is Here to Stay; Rutabaga Rag; Although I Dropped $100,000; Boogie Woogie Bakery Man; Rock Rumble and Roar

**Notes**   Animated cartoon.

## 5989 ✦ SYNCOPATION (1929)
### RKO, 1929

**Producer(s)**   Kane, Robert T.
**Director(s)**   Glennon, Bert; Harrison, Bertram; Seymour, James
**Screenwriter(s)**   Haschke, Paul S.; Agnew, Frances
**Source(s)**   *Stepping High* (novel) Markey, Gene

**Cast**   Bennett, Barbara; Watson, Bobby; Downey, Morton; Hunter, Ian; Lee, Dorothy; Perkins, Osgood; Teasdale, Verree; Fred Waring and His Pennsylvanians

**Song(s)**   Jericho [1] (C: Myers, Richard; L: Robin, Leo); Mine Alone (C/L: Myers, Richard); Do Something (C/L: Green, Bud; Stept, Sam H.); I'll Always Be in Love with You (C/L: Green, Bud; Stept, Sam H.; Ruby, Herman); Tin Pan Parade (C/L: Unknown)

**Notes**   No cue sheet available. The first Radio Picture. [1] Also in I DOOD IT (MGM).

## 5990 ✦ SYNCOPATION (1942)
### RKO, 1942

**Composer(s)**   Stevens, Leith

**Producer(s)**   Dieterle, William
**Director(s)**   Dieterle, William
**Screenwriter(s)**   Yordan, Philip; Cavett, Frank
**Source(s)**   "The Band Played On" (story) Davies, Valentine

**Cast**   Cooper, Jackie [1]; Granville, Bonita; Duncan, Todd [2]; James, Harry; Goodman, Benny; Barnet, Charlie; Venuti, Joe; Krupa, Gene; Boswell, Connee; The Hall Johnson Choir; Menjou, Adolphe; Bancroft, George

**Song(s)**   Goin' Up the River (L: Torbett, Dave); Only Worry for a Pillow (inst.); Chicago Ragtime (inst.); Under a Falling Star (L: Hall, Rich); Slave Market (C/L: Johnson, Hall)

**Notes**   No cue sheet available. [1] Trumpet playing dubbed by Rex Stewart. [2] Playing dubbed by Bunny Berigan. There were additional instrumentals.

**5991** ✦ **SYNTHETIC SIN**
Warner Brothers–First National, 1929

**Producer(s)**  McCormick, John
**Director(s)**  Seiter, William A.
**Screenwriter(s)**  Geraghty, Tom J.; Reed, Tom
**Source(s)**  *Synthetic Syn* (play) Hatton, Fanny; Hatton, Frederic

**Cast**  Moore, Colleen; Moreno, Antonio; Chapman, Edythe; McGuire, Kathryn; Howard, Gertrude; Astor, Gertrude; Turner, Raymond; Love, Montagu

**Song(s)**  Betty (C: Shilkret, Nathaniel; L: Christy, Harold)

**Notes**  No cue sheet available.

# T

## 5992 ✦ TAFFY AND THE JUNGLE HUNTER
Allied Artists, 1965

**Musical Score** Rogers, Milton "Shorty"

**Producer(s)** Faris, William
**Director(s)** Morse, Terry O.
**Screenwriter(s)** Hoerl, Arthur

**Cast** Bergerac, Jacques; Padilla, Manuel; Marshall, Shary; Rhodes, Hari

**Song(s)** Taffy (C: Rogers, Milton "Shorty"; L: Zimbalist, Al)

**Notes** No cue sheet available.

## 5993 ✦ TAHITI HONEY
Republic, 1943

**Composer(s)** Pollack, Lew
**Lyricist(s)** Newman, Charles

**Producer(s)** Auer, John H.
**Director(s)** Auer, John H.
**Screenwriter(s)** Kimble, Lawrence; Kohner, Frederick; Hanemann, H.W.

**Cast** Simon, Simone; O'Keefe, Dennis; Stander, Lionel; Seymour, Danny; Seidel, Tom; Vernon, Wally

**Song(s)** Tahiti Honey [1] (C: Styne, Jule; L: Meyer, Sol; Brown, George); Any Old Port in a Storm; Koni Plenty Hu-Hu; I'm a Cossack; You Could Hear a Pin Drop [2]; This Gets Better Every Minute; In a Ten Gallon Hat [3]

**Notes** There is also a vocal of "Clap Hands Here Comes Charley" by Billy Rose, Ballard Macdonald and Joseph Meyer. [1] Also in MELODY AND MOONLIGHT. [2] Also in PISTOL PACKIN' MAMA. [3] Sheet music only.

## 5994 ✦ TAHITI, MY ISLAND
Shoestring Productions, 1951

**Producer(s)** Long, Dwight
**Director(s)** Long, Dwight

**Cast** Moe, Paul; Tetahamaui, Adeline

**Song(s)** Tahiti, My Island (C: Young, Victor; L: David, Mack; Rogers, Lela)

## 5995 ✦ TAHITI NIGHTS
Columbia, 1945

**Composer(s)** Owens, Harry
**Lyricist(s)** Owens, Harry

**Producer(s)** White, Sam
**Director(s)** Jason, Will
**Screenwriter(s)** Hayward, Lillie

**Cast** Falkenburg, Jinx; O'Brien, Dave; Treen, Mary; Bates, Florence

**Song(s)** Let Me Love You Tonight (C: Touzet, Rene; L: Parrish, Mitchell); Cockeyed Mayor of Kaunakakai (C: Anderson, A.; L: Anderson, A.; Stillman, Al)

**Notes** No cue sheet available.

## 5996 ✦ A TAIL OF TWO CRITTERS
Disney, 1977

**Musical Score** Baker, Buddy

**Producer(s)** Miller, Ron
**Director(s)** Speirs, Jack
**Screenwriter(s)** Speirs, Jack

**Song(s)** Travelin' On (C/L: Borgeson, Erika; Speirs, Jack; Baker, Buddy)

## 5997 ✦ TAIL SPIN
Twentieth Century–Fox, 1939

**Producer(s)** Zanuck, Darryl F.
**Director(s)** Del Ruth, Roy
**Screenwriter(s)** Wead, Frank

**Cast** Faye, Alice; Bennett, Constance; Kelly, Nancy; Davis, Joan; Farrell, Charles; Wyman, Jane; Davenport, Harry

**Song(s)** Are You in the Mood for Mischief? (C: Revel, Harry; L: Gordon, Mack); Go in and Out the Window [1] (C: Pollack, Lew; L: Bullock, Walter)

**Notes** [1] Recorded but not used.

## 5998 ◆ THE TAKE
Columbia, 1974

**Musical Score**   Karlin, Fred
**Composer(s)**   Karlin, Fred
**Lyricist(s)**   Karlin, Fred

**Producer(s)**   Brandy, Howard
**Director(s)**   Hartford-Davis, Robert
**Screenwriter(s)**   Reisman, Del; Coen, Franklin
**Source(s)**   *Sir You Bastard* (novel) Newman, G.F.

**Cast**   Williams, Billy Dee; Albert, Eddie; Avalon, Frankie; Booke, Sorrell; Reed, Tracy; Salmi, Albert; Morrow, Vic; Luisi, James

**Song(s)**   Over and Over Again; This Time's Going to Be the Last Time; Take It As It Comes

## 5999 ◆ TAKE A CHANCE
Paramount, 1933

**Producer(s)**   DeSylva, B.G.
**Director(s)**   Brice, Monte; Schwab, Laurence
**Screenwriter(s)**   Brice, Monte; Schwab, Laurence; DeSylva, B.G.
**Source(s)**   *Take a Chance* (musical) Brown, Nacio Herb; Whiting, Richard A.; DeSylva, B.G.; Schwab, Laurence

**Cast**   Knight, June; Roth, Lillian; Dunn, James; Rogers, Charles "Buddy"; Edwards, Cliff; Bond, Lillian; Andre, Lona; Lee, Dorothy; Gleckler, Robert

**Song(s)**   Come Up and See Me Sometime (C: Alter, Louis; L: Swanstrom, Arthur); (I'm a) Night Owl (C/L: Hupfeld, Herman); Should I Be Sweet [1] [4] (C: Youmans, Vincent; L: DeSylva, B.G.); New Deal Rhythm (C: Edens, Roger; L: Harburg, E.Y.); Eadie Was a Lady [1] [3] (C: Brown, Nacio Herb; Whiting, Richard A.; L: DeSylva, B.G.); It's Only a Paper Moon [2] (C: Arlen, Harold; L: Harburg, E.Y.; Rose, Billy)

**Notes**   [1] From original Broadway show. [2] Originally in the show THE GREAT MAGOO. Also in FUNNY LADY. [3] Roger Edens not credited on cue sheets though he is in some sources. Maybe he added lyrics to another version. Also in film EADIE WAS A LADY (Columbia). [4] Used instrumentally only apparently.

## 6000 ◆ TAKE A GIANT STEP
United Artists, 1959

**Musical Score**   Marshall, Jack

**Producer(s)**   Epstein, Julius J.
**Director(s)**   Leacock, Philip
**Screenwriter(s)**   Peterson, Louis S.; Epstein, Julius J.
**Source(s)**   (play) Peterson, Louis S.

**Cast**   Nash, Johnny; Hemsley, Estelle; Dee, Ruby; O'Neal, Frederick

**Song(s)**   Take a Giant Step [1] (C/L: Livingston, Jay; Evans, Ray)

**Notes**   [1] Used instrumentally only.

## 6001 ◆ TAKE CARE OF MY LITTLE GIRL
Twentieth Century–Fox, 1951

**Composer(s)**   Darby, Ken
**Lyricist(s)**   Darby, Ken

**Producer(s)**   Blaustein, Julian
**Director(s)**   Negulesco, Jean
**Screenwriter(s)**   Epstein, Julius J.; Epstein, Philip G.
**Source(s)**   *Take Care of My Little Girl* (novel) Goodin, Peggy

**Cast**   Crain, Jeanne; Robertson, Dale; Gaynor, Mitzi; Peters, Jean; Hunter, Jeffrey; Lynn, Betty; Westcott, Helen; Schafer, Natalie

**Song(s)**   The Old Maine Bell; Crown Us Gently, Gently; The Clasp of Hands (L: Darby, Ken; Goodin, Peggy); Sweet Dreams to You, Tri-U (L: Darby, Ken; Goodin, Peggy); Goodbye My Lover Goodbye [1] (C: Allen, T.H.); Juanita [1] (C: Traditional); Star of Kappa Delta; Night Night, Delta Mu; Here's to Our Lizzie (L: Darby, Ken; Goodin, Peggy); When You See a Donkey [1] (C: Traditional); Genevieve, Sweet Genevieve [1] (C: Tucker, Henry)

**Notes**   [1] An old public domain tune with new Darby lyrics.

## 6002 ◆ TAKE DOWN
American Film Consortium, 1979

**Musical Score**   Jenson, Merrill B.

**Producer(s)**   Merrill, Keith
**Director(s)**   Merrill, Keith
**Screenwriter(s)**   Merrill, Keith; Hendershot, Eric

**Cast**   Herrmann, Edward; Lloyd, Kathleen; Lamas, Lorenzo; McCormick, Maureen; Furst, Stephen

**Song(s)**   I'll Try for You (C/L: Lamas, Lorenzo)

**Notes**   No cue sheet available.

## 6003 ◆ TAKE HER SHE'S MINE
Twentieth Century–Fox, 1963

**Musical Score**   Goldsmith, Jerry

**Producer(s)**   Koster, Henry
**Director(s)**   Koster, Henry
**Screenwriter(s)**   Johnson, Nunnally
**Source(s)**   *Take Her, She's Mine* (play) Ephron, Phoebe; Ephron, Henry

**Cast**   Stewart, James; Dee, Sandra; Meadows, Audrey; Morley, Robert; Forquet, Philippe; McGiver, John; Denver, Robert; Pepper, Cynthia

**Song(s)** Fa La La La [1] (C: Traditional; L: Sheldon, Ernie); Here's to the Girl Who Steals a Kiss [2] (C: Traditional; L: Sheldon, Ernie); Chantez, Chantez (C/L: Fields, Irving; Gamse, Albert)

**Notes** [1] Music based on "Vive L'Amour." [2] Music based on "Landlord Fill the Flowing Bowl."

## 6004 ✦ TAKE IT ALL
### United Artists, 1965

**Musical Score** Cousineau, Jean

**Director(s)** Jutra, Claude
**Screenwriter(s)** Jutra, Claude

**Cast** Jutra, Claude; Johanne

**Song(s)** My Youth (C/L: Blackburn, Maurice)

**Notes** French title: A TOUT PRENDRE.

## 6005 ✦ TAKE IT BIG
### Paramount, 1944

**Composer(s)** Lee, Lester
**Lyricist(s)** Seelen, Jerry

**Producer(s)** Pine, William; Thomas, William
**Director(s)** McDonald, Frank
**Screenwriter(s)** Green, Howard J.; Bigelow, Joe

**Cast** Haley, Jack; Hilliard, Harriet; Nelson, Ozzie

**Song(s)** Love and Learn; Lucky, Lucky Boy; Take It Big; I'm a Big Success (with You); Sunday, Monday or Always [1] (C: Van Heusen, James; L: Burke, Johnny); Life Can Be Beautiful [2]; Can Anyone Use a Dream [2] (L: Seelen, Jerry; Nelson, Ozzie)

**Notes** Formerly titled RHYTHM RANCH. [1] Also in DIXIE and ROAD TO UTOPIA. [2] Special lyric written by Ozzie Nelson.

## 6006 ✦ TAKE ME BACK TO OKLAHOMA
### Studio Unknown, 1930

**Composer(s)** Wills, Bob
**Lyricist(s)** Wills, Bob

**Song(s)** Village Blacksmith (C: Lange, Johnny; L: Porter, Lew); Kalamity Kate (C: Lange, Johnny; L: Porter, Lew); Good Old Oklahoma; Take Me Back to Tulsa; Lone Star Rag; Going Indian; Bob Wills Special

**Notes** No other information available.

## 6007 ✦ TAKE ME OUT TO THE BALL GAME (1947)
### Metro–Goldwyn–Mayer, 1947 unproduced

**Composer(s)** Warren, Harry
**Lyricist(s)** Blane, Ralph

**Song(s)** Someone Like You [3]; Me-O-My; If It Weren't for the Irish; Puttin' on Airs [1]; I've Got a Funny Feeling [2]; The Boy in the Celluloid Collar; Ride-Ride-Ride

**Notes** [1] Originally written for HUCKLEBERRY FINN. [2] Used in SKIRTS AHOY. [3] Used in MY DREAM IS YOURS.

## 6008 ✦ TAKE ME OUT TO THE BALL GAME (1949)
### Metro–Goldwyn–Mayer, 1949

**Musical Score** Edens, Roger
**Composer(s)** Edens, Roger
**Lyricist(s)** Comden, Betty; Green, Adolph
**Choreographer(s)** Kelly, Gene; Donen, Stanley

**Producer(s)** Freed, Arthur
**Director(s)** Berkeley, Busby
**Screenwriter(s)** Tugend, Harry; Wells, George

**Cast** Sinatra, Frank; Williams, Esther; Kelly, Gene; Garrett, Betty; Arnold, Edward; Munshin, Jules; Lane, Richard

**Song(s)** Yes, Indeedy; K.C. Higgins (L: Edens, Roger); O'Brien to Ryan to Goldberg; The Right Girl for Me; It's Fate Baby, It's Fate; Strictly U.S.A. (L: Edens, Roger); Boys and Girls Like You and Me [1] (C: Rodgers, Richard; L: Hammerstein II, Oscar); Sand Man [4]; Hayride [2] (C: Warren, Harry; L: Mercer, Johnny); Baby Doll [3] [4] (C: Warren, Harry; L: Mercer, Johnny)

**Notes** Released overseas as EVERYBODY'S CHEERING. There are also vocals of "Take Me Out to the Ball Game" by Albert Von Tilzer and Jack Norworth and "The Hat My Father Wore Upon St. Patrick's Day" by Jean Schwartz and William Jerome. [1] Deleted from final print. Also deleted from MEET ME IN ST. LOUIS. Originally written for stage production of SOUTH PACIFIC. [2] Not used. Also not used in THE HARVEY GIRLS (1946). Later the music was used for the song "The House of Singing Bamboo" in PAGAN LOVE SONG (1950). [3] Deleted from final print. Song (not filmed sequence) used in THE BELLE OF NEW YORK (1952). [4] Not used.

## 6009 ✦ TAKE ME TO TOWN
### Universal, 1953

**Choreographer(s)** Belfer, Harold

**Producer(s)** Hunter, Ross
**Director(s)** Sirk, Douglas
**Screenwriter(s)** Morris, Richard

**Cast** Sheridan, Ann; Hayden, Sterling; Reed, Philip; Patrick, Lee; Asker, Lee; Gates, Larry; Stanley, Phyllis

**Song(s)** The Tale of Vermillion O'Toole [1] (C: Traditional; L: Herbert, Frederick); Oh You Red Head (C: Rosen, Milton; L: Herbert, Frederick); Take Me to Town [2] (C/L: Shapiro, Dan; Lee, Lester)

**Notes** [1] Based on "On Top of Old Smokey." [2] Also in A DAY OF FURY and WYOMING MAIL.

## 6010 ◆ TAKE THE AIR
Warner Brothers, 1940

**Musical Score** Jackson, Howard

**Song(s)** What Does It Take? (C: Jerome, M.K.; L: Scholl, Jack)

**Notes** Short subject.

## 6011 ◆ TAKE THE HEIR
Big 4 Corp., 1930

**Musical Score** Coopersmith, J.M.

**Producer(s)** Freuler, John R.; Stimson, C.A.
**Director(s)** Ingraham, Lloyd
**Screenwriter(s)** Van, Beatrice; Siegler, Al

**Cast** Horton, Edward Everett; Devore, Dorothy; Elliott, Frank; Chapman, Edythe; Harlan, Otis; Deslys, Kay

**Song(s)** I Always Knew It Would Be You (C: Coopersmith, J.M.; L: Hess, Cliff)

**Notes** No cue sheet available.

## 6012 ◆ TAKE THE HIGH GROUND
Metro–Goldwyn–Mayer, 1953

**Musical Score** Tiomkin, Dimitri

**Producer(s)** Schary, Dore
**Director(s)** Brooks, Richard
**Screenwriter(s)** Kaufman, Millard

**Cast** Widmark, Richard; Malden, Karl; Stewart, Elaine; Carpenter, Carleton; Tamblyn, Russ; Courtland, Jerome; Forrest, Steve; Arthur, Robert

**Song(s)** Take the High Ground (C: Tiomkin, Dimitri; L: Washington, Ned); Julie (C: Tiomkin, Dimitri; L: Wolcott, Charles)

## 6013 ◆ TAKE THIS JOB AND SHOVE IT
Avco Embassy, 1981

**Musical Score** Sherrill, Billy
**Composer(s)** Kasha, Al; Hirschhorn, Joel; Lloyd, Michael
**Lyricist(s)** Kasha, Al; Hirschhorn, Joel; Lloyd, Michael

**Producer(s)** Blackwell, Greg
**Director(s)** Trikonis, Gus
**Screenwriter(s)** Schneider, Barry
**Source(s)** "Take This Job and Shove It" (song) Coe, David Allan

**Cast** Hays, Robert; Carney, Art; Hershey, Barbara; Keith, David; Thomerson, Tim; Mull, Martin; Albert,

Eddie; Milford, Penelope; Coe, David Allan; Rich, Charlie; Lindsay, George; Paycheck, Johnny; Dano, Royal

**Song(s)** You Can Count on Beer; How Good It Used to Be; The Road Song (C/L: Sherrill, Billy); You Made It Beautiful (C/L: Sherrill, Billy; Davis, Steve; Sutton, Glenn)

**Notes** No cue sheet available.

## 6014 ◆ TALENT SCOUT
Warner Brothers–First National, 1937

**Composer(s)** Jerome, M.K.
**Lyricist(s)** Scholl, Jack

**Producer(s)** Foy, Bryan
**Director(s)** Clemens, William
**Screenwriter(s)** Bilson, George

**Cast** Woods, Donald; Madden, Jeanne; Lawrence, Fred; Marquis, Rosalind; Hart, Teddy; Treen, Mary; Faylen, Frank; Fox, Harry; Crehan, Joseph

**Song(s)** In the Silent Picture Days; I Am a Singer; Born to Love; I Was Wrong

**Notes** Released in Great Britain as STUDIO ROMANCE.

## 6015 ◆ TALE OF A MOUSE
Disney, 1973 unproduced

**Composer(s)** Evans, Ray; Livingston, Jay
**Lyricist(s)** Evans, Ray; Livingston, Jay

**Song(s)** The Heebie Jeebie River; My Compliments to the Chef; Mister Misbehave; Sometimes There's a Moment; That's the Way to Go; This Is Home

**Notes** Unproduced. Originally titled THE TALE OF TWO MICE and also CITY MOUSE COUNTRY MOUSE.

## 6016 ◆ A TALE OF TWO CITIES
Paramount, 1946

**Composer(s)** Wayne, Bernie
**Lyricist(s)** Raleigh, Ben

**Producer(s)** Templeton, George
**Director(s)** Templeton, George
**Screenwriter(s)** Rosenwald, Franz
**Source(s)** story by Gibbs, Anthony

**Cast** The Four V's; Graham, Bob; Myrtil, Odette; Porter, Dorothy; Faylen, Frank

**Song(s)** What a Wonderful Evening; Soon We'll Be Together; Swingin' the Beans [1] (C/L: Kelly, Willie; Whittaker, Verne; Glascow, Anna)

**Notes** Vocals of "Hit the Road to Dreamland" by Johnny Mercer and Harold Arlen and "Beyond the Blue Horizon" by Richard Whiting, Leo Robin and W. Franke Harling are also used. [1] Not used

# 6017 ◆ TALES OF BEATRIX POTTER

See PETER RABBIT AND TALES OF BEATRIX POTTER.

# 6018 ◆ TALES OF MANHATTAN
### Twentieth Century–Fox, 1942

**Musical Score** Kaplan, Sol
**Composer(s)** Rainger, Ralph
**Lyricist(s)** Robin, Leo

**Producer(s)** Morros, Boris; Eagle, S.P.
**Director(s)** Duvivier, Julien
**Screenwriter(s)** Hecht, Ben; Molnar, Ferenc; Stewart, Donald Ogden; Hoffenstein, Samuel; Campbell, Alan; Fodor, Ladislas; Vadnay, Laslo; Gorog, Laszlo; Trotti, Lamar; Blankfort, Henry

**Cast** Boyer, Charles; Hayworth, Rita; Rogers, Ginger; Fonda, Henry; Laughton, Charles; Robinson, Edward G.; Robeson, Paul; Waters, Ethel; Anderson, Eddie "Rochester"; Mitchell, Thomas; Pallette, Eugene; Romero, Cesar; Patrick, Gail; Young, Roland; Lanchester, Elsa; Sanders, George; Gleason, James; Davenport, Harry

**Song(s)** Glory Day; Better Behave My Heart [1]; Choppa Down a Chris-A-Mus Tree [1]; Fare Thee Well to El Dorado [2] (C: Kaplan, Sol; L: Webster, Paul Francis); Journey to Your Lips [2] (C: Kaplan, Sol; L: Webster, Paul Francis); Tale of Manhattan [2] (C: Kaplan, Sol; L: Webster, Paul Francis)

**Notes** [1] Not used. [2] Sheet music only.

# 6019 ◆ TALK ABOUT A LADY
### Columbia, 1946

**Composer(s)** Roberts, Allan; Fisher, Doris
**Lyricist(s)** Roberts, Allan; Fisher, Doris

**Producer(s)** Kraike, Michel
**Director(s)** Sherman, George
**Screenwriter(s)** Weil, Richard; Thomas, Ted

**Cast** Falkenburg, Jinx; Tucker, Forrest; Besser, Joe; Marshall, Trudy; Lane, Richard; Sully, Frank; Stan Kenton and His Orchestra

**Song(s)** You Gotta Do Whatcha Gotta Do [2]; Avocado; I Never Had a Dream Come True; A Mist Is Over the Moon [1] (C: Oakland, Ben; L: Hammerstein II, Oscar)

**Notes** No cue sheet available. [1] Also used in THE LADY OBJECTS. [2] Also in BETTY CO-ED.

# 6020 ◆ TALK RADIO
### Universal, 1989

**Musical Score** Copeland, Stewart

**Producer(s)** Stone, Oliver
**Director(s)** Stone, Oliver

**Screenwriter(s)** Bogosian, Eric; Stone, Oliver
**Source(s)** *Talk Radio* (play) Bogosian, Eric; Savinar, Tad; *Talked to Death: The Life and Murder of Alan Berg* (book) Singular, Stephen

**Cast** Bogosian, Eric; Baldwin, Alec; Greene, Ellen; Hope, Leslie; McGinley, John C.; Pankow, Michael

**Song(s)** Bad to the Bone (C/L: Thorogood, George); Disco Inferno (C/L: Kersey, Ron "Have Mercy"; Green, Leroy); Mr. Toaster (C/L: Farlerg, William; Bovell, Dennis)

# 6021 ◆ TALL DARK AND HANDSOME
### Twentieth Century–Fox, 1941

**Composer(s)** Rainger, Ralph
**Lyricist(s)** Robin, Leo

**Producer(s)** Kohlmar, Fred
**Director(s)** Humberstone, H. Bruce
**Screenwriter(s)** Tunberg, Karl; Ware, Darrell

**Cast** Romero, Cesar; Gilmore, Virginia; Greenwood, Charlotte; Berle, Milton; Leonard, Sheldon; Clements, Stanley; Jenks, Frank; Lawrence, Marc; Caruso, Anthony

**Song(s)** I'm Alive and Kickin'; Hello Ma—I Done It Again; Wishful Thinking; Did I Have Fun? [1]

**Notes** [1] Not used.

# 6022 ◆ TALL MAN RIDING
### Warner Brothers, 1955

**Musical Score** Sawtell, Paul

**Producer(s)** Weisbart, David
**Director(s)** Selander, Lesley
**Screenwriter(s)** Hoffman, Joseph
**Source(s)** *Tall Man Riding* (novel) Fox, Norman A.

**Cast** Scott, Randolph; Malone, Dorothy; Castle, Peggie; Ching, William; Baragrey, John; Barrat, Robert; Dehner, John; Richards, Paul; Chandler, Lane; Simpson, Mickey; Bassett, Joe; Watts, Charles; Conway, Russ

**Song(s)** It Looks Like a Big Night Tonight (C: Van Alstyne, Egbert; L: Williams, Harry); Oh! It Looked Like He Might Buy Wine [1] (C: Heindorf, Ray; L: Cahn, Sammy); As the Brass Band Played [2] (C: Heindorf, Ray; L: Scholl, Jack)

**Notes** [1] Background vocal only. [2] Also used in SOUTH OF ST. LOUIS.

# 6023 ◆ THE TALL MEN
### Twentieth Century–Fox, 1955

**Musical Score** Young, Victor

**Producer(s)** Bacher, William A.; Hawks, William B.
**Director(s)** Walsh, Raoul
**Screenwriter(s)** Boehm, Sydney; Nugent, Frank
**Source(s)** *The Tall Men* (novel) Fisher, Clay

**Cast** Gable, Clark; Russell, Jane; Ryan, Robert; Mitchell, Cameron; Garcia, Juan; Shannon, Harry; Meyer, Emile; Darrell, Steve; Wright, Will; Marsh, Mae

**Song(s)** Tall Men [1] (C/L: Darby, Ken); Night Camp (C: Young, Victor; L: Darby, Ken); Cancion Mixteca (C/L: Alaves, Jose Lopez)

**Notes** [1] Adapted from "Cindy."

## 6024 ✦ TALL STORY
Warner Brothers, 1960

**Musical Score** Mockridge, Cyril J.

**Producer(s)** Logan, Joshua
**Director(s)** Logan, Joshua
**Screenwriter(s)** Epstein, Julius J.
**Source(s)** *Tall Story* (play) Lindsay, Howard; Crouse, Russel

**Cast** Perkins, Anthony; Fonda, Jane; Walston, Ray; Connelly, Marc; Jackson, Anne; Hamilton, Murray; Wright, Bob

**Song(s)** Custer Song (C: Weeks, Paul; L: Miller, Sy); Tall Story [1] (C: Previn, Andre; Manne, Shelly; L: Langdon, Dory)

**Notes** "Cuddle Up a Little Closer, Lovey Mine" by Karl Hoschna and Otto Harbach is used as a visual vocal. [1] Background vocal only.

## 6025 ✦ TAMAHINE
Metro–Goldwyn–Mayer, 1965

**Musical Score** Arnold, Malcolm

**Producer(s)** Bryan, John
**Director(s)** Leacock, Philip
**Screenwriter(s)** Cannan, Denis
**Source(s)** *Tamahine* (novel) Niklaus, Thelma

**Cast** Kwan, Nancy; Fraser, John; Price, Dennis; Browne, Coral; Nimmo, Derek; Gough, Michael

**Song(s)** School Song 1 (C/L: Arnold, Malcolm); School Song 2 (C/L: Arnold, Malcolm)

## 6026 ✦ TAMMY AND THE BACHELOR
Universal, 1957

**Musical Score** Skinner, Frank

**Producer(s)** Hunter, Ross
**Director(s)** Pevney, Joseph
**Screenwriter(s)** Brodney, Oscar
**Source(s)** (novel) Sumner, Cid Ricketts

**Cast** Reynolds, Debbie; Nielsen, Leslie; Brennan, Walter; Wray, Fay; Blackmer, Sidney; Natwick, Mildred; Powers, Mala; Beavers, Louise

**Song(s)** Tammy (C/L: Livingston, Jay; Evans, Ray)

**Notes** Titled TAMMY overseas.

## 6027 ✦ TAMMY TELL ME TRUE
Universal, 1961

**Musical Score** Faith, Percy

**Producer(s)** Hunter, Ross
**Director(s)** Keller, Harry
**Screenwriter(s)** Brodney, Oscar
**Source(s)** *Tammy Tell Me True* (novel) Sumner, Cid Ricketts

**Cast** Dee, Sandra; Gavin, John; Drake, Charles; Meade, Julia; Grey, Virginia; Bondi, Beulah; Kellaway, Cecil; Perreau, Gigi

**Song(s)** Tammy Tell Me True (C/L: Squires, Dorothy)

## 6028 ✦ TANGANYIKA
Universal, 1954

**Musical Score** Salter, Hans J.
**Composer(s)** Hairston, Jester
**Lyricist(s)** Hairston, Jester

**Producer(s)** Cohen, Albert J.
**Director(s)** De Toth, Andre
**Screenwriter(s)** Sackheim, William; Simmons, Richard Alan

**Cast** Heflin, Van; Morrow, Jeff; Duff, Howard; Roman, Ruth; Corcoran, Noreen; Marshall, Gregory

**Song(s)** Funeral Chant; Native Chant and Drums; Nukumbi Warriors Song; Nukumbi Dance Song

## 6029 ✦ TANGIER
Universal, 1946

**Musical Score** Rosen, Milton
**Choreographer(s)** Horton, Lester

**Producer(s)** Malvern, Paul
**Director(s)** Waggner, George
**Screenwriter(s)** Collins, Monty; Musselman, M.M.

**Cast** Sabu; Montez, Maria; Paige, Robert; Foster, Preston; Allbritton, Louise; Taylor, Kent; Bromberg, J. Edward; Denny, Reginald; Judels, Charles

**Song(s)** Love Me Tonight (C: Ruiz, Gabriel; L: Waggner, George)

## 6030 ✦ TANK
Universal, 1984

**Musical Score** Schifrin, Lalo
**Composer(s)** Schifrin, Lalo

**Producer(s)** Yablans, Irwin
**Director(s)** Chomsky, Marvin J.
**Screenwriter(s)** Gordon, Dan

**Cast** Garner, James; Jones, Shirley; Howell, C. Thomas; Herrier, Mark; Ward, Sandy; Harewood, Dorian

**Song(s)** The Girl's Got a Hold on Your Heart (L: Tucker, Elliot); Saturday Girl (L: Schifrin, Donna)

## 6031 ✦ TANNED LEGS
### RKO, 1929

**Composer(s)** Levant, Oscar
**Lyricist(s)** Clare, Sidney

**Producer(s)** Seracky, Louis
**Director(s)** Neilan, Marshall
**Screenwriter(s)** Geraghty, Tom J.

**Cast** Pennington, Ann; Lake, Arthur; Revier, Dorothy; Blane, Sally; Clyde, June; Gran, Albert; Kearns, Allen

**Song(s)** Come On In; You're Responsible; Tanned Legs; With You—With Me; Love to Take a Lesson in Love [1]

**Notes** [1] Used instrumentally only.

## 6032 ✦ TAPEHEADS
### Avenue/NBC, 1988

**Musical Score** Fishbone
**Composer(s)** Taylor, Sam
**Lyricist(s)** Taylor, Sam

**Producer(s)** MacCarthy, Peter
**Director(s)** Fishman, Bill
**Screenwriter(s)** Fishman, Bill; McCarthy, Peter

**Cast** Cusack, John; Robbins, Tim; Crosby, Mary; Gulager, Clu; Boyer, Katy; Walter, Jessica; Moore, Sam; Walker, Junior; Tyrrell, Susan; McClure, Doug; Stevens, Connie; King Cotton; Alzado, Lyle

**Song(s)** Betcher Bottom Dollar (C/L: Adler, Brian); Live and Learn; Roscoe's Rap (C: King Cotton; Nelson, Dennis; Holloway, Danny; L: Fishman, Bill; Fishman, Jim); Repave Amerika (C/L: Robbins, Tim); You Hooked Me Baby; That's Enough (C: Vice, Michele; L: Treadwell, Larry); Audience for My Pain (C: Goffin, Gerry; L: Goldberg, Barry); Language of Love (C/L: Sabatino, Chuck); Ordinary Man (C/L: Adler, Brian); Now That You're Gone (C: Sales, Hunt; L: Sales, Tony)

**Notes** No cue sheet available.

## 6033 ✦ TAPS
### Twentieth Century–Fox, 1981

**Producer(s)** Jaffe, Stanley R.; Jaffe, Howard B.
**Director(s)** Becker, Harold
**Screenwriter(s)** Ponicsan, Darryl; Kamen, Robert Mark
**Source(s)** *Father Sky* (novel) Freeman, Devery

**Cast** Scott, George C.; Hutton, Timothy; Cox, Ronny; Penn, Sean; Cruise, Tom; Wood, Brendan

**Song(s)** I Don't Want to Be in This Movie (C/L: Neary, Brian; Photoglo, James); Stop Draggin' My Heart (C/L: Campbell, Mike; Petty, Tom); Slow Hand (C/L: Clark, Mike; Bettis, John)

## 6034 ✦ TARAS BULBA
### United Artists, 1962

**Musical Score** Waxman, Franz
**Composer(s)** Waxman, Franz
**Lyricist(s)** David, Mack

**Producer(s)** Hecht, Harold
**Director(s)** Thompson, J. Lee
**Screenwriter(s)** Salt, Waldo; Turnberg, Karl
**Source(s)** *Taras Bulba* (novel) Gogol, Nikolai

**Cast** Brynner, Yul; Curtis, Tony; Kaufmann, Christine; Lopez, Perry; Sokoloff, Vladimir

**Song(s)** Zaparozhti; Rise Ye Shepherds; Pastoral; Gypsy Camp; Fanfare and Drums; Celebration #1; Wishing Star [1]

**Notes** [1] Used instrumentally only.

## 6035 ✦ TARGET UNKNOWN
### Universal, 1951

**Producer(s)** Schenck, Aubrey
**Director(s)** Sherman, George
**Screenwriter(s)** Medford, Harold

**Cast** Stevens, Mark; Nicol, Alex; Taylor, Don; Best, James; Carlyle, Richard; Sands, Johnny; Young, James; Dalbert, Suzanne

**Song(s)** Danse Avec Moi [1] (C/L: Lopez, Francis; Harvey, Andre)

**Notes** [1] Also in THE LAST TIME I SAW PARIS.

## 6036 ✦ TARNISHED ANGEL
### RKO, 1938

**Musical Score** Tours, Frank

**Producer(s)** Fineman, B.P.
**Director(s)** Goodwins, Leslie
**Screenwriter(s)** Pagano, Jo

**Cast** Eilers, Sally; Bowman, Lee; Miller, Ann; Kruger, Alma; Guilfoyle, Paul; Hale, Jonathan; Arnold, Jack; Kellaway, Cecil; Dempsey, Janet; MacFadden, Hamilton; Foulger, Byron

**Song(s)** It's the Doctor's Orders (C: Fain, Sammy; L: Brown, Lew)

## 6037 ✦ TARS AND SPARS
### Columbia, 1946

**Composer(s)** Styne, Jule
**Lyricist(s)** Cahn, Sammy
**Choreographer(s)** Cole, Jack

**Producer(s)** Bren, Milton
**Director(s)** Green, Alfred E.
**Screenwriter(s)** Jacoby, John; Tobias, Sarett; Dunning, Decla

**Cast** Drake, Alfred; Blair, Janet; Platt, Marc; Caesar, Sid; Donnell, Jeff; Walker, Ray; Flavin, James

**Song(s)** Kiss Me Hello Baby; He's a Hero; I'm Glad I Waited for You; Love Is a Merry-Go-Round; I Love Eggs; Don't Call on Me [1]; I Always Meant to Tell You [1]; I Have a Love in Every Port [1]; When I Get to Town [1]

**Notes** [1] Not used.

## 6038 ✦ TARZAN AND THE MERMAIDS
RKO, 1948

**Musical Score** Tiomkin, Dimitri
**Composer(s)** Sir Lancelot
**Lyricist(s)** Sir Lancelot

**Producer(s)** Lesser, Sol
**Director(s)** Florey, Robert
**Screenwriter(s)** Young, Carroll

**Cast** Wagner, Fernando; Christian, Linda; Weissmuller, Johnny; Joyce, Brenda; Zucco, George; Palma, Andrea; Ashley, Edward

**Song(s)** Benji's Song; Cheer Up My Friends; Dearest Mara, Farewell; Sleeping Mermaid Song; My Guitar (C/L: Myers, Harlan; Brady, Ben)

## 6039 ✦ TARZAN, THE APE MAN
Metro–Goldwyn–Mayer, 1959

**Musical Score** Rogers, Milton "Shorty"

**Producer(s)** Zimbalist, Al
**Director(s)** Newman, Joseph
**Screenwriter(s)** Hill, Robert
**Source(s)** characters by Burroughs, Edgar Rice

**Cast** Miller, Denny; Danova, Cesare; Barnes, Joanna; Douglas, Robert

**Song(s)** Liabango (C/L: Yangha, Thomas)

## 6040 ✦ THE TATTLER

See HERE COMES CARTER.

## 6041 ✦ THE TATTOOED POLICE HORSE
Disney, 1964

**Musical Score** Lava, William

**Producer(s)** Lansburgh, Larry
**Director(s)** Lansburgh, Larry
**Screenwriter(s)** Lansburgh, Janet

**Cast** Skiles, Shirley; Sanders, Sandy; Seel, Charles; Andes, Keith

**Song(s)** Things I Love to Share (C: Lava, William; L: Jackman, Bob)

## 6042 ✦ TEA AND SYMPATHY
Metro–Goldwyn–Mayer, 1956

**Musical Score** Deutsch, Adolph

**Producer(s)** Berman, Pandro S.
**Director(s)** Minnelli, Vincente
**Screenwriter(s)** Anderson, Robert
**Source(s)** *Tea and Sympathy* (play) Anderson, Robert

**Cast** Kerr, Deborah [1]; Kerr, John [1]; Erickson, Leif [1]; Andrews, Edward; Hickman, Darryl; Crane, Norma; Jones, Dean; de Wit, Jacqueline; Laughlin, Tom

**Song(s)** The Joys of Love [2] (C: Martini, G.B.; L: Dyer-Bennett; Anderson)

**Notes** [1] From Broadway production. [2] Based on "Plaisir d'Amour."

## 6043 ✦ TEACHERS
MGM/UA, 1984

**Producer(s)** Russo, Aaron
**Director(s)** Hiller, Arthur
**Screenwriter(s)** McKinney, W.R.

**Cast** Nolte, Nick; Williams, Jobeth; Macchio, Ralph; Dano, Royal; Dern, Laura; Freeman, Morgan; Glover, Crispin; Hill, Steven; Lampert, Zohra; Schallert, William; Grant, Lee; Mulligan, Richard

**Song(s)** Teacher Teacher (C/L: Adams, Bryan; Vallance, Jim); Foolin' Around (C/L: Mercury, Freddie); Cheap Sunglasses (C/L: Gibbons; Hill; Beard); I Can't Stop the Fire (C/L: Martin; Schon; Fanucci; Elson); (I'm the) Teacher (C/L: Hunter, Ian; Ronson, Mick); One Foot Back in Your Door (C/L: Lange, Robert John); Edge of a Dream (C/L: Adams, Bryan; Vallance, Jim); Interstate Love Affiar (C/L: Blades, Jack); In the Jungle (Concrete Jungle) (C/L: Motels, The); Understanding (C/L: Seger, Bob)

**Notes** It is not known if any of these were written for this picture.

## 6044 ✦ TEACHER'S PET
Paramount, 1957

**Musical Score** Webb, Roy
**Composer(s)** Lubin, Joe
**Lyricist(s)** Lubin, Joe

**Producer(s)** Perlberg, William
**Director(s)** Seaton, George
**Screenwriter(s)** Kanin, Fay; Kanin, Michael

**Cast** Adams, Nick; Gable, Clark; Day, Doris; Nathan, Vivian; Lane, Charles; Ross, Marion; Albertson, Jack; Ames, Florenz

**Song(s)** Teacher's Pet; The Girl Who Invented Rock and Roll

## 6045 ✦ TEA FOR TWO
### Warner Brothers, 1950

**Composer(s)** Jerome, M.K.
**Lyricist(s)** Scholl, Jack
**Choreographer(s)** Prinz, LeRoy

**Producer(s)** Jacobs, William
**Director(s)** Butler, David
**Screenwriter(s)** Clork, Harry
**Source(s)** *No, No, Nanette* (musical) Mandel, Frank; Harbach, Otto; Caesar, Irving; Youmans, Vincent

**Cast** Day, Doris; MacRae, Gordon; De Wolfe, Billy; Sakall, S.Z.; Goodwin, Bill; Wymore, Patrice; Gibson, Virginia; Arden, Eve; Kent, Crauford; Nelson, Gene

**Song(s)** Atlantic City; Sunburn Lotion

**Notes** Songs include those written for stage musical NO NO NANETTE including: "Tea for Two," "I Want to Be Happy" and "Call of the Sea" by Vincent Youmans and Irving Caesar and "No No Nanette" by Vincent Youmans and Otto Harbach. Other vocals include: "I Know That You Know" by Vincent Youmans and Anne Caldwell; "Crazy Rhythm" by Joseph Meyer, Roger Wolfe Kahn and Irving Caesar; "I Only Have Eyes for You" by Harry Warren and Al Dubin; "Do Do Do" by George and Ira Gershwin and "Oh Me Oh My" by Vincent Youmans and Arthur Francis (Ira Gershwin). Some of these songs are presented in medleys.

## 6046 ✦ TEAR GAS SQUAD
### Warner Brothers, 1940

**Composer(s)** Jerome, M.K.
**Lyricist(s)** Scholl, Jack

**Producer(s)** Foy, Bryan
**Director(s)** Morse, Terry O.
**Screenwriter(s)** Belden, Charles; Gamet, Kenneth; Ryan, Don
**Source(s)** "The State Cop" (story) Belden, Charles; Gamet, Kenneth; Ryan, Don

**Cast** Morgan, Dennis; Payne, John; Dickson, Gloria; Reeves, George; Wilcox, Frank; Shannon, Harry; Stevens, Julie; Buchanan, Edgar; Hopper, DeWolf

**Song(s)** I'm an Officer of the Law; You You Darlin'; The Song Is the Thing

**Notes** "When Irish Eyes Are Smiling" by Ernest Ball and Chauncey Olcott is also used.

## 6047 ✦ TEENAGE MILLIONAIRE
### United Artists, 1961

**Producer(s)** Kreitsek, Howard B.
**Director(s)** Dohen, Lawrence F.
**Screenwriter(s)** Gross, H.B.

**Cast** Clanton, Jimmy; Jergens, Diane; Graziano, Rocky; Tabor, Joan

**Song(s)** Teenage Millionaire (C: May, Billy; L: Cross, H.B.; Loose, Bill); Green Light (C/L: Clanton, Jimmy); Smokey, Part 2 (C/L: Black, Bill); The Way I Am (C/L: Udell, Peter; Geld, Gary); Somebody Nobody Wants (C/L: Dee, Sylvia; Goehring, George); Show Me (C/L: Gordy Jr., Berry); Hello Mr. Dream (C/L: Bare, Bobby); The Jet (C/L: Mann, Kal); Back to School Blues (C/L: Bare, Bobby; Bell, Louise); Kissin' Game (C/L: Vance, Jerry; Philips, Terry); I Wait (C/L: Spencer, Vicki); Let's Twist Again (C/L: Mann, Kal; Appell, Dave); Oh Mary (C/L: Gordy Jr., Berry; Stevenson, W.); Lonely Life (C/L: Kasha, Al; Thomas, Alan); Dance the Mess Around (C/L: Mann, Kal; Appell, Dave); Twistin' U.S.A. [1] (C/L: Mann, Kal); Possibility (C/L: Clanton, Jimmy)

**Notes** It is not known if any of the above (other than the title song) were written for this film. [1] Also in TWIST AROUND THE CLOCK.

## 6048 ✦ TEENAGE REBEL
### Twentieth Century–Fox, 1956

**Musical Score** Harline, Leigh

**Producer(s)** Brackett, Charles
**Director(s)** Goulding, Edmund
**Screenwriter(s)** Reisch, Walter; Brackett, Charles
**Source(s)** *A Roomful of Roses* (play) Sommer, Edith

**Cast** Rogers, Ginger; Rennie, Michael; Natwick, Mildred; Keim, Betty Lou; Berlinger, Warren; Jergens, Diane

**Song(s)** Dodie (Teenage Love) (C: Goulding, Edmund; L: Freed, Ralph); Cool It, Baby! [1] (C: Newman, Lionel; L: Coates, Carroll)

**Notes** [1] Also in THE GIRL CAN'T HELP IT.

## 6049 ✦ TEENAGE REBELLION

See MONDO TEENO.

## 6050 ✦ TEEN WOLF
### Atlantic, 1985

**Musical Score** Goodman, Miles
**Composer(s)** Goodman, Miles
**Lyricist(s)** Brayfield, Douglas

**Producer(s)** Levinson, Mark; Rosenfelt, Scott M.
**Director(s)** Daniel, Rod
**Screenwriter(s)** Loeb III, Joseph; Weisman, Matthew

**Cast** Fox, Michael J.; Hampton, James; Ursitti, Susan; Levine, Jerry; MacKrell, Jim; Griffin, Lorie; Tarses, Jay

**Song(s)** Good News; Silhouette; Way to Go; Big Bad Wolf; Flesh on Fire; Win in the End; Shooting for the Moon

**Notes** No cue sheet available.

## 6051 ✦ TELEFON
### Metro–Goldwyn–Mayer, 1977

**Musical Score**   Schifrin, Lalo

**Producer(s)**   Harris, James B.
**Director(s)**   Siegel, Don
**Screenwriter(s)**   Hyams, Peter; Silliphant, Stirling
**Source(s)**   *Telefon* (novel) Wager, Walter

**Cast**   Bronson, Charles; Remick, Lee; Daly, Tyne; Badel, Alan; Magee, Patrick; North, Sheree; Pleasence, Donald

**Song(s)**   Is the End Coming Near? (C/L: Siegel, Nowell Samuel)

## 6052 ✦ TELL IT TO A STAR
### Republic, 1945

**Producer(s)**   Goetz, Walter
**Director(s)**   MacDonald, Frank
**Screenwriter(s)**   Butler, John K.

**Cast**   Terry, Ruth; Livingston, Robert; Mowbray, Alan

**Song(s)**   You're So Good to Me [1] (C: Styne, Jule; L: Cahn, Sammy); Tell It to a Star (C/L: Botwin, Shirley); A Batacuda Comecou (C/L: Barroso, Ary)

**Notes**   There is also a vocal of "Love Me or Leave Me" by Gus Kahn and Walter Donaldson. [1] Also in HERE COMES ELMER and YOUTH ON PARADE.

## 6053 ✦ TELL ME THAT YOU LOVE ME, JUNIE MOON
### Paramount, 1970

**Musical Score**   Springer, Phil
**Composer(s)**   Springer, Phil
**Lyricist(s)**   Levitt, Estelle

**Producer(s)**   Preminger, Otto
**Director(s)**   Preminger, Otto
**Screenwriter(s)**   Kellogg, Marjorie
**Source(s)**   *Tell Me That You Love Me, Junie Moon* (novel) Kellogg, Marjorie

**Cast**   Minnelli, Liza; Howard, Ken; Moore, Robert; Coco, James; Thompson, Kay; Williamson, Fred; Seeger, Pete

**Song(s)**   Work Your Show; The Rake; Love Your Neighbor (L: Kellogg, Marjorie); Tell Me That You Love Me, Junie Moon [1] (L: Springer, Phil)

**Notes**   [1] Sheet music only.

## 6054 ✦ TEMPEST
### Paramount, 1959

**Producer(s)**   De Laurentiis, Dino
**Director(s)**   Lattuada, Alberto
**Screenwriter(s)**   Lattuada, Alberto; Peterson, Louis S.

**Source(s)**   *The Captain's Daughter* (novel) Pushkin, Alexander

**Cast**   Heflin, Van; Mangano, Silvana; Lindfors, Viveca; Horne, Geoffrey; Homolka, Oscar; Gassman, Vittorio; Moorehead, Agnes; Dantine, Helmut

**Song(s)**   Tempest [1] (C/L: Wolfson, Mark; White, Eddie)

**Notes**   [1] Written for exploitation only.

## 6055 ✦ TEMPO OF TOMORROW
### Paramount, 1939

**Cast**   Richard Himber and His Orchestra

**Song(s)**   The Prom Waltz [1] (C: Rainger, Ralph; L: Robin, Leo); Listen to My Heart (C/L: Silver, Abner; Ross, Lanny; Neiburg, Al J.); Gettin' Off (C: Lawnhurst, Vee; L: Seymour, Tot); Alone in the Station (C/L: Shaw, Naomi; Himber, Richard)

**Notes**   Short subject. No cue sheet available. [1] Not used in COLLEGE HOLIDAY.

## 6056 ✦ 10
### Orion, 1979

**Musical Score**   Mancini, Henry
**Composer(s)**   Mancini, Henry
**Lyricist(s)**   Wells, Robert

**Producer(s)**   Edwards, Blake; Adams, Tony
**Director(s)**   Edwards, Blake
**Screenwriter(s)**   Edwards, Blake

**Cast**   Moore, Dudley; Andrews, Julie; Derek, Bo; Webber, Robert; Wallace, Dee; Jones, Sam; Dennehy, Brian; Showalter, Max; Daly, Red; Rush, Deborah

**Song(s)**   Don't Call It Love (L: Sager, Carole Bayer); He Pleases Me; It's Easy to Say; I Have an Ear for Love; Estanoche La Paso Contigo (C/L: Llanos, Laura Gomez)

**Notes**   "I Give My Heart to You" (from the operetta THE DUBARRY) by Theo Mackeben after Carl Millocker; Paul Knepler; J.M. Wellemsky; Rowland Leigh and Desmond Carter is used as a visual vocal also. It is not known if the Llanos song was written for the film.

## 6057 ✦ TEN CENTS A DANCE
### Columbia, 1945

**Producer(s)**   Kraike, Michel
**Director(s)**   Jason, Will
**Screenwriter(s)**   Grant, Morton

**Cast**   Calvert, John; Johnson, Marilyn; Lloyd, Jimmy; Mathews, Carole; McGowan, Jewel; Scott, Robert; Frazee, Jane; Winters, Shirley [3]; Stanwyck, Barbara [4]

**Song(s)**   Ten Cents a Dance [1] [2] (C: Rodgers, Richard; L: Hart, Lorenz); Someday Somewhere [1]

(C/L: Brooks, Joan; Segal, Jack; Miles, Dick); It Must Be Jelly [1] (C/L: MacGregor, Chummy; Williams, George; Skylar, Sunny); Michael the Bicycle Rider (C: Chaplin, Saul; L: Cahn, Sammy); This Is Love (C/L: Winslow, Alfred)

**Notes** [1] Not written for picture. [2] From Broadway musical SIMPLE SIMON. [3] Shelley Winters. [4] Dubbed by Virginia Verrill.

## 6058 ✦ THE TEN COMMANDMENTS
Paramount, 1956

**Musical Score** Bernstein, Elmer
**Composer(s)** Bernstein, Elmer
**Choreographer(s)** Prinz, LeRoy; Godfrey, Ruth

**Producer(s)** De Mille, Cecil B.
**Director(s)** De Mille, Cecil B.
**Screenwriter(s)** MacKenzie, Aeneas; Lasky Jr., Jesse; Gariss, Jack; Frank, Fredric M.
**Source(s)** Holy Scriptures (Scriptures); *Prince of Egypt* (book) Wilson, Dorothy Clarke; *Pillar of Fire* (book) Ingraham, Rev. J.H.; *On Eagle's Wings* (book) Southon, Rev. A.E.; Ancient Texts (texts) Josephus, Eusebius, Philo

**Cast** Heston, Charlton; Brynner, Yul; Baxter, Anne; Robinson, Edward G.; De Carlo, Yvonne; Paget, Debra; Derek, John; Hardwicke, Sir Cedric; Foch, Nina; Scott, Martha; Anderson, Judith; Price, Vincent; Carradine, John; Dumbrille, Douglass; Wilcoxon, Henry; Franz, Eduard; Warner, H.B.; Deering, Olive; De Kova, Frank; Curtis, Donald; Dobkin, Lawrence; Faye, Julia; Mitchell, Lisa; Merlin, Joanna; Vanderveen, Joyce; Hall, Diane; Richard, Pat; Williams, Noelle; El Boughdadly, Abbas; Heston, Fraser; Miljan, John; Duran, Tommy; McDonald, Francis; Mazzola, Eugene; Keith, Ian; Hill, Ramsay; De Rolf, Paul; Strode, Woody [4]; Woodbury, Joan; Brown, Esther; Abaza, Rushti; Adams, Dorothy; Elden, Eric; Andre, E.J.; Bain, Babette; Barron, Baynes; Bell, Kay; Bendt, Mary; Brandon, Henry; Carson, Robert; Clark, Robert; Conklin, Russ; Connors, Touch; Gordon, Henry; Cooper, Edna May; Dibbs, Kem; Fealy, Maude; Gibson, Mimi; Gump, Diane; Hale, Nancy; Jocelyn, June; Kean, Richard; Kobe, Gail; Kohler Jr., Fred; MacDonald, Kenneth; Mamakos, Peter; Martin, Irene; Melford, George; Merton, John; Mohamed, Amena; Morgan, Paula; Neumann, Dorothy; Parrish, John; Redwing, John; Redwing, Rodd; Richards, Addison; Richards, Keith; Starr, Marcoreta; Stevens, Onslow; Walker, Clint; Webb, Amanda; Wilcox, Frank; Wood, Jeane

**Song(s)** Moses Crosses Desert (L: Bernstein, Elmer); Sethi's Death Chant (L: Bernstein, Elmer); The Shrine of the River Gods (L: Noerdlinger, Henry); Lilia's Song (L: Wilcoxon, Henry); Prayer for Passover Scene [1] (L: Traditional); Song of Joseph (L: Noerdlinger, Henry); Chant of Praise [2] (L: Traditional); Chant of Priests and Priestesses at the Sickbed of the Son of Rameses [3] (L:

Noerdlinger, Henry); Drinking Song - Bacchanal [3] (L: Bernstein, Elmer)

**Notes** [1] Words from "91st Psalm." [2] Words from the Bible. [3] Not used or called something else on the cue sheet. [4] Billed as Woodrow Strode.

## 6059 ✦ TENDER FLESH
Warner Brothers, 1976

**Musical Score** Camillo, Tony

**Producer(s)** Cushingham, Jack
**Director(s)** Harvey, Laurence
**Screenwriter(s)** Bennett, Wallace C.

**Cast** Harvey, Laurence; Pettet, Joanna; Whitman, Stuart; Ireland, John; Foster, Meg

**Song(s)** Who Can Tell Us Why (C: Keyes, Bert; Barrie, George; L: Cahn, Sammy)

**Notes** No cue sheet available.

## 6060 ✦ TENDER IS THE NIGHT
Twentieth Century–Fox, 1961

**Producer(s)** Weinstein, Henry T.
**Director(s)** King, Henry
**Screenwriter(s)** Moffat, Ivan
**Source(s)** *Tender Is the Night* (novel) Fitzgerald, F. Scott

**Cast** Jones, Jennifer; Robards Jr., Jason; Fontaine, Joan; Ewell, Tom; Danova, Cesare; St. John, Jill; Lukas, Paul

**Song(s)** Tender Is the Night [1] (C: Fain, Sammy; L: Webster, Paul Francis)

**Notes** [1] There was an earlier rejected version with lyrics by Harry Harris.

## 6061 ✦ TENDER MERCIES
Universal, 1983

**Producer(s)** Hobel, Philip S.
**Director(s)** Beresford, Bruce
**Screenwriter(s)** Foote, Horton

**Cast** Duvall, Robert; Harper, Tess; Buckley, Betty; Brimley, Wilford; Barkin, Ellen; Hubbard, Allan

**Song(s)** Fool's Waltz (C/L: Duvall, Robert); I've Decided to Leave Here Forever (C/L: Duvall, Robert); The Best Bedroom in Town (C/L: Craig, Charlie); Over You (C/L: Roberts, Austin; Hart, Bobby); Overnight Sensation (C/L: Bickhardt, Craig); Oklahoma Twister (C/L: Barnes, Max D.); I'm Not Strong Like I Used to Be (C/L: Gorden, Kelly; Marable, Abby); Wings of a Dove (C/L: Ferguson, Bob); If You'll Hold the Ladder (C/L: Rabin, Buzz; B., Sara); Champagne Ladies (C/L: Craig, Charlie); Midnight Tennessee Woman (C/L: Craig, Charlie); Off on Wednesdays (C/L: Craig,

Charlie); You Are What Love Means to Me (C/L: Bickhardt, Craig)

**Notes** The cue sheet does not indicate which are instrumental cues, which are vocals or which were written for this picture.

### 6062 ✦ THE TENDER TRAP
Metro–Goldwyn–Mayer, 1955

**Musical Score** Alexander, Jeff

**Producer(s)** Weingarten, Lawrence
**Director(s)** Walters, Charles
**Screenwriter(s)** Epstein, Julius J.
**Source(s)** *The Tender Trap* (play) Shulman, Max; Smith, Robert Paul

**Cast** Sinatra, Frank; Reynolds, Debbie; Wayne, David; Holm, Celeste; Lewis, Jarma; Albright, Lola; Jones, Carolyn; St. John, Howard; Faye, Joey

**Song(s)** (Love Is) The Tender Trap (C: Van Heusen, James; L: Cahn, Sammy)

### 6063 ✦ TEN GENTLEMEN FROM WEST POINT
Twentieth Century–Fox, 1942

**Producer(s)** Perlberg, William
**Director(s)** Hathaway, Henry
**Screenwriter(s)** Maibaum, Richard

**Cast** Montgomery, George; O'Hara, Maureen; Sutton, John; Cregar, Laird; Shepperd, John; Francen, Victor; Bond, Ward; Dumbrille, Douglass; Brown Jr., Joe

**Song(s)** Blind Man's Buff (C/L: Newman, Lionel)

### 6064 ✦ TENNESSEE CHAMP
Metro–Goldwyn–Mayer, 1954

**Musical Score** Salinger, Conrad

**Producer(s)** Fielding, Sol Baer
**Director(s)** Wilcox, Fred M.
**Screenwriter(s)** Cohn, Art
**Source(s)** "The Lord in His Corner" (story) Cockrell, Eustace

**Cast** Winters, Shelley; Wynn, Keenan; Martin, Dewey; Holliman, Earl; O'Brien, Dave; Buchinsky, Charles; Dugay, Yvette

**Song(s)** The Weary Blues [1] (C: Warren, Harry; L: Blane, Ralph)

**Notes** [1] Used instrumentally only.

### 6065 ✦ TENNESSEE'S PARTNER
RKO, 1955

**Musical Score** Forbes, Louis

**Producer(s)** Bogeaus, Benedict
**Director(s)** Dwan, Allan

**Screenwriter(s)** Krims, Milton; Beauchamp, D.D.; Baker, Graham; Sherman, Teddi
**Source(s)** "Tennessee's Partner" (story) Harte, Bret

**Cast** Payne, John; Reagan, Ronald; Gray, Coleen; Fleming, Rhonda; Caruso, Anthony; Ankrum, Morris; Gordon, Leo

**Song(s)** Heart of Gold (C: Forbes, Louis; L: Franklin, Dave)

### 6066 ✦ TENSION AT TABLE ROCK
RKO, 1956

**Musical Score** Tiomkin, Dimitri

**Producer(s)** Wiesenthal, Sam
**Director(s)** Warren, Charles Marquis
**Screenwriter(s)** Miller, Winston
**Source(s)** *Bitter Sage* (novel) Gruber, Frank

**Cast** Egan, Richard; Malone, Dorothy; Mitchell, Cameron; Chapin, Billy; Dano, Royal; Andrews, Edward; Dehner, John; Kelley, DeForest; DeSantis, Joe; Dickinson, Angie

**Song(s)** The Ballad of Wes Tancred (C: Myrow, Josef; L: Wells, Robert); Wait for Love [1] (C: Myrow, Josef; L: Wells, Robert)

**Notes** [1] Sheet music only.

### 6067 ✦ TENTH AVENUE KID
Republic, 1938

**Producer(s)** Siegel, Sol
**Director(s)** Vorhaus, Bernard
**Screenwriter(s)** Kahn, Gordon

**Cast** Cabot, Bruce; Roberts, Beverly; Ryan, Tommy; Weldon, Ben; MacMahon, Horace; Novello, Jay

**Song(s)** We Walk Alone [1] (C: Traditional; L: Cherkose, Eddie); Mama I Wanna Make Rhythm [2] (C/L: Jerome, Jerome; Byron, Richard; Kent, Walter)

**Notes** [1] Based on tune "Londonderry Air." [2] Also in BEAUTIFUL BUT BROKE (Columbia) and MANHATTAN MERRY-GO-ROUND.

### 6068 ✦ 10:30 P.M. SUMMER
United Artists, 1966

**Musical Score** Halffter, Cristobal

**Producer(s)** Dassin, Jules; Litvak, Anatole
**Director(s)** Dassin, Jules
**Screenwriter(s)** Duras, Marguerite; Dassin, Jules
**Source(s)** *10:30 p.m. on a Summer Night* (novel) Duras, Marguerite

**Cast** Mercouri, Melina; Finch, Peter; Schneider, Romy; Mateos, Julian

**Song(s)** Judith Has a Baby (C/L: Dassin, Jules); Farmerman Farmerman (C: Traditional; L: Dassin, Jules)

**Notes** There are also several folksongs and "Avec ses Castagnettes" by Etienne Lorin and Bourvil.

## 6069 ✦ TEN THOUSAND BEDROOMS
Metro–Goldwyn–Mayer, 1957

**Composer(s)** Brodszky, Nicholas
**Lyricist(s)** Cahn, Sammy
**Choreographer(s)** Baker, Jack

**Producer(s)** Pasternak, Joe
**Director(s)** Thorpe, Richard
**Screenwriter(s)** Vadnay, Laslo; Cohn, Art

**Cast** Martin, Dean; Alberghetti, Anna Maria; Bartok, Eva; Martin, Dewey; Slezak, Walter; Henreid, Paul; Munshin, Jules; Varden, Evelyn; Dalio, Marcel; Montell, Lisa [1]; Jones, Dean; Van Vooren, Monique

**Song(s)** Ten Thousand Bedrooms; Only Trust Your Heart; No One But You [2] (L: Lawrence, Jack); You I Love; Money Is a Problem; Man Who Plays the Mandolin (C: Faniciulli, G.; Bergman, Andrew; Bergman, Marilyn)

**Notes** There is also a vocal of "Rock Around the Clock" by Max C. Freedman and Jimmy DeKnight. [1] Dubbed by Betty Wand. [2] Also in FLAME AND THE FLESH.

## 6070 ✦ TENTING TONIGHT ON THE OLD CAMP GROUND
Universal, 1942

**Producer(s)** Drake, Oliver
**Director(s)** Collins, Lewis D.
**Screenwriter(s)** Beecher, Elizabeth

**Cast** Brown, Johnny Mack; Ritter, Tex

**Song(s)** The Drinks Are on the House (C: Rosen, Milton; L: Carter, Everett); Ridin' Home [1] (C: McHugh, Jimmy; L: Adamson, Harold)

**Notes** There is also a vocal of "Tenting Tonight on the Old Camp Ground" by Walter Kitteridge. [1] Also in DESPERATE TRAILS (1939), ROAD AGENT, THE ROAD TO RENO and STRICTLY IN THE GROOVE.

## 6071 ✦ TEN WHO DARED
Disney, 1960

**Musical Score** Wallace, Oliver

**Producer(s)** Algar, James
**Director(s)** Beaudine, William
**Screenwriter(s)** Watkin, Lawrence Edward
**Source(s)** (journal) Powell, John Wesley

**Cast** Keith, Brian; Beal, John; Drury, James; Armstrong, R.G.; Johnson, Ben

**Song(s)** The Jolly Rovers (C: Jones, Stan; L: Watkin, Lawrence Edward); Roll Along (Unto the Sea) [2]

(C/L: Jones, Stan); Ten Who Dared [1] (C/L: Jones, Stan)

**Notes** [1] Sheet music only. [2] Sheet music may also credit Watkin.

## 6072 ✦ TE QUIERO CON LOCURA
Fox, 1935

**Composer(s)** Roulien, Raul
**Lyricist(s)** Roulien, Raul

**Song(s)** No Estan Todos Los Que Son; Do Re Me Fa Sol - Por Ti; Suenos de Princesa (C: Sanders, Troy; L: Rubio, Jose Lopez); La Locumba [1]; No Estan Todos Los Dos

**Notes** No other information available. [1] Also in MUSIC IS MAGIC with lyrics by Sidney Clare.

## 6073 ✦ TEQUILA SUNRISE
Warner Brothers, 1988

**Musical Score** Grusin, Dave

**Producer(s)** Mount, Thom
**Director(s)** Towne, Robert
**Screenwriter(s)** Towne, Robert

**Cast** Gibson, Mel; Pfeiffer, Michelle; Russell, Kurt; Julia, Raul; Howard, Arliss; Gross, Arye; Magnuson, Ann; Boetticher, Budd

**Song(s)** Surrender to Me (C/L: Marx, Richard; Vanelli, Ross)

**Notes** No cue sheet available.

## 6074 ✦ TERESA
Metro–Goldwyn–Mayer, 1950

**Musical Score** Applebaum, Louis

**Producer(s)** Loew Jr., Arthur M.
**Director(s)** Zinnemann, Fred
**Screenwriter(s)** Stern, Stewart

**Cast** Angeli, Pier; Ericson, John; Collinge, Patricia; Mauldin, Bill; Garner, Peggy Ann; Steiger, Rod

**Song(s)** Teresa [1] (C: Livingston, Jerry; L: David, Mack)

**Notes** [1] Written for exploitation only.

## 6075 ✦ THE TERROR OF TINY TOWN
Columbia, 1938

**Composer(s)** Porter, Lew
**Lyricist(s)** Porter, Lew

**Producer(s)** Buell, Jed
**Director(s)** Newfield, Sam
**Screenwriter(s)** Myton, Fred; Marks, Clarence

**Cast**    Little Billy; Curtis, Billy; Moray, Yvonne; Platt, Billy; Bambary, Johnny; Becker, Charles

**Song(s)**    Laugh Your Troubles Away; Hey Look Out (C/L: Porter, Lew; Stern, Phil); She's the Daughter of Sweet Caroline; Down on the Sunset Trail; The Wedding of Jack and Jill

### 6076 ◆ TERROR TRAIN
United Artists, 1980

**Musical Score**    Cockell, John Mills
**Composer(s)**    Cohen, Larry
**Lyricist(s)**    Cohen, Larry

**Producer(s)**    Greenberg, Harold
**Director(s)**    Spottiswoode, Roger
**Screenwriter(s)**    Drake, Tom

**Cast**    Johnson, Ben; Curtis, Jamie Lee; Bochner, Hart; Copperfield, David; MacKinnon, Derek

**Song(s)**    Title (C/L: Cockell, John Mills); Heroes; Funky Love; Love or Blues; Broken Man

### 6077 ◆ TERRYTOON CARTOONS
Studio Unknown, 1942

**Composer(s)**    Scheib, Philip A.
**Lyricist(s)**    Scheib, Philip A.

**Song(s)**    Five Little Reasons; In Old Havana; Working for Defense; Have Y'Got Any Scrap?; Keep 'Em Growing

**Notes**    No other information available.

### 6078 ◆ TEST PILOT
Metro–Goldwyn–Mayer, 1938

**Musical Score**    Waxman, Franz

**Producer(s)**    Lighton, Louis D.
**Director(s)**    Fleming, Victor
**Screenwriter(s)**    Lawrence, Vincent; Young, Waldemar

**Cast**    Loy, Myrna; Gable, Clark; Tracy, Spencer; Barrymore, Lionel; Hinds, Samuel S.; Main, Marjorie; Heydt, Louis Jean; Grey, Virginia

**Song(s)**    Yours and Mine [1] (C: Brown, Nacio Herb; L: Freed, Arthur)

**Notes**    [1] Also in BROADWAY MELODY OF 1938.

### 6079 ◆ THE TEXAN
Paramount, 1930

**Composer(s)**    Baer, Abel
**Lyricist(s)**    Gilbert, L. Wolfe

**Producer(s)**    Selznick, David O.
**Director(s)**    Cromwell, John
**Screenwriter(s)**    Rubin, Daniel Nathan
**Source(s)**    "The Double-dyed Deceiver" (story) Henry, O.

**Cast**    Cooper, Gary; Wray, Fay; Apfel, Oscar; Dunn, Emma; Marcus, James; Reed, Donald

**Song(s)**    Chico; To Hold You [1]; Over the Plains [2]

**Notes**    [1] Used instrumentally only but recorded as a vocal. [2] Not used.

### 6080 ◆ THE TEXANS
Paramount, 1938

**Producer(s)**    Hubbard, Lucien
**Director(s)**    Hogan, James
**Screenwriter(s)**    Millhauser, Bertram; Sloane, Paul; Haines, William Wister
**Source(s)**    *North of '36* (novel) Hough, Emerson

**Cast**    Bennett, Joan; Scott, Randolph; Cummings, Robert; Brennan, Walter

**Song(s)**    Silver on the Sage [2] (C: Rainger, Ralph; L: Robin, Leo); I'll Come to the Wedding [1] (C: Traditional; L: Loesser, Frank)

**Notes**    The score also includes vocal renditions of the following songs: Owen Wister's "Ten Thousand Cattle," "Noah's Ark" and Will S. Hays' "Roll Out Heave That Cotton." [1] To the tune of "Buffalo Gals." [2] Also in SILVER ON THE SAGE.

### 6081 ◆ TEXANS NEVER CRY
Columbia, 1951

**Producer(s)**    Schaefer, Armand
**Director(s)**    McDonald, Frank
**Screenwriter(s)**    Hall, Norman S.

**Cast**    Autry, Gene; Buttram, Pat; Davis, Gail; Castle, Mary; Haydn, Russell; Powers, Richard [1]

**Song(s)**    Ride, Ranger, Ride [2] (C/L: Spencer, Tim); Texans Never Cry (C/L: Autry, Gene; Haldeman, Oakley; Fort, Hank)

**Notes**    No cue sheet available. [1] Tom Keene. [2] Also in GANGSTERS OF THE FRONTIER (PRC) and the Republic pictures THE BIG SHOW, KING OF THE COWBOYS and RIDE, RANGER, RIDE.

### 6082 ◆ TEXAS ACROSS THE RIVER
Universal, 1966

**Musical Score**    De Vol, Frank

**Producer(s)**    Keller, Harry
**Director(s)**    Gordon, Michael
**Screenwriter(s)**    Root, Wells; Greene, Harold; Starr, Ben

**Cast**    Martin, Dean; Delon, Alain; Marquand, Tina; Ansara, Michael; Chiles, Linden; Forsyth, Rosemary

**Song(s)**    Texas Across the River (C: Van Heusen, James; L: Cahn, Sammy)

## 6083 ✦ TEXAS CARNIVAL
### Metro–Goldwyn–Mayer, 1951

**Musical Score**   Rose, David
**Composer(s)**   Warren, Harry
**Lyricist(s)**   Fields, Dorothy
**Choreographer(s)**   Pan, Hermes

**Producer(s)**   Cummings, Jack
**Director(s)**   Walters, Charles
**Screenwriter(s)**   Kingsley, Dorothy

**Cast**   Williams, Esther; Skelton, Red; Keel, Howard; Miller, Ann; Raymond, Paula; Wynn, Keenan; Tully, Tom

**Song(s)**   Cornie's Pitch; Whoa Emma; It's Dynamite; Clap Your Hands (C: Rose, David; L: Brent, Earl; Pan, Hermes); Young Folks Should Get Married; Love Is a Lovely Word [1]; You've Got a Face Full of Wonderful Things [1]

**Notes**   [1] Not used.

## 6084 ✦ TEXAS JOHN SLAUGHTER
### Disney, 1960

**Musical Score**   Dubin, Joseph S.; Baker, Buddy

**Producer(s)**   Pratt, James
**Director(s)**   Keller, Harry
**Screenwriter(s)**   Gilroy, Frank D.; Lewin, Albert; Styler, Burt

**Cast**   Tryon, Tom; Middleton, Robert; Moore, Norma; Carey Jr., Harry; Pratt, Judson; Platt, Edward

**Song(s)**   Texas John Slaughter [2] (C/L: Jones, Stan); Song of the Texas Rangers [1] (C: Dubin, Joseph S.; L: Jackman, Bob)

**Notes**   [1] Also in GERONIMO'S REVENGE and GUNFIGHT AT SANDOVAL. [2] Also in GUNFIGHT AT SANDOVAL.

## 6085 ✦ THE TEXAS RANGERS
### Paramount, 1936

**Producer(s)**   Vidor, King
**Director(s)**   Vidor, King
**Screenwriter(s)**   Stevens, Louis
**Source(s)**   *The Texas Rangers* (book) Webb, Walter Prescott

**Cast**   MacMurray, Fred; Oakie, Jack; Nolan, Lloyd; Parker, Jean

**Song(s)**   Texas Ranger Song (C: Coslow, Sam; L: Behn, Harry); I Can't Play the Banjo with Susannah on My Knee [2] (C: Boutelje, Phil; L: Scholl, Jack); Purple Shadows [1] (C: Boutelje, Phil; L: Behn, Harry)

**Notes**   There are also vocal renditions of "Bury Me Not on the Lone Prairie," "Alla En Rancho Grande" by Silvano Ramos and J.D. del Morel and "Root Hog or

Die." [1] Not used. [2] Also used in SECRETS OF THE WASTELANDS and considered but not used in RHYTHM ON THE RANGE.

## 6086 ✦ TEXAS TERRORS
### Republic, 1940

**Producer(s)**   Sherman, George
**Director(s)**   Sherman, George
**Screenwriter(s)**   Coldeway, Anthony; Schroeder, Doris

**Cast**   Barry, Donald; Duncan, Julie; Loft, Arthur; St. John, Al; Walker, Eddy; Ruhl, William; Pennington, Ann; Jimmy Wakely and His Roughriders

**Song(s)**   Listen to the Rhythm of the Range [1] (C/L: Autry, Gene; Marvin, Johnny)

**Notes**   [1] Also in UNDER WESTERN STARS.

## 6087 ✦ TEXAS TRAIL
### Paramount, 1937

**Producer(s)**   Sherman, Harry
**Director(s)**   Selman, David
**Screenwriter(s)**   O'Donnell, Jack

**Cast**   Boyd, William; Hayden, Russell; Hayes, George "Gabby"; Allen, Judith

**Song(s)**   Mountain Moon [1] (C: Stern, Jack; L: Tobias, Harry)

**Notes**   Film formerly titled MEN MUST FIGHT. [1] Not used in picture.

## 6088 ✦ TEXAS TROUBLE SHOOTERS
### Monogram, 1968

**Musical Score**   Sanucci, Frank

**Cast**   King, John

**Song(s)**   Under the Western Skies (C/L: Tobias, Harry)

**Notes**   No other information available. There is also a vocal of "Deep in the Heart of Texas" by June Hershey and Don Swander.

## 6089 ✦ THANK GOD IT'S FRIDAY
### Casablanca/Motown/Columbia, 1978

**Producer(s)**   Cohen, Rob
**Director(s)**   Klane, Robert
**Screenwriter(s)**   Bernstein, Barry Armyan

**Cast**   Vennera, Chick; Landsburg, Valerie; Nunn, Terri; Summer, Donna; Adams, Phil; Vitte, Ray; Lonow, Mark; Howard, Andrea; The Commodores

**Song(s)**   After Dark (C/L: Soussan, Simon; Soussan, Sabrina); Find My Way (C: Melfi, J.); It's Serious (C/L: Johnson, Gregory; Blackman, Larry); Let's Make a Deal (C/L: Smith, Michael); Romeo and Juliet (C/L:

Costadinos, Alec R.); You're the Reason I Feel Like Dancing (C/L: Johnson, H.); From Here to Eternity (C/L: Moroder, Giorgio; Bellotte, Pete); Dance All Night (C/L: Hutch, Willie ); Love Masterpiece (C/L: Davis, H.; Powell, J.; Posey, Art); I'm Here Again (C/L: Sutton, B.; Sutton, Michael; Wakefield, Kathy); Disco Queen (C/L: Jabara, Paul); Trapped in a Stairway (C/L: Jabara, Paul; Esty, Bob); Do You Want the Real Thing (C/L: LaRue, D.C.; Esty, Bob); You Can Always Tell a Lady by the Company She Keeps (C/L: LaRue, D.C.; Esty, Bob); Thank God It's Friday (C/L: Costadinos, Alec R.); You Are the Most Precious Thing in My Life (C/L: Costadinos, Alec R.); I Wanna Dance (C/L: Bellotte, P.); Meco's Theme (inst.) (C: Wheeler, Harold); Floyd's Theme (inst.) (C: St. Nicklaus, D.); Down to Lovetown (C/L: Daniels, Don; Sutton, Michael; Wakefield, Kathy); Lovin', Livin', and Givin' (C/L: Stover, Kenneth; Davis, Pam); Sevilla Nights (C/L: Skorsky, N.; Descarano, J.M.; Petit, J.C.); Love to Love You Baby (C/L: Moroder, Giorgio; Summer, Donna); Try with Your Love (C/L: Moroder, Giorgio; Summer, Donna); Je T'Aime (C/L: Gainsbourg, Serge)

**Notes**   No cue sheet available.

### 6090   ✦   THANKS A MILLION
Twentieth Century–Fox, 1935

**Composer(s)**   Johnston, Arthur
**Lyricist(s)**   Kahn, Gus

**Producer(s)**   Zanuck, Darryl F.
**Director(s)**   Del Ruth, Roy
**Screenwriter(s)**   Johnson, Nunnally

**Cast**   Powell, Dick; Dvorak, Ann; Allen, Fred; Kelly, Patsy; Walburn, Raymond; Baker, Benny; Dinehart, Alan; Tombes, Andrew; Harvey, Paul; Richman, Charles; Paul Whiteman and His Band; Rubinoff, Ramona; The Yacht Club Boys

**Song(s)**   Thanks a Million [1]; I've Got a Pocket Full of Sunshine; Square Deal Party (C/L: The Yacht Club Boys); Alphabet Song (C/L: The Yacht Club Boys); Sugar Plum; I'm Sittin' High on a Hill Top; New O'leans

**Notes**   [1] Also in SING BABY SING.

### 6091   ✦   THANKS FOR EVERYTHING
Twentieth Century–Fox, 1938

**Composer(s)**   Revel, Harry
**Lyricist(s)**   Gordon, Mack

**Producer(s)**   Zanuck, Darryl F.
**Director(s)**   Seiter, William A.
**Screenwriter(s)**   Tugend, Harry

**Cast**   Menjou, Adolphe; Oakie, Jack; Haley, Jack; Whelan, Arleen; Martin, Tony; Barnes, Binnie; Barbier, George; Hymer, Warren; Gaye, Gregory; Tombes, Andrew; Lane, Charles; Sully, Frank

**Song(s)**   Puff-A-Puff; Three Cheers for Henry Smith; Thanks for Everything; You're the World's Fairest; Here Am I Doing It [1]

**Notes**   [1] Instrumental use only.

### 6092   ✦   THANKS FOR THE MEMORY
Paramount, 1938

**Producer(s)**   Shauer, Mel
**Director(s)**   Archainbaud, George
**Screenwriter(s)**   Starling, Lynn
**Source(s)**   *Up Pops the Devil* (play) Hackett, Albert; Goodrich, Frances

**Cast**   Hope, Bob; Ross, Shirley; Butterworth, Charles; Hopper, Hedda; Kruger, Otto; Crews, Laura Hope; Anderson, Eddie "Rochester"

**Song(s)**   Two Sleepy People (C: Carmichael, Hoagy; L: Loesser, Frank); Thanks for the Memory [1] (C: Rainger, Ralph; L: Robin, Leo)

**Notes**   [1] From THE BIG BROADCAST OF 1938.

### 6093   ✦   THANK YOUR LUCKY STARS
Warner Brothers, 1943

**Composer(s)**   Schwartz, Arthur
**Lyricist(s)**   Loesser, Frank
**Choreographer(s)**   Prinz, LeRoy

**Producer(s)**   Hellinger, Mark
**Director(s)**   Butler, David
**Screenwriter(s)**   Panama, Norman; Frank, Melvin; Kern, James V.

**Cast**   Bogart, Humphrey; Cantor, Eddie; Davis, Bette; de Havilland, Olivia; Flynn, Errol; Garfield, John; Leslie, Joan; Lupino, Ida; Morgan, Dennis; Sheridan, Ann; Shore, Dinah; Smith, Alexis; Carson, Jack; Hale, Alan; Tobias, George; Horton, Edward Everett; Sakall, S.Z.; McDaniel, Hattie; Donnelly, Ruth; Wilson, Don; Best, Willie; Armetta, Henry; Reynolds, Joyce; Spike Jones and His City Slickers

**Song(s)**   Thank Your Lucky Stars; Riding for a Fall; We're Staying Home Tonight (My Baby and Me) [1]; I'm Going North; Love Isn't Born; No You No Me; The Dreamer; Ice Cold Katy; Good Night Good Neighbor; How Sweet You Are; That's What You Jolly Well Get; They're Either Too Young or Too Old

**Notes**   "Now's the Time to Fall in Love" by Al Sherman and Al Lewis is used as a visual vocal and "Blues in the Night" by Harold Arlen and Johnny Mercer is heard briefly. [1] Used for 4 seconds in HOLLYWOOD CANTEEN.

### 6094   ✦   THANK YOUR STARS

See SHOOT THE WORKS.

## 6095 ◆ THAT CERTAIN AGE
Universal, 1938

**Composer(s)** McHugh, Jimmy
**Lyricist(s)** Adamson, Harold

**Producer(s)** Pasternak, Joe
**Director(s)** Ludwig, Edward
**Screenwriter(s)** Manning, Bruce; Brackett, Charles; Wilder, Billy

**Cast** Durbin, Deanna; Douglas, Melvyn; Cooper, Jackie; Rich, Irene; Halliday, John; Carroll, Nancy; Quigley, Juanita; Searl, Jackie; Coleman, Charles; Stewart, Peggy

**Song(s)** That Certain Age; Be a Good Scout; You're As Pretty As a Picture; My Own; Daydreams [2] (C: Gounod, Charles; L: Ronell, Ann); Girls of Cadiz [1] (C: Delibes, Leo; L: Ronell, Ann); Romeo and Juliet Waltz [2] (C: Gounod, Charles; L: Ronell, Ann)

**Notes** There is also a vocal of "Les Filles de Cadiz" by Leo Delibes. [1] Sheet music only—see note above. [2] Sheet music only.

## 6096 ◆ THAT DARN CAT
Disney, 1965

**Musical Score** Brunner, Robert F.

**Producer(s)** Miller, Ron; Walsh, Bill
**Director(s)** Stevenson, Robert
**Screenwriter(s)** Gordons, The; Walsh, Bill
**Source(s)** *Undercover Cat* (novel) Gordons, The

**Cast** Mills, Hayley; Jones, Dean; Provine, Dorothy; McDowall, Roddy; Brand, Neville; Lanchester, Elsa; Demarest, William; Gorshin, Frank; Hall, Grayson; Eastham, Richard; Adrian, Iris; Deacon, Richard; Wynn, Ed

**Song(s)** That Darn Cat (C/L: Sherman, Robert B.; Sherman, Richard M.); Ten Foot Surf (C/L: Brunner, Robert F.)

## 6097 ◆ THAT FUNNY FEELING
Universal, 1965

**Musical Score** Darin, Bobby

**Producer(s)** Keller, Harry
**Director(s)** Thorpe, Richard
**Screenwriter(s)** Schwartz, David R.

**Cast** Dee, Sandra; Darin, Bobby; O'Connor, Donald; Talbot, Nita; Storch, Larry

**Song(s)** Funny Feeling (C/L: Darin, Bobby)

## 6098 ◆ THAT GIRL FROM PARIS
RKO, 1936

**Composer(s)** Schwartz, Arthur
**Lyricist(s)** Heyman, Edward

**Producer(s)** Berman, Pandro S.
**Director(s)** Jason, Leigh
**Screenwriter(s)** Wolfson, P.J.; Yost, Dorothy
**Source(s)** "The Viennese Charmer" (story) Wonderly, William Carey

**Cast** Oakie, Jack; Pons, Lily; Raymond, Gene; Bing, Herman; Auer, Mischa; Ball, Lucille; Jenks, Frank

**Song(s)** Comme un Oiseau (L: De Gombert, G.); The Call to Arms; Love and Learn; Seal It with a Kiss; My Nephew from Nice; The Beautiful Blue Danube (C: Strauss, Johann; L: De Gombert, G.); Moon Face

## 6099 ◆ THAT KIND OF WOMAN
Paramount, 1959

**Producer(s)** Ponti, Carlo; Girosi, Marcello
**Director(s)** Lumet, Sidney
**Screenwriter(s)** Bernstein, Walter

**Cast** Loren, Sophia; Hunter, Tab; Warden, Jack; Nichols, Barbara; Wynn, Keenan; Sanders, George

**Song(s)** That Kind of Woman [1] (C: Bacharach, Burt; L: David, Hal)

**Notes** [1] Written for exploitation only.

## 6100 ◆ THAT LADY FROM PEKING
Commonwealth United

**Musical Score** Young, Robert

**Producer(s)** Davis, Eddie
**Director(s)** Davis, Eddie

**Cast** Rydell, Bobby; Betz, Carl; Kwan, Nancy

**Song(s)** Target for Tonight (C: Oakland, Ben; L: Elliott, Jack); Talk to Me Softly (C: Young, Bob; L: Denton, Kit)

## 6101 ◆ THAT LADY IN ERMINE
Twentieth Century–Fox, 1948

**Musical Score** Newman, Alfred
**Composer(s)** Hollander, Frederick
**Lyricist(s)** Robin, Leo
**Choreographer(s)** Pan, Hermes

**Producer(s)** Lubitsch, Ernst
**Director(s)** Lubitsch, Ernst
**Screenwriter(s)** Raphaelson, Samson

**Cast** Grable, Betty; Fairbanks Jr., Douglas; Romero, Cesar; Abel, Walter; Gardiner, Reginald; Davenport, Harry; Bissell, Whit

**Song(s)** This Is the Moment [1]; There's Something About Midnight; What a Crisis; What Do You See; Ooh! What I'll Do (To That Wild Hungarian); The Jester's Song (The Jester and Me); The Melody Has to Be Right; The Colonel's Waltz (Inst.); Hurry Up! (Alberto's Lullaby) [2]; It's Always a Beautiful Day [2] (C: Lubitsch, Ernst)

**Notes**  [1] Robin wrote a song of the same name to music by Ralph Rainger for the Paramount films THE VIRTUOUS SIN and THE WOLF OF WALL STREET. [2] Not used.

## 6102  ◆  THAT MAN BOLT
### Universal, 1973

**Musical Score**  Bernstein, Charles

**Producer(s)**  Schwartz, Bernard
**Director(s)**  Levin, Henry; Rich, David Lowell
**Screenwriter(s)**  Wert, Quentin; Johnson, Charles

**Cast**  Williamson, Fred; Webster, Byron; Graves, Teresa; Ging, Jack; Lambrinos, Vassili

**Song(s)**  That'll Be Never (C/L: Paich, David)

## 6103  ◆  THAT MIDNIGHT KISS
### Metro–Goldwyn–Mayer, 1949

**Musical Score**  Previn, Charles

**Producer(s)**  Pasternak, Joe
**Director(s)**  Taurog, Norman
**Screenwriter(s)**  Manning, Bruce; Hovey, Tamara

**Cast**  Grayson, Kathryn; Iturbi, Jose; Barrymore, Ethel; Wynn, Keenan; Naish, J. Carrol; Munshin, Jules; Gomez, Thomas; Reynolds, Marjorie; Iturbi, Amparo; Lanza, Mario

**Song(s)**  I Know, I Know, I Know (C: Kaper, Bronislau; L: Russell, Bob); Love Is Music (C: Tchaikovsky, Peter; Previn, Charles; L: Katz, William)

**Notes**  Originally titled THIS SUMMER IS YOURS. There are also vocals of "Caro Nome Che Il Mio Cor" from RIGOLETTO by Verdi; "Duet Finale Act I" of LUCIA DI LAMMERMOOR by Donizetti; "Mama Mia, Che Vo Sape!" by Nutile and Russo; "O Sole Mio" [1] by Di Capua; "Down Among the Sheltering Palms" by Abe Olman and James Brockman; "Una Furtiva Lagrima" from L'ElISIR D'AMORE by Donizetti; "Celeste Aida" by Verdi; "They Didn't Believe Me" by Jerome Kern and Herbert Reynolds; "Russian Nightingale" by Alabieff; and "Three O'Clock in the Morning" by Julian Robledo and Dorothy Terris (Theodora Morse). [1] Replaced outside the United States by "Santa Lucia" by Cottrau.

## 6104  ◆  THAT NIGHT IN RIO
### Twentieth Century–Fox, 1941

**Composer(s)**  Warren, Harry
**Lyricist(s)**  Gordon, Mack
**Choreographer(s)**  Pan, Hermes

**Producer(s)**  Zanuck, Darryl F.
**Director(s)**  Cummings, Irving
**Screenwriter(s)**  Seaton, George; Meredyth, Bess; Long, Hal; Hoffenstein, Samuel

**Source(s)**  *The Black Cat* (play) Lothar, Rudolph; Adler, Hans

**Cast**  Faye, Alice; Ameche, Don; Miranda, Carmen; Sakall, S.Z.; Naish, J. Carrol; Bois, Curt; Kinskey, Leonid; Montez, Maria; Bonanova, Fortunio; The Flores Brothers

**Song(s)**  Chica Chica Boom Chic; The Baron Is in Conference; The Conference; Boa Noite (Good Night); They Met in Rio (A Midnight Serenade) [2]; I Yi, Yi, Yi, Yi (I Like You Very Much) [2]; Cae Cae [1] (C/L: Martins, Roberto)

**Notes**  [1] Also in NANCY GOES TO RIO (MGM) with lyrics by John Latouche. [2] Also in CHARLIE CHAN IN RIO.

## 6105  ◆  THAT NIGHT WITH YOU
### Universal, 1945

**Lyricist(s)**  Brooks, Jack
**Choreographer(s)**  Da Pron, Louis; Horton, Lester

**Producer(s)**  Fessier, Michael; Pagano, Ernest
**Director(s)**  Seiter, William A.
**Screenwriter(s)**  Fessier, Michael; Pagano, Ernest

**Cast**  Foster, Susanna; Tone, Franchot; Bruce, David

**Song(s)**  Sextette from Lucia (C: Donizetti, G.); Nutcracker Suite (C: Tchaikovsky, Peter); Once Upon a Dream (C: Salter, Hans J.); Barber of Seville (C: Rossini, Giacomo); Romeo and Juliet (C: Tchaikovsky, Peter)

## 6106  ◆  THAT'S DANCING
### Metro–Goldwyn–Mayer, 1985

**Musical Score**  Mancini, Henry

**Producer(s)**  Niven Jr., David
**Director(s)**  Haley Jr., Jack
**Screenwriter(s)**  Haley Jr., Jack

**Cast**  Baryshnikov, Mikhail; Bolger, Ray; Davis Jr., Sammy; Kelly, Gene; Minnelli, Liza

**Song(s)**  That's Dancing (C/L: Mancini, Henry; Grossman, Larry; Fitzhugh, Ellen); Invitation to Dance (C/L: Carnes, Kim; Page, Martin; Fairweather, Brian; Ellinson, David)

**Notes**  Only original songs listed. This is a compilation of dance numbers in various movie musicals. The credits above refer to this film and not the clips included. The film contains the uncut "If I Only Had a Brain" sequence from THE WIZARD OF OZ.

## 6107  ◆  THAT'S ENTERTAINMENT, PART 2
### Metro–Goldwyn–Mayer, 1976

**Producer(s)**  Chaplin, Saul; Melnick, Daniel
**Director(s)**  Kelly, Gene
**Screenwriter(s)**  Gershe, Leonard

**Cast**  Astaire, Fred; Kelly, Gene

**Song(s)**  That's Entertainment [1] (C: Schwartz, Arthur; L: Dietz, Howard; Chaplin, Saul)

**Notes**  This is a compilation of scenes from past films. The credits above refer to this picture, not the clips. [1] Additional lyrics were added for this film by Saul Chaplin. The song was written for the film THE BAND WAGON.

## 6108  ✦  THAT'S LIFE
### Columbia, 1986

**Musical Score**  Mancini, Henry

**Producer(s)**  Adams, Tony
**Director(s)**  Edwards, Blake
**Screenwriter(s)**  Edwards, Blake; Wexler, Milton

**Cast**  Lemmon, Jack; Andrews, Julie; Kellerman, Sally; Loggia, Robert; Edwards, Jennifer; Knepper, Rob; Lattanzi, Matt; Lemmon, Chris; Walton, Emma; Farr, Felicia; Sikes, Cynthia

**Song(s)**  Life in a Looking Glass (C: Mancini, Henry; L: Bricusse, Leslie)

## 6109  ✦  THAT'S MY BABY
### Republic, 1946

**Musical Score**  Chernis, Jay

**Producer(s)**  Colmes, Walter
**Director(s)**  Berke, William
**Screenwriter(s)**  Tunberg, William; Barrows, Nicholas T.

**Cast**  Arlen, Richard; Drew, Ellen; Kinskey, Leonid; Bailey, Richard; Watson, Minor

**Song(s)**  Crying (C/L: Chernis, Jay); Jachanka (C/L: Kuznetzoff, Aida)

## 6110  ✦  THAT'S MY BOY
### Paramount, 1951

**Musical Score**  Harline, Leigh

**Producer(s)**  Wallis, Hal B.
**Director(s)**  Walker, Hal
**Screenwriter(s)**  Howard, Cy

**Cast**  Martin, Dean; Lewis, Jerry; Hussey, Ruth; Marshall, Marion; Bergen, Polly; Mayehoff, Eddie

**Song(s)**  Ridgeville Fight Song (C/L: Livingston, Jay; Evans, Ray)

**Notes**  Formerly titled JUNIOR. There are also vocals of "Ballin' the Jack" by Chris Smith and Jim Burris and "I'm in the Mood for Love" by Jimmy McHugh and Dorothy Fields. The latter has also been used in ABOUT MRS. LESLIE, EVERY NIGHT AT EIGHT and PEOPLE ARE FUNNY.

## 6111  ✦  THAT'S MY GAL
### Republic, 1946

**Composer(s)**  Elliott, Jack
**Lyricist(s)**  Elliott, Jack

**Producer(s)**  Schaefer, Armand
**Director(s)**  Blair, George
**Screenwriter(s)**  Hoffman, Joseph

**Cast**  Roberts, Lynne; Barry, Donald; Lee, Pinky; Jenks, Frank; Gargan, Edward; Clark, Judy

**Song(s)**  That's My Gal; The Music in My Heart Is You [1]; Take It Away

**Notes**  There is also a vocal of "A Gay Ranchero" by J.J. Espinosa, Abe Tuvim and Francia Luban. [1] Also in SWINGIN' ON A RAINBOW.

## 6112  ✦  THAT'S RIGHT—YOU'RE WRONG
### RKO, 1939

**Choreographer(s)**  Prinz, Eddie

**Producer(s)**  Butler, David
**Director(s)**  Butler, David
**Screenwriter(s)**  Conselman, William; Kern, James V.

**Cast**  Kay Kyser and His Band; Simms, Ginny; Babbitt, Harry; Mason, Sully; Kabibble, Ish; Menjou, Adolphe; Robson, May; Ball, Lucille; O'Keefe, Dennis; Horton, Edward Everett; Karns, Roscoe; Olsen, Moroni; Cavanaugh, Hobart

**Song(s)**  The Answer Is Love (C: Stept, Sam H.; L: Newman, Charles); Happy Birthday to Love (C/L: Franklin, Dave); The Little Red Fox (C: Porter, Lew; L: Kern, James V.; Lange, Johnny; Heath, Hy); Chatterbox (C: Brainin, Jerome; L: Roberts, Allan); Fit to Be Tied (C/L: Donaldson, Walter); Scatterbrain [1] (C: Bean, Keene; Masters, Frankie; L: Burke, Johnny)

**Notes**  There are other very short vocals. [1] Sheet music only.

## 6113  ✦  THAT'S THE SPIRIT
### Universal, 1945

**Composer(s)**  Miller, Sidney; James, Inez
**Lyricist(s)**  Miller, Sidney; James, Inez
**Choreographer(s)**  Da Pron, Louis; Romero, Carlos

**Producer(s)**  Fessier, Michael; Pagano, Ernest
**Director(s)**  Lamont, Charles
**Screenwriter(s)**  Fessier, Michael; Pagano, Ernest

**Cast**  Oakie, Jack; Ryan, Peggy; Lockhart, Gene; Vincent, June

**Song(s)**  The Fella with the Flute; Oh! Oh! Oh!; No Matter Where You Are (C: Salter, Hans J.; L: Brooks, Jack); Evening Star [1] (C: Wagner, Richard; L: Brooks, Jack)

**Notes** There are also vocals of "Baby, Won't You Please Come Home" by Charles Warfield and Clarence Williams and "How Come You Do Me Like You Do" by Gene Austin and Roy Bergere. [1] Same music used in MGM's THE CHOCOLATE SOLDIER for song with same name with lyrics by Gus Kahn.

### 6114 ✦ THAT'S US IN THE U.S.A.
Warner Brothers, 1976

**Composer(s)** Adlam, Basil
**Lyricist(s)** Hendricks, William L.

**Song(s)** That's Us in the U.S.A. [2]; Climb Upon a Mountain [1]; Long Time Ago (C: Roemheld, Heinz); Winning of the Land; Ho! to the West (C: Gould, Danny); Civil War [1]; Wait for Me (C: Gould, Danny); The Iron Horse [1]; Freedom's Flame; Look to the Stars [2]; We'll Saddle a Rocket and Ride [2]

**Notes** Short subject. Many of these songs were written for other projects. This is a documentary for the Department of Defense. All these are background instrumentals. [1] Also in A FREE PEOPLE. [2] Also in ONE GIANT LEAP.

### 6115 ✦ THAT TENNESSEE BEAT
Twentieth Century–Fox, 1966

**Producer(s)** Brill, Richard
**Director(s)** Brill, Richard
**Screenwriter(s)** Schneider, Paul

**Cast** DeBord, Sharon; Richards, Earl; Faith, Dolores; Pearl, Minnie; Travis, Merle; Hardin, Rink; Lightnin' Chance; The Statler Brothers; Randolph, Boots; The Stony Mt. Cloggers

**Song(s)** That Tennessee Beat (C/L: Travis, Merle); I'm Sorry (C/L: Travis, Merle)

**Notes** No cue sheet available.

### 6116 ✦ THAT WAS THEN . . . THIS IS NOW
Paramount, 1985

**Musical Score** Olsen, Keith; Cuomo, Bill
**Composer(s)** Olsen, Keith; Cuomo, Bill

**Producer(s)** Lindberg, Gary R.; Ondov, John M.
**Director(s)** Cain, Christopher
**Screenwriter(s)** Estevez, Emilio
**Source(s)** (novel) Hinton, S.E.

**Cast** Estevez, Emilio; Sheffer, Craig; Delaney, Kim; Babcock, Barbara; Freeman, Morgan

**Song(s)** That Was Then . . . This Is Now (L: Wayne, Randy; Hill, Carroll Sue); I Don't Care (L: Wayne, Randy); Sly (C/L: Lipsker, Scott; Kapitan, Michael)

### 6117 ✦ THEATRE ROYAL
Republic, 1943

**Composer(s)** Russell, Kennedy
**Lyricist(s)** O'Connor, Desmond

**Producer(s)** Baxter, John
**Director(s)** Baxter, John
**Screenwriter(s)** Blanagan, Bud; Melford, Austin; Orme, Geoffrey

**Cast** Flanagan, Bud; Allen, Chesney; Dexter, Peggy; Sherwood, Lydia; Kenney, Horace; Rhodes, Marjorie; Currie, Finlay; Victor Feldman Trio, The

**Song(s)** One of the Boys in Town; Roll on Tomorrow; I Know I Must be Dreaming; I'll Always Have Time for You; Jealousy (C: Cade, J.; L: May, W.)

**Notes** A British picture distributed by Republic.

### 6118 ✦ THEIR OWN DESIRE
Metro–Goldwyn–Mayer, 1929

**Director(s)** Hopper, E. Mason
**Screenwriter(s)** Marion, Frances; Forbes, James
**Source(s)** *Their Own Desire* (novel) Fuller, Sarita

**Cast** Shearer, Norma; Bennett, Belle; Stone, Lewis; Montgomery, Robert

**Song(s)** Blue Is the Night (C/L: Fisher, Fred); Boy Friend Blues (C: Ward, Edward; L: Montgomery, Reggie)

### 6119 ✦ THERE'S A GIRL IN MY HEART
Allied Artists, 1950

**Composer(s)** Bilder, Robert
**Lyricist(s)** Bilder, Robert

**Producer(s)** Dreifuss, Arthur
**Director(s)** Dreifuss, Arthur
**Screenwriter(s)** Hoerl, Arthur; Hasty, John Eugene

**Cast** Bowman, Lee; Knox, Elyse; Adrian, Iris; Jean, Gloria; Ryan, Peggy; mcDonald, Ray; Chaney, Lon; Donath, Ludwig; Marston, Joel; Ryan, Irene

**Song(s)** There's a Girl in My Heart (C: Bilder, Robert; L: Dreifuss, Arthur); The Roller Skating Song; Be Careful of the Tidal Wave; We Are the Main Attraction; Any Old Street

**Notes** No cue sheet available. There are also vocals of "Daisy Bell" by Harry Dacre and "After the Ball" by Charles K. Harris.

### 6120 ✦ THERE'S MAGIC IN MUSIC
Paramount, 1941

**Composer(s)** Ronell, Ann
**Lyricist(s)** Ronell, Ann

**Producer(s)** Stone, Andrew L.
**Director(s)** Stone, Andrew L.
**Screenwriter(s)** Jackson, Frederick

**Cast** Jones, Allan; Foster, Susanna; Lindsay, Margaret; Overman, Lynne

**Song(s)** Fireflies on Parade; The Mountain Song (Concerto in A Minor) (C: Grieg, Edvard); There's Magic in Music [1]; Interlochen Here We Come (National Emblem March) [1] (C: Bagley, E.E.); Stars and Stripes [1] (C: Sousa, John Philip); Toodles Imitation (C: Boutelje, Phil; L: Loesser, Frank); Twilight, Twilight (Elegy) [1] (C: Massenet, Jules); Let's Go Out in the Open Air [1]; The Music Master [1]; There's Jam on the Moon [1]; Beautiful Night (Barcarolle from Tales of Hoffman) [1] (C: Offenbach, Jacques); Awake and Sing [1]; The Lullaby of Love [1]; Evening Bells (Kamenoi-Ostrow) [1] (C: Rubenstein, Anton); Sunshine Bugle Call [1]; Bright Indian Pine (Sakuntala Overture) [1] (C: Unknown); Drifting Moonlight [1]; My Own America [1] (C: Young, Victor); On Wings of Song [1] (C: Mendelssohn, Felix; L: Loesser, Frank); Opera Wrangle (Trio from FAUST) - (Toreador Song from CARMEN) (C: Gounod; Bizet; L: Lester, Edwin); You Tell Her I Stutter Introduction [1] (C/L: Loesser, Frank); To Hear Your Voice Again (Romance) (C: Rubenstein, Anton)

**Notes** Formerly titled INTERLOCHEN. The movie is also known as THE HARDBOILED CANARY. There are also renditions of Meyerbeer's "Shadow Song;" Johann Strauss' "Voices of Spring;" The traditional song "The Animal Fair;" John Philip Sousa's "Stars and Stripes" (with Sousa's lyrics); the folk song "Jesse James;" Boisdeffre's "By the Brook;" Bizet's CARMEN excerpts and excerpts from Gounod's FAUST. Suzanne Foster was to imitate popular performers with their specialties. These were Allan Jones singing "Donkey Serenade;" Judy Garland singing "You Made Me Love You" including "Dear Mr. Gable" (this was recorded, though not used); Bonnie Baker singing "Oh Johnnie;" Joan Davis performing "You-u-u-u-u Tell Her Because I-I-I-I-I Stutter;" and "Falling in Love Again" by Marlene Dietrich. Only "Falling in Love Again," "Oh Johnny" and "Jesse James" are used. [1] Not used.

## 6121 ✦ THERE'S NO BUSINESS LIKE SHOW BUSINESS
### Twentieth Century–Fox, 1954

**Composer(s)** Berlin, Irving
**Lyricist(s)** Berlin, Irving
**Choreographer(s)** Alton, Robert

**Producer(s)** Siegel, Sol C.
**Director(s)** Lang, Walter
**Screenwriter(s)** Ephron, Phoebe; Ephron, Henry

**Cast** Merman, Ethel; O'Connor, Donald; Monroe, Marilyn; Dailey, Dan; Ray, Johnnie; Gaynor, Mitzi; Eastham, Richard; O'Brian, Hugh; McHugh, Frank; Williams, Rhys; Patrick, Lee; Miller, Eve

**Song(s)** A Sailor's Not a Sailor ('Til a Sailor's Been Tattooed); A Man Chases a Girl [1]; If You Believe; But I Ain't Got a Man [2]; I Can Make You Laugh [2]

**Notes** There are also vocals of the following Berlin songs: "There's No Business Like Show Business" (from ANNIE GET YOUR GUN); "Remember" (also in ALEXANDER'S RAGTIME BAND); "When the Midnight Choo Choo Leaves for Alabam'" (also in ALEXANDER'S RAGTIME BAND and EASTER PARADE); "Play a Simple Melody;" "A Pretty Girl Is Like a Melody" (also in BLUE SKIES and ALEXANDER'S RAGTIME BAND); "You'd Be Surprised" (also in BLUE SKIES); "Let's Have Another Cup of Coffee;" "Alexander's Ragtime Band" (also in ALEXANDER'S RAGTIME BAND); "After You Get What You Want, You Don't Want It;" "Marie;" "Lazy" and "Heat Wave" (From stage musical AS THOUSANDS CHEER. Also in films BLUE SKIES and ALEXANDER'S RAGTIME BAND). Dolores Gray sang Marilyn Monroe's songs on the soundtrack album because of record company contractual problems. [1] Considered for WHITE CHRISTMAS but not used. This song was written in 1948. [2] Deleted before release.

## 6122 ✦ THERE'S ONE BORN EVERY MINUTE
### Universal, 1942

**Musical Score** Skinner, Frank

**Producer(s)** Goldsmith, Ken
**Director(s)** Young, Harold
**Screenwriter(s)** Hunt, Robert B.; Weisberg, Brenda
**Source(s)** "Man or Mouse?" (story) Hunt, Robert B.

**Cast** Herbert, Hugh; Moran, Peggy; Brown, Tom; Kibbee, Guy; Kennedy, Edgar; Doucet, Catherine; Jordan, Scott; Switzer, Carl "Alfalfa"

**Song(s)** Twine for Mayor (C: Berens, Norman; L: Brooks, Jack)

## 6123 ✦ THERE WAS A CROOKED MAN
### Warner Brothers, 1970

**Musical Score** Strouse, Charles

**Producer(s)** Mankiewicz, Joseph L.
**Director(s)** Mankiewicz, Joseph L.
**Screenwriter(s)** Newman, David; Benton, Robert
**Source(s)** "Prison Story" (story) Newman, David; Benton, Robert

**Cast** Douglas, Kirk; Fonda, Henry; Cronyn, Hume; Oates, Warren; Meredith, Burgess; Grant, Lee; O'Connell, Arthur; Gabel, Martin; Randolph, John; Blodgett, Michael; McNeil, Claudia; Hale, Alan; French, Victor

**Song(s)** There Was A Crooked Man (C: Strouse, Charles; L: Adams, Lee)

### 6124 ✦ THESE GLAMOUR GIRLS
Metro–Goldwyn–Mayer, 1939

**Musical Score**   Ward, Edward; Snell, Dave

**Producer(s)**   Zimbalist, Sam
**Director(s)**   Simon, S. Sylvan
**Screenwriter(s)**   Hall, Jane; Parsonnet, Marion
**Source(s)**   (story) Hall, Jane

**Cast**   Ayres, Lew; Turner, Lana; Brown, Tom; Carlson, Richard; Bryan, Jane; Louise, Anita; Hunt, Marsha; Rutherford, Ann; Hughes, Mary Beth; Davis Jr., Owen; Truex, Ernest

**Song(s)**   Loveliness (C: Ward, Edward; L: Wright, Bob; Forrest, Chet)

### 6125 ✦ THESE THOUSAND HILLS
Twentieth Century–Fox, 1959

**Musical Score**   Harline, Leigh

**Producer(s)**   Weisbart, David
**Director(s)**   Fleischer, Richard
**Screenwriter(s)**   Hayes, Alfred
**Source(s)**   *These Thousand Hills* (novel) Guthrie Jr., A.B.

**Cast**   Murray, Don; Egan, Richard; Remick, Lee; Owens, Patricia; Whitman, Stuart; Dekker, Albert; Stone, Harold J.; Dano, Royal; Knight, Fuzzy; Morrison, Barbara

**Song(s)**   These Thousand Hills (C: Warren, Harry; L: Washington, Ned)

### 6126 ✦ THEY ALL LAUGHED
PSO/Moon, 1981

**Musical Score**   Ball, Earl Poole

**Producer(s)**   Morfogen, George; Novak, Blaine
**Director(s)**   Bogdanovich, Peter
**Screenwriter(s)**   Bogdanovich, Peter

**Cast**   Hepburn, Audrey; Gazzara, Ben; Ritter, John; Camp, Colleen; Stratten, Dorothy; Hansen, Patti

**Song(s)**   One Day Since Yesterday (C: Ball, Earl Poole; L: Bogdanovich, Peter); Kentucky Nights (C/L: Kaz, Eric)

**Notes**   No cue sheet available.

### 6127 ✦ THEY CALL IT SIN
Warner Brothers–First National, 1932

**Producer(s)**   Wallis, Hal B.
**Director(s)**   Freeland, Thornton
**Screenwriter(s)**   Hayward, Lillie; Green, Howard J.
**Source(s)**   (novel) Eagan, Alberta Stedman

**Cast**   Young, Loretta; Brent, George; Merkel, Una; Manners, David; Vinson, Helen; Calhern, Louis; Walker, Nella

**Song(s)**   Where Are You (C: Gorney, Jay; L: Harburg, E.Y.)

**Notes**   Released in Great Britain as THE WAY OF LIFE.

### 6128 ✦ THEY CALL ME BRUCE
Film Ventures, 1982

**Musical Score**   Vig, Tommy

**Producer(s)**   Hong, Elliott
**Director(s)**   Hong, Elliott
**Screenwriter(s)**   Randolph, David; Yune, Johnny; Hong, Elliott; Clawson, Tim

**Cast**   Yune, Johnny; Hemingway, Margaux; Huntington, Pam; Mauro, Ralph

**Song(s)**   Oriental Boy (C/L: Vig, Tommy)

**Notes**   No cue sheet available.

### 6129 ✦ THEY GAVE HIM A GUN
Metro–Goldwyn–Mayer, 1937

**Musical Score**   Romberg, Sigmund

**Director(s)**   Van Dyke II, W.S.
**Screenwriter(s)**   Hume, Cyril; Maibaum, Richard; Rapf, Maurice
**Source(s)**   *They Gave Him a Gun* (novel) Cowen, William Joyce

**Cast**   Tracy, Spencer; George, Gladys; Tone, Franchot; Edwards, Cliff; Treen, Mary

**Song(s)**   A Love Song of Long Ago (C: Romberg, Sigmund; L: Kahn, Gus)

### 6130 ✦ THEY GOT ME COVERED
Goldwyn, 1942

**Musical Score**   Harline, Leigh

**Producer(s)**   Goldwyn, Samuel
**Director(s)**   Butler, David
**Screenwriter(s)**   Kurnitz, Harry; Fenton, Frank; Root, Lynn

**Cast**   Hope, Bob; MacBride, Donald; Lamour, Dorothy; Preminger, Otto; Ciannelli, Eduardo; Martin, Marion; Meek, Donald; Aubert, Lenore; Ruth, Phyllis; Ahn, Philip; Treen, Mary; Catlett, Walter

**Song(s)**   Palsy Walsy (C: Arlen, Harold; L: Mercer, Johnny)

### 6131 ✦ THEY HAD TO SEE PARIS
Fox, 1929

**Director(s)**   Borzage, Frank; Steele, Bernard
**Screenwriter(s)**   Davis, Owen
**Source(s)**   *They Had to See Paris* (novel) Croy, Homer

**Cast** Rogers, Will; Rich, Irene; Davis Jr., Owen; Churchill, Marguerite; D'Orsay, Fifi; Bell, Rex; Lebedeff, Ivan; Kennedy, Edgar

**Song(s)** I Could Do It For You (C/L: Conrad, Con; Gottler, Archie; Mitchell, Sidney D.)

**Notes** "Madelon" by Camille Robert and Louis Bousquet is also used.

## 6132 ✦ THEY LEARNED ABOUT WOMEN
### Metro–Goldwyn–Mayer, 1930

**Composer(s)** Ager, Milton
**Lyricist(s)** Yellen, Jack

**Director(s)** Conway, Jack; Wood, Sam
**Screenwriter(s)** Baer, Arthur "Bugs"

**Cast** Van, Gus; Schenck, Joseph T.; Love, Bessie; Rubin, Benny; Nugent, J.C.; Doran, Mary; Bushman Jr., Francis X.

**Song(s)** Harlem Madness; He's That Kind of Pal; Ain't You Baby [1]; A Man of My Own; Does My Baby Love (Nobody but Me); There'll Never Be Another Mary; Ten Sweet Mamas; Daugherty Is My Name [2]; I'm an Old Fashioned Guy [2]; I've Got to See My Partner [2] [3]

**Notes** [1] Used instrumentally only. [2] Gus Van and Joe Schenck also credited by ASCAP. They probably contributed additional lyrics. [3] Not used.

## 6133 ✦ THEY LIVE BY NIGHT
### RKO, 1949

**Musical Score** Harline, Leigh

**Producer(s)** Houseman, John
**Director(s)** Ray, Nicholas
**Screenwriter(s)** Schnee, Charles
**Source(s)** *Thieves Like Us* (novel) Anderson, Edward

**Cast** Granger, Farley; O'Donnell, Cathy; Da Silva, Howard; Flippen, Jay C.; Craig, Helen; Wright, Will; Bryant, Marie; Wolfe, Ian

**Song(s)** Your Red Wagon (C: de Paul, Gene; L: Raye, Don)

**Notes** Remade in 1974 as THIEVES LIKE US.

## 6134 ✦ THEY MEET AGAIN
### RKO, 1941

**Musical Score** Bakaleinikoff, Constantin

**Producer(s)** Stephens, William
**Director(s)** Kenton, Erle C.
**Screenwriter(s)** Milne, Peter; Leo, Maurice

**Cast** Hersholt, Jean; Lovett, Dorothy; Eburne, Maude; Baldwin, Robert; Hamilton, Neil

**Song(s)** Rhythm Is Red & White & Blue (C: Moss, Al; L: Greggory, David); In the Make Believe Land of

Dreams (C/L: Owens, Jack); When Love Is New (C: Sweeton, Claude; L: Owens, Jack)

**Notes** Some sources also list the song "Get Alive" by Jack Owens.

## 6135 ✦ THEY MET IN ARGENTINA
### RKO, 1941

**Composer(s)** Rodgers, Richard
**Lyricist(s)** Hart, Lorenz
**Choreographer(s)** Veloz, Frank

**Producer(s)** Brock, Lou
**Director(s)** Hively, Jack; Goodwins, Leslie
**Screenwriter(s)** Cady, Jerry

**Cast** O'Hara, Maureen; Ellison, James; Vila, Alberto; Ebsen, Buddy; Barrat, Robert; Buloff, Joseph; Costello, Diosa; Cordova, Victoria; Moreno, Antonio; Middlemass, Robert; Bonanova, Fortunio; Alberni, Luis

**Song(s)** North America Meets South America; Contrapunto [3]; Amarillo; Carefree Carretero; You've Got the Best of Me; Lolita [5]; Cutting the Game; Never Go to Argentina; Simpatica [1]; I Congratulate You Mr. Cowboy [2]; We're on the Track [4]; Encanto [4]

**Notes** [1] Used instrumentally only in American prints. Used vocally in foreign prints. Other sources say it was in all prints but this isn't the case on the cue sheets or scripts I saw. [2] Not on cue sheet. It may be considered part of "North America Meets South America." [3] Kimble's Lorenz Hart book says it was dropped from the film but it appears in the cue sheet I saw. [4] Not used. [5] Also in SUNSET PASS.

## 6136 ✦ THEY'RE OFF

See STRAIGHT, PLACE AND SHOW.

## 6137 ✦ THEY SHALL HAVE FAITH
### Monogram, 1944

**Producer(s)** Bernerd, Jeffrey
**Director(s)** Nigh, William
**Screenwriter(s)** Nigh, William; Sayre, George W.

**Cast** Storm, Gale; Smith, Sir C. Aubrey; Brown, Johnny Mack; Nagel, Conrad; Boland, Mary; Craven, Frank; Downs, Johnny; Jackson, Selmer

**Song(s)** Close Your Eyes and Just Pretend (C/L: Jaxton, Al; Rau, Neil); You're the Answer (C/L: Watson, Robert)

**Notes** No cue sheet available.

## 6138 ✦ THEY SHALL HAVE MUSIC
### United Artists, 1939

**Producer(s)** Goldwyn, Samuel
**Director(s)** Mayo, Archie
**Screenwriter(s)** Lawson, John Howard

**Cast** Heifitz, Jascha; Reynolds, Gene; Brennan, Walter; Leeds, Andrea; McCrea, Joel; Hall, Porter; Kilburn, Terry; Peter Meremblum California Junior Symphony; Loehr, Dolly [1]

**Notes** No cue sheet available. Titled MELODY OF YOUTH overseas. There are no vocals in this film. Instrumentals include "The Rondo Capriceioso" by Saint-Saens; "Souvenir d'un Lieu Cher" opus 42 by Tchaikovsky; "Hora Stacato" by Dinico and Heifitz; "Concerto in E Minor for Violin and Orchestra" (3rd Movement) by Mendelssohn; "Waltz in D Flat" Opus 64. No. 1 ("The Minute Waltz") by Chopin. [1] Diana Lynn.

## 6139 ◆ THEY WERE EXPENDABLE
### Metro–Goldwyn–Mayer, 1945

**Musical Score** Stothart, Herbert

**Director(s)** Ford, John
**Screenwriter(s)** Wead, Frank
**Source(s)** *They Were Expendable* (book) White, William L.

**Cast** Montgomery, Robert; Wayne, John; Reed, Donna; Holt, Jack; Bond, Ward; Pennick, Jack; Thompson, Marshall; Mitchell, Cameron; Heydt, Louis Jean; Ames, Leon; Barat, Robert

**Song(s)** To the End of the End of the World (C: Stothart, Herbert; L: Brent, Earl); Marcheta [1] (C/L: Schertzinger, Victor)

**Notes** When John Ford took ill Robert Montgomery directed some of the scenes. [1] Sheet music only.

## 6140 ◆ THIEF
### United Artists, 1981

**Musical Score** Radami, Robert

**Producer(s)** Bruckheimer, Jerry; Caan, Ronnie
**Director(s)** Mann, Michael
**Screenwriter(s)** Mann, Michael
**Source(s)** *The Home Invaders* (novel) Hohimer, Frank

**Cast** Caan, James; Weld, Tuesday; Nelson, Willie; Belushi, James; Prosky, Robert; Signorelli, Tom; Farina, Dennis

**Song(s)** Turning Point (C/L: Graham, Leo)

## 6141 ◆ THIEF OF BAGDAD
### Metro–Goldwyn–Mayer, 1961

**Musical Score** Luttazzi, Lelio

**Producer(s)** Vailati, Bruno
**Director(s)** Lubin, Arthur
**Screenwriter(s)** Frassinetti, Augusto; Sanjust, Filippo; Vailati, Bruno

**Cast** Reeves, Steve; Moll, Georgia; Vessel, Edy; Dominici, Arturo; Vargas, Daniele

**Song(s)** Zebra a "Pois" (C/L: Ciorciolini-Verde; Luttazzi, Lelio)

## 6142 ◆ THIEF OF HEARTS
### Paramount, 1984

**Musical Score** Faltermeyer, Harold
**Composer(s)** Faltermeyer, Harold

**Producer(s)** Simpson, Don; Bruckheimer, Jerry
**Director(s)** Stewart, Douglas Day
**Screenwriter(s)** Stewart, Douglas Day

**Cast** Bauer, Steven; Williams, Barbara; Getz, John; Wendt, George; Caruso, David; Ebersole, Christine

**Song(s)** Just Imagine (Way Beyond Fear) [1] (L: Forsey, Keith); Love in the Shadows [1] (L: Daily, Elizabeth); Passion Play [1] (L: Lewin, Annabella); Thief of Hearts [1] (L: Manchester, Melissa; Forsey, Keith)

**Notes** [1] Background vocal use only.

## 6143 ◆ THIEVES
### Paramount, 1977

**Producer(s)** Barrie, George
**Director(s)** Berry, John
**Screenwriter(s)** Gardner, Herb
**Source(s)** *Thieves* (play) Gardner, Herb

**Cast** Thomas, Marlo [2]; Grodin, Charles [3]; Corey, Irwin [2]; Elizondo, Hector; McCambridge, Mercedes; McMartin, John; Merrill, Gary; Wedgeworth, Ann [2]; Fosse, Bob; Matlock, Norman; Dixon, MacIntyre; Scooler, Zvee; Wallace, Lee

**Song(s)** The Kaminsky Rag [1] (Inst) (C: Styne, Jule); Thieves [4] (C: Barrie, George; L: Cahn, Sammy)

**Notes** [1] Played by Styne on soundtrack. [2] Repeating Broadway role. [3] Director of stage version. [4] Sheet music only.

## 6144 ◆ THINGS ARE TOUGH ALL OVER
### Columbia, 1982

**Musical Score** Delorme, Gaye

**Producer(s)** Brown, Howard
**Director(s)** Avildsen, Thomas K.
**Screenwriter(s)** Marin, Richard "Cheech"; Chong, Thomas

**Cast** Chong, Thomas; Marin, Richard "Cheech"; Rayford III, Ernest; Taylor, Rip; Wallace, George

**Song(s)** Chilly Winds of Chicago (C: Marin, Richard "Cheech"; Chong, Thomas; L: Delorme, Gaye); Me and My Old Lady (C/L: Marin, Richard "Cheech"; Chong, Shelby; L: Delorme, Gaye)

**Notes** No cue sheet available.

## 6145 ✦ THIN ICE
### Twentieth Century–Fox, 1937

**Composer(s)** Pollack, Lew
**Lyricist(s)** Mitchell, Sidney D.
**Choreographer(s)** Losee, Harry

**Producer(s)** Zanuck, Darryl F.
**Director(s)** Lanfield, Sidney
**Screenwriter(s)** Ingster, Boris; Sperling, Milton
**Source(s)** *Der Komet* (play) Obok, Attila

**Cast** Henie, Sonja; Power, Tyrone; Treacher, Arthur; Walburn, Raymond; Davis, Joan; Rumann, Sig; Hale, Alan; Ray, Leah; Cooper, Melville; Givot, George; Chaney Jr., Lon; Brecher, Egon

**Song(s)** Over Night; My Secret Love Affair; My Swiss Hill Billy; I'm Olga from the Volga (C: Revel, Harry; L: Gordon, Mack)

## 6146 ✦ THINK DIRTY
### Quartet, 1982

**Musical Score** Cameron, John

**Producer(s)** Sherrin, Ned
**Director(s)** Clark, Jim
**Screenwriter(s)** Feldman, Marty; Took, Barry; Norden, Denis

**Cast** Feldman, Marty; Cornwall, Judy; Berman, Shelley; Hazell, Hy; Ege, Julie; Keith, Penelope; Elwes, Mark; Landen, Dinsdale; De La Tour, Francis; Cargill, Patrick

**Song(s)** Think Dirty (C/L: Brahms, Caryl; Sherrin, Ned)

**Notes** No cue sheet available.

## 6147 ✦ THINK FAST, MR. MOTO
### Twentieth Century–Fox, 1937

**Composer(s)** Akst, Harry

**Producer(s)** Wurtzel, Sol M.
**Director(s)** Foster, Norman
**Screenwriter(s)** Smith, Howard Ellis; Foster, Norman
**Source(s)** *That Girl and Mr. Moto* (novel) Marquand, J.P.

**Cast** Lorre, Peter; Field, Virginia; Beck, Thomas; Rumann, Sig; Kinnell, Murray; Rogers, John; Naish, J. Carrol

**Song(s)** Improvisation (C: Akst, Harry; Clare, Sidney; L: Foster, Norman); Shy Violet (L: Clare, Sidney)

## 6148 ✦ THE THIRD DAY
### Warner Brothers, 1965

**Musical Score** Faith, Percy

**Producer(s)** Smight, Jack
**Director(s)** Smight, Jack

**Screenwriter(s)** Wohl, Burton; Presnell Jr., Robert
**Source(s)** *The Third Day* (novel) Hayes, Joseph

**Cast** Peppard, George; Ashley, Elizabeth; McDowall, Roddy; O'Connell, Arthur; Washbourne, Mona; Marshall, Herbert; Webber, Robert; Drake, Charles; Johnson, Arte; Walker, Bill; Gardenia, Vincent; Gray, Janine

**Song(s)** Love Me Now (C: Faith, Percy; L: Livingston, Jay; Evans, Ray)

## 6149 ✦ THIRD FINGER LEFT HAND
### Metro–Goldwyn–Mayer, 1940

**Musical Score** Snell, Dave

**Producer(s)** Considine Jr., John W.
**Director(s)** Leonard, Robert Z.
**Screenwriter(s)** Houser, Lionel

**Cast** Loy, Myrna; Douglas, Melvyn; Walburn, Raymond; Bowman, Lee; Granville, Bonita; Bressart, Felix

**Song(s)** The Riddle (C: Snell, Dave; L: Brent, Earl)

## 6150 ✦ THIRD MAN ON THE MOUNTAIN
### Disney, 1959

**Musical Score** Alwyn, William
**Composer(s)** Stark, Frederick
**Lyricist(s)** Adair, Tom

**Producer(s)** Anderson, William H.
**Director(s)** Annakin, Ken
**Screenwriter(s)** Griffin, Eleanore
**Source(s)** *Banner in the Sky* (book) Ullman, James Ramsey

**Cast** Rennie, Michael; MacArthur, James; Munro, Janet; Donald, James; Lom, Herbert; Naismith, Laurence

**Song(s)** Climb the Mountain [2] (C: Marks, Franklyn; L: Dunham, "By"); Sentiers Valaisans (Goodnight Valais) (C: Haenni, Georges); Banner in the Sky Polka [1]; The Mountains Are My Happy Home [1]; Oom-Pah-Pah [1] (L: George, Gil; Sykes, Sam); Two Hearts A Singing [1] (L: Marks, Franklyn); Up in the Mountain [1] (L: George, Gil; Sykes, Sam); What a Happy Day [1] (C: Marks, Franklyn); Where Dreamers Go [1] (C: Orlenica, Steve; L: Jackman, Bob)

**Notes** There are also two Swiss songs used vocally. [1] Not used. [2] Also in GALA DAY AT DISNEYLAND.

## 6151 ✦ -30-
### Warner Brothers, 1959

**Musical Score** Heindorf, Ray

**Producer(s)** Webb, Jack
**Director(s)** Webb, Jack
**Screenwriter(s)** Bowers, William

**Cast** Webb, Jack; Conrad, William; Nelson, David; Blake, Whitney; Lorimer, Louise; Bell, James; Valentine, Nancy; Flynn, Joe

**Song(s)** Boy [1] (C: Ralke, Don; L: Bowers, William)

**Notes** Released in Great Britain as DEADLINE MIDNIGHT. [1] Sheet music also credits N. Beckman and B. Rosen.

## 6152 ✦ THIRTY SECONDS OVER TOKYO
Metro–Goldwyn–Mayer, 1944

**Musical Score** Stothart, Herbert

**Producer(s)** Zimbalist, Sam
**Director(s)** LeRoy, Mervyn
**Screenwriter(s)** Trumbo, Dalton
**Source(s)** *Thirty Seconds Over Tokyo* (book) Lawson, Ted W.; Considine, Robert

**Cast** Johnson, Van; Walker, Robert; Thaxter, Phyllis; Murdock, Tim; McKay, Scott; McDonald, Gordon; DeFore, Don; Mitchum, Robert; Reilly, John R.; McNally, Horace; Tracy, Spencer

**Song(s)** I Love You, I Love You, I Love You Sweetheart of All My Dreams (C/L: Fitch, Kay; Fitch, Art; Lowe, Bert)

**Notes** There are other brief vocals of popular tunes.

## 6153 ✦ THIS COULD BE THE NIGHT
Metro–Goldwyn–Mayer, 1957

**Composer(s)** Brodszky, Nicholas
**Lyricist(s)** Cahn, Sammy
**Choreographer(s)** Baker, Jack

**Producer(s)** Pasternak, Joe
**Director(s)** Wise, Robert
**Screenwriter(s)** Lennart, Isobel
**Source(s)** stories by Gross, Cordilia Baird

**Cast** Simmons, Jean; Douglas, Paul; Franciosa, Anthony; Wilson, Julie; Adams, Neile; Blondell, Joan; Naish, J. Carrol; Campos, Rafael; Pitts, ZaSu; Helmore, Tom; Vye, Murvyn; Ray Anthony and His Orchestra

**Song(s)** This Could Be the Night; I'm Gonna Live 'Till I Die [1] (C: Kent, Walter; L: Hoffman, Al; Curtis, Mann); Club Tonic Blues (C/L: Wright, Marvin; Baker, Jack; Mills, Jack); Hustlin' Newsgal (C/L: Stoll, George); Sadie Green, the Vamp of New Orleans [2] (C: Wells, Gilbert; Dunn, Johnny; Martin, Lloyd "Skip")

**Notes** There is also a vocal of "Taking a Chance on Love" by Vernon Duke, John Latouche and Ted Fetter and one of "I Got It Bad and That Ain't Good" by Duke Ellington and Paul Francis Webster. [1] Also in OCEAN'S ELEVEN (Warner). Sometimes referred to as "I'm Gonna Live, Live, Live Until I Die." The song was written in 1950. [2] Martin is not listed on soundtrack LP.

## 6154 ✦ THIS EARTH IS MINE
Universal, 1959

**Musical Score** Friedhofer, Hugo

**Producer(s)** Robinson, Casey; Heilman, Claude
**Director(s)** King, Henry
**Screenwriter(s)** Robinson, Casey
**Source(s)** *The Cup and the Sword* (novel) Hobart, Alice Tisdale

**Cast** Hudson, Rock; Simmons, Jean; McGuire, Dorothy; Smith, Kent; Rains, Claude

**Song(s)** This Earth Is Mine (C: Van Heusen, Jimmy; L: Cahn, Sammy); Amor (C/L: Mendez, Richard Lopez; Ruiz, Gabriel); Brindisi (C: Friedhofer, Hugo; L: Perry, Alfred)

## 6155 ✦ THIS GUN FOR HIRE
Paramount, 1942

**Musical Score** Buttolph, David
**Composer(s)** Press, Jacques
**Lyricist(s)** Loesser, Frank

**Producer(s)** Blumenthal, Richard
**Director(s)** Tuttle, Frank
**Screenwriter(s)** Maltz, Albert; Burnett, W.R.
**Source(s)** *A Gun for Sale* (novel) Greene, Graham

**Cast** Lake, Veronica [2]; Ladd, Alan; Preston, Robert; Cregar, Laird; Marshall, Tully; Lawrence, Marc

**Song(s)** Now You See It, Now You Don't; I've Got You; I'm Amazed at You [1] (C: Spina, Harold)

**Notes** [1] Not used. [2] Dubbed by Martha Mears.

## 6156 ✦ THIS HAPPY FEELING
Universal, 1958

**Musical Score** Skinner, Frank

**Producer(s)** Hunter, Ross
**Director(s)** Edwards, Blake
**Screenwriter(s)** Edwards, Blake
**Source(s)** *For Love of Money* (play) Herbert, F. Hugh

**Cast** Reynolds, Debbie; Jurgens, Curt; Saxon, John; Smith, Alexis; Winwood, Estelle; Astor, Mary; Donahue, Troy; Rorke, Hayden

**Song(s)** This Happy Feeling (C/L: Livingston, Jay; Evans, Ray)

## 6157 ✦ THIS IS HEAVEN
United Artists, 1929

**Musical Score** Riesenfeld, Dr. Hugo

**Producer(s)** Goldwyn, Samuel
**Director(s)** Santell, Alfred
**Screenwriter(s)** Loring, Hope; Marion Jr., George

**Cast** Banky, Vilma; Hall, James; Ridgeway, Fritzi; Littlefield, Lucien; Tucker, Richard

**Song(s)** This Is Heaven (C: Akst, Harry; L: Yellen, Jack); Tell Me Daisy (C: Reisenfeld, Hugo; L: Smith, Harry B.)

**Notes** No cue sheet available.

## 6158 ✦ THIS IS MY AFFAIR
Twentieth Century–Fox, 1937

**Composer(s)** Revel, Harry
**Lyricist(s)** Gordon, Mack

**Producer(s)** Macgowan, Kenneth
**Director(s)** Seiter, William A.
**Screenwriter(s)** Trotti, Lamar; Rivkin, Allen

**Cast** Taylor, Robert; Stanwyck, Barbara; McLaglen, Victor; Donlevy, Brian; Blackmer, Sidney; Carradine, John; Dinehart, Alan; Fowley, Douglas; Rumann, Sig; Weaver, Marjorie; Nugent, J.C.

**Song(s)** Put Down Your Glass (Pick Up Your Girl and Dance); I Hum a Waltz; Fill It Up

**Notes** There are also vocals of "While Strolling Through the Park One Day" and "Just Because She Made Those Goo Goo Eyes" by Hughie Cannon and John Queen and "Strike Up the Band—Here Comes a Sailor" by Charles B. Ward and Andrew B. Sterling.

## 6159 ✦ THIS IS MY LOVE
RKO, 1954

**Musical Score** Waxman, Franz

**Producer(s)** Brooke, Hugh
**Director(s)** Heisler, Stuart
**Screenwriter(s)** Wilde, Hagar; Brooke, Hugh
**Source(s)** "Fear Has Black Wings" (story) Brooke, Hugh

**Cast** Darnell, Linda; Jason, Rick; Duryea, Dan; Domergue, Faith; Russell, Connie; Mathers, Jerry; Hopper, William; Switzer, Carl "Alfalfa"

**Song(s)** This Is My Love (C: Waxman, Franz; L: Brooke, Hugh)

## 6160 ✦ THIS IS SPINAL TAP
Embassy, 1984

**Producer(s)** Murphy, Karen
**Director(s)** Reiner, Rob
**Screenwriter(s)** Guest, Christopher; McKean, Michael; Shearer, Harry; Reiner, Rob

**Cast** Reiner, Rob; McKean, Michael; Guest, Christopher; Shearer, Harry; Parnell, R.J.; Kaff, David; Hendra, Tony; Kirby, Bruno; Begley Jr., Ed; MacNee, Patrick; Carvey, Dana; Crystal, Billy; Hesseman, Howard; Shaffer, Paul; Huston, Anjelica

**Song(s)** Hell Hole (C/L: Guest, Christopher; McKean, Michael; Shearer, Harry; Reiner, Rob); Tonight I'm Going to Rock You Tonight (C/L: Guest, Christopher; McKean, Michael; Shearer, Harry; Reiner, Rob)

**Notes** No cue sheet available.

## 6161 ✦ THIS IS THE ARMY
Warner Brothers, 1943

**Composer(s)** Berlin, Irving
**Lyricist(s)** Berlin, Irving
**Choreographer(s)** Prinz, LeRoy; Sidney, Robert

**Producer(s)** Wallis, Hal B.
**Director(s)** Curtiz, Michael
**Screenwriter(s)** Robinson, Casey; Binyon, Claude
**Source(s)** *This Is the Army* (musical) Berlin, Irving

**Cast** Berlin, Irving; Murphy, George; Leslie, Joan; Tobias, George; Hale, Alan; Butterworth, Charles; Costello, Dolores; Merkel, Una; Ridges, Stanley; De Camp, Rosemary; Donnelly, Ruth; Peterson, Dorothy; Langford, Frances; Niesen, Gertrude; Smith, Kate; Gurning, Ilka; Reagan, Ronald; Louis, Joe; D'Andrea, Tom; Oshins, Julie; Shanley, Robert; Stone, Ezra; Truex, Philip; Cook Jr., Joe; Weeks, Larry

**Song(s)** For Your Country and My Country [1] [4]; My Sweetie [1]; Poor Little Me I'm on K.P.; Oh How I Hate to Get Up in the Morning; God Bless America [2]; We're on Our Way to France [1] [4]; Good-bye France [1]; In the YMCA [1]; What Does He Look Like That Boy of Mine; This Is the Army, Mr. Jones; I'm Getting Tired So I Can Sleep; Mandy [3]; Ladies of the Chorus; That's What the Well-Dressed Man in Harlem Will Wear [5]; How About a Cheer for the Navy; Canteen Number [1]; I Left My Heart at the Stagedoor Canteen; With My Head in the Clouds; American Eagles; This Time (Is the Last Time); Dressed Up to Win [1]

**Notes** [1] Written for film version. [2] Not in original version. [3] Originally in YIP YIP YAPHANK and ZIEGFELD FOLLIES OF 1919. Also in stage version of THIS IS THE ARMY and in film KID MILLIONS. [4] Also in ALEXANDER'S RAGTIME BAND. [5] Also in BANDS ACROSS THE SEA.

## 6162 ✦ THIS IS THE LIFE (1935)
Twentieth Century–Fox, 1935

**Composer(s)** Stept, Sam H.
**Lyricist(s)** Clare, Sidney

**Producer(s)** Engel, Joseph
**Director(s)** Neilan, Marshall
**Screenwriter(s)** Trotti, Lamar; Horman, Arthur T.

**Cast** Withers, Jane; McGuire, John; Blane, Sally; Toler, Sidney; Roy, Gloria; Westcott, Gordon; Ford, Francis; Lucas, Nick; Hovig, Jayne

**Song(s)** Sandy and Me; Got a New Kind-a Rhythm; Fresh from the Country

## 6163 ✦ THIS IS THE LIFE (1943)
### Universal, 1943

**Composer(s)** Pepper, Buddy; James, Inez
**Lyricist(s)** Pepper, Buddy; James, Inez
**Choreographer(s)** Da Pron, Louis

**Producer(s)** Burton, Bernard W.
**Director(s)** Feist, Felix E.
**Screenwriter(s)** Tuchock, Wanda
**Source(s)** *Angela at 22* (play) Lewis, Sinclair; Wray, Fay

**Cast** O'Connor, Donald; Foster, Susanna; Knowles, Patric; Ray Eberle and His Orchestra; The Bobby Brooks Quartet; Allbritton, Louise; Peterson, Dorothy; Ryan, Peggy; Hale, Jonathan; Quillan, Eddie; Brissac, Virginia; Nichols, Richard; Jenks, Frank

**Song(s)** You're a La La Palooza (C: Shannon, Grace; L: Crago, Bill); Now That You've Gone; All or Nothing At All (C/L: Lawrence, Jack; Altman, Arthur); Yippi-I-Voot (C/L: Pepper, Buddy; James, Inez; Miller, Sidney); The Gremlin Walk; Girl of a Soldier's Heart

**Notes** There are also vocals of "L'Amour, Toujours L'Amour" by Catherine C. Cushing and Rudolf Friml; "At Sundown" by Walter Donaldson; "Ouvre Ton Coeur" by Georges Bizet and "With a Song in My Heart" by Richard Rodgers and Lorenz Hart.

## 6164 ✦ THIS IS THE NIGHT
### Paramount, 1932

**Composer(s)** Rainger, Ralph
**Lyricist(s)** Marion Jr., George

**Director(s)** Tuttle, Frank
**Screenwriter(s)** Marion Jr., George
**Source(s)** *Naughty Cinderella* (musical) Hopwood, Avery

**Cast** Grant, Cary; Damita, Lily; Ruggles, Charles; Young, Roland; Todd, Thelma

**Song(s)** Madame Has Lost Her Dress; My Girl Is Named Yvonne; This Is the Night [1] (L: Coslow, Sam); Tonight Is All a Dream (L: Coslow, Sam); Boswell Weeps [2] (L: Robin, Leo); Dream of All My Dreams [2]

**Notes** Formerly named HE MET A FRENCH GIRL. [1] Also in INTERNATIONAL HOUSE and HOT SATURDAY. [2] Not used.

## 6165 ✦ THIS LAND IS MINE
### RKO, 1943

**Musical Score** Perl, Lothar

**Producer(s)** Renoir, Jean; Nichols, Dudley
**Director(s)** Renoir, Jean
**Screenwriter(s)** Nichols, Dudley

**Cast** Laughton, Charles; O'Hara, Maureen; Sanders, George; Slezak, Walter; Smith, Kent; O'Connor, Una; Merivale, Philip; Hall, Thurston; Coulouris, George; Gates, Nancy

**Song(s)** School Song (C/L: Perl, Lothar)

## 6166 ✦ THIS'LL MAKE YOU WHISTLE
### Republic, 1936

**Composer(s)** Goodhart, Al; Hoffman, Al
**Lyricist(s)** Sigler, Maurice

**Producer(s)** Wilcox, Herbert
**Director(s)** Wilcox, Herbert
**Screenwriter(s)** Bolton, Guy; Thompson, Paul
**Source(s)** (play) Bolton, Guy; Thompson, Paul

**Cast** Buchanan, Jack; Randolph, Elsie; Gillie, Jean; Kendall, William

**Song(s)** There Isn't Any Limit to My Love; Black Baby Sequence (C/L: Windeatt, G.); Dancing Mood; This'll Make You Whistle; Keep Your Eye on the Sky [1]; Without Rhythm [1]; Crazy with Love [1]; I'm Never Too Busy for You [1]; You've Got the Wrong Rhumba [1]; Red Letter Day [1]

**Notes** A General Film Distributors (British) production. [1] I believe this is only used instrumentally.

## 6167 ✦ THIS LOVE OF OURS
### Universal, 1945

**Musical Score** Salter, Hans J.
**Lyricist(s)** Brooks, Jack

**Producer(s)** Benedict, Howard
**Director(s)** Dieterle, William
**Screenwriter(s)** Manning, Bruce; Klorer, John; Lee, Leonard
**Source(s)** *Come Prima Meglio de Prima* (play) Pirandello, Luigi

**Cast** England, Sue; Oberon, Merle; Rains, Claude; Korvin, Charles; Barker, Jess; Davenport, Harry; Morgan, Ralph

**Song(s)** They Went to Get Married [1] (C: Unknown); Dance with Me [2] (C: Traditional)

**Notes** A remake of AS YOU DESIRE ME (C1932). [1] Based on "Aupres de Ma Blonde." [2] Based on "Le Pont D'Avignon."

## 6168 ✦ THIS PROPERTY IS CONDEMNED
### Paramount, 1966

**Musical Score** Hopkins, Kenyon

**Producer(s)** Houseman, John
**Director(s)** Pollack, Sydney

**Screenwriter(s)** Coppola, Francis Ford; Coe, Fred; Sommer, Edith
**Source(s)** (play) Williams, Tennessee

**Cast** Wood, Natalie; Redford, Robert; Bronson, Charles; Reid, Kate; Coleman, Dabney; Blake, Robert; Provost, Jon

**Song(s)** Wish Me a Rainbow (C/L: Livingston, Jay; Evans, Ray)

## 6169 ✦ THIS RECKLESS AGE
### Paramount, 1932

**Director(s)** Tuttle, Frank
**Screenwriter(s)** Mankiewicz, Joseph L.

**Cast** Bennett, Richard; Starr, Frances; Rogers, Charles "Buddy"; Dee, Frances; Ruggles, Charles

**Song(s)** Just One More Chance [1] (C: Johnston, Arthur; L: Coslow, Sam)

**Notes** [1] Also in COUNTRY MUSIC HOLIDAY, LEMON DROP KID (1934) and THE MAGNIFICENT LIE.

## 6170 ✦ THIS TIME FOR KEEPS
### Metro–Goldwyn–Mayer, 1947

**Choreographer(s)** Donen, Stanley

**Producer(s)** Pasternak, Joe
**Director(s)** Thorpe, Richard
**Screenwriter(s)** Lehman, Gladys

**Cast** Williams, Esther; Durante, Jimmy; Melchior, Lauritz; Johnston, Johnnie; Xavier Cugat and His Orchestra; Whitty, Dame May; McManus, Sharon; Simmons, Dick; Stuart, Mary; Stossel, Ludwig; Porter, Dorothy; Wonder, Tommy

**Song(s)** A Little Bit This and A Little Bit That (C/L: Durante, Jimmy); I Love to Dance (C: Lane, Burton; L: Freed, Ralph); Why Don't They Let Me Sing a Love Song? (C: Akst, Harry; L: Davis, Benny); Martha (C: Flotow, Frederich; L: Donen, Stanley); Ten Percent Off (C: Fain, Sammy; L: Freed, Ralph); Inka Dinka Doo (C/L: Durante, Jimmy); S'No Wonder They Fell in Love (C: Fain, Sammy; L: Freed, Ralph); The Lost Chord (C/L: Brent, Earl; Durante, Jimmy); When It's Lilac Time on Mackinac Island (C/L: Kirk, Lesley); Un Poquito de Amor (C: Soler, Raoul; Cugat, Xavier; L: Freed, Ralph); Hokey Joe [1] (C: Swan, Don; L: Ricardo, Juan)

**Notes** There are also vocals of "Easy to Love" by Cole Porter; "Main Title Opera" based on music by Bizet; "I Det Fri" by Anderson; "M'Appari" by Flotow; "I'll Be with You in Apple Blossom Time" by Albert Von Tilzer and Neville Fleeson; "Ora e Per Sempre Addio" by Verdi; "Enlloro" by Obdulio Morales and Blanco; and "Chiquita Banana" by William Wirges, Garth Montgomery and Len McKenzie. [1] Sheet music only.

## 6171 ✦ THIS WAS PARIS
### Warner Brothers, 1942

**Musical Score** Beaver, Jack

**Director(s)** Harlow, John
**Screenwriter(s)** Williams, Brock; Dryhurst, Edward

**Cast** Dvorak, Ann; Lyon, Ben; Jones, Griffith; Maguire, Mary; Morley, Robert; Welchman, Harry; Miles, Bernard; Huth, Harold

**Song(s)** There's a Boy in Harlem [1] (C: Rodgers, Richard; L: Hart, Lorenz); What Goes Up Must Come Down (And Baby, You've Been Flyin' Too High) [2] (C: Bloom, Rube; L: Koehler, Ted)

**Notes** [1] Also in FOOLS FOR SCANDAL. [2] Originally in COTTON CLUB PARADE OF 1939 (show).

## 6172 ✦ THIS WAY PLEASE
### Paramount, 1937

**Lyricist(s)** Coslow, Sam

**Producer(s)** Shauer, Mel
**Director(s)** Florey, Robert
**Screenwriter(s)** Garrett, Grant; Owen, Seena; Green, Howard J.

**Cast** Rogers, Charles "Buddy"; Grable, Betty; Bowman, Lee; Sparks, Ned; Vernon, Wally; Livingstone, Mary

**Song(s)** This Way Please (C/L: Coslow, Sam; Siegel, Al); (Is It) Love or Infatuation [3] (C: Hollander, Frederick); Delighted to Meet You (C: Coslow, Sam); Voom Voom [2] (C: Coslow, Sam); I'm the Sound Effects Man [5] (C: "Jock" [4]; L: Gray, George); Speaking of Love [1] (C: Lane, Burton; L: Freed, Ralph); Play My Request [1] (C: Coslow, Sam)

**Notes** [1] Not used. [2] Based on an idea by Al Siegel. Written for THE BIG BROADCAST OF 1937 but not used. Also not used in DOUBLE OR NOTHING. [3] Written for THE NEW DIVORCE. [4] Pseudonym for Jack Rock. [5] Also in RADIO STARS ON PARADE (RKO).

## 6173 ✦ THIS WOMAN IS MINE
### Universal, 1941

**Musical Score** Hageman, Richard
**Composer(s)** Hageman, Richard
**Lyricist(s)** Grossman, Bernie

**Producer(s)** Lloyd, Frank
**Director(s)** Lloyd, Frank
**Screenwriter(s)** Miller, Seton I.
**Source(s)** *I, James Lewis* (novel) Gabriel, Gilbert Wolff

**Cast** Tone, Franchot; Rumann, Sig; Carroll, John; Bruce, Carol; Bruce, Nigel; Carroll, Leo G.; Brennan, Walter; Conroy, Frank; Hurst, Paul; Biberman, Abner

**Song(s)**   I Am Far Too Young to Marry; We'll Be Crossing the Bar in the Morning

## 6174 ✦ THOMAS CROWN AFFAIR
United Artists, 1968

**Musical Score**   Legrand, Michel

**Producer(s)**   Jewison, Norman
**Director(s)**   Jewison, Norman
**Screenwriter(s)**   Trustman, Alan R.

**Cast**   McQueen, Steve; Dunaway, Faye; Burke, Paul; Weston, Jack

**Song(s)**   The Windmills of Your Mind (C: Legrand, Michel; L: Bergman, Marilyn; Bergman, Alan); His Eyes Her Eyes [1] (C: Legrand, Michel; L: Bergman, Alan; Bergman, Marilyn)

## 6175 ✦ THOROUGHBREDS DON'T CRY
Metro–Goldwyn–Mayer, 1937

**Producer(s)**   Rapf, Harry
**Director(s)**   Green, Alfred E.
**Screenwriter(s)**   Hazard, Lawrence

**Cast**   Garland, Judy; Rooney, Mickey; Sinclair, Ronald; Smith, C. Aubrey; Tucker, Sophie; Harvey, Forrester

**Song(s)**   Got a Pair of New Shoes [1] (C: Brown, Nacio Herb; L: Freed, Arthur)

**Notes**   [1] Deleted from BROADWAY MELODY OF 1938 without Edens lyric.

## 6176 ✦ THOROUGHLY MODERN MILLIE
Universal, 1967

**Musical Score**   Bernstein, Elmer
**Composer(s)**   Van Heusen, James
**Lyricist(s)**   Cahn, Sammy
**Choreographer(s)**   Layton, Joe

**Producer(s)**   Hunter, Ross
**Director(s)**   Hill, George Roy
**Screenwriter(s)**   Morris, Richard

**Cast**   Moore, Mary Tyler; Andrews, Julie; Lillie, Beatrice; Channing, Carol; Fox, James; Gavin, John; Soo, Jack; Morita, Pat; Dee, Ann

**Song(s)**   Thoroughly Modern Millie; The Tapioca; Trinkt le Chaim (C/L: Neufeld, Sylvia); Jimmy (C/L: Thompson, Jay)

**Notes**   There are also vocals of "Looking at the World Thru Rose Colored Glasses" by Tommy Malie and Jimmy Steiger; "I Can't Believe That You're in Love with Me" by Clarence Gaskill and Jimmy McHugh; "Baby Face" by Benny Davis and Harry Akst; "Mazel Tov" and "Freilachs" (two traditional songs); "Jazz Baby" by Blanche Merrill and M.K. Jerome; "Ah, Sweet Mystery of Life" by Victor Herbert and Rida Johnson Young; "Do It Again" by George Gershwin and B.G.

DeSylva; "Poor Butterfly" by John L. Golden and Raymond Hubbell and "Rose of Washington Square" by Ballard Macdonald and James F. Hanley.

## 6177 ✦ THOSE CALLOWAYS
Disney, 1964

**Musical Score**   Steiner, Max
**Composer(s)**   Sherman, Richard M.; Sherman, Robert B.
**Lyricist(s)**   Sherman, Richard M.; Sherman, Robert B.

**Producer(s)**   Hibler, Winston
**Director(s)**   Tokar, Norman
**Screenwriter(s)**   Pelletier, Louis
**Source(s)**   *Swiftwater* (novel) Annixter, Paul

**Cast**   Keith, Brian; Miles, Vera; de Wilde, Brandon; Brennan, Walter; Wynn, Ed; Evans, Linda; Abbott, Philip

**Song(s)**   Angel (C: Steiner, Max; L: Livingston, Jay; Evans, Ray); The Cabin Raising Song; Rhyme-Around

**Notes**   Originally titled WILD GOOSE STOP. This was serialized on TV. There are also vocals of "You Were Meant for Me" by Arthur Freed and Nacio Herb Brown; "Little Town of Bethlehem" by Phillips Brooks and Lewis H. Redner and "Silent Night" by Franz Gruber and Joseph Mohr.

## 6178 ✦ THOSE DARING YOUNG MEN IN THEIR JAUNTY JALOPIES
Paramount, 1969

**Musical Score**   Goodwin, Ron

**Producer(s)**   Annakin, Ken
**Director(s)**   Annakin, Ken
**Screenwriter(s)**   Annakin, Ken; Davies, Jack

**Cast**   Bourvil; Buzzanca, Lando; Chiari, Walter; Cook, Peter; Curtis, Tony; Carc, Mireille; Dubois, Marie; Frobe, Gert; Hawkins, Jack; Moore, Dudley; Terry-Thomas; Sykes, Eric; Hampshire, Susan; Machiavelli, Nicoletta; Schmidt, Peer

**Song(s)**   Those Daring Young Men in Their Jaunty Jalopies [1] (C/L: Goodwin, Ron); They're Playing Chester's Song [2] (C/L: Goodwin, Ron)

**Notes**   Titled MONTE CARLO OR BUST in the United Kingdom. [1] Background use only. [2] Not used.

## 6179 ✦ THOSE GOOD OLD DAYS
Warner Brothers, 1941

**Composer(s)**   Jerome, M.K.
**Lyricist(s)**   Scholl, Jack

**Song(s)**   My Old Shack in Dixie; Who's Your Honey Lamb [2]; Seaside Finale [1]; Seaside Finale No. 2

**Notes**   Short subject. [1] Also in HORSE AND BUGGY DAYS. [2] Also in SHINE ON HARVEST MOON.

## 6180 ✦ THOSE MAGNIFICENT MEN IN THEIR FLYING MACHINES OR HOW I FLEW FROM LONDON TO PARIS IN 25 HOURS AND 11 MINUTES
Twentieth Century–Fox, 1966

**Musical Score**   Goodwin, Ron

**Producer(s)**   Margulies, Stan
**Director(s)**   Annakin, Ken
**Screenwriter(s)**   Davies, Jack; Annakin, Ken

**Cast**   Whitman, Stuart; Miles, Sarah; Fox, James; Sordi, Alberto; Morley, Robert; Frobe, Gert; Cassel, Jean-Pierre; Sykes, Eric; Terry-Thomas; Skelton, Red; Demick, Irina; Hill, Benny; Ishihara, Yujiro; Robson, Flora; Vogler, Karl Michael; Wanamaker, Sam; Hancock, Tony

**Song(s)**   Those Magnificent Men in Their Flying Machines (C/L: Goodwin, Ron)

## 6181 ✦ THOSE REDHEADS FROM SEATTLE
Paramount, 1953

**Musical Score**   Shuken, Leo; Cutner, Sidney
**Choreographer(s)**   Baker, Jack

**Producer(s)**   Pine, William; Thomas, William
**Director(s)**   Foster, Lewis R.
**Screenwriter(s)**   Foster, Lewis R.; Homes, Geoffrey; Yates, George Worthing

**Cast**   Fleming, Rhonda; Barry, Gene; Moorehead, Agnes; Brewer, Teresa; Mitchell, Guy; The Bell Sisters; Parker, Jean; Ates, Roscoe

**Song(s)**   Baby, Baby, Baby (C: Livingston, Jerry; L: David, Mack); Chick-A-Boom [3] (C/L: Merrill, Bob); I Guess It Was You All the Time [2] (C: Carmichael, Hoagy; L: Mercer, Johnny); Mr. Banjo Man (C/L: Livingston, Jay; Evans, Ray); Once More [1] (C: Shuken, Leo; L: Blake, Bebe)

**Notes**   Originally titled THOSE SISTERS FROM SEATTLE. [1] Lyrics written for exploitation only. "Take Back Your Gold" by M.H. Rosenfeld and Louis W. Pritzkow was written in 1897 and also given a vocal treatment in this movie. [2] Originally written for THE KEYSTONE GIRL. [3] Not written for this film.

## 6182 ✦ THOSE THREE FRENCH GIRLS
Metro–Goldwyn–Mayer, 1930

**Composer(s)**   Meyer, Joseph
**Lyricist(s)**   Freed, Arthur
**Choreographer(s)**   Lee, Sammy

**Director(s)**   Beaumont, Harry
**Screenwriter(s)**   Wodehouse, P.G.

**Cast**   D'Orsay, Fifi; Edwards, Cliff; Ravel, Sandra; Denny, Reginald; d'Avril, Yola; Grossmith, George

**Song(s)**   We Are Six Poor Mortals; You're Simply Delish; I'd be So Happy with You [1]; In Good Old Paree [1]; The Moment We Met [1]; Rattling Along [1]; The Right Way to Love [1]

**Notes**   [1] Not used.

## 6183 ✦ THOSE WERE THE DAYS

See AT GOOD OLD SIWASH.

## 6184 ✦ A THOUSAND CLOWNS
United Artists, 1966

**Musical Score**   Walker, Don

**Producer(s)**   Coe, Fred
**Director(s)**   Coe, Fred
**Screenwriter(s)**   Gardner, Herb
**Source(s)**   *A Thousand Clowns* (play) Gardner, Herb

**Cast**   Robards Jr., Jason; Harris, Barbara; Balsam, Martin; Gordon, Barry; Saks, Gene; Daniels, William

**Song(s)**   A Thousand Clowns (C: Mulligan, Gerry; L: Holliday, Judy)

## 6185 ✦ THOUSANDS CHEER
Metro–Goldwyn–Mayer, 1943

**Producer(s)**   Pasternak, Joe
**Director(s)**   Sidney, George
**Screenwriter(s)**   Jarrico, Paul; Collins, Richard
**Source(s)**   "Private Miss Jones" (story) Jarrico, Paul; Collins, Richard

**Cast**   Iturbi, Jose; Grayson, Kathryn; Kelly, Gene; Astor, Mary; Boles, John; Blue, Ben; Rafferty, Frances; Elliott, Mary; Jenks, Frank; Sully, Frank; Simmons, Dick; Lessy, Ben; Rooney, Mickey; Garland, Judy; Skelton, Red; Powell, Eleanor; Sothern, Ann; Ball, Lucille; O'Brien, Virginia; Morgan, Frank; Horne, Lena; Hunt, Marsha; Maxwell, Marilyn; Reed, Donna; O'Brien, Margaret; Allyson, June; De Haven, Gloria; Conte, John; Haiden, Sara; Loper, Don; Barrat, Maxine; Kay Kyser and His Orchestra; Bob Crosby and His Orchestra; Henry Carter and His Band; The M-G-M Dancing Girls

**Song(s)**   Main Title (C: Stothart, Herbert; Brent, Earl; L: Harburg, E.Y.; Stothart, Herbert); Let There Be Music (C: Brent, Earl; L: Harburg, E.Y.); Daybreak (C: Grofe, Ferde; L: Adamson, Harold); Three Letters in the Mailbox (C: Jurmann, Walter; L: Webster, Paul Francis); I Dug a Ditch (C: Lane, Burton; L: Brown, Lew; Freed, Ralph); Should I Reveal (C: Brown, Nacio Herb; L: Freed, Arthur); The Joint Is Really Jumpin' (C/L: Edens, Roger; Blane, Ralph; Martin, Hugh); United Nations [2] (C: Shostakovitch, Dimitri; L: Stothart, Herbert; Rome, Harold; Harburg, E.Y.); Just As Long As I Know Katie's Waitin [1] (C: Brown, George; L: Brown, Lew; Freed, Ralph)

**Notes** There are also vocals of "In a Little Spanish Town" by Mabel Wayne, Joe Young and Sam M. Lewis and "Honeysuckle Rose" by Andy Razaf and Fats Waller. [1] Sheet music only under the film title PRIVATE MISS JONES. Ralph Freed apparently contributed to lyrics before the song was cut from THOUSANDS CHEER. [2] Rome alone is credited with lyrics on sheet music.

### 6186 ✦ THRASHIN'
Fries Entertainment, 1986

**Producer(s)** Sacks, Alan
**Director(s)** Winters, David
**Screenwriter(s)** Brown, Paul; Sacks, Alan

**Cast** Brolin, Josh; Rusler, Robert; Gidley, Pamela; McCarter Jr., Brooke; McCann, Chuck

**Song(s)** Thrashin' (C: Lee, Larry; L: Sacks, Alan; Michel, Jodi Sacks); That's Good (C/L: Casale, Gerald V.; Mothersbaugh, Alan; Mothersbaugh, Mark); Tequila (C/L: Rio, Chuck); Arrow Through My Heart (C/L: Piccirillo, Mike; Goetzman, Gary)

**Notes** No cue sheet available.

### 6187 ✦ THE THREAT
Warner Brothers, 1960

**Musical Score** Stein, Ronald
**Composer(s)** Stein, Ronald
**Lyricist(s)** Stein, Ronald

**Producer(s)** Rondeau, Charles R.
**Director(s)** Rondeau, Charles R.
**Screenwriter(s)** Hiems, Jo

**Cast** Knapp, Robert; Lawson, Linda; Hush, Lisabeth; Seay, James; Castle, Mary; Brown, Lew; King, Nicholas

**Song(s)** Destiny of Love; In Love Before

### 6188 ✦ THREE AMIGOS
Orion, 1986

**Musical Score** Bernstein, Elmer
**Composer(s)** Newman, Randy
**Lyricist(s)** Newman, Randy

**Producer(s)** Michaels, Lorne; Folsey Jr., George
**Director(s)** Landis, John
**Screenwriter(s)** Martin, Steve; Michaels, Lorne; Newman, Randy

**Cast** Chase, Chevy; Martin, Steve; Short, Martin; Arau, Alfonso; Plana, Tony; Martinez, Patrice; Mantegna, Joe; Lovitz, Jon

**Song(s)** The Ballad of the Three Amigos; My Little Buttercup; Blue Shadows

**Notes** No cue sheet available.

### 6189 ✦ THREE BITES OF THE APPLE
Metro–Goldwyn–Mayer, 1967

**Musical Score** Manson, Eddy
**Composer(s)** McCallum, David; Manson, Eddy
**Lyricist(s)** Webster, Paul Francis

**Producer(s)** Ganzer, Alvin
**Director(s)** Ganzer, Alvin
**Screenwriter(s)** Wells, George

**Cast** McCallum, David; Koscina, Sylva; Grimes, Tammy; Modugno, Domenico; Angers, Avril; Fabrizi, Aldo

**Song(s)** In the Garden—Under the Tree (C: McCallum, David; L: Webster, Paul Francis); The Serpent [1]; The Swindle [1]; Mr. Thrumm's Chase [1]

**Notes** [1] Not on cue sheets (as songs anyway).

### 6190 ✦ THE THREE CABALLEROS
Disney, 1944

**Musical Score** Wolcott, Charles; Smith, Paul J.; Plumb, Ed
**Lyricist(s)** Gilbert, Ray
**Choreographer(s)** Daniels, Billy; Oliveira, Aloysio; Maracci, Carmelita

**Producer(s)** Ferguson, Norman
**Director(s)** Geronimi, Clyde; Kinney, Jack; Roberts, Bill; Ferguson, Norman
**Screenwriter(s)** Brightman, Homer; Terrazas, Ernest; Sears, Ted; Peet, Bill; Wright, Ralph; Plummer, Elmer; Williams, Roy; Cottrell, William; Connell, Del; Bodrero, James

**Cast** Holloway, Sterling; Miranda, Aurora; Molina, Carmen; Nash, Clarence; Garay, Joaquin; Oliveira, Jose; Graham, Frank; Shields, Fred; Amaral, Nestor; Almirante; The Trio Calaveras; Ascencio Del Rio Trio; The Padua Hills Players

**Song(s)** The Three Caballeros (C: Esperon, Manuel); Baia (Na Baixia do Sapateiro) (C: Barroso, Ary); Have You Ever Been to Baia (Voce Ja Foi a Baia?) (C: Caymmi; L: Ferguson, Norman); Cookie Peddler's Call (C/L: Oliveira, Louis); Os Quindins De Ya-Ya (C/L: Barroso, Ary); Pregos Cariocas (C/L: Braja, Carlos); Mexico (C: Wolcott, Charles; L: Gilbert, Ray; Santos, Edmundo); Lilongo (C/L: Gill, Charo); Solamente Una Vez (You Belong to My Heart) [4] (C: Lara, Augustin); Hey! Mr. Sunshine [1] (C: Wolcott, Charles); Joe Carioca [2] (C: Wolcott, Charles; L: Heyman, Edward); Latin for a Day [3] (C: Wolcott, Charles); Angel May Care [5] (C: Barroso, Ary; L: Drake, Ervin); Jesusita en Chihuahua (Cactus Polka) [5] (C: Plumb, Edward; L: Drake, Ervin); Arroz con Leche [5] (C/L: Smith, Paul J.)

**Notes** Live action and animated feature. The cast list includes cast as well as voices. [1] Used instrumentally only. [2] Written for exploitation only. [3] Not used. Also not used in the unproduced short LATIN FOR A

DAY. [4] Also in MR. IMPERIUM (MGM), THE BIG SOMBRERO (Columbia) and THE GAY RANCHERO (Republic). [5] Sheet music only.

## 6191 ✦ THREE CHEERS FOR LOVE
### Paramount, 1936

**Composer(s)** Rainger, Ralph
**Lyricist(s)** Robin, Leo

**Producer(s)** Botsford, A.M.
**Director(s)** McCarey, Ray
**Screenwriter(s)** Trivers, Barry

**Cast** Cummings, Robert; Whitney, Eleanore; Halliday, John

**Song(s)** Learn to Be Lovely [4] (C: Revel, Harry; L: Gordon, Mack); Hail to Chester; Where Is My Heart; Long Ago and Far Away; Tap Your Feet [1]; Swing Tap [2] [3]; You're a Four Star Picture to Me [1]; Light Up Your Face [1]; Three Cheers for Love [1]; Those Bootblack Blues [1] [3] (L: Rainger, Ralph)

**Notes** [1] Not used. [2] Used instrumentally only. Not used in BIG BROADCAST OF 1937. [3] Same music. [4] Used as instrumental background only in COLLEGIATE.

## 6192 ✦ THREE CHEERS FOR THE GIRLS
### Warner Brothers, 1943

**Song(s)** Floradora Chorus of the Screen (C: Jerome, M.K.; L: Scholl, Jack)

**Notes** Short subject.

## 6193 ✦ THREE COINS IN THE FOUNTAIN
### Twentieth Century–Fox, 1954

**Musical Score** Young, Victor

**Producer(s)** Siegel, Sol C.
**Director(s)** Negulesco, Jean
**Screenwriter(s)** Patrick, John
**Source(s)** *Coins in the Fountain* (novel) Secondari, John H.

**Cast** Webb, Clifton; McGuire, Dorothy; Peters, Jean; Jourdan, Louis; McNamara, Maggie; Brazzi, Rossano; St. John, Howard; Givney, Kathryn; Nesbitt, Cathleen; Siletti, Mario

**Song(s)** Three Coins in the Fountain (C: Styne, Jule; L: Cahn, Sammy); Anema e Core (C: D'Esposito, Salve; L: Manlio, Tito); Nanni (C/L: Silvestri, Franco); 'O Ciucciariello (C: Oliviero, Nino; L: Murolo, Roberto)

## 6194 ✦ THREE COMRADES
### Metro–Goldwyn–Mayer, 1938

**Musical Score** Waxman, Franz
**Composer(s)** Waxman, Franz
**Lyricist(s)** Wright, Bob; Forrest, Chet

**Producer(s)** Mankiewicz, Joseph L.
**Director(s)** Borzage, Frank
**Screenwriter(s)** Fitzgerald, F. Scott; Paramore Jr., Edward E.
**Source(s)** *Three Comrades* (novel) Remarque, Erich Maria

**Cast** Taylor, Robert; Sullavan, Margaret; Tone, Franchot; Young, Robert; Kibbee, Guy; Atwill, Lionel; Hull, Henry; Grapewin, Charley; Woolley, Monty

**Song(s)** The Comrade Song; Forever Follow Truth; Mighty Forest (C: Waxman, Franz; Mendelssohn, Felix); How Can I Leave Thee; The Yankee Ragtime College Jazzes

## 6195 ✦ THREE DARING DAUGHTERS
### Metro–Goldwyn–Mayer, 1947

**Musical Score** Stothart, Herbert; Perl, Lothar

**Producer(s)** Pasternak, Joe
**Director(s)** Wilcox, Fred M.
**Screenwriter(s)** Mannheimer, Albert; Kohner, Frederick; Levien, Sonya; Meehan, John

**Cast** MacDonald, Jeanette; Iturbi, Jose; Powell, Jane; Arnold, Edward; Davenport, Harry; MacGill, Moyna; Adler, Larry; Donahue, Mary; Todd, Ann

**Song(s)** Hail to Thee, Dear Alma Mater (C: Stoll, George; L: Katz, William); The Dickey-Bird Song (C: Fain, Sammy; L: Dietz, Howard); Where There's Love (C: Strauss, Richardrent, Earl)

**Notes** Originally titled BIRDS AND THE BEES which is also its international title. There are also vocals of "Route 66" by Bobby Troup; "Passepied" by Delibes and Eristoff; "You Made Me Love You" by James V. Monaco and Joseph McCarthy; "Mulatta Likes the Rhumba" by Rodriguiz and Sunshine; "Je Veux Vivre" from ROMEO AND JULIET by Gounod; "Sweethearts" by Victor Herbert, Wright and Forrest; "Fleurette" by Victor Herbert and Ralph Freed and "Springtide" by Grieg and Dole.

## 6196 ✦ THREE DAYS OF THE CONDOR
### Paramount, 1975

**Musical Score** Grusin, Dave

**Producer(s)** Schneider, Stanley
**Director(s)** Pollack, Sydney
**Screenwriter(s)** Semple Jr., Lorenzo; Rayfiel, David
**Source(s)** *Six Days of the Condor* (novel) Grady, James

**Cast** Redford, Robert; Dunaway, Faye; Robertson, Cliff; Von Sydow, Max; Chen, Tina; Houseman, John

**Song(s)** I've Got You Where I Want You [1] (C: Grusin, Dave; L: Bahler, Tom)

**Notes** [1] Background vocal only.

## 6197 ✦ THE THREE FACES OF EVE
Twentieth Century–Fox, 1957

**Musical Score** Dolan, Robert Emmett

**Producer(s)** Johnson, Nunnally
**Director(s)** Johnson, Nunnally
**Screenwriter(s)** Johnson, Nunnally
**Source(s)** *A Case of Multiple Personality* (book)
Thigpen M.D., Corbett H.; Cleckley M.D., Hervey M.

**Cast** Woodward, Joanne; Wayne, David; Cobb, Lee J.;
Jerome, Edwin; Murray, Alena; Kulp, Nancy

**Song(s)** Hold Me [1] (C/L: Little, Little Jack;
Oppenheim, Dave; Schuster, Ira); I Never Knew [2]
(C/L: Pitts, Tom; Egan, Raymond B.; Marsh, Roy)

**Notes** [1] Also in PEG O' MY HEART (1933)
(MGM). [2] Also in the THE CLOWN (MGM) and the
Universal films THE CRIMSON CANARY and
STRICTLY IN THE GROOVE.

## 6198 ✦ THREE FOR THE SHOW
Columbia, 1954

**Musical Score** Duning, George
**Choreographer(s)** Cole, Jack

**Producer(s)** Taps, Jonie
**Director(s)** Potter, H.C.
**Screenwriter(s)** Hope, Edward; Stern, Leonard
**Source(s)** *Too Many Husbands* (play) Maugham, W.
Somerset

**Cast** Grable, Betty; Lemmon, Jack; Champion, Marge;
Champion, Gower; McCormick, Myron; Harvey, Paul

**Song(s)** Down Boy [1] (C: Carmichael, Hoagy; L:
Adamson, Harold); I've Been Kissed Before [2] (C: Lee,
Lester; L: Russell, Bob); Which One (C: Lee, Lester; L:
Washington, Ned)

**Notes** A remake of TOO MANY HUSBANDS (1942).
There are also vocals of "Someone to Watch Over Me"
and "I've Got a Crush on You" by George and Ira
Gershwin and "How Come You Do Me Like You Do"
by Gene Austin and Roy Bergere. [1] Written for but
not used in film version of GENTLEMEN PREFER
BLONDES. [2] Written for AFFAIR IN TRINIDAD.

## 6199 ✦ 365 NIGHTS IN HOLLYWOOD
Fox, 1934

**Composer(s)** Whiting, Richard A.
**Lyricist(s)** Clare, Sidney
**Choreographer(s)** Lee, Sammy

**Producer(s)** Wurtzel, Sol M.
**Director(s)** Marshall, George
**Screenwriter(s)** Conselman, William; Johnson, Henry
**Source(s)** "365 Nights in Hollywood" (stories) Starr,
James A.

**Cast** Dunne, James; Faye, Alice; Mitchell, Frank;
Durant, Jack; Melton, Frank

**Song(s)** She Learned About Sailors [1]; Yes to You;
Good Morning; My Future Star

**Notes** There are also vocals of "Yip-I-Addy-I-Ay!" by
Will D. Cobb and J.H. Flynn; "Hold Your Man" by
Nacio Herb Brown and Arthur Freed and "Where the
Blue of the Night" by Roy Turk, Bing Crosby and Fred
E. Ahlert. [1] Also in SHE LEARNED ABOUT
SAILORS.

## 6200 ✦ THREE IN THE SADDLE
PRC, 1945

**Producer(s)** Alexander, Arthur
**Director(s)** Fraser, Harry
**Screenwriter(s)** Clifton, Elmer

**Cast** O'Brien, Dave; Ritter, Tex; Wilkerson, Guy;
Miller, Lorraine; King, Charles

**Song(s)** Try Me One More Time (C/L: Tubb, Ernest);
I've Done the Best I Could (C/L: Harford, Frank;
Ritter, Tex)

**Notes** The cue sheet doesn't differentiate between
vocals and instrumentals.

## 6201 ✦ THREE INTO TWO WON'T GO
Universal, 1969

**Musical Score** Lai, Francis

**Producer(s)** Blaustein, Julian
**Director(s)** Hall, Peter
**Screenwriter(s)** O'Brien, Edna
**Source(s)** (novel) Newman, Andrea

**Cast** Steiger, Rod; Bloom, Claire; Geeson, Judy;
Ashcroft, Peggy; Bloom, Dame Peggy; Rogers, Paul

**Song(s)** Untamed Honey (C/L: Cole, Tony)

## 6202 ✦ THREE KINDS OF HEAT
Cannon, 1987

**Musical Score** Bishop, Michael; Page, Scott

**Producer(s)** Kagan, Michael J.
**Director(s)** Stevens, Leslie
**Screenwriter(s)** Stevens, Leslie

**Cast** Ginty, Robert; Barrett, Victoria; Shakti; McCoy,
Sylvester; Foster, Barry

**Song(s)** Spin (C/L: Bishop, Michael); Blast (C/L:
Bates, Steve); 3 Kinds of Hate (C/L: Bishop, Michael)

**Notes** No cue sheet available.

## 6203 ✦ THREE LITTLE BOPS
Warner Brothers, 1957

**Musical Score** Rogers, Milton "Shorty"

**Director(s)** Freling, Friz
**Screenwriter(s)** Foster, Warren

**Cast** Freberg, Stan

**Song(s)** Three Little Bops (C: Rogers, Milton "Shorty"; L: Foster, Warren)

**Notes** Looney Tune.

## 6204 ♦ THREE LITTLE GIRLS IN BLUE
### Twentieth Century–Fox, 1946

**Composer(s)** Myrow, Josef
**Lyricist(s)** Gordon, Mack
**Choreographer(s)** Felix, Seymour; Pearce, Babe

**Producer(s)** Gordon, Mack
**Director(s)** Humberstone, H. Bruce
**Screenwriter(s)** Davies, Valentine
**Source(s)** (play) Powys, Stephen

**Cast** Vera-Ellen [2]; Montgomery, George [3]; Blaine, Vivian; Haver, June; Smith, Charlie [4]; Holm, Celeste; Latimore, Frank [5]; Dandridge, Ruby; Hall, Thurston; Smith, Charles

**Song(s)** Three Little Girls in Blue; A Farmer's Life Is a Very Merry Life; On the Boardwalk (In Atlantic City); Three Little Girls in Blue—Prayer Sequence; Oh! My Love (C: Monaco, James V.; L: McCarthy, Joseph); I Like Mike; Somewhere in the Night; If You Can't Get a Girl in the Summertime (You'll Never Get a Girl at All) (C: Tierney, Harry; L: Kalmar, Bert); You Make Me Feel So Young; Always the Lady; Rio [1] [7] (C/L: Barroso, Ary); Love Theme [1] (C/L: Barroso, Ary); Torch Song [1] (Inst.) (C: Barroso, Ary); Assubia um Samba [1] (C/L: Barroso, Ary); When a Ya-Ya Meets a Yo-Yo (Inst.) [1] (C: Barroso, Ary); Pam [1] (Inst.) (C: Barroso, Ary); Oomba-Ba-Ga [1] (C/L: Barroso, Ary); Additional Samba [1] (Inst.) (C: Barroso, Ary); This Is Always [6] (C: Warren, Harry)

**Notes** Originally titled RIO CABANA with a score to be written by Ary Barroso and Mack Gordon. The Brazilian locale was changed and Gordon never wrote any English lyrics. [1] These are the tunes and songs Barroso wrote that weren't used. [2] Dubbed by Carol Stewart. [3] Dubbed by Ben Gage. [4] Dubbed by Del Porter. [5] Dubbed by Bob Scott. [6] Vocal cut from final print. Recorded by June Haver and Ben Gage (for George Montgomery). [7] Used in HOLIDAY FOR LOVERS.

## 6205 ♦ THREE LITTLE PIGS
### Disney, 1933

**Musical Score** Churchill, Frank E.

**Song(s)** Who's Afraid of the Big Bad Wolf [1] (C/L: Churchill, Frank E.)

**Notes** Animated cartoon. No credits sheet available. [1] According to a Disney memo: "Ann Ronnell, who claimed to have written the lyrics and song 'Who's Afraid of the Big Bad Wolf,' lost the case; therefore the cue sheet should read: Words and Music: Frank Churchill."

Other sources say Ronnell contributed "Additional Lyrics." Also in SHIP CAFE.

## 6206 ♦ THREE LITTLE SISTERS
### Republic, 1944

**Composer(s)** Kent, Walter
**Lyricist(s)** Gannon, Kim

**Producer(s)** Grey, Harry
**Director(s)** Santley, Joseph
**Screenwriter(s)** Cooper, Olive

**Cast** Lee, Mary; Terry, Ruth; Walker, Cheryl; Terry, William; Moran, Jackie; Arnt, Charles; Jenks, Frank; London, Tom; Richards, Addison

**Song(s)** Three Little Sisters (C: Mizzy, Vic; L: Taylor, Irving); Little Old Fashioned Looking Glass; Khaki Wacky Sue; Sweet Dreams, Sweetheart; Don't Forget the Girl Back Home

## 6207 ♦ THREE LITTLE WORDS
### Metro–Goldwyn–Mayer, 1950

**Choreographer(s)** Pan, Hermes

**Producer(s)** Cummings, Jack
**Director(s)** Thorpe, Richard
**Screenwriter(s)** Wells, George

**Cast** Astaire, Fred; Skelton, Red; Vera-Ellen [1]; Dahl, Arlene; Wynn, Keenan; Robbins, Gale; De Haven, Gloria; Regan, Phil; Shannon, Harry; Reynolds, Debbie [2]; Carpenter, Carleton

**Notes** This film is based on the lives of and featured the songs of Harry Ruby and Burt Kalmar. There were no songs written for this film. Songs include "Where Did You Get That Girl" by Harry Puck and Kalmar; "She's Mine, All Mine" and "My Sunny Tennessee" by Kalmar, Ruby and Herman Ruby; "Three Little Words," "So Long! Oo-Long" and "Who's Sorry Now?" with music by Ted Snyder; "Come on Papa" with lyrics by Edgar Leslie; "Nevertheless (I'm in Love with You)," "All Alone Monday," "You Smiled at Me," and "I Wanna Be Loved By You" with music by Ruby and Herbert Stothart; "Up in the Clouds," "Thinking of You," "Hooray for Captain Spaulding," "I Love You So Much" and "You Are My Lucky Star" by Arthur Freed and Nacio Herb Brown. [1] Dubbed by Anita Ellis. [2] Dubbed by Helen Kane (whom she was portraying) for "I Wanna Be Loved By You."

## 6208 ♦ THE THREE LIVES OF THOMASINA
### Disney, 1963

**Musical Score** Smith, Paul J.

**Producer(s)** Attwooll, Hugh
**Director(s)** Chaffey, Don
**Screenwriter(s)** Westerby, Robert
**Source(s)** *Thomasina* (novel) Gallico, Paul

**Cast** McGoohan, Patrick; Hampshire, Susan; Naismith, Laurence; Brambell, Wilfrid; Anderson, Jean; Currie, Finlay

**Song(s)** Thomasina (C/L: Gilkyson, Terry)

## 6209 ◆ THREE MEN AND A BABY
Touchstone, 1987

**Musical Score** Hamlisch, Marvin

**Producer(s)** Field, Ted; Cort, Robert W.
**Director(s)** Nimoy, Leonard
**Screenwriter(s)** Orr, James; Cruickshank, Jim
**Source(s)** *Trois Hommes Et Un Couffin* (film) Serreau, Coline

**Cast** Selleck, Tom; Guttenberg, Steve; Danson, Ted; Colin, Margaret; Holm, Celeste; Travis, Nancy; Bosco, Philip

**Song(s)** The Minute I Saw You (C/L: Hamlisch, Marvin; Foster, David; Sager, Carole Bayer; Parr, John); Goodnight Sweetheart Goodnight (C/L: Hudson, James; Carter, Calvin); Conga (C/L: Garcia, Enrique); My Girl (C/L: Robinson, William; White, Ronald); Bad Boy (C/L: Dermer, Larry; Galdo, Joe; Vigil, Rafael); Good Lovin' (C/L: Clark, Rudy; Resnick, Arthur); Daddy's Girl (C/L: Goldenberg, Mark; Cetera, Peter); The Right Thing (C/L: Hucknall, Mick)

## 6210 ◆ THREE MEN AND A GIRL

See KENTUCKY MOONSHINE.

## 6211 ◆ THE THREE MUSKETEERS (1933)
Mascot, 1933

**Composer(s)** Zahler, Lee
**Lyricist(s)** Gittens

**Song(s)** The Legioneers; Song of Three Musketeers

**Notes** No other information available.

## 6212 ◆ THE THREE MUSKETEERS (1939)
Twentieth Century–Fox, 1939

**Composer(s)** Pokrass, Sam
**Lyricist(s)** Bullock, Walter

**Producer(s)** Griffith, Raymond
**Director(s)** Dwan, Allan
**Screenwriter(s)** Musselman, M.M.; Drake, William A.; Hellman, Sam
**Source(s)** *The Three Musketeers* (novel) Dumas, Alexandre

**Cast** Ameche, Don; The Ritz Brothers; Barnes, Binnie; Atwill, Lionel; Stuart, Gloria; Moore, Pauline; Schildkraut, Joseph; Carradine, John; King, John; Mander, Miles; Dumbrille, Douglass; Hicks, Russell; Brecher, Egon

**Song(s)** Voila; Doin' the Nimble Cymbal [1] (C/L: Pokrass, Sam; Golden, Ray; Kuller, Sid); Plucking Song (L: Golden, Ray; Kuller, Sid); Song of the Musketeers; My Lady; A Heart That's Free [2] (C: Robyn, Alfred George; L: Railey, Thomas T.; Golden, Ray; Kuller, Sid)

**Notes** [1] Instrumental use only. [2] Kuller and Golden wrote parody lyrics to this tune.

## 6213 ◆ THREE O'CLOCK HIGH
Universal, 1987

**Musical Score** Levay, Sylvester; Tangerine Dream

**Producer(s)** Vogel, David E.
**Director(s)** Joanou, Phil
**Screenwriter(s)** Matheson, Richard; Szollosi, Thomas

**Cast** Siemaszko, Casey; Ryan, Anne; Tyson, Richard; Glick, Stacey

**Song(s)** Something to Remember Me By (C/L: Walker, Jim)

## 6214 ◆ THREE ON A COUCH
Columbia, 1966

**Musical Score** Brown, Louis Yule

**Producer(s)** Lewis, Jerry
**Director(s)** Lewis, Jerry
**Screenwriter(s)** Ross, Bob; Taylor, Samuel A.

**Cast** Lewis, Jerry; Leigh, Janet; Best, James; Mobley, Mary Ann; Golan, Gila; Parrish, Leslie; Freeman, Kathleen; Lester, Buddy; Feld, Fritz

**Song(s)** A Now and a Later Love (C: Brown, Louis Yule; L: Mattis, Lil; Lewis, Jerry)

## 6215 ◆ THREE ON A HONEYMOON
Fox, 1934

**Producer(s)** Stone, John
**Director(s)** Tinling, James
**Screenwriter(s)** Lowe, Edward T.; Van Sickle, Raymond
**Source(s)** *Promenade Deck* (novel) Ross, Isabel

**Cast** Eilers, Sally; Brown, Johnny Mack; Starrett, Charles; Pitts, ZaSu

**Song(s)** Desert Nights (C/L: Kernell, William); Stay Away Girls from Sailors Deep (C/L: Tinling, James)

## 6216 ◆ THREE RING CIRCUS
Paramount, 1954

**Musical Score** Scharf, Walter
**Choreographer(s)** Castle, Nick

**Producer(s)** Wallis, Hal B.
**Director(s)** Pevney, Joseph
**Screenwriter(s)** McGuire, Don

**Cast**    Martin, Dean; Lewis, Jerry; Dru, Joanne; Gabor, Zsa Zsa; Ford, Wallace; Rumann, Sig; Sheldon, Gene; Cravat, Nick; Lanchester, Elsa

**Song(s)**    It's a Big, Wide Wonderful World [1] (C/L: Rox, John); Hey, Punchinello (C/L: Livingston, Jay; Evans, Ray); Three Ring Circus [2] (C: Scharf, Walter; L: Stone, Wilson)

**Notes**    [1] Also in SWEET BIRD OF YOUTH (MGM). Originally written for ALL IN FUN (Broadway revue). [2] Lyric written for exploitation only.

### 6217    ♦    THREE SAILORS AND A GIRL
Warner Brothers, 1953

**Composer(s)**    Fain, Sammy
**Lyricist(s)**    Cahn, Sammy
**Choreographer(s)**    Prinz, LeRoy

**Producer(s)**    Cahn, Sammy
**Director(s)**    Del Ruth, Roy
**Screenwriter(s)**    Kibbee, Roland; Freeman, Devery
**Source(s)**    *The Butter and Egg Man* (play) Kaufman, George S.

**Cast**    Powell, Jane; MacRae, Gordon; Nelson, Gene; Levene, Sam; Givot, George; Borg, Veda Ann; MacDonald, Archer; Greenleaf, Raymond; Slate, Henry; Leonard, Jack E.

**Song(s)**    My Heart Is a Singing Heart; You're But Oh So Right; Kiss Me or I'll Scream; Face to Face; The Lately Song; There Must Be a Reason; When It's Love (C: Brent, Earl); Show Me a Happy Woman (And I'll Show You a Miserable Man); It's Gonna Be a Big Hit; Here Comes the Navy; Home Is Where the Heart Is; I Made Myself a Promise [1]; The Five Senses [1]; I Got Butterflies [1]; Home Is Where the Heart Is [2]

**Notes**    The play was made into a number of movies: in 1928, 1932 (THE TENDERFOOT), 1937 (DANCE, CHARLIE, DANCE) and 1940 (AN ANGEL FROM TEXAS). [1] In Hirschhorn but not on cue sheet. [2] Sheet music only.

### 6218    ♦    THE 3 SISTERS
Fox, 1930

**Composer(s)**    Kay, Arthur
**Lyricist(s)**    Severi

**Director(s)**    Sloane, Paul
**Screenwriter(s)**    Brooks, George; McGuinness, James Kevin

**Cast**    Dresser, Louise; Patricola, Tom; MacKenna, Kenneth; Compton, Joyce; Collyer, June; McPhail, Addie; Saum, Cliff

**Song(s)**    Ella Bella Cigucini; La Marianna; Passionate Night Serenade (C/L: Schultheis, G.H.); Addio, My Darling; Italian Kisses (C: Baer, Abel; L: Gilbert, L. Wolfe)

### 6219    ♦    THREE SMART GIRLS
Universal, 1936

**Composer(s)**    Jurmann, Walter; Kaper, Bronislau
**Lyricist(s)**    Kahn, Gus

**Producer(s)**    Pasternak, Joe
**Director(s)**    Koster, Henry
**Screenwriter(s)**    Comandini, Adele; Parker, Austin

**Cast**    Durbin, Deanna; Grey, Nan; Read, Barbara; Barnes, Binnie; Walker, Nella; Winninger, Charles; Milland, Ray; Brady, Alice; Auer, Mischa; Cavanaugh, Hobart; Pangborn, Franklin

**Song(s)**    My Heart Is Singing; Someone to Care for Me

**Notes**    Remade as THREE DARING DAUGHTERS. This is Deanna Durbin's screen debut. There is also a vocal of "Il Bacio" by Arditi.

### 6220    ♦    THREE SMART GIRLS GROW UP
Universal, 1938

**Producer(s)**    Pasternak, Joe
**Director(s)**    Koster, Henry
**Screenwriter(s)**    Manning, Bruce; Jackson, Felix

**Cast**    Durbin, Deanna; Grey, Nan; Parrish, Helen; Cummings, Robert; Lundigan, William

**Song(s)**    Invitation to the Dance (C: Von Weber, Carl; L: Henderson, Charles); The Wren (C: Benedict, J.; Johnson, Howard)

**Notes**    No cue sheet available. There are vocals of "Because" by Guy d'Hartelot and Edward Teschemacher and "The Last Rose of Summer" by Thomas Moore and Richard Alfred Milliken.

### 6221    ♦    THREE SONS
RKO, 1939

**Musical Score**    Webb, Roy

**Producer(s)**    Sisk, Robert
**Director(s)**    Hively, Jack
**Screenwriter(s)**    Twist, John
**Source(s)**    *Sweepings* (novel) Cohen, Lester

**Cast**    Ellis, Edward; Gargan, William; Taylor, Kent; Bromberg, J. Edward; Alexander, Katherine; Vale, Virginia; Stanton, Robert; Sutton, Grady; Pearce, Adele

**Song(s)**    Tootin' Down to Tennessee (C: Dreyer, Dave; L: Ruby, Herman)

### 6222    ♦    3:10 TO YUMA
Columbia, 1957

**Musical Score**    Duning, George

**Producer(s)**    Heilwell, David
**Director(s)**    Daves, Delmer
**Screenwriter(s)**    Welles, Halsted
**Source(s)**    (story) Leonard, Elmore

**Cast** Ford, Glenn; Heflin, Van; Farr, Felicia; Dana, Leora; Jones, Henry; Jaeckel, Richard

**Song(s)** 3:10 to Yuma (C: Duning, George; L: Washington, Ned)

## 6223 ◆ THREE TOUGH GUYS
### Paramount, 1974

**Musical Score** Hayes, Isaac

**Producer(s)** De Laurentiis, Dino
**Director(s)** Tessari, Duccio
**Screenwriter(s)** Vincenzoni, Luciano; Badalucco, Nicola

**Cast** Ventura, Lina; Hayes, Isaac; Williamson, Fred; Kelly, Paula

**Song(s)** Title Theme [1] (C/L: Hayes, Isaac); Ain't No Secret (C/L: Hayes, Isaac)

**Notes** [1] Background vocal only.

## 6224 ◆ THREE VIOLENT PEOPLE
### Paramount, 1956

**Musical Score** Scharf, Walter

**Producer(s)** Brown, Hugh
**Director(s)** Mate, Rudolph
**Screenwriter(s)** Grant, James Edward

**Cast** Heston, Charlton; Baxter, Anne; Roland, Gilbert; Tucker, Forrest; Tryon, Tom; Bennett, Bruce; Stritch, Elaine; MacLane, Barton; Blake, Bobby

**Song(s)** Una Momento (C: Martita; L: David, Mack); My Wild and Reckless Heart [1] (C: Scharf, Walter; L: Blake, Bebe)

**Notes** [1] Used instrumentally only.

## 6225 ◆ 3 WOMEN
### Twentieth Century–Fox, 1977

**Musical Score** Busby, Gerald
**Composer(s)** Nicholls, Allan
**Lyricist(s)** Nicholls, Allan

**Producer(s)** Altman, Robert
**Director(s)** Altman, Robert
**Screenwriter(s)** Altman, Robert

**Cast** Duvall, Shelley; Spacek, Sissy; Rule, Janice; Fortier, Robert; Nelson, Ruth; Cromwell, John; Nelson, Craig Richard

**Song(s)** Drink Until I Drop; Keep On Walking; Dessert Center Country Radio; I Love How You Love Me; When You Can't Find Love; I Need Your Love Today; Loaded

## 6226 ◆ THREE WORLDS OF GULLIVER
### Columbia, 1961

**Musical Score** Herrmann, Bernard
**Composer(s)** Duning, George
**Lyricist(s)** Washington, Ned

**Producer(s)** Schneer, Charles H.
**Director(s)** Sher, Jack
**Screenwriter(s)** Ross, Arthur; Sher, Jack
**Source(s)** "Gulliver's Travels" (story) Swift, Jonathan

**Cast** Mathews, Kerwin; Morrow, Jo; Thorburn, June; Alberoni, Sherry; Patterson, Lee; Sydney, Basil

**Song(s)** Wonderful Wonderful Gulliver; Gentle Love

## 6227 ◆ THREE YOUNG TEXANS
### Twentieth Century–Fox, 1954

**Producer(s)** Goldstein, Leonard
**Director(s)** Levin, Henry
**Screenwriter(s)** Adams, Gerald Drayson

**Cast** Gaynor, Mitzi; Brasselle, Keefe; Hunter, Jeffrey; Stephens, Harvey; Riss, Dan; Ansara, Michael; Spelling, Aaron; Wilcox, Frank

**Song(s)** Just Let Me Love You (C: Newman, Lionel; L: Daniel, Eliot)

## 6228 ◆ THRILL OF A LIFETIME
### Paramount, 1937

**Composer(s)** Hollander, Frederick
**Lyricist(s)** Coslow, Sam

**Producer(s)** Roger, Fanchon
**Director(s)** Archainbaud, George
**Screenwriter(s)** Garrett, Grant; Owen, Seena; Smith, Paul Gerard

**Cast** The Yacht Club Boys [2]; Erickson, Leif; Grable, Betty; Lamour, Dorothy; Canova, Judy; Crabbe, Buster; Downs, Johnny; Whitney, Eleanore; Blue, Ben; Pangborn, Franklin; Wonder, Tommy

**Song(s)** Merry Go Round (C/L: The Yacht Club Boys [2]); It's Been a Whole Year (C/L: The Yacht Club Boys [2]); Sweetheart Time; Thrill of a Lifetime [6]; Nobody's Darling (C/L: Davis, Jimmie); Paris in Swing; If We Could Run the Country for a Day (C/L: The Yacht Club Boys [2]); Blow the Whistle [3] (C/L: McClintock, Harry; Sherwin, Sterling); My Mistake [1] [7] (C/L: Coslow, Sam); Keeno, Screeno and You; I'll Follow My Baby; Let Down Your Hair [1] [4] (C/L: Coslow, Sam); Along the Broadway Trail [1] [5] (C: Trivers, Barry; L: Coslow, Sam)

**Notes** Formerly titled SUMMER ROMANCE. [1] Not used. [2] George Kelly, Charles Adler, William B. Mann and James V. Kern. [3] Not written for film. Used in the Republic picture OKLAHOMA ANNIE. [4] Written for SWING HIGH, SWING LOW. [5] Written for EVERY DAY'S A HOLIDAY (1936). [6] Carmen Lombardo and Dave Franklin wrote another song titled "Thrill of a Lifetime." In order for Paramount to use the title they bought the Lombardo and Franklin song and in exchange for Lombardo's agreement to not use his song they put his name on this song from the movie even though he had nothing to do with its composition. [7] From unproduced movie SHADOW OF GLORY.

## 6229 ◆ THRILL OF A ROMANCE
Metro–Goldwyn–Mayer, 1945

**Musical Score** Stoll, George; Jackson, Calvin

**Producer(s)** Pasternak, Joe
**Director(s)** Thorpe, Richard
**Screenwriter(s)** Connell, Richard; Lehman, Gladys

**Cast** Johnson, Van; Williams, Esther; Gifford, Frances; Travers, Henry; Byington, Spring; Melchior, Lauritz; Tommy Dorsey and His Orchestra

**Song(s)** I Should Care (C: Stordahl, Axel; Weston, Paul; L: Cahn, Sammy); Hungarian Rhapsody (C: Liszt, Franz; L: Brent, Earl); Serenade (C: Schubert, Franz; L: Meskill, Jack; Brent, Earl); Please Don't Say No (C: Fain, Sammy; L: Freed, Ralph); Vive L'Amour (C: Traditional; L: Stoll, George; Blane, Ralph; Thompson, Kay); Lonely Night (C: Traditional; L: Connell, Richard)

**Notes** There are also vocals of "Mattinata" and "Vesti La Giubba" by Leoncavallo; "Ich Liebe Dich" by Grieg, Anderson and Forstier; "Because" by Guy d'Hardelot and Edward Teschemacher; and "I Want What I Want When I Want It" by Victor Herbert and Henry Blossom.

## 6230 ◆ THRILL OF BRAZIL
Columbia, 1946

**Composer(s)** Fisher, Doris; Roberts, Allan
**Lyricist(s)** Fisher, Doris; Roberts, Allan
**Choreographer(s)** Cole, Jack; Loring, Eugene

**Producer(s)** Biddell, Sidney
**Director(s)** Simon, S. Sylvan
**Screenwriter(s)** Rivkin, Allen; Clork, Harry; Freeman, Devery

**Cast** Wynn, Keenan; Joslyn, Allyn; Keyes, Evelyn; Miller, Ann; Guizar, Tito; Veloz and Yolanda

**Song(s)** Copacabana [1]; Mucho Dinero (C/L: Madriguera, Enric); Minute Samba (C/L: Madriguera, Enric); A Man Is Brother to a Mule [3]; Linda Mujer (You Never Say Yes) [2] (C/L: Duchesne, Raphael); Thrill of Brazil; That's Good Enough for Me [4]

**Notes** [1] Also in HOLIDAY IN HAVANA. [2] Used with an Irving Caesar lyric in GAY SENORITA. [3] Also in LITTLE MISS BROADWAY (1947) and SINGING SPURS. [4] Sheet music only.

## 6231 ◆ THE THRILL OF IT ALL
Universal, 1963

**Musical Score** De Vol, Frank
**Choreographer(s)** Walters, Charles

**Producer(s)** Hunter, Ross; Melcher, Martin
**Director(s)** Jewison, Norman
**Screenwriter(s)** Reiner, Carl

**Cast** Day, Doris; Garner, James; Francis, Arlene; Andrews, Edward; Pitts, ZaSu; Owen, Reginald; Reid, Elliott; Landau, Lucy; Pearce, Alice; Curran, Pamela; Karath, Kym; Nash, Brian

**Song(s)** The Thrill of It All (C: Schwarzwald, Milton; L: Herbert, Frederick)

## 6232 ◆ THROUGH THE COLORADO ROCKIES
Metro–Goldwyn–Mayer, 1943

**Musical Score** Nussbaum, Joseph; Zeisl, Eric

**Producer(s)** FitzPatrick, James A.

**Cast** FitzPatrick, James A.

**Song(s)** Dear Old Home in Colorado (C/L: Kirk, Lesley)

**Notes** This is a FitzPatrick Traveltalk.

## 6233 ◆ THRU DIFFERENT EYES
Fox, 1929

**Director(s)** Blystone, John; Van Buren, A.H.
**Screenwriter(s)** Barry, Tom; Gropper, Milton Herbert

**Cast** Duncan, Mary; Baxter, Warner; Lowe, Edmund; Sydney, Sylvia; Moorhead, Natalie; Foxe, Earle; Gallagher, Donald; Lake, Florence; Pratt, Purnell; Fetchit, Stepin; Erwin, Stuart

**Song(s)** I'm Savin' All My Lovin' (C/L: Kernell, William; Stamper, Dave)

**Notes** Stuart Erwin has a small role as a reporter.

## 6234 ◆ THUMBS UP
Republic, 1943

**Composer(s)** Styne, Jule
**Lyricist(s)** Cahn, Sammy

**Producer(s)** Cohen, Albert J.
**Director(s)** Santley, Joseph
**Screenwriter(s)** Gill, Frank, Jr.

**Cast** Fraser, Richard; Joyce, Brenda; Lanchester, Elsa; Margetson, Arthur; O'Malley, J. Pat; Leonard, Queenie

**Song(s)** From Here On In; Who Are the British?; Love Is a Corny Thing [1]; Love Is a Balmy Thing; Who Took Me Home Last Night (L: Adamson, Harold) [2]

**Notes** There is also a vocal of "Thumbs Up" by Moe Jaffe, Bert Lee and Jack O'Brien. [1] Also in PISTOL PACKIN' MAMA. [2] Also in CASANOVA IN BURLESQUE, CHANGE OF HEART, HIT PARADE OF 1943 and THE PHANTOM SPEAKS.

## 6235 ◆ THUNDER ALLEY
### Cannon, 1986

**Musical Score**  Folk, Robert

**Producer(s)**  Ewing, Bill
**Director(s)**  Cardone, J.S.
**Screenwriter(s)**  Cardone, J.S.

**Cast**  Wilson, Roger; Schoelen, Jill; McGinnis, Scott; Eilbacher, Cynthia; Garrett, Leif; Brown, Clancy

**Song(s)**  Thunder Alley (C/L: Shelly, Scott; Robinson, Peter)

**Notes**  No cue sheet available.


## 6236 ◆ THUNDERBALL
### United Artists, 1966

**Musical Score**  Barry, John

**Producer(s)**  Broccoli, Albert R.; Saltzman, Harry
**Director(s)**  Young, Terence
**Screenwriter(s)**  McClory, Kevin; Whittingham, Jack
**Source(s)**  *Thunderball* (novel) Fleming, Ian

**Cast**  Connery, Sean; Auger, Claudine; Celi, Adolfo; Lee, Bernard; Maxwell, Lois

**Song(s)**  Thunderball (C: Barry, John; L: Black, Don); Mister Kiss Kiss Bang Bang [1] (C: Barry, John; L: Bricusse, Leslie)

**Notes**  [1] Sheet music only.


## 6237 ◆ THUNDER BELOW
### Paramount, 1932

**Director(s)**  Wallace, Richard
**Screenwriter(s)**  Lovett, Josephine; Buckman, Sidney
**Source(s)**  (novel) Rourke, Thomas

**Cast**  Bankhead, Tallulah; Bickford, Charles; Lukas, Paul; Pallette, Eugene; Finlayson, James; Fenton, Leslie; Forbes, Ralph

**Song(s)**  Mona (C: Johnston, Arthur; L: Molino, Carlos); It Had to Be That Way [1] (C/L: Coslow, Sam)

**Notes**  "I'll Be Glad When You're Dead You Rascal You" by Charles Davenport is also used vocally. [1] Not used in TOO MUCH HARMONY.


## 6238 ◆ THUNDERBOLT
### Paramount, 1929

**Producer(s)**  Fineman, B.P.
**Director(s)**  von Sternberg, Josef
**Screenwriter(s)**  Furthman, Jules; Mankiewicz, Herman J.

**Cast**  Bancroft, George; Arlen, Richard; Wray, Fay; Kohler, Fred; Marshall, Tully; Irving, George

**Song(s)**  Daddy Won't You Please Come Home (C: Spier, Larry; L: Coslow, Sam); Sittin' Around Thinkin' About My Baby [1] (C/L: Coslow, Sam)

**Notes**  There are also vocal renditions of "Sweet Adeline" by Richard H. Gerard and Henry W. Armstrong; "Rock a Bye Baby" by Robert Burdette and Effie Canning; Jack Norworth and Albert Von Tilzer's "Take Me Out to the Ball Game;" "When the Midnight Choo Choo Leaves for Alabam'" by Irving Berlin; "Summertime" by Harry Von Tilzer; "Here Am I - Brokenhearted" by B.G. DeSylva, Lew Brown and Ray Henderson; "Roll Jordan Roll" and "All God's Chillun Got Wings." [1] Sheet music only.


## 6239 ◆ THUNDERBOLT AND LIGHTFOOT
### United Artists, 1974

**Musical Score**  Barton, Dee

**Producer(s)**  Daley, Robert
**Director(s)**  Cimino, Michael
**Screenwriter(s)**  Cimino, Michael

**Cast**  Eastwood, Clint; Bridges, Jeff; Kennedy, George; Lewis, Geoffrey

**Song(s)**  Where Do I Go From Here (C/L: Williams, Paul)


## 6240 ◆ THUNDERING HOOFS
### RKO, 1941

**Musical Score**  Dreyer, Dave; Sawtell, Paul
**Composer(s)**  Whitley, Ray; Rose, Fred
**Lyricist(s)**  Whitley, Ray; Rose, Fred

**Producer(s)**  Gilroy, Bert
**Director(s)**  Selander, Lesley
**Screenwriter(s)**  Franklin, Paul

**Cast**  Holt, Tim; Whitley, Ray; White, Lee "Lasses"; Walters, Luana; Twitchell, Archie

**Song(s)**  Ramble On; Thundering Hoofs; As Along the Trail I Ride


## 6241 ◆ THUNDERING JETS
### Twentieth Century–Fox, 1958

**Producer(s)**  Leewood, Jack
**Director(s)**  Dantine, Helmut
**Screenwriter(s)**  Landis, James

**Cast**  Reason, Rex; Foran, Dick; Dalton, Audrey; Coe, Barry; Class, Buck; Melton, Sid; Conrad, Robert

**Song(s)**  Lonely Love [1] (C: Gertz, Irving; L: Stewart, Larry); Don't Be Afraid [1] (C/L: Gertz, Irving); Blast Off (The Song of the Jet Command) (C/L: Kent, Walter; Walton, Tom)

**Notes**  [1] Instrumental use only.

**6242 ✦ THUNDER IN GOD'S COUNTRY**
Republic, 1951

**Producer(s)**   Tucker, Melville
**Director(s)**   Blair, George
**Screenwriter(s)**   Orloff, Arthur

**Cast**   Allen, Rex; Koko; Kay, Mary Ellen; Ebsen, Buddy; Harvey, Paul

**Song(s)**   Melody of the Plains [1] (C/L: Berlau, Irving; Sive, Leonard M.)

**Notes**   [1] Not written for this film.

**6243 ✦ THUNDERING TRAILS**
Republic, 1942

**Producer(s)**   Gray, Louis
**Director(s)**   English, John
**Screenwriter(s)**   Hall, Norman S.; Yost, Robert
**Source(s)**   characters by MacDonald, William Colt

**Cast**   Tyler, Tom; Steele, Bob; Dodd, Jimmy; Miller, Charles; James, Johnny; Flint, Sam; Taylor, Forrest

**Song(s)**   Minstrel Medicine Man (C/L: Dodd, Jimmy)

**6244 ✦ THUNDER IN THE EAST**
Paramount, 1953

**Musical Score**   Friedhofer, Hugo

**Producer(s)**   Riskin, Everett
**Director(s)**   Vidor, Charles
**Screenwriter(s)**   Swerling, Jo
**Source(s)**   *Rage of the Vultures* (novel) Moorehead, Alan

**Cast**   Ladd, Alan; Kerr, Deborah; Boyer, Charles; Calvet, Corinne; Kellaway, Cecil; Bourneuf, Philip

**Song(s)**   The Ruby and the Pearl [1] (C/L: Livingston, Jay; Evans, Ray); We're Going to See Matilda May [2] (C/L: Boutelje, Phil)

**Notes**   First titled RAGE OF THE VULTURE. [1] Used instrumentally only. [2] Based on "Here We Go Round the Mulberry Bush."

**6245 ✦ THUNDER IN THE SUN**
Paramount, 1959

**Musical Score**   Mockridge, Cyril J.
**Composer(s)**   Mockridge, Cyril J.
**Lyricist(s)**   Washington, Ned

**Producer(s)**   Greene, Clarence
**Director(s)**   Rouse, Russell
**Screenwriter(s)**   Rouse, Russell

**Cast**   Hayward, Susan; Chandler, Jeff; Bergerac, Jacques

**Song(s)**   Thunder in the Sun; Mon Petit [1]

**Notes**   [1] Used instrumentally only.

**6246 ✦ THUNDER RIVER FEUD**
Monogram, 1942

**Musical Score**   Sanucci, Frank

**Producer(s)**   Weeks, George W.
**Director(s)**   Luby, S. Roy
**Screenwriter(s)**   Snell, Earle

**Cast**   Corrigan, Ray; King, John; Terhune, Max; Wiley, Jan; Holmes, Jack H.; Chesebro, George

**Song(s)**   What a Wonderful Day (C/L: George, Jean [1])

**Notes**   [1] Pseudonym for Lucille Nolte.

**6247 ✦ THUNDER ROAD**
United Artists, 1958

**Musical Score**   Marshall, Jack

**Director(s)**   Ripley, Arthur
**Screenwriter(s)**   Phillips, James Atlee; Wise, Walter

**Cast**   Mitchum, Robert; Barry, Gene; Smith, Keely; Mitchum, Jim

**Song(s)**   Thunder Road (C: Marshall, Jack; L: Raye, Don); Whipporwill (C: Mitchum, Robert; L: Raye, Don);

**6248 ✦ THUNDER RUN**
Cannon, 1986

**Musical Score**   Levy, Jay; MacCauley, Matthew

**Producer(s)**   Lynn, Carol
**Director(s)**   Hudson, Gary
**Screenwriter(s)**   Wenger Sr., Clifford; Lynn, Carol

**Cast**   Tucker, Forrest; Ireland, John; Shepherd, John; Whitlow, Jill; Ward, Wally; Lynn, Cheryl M.

**Song(s)**   Born to Rock [1] (C/L: Levy, Jay; Shaddick, Terry); Thunder Run (C/L: Levy, Jay; McCauley, Matthew)

**Notes**   No cue sheet available. [1] Also in PRETTY SMART though credited to Jay Levy and Terry Shaddick.

**6249 ✦ THUNDER TOWN**
PRC, 1946

**Musical Score**   Zahler, Lee

**Producer(s)**   Alexander, Arthur
**Director(s)**   Fraser, Harry
**Screenwriter(s)**   Oliver, James

**Cast**   Steele, Bob; Saylor, Syd; Hall, Ellen; King, Charles; Geary, Bud

**Song(s)**   Trying So Hard to Forget (C/L: Weston, Don)

**6250 ✦ A TICKET TO TOMAHAWK**
Twentieth Century–Fox, 1950

**Musical Score**   Mockridge, Cyril J.
**Choreographer(s)**   Williams, Kenny

**Producer(s)** Bassler, Robert
**Director(s)** Sale, Richard
**Screenwriter(s)** Loos, Mary; Sale, Richard

**Cast** Dailey, Dan; Baxter, Anne; Calhoun, Rory; Brennan, Walter; Kemper, Charles; Gilchrist, Connie; Hunnicutt, Arthur; Wright, Will; Yawlachie, Chief; Sen Yung, Victor

**Song(s)** A Ticket to Tomahawk (On the Colorado Trail) (C: Warren, Harry; L: Gordon, Mack); Time Again (C/L: Sale, Richard); Oh, What a Forward Young Man You Are [1] (C: Read, John; L: Read, John; Darby, Ken); Paddy Works on the Erie (C/L: Sale, Richard)

**Notes** [1] Special lyric written by Darby.

## 6251 ◆ TICKLE ME
### Allied Artists, 1965

**Choreographer(s)** Winters, David

**Producer(s)** Schwalb, Ben
**Director(s)** Taurog, Norman
**Screenwriter(s)** Ullman, Elwood; Bernds, Edward

**Cast** Presley, Elvis; Lane, Jocelyn; Adams, Julie; Mullaney, Jack; Anders, Merry; Williams, Bill; Faulkner, Edward; Gilchrist, Connie

**Song(s)** It's a Long, Lonely Highway (C/L: Pomus, Doc; Shuman, Mort); It Feels So Right (C/L: Weisman, Ben; Wise, Fred); (Such an) Easy Question (C/L: Blackwell, Otis; Scott, Winfield); Dirty, Dirty Feeling (C/L: Leiber, Jerry; Stoller, Mike); Put the Blame on Me (C/L: Blagman, Norman; Wise, Fred; Twomey, Kay); I'm Yours (C/L: Robertson, Don; Blair, Hal); Night Rider (C/L: Pomus, Doc; Shuman, Mort); I Feel That I've Known You Forever (C/L: Pomus, Doc; Jeffreys, Alan); Slowly but Surely (C/L: Wayne, Sid; Weisman, Ben)

**Notes** No cue sheet available.

## 6252 ◆ A TICKLISH AFFAIR
### Metro–Goldwyn–Mayer, 1964

**Musical Score** Stoll, George; Van Eps, Robert
**Composer(s)** Stoll, George; Van Eps, Robert
**Lyricist(s)** Adamson, Harold; Pasternak, Joe [2]

**Producer(s)** Pasternak, Joe
**Director(s)** Sidney, George
**Screenwriter(s)** Flippen, Ruth Brooks
**Source(s)** "Moon Walk" (story) Luther, Barbara

**Cast** Jones, Shirley; Young, Gig; Buttons, Red; Jones, Carolyn; Buchanan, Edgar; Applegate, Eddie; Platt, Edward; Mumy, Billy; Russell, Bryan; Foulk, Robert; Frome, Milton; Robbins, Peter

**Song(s)** Love Is a Ticklish Affair; Tandy [1]

**Notes** [1] Used instrumentally only. [2] Credited on cue sheets not screen credits or sheet music.

## 6253 ◆ . . . TICK . . . TICK . . . TICK . . .
### Metro–Goldwyn–Mayer, 1970

**Musical Score** Jackson, Calvin

**Producer(s)** Nelson, Ralph; Barrett, James Lee
**Director(s)** Nelson, Ralph
**Screenwriter(s)** Barrett, James Lee

**Cast** Brown, Jim; Kennedy, George; March, Fredric; Carlin, Lynn; Stroud, Don; James, Clifton

**Song(s)** Black Magnolia (C/L: Karliski, Steve; Kolber, Larry); Old Before My Time [1] (C/L: Karliski, Steve); Money Can't Buy You Happiness (C/L: Karliski, Steve)

**Notes** There are also vocals of "I'm a Long Gone Daddy" by Hank Williams Sr.; "Tie a Tiger Down" by Sheb Wooley and "Give Me the Hummingbird Line" by Hank Williams Jr. [1] Also in A TIME TO SING.

## 6254 ◆ TIDE OF EMPIRE
### Metro–Goldwyn–Mayer, 1929

**Director(s)** Dwan, Allan
**Screenwriter(s)** Young, Waldemar
**Source(s)** *Tide of Empire* (novel) Kine, Peter Bernard

**Cast** Adoree, Renee; Duryea, George; Kohler, Fred; Collier Jr., William

**Song(s)** Josephita (C: Greer, Jesse; L: Klages, Raymond)

## 6255 ◆ TIGER BY THE TAIL

See CROSS-UP.

## 6256 ◆ TIGER ROSE
### Warner Brothers, 1929

**Director(s)** Fitzmaurice, George
**Screenwriter(s)** Rigby, Gordon; Thew, Harvey
**Source(s)** *Tiger Rose* (play) Mack, Willard

**Cast** Blue, Monte; Velez, Lupe; Withers, Grant; Rin-Tin-Tin; Warner, H.B.; Glass, Gaston; Montana, Bull; Summerville, Slim; Conklin, Heinie; Marshall, Tully

**Song(s)** The Day You Fall in Love (C: Cleary, Michael; L: Magidson, Herb; Washington, Ned)

**Notes** No cue sheet available. A remake of a 1923 film.

## 6257 ◆ THE TIGER WOMAN
### Republic, 1945

**Producer(s)** McGowan, Stuart; McGowan, Dorrell
**Director(s)** Ford, Philip
**Screenwriter(s)** Brown, George Carleton
**Source(s)** "Tale the Dead Man Told" (radio script from the Whistler series) Dunkel, John A.

**Cast** Mara, Adele; Richmond, Kane; Fraser, Richard; Stewart, Peggy; Richards, Addison

**Song(s)** Who Am I [1] (C: Styne, Jule; L: Bullock, Walter)

**Notes**   [1] Also in HIT PARADE OF 1941 and RIDIN' DOWN THE CANYON.

## 6258 ✦ TIGHT SHOES
Universal, 1941

**Musical Score**   Skinner, Frank

**Producer(s)**   Levey, Jules
**Director(s)**   Rogell, Albert S.
**Screenwriter(s)**   Spigelgass, Leonard
**Source(s)**   (story) Runyon, Damon

**Cast**   Howard, John; Crawford, Broderick; Lane, Richard; Carrillo, Leo; Gwynne, Anne; Barnes, Binnie; Hinds, Samuel S.; Howard, Shemp; Gargan, Edward

**Song(s)**   Carmenita McCoy [1] (C: Skinner, Frank; L: Lerner, Sam); Remlo Toothpaste Song (C: Salter, Hans J.; L: Previn, Charles)

**Notes**   There is also a vocal of "You're a Sweetheart" by Harold Adamson and Jimmy McHugh. [1] Also in LA CONGA NIGHTS.

## 6259 ✦ TILL MARRIAGE DO US PART
Franklin Media, 1979

**Musical Score**   Carpi, Fiorenzo

**Producer(s)**   Angelleti, Pio; De Micheli, Adriano
**Director(s)**   Comencini, Luigi
**Screenwriter(s)**   Comencini, Luigi; Perilli, Ivo

**Cast**   Antonelli, Laura; Lionello, Alberto; Placido, Michele; Rochefort, Jean; Schubert, Karin

**Song(s)**   For the Love of Love (C/L: Chalif, Jamie)

**Notes**   No cue sheet available.

## 6260 ✦ TILL THE CLOUDS ROLL BY
Metro–Goldwyn–Mayer, 1946

**Choreographer(s)**   Alton, Robert

**Producer(s)**   Freed, Arthur
**Director(s)**   Whorf, Richard
**Screenwriter(s)**   Connolly, Myles; Holloway, Jean

**Cast**   Allyson, June; Bremer, Lucille [1]; Garland, Judy; Grayson, Kathryn; Heflin, Van; Horne, Lena; Johnson, Van; Martin, Tony; Shore, Dinah; Sinatra, Frank; Walker, Robert; Champion, Gower; Charisse, Cyd; Hayden, Harry; Lansbury, Angela; McDonald, Ray; O'Brien, Virginia; The Wilde Twins

**Notes**   Based on the life of Jerome Kern. Judy Garland's numbers were directed by Vincente Minnelli. There are no original songs in this film. All songs had music by Jerome Kern. Vocals include "Opening Act 1 Show Boat," "Make Believe," "Life Upon the Wicked Stage," "Can't Help Lovin' Dat Man," "The Last Time I Saw Paris," "Ol' Man River," "One More Dance," "All the Things You Are" and "Why Was I Born" with lyric by Oscar Hammerstein II; "How'd You Like to Spoon with Me" with lyric by Edward Laska; "They Didn't Believe Me" with lyric by Herbert Reynolds; "Till the Clouds Roll By" with lyric by Kern, P.G. Wodehouse and Guy Bolton; "The Crickets Are Calling," "Go Little Boat," "Land Where the Good Songs Go," "Siren's Song," "Leave It to Jane," and "Cleopatterer" with lyric by P.G. Wodehouse; "Look for the Silver Lining" with lyric by B.G. DeSylva; "Who" and "Sunny" with lyric by Otto Harbach and Oscar Hammerstein II; "I Won't Dance" with lyric by Oscar Hammerstein II, Otto Harbach, Dorothy Fields and Jimmy McHugh; "She Didn't Say Yes," "Yesterdays" and "Smoke Gets in Your Eyes" with lyric by Harbach; "Long Ago (And Far Away)" with lyric by Ira Gershwin and "A Fine Romance" with lyric by Dorothy Fields. Deleted from the final print were vocals of "Bill" with lyric by P.G. Wodehouse and Oscar Hammerstein II; "Lovely to Look At" with lyric by Dorothy Fields, "I've Told Ev'ry Little Star" with lyric by Oscar Hammerstein II, "The Song Is You" with lyric by Oscar Hammerstein II, "D' Ye Love Me?" with lyric by Oscar Hammerstein II and Otto Harbach and "Dearly Beloved" with lyric by Johnny Mercer. "The Sun Shines Brighter" was recorded but not used. [1] Dubbed by Trudy Erwin.

## 6261 ✦ TILL THE END OF TIME
RKO, 1946

**Producer(s)**   Schary, Dore
**Director(s)**   Dmytryk, Edward
**Screenwriter(s)**   Rivkin, Allen
**Source(s)**   *They Dream of Home* (novel) Busch, Niven

**Cast**   McGuire, Dorothy; Madison, Guy; Mitchum, Robert; Williams, Bill; Tully, Tom; Gargan, William; Porter, Jean; Royle, Selena; Von Zell, Harry

**Song(s)**   Till the End of Time [1] (C/L: Kaye, Buddy; Moseman, Ted)

**Notes**   [1] Based on Chopin's "Polonaise."

## 6262 ✦ TILT
Warner Brothers, 1979

**Musical Score**   Holdridge, Lee
**Composer(s)**   Wray, Bill
**Lyricist(s)**   Wray, Bill

**Producer(s)**   Durand, Rudy
**Director(s)**   Durand, Rudy
**Screenwriter(s)**   Durand, Rudy; Cammell, Donald

**Cast**   Shields, Brooke; Marshall, Ken; Durning, Charles; Crawford, John

**Song(s)**   Long Road to Texas [1] (C/L: Neely, Sam; Durand, Rudy); Rock 'N' Roll Rodeo; Melody Man; Where Were You?; Don't Let the Rain Get to You (C/L: Bishop, Randy; Gwinn, Marty); My Lady [1] (C/L: Marshall; Stoddard; Morgan); You Really Didn't Have to

Do It (C/L: Bishop, Randy; Gwinn, Marty); Friends; Don't Stop the Music; My Music; Pinball, That's All

**Notes** [1] Visual vocal use. All others background vocals.

## 6263 ✦ 'TIL WE MEET AGAIN
### Warner Brothers–First National, 1940

**Musical Score** Roemheld, Heinz

**Producer(s)** Warner, Jack L.; Wallis, Hal B.
**Director(s)** Goulding, Edmund
**Screenwriter(s)** Duff, Warren
**Source(s)** "S.S. Atlantic" (story) Lord, Robert

**Cast** Oberon, Merle; Brent, George; O'Brien, Pat; Fitzgerald, Geraldine; Barnes, Binnie; McHugh, Frank; Blore, Eric; O'Neill, Henry; Reeves, George; Wilcox, Frank; Lloyd, Doris; Gateson, Marjorie; Toomey, Regis

**Song(s)** If I Had My Way (C/L: Kendis, James; Klein, James); Where Was I (C: Harling, W. Franke; L: Dubin, Al)

**Notes** A remake of the 1932 film ONE WAY PASSAGE. "Aloha Oe" by Queen Liliuokalini is used as a visual vocal. There is also a vocal of "Song of the Islands" by Charles E. King.

## 6264 ✦ TIMBERJACK
### Republic, 1955

**Composer(s)** Carmichael, Hoagy

**Producer(s)** Kane, Joseph
**Director(s)** Kane, Joseph
**Screenwriter(s)** Rivkin, Allen
**Source(s)** *Timberjack* (novel) Cushman, Dan

**Cast** Hayden, Sterling; Ralston, Vera Hruba; Brian, David; Menjou, Adolphe; Carmichael, Hoagy; Wills, Chill; Cook Jr., Elisha

**Song(s)** What Ev'ry Young Girl Should Know (L: Webster, Paul Francis); He's Dead But He Won't Lie Down [2] (L: Mercer, Johnny); The Tambourine Waltz [1] (L: Webster, Paul Francis); Timberjack (C: Young, Victor; L: Washington, Ned)

**Notes** [1] Used instrumentally only. [2] Also used in THE KEYSTONE GIRL (Paramount).

## 6265 ✦ TIMBER QUEEN
### Paramount, 1944

**Producer(s)** Pine, William; Thomas, William
**Director(s)** McDonald, Frank
**Screenwriter(s)** Shane, Maxwell; Lowe, Edward T.

**Cast** Arlen, Richard; Hughes, Mary Beth; Havoc, June

**Song(s)** You're the One for Me [1] (C: McHugh, Jimmy; L: Mercer, Johnny)

**Notes** [1] Also in YOU'RE THE ONE.

## 6266 ✦ TIMBER TRAIL
### Republic, 1948

**Producer(s)** Tucker, Melville
**Director(s)** Ford, Philip
**Screenwriter(s)** Williams, Bob

**Cast** Hale, Monte; Roberts, Lynne; Burke, James; Barcroft, Roy; Acuff, Eddie

**Song(s)** The Timber Trail [1] (C/L: Spencer, Tim); When Your Heart's on Easy Street [2] (C: Ohman, Phil; L: Washington, Ned)

**Notes** There is also a vocal of "Nelly Bly" by Stephen Foster. [1] Also in YELLOW ROSE OF TEXAS. [2] Also in HANDS ACROSS THE BORDER.

## 6267 ✦ TIME BANDITS
### Avco Embassy, 1981

**Musical Score** Moran, Mike

**Producer(s)** Gilliam, Terry
**Director(s)** Gilliam, Terry
**Screenwriter(s)** Palin, Michael; Gilliam, Terry

**Cast** Cleese, John; Connery, Sean; Duvall, Shelley; Helmond, Katherine; Holm, Ian; Palin, Michael; Richardson, Ralph; Vaughn, Peter; Warner, David; Rapporport, David; Warnock, Craig

**Song(s)** Dreamaway (C/L: Harrison, George)

**Notes** No cue sheet available.

## 6268 ✦ TIME OUT FOR RHYTHM
### Columbia, 1941

**Composer(s)** Chaplin, Saul
**Lyricist(s)** Cahn, Sammy
**Choreographer(s)** Prinz, LeRoy; Da Pron, Louis

**Producer(s)** Starr, Irving
**Director(s)** Salkow, Sidney
**Screenwriter(s)** Hartmann, Edmund L.; Lawrence, Bert
**Source(s)** (play) Ruben, Alex

**Cast** Vallee, Rudy; The Three Stooges [1]; Glen Gray and His Casa Loma Band; Merrill, Joan; Miller, Ann; Jenkins, Allen; Lane, Rosemary; Brenda and Cobina [2]; Andrews, Stanley; Six Hits and a Miss; Eddie Durant's Rhumba Orchestra

**Song(s)** Did Anyone Ever Tell You; Boogie Woogie Man; Time Out for Rhythm; Twiddlin' My Thumbs; Obviously the Gentleman Prefers to Dance; As If You Didn't Know; The Rio De Janeiro; Shows How Wrong a Gal Can Be [3]

**Notes** Originally titled SHOW BUSINESS. [1] Moe Howard, Larry Fine and Jerry Howard. [2] Blanche Stewart and Elvis Allman. [3] Not used.

**6269 ◆ TIMES SQUARE**
AFD, 1980

**Lyricist(s)**   Brackman, Jacob

**Producer(s)**   Stigwood, Robert; Brackman, Jacob
**Director(s)**   Moyle, Alan
**Screenwriter(s)**   Brackman, Jacob

**Cast**   Curry, Tim; Alvarado, Trini; Johnson, Robin; Coffield, Peter; Berghof, Herbert; Margulies, David; Pinero, Miguel; Stevens, Ronald "Smokey"

**Song(s)**   Damn Dog (C: Mernit, Billy); Your Daughter Is One (C: Mernit, Billy; Ross, Norman); Help Me (C/L: Gibb, Robin; Weaver, Blue)

**Notes**   No cue sheet available.

**6270 ◆ TIMES SQUARE LADY**
Metro–Goldwyn–Mayer, 1935

**Musical Score**   Ward, Edward
**Composer(s)**   Tomlin, Pinky
**Lyricist(s)**   Grier, Jimmy; Poe, Coy

**Producer(s)**   Hubbard, Lucien
**Director(s)**   Seitz, George B.
**Screenwriter(s)**   Cohen, Albert J.; Shannon, Robert T.

**Cast**   Taylor, Robert; Bruce, Virginia; Tomlin, Pinky; Twelvetrees, Helen; Jewell, Isabel; Pendleton, Nat; Kolker, Henry; LaRue, Jack; Hatton, Raymond; Hopton, Russell; Kohler, Fred; Elliott, Robert

**Song(s)**   The Object of My Affection; What's the Reason [1]

**Notes**   [1] Earl Hatch also credited with music on sheet music.

**6271 ◆ TIMES SQUARE PLAYBOY**
Warner Brothers, 1936

**Producer(s)**   Foy, Bryan
**Director(s)**   McGann, William
**Screenwriter(s)**   Chanslor, Roy
**Source(s)**   *The Hometowners* (play) Cohan, George M.

**Cast**   William, Warren; Travis, June; MacLane, Barton; Lockhart, Gene; Lockhart, Kathleen; Purcell, Dick; Reynolds, Craig; Bates, Granville; Vaughan, Dorothy

**Song(s)**   Looking for Trouble (C: Jerome, M.K.; L: Jasmyn, Joan)

**Notes**   Released in Great Britain as HIS BEST MAN. A remake of a 1928 picture.

**6272 ◆ THE TIME, THE PLACE, AND THE GIRL (1929)**
Warner Brothers, 1929

**Director(s)**   Bretherton, Howard
**Screenwriter(s)**   Lord, Robert

**Source(s)**   *The Time, the Place, and the Girl* (musical) Hough, Will M.; Adams, Frank R.; Howard, Joseph E.

**Cast**   Withers, Grant; Compson, Betty; Kirkwood, James; Oakland, Vivian; Hartman, Gretchen; Haisman, Irene; Davidson, John; King, Gerald; Roach, Bert

**Song(s)**   I Wonder Who's Kissing Her Now [1] (C: Howard, Joseph E.; L: Hough, Will M.; Adams, Frank R.); Collegiate (C/L: Bonx, Nat; Jaffe, Moe); Collegiana (C: McHugh, Jimmy; L: Fields, Dorothy); Doin' the Raccoon (C: Coots, J. Fred; L: Klages, Raymond; Magidson, Herb); Fashionette (C: King, Robert; L: Glogau, Jack); Jack and Jill (C: Spier, Larry; L: Coslow, Sam); How Many Times (C/L: Berlin, Irving); Everything I Do I Do For You (C/L: Sherman, Al); If You Could Care (C/L: Goetz, E. Ray; Wimperis, Arthur; Darewski, Herman); Honeymoon (C: Howard, Joseph E.; L: Hough, Will M.; Adams, Frank R.)

**Notes**   No cue sheet available. [1] From 1909 musical THE PRINCE OF TONIGHT.

**6273 ◆ THE TIME, THE PLACE AND THE GIRL (1946)**
Warner Brothers, 1946

**Musical Score**   Hollander, Frederick
**Composer(s)**   Schwartz, Arthur
**Lyricist(s)**   Robin, Leo
**Choreographer(s)**   Prinz, LeRoy

**Producer(s)**   Gottlieb, Alex
**Director(s)**   Butler, David
**Screenwriter(s)**   Swann, Francis; Johnston, Agnes Christine; Starling, Lynn

**Cast**   Morgan, Dennis; Carson, Jack; Paige, Janis; Vickers, Martha [1]

**Song(s)**   I Happened to Walk Down First Street; A Solid Citizen of the Solid South; Oh But I Do; Through a Thousand Dreams; A Gal in Calico; A Rainy Night in Rio

**Notes**   [1] Dubbed by Sally Mueller.

**6274 ◆ A TIME TO LOVE AND A TIME TO DIE**
Universal, 1958

**Musical Score**   Rozsa, Miklos

**Producer(s)**   Arthur, Robert
**Director(s)**   Sirk, Douglas
**Screenwriter(s)**   Jannings, Orin
**Source(s)**   *Time to Love and a Time to Die* (novel) Remarque, Erich Maria

**Cast**   Pulver, Lilo; Gavin, John; Wynn, Keenan; Mahoney, Jock; DeFore, Don; Remarque, Erich Marie; Borsche, Dieter; Wieck, Dorothea; Kinski, Klaus

**Song(s)**   A Time to Love (C: Rozsa, Miklos; L: Henderson, Charles)

### 6275 ✦ A TIME TO SING
Metro–Goldwyn–Mayer, 1968

**Musical Score** Karger, Fred

**Producer(s)** Katzman, Sam
**Director(s)** Dreifuss, Arthur
**Screenwriter(s)** Kent, Robert E.; Hampton, Orville H.

**Cast** Williams Jr., Hank; Fabares, Shelley; Begley, Ed; Robinson, Charles; Martin, D'Urville; Woods, Donald; Ward, Clara; Haymes, Dick; The X-L's

**Song(s)** Soon One Morning (C/L: Ward, Clara); A Time to Sing (C/L: Scoggins, John); Old Before My Time [1] (C/L: Karliski, Steve); Next Time I Say Goodbye I'm Leavin' (C/L: Kusik, Larry; Snyder, Eddie); Summer Love in the Sand (C/L: Guy, Robert; Martin, Gary); Rock in My Shoe (C/L: Williams Jr., Hank); Money Can't Buy Happiness (C/L: Karliski, Steve); A Man Is On His Own (C/L: Williams Jr., Hank; Scoggins, John); There's Gotta Be Much More to Life than You (C/L: Karliski, Steve); It's All Over but the Crying (C/L: Williams Jr., Hank); Give Me the Humming Bird Line (C/L: Williams Jr., Hank)

**Notes** [1] Also in . . . TICK . . . TICK . . . TICK . . .

### 6276 ✦ TIN MEN
Touchstone, 1986

**Musical Score** Steele, David; Cox, Andy
**Composer(s)** Steele, David
**Lyricist(s)** Gift, Roland

**Producer(s)** Johnson, Mark
**Director(s)** Levinson, Barry
**Screenwriter(s)** Levinson, Barry

**Cast** Dreyfuss, Richard; DeVito, Danny; Hershey, Barbara; Mahoney, John; Brock, Stanley; Cassel, Seymour; Kirby, Bruno; Gayle, Jackie; Walsh, J.T.; Tucker, Michael; Craven, Matt; Willis, Michael S.; Billings, Josh; Rappaport, Barbara

**Song(s)** Good Thing; As Hard As It Is; Social Securtiy; Tell Me What

### 6277 ✦ TIN PAN ALLEY
Twentieth Century–Fox, 1940

**Choreographer(s)** Felix, Seymour

**Producer(s)** Zanuck, Darryl F.
**Director(s)** Lang, Walter
**Screenwriter(s)** Logue, Helen; Ellis, Robert

**Cast** Faye, Alice; Grable, Betty; Oakie, Jack; Payne, John; Jenkins, Allen; Ralston, Esther; Loder, John; Cook Jr., Elisha; Keating, Fred; Gilbert, Billy; The Nicholas Brothers

**Song(s)** K-K-K-Katy [1] (C: O'Hara, Geoffrey; L: O'Hara, Geoffrey; Gordon, Mack); Old Folks at Home [1] (C: Foster, Stephen; L: Foster, Stephen; Gordon, Mack); You Say the Sweetest Things Baby (C: Warren, Harry; L: Gordon, Mack); Harem Days (C/L: Rainger, Ralph); The Sheik of Araby [2] (C: Snyder, Ted; L: Smith, Harry B.; Wheeler, Francis; Robin, Leo; Henderson, Charles)

**Notes** Tin Pan Alley tunes, not written for this picture, which are given vocal treatments of more than a minute include: "Moonlight Bay" by Percy Wenrich and Edward Madden; "Honeysuckle Rose" by Thomas "Fats" Waller and Andy Razaf; "Moonlight and Roses" by Edwin Lemare, Ben Black and Neil Moret; "I Want a Girl—Just Like the Girl That Married Dear Old Dad" by William Dillon and Harry Von Tilzer; "America I Love You" by Archie Gottler and Edgar Leslie and "Goodbye Broadway Hello France" by Billy Baskette, C. Francis Reisner and Benny Davis. "Get Out and Get Under" by Grant Clarke, Edgar Leslie and Maurice Abrahams was recorded but not used. [1] Gordon contributed the special lyrics. [2] Henderson and Robin contributed special lyrics.

### 6278 ✦ TIN PAN ALLEY TEMPOS
Universal, 1945

**Song(s)** Swingin' for My Supper (C/L: Dodd, Jimmy); Popcorn Poppin' Time (C/L: Dodd, Jimmy)

**Notes** Short subject. Only original songs listed for this short.

### 6279 ✦ THE TIN STAR
Paramount, 1957

**Musical Score** Bernstein, Elmer

**Producer(s)** Perlberg, William; Seaton, George
**Director(s)** Mann, Anthony
**Screenwriter(s)** Nichols, Dudley

**Cast** Fonda, Henry; Perkins, Anthony; Palmer, Betsy; Ray, Michael; Brand, Neville; McIntire, John; Van Cleef, Lee

**Song(s)** The Tin Star [1] (C: Bernstein, Elmer; L: Brooks, Jack)

**Notes** [1] Instrumental use only.

### 6280 ✦ TINTORERA
Hemdale Leidsure-Conacine, 1978

**Musical Score** Poledouris, Basil

**Producer(s)** Green, Gerald
**Director(s)** Cardona Jr., Rene
**Screenwriter(s)** Bravo, Ramon; Cardona Jr., Rene
**Source(s)** (novel) Bravo, Ramon

**Cast** George, Susan; Lewis, Fiona; Ashley, Jennifer; Stiglitz, Hugo; Garcia, Andres

**Song(s)** Main title (C: Poledouris, Basil; L: Connors, Carol; Robbins, Ayn); Incidental Music (C/L: Poledouris, Basil)

**Notes** No cue sheet available.

## 6281 ✦ THE TIOGA KID
Pathe, 1948

**Musical Score** Greene, Walter

**Producer(s)** Thomas, Jerry
**Director(s)** Taylor, Ray
**Screenwriter(s)** Repp, Ed Earl

**Cast** Dean, Eddie; Ates, Roscoe; Holt, Jennifer; Bennett, Lee; Moore, Dennis; Andy Parker and His Plainsmen

**Song(s)** Way Back in Oklahoma [1] (C/L: Dean, Eddie; Bond, Johnny)

**Notes** Vocals and instrumentals are not indicated on the cue sheet. [1] Also in TUMBLEWEED TRAIL (PRC) and, with credit to Johnny Bond only, SIX LESSONS FROM MADAME LA ZONGA (Universal).

## 6282 ✦ THE TOAST OF NEW ORLEANS
Metro–Goldwyn–Mayer, 1950

**Musical Score** Stoll, George; Sendrey, Al
**Composer(s)** Brodszky, Nicholas
**Lyricist(s)** Cahn, Sammy
**Choreographer(s)** Loring, Eugene

**Producer(s)** Pasternak, Joe
**Director(s)** Taurog, Norman
**Screenwriter(s)** Gomberg, Sy; Wells, George

**Cast** Grayson, Kathryn; Lanza, Mario; Niven, David; Naish, J. Carrol; Mitchell, James; Hageman, Richard; Sundberg, Clinton; Arno, Sig; Moreno, Rita; Vincent, Romo

**Song(s)** The Toast of New Orleans; Be My Love [1]; The Tina-Lina; I'll Never Love You; Bayou Lullaby; Boom Biddy Boom Boom [2]; Brindisi [2] (C: Verdi, Giuseppe; L: Hirsch, Walter); La Fleur Que Tu M'Avais Jetee [2] (C: Bizet, Georges; L: Davies, Carolyn); O Paradis Sorti de Londe [3] (C: Meyerbeer, Giacomo; L: Hirsch, Walter)

**Notes** There are also vocals of "Ave Maris Stella" and "O Luce di Quest' Anima" from LINDA DI CHAMOUNIX by Donizetti; "Je Suis Titania" from MIGNON by Thomas; "La Ci Darem la Mano" from DON GIOVANNI by Mozart; "Flower Song" from CARMEN by Bizet; "Regnava nel Silenzio" from LUCIA DI LAMMERMOOR by Donizetti; "O Paradiso" from L'AFRICAINE by Meyerbeer; "Shadow Song" from DINORAH by Meyerbeer; "M'Appari" from MARTHA by Flotow; "Libiamo" from LA TRAVIATA by Verdi and "Duet - Finale Act I" from

MME. BUTTERFLY by Puccini. [1] Also in BECAUSE OF YOU and LOOKING FOR LOVE. [2] Sheet music only. [3] Used but without the Hirsch lyrics.

## 6283 ✦ TOAST OF NEW YORK
RKO, 1937

**Musical Score** Shilkret, Nathaniel
**Composer(s)** Shilkret, Nathaniel
**Lyricist(s)** Wrubel, Allie

**Producer(s)** Small, Edward
**Director(s)** Lee, Rowland V.
**Screenwriter(s)** Nichols, Dudley; Twist, John; Sayre, Joel
**Source(s)** *Book of Daniel Drew* (novel) White, Bouck; "Robber Barons" (story) Josephson, Matthew

**Cast** Arnold, Edward; Grant, Cary; Farmer, Frances; Oakie, Jack

**Song(s)** Ooh! La! La! [2]; The First Time I Saw You [1]; Temptation Waltz (L: Gilbert, L. Wolfe)

**Notes** [1] Also in THE FALCON TAKES OVER, LAW OF THE UNDERWORLD and OUT OF THE PAST. [2] Also in CODE OF THE WEST.

## 6284 ✦ TO BEAT THE BAND
RKO, 1935

**Composer(s)** Malneck, Matty
**Lyricist(s)** Mercer, Johnny
**Choreographer(s)** White, Sam

**Producer(s)** Myers, Zion
**Director(s)** Stoloff, Benjamin
**Screenwriter(s)** James, Rian

**Cast** Herbert, Hugh; Broderick, Helen; Pryor, Roger; Keating, Fred; Blore, Eric; Brooks, Phyllis; Poe, Evelyn; Mercer, Johnny; Mayer, Ray; Hodges, John; Lamont, Sonny; Graham, Ronny [1]; The Original California Collegians

**Song(s)** I Saw Her at Eight O'Clock; Santa Claus Came in the Spring (C: Mercer, Johnny); Eeny Meeny Miney Mo; If You Were Mine; Meet Miss America

**Notes** Billed as Ronald Graham.

## 6285 ✦ TO BE OR NOT TO BE
Twentieth Century–Fox, 1983

**Musical Score** Morris, John

**Producer(s)** Brooks, Mel
**Director(s)** Johnson, Alan
**Screenwriter(s)** Meehan, Thomas; Graham, Ronny

**Cast** Brooks, Mel; Bancroft, Anne; Matheson, Tim; Durning, Charles; Ferrer, Jose; Gaynes, George; Lloyd, Christopher; Stadlen, Lewis J.; Haake, James; Graham, Ronny; Reiner, Estelle

**Song(s)** Ladies (C/L: Brooks, Mel; Graham, Ronny); A Little Peace (C/L: Brooks, Mel; Graham, Ronny)

**Notes** No cue sheet available. A remake of the 1942 film.

## 6286 ✦ TOBY TYLER OR TWO WEEKS WITH A CIRCUS
### Disney, 1959

**Musical Score** Baker, Buddy
**Composer(s)** Baker, Buddy
**Lyricist(s)** Jackman, Bob

**Producer(s)** Walsh, Bill
**Director(s)** Barton, Charles
**Screenwriter(s)** Walsh, Bill; Hayward, Lillie
**Source(s)** *Toby Tyler* (novel) Kaler, James Otis

**Cast** Corcoran, Kevin; Calvin, Henry; Sheldon, Gene; Sweeney, Bob; Eastham, Richard; Mr. Stubbs; Wallace, Oliver

**Song(s)** Biddle Dee Dee (I Go My Way) (The Bindle Stick Song) (C/L: Lampert, Diane; Loring, Richard); Little Toby [1]; Fi-Fi [1]

**Notes** [1] Used instrumentally only.

## 6287 ✦ TO CATCH A THIEF
### Paramount, 1955

**Musical Score** Murray, Lyn

**Producer(s)** Hitchcock, Alfred
**Director(s)** Hitchcock, Alfred
**Screenwriter(s)** Hayes, John Michael
**Source(s)** *To Catch a Thief* (novel) Dodge, David

**Cast** Grant, Cary; Kelly, Grace; Vanel, Charles; Landis, Jessie Royce; Martinelli, Jean; Williams, John; Anys, Georgette

**Song(s)** Your Kiss [1] (C/L: Auld, Georgie; Auld, Pat; Cates, George); Unexpectedly [2] (C: Murray, Lyn; Heymann, Werner)

**Notes** [1] Song used instrumentally only. [2] Sheet music only.

## 6288 ✦ TODAY WE LIVE
### Metro–Goldwyn–Mayer, 1933

**Director(s)** Hawks, Howard
**Screenwriter(s)** Faulkner, William; Fitzgerald, Edith; Taylor, Dwight

**Cast** Crawford, Joan; Cooper, Gary; Young, Robert; Tone, Franchot; Karns, Roscoe; Hale, Louise Closser

**Song(s)** The Young Observer [1] (C: Traditional; L: Snell, Dave)

**Notes** [1] To the tune of "My Bonnie."

## 6289 ✦ TO DOROTHY, A SON

See CASH ON DELIVERY.

## 6290 ✦ TO EACH HIS OWN
### Paramount, 1946

**Producer(s)** Brackett, Charles
**Director(s)** Leisen, Mitchell
**Screenwriter(s)** Brackett, Charles; Thery, Jacques

**Cast** de Havilland, Olivia; Lund, John; Culver, Roland; Anderson, Mary; Terry, Phillip; Welles, Virginia; Goodwin, Bill; Faylen, Frank

**Song(s)** To Each His Own [1] (C/L: Livingston, Jay; Evans, Ray)

**Notes** [1] Not used in picture. It was used instrumentally and sometimes vocally in THE BIRDS AND THE BEES, THE LEATHER SAINT, THE SEARCH FOR BRIDEY MURPHY and I MARRIED A MONSTER FROM OUTER SPACE.

## 6291 ✦ TOGETHER?
### Leisure Entertainment, 1979

**Musical Score** Bacharach, Burt
**Composer(s)** Bacharach, Burt
**Lyricist(s)** Anka, Paul

**Producer(s)** Bozzacchi, Gianni
**Director(s)** Balducci, Armenia
**Screenwriter(s)** Balducci, Armenia; De Concini, Ennio

**Cast** Bisset, Jacqueline; Schell, Maximilian; Guerrtore, Monica; Stamp, Terence

**Song(s)** I've Got My Mind Made Up; I Don't Need You Anymore; Find Love; In Tune (L: Titus, Libby)

**Notes** No cue sheet available.

## 6292 ✦ TO HARE IS HUMAN
### Warner Brothers, 1956

**Musical Score** Franklyn, Milton J.

**Director(s)** Jones, Chuck

**Cast** Bunny, Bugs; Coyote, Wile E.

**Song(s)** Carrots Wait for No One (C: Franklyn, Milton J.; L: Foster, Warren)

**Notes** Merrie Melodie.

## 6293 ✦ TO HAVE AND HAVE NOT
### Warner Brothers, 1945

**Composer(s)** Carmichael, Hoagy

**Producer(s)** Hawks, Howard
**Director(s)** Hawks, Howard
**Screenwriter(s)** Furthman, Jules; Faulkner, William

**Source(s)**   *To Have and Have Not* (novel) Hemingway, Ernest

**Cast**   Bogart, Humphrey; Brennan, Walter; Bacall, Lauren; Moran, Dolores; Carmichael, Hoagy; Molnar, Walter; Leonard, Sheldon; Seymour, Dan

**Song(s)**   How Little We Know (L: Mercer, Johnny); Behold How Beautiful (L: Adams, Stanley); Hong Kong Blues (L: Carmichael, Hoagy); Baltimore Oriole [1] (L: Webster, Paul Francis)

**Notes**   There is also a vocal of "Am I Blue" by Harry Akst and Grant Clarke. [1] Sheet music only.

## 6294 ✦ TO HELL AND BACK
### Universal, 1955

**Producer(s)**   Rosenberg, Aaron
**Director(s)**   Hibbs, Jesse
**Screenwriter(s)**   Doud, Gil
**Source(s)**   *To Hell and Back* (book) Murphy, Audie

**Cast**   Murphy, Audie; Thompson, Marshall; Palmer, Gregg; Drake, Charles; Kelly, Jack; Kohner, Susan; Castle, Richard; Field, Mary

**Song(s)**   Dog Face Soldier [1] (C/L: Gold, Bert; Hart, Ken)

**Notes**   [1] Jack Dolph also credited on cue sheet.

## 6295 ✦ TO KILL A DRAGON
### United Artists, 1967

**Musical Score**   Springer, Phil
**Composer(s)**   Springer, Phil
**Lyricist(s)**   Kaye, Buddy

**Producer(s)**   Schenck, Aubrey
**Director(s)**   Moore, Michael
**Screenwriter(s)**   Schenk, George; Marks, William

**Cast**   Palance, Jack; Lamas, Fernando; Ray, Aldo; Gur, Alizia

**Song(s)**   Kill a Dragon; There's Love in Your Eyes [1]

**Notes**   [1] It is not known if this is performed instrumentally or vocally.

## 6296 ✦ TOKYO AFTER DARK
### Paramount, 1959

**Musical Score**   Courage, Alexander

**Producer(s)**   Herman, Norman T.; Segal, Marvin
**Director(s)**   Herman, Norman T.
**Screenwriter(s)**   Herman, Norman T.; Segal, Marvin

**Cast**   Kobi, Michi; Long, Richard; Dobkin, Lawrence; Dubov, Paul; Shimada, Teru

**Song(s)**   Honto Ni (Honestly) (C/L: Courage, Alexander)

**Notes**   The film was orginally titled DATELINE TOKYO. The Japanese folk song "Soran Bushi" was adapted by Alexander Courage and Michi Kobi and used vocally.

## 6297 ✦ TOKYO FILE NO. 212
### RKO, 1951

**Musical Score**   Glasser, Albert

**Producer(s)**   Breakston, George; McGowan, Dorrell
**Director(s)**   McGowan, Dorrell; McGowan, Stuart
**Screenwriter(s)**   McGowan, Dorrell; McGowan, Stuart

**Cast**   Payton, Robert [1]; Marly, Florence; Haida, Katsuhaiko; Otani, Reiko; Saito, Tatsuo; Nakamura, Satoshi

**Song(s)**   Oyedo Boogie Woogie (C/L: Yoshikawa, Shisuo); Yankee Doodle Parody (C/L: McGowan, Stuart)

**Notes**   [1] Name changed from Lee Frederick.

## 6298 ✦ TO LIVE AND DIE IN L.A.
### MGM/UA, 1985

**Musical Score**   Feldman, Nicholas; Hues, Jack
**Composer(s)**   Feldman, Nicholas; Hues, Jack
**Lyricist(s)**   Feldman, Nicholas; Hues, Jack

**Producer(s)**   Levin, Irving H.
**Director(s)**   Friedkin, William
**Screenwriter(s)**   Friedkin, William; Petievich, Gerald
**Source(s)**   (novel) Petievich, Gerald

**Cast**   Petersen, William L.; Dafoe, Willem; Pankow, John; Feuer, Debra

**Song(s)**   To Live and Die in L.A.; Coyote (C/L: Kinman, Tony; Kinman, Chip); Cold Day in Hell (C/L: Rush, Otis); Flashing Back to Happiness; Lullaby; The Red Stare; Uphill Climb to the Bottom (C/L: Envil, F.); Laudy! Laudy! (C/L: Wells, Junior); The Conductor Wore Black (C/L: Kinman, Tony; Kinman, Chip); Rank & File (C/L: Kinman, Tony; Escovedo, Alejandro); Dance Hall Days; Wake Up Stop Dreaming' L.A. L.A. (C/L: Leiber, Jerry; Leiber, Jed); Independent Intavenshan (C/L: Johnson, Lynton Kwesi); Wait

## 6299 ✦ TOMBOY AND THE CHAMP
### Universal, 1961

**Musical Score**   Shores, Richard
**Composer(s)**   Reynolds, Tommy; Lightfoot, William
**Lyricist(s)**   Reynolds, Tommy; Lightfoot, William

**Producer(s)**   Reynolds, Tommy; Lightfoot, William
**Director(s)**   Lyon, Francis D.
**Screenwriter(s)**   Cooke, Virginia M.

**Cast**   Moore, Candy; Johnson, Ben; White, Jesse; Kirkpatrick, Jess; Smith, Christine; Bernath, Paul; Sherry, Norman; Allen, Rex; Tibbs, Casey; Naill, Jerry

**Song(s)** Get Ready with the Ribbon Judge; Who Says Animals Don't Cry; Barbecue Rock (C/L: Wilkes, Elsie Pierce)

**Notes** No cue sheet available.

### 6300 ✦ TOM, DICK AND HARRY
RKO, 1941

**Musical Score** Webb, Roy

**Producer(s)** Sisk, Robert
**Director(s)** Kanin, Garson
**Screenwriter(s)** Jarrico, Paul

**Cast** Rogers, Ginger; Murphy, George; Marshal, Alan; Meredith, Burgess; Silvers, Phil; Cunningham, Joe; Seymour, Jane; Lonergan, Lenore; Lester, Vicki

**Song(s)** Tom Collins (C/L: Webb, Roy; Rose, Gene)

### 6301 ✦ TOMMY
Columbia, 1975

**Composer(s)** Townsend, Pete
**Lyricist(s)** Townsend, Pete
**Choreographer(s)** Gregory, Gillian

**Producer(s)** Stigwood, Robert; Russell, Ken
**Director(s)** Russell, Ken
**Screenwriter(s)** Russell, Ken
**Source(s)** *Tommy* (record album) Townsend, Pete

**Cast** Ann-Margaret; Reed, Oliver; Daltrey, Roger; John, Elton; Clapton, Eric; Moon, Keith; Nicholson, Jack; Powell, Robert; Nicholas, Paul; Turner, Tina; Russell, Victoria

**Song(s)** Captain Walker; It's a Boy; Bernie's Holiday Camp; What About the Boy; Amazing Journey; Christmas; Eyesight to the World (C/L: Williamson, Willie "Sonny Boy"); Acid Queen; Do You Think It's Allright; Cousin Kevin (C/L: Entwistle, J.); Fiddle About (C/L: Entwistle, J.); Sparks; Extra! Extra!; Pinball Wizard; Champagne; There's a Doctor I've Found; Rex Beans; Go to the Mirror; Tommy Can You Hear Me; Smash the Mirror; I'm Free; Miracle Cure; Sally Simpson; Mother and Son; I'm a Sensation; Welcome; Hell's Angels; Tommy's Holiday Camp (C/L: Moon, Keith); We're Not Gonna Take It; Deceived; See Me, Feel Me; Listening to You

### 6302 ✦ TOMORROW IS FOREVER
RKO, 1946

**Musical Score** Steiner, Max

**Producer(s)** Lewis, David
**Director(s)** Pichel, Irving
**Screenwriter(s)** Coffee, Lenore
**Source(s)** *Tomorrow Is Forever* (novel) Bristow, Gwen

**Cast** Wood, Natalie [1]; Welles, Orson; Colbert, Claudette; Brent, George; Long, Richard; Watson, Lucile; Wood, Douglas; Howe, Sonny

**Song(s)** Tomorrow Is Forever (C: Steiner, Max; L: Tobias, Charles)

**Notes** There is also a vocal of "Till We Meet Again" by Raymond Egan and Richard Whiting. [1] Film debut.

### 6303 ✦ TOM SAWYER
United Artists, 1973

**Musical Score** Sherman, Richard M.; Sherman, Robert B.
**Composer(s)** Sherman, Richard M.; Sherman, Robert B.
**Lyricist(s)** Sherman, Robert B.; Sherman, Richard M.
**Choreographer(s)** Daniels, Danny

**Producer(s)** Jacobs, Arthur P.
**Director(s)** Taylor, Don
**Screenwriter(s)** Sherman, Robert B.; Sherman, Richard M.
**Source(s)** *The Adventures of Tom Sawyer* (novel) Twain, Mark

**Cast** Whitaker, Johnny; East, Jeff; Holm, Celeste; Oates, Warren; Foster, Jodie

**Song(s)** Tom Sawyer; Gratification; Man's Gotta Be; How Come; If'n I Was God; River Song; Free Bootin'; Soliloquy; Hannibal Mo-Zou-ree [1]

**Notes** [1] Sheet music only.

### 6304 ✦ TOM THUMB
Metro–Goldwyn–Mayer, 1959

**Musical Score** Jones, Kenneth V.; Gamley, Douglas
**Composer(s)** Spielman, Fred
**Lyricist(s)** Torre, Janice
**Choreographer(s)** Romero, Alex

**Producer(s)** Pal, George
**Director(s)** Pal, George
**Screenwriter(s)** Fodor, Ladislas
**Source(s)** "Tom Thumb" (fairy tale) The Grimm Brothers
**Voices** Freberg, Stan; McKennon, Dallas

**Cast** Tamblyn, Russ; Terry-Thomas; Sellers, Peter; Young, Alan; Thorburn, June; Matthews, Jessie; Miles, Bernard; Wallace, Ian; Butterworth, Peter; Bull, Peter; The Puppetoons

**Song(s)** Tom Thumb's Tune (C/L: Lee, Peggy); After All These Years; Talented Shoes; The Yawning Song (L: Goell, Kermit); Are You a Dream (C/L: Lee, Peggy)

### 6305 ✦ TONIGHT AND EVERY NIGHT
Columbia, 1945

**Composer(s)** Styne, Jule
**Lyricist(s)** Cahn, Sammy
**Choreographer(s)** Cole, Jack; Raset, Val

**Producer(s)**    Saville, Victor
**Director(s)**    Saville, Victor
**Screenwriter(s)**    Samuels, Lesser; Finkel, Abem
**Source(s)**    *Heart of a City* (play) Storm, Lesley

**Cast**    Hayworth, Rita [1]; Bowman, Lee; Platt, Marc; Lamberti, Professor; Crane, Stephen; Bannon, Jim; Johnson, Marilyn; Law, Mildred; Blair, Janet; Winters, Shelley; Anderson, Dusty; Brooks, Leslie; Cole, Jack; Cossart, Ernest; Bates, Florence; Haydn, Richard; Merivale, Philip; Bevan, Billy

**Song(s)**    What Does an English Girl Think of a Yank; You Excite Me; Anywhere; Tonight and Every Night; Ladies Don't Have Fun [2]; As You Were [2]; The Girl in Nottingham Lace [2]; What Did I Do? [2]; Mad [2]; The Boy I Left Behind; Cry and You Cry Alone

**Notes**    [1] Dubbed by Martha Mears. [2] Not used

## 6306  ✦  TONIGHT'S THE NIGHT
### Republic, 1954

**Musical Score**    Black, Stanley

**Producer(s)**    Zampi, Mario
**Director(s)**    Zampi, Mario
**Screenwriter(s)**    Pertwee, Michael; Davies, Jack

**Cast**    Niven, David; de Carlo, Yvonne; Fitzgerald, Barry; Cole, George; Urquhart, Robert

**Song(s)**    My Heart Is Irish (C/L: Carr, Michael)

**Notes**    A British film titled HAPPY EVER AFTER. Released in U.S. by Republic.

## 6307  ✦  TONIGHT WE SING
### Twentieth Century–Fox, 1953

**Choreographer(s)**    Lichine, David

**Producer(s)**    Jessel, George
**Director(s)**    Leisen, Mitchell
**Screenwriter(s)**    Kurnitz, Harry; Oppenheimer, George
**Source(s)**    *Impressario* (book) Hurok, Sol; Goode, Ruth

**Cast**    Bancroft, Anne; Pinza, Ezio; Toumanova, Tamara; Stern, Isaac; Wayne, David; Palmer, Byron [1]; Peters, Robert; Karlweis, Oscar; Rasumny, Mikhail; Geray, Steven; King, Walter Woolf; Meek, John

**Notes**    No cue sheet available. There are no original songs in this film. Vocals and instrumentals include "Le Cygne" by Saint-Saens; "Sempre Libera" from Verdi's LA TRAVIATA; "Jewel Song" and "Qu'Attendez-Vous Encore" from Gounod's FAUST; "Love Duet" from Act I of Puccini's MADAMA BUTTERFLY; and "Andante le Triste Vero" and "Addio Fiorito Asil" from MADAMA BUTTERFLY; "Mattinata" by Leoncavallo; "Valse Caprice in E Flat" by Anton Rubenstein and "Processional" by Mussorgsky.

## 6308  ✦  TONKA
### Disney, 1958

**Musical Score**    Wallace, Oliver

**Producer(s)**    Pratt, James
**Director(s)**    Foster, Lewis R.
**Screenwriter(s)**    Hayward, Lillie; Foster, Lewis R.
**Source(s)**    *Comanche* (novel) Appel, David

**Cast**    Mineo, Sal; Carey, Philip; Courtland, Jerome; Wynant, H.M.; Lomond, Britt; Page, Joy; Campos, Rafael

**Song(s)**    Tonka (C: Bruns, George; L: George, Gil)

## 6309  ✦  TONTO BASIN OUTLAWS
### Monogram, 1941

**Musical Score**    Sanucci, Frank

**Producer(s)**    Weeks, George W.
**Director(s)**    Luby, S. Roy
**Screenwriter(s)**    Snell, Earle

**Cast**    King, John; Corrigan, Ray; Terhune, Max; Wiley, Jan; Coffin, Tristram; Cobb, Edmund

**Song(s)**    Cabin of My Dreams (C: George, Jean [1]; L: King, John)

**Notes**    [1] Pseudonym for Lucille Nolte.

## 6310  ✦  TONY ROME
### Twentieth Century–Fox, 1967

**Musical Score**    May, Billy
**Composer(s)**    May, Billy
**Lyricist(s)**    Newman, Randy

**Producer(s)**    Rosenberg, Aaron
**Director(s)**    Douglas, Gordon M.
**Screenwriter(s)**    Breen, Richard L.
**Source(s)**    *Miami Mayhem* (novel) Albert, Marvin H.

**Cast**    Sinatra, Frank; St. John, Jill; Conte, Richard; Rowlands, Gena; Oakland, Simon; Lynn, Jeffrey; Bochner, Lloyd; Wilke, Robert J.; Lyon, Sue

**Song(s)**    Something Here Inside Me; Tony Rome (C/L: Hazlewood, Lee); Hard Times

## 6311  ✦  TOO HOT TO HANDLE
### New World, 1977

**Musical Score**    Montenegro, Hugo

**Producer(s)**    Desiderio, Ralph T.
**Director(s)**    Schain, Don
**Screenwriter(s)**    Sherman, J. Michael; Buday, Don

**Cast**    Caffaro, Cheri; Ipale, Aharon; Diaz, Vic; Calvet, Corinne

**Song(s)**    Lady Samantha (C: Montenegro, John; L: Justin, Michael)

**Notes**    No cue sheet available.

## 6312 ✦ TOO LATE BLUES
Paramount, 1962

**Musical Score** Raksin, David
**Composer(s)** Raksin, David
**Lyricist(s)** Raksin, David

**Producer(s)** Cassavetes, John
**Director(s)** Cassavetes, John
**Screenwriter(s)** Carr, Richard; Cassavetes, John

**Cast** Darin, Bobby; Stevens, Stella [3]; Chambers, Everett; Dennis, Nick; Edwards, Vince; Avery, Val; Clark, Marilyn; Joyce, James; Crosse, Rupert

**Song(s)** Something Like That; Too Late Blues [1] (C: Raksin, David); When Your Time Comes [2] (C: Raksin, David); Bass Canard (inst.); Those Bad Old Days [4] (inst.); Blues for Tomorrow; Ciudad de Mexico (inst.); Danzon (inst.); Look Inward, Angel (inst.); The Rim Shot Heard Round the World (inst.); Sambalero (inst.); Sax Raises Its Ugly Head (inst.); How Shall We Begin [5] (inst.)

**Notes** The jazz instrumentals were recorded for the soundtrack by Shelly Manne, Red Mitchell, Jimmy Rowles, Benny Carter, Uan Rasey and Milt Bernhardt. [1] Originally titled "A Song After Sundown." Livingston and Evans wrote lyrics for this song but they were not used. [2] Not used but recorded by Jean Sewell and Jerry West. [3] Dubbed by Loulie Jean Norman. [4] Originally titled "Benny Splits While Jimmy Rowles." [5] Titled originally "Some Other Time."

## 6313 ✦ TOO MANY BLONDES
Universal, 1941

**Musical Score** Skinner, Frank
**Composer(s)** Rosen, Milton
**Lyricist(s)** Carter, Everett

**Producer(s)** Sandford, Joseph G.
**Director(s)** Freeland, Thornton
**Screenwriter(s)** Shane, Maxwell; Kaye, Louis S.

**Cast** Vallee, Rudy; Parrish, Helen; Adrian, Iris; Chaney Jr., Lon; Humberto Herrera and His Orchestra

**Song(s)** Don't Mind If I Do; Let's Love Again [2]; Whistle Your Blues to a Bluebird [1]; Chick Qui Boom (C/L: Herrera, Humberto; Brazil, P.)

**Notes** There is also a vocal of "The Man on the Flying Trapeze" by Walter O'Keefe. [1] Also in COWBOY IN MANHATTAN and the short IN THE GROOVE. [2] Also in STARS AND VIOLINS and TWILIGHT ON THE PRAIRIE.

## 6314 ✦ TOO MANY GIRLS
RKO, 1940

**Composer(s)** Rodgers, Richard
**Lyricist(s)** Hart, Lorenz
**Choreographer(s)** Prinz, LeRoy

**Producer(s)** Abbott, George
**Director(s)** Abbott, George
**Screenwriter(s)** Twist, John
**Source(s)** *Too Many Girls* (musical) Marion Jr., George; Rodgers, Richard; Hart, Lorenz

**Cast** Ball, Lucille [1]; Carlson, Richard; Miller, Ann; Bracken, Eddie [2]; Langford, Frances; Arnaz, Desi [2]; LeRoy, Hal [2]; Bennett, Libby; Shannon, Harry; Walton, Douglas; Johnson, Van [2]; Sutton, Grady; Scott, Ivy [2]; Shores, Byron [2]

**Song(s)** Heroes in the Fall [2] (L: Rodgers, Richard); You're Nearer [3]; Pottawatomie [2]; 'Cause We All Got Cake [2]; Spic and Spanish [2]; Love Never Went to College [2]; Look Out [2]; I Didn't Know What Time It Was [2] [4]

**Notes** [1] Dubbed by Trudy Erwin. [2] From Broadway version. [3] All numbers but "You're Nearer" are from the Broadway original. [4] Also in film version of PAL JOEY (Columbia).

## 6315 ✦ TOO MANY PARENTS
Paramount, 1936

**Producer(s)** Botsford, A.M.
**Director(s)** McGowan, Robert F.
**Screenwriter(s)** Van Upp, Virginia; Malloy, Doris
**Source(s)** "Not Wanted" (story) Williams, Jesse Lynch; "Too Many Parents" (story) Templeton, George

**Cast** Farmer, Frances; Matthews, Lester; Lee, Billy

**Song(s)** A Little White Gardenia [1] (C/L: Coslow, Sam)

**Notes** [1] Also in ALL THE KING'S HORSES.

## 6316 ✦ TOO MUCH HARMONY
Paramount, 1933

**Composer(s)** Johnston, Arthur
**Lyricist(s)** Coslow, Sam

**Producer(s)** LeBaron, William
**Director(s)** Sutherland, Edward
**Screenwriter(s)** Ruskin, Harry

**Cast** Crosby, Bing; Oakie, Jack; Gallagher, Skeets; Allen, Judith; Tashman, Lilyan

**Song(s)** Learn to Croon [4]; Two Aristocrats; The Day You Came Along; Boo Boo Boo; Thanks; Black Moonlight; Cradle Me with a Ha Cha Lullaby; Where Have I Heard that Melody [5]; Buckin' the Wind; Music to My Ears [1]; It Had to Be that Way [1] [3]; I'm a Bachelor of the Art of Ha Cha Cha [2]

**Notes** Formerly titled FALL IN LOVE. During the "Black Moonlight" and "Boo Boo Boo" rehearsal scene Harry Akst is seen playing the piano which he actually is doing. [1] Not used. [2] Used instrumentally only. Also used instrumentally in COLLEGE HUMOR. [3] Recorded. Used in THUNDER BELOW. [4] Also in

COLLEGE HUMOR and HELL AND HIGH WATER. [5] Also in HER BODYGUARD.

## 6317 ✦ TOO SCARED TO SCREAM
### Movie Store, 1985

**Musical Score**   Garvarentz, Georges

**Producer(s)**   Connors, Michael
**Director(s)**   LoBianco, Tony
**Screenwriter(s)**   Barbera, Neal; Leopold, Glenn

**Cast**   Connors, Michael; Archer, Anne; Kennedy, Leon Isaac; McShane, Ian; Ford, Ruth; Heard, John; Nye, Carrie; O'Sullivan, Maureen; Hamilton, Murray

**Song(s)**   I'll Be There (C: Garaventz, George; L: Aznavour, Charles; Kretzmer, Herbert)

**Notes**   No cue sheet available.

## 6318 ✦ TOOTSIE
### Columbia, 1982

**Musical Score**   Grusin, Dave
**Composer(s)**   Grusin, Dave
**Lyricist(s)**   Bergman, Alan; Bergman, Marilyn

**Producer(s)**   Pollack, Sydney; Richards, Dick
**Director(s)**   Pollack, Sydney
**Screenwriter(s)**   Gelbart, Larry; Schisgal, Murray

**Cast**   Hoffman, Dustin; Lange, Jessica; Garr, Teri; Coleman, Dabney; Durning, Charles; Murray, Bill; Pollack, Sydney; Gaynes, George; Davis, Geena; Foley, Ellen; Thigpen, Lynne

**Song(s)**   Tootsie; It Might Be You; That's All [1] (C/L: Brandt, Alan; Haymes, Bob)

**Notes**   [1] Sheet music only.

## 6319 ✦ TOOT, WHISTLE PLUNK AND BOOM
### Disney, 1953

**Musical Score**   Dubin, Joseph S.
**Composer(s)**   Dubin, Joseph S.
**Lyricist(s)**   Huemer, Dick

**Producer(s)**   Disney, Walt
**Director(s)**   Nichols, C. August; Kimball, Ward
**Screenwriter(s)**   Huemer, Dick

**Song(s)**   Toot, Whistle, Plunk and Boom (C: Burke, Sonny; L: Elliott, Jack); Opening Chorus; Caveman Chant; The River Nile; First You Take the Bow

**Notes**   Animated short.

## 6320 ✦ TOP BANANA
### United Artists, 1953

**Composer(s)**   Mercer, Johnny
**Lyricist(s)**   Mercer, Johnny

**Producer(s)**   Zugsmith, Albert; Peskay, Ben
**Director(s)**   Green, Alfred E.
**Screenwriter(s)**   Towne, Gene
**Source(s)**   *Top Banana* (musical) Mercer, Johnny; Kraft, Hy

**Cast**   Silvers, Phil; Lynn, Judy; Scholl, Danny; Rose Marie; Albertson, Jack; Coy, Johnny; Faye, Herbie; Faye, Joey; Wahl, Walter Dare; Hatton, Bradford; Dana, Dick

**Song(s)**   He's the Man of the Year; You're So Beautiful; Top Banana; Going Up; The Slogan Song; Meet Miss Blendo; Be My Guest; Sans Souci; Girl of All Nations

**Notes**   This is basically a film of the stage show shot from the audience at the Winter Garden Theatre. All songs are from the Broadway original.

## 6321 ✦ TOP GUN
### Paramount, 1986

**Musical Score**   Faltermeyer, Harold
**Composer(s)**   Moroder, Giorgio
**Lyricist(s)**   Whitlock, Tom

**Producer(s)**   Simpson, Don; Bruckheimer, Jerry
**Director(s)**   Scott, Tony
**Screenwriter(s)**   Cash, Jim; Epps Jr., Jack

**Cast**   Cruise, Tom; McGillis, Kelly; Kilmer, Val; Edwards, Anthony; Skerritt, Tom

**Song(s)**   Memories (inst.) [1] [2] (C: Faltermeyer, Harold); Heaven In Your Eyes [1] (C/L: Dean, Paul; Reno, Mike; Dexter, John; Moore, Mae); Radar Radio [1]; Mighty Wings [1] (C: Faltermeyer, Harold; L: Spiro, Mark); Take My Breath Away [1]; Top Gun Anthem (inst) [1] (C: Faltermeyer, Harold); Lead Me On [1]; Through the Fire [1]; Destination Unknown [1] (C/L: Golde, Franne; Fox, Paul; Hooker, Jake); Playing with the Boys [1] (C/L: Loggins, Kenny; Wolf, Peter; Wolf, Ina); Hot Summer Nights [1] (C/L: Jay, Michael; Scott, Alan Roy; Freedland, Roy); Danger Zone (C: Moroder, Giorgio; L: Whitlock, Tom)

**Notes**   [1] All these are background instrumentals. [2] Originally titled "Goose's Theme."

## 6322 ✦ TOP HAT
### RKO, 1935

**Composer(s)**   Berlin, Irving
**Lyricist(s)**   Berlin, Irving
**Choreographer(s)**   Pan, Hermes

**Producer(s)**   Berman, Pandro S.
**Director(s)**   Sandrich, Mark
**Screenwriter(s)**   Taylor, Dwight; Scott, Allan

**Cast**   Astaire, Fred; Rogers, Ginger; Horton, Edward Everett; Rhodes, Erik; Blore, Eric; Broderick, Helen

**Song(s)**   No Strings; Isn't This a Lovely Day; Top Hat, White Tie and Tails; Cheek to Cheek [1]; Get Thee Behind Me Satan [2]; The Piccolino; Wild About You [3]

**Notes**  [1] Also in ALEXANDER'S RAGTIME BAND. [2] Not used. Later in FOLLOW THE FLEET. [3] Not used.

## 6323 ◆ TOPKAPI
United Artists, 1964

**Musical Score**  Hadjidakis, Manos

**Producer(s)**  Dassin, Jules
**Director(s)**  Dassin, Jules
**Screenwriter(s)**  Danischewsky, Monja
**Source(s)**  *The Light of Day* (novel) Ambler, Eric

**Cast**  Mercouri, Melina; Ustinov, Peter; Schell, Maximilian; Morley, Robert; Tamiroff, Akim; Segal, Gilles

**Song(s)**  Astro Tis Anatilis (C: Hadjidakis, Manos; L: Gatsos, Nikos); Topkapi [1] (C: Hadjidakis, Manos; L: Sherman, Noel)

**Notes**  [1] Not used.

## 6324 ◆ TOP MAN
Universal, 1943

**Composer(s)**  James, Inez; Pepper, Buddy
**Lyricist(s)**  James, Inez; Pepper, Buddy

**Producer(s)**  Schwarzwald, Milton
**Director(s)**  Lamont, Charles
**Screenwriter(s)**  Gold, Zachary

**Cast**  O'Connor, Donald; Ryan, Peggy; Gwynne, Anne; Dix, Richard; Gish, Lillian; Foster, Susanna; Count Basie and His Band; Borrah Minnevitch and His Harmonica Rascals; Holt, David; Beery Jr., Noah; Jones, Marcia Mae; Beavers, Louise; Hinds, Samuel S.

**Song(s)**  Wishing (C/L: James, Inez; Pepper, Buddy; Schwarzwald, Milton); Samba Sue; The Road Song

**Notes**  Released as MAN OF THE FAMILY overseas. There are also vocals of "Jurame" by Maria Grever and "Wrap Your Troubles in Dreams" by Ted Koehler, Billy Moll and Harry Barris.

## 6325 ◆ TOP OF THE TOWN
Universal, 1937

**Composer(s)**  McHugh, Jimmy
**Lyricist(s)**  Adamson, Harold

**Producer(s)**  Brock, Lou
**Director(s)**  Murphy, Ralph
**Screenwriter(s)**  Holmes, Brown; Grayson, Charles

**Cast**  Nolan, Doris; Niesen, Gertrude; Logan, Ella; The Three Sailors; Auer, Mischa; Ryan, Peggy; Ratoff, Gregory; Murphy, George; Herbert, Hugh; Armetta, Henry; Gillingwater, Claude; Soccart, Ernest; The Californian Collegians; The Four Esquires

**Song(s)**  Where Are You? [1]; Top of the Town; Blame It on the Rhumba; (That) Foolish Feeling; Fireman Save

My Child; There's No Two Ways About It; Jamboree; Hamlet's Soliloquy (C: Henderson, Charles; L: Shakespeare, William); Ballet Moderne (Inst.) (C: McHugh, Jimmy; Skinner, Frank)

**Notes**  [1] Also used in DANGER ON THE AIR.

## 6326 ◆ TOP O' THE MORNING
Paramount, 1949

**Composer(s)**  Van Heusen, James
**Lyricist(s)**  Burke, Johnny

**Producer(s)**  Welch, Robert L.
**Director(s)**  Miller, David
**Screenwriter(s)**  Beloin, Edmund; Breen, Richard L.

**Cast**  Crosby, Bing; Fitzgerald, Barry; Blyth, Ann; Cronyn, Hume; Crowe, Eileen; McIntire, John

**Song(s)**  Top o' the Morning; You're in Love with Someone

**Notes**  Formerly titled DIAMOND IN A HAYSTACK. There are also vocal renditions of "My Lagen Love" by Hamilton Harty and Seosamh MacCathmhaoil; "Oh, 'Tis Sweet to Think" by Thomas Moore; the traditional Irish air "The Leprechan"; "My Beautiful Kitty" by Edward Lysaght to a traditional Irish melody; "The Donovans" by Francis Fahy and Alicia Needham and "When Irish Eyes Are Smiling" by Ernest Ball, Chauncey Olcott and George Graff, Jr. Burke and Van Heusen may have had something to do with the writing of "Oh, 'Tis Sweet to Think," although the signed certificate and cue sheet do not credit them. However, a publishing contract lists the song under their authorship.

## 6327 ◆ TOPPER
Metro–Goldwyn–Mayer, 1937

**Producer(s)**  Roach, Hal
**Director(s)**  McLeod, Norman Z.
**Screenwriter(s)**  Jevne, Jack; Hatch, Eric; Moran, Eddie
**Source(s)**  *Topper* (novel) Smith, Thorne

**Cast**  Bennett, Constance; Grant, Cary; Young, Roland; Burke, Billie; Mowbray, Alan; Pallette, Eugene

**Song(s)**  Old Man Moon (C/L: Carmichael, Hoagy)

**Notes**  No cue sheet available.

## 6328 ◆ TOP SECRET
Paramount, 1984

**Musical Score**  Jarre, Maurice

**Producer(s)**  Lowry, Hunt; Davison, Jon
**Director(s)**  Abrahams, Jim; Zucker, David; Zucker, Jerry
**Screenwriter(s)**  Abrahams, Jim; Zucker, David; Zucker, Jerry; Burke, Martyn

**Cast**  Kilmer, Val; Gutteridge, Lucy; Sharif, Omar

**Song(s)** Spend This Night with Me (C: Moran, Mike; L: Abrahams, Jim; Zucker, David; Zucker, Jerry); Straighten Out the Rug (C/L: Hudson, Paul); How Silly Can You Get (C/L: Pickett, Phil); Skeet Surfin' [1]; Hymn (C/L: Smith, Sandy)

**Notes** Kilmer also sings "Tutti Frutti" by Richard Penniman (Little Richard) and Dorothy LaBostrie and "Are You Lonesome Tonight" by Roy Turk and Lou Handman. [1] Based on the Beach Boys songs "Surfin' U.S.A." by Brian Wilson and Chuck Berry; "Fun, Fun, Fun" and "Little Honda" by Brian Wilson and Michael Love, and "California Girls" and "Hawaii" by Brian Wilson.

---

**6329 ✦ TOP SERGEANT MULLIGAN**
Monogram, 1941

**Producer(s)** Parsons, Lindsley
**Director(s)** Yarbrough, Jean
**Screenwriter(s)** Kelso, Edmund

**Cast** Pendleton, Nat; Hughes, Carol; Holloway, Sterling; Reynolds, Marjorie; Faylen, Frank; Hall, Charles; Neal, Tom; Blythe, Betty; Elliott, Dick; Smith, Wonderful

**Song(s)** $21.00 a Day - Once a Month (C/L: Klages, Raymond; Bernard, Felix); That's What I Think about You (C/L: Kay, Edward J.; Tobias, Harry)

**Notes** No cue sheet available.

---

**6330 ✦ TOPS IS THE LIMIT**

See ANYTHING GOES (1936).

---

**6331 ✦ TOP SPEED**
Warner Brothers–First National, 1930

**Composer(s)** Burke, Joe
**Lyricist(s)** Dubin, Al
**Choreographer(s)** Ceballos, Larry

**Director(s)** LeRoy, Mervyn
**Screenwriter(s)** Pearson, Humphrey; McCarty, Henry
**Source(s)** *Top Speed* (musical) Ruby, Harry; Kalmar, Bert; Bolton, Guy

**Cast** Brown, Joe E.; Claire, Bernice; Whiting, Jack; McHugh, Frank; Lee, Laura; Breese, Edmund; Flynn, Rita; Maxwell, Edwin; Ring, Cyril; Boteler, Wade

**Song(s)** Looking for the Lovelight in the Dark; If You Were a Traveling Salesman; Knock Knees; As Long As I Have You; Goodness Gracious [1] (C: Ruby, Harry; L: Kalmar, Bert); I'll Know and She'll Know [1] (C: Ruby, Harry; L: Kalmar, Bert); Keep Your Undershirt On [1] (C: Ruby, Harry; L: Kalmar, Bert); What Would I Care? [1] (C: Ruby, Harry; L: Kalmar, Bert); Sweeter than You [1] (C: Ruby, Harry; L: Kalmar, Bert)

**Notes** [1] In some sources but not on cue sheets. One book (probably Burton's *Blue Book of Hollywood Musicals*) first listed the songs and everyone else copied. The songs appeared in the stage musical TOP SPEED.

---

**6332 ✦ TORCH SINGER**
Paramount, 1933

**Composer(s)** Rainger, Ralph
**Lyricist(s)** Robin, Leo

**Producer(s)** Lewis, Albert
**Director(s)** Hall, Alexander; Somnes, George
**Screenwriter(s)** Starling, Lynn; Coffee, Lenore

**Cast** Colbert, Claudette; Cortez, Ricardo; Manners, David; Roberti, Lyda; Eddy, Helen Jerome; Burke, Kathleen

**Song(s)** Give Me Liberty or Give Me Love; Don't Be a Cry Baby; It's a Long, Dark Night; Here Lies Love [3]; The Torch Singer [1]; The Slumber Boat [2] (C: Gaynor, Jessie L.; L: Riley, Alice C.D.)

**Notes** [1] Not used. [2] Not used in THE MILKY WAY. [3] Also in THE BIG BROADCAST (1932) and INTERNATIONAL HOUSE.

---

**6333 ✦ TORCH SONG (1953)**
Metro–Goldwyn–Mayer, 1953

**Choreographer(s)** Walters, Charles

**Producer(s)** Berman, Henry; Franklin Jr., Sidney
**Director(s)** Walters, Charles
**Screenwriter(s)** Hayes, John Michael; Lustig, Jan

**Cast** Crawford, Joan [1]; Wilding, Michael; Young, Gig; Rambeau, Marjorie; Morgan, Henry; Patrick, Dorothy; Todd, James; Loring, Eugene; Guilfoyle, Paul; Rubin, Benny

**Song(s)** Follow Me (C/L: Deutsch, Adolph); Two-Faced Woman [2] (C: Schwartz, Arthur; L: Dietz, Howard); You Won't Forget Me (C: Spielman, Fred; L: Goell, Kermit); Tenderly (C: Gross, Walter; Lawrence, Jack)

**Notes** [1] Dubbed by India Adams. [2] This vocal (by India Adams) was originally recorded for THE BAND WAGON (1953) but deleted from the final print.

---

**6334 ✦ TORCHY BLANE IN PANAMA**
Warner Brothers–First National, 1938

**Musical Score** Jackson, Howard

**Producer(s)** Foy, Bryan
**Director(s)** Clemens, William
**Screenwriter(s)** Bricker, George
**Source(s)** characters by Nebel, Frederick

**Cast** Lane, Lola; Kelly, Paul; Kennedy, Tom; Williams, Larry; Compson, Betty; Averill, Anthony; Conlin, Jimmy

**Song(s)** Song of the Leopards (C: Jerome, M.K.; L: Scholl, Jack)

**Notes** There is also a vocal of "California Here I Come."

### 6335 ✦ TORMENTED
Allied Artists, 1960

**Musical Score** Glasser, Albert

**Producer(s)** Gordon, Bert I.; Steinberg, Joe
**Director(s)** Gordon, Bert I.
**Screenwriter(s)** Yates, George Worthing

**Cast** Carlson, Richard; Reding, Juli; Gordon, Susan; Sanders, Lugene

**Song(s)** Tormented (C: Glasser, Albert; L: Meltzer, Lewis)

**Notes** No cue sheet available.

### 6336 ✦ TORNADO
Paramount, 1943

**Composer(s)** Hollander, Frederick

**Producer(s)** Pine, William; Thomas, William
**Director(s)** Berke, William
**Screenwriter(s)** Shane, Maxwell

**Cast** Morris, Chester; Kelly, Nancy; Henry, William; McDonald, Marie

**Song(s)** There Goes My Dream [2] (L: Loesser, Frank); I'm Afraid of You [3] (L: Freed, Ralph); Whodunit [1] (C: Carmichael, Hoagy; L: Loesser, Frank)

**Notes** [1] May have been written for A NIGHT AT EARL CARROLL'S. Not used in SOME LIKE IT HOT. [2] Not used. Used in A NIGHT IN EARL CARROLL'S. [3] Not used in ST. LOUIS BLUES.

### 6337 ✦ TORNADO RANGE
Eagle Lion, 1948

**Producer(s)** Thomas, Jerry
**Director(s)** Taylor, Ray
**Screenwriter(s)** Lively, William

**Cast** Dean, Eddie; Ates, Roscoe; Holt, Jennifer; Chesebro, George; Slaven, Brad; Arms, Russell

**Song(s)** Little Ranch Upon the Hill (C/L: Massey, Curt; Massey, Allen); Song of the Range (C/L: Dean, Eddie; Greene, Walter; Blair, Hal)

### 6338 ✦ TORPEDO BOAT
Paramount, 1942

**Producer(s)** Pine, William; Thomas, William
**Director(s)** McDonald, Frank
**Screenwriter(s)** Sloane, Maxwell

**Cast** Arlen, Richard; Parker, Jean; Purcell, Dick; Terry, Phillip

**Song(s)** Heaven Is a Moment in Your Arms (C: Boyle, Marian; L: Winecoff, Nat)

### 6339 ✦ TORRID ZONE
Warner Brothers, 1940

**Musical Score** Deutsch, Adolph

**Producer(s)** Warner, Jack L.; Wallis, Hal B.
**Director(s)** Keighley, William
**Screenwriter(s)** Wald, Jerry; Macaulay, Richard

**Cast** Cagney, James; Sheridan, Ann; O'Brien, Pat; Devine, Andy; Vinson, Helen; Cowan, Jerome; Tobias, George; Reeves, George; Sutton, Grady

**Song(s)** Mi Cabellero (C: Jerome, M.K.; L: Scholl, Jack)

### 6340 ✦ TORTILLA FLAT
Metro–Goldwyn–Mayer, 1942

**Musical Score** Waxman, Franz

**Producer(s)** Zimbalist, Sam
**Director(s)** Fleming, Victor
**Screenwriter(s)** Mahin, John Lee; Glazer, Benjamin
**Source(s)** *Tortilla Flat* (novel) Steinbeck, John

**Cast** Tracy, Spencer; Lamarr, Hedy; Garfield, John; Morgan, Frank; Tamiroff, Akim; Leonard, Sheldon; Qualen, John; Meek, Donald; Gilchrist, Connie; Jenkins, Allen; O'Neill, Henry

**Song(s)** Ai Paisano (C: Traditional; L: Loesser, Frank)

### 6341 ✦ TO SIR WITH LOVE
Columbia, 1967

**Musical Score** Grainer, Ron
**Composer(s)** London, Mark

**Producer(s)** Clavell, James
**Director(s)** Clavell, James
**Screenwriter(s)** Clavell, James
**Source(s)** *To Sir, With Love* (novel) Braithwaite, E.R.

**Cast** Poitier, Sidney; Roberts, Christian; Geeson, Judy; Kendall, Suzy; Brook, Faith; Chittell, Christopher; Lulu

**Song(s)** To Sir with Love (L: Black, Don); Stealing My Love From Me (L: London, Marc); Off and Running (C: Wine, Toni; L: Sager, Carole Bayer); Getting Harder All the Time (C: Albertine, Charles; L: Raleigh, Ben)

### 6342 ✦ TO THE COAST OF DEVON
Metro–Goldwyn–Mayer, 1947

**Producer(s)** FitzPatrick, James A.

**Cast** FitzPatrick, James A.

**Song(s)** The Torquay Waltz (C/L: Kirk, Lesley; Gould, Clara)

**Notes** A FitzPatrick Traveltalk.

## 6343 ✦ THE TOUCHABLES
Twentieth Century–Fox, 1968

**Musical Score**    Thorne, Ken

**Producer(s)**    Bryan, John
**Director(s)**    Freeman, Robert
**Screenwriter(s)**    La Frenais, Ian

**Cast**    Huxtable, Judy; Anderson, Esther; Rickard, Marilyn; Simmonds, Kathy

**Song(s)**    All of Us (C/L: Spyropoulos, Alex; Campbell-Lyons, Patrick)

**Notes**    There is also a vocal of "Good Day Sunshine" by John Lennon and Paul McCartney and one of "Respect" by Otis Redding.

## 6344 ✦ TOUCHDOWN
Paramount, 1931

**Producer(s)**    Lighton, Louis D.
**Director(s)**    McLeod, Norman Z.
**Screenwriter(s)**    McNutt, William Slavens; Jones, Grover
**Source(s)**    *Stadium* (novel) Wallace, Francis

**Cast**    Arlen, Richard; Oakie, Jack; Shannon, Peggy; Toomey, Regis

**Song(s)**    There I Go Again [1] (C: Mann, Stephen; Weiss, Stephan; L: Lawrence, Jack)

**Notes**    Formerly titled SENTIMENTAL ME. Titled PLAYING THE GAME in Great Britain. [1] Not used.

## 6345 ✦ TOUCHED
Lorimar, 1983

**Musical Score**    Walker, Shirley

**Producer(s)**    Petersmann, Dirk; Lottimer, Barclay
**Director(s)**    Flynn, John
**Screenwriter(s)**    Kessler, Kyle

**Cast**    Hays, Robert; Beller, Kathleen; Beatty, Ned; Lewis, Gilbert; Kessler, Kyle

**Song(s)**    Find Me (C/L: Connors, Carol; Shire, David)

**Notes**    No cue sheet available.

## 6346 ✦ TOUGH ENOUGH
Twentieth Century–Fox, 1983

**Musical Score**    Lloyd, Michael

**Producer(s)**    Gilmore, William S.
**Director(s)**    Fleischer, Richard
**Screenwriter(s)**    Leone, John

**Cast**    Quaid, Dennis; Watkins, Carlene; Shaw, Stan; Grier, Pam; Oates, Warren; McGill, Bruce; Brimley, Wilford

**Song(s)**    Tough Enough (C/L: Bresh, Thom; Brody, Lane); Don't They Know Who I'm Gonna Be (C/L: Lloyd, Michael; Cymbal, Johnny; Holmes, Bill); More

Nights (C/L: Morrison, Bob); The Jungle (C/L: Quaid, Dennis); Rainbows Never Touch the Ground (C/L: Bruce, Ed; Bruce, Patty; Rogers, Ronnie); Don't Let Me Dream Alone (C: Lloyd, Michael; L: Fleischer, Mark)

## 6347 ✦ TOUGHEST MAN ALIVE
Allied Artists, 1955

**Producer(s)**    Broidy, William F.
**Director(s)**    Salkow, Sidney
**Screenwriter(s)**    Fisher, Steve

**Cast**    Clark, Dane; Milan, Lita; Caruso, Anthony; Elliott, Rose; Dell, Myrna

**Song(s)**    I Hear a Rhapsody (C/L: Gasparre, Dick; Baker, Jack; Fragos, George); You Walk By (C: Raleigh, Ben; L: Wayne, Bernie)

**Notes**    No cue sheet available.

## 6348 ✦ THE TOUGHEST MAN IN ARIZONA
Republic, 1952

**Producer(s)**    Picker, Sidney
**Director(s)**    Springsteen, R.G.
**Screenwriter(s)**    Butler, John K.; Horman, Arthur T.
**Source(s)**    "The Toughest Man in Arizona" (story) Pinkerton, Robert E.

**Cast**    Monroe, Vaughn; Leslie, Joan; Parker, Jean; Buchanan, Edgar; Jory, Victor

**Song(s)**    Hound Dog (Bay at the Moon) (C/L: Smith, James; Hickman, William; Lee, Katie); A Man's Best Friend Is His Horse (C/L: Vann, Al; Moore, Wilton; Lubin, Joe); The Man Don't Live Who Can Die Alone (C: Sherwood, Bobby; L: Schram, Johnny)

## 6349 ✦ TOUGH GUYS
Disney, 1986

**Musical Score**    Howard, James Newton

**Producer(s)**    Wizan, Joe
**Director(s)**    Kanew, Jeff
**Screenwriter(s)**    Orr, James; Cruickshank, Jim

**Cast**    Lancaster, Burt; Douglas, Kirk; Durning, Charles; Smith, Alexis; Garvey, Dana; Fluegel, Darlanne; Wallach, Eli

**Song(s)**    They Don't Make 'Em Like They Used To (C: Bacharach, Burt; L: Sager, Carole Bayer)

## 6350 ✦ TOUGH GUYS DON'T DANCE
Cannon, 1987

**Musical Score**    Badalamenti, Angelo

**Producer(s)**    Golan, Menahem; Globus, Yoram
**Director(s)**    Mailer, Norman
**Screenwriter(s)**    Mailer, Norman
**Source(s)**    *Tough Guys Don't Dance* (novel) Mailer, Norman

**Cast** O'Neal, Ryan; Rossellini, Isabella; Sandlund, Debra; Hauser, Wings; Tierney, Lawrence; Jillette, Penn; Williams III, Clarence

**Song(s)** You'll Come Back to Me (You Always Do) (C: Badalamenti, Angelo; L: Mailer, Norman; Badalamenti, Angelo); Real Man (C: Badalamenti, Angelo; L: Badalamenti, Danielle)

**Notes** No cue sheet available.

## 6351 ✦ TOUGH KID
Monogram, 1939

**Producer(s)** Dunlap, Scott R.
**Director(s)** Bretherton, Howard
**Screenwriter(s)** Totman, Wellyn

**Cast** Darro, Frankie; Purcell, Dick; Allen, Judith; Elliott, Lillian; Rowan, Don; Ruhl, William; Mack, Wilbur

**Song(s)** All for You (C/L: Rosoff, Charles)

**Notes** No cue sheet available.

## 6352 ✦ THE TOWERING INFERNO
Twentieth Century–Fox/Warner Brothers, 1974

**Musical Score** Williams, John

**Producer(s)** Allen, Irwin
**Director(s)** Guillermin, John
**Screenwriter(s)** Silliphant, Stirling
**Source(s)** *The Tower* (novel) Stern, Richard Martin; *The Glass Inferno* (novel) Scortia, Thomas; Robinsin, Frank M.

**Cast** Newman, Paul; Dunaway, Faye; Chamberlain, Richard; Blakely, Susan; Vaughn, Robert; Wagner, Robert; Astaire, Fred; Jones, Jennifer; McQueen, Steve; Holden, William; Simpson, O.J.; Flannery, Susan

**Song(s)** We May Never Love Like This Again (C/L: Kasha, Al; Hirschhorn, Joel)

## 6353 ✦ TOWN TAMER
Paramount, 1965

**Musical Score** Haskell, Jimmie

**Producer(s)** Lyles, A.C.
**Director(s)** Selander, Lesley
**Screenwriter(s)** Gruber, Frank
**Source(s)** *Town Tamer* (novel) Gruber, Frank

**Cast** Andrews, Dana; Moore, Terry; O'Brien, Pat; Chaney, Lon; Cabot, Bruce; Bettger, Lyle; Arlen, Richard; MacLane, Barton; Jaeckel, Richard; Carey, Philip; Tufts, Sonny; Gray, Coleen; Cagney, Jeanne; Steele, Bob; Kelley, DeForest

**Song(s)** Town Tamer [2] (C: Haskell, Jimmie; L: Dunham, "By" [1])

**Notes** [1] Pen name for William D. Dunham. [2] Used as background vocal only.

## 6354 ✦ TOWN WITHOUT PITY
United Artists, 1961

**Musical Score** Tiomkin, Dimitri

**Producer(s)** Reinhardt, Gottfried
**Director(s)** Reinhardt, Gottfried
**Screenwriter(s)** Reinhardt, Silvia; Hurdalek, George
**Source(s)** *The Verdict* (novel) Gregor, Manfred

**Cast** Douglas, Kirk; Marshall, E.G.; Sutton, Frank; Kaufmann, Christine; Blake, Robert; Jaeckel, Richard; Sondock, Mal

**Song(s)** Town Without Pity (C: Tiomkin, Dimitri; L: Washington, Ned)

## 6355 ✦ THE TOY
Columbia, 1982

**Musical Score** Williams, Patrick

**Producer(s)** Feldman, Phil
**Director(s)** Donner, Richard
**Screenwriter(s)** Sobieski, Carol
**Source(s)** *Le Jouet* (film) Veber, Francis

**Cast** Pryor, Richard; Gleason, Jackie; Beatty, Ned; Schwartz, Scott; Ganzel, Teresa; Hyde-White, Wilfrid; Chase, Annazette; Capers, Virginia

**Song(s)** I Just Want to Be Your Friend (C/L: Lawrence, Trevor; Musker, Frank)

## 6356 ✦ THE TOYLAND BROADCAST
Metro–Goldwyn–Mayer, 1934

**Song(s)** Beep Beep-ie Daddle (C/L: Keyes, Baron)

**Notes** Animated cartoon. There are also vocals of "When the Moon Comes Over the Mountain" by Howard Johnson and Harry Woods; "Trees" by Joyce Kilmer and Oscar Rasbach and "Jungle Fever" by Walter Donaldson.

## 6357 ✦ TOY WIFE
Metro–Goldwyn–Mayer, 1938

**Song(s)** Dancing By the Moonlight (C/L: Wright, Robert; Forrest, Chet)

**Notes** No cue sheet available.

## 6358 ✦ TRACKDOWN
United Artists, 1976

**Musical Score** Bernstein, Charles

**Producer(s)** Schwartz, Bernard
**Director(s)** Heffron, Richard T.
**Screenwriter(s)** Edwards, Paul

**Cast** Mitchum, Jim; Lamm, Karen; Archer, Anne; Estrada, Erik; Crosby, Cathy Lee; Cannon, Vince

**Song(s)** I Ain't Got Nobody (C/L: Butler, Larry; Bowling, Roger); Runaway Girl (C/L: Butler, Larry;

Richey, George); Por Increible Que Parezca (C/L: Ned, Nelson)

## 6359 ✦ TRAGEDY AT MIDNIGHT
Republic, 1942

**Producer(s)** North, Robert
**Director(s)** Santley, Joseph
**Screenwriter(s)** Dawn, Isabel

**Cast** Howard, John; Lindsay, Margaret; Karns, Roscoe; Luke, Keye; Barrie, Mona; Mander, Miles; Bond, Lillian; Cavanaugh, Hobart

**Song(s)** From You [1] (C: Styne, Jule; L: Meyer, Sol; Brown, George)

**Notes** [1] Also in MOUNTAIN MAGIC.

## 6360 ✦ TRAIL DUST
Paramount, 1936

**Composer(s)** Stern, Jack
**Lyricist(s)** Tobias, Harry

**Producer(s)** Sherman, Harry
**Director(s)** Watt, Nate
**Screenwriter(s)** Martin, Al

**Cast** Boyd, William; Ellison, James; Hayes, George "Gabby"

**Song(s)** Beneath a Western Sky; Take Me Back to Those Wide Open Spaces; Trail Dust (C/L: Humphrey, Claudia)

## 6361 ✦ TRAILING DOUBLE TROUBLE
Monogram, 1940

**Musical Score** Sanucci, Frank

**Producer(s)** Weeks, George W.
**Director(s)** Luby, S. Roy
**Screenwriter(s)** Drake, Oliver

**Cast** King, John; Terhune, Max; Corrigan, Ray; Conway, Lita; King, Nancy Louise; Barcroft, Roy; Taylor, Forrest

**Song(s)** Western Skies (C: Lange, Johnny; L: Porter, Lew); Breakdown [1] (C: Lange, Johnny; L: Porter, Lew)

**Notes** [1] Used instrumentally only.

## 6362 ✦ TRAILIN' WEST
Warner Brothers–First National, 1936

**Musical Score** Jackson, Howard
**Composer(s)** Jerome, M.K.
**Lyricist(s)** Scholl, Jack

**Producer(s)** Foy, Bryan
**Director(s)** Smith, Noel
**Screenwriter(s)** Coldeway, Anthony
**Source(s)** "On Secret Service" (story) Coldeway, Anthony

**Cast** Foran, Dick; Stone, Paula; Elliott, Gordon; Richards, Addison; Barrat, Robert; Crehan, Joseph; Lawrence, Fred; Shubert, Eddie; Otho, Henry; Holmes, Stuart; Saum, Cliff

**Song(s)** Drums of Glory; Moonlight Valley

**Notes** Released in Great Britain as ON SECRET SERVICE.

## 6363 ✦ THE TRAIL OF '98
Metro–Goldwyn–Mayer, 1929

**Musical Score** Axt, William

**Director(s)** Brown, Clarence
**Screenwriter(s)** Glazer, Benjamin; Young, Waldemar
**Source(s)** *The Trail of '98* (novel) Service, Robert

**Cast** Del Rio, Dolores; Forbes, Ralph; Dane, Karl; Carey, Harry; Marshall, Tully

**Song(s)** I Found Gold When I Found You [1] (C: Axt, William; L: Lyn, Evelyn; Mooney, Hazel)

**Notes** [1] Cue sheet indicates instrumental use only.

## 6364 ✦ TRAIL OF ROBIN HOOD
Republic, 1950

**Producer(s)** White, Edward J.
**Director(s)** Witney, William
**Screenwriter(s)** Geraghty, Gerald

**Cast** Rogers, Roy; Trigger; Edwards, Penny; Jones, Gordon; Allen, Rex; Lane, Allan; Hale, Monte; Franum, William; Tyler, Tom; Corrigan, Ray; Maynard, Kermit; Keene, Tom; Holt, Jack; Foy Willing and the Riders of the Purple Sage

**Song(s)** Get a Christmas Tree for Johnny (C/L: Elliott, Jack); Ev'ry Day Is Christmas in the West (C/L: Elliott, Jack); Trail of Robin Hood [1] (C/L: Elliott, Jack); Home Town Jubilee [1] (C/L: Willing, Foy; Gonzales, Aaron)

**Notes** [1] Sheet music only.

## 6365 ✦ THE TRAIL OF THE LONESOME PINE
Paramount, 1936

**Composer(s)** Alter, Louis
**Lyricist(s)** Mitchell, Sidney D.

**Producer(s)** Wanger, Walter
**Director(s)** Hathaway, Henry
**Screenwriter(s)** Jones, Grover; Thew, Harvey; McCoy, Horace
**Source(s)** *The Trail of the Lonesome Pine* (novel) Fox Jr., John

**Cast** MacMurray, Fred; Sidney, Sylvia; Fonda, Henry; Stone, Fred; Barrat, Robert; Baxter, Alan; Bruce, Nigel; Bondi, Beulah; Knight, Fuzzy

**Song(s)** Twilight on the Trail [2]; The Poorest Man in Town (L: Knight, Fuzzy); A Melody from the Sky;

Stackolee Blues [1] (C/L: Lopez, Ray); Trail of the Lonesome Pine [3] (C: Carroll, Harry; L: Macdonald, Ballard)

**Notes**   [1] Based on the traditional song "Stackolee Staggerlee." [2] Also in TWILIGHT ON THE TRAIL. [3] Sheet music only.

## 6366 ✦ TRAIL OF THE SILVER SPURS
Monogram, 1941

**Musical Score**   Sanucci, Frank

**Producer(s)**   Weeks, George W.
**Director(s)**   Luby, S. Roy
**Screenwriter(s)**   Snell, Earle

**Cast**   King, John; Corrigan, Ray; Terhune, Max; Jolley, I. Stanford; Short, Dorothy; Dean, Eddie; Chesebro, George

**Song(s)**   A Rainbow Is Riding the Range (C: Lange, Johnny; L: Porter, Lew)

## 6367 ✦ TRAIL STREET
RKO, 1947

**Musical Score**   Sawtell, Paul; Webb, Roy

**Producer(s)**   Holt, Nat
**Director(s)**   Enright, Ray
**Screenwriter(s)**   Lewis, Gene; Houston, Norman
**Source(s)**   *Golden Horizons* (novel) Corcoran, William

**Cast**   Scott, Randolph; Ryan, Robert; Jeffreys, Anne; Hayes, George "Gabby"; Meredith, Madge; Brodie, Steve; Robards, Jason

**Song(s)**   You May Not Remember [1] (C: Oakland, Ben; L: Jessel, George); You're Not the Only Pebble on the Beach (C/L: Carter, Stanley; Braistead, Harry)

**Notes**   [1] Also in RIO GRANDE PATROL and SHOW BUSINESS.

## 6368 ✦ TRAIL TO GUNSIGHT
Universal, 1944

**Producer(s)**   Drake, Oliver
**Director(s)**   Keays, Vernon
**Screenwriter(s)**   Cohen, Bennett R.; Harper, Patricia

**Cast**   Dew, Eddie; Knight, Fuzzy; Wrixon, Maris

**Song(s)**   Slumbertime Out on the Prairie (C/L: Drake, Oliver); Chuck Wagon Blues (C/L: Jackson, Betty; Walters, Harry; Lillie, Jessie); Old Nevada Trail (C/L: Carol, Joe); I Ain't Got a Gal to Come Home To (C/L: Drake, Oliver)

## 6369 ✦ TRAIL TO SAN ANTONE
Republic, 1947

**Producer(s)**   Schaefer, Armand
**Director(s)**   English, John
**Screenwriter(s)**   Natteford, Jack; Ward, Luci

**Cast**   Autry, Gene; Champion; Stewart, Peggy; Holloway, Sterling; Henry, William; The Cass County Boys

**Song(s)**   Down the Trail to San Antone (C/L: Spiggins, Deuce); Cowboy Blues [1] (C/L: Autry, Gene; Walker, Cindy); Shame on You (C/L: Cooley, Spade); That's My Home (C/L: Robin, Sid); By the River of Roses (C/L: Burke, Joe; Symes, Marty)

**Notes**   No cue sheet available. [1] Also in WINNING OF THE WEST (Columbia).

## 6370 ✦ TRAIL TO VENGEANCE
Universal, 1945

**Composer(s)**   Rosen, Milton
**Lyricist(s)**   Carter, Everett

**Producer(s)**   Fox, Wallace W.
**Director(s)**   Fox, Wallace W.
**Screenwriter(s)**   Williams, Bob

**Cast**   Grant, Kirby; Knight, Fuzzy; Adams, Poni

**Song(s)**   On the Trail of Tomorrow [2]; Huckleberry Pie [1]

**Notes**   [1] Also in RAWHIDE RANGERS. [2] Also in ARIZONA CYCLONE (1942) and WEST OF CARSON CITY.

## 6371 ✦ TRANSATLANTIC MERRY-GO-ROUND
United Artists, 1934

**Composer(s)**   Whiting, Richard A.
**Lyricist(s)**   Clare, Sidney

**Producer(s)**   Small, Edward
**Director(s)**   Stoloff, Benjamin
**Screenwriter(s)**   March, Joseph Moncure; Conn, Harry W.

**Cast**   Benny, Jack; Carroll, Nancy; Green, Mitzi; Parker, Frank; The Boswell Sisters; Silvers, Sid; Jimmy Grier and His Orchestra; Grey, Shirley; Morgan, Ralph; Blackmer, Sidney; Raymond, Gene; Elliott, Robert; Hardy, Sam; Boyd, William; Moore, Carlyle

**Song(s)**   It Was Sweet of You; Rock and Roll; Oh, Leo, It's Love; Moon Over Monte Carlo; If I Had a Million Dollars (C: Malneck, Matty; L: Mercer, Johnny)

**Notes**   No cue sheet available.

## 6372 ✦ TRAPPED IN TANGIERS
Twentieth Century–Fox, 1960

**Musical Score**   Luttazzi, Lelio

**Producer(s)**   Freda, Riccardo
**Director(s)**   Cervi, Antonio
**Screenwriter(s)**   Continenza, Allessandro; Petrilli, Vittoriano; Spinola, Paolo; Freda, Riccardo

**Cast**   Purdom, Edmund; Page, Genevieve; Molino, Gino

**Song(s)**   The Last Phone Call (C/L: Brody, Edward)

**Notes**   No cue sheet available.

## 6373 ✦ THE TRAPP FAMILY
Twentieth Century–Fox, 1961

**Composer(s)**   Grothe, Franz
**Lyricist(s)**   Dehmel, Willy

**Producer(s)**   Reinhardt, Wolfgang
**Director(s)**   Liebeneiner, Wolfgang
**Screenwriter(s)**   Hurdalek, George
**Source(s)**   material by von Trapp, Baroness Maria

**Cast**   Leuwerik, Ruth; Holt, Hans; Holst, Maria; Meinrad, Josef; Domin, Friedrich

**Song(s)**   Kein Schoner Land; Wenn All Brunnlein FileBen; Ich Wollt', Ich Hatt' Eine Fiedel; Jagdlled der Kinder; Geschichten Aus Dem Wienerwald (C: Strauss, Johann); Wir Bauen uns Ein Hauschen; Geschichten aus dem Wienerwald (C: Strauss, Johann)

**Notes**   This is two films joined together for release in America. There is also a vocal of "Old Black Joe" by Stephen Foster with German lyrics by Dehmel.

## 6374 ✦ TRAVELING HUSBANDS
RKO, 1941

**Producer(s)**   Connolly, Myles
**Director(s)**   Sloane, Paul
**Screenwriter(s)**   Pearson, Humphrey

**Cast**   Brent, Evelyn; Albertson, Frank; Cummings, Constance; Herbert, Hugh; Peterson, Dorothy; McHugh, Frank; Fields, Stanley

**Song(s)**   There's a Sob in My Heart (C: Steiner, Max; L: Pearson, Humphrey)

## 6375 ✦ THE TRAVELING SALESWOMAN
Columbia, 1949

**Composer(s)**   Lee, Lester
**Lyricist(s)**   Roberts, Allan

**Producer(s)**   Owen, Tony
**Director(s)**   Riesner, Charles F.
**Screenwriter(s)**   Dimsdale, Howard

**Cast**   Davis, Joan; Devine, Andy; Jergens, Adele; Riesner, Dean; Cason, John; Sawyer, Joe; Urecal, Minerva

**Song(s)**   Every Baby Needs a Da-Da-Daddy [1]; He Died with His Boots On

**Notes**   [1] Also used in LADIES OF THE CHORUS.

## 6376 ✦ TRAVELS WITH ANITA

See A TRIP WITH ANITA.

## 6377 ✦ TRAVELS WITH MY AUNT
Metro–Goldwyn–Mayer, 1973

**Musical Score**   Hatch, Tony

**Producer(s)**   Fryer, Robert; Cresson, James
**Director(s)**   Cukor, George
**Screenwriter(s)**   Allen, Jay Presson; Wheeler, Hugh
**Source(s)**   *Travels with My Aunt* (novel) Greene, Graham

**Cast**   Smith, Maggie; McCowen, Alec; Gossett, Lou; Stephens, Robert; Williams, Cindy; Fleming, Robert; Luis, Jose; Vazquez, Lopez

**Song(s)**   Serenade of Love (C: Hatch, Tony; L: Trent, Jackie)

## 6378 ✦ T.R. BASKIN
Paramount, 1971

**Musical Score**   Elliott, Jack
**Composer(s)**   Elliott, Jack
**Lyricist(s)**   Jackson, June

**Producer(s)**   Hyams, Peter
**Director(s)**   Ross, Herbert
**Screenwriter(s)**   Hyams, Peter

**Cast**   Bergen, Candice; Boyle, Peter; Rodd, Marcia; Caan, James

**Song(s)**   I Got a Feeling [1]; It's a Mixed Up World [1]; Love Is All [2] (L: Gimbel, Norman); Waitin' for a Date [3] (L: Elliott, Jack); It's So Hard to Do [4]

**Notes**   [1] Background use only. [2] Lyric used for exploitation only. [3] Background use only for 22 seconds. [4] Not used.

## 6379 ✦ TREACHERY RIDES THE RANGE
Warner Brothers, 1936

**Musical Score**   Jackson, Howard
**Composer(s)**   Jerome, M.K.
**Lyricist(s)**   Scholl, Jack

**Producer(s)**   Foy, Bryan
**Director(s)**   McDonald, Frank
**Screenwriter(s)**   Jacobs, William

**Cast**   Foran, Dick; Stone, Paula; Reynolds, Craig; Blue, Monte; Moore Jr., Carlyle; Montague, Monte; Thorpe, Jim

**Song(s)**   Leather and Steel; Ridin' Home

## 6380 ✦ TREASURE OF MATECUMBE
Disney, 1976

**Musical Score**   Baker, Buddy

**Producer(s)**   Anderson, Bill
**Director(s)**   McEveety, Vincent
**Screenwriter(s)**   Tait, Don
**Source(s)**   *A Journey to Matecumbe* (novel) Taylor, Robert Lewis

Cast   Foxworth, Robert; Hackett, Joan; Ustinov, Peter; Morrow, Vic; Doran, Johnny; Wyatt, Jane; Attmore, Billy

Song(s)   Matecumbe (C/L: Tatum, Shane; L: McKinley, Richard)

### 6381 ◆ TREMORS
Universal, 1990

Musical Score   Troost, Ernest; Fox, Robert

Producer(s)   Wilson, S.S.; Maddock, Brent
Director(s)   Underwood, Ron
Screenwriter(s)   Wilson, S.S.; Maddock, Brent

Cast   Bacon, Kevin; Ward, Fred; Carter, Finn; Gross, Michael; McEntire, Reba

Song(s)   You Are the One (C/L: Lorber, Andrew; Lorber, William; Singh, Jay; Rastorfer, Daniel); It's a Cowboy Lovin' Night (C/L: Rogers, Ronnie); Heart of a Working Man (C/L: Russell, Tom); Drop Kick Me Jesus (C/L: Craft, Paul); Why Not Tonight (C/L: Montgomery, Nancy; Stringfellow, David; Vezner, John)

### 6382 ◆ THE TRESPASSER (1929)
United Artists, 1929

Producer(s)   Kennedy, Joseph P.
Director(s)   Goulding, Edmund
Screenwriter(s)   Goulding, Edmund

Cast   Swanson, Gloria; Ames, Robert; Pratt, Purnell; Walthall, Henry B.; Albright Jr., Wally; Holden, William; Frederici, Blanche

Song(s)   Love, Your Magic Spell Is Everywhere (C/L: Goulding, Edmund; Janis, Elsie); Serenade [1] (C: Tosell, Enrico; L: Spaeth, Sigmund)

Notes   No cue sheet available.

### 6383 ◆ THE TRESPASSER (1947)
Republic, 1947

Producer(s)   O'Sullivan, William J.
Director(s)   Blair, George
Screenwriter(s)   Gruskin, Jerry

Cast   Martin, Janet; Douglas, Warren; Evans, Dale; Fowley, Douglas; Mara, Adele

Song(s)   It's Not the First Love [1] (C: Scott, Nathan; L: Maxwell, Eddie)

Notes   [1] Also in I COVER THE WATERFRONT and ROSE OF THE YUKON.

### 6384 ◆ THE TRIAL OF VIVIENNE WARE
Fox, 1932

Director(s)   Howard, William K.
Screenwriter(s)   Klein, Philip; Connors, Barry
Source(s)   (novel) Ellis, Kenneth M.

Cast   Bennett, Joan; Cook, Donald; Gallagher, Skeets; Pitts, ZaSu; Bond, Lillian; Dinehart, Alan; Mundin, Herbert; Selwyn, Ruth

Song(s)   Together Again (C: Hanley, James F.; L: Freed, Ralph); If I Were Adam and You Were Eve [1] (C/L: Hanley, James F.)

Notes   [1] Sheet music only.

### 6385 ◆ TRIBUTE
Twentieth Century–Fox, 1981

Musical Score   Wannberg, Ken

Producer(s)   Michaels, Joel B.; Drabinsky, Garth
Director(s)   Clark, Bob
Screenwriter(s)   Slade, Bernard
Source(s)   Tribute (play) Slade, Bernard

Cast   Lemmon, Jack; Benson, Robby; Remick, Lee; Dewhurst, Colleen; Cattrall, Kim; Garnett, Gale; Marley, John

Song(s)   It's All for the Best (C: Lemmon, Jack; L: Lerner, Alan Jay); We Still Have Time (C: Manilow, Barry; L: Feldman, Jack; Sussman, Bruce)

### 6386 ◆ TRIBUTE TO A BAD MAN
Metro–Goldwyn–Mayer, 1956

Musical Score   Rozsa, Miklos

Producer(s)   Zimbalist, Sam
Director(s)   Wise, Robert
Screenwriter(s)   Blankfort, Michael
Source(s)   "Jeremy Rodock" [1] (story) Schaefer, Jack

Cast   Cagney, James; Dubbins, Don; McNally, Stephen; Morrow, Vic; Papas, Irene; Griffith, James; Nolan, Jeanette; Van Cleef, Lee; Dano, Royal

Song(s)   Rough Wrangler (C/L: Jones, Stan)

Notes   Spencer Tracy began the filming of this picture but quit and was replaced by Cagney. [1] Also published under the title "Hanging's for the Lucky."

### 6387 ◆ TRICK OR TREAT (1952)
Disney, 1952

Musical Score   Smith, Paul J.

Director(s)   Hannah, Jack
Screenwriter(s)   Wright, Ralph

Song(s)   Trick or Treat (C/L: David, Mack; Hoffman, Al; Livingston, Jerry)

Notes   Cartoon short.

### 6388 ◆ TRICK OR TREAT (1986)
De Laurentiis Entertainment, 1986

Musical Score   Young, Christopher

Producer(s)   Murphey, Michael S.; Soisson, Joel
Director(s)   Smith, Charles Martin

**Screenwriter(s)** Murphey, Michael S.; Soisson, Joel; Topham, Rhet

**Cast** Price, Marc; Fields, Tony; Orgolini, Lisa; Savant, Doug; Joyce, Elaine; Simmons, Gene; Osbourne, Ozzy

**Song(s)** Stand Up (C/L: Fastway); Tear It Down (C/L: Fastway); Trick or Treat (C/L: Fastway)

**Notes** No cue sheet available.

## 6389 ✦ TRIGGER JR.
### Republic, 1950

**Producer(s)** White, Edward J.
**Director(s)** Witney, William
**Screenwriter(s)** Geraghty, Gerald

**Cast** Rogers, Roy; Trigger; Evans, Dale; Brady, Pat; Jones, Gordon; Withers, Grant; Miles, Peter; Cleveland, George; Foy Willing and the Riders of the Purple Sage

**Song(s)** The Big Rodeo [1] (C/L: Willing, Foy); May the Good Lord Take a Liking to You [2] (C/L: Tinturin, Peter); Stampede (C/L: Rice, Darol; Willing, Foy)

**Notes** [1] Spanish lyrics by Aaron Gonzalez. [2] Sheet music also credits Roy Rogers.

## 6390 ✦ TRIGGER TRAIL
### Universal, 1944

**Producer(s)** Drake, Oliver
**Director(s)** Collins, Lewis D.
**Screenwriter(s)** Repp, Ed Earl; Harper, Patricia

**Cast** Cameron, Rod; Austin, Vivian

**Song(s)** Trail Dreamin' [1] (C: Rosen, Milton; L: Drake, Oliver; Wakely, Jimmy); I'm Headin' for My Oklahoma Home (C/L: Hamilton, Albert; Mays, Muriel); Twilight on the Prairie [2] (C/L: Whitley, Ray); 'Long About Sundown (C/L: Marvin, Johnny)

**Notes** [1] Also in BOSS OF HANGTOWN MESA and THE LONE STAR TRAIL. [2] Also credited to Fred Rose in the RKO pictures THE FARGO KID and RED RIVER ROBIN HOOD.

## 6391 ✦ TRIPLE CROSS
### Warner Brothers, 1967

**Musical Score** Garvarentz, Georges

**Producer(s)** Bertrand, Jacques-Paul
**Director(s)** Young, Terence
**Screenwriter(s)** Hardy, Rene; Marchant, William
**Source(s)** *The Eddie Chapman Story* (book) Owen, Frank; Chapman, Eddie

**Cast** Plummer, Christopher; Schneider, Romy; Howard, Trevor; Frobe, Gert; Auger, Claudine; Brynner, Yul; Mayen, Harry

**Song(s)** Triple Cross (C: Garvarentz, Georges; L: Kaye, Buddy)

## 6392 ✦ TRIPLE DECEPTION
### United Artists, 1957

**Musical Score** Clifford, Hubert

**Producer(s)** Wintle, Julian; Cox, Vivian A.
**Director(s)** Green, Guy
**Screenwriter(s)** Buckner, Robert; Forbes, Bryan
**Source(s)** *Storm Over Paris* (novel) Noel, Sterling

**Cast** Craig, Michael; Arnall, Julia; De Banzie, Brenda; Bates, Barbara; Kossoff, David; Oury, Gerard

**Song(s)** Mon Amour Parisien (C: Green, Philip; L: Stellman, Marcel)

**Notes** Titled HOUSE OF SECRETS in Great Britain.

## 6393 ✦ TRIPLE JUSTICE
### RKO, 1940

**Musical Score** Dreyer, Dave; Sawtell, Paul

**Producer(s)** Gilroy, Bert
**Director(s)** Howard, David
**Screenwriter(s)** Jones, Arthur V.; Grant, Morton

**Cast** O'Brien, George; Vale, Virginia; Shannon, Peggy; Woods, Harry; Fix, Paul; Strange, Glenn; The Lindeman Sisters

**Song(s)** Lonely Rio (C/L: Whitley, Ray; Rose, Fred)

## 6394 ✦ A TRIP WITH ANITA
### United Artists, 1978

**Musical Score** Morricone, Ennio; Travia, Maria

**Producer(s)** Grimaldi, Alberto
**Director(s)** Monicelli, Mario
**Screenwriter(s)** Benvenuti, Leo; de Barnardi, Piero; Pinelli, Tulio; Zimmerman, Paul; Monicelli, Mario

**Cast** Giannini, Giancarlo; Hawn, Goldie; Auger, Claudine; Clement, Aurore; Montagnani, Renzo

**Song(s)** Move (C/L: Morricone, Ennio; Travia, Maria; L: Fraser)

**Notes** Italian title: VIAGGIO CON ANITA. Also known as TRAVELS WITH ANITA and also LOVERS AND LIARS.

## 6395 ✦ TROCADERO
### Republic, 1944

**Musical Score** Chernis, Jay

**Producer(s)** Colmes, Walter
**Director(s)** Nigh, William
**Screenwriter(s)** Gale, Allen

**Cast** Lane, Rosemary; Downs, Johnny; Morgan, Ralph; Purcell, Dick; Nazarro, Cliff; Nazarro, Sheldon; Manners, Marjorie; Johnson, Erskine; Fleischer, Dave; Robinson, Dewey

**Song(s)** Bull Frog Jump (C/L: Porter, Lew); Roundabout Way (C/L: Porter, Lew; Clare, Evelyn; Urban, B.); Louisiana Lulu (C/L: Porter, Lew; Mitchell, T.P.); The King Was Doing the Rhumba (C: Chernis, Jay; L: Porter, Lew); How Could You Do That to Me (C/L: Porter, Lew); Can't Take the Place of You (C/L: Colmes, Walter; Porter, Lew); Trying to Forget (C/L: Romano, Tony); Shoo Shoo Baby [1] (C/L: Moore, Phil); The Trocadero [2] (C/L: Porter, Lew)

**Notes** "The Music Goes Round and Round" by Red Hodgson, Michael Riley and Edward Farley is also used as a vocal. It is also in SING BABY SING (20th) and THE MUSIC GOES ROUND (Columbia). [1] Also used in BEAUTIFUL BUT BROKE (Columbia), BIG CITY (1948) and SOUTH OF DIXIE (Universal). [2] Sheet music only.

### 6396 ♦ TRON
Disney, 1982

**Musical Score** Carlos, Wendy

**Producer(s)** Kushner, Donald
**Director(s)** Lisberger, Steven
**Screenwriter(s)** Lisberger, Steven

**Cast** Bridges, Jeff; Boxleitner, Bruce; Warner, David; Morgan, Cindy; Hughes, Barnard; Shor, Dan

**Song(s)** 1990's Theme (Inst.) (C: Schon, Neal; Cain, Jonathan); Only Solutions (C/L: Perry, Steve; Schon, Neal; Cain, Jonathan)

**Notes** The songwriters were members of the band Journey.

### 6397 ♦ TROOPER HOOK
United Artists, 1957

**Musical Score** Fried, Gerald

**Producer(s)** Fielding, Sol Baer
**Director(s)** Warren, Charles Marquis
**Screenwriter(s)** Warren, Charles Marquis; Vistor, David; Little, Herbert

**Cast** McCrea, Joel; Stanwyck, Barbara; Lawrence, Terry; Dehner, John

**Song(s)** Trooper Hook (C: Fried, Gerald; L: Cummings, Mitzi)

### 6398 ♦ TROOPERS THREE
Tiffany, 1930

**Composer(s)** Silver, Abner
**Lyricist(s)** Waggner, George

**Producer(s)** Empey, Arthur Guy
**Director(s)** Taurog, Norman; Eason, B. Reeves
**Screenwriter(s)** Natteford, Jack

**Cast** Lease, Rex; Gulliver, Dorothy; Karns, Roscoe; Summerville, Slim; London, Tom; Girard, Joseph; Perry, Walter

**Song(s)** As Long As You Love Me; Please Be Good to Me; The Girl from Oscaloosa

**Notes** No cue sheet available.

### 6399 ♦ TROPICAL HEAT WAVE
Republic, 1952

**Musical Score** Wilson, Stanley

**Producer(s)** Picker, Sidney
**Director(s)** Springsteen, R.G.

**Cast** Rodriguez, Estelita; Hutton, Robert; Withers, Grant; Miller, Kristine

**Song(s)** My Lonely Heart and I (C/L: Wilson, Stanley; Horman, Arthur T.); I Want to Be Kissed (C: Amaral, Nestor; L: Wilson, Stanley); What Should Happen to You (C/L: Wilson, Stanley)

### 6400 ♦ TROPICAL MASQUERADE
Paramount, 1948

**Producer(s)** Grey, Harry
**Director(s)** Ganzer, Alvin

**Cast** Guizar, Tito

**Song(s)** Morena (C/L: Del Moral, Jorge); Tonight Will Live (Oracion Caribe) [1] (C: Lara, Augustin; L: Lara, Augustin; Washington, Ned); Rosa (C/L: Lara, Augustin)

**Notes** Short subject. [1] Also in CARIBBEAN ROMANCE and TROPIC HOLIDAY.

### 6401 ♦ TROPICANA

See THE HEAT'S ON.

### 6402 ♦ TROPIC HOLIDAY
Paramount, 1938

**Composer(s)** Lara, Augustin
**Lyricist(s)** Washington, Ned; Lara, Augustin

**Producer(s)** Hornblow Jr., Arthur
**Director(s)** Reed, Theodore
**Screenwriter(s)** Hartman, Don; Butler, Frank; Moffitt, John C.; Atteberry, Duke

**Cast** Lamour, Dorothy; Milland, Ray; Raye, Martha; Burns, Bob

**Song(s)**   The Lamp on the Corner (Farolito) [4]; On a Tropic Night (Noche De Vera Cruz); My First Love (Mujer) [2] (L: Lara, Augustin); Tonight Will Live (Oracion Caribe) [5]; Havin' Myself a Time (C: Rainger, Ralph; L: Robin, Leo); Ensenada Nights [1]; On the Wings of a Breeze [1] (L: Washington, Ned); The Hot Tamale Man [1] (L: Washington, Ned); Como Me Gusto [1] (L: Lara, Augustin); Janitzio [1] (L: Lara, Augustin); The Song of the Fishermen (Ay Ay Ay) [1] (L: Washington, Ned); This Time of the Year [1] [3] (L: Washington, Ned); Serenade for Two [1] (L: Washington, Ned); Tropic Night [1] (L: Washington, Ned)

**Notes**   Formerly titled ENSENADA and then MANANA. The titles in parenthesis are the original Spanish titles by Augustin Lara. If no Spanish name appears the song was probably just a tune which Washington put lyrics to. [1] Not used. [2] Apparently Ned Washington wrote English lyrics but only the Spanish were used. [3] Only song with both words by Washington and music by Lara to be written for the film. [4] Also in LAS VEGAS NIGHTS and CHAMPAGNE FOR TWO. [5] Also in CARIBBEAN ROMANCE and TROPICAL MASQUERADE.

## 6403  ◆  TROPIC OF CANCER
### Paramount, 1970

**Musical Score**   Myers, Stanley

**Producer(s)**   Strick, Joseph
**Director(s)**   Strick, Joseph
**Screenwriter(s)**   Strick, Joseph; Botley, Betty
**Source(s)**   *Tropic of Cancer* (novel) Miller, Henry

**Cast**   Torn, Rip; Bauer, David; Brown, Phil; Burstyn, Ellen; Callahan, James; Ligneres, Laurence

**Song(s)**   Germaine [1] (C: Myers, Stanley; L: Darrow, Jay)

**Notes**   [1] Song used for exploitation only.

## 6404  ◆  TROPIC ZONE
### Paramount, 1953

**Musical Score**   Cailliet, Lucien

**Producer(s)**   Pine, William; Thomas, William
**Director(s)**   Foster, Lewis R.
**Screenwriter(s)**   Foster, Lewis R.
**Source(s)**   *Gentleman of the Jungle* (novel) Gill, Tom

**Cast**   Reagan, Ronald; Fleming, Rhonda; Estelita; Beery Jr., Noah; Withers, Grant

**Song(s)**   I'll Always Love You [1] (C/L: Livingston, Jay; Evans, Ray)

**Notes**   [1] Also in MY FRIEND IRMA GOES WEST.

## 6405  ◆  TROUBLE ALONG THE WAY
### Warner Brothers, 1953

**Musical Score**   Steiner, Max

**Producer(s)**   Shavelson, Melville
**Director(s)**   Curtiz, Michael
**Screenwriter(s)**   Shavelson, Melville; Rose, Jack
**Source(s)**   "It Figures" (story) Morrow, Douglas; Andrews, Robert H.

**Cast**   Wayne, John; Reed, Donna; Coburn, Charles; Tully, Tom; Jackson, Sherry; Windsor, Marie; Helmore, Tom; Greer, Dabbs; Erickson, Leif; Connors, Chuck

**Song(s)**   St. Anthony's Alma Mater Hymn (C: Steiner, Max; L: Cahn, Sammy); When the Roll Is Called Alma Mater [1] (C: Fain, Sammy; L: Kahal, Irving)

**Notes**   A brief rendition of "Mother Machree" by Chauncey Olcott, Ernest R. Ball and Rida Johnson Young is used. [1] Also in GENTLEMEN ARE BORN.

## 6406  ◆  TROUBLE IN MIND
### Alive, 1985

**Musical Score**   Isham, Mark

**Producer(s)**   Pfeiffer, Carolyn; Blocker, David
**Director(s)**   Rudolph, Alan
**Screenwriter(s)**   Rudolph, Alan

**Cast**   Kristofferson, Kris; Carradine, Keith; Singer, Lori; Bujold, Genevieve; Morton, Joe; Divine; Kirby, George; Considine, John; Blocker, Dirk

**Song(s)**   El Bavilan (C: Isham, Mark; L: Kristofferson, Kris); True Love (C/L: Shallat, Phil; Engerman, John)

**Notes**   No cue sheet available.

## 6407  ◆  TROUBLE IN PARADISE
### Paramount, 1932

**Composer(s)**   Harling, W. Franke
**Lyricist(s)**   Robin, Leo

**Producer(s)**   Lubitsch, Ernst
**Director(s)**   Lubitsch, Ernst
**Screenwriter(s)**   Raphaelson, Samson
**Source(s)**   *The Honest Finder* (play) Lazlo, Aladar

**Cast**   Marshall, Herbert; Francis, Kay; Hopkins, Miriam; Ruggles, Charles; Horton, Edward Everett; Smith, C. Aubrey; Greig, Robert; Kinskey, Leonid

**Song(s)**   Trouble in Paradise; Colet and Company; Grand Opera Sequence; You'll Fall in Love in Venice [1] [3] (L: Coslow, Sam); I'm Afraid to Waltz with You [1] [2] (L: Coslow, Sam)

**Notes**   Formerly titled THE HONEST FINDER. [1] Not used. [2] Also not used in EL PRINCIPE GONDOLERO and FOUR HOURS TO KILL. [3] In EL PRINCIPE GONDOLERO.

## 6408 ♦ TROUBLE IN STORE
United Artists, 1953

**Musical Score** Spoliansky, Mischa

**Producer(s)** Cowan, Maurice
**Director(s)** Carstairs, John Paddy
**Screenwriter(s)** Carstairs, John Paddy; Cowan, Maurice; Willis, Ted

**Cast** Wisdom, Norman; Morris, Lana; Rutherford, Margaret; Lister, Moira; Bond, Derek; Demonde, Jerry

**Song(s)** I'd Like to Put on Record (C: Spoliansky, Mischa; L: Arkell, David); Don't Laugh at Me ('Cos I'm a Fool) [1] (C/L: Wisdom, Norman; Tremayne, June)

**Notes** [1] Also in AS LONG AS THEY'RE HAPPY (with music credited to Stanley Black) and UP IN THE WORLD.

## 6409 ♦ TROUBLE IN SUNDOWN
RKO, 1939

**Musical Score** Webb, Roy

**Producer(s)** Gilroy, Bert
**Director(s)** Howard, David
**Screenwriter(s)** Drake, Oliver; McGowan, Dorrell; McGowan, Stuart

**Cast** O'Brien, George; Meith, Rosalind; Whitley, Ray; Wills, Chill; Bond, Ward; Kendall, Cyrus W.; Montague, Monte

**Song(s)** Prairie Winds (C/L: Whitley, Ray); Home on the Prairie (C/L: Whitley, Ray)

## 6410 ♦ TROUBLE IN THE GLEN
Republic, 1954

**Musical Score** Young, Victor

**Producer(s)** Wilcox, Herbert
**Director(s)** Wilcox, Herbert
**Screenwriter(s)** Nugent, Frank S.
**Source(s)** *Trouble in the Glen* (novel) Walsh, Maurice

**Cast** Lockwood, Margaret; Welles, Orson; Tucker, Forrest; McLaglen, Victor; McCallum, John; Byrne, Eddie

**Song(s)** Song of the Broken Claw (C/L: Collins, Anthony); Just a Wee Drap Oot the Bottle (C/L: McKay, Jock)

## 6411 ♦ TROUBLE MAN
Twentieth Century–Fox, 1972

**Musical Score** Gaye, Marvin

**Producer(s)** Freeman, Joel D.
**Director(s)** Dixon, Ivan
**Screenwriter(s)** Black, John D.F.

**Cast** Hooks, Robert; Winfield, Paul; Waite, Ralph; Kelly, Paula; Capers, Virginia

**Song(s)** Trouble Man (C/L: Gaye, Marvin)

## 6412 ♦ THE TROUBLE WITH GIRLS
Metro–Goldwyn–Mayer, 1969

**Choreographer(s)** Lucas, Jonathan

**Producer(s)** Welch, Lester
**Director(s)** Tewksbury, Peter
**Screenwriter(s)** Peyser, Arnold; Peyser, Lois
**Source(s)** *Chautauqua* (novel) Keene, Day; Babcock, Dwight

**Cast** Presley, Elvis; Mason, Marlyn; North, Sheree; Andrews, Edward; Carradine, John; Jones, Anissa; Jaffe, Nicole; Brown, Pepe; Coleman, Dabney; Nichols, Robert; Price, Vincent; Van Patten, Joyce

**Song(s)** Doodle Doo Doo (C/L: Kassel, Art; Stitzel, Mel); Clean Up Your Own Backyard (C/L: Strange, Billy; Davis, Scott); Signs of the Zodiac (C/L: Kaye, Buddy; Weisman, Ben); Almost (C/L: Kaye, Buddy; Weisman, Ben); Chatauqua March [1] (C/L: Kaye, Buddy; Weisman, Ben)

**Notes** There are also vocals of "Exulstate Justi" by L. DaViadana; "When You Wore a Tulip" by Percy Wenrich and Jack Mahoney; "Toot Toot Tootsie" by Gus Kahn, Ernie Erdman and Dan Russo; "Darktown Strutter's Ball" by Shelton Brooks; "Bell Song" by Delibes; "Ah Fors'e Lui" from LA TRAVIATA by Verdi; "Swing Down, Sweet Chariot," "Lord High Executioner" and "The Moon and I" from THE MIKADO and "Captain of the Pinafore" and "Three Little Maids Are We" from H.M.S. PINAFORE both by Gilbert and Sullivan; "A-Roving," "Frere Jacques," "Blow the Man Down," "Mademoiselle from Armentieres," "Row, Row, Row Your Boat," "Rocked in the Cradle of the Deep" and "Violets" by H.V. Hill and H.R. Green; "Rambling Boy," "Cripple Creek" and "I'm Nobody's Baby" by Milton Ager, Lester Santly and Benny Davis and many other popular and folk tunes in renditions of less than a minute. [1] Used instrumentally only.

## 6413 ♦ THE TROUBLE WITH HARRY
Paramount, 1955

**Musical Score** Herrmann, Bernard

**Producer(s)** Hitchcock, Alfred
**Director(s)** Hitchcock, Alfred
**Screenwriter(s)** Hayes, John Michael
**Source(s)** (novel) Story, Jack Trevor

**Cast** Gwenn, Edmund; Forsythe, John; Natwick, Mildred; Dunnock, Mildred; Mathers, Jerry; Dano, Royal; Fennelly, Parker; MacLaine, Shirley

**Song(s)**    Flaggin' the Train to Tuscaloosa [1] (C: Scott, Raymond; L: David, Mack); The Trouble with Harry (1) [2] (C/L: Loesser, Frank); The Trouble with Harry (2) [2] (C: McIntyre, Mark; L: Huddleston, Floyd; Eiseman, H.)

**Notes**    [1] Not written for the film. The music was taken from the Lucky Strike Cigarettes theme written by Raymond Scott. Mack David added new lyrics for this picture. [2] Written and used for exploitation only.

## 6414 ✦ THE TROUBLE WITH WOMEN
### Paramount, 1947

**Producer(s)**    Tugend, Harry
**Director(s)**    Lanfield, Sidney
**Screenwriter(s)**    Sheekman, Arthur

**Cast**    Milland, Ray; Wright, Teresa; Donlevy, Brian

**Song(s)**    Trap that Wolf (C: Wayne, Bernie; L: Raleigh, Ben)

**Notes**    Originally titled TOO TRUE TO BE GOOD.

## 6415 ✦ THE TRUCK THAT FLEW
### Paramount, 1943

**Producer(s)**    Pal, George
**Director(s)**    Pal, George

**Song(s)**    Moonlight Holiday (C: de Packh, Maurice; L: Porter, Del)

**Notes**    No cue sheet available. Sheet music only. This is a George Pal Puppetoon short.

## 6416 ✦ TRUE CONFESSION
### Paramount, 1937

**Producer(s)**    Lewis, Albert
**Director(s)**    Ruggles, Wesley
**Screenwriter(s)**    Binyon, Claude
**Source(s)**    *Mon Crime* (play) Verneuil, Louis; Berr, Georges

**Cast**    Lombard, Carole; MacMurray, Fred; Merkel, Una; Barrymore, John; Overman, Lynne; Kennedy, Edgar; Hall, Porter; Feld, Fritz; McDaniel, Hattie

**Song(s)**    True Confession [1] (C: Hollander, Frederick; L: Coslow, Sam)

**Notes**    [1] Used instrumentally only.

## 6417 ✦ TRUE GRIT
### Paramount, 1969

**Musical Score**    Bernstein, Elmer
**Composer(s)**    Bernstein, Elmer
**Lyricist(s)**    Black, Don

**Producer(s)**    Wallis, Hal B.
**Director(s)**    Hathaway, Henry

**Screenwriter(s)**    Roberts, Marguerite
**Source(s)**    *True Grit* (novel) Portis, Charles

**Cast**    Wayne, John; Campbell, Glen; Darby, Kim; Slate, Jeremy; Duvall, Robert; Martin, Strother

**Song(s)**    True Grit [1]; Where Is the Willow [2]; The Eyes of the Young [2]

**Notes**    [1] Used as background vocal only. [2] Not used.

## 6418 ✦ TRUE STORIES
### Warner Brothers, 1986

**Composer(s)**    Byrne, David
**Lyricist(s)**    Byrne, David

**Producer(s)**    Kirfirst, Gary
**Director(s)**    Byrne, David
**Screenwriter(s)**    Tobolowsky, Stephen; Henley, Beth; Byrne, David

**Cast**    Goodman, John; McEnroe, Annie; Allen, Jo Harvey; Gray, Spalding; Byrne, David; Kurtz, Swoosie

**Song(s)**    Cocktail Desperado (C/L: Byrne, David; Allen, Terry); Mall Melodies; Wild Wild Life; Love for Sale; City of Dreams; People Like Us; Dream Operator; Radio Head; Papa Legba

**Notes**    No cue sheet available.

## 6419 ✦ THE TRUE STORY OF JESSE JAMES
### Twentieth Century–Fox, 1957

**Producer(s)**    Swope Jr., Herbert B.
**Director(s)**    Ray, Nicholas
**Screenwriter(s)**    Newman, Walter

**Cast**    Wagner, Robert; Hunter, Jeffrey; Lange, Hope; Moorehead, Agnes; Hale, Alan; Baxter, Alan; Carradine, John; Seldes, Marian

**Song(s)**    Black Girl (C/L: Ray, Nicholas; Darby, Ken)

## 6420 ✦ TRUE TO LIFE
### Paramount, 1943

**Composer(s)**    Carmichael, Hoagy
**Lyricist(s)**    Mercer, Johnny

**Producer(s)**    Jones, Paul
**Director(s)**    Marshall, George
**Screenwriter(s)**    Hartman, Don; Tugend, Harry

**Cast**    Martin, Mary; Powell, Dick; Moore, Victor; Paige, Mabel; Demarest, William

**Song(s)**    Mister Pollyanna; Sudsy Suds Theme Song; The Old Music Master [3]; There She Was (L: Carmichael, Hoagy); Moments Like This [1] (C: Lane, Burton; L: Loesser, Frank); When Love Walks By [2]; My Daddy Told Me [2] [4] (C: Press, Jacques; L: Cherkose, Eddie)

**Notes** [1] Not used but recorded. Used in COLLEGE SWING, LAS VEGAS NIGHTS and MONEY FROM HOME. [2] Not used. [3] Called "Mr. Music Master" on cue sheet. [4] Used in STAR BRIGHT.

### 6421 ✦ TRUE TO THE ARMY
Paramount, 1942

**Composer(s)**   Spina, Harold
**Lyricist(s)**   Loesser, Frank

**Producer(s)**   Siegel, Sol C.
**Director(s)**   Rogell, Albert S.
**Screenwriter(s)**   Arthur, Art; Ropes, Bradford
**Source(s)**   *She Loves Me Not* (novel) Coffey Jr., Edward Hope; *She Loves Me Not* (play) Lindsay, Howard

**Cast**   Canova, Judy; Hopkins, Miriam; Jones, Allan; Miller, Ann

**Song(s)**   In the Army; Spangles on My Tights; I Can't Give You Anything but Love [1] (C: McHugh, Jimmy; L: Fields, Dorothy); Need I Speak?; Swing in Line (C: Lilley, Joseph J.); Jitterbug's Lullaby; Wacki for Khaki; Tin Horn (inst.) [1] [2]; We're Building Men [1]; Ophelia [1]

**Notes**   [1] Not used. [2] Recorded.

### 6422 ✦ TRUE TO THE NAVY
Paramount, 1930

**Director(s)**   Tuttle, Frank
**Screenwriter(s)**   Thompson, Keene; Anderson, Doris; Mankiewicz, Herman J.

**Cast**   Bow, Clara; March, Fredric; Green, Harry; Bell, Rex; Fetherston, Eddie; Dunn, Eddie; Hardy, Sam; Prouty, Jed

**Song(s)**   There's Only One (Who Matters to Me) (C: Baer, Abel; L: Gilbert, L. Wolfe)

### 6423 ✦ THE TRUMPET BLOWS
Paramount, 1934

**Composer(s)**   Rainger, Ralph
**Lyricist(s)**   Robin, Leo

**Director(s)**   Roberts, Stephen
**Screenwriter(s)**   Cormack, Bartlett; Smith, Wallace
**Source(s)**   "The Return of the Bad Man" (story) Browne, Porter Emerson; Read Jr., J. Parker

**Cast**   Raft, George; Menjou, Adolphe; Drake, Frances

**Song(s)**   Pancho; This Night [2]; My Heart Does a Rumba [1]; The Red Cape (inst.)

**Notes**   [1] Used instrumentally only. [2] Not used in SOULS AT SEA.

### 6424 ✦ THE TRUTH ABOUT MOTHER GOOSE
Disney, 1957

**Musical Score**   Bruns, George
**Composer(s)**   Bruns, George
**Lyricist(s)**   Adair, Tom

**Director(s)**   Reitherman, Wolfgang; Justice, Bill
**Screenwriter(s)**   Peet, Bill

**Cast**   The Page Cavanaugh Trio

**Song(s)**   The Truth About Mother Goose; London Bridge Rock and Roll

**Notes**   Animated cartoon.

### 6425 ✦ TUCKER: THE MAN AND HIS DREAM
Paramount, 1988

**Musical Score**   Jackson, Joe

**Producer(s)**   Roos, Fred; Fuchs, Fred
**Director(s)**   Coppola, Francis Ford
**Screenwriter(s)**   Schulman, Arnold; Seidler, David

**Cast**   Bridges, Jeff; Allen, Joan; Landau, Martin; Forrest, Frederic; Mako; Stockwell, Dean; Slater, Christian; Donat, Peter; Sanders, Jay O.; Novello, Don

**Song(s)**   Tucker Jingle (C: Coppola, Carmine; L: Schulman, Arnold)

**Notes**   "Tiger Rag" by Harry DeCosta, Edwin B. Edwards, D. James LaRocca, Anthony Sbarbaro and Larry Shields (Original Dixieland Jazz Band) was used extensively in the score.

### 6426 ✦ TUCSON
Twentieth Century–Fox, 1949

**Musical Score**   Calker, Darrell
**Composer(s)**   Kornblum, I.B.
**Lyricist(s)**   Gilbert, L. Wolfe

**Producer(s)**   Wurtzel, Sol M.
**Director(s)**   Claxton, William F.
**Screenwriter(s)**   Belgard, Arnold

**Cast**   Lydon, Jimmy; Edwards, Penny; Wayne, Deanna; Russell, Charles; Sawyer, Joe; Stratton, Gil; Lauter, Harry

**Song(s)**   Ringin' the New Year In; Nobody's Lost on the Lonesome Trail

### 6427 ✦ TUGBOAT GRANNY
Warner Brothers, 1956

**Musical Score**   Franklyn, Milton J.

**Director(s)**   Freling, Friz

**Cast**    Tweety; Sylvester; Granny

**Song(s)**    Chugga-Chugga-Chug (C: Franklyn, Milton J.; L: Foster, Warren)

**Notes**    Merrie Melodie.

## 6428 ✦ TULIP TIME IN MICHIGAN
### Studio Unknown, 1942

**Lyricist(s)**    Freed, Ralph

**Song(s)**    Tulip Time (L: Lane, Burton; L: Freed, Ralph); Cradle Song (C: Mozart, Wolfgang Amadeus; L: Freed, Ralph; Brent, Earl); Dreamer's Lullaby (C: Mozart, Wolfgang Amadeus)

**Notes**    No other information available.

## 6429 ✦ TULSA
### Eagle Lion, 1949

**Musical Score**    Skinner, Frank

**Producer(s)**    Wanger, Walter
**Director(s)**    Heisler, Stuart
**Screenwriter(s)**    Nugent, Frank; Kenyon, Curtis

**Cast**    Hayward, Susan; Preston, Robert; Armendariz, Pedro; Gough, Lloyd; Wills, Chill; Begley, Ed

**Song(s)**    Tulsa (C: Wrubel, Allie; Greene, Mort)

**Notes**    No cue sheet available.

## 6430 ✦ TUMBLEDOWN RANCH IN ARIZONA
### Monogram, 1941

**Musical Score**    Sanucci, Frank
**Composer(s)**    Steiner, Howard
**Lyricist(s)**    Watters, Bill

**Producer(s)**    Weeks, George W.
**Director(s)**    Luby, S. Roy
**Screenwriter(s)**    Raison, Milton

**Cast**    Corrigan, Ray; King, John; Terhune, Max; Darcy, Sheila; Kerby, Marion

**Song(s)**    Tumbledown Ranch in Arizona; Wake Up with the Dawn

## 6431 ✦ TUMBLEWEED TRAIL
### PRC, 1947

**Musical Score**    Hajos, Karl

**Producer(s)**    Tansey, Robert Emmett
**Director(s)**    Tansey, Robert Emmett
**Screenwriter(s)**    Kavanaugh, Frances

**Cast**    Dean, Eddie; Ates, Roscoe; Patterson, Shirley; McGovern, Johnny; Duncan, Bob; Adams, Ted;

Maynard, Kermit; Fawcett, William; The Sunshine Boys [1]

**Song(s)**    Sands of the Rio Grande [2] (C/L: Dean, Eddie; Strange, Glenn); Way Back in Oklahoma [3] (C/L: Dean, Eddie; Bond, Johnny); 1501 Miles of Heaven (C/L: Dean, Eddie); Stars Over Texas [2] (C/L: Dean, Eddie; Blair, Hal)

**Notes**    [1] Consisted of M.H. Richman, J.O. Smith, A.L. Smith and Edward F. Wallace. [2] Also in STARS OVER TEXAS. [3] Also in THE TIOGA KID (Pathe) and, without Eddie Dean credit, in SIX LESSONS FROM MADAME LA ZONGA (Universal).

## 6432 ✦ TUMBLING TUMBLEWEEDS
### Republic, 1935

**Composer(s)**    Burnette, Smiley
**Lyricist(s)**    Burnette, Smiley

**Producer(s)**    Levine, Nat
**Director(s)**    Kane, Joseph
**Screenwriter(s)**    Beebe, Ford

**Cast**    Autry, Gene; Burnette, Smiley; Browne, Lucille; Taylor, Norma; Hayes, George "Gabby"; Chesebro, George; King, Charles

**Song(s)**    Cornfed and Rusty; The Old Covered Wagon; Ridin' Down the Canyon [1] (C/L: Burnette, Smiley); Tumbling Tumbleweeds [2] (C/L: Nolan, Bob); That Silver Haired Daddy of Mine (C/L: Autry, Gene; Long, Jimmy)

**Notes**    No cue sheet available. Autry's first starring film. [1] Also in RIDIN' DOWN THE CANYON and SILVER CANYON (Columbia). Gene Autry is listed as the coauthor of this song but he did not contribute to it. [2] Also in RHYTHM ROUND-UP (Columbia), DON'T FENCE ME IN, IN OLD MONTEREY, SILVER SPURS and HOLLYWOOD CANTEEN (Warner).

## 6433 ✦ TUNNEL OF LOVE
### Metro–Goldwyn–Mayer, 1958

**Musical Score**    Sack, Al

**Producer(s)**    Fields, Joseph; Melcher, Martin
**Director(s)**    Kelly, Gene
**Screenwriter(s)**    Fields, Joseph
**Source(s)**    *Tunnel of Love* (play) Fields, Joseph; De Vries, Peter

**Cast**    Day, Doris; Widmark, Richard; Young, Gig; Scala, Gia; Fraser, Elisabeth; Wilson, Elizabeth; Weaver, Doodles; The Esquire Trio

**Song(s)**    Have Lips, Will Kiss in the Tunnel of Love (C/L: Roberts, Bob; Fisher, Patty); Runaway, Skidaddle, Skidoo (C/L: Roberts, Ruth; Katz, Bill)

## 6434 ◆ TURK 182
Twentieth Century–Fox, 1985

**Musical Score** Zaza, Paul; Zittner, Carl

**Producer(s)** Field, Ted; Dupont, Rene
**Director(s)** Clark, Bob
**Screenwriter(s)** Kingston, James Gregory; Hamill, Denis; Hamill, John

**Cast** Hutton, Timothy; Urich, Robert; Cattrall, Kim; Culp, Robert; McGavin, Darren; Keats, Steven; Sorvino, Paul

**Song(s)** Burning Down the House [1] (C/L: Frantz, Chris; Byrne, David; Weymouth, Tina; Harrison, Jerry); Down by the Station (C/L: Ricks, Lee; Gaillard, Slim)

**Notes** There is also a vocal of "Mack the Knife" by Kurt Weill, Marc Blitzstein and Bertolt Brecht. [1] Also in REVENGE OF THE NERDS where the credit is for David Byrne only.

## 6435 ◆ TURN BACK THE CLOCK
Metro–Goldwyn–Mayer, 1933

**Musical Score** Stothart, Herbert

**Producer(s)** Rapf, Harry
**Director(s)** Selwyn, Edgar
**Screenwriter(s)** Selwyn, Edgar; Hecht, Ben

**Cast** Tracy, Lee; Clarke, Mae; Kruger, Otto; Barbier, George; Blandick, Clara

**Song(s)** Tony's Wife (C: Lane, Burton; L: Adamson, Harold)

## 6436 ◆ TURN OFF THE MOON
Paramount, 1937

**Composer(s)** Coslow, Sam
**Lyricist(s)** Coslow, Sam

**Producer(s)** Roger, Fanchon
**Director(s)** Seiler, Lewis
**Screenwriter(s)** Ware, Harlan; Roberts, Marguerite; Smith, Paul Gerard

**Cast** Ruggles, Charles; Baker, Kenny; Whitney, Eleanore; Downs, Johnny

**Song(s)** Turn Off the Moon; Easy on the Eyes; That's Southern Hospitality [2]; Jammin'; The Little Wooden Soldier (and the Walking, Talking Doll) [1]

**Notes** [1] Not used. [2] Also briefly in LAS VEGAS NIGHTS.

## 6437 ◆ THE TUTTLES OF TAHITI
RKO, 1942

**Musical Score** Webb, Roy
**Composer(s)** Goupil, Augie
**Lyricist(s)** Goupil, Augie

**Producer(s)** Lesser, Sol
**Director(s)** Vidor, Charles
**Screenwriter(s)** Meltzer, Lewis; Carson, Robert
**Source(s)** *No More Gas* (novel) Nordhoff, Charles; Hall, James Norman

**Cast** Laughton, Charles; Hall, Jon; Drake, Peggy; Francen, Victor; Reynolds, Gene; Bates, Florence; Bois, Curt

**Song(s)** Uahiti O Te Ra (C/L: Webb, Roy; Goupil, Augie; Ruby, Herman); Ro Ri Ete Ro Ri Hi; Tuatira Mot E; Ua Tua Ti Ti Nia

## 6438 ◆ TUXEDO JUNCTION
Republic, 1941

**Producer(s)** Schaefer, Armand
**Director(s)** McDonald, Frank
**Screenwriter(s)** McGowan, Stuart; McGowan, Dorrell

**Cast** Weaver, Leon; Weaver, June; Weaver, Frank; Hall, Thurston; Darro, Frankie; Payne, Sally; Moore, Clayton; The Little Vagabonds

**Song(s)** Tuxedo Junction (C: Hawkins, Erskine; Johnson, William; Dash, Julian; L: Fayne, Buddy)

**Notes** This song wasn't written for this film. Originally an instrumental (written in 1939), lyrics were added in 1940.

## 6439 ◆ TWEETIE PIE
Warner Brothers, 1947

**Musical Score** Stalling, Carl

**Director(s)** Freling, Friz

**Cast** Tweety; Sylvester

**Song(s)** He'll Do Me No Harm (C/L: Stalling, Carl)

**Notes** Merrie Melodie. Warner's first Academy Award winning cartoon.

## 6440 ◆ TWEET TWEET TWEETY
Warner Brothers, 1951

**Musical Score** Stalling, Carl

**Director(s)** Freling, Friz
**Screenwriter(s)** Foster, Warren

**Cast** Tweety; Sylvester

**Song(s)** Tweety's Lament (C/L: Stalling, Carl)

**Notes** Looney Tune.

## 6441 ◆ TWENTY-FOUR HOURS
Paramount, 1931

**Director(s)** Gering, Marion
**Screenwriter(s)** Weitzenkorn, Louis
**Source(s)** (novel) Bromfield, Louis

**Cast**   Hopkins, Miriam; Brook, Clive; Toomey, Regis; Francis, Kay; Granville, Charlotte; Barbier, George; Ames, Adrienne; Watson, Minor; LaVerne, Lucille; Jackson, Thomas

**Song(s)**   You're the One I Crave (C/L: King, Jack); It's No Use Trying to Leave That Man (C: King, Jack; L: Coslow, Sam); All I Need Is Your Love [1] (C: King, Jack; L: Coslow, Sam)

**Notes**   Released as THE HOURS BETWEEN in Great Britain. [1] Not used.

## 6442 ✦ TWENTY MILLION SWEETHEARTS
### Warner Brothers, 1934

**Composer(s)**   Warren, Harry
**Lyricist(s)**   Dubin, Al

**Producer(s)**   Bischoff, Sam
**Director(s)**   Enright, Ray
**Screenwriter(s)**   Duff, Warren; Sauber, Larry
**Source(s)**   "Hot Air" (story) Moss, Paul Finder; Wald, Jerry

**Cast**   O'Brien, Pat; Powell, Dick; Rogers, Ginger; The Four Mills Brothers; Ted Fiorito and His Band; Jenkins, Allen; Mitchell, Grant; Cawthorn, Joseph; Wheeler, Joan; O'Neill, Henry; Arthur, Johnny

**Song(s)**   Out for No Good; I Heard (C/L: Redman, Don); How'm I Doin (C/L: Redman, Don); I'll String Along with You; Fair and Warmer; What Are Your Intentions

**Notes**   It is not known if the Redman songs were written for the picture. There are also brief renditions of "Carolina Moon" by Joe Burke; "Marta" by L. Wolfe Gilbert and Moises Simons; "My Time Is Your Time" by Dance; "When the Blue of the Night" by Fred Ahlert and several complete renditions of "Man on the Flying Trapeze" by O'Keefe and Billy Hill's "The Last Round Up" with parody lyrics.

## 6443 ✦ 20,000 LEAGUES UNDER THE SEA
### Disney, 1955

**Musical Score**   Smith, Paul J.

**Director(s)**   Fleischer, Richard
**Screenwriter(s)**   Felton, Earl
**Source(s)**   *20,000 Leagues Under the Sea* (novel) Verne, Jules

**Cast**   Douglas, Kirk; Mason, James; Lukas, Paul; Lorre, Peter

**Song(s)**   A Whale of a Tale (C/L: Hoffman, Al; Gimbel, Norman)

## 6444 ✦ 23 1/2 HOURS LEAVE
### Grand National, 1937

**Composer(s)**   Stept, Sam H.
**Lyricist(s)**   Koehler, Ted

**Producer(s)**   MacClean, Douglas
**Director(s)**   Blystone, John
**Screenwriter(s)**   Ruskin, Harry; McCarty, Henry; Warshawsky, Samuel J.

**Cast**   Ellison, James; Walker, Terry; Hill, Morgan; Lake, Arthur; Harvey, Paul; Gleason, Pat; Bond, Ward

**Song(s)**   Good Night My Lucky Day; Now You're Talking My Language (C/L: Koehler, Ted; Mitchell, Sidney D.); It Must Be Love; We Happen to Be in the Army

**Notes**   No cue sheet available.

## 6445 ✦ TWICE IN A LIFETIME
### Bud Yorkin Company, 1985

**Musical Score**   Metheny, Pat

**Producer(s)**   Yorkin, Bud
**Director(s)**   Yorkin, Bud
**Screenwriter(s)**   Welland, Colin

**Cast**   Hackman, Gene; Ann-Margaret; Burstyn, Ellen; Madigan, Amy; Sheedy, Ally; Dennehy, Brian; Lang, Stephen

**Song(s)**   Twice in a Lifetime (C/L: McCartney, Paul)

**Notes**   No cue sheet available.

## 6446 ✦ TWICE UPON A TIME
### Ladd Company, 1983

**Musical Score**   Atkinson, Dawn; Melville, Ken

**Producer(s)**   Couturie, Bill
**Director(s)**   Korty, John; Swenson, Charles
**Screenwriter(s)**   Korty, John; Swenson, Charles; Kennedy, Suella; Couturie, Bill
**Source(s)**   "The Rushers of Din" (story) Korty, John; Couturie, Bill
**Narrator(s)**   Frees, Paul

**Song(s)**   Twice Upon a Time (C/L: Atkinson, Dawn; Ferguson, Tom; McDonald, Michael); Life Is But a Dream (C/L: Atkinson, Dawn; Ferguson, Tom; McDonald, Michael); Out on My Own (C/L: McDonald, Maureen; Ferguson, Tom; Moordigian, David); Heartbreak Town (C/L: Hornsby, Bruce; Hornsby, Jon)

**Notes**   Animated feature. No cue sheet available.

## 6447 ✦ TWILIGHT IN THE SIERRAS
### Republic, 1950

**Composer(s)**   Willing, Foy
**Lyricist(s)**   Robin, Sid

**Producer(s)**   White, Edward J.
**Director(s)**   Witney, William
**Screenwriter(s)**   Nibley, Sloan

**Cast**   Rogers, Roy; Trigger; Evans, Dale

**Song(s)**   Rootin' Tootin' Cowboy; Pancho's Rancho; It's One Wonderful Day; Twilight in the Sierras

## 6448 ✦ TWILIGHT ON THE PRAIRIE
### Universal, 1944

**Composer(s)**   Rosen, Milton
**Lyricist(s)**   Carter, Everett

**Producer(s)**   Wilson, Warren
**Director(s)**   Yarbrough, Jean
**Screenwriter(s)**   Bruckman, Clyde

**Cast**   Austin, Vivian; Errol, Leon; Quillan, Eddie; Jack Teagarden and His Orchestra

**Song(s)**   I Get Mellow in the Yellow of the Moon [1] (C/L: Dodd, Jimmy); The Sip Nip Song (C/L: George, Don; Weisberg, Brenda); Where the Prairie Meets the Sky [4]; The Blues (C/L: Teagarden, Jack); Let's Love Again [2]; Salt Water Cowboy (C/L: Evans, Redd); Need I Say More? [3]; Don't You Ever Be a Cowboy; No Letter Today (C/L: Brown, Frankie); Texas Polka (C/L: Knight, Vick; Haldeman, Oakley; Porter, Lew)

**Notes**   [1] Also in THE MYSTERY OF THE RIVER BOAT. [2] Also in STARS AND VIOLINS and TOO MANY BLONDES. [3] Also in COWOBY IN MANHATTAN. [4] Also in BAD MAN FROM RED BUTTE, ESCAPE FROM HONG KONG, FRONTIER LAW and I'LL TELL THE WORLD.

## 6449 ✦ TWILIGHT ON THE RIO GRANDE
### Republic, 1947

**Composer(s)**   Elliott, Jack
**Lyricist(s)**   Elliott, Jack

**Producer(s)**   Schaefer, Armand
**Director(s)**   McDonald, Frank
**Screenwriter(s)**   McGowan, Dorrell; McGowan, Stuart

**Cast**   Autry, Gene; Champion; Holloway, Sterling; Mara, Adele; Steele, Bob; Evans, Charles; Cass County Boys, The

**Song(s)**   The Pretty Knife Grinder [1]; The Old Lamplighter (C/L: Simon, Nat; Tobias, Charles); Twilight on the Rio Grande

**Notes**   No cue sheet available. [1] Spanish lyrics by Aaron Gonzales.

## 6450 ✦ TWILIGHT ON THE TRAIL
### Paramount, 1941

**Producer(s)**   Sherman, Harry
**Director(s)**   Bretherton, Howard
**Screenwriter(s)**   Cheney, J. Benton; Kramer, Cecile; Corby, Ellen

**Cast**   Boyd, William; King, Brad; McKay, Wanda; Clyde, Andy

**Song(s)**   The Funny Old Hills [2] (C: Rainger, Ralph; L: Robin, Leo); Twilight on the Trail [2] (C: Alter, Louis; L: Mitchell, Sidney D.); Cimarron (Roll On) [1] (C/L: Bond, Johnny)

**Notes**   [1] Also in HEART OF THE RIO GRANDE (Republic). [2] Also in PARIS HONEYMOON. [3] Also in THE TRAIL OF THE LONESOME PINE.

## 6451 ✦ TWILIGHT ZONE
### Warner Brothers, 1983

**Musical Score**   Goldsmith, Jerry

**Producer(s)**   Spielberg, Steven; Landis, John
**Director(s)**   Landis, John; Spielberg, Steven; Dante, Joe; Miller, George
**Screenwriter(s)**   Landis, John; Johnson, George Clayton; Matheson, Richard; Rogan, Josh

**Cast**   Aykroyd, Dan; Brooks, Albert; Morrow, Vic; McGrath, Doug; Crothers, Benjamin "Scatman"; Quinn, Bill; Diamond, Selma; Garner, Martin; Pointer, Priscilla; Quinlan, Kathleen; Licht, Jeremy; McCarthy, Kevin; Schallert, William; Lithgow, John; Lane, Abbe; Dixon, Donna

**Song(s)**   Nights Are Forever (C: Goldsmith, Jerry; L: Bettis, John); Anesthesia (C/L: Williams, Joseph; Gordon, Paul)

**Notes**   This movie consisted of four different segments.

## 6452 ✦ TWIN BEDS
### Warner Brothers–First National, 1929

**Director(s)**   Santell, Alfred
**Screenwriter(s)**   Willis, F. McGrew
**Source(s)**   (play) Mayo, Margaret; Fields, Salisbury

**Cast**   Mulhall, Jack; Miller, Patsy Ruth; Kaliz, Armand; Chapman, Edythe; Astor, Gertrude; Lake, Alice; Gribbon, Eddie; Lee, Jocelyn; Erickson, Knute; Martan, Nita; Pitts, ZaSu; Roach, Bert

**Song(s)**   If You Were Mine (C: Meyer, George W.; L: Bryan, Al); Chicken Walk (C: Meyer, George W.; L: Bryan, Alfred)

**Notes**   No cue sheet available. A remake of the 1920 film of the same title.

## 6453 ✦ TWINKLE AND SHINE

See IT HAPPENED TO JANE.

## 6454 ✦ THE TWINKLE IN GOD'S EYE
### Republic, 1955

**Producer(s)**   Rooney-Duke Enterprises
**Director(s)**   Blair, George
**Screenwriter(s)**   Wolfson, P.J.

**Cast**    Rooney, Mickey; Gray, Coleen; O'Brian, Hugh; Forman, Joey; Barry, Donald; Hatton, Raymond; Lee, Ruta

**Song(s)**    The Twinkle in God's Eye (C/L: Rooney, Mickey); I'm So Lonesome (C/L: Rooney, Mickey)

### 6455 ✦ TWINKLE TWINKLE "KILLER" KANE
Warner Brothers, 1980

**Musical Score**    De Vorzon, Barry

**Producer(s)**    Blatty, William Peter
**Director(s)**    Blatty, William Peter
**Screenwriter(s)**    Blatty, William Peter
**Source(s)**    *The Ninth Configuration* (novel) Blatty, William Peter

**Cast**    Keach, Stacy; Wilson, Scott; Miller, Jason; Flanders, Ed; Brand, Neville; Dicenzo, George; Gunn, Moses; Loggia, Robert; Spinell, Joe; Rey, Alejandro

**Song(s)**    Dancing in the Night (C/L: De Vorzon, Barry)

**Notes**    Background vocal.

### 6456 ✦ TWINS
Universal, 1988

**Musical Score**    Edelman, Randy; Delerue, Georges

**Producer(s)**    Reitman, Ivan
**Director(s)**    Reitman, Ivan
**Screenwriter(s)**    Davies, William; Osborne, William; Harris, Timothy; Weingrod, Herschel

**Cast**    Schwarzenegger, Arnold; DeVito, Danny; Preston, Kelly; Webb, Chloe; Bartlett, Bonnie; Bell, Marshall; Persoff, Nehemiah

**Song(s)**    Turtle Shoes (C/L: McFerrin, Bobby; Hancock, Herbie); I'd Die for This Dance (C/L: Clark, Tena; Prim, Gary); Brother to Brother (C/L: Kimmel, Tim; Vidal, Elizabeth); Twins (C/L: Scarborough, Skip; Bates, Lorrin "Smokey")

### 6457 ✦ TWIST AROUND THE CLOCK
Columbia, 1961

**Composer(s)**    Springer, Phil
**Lyricist(s)**    Cole, Clay; Kaye, Buddy

**Producer(s)**    Katzman, Sam
**Director(s)**    Rudolph, Oscar
**Screenwriter(s)**    Gordon, James B.

**Cast**    Checker, Chubby; Dion and the Belmonts; Spencer, Vicki; Cole, Clay; Moore, Alvy; Parker, Jeff; The Marcels

**Song(s)**    Twist Around the Clock; The Twist Is Here to Stay (C: Karger, Fred; L: Cole, Clay); Don't Twist With Anyone Else But Me; The Wanderer (C/L: Meresca, E.); Here There Everywhere (C/L: Van, Teddy); Twistin' U.S.A. [1] (C/L: Mann, Kal); Your Lips and Mine (C/L: Mann, Kal; Appell, Dave); Run Around Sue (C/L: Meresca, E.; Dimucci, D.); Too Many Boyfriends (C/L: Spencer, Vicki); The Majestic (C/L: Jones, B.L.; Young, Wilton); Merry Twist-Mas (C/L: Wolfson, Mack; Hall, Wally; Singleton, Charles); He's So Sweet (C/L: Tucker, A.; Elias, G.; Evans, G.); Twist Along (C/L: Mann, Kal; Appell, Dave)

**Notes**    Other than the Clay Cole songs it is not known if any were written for the film. [1] Also in TEENAGE MILLIONAIRE (UA).

### 6458 ✦ TWIST OF FATE
United Artists, 1954

**Musical Score**    Arnold, Malcolm

**Director(s)**    Miller, David
**Screenwriter(s)**    Westerby, Robert; Nystrom, Carl

**Cast**    Rogers, Ginger; Bergerac, Jacques; Baker, Stanley; Lom, Herbert; Rawlings, Margaret; Byrne, Eddie; Browne, Coral

**Song(s)**    Love Is a Beautiful Stranger (C: Ferrer, Jose; L: Frings, Ketti)

**Notes**    Originally released in Britain as BEAUTIFUL STRANGER.

### 6459 ✦ TWO AGAINST THE WORLD
Warner Brothers–First National, 1936

**Producer(s)**    Foy, Bryan
**Director(s)**    McGann, William
**Screenwriter(s)**    Jacoby, Michel
**Source(s)**    *Five Star Final* (play) Weitzenkorn, Louis

**Cast**    Perry, Linda; Bogart, Humphrey; Roberts, Beverly; O'Neill, Henry; MacKellar, Helen; Dodd, Claire; Cavanaugh, Hobart; Wood, Douglas; Stone, Paula

**Song(s)**    The Moon Does Things to Me (C: Jerome, M.K.; L: Scholl, Jack)

**Notes**    Remake of 1931 film FIVE STAR FINAL. Released in Great Britain as THE CASE OF MRS. PEMBROOK.

### 6460 ✦ TWO A PENNY
Universal, 1968

**Musical Score**    Leander, Mike

**Producer(s)**    Jacobson, Frank R.
**Director(s)**    Collier, James F.
**Screenwriter(s)**    Linden, Stella

**Cast**    Richard, Cliff; Bryan, Dora; Angers, Avril; Holloway, Ann; Bayldon, Geoffrey; Washbourne, Mona

**Song(s)**    Two a Penny (C/L: Richard, Cliff); Questions, Questions (C/L: Richard, Cliff; Collier, James F.); Love You Forever, Today (C/L: Richard, Cliff; Collier, James F.)

**Notes**    A World Wide Films British production.

## 6461 ✦ TWO ARE GUILTY
### Metro–Goldwyn–Mayer, 1964

**Musical Score** Louiguy
**Composer(s)** Louiguy
**Lyricist(s)** Louiguy

**Producer(s)** Poire, Alain
**Director(s)** Cayatte, Andre
**Screenwriter(s)** Jeanson, Henri

**Cast** Perkins, Anthony; Brialy, Jean-Claude; Salvatori, Renato; Audret, Pascale

**Song(s)** Amor Mio; Mo Lily; I Sing the Blues (L: Brown, Ruth); I'm Dreaming of You (Je Reve de Vous) (L: Vaudrey, M.)


## 6462 ✦ TWO BLONDES AND A REDHEAD
### Columbia, 1947

**Composer(s)** Roberts, Allan; Fisher, Doris
**Lyricist(s)** Roberts, Allan; Fisher, Doris
**Choreographer(s)** Brier, Audrene

**Producer(s)** Katzman, Sam
**Director(s)** Dreifuss, Arthur
**Screenwriter(s)** McLeod, Victor; Brewer, Jameson

**Cast** Porter, Jean; Lloyd, Jimmy; Preisser, June; Clark, Judy; Tony Pastor and His Orchestra

**Song(s)** It's So Easy; The Si Si Song (All I Know Is Si Si) [2]; Nothin' Boogie from Nowhere [1] (C/L: Chaplin, Saul)

**Notes** There is also a vocal of "On the Sunny Side of the Street" by Jimmy McHugh and Dorothy Fields. [1] Also in KANSAS CITY KITTY. [2] Also in SMOKY RIVER SERENADE.


## 6463 ✦ TWO CROWS FROM TACOS
### Warner Brothers, 1956

**Musical Score** Stalling, Carl

**Director(s)** Freling, Friz
**Screenwriter(s)** Pierce, Ted

**Song(s)** The Peon (C/L: Stalling, Carl)

**Notes** Merrie Melodie.


## 6464 ✦ TWO FOR THE ROAD
### Twentieth Century–Fox, 1967

**Musical Score** Mancini, Henry

**Producer(s)** Donen, Stanley
**Director(s)** Donen, Stanley
**Screenwriter(s)** Raphael, Frederic

**Cast** Hepburn, Audrey; Finney, Albert; Daniels, William; Bron, Eleanor; Dauphin, Claude; Middleton, Gabrielle; Jones, Cathy

**Song(s)** Two for the Road [1] (C: Mancini, Henry; L: Bricusse, Leslie)

**Notes** [1] Lyric added for exploitation only.


## 6465 ✦ TWO FOR THE SEESAW
### United Artists, 1962

**Musical Score** Previn, Andre

**Producer(s)** Mirisch, Walter
**Director(s)** Wise, Robert
**Screenwriter(s)** Lennart, Isobel
**Source(s)** Two for the Seesaw (play) Gibson, William

**Cast** Mitchum, Robert; MacLaine, Shirley; Ryan, Edmon; Fraser, Elisabeth; Firestone, Eddie; Gray, Billy

**Song(s)** Gitana (C/L: Lundin, Vic); A Second Chance (C: Previn, Andre; L: Langdon, Dory)


## 6466 ✦ TWO FOR TONIGHT
### Paramount, 1935

**Composer(s)** Revel, Harry
**Lyricist(s)** Gordon, Mack

**Producer(s)** MacLean, Douglas
**Director(s)** Tuttle, Frank
**Screenwriter(s)** Marion Jr., George; Storm, Jane; Ruskin, Harry

**Cast** Crosby, Bing; Bennett, Joan; Boland, Mary; Overman, Lynne

**Song(s)** Two for Tonight (1); Takes Two to Make a Bargain (What's the Answer—What's the Verdict—How's About It Baby); Did You Ever See a Dream Walking? [1] [5]; From the Top of Your Head to the Tip of Your Toes; I Wish I Were Aladdin; Without a Word of Warning; Start My Heart Again [2] (C: Coslow, Sam; L: Marion Jr., George); Love Can Be Fun [2] (C: Coslow, Sam; L: Marion Jr., George); Keep Your Fingers Crossed [2] [3] (C/L: Coslow, Sam); May I Have the Next Dream with You? [2] [4] (C: Coslow, Sam; L: Marion Jr., George); Two for Tonight (2) [2] (C/L: Coslow, Sam)

**Notes** [1] Not written for this film. [2] Not used. [3] Written for ALL THE KING'S HORSES. Used for CORONADO with Richard A. Whiting music. [4] Written for WAIKIKI WEDDING. [5] Also in SITTING PRETTY.


## 6467 ✦ TWO GIRLS AND A SAILOR
### Metro–Goldwyn–Mayer, 1944

**Composer(s)** McHugh, Jimmy
**Lyricist(s)** Freed, Ralph
**Choreographer(s)** Lee, Sammy

**Producer(s)**    Pasternak, Joe
**Director(s)**    Thorpe, Richard
**Screenwriter(s)**    Connell, Richard; Lehman, Gladys

**Cast**    Allyson, June; De Haven, Gloria; Johnson, Van; Drake, Tom; Stephenson, Henry; Blue, Ben; Sully, Frank; Meek, Donald; Novarro, Amparo; Coates, Albert; Ramirez, Carlos; O'Neill, Henry; Iturbi, Jose; Durante, Jimmy; Allen, Gracie; Horne, Lena; O'Brien, Virginia; The Wilde Twins; Harry James and His Music Makers; Forrest, Helen; Xavier Cugat and His Orchestra; Romay, Lina

**Song(s)**    Did You Ever Have the Feeling (C/L: Durante, Jimmy); Who Will Be With You When I'm Far Away (C/L: Farrell); A Love Like Ours (C: Nichols, Alberta; L: Holiner, Mann); My Mother Told Me; Take It Easy (C/L: Brent, Earl); In a Moment of Madness; Young Man with a Horn [2] (C: Stoll, George); You Dear (C: Fain, Sammy); Inka Dinka Doo (C/L: Durante, Jimmy); Sweet and Lovely [1] (C/L: Arnheim, Gus; Lemare, Jules; Tobias, Harry); Take It Easy (C/L: de Bru, Albert; Taylor, Irving; Mizzy, Vic); La Mulata Rumbero [3] (C/L: Rodriguez, Alejandro); I Found Out This Morning that I Fell in Love Last Night [4]; I've Got My Mind Set On You [4]; You Slipped Right Through My Fingers [4]

**Notes**    This film may have once been titled TWO SISTERS AND A SAILOR. There are also vocals of "A Tisket A Tasket" by Ella Fitzgerald and Al Feldman; "Rumba Rumba" by Jose Parfumay and Valencia; "Granada" by Augustin Lara and Dorothy Dodd; "Estrellita" by Manuel Ponce; "Babalu" by Marguerita Lecuona and "Paper Doll" by Johnny S. Black. [1] Also in BEAST OF THE CITY. [2] Vocal arranger Kay Thompson may have contributed lyrics to this number. Also in THE OPPOSITE SEX. [3] Sheet music only. [4] Not used.

### 6468 ◆ TWO GIRLS ON BROADWAY
Metro–Goldwyn–Mayer, 1940

**Choreographer(s)**    Connolly, Bobby; Larkin, Eddie

**Producer(s)**    Cummings, Jack
**Director(s)**    Simon, S. Sylvan
**Screenwriter(s)**    Fields, Joseph; Chodorov, Jerome

**Cast**    Turner, Lana; Blondell, Joan; Murphy, George; Taylor, Kent; Wilson, Don

**Song(s)**    My Wonderful One Let's Dance (C/L: Edens, Roger; Brown, Nacio Herb; Freed, Arthur); Broadway's Still Broadway [2] (C: Revel, Harry; L: Fetter, Ted); Rancho Santa Fe [1] (C: Donaldson, Walter; L: Kahn, Gus); True Love [1] (C: Donaldson, Walter; L: Kahn, Gus); Maybe It's the Moon [3] (C: Donaldson, Walter; L: Wright, Robert; Forrest, Chet)

**Notes**    A remake of BROADWAY MELODY. Titled CHOOSE YOUR PARTNERS internationally. [1] Used instrumentally only. [2] Also in GRAND CENTRAL MURDER. [3] Sheet music only.

### 6469 ◆ TWO GUN GOOFY
Disney, 1952

**Musical Score**    Smith, Paul J.

**Cast**    Goofy

**Song(s)**    I'm a Ropin' and a Ridin' (C/L: Smith, Paul J.)

**Notes**    Cartoon short. No credit sheet available.

### 6470 ◆ TWO GUN RUSTY
Paramount, 1944

**Musical Score**    de Packh, Maurice

**Producer(s)**    Pal, George
**Director(s)**    Pal, George

**Song(s)**    Down in Santa Fe (C: de Packh, Maurice; L: Sooter, Rudy)

**Notes**    Short subject. This is a Puppetoon.

### 6471 ◆ TWO GUYS FROM MILWAUKEE
Warner Brothers, 1946

**Musical Score**    Hollander, Frederick

**Producer(s)**    Gottlieb, Alex
**Director(s)**    Butler, David
**Screenwriter(s)**    Hoffman, Charles; Diamond, I.A.L.
**Source(s)**    "Royal Welcome" (story) Hoffman, Charles; Diamond, I.A.L.

**Cast**    Morgan, Dennis; Carson, Jack; Leslie, Joan; Paige, Janis; Sakall, S.Z.; Brady, Patti; D'Andrea, Tom; De Camp, Rosemary; Ridgely, John; McVey, Patrick; Pangborn, Franklin

**Song(s)**    And Her Tears Flowed Like Wine [1] (C/L: Kenton, Stanley; Greene, Joe; Lawrence, Charles)

**Notes**    There is a cameo appearance by Humphrey Bogart and Lauren Bacall. [1] Also in THE BIG SLEEP.

### 6472 ◆ TWO GUYS FROM TEXAS
Warner Brothers, 1948

**Musical Score**    Hollander, Frederick
**Composer(s)**    Styne, Jule
**Lyricist(s)**    Cahn, Sammy
**Choreographer(s)**    Prinz, LeRoy

**Producer(s)**    Gottlieb, Alex
**Director(s)**    Butler, David
**Screenwriter(s)**    Diamond, I.A.L.; Boretz, Allen
**Source(s)**    *Howdy Stranger* (play) Pelletier Jr., Louis; Sloane, Robert

**Cast**    Morgan, Dennis; Carson, Jack; Malone, Dorothy; Edwards, Penny; Tucker, Forrest; Mohr, Gerald; Alvin, John; Tombes, Andrew; Blue, Monte

**Song(s)**    There's Music in the Land; I Don't Care If It Rains All Night; I Never Met a Texan; Ev'ry Day I Love You (Just a Little Bit More); I Wanna Be a Cowboy in the Movies; Hankerin'; At the Rodeo

**6473 ✦ 200 MOTELS**
United Artists, 1971

**Musical Score**   Zappa, Frank
**Composer(s)**   Zappa, Frank
**Lyricist(s)**   Zappa, Frank

**Producer(s)**   Good, Jerry; Cohen, Herb
**Director(s)**   Zappa, Frank
**Screenwriter(s)**   Zappa, Frank

**Cast**   Zappa, Frank; The Mothers of Invention; Bikel, Theodore; Starr, Ringo; Ferguson, Janet; Offerall, Lucy

**Notes**   Songs are not deliniated on cue sheet.

**6474 ✦ TWO KINDS OF WOMAN**
Paramount, 1932

**Director(s)**   de Mille, William C.
**Screenwriter(s)**   Glazer, Benjamin
**Source(s)**   (play) Sherwood, Robert E.

**Cast**   Pichel, Irving; Holmes, Phillips; Gibson, Wynne; Erwin, Stuart; Dodd, Claire; Osborne, Vivienne; Fields, Stanley; Crane, James; Taylor, Kent; Dunn, Josephine; Ames, Adrienne

**Song(s)**   Who Was Made for Who (C/L: Grier, Jimmy; Coslow, Sam); Miserable Me (C/L: Rainger, Ralph); My Hour Has Come [1] (C/L: Rainger, Ralph)

**Notes**   [1] Not used. Also not used in DANCERS IN THE DARK.

**6475 ✦ TWO LATINS FROM MANHATTAN**
Columbia, 1941

**Composer(s)**   Chaplin, Saul
**Lyricist(s)**   Cahn, Sammy

**Producer(s)**   MacDonald, Wallace
**Director(s)**   Barton, Charles
**Screenwriter(s)**   Duffy, Albert

**Cast**   Davis, Joan; Beddoe, Don; Bridges, Lloyd; Falkenburg, Jinx; Woodbury, Joan; Bonanova, Fortunio; Storm, Rafael; Arno, Sig; Davis, Boyd

**Song(s)**   Daddy [1] (C/L: Troup, Bobby); How Do You Say It; The Kid with the Drum

**Notes**   Originally titled GIRLS FROM PANAMA. [1] Not written for film.

**6476 ✦ THE TWO LITTLE BEARS**
Twentieth Century–Fox, 1961

**Musical Score**   Vars, Henry

**Producer(s)**   George, George W.
**Director(s)**   Hood, Randall F.
**Screenwriter(s)**   George, George W.

**Cast**   Albert, Eddie; Wyatt, Jane; Carter, Donnie; Patrick, Butch; Lee, Brenda; Kulp, Nancy; Sales, Soupy

**Song(s)**   Honey Bear (C/L: Livingston, Jay; L: Evans, Ray); Speak to Me Pretty (C: Vars, Henry; L: Dunham, "By")

**6477 ✦ TWO LOVERS**
United Artists, 1928

**Musical Score**   Riesenfeld, Hugo

**Producer(s)**   Goldwyn, Samuel
**Director(s)**   Niblo, Fred
**Screenwriter(s)**   Colton, John
**Source(s)**   *Leatherface* (novel) Orczy, Emmuska

**Cast**   Colman, Ronald; Banky, Vilma; Beery, Noah; De Brulier, Nigel; Bradford, Virginia; Eddy, Helen Jerome; Besserer, Eugenie; Lukas, Paul

**Song(s)**   Grieving (C/L: Axtell, Wayland); Lenora (C: Riesenfeld, Hugo; L: Gilbert, L. Wolfe)

**Notes**   No cue sheet available.

**6478 ✦ TWO LOVES**
Metro–Goldwyn–Mayer, 1961

**Musical Score**   Kaper, Bronislau
**Composer(s)**   Kaper, Bronislau
**Lyricist(s)**   Ihaka, Kingi

**Producer(s)**   Blaustein, Julian
**Director(s)**   Walters, Charles
**Screenwriter(s)**   Maddow, Ben
**Source(s)**   *Two Loves* (novel) Ashton-Warner, Sylvia

**Cast**   MacLaine, Shirley; Harvey, Laurence; Hawkins, Jack; McCarthy, Nobu; Long, Ronald; Howard, Norah; Hernandez, Juano

**Song(s)**   Ta-Hu-Ri-Mai Ki Au (C: Kaper, Bronislau; Armbruster, Robert); Lullaby; Children's Picnic Song [1]; Funeral Hymn

**Notes**   Originally titled THE SPINSTER, the title by which it was released internationally. [1] Sheet music credits Walton Farrar with lyrics.

**6479 ✦ TWO MEN AND A MAID**
Tiffany–Stahl, 1929

**Musical Score**   Riesenfeld, Hugo

**Director(s)**   Archainbaud, George
**Screenwriter(s)**   Hatton, Frederic; Hatton, Fanny

**Cast**   Collier Jr., William; Bennett, Alma; Gribbon, Eddie; Stone, George E.; Quimby, Margaret

**Song(s)**   Love Will Find You (C: Baer, Abel; L: Gilbert, L. Wolfe); Rose of Algiers (C: Shapiro, Ted; L: Rafael, John)

**Notes**   No cue sheet available.

## 6480 ✦ THE TWONKY
United Artists, 1953

**Musical Score**  Meakin, Jack

**Producer(s)**  Oboler, Arch
**Director(s)**  Oboler, Arch
**Screenwriter(s)**  Oboler, Arch

**Cast**  Conried, Hans; Lynn, Billy; Blondell, Gloria; Warren, Janet; Max, Ed

**Song(s)**  Oh Death Where Is Thy Sting (C: Meakin, Jack; L: Oboler, Arch)

## 6481 ✦ TWO OF A KIND
Twentieth Century–Fox, 1983

**Musical Score**  Williams, Patrick

**Producer(s)**  Rothstein, Roger M.
**Director(s)**  Rothstein, Roger M.
**Screenwriter(s)**  Herzfeld, John

**Cast**  Travolta, John; Newton-John, Olivia; Reed, Oliver; Straight, Beatrice; Crothers, Benjamin "Scatman"; Guerra, Castulo

**Song(s)**  (Living In) Desperate Times (C/L: Snow, Tom; Alfonso, Barry); Ask the Lonely (C/L: Perry, Steve; Cain, Jonathan); Twist of Fate (C/L: Kipner, Steve; Beckett, Peter); The Perfect One (C/L: Scaggs, Boz; Foster, David); Shakin' You (C/L: Foster, David; Gordon, Paul; Keane, Tom); Rain (C/L: McCartney, Paul; Lennon, John); Take a Chance [1] (C/L: Foster, David; Lukather, Steve; Newton-John, Olivia)

**Notes**  It is not known if any of these were written for the film. [1] Sheet music only.

## 6482 ✦ TWO ON A GUILLOTINE
Warner Brothers, 1965

**Musical Score**  Steiner, Max

**Producer(s)**  Conrad, William
**Director(s)**  Conrad, William
**Screenwriter(s)**  Slesar, Henry; Kneubuhl, John

**Cast**  Stevens, Connie; Jones, Dean; Romero, Cesar; Baer, Parley; Gregg, Virginia; Gilchrist, Connie; Hoyt, John

**Song(s)**  My Little Monkey (C/L: Hamilton, George; Brown, Teddy; Carter, Thomas; Sartuche, David; Sareo, Rodger; Martini, Gerry); The Right to Love [1] (C: Steiner, Max; L: Drake, Ervin)

**Notes**  [1] Sheet music only.

## 6483 ✦ TWO PEOPLE
Universal, 1973

**Musical Score**  Shire, David
**Composer(s)**  Shire, David
**Lyricist(s)**  Maltby Jr., Richard

**Producer(s)**  Wise, Robert
**Director(s)**  Wise, Robert
**Screenwriter(s)**  De Roy, Richard

**Cast**  Fonda, Peter; Wagner, Lindsay; Fudge, Alan; Horne, Geoffrey; Sternhagen, Frances; Parsons, Estelle

**Song(s)**  Baby I Think I Love You Too Much; Maintenant; Time Will Tell [1]

**Notes**  [1] Sheet music only.

## 6484 ✦ TWO SECONDS
Warner Brothers–First National, 1932

**Producer(s)**  Wallis, Hal B.
**Director(s)**  LeRoy, Mervyn
**Screenwriter(s)**  Thew, Harvey
**Source(s)**  (play) Elliott, Lester

**Cast**  Robinson, Edward G.; Osborne, Vivienne; Kibbee, Guy; Foster, Preston; Naish, J. Carrol; Walker, Walter; Churchill, Berton

**Song(s)**  Why Did It Have to Be Me (C: Stept, Sam H.; L: Green, Bud; Lombardo, Carmen)

## 6485 ✦ TWO SILHOUETTES
Disney, 1946

**Song(s)**  Two Silhouettes (C: Wolcott, Charles; L: Gilbert, Ray)

**Notes**  This animated short is part of MAKE MINE MUSIC.

## 6486 ✦ TWO SISTERS FROM BOSTON
Metro–Goldwyn–Mayer, 1946

**Composer(s)**  Fain, Sammy
**Lyricist(s)**  Freed, Ralph
**Choreographer(s)**  Donohue, Jack

**Producer(s)**  Pasternak, Joe
**Director(s)**  Koster, Henry
**Screenwriter(s)**  Connolly, Myles; O'Hanlon, James; Crane, Harry

**Cast**  Grayson, Kathryn; Allyson, June; Melchior, Lauritz; Durante, Jimmy; Lawford, Peter; Blue, Ben; Elsom, Isobel; Hayden, Harry; Hall, Thurston; Walker, Nella

**Song(s)**  Hello, Hello, Hello (C/L: Durante, Jimmy); There Are Two Sides to Ev'ry Girl; Nellie Martin; The Firechief's Daughter; G'Wan Home Your Mudder's Callin'; Opera Sequence (C: Liszt, Franz; Previn, Charles); Down By the Ocean; Vales Lente [1] (C: Delibes, Leo; L: Brent, Earl); After the Show; Opera Sequence No. 2 (C: Mendelssohn, Felix; Previn, Charles; L: Brent, Earl); When Romance Passes By [1] [2] (C: Delibes, Leo; L: Brent, Earl); Autumn Twilight [3]; Indian Holiday [3]; Lanterns in the Sky [3]; More Than Ever [3]; Seattle [3]

**Notes** There are also vocals of "An excerpt from Lohengrin" by R. Wagner and Wilhelm von Wymetal; "Preislied" from DIE MEISTERSINGER by Wagner and "O Sole Mio" by Di Capua. [1] These might be the same song. [2] Sheet music only. [3] Not used.

## 6487 ✦ TWO SMART PEOPLE
Metro–Goldwyn–Mayer, 1946

**Musical Score** Bassman, George

**Producer(s)** Wheelwright, Ralph
**Director(s)** Dassin, Jules
**Screenwriter(s)** Hill, Ethel; Charteris, Leslie

**Cast** Ball, Lucille; Hodiak, John; Nolan, Lloyd; Haas, Hugo; Ulric, Lenore; Cook Jr., Elisha; Corrigan, Lloyd; Sokoloff, Vladimir

**Song(s)** Dangerous (Peligrosa) (C: Bassman, George; Blane, Ralph; L: Blane, Ralph)

## 6488 ✦ 2,000 YEARS LATER
Warner Brothers, 1969

**Musical Score** Phillips, Stu
**Composer(s)** Phillips, Stu
**Lyricist(s)** Sedacca, Chuck

**Producer(s)** Tanzer, Bert
**Director(s)** Tanzer, Bert
**Screenwriter(s)** Tanzer, Bert

**Cast** Terry-Thomas; Horton, Edward Everett; Harrington, Pat; Seagram, Lisa; Abbott, John; Rock III, Monti; Kasem, Casey; Gernreich, Rudi

**Song(s)** Two Thousand Years Later; Step Aside You're Crushing All the Flowers; The Ballad of Super Dude; Funsville, U.S.A.

## 6489 ✦ TWO TICKETS TO BROADWAY
RKO, 1951

**Musical Score** Scharf, Walter
**Composer(s)** Styne, Jule
**Lyricist(s)** Robin, Leo
**Choreographer(s)** Berkeley, Busby; Castle, Nick [2]; Ceballos, Larry

**Producer(s)** Wald, Jerry; Krasna, Norman
**Director(s)** Kern, James V.
**Screenwriter(s)** Silvers, Sid; Kanter, Hal

**Cast** Leigh, Janet; Martin, Tony; Miller, Ann; De Haven, Gloria; Lawrence, Barbara; Bracken, Eddie; Crosby, Bob; Smith and Dale; Holmes, Taylor; Baer, Buddy; The Charlivels

**Song(s)** Pelican Falls High; There's No Tomorrow (C/L: Hoffman, Al; Corday, Leo; Carr, Leon); Are You Just a Beautiful Dream; Baby You'll Never Be Sorry; The Closer You Are; Let the Worry Bird Worry for You; Let's Make Comparisons (C: Crosby, Bob; L: Cahn, Sammy);

Big Chief Hole in the Ground; It Began in Yucatan [1]; Let's Do Something New [3]; New York (Let Me Sing) [3]; That's the Tune [3]; Two Tickets to Broadway [3]; Way Down South of Dixie [3]

**Notes** There is also a vocal of "Manhattan" by Richard Rodgers and Lorenz Hart and "When I'm President" by Sherman and Lewis. [1] Used instrumentally only. [2] Nick Castle may not have contributed choreography. He isn't listed in all sources. [3] Not used.

## 6490 ✦ TWO TICKETS TO LONDON
Universal, 1943

**Musical Score** Skinner, Frank

**Producer(s)** Marin, Edwin L.
**Director(s)** Marin, Edwin L.
**Screenwriter(s)** Reed, Tom

**Cast** Curtis, Alan; Morgan, Michele; Smith, C. Aubrey

**Song(s)** You Don't Know What Love Is [1] (C: de Paul, Gene; L: Raye, Don)

**Notes** [1] Also in BUTCH MINDS THE BABY.

## 6491 ✦ TWO TICKETS TO PARIS
Columbia, 1962

**Composer(s)** Gohman, Don
**Lyricist(s)** Hackady, Hal

**Producer(s)** Romm, Harry
**Director(s)** Garrison, Greg
**Screenwriter(s)** Hackady, Hal

**Cast** Joey Dee and the Starlighters; Medford, Kay; Crosby, Gary; Fraser, Jeri Lynne; Reilly, Charles Nelson; James, Lisa

**Song(s)** Two Tickets to Paris; Everytime (I Think About You) (C/L: Taylor, Sam; Glover, Henry; Levy, Morris); This Boat [2] (C/L: Glover, Henry; Levy, Morris; Dee, Joey); The Lady Wants to Twist (C/L: Leiber, Jerry; Stoller, Mike); Willy, Willy (C/L: Glover, Henry; Levy, Morris); Instant Men [2] (L: Hackady, Hal; Dee, Joey); What Kind of Love Is This (C/L: Nash, Johnny); Teenage Vamp (C/L: Seigal, Albert); Twistin' on a Liner [2] (C/L: Glover, Henry; Levy, Morris; Dee, Joey); C'est La Vie (C/L: White, Edward R.; Wolfson, Mack); Baby, Won't You Please Come Home (C/L: Williams, Clarence; Warfield, Charles); C'est Si Bon [1] (C: Betti, Henri; L: Seelen, Jerry)

**Notes** It is not known which of these songs other than the Gohman/Hackady ones, were written for the picture. Morris Levy's songwriter credits are suspect. It is likely that he is a member of the club, including Al Jolson, Billy Rose, Irving Mills and Gene Autry, who had their names put on song which they made no contribution. [1] Original French lyrics by Andre Hornez. [2] Cue sheet does not credit Dee, however soundtrack album does.

## 6492 ✦ TWO WEEKS IN SEPTEMBER
### Paramount, 1967

**Musical Score**  Magne, Michel
**Composer(s)**  Magne, Michel
**Lyricist(s)**  Tulipe, Corinne

**Producer(s)**  Harper, Kenneth; Cosne, Francis
**Director(s)**  Bourguignon, Serge
**Screenwriter(s)**  Katcha, Vahe; Jardin, Pascal; Bourguignon, Serge

**Cast**  Bardot, Brigitte; Terzieff, Laurent; Sarne, Michael; Ward, Georgina; Justice, James Robertson

**Song(s)**  In My Small Country [1]; Do You Want to Marry Me? [1]

**Notes**  The screenplay's English adaptation is by Sean Graham. [1] Used as background vocal only.

## 6493 ✦ TWO WEEKS OFF
### Warner Brothers–First National, 1929

**Director(s)**  Beaudine, William
**Screenwriter(s)**  Willis, F. McGrew; Poland, Joseph; Weil, Richard
**Source(s)**  (play) Nicholson, Kenyon; Barrows, Thomas

**Cast**  Mackaill, Dorothy; Mulhall, Jack; Astor, Gertrude; Finlayson, James; Price, Kate; Gribbon, Eddie; Gay, Dixie; Messinger, Gertrude; Prouty, Jed

**Song(s)**  Love Thrills (C: Meyer, George W.; L: Bryan, Alfred)

**Notes**  No cue sheet available.

## 6494 ✦ TWO WEEKS—WITH LOVE
### Metro–Goldwyn–Mayer, 1950

**Choreographer(s)**  Berkeley, Busby

**Producer(s)**  Cummings, Jack
**Director(s)**  Rowland, Roy
**Screenwriter(s)**  Larkin, John; Kingsley, Dorothy

**Cast**  Powell, Jane; Montalban, Ricardo; Calhern, Louis; Harding, Ann; Kirk, Phyllis; Carpenter, Carleton; Reynolds, Debbie; Sundberg, Clinton; Rettig, Tommy

**Song(s)**  Aba Daba Honeymoon (C/L: Donovan, Walter; Fields, Arthur)

**Notes**  It is not known if the above song was written for this film. There are also vocals of "A Heart That's Free" by Alfred George Robyn and Railey; "That's How I Need You" by Joseph McCarthy, Joe Goodwin and Al Piantadosi; "Oceana Roll" by Lucien Denni and Roger Lewis; "By the Light of the Silvery Moon" by Gus Edwards and Edward Madden; "Beautiful Lady" by Ivan Caryll and McClellan; "My Hero" by Oscar Straus and Stanislaus Stange and "Row, Row, Row" by James V. Monaco and William Jerome.

## 6495 ✦ TWO YANKS IN TRINIDAD
### Columbia, 1942

**Producer(s)**  Bischoff, Sam
**Director(s)**  Ratoff, Gregory
**Screenwriter(s)**  Bartlett, Sy; Carroll, Richard; Segall, Harry; Henley, Jack

**Cast**  O'Brien, Pat; Donlevy, Brian; Blair, Janet; Clark, Roger; Borg, Veda Ann; Sully, Frank; MacBride, Donald; Emery, John; Arno, Sig

**Song(s)**  Trinidad (C: Chaplin, Saul; L: Cahn, Sammy)

## 6496 ✦ TWO YEARS BEFORE THE MAST
### Paramount, 1946

**Producer(s)**  Miller, Seton I.
**Director(s)**  Farrow, John
**Screenwriter(s)**  Miller, Seton I.; Bruce, George
**Source(s)**  *Two Years Before the Mast* (book) Dana Jr., Richard Henry

**Cast**  Donlevy, Brian; Da Silva, Howard; Ladd, Alan; Bendix, William; Fitzgerald, Barry; Dekker, Albert; Collins, Ray; Fernandez, Esther; Hickman, Darryl; Bohnen, Roman

**Song(s)**  Johnnie Chantey-Man (C: Traditional; L: Adams, B.M.)

## 6497 ✦ TYPHOON
### Paramount, 1940

**Producer(s)**  Veiller, Anthony
**Director(s)**  King, Louis
**Screenwriter(s)**  Rivkin, Allen

**Cast**  Lamour, Dorothy; Preston, Robert; Overman, Lynne; Naish, J. Carrol; Carson, Jack; Reicher, Frank; Harvey, Paul; Nelson, Norma; Chief Thundercloud

**Song(s)**  Palms of Paradise (C: Hollander, Frederick; L: Loesser, Frank)

**Notes**  First titled SARONG then SOUTH OF SAMOA.

# U

## 6498 ✦ UFORIA
Universal, 1985

**Musical Score**  Baskin, Richard

**Producer(s)**  Wolf, Gordon
**Director(s)**  Binder, John
**Screenwriter(s)**  Binder, John

**Cast**  Williams, Cindy; Stanton, Harry Dean; Ward, Fred; Atkinson, Beverly Hope; Carey Jr., Harry; Diefendorf, Diane

**Song(s)**  I've Always Been Crazy (C/L: Jennings, Waylon); I Do What It Takes to Get By (C/L: Wilson, Johnny; Bomar, Woody); Euphoria (C/L: Remaily, Robin); Crazy with the Heat (C/L: Welch, Kevin; Paden, Mark); Stoned Again (C/L: Bryant, Boudleaux; Bryant, Felice); I Gotta Outrun the Blues (C/L: Brooks, Jake); When Two Worlds Collide (C/L: Miller, Roger; Anderson, Bill); Break It to Me Gently (C/L: Lampert, Diane; Seneca, Joe); It's Happening to You (C/L: Prine, John; Burns, John); Hollywood Get Ready (C/L: Cason, James); Good Hearted Woman (C/L: Jennings, Waylon; Nelson, Willie); I Know an Ending (C/L: Cochran, Hank); Quicksand (C/L: Burnett, T-Bone)

**Notes**  It is not known which of these were written especially for this picture.

## 6499 ✦ THE ULTIMATE SOLUTION OF GRACE QUIGLEY
Cannon, 1985

**Musical Score**  Addison, John

**Producer(s)**  Golan, Menahem; Globus, Yoram
**Director(s)**  Harvey, Anthony
**Screenwriter(s)**  Zweiback, A. Martin

**Cast**  Hepburn, Katharine; Nolte, Nick; Wilson, Elizabeth; Zien, Chip; Le Fever, Kit; Duell, William; Abel, Walter; Gaige, Truman

**Song(s)**  So Much More (C/L: Herrey, Michel)

**Notes**  No cue sheet available.

## 6500 ✦ ULYSSES
Paramount, 1955

**Musical Score**  Cicognini, Alessandro

**Producer(s)**  De Laurentiis, Dino; Ponti, Carlo; Schorr, William W.
**Director(s)**  Camerini, Mario
**Screenwriter(s)**  Brusati, Franco; Camerini, Mario; De Concini, Ennio; Gray, Hugh; Hecht, Ben; Perilli, Ivo; Shaw, Irwin
**Source(s)**  "Ulysses" (poem) Homer

**Cast**  Douglas, Kirk; Mangano, Silvana; Quinn, Anthony; Podesta, Rossana; Sylvie; Ivernel, Daniel; Dumesnil, Jacques

**Song(s)**  Sirens, Close (C: Cicognini, Alessandro; L: Fange, Angelo)

## 6501 ✦ UMBRELLAS OF CHERBOURG
Twentieth Century–Fox, 1964

**Composer(s)**  Legrand, Michel
**Lyricist(s)**  Demy, Jacques

**Director(s)**  Demy, Jacques
**Screenwriter(s)**  Demy, Jacques

**Cast**  Deneuve, Catherine; Castelnuovo, Nino; Vernon, Anne; Michel, Marc; Perrey, Mirelle; Farmer, Ellen

**Song(s)**  I'm Falling in Love Again (L: Barberis, Billy; Randazzo, Teddy); I Will Wait for You (L: Gimbel, Norman); Watch What Happens (L: Gimbel, Norman); Where's the Love (L: Weinstein, Bobby); Day They Closed the Carousel (L: Allison, Ruth); Two Voices (L: Barberis, Billy; Randazzo, Teddy)

**Notes**  The entire picture is scored therefore the cue sheet did not list individual numbers. The song titles and English language authors (film is entirely in French) are listed above. French title: LES PARAPLUIES DE CHERBOURG.

## 6502 ✦ THE UMPIRE'S DAUGHTER
Paramount, 1945 unproduced

**Composer(s)**  Styne, Jule
**Lyricist(s)**  Cahn, Sammy

**Song(s)**  I Gotta Gal I Love (In North and South Dakota) [1]; Every So Often; What's He Got?

**Notes**  [1] Later in LADIES' MAN.

## 6503 ♦ UNASHAMED
Cine Grand Films, 1938

**Director(s)**  Stuart, Allen
**Screenwriter(s)**  Lively, William

**Cast**  Kidd, Rae; Stanley, Robert; Shearer, Lucille; Todd, Emily; Girard, Joseph; McGillicudddy, Woody

**Song(s)**  Back to Nature (C/L: Gump, Richard; Sprague, Howard)

**Notes**  No cue sheet available.

## 6504 ♦ UN CAPITAN DE COSACOS
Fox, 1934

**Composer(s)**  Sanders, Troy
**Lyricist(s)**  Mojica, Jose

**Song(s)**  El Boyardo; Besame La Ultima Vez (C: Reinhardt); Pequinteselo a Ellas; Polinka Se Casa; Moon Dreams (C: Seaver, Blanche)

**Notes**  No other information available.

## 6505 ♦ UNCENSORED
Gainsborough, 1942

**Producer(s)**  Black, Edward
**Director(s)**  Asquith, Anthony
**Screenwriter(s)**  Ackland, Rodney; Rattigan, Terence
**Source(s)**  (book) Millard, Oscar

**Cast**  Portman, Eric; Calvert, Phyllis; Jones, Griffith; Lovell, Raymond; Glenville, Peter; Culley, Frederick

**Song(s)**  With the Little Bear Behind (C/L: Haines, Will E.; Castling, Harry); Drink to the Ladies (C/L: May, Hans); It Lowers the Tone of the Place (C/L: Haines, Will E.; Harper, Jimmy; Long, J.P.); Waltzing in the Shadows (C/L: May, Hans)

**Notes**  Distributed by Twentieth Century–Fox.

## 6506 ♦ THE UNCERTAIN LADY
Universal, 1934

**Producer(s)**  Van Every, Dale
**Director(s)**  Freund, Karl
**Screenwriter(s)**  O'Neil, George; Anderson, Doris
**Source(s)**  *Behaviour of Mrs. Crane* (play) Segall, Harry

**Cast**  Horton, Edward Everett; Tobin, Genevieve; Gadd, Renee; Meeker, George

**Song(s)**  Tonight May Never Come Again (C: Cowan, Lynn; L: Klatzkin, D.)

## 6507 ♦ UNCOMMON VALOR
Paramount, 1983

**Musical Score**  Horner, James

**Producer(s)**  Milius, John; Feitshans, Buzz
**Director(s)**  Kotcheff, Ted
**Screenwriter(s)**  Gayton, Joe

**Cast**  Hackman, Gene; Ward, Fred; Brown, Reb; Cobb, Randall "Tex"; Swayze, Patrick; Sylvester, Harold; Thomerson, Tim; Stack, Robert

**Song(s)**  Badman [1] (C/L: Kennedy, Ray); Brothers in the Night [1] (C/L: Kennedy, Ray; Ritz, David; Dukes, Kevin)

**Notes**  [1] Background vocal use only.

## 6508 ♦ UNCONQUERED
Paramount, 1947

**Choreographer(s)**  Crosby, Jack

**Producer(s)**  De Mille, Cecil B.
**Director(s)**  De Mille, Cecil B.
**Screenwriter(s)**  Bennett, Charles; Frank, Fredric M.; Lasky Jr, Jesse
**Source(s)**  *The Judas Tree* (novel) Swanson, Neil

**Cast**  Cooper, Gary; Da Silva, Howard; de Mille, Katherine; Karloff, Boris; Kellaway, Cecil; Wilcoxon, Henry; Bond, Ward; Smith, Sir C. Aubrey; Varconi, Victor; Grey, Virginia; Hall, Porter; Napier, Alan; Lawrence, Marc

**Song(s)**  Whippoorwill's a Singin' (C: Young, Victor; Boutelje, Phil; L: Livingston, Jay; Evans, Ray); Marsa's Come Home to Stay [1] (C: Young, Victor; L: Livingston, Jay; Evans, Ray)

**Notes**  [1] Not used.

## 6509 ♦ UNDER A TEXAS MOON
Warner Brothers, 1930

**Director(s)**  Curtiz, Michael
**Screenwriter(s)**  Rigby, Gordon

**Cast**  Fay, Frank; Torres, Raquel; Loy, Myrna; Armida; Beery, Noah

**Song(s)**  Under a Texas Moon (C/L: Perkins, Ray)

**Notes**  No cue sheet available.

## 6510 ♦ UNDER CALIFORNIA STARS
Republic, 1948

**Composer(s)**  Elliott, Jack
**Lyricist(s)**  Elliott, Jack

**Producer(s)**  White, Eddy
**Director(s)**  Witney, William
**Screenwriter(s)**  Gangelin, Paul; Nibley, Sloan

**Cast**    Rogers, Roy; Trigger; Frazee, Jane; Devine, Andy; Lloyd, George H.; Crosby, Wade; Bob Nolan and the Sons of the Pioneers

**Song(s)**    Rogers, King of the Cowboys; Under California Stars [1]; Serenade to a Coyote (C/L: Parker, Andy); Dust (C/L: Marvin, Johnny); Little Saddle Pal

**Notes**    [1] Also in COLORADO SUNDOWN.

### 6511 ◆ UNDER COLORADO SKIES
Republic, 1947

**Producer(s)**    Tucker, Melville
**Director(s)**    Springsteen, R.G.
**Screenwriter(s)**    Rousseau, Louise

**Cast**    Hale, Monte; Booth, Adrian; Foy Willing and the Riders of the Purple Sage

**Song(s)**    San Antonio Rose [1] (C/L: Wills, Bob); Holiday for the Blues (C: Willing, Foy; L: Robin, Sid); Wait for the Wagon [2] (C: Traditional; L: Robin, Sid)

**Notes**    There are also vocals of "Jim Crack Corn," "Wait for the Wagon," "Old Chisholm Trail" and "I Ride an Old Paint." [1] Also in RHYTHM ROUND-UP (Columbia), SAN ANTONIO ROSE (Universal), BOB WILLS AND HIS TEXAS PLAYBOYS (Warner) and HONKYTONK MAN (Warner). [2] Traditional song used as basis for Johnny Mercer rewrite for HOW THE WEST WAS WON (MGM).

### 6512 ◆ UNDER COVER
Cannon, 1987

**Musical Score**    Rundgren, Todd

**Producer(s)**    Golan, Menahem; Globus, Yoram
**Director(s)**    Stockwell, John
**Screenwriter(s)**    Stockwell, John; Fields, Scott

**Cast**    Neidorf, David; Leigh, Jennifer Jason; Corbin, Barry; Harris, David; Wilhoite, Kathleen

**Song(s)**    Gotta Have You (C/L: Bishop, Michael; Page, Scott)

**Notes**    No cue sheet available.

### 6513 ◆ UNDERCOVER GIRL
Universal, 1950

**Producer(s)**    Schenck, Aubrey
**Director(s)**    Pevney, Joseph
**Screenwriter(s)**    Essex, Harry; Rosenwald, Francis

**Cast**    Smith, Alexis; Brady, Scott; Egan, Richard; George, Gladys; Ryan, Edmon; Mohr, Gerald; Dano, Royal

**Song(s)**    He's My Guy [1] (C: de Paul, Gene; L: Raye, Don)

**Notes**    [1] Also in HI 'YA CHUM and HE'S MY GUY.

### 6514 ◆ UNDER FIESTA STARS
Republic, 1941

**Producer(s)**    Grey, Harry
**Director(s)**    McDonald, Frank
**Screenwriter(s)**    Brown, Karl; Gibbons, Eliot

**Cast**    Autry, Gene; Burnette, Smiley; Hughes, Carol; Darien, Frank; Strauch Jr., Joe

**Song(s)**    Keep It in the Family (C/L: Burnette, Smiley); Purple Sage in the Twilight (C: Styne, Jule; L: Meyer, Sol); Under Fiesta Stars (C/L: Autry, Gene; Rose, Fred)

**Notes**    There are also vocals of "When You're Smilin'" by Mark Fisher, Joe Goodwin and Larry Shay; "The Man on the Flying Trapeze" by Walter O'Keefe and "I've Got No Use for Women."

### 6515 ◆ UNDER FIRE
Twentieth Century–Fox, 1957

**Musical Score**    Dunlap, Paul

**Producer(s)**    Skouras, Plato
**Director(s)**    Clark, James B.
**Screenwriter(s)**    Landis, James

**Cast**    Reason, Rex; Morgan, Henry; Brodie, Steve; Walker, Peter; Levin, Robert; Locke, Jon; Allyn, William

**Song(s)**    Ich Moecht So Gern Treu Sein (C: Dunlap, Paul; L: Colpet, Max)

**Notes**    There is also a vocal of "Don't Fence Me In" by Cole Porter. In German!

### 6516 ◆ UNDERGROUND RUSTLERS
Monogram, 1942

**Musical Score**    Sanucci, Frank

**Producer(s)**    Weeks, George W.
**Director(s)**    Luby, S. Roy
**Screenwriter(s)**    Tuttle, Bud

**Cast**    Corrigan, Ray; King, John; Terhune, Max; Gaze, Gwen; Blair, Robert; Taylor, Forrest

**Song(s)**    Sweethearts of the Range (C/L: Tobias, Harry; Ingraham, Roy; Ford, Mickey); Following the Trail (C/L: Unknown)

### 6517 ◆ UNDER MEXICALI STARS
Republic, 1950

**Producer(s)**    Tucker, Melville
**Director(s)**    Blair, George
**Screenwriter(s)**    Williams, Bob

**Cast**    Allen, Rex; Koko; Patrick, Dorothy; Barcroft, Roy; Ebsen, Buddy; Helton, Percy; Coy, Walter

**Song(s)** Old Black Mountain Trail (C/L: Howard, Fred; Vincent, Fred); Born to the Saddle [1] (C/L: Cherkose, Eddie)

**Notes** [1] Also in BILLY THE KID RETURNS and PHANTOM STALLION.

## 6518 ✦ UNDER MY SKIN
Twentieth Century–Fox, 1950

**Musical Score** Amfitheatrof, Daniele
**Composer(s)** Newman, Alfred

**Producer(s)** Robinson, Casey
**Director(s)** Negulesco, Jean
**Screenwriter(s)** Robinson, Casey
**Source(s)** "My Old Man" (story) Hemingway, Ernest

**Cast** Garfield, John; Presle, Micheline; Adler, Luther; Lindgren, Orley; Drayton, Noel; Merola, A.A.

**Song(s)** Stranger in the Night [1] (L: Gordon, Mack; Chandler, Tanis); Viendras Tu Ce Soir [3] (L: Surmagne, Jacques); The River Seine [2] (C: LaFarge, Guy; L: Monod, Flavien; LaFarge, Guy; Parsons, Geoffrey)

**Notes** [1] French lyrics by Tanis Chandler. [2] English version by Geoffrey Parsons. Also in THE GREEN BERETS (Warner) but with different English lyrics. [3] Also in ON THE RIVIERA.

## 6519 ✦ UNDER NEVADA SKIES
Republic, 1946

**Composer(s)** Elliott, Jack
**Lyricist(s)** Elliott, Jack

**Producer(s)** White, Eddy
**Director(s)** MacDonald, Frank
**Screenwriter(s)** Cheney, J. Benton; Gangelin, Paul

**Cast** Rogers, Roy; Trigger; Hayes, George "Gabby"; Evans, Dale; Sons of the Pioneers

**Song(s)** Under Nevada Skies; Ne-Hah-Ne (C/L: Nolan, Bob); I Want to Go West; Sea Goin' Cowboy (C/L: Forster, Gordon); Any Time That I'm with You

## 6520 ✦ THE UNDER-PUP
Universal, 1939

**Lyricist(s)** Freed, Ralph

**Producer(s)** Pasternak, Joe
**Director(s)** Wallace, Richard
**Screenwriter(s)** Jones, Grover

**Cast** Jean, Gloria; Cummings, Robert; Grey, Nan; Smith, C. Aubrey; Bondi, Beulah; Weidler, Virginia; Lindsay, Margaret; Walburn, Raymond; Gillis, Ann; Cavanagh, Pat; Gilbert, Billy

**Song(s)** I'm Like a Bird (French Gergerette) (C: Previn, Charles; L: Adamson, Harold); Shepherd Lullaby

(C: Mozart, W.A.); The Shepherd (C: Skinner, Frank); High School Cadets [1] (C: Sousa, John Philip); Wer Hat Die Schonsten Schafchen (C: Reinicke, C.)

**Notes** This was Gloria Jean's screen debut. There is also a vocal of "Annie Laurie" by Lady John Scott. [1] Also in A LITTLE BIT OF HEAVEN.

## 6521 ✦ UNDERSEA GIRL
Allied Artists, 1957

**Musical Score** Courage, Alexander

**Producer(s)** Yokoseki, David T.
**Director(s)** Peyser, John
**Screenwriter(s)** Jones, Arthur V.

**Cast** Corday, Mara; Conway, Pat; Marly, Florence; Seymour, Dan; Clanton, Ralph

**Song(s)** Daydreams (C: Courage, Alexander; L: Unknown)

**Notes** No cue sheet available.

## 6522 ✦ UNDER SUSPICION
Twentieth Century–Fox, 1931

**Composer(s)** Hanley, James F.
**Lyricist(s)** McCarthy, Joseph

**Director(s)** Erickson, A.F.
**Screenwriter(s)** Barry, Tom

**Cast** Murray, J. Harold; Moran, Lois; Kerrigan, J.M.; Brent, George; Saxon, Marie

**Song(s)** Saskatcha; Here's to the Folks Back Home; Whisper to the Whispering Pines; Round My Kingdom's Door; When You Don't Know What to Do With It [1]

**Notes** Previously titled TONIGHT AND YOU. [1] Used instrumentally only.

## 6523 ✦ UNDER TEN FLAGS
Paramount, 1959

**Producer(s)** De Laurentiis, Dino
**Director(s)** Coletti, Duilio
**Screenwriter(s)** Coletti, Duilio; Mohr, Ulrich

**Cast** Heflin, Van; Laughton, Charles; Demongeot, Mylene; Ericson, John; Lulli, Folco; Parker, Cecil

**Song(s)** Under Ten Flags [1] (C/L: Roberts, Ruth; Katz, William)

**Notes** [1] Written for exploitation only.

## 6524 ✦ UNDER TEXAS SKIES
Republic, 1940

**Producer(s)** Grey, Harry
**Director(s)** Sherman, George
**Screenwriter(s)** Burbridge, Betty; Coldeway, Anthony
**Source(s)** characters by MacDonald, William Colt

**Cast** Livingston, Robert; Steele, Bob; Davis, Rufe; Ranson, Lois; Brandon, Henry; Boteler, Wade; Lease, Rex; Canutt, Yakima

**Song(s)** Let's Make a Deal (C/L: Burnette, Smiley)

#### 6525 ◆ UNDER THE PAMPAS MOON
Fox, 1935

**Producer(s)** DeSylva, B.G.
**Director(s)** Tinling, James
**Screenwriter(s)** Pascal, Ernest; King, Bradley; Johnson, Harry

**Cast** Baxter, Warner; Gallian, Ketti; Veloz and Yolanda; Miljan, John; Naish, J. Carrol; Jimenez, Soledad; Armida

**Song(s)** The Gaucho (C: Samuels, Walter G.; L: DeSylva, B.G.); Love Song of the Pampas (C: Mockridge, Cyril J.; L: Stuart, Allan); Zamba (C/L: Smith; L: Zarraga); Je T'Adore [2] (C: Akst, Harry; L: Grossman, Bernie); Veredita [1] (C/L: Guizar, Tito); China de Mi Amor [3] (C: Canaro, Francisco; L: Caruso, Juan A.)

**Notes** [1] In foreign prints only. [2] Not used in MARIE GALANTE. [3] Not used.

#### 6526 ◆ UNDER THE RED ROBE
Twentieth Century–Fox, 1937

**Musical Score** Benjamin, Arthur

**Producer(s)** Kane, Robert T.
**Director(s)** Seastrom, Victor
**Screenwriter(s)** Biro, Lajos; Lindsay, Philip; Hudson, J.L.
**Source(s)** *Under the Red Robe* (play) Rose, Edward

**Cast** Veidt, Conrad; Annabella; Massey, Raymond; Brent, Romney; Stewart, Sophie; Goldio, F. Wyndham

**Song(s)** There Stands a Palace (C: Benjamin, Arthur; L: Unknown)

**Notes** The play is based on a novel by Stanley J. Weyman.

#### 6527 ◆ UNDER THE YUM YUM TREE
Columbia, 1963

**Musical Score** De Vol, Frank

**Producer(s)** Brisson, Frederick
**Director(s)** Swift, David
**Screenwriter(s)** Roman, Lawrence; Swift, David
**Source(s)** *Under the Yum Yum Tree* (play) Roman, Lawrence

**Cast** Lemmon, Jack; Jones, Dean; Adams, Edie; Darren, James; Coca, Imogene; Lynley, Carol; Lynde, Paul; Lansing, Robert; Bixby, Bill

**Song(s)** Under the Yum Yum Tree (C: Van Heusen, James; L: Cahn, Sammy)

#### 6528 ◆ UNDER TWO FLAGS
Twentieth Century–Fox, 1936

**Producer(s)** Zanuck, Darryl F.
**Director(s)** Lloyd, Frank
**Screenwriter(s)** Lipscomb, W.P.; Ferris, Walter

**Cast** Colman, Ronald; Colbert, Claudette; McLaglen, Victor; Russell, Rosalind; Ratoff, Gregory; Bruce, Nigel; Gordon, C. Henry; Mundin, Herbert; Carradine, John; Hare, Lumsden; Bromberg, J. Edward

**Song(s)** One-Two-Three-Four Hey! (C: Pollack, Lew; L: Mitchell, Sidney D.)

#### 6529 ◆ UNDER WESTERN SKIES
Universal, 1945

**Musical Score** Sawtell, Paul
**Composer(s)** Rosen, Milton
**Lyricist(s)** Carter, Everett

**Producer(s)** Siegel, Sol C.
**Director(s)** Kane, Joseph
**Screenwriter(s)** McGowan, Dorrell; McGowan, Stuart; Burbridge, Betty

**Cast** O'Driscoll, Martha; Beery Jr., Noah; Carrillo, Leo

**Song(s)** Under Western Skies; Don't Go Making Speeches; Oh, You Kid!; An Old Fashioned Girl; A Cowboy's Prayer; In an Open Shay [1]

**Notes** [1] Used instrumentally only.

#### 6530 ◆ UNDER WESTERN STARS
Republic, 1938

**Composer(s)** Tinturin, Peter
**Lyricist(s)** Tinturin, Peter; Lawrence, Jack

**Producer(s)** Siegel, Sol C.
**Director(s)** Kane, Joseph
**Screenwriter(s)** McGowan, Stuart; McGowan, Dorrell; Burbridge, Betty

**Cast** Rogers, Roy; Burnette, Smiley; Hughes, Carol; Usher, Guy; Harlan, Kenneth; The Maple City Four

**Song(s)** Send My Mail to the County Jail; Campaign Song (C/L: Cherkose, Eddie; Rosoff, Charles); That Pioneer Mother of Mine (C/L: Spencer, Tim); Back to the Backwoods; Dust (C/L: Marvin, Johnny); Dust Over the West; Listen to the Rhythm of the Range [1] (C/L: Marvin, Johnny; Autry, Gene); When a Cowboy Sings a Song

**Notes** [1] Also in TEXAS TERRORS.

#### 6531 ◆ UNDER YOUR SPELL
Twentieth Century–Fox, 1936

**Composer(s)** Schwartz, Arthur
**Lyricist(s)** Dietz, Howard

**Producer(s)** Stone, John
**Director(s)** Preminger, Otto
**Screenwriter(s)** Hyland, Frances; Elkins, Saul

**Cast** Tibbett, Lawrence; Barrie, Wendy; Ratoff, Gregory; Treacher, Arthur; Gaye, Gregory; Churchill, Berton; Prouty, Jed; Richman, Charles

**Song(s)** Under Your Spell; My Little Mule Wagon; Amigo

# 6532 ✦ UNEXPECTED FATHER
## Universal, 1939

**Producer(s)** Goldsmith, Ken
**Director(s)** Lamont, Charles
**Screenwriter(s)** Spigelgass, Leonard; Grayson, Charles

**Cast** O'Keefe, Dennis; Henville, Sandra Lee; Auer, Mischa; Ross, Shirley; Hodges, Joy; Methot, Mayo; Gwynne, Anne

**Song(s)** Sweet and Low (C/L: Barnby, J.)

# 6533 ✦ UNFAITHFUL
## Paramount, 1931

**Director(s)** Cromwell, John
**Screenwriter(s)** van Druten, John

**Cast** Chatterton, Ruth; Lukas, Paul; Cook, Donald; Compton, Juliette

**Song(s)** Mama's in the Dog House Now (C/L: Coslow, Sam); I'm True to the Navy Now [1] (C: King, Jack; L: Janis, Elsie)

**Notes** Formerly called NEW MORALS. [1] Also in PARAMOUNT ON PARADE.

# 6534 ✦ UNFAITHFULLY YOURS
## Twentieth Century–Fox, 1984

**Producer(s)** Worth, Marvin; Wizan, Joe
**Director(s)** Zieff, Howard
**Screenwriter(s)** Curtin, Valerie; Levinson, Barry; Klane, Robert

**Cast** Moore, Dudley; Kinski, Nastassia; Assante, Armand; Brooks, Albert; Yates, Cassie; Libertini, Richard; Shull, Richard B.; Triska, Jan

**Song(s)** Unfaithfully Yours (One Love) (C/L: Bishop, Stephen)

**Notes** A remake of the Preston Sturges film.

# 6535 ✦ UNFINISHED BUSINESS
## Universal, 1941

**Producer(s)** La Cava, Gregory
**Director(s)** La Cava, Gregory
**Screenwriter(s)** Thackeray, Eugene

**Cast** Dunne, Irene; Foster, Preston; Montgomery, Robert; Pallette, Eugene; Catlett, Walter; Foran, Dick; Hinds, Samuel S.; Clyde, June

**Song(s)** Cafe Kohinor (C: Todd, Dave; L: La Cava, Gregory); Finale Act 3 [1] (C: Flotow, Frederich; L: MacFarren, Natalie)

**Notes** [1] From the opera MARTHA by Von Flotow. There is also a vocal of "Ich Liebe Dich" by Edvard Grieg with English lyrics by Henry Chapman titled "I Love Thee."

# 6536 ✦ THE UNFINISHED DANCE
## Metro–Goldwyn–Mayer, 1947

**Musical Score** Stothart, Herbert
**Choreographer(s)** Lichine, David

**Producer(s)** Pasternak, Joe
**Director(s)** Koster, Henry
**Screenwriter(s)** Connolly, Myles
**Source(s)** "La Mort du Cygne" (story) Morand, Paul

**Cast** O'Brien, Margaret; Charisse, Cyd; Booth, Karin; Dale, Esther; Hall, Thurston; Thomas, Danny

**Song(s)** Watch Song (C: Stothart, Herbert; L: Perl, Lothar); Minor Melody (C/L: Jacobs, Ray; Thomas, Danny); I Went Merrily Merrily on My Way (C: Fain, Sammy; L: Kahal, Irving)

# 6537 ✦ THE UNHOLY WIFE
## RKO, 1957

**Musical Score** Amfitheatrof, Daniele

**Producer(s)** Farrow, John
**Director(s)** Farrow, John
**Screenwriter(s)** Latimer, Jonathan

**Cast** Steiger, Rod; Tryon, Tom; Bondi, Beulah; Windsor, Marie; Franz, Arthur; Van Rooten, Luis

**Song(s)** Eyes of the Night [1] (C: Amfitheatrof, Daniele; L: David, Mack)

**Notes** There is also a brief vocal of "One for My Baby" by Harold Arlen and Johnny Mercer. [1] Used instrumentally only.

# 6538 ✦ THE UNINVITED
## Paramount, 1944

**Producer(s)** Brackett, Charles
**Director(s)** Allen, Lewis
**Screenwriter(s)** Smith, Dodie; Partos, Frank
**Source(s)** *Uneasy Freehold* (novel) Macardle, Dorothy

**Cast** Milland, Ray; Hussey, Ruth; Russell, Gail; Crisp, Donald; Skinner, Cornelia Otis; Stickney, Dorothy; Everest, Barbara; Napier, Alan

**Song(s)** Stella By Starlight (C: Young, Victor; L: Washington, Ned)

## 6539 ✦ UNION PACIFIC
Paramount, 1939

**Choreographer(s)** Prinz, LeRoy

**Producer(s)** De Mille, Cecil B.
**Director(s)** De Mille, Cecil B.
**Screenwriter(s)** Sullivan, C. Gardner; De Leon, Walter; Lasky Jr., Jesse
**Source(s)** *Trouble Shooter* (novel) Haycox, Ernest

**Cast** McCrea, Joel; Lamour, Dorothy; Stanwyck, Barbara; Preston, Robert; Donlevy, Brian; Tamiroff, Akim; Keyes, Evelyn; Overman, Lynne; Ridges, Stanley; Quinn, Anthony; Toomey, Regis; Chaney Jr., Lon; Barrat, Robert

**Song(s)** The Rose of St. Louis [1] (C/L: Pasternacki, Stephen; Krumgold, Sigmund)

**Notes** [1] This song resembles "My Gal Sal" by Paul Dresser.

## 6540 ✦ UNION STATION
Paramount, 1950

**Producer(s)** Schermer, Jules
**Director(s)** Mate, Rudolph
**Screenwriter(s)** Boehm, Sydney
**Source(s)** (story) Walsh, Thomas

**Cast** Holden, William; Olson, Nancy; Fitzgerald, Barry; Bettger, Lyle; Sterling, Jan

**Song(s)** You're Wonderful [1] (C: Young, Victor; L: Livingston, Jay; Evans, Ray)

**Notes** [1] Used instrumentally only.

## 6541 ✦ THE UNKNOWN RANGER
Columbia, 1937

**Composer(s)** Zahler, Lee
**Lyricist(s)** Wood, John Hickory

**Director(s)** Bennett, Spencer Gordon
**Screenwriter(s)** Gatzert, Nate

**Cast** Allen, Bob; Tibbetts, Martha; Woods, Harry; Taliaferro, Hal

**Song(s)** Frankie's Flamin' Fandango (C/L: Zahler, Lee; Wheeler; Pense, Raphael); Cowboy, Where You Been [1]; I Lost My Heart on the Lone Prairie [1] (L: Pense, Raphael); Anthem Song [1]

**Notes** Previously titled THE PHANTOM FIGHTER. [1] Used instrumentally only.

## 6542 ✦ UNKNOWN TERROR
Twentieth Century–Fox, 1957

**Producer(s)** Stabler, Robert W.
**Director(s)** Warren, Charles Marquis
**Screenwriter(s)** Higgins, Kenneth C.

**Cast** Howard, John; Powers, Mala; Richards, Paul; Wynn, May; Milton, Gerald; Gray, Duane; Sir Lancelot

**Song(s)** Jump Up and Shake (C/L: Sir Lancelot); The Bottomless Cave (C: Sir Lancelot; L: Higgins, Kenneth C.)

## 6543 ✦ UNMARRIED
Paramount, 1939

**Director(s)** Neumann, Kurt
**Screenwriter(s)** Hayward, Lillie; Marlow, Brian

**Cast** Twelvetrees, Helen; Jones, Buck; O'Connor, Donald

**Song(s)** Everyone Knows It but You [1] (C: Johnston, Arthur; L: Coslow, Sam)

**Notes** Formerly titled NIGHT SPOT HOSTESS. Titled NIGHT CLUB HOSTESS in Great Britain. [1] Also used in LADY AND GENT.

## 6544 ✦ AN UNMARRIED WOMAN
Twentieth Century–Fox, 1978

**Musical Score** Conti, Bill

**Producer(s)** Mazursky, Paul; Ray, Tony
**Director(s)** Mazursky, Paul
**Screenwriter(s)** Mazursky, Paul

**Cast** Clayburgh, Jill; Bates, Alan; Murphy, Michael; Gorman, Cliff; Quinn, Pat; Bishop, Kelly; Duncan, Andrew; Mazursky, Paul; Ultra Violet

**Song(s)** Maybe I'm Amazed (C/L: McCartney, Paul); An Unmarried Woman [1] (C: Conti, Bill; L: Wiley, Michelle)

**Notes** There is also a vocal of "I'm Yours" by Johnny Green and E.Y. Harburg.

## 6545 ✦ UNSEEN ENEMY
Universal, 1942

**Producer(s)** Grant, Marshall
**Director(s)** Rawlins, John
**Screenwriter(s)** Chanslor, Roy; Rubin, Stanley

**Cast** Carrillo, Leo; Devine, Andy; Terry, Don; Hervey, Irene; Royce, Lionel; Bey, Turhan; Giermann, Frederick

**Song(s)** I've Been Around (C/L: Meskill, Jack; Stern, Jack)

## 6546 ✦ THE UNSINKABLE MOLLY BROWN
### Metro–Goldwyn–Mayer, 1964

**Composer(s)**   Willson, Meredith
**Lyricist(s)**   Willson, Meredith
**Choreographer(s)**   Gennaro, Peter

**Producer(s)**   Weingarten, Lawrence
**Director(s)**   Walters, Charles
**Screenwriter(s)**   Deutsch, Helen
**Source(s)**   *The Unsinkable Molly Brown* (musical) Willson, Meredith; Morris, Richard

**Cast**   Reynolds, Debbie; Presnell, Harve [1]; Begley, Ed; Kruschen, Jack; Baddeley, Hermione; Lambrinos, Vassili; Hunt, Martita; Dale, Grover; Karnilova, Maria; Christie, Audrey; Trikonis, Gus; Lembeck, Harvey; Rorke, Hayden

**Song(s)**   Belly Up to the Bar, Boys; I Ain't Down Yet; Colorado, My Home; I'll Never Say No; He's My Friend [1]; Leadville Johnny Brown (Soliloquy); Dignity (We've Got to Get Us Some) [1]

**Notes**   All songs but [1] from Broadway original.


## 6547 ✦ UNTAMED (1929)
### Metro–Goldwyn–Mayer, 1929

**Director(s)**   Conway, Jack
**Screenwriter(s)**   Thalberg, Sylvia; Butler, Frank

**Cast**   Crawford, Joan; Montgomery, Robert; Torrence, Ernest; Herbert, Holmes; Miljan, John; Nugent, Edward; Astor, Gertrude; Lee, Gwen

**Song(s)**   Chant of the Jungle (C: Brown, Nacio Herb; L: Freed, Arthur); That Wonderful Something Is Love (C: Alter, Louis; L: Goodwin, Joe)


## 6548 ✦ UNTAMED (1940)
### Paramount, 1940

**Producer(s)**   Jones, Paul
**Director(s)**   Archainbaud, George
**Screenwriter(s)**   Brennan, Frederick Hazlitt; Butler, Frank
**Source(s)**   *Mantrap* (novel) Lewis, Sinclair

**Cast**   Milland, Ray; Morison, Patricia; Tamiroff, Akim

**Song(s)**   Shake Hands with Your Neighbor [1] (C: Young, Victor; L: Loesser, Frank)

**Notes**   [1] Not used in AND THE ANGELS SING.


## 6549 ✦ UNTAMED HEIRESS
### Republic, 1954

**Producer(s)**   Picker, Sidney
**Director(s)**   Witney, William
**Screenwriter(s)**   Shipman, Barry

**Cast**   Canova, Judy; Barry, Donald; Cleveland, George; Holmes, Taylor; Chandler, Chick

**Song(s)**   Welcome (C/L: Elliott, Jack); A Dream for Sale (C/L: Elliott, Jack; Kahn, Donald); Sugar Daddy (C/L: Kahn, Donald; Elliott, Jack)


## 6550 ✦ UNTAMED YOUTH
### Warner Brothers, 1957

**Musical Score**   Baxter, Les
**Composer(s)**   Baxter, Les
**Lyricist(s)**   Baxter, Les

**Producer(s)**   Schenck, Aubrey
**Director(s)**   Koch, Howard W.
**Screenwriter(s)**   Higgins, John C.

**Cast**   Van Doren, Mamie; Nelson, Lori; Russell, John; Burnett, Don; Cochran, Eddie; Tuttle, Lurene; Wally Brown and the Hollywood Rock and Rollers; Lucita; Richards, Keith; Reynolds, Valerie

**Song(s)**   Cottonpicker; Salamander; Go, Go Go, Calypso; Rolling Stone (L: Adelson, Lenny); Oobala Baby (L: Adelson, Lenny; Cochran, Eddie; Capehart, Jerry)

**Notes**   No cue sheet available.


## 6551 ✦ UNTIL THEY SAIL
### Metro–Goldwyn–Mayer, 1957

**Musical Score**   Raksin, David

**Producer(s)**   Schnee, Charles
**Director(s)**   Wise, Robert
**Screenwriter(s)**   Anderson, Robert
**Source(s)**   "Return to Paradise" (story) Michener, James A.

**Cast**   Simmons, Jean; Fontaine, Joan; Newman, Paul; Laurie, Piper; Drake, Charles; Dee, Sandra; Napier, Alan; Shaughnessy, Mickey

**Song(s)**   Until They Sail (C: Raksin, David; L: Cahn, Sammy)


## 6552 ✦ THE UNTOUCHABLES
### Paramount, 1987

**Musical Score**   Morricone, Ennio

**Producer(s)**   Linson, Art
**Director(s)**   De Palma, Brian
**Screenwriter(s)**   Mamet, David

**Cast**   Kostner, Kevin; Smith, Charles Martin; Garcia, Andy; De Niro, Robert; Connery, Sean

**Song(s)**   Untouchable [1] (C: Morricone, Ennio; L: Crewe, Bob; Corbetta, Jerry)

**Notes**   [1] Lyric added for exploitation only. Based on cue titled "Ness and His Family."

## 6553 ✦ UP FOR MURDER
### Universal, 1931

**Musical Score** Roemheld, Heinz

**Director(s)** Bell, Monta
**Screenwriter(s)** Bell, Monta

**Cast** Ayres, Lew; Tobin, Genevieve; Pratt, Purnell; McHugh, Frank; Tucker, Richard; Beavers, Louise; Burt, Frederick; Peterson, Dorothy

**Song(s)** There Must Be Somebody for Me (C: Ryan, Ben; Handman, Lou); Waitin' Around the Corner (C/L: Foley, Jack)

**Notes** A remake of MAN, WOMAN AND SIN (1927).

## 6554 ✦ UP FROM THE BEACH
### Twentieth Century–Fox, 1965

**Musical Score** Cosma, Edgar

**Producer(s)** Graetz, Paul
**Director(s)** Parrish, Robert
**Screenwriter(s)** Mann, Stanley; Clewes, Howard
**Source(s)** *Epitaph for an Enemy* (novel) Barr, George

**Cast** Robertson, Cliff; Buttons, Red; Demick, Irina; Goring, Marius; Pickens, Slim; Robertston-Justice, James; Crawford, Broderick; Rosay, Francoise

**Song(s)** No Time to Love [1] (C: Cosma, Edgar; L: Williams, Lorraine)

**Notes** [1] Used instrumentally only.

## 6555 ✦ UP IN ARMS
### RKO, 1944

**Musical Score** Forbes, Louis
**Composer(s)** Arlen, Harold
**Lyricist(s)** Koehler, Ted
**Choreographer(s)** Dare, Danny

**Producer(s)** Goldwyn, Samuel
**Director(s)** Nugent, Elliott
**Screenwriter(s)** Hartman, Don; Boretz, Allen; Pirosh, Robert
**Source(s)** *The Nervous Wreck* (play) Davis, Owen

**Cast** Kaye, Danny [1]; Shore, Dinah; Andrews, Dana; Dowling, Constance; Calhern, Louis; Mathews, George; Baker, Benny; Cook Jr., Elisha; Talbot, Lyle; Catlett, Walter; Meeker, George; Dumont, Margaret; Arnt, Charles; Friml Jr., Rudolf; Arno, Sig

**Song(s)** Lobby Number (C/L: Fine, Sylvia); Conga (C/L: Fine, Sylvia); Cherry Blossom Time (C/L: Fine, Sylvia); Now I Know; All Out for Freedom; Tess's Torch Song; Melody in 4F (C/L: Fine, Sylvia); The Skaddle (C/L: Fine, Sylvia); The Jive Number (C/L: Fine, Sylvia)

**Notes** The source is also the basis for the stage musical WHOOPEE. [1] Kaye's film debut.

## 6556 ✦ UP IN CENTRAL PARK
### Universal, 1948

**Musical Score** Green, Johnny
**Composer(s)** Romberg, Sigmund
**Lyricist(s)** Fields, Dorothy
**Choreographer(s)** Tamiris, Helen

**Producer(s)** Tunberg, Karl
**Director(s)** Seiter, William A.
**Screenwriter(s)** Tunberg, Karl
**Source(s)** *Up in Central Park* (musical) Romberg, Sigmund; Fields, Dorothy; Fields, Herbert

**Cast** Durbin, Deanna; Sharple, Albert; Haymes, Dick; Price, Vincent; Powers, Tom; Hall, Thurston; Cavanaugh, Hobart; Pedi, Tom

**Song(s)** Boss Tweed; Oh! Say Can You See? [2]; Carousel in the Park; When She Walks in the Room; Currier & Ives [1]; It Doesn't Cost You Anything to Dream [1]

**Notes** Deanna Durbin's last film. There is also a vocal of "Pace Mio Dio" from Verdi's LA FORZA DEL DESTINO. All songs but [3] from Broadway original. [1] Performed instrumentally in the ice ballet. [2] Written for film.

## 6557 ✦ UP IN SMOKE
### Paramount, 1978

**Producer(s)** Adler, Lou; Lombardo, Lou
**Director(s)** Adler, Lou
**Screenwriter(s)** Chong, Thomas; Marin, Cheech

**Cast** Marin, Richard "Cheech"; Chong, Thomas; Skerritt, Tom; Adams, Edie; Martin, Strother; Moritz, Louisa; Buzby, Zane; Keach, Stacy

**Song(s)** Up in Smoke (C/L: Chong, Thomas; Marin, Richard "Cheech"); Low Rider (C/L: Allen, S.; Brown, H.R.; Kickerson, M.; Jordon, L.; Miller, C.W.; Oskar, Lee; Scott, H.; Goldstein); Framed (C/L: Lieber, Jerry; Stoller, Mike); Searchin' (C/L: Lieber, Jerry; Stoller, Mike); Blind Man (C/L: Foster, David; Chong, Thomas); Rock Fight (C/L: Kortchmar, Danny; Wachtel, Robert; Chong, Thomas; Marin, Richard "Cheech"); Earache My Eye (C/L: Chong, Thomas; Marin, Richard "Cheech"; De Lorme, Gay)

**Notes** Also known as CHEECH AND CHONG'S UP IN SMOKE.

## 6558 ✦ UP IN THE WORLD
### United Artists, 1956

**Musical Score** Green, Philip

**Producer(s)** Stewart, Hugh
**Director(s)** Carstairs, John Paddy

**Screenwriter(s)** Davies, Jack; Blyth, Henry E.; Blackmore, Peter

**Cast** Wisdom, Norman; Swanson, Maureen; Desmonde, Jerry

**Song(s)** Up in the World (C/L: Wisdom, Norman); Don't Laugh At Me [1] (C/L: Wisdom, Norman; Tremayne, June); Talent (C: Green, Philip; L: Stollman, Marcel)

**Notes** A Rank Organisation film. [1] Also in AS LONG AS THEY'RE HAPPY (with music credited to Stanley Black) and TROUBLE IN STORE.

## 6559 ✦ UPSTAIRS AND DOWNSTAIRS
J. Arthur Rank, 1959

**Musical Score** Green, Philip

**Producer(s)** Box, Betty E.
**Director(s)** Thomas, Ralph
**Screenwriter(s)** Harvey, Frank
**Source(s)** *Upstairs and Downstairs* (novel) Thorne, Ronald Scott

**Cast** Craig, Michael; Heywood, Anne; Demongeot, Mylene; Justice, James Robertson; Massey, Daniel; Cardinale, Claudia; Hickson, Joan

**Song(s)** In a House with an Upstairs and Downstairs (C: Green, Philip; L: Miller, Sonny)

**Notes** A Rank film distributed by Twentieth Century–Fox.

## 6560 ✦ UP THE JUNCTION
Paramount, 1968

**Musical Score** Hugg, Mike
**Composer(s)** Hugg, Mike
**Lyricist(s)** Hugg, Mike

**Producer(s)** Brabourne, John; Havelock-Allan, Anthony
**Director(s)** Collinson, Peter
**Screenwriter(s)** Smith, Roger
**Source(s)** (book) Dunn, Nell

**Cast** Kendall, Suzy; Waterman, Dennis; Posta, Adrienne; Lipman, Maureen; Bass, Alfie

**Song(s)** Up the Junction; Standing There Alone; Walking Round; Sing Songs of Love (C/L: Hugg, Mike; Gill, Michael; Hugg, Brian); Girl You've Got My Life (C/L: McBride, Michael); I Need Your Love; Just For Me; Love Theme (inst.) (C/L: Mann, Manfred; Hugg, Mike); Scotswood Bridge Blues [1] (C/L: McBride, Michael); Sheila's Dance (inst.) (C/L: Mann, Manfred; Hugg, Mike); Belgravia (inst.) (C/L: Mann, Manfred; Hugg, Mike); Wailing Horn (inst.) (C/L: Mann, Manfred; Hugg, Mike)

**Notes** Some of these are background vocals. [1] Not used.

## 6561 ✦ UP THE RIVER (1930)
Fox, 1930

**Director(s)** Ford, John; Collier Jr., William
**Screenwriter(s)** Watkins, Maurine

**Cast** Tracy, Spencer; Luce, Claire; Hymer, Warren; Bogart, Humphrey; MacFarlane, George

**Song(s)** Sunshine in the Soul (C/L: Sweney, J.R.); Prison College Song (C/L: Hanley, James F.)

**Notes** Also given vocals are "M-O-T-H-E-R" by Howard Johnson and Theodore Morse and "Girl of My Dreams" by Sunny Clapp. Collier Jr. was credited with the staging.

## 6562 ✦ UP THE RIVER (1938)
Twentieth Century–Fox, 1938

**Composer(s)** Akst, Harry
**Lyricist(s)** Clare, Sidney

**Producer(s)** Wurtzel, Sol M.
**Director(s)** Werker, Alfred
**Screenwriter(s)** Patrick, John; Breslow, Lou

**Cast** Foster, Preston; Martin, Tony; Brooks, Phyllis; Summerville, Slim; Treacher, Arthur; Dinehart, Alan; Collins, Eddie; Darwell, Jane; Toler, Sidney; Robinson, Bill; Gargan, Edward; Dearing, Dorothy

**Song(s)** Rhythmettes (L: Breslow, Lou; Patrick, John); It's the Strangest Thing; Song of Rockwell; Old Soldiers Never Die (C/L: Conrad, Con; Mitchell, Sidney D.; Gottler, Archie)

## 6563 ✦ UP TIGHT
Paramount, 1968

**Musical Score** Jones, Booker T.
**Composer(s)** Jones, Booker T.
**Lyricist(s)** Jones, Booker T.

**Producer(s)** Dassin, Jules
**Director(s)** Dassin, Jules
**Screenwriter(s)** Dassin, Jules; Dee, Ruby; Mayfield, Julian
**Source(s)** *The Informer* (novel) O'Flaherty, Liam

**Cast** St. Jacques, Raymond; Dee, Ruby; Silvera, Frank; Browne, Roscoe Lee; Mayfield, Julian

**Song(s)** Johnny, I Love You; Children Don't Get Weary [1] (C/L: Williams, Frank); Down At Ralph's Joint; Time Is Tight [2]

**Notes** The score is performed by Booker T. and the M.G.s. [1] Not written for picture. [2] Sheet music only.

## 6564 ♦ URBAN COWBOY
Paramount, 1980

**Producer(s)** Evans, Robert; Azoff, Irving
**Director(s)** Bridges, James
**Screenwriter(s)** Bridges, James; Latham, Aaron
**Source(s)** "The Ballad of the Urban Cowboy" (article) Latham, Aaron

**Cast** Travolta, John; Winger, Debra; Glenn, Scott; Smith, Madolyn; Alderson, Brooke; Huckabee, Cooper

**Song(s)** Look What You've Done to Me (C/L: Scaggs, Boz; Foster, David); Lookin' for Love (C/L: Mallette, Wanda; Ryan, Patti; Morrison, Bob); Hearts Against the Wind (C/L: Sother, J.D.); All Night Long (C/L: Walsh, Joe); Love the World Away (C/L: Morrison, Bob: Wilson, Johnny); Could I Have This Dance (C/L: Holyfield, Wayland; House, Bob); Hello Texas [1] (C/L: Collins, Brian; Campbell, Robby)

**Notes** [1] Sheet music only.

## 6565 ♦ USED CARS
Columbia, 1980

**Musical Score** Williams, Patrick

**Producer(s)** Gale, Bob
**Director(s)** Zemeckis, Robert
**Screenwriter(s)** Zemeckis, Robert; Gale, Bob

**Cast** Russell, Kurt; Warden, Jack; Graham, Gerrit; McRae, Frank; Harmon, Deborah

**Song(s)** Used Cars (C: Williams, Patrick; L: Gimbel, Norman)

## 6566 ♦ UTAH
Republic, 1945

**Choreographer(s)** Ceballos, Larry

**Producer(s)** Brown, Donald H.
**Director(s)** English, John
**Screenwriter(s)** Townley, Jack; Butler, John K.

**Cast** Rogers, Roy; Trigger; Hayes, George "Gabby"; Evans, Dale; Stewart, Peggy; Lloyd, Beverly; Withers, Grant; Bob Nolan and the Sons of the Pioneers

**Song(s)** Thank Dixie for Me (C/L: Franklin, Dave); Utah Trail (C/L: Palmer, Bob); Welcome Home, Miss Bryant (C/L: Carson, Ken); Five Little Miles [1] (C/L: Nolan, Bob); Beneath a Utah Sky (C/L: Spencer, Glenn); Utah [2] (C/L: Henderson, Charles); The Lonesome Cowboy Blues (C/L: Spencer, Tim)

**Notes** [1] The final reprise of the song has special lyrics by Jack Elliott. [2] A song of the same title but without songwriter credits appeared in HILLS OF UTAH, a Gene Autry Columbia picture.

## 6567 ♦ UTAH WAGON TRAIN
Republic, 1951

**Producer(s)** Tucker, Melville
**Director(s)** Ford, Philip
**Screenwriter(s)** Butler, John K.

**Cast** Allen, Rex; Koko; Edwards, Penny; Ebsen, Buddy; Barcroft, Roy; Padden, Sarah; Withers, Grant

**Song(s)** Toolie Rollum [1] (C/L: Allen, Rex); The Colorado Trail (C/L: Traditional; L: Allen, Rex)

**Notes** There are also vocals of "The Streets of Laredo" and "The Big Corral." [1] Also in THE ARIZONA COWBOY, RODEO KING AND THE SENORITA, SHADOWS OF TOMBSTONE and SILVER CITY BONANZA.

# V

## 6568 ✦ VACATION FROM LOVE
### Metro–Goldwyn–Mayer, 1938

**Musical Score**   Ward, Edward

**Producer(s)**   Dull, Orville O.
**Director(s)**   Fitzmaurice, George
**Screenwriter(s)**   McNutt, Patterson; Ware, Harlan

**Cast**   O'Keefe, Dennis; Rice, Florence; Owen, Reginald; Knight, June

**Song(s)**   Let's Pretend It's True (C: Ward, Edward; L: Wright, Bob; Forrest, Chet)

## 6569 ✦ THE VAGABOND KING (1930)
### Paramount, 1930

**Composer(s)**   Friml, Rudolf

**Director(s)**   Berger, Ludwig
**Screenwriter(s)**   Mankiewicz, Herman J.
**Source(s)**   *The Vagabond King* (musical) Janney, Russell; Post, William; Hooker, Brian; Friml, Rudolf

**Cast**   MacDonald, Jeanette; King, Dennis; Heggie, O.P.; Roth, Lillian; Oland, Warner; Davidson, Lawford; Stone, Arthur

**Song(s)**   Song of the Vagabonds [1]; King Louie [3] (C: Chase, Newell; L: Robin, Leo); Mary, Queen of Heaven (C: Chase, Newell; L: Robin, Leo); Some Day [1]; If I Were King [4] (C: Coslow, Sam; Chase, Newell; L: Robin, Leo); Opening Chorus [1]; What France Needs (C: Chase, Newell; L: Robin, Leo); Only a Rose [1]; Huguette Waltz [1]; Love Me Tonight [1]; Nocturne [1]; Death March (C: Chase, Newell; L: Robin, Leo); Arise (Clock Song) [2] (C: Chase, Newell; L: Robin, Leo); Vagabond King Opening Chorus [2] [5] (C: Chase, Newell; L: Robin, Leo)

**Notes**   Paramount wanted Friml to write the additional numbers for the film but the composer was in Europe and not expected back for six months and the production couldn't be held up. Three instrumental pieces from the film were published. All were by Newell Chase. These are "Tiddly Winks," "Trickette" and "Conversational." Songs from the original score which were recorded but not used in the finished picture include "Tavern Scene" and "Nocturne." Burton lists the song "Love for Sale" but it doesn't appear on cue sheets or any lists. [1] From

Broadway stage version. [2] Not used. [3] Also titled "Opening Patter." [4] The French lyrics (Si J'Etais Roi) were by Battaille-Henri. [5] Recorded.

## 6570 ✦ THE VAGABOND KING (1956)
### Paramount, 1956

**Musical Score**   Young, Victor
**Composer(s)**   Friml, Rudolf
**Lyricist(s)**   Hooker, Brian
**Choreographer(s)**   Holm, Hanya

**Producer(s)**   Duggan, Pat
**Director(s)**   Curtiz, Michael
**Screenwriter(s)**   Englund, Ken; Langley, Noel
**Source(s)**   (musical) Janney, Russell; Post, William; Hooker, Brian; Friml, Rudolf

**Cast**   Oreste [3]; Grayson, Kathryn; Moreno, Rita; Hampden, Walter; Hardwicke, Sir Cedric; Nielsen, Leslie; Prince, William; Lord, Jack

**Song(s)**   Bon Jour (L: Burke, Johnny); Lord, I'm Glad That I Know Thee [6] (C: Giovane, V.; L: Rogan, K.C.); Vive La You! (L: Burke, Johnny); Some Day [1] [4]; Comparisons (L: Burke, Johnny); Huguette Waltz [1]; Only a Rose [1] [8]; This Same Heart (L: Burke, Johnny); Watch Out for the Devil (L: Burke, Johnny); Song of the Vagabonds [1]; If a Vagabond Were King [5] (L: Burke, Johnny; Hooker, Brian); Love That Cannot Be [2] (L: Janney, Russell); The Love Song of a Thief [2] (L: Janney, Russell); The Merry Gallows [2] (L: Janney, Russell); Lady Mary's Song to Taberie [2] (L: Janney, Russell); A Harp and a Fiddle and a Flute [7] (L: Burke, Johnny); One, Two, Three, Pause [7] (L: Burke, Johnny)

**Notes**   "Love for Sale!" from the original production was disapproved by the censors and so was not used. [1] From original production. [2] These were songs written by Friml and Janney in 1954 for use in a possible Paris production. Janney wanted Paramount to use the songs in the picture but they refused. Janney didn't think much of Johnny Burke's new lyrics. Janney's lyrics, included in Janney's letter to Paramount, were second-rate. All but "Lady Mary's Song" were composed for the character of Villon. Janney wrote that he had even contributed some lyrics to the original production. Friml denied this.

Whether Janney (the original producer fronting for the Shuberts) actually contributed to the libretto was doubted by Paramount. In fact, Janney did not receive credit on the title cards for his contributions to the original production. [3] Real name Oreste Kirkop. [4] The change in lyric from the word "you" to "he" was done at the request of Kathryn Grayson. [5] This is based on the "Song of the Vagabonds" with additional lyrics and new title by Johnny Burke. It was not used but was recorded. [6] K.C. Rogan is Johnny Burke and V. Giovane is Victor Young. Pseudonyms were used since at the time Friml was not to know about the number. The piece is based on "Preludio VIII from Well-Tempered Clavichord" by Johann Sebastian Bach. [7] Not used but recorded and probably filmed. [8] A new verse was written by Burke but probably not used as he is not credited on the cue sheet.

## 6571 ✦ THE VAGABOND LOVER
### RKO, 1929

**Producer(s)** Sarecky, Louis
**Director(s)** Neilan, Marshall
**Screenwriter(s)** Creelman, James Ashmore

**Cast** Vallee, Rudy; Blane, Sally; Dressler, Marie; Sellon, Charles; Nugent, Eddie; Walker, Nella

**Song(s)** A Little Kiss Each Morning (C/L: Woods, Harry); I'm Just a Vagabond Lover [3] (C/L: Vallee, Rudy; Zimerman, Leon); Sweetheart We Need Each Other [4] (C: Tierney, Harry; L: McCarthy, Joseph); Dream of My Heart [1] (C: Boutelje, Phil; L: Cowan, Ruby; Bartholomae, Philip); Then I'll Be Reminded of You (C: Smith, Ken; L: Heyman, Edward); Heigh Ho, Everybody [2] (C/L: Woods, Harry); Piccolo Pete [2] (C/L: Baxter, Phil)

**Notes** The cue sheet doesn't differentiate between vocals and instrumentals. There is also a vocal of "If You Were the Only Girl in the World" by Nat D. Ayer and Clifford Grey. Foreign prints contain a vocal of "You're Nobody's Sweetheart Now" by Kahn and Erdman. [1] Also called "I Love You, Believe Me, I Love You?" [2] Not on cue sheet but in some sources. [3] Also in GLORIFYING THE AMERICAN GIRL (Paramount). [4] Also in RIO RITA.

## 6572 ✦ VALENTINO
### Columbia, 1951

**Musical Score** Roemheld, Heinz
**Choreographer(s)** Ceballos, Larry

**Producer(s)** Small, Edward
**Director(s)** Allen, Lewis
**Screenwriter(s)** Bruce, George

**Cast** Parker, Eleanor; Dexter, Anthony; Drake, Dona; Carlson, Richard; Medina, Patricia; Kruger, Otto

**Song(s)** Valentino Tango (C: Roemheld, Heinz; L: Lawrence, Jack)

## 6573 ✦ VALLEY OF FIRE
### Columbia, 1951

**Producer(s)** Schaefer, Armand
**Director(s)** English, John
**Screenwriter(s)** Geraghty, Gerald
**Source(s)** "Valley of Fire" (story) Harrison, C. William

**Cast** Autry, Gene; Champion; Lauter, Harry; Buttram, Pat; Davis, Gail; Hayden, Russell

**Song(s)** Here's to the Ladies (C/L: Autry, Gene; Walker, Cindy)

## 6574 ✦ VALLEY OF MYSTERY
### Universal, 1966

**Musical Score** Elliott, Jack

**Producer(s)** Tatelman, Harry
**Director(s)** Leyles, Joseph
**Screenwriter(s)** Neal, Richard; Barrington, Lowell

**Cast** Egan, Richard; Graves, Peter; Guardino, Harry; Baker, Joby; Nettleton, Lois; Adams, Julie; Lamas, Fernando

**Song(s)** A Long Way from Home (C/L: Coster, Irwin; Wilson, Stanley)

## 6575 ✦ VALLEY OF THE DOLLS
### Twentieth Century–Fox, 1967

**Musical Score** Williams, John
**Composer(s)** Previn, Andre
**Lyricist(s)** Previn, Dory
**Choreographer(s)** Sidney, Robert

**Producer(s)** Weisbart, David
**Director(s)** Robson, Mark
**Screenwriter(s)** Deutsch, Helen; Kingsley, Dorothy
**Source(s)** *Valley of the Dolls* (novel) Susann, Jacqueline

**Cast** Duke, Patty [1]; Parkins, Barbara; Burke, Paul; Tate, Sharon; Scotti, Tony; Milner, Martin; Drake, Charles; Davion, Alex; Grant, Lee; Stevens, Naomi; Susann, Jacqueline; Hayward, Susan [2]

**Song(s)** Come Live with Me; Give a Little More; I'll Plant My Own Tree; It's Impossible; Theme from Valley of the Dolls

**Notes** Judy Garland who was replaced, did record "I'll Plant My Own Tree." [1] Dubbed by Gail Heideman. [2] Dubbed by Margaret Whiting, however, because of contractual problems, Eileen Wilson provided the vocals on the soundtrack album.

# 6576 ◆ VALLEY OF THE KINGS
Metro–Goldwyn–Mayer, 1954

**Musical Score**   Rozsa, Miklos
**Composer(s)**   Nouera, Abdel Halim
**Lyricist(s)**   el Saftawi, Imam

**Director(s)**   Pirosh, Robert
**Screenwriter(s)**   Pirosh, Robert; Tunberg, Karl
**Source(s)**   *Gods, Graves and Scholars* (book) Ceram, C.W.

**Cast**   Taylor, Robert; Parker, Eleanor; Thompson, Carlos; Kasznar, Kurt; Jory, Victor; Askin, Leon; Silvani, Aldo; Gamal, Sania

**Song(s)**   Song of the Boat (The Big One); Song of the Boat (The Small One) (Ah Yafara Hel Mawod); Song of the Camel Boy (How Wa Be E No); Song of Sakkara's Workers (Idak Wayana Ya Raes)

# 6577 ◆ VALLEY SERENADE
Twentieth Century–Fox, 1941

**Composer(s)**   Warren, Harry
**Lyricist(s)**   Gordon, Mack
**Choreographer(s)**   Pan, Hermes

**Producer(s)**   Sperling, Milton
**Director(s)**   Humberstone, H. Bruce
**Screenwriter(s)**   Ellis, Robert; Logan, Helen

**Cast**   Bari, Lynn [2]; Kelly, Paula; Eberle, Ray; The Modernaires; Tilton, Martha; Henie, Sonja; Payne, John; Miller, Glenn; Berle, Milton; Davis, Joan; The Nicholas Brothers; Davidson, William B.; Dandridge, Dorothy; Murray, Forbes

**Song(s)**   It Happened in Sun Valley; I Know Why (And So-Do-You); The Kiss Polka; At Last [1]; Chattanooga Choo Choo; In the Mood (Inst.) (C: Garland, Joe)

**Notes**   [1] Latter featured in ORCHESTRA WIVES. [2] Dubbed by Pat Friday.

# 6578 ◆ VALUE FOR MONEY
United Artists, 1955

**Musical Score**   Arnold, Malcolm
**Composer(s)**   Pritchett, John
**Lyricist(s)**   Pritchett, John

**Producer(s)**   Nolbandov, Sergei
**Director(s)**   Annakin, Ken
**Screenwriter(s)**   Delderfield, R.F.; Fairfield, William
**Source(s)**   *Value for Money* (novel) Boothroyd, Derrick

**Cast**   Gregson, John; Dors, Diana; Stephen, Susan; Farr, Derek; Pettingell, Frank; Adams, Jill; Victor, Charles

**Song(s)**   Dolls for Gentlemen; Dolly Polka

**Notes**   There is also a vocal of "Is You Is or Is You Ain't My Baby" by Billy Austin and Louis Jordan.

# 6579 ◆ VAMP
New World, 1986

**Musical Score**   Elias, Jonathan

**Producer(s)**   Borchers, Donald P.
**Director(s)**   Wenk, Richard
**Screenwriter(s)**   Wenk, Richard

**Cast**   Makepeace, Chris; Baron, Sandy; Rusler, Robert; Pfeiffer, Dedee; Watanabe, Gedde; Jones, Grace

**Song(s)**   Vamp (C/L: Elias, Jonathan; Jones, Grace)

**Notes**   No cue sheet available.

# 6580 ◆ VANISHING POINT
Twentieth Century–Fox, 1971

**Composer(s)**   Settle, Mike
**Lyricist(s)**   Settle, Mike

**Producer(s)**   Spencer, Norman
**Director(s)**   Sarafian, Richard C.
**Screenwriter(s)**   Colin, Guillermo

**Cast**   Newman, Barry; Little, Cleavon; Jagger, Dean; Medlin, Victoria; Donner, Bob

**Song(s)**   (The Girl Done) Got It Together; Where Do We Go From Here; Love Theme (C/L: Bowen, Jimmy; Carpenter, Pete); You Got to Believe (C/L: Bramlett, Delaney); So Tired (C/L: Temmer; Creamer; Silwin); Dear Jesus God (C/L: Segarini, Bob; Bishop, Randy); Mississippi Queen (C/L: West; Laing; Pappalardi; Rea); Sweet Jesus (C/L: Steagall, Red); Sing Out for Jesus (C/L: Carnes, Kim); Over Me (C/L: Segarini, Bob; Bishop, Randy); Nobody Knows

# 6581 ◆ THE VANISHING PRAIRIE
Disney, 1954

**Musical Score**   Smith, Paul J.
**Composer(s)**   Smith, Paul J.
**Lyricist(s)**   George, Gil

**Producer(s)**   Sharpsteen, Ben
**Director(s)**   Algar, James
**Screenwriter(s)**   Algar, James; Hibler, Winston; Sears, Ted
**Narrator(s)**   Hibler, Winston

**Song(s)**   Prairie Home [1]; If You're Happy [2]

**Notes**   [1] Used in WESTWARD HO THE WAGONS as "Pioneer Prayer." [2] Used instrumentally only. Based on "Wedding Waltz Sequence."

# 6582 ◆ THE VANISHING PRIVATE
Disney, 1942

**Musical Score**   Wallace, Oliver

**Song(s)**   The Army's Not the Army Anymore [1] (C: Harline, Leigh; L: Quenzer, Arthur)

**Notes** Short subject. No credit sheet available. [1] Also used in DONALD GETS DRAFTED.

## 6583 ✦ THE VANISHING VIRGINIAN
Metro–Goldwyn–Mayer, 1941

**Musical Score** Snell, Dave

**Producer(s)** Knopf, Edwin H.
**Director(s)** Borzage, Frank
**Screenwriter(s)** Fortune, Jan
**Source(s)** *Father Was a Handful* (book) Yancey Williams, Rebecca

**Cast** Morgan, Frank; Grayson, Kathryn; Byington, Spring; Thompson, Natalie; Daniels, Mark; Newland, Douglass; Patterson, Elizabeth; Beavers, Louise; Beckett, Scotty

**Song(s)** The World Was Made for You [1] (C: Strauss, Johann; L: White, Minneletha)

**Notes** This is the story of Cap'n Bob Yancey. [1] Earl Brent credited with lyrics on sheet music.

## 6584 ✦ VARIETY GIRL
Paramount, 1947

**Musical Score** Lilley, Joseph J.
**Composer(s)** Loesser, Frank
**Lyricist(s)** Loesser, Frank
**Choreographer(s)** Daniels, Billy; Pearce, Bernard

**Producer(s)** Dare, Danny
**Director(s)** Marshall, George
**Screenwriter(s)** Hartmann, Edmund L.; Tashlin, Frank; Walsh, Robert; Brice, Monte

**Cast** Hatcher, Mary; San Juan, Olga; Crosby, Bing; Hope, Bob; Cooper, Gary; Milland, Ray; Ladd, Alan; Stanwyck, Barbara; Goddard, Paulette; Lamour, Dorothy; Tufts, Sonny; Caulfield, Joan; Holden, William; Scott, Lizabeth; Lancaster, Burt; Russell, Gail; Lynn, Diana; Hayden, Sterling; Preston, Robert; Lake, Veronica; Lund, John; Bendix, William; Fitzgerald, Barry; Daley, Cass; Da Silva, Howard; Carey, Macdonald; De Wolfe, Billy; Knowles, Patric; Demarest, William; Freeman, Mona; Kellaway, Cecil; Field, Virginia; Webb, Richard; Faylen, Frank; Kelley, DeForest; Bailey, Pearl; Spike Jones and His City Slickers; De Mille, Cecil B.; Leisen, Mitchell; Marshall, George; Butler, Frank

**Song(s)** Your Heart Calling Mine; Tallahassee; Tired (C/L: Roberts, Allan; Fisher, Doris); He Can Waltz; Harmony [4] (C: Van Heusen, James; L: Burke, Johnny); We French Get So Excited [1]; Romeow and Julicat [2] (C/L: Plumb, Ed); I Must Have Been Madly in Love [3]; The Fireman's Ball [5]; I Want My Money Back [5]; Tunnel of Love [5] [6]; Impossible Things [3]; Grauman's Chinese Sequence [5]

**Notes** [1] Only used instrumentally but recorded vocally. Also called "The French They Get So Excited." [2] Used for the Puppetoon sequence. [3] Not used but recorded. [4] From the Broadway musical NELLIE BLY. [5] Not used. [6] Used in LET'S DANCE.

## 6585 ✦ VARIETY TIME
RKO, 1948

**Producer(s)** Bilson, George
**Director(s)** Yates, Hal [2] [3]
**Screenwriter(s)** Solomon, Leo [1]; Quillan, Joseph [1]; Law, Hal [2]; Yates, Hal [3]

**Cast** Kennedy, Edgar; Errol, Leon; Frankie Carle and His Orchestra; Rooney, Pat; Valdes, Miguelito; Harold and Lola; Jesse & James; Lynn, Royce & Vanya; Conried, Hans; Granger, Dorothy; Norton, Jack; Urecal, Minerva; Lake, Florence; Rice, Jack; Farley, Dot; Paar, Jack

**Song(s)** Carle Boogie (Inst.) (C: Carle, Frankie); C'est Mon Couer [4] (C/L: Morgan, Stephen)

**Notes** There is also a vocal of "Babalu" by M. Lecuona. [1] Jack Paar material. [2] Leon Errol material. [3] Edgar Kennedy material. [4] Also in GANGWAY FOR TOMORROW and JOURNEY INTO FEAR.

## 6586 ✦ VARSITY
Paramount, 1928

**Director(s)** Tuttle, Frank
**Screenwriter(s)** Root, Wells; Estabrook, Howard

**Cast** Rogers, Charles "Buddy"; Conklin, Chester; Brian, Mary; Holmes, Phillips; Ellis, Robert; Westwood, John

**Song(s)** My Varsity Girl, I'll Cling to You (C: Harling, W. Franke; L: Bryan, Alfred)

**Notes** This is a part talkie. This was Phillips Holmes' first picture.

## 6587 ✦ VARSITY SHOW
Warner Brothers, 1937

**Composer(s)** Whiting, Richard A.
**Lyricist(s)** Mercer, Johnny
**Choreographer(s)** Berkeley, Busby

**Director(s)** Keighley, William
**Screenwriter(s)** Wald, Jerry; Macaulay, Richard; Herzig, Sig; Duff, Warren

**Cast** Powell, Dick; Waring, Fred; Lane, Priscilla; Catlett, Walter; Healy, Ted; Lane, Rosemary; Davis, Johnnie; Dixon, Lee; Todd, Mabel; MacFarlane, George; Hobbes, Halliwell; Brophy, Edward S.; Dunn, Emma; Buck and Bubbles; Holloway, Sterling

Song(s)   Have You Got Any Castles, Baby?; Love Is on the Air Tonight; Moonlight on the Campus; Old King Cole; On with the Dance; We're Working Our Way through College [1]; You've Got Something There; When Your College Days Are Gone; Give Us a Drink (C/L: Ballard, Pat; Henderson, Charles; Waring, Tom); I'm Dependable (C: Waring, Tom; L: Raye, Don); Let that Be a Lesson to You; Little Fraternity Pin (C: Ringwald, Roy; L: Gibbons, Paul); Gasoline Gypsies

Notes   No cue sheet available. [1] Also in SHE'S WORKING HER WAY THROUGH COLLEGE.

## 6588 ✦ VASECTOMY, A DELICATE MATTER
Seymour Borde, 1986

Musical Score   Karlin, Fred

Producer(s)   Burge, Robert A.
Director(s)   Burge, Robert A.
Screenwriter(s)   Hilliard, Robert; Burge, Robert A.

Cast   Sorvino, Paul; Edwards, Cassandra; D'John, Leonard; Vigoda, Abe; Greene, Lorne; Balin, Ina; Powers, Wayne

Song(s)   Love Says It All (C: Karlin, Fred; L: Robbins, Ayn)

Notes   No cue sheet available.

## 6589 ✦ THE VELVET TOUCH
RKO, 1948

Musical Score   Harline, Leigh

Producer(s)   Brisson, Frederick
Director(s)   Gage, John
Screenwriter(s)   Rosten, Leo

Cast   Russell, Rosalind; Genn, Leo; Trevor, Claire; Greenstreet, Sydney; Ames, Leon; McHugh, Frank; Kingsford, Walter; Westman, Nydia

Song(s)   The Velvet Touch (C: Harline, Leigh; L: Greene, Mort)

## 6590 ✦ THE VENETIAN AFFAIR
Metro–Goldwyn–Mayer, 1966

Musical Score   Schifrin, Lalo

Producer(s)   Thorpe, Jerry; Neuman, E. Jack
Director(s)   Thorpe, Jerry
Screenwriter(s)   Neuman, E. Jack
Source(s)   *The Venetian Affair* (novel) MacInnes, Helen

Cast   Vaughn, Robert; Sommer, Elke; Farr, Felicia; Boehm, Karl; Karloff, Boris; Carmel, Roger C.; Asner, Edward

Song(s)   Our Venetian Affair (C: Schifrin, Lalo; L: Winn, Hal)

## 6591 ✦ THE VENGEANCE OF FU MANCHU
Warner Brothers, 1968

Musical Score   Lockyer, Malcolm

Producer(s)   Towers, Harry Alan
Director(s)   Summers, Jeremy
Screenwriter(s)   Welbeck, Peter

Cast   Lee, Christopher; Ferrer, Tony; Chin, Tsal; Wilmer, Douglas

Song(s)   Where Are the Men (C: Lockyer, Malcolm; L: Black, Don)

Notes   No cue sheet available.

## 6592 ✦ VERA CRUZ
United Artists, 1954

Musical Score   Friedhofer, Hugo

Producer(s)   Hill, James
Director(s)   Aldrich, Robert
Screenwriter(s)   Kibbee, Roland; Webb, James R.

Cast   Cooper, Gary; Lancaster, Burt; Darcel, Denise; Romero, Cesar; Montiel, Sarita; Macready, George; Borgnine, Ernest

Song(s)   Vera Cruz [1] (C: Friedhofer, Hugo; L: Cahn, Sammy)

Notes   [1] Used instrumentally only.

## 6593 ✦ VERBOTEN
RKO, 1958

Musical Score   Sukman, Harry

Producer(s)   Fuller, Samuel
Director(s)   Fuller, Samuel
Screenwriter(s)   Fuller, Samuel

Cast   Best, James; Cummings, Susan; Pittman, Tom; Dubov, Paul; Daye, Harold; Kallman, Dick; Randall, Stuart; Geray, Steven

Song(s)   Verboten (C: Sukman, Harry; L: David, Mack)

## 6594 ✦ VERTIGO
Paramount, 1958

Producer(s)   Hitchcock, Alfred
Director(s)   Hitchcock, Alfred
Screenwriter(s)   Coppel, Alec; Taylor, Samuel
Source(s)   *D'Entre Les Morts* (novel) Boileau, Pierre; Narcejac, Thomas

Cast   Stewart, James; Novak, Kim; Bel Geddes, Barbara; Helmore, Tom; Bailey, Raymond; Corby, Ellen; Patrick, Lee

Song(s)   Madeleine [2] (C: Herrmann, Bernard; Alexander, Jeff; L: Orenstein, Larry); Vertigo [1] (C/L: Livingston, Jay; Evans, Ray)

**Notes** [1] Written for exploitation only. [2] Based on a theme by Herrmann. Written for exploitation only.

## 6595 ◆ A VERY PRIVATE AFFAIR
Metro–Goldwyn–Mayer, 1965

**Musical Score** Carpi, Fiorenzo

**Producer(s)** Gouze-Renal, Christine
**Director(s)** Malle, Louis
**Screenwriter(s)** Rappeneau, Jean-Paul; Malle, Louis

**Cast** Bardot, Brigitte; Mastroianni, Marcello; Bataille, Nicolas; Sanders, Dirk

**Song(s)** Sidonie (C: Spanos, Jean; Riviere, Jean-Max; L: Cros, Charles)

## 6596 ◆ VIAGGIO CON ANITA

See A TRIP WITH ANITA.

## 6597 ◆ VIBES
Columbia, 1988

**Musical Score** Horner, James

**Producer(s)** Blum, Deborah; Ganz, Tony
**Director(s)** Kwapis, Ken
**Screenwriter(s)** Ganz, Lowell; Mandel, Babaloo

**Cast** Lauper, Cyndi; Goldblum, Jeff; Sands, Julian; Gress, Googy; Pena, Elizabeth; Lerner, Michael

**Song(s)** I've Got a Hole in My Heart (C/L: Orange, Richard)

**Notes** No cue sheet available.

## 6598 ◆ VICE AND VIRTUE
Metro–Goldwyn–Mayer, 1966

**Musical Score** Magne, Michel
**Composer(s)** Magne, Michel
**Lyricist(s)** Magne, Michel

**Producer(s)** Poire, Alain
**Director(s)** Vadim, Roger
**Screenwriter(s)** Vailland, Roger; Vadim, Roger; Choublier, Claude

**Cast** Girardot, Annie; Hossein, Robert; Deneuve, Catherine; Hasse, O.E.

**Song(s)** Pour un Jour, Pour un An; Pour la Vie; Vent Un Jour on Iva; Pent Etre un Jour

## 6599 ◆ VICE SQUAD
Avco Embassy, 1982

**Producer(s)** Frankish, Brian
**Director(s)** Sherman, Gary A.

**Screenwriter(s)** Howard, Sandy; O'Neil, Robert Vincent; Peters, Kenneth

**Cast** Hubley, Season; Swanson, Gary; Hauser, Wings; Serna, Pepe; Todd, Beverly

**Song(s)** Neon Slime (C: Renzetti, Joe; L: Stokes, Simon); Red Light Lover (C/L: Sabu, Paul)

**Notes** No cue sheet available.

## 6600 ◆ VICE VERSA
Columbia, 1988

**Musical Score** Shire, David

**Producer(s)** Clement, Dick; La Frenais, Ian
**Director(s)** Gilbert, Brian
**Screenwriter(s)** Clement, Dick; La Frenais, Ian

**Cast** Reinhold, Judge; Savage, Fred; Bohrer, Corinne; Kurtz, Swoosie; Kaczmarek, Jane; Proval, David; Prince, William

**Song(s)** Crazy in the Night (C/L: Zane, Mick; Behn, Mark; Neal, James); Vice Versa (C/L: Zane, Mick; Behn, Mark; Neal, James)

**Notes** No cue sheet available.

## 6601 ◆ VICKI
Twentieth Century–Fox, 1953

**Musical Score** Harline, Leigh

**Producer(s)** Goldstein, Leonard
**Director(s)** Horner, Harry
**Screenwriter(s)** Taylor, Dwight
**Source(s)** *I Wake Up Screaming* (novel) Fisher, Steve

**Cast** Crain, Jeanne; Peters, Jean; Reid, Elliott; Boone, Richard; Adams, Casey; D'Arcy, Alexander; Betz, Carl; Spelling, Aaron; Engel, Roy

**Song(s)** Vicki [1] (C: Showalter, Max; L: Darby, Ken)

**Notes** There are also vocals of "I Know Why (And So Do You)" by Harry Warren and Mack Gordon and "How Many Times Do I Have to Tell You" by Jimmy McHugh and Harold Adamson. [1] Used instrumentally only.

## 6602 ◆ VICTOR/VICTORIA
Metro–Goldwyn–Mayer, 1982

**Musical Score** Mancini, Henry
**Composer(s)** Mancini, Henry
**Lyricist(s)** Bricusse, Leslie
**Choreographer(s)** Stone, Paddy

**Producer(s)** Edwards, Blake; Adams, Tony
**Director(s)** Edwards, Blake
**Screenwriter(s)** Edwards, Blake
**Source(s)** *Viktor und Viktoria* (film) Schunzel, Reinhold

**Cast**  Garner, James; Andrews, Julie; Preston, Robert; Warren, Lesley Ann; Karras, Alex; Rhys-Davies, John

**Song(s)**  Gay Paree; Le Jazz Hot; The Shady Dame from Seville; Chicago, Illinois; You and Me; Crazy World

## 6603 ✦ VICTORY VEHICLES
### Disney, 1943

**Song(s)**  Hop On Your Pogo Stick (C: Wallace, Oliver; L: Washington, Ned)

**Notes**  Cartoon.

## 6604 ✦ VIENNA SOUVENIR
### Studio Unknown, 1940

**Composer(s)**  Strauss, Johann
**Lyricist(s)**  Drake, Milton

**Song(s)**  Voices of Spring; Vienna Life; Southern Roses; Beautiful Blue Danube; Woods of Vienna

**Notes**  No other information available.

## 6605 ✦ VIENNESE NIGHTS
### Warner Brothers, 1930

**Composer(s)**  Romberg, Sigmund
**Lyricist(s)**  Hammerstein II, Oscar
**Choreographer(s)**  Haskell, Jack

**Director(s)**  Crosland, Alan
**Screenwriter(s)**  Hammerstein II, Oscar

**Cast**  Gray, Alexander; Segal, Vivienne; Pidgeon, Walter; Roach, Bert; Douglas, Milton; Hersholt, Jean; Purcell, June; Fazenda, Louise

**Song(s)**  Wake Up; Oli, Oli, Oli; You Will Remember Vienna; Brass Band March; Regimental March; Goodbye, My Love; Here We Are; When You Have No Man to Love; I Bring a Love Song; Ja, Ja, Ja!; Pretty Gypsy; Waiting; I'm Lonely

**Notes**  No cue sheet available.

## 6606 ✦ A VIEW TO A KILL
### United Artists, 1985

**Musical Score**  Barry, John

**Producer(s)**  Broccoli, Albert R.; Wilson, Michael G.
**Director(s)**  Glen, John
**Screenwriter(s)**  Maibaum, Richard; Wilson, Michael G.
**Source(s)**  characters by Fleming, Ian

**Cast**  Moore, Roger; Walken, Christopher; Roberts, Tanya; Jones, Grace; MacNee, Patrick; Bauchau, Patrick

**Song(s)**  A View to a Kill (C: Barry, John; L: Duran Duran)

## 6607 ✦ VIGILANTE FORCE
### United Artists, 1977

**Musical Score**  Fried, Gerald

**Producer(s)**  Corman, Gene
**Director(s)**  Armitage, George
**Screenwriter(s)**  Armitage, George

**Cast**  Kristofferson, Kris; Vincent, Jan-Michael; Principal, Victoria; Peters, Bernadette; Dexter, Brad

**Song(s)**  Alone in Carnegie Hall (C: Armitage, George; L: Peters, Bernadette); Take Me to Morning (C: Armitage, George; L: Hilton, Hermine)

## 6608 ✦ THE VIGILANTES RETURN
### Universal, 1947

**Musical Score**  Skinner, Frank

**Producer(s)**  Welsch, Howard
**Director(s)**  Taylor, Ray
**Screenwriter(s)**  Chanslor, Roy

**Cast**  Hall, Jon; Lindsay, Margaret; Devine, Andy; Drew, Paula; Wilcox, Robert

**Song(s)**  One Man Woman [1] (C: Schwarzwald, Milton; L: Brooks, Jack)

**Notes**  [1] Also in SOUTH SEA SINNER.

## 6609 ✦ VILLA!!
### Twentieth Century–Fox, 1958

**Musical Score**  Sawtell, Paul; Shefter, Bert

**Producer(s)**  Skouras, Plato
**Director(s)**  Clark, James B.
**Screenwriter(s)**  Vittes, Louis

**Cast**  Keith, Brian; Romero, Cesar; Dean, Margia; Hoyos, Rodolfo; Monteros, Rosenda; Wright, Ben

**Song(s)**  A Lonely Kind of Love [1] (C: Traditional; L: Dean, Margia); Sin-Decirte-Adios (C/L: Espinosa, J.J.); Farruca Jerezana (C/L: Millet, Paco); Men-Men-Men (C: Newman, Lionel; L: Darby, Ken; Dean, Margia); Just Between Friends (C/L: Kent, Walter; Walton, Tom)

**Notes**  [1] Based on the Mexican folk song "Las Mananitas."

## 6610 ✦ VILLAGE BARN DANCE
### Republic, 1940

**Producer(s)**  Schaefer, Armand
**Director(s)**  McDonald, Frank
**Screenwriter(s)**  McGowan, Dorrell; McGowan, Stuart

**Cast**  Cromwell, Richard; Day, Doris; Barbier, George; Dale, Esther; Tombes, Andrew; Lulu Belle and Scotty; Wilson, Don; The Kidoodlers; The Texas Wanderers

**Song(s)** Hail to Lyndale (C: Kraushaar, Raoul; L: Cherkose, Eddie); Howdy Neighbor (C/L: Cherkose, Eddie); Nobody's Business but Our Own (C/L: Lair, John; Wiseman, Scott); When the Circus Came to Town [1] (C/L: Eaton, Jimmy; Shand, Terry); What Are Little Girls Made Out Of (C/L: Lair, John; Wiseman, Scott)

**Notes** There is also a vocal of "When I Yoo Hoo in the Valley." [1] Also in BELLS OF ROSARITA.

## 6611 ✦ VILLAGE OF THE GIANTS
### Embassy, 1965

**Musical Score** Nitzsche, Jack

**Producer(s)** Gordon, Bert I.
**Director(s)** Gordon, Bert I.
**Screenwriter(s)** Caillou, Alan
**Source(s)** *The Food of the Gods* (novel) Wells, H.G.

**Cast** Kirk, Tommy; Crawford, Johnny; Bridges, Beau; Howard, Ron; Harmoon, Joy; Random, Bob; Sterling, Tisha

**Song(s)** Woman (C/L: Elliott, Ron); When It Comes to Your Love (C/L: Elliott, Ron); Little Bitty Corrine (C/L: Slay, Frank; Picariello, Frederic A.); Marianne (C: Nitzsche, Jack; L: Titleman, Russ); Nothing Can Stand in My Way (C: Nitzsche, Jack; L: Titleman, Russ)

**Notes** No cue sheet available.

## 6612 ✦ THE VILLAIN STILL PURSUED HER
### RKO, 1940

**Musical Score** Tours, Frank

**Producer(s)** Franklin, Harold B.
**Director(s)** Cline, Edward F.
**Screenwriter(s)** Franklin, Elbert

**Cast** Louise, Anita; Mowbray, Alan

**Song(s)** Our Home Is Happy Again (C/L: Tours, Frank); The Villain Still Pursued Her [1] (C/L: Simon, Nat; Tobias, Harry; Tobias, Charles)

**Notes** [1] Sheet music only.

## 6613 ✦ THE VILLAIN
### Columbia, 1979

**Musical Score** Justis, Bill

**Producer(s)** Engelberg, Mort
**Director(s)** Needham, Hal
**Screenwriter(s)** Kane, Robert G.

**Cast** Douglas, Kirk; Lynde, Paul; Ann-Margaret; Schwarzenegger, Arnold; Brooks, Foster; Buzzi, Ruth; Elam, Jack; Martin, Strother; Tillis, Mel

**Song(s)** Cactus Jack Slade (C/L: Cannon, Buddy; Younts, Bob; Williams, Billy); Charmin (C/L: Cannon, Buddy; Starr, Kenny; Younts, Bob; Darrell, Jimmy);

Handsome Stranger (C/L: Darrell, Jimmy; Smartt, Joe); The Villain (C/L: Rabin, Buzz; Tillis, Mel)

**Notes** No cue sheet available.

## 6614 ✦ THE VIOLENT FOUR
### Paramount, 1969

**Musical Score** Ortolani, Riz

**Producer(s)** De Laurentiis, Dino
**Director(s)** Lizzani, Carlo
**Screenwriter(s)** Maiuri, Dino; De Ritz, Massimo; Lizzani, Carlo

**Cast** Volonte, Gian Maria; Milian, Thomas; Lee, Margaret; Gravins, Carla; Backy, Don; Lovelock, Ray

**Song(s)** Black Skin (C/L: Ferrer, Nino); Strange World (C: Ortolani, Riz; L: Newell, Norman)

**Notes** The film is titled BANDITI A MILANO in Italy.

## 6615 ✦ THE VIOLENT ONES
### Madison/Harold Goldman, 1967

**Musical Score** Skiles, Marlin

**Producer(s)** Stabler, Robert W.
**Director(s)** Lamas, Fernando
**Screenwriter(s)** Wilson, Doug; Davis, Charles

**Cast** Lamas, Fernando; Ray, Aldo; Sands, Tommy; Carradine, David; Gaye, Lisa

**Song(s)** The Violent Ones (C: Skiles, Marlin; L: Harris, Albert); He Was a Beeg Man (C: Stabler, Robert W.; L: Miller, Herman)

## 6616 ✦ VIOLENT PLAYGROUND
### United Artists, 1958

**Musical Score** Green, Philip

**Producer(s)** Relph, Michael
**Director(s)** Dearden, Basil
**Screenwriter(s)** Kennaway, James
**Source(s)** (novel) Kennaway, James

**Cast** Baker, Stanley; Heywood, Anne; McCallum, David; Cushing, Peter

**Song(s)** Play Rough (C: Green, Philip; L: Roberts, Paddy)

## 6617 ✦ VIOLETS ARE BLUE
### Columbia, 1986

**Musical Score** Williams, Patrick

**Producer(s)** Powell, Marykay
**Director(s)** Fisk, Jack
**Screenwriter(s)** Foner, Naomi

**Cast**   Spacek, Sissy; Kline, Kevin; Bedelia, Bonnie; Kellogg, John

**Song(s)**   One Day (C: Williams, Patrick; L: Jennings, Will)

## 6618 ✦ VIOLETS IN SPRING
Metro–Goldwyn–Mayer, 1936

**Musical Score**   Vaughan, C.
**Composer(s)**   Jason, Will; Burton, Val
**Lyricist(s)**   Jason, Will; Burton, Val

**Director(s)**   Neumann, Kurt
**Screenwriter(s)**   Burton, Val; Jason, Will; Rauh, Stanley

**Cast**   Murphy, George; Grey, Virginia

**Song(s)**   Opening Sequence; Let's Keep on Dancing; Violets in Spring

**Notes**   Short subject.

## 6619 ✦ THE VIRGINIAN
Paramount, 1929

**Composer(s)**   Hajos, Karl

**Producer(s)**   Lighton, Louis D.
**Director(s)**   Fleming, Victor
**Screenwriter(s)**   Estabrook, Howard; Paramore Jr., Edward E.
**Source(s)**   *The Virginian* (play) LaShelle, Kirke; *The Virginian* (novel) Wister, Owen

**Cast**   Cooper, Gary; Huston, Walter; Arlen, Richard; Brian, Mary; Conklin, Chester; Pallette, Eugene; Calvert, E.H.; Ware, Helen

**Song(s)**   I Had a Gal; Take Me Home [1]; Sweet Annie [1]; Old Pete [1]; Give Me a Buckin' Broncho [1]; A Cowboy's Life [1]; In Wyoming [1]; So Long Cowboys [1] (C/L: Coslow, Sam); I Ain't Got No Home [1] (C/L: Chase, Newell); And She Never Came Home Any More [2]

**Notes**   There are several traditional songs rendered vocally also. [1] Not used. [2] Used instrumentally only.

## 6620 ✦ THE VIRTUOUS SIN
Paramount, 1930

**Lyricist(s)**   Robin, Leo

**Director(s)**   Cukor, George; Gasnier, Louis
**Screenwriter(s)**   Brown, Martin
**Source(s)**   *The General* (novel) Zilahy, Lajos

**Cast**   Francis, Kay; Huston, Walter; MacKenna, Kenneth; Howland, Jobyna

**Song(s)**   Who Wants a Girl Like Me (C: Jackson, Howard); This Is the Moment [1] (C: Whiting, Richard A.); [2] Just to Hear You Say I Love You [2] (C: unknown)

**Notes**   [1] Based on Serge Malavsky's adaptation of a Russian folk song which he titled "Ia Tak Hochu Chtos Te Bel So Mriou" ("I Always Long for You to Be with Me"). Also in THE WOLF OF WALL STREET. See under that title for more information. [2] Not used.

## 6621 ✦ THE VISIT
Twentieth Century–Fox, 1967

**Musical Score**   Majewski, Hans-Martin; Arnell, Richard

**Producer(s)**   Derode, Julien; Quinn, Anthony
**Director(s)**   Wicki, Bernhard
**Screenwriter(s)**   Barzman, Ben
**Source(s)**   *The Visit* (play) Duerrenmatt, Friedrich

**Cast**   Bergman, Ingrid; Quinn, Anthony; Demick, Irina; Stoppa, Paolo; Blech, Hans-Cristian; Dauphin, Claude; Cortese, Valentina; Ciannelli, Eduardo

**Song(s)**   Welcome Karla (C: Majewski, Hans-Martin; L: Williams, Elmo)

## 6622 ✦ VIVACIOUS LADY
RKO, 1938

**Musical Score**   Webb, Roy

**Producer(s)**   Stevens, George
**Director(s)**   Stevens, George
**Screenwriter(s)**   Wolfson, P.J.; Pagano, Ernest

**Cast**   Rogers, Ginger; Stewart, James; Ellison, James; Coburn, Charles; Bondi, Beulah; Mercer, Frances; Kennedy, Phyllis; Pangborn, Franklin; Sutton, Grady

**Song(s)**   You'll Be Reminded of Me (C/L: Jessel, George; Meskill, Jack; Shapiro, Ted)

## 6623 ✦ VIVA CISCO KID
Twentieth Century–Fox, 1940

**Producer(s)**   Wurtzel, Sol M.
**Director(s)**   Foster, Norman
**Screenwriter(s)**   Engel, Samuel G.; Long, Hal
**Source(s)**   character Henry, O.

**Cast**   Romero, Cesar; Rogers, Jean; Martin, Chris-Pin; Watson, Minor; Fields, Stanley

**Song(s)**   Lord, I'm Going to My Home (C: Ricardi, Enrico; L: Engel, Samuel G.; Long, Hal)

## 6624 ✦ VIVA LAS VEGAS (1956)

See MEET ME IN LAS VEGAS.

## 6625 ✦ VIVA LAS VEGAS (1965)
Metro–Goldwyn–Mayer, 1965

**Musical Score**   Stoll, George; Van Eps, Robert
**Choreographer(s)**   Winters, David

**Producer(s)**   Cummings, Jack
**Director(s)**   Sidney, George
**Screenwriter(s)**   Benson, Sally

**Cast**   Presley, Elvis; Ann-Margaret; Danova, Cesare; Demarest, William; Blair, Nicky

**Song(s)**   Viva, Las Vegas (C: Pomus, Doc; L: Shuman, Mort); C'mon Everybody (C/L: Byers, Joy); Today, Tomorrow and Forever (C/L: Giant, Bill; Baum, Bernie; Kaye, Florence); The Climb (C/L: Leiber, Jerry; Stoller, Mike); What'd I Say [1] (C/L: Charles, Ray); If You Think I Don't Need You (C/L: West, Bob "Red"; Cooper, Joe); Appreciation (C/L: Wayne, Bernie; Moore, Marvin); I Need Somebody to Lean On (C: Pomus, Doc; L: Shuman, Mort); My Rival (C/L: Wayne, Bernie; Moore, Marvin)

**Notes**   Released overseas as LOVE IN LAS VEGAS. There are also vocals of "The Yellow Rose of Texas" by J.K. and adapted by Don George; "Santa Lucia" and "The Eyes of Texas" by John Lang Sinclair. [1] Also in the Fox films BLUES FOR LOVERS and SWINGIN' ALONG.

### 6626 ◆ VIVA MARIA!
United Artists, 1966

**Musical Score**   Delerue, Georges
**Composer(s)**   Delerue, Georges
**Lyricist(s)**   Carriere, John-Claude; Malle, Louis

**Producer(s)**   Malle, Louis; Dancigers, Oscar
**Director(s)**   Malle, Louis
**Screenwriter(s)**   Carriere, Jean-Claude; Malle, Louis

**Cast**   Moreau, Jeanne; Bardot, Brigitte; Hamilton, George; von Rezzori, Gregor; Dubost, Paulette; Brook, Claudio; Montezuma, Carlos Lopez

**Song(s)**   Paris, Paris, Paris; Ah Le P'tites Femmes; Maria Maria; L'Irlandaise; Viva Maria [1] (C/L: Delerue, Georges; Holmes, Leroy; Sherman, Noel)

**Notes**   This cue sheet does not differentiate between vocals and instrumentals. [1] Sheet music only.

### 6627 ◆ VIVA VILLA!
Metro–Goldwyn–Mayer, 1934

**Musical Score**   Stothart, Herbert

**Producer(s)**   Selznick, David O.
**Director(s)**   Conway, Jack
**Screenwriter(s)**   Hecht, Ben
**Source(s)**   (book) Pinchon, Edgcumb; Stade, O.B.

**Cast**   Beery, Wallace; Carrillo, Leo; Cook, Donald; Walthall, Henry B.; de Mille, Katherine; Wray, Fay; Erwin, Stuart; Schildkraut, Joseph; Stone, George E.; Bushman Jr., Francis X.; Armetta, Henry

**Song(s)**   Madre Mia (C: Stothart, Herbert; L: Tobias); La Cucaracha [1] (C: Savino, Domenico; L: Washington, Ned)

**Notes**   Lee Tracy began filming but was replaced by Stuart Erwin. Howard Hawks began the direction but was replaced by Jack Conway. [1] Sheet music only.

### 6628 ◆ VIVRE POUR VIVRE

See LIVE FOR LIFE.

### 6629 ◆ VOGUES OF 1938
United Artists, 1938

**Producer(s)**   Wanger, Walter
**Director(s)**   Cummings, Irving
**Screenwriter(s)**   Spewack, Sam; Spewack, Bella

**Cast**   Baxter, Warner; Bennett, Joan; Vinson, Helen; Auer, Mischa; Cowan, Jerome; Gateson, Marjorie; Verrill, Virginia

**Song(s)**   (Turn On That) Red Hot Heat (C: Alter, Louis; L: Webster, Paul Francis); That Old Feeling (C: Fain, Sammy; L: Brown, Lew); Lovely One (C: Sherwin, Manning; L: Loesser, Frank); Lady of the Evening (C: Alter, Louis; L: Webster, Paul Francis); King of Jam (inst.) (C: Alter, Louis)

### 6630 ◆ VOICE IN THE MIRROR
Universal, 1958

**Musical Score**   Mancini, Henry

**Producer(s)**   Kay, Gordon
**Director(s)**   Keller, Harry
**Screenwriter(s)**   Marcus, Lawrence B.

**Cast**   Egan, Richard; London, Julie; Matthau, Walter; O'Connell, Arthur; Donahue, Troy; Doran, Ann; Converse, Peggy; Clarke, Mae

**Song(s)**   Voice in the Mirror (C/L: Troup, Bobby; London, Julie)

### 6631 ◆ VOICES
Metro–Goldwyn–Mayer, 1978

**Musical Score**   Webb, Jimmy
**Composer(s)**   Webb, Jimmy
**Lyricist(s)**   Webb, Jimmy

**Producer(s)**   Wizan, Joe
**Director(s)**   Markowitz, Robert
**Screenwriter(s)**   Herzfeld, John

**Cast**   Irving, Amy; Rocco, Alex; Miller, Barry; Berghof, Herbert; Lindfors, Viveca; Rich, Allan

**Song(s)**   I Will Always Wait for You; Drunk As a Punk; Champagne Jam (C/L: Buie, Buddy; Nix, Robert; Cobb, J.R.); On a Stage; The Coffee Is Good; Bubbles in My Beer (C/L: Duncan, Tommy; Walker, Cindy; Wills, Bob); Anything That's Rock 'N' Roll (C/L: Petty, Tom); The Children's Song; Disco If You Want To [1]

**Notes**    [1] Sheet music only.

## 6632 ✦ VON DRAKE IN SPAIN
Disney, 1962

**Musical Score**    Baker, Buddy

**Song(s)**    Flamenco (C/L: Leven, Mel)

**Notes**    Animated short. No credit sheet available.

## 6633 ✦ VON RICHTHOFEN AND BROWN
United Artists, 1971

**Musical Score**    Friedhofer, Hugo

**Producer(s)**    Corman, Gene
**Director(s)**    Corman, Roger
**Screenwriter(s)**    Corrington, John

**Cast**    Law, John Phillip; Stroud, Don; Primus, Barry; Redgrave, Corin

**Song(s)**    Ilse's Theme (C/L: Booth, Tim)

**Notes**    Titled THE RED BARON internationally.

## 6634 ✦ VOYAGE TO THE BOTTOM OF THE SEA
Twentieth Century–Fox, 1961

**Musical Score**    Sawtell, Paul; Shefter, Bert

**Producer(s)**    Allen, Irwin
**Director(s)**    Allen, Irwin
**Screenwriter(s)**    Allen, Irwin; Bennett, Charles

**Cast**    Pidgeon, Walter; Fontaine, Joan; Eden, Barbara; Lorre, Peter; Sterling, Robert; Ansara, Michael; Avalon, Frankie

**Song(s)**    Voyage to the Bottom of the Sea (C/L: Faith, Russell)

## 6635 ◆ WABASH AVENUE
Twentieth Century–Fox, 1950

**Composer(s)** Myrow, Josef
**Lyricist(s)** Gordon, Mack
**Choreographer(s)** Daniels, Billy

**Producer(s)** Perlberg, William
**Director(s)** Koster, Henry
**Screenwriter(s)** Tugend, Harry; Lederer, Charles

**Cast** Grable, Betty; Mature, Victor; Harris, Phil; Gardiner, Reginald; Barton, James; Kelley, Barry; Hamilton, Margaret; Pope, Alexander

**Song(s)** Down on Wabash Avenue; May I Tempt You with a Big Red Rosy Apple; Baby Won't You Say You Love Me; Joe, Jack, Moe and Mack; Wilhelmina; Clean Up Chicago [1]

**Notes** There are also vocals of "I Wish I Could Shimmy Like My Sister Kate" by A.J. Piron and with additional music and lyrics by Ken Darby and Max Gordon; "In the Shade of the Old Apple Tree" by Egbert Van Alstyne and Harry Williams; "Honey Man (My Little Lovin' Honey Man)" by Al Piantadosi and Joseph McCarthy; "Are You From Dixie? (Cause I'm From Dixie Too)" by George L. Cobb and Jack Yellen; "When You Wore a Tulip and I Wore a Big Red Rose" by Percy Wenrich and Jack Mahoney; "I've Been Floating Down the Old Green River" by Joe Cooper and Bert Kalmar; "I Remember You" by Harry Von Tilzer and Vincent Bryan and "Billy (I Always Dream of Bill)" by James Kendis and Herman Paley and Joe Goodwin. [1] Not used but recorded.

## 6636 ◆ THE WAC FROM WALLA WALLA
Republic, 1952

**Musical Score** Butts, Dale
**Composer(s)** Elliott, Jack
**Lyricist(s)** Elliott, Jack

**Producer(s)** Picker, Sidney
**Director(s)** Witney, William
**Screenwriter(s)** Horman, Arthur T.

**Cast** Canova, Judy; Dunne, Stephen; Cleveland, George; Vincent, June; Ryan, Irene; Barcroft, Roy; Jenkins, Allen

**Song(s)** Song of the Women's Army Corps (C: Spina, Harold; L: Elliott, Jack); Boy Oh Boy; Lovey; If Only Dreams Came True

## 6637 ◆ WACO
Paramount, 1966

**Musical Score** Haskell, Jimmie
**Composer(s)** Haskell, Jimmie
**Lyricist(s)** Blair, Hal

**Producer(s)** Lyles, A.C.
**Director(s)** Springsteen, R.G.
**Screenwriter(s)** Fisher, Steve
**Source(s)** *Emporia* (novel) Sanford, Harry; Lamb, Max

**Cast** Keel, Howard; Russell, Jane; Donlevy, Brian; Corey, Wendell; Smith, John; Moore, Terry; Agar, John; Arlen, Richard; Kelley, DeForest; Seymour, Anne; Knight, Fuzzy

**Song(s)** Waco; All but the Remembering [1]

**Notes** [1] Used instrumentally only.

## 6638 ◆ WAGON MASTER
RKO, 1950

**Musical Score** Hageman, Richard
**Composer(s)** Jones, Stan
**Lyricist(s)** Jones, Stan

**Producer(s)** Cooper, Merian C.
**Director(s)** Ford, John
**Screenwriter(s)** Nugent, Frank; Ford, Patrick

**Cast** Arness, James; Thorpe, Jim; Mowbray, Alan; Darwell, Jane; O'Malley, Kathleen; Johnson, Ben; Dru, Joanne; Carey Jr., Harry; Bond, Ward

**Song(s)** Wagons West; Song of the Wagon Master (White Tops); Shadows in the Dust; Chuckawalla Swing; Rollin' Dust [1]

**Notes** [1] Sheet music only.

## 6639 ◆ WAGON TRAIN
RKO, 1940

**Musical Score** Dreyer, Dave; Sawtell, Paul
**Composer(s)** Whitley, Ray; Rose, Fred
**Lyricist(s)** Whitley, Ray; Rose, Fred

**Producer(s)** Gilroy, Bert
**Director(s)** Killy, Edward
**Screenwriter(s)** Grant, Morton

**Cast** Holt, Tim; Whitley, Ray; Lynn, Emmett; O'Driscoll, Martha; McTaggart, Malcolm; Clark, Cliff; Lowe, Ellen; Montague, Monte; Strange, Glenn

**Song(s)** Wagon Train [1]; Why Shore; Farewell

**Notes** [1] Also in BULLET CODE but without Fred Rose credit.

## 6640 ✦ WAGON WHEELS
Paramount, 1934

**Producer(s)** Hurley, Harold
**Director(s)** Barton, Charles
**Screenwriter(s)** Cunningham, Jack
**Source(s)** *Fighting Caravans* (novel) Grey, Zane

**Cast** Scott, Randolph; Patrick, Gail; Blue, Monte

**Song(s)** Wagon Wheels [1] (C: de Rose, Peter; L: Hill, Billy)

**Notes** [1] One source also credits Harlan Thompson with lyrics. Since Paramount had new lyrics written he might have done them. This song was originally in the ZIEGFELD FOLLIES OF 1934. It also appears in the film THE CARAVAN TRAIL (PRC).

## 6641 ✦ WAIKIKI WEDDING
Paramount, 1937

**Composer(s)** Rainger, Ralph
**Lyricist(s)** Robin, Leo
**Choreographer(s)** Prinz, LeRoy

**Producer(s)** Hornblow Jr., Arthur
**Director(s)** Tuttle, Frank
**Screenwriter(s)** Butler, Frank; Hartman, Don; De Leon, Walter; Martin, Francis

**Cast** Crosby, Bing; Ross, Shirley; Burns, Bob; Raye, Martha; Erickson, Leif; Barbier, George; Bates, Granville; Quinn, Anthony; Sutton, Grady; Lewis, Mitchell

**Song(s)** Blue Hawaii [5]; In a Little Hula Heaven; Lani's Song (L: Lowell, Jimmy); Nani Ona Pua (L: Lowell, Jimmy); Aloha [1] (C/L: Liliuokalani, Queen); Momi Pele (L: Lowell, Jimmy); Sweet Leilani [2] (C/L: Owens, Harry); Okolehao (C/L: Rainger, Ralph; Robin, Leo; Hartman, Don); Sweet Is the Word for You; May I Have the Next Dream with You? [3] [7] (C: Coslow, Sam; L: Marion Jr., George); My Secret Song [3] (C: Coslow, Sam; L: Marion Jr., George); The Tropical [3] (C: Coslow, Sam; L: Marion Jr., George); I Have Eyes [3] [6]; You're a Blessing to Me [3] [4]; Live a Love-Dream [3]; What Aloha Means [3]; Maile Dance [3] (L: Lowell, Jimmy; Robin, Leo)

**Notes** [1] Not written for picture. [2] Hawaiian lyrics by Jimmy Lowell. [3] Not used. [4] Also not used in the following films: COCOANUT GROVE, FOUR HOURS TO KILL, GIVE ME A SAILOR and HERE IS MY HEART. [5] Also in BLUE HAWAII. [6] Not used also in ARTISTS AND MODELS but used in PARIS HONEYMOON. [7] Also not used in TWO FOR TONIGHT.

## 6642 ✦ WAIT TILL THE SUN SHINES NELLIE
Twentieth Century–Fox, 1952

**Musical Score** Newman, Alfred

**Producer(s)** Jessel, George
**Director(s)** King, Henry
**Screenwriter(s)** Scott, Allan
**Source(s)** (novel) Reyher, Ferdinand

**Cast** Wayne, David; Peters, Jean; Marlowe, Hugh; Dekker, Albert; Stanley, Helene; Morton, Tom; Hale Jr., Alan; Anders, Merry

**Song(s)** Open the Door (C: Daniel, Eliot; L: Reyher, Ferdinand)

**Notes** There are also vocals of "Wait Till the Sun Shines Nellie" by Harry Von Tilzer and Andrew B. Sterling; "On the Banks of the Wabash, Far Away" by Paul Dresser; "Good-Bye Dolly Gray" by Paul Barnes; "Listen to the Mocking Bird" by Alice Hawthorn; "Break the News to Mother" by Charles K. Harris; "Love's Old Sweet Song (Just a Song at Twilight)" by J.L. Molloy and G. Clifton Bingham; "Smiles" by Lee S. Roberts and J. Will Callahan; and "Pack Up Your Troubles in Your Old Kit Bag" by Felix Powell and George Asaf.

## 6643 ✦ WAIT UNTIL DARK
Warner Brothers, 1967

**Musical Score** Mancini, Henry

**Producer(s)** Ferrer, Mel
**Director(s)** Young, Terence
**Screenwriter(s)** Carrington, Robert; Carrington, Jane-Howard
**Source(s)** *Wait Until Dark* (play) Knott, Frederick

**Cast** Hepburn, Audrey; Arkin, Alan; Crenna, Richard; Zimbalist Jr., Efrem; Weston, Jack; Jones, Samantha; Herrod, Julie; Morgan, Gary

**Song(s)** Wait Until Dark (C: Mancini, Henry; L: Livingston, Jay; Evans, Ray)

## 6644 ✦ WAKE ISLAND
Paramount, 1942

**Producer(s)** Sistrom, Joseph
**Director(s)** Farrow, John
**Screenwriter(s)** Burnett, W.R.; Butler, Frank

**Cast** Preston, Robert; Donlevy, Brian; Bendix, William; Carey, Macdonald; Dekker, Albert; Abel, Walter;

Cameron, Rod; Terry, Phillip; Albertson, Frank; Britton, Barbara

**Song(s)**   Wake Island [1] (C: Young, Victor; L: Frey, Fran)

**Notes**   [1] Not used.

## 6645 ◆ WAKE ME WHEN IT'S OVER
### Twentieth Century–Fox, 1960

**Musical Score**   Mockridge, Cyril J.

**Producer(s)**   LeRoy, Mervyn
**Director(s)**   LeRoy, Mervyn
**Screenwriter(s)**   Breen, Richard L.

**Cast**   Kovacs, Ernie; Moore, Margo; Warden, Jack; McCarthy, Nobu; Shawn, Dick

**Song(s)**   Wake Me When It's Over (C: Van Heusen, James; L: Cahn, Sammy); Chant of Shima (C/L: Shindo, Tak)

**Notes**   There are also vocal renditions of "Should I" by Arthur Freed and Nacio Herb Brown and "You Make Me Feel So Young" by Josef Myrow and Mack Gordon.

## 6646 ◆ WAKE UP AND DREAM (1934)
### Universal, 1934

**Musical Score**   Jackson, Howard
**Composer(s)**   Columbo, Russ; Stern, Jack; Grossman, Bernie
**Lyricist(s)**   Columbo, Russ; Stern, Jack; Grossman, Bernie

**Producer(s)**   Zeidman, B.F.
**Director(s)**   Neumann, Kurt
**Screenwriter(s)**   Meehan Jr., John

**Cast**   Columbo, Russ; Pryor, Roger; Knight, June; Doucet, Catherine; Armetta, Henry; Devine, Andy; Charters, Spencer; Shaw, Winifred

**Song(s)**   Opening Vaudeville Act (C/L: Stern, Jack; Grossman, Bernie); Let's Pretend There's a Moon (C/L: Columbo, Russ; Stern, Jack; Grossman, Bernie; Hamilton, Grace); Where Will I Find the One (C/L: Clifford, Gordon; Cutner, Sidney); Too Beautiful for Words; When You're in Love

**Notes**   Colombo's last film.

## 6647 ◆ WAKE UP AND DREAM (1942)

See WHAT'S COOKIN'.

## 6648 ◆ WAKE UP AND DREAM (1946)
### Twentieth Century–Fox, 1946

**Composer(s)**   Bloom, Rube
**Lyricist(s)**   Ruby, Harry

**Producer(s)**   Morosco, Walter
**Director(s)**   Bacon, Lloyd

**Screenwriter(s)**   Moll, Elick
**Source(s)**   *The Enchanted Voyage* (novel) Nathan, Robert

**Cast**   Payne, John; Haver, June; Greenwood, Charlotte; Marshall, Connie; Ireland, John; Bevans, Clem; Russell, Charles; Patrick, Lee; Brown, Charles D.; Bacon, Irving; Urecal, Minerva; Acuff, Eddie

**Song(s)**   Give Me the Simple Life; I Wish I Could Tell You; Bell Bottom Trousers (C/L: Jaffe, Moe); Into the Sun [1]

**Notes**   [1] Sheet music only.

## 6649 ◆ WAKE UP AND LIVE
### Twentieth Century–Fox, 1937

**Composer(s)**   Revel, Harry
**Lyricist(s)**   Gordon, Mack

**Producer(s)**   Zanuck, Darryl F.
**Director(s)**   Lanfield, Sidney
**Screenwriter(s)**   Tugend, Harry; Yellen, Jack
**Source(s)**   (book) Brande, Dorthea

**Cast**   Winchell, Walter; Bernie, Ben; Faye, Alice; Kelly, Patsy; Sparks, Ned; Haley, Jack [1]; Catlett, Walter; Bradley, Grace; Davis, Joan; Ray, Leah; Mander, Miles; Girardot, Etienne

**Song(s)**   It's Swell of You; Ooh, But I'm Happy; I'm Bubbling Over; Wake Up and Live; Red Seal Malt; Never in a Million Years; I Love You Much Too Much Muchacha; There's a Lull in My Life [2]

**Notes**   [1] Dubbed by Buddy Clark. [2] Also in DANCE HALL.

## 6650 ◆ WALK, DON'T RUN
### Columbia, 1966

**Musical Score**   Jones, Quincy
**Composer(s)**   Jones, Quincy
**Lyricist(s)**   Lee, Peggy

**Producer(s)**   Siegel, Sol C.
**Director(s)**   Walters, Charles
**Screenwriter(s)**   Saks, Sol

**Cast**   Grant, Cary; Eggar, Samantha; Hutton, Jim; Standing, John; Taka, Miiko; Hartley, Ted

**Song(s)**   Stay With Me [1]; Happy Feet [1]

**Notes**   [1] Used instrumentally only.

## 6651 ◆ WALKER
### Universal, 1988

**Musical Score**   Strummer, Joe

**Producer(s)**   Marini, Angel Flores; O'Brien, Lorenzo
**Director(s)**   Cox, Alex
**Screenwriter(s)**   Wurlitzer, Rudy

**Cast** Harris, Ed; Matlin, Marlee; Masur, Richard; Auberjonois, Rene; Szarabajka, Keith; Richardson, Sy; Diehl, John; Armendariz, Pedro; Graham, Gerrit

**Song(s)** Tennessee Rain (C/L: Strummer, Joe); Unknown Immortal (C/L: Strummer, Joe)

## 6652 ◆ WALKING DOWN BROADWAY
### Twentieth Century–Fox, 1938

**Producer(s)** Wurtzel, Sol M.
**Director(s)** Foster, Norman
**Screenwriter(s)** Chapin, Robert; De Wolf, Karen

**Cast** Trevor, Claire; Brooks, Phyllis; Ray, Leah; Dunbar, Dixie; Bari, Lynn; Regan, Jayne; Whalen, Michael; King, Walter Woolf; Prouty, Jed; Kellard, Robert; Carol, Joan; Ames, Leon; Benedict, William

**Song(s)** Goodbye My Heart (C: Akst, Harry; L: Clare, Sidney)

## 6653 ◆ WALKING MY BABY BACK HOME
### Universal, 1953

**Musical Score** Mancini, Henry
**Lyricist(s)** Herbert, Frederick
**Choreographer(s)** Da Pron, Louis

**Producer(s)** Richmond, Ted
**Director(s)** Bacon, Lloyd
**Screenwriter(s)** McGuire, Don; Brodney, Oscar

**Cast** O'Connor, Donald; Leigh, Janet [1]; Hackett, Buddy; Crothers, Benjamin "Scatman"; Nelson, Lori; Lockhart, Kathleen; Cleveland, George; Hubbard, John; Kelly, Paula; The Sportsmen; The Modernaires

**Song(s)** Down in the South (C: Scott, Johnny); Hop on the Band Wagon (C: Hughes, Arnold); A Man's Gotta Eat (C/L: Miller, F.E.; Crothers, Benjamin "Scatman")

**Notes** Vocals also include "Glow Worm" by Johnny Mercer and Paul Lincke; "You Tell Me Your Dream" (Traditional); "Hi-Lee, Hi-Lo" by Eugene West and Ira Schuster; "Camptown Races" by Stephen Foster; "Walkin' My Baby Back Home" by Fred Ahlert and Roy Turk and "South Rampart Street Parade" by Ray Bauduc, Bob Haggart and Steve Allen. [1] Dubbed by Paula Kelly.

## 6654 ◆ WALKING ON AIR
### RKO, 1936

**Composer(s)** Ruby, Harry
**Lyricist(s)** Kalmar, Bert; Silvers, Sid

**Producer(s)** Kaufman, Edward
**Director(s)** Santley, Joseph
**Screenwriter(s)** Kalmar, Bert; Ruby, Harry; Shore, Viola Brothers

**Cast** Raymond, Gene; Sothern, Ann; Stephenson, Henry; Ralph, Jessie; Meeker, George; Jones, Gordon; Jennings, Maxine; Curtis, Alan; Colby, Anita

**Song(s)** Cabin on the Hilltop (L: Kalmar, Bert); My Heart Wants to Dance; Let's Make a Wish; Spring Prelude [1] (L: Shilkret, Nathaniel; Kalmar, Bert)

**Notes** [1] Not used.

## 6655 ◆ THE WALKING STICK
### Metro–Goldwyn–Mayer, 1970

**Musical Score** Myers, Stanley

**Producer(s)** Ladd Jr., Alan
**Director(s)** Till, Eric
**Screenwriter(s)** Bluestone, George

**Cast** Hemmings, David; Eggar, Samantha; Williams, Emlyn; Calvert, Phyllis; Mayne, Ferdy; Sutton, Dudley; Anis, Francesca; Cherrell, Gwen

**Song(s)** Dance the Night Away (C/L: Curb, Mike; Hatcher, Harley)

**Notes** There is also a vocal of "Ebb Tide" by Robert Maxwell and Carl Sigman. It is not known if the song was written for the picture.

## 6656 ◆ A WALK IN THE SUN
### Twentieth Century–Fox, 1945

**Composer(s)** Robinson, Earl
**Lyricist(s)** Lampell, Millard

**Producer(s)** Milestone, Lewis
**Director(s)** Milestone, Lewis
**Screenwriter(s)** Rossen, Robert

**Cast** Andrews, Dana; Conte, Richard; Tyne, George; Ireland, John; Bridges, Lloyd; Holloway, Sterling; Lloyd, Norman; Rudley, Herbert; Hall, Huntz

**Song(s)** It Was Just a Little Walk in the Sun; This Is the Story of One Little Job; Waiting; These Are the Men of the Texas Division; Trouble [1]

**Notes** [1] Not on cue sheets.

## 6657 ◆ WALK LIKE A DRAGON
### Paramount, 1960

**Musical Score** Dunlap, Paul

**Producer(s)** Clavell, James
**Director(s)** Clavell, James
**Screenwriter(s)** Clavell, James; Mainwaring, Daniel

**Cast** Lord, Jack; McCarthy, Nobu; Shigeta, James; Torme, Mel; Hutchinson, Josephine; Fong, Benson; Pate, Michael; Acosta, Rodolfo

**Song(s)** Walk Like a Dragon (C/L: Torme, Mel)

### 6658 ✦ WALK ON THE WILD SIDE
Columbia, 1962

**Musical Score** Bernstein, Elmer
**Composer(s)** Bernstein, Elmer
**Lyricist(s)** David, Mack

**Producer(s)** Feldman, Charles K.
**Director(s)** Dmytryk, Edward
**Screenwriter(s)** Fante, John; Morris, Edmund
**Source(s)** *Walk on the Wild Side* (novel) Algren, Nelson

**Cast** Harvey, Laurence; Capucine; Fonda, Jane; Baxter, Anne; Stanwyck, Barbara; Moore, Joanna; Rust, Richard

**Song(s)** Walk on the Wild Side; Somewhere in the Used to Be [1]

**Notes** [1] Instrumental use only.

### 6659 ✦ WALK PROUD
Universal, 1979

**Musical Score** Benson, Robby; Peake, Don
**Lyricist(s)** Segal, Jerry

**Producer(s)** Turman, Lawrence
**Director(s)** Collins, Robert
**Screenwriter(s)** Hunter, Evan

**Cast** Benson, Robby; Holcomb, Sarah; De Bari, Irene; Sullivan, Brad; Darrow, Henry; Serna, Pepe; Pressman, Lawrence

**Song(s)** Blessed Virgin (C/L: Coster, Irwin); Adios Yesterday (C: Benson, Robby); Memories of Sarah [1] (C: Benson, Robby; Peake, Don)

**Notes** [1] Used instrumentally only.

### 6660 ✦ A WALK WITH LOVE AND DEATH
Twentieth Century–Fox, 1969

**Musical Score** Delerue, Georges
**Composer(s)** Delerue, Georges
**Lyricist(s)** Hill, Gladys

**Producer(s)** De Haven, Carter
**Director(s)** Huston, John
**Screenwriter(s)** Wasserman, Dale
**Source(s)** (novel) Koningsberger, Hans

**Cast** Huston, Anjelica; Dayan, Assaf; Corlan, Anthony; Hallam, John; Lang, Robert; Gough, Michael

**Song(s)** Hymn; I Went Down When Twilight Fell; The Long Road Leads Us On to Death; The World Is Near Its End; My Love Has Gone from Me

### 6661 ✦ WALLFLOWER
Warner Brothers, 1947

**Musical Score** Hollander, Frederick

**Producer(s)** Gottlieb, Alex
**Director(s)** de Cordova, Frederick

**Screenwriter(s)** Ephron, Phoebe; Ephron, Henry
**Source(s)** (play) Orr, Mary; Denham, Reginald

**Cast** Hutton, Robert; Reynolds, Joyce; Paige, Janis; Arnold, Edward; Brown, Barbara; Cowan, Jerome; McGuire, Don; Shoemaker, Ann; Stein, Lotte

**Song(s)** I May Be Wrong But I Think You're Wonderful [2] (C/L: Sullivan, Henry; Ruskin, Harry); Ask Anyone Who Knows [1] (C/L: Kaufman, Al; Marcus, Sol; Seiler, Eddie)

**Notes** [1] Background instrumental use only. [2] Also used in SWINGTIME JOHNNY (Universal) and YOUNG MAN WITH A HORN.

### 6662 ✦ WALL STREET
Twentieth Century–Fox, 1987

**Musical Score** Copeland, Stewart

**Producer(s)** Pressman, Edward R.
**Director(s)** Stone, Oliver
**Screenwriter(s)** Weiser, Stanley; Stone, Oliver

**Cast** Douglas, Michael; Sheen, Charlie; Hannah, Daryl; Sheen, Martin; Holbrook, Hal; Young, Sean; McGinley, John C.; Rubinek, Saul; Spader, James; Mostel, Josh; Sherman, Martin; O'Donoghue, Michael

**Song(s)** On Your Way to Heaven (C: Copeland, Stewart; L: Copeland, Stewart; Holland, Deborah)

**Notes** No cue sheet available.

### 6663 ✦ WALL STREET COWBOY
Republic, 1939

**Composer(s)** Samuels, Walter G.
**Lyricist(s)** Samuels, Walter G.

**Producer(s)** Kane, Joseph
**Director(s)** Kane, Joseph
**Screenwriter(s)** Geraghty, Gerald; Hall, Norman S.

**Cast** Rogers, Roy; Hayes, George "Gabby"; Hatton, Raymond; Baldwin, Ann; Watkin, Pierre; Louisiana Lou

**Song(s)** Ride 'Em Cowboy; Ridin' Down Rainbow Trail; That's My Louisiana; Me and the Rolling Hills

### 6664 ✦ WALTZ TIME (1945)
Republic, 1945

**Musical Score** May, Hans
**Composer(s)** May, Hans
**Lyricist(s)** Stranks, Alan

**Producer(s)** Jackson, Louis H.
**Director(s)** Stein, Paul
**Screenwriter(s)** Tully, Montgomery; Whittingham, Jack

**Cast** Raye, Carol; Graves, Peter; Medina, Patricia; Booth, Webster; Ziegler, Anne; Tauber, Richard; Dandler, Albert; Robey, George

**Song(s)** Waltz Time; Only to You; Return to Vienna; Land of Mine; Call to Arms; Little White Horse; Heavenly Waltz; Break of Day

**Notes** A British National picture.

## 6665 ✦ WALTZ TIME (1946)
### British National, 1946

**Composer(s)** May, Hans
**Lyricist(s)** Stranks, Alan

**Producer(s)** Jackson, Louis H.
**Director(s)** Stein, Paul
**Screenwriter(s)** Tully, Montgomery; Whittingham, Jack

**Cast** Booth, Webster; Tauber, Richard; Ziegler, Anne; Sandler, Albert; Raye, Carol; Graves, Peter; Medina, Patricia; Robey, George; Kendall, Kay

**Song(s)** Waltz Time; Return to Vienna; Only to You; Land of Mine; Heavenly Waltz; Call to Arms; Break of Day; Little White Horse Polka

**Notes** A British National film distributed by Fox. Kendall plays a lady in waiting.

## 6666 ✦ WANDA NEVADA
### United Artists, 1979

**Musical Score** Lauber, Ken
**Composer(s)** Lauber, Ken

**Producer(s)** Dobrofsky, Neal; Hackin, Dennis
**Director(s)** Fonda, Peter
**Screenwriter(s)** Hackin, Dennis

**Cast** Lewis, Fiona; Askew, Luke; Markland, Ted; Darden, Severn; Fix, Paul; Fonda, Henry; Fonda, Peter; Shields, Brooke

**Song(s)** Wanda's Wish (L: McElwee, John); Gonna Find Me a Woman (L: Lauber, Ken; Benson, Ray); Lookin' Out from Behind Shadowed Walls (L: Lauber, Ken)

**Notes** No cue sheet available.

## 6667 ✦ WANTED FOR MURDER
### Twentieth Century–Fox, 1946

**Musical Score** Spoliansky, Mischa
**Composer(s)** Spoliansky, Mischa
**Lyricist(s)** Spoliansky, Mischa

**Producer(s)** Hellman, Marcel
**Director(s)** Huntington, Lawrence
**Screenwriter(s)** Pressburger, Emeric; Ackland, Rodney; Cowan, Maurice
**Source(s)** (play) Robinson, Percy; de Marney, Terence

**Cast** Portman, Eric; Gray, Dulcie; Farr, Derek; Culver, Roland; Holloway, Stanley; Everest, Barbara

**Song(s)** You and You Again; A Voice in the Night; Medley; Far Far Away

**Notes** A British film released by Fox.

## 6668 ✦ WAR AND PEACE
### Paramount, 1956

**Musical Score** Rota, Nino

**Producer(s)** Ponti, Carlo; De Laurentiis, Dino
**Director(s)** Vidor, King
**Screenwriter(s)** Vidor, King; Boland, Bridget; Westerby, Robert; Camerini, Mario; De Concini, Ennio; Perilli, Ivo
**Source(s)** *War and Peace* (novel) Tolstoy, Leo

**Cast** Hepburn, Audrey; Fonda, Henry; Ferrer, Mel; Prince Andrei; Lom, Herbert; Mills, John; Gassman, Vittorio; Homolka, Oscar; Dantine, Helmut; Ekberg, Anita; Jones, Barry; Carminati, Tullio; Britt, May

**Song(s)** War and Peace [1] (C: Rota, Nino; L: Stone, Wilson)

**Notes** [1] Lyric written for exploitation only.

## 6669 ✦ WARGAMES
### MGM/UA, 1983

**Musical Score** Rubinstein, Arthur B.

**Producer(s)** Schneider, Harold
**Director(s)** Badham, John
**Screenwriter(s)** Lasker, Lawrence; Parkus, Walter F.

**Cast** Broderick, Matthew; Coleman, Dabney; Wood, John; Sheedy, Ally

**Song(s)** Video Fever (C: Rubinstein, Arthur B.; L: Morrow, Cynthia)

## 6670 ✦ WARMING UP
### Paramount, 1928

**Director(s)** Newmeyer, Fred
**Screenwriter(s)** Harris, Ray

**Cast** Dix, Richard; Arthur, Jean; Karns, Roscoe; King, Claude; McCullough, Philo; Schaefer, Billy Kent; Ready, Mike; Thomas, Chet; Pirrone, Joe; Hood, Wally; Murray, Bob; Hannah, Truck

**Song(s)** Out of the Dawn (C/L: Donaldson, Walter)

**Notes** No cue sheet available. Some of the cast are famous baseball players of the time.

## 6671 ✦ WAR OF THE WILDCATS
### Republic, 1956

**Musical Score** Scharf, Walter

**Song(s)** Then I'd Be Satisfied All Right (C: Scharf, Walter; L: Meyer, Sol)

**Notes** No other information available. There are also vocals of "Put Your Arms Around Me Honey" by Junie McCreee and Albert Von Tilzer; "In My Merry Oldsmobile" by Vincent Bryan and Gus Edwards; "Red

Wing" by Thurland Chattaway and Kerry Mills and "Down By the Old Mill Stream" by Tell Taylor.

## 6672 ◆ WAR PAINT
### United Artists, 1953

**Musical Score**   Lange, Arthur

**Producer(s)**   Koch, Howard W.
**Director(s)**   Selander, Lesley
**Screenwriter(s)**   Simmons, Richard Alan; Berkeley, Martin

**Cast**   Stack, Robert; Taylor, Joan; McGraw, Charles; Graves, Peter; Larsen, Keith; Pullen, William; Cutting, Richard

**Song(s)**   Elaine (C: Newman, Emil; L: Lehman, Johnny)

## 6673 ◆ THE WARRIORS
### Paramount, 1979

**Musical Score**   De Vorzon, Barry

**Producer(s)**   Gordon, Lawrence
**Director(s)**   Hill, Walter
**Screenwriter(s)**   Shaber, David; Hill, Walter
**Source(s)**   (novel) Yurick, Sol

**Cast**   Beck, Michael; Remar, James; Wright, Dorsey; Tyler, Brian; Harris, David; McKitterick, Tom; Sanchez, Marcelino; Thigpen, Lynne; Kelly, David Patrick

**Song(s)**   Love Is a Fire (C/L: Poncia, Vincent; Vastano, Johnny); You're Movin' Too Slow (C/L: Mercury, Eric; Smith, William); In the City (C/L: Walsh, Joe; De Vorzon, Barry)

**Notes**   No cue sheet available.

## 6674 ◆ THE WARRIOR'S HUSBAND
### Fox, 1933

**Producer(s)**   Lasky, Jesse L.
**Director(s)**   Lang, Walter
**Screenwriter(s)**   Spence, Ralph
**Source(s)**   *The Warrior's Husband* (play) Thompson, Julian

**Cast**   Landi, Elissa; Manners, David; Truex, Ernest; Rambeau, Marjorie; Ware, Helen; Eburne, Maude; Belmore, Lionel

**Song(s)**   Amazon Blues (C: Lange, Arthur; L: Burton, Val; Jason, Will); Pocus Recites (C: De Francesco, Louis E.; L: Spence)

## 6675 ◆ THE WAR WAGON
### Universal, 1967

**Musical Score**   Tiomkin, Dimitri

**Producer(s)**   Schwartz, Marvin
**Director(s)**   Kennedy, Burt

**Screenwriter(s)**   Huffaker, Clair
**Source(s)**   *Badman* (novel) Huffaker, Clair

**Cast**   Wayne, John; Douglas, Kirk; Cabot, Bruce; Keel, Howard; Walker, Robert; Wynn, Keenan; Antonio, Marco; Barnes, Joanna; Evans, Gene; Dern, Bruce

**Song(s)**   Ballad of the War Wagon (C: Tiomkin, Dimitri; L: Washington, Ned)

## 6676 ◆ WASHINGTON MELODRAMA
### MGM, 1941

**Musical Score**   Snell, Dave
**Choreographer(s)**   Lee, Sammy

**Producer(s)**   Selwyn, Edgar
**Director(s)**   Simon, S. Sylvan
**Screenwriter(s)**   Parsonnet, Marion; Chanslor, Roy

**Cast**   Morgan, Frank; Rutherford, Ann; Taylor, Kent; Dailey, Dan; Bowman, Lee; Holden, Fay; Grey, Virginia; Dumbrille, Douglass; Crehan, Joseph; Brissac, Virginia; Hall, Thurston

**Song(s)**   Fishing for Suckers (C/L: Brent, Earl)

**Notes**   No cue sheet available.

## 6677 ◆ WATER
### Atlantic, 1986

**Musical Score**   Moran, Mike

**Producer(s)**   La Frenais, Ian
**Director(s)**   Clement, Dick
**Screenwriter(s)**   Clement, Dick; La Frenais, Ian; Persky, Bill

**Cast**   Caine, Michael; Perrine, Valerie; Vaccaro, Brenda; Connolly, Billy; Rossiter, Leonard; Dugan, Dennis; Walker, Jimmie

**Song(s)**   Water (C/L: Grant, Eddy); Casacara National Anthem (C: Moran, Mike; L: Clement, Dick; La Frenais, Ian; Persky, Bill)

**Notes**   No cue sheet available.

## 6678 ◆ WATERFRONT LADY
### Mascot, 1935

**Composer(s)**   Burnette, Smiley
**Lyricist(s)**   Burnette, Smiley

**Producer(s)**   Clark, Colbert
**Director(s)**   Totman, Weilyn
**Screenwriter(s)**   Santley, Joseph

**Cast**   Rutherford, Ann; Albertson, Frank; MacDonald, J. Farrell; Pepper, Barbara; Withers, Grant; LaRue, Jack

**Song(s)**   Why Can't We Love Forever [3] (C/L: Rosoff, Charles); Should You (C/L: Wallace, Oliver); My Sweet Jeannette (C/L: Allen, Wayne); Moonlight and

Moonbeams (C/L: Rosoff, Charles); There's Life in Music [2] (C/L: Rosoff, Charles); Are You Mine [1] (C/L: Rosoff, Charles); What Wouldn't I Do for a Girl Like You; Deep Dark River; Bells of Satan; Dagger Waltz; Alphabet Rag; What Do You Think

**Notes**   No cue sheet available. These songs were purchased for the picture. It is not known which, if any, were used. [1] Used instrumentally in ABOVE THE CLOUDS and BEYOND THE LAW (1934), both from Columbia. [2] Used instrumentally in the Columbia films ANN CARVER'S PROFESSION and THE CRIME OF HELEN STANLEY. [3] Also used instrumentally in ANN CARVER'S PROFESSION.

## 6679  ✦  WATERHOLE #3
### Paramount, 1967

**Musical Score**   Grusin, Dave

**Producer(s)**   Steck, Joseph T.
**Director(s)**   Graham, William
**Screenwriter(s)**   Steck, Joseph T.; Young, R.R.

**Cast**   Coburn, James; O'Connor, Carroll; Blye, Maggie; Akins, Claude; Carey, Timothy; Dern, Bruce; Davis, Harry; Blondell, Joan; Whitmore, James

**Song(s)**   The Ballad of Waterhole #3 (Code of the West) (C: Grusin, Dave; L: Wells, Robert); Durango (C/L: Coburn, James; Graham, William; Steck, Joseph T.; Young, Robert R.); Rainbow Valley [1] (C: Grusin, Dave; L: Wells, Robert)

**Notes**   [1] Used instrumentally only.

## 6680  ✦  WATERMELON MAN
### Columbia, 1970

**Musical Score**   Van Peebles, Melvin
**Composer(s)**   Van Peebles, Melvin
**Lyricist(s)**   Van Peebles, Melvin

**Producer(s)**   Bennett, John B.
**Director(s)**   Van Peebles, Melvin
**Screenwriter(s)**   Raucher, Herman

**Cast**   Cambridge, Godfrey; Parsons, Estelle; Caine, Howard; Martin, D'urville; Moreland, Mantan; Moran, Erin

**Song(s)**   Love, That's America; Where Are the Children

## 6681  ✦  WATERSHIP DOWN
### Avco Embassy, 1978

**Musical Score**   Morley, Angela; Williamson, Malcolm

**Producer(s)**   Rosen, Martin
**Director(s)**   Rosen, Martin
**Screenwriter(s)**   Rosen, Martin
**Source(s)**   *Watership Down* (novel) Adams, Richard
**Voices**   Hurt, John; Briers, Richard; Graham-Cox, Michael; Bennett, John; Cadell, Simon; Kinnear, Roy;

Rigby, Terence; Richardson, Ralph; O'Callaghan, Richard; Elliott, Denholm; Mostel, Zero; Andrews, Harry; Hawthorne, Nigel; Hordern, Michael; Ackland, Joss

**Song(s)**   Bright Eyes (C/L: Batt, Michael)

**Notes**   An animated feature. No cue sheet available.

## 6682  ✦  A WAVE, A WAC, AND A MARINE
### Monogram, 1944

**Musical Score**   Rich, Freddie
**Composer(s)**   Cherkose, Eddie
**Lyricist(s)**   Press, Jacques

**Producer(s)**   Cristillo, Sebastian
**Director(s)**   Karlson, Phil
**Screenwriter(s)**   Fimberg, Hal

**Cast**   Knox, Elyse; Gillis, Ann; Eilers, Sally; Lane, Richard; Youngman, Henny; Freddie Rich and His Orchestra

**Song(s)**   Time Will Tell (C: Cherkose, Eddie; Rich, Freddie); G.I. Guy; Carry On; We Stopped for a Kiss [1] (C/L: Denni, Lucien); You Have Me So Excited [1] (C: Denni, Lucien; L: Denni, Gwynne)

**Notes**   [1] Sheet music only.

## 6683  ✦  WAY DOWN SOUTH
### RKO, 1939

**Musical Score**   Young, Victor
**Composer(s)**   Muse, Clarence; Hughes, Langston
**Lyricist(s)**   Muse, Clarence; Hughes, Langston

**Producer(s)**   Lesser, Sol
**Director(s)**   Vorhaus, Bernard
**Screenwriter(s)**   Muse, Clarence; Hughes, Langston

**Cast**   Breen, Bobby; Mowbray, Alan; Maxwell, Edwin; Greig, Robert; Morgan, Ralph; Muse, Clarence; Duna, Steffi; Blane, Sally; Middleton, Charles; Yarbo, Lilian; Beard, Stymie; Carr, Jack; The Hall Johnson Choir

**Song(s)**   Good Ground; Louisiana

## 6684  ✦  WAY OF A GAUCHO
### Twentieth Century–Fox, 1952

**Musical Score**   Kaplan, Sol

**Producer(s)**   Dunne, Philip
**Director(s)**   Tourneur, Jacques
**Screenwriter(s)**   Dunne, Philip
**Source(s)**   *Gaucho* (novel) Childs, Herbert

**Cast**   Calhoun, Rory; Tierney, Gene; Boone, Richard; Marlowe, Hugh; Sloane, Everett

**Song(s)**   La Huella, Huella (C: Palorma, Felix R.; L: Dunne, Philip); A Lonely Voice [1] (C/L: Kaplan, Sol)

**Notes** [1] No lyrics. Just the words "Baheeah" or "Bayeeah" repeated to the music.

## 6685 ✦ WAY OUT WEST
### Metro–Goldwyn–Mayer, 1930

**Director(s)** Niblo, Fred
**Screenwriter(s)** Morgan, Byron; Block, Alfred; Farnham, Joe

**Cast** Haines, William; Hyams, Leila; Moran, Polly; Edwards, Cliff; Bushman Jr., Francis X.; Middleton, Charles; Marsh, Vera; Spence, Ralph

**Song(s)** Singing a Song to the Stars (C: Meyer, Joseph; L: Johnson, Howard)

## 6686 ✦ THE WAY TO LOVE
### Paramount, 1933

**Composer(s)** Rainger, Ralph
**Lyricist(s)** Robin, Leo

**Director(s)** Taurog, Norman
**Screenwriter(s)** Glazer, Benjamin; Fowler, Gene

**Cast** Chevalier, Maurice; LeRoy, Baby; Dvorak, Ann; Horton, Edward Everett; Gombell, Minna; Dumbrille, Douglass; Toler, Sidney

**Song(s)** There's a Lucky Guy; I'm a Lover of Paree; In a One Room Flat and a Two Pants Suit; It's Oh, It's Ah! It's Wonderful [1] [4]; My Future Wife [2]; Just Follow the Sun [2] [3] [4] (C: Donaldson, Walter; L: Kahn, Gus); The Way to Love (1) [2] (C: Johnston, Arthur; L: Coslow, Sam); Be Optimistic [2]; Turn that Frown Upside Down [2]; Laugh, You Son of a Gun [2]; I Have to Laugh [2]; For Laughing Out Loud [2]; Snap Out of It [2]; The Way to Love (2) [2] [4]

**Notes** [1] Instrumental use only in American prints. However the song is used with a translated lyric in French prints. [2] Not used. [3] Not written for this film. [4] Recorded.

## 6687 ✦ WAY TO THE GOLD
### Twentieth Century–Fox, 1957

**Musical Score** Newman, Lionel
**Composer(s)** Newman, Lionel
**Lyricist(s)** Coates, Carroll

**Producer(s)** Weisbart, David
**Director(s)** Webb, Robert D.
**Screenwriter(s)** Mayes, Wendell
**Source(s)** *The Way to the Gold* (novel) Steele, Wilbur Daniel

**Cast** Hunter, Jeffrey; North, Sheree; Sullivan, Barry; Brennan, Walter; Brand, Neville; Aubuchon, Jacques; Donnelly, Ruth; Ahn, Philip

**Song(s)** Strange Weather

## 6688 ✦ WAY . . . WAY OUT
### Twentieth Century–Fox, 1966

**Musical Score** Schifrin, Lalo

**Producer(s)** Stuart, Malcolm
**Director(s)** Douglas, Gordon M.
**Screenwriter(s)** Bowers, William; Vadnay, Laslo

**Cast** Lewis, Jerry; Stevens, Connie; Morley, Robert; Weaver, Dennis; Morris, Howard; Keith, Brian; Shawn, Dick; Ekberg, Anita; Lewis, Bobo

**Song(s)** Way Way Out (C: Schifrin, Lalo; L: Winn, Hal)

## 6689 ✦ THE WAY WE LIVE NOW
### United Artists, 1970

**Musical Score** Sassover, Nate
**Composer(s)** Sassover, Nate
**Lyricist(s)** Tamkus, Daniel

**Producer(s)** Brown, Barry; Lapidus, Saul
**Director(s)** Brown, Barry
**Screenwriter(s)** Brown, Barry; Newman, Chris
**Source(s)** (novel) Miller, Warren

**Cast** Pryor, Nicholas; Simon, Linda; Miles, Joanna; McAneny, Patricia; Drake, Rebecca; Walker, Sydney; Smith, Lois

**Song(s)** And Now's the Time; The Way We Live Now

## 6690 ✦ THE WAY WEST
### United Artists, 1967

**Musical Score** Kaper, Bronislau

**Producer(s)** Hecht, Harold
**Director(s)** McLaglen, Andrew V.
**Screenwriter(s)** Maddow, Ben; Lindemann, Mitch
**Source(s)** *The Way West* (novel) Guthrie Jr., A.B. [1]

**Cast** Douglas, Kirk; Mitchum, Robert; Widmark, Richard; Albright, Lola; Field, Sally; Whitney, Michael

**Song(s)** The Way West (C: Kaper, Bronislau; L: David, Mack); Mercy McBee (C/L: Kaper, Bronislau; L: David, Mack)

**Notes** [1] Billed as Albert Bertram Guthrie Jr.

## 6691 ✦ THE WAY WE WERE
### Columbia, 1973

**Musical Score** Hamlisch, Marvin

**Producer(s)** Stark, Ray
**Director(s)** Pollack, Sydney
**Screenwriter(s)** Laurents, Arthur
**Source(s)** *The Way We Weren* (novel) Laurents, Arthur

**Cast** Streisand, Barbra; Redford, Robert; Dillman, Bradford; Chiles, Lois; O'Neal, Patrick; Lindfors, Viveca; McLerie, Allyn Ann; Hamilton, Murray; Edelman, Herb

**Song(s)**   The Way We Were (C: Hamlisch, Marvin; L: Bergman, Alan; Bergman, Marilyn)

## 6692 ✦ WEARY RIVER
### Warner Brothers–First National, 1929

**Director(s)**   Lloyd, Frank
**Screenwriter(s)**   King, Bradley; Geraghty, Tom J.

**Cast**   Barthelmess, Richard [1]; Compson, Betty; Holden, William; Natheaux, Louis; Turner, Raymond; Stone, George E.; James, Gladden

**Song(s)**   Weary River (C: Silvers, Louis; L: Clarke, Grant); It's Up to You (C: Silvers, Louis; L: Clarke, Grant)

**Notes**   No cue sheet available. [1] Dubbed by John Murray for singing and by Frank Churchill for piano playing.

## 6693 ✦ WEDDING BELLS

See ROYAL WEDDING.

## 6694 ✦ THE WEDDING MARCH
### Paramount, 1928

**Musical Score**   Zamecnik, J.S.

**Producer(s)**   Powers, P.A.
**Director(s)**   von Stroheim, Erich
**Screenwriter(s)**   von Stroheim, Erich; Carr, Harry

**Cast**   Fawcett, George; von Stroheim, Erich; Pitts, ZaSu; George, Maude; Nichols, George; Mack, Hughie; Betz, Matthew; Gravina, Cesare; Wray, Fay; Fuller, Dale

**Song(s)**   Paradise (C: Zamecnik, J.S.; L: Kerr, Harry D.)

## 6695 ✦ THE WEDDING PRESENT
### Paramount, 1936

**Producer(s)**   Schulberg, B.P.
**Director(s)**   Wallace, Richard
**Screenwriter(s)**   Anthony, Joseph

**Cast**   Grant, Cary; Bennett, Joan; Bancroft, George; Lockhart, Gene; Demarest, William; Courtney, Inez; Meeker, George; Nagel, Conrad; Wilson, Lois

**Song(s)**   Schnitzel Bank (C: Traditional; L: Anthony, Joseph)

## 6696 ✦ WEDDING RINGS
### Warner Brothers–First National, 1929

**Director(s)**   Beaudine, William
**Screenwriter(s)**   Harris, Ray
**Source(s)**   *The Dark Swan* (novel) Pascal, Ernest

**Cast**   Wilson, Lois; Warner, H.B.; Borden, Olive; Williams, Kathlyn; Manning, Aileen; Cooley, Hallam; Ford, James

**Song(s)**   Love Will Last Forever If It's True (C: Ward, Edward; L: Bryan, Alfred); That's My Business (C: Ward, Edward; L: Bryan, Alfred)

**Notes**   No cue sheet available.

## 6697 ✦ WEEKEND AT DUNKIRK
### Twentieth Century–Fox, 1966

**Musical Score**   Jarre, Maurice

**Producer(s)**   Hakim, Robert; Hakim, Raymond
**Director(s)**   Verneuil, Henri
**Screenwriter(s)**   Boyer, Francois
**Source(s)**   *Weekend at Zuydcoote* (novel) Merle, Robert

**Cast**   Belmondo, Jean-Paul; Spaak, Catherine; Geret, George; Marielle, Jean-Pierre

**Song(s)**   Je T'Attendrai (C/L: Oliveri, Portera)

## 6698 ✦ WEEKEND AT THE WALDORF
### Metro–Goldwyn–Mayer, 1945

**Musical Score**   Green, Johnny
**Choreographer(s)**   Walters, Charles

**Producer(s)**   Hornblow Jr., Arthur
**Director(s)**   Leonard, Robert Z.
**Screenwriter(s)**   Spewack, Sam; Spewack, Bella
**Source(s)**   *Grand Hotel* (play) Baum, Vicki

**Cast**   Rogers, Ginger; Turner, Lana; Pidgeon, Walter; Johnson, Van; Arnold, Edward; Wynn, Keenan; Benchley, Robert; Thaxter, Phyllis; Ames, Leon; Romay, Lina; Hall, Porter; Mander, Miles; Xavier Cugat and His Orchestra; Hinds, Samuel S.

**Song(s)**   And There You Are (C: Fain, Sammy; L: Koehler, Ted); Guadalajara [1] (C/L: Guizar, Pepe)

**Notes**   [1] Also used in FUN IN ACAPULCO (Paramount); MEXICANA (Republic) and PAN AMERICANA (RKO).

## 6699 ✦ WEEKEND IN HAVANA
### Twentieth Century–Fox, 1941

**Composer(s)**   Warren, Harry
**Lyricist(s)**   Gordon, Mack
**Choreographer(s)**   Pan, Hermes

**Producer(s)**   LeBaron, William
**Director(s)**   Lang, Walter
**Screenwriter(s)**   Tunberg, Karl; Ware, Darrell

**Cast**   Faye, Alice; Miranda, Carmen; Payne, John; Romero, Cesar; Wright Jr., Cobina; Barbier, George; Leonard, Sheldon; Kinskey, Leonid; Gilbert, Billy; Martin, Billy-Pin

**Song(s)**   The Man with the Lollypop Song; The Nango; Tropical Magic; A Weekend in Havana; When I Love, I Love; Rebola Boal (Embolda) (C: Oliveira, Aloysio; Amaral, Nestor; L: Horta, Francisco Eugenio Brant);

Romance and Rhumba (C: Monaco, James V.); Maria Inez [1] (C: Grenet, Eliseo; L: Gilbert, L. Wolfe)

**Notes** "Chica Chica Boom Chic" by Harry Warren and Mack Gordon was recorded but not used. [1] Not on cue sheet but in some sources.

## 6700 ◆ WEEK-END PASS (1944)
### Universal, 1944

**Musical Score** Skinner, Frank
**Composer(s)** Rosen, Milton
**Lyricist(s)** Carter, Everett

**Producer(s)** Wilson, Warren
**Director(s)** Yarbrough, Jean
**Screenwriter(s)** Bruckman, Clyde

**Cast** Beery Jr., Noah; The Delta Rhythm Boys

**Song(s)** We Build 'Em, You Sail 'Em; I Am, Are You? [1]; I Like to Be Loved [2]; She's a Girl a Man Can Dream Of

**Notes** There is also a vocal of "All or Nothing at All" by Jack Lawrence and Arthur Altman. [1] Also in THE MYSTERY OF THE RIVER BOAT. [2] Also in THE MYSTERY OF THE RIVER BOAT and MELODY GARDEN.

## 6701 ◆ WEEKEND PASS (1984)
### Crown International, 1984

**Musical Score** Baer, John
**Composer(s)** Baer, John
**Lyricist(s)** Baer, Robbie

**Producer(s)** Tenser, Marilyn J.
**Director(s)** Bassoff, Lawrence
**Screenwriter(s)** Bassoff, Lawrence

**Cast** Brown, D.W.; Ellenstein, Peter; Houser, Patrick; McAllister, Chip

**Song(s)** Weekend Pass; All Night Love; Hard As a Rock; Beach Nut; L.A. Xtra (Read About Me); Free Me from the Night Life

**Notes** No cue sheet available.

## 6702 ◆ WEIRD SCIENCE
### Universal, 1985

**Musical Score** Newborn, Ira

**Producer(s)** Silver, Joel
**Director(s)** Hughes, John
**Screenwriter(s)** Hughes, John

**Cast** Hall, Anthony Michael; Le Brock, Kelly; Mitchell-Smith, Ian; Paxton, Bill; Snyder, Suzanne; Aronson, Judie; Downey, Robert; Rusler, Robert; Lang, Barbara

**Song(s)** Weird Science (C/L: Elfman, Danny); Turn It On (C/L: Chapman, Mike; Knight, Holly); Deep in the Jungle (C/L: Moreland, Bruce; Moreland, Marc; Gray, Charles T.); A Nerd Named Wyatt (C/L: Newborn, Ira); Tesla Girls (C/L: McCluskey, Andy; Humphreys, Paul David); Oh, Pretty Woman (C/L: Orbison, Roy; Dees, William); Private Joy (C/L: Prince); Wanted Man (C/L: Crosby, Robin; Pearcy, Stephen; Cristofanelli, Joseph); Don't Worry About Baby (C/L: Rosas, Cesar; Perez, Louis; Burnett, T-Bone); Forever (C/L: Payne, C.; Nead, Jeff); Method to My Madness (C/L: Bator, Stiv; James, Brian); Eighties (C/L: Killing Joke); Do Not Disturb (C/L: Thunder; Ragg); Why Don't Pretty Girls Look at Me? (C/L: Wainwright, Zowie; Wainwright, Bob; Peacock, Daniel; Smith, Simon; Bodymead, Tony); Nervous and Shaky (C/L: Zanes, D.; Morrell, S.); The Circle (C/L: Pasqua, Allan; Carl, Max); Wyatt and Hilly (C/L: Newborn, Ira); Tenderness (C/L: Charlery, Roger; Billingham, Mickey; Wakeling, David)

**Notes** It is not known which of these were written for this film.

## 6703 ◆ WELCOME DANGER
### Paramount, 1929

**Director(s)** Bruckman, Clyde
**Screenwriter(s)** Smith, Paul Gerard

**Cast** Lloyd, Harold; Kent, Barbara; Young, Noah; Middleton, Charles; Walling, William; Wang, James; Haig, Douglas

**Song(s)** Billie (C/L: Cowan, Lynn); When You Are Mine (C/L: Titsworth, Paul)

**Notes** No cue sheet available.

## 6704 ◆ WELCOME HOME
### Fox, 1935

**Producer(s)** DeSylva, B.G.
**Director(s)** Tinling, James
**Screenwriter(s)** Orth, Marion; Horman, Arthur T.

**Cast** Dunn, James; Judge, Arline

**Song(s)** Hail Hail Hail to Ellumdale (C/L: DeSylva, B.G.)

## 6705 ◆ WELCOME HOME SOLDIER BOYS
### Twentieth Century–Fox, 1972

**Musical Score** Wannberg, Ken
**Composer(s)** Blakley, Ronee
**Lyricist(s)** Blakley, Ronee

**Producer(s)** Schwartz, Marvin
**Director(s)** Compton, Richard
**Screenwriter(s)** Trueblood, Guerdon

**Cast** Baker, Joe Don; Koslo, Paul; Vint, Alan; Billingsley, Jennifer; Chapman, Lonny

**Song(s)** Double Crossed (C/L: Meader, Vaughn); As I Lay Dying; Dues [1]; Black Bug Blues (C/L: Chadwick, Bill); Bluebird [1]; Sweet Mystery

**Notes** [1] Also in NASHVILLE.

## 6706 ✦ WELCOME STRANGER
Paramount, 1947

**Musical Score** Dolan, Robert Emmett
**Composer(s)** Van Heusen, James
**Lyricist(s)** Burke, Johnny
**Choreographer(s)** Daniels, Billy

**Producer(s)** Siegel, Sol C.
**Director(s)** Nugent, Elliott
**Screenwriter(s)** Sheekman, Arthur

**Cast** Fitzgerald, Barry; Crosby, Bing; Caulfield, Joan; Hendrix, Wanda; Faylen, Frank; Kilbride, Percy

**Song(s)** Smack in the Middle of Maine [1]; Smile Right Back at the Sun; Country Style; My Heart Is a Hobo [2]; As Long As I'm Dreaming; My Girl Ain't Mean or Vain [1] (C: Unknown; L: Nugent, Elliott)

**Notes** [1] Not used. [2] Lyrics almost identical to a song Burke wrote with James V. Monaco for RHYTHM ON THE RIVER. They were not used in that film.

## 6707 ✦ WELCOME TO L.A.
Lion's Gate, 1977

**Musical Score** Baskin, Richard
**Composer(s)** Baskin, Richard
**Lyricist(s)** Baskin, Richard

**Producer(s)** Altman, Robert
**Director(s)** Rudolph, Alan
**Screenwriter(s)** Rudolph, Alan

**Cast** Carradine, Keith; Kellerman, Sally; Chaplin, Geraldine; Keitel, Harvey; Hutton, Lauren; Lindfors, Viveca; Spacek, Sissy; Pyle, Denver; Considine, John; Baskin, Richard

**Song(s)** Welcome to L.A.; City of the One Night Stands; The Best Temptation of All; Night Time; Arrow (When the Arrow Flies); At the Door; After the End

**Notes** No cue sheet available.

## 6708 ✦ WELLS FARGO
Paramount, 1937

**Musical Score** Morros, Boris

**Producer(s)** Lloyd, Frank
**Director(s)** Lloyd, Frank
**Screenwriter(s)** Schofield, Paul; Geraghty, Gerald; Jackson, Frederick

**Cast** McCrea, Joel; Burns, Bob; Dee, Frances; Nolan, Lloyd; O'Neill, Henry

**Song(s)** Where I Ain't Been Before [1] (C: Lane, Burton; L: Freed, Ralph)

**Notes** [1] Hugh Fordin's *The World of Entertainment* says Arthur Freed and Nacio Herb Brown wrote the above song. The cue sheet and sheet music disagree.

## 6709 ✦ WE'LL SMILE AGAIN
Republic, 1942

**Musical Score** Russell, Kennedy
**Composer(s)** Russell, Kennedy
**Lyricist(s)** O'Connor, Desmond

**Producer(s)** Baxter, John
**Director(s)** Baxter, John
**Screenwriter(s)** Melford, Austin; Emary, Barbara K.; Flanagan, Bud

**Cast** Flanagan, Bud; Allen, Chesney; Stanley, Phyllis; Kenney, Horace; Mayerl, Billy

**Song(s)** Tonight You're Mine; We'll Smile Again; Waltz of Delight

**Notes** A British National Films picture.

## 6710 ✦ WE MUST HAVE MUSIC
Metro–Goldwyn–Mayer, 1942

**Cast** Garland, Judy

**Notes** This short subject contains an outake from ZIEGFELD GIRL.

## 6711 ✦ WE'RE GOING TO BE RICH
Twentieth Century–Fox, 1938

**Producer(s)** Engel, Samuel G.
**Director(s)** Banks, Monty
**Screenwriter(s)** Hellman, Sam; Siegel, Rohama

**Cast** Fields, Gracie; McLaglen, Victor; Donlevy, Brian; Browne, Coral; Smith, Ted; Payne, Tom

**Song(s)** The Sweetest Song in the World (C/L: Parr-Davies, Harry); Oh You Naughty Men (C/L: Haines, Will E.; Harper, Jimmy; Parr-Davies, Harry); Walter, Walter (Lead Me to the Alter) (C/L: Haines, Will E.; Harper, Jimmy; Forrester, Noel); The Trek Song [1] (C/L: Parr-Davies, Harry)

**Notes** Vocal renditions also include: the nursery rhyme "In and Out the Window;" "Ee By Gum" by Ralph Butler and Howard Flynn; "Don't 'Ang My 'Arry" by Greatrix Newman and "There Is a Tavern in the Town" by William Hills. [1] Sheet music only.

## 6712 ✦ WE'RE IN THE MONEY
Warner Brothers, 1935

**Producer(s)** Brown, Harry Joe
**Director(s)** Enright, Ray; Lewis, Gene
**Screenwriter(s)** Herbert, F. Hugh; Holmes, Brown

**Cast** Blondell, Joan; Farrell, Glenda; Herbert, Hugh; Alexander, Ross; Cavanaugh, Hobart; Regan, Phil; Kerry, Anita; O'Neill, Henry; Dean, Man Mountain; Stander, Lionel; Gargan, Edward; Clive, E.E.; Cox, Myron; Chief Little Wolf

**Song(s)** So Nice Seeing You Again (C: Wrubel, Allie; L: Dixon, Mort)

## 6713 ♦ WE'RE NO ANGELS
### Paramount, 1955

**Musical Score** Hollander, Frederick

**Producer(s)** Duggan, Pat
**Director(s)** Curtiz, Michael
**Screenwriter(s)** MacDougall, Ranald
**Source(s)** *Cuisine des Anges* (play) Husson, Albert

**Cast** Bogart, Humphrey; Ray, Aldo; Ustinov, Peter; Bennett, Joan; Rathbone, Basil; Carroll, Leo G.

**Song(s)** Ma France Bien Aimee [1] (C: Martini, G.B.; L: Wagner, Roger); Sentimental Moments (C: Hollander, Frederick; L: Freed, Ralph); Three Angels [2] (C: Hopkins, Edward J.; L: Sanders, Troy)

**Notes** [1] Based on "Plaisir D'Amour." [2] Adapted from "Saint Atanasius."

## 6714 ♦ WE'RE NOT DRESSING
### Paramount, 1934

**Composer(s)** Revel, Harry
**Lyricist(s)** Gordon, Mack

**Director(s)** Taurog, Norman
**Screenwriter(s)** Jackson, Horace; Martin, Francis; Marion Jr., George

**Cast** Crosby, Bing; Merman, Ethel; Errol, Leon; Burns, George; Allen, Gracie; Lombard, Carole; Milland, Ray

**Song(s)** Sailor's Chanty (It's a Lie); It's Just a New Spanish Custom [1]; Good Night Lovely Little Lady; I Positively Refuse to Sing; May I?; She Reminds Me of You [7]; Love Thy Neighbor; Once in a Blue Moon; Finale Sequence; It's the Animal in Me [3]; The Rhythm of the Moon [2] [6] (C: Rainger, Ralph; L: Robin, Leo); When the Golden Gate Was Silver [2] (C: Rainger, Ralph; L: Robin, Leo); Live and Love Tonight [2] [5] (C: Johnston, Arthur; L: Coslow, Sam); My Gigolo [2] (C: Johnston, Arthur; L: Coslow, Sam); Dreaming Out Loud [2] [4] (C: Rainger, Ralph; L: Robin, Leo)

**Notes** [1] Almost identical to the song "It's an Old Spanish Custom" from the musical SMILING FACES by Harry Revel and Mack Gordon. [2] Not used. [3] Used briefly in the finale although sequence cut from film. The complete number with Ethel Merman singing was inserted into the BIG BROADCAST OF 1936. [4] Also not used in PALM SPRINGS. [5] Used in MURDER AT THE VANITIES and not used in DANCERS IN THE DARK. [6] Also not used for BLOSSOMS ON BROADWAY. [7] Not used in SITTING PRETTY.

## 6715 ♦ WE'RE NOT MARRIED
### Twentieth Century–Fox, 1952

**Producer(s)** Johnson, Nunnally
**Director(s)** Goulding, Edmund
**Screenwriter(s)** Johnson, Nunnally

**Cast** Rogers, Ginger; Allen, Fred; Moore, Victor; Monroe, Marilyn; Wayne, David; Arden, Eve; Douglas, Paul; Bracken, Eddie; Gaynor, Mitzi; Calhern, Louis; Gabor, Zsa Zsa; Gleason, James; Stewart, Paul

**Song(s)** Cuddles (C/L: Goulding, Edmund)

## 6716 ♦ WE'RE RICH AGAIN
### RKO, 1934

**Producer(s)** Allvine, Glendon
**Director(s)** Seiter, William A.
**Screenwriter(s)** Harris, Ray
**Source(s)** *And Let Who Will Be Clever* (play) Nash, Alden

**Cast** Oliver, Edna May; Burke, Billie; Nixon, Marian; Denny, Reginald; Marsh, Joan; Crabbe, Buster [1]; Mitchell, Grant

**Song(s)** Senorita [2] (C/L: Malotte, Albert Hay)

**Notes** [1] Billed as Larry "Buster" Crabbe. [2] Also in THE RENEGADE RANGER.

## 6717 ♦ WEST COAST THEATERS
### Fox, 1930

**Song(s)** You Can Have It—I Don't Want It, Daylight Saving Time (C: Monaco, James V.; L: Friend, Cliff)

**Notes** No cue sheet available. This might have been a promotional short subject.

## 6718 ♦ WESTERN DAZE
### Paramount, 1941

**Musical Score** Raksin, David

**Producer(s)** Pal, George
**Director(s)** Pal, George

**Song(s)** I've Got No Cares (C/L: Raksin, David)

**Notes** This is a Puppetoon short.

## 6719 ♦ WESTERN GRANDEUR
### Twentieth Century–Fox, 1937

**Song(s)** Home Folks (C: Hanley, James F.; L: Lehr, Lew)

**Notes** This is a Lowell Thomas Magic Carpet of Movietone travelogue.

## 6720 ✦ WESTERN JAMBOREE
Republic, 1938

**Producer(s)**  Grey, Harry
**Director(s)**  Staub, Ralph
**Screenwriter(s)**  Geraghty, Gerald

**Cast**  Autry, Gene; Burnette, Smiley; Rouverol, Jean; Muir, Esther; Frisco, Joe; Darien, Frank; Armstrong, Margaret

**Song(s)**  Balloon Song (C/L: Cherkose, Eddie; Marvin, Johnny); I Love the Morning (C/L: Autry, Gene; Rose, Fred; Marvin, Johnny); Old November Moon [5] (C/L: Marvin, Johnny); Cowboys Don't Milk Cows (C/L: Burnette, Smiley); Seven Years (with the Wrong Woman) [4] (C/L: Nolan, Bob); Poor Little Doggie [3] (C/L: Marvin, Johnny; Rose, Fred); The Merry Old Way Back Home (C/L: Samuels, Walter G.); Beautiful Isle of Somewhere (C/L: Hamer, Billy); Autry's Your Man [1] (C/L: Samuels, Walter G.); Colorado Sunset [2] (C: Conrad, Con; L: Gilbert, L. Wolfe); Paradise in the Moonlight (C/L: Rose, Fred; Autry, Gene)

**Notes**  No cue sheet available. [1] May have been intended for EL RANCHO GRANDE. [2] Also in COLORADO SUNSET. [3] There is a similarly titled song, "Get Along Little Dogies" in COLORADO SUNSET. The writer is Fred Rose. [4] Also in COLORADO SUNSET. [5] Sheet music also credits Gene Autry.

## 6721 ✦ WEST OF CARSON CITY
Universal, 1940

**Composer(s)**  Rosen, Milton
**Lyricist(s)**  Carter, Everett

**Director(s)**  Taylor, Ray
**Screenwriter(s)**  Raison, Milton; Lowe, Sherman; Bernhard, Jack

**Cast**  Brown, Johnny Mack; Moran, Peggy; Baker, Bob; Knight, Fuzzy

**Song(s)**  Let's Go [1]; Git-A-Long; On the Trail of Tomorrow [2]

**Notes**  [1] Also in ARIZONA CYCLONE (1942) and ARIZONA TRAIL. [2] Also in ARIZONA CYCLONE (1942) and TRAIL TO VENGEANCE.

## 6722 ✦ WEST OF CIMARRON
Republic, 1941

**Producer(s)**  Gray, Louis
**Director(s)**  Orlebeck, Lester
**Screenwriter(s)**  De Mond, Albert; Ryan, Don
**Source(s)**  characters by MacDonald, William Colt

**Cast**  Steele, Bob; Tyler, Tom; Davis, Rufe; Collier, Lois; Bush, James; Usher, Guy; Prosser, Hugh

**Song(s)**  Wa Wa Watermelon (C: Styne, Jule; L: Meyer, Sol)

## 6723 ✦ WEST OF PINTO BASIN
Monogram, 1940

**Musical Score**  Sanucci, Frank

**Producer(s)**  Weeks, George W.
**Director(s)**  Luby, S. Roy
**Screenwriter(s)**  Snell, Earle

**Cast**  Terhune, Max; King, John; Corrigan, Ray; Gaze, Gwen; Coffin, Tristram; Chesebro, George

**Song(s)**  That Little Prairie Gal of Mine (C: Lange, Johnny; L: Porter, Lew); I'm Ridin' the Trail (C/L: Smith, Jerry)

## 6724 ✦ WEST OF THE ROCKIES
Warner Brothers

**Musical Score**  Lava, William
**Composer(s)**  Jerome, M.K.
**Lyricist(s)**  Scholl, Jack

**Song(s)**  Bunk-House Boys [1]; West of the Great Divide [1]; Finale; My Texas Home [5]; My Little Buckaroo [4]; The Circle Bar [2]; I Gotta Get Back to My Gal [3]

**Notes**  Short subject. Many of these are used briefly in a medley. [1] Also in SONGS OF THE RANGE. [2] Also in THE LAND BEYOND THE LAW. [3] Also in EMPTY HOLSTERS, GOLD IS WHERE YOU FIND IT and SONGS OF THE RANGE. [4] Also in DON'T FENCE ME IN (Republic), BROTHER ORCHID, THE CHEROKEE STRIP and SONGS OF THE RANGE. [5] Also used in DEVIL'S SADDLE LEGION and SONGS OF THE RANGE.

## 6725 ✦ WEST OF TOMBSTONE
Columbia, 1942

**Producer(s)**  Berke, William
**Director(s)**  Bretherton, Howard
**Screenwriter(s)**  Geraghty, Maurice

**Cast**  Starrett, Charles; Edwards, Cliff; DeMain, Gordon; Hayden, Russell; Martin, Marcelle

**Song(s)**  Get Along Little Pony (C/L: Unknown); Midnight Blues (C/L: Unknown); We'll All Be Together (C/L: Unknown)

**Notes**  No cue sheet available.

## 6726 ✦ THE WEST POINT STORY
Warner Brothers, 1950

**Musical Score**  Jackson, Howard
**Composer(s)**  Styne, Jule
**Lyricist(s)**  Cahn, Sammy
**Choreographer(s)**  Prinz, LeRoy; Boyle Jr., Johnny

**Producer(s)**    Edelman, Louis F.
**Director(s)**    Del Ruth, Roy
**Screenwriter(s)**    Monks Jr., John; Hoffman, Charles; Wallace, Irving
**Source(s)**    "Classmates" (story) Wallace, Irving

**Cast**    Cagney, James; Mayo, Virginia [1]; Day, Doris; MacRae, Gordon; Nelson, Gene; Hale Jr., Alan; Winters, Roland; Roe, Raymond; Graff, Wilton; Cowan, Jerome; Ferguson, Frank

**Song(s)**    It's Raining Sundrops; One Hundred Days 'Til June (C/L: Resta, Francis E.); By the Kissing Rock; Long Before I Knew You; This is the Finale; Ten Thousand Four Hundred Thirty Two Sheep; The Military Polka; You Love Me; The Corps (C: Harling, W. Franke; L: Shipman, Herbert); B 'Postrophe K No 'Postrophe Lyn; It Could Only Happen in Brooklyn

**Notes**    Released in Great Britain as FINE AND DANDY. [1] Dubbed by Bonnie Lou Williams.

## 6727 ◆ WEST SIDE STORY
United Artists, 1961

**Composer(s)**    Bernstein, Leonard
**Lyricist(s)**    Sondheim, Stephen
**Choreographer(s)**    Robbins, Jerome

**Producer(s)**    Wise, Robert
**Director(s)**    Wise, Robert; Robbins, Jerome
**Screenwriter(s)**    Lehman, Ernest
**Source(s)**    *West Side Story* (musical) Laurents, Arthur; Sondheim, Stephen; Bernstein, Leonard

**Cast**    Wood, Natalie [2]; Beymer, Richard [1]; Tamblyn, Russ; Moreno, Rita [3]; Chakiris, George; Smith, Tucker; Oakes, Sue; Oakland, Simon; Mordente, Tony; Feld, Eliot; Winters, David [6]; Michaels, Burt; Banas, Robert; Teague, Anthony "Scooter"; Abbott, Tom [5] [6]; Evans, Harvey [4]; Trikonis, Gina; D'Andrea, Carole; De Vega, Joe; Trikonis, Gus; Rogers, Jaime; Bramley, Bill; Glass, Ned; Astin, John

**Song(s)**    Jet Song; Something's Comin'; Maria; America; Tonight; Gee Officer Krupke; I Feel Pretty; One Hand One Heart; Quintet; Somewhere; Cool; A Boy Like That; I Have a Love

**Notes**    All songs written for Broadway original. [1] Dubbed by Jimmy Bryant. [2] Dubbed by Marni Nixon. [3] Dubbed by Betty Wand. [4] Billed as Harvey Hohnecker. [5] Billed as Tommy Abbott. [6] From Broadway cast.

## 6728 ◆ WEST TO GLORY
PRC, 1947

**Musical Score**    Hajos, Karl

**Producer(s)**    Thomas, Jerry
**Director(s)**    Taylor, Ray
**Screenwriter(s)**    Clifton, Elmer; Churchill, Robert B.

**Cast**    Dean, Eddie; Ates, Roscoe; Castle, Delores; Barton, Gregg; Martin, Jimmie

**Song(s)**    Cry, Cry, Cry (C/L: Dean, Eddie); In the Shadow of the Mission (C/L: Gates, V.W.); West to Glory (C/L: Dean, Eddie)

## 6729 ◆ WESTWARD HO THE WAGONS!
Disney, 1956

**Musical Score**    Bruns, George
**Composer(s)**    Bruns, George
**Lyricist(s)**    Blackburn, Tom

**Producer(s)**    Walsh, Bill
**Director(s)**    Beaudine, William
**Screenwriter(s)**    Blackburn, Tom
**Source(s)**    *The Children of the Covered Wagon* (novel) Carr, Mary Jane

**Cast**    Parker, Fess; Crowley, Kathleen; York, Jeff; Stollery, David; Cabot, Sebastian; Reeves, George; Tracey, Doreen; O'Brien, Cubby; Cody, Iron Eyes

**Song(s)**    Westward Ho! The Wagons; The Ballad of John Colter; Wringle Wrangle (C/L: Jones, Stan); Pioneer's Prayer [1] (C: Smith, Paul J.; L: George, Gil); Green Grow the Lilacs [2] (C/L: Ritter, Tex)

**Notes**    [1] From THE VANISHING PRAIRIE as "Prairie Home." [2] Sheet music only.

## 6730 ◆ THE WESTWARD TRAIL
PRC, 1947

**Musical Score**    Greene, Walter

**Producer(s)**    Thomas, Jerry
**Director(s)**    Taylor, Ray
**Screenwriter(s)**    Miller, Arthur Alan

**Cast**    Dean, Eddie; Ates, Roscoe; Planchard, Phyllis; Hardin, Eileen; Whitaker, Slim; Andy Parker and His Plainsmen

**Song(s)**    Cathy (C/L: Gates, Pete); Courtin' Time (C/L: Dean, Eddie; Blair, Hal); When Shorty Plays the Schottische (C/L: Gates, Pete)

## 6731 ◆ WE'VE NEVER BEEN LICKED
Universal, 1943

**Producer(s)**    Wanger, Walter
**Director(s)**    Rawlins, John
**Screenwriter(s)**    Raine, Norman Reilly; Grinde, Nick

**Cast**    Quine, Richard; Beery Jr., Noah; Gwynne, Anne; O'Driscoll, Martha; Frawley, William; Davenport, Harry

**Song(s)**    Spirit of Aggie Land (C/L: Mimms, Marvin H.; Dunn, Richard J.); Me for You, Forever! (C: Revel, Harry; L: Webster, Paul Francis)

**Notes**    There is also a vocal of the "Aggie War Hymn" by J.V. Wilson and George Fairleigh.

## 6732 ✦ WE WHO ARE ABOUT TO DIE
### RKO, 1936

**Musical Score**   Steiner, Max

**Producer(s)**   Small, Edward
**Director(s)**   Cabanne, Christy
**Screenwriter(s)**   Twist, John
**Source(s)**   *We Who Are About to Die* (book) Lamson, David

**Cast**   Foster, Preston; Dvorak, Ann; Beal, John; Mayer, Ray; Jones, Gordon; Hopton, Russell; Naish, J. Carrol; Hurst, Paul; Jenks, Frank; Wray, John

**Song(s)**   My Heart's on the Trail [1] (C: Shilkret, Nathaniel; L: Luther, Frank)

**Notes**   Originally titled CONDEMNED ROW. [1] Also in THE LAST OUTLAW.

## 6733 ✦ THE WHALE WHO WANTED TO SING AT THE MET
### Disney, 1946

**Musical Score**   Darby, Ken
**Composer(s)**   Darby, Ken; Paxton, Theodore
**Lyricist(s)**   Darby, Ken; Paxton, Theodore

**Director(s)**   Luske, Hamilton; Geronimi, Clyde
**Screenwriter(s)**   Hee, T.; Kelsey, Richmond
**Source(s)**   "Willie the Operatic Whale" (story) Graham, Irvin
**Narrator(s)**   Eddy, Nelson

**Song(s)**   Clown Song; Mephisto Song

**Notes**   This cartoon is a part of MAKE MINE MUSIC. There are also several brief operatic excerpts. See MAKE MINE MUSIC for other credits.

## 6734 ✦ WHARF ANGEL
### Paramount, 1934

**Producer(s)**   Lewis, Albert
**Director(s)**   Menzies, William Cameron
**Screenwriter(s)**   Hoffenstein, Samuel; Partos, Frank; Avery, Stephen Morehouse
**Source(s)**   *The Man Who Brooke His Heart* (play) Schlick, Frederick

**Cast**   Dell, Dorothy; McLaglen, Victor; Foster, Preston; Skipworth, Alison

**Song(s)**   While the Sun Is Going Down (Down Home) (C: Rainger, Ralph; L: Robin, Leo)

**Notes**   Formerly titled MAN WHO BROKE HIS HEART.

## 6735 ✦ WHAT A BLONDE
### RKO, 1946

**Musical Score**   Harline, Leigh

**Producer(s)**   Stoloff, Ben
**Director(s)**   Goodwins, Leslie
**Screenwriter(s)**   Roberts, Charles E.

**Cast**   Errol, Leon; Lane, Richard; St. Angel, Michael; Riley, Elaine; Borg, Veda Ann; Kolb, Clarence

**Song(s)**   I Haven't a Thing to Wear [1] (C: Revel, Harry; L: Greene, Mort)

**Notes**   [1] Also in FOUR JACKS AND A JILL.

## 6736 ✦ WHAT A WAY TO GO
### Twentieth Century–Fox, 1964

**Musical Score**   Riddle, Nelson
**Composer(s)**   Styne, Jule
**Lyricist(s)**   Comden, Betty; Green, Adolph

**Producer(s)**   Jacobs, Arthur P.
**Director(s)**   Thompson, J. Lee
**Screenwriter(s)**   Comden, Betty; Green, Adolph

**Cast**   MacLaine, Shirley; Newman, Paul; Mitchum, Robert; Martin, Dean; Kelly, Gene; Cummings, Robert; Van Dyke, Dick; Gardiner, Reginald; Dumont, Margaret; Nova, Lou; D'Orsay, Fifi

**Song(s)**   A Cup of Coffee; I Think That You and I Should Get Acquainted; The Story of My Life; Good Morning Mrs. Benson; On Our Houseboat in the Hudson; I Love Louisa [2]; Louisa March; What a Way to Go [1]

**Notes**   Original title: I LOVE LOUISA. [1] Not used. Written for exploitation only. [2] Not used.

## 6737 ✦ WHAT A WIDOW!
### United Artists, 1930

**Composer(s)**   Youmans, Vincent
**Lyricist(s)**   Robinson, J. Russel; Waggner, George

**Producer(s)**   Swanson, Gloria; Kennedy, Joseph P.
**Director(s)**   Dwan, Allan
**Screenwriter(s)**   Seymour, James; Gleason, James

**Cast**   Swanson, Gloria; Moore, Owen; Gaye, Gregory; Braggiotti, Herbert; Cody, Lew; Livingston, Margaret; Holden, William; Walker, Nella

**Song(s)**   Love, Your Magic Spell Is Everywhere (C/L: Goulding, Edmund); Love Is Like a Song; Say Oui, Cherie; You're the One

**Notes**   No cue sheet available.

## 6738 ✦ WHAT DID YOU DO IN THE WAR, DADDY?
### United Artists, 1966

**Musical Score**   Mancini, Henry

**Producer(s)**   Edwards, Blake
**Director(s)**   Edwards, Blake
**Screenwriter(s)**   Blatty, William Peter

**Cast**   Coburn, James; Shawn, Dick; Fantoni, Sergio; Ralli, Giovanna; Ray, Aldo; Morgan, Harry; O'Connor, Carroll

**Song(s)**   In the Arms of Love (C: Mancini, Henry; L: Livingston, Jay; Evans, Ray)

**6739 ◆ WHAT DO YOU SAY TO A NAKED LADY?**
United Artists, 1970

**Musical Score** Karmen, Steve
**Composer(s)** Karmen, Steve
**Lyricist(s)** Karmen, Steve

**Producer(s)** Funt, Allen
**Director(s)** Funt, Allen
**Screenwriter(s)** Funt, Allen

**Song(s)** Let's Get Down to It!; What Do You Say to a Naked Lady?; Hail to Humanity; Pardon Me; The Tailor Song; The Follow Song; Just a Little Mystery; Too Bad You Can't Read My Mind; Rape Is Not as Easy as It Looks; Kids

**Notes** This film is composed of CANDID CAMERA-type segments.

**6740 ◆ WHATEVER HAPPENED TO BABY JANE**
Warner Brothers, 1970

**Musical Score** De Vol, Frank

**Producer(s)** Aldrich, Robert
**Director(s)** Aldrich, Robert
**Screenwriter(s)** Heller, Lukas

**Cast** Davis, Bette; Crawford, Joan; Buono, Victor; Addy, Wesley; Allred, Julie; Barton, Ann; Bennett, Marjorie; Freed, Bert; Lee, Anna; Norman, Maidie; Willock, Dave; Burton, Debby [1]

**Song(s)** I've Written a Letter to Daddy (If I Had My Life to Live Over) [2] (C/L: Vincent, Larry; Tobias, Henry; Jaffe, Moe); Whatever Happened to Baby Jane [3] (C/L: De Vol, Frank; Helfer, Bobby)

**Notes** [1] Singing voice of Baby Jane. [2] Later in THE ROSE. [3] Lyric added for exploitation only.

**6741 ◆ WHAT LOLA WANTS**

See DAMN YANKEES.

**6742 ◆ WHAT PRICE GLORY?**
Twentieth Century–Fox, 1952

**Composer(s)** Livingston, Jay; Evans, Ray
**Lyricist(s)** Livingston, Jay; Evans, Ray

**Producer(s)** Siegel, Sol C.
**Director(s)** Ford, John
**Screenwriter(s)** Ephron, Phoebe; Ephron, Henry
**Source(s)** *What Price Glory?* (play) Stallings, Laurence; Anderson, Maxwell

**Cast** Cagney, James; Calvet, Corinne; Dailey, Dan; Demarest, William; Hill, Craig; Wagner, Robert; Pavan, Marisa; Gleason, James

**Song(s)** My Love, My Life; The Marines' Drill [1] (C: Newman, Lionel); All My Life

**Notes** [1] Lyrics assigned under the title "You and Me Together."

**6743 ◆ WHAT'S BUZZIN' COUSIN?**
Columbia, 1943

**Composer(s)** Pollack, Lew
**Lyricist(s)** Newman, Charles
**Choreographer(s)** Castle, Nick; Raset, Val

**Producer(s)** Fier, Jack
**Director(s)** Barton, Charles
**Screenwriter(s)** Sauber, Harry; Medbury, John P.

**Cast** Anderson, Eddie "Rochester"; Miller, Ann; Hubbard, John; Brooks, Leslie; Donnell, Jeff; Freddy Martin and His Orchestra; Brier, Audrene; Harris, Theresa

**Song(s)** Mister President (C/L: Samuels, Walter G.); Short, Fat and 4F (C: de Paul, Gene; L: Raye, Don); Nevada (C: Donaldson, Walter; L: Greene, Mort); Three Little Mosquitoes; Knocked Out Nocturne (C: Press, Jacques; L: Cherkose, Eddie); Ain't That Just Like a Man (C: de Paul, Gene; L: Raye, Don); In Grandpaw's Beard; They're Countin' in the Mountains; Where Am I Without You (C: de Paul, Gene; L: Raye, Don); Eighteen Seventy-Five (C/L: Anderson, Wally); Blue Ridge Mountain Blues [1] (C: de Paul, Gene; L: Raye, Don)

**Notes** [1] Sheet music only.

**6744 ◆ WHAT'S COOKIN'**
Universal, 1942

**Choreographer(s)** Mattison, John

**Producer(s)** Goldsmith, Ken
**Director(s)** Cline, Edward F.
**Screenwriter(s)** Cady, Jerry; Roberts, Stanley

**Cast** Jean, Gloria; O'Connor, Donald; McDonald, Grace; Ryan, Peggy; Frazee, Jane; The Andrews Sisters; Woody Herman and His Band; Butterworth, Charles; Carrillo, Leo; Burke, Billie; Pangborn, Franklin; The Jivin' Jacks and Jills; Paige, Robert; Levine, Susan

**Song(s)** Gee, But It's Great to Meet a Friend from Your Home Town (C: McGavisk, James; Fisher, Fred; L: Tracey, William); You Can't Hold a Memory in Your Arms (C: Altman, Arthur; L: Zaret, Hy); What to Do (C/L: Robin, Sid); If (C: de Paul, Gene; L: Raye, Don); Love Laughs at Anything (C: de Paul, Gene; L: Raye, Don); Amen (C/L: Schoen, Vic; Segure, Roger); I'll Pray for You (C: Altman, Arthur; L: Gannon, Kim)

**Notes** Released as WAKE UP AND DREAM internationally. There are also vocals of "Believe Me If All Those Endearing Young charms" by Thomas Moore; "Il Bacio" by L. Arditi; "Pack Up Your Troubles in Your Old Kit Bag and Smile, Smile, Smile" by George Asaf and Felix Powell and "Lo! Hear the Gentle Lark" by Sir Henry R. Bishop. Sid Robin is credited with the song

"One Kiss-Il Bacio" in sheet music, but it is uncertain whether his lyrics were used in the film.

## 6745 ✦ WHAT'S GOOD FOR THE GOOSE
### National Showmanship, 1969

**Musical Score**   Tilsley, Reg
**Composer(s)**   Pretty Things, The
**Lyricist(s)**   Pretty Things, The

**Producer(s)**   Tenser, Tony
**Director(s)**   Golan, Menahem
**Screenwriter(s)**   Golan, Menahem

**Cast**   Wisdom, Norman; Geeson, Sally; Alexander, Terrence

**Song(s)**   What's Good for the Goose (C: Tilsley, Reg; L: Blaikley, Howard); Never Be Me; Alexandra; Eagle's Sun

**Notes**   No cue sheet available.

## 6746 ✦ WHAT'S NEW PUSSYCAT?
### United Artists, 1965

**Musical Score**   Bacharach, Burt
**Composer(s)**   Bacharach, Burt
**Lyricist(s)**   David, Hal

**Producer(s)**   Feldman, Charles K.
**Director(s)**   Donner, Clive
**Screenwriter(s)**   Allen, Woody

**Cast**   Sellers, Peter; O'Toole, Peter; Schneider, Romy; Prentiss, Paula; Capucine; Allen, Woody; Andress, Ursula

**Song(s)**   What's New Pussycat; Dance Mamma, Dance Pappa, Dance; Here I Am; My Little Red Book; Downhill and Shady

**Notes**   No cue sheet available.

## 6747 ✦ WHAT'S OPERA, DOC?
### Warner Brothers, 1957

**Musical Score**   Franklyn, Milton J.

**Director(s)**   Jones, Chuck
**Screenwriter(s)**   Maltese, Michael

**Cast**   Bunny, Bugs; Fudd, Elmer

**Song(s)**   Mighty Hunter (C/L: Franklyn, Milton J.); Return My Love (C: Wagner, Richard; L: Maltese, Michael)

**Notes**   Merrie Melodie. Other selections from the "Ring Cycle" by Richard Wagner were used.

## 6748 ✦ WHAT'S SO BAD ABOUT FEELING GOOD?
### Universal, 1972

**Musical Score**   De Vol, Frank
**Composer(s)**   Keller, Jerry; Blume, Dave
**Lyricist(s)**   Keller, Jerry; Blume, Dave

**Producer(s)**   Seaton, George
**Director(s)**   Seaton, George
**Screenwriter(s)**   Seaton, George; Pirosh, Robert
**Source(s)**   *I Am Thinking About My Darling* (novel) McHugh, Vincent

**Cast**   Peppard, George; Moore, Mary Tyler; DeLuise, Dom; McMartin, John; Gumeny, Peter; Stroud, Don; Ritter, Thelma

**Song(s)**   What's So Bad About Feeling Good?; Blue Black & Grey; I'm Bubblin' Over

## 6749 ✦ WHAT'S UP DOC
### Warner Brothers, 1950

**Musical Score**   Stalling, Carl
**Composer(s)**   Stalling, Carl
**Lyricist(s)**   Stalling, Carl

**Director(s)**   McKimson, Robert

**Cast**   Bunny, Bugs; Fudd, Elmer

**Song(s)**   Boys of the Chorus; What's Up Doc

**Notes**   Looney Tune.

## 6750 ✦ THE WHEELER DEALERS
### Metro–Goldwyn–Mayer, 1964

**Musical Score**   De Vol, Frank

**Producer(s)**   Ransohoff, Martin
**Director(s)**   Hiller, Arthur
**Screenwriter(s)**   Goodman, George J.W.; Wallach, Ira
**Source(s)**   *The Wheeler Dealers* (novel) Goodman, George J.W.

**Cast**   Garner, James; Remick, Lee; Harris, Phil; Wills, Chill; Backus, Jim; Nye, Louis; Astin, John; Reid, Elliott; Harrington Jr., Pat; Forman, Joey; Crowley, Pat

**Song(s)**   The Wheeler Dealers (C/L: Sparks, Randy)

**Notes**   Titled SEPARATE BEDS outside the U.S.

## 6751 ✦ WHEEL OF FORTUNE

See A MAN BETRAYED.

## 6752 ✦ THE WHEEL OF LIFE
### Paramount, 1929

**Director(s)**   Schertzinger, Victor
**Screenwriter(s)**   Johnson, Julian
**Source(s)**   *The Wheel of Life* (play) Fagan, James Bernard

**Cast**   Ralston, Esther; Dix, Richard; Heggie, O.P.; Hoyt, Arthur; Stedman, Myrtle; Toomey, Regis

**Song(s)**   I Wonder Why You Love Me (C/L: Schertzinger, Victor)

## 6753 ✦ WHEN A GIRL'S BEAUTIFUL
Columbia, 1947

**Composer(s)** Lee, Lester
**Lyricist(s)** Roberts, Allan

**Producer(s)** MacDonald, Wallace
**Director(s)** McDonald, Frank
**Screenwriter(s)** Weisberg, Brenda

**Cast** Jergens, Adele [1]; White, Patricia [2]; Platt, Marc [3]; Leonard, Jack; Barrie, Mona; Harvey, Paul; Geray, Steven

**Song(s)** When a Girl Is Beautiful; I'm Sorry I Didn't Say I'm Sorry [4]; As Long As You Belong to Me

**Notes** [1] Dubbed by Suzanne Ellers. [2] Dubbed by Jewel Eberly. [3] Dubbed by Ken Harvey. [4] Also in MARY LOU.

## 6754 ✦ WHEN A STRANGER CALLS
Columbia, 1979

**Musical Score** Kaproff, Dana

**Producer(s)** Feke, Steve; Chapin, Doug
**Director(s)** Walton, Fred
**Screenwriter(s)** Feke, Steve; Walton, Fred

**Cast** Kane, Carol; Alda, Rutanya; Argenziano, Carmen; Larkin, Kirsten; Durning, Charles

**Song(s)** Space Race (C/L: Preston, Billy)

## 6755 ✦ WHEN JOHNNY COMES MARCHING HOME
Universal, 1942

**Producer(s)** Burton, Bernard W.
**Director(s)** Lamont, Charles
**Screenwriter(s)** Brodney, Oscar; Bennett, Dorothy

**Cast** Jones, Allan; Frazee, Jane; Jean, Gloria; O'Connor, Donald; Ryan, Peggy; The Step Brothers

**Song(s)** One of Us Has Gotta Go (C: Pepper, Buddy; L: James, Inez); This Is It (C: de Paul, Gene; L: Raye, Don); Say It with Dancing (C: de Paul, Gene; L: Raye, Don)

**Notes** There are also vocals of "Romance" by Edgar Leslie and Walter Donaldson; "Green Eyes" by Adolfo Utera and Nilo Menendez; "This Is Worth Fighting For" by Eddie de Lange and Sam H. Stept; "You and the Night and the Music" by Arthur Schwartz and Howard Dietz; "My Little Dream Girl" by Anatol Friedland and L. Wolfe Gilbert; "The Yanks Are Coming Again" by Harry Seymour and "We Must be Vigilant" by Edgar Leslie and Joe Burke.

## 6756 ✦ WHEN LOVE IS YOUNG
Universal, 1937

**Composer(s)** McHugh, Jimmy
**Lyricist(s)** Adamson, Harold

**Producer(s)** Presnell, Robert
**Director(s)** Mohr, Hal
**Screenwriter(s)** Green, Eve; Fields, Joseph
**Source(s)** "Class Prophecy" (story) Griffin, Eleanore

**Cast** Bruce, Virginia; Taylor, Kent; Tannen, William; Brennan, Walter; Holloway, Sterling

**Song(s)** I'm Hittin' the Hot Spots [1]; Did Anyone Ever Tell You; When Love Is Young [2]; The Red and White of Santa Clara [3]

**Notes** [1] Also in BREEZING HOME and MISSISSIPPI GAMBLER (1942). [2] Also in SMASH-UP. [3] Not used.

## 6757 ✦ WHEN MY BABY SMILES AT ME
Twentieth Century–Fox, 1948

**Composer(s)** Myrow, Josef
**Lyricist(s)** Gordon, Mack
**Choreographer(s)** Felix, Seymour; Williams, Kenny

**Producer(s)** Jessel, George
**Director(s)** Lang, Walter
**Screenwriter(s)** Trotti, Lamar
**Source(s)** *Burlesque* (play) Watters, George Manker; Hopkins, Arthur

**Cast** Grable, Betty; Dailey, Dan; Oakie, Jack; Havoc, June; Arlen, Richard; Gleason, James; Wade, Vanita; Keane, Robert Emmett

**Song(s)** The Belles of Gay Paree; By the Way; Shine Yo' Shoes; What Did I Do?; Belles of Gay Madrid

**Notes** There are also vocals of "Oui, Oui, Marie" by Alfred Bryan, Fred Fisher and Joseph McCarthy; "Bye Bye Blackbird" by Ray Henderson and Mort Dixon; "Don't Bring Lulu" by Ray Henderson, Billy Rose and Lew Brown; "Bam Bam Bamy Shore" by Ray Henderson and Mort Dixon; "Ain't We Got Fun" by Richard A. Whiting, Gus Kahn and Raymond B. Egan; "Birth of the Blues" by Ray Henderson, B.G. DeSylva and Lew Brown; "When My Baby Smiles at Me" by Bill Munro, Andrew B. Sterling and Ted Lewis; "The Daughter of Rosie O'Grady" by Walter Donaldson and Monte C. Brice; "Sweet Georgia Brown" by Ben Bernie, Maceo Pinkard and Kenneth Casey and "Say Si Si" by Ernesto Lecuona.

## 6758 ✦ WHEN'S YOUR BIRTHDAY
RKO, 1937

**Producer(s)** Loew, David L.
**Director(s)** Beaumont, Harry
**Screenwriter(s)** Clork, Harry
**Source(s)** (play) Ballard, Fred

**Cast** Brown, Joe E.; Marsh, Marian; Kaaren, Suzanne; Keating, Fred; Kennedy, Edgar; Eburne, Maude; Hamilton, Margaret; Watson, Minor; Jenks, Frank; Judels, Charles; Montana, Bull; Corky

**Song(s)** From Coast to Coast (C/L: Stillman, Al; Hyde, Alex; Adlam, Basil)

**Notes** There is a cartoon segment produced by Leon Schlesinger.

## 6759 ◆ WHEN THE BOYS MEET THE GIRLS
### Metro–Goldwyn–Mayer, 1966

**Musical Score** Karger, Fred

**Producer(s)** Katzman, Sam
**Director(s)** Ganzer, Alvin
**Screenwriter(s)** Kent, Robert E.

**Cast** Francis, Connie; Presnell, Harve; Herman's Hermits; Armstrong, Louis; Liberace; Langdon, Sue Ane; Clark, Fred; Faylen, Frank

**Song(s)** When the Boys Meet the Girls (C/L: Keller, Jack; Greenfield, Howard); Throw It Out of Your Mind (C/L: Armstrong, Louis; Kyle, Billy); Mail Call (C/L: Karger, Fred; Weisman, Ben; Wayne, Sid); Listen People (C/L: Gouldman, Graham); It's All in Your Mind (C/L: Karger, Fred; Weisman, Ben; Wayne, Sid); Aurba Liberace (C/L: Liberace, Lee)

**Notes** A remake of GIRL CRAZY. There are also vocals of "Treat Me Rough," "Embraceable You," "Bidin' My Time," "I Got Rhythm" and "But Not for Me" by George and Ira Gershwin.

## 6760 ◆ WHEN THE LEGENDS DIE
### Twentieth Century–Fox, 1972

**Composer(s)** Paxton, Glenn
**Lyricist(s)** Goldman, Bo

**Producer(s)** Millar, Stuart
**Director(s)** Millar, Stuart
**Screenwriter(s)** Dozier, Robert
**Source(s)** *When the Legends Die* (novel) Borland, Hal

**Cast** Widmark, Richard; Forrest, Frederic; Anders, Luana; Scotti, Vito; Wilson, Herbert

**Song(s)** When You Speak to the Kids; The Riderless Wagon; Summer Storm

## 6761 ◆ WHEN THE LIGHTS GO ON AGAIN
### PRC, 1944

**Musical Score** Harling, W. Franke

**Producer(s)** Fromkess, Leon
**Director(s)** Howard, William K.
**Screenwriter(s)** Lazarus, Milton

**Cast** Lydon, James; Toomey, Regis; Cleveland, George; Mitchell, Grant; Peterson, Dorothy; Shannon, Harry; Littlefield, Lucien; Alberni, Luis; Crehan, Joseph

**Song(s)** When the Lights Go on Again (C/L: Benjemen, Benny; Marcus, Sol; Morrison, Alec; Seiler, Eddie)

**Notes** No cue sheet available.

## 6762 ◆ WHEN TOMORROW COMES
### Universal, 1939

**Producer(s)** Stahl, John M.
**Director(s)** Stahl, John M.
**Screenwriter(s)** Taylor, Dwight
**Source(s)** *A Modern Cinderella* (novel) Cain, James M.

**Cast** Dunne, Irene; Boyer, Charles; O'Neil, Barbara; Stevens, Onslow; Westman, Nydia; Feld, Fritz; Walker, Nella

**Song(s)** Serenade (C: Schubert, Franz; L: Pinkerton, Percy)

**Notes** Remade as INTERLUDE (1957).

## 6763 ◆ WHEN WILLIE COMES MARCHING HOME
### Twentieth Century–Fox, 1950

**Producer(s)** Kohlmar, Fred
**Director(s)** Ford, John
**Screenwriter(s)** Loos, Mary; Sale, Richard

**Cast** Dailey, Dan; Calvet, Corinne; Townsend, Coleen; Demarest, William; Lydon, Jimmy [1]; Corrigan, Lloyd; Varden, Evelyn; Marsh, Mae

**Song(s)** You've Got Me This Way [2] (C: McHugh, Jimmy; L: Mercer, Johnny); Somebody Stole My Gal [3] (C/L: Wood, Leo)

**Notes** [1] Billed as James Lydon. [2] Also in YOU'LL FIND OUT (RKO). [3] Sheet music only.

## 6764 ◆ WHEN WORLDS COLLIDE
### Paramount, 1951

**Musical Score** Stevens, Leith

**Producer(s)** Pal, George
**Director(s)** Mate, Rudolph
**Screenwriter(s)** Boehm, Sydney
**Source(s)** (novel) Wylie, Philip; Balmer, Edwin

**Cast** Derr, Richard; Rush, Barbara; Hanson, Peter; Hoty, John; Keating, Larry; Ames, Judith; Chase, Stephen; Cady, Frank; Rorke, Hayden; Giglio, Sandro

**Song(s)** When Worlds Collide (C: Stevens, Leith; L: Livingston, Jay; Evans, Ray)

## 6765 ◆ WHEN YOU'RE IN LOVE
### Columbia, 1937

**Composer(s)** Kern, Jerome
**Lyricist(s)** Fields, Dorothy
**Choreographer(s)** Leonidoff, Leon

**Producer(s)** Riskin, Everett
**Director(s)** Lachman, Harry; Riskin, Robert
**Screenwriter(s)** Riskin, Robert

**Cast** Moore, Grace; Grant, Cary; Mitchell, Thomas; Smith, Gerald Oliver; MacMahon, Aline; Kennedy, Edgar; Alberni, Luis

**Song(s)** Whistling Boy; Our Song

**Notes** Vocal renditions included "Minnie the Moocher" by Cab Calloway, Irving Mills and Clarence Gaskill; "In the Gloaming" by Annie Harrison; "One Fine Day" by Puccini; "O Sole Mio" by G. Capurro and E. DiCapua; "Vissi D'Arte" by Puccini; "M'Appari" by F. Von Flotow; "Siboney" by Ernest Lecuona and "Serenade" by Franz Schubert with English lyric by Henry G. Chapman.

### 6766 ♦ WHEN YOU'RE SMILING
Columbia, 1950

**Producer(s)** Taps, Jonie
**Director(s)** Santley, Joseph
**Screenwriter(s)** De Wolf, Karen; Roberts, John R.

**Cast** Courtland, Jerome; Laine, Frankie; Albright, Lola; Cowan, Jerome; Wood, Margo; Otis, Don; Earle, Edward; Crosby, Bob; The Mills Brothers; The Modernaires; Starr, Kay; Daniels, Billy

**Song(s)** When the Wind Was Green (C/L: Hunt, Don)

**Notes** No cue sheet available. Vocals also include: "When You're Smiling" by Mark Fisher, Joe Goodwin, and Larry Shay; "That Old Black Magic" by Harold Arlen and Johnny Mercer; "Georgia on My Mind" by Hoagy Carmichael and Stuart Garrell; "Up a Lazy River" by Hoagy Carmichael and Sidney Arodin; "Deed I Do" by Walter Hirsch and Fred Rose; "Juke Box Saturday Night" by Al Stillman and Paul McGrane; "Mama Goes Where Papa Goes" and "If You Can't Get a Drum with a Boom, Boom, Boom."

### 6767 ♦ WHERE ANGELS GO . . . TROUBLE FOLLOWS!
Columbia, 1968

**Musical Score** Schifrin, Lalo

**Producer(s)** Frye, William
**Director(s)** Neilson, James
**Screenwriter(s)** Hanalis, Blanche

**Cast** Russell, Rosalind; Stevens, Stella; Barnes, Binnie; Wickes, Mary; Sutton, Dolores; Berle, Milton; Godfrey, Arthur; Johnson, Van; Taylor, Robert; Saint James, Susan; Hunter, Barbara

**Song(s)** Where Angels Go, Trouble Follows (C: Schifrin, Lalo; L: Boyce, Tommy; Hart, Bobby)

### 6768 ♦ WHERE DANGER LIVES
RKO, 1950

**Musical Score** Webb, Roy

**Producer(s)** Cummings Jr., Irving
**Director(s)** Farrow, John
**Screenwriter(s)** Bennett, Charles

**Cast** Mitchum, Robert; Domergue, Faith; Rains, Claude; O'Sullivan, Maureen; Kemper, Charles; Dumke, Ralph

**Song(s)** I'm Living in a Great Big Way [1] (C: McHugh, Jimmy; L: Fields, Dorothy); Margot [2] (C: Webb, Roy; L: Carter, Ray)

**Notes** [1] Also in HOORAY FOR LOVE. [2] Sheet music only.

### 6769 ♦ WHERE DID YOU GET THAT GIRL
Universal, 1940

**Composer(s)** Rosen, Milton
**Lyricist(s)** Carter, Everett

**Producer(s)** Sandford, Joseph G.
**Director(s)** Lubin, Arthur
**Screenwriter(s)** Dratler, Jay; Franklin, Paul; Rubin, Stanley Crea

**Cast** Errol, Leon; Parrish, Helen; Quillan, Eddie; Pangborn, Franklin

**Song(s)** Rug Cuttin' Romeo [1]; Sergeant Swing

**Notes** There is also a vocal of "Where Did You Get that Girl" by Bert Kalmar and Harry Puck. [1] Also in IN THE GROOVE, SING ANOTHER CHORUS and SWING IT SISTER.

### 6770 ♦ WHERE DO WE GO FROM HERE
Twentieth Century–Fox, 1945

**Composer(s)** Weill, Kurt
**Lyricist(s)** Gershwin, Ira
**Choreographer(s)** Fanchon

**Producer(s)** Perlberg, William
**Director(s)** Ratoff, Gregory
**Screenwriter(s)** Ryskind, Morrie

**Cast** MacMurray, Fred; Leslie, Joan; Haver, June; Sheldon, Gene; Quinn, Anthony; Ramirez, Carlos; Mowbray, Alan; Bonanova, Fortunio; Bing, Herman; Davidson, John

**Song(s)** Song of the Rhineland (Trenton Bieretuse); All At Once; If Love Remains; That's How It Is [1]; (Woo Woo Woo Woo) Manhattan [1]; (It Could Have Happened to Anyone) It Happened to Happen to Me [1]; Morale; Where Do We Go from Here; The Nina, the Pinta, the Santa Maria (Columbus); Telephone Scene [1]

**Notes** [1] Not used.

### 6771 ♦ WHERE LOVE HAS GONE
Paramount, 1964

**Musical Score** Scharf, Walter

**Producer(s)** Levine, Joseph E.
**Director(s)** Dmytryk, Edward
**Screenwriter(s)** Hayes, John Michael

**Source(s)** *Where Love Has Gone* (novel) Robbins, Harold

**Cast** Hayward, Susan; Davis, Bette; Connors, Michael; Heatherton, Joey; Greer, Jane; Kelley, DeForest; Seymour, Anne; Bissell, Whit

**Song(s)** Where Love Has Gone (C: Van Heusen, James; L: Cahn, Sammy)

## 6772 ◆ WHERE'S CHARLEY?
Warner Brothers, 1952

**Composer(s)** Loesser, Frank
**Lyricist(s)** Loesser, Frank
**Choreographer(s)** Kidd, Michael

**Director(s)** Butler, David
**Screenwriter(s)** Monks Jr., John
**Source(s)** *Where's Charley* (musical) Abbott, George; Loesser, Frank

**Cast** Bolger, Ray [1]; McLerie, Allyn Ann [1]; Shackleton, Robert; Germaine, Mary; Cooper, Horace; Scott, Margaretta; Crawford, Howard Marion; Hewitt, Henry; Stoker, H.G.; Miller, Martin

**Song(s)** My Darling, My Darling; Where's Charley; The Years Before Us; Better Get Out of Here; New Ashmolean Marching Society and Student Conservatory Band; Make a Miracle; Serenade with Asides; Once in Love with Amy; At the Red Rose Cotillion

**Notes** All songs from Broadway production. [1] From Broadway production.

## 6773 ◆ WHERE'S JACK?
Paramount, 1969

**Musical Score** Bernstein, Elmer
**Composer(s)** Bernstein, Elmer
**Lyricist(s)** Black, Don

**Producer(s)** Baker, Stanley
**Director(s)** Clavell, James
**Screenwriter(s)** Newhouse, Rafe; Newhouse, David

**Cast** Steele, Tommy; Baker, Stanley; Byrne, Eddie; Lewis, Fiona; Badel, Alan; Foster, Dudley

**Song(s)** Where's Jack?; Ballad of Jack Shepherd

## 6774 ◆ WHERE'S POPPA?
United Artists, 1970

**Musical Score** Elliott, Jack Z.
**Composer(s)** Elliott, Jack Z.
**Lyricist(s)** Gimbel, Norman

**Producer(s)** Tokofsky, Jerry; Worth, Marvin
**Director(s)** Reiner, Carl
**Screenwriter(s)** Klane, Robert
**Source(s)** (novel) Klane, Robert

**Cast** Gordon, Ruth; Segal, George; Leibman, Ron; Van Devere, Trish; Hughes, Barnard; Gardenia, Vincent; Sorvino, Paul

**Song(s)** Where's Poppa; Move It Out of Here; Freedom; Pleasure Palace; The Goodbye Song

## 6775 ◆ WHERE THE BOYS ARE
Metro–Goldwyn–Mayer, 1960

**Musical Score** Stoll, George
**Composer(s)** Sedaka, Neil
**Lyricist(s)** Greenfield, Howard
**Choreographer(s)** Sidney, Robert

**Producer(s)** Pasternak, Joe
**Director(s)** Levin, Henry
**Screenwriter(s)** Wells, George
**Source(s)** *Where the Boys Are* (novel) Swarthout, Glendon

**Cast** Hart, Dolores; Hamilton, George; Mimieux, Yvette; Hutton, Jim; Nichols, Barbara; Prentiss, Paula; Wills, Chill; Gorshin, Frank; Harrity, Rory; Berger, Ted; Francis, Connie

**Song(s)** Where the Boys Are; Limbo-Rak-Dance (C/L: Pinder, Adney H.); Turn on the Sunshine; Have You Met Miss Fandango (C: Young, Victor; L: Unger, Stella)

## 6776 ◆ WHERE THE BUFFALO ROAM
Monogram, 1938

**Producer(s)** Finney, Edward
**Director(s)** Herman, Al
**Screenwriter(s)** Emmett, Robert

**Cast** Ritter, Tex; Short, Dorothy; Murphy, Horace; Pollard, Snub; King Jr., Charles; Louise Massey's Westerners

**Song(s)** In the Heart of the West (C/L: Smith, J.W.); Where the Buffalo Roam (C/L: Harford, Frank; Sanucci, Frank); Troubador of the Prairie (C/L: Harford, Frank); In the Heart of the Prairie (C/L: Massey, Louise; Wollington, Larry); Bunkhouse Jamboree (C/L: Massey, Louise; Wollington, Larry)

**Notes** No cue sheet available.

## 6777 ◆ WHERE THE BULLETS FLY
Embassy, 1966

**Musical Score** Graham, Kenny

**Producer(s)** Ward, James
**Director(s)** Gilling, John
**Screenwriter(s)** Pittock, Michael

**Cast** Adams, Tom; Addams, Dawn; Barett, Tim; Ripper, Michael

**Song(s)** Where the Bullets Fly (C: Kingston, Bob; L: Bridges, Ronald)

**Notes** No cue sheet available.

## 6778 ✦ WHERE THE HOT WIND BLOWS
Metro–Goldwyn–Mayer, 1960

**Musical Score**  Vlad, Roman

**Producer(s)**  Bar, Jacques
**Director(s)**  Dassin, Jules
**Screenwriter(s)**  Dassin, Jules; Giroud, Francoise
**Source(s)**  *The Law* (novel) Valland, Roger

**Cast**  Lollobrigida, Gina; Brasseur, Pierre; Mastroianni, Marcello; Mercouri, Melina; Montand, Yves; Stoppa, Paolo; Mattoli, Raf

**Song(s)**  Where the Hot Wind Blows (C: McHugh, Jimmy; L: Kaye, Buddy)

**Notes**  No cue sheet available.

## 6779 ✦ WHERE THE LILLIES BLOOM
United Artists, 1974

**Producer(s)**  Radnitz, Robert B.
**Director(s)**  Graham, William
**Screenwriter(s)**  Hammer, Earl, Jr.
**Source(s)**  *Where the Lillies Bloom* (novel) Cleaver, Bill; Cleaver, Vera

**Cast**  Gholson, Julie; Smithers, Jan; Burrill, Matthew; Harmon, Helen; Stanton, Harry Dean; Howard, Rance; Bond, Sudie

**Song(s)**  Where the Lilies Bloom (C/L: Mauritz, Barbara); All the Things Inside of Me (C/L: Mauritz, Barbara)

**Notes**  There are also vocals of the public domain songs "I Love My Love" and "Been a Long Time Traveling."

## 6780 ✦ WHERE TURF MEETS SURF
Metro–Goldwyn–Mayer, 1939

**Producer(s)**  Lewyn, Louis
**Director(s)**  Lee, Sammy
**Screenwriter(s)**  Mack, Marion

**Cast**  Payne, Sally; Treen, Mary; Hernandez, Joe; Crosby, Bing; Pendleton, Nat

**Song(s)**  Where the Turf Meets the Surf (C: Monaco, James V.; L: Burke, Johnny)

**Notes**  Short subject.

## 6781 ✦ WHERE WERE YOU WHEN THE LIGHTS WENT OUT
Metro–Goldwyn–Mayer, 1968

**Musical Score**  Grusin, Dave

**Producer(s)**  Freeman, Everett; Melcher, Martin
**Director(s)**  Averback, Hy
**Screenwriter(s)**  Freeman, Everett; Tunberg, Karl
**Source(s)**  *Monsieur Masure* (play) Magnier, Claude

**Cast**  Day, Doris; Morse, Robert; Terry-Thomas; O'Neal, Patrick; Albright, Lola; Allen, Steve; Backus, Jim; Blue, Ben; Paulsen, Pat; Malone, Dale

**Song(s)**  Where Were You When the Lights Went Out (C: Grusin, Dave; L: Gordon, Kelly)

## 6782 ✦ WHICH WAY IS UP?
Universal, 1977

**Musical Score**  Davis, Mark

**Producer(s)**  Krantz, Steve
**Director(s)**  Schultz, Michael
**Screenwriter(s)**  Gottlieb, Carl; Brown, Cecil

**Cast**  Pryor, Richard; McKee, Lonette; Avery, Margaret; Woodward, Morgan

**Song(s)**  Which Way Is Up? (C/L: Whitfield, Norman)

**Notes**  A remake of THE SEDUCTION OF MIMI (1974).

## 6783 ✦ WHIFFS
Twentieth Century–Fox, 1975

**Musical Score**  Cameron, John
**Composer(s)**  Barrie, George
**Lyricist(s)**  Cahn, Sammy

**Producer(s)**  Barrie, George
**Director(s)**  Post, Ted
**Screenwriter(s)**  Marmorstein, Malcolm

**Cast**  Gould, Elliott; Albert, Eddie; Guardino, Harry; Cambridge, Godfrey; O'Neill, Jennifer; Masur, Richard; Hesseman, Howard

**Song(s)**  If You Do It Without the Army; Now That We're in Love

## 6784 ✦ WHILE NEW YORK SLEEPS
Twentieth Century–Fox, 1938

**Producer(s)**  Wurtzel, Sol M.
**Director(s)**  Humberstone, H. Bruce
**Screenwriter(s)**  Hyland, Frances; Ray, Albert

**Cast**  Whalen, Michael; Rogers, Jean; Chandler, Chick; Kellard, Robert; Woodbury, Joan; Huber, Harold; Demarest, William; Blackmer, Sidney; Lawrence, Marc; Gargan, Edward; Watson, Minor

**Song(s)**  Ain't He Good Lookin' [1] (C/L: Clare, Sidney); I'll Never Change (C: Johnston, Arthur; L: Clare, Sidney)

**Notes**  [1] Not used in SONG AND DANCE MAN though written for that film.

## 6785 ✦ WHILE PARIS SLEEPS
Fox, 1932

**Director(s)**  Dwan, Allan
**Screenwriter(s)**  Woon, Basil

**Cast**  McLaglen, Victor; Mack, Helen; LaRue, Jack; La Roy, Rita

**Song(s)** Cherie Paree Is Mine [1] (C/L: Hanley, James F.)

**Notes** [1] French lyrics by Silver.

## 6786 ✦ WHILE THE CITY SLEEPS
### RKO, 1955

**Musical Score** Gilbert, Herschel Burke

**Producer(s)** Friedlob, Bert
**Director(s)** Lang, Fritz
**Screenwriter(s)** Robinson, Casey
**Source(s)** *The Bloody Spur* (novel) Einstein, Charles

**Cast** Andrews, Dana; Fleming, Rhonda; Sanders, George; Duff, Howard; Mitchell, Thomas; Price, Vincent; Forrest, Sally; Barrymore Jr., John; Craig, James; Lupino, Ida; Marsh, Mae

**Song(s)** While the City Sleeps [1] (C: Gilbert, Herschel Burke; L: Mullendore, Joseph); The Lazy Piano Blues [1] (C/L: Gilbert, Herschel Burke); I'll Know [1] (C/L: Gilbert, Herschel Burke)

**Notes** [1] All songs used instrumentally only.

## 6787 ✦ WHIPLASH
### Warner Brothers, 1949

**Musical Score** Waxman, Franz

**Producer(s)** Jacobs, William
**Director(s)** Seiler, Lewis
**Screenwriter(s)** Geraghty, Maurice; Frank Jr., Harriet

**Cast** Clark, Dane; Smith, Alexis; Scott, Zachary; Arden, Eve; Lynn, Jeffrey; Sakall, S.Z.; Hale, Alan; Kennedy, Douglas; Sherman, Ransom; McGuire, Don

**Song(s)** Just for Now (C/L: Redmond, Dick)

## 6788 ✦ WHIRLWIND
### Columbia, 1951

**Producer(s)** Schaefer, Armand
**Director(s)** English, John
**Screenwriter(s)** Hall, Norman S.

**Cast** Autry, Gene; Champion; Davis, Gail; Hall, Thurston; Lauter, Harry; Curtis, Dick; Harvey, Harry; Barton, Gregg; Burnette, Smiley

**Song(s)** Whirlwind (C/L: Jones, Stan); As Long As I Have My Horse (C/L: Autry, Gene; Rose, Fred)

**Notes** Previously in the Republic picture GOLD MINE IN THE SKY but with additional credit to Johnny Marvin.

## 6789 ✦ THE WHISPERING SKULL
### PRC, 1944

**Producer(s)** Alexander, Arthur
**Director(s)** Clifton, Elmer
**Screenwriter(s)** Fraser, Harry

**Cast** Ritter, Tex; O'Brien, Dave; Wilkerson, Guy; Burke, Denny; Jolley, I. Stanford; Hall, Henry

**Song(s)** In Case You Change Your Mind, It's Never Too Late (C/L: Ritter, Tex; Harford, Frank)

**Notes** No cue sheet available.

## 6790 ✦ WHISPERING SMITH
### Paramount, 1948

**Producer(s)** Epstein, Mel
**Director(s)** Fenton, Leslie
**Screenwriter(s)** Butler, Frank; Lamb, Karl
**Source(s)** *Whispering Smith* (novel) Spearman, Frank H.

**Cast** Ladd, Alan; Preston, Robert; Marshall, Brenda; Crisp, Donald; Demarest, William; Holden, Fay; Faylen, Frank; Vye, Murvyn

**Song(s)** Laramie (C/L: Livingston, Jay; Evans, Ray)

## 6791 ✦ WHISPERING WINDS
### Tiffany–Stahl, 1929

**Musical Score** Rapee, Erno

**Director(s)** Flood, James
**Screenwriter(s)** Logue, Charles

**Cast** Miller, Patsy Ruth; Besserer, Eugenie; McGregor, Malcolm; Marcus, James; Southern, Eve

**Song(s)** When I Think of You (C: Tandler, H.J.; L: Kerr, Harry D.)

**Notes** No cue sheet available.

## 6792 ✦ WHITE CHRISTMAS
### Paramount, 1954

**Composer(s)** Berlin, Irving
**Lyricist(s)** Berlin, Irving
**Choreographer(s)** Alton, Robert

**Producer(s)** Dolan, Robert Emmett
**Director(s)** Curtiz, Michael
**Screenwriter(s)** Panama, Norman; Frank, Melvin; Krasna, Norman

**Cast** Crosby, Bing; Kaye, Danny; Brascia, John; Vera-Ellen [6]; Clooney, Rosemary; Jagger, Dean; Wickes, Mary; Chakiris, George; Sutton, Grady; Rumann, Sig; Whitfield, Anne; Chase, Barrie

**Song(s)** Santa Claus [3]; The Old Man [8]; The Best Things Happen When You're Dancing; Sisters; Snow; I'd Rather See a Minstrel Show; Count Your Blessings Instead of Sheep; Choreography; Love, You Didn't Do Right By Me; What Can You Do with a General [2]; Gee, I Wish I Was Back in the Army; A Crooner—a Comic [1]; A Man Chases a Girl [5] [7]; What Does a Soldier Want for Christmas [5]; Abraham [4]; Bells [5]; I've Got My Love to Keep Me Warm [5]

**Notes** There are also vocals of the Irving Berlin songs "White Christmas" (originally in HOLIDAY INN) and

"Mandy" (from stage revue ZIEGFELD FOLLIES OF 1919. Also in KID MILLIONS and THIS IS THE ARMY.). Brief renditions of "Heat Wave" "Let Me Sing and I'm Happy" and "Blue Skies" are also used in the production. Rosemary Clooney could not appear on the soundtrack album because of record company feuds so she was replaced on the album by Peggy Lee. [1] Not used. First written as "A Singer—A Dancer" when film was to star Crosby and Astaire. (Donald O'Connor replaced Astaire but he was later injured and was replaced in turn by Kaye). [2] Written in 1948 for show STARS ON MY SHOULDERS (unproduced). [3] Used instrumentally only. [4] This was presented instrumentally as a dance number for Vera-Ellen and Johnny Braschia. [5] Not used. [6] Dubbed by Trudy Stevens. [7] Used in THERE'S NO BUSINESS LIKE SHOW BUSINESS (20th). [8] Written in 1948.

### 6793 ✦ WHITE FANG
Twentieth Century–Fox, 1936

**Producer(s)**  Zanuck, Darryl F.
**Director(s)**  Butler, David
**Screenwriter(s)**  Long, Hal; Duncan, S.G.
**Source(s)**  "White Fang" (story) London, Jack

**Cast**  Whalen, Michael; Muir, Jean; Summerville, Slim; Winninger, Charles; Darwell, Jane; Carradine, John; Beck, Thomas

**Song(s)**  The Church Bells Are Ringing for Mary [1] (C/L: Colby, Elmer); Creole Belle [2] (C: Lampe, J. Bodewalt; L: Sidney, George)

**Notes**  [1] Not written for this picture. [2] Not used.

### 6794 ✦ WHITE HUNTER
Twentieth Century–Fox, 1936

**Composer(s)**  Treatt, C. Court
**Lyricist(s)**  Treatt, C. Court

**Producer(s)**  Zanuck, Darryl F.
**Director(s)**  Cummings, Irving
**Screenwriter(s)**  Duncan, Sam; Earl, Kenneth

**Cast**  Baxter, Warner; Lang, June; Patrick, Gail; Skipworth, Alison; Lawson, Wilfred; Hassell, George

**Song(s)**  Swahili Hunt Song [1] [2]; Swahili Laboring Song [1]; Swahili Lament (M'Ke Malea) [1]

**Notes**  [1] Based on traditional Swahili chants. [2] Also in SNOWS OF KILIMANJARO.

### 6795 ✦ WHITE LINE FEVER
Columbia, 1975

**Musical Score**  Nichtern, David

**Producer(s)**  Kemeny, John
**Director(s)**  Kaplan, Jonathan
**Screenwriter(s)**  Friedman, Ken; Kaplan, Jonathan

**Cast**  Vincent, Jan-Michael; Lenz, Kay; Pickens, Slim; Jones, L.Q.; Porter, Don; Laws, Sam; McGhee, Johnny Ray; Kove, Martin

**Song(s)**  Drifting and Dreaming of You (C/L: Nichtern, David)

### 6796 ✦ WHITE MISCHIEF
Columbia, 1988

**Musical Score**  Fenton, George

**Producer(s)**  Perry, Simon
**Director(s)**  Radford, Michael
**Screenwriter(s)**  Radford, Michael; Gems, Jonathan
**Source(s)**  *White Mischief* (book) Fox, James

**Cast**  Scacchi, Greta; Dance, Charles; Ackland, Joss; Miles, Sarah; Chaplin, Geraldine; McAnally, Ray; Head, Murray; Hurt, John; Howard, Trevor; Grant, Hugh

**Song(s)**  White Mischief (C/L: Finn, Tom)

**Notes**  No cue sheet available.

### 6797 ✦ WHITE NIGHTS
Columbia, 1985

**Musical Score**  Colombier, Michel

**Producer(s)**  Hackford, Taylor; Gilmore, William S.
**Director(s)**  Hackford, Taylor
**Screenwriter(s)**  Goldman, James

**Cast**  Baryshnikov, Mikhail; Hines, Gregory; Skolimowski, Jerzy; Mirren, Helen; Page, Geraldine; Rossellini, Isabella; Glover, John

**Song(s)**  My Love Is Chemical (C/L: Aldridge, Walt); People on a String (C: Colombier, Michel; L: Wakefield, Kathy); People Have Got to Move (C/L: Rodgers, Nile); The Other Side of the World (C/L: Rutherford, Michael; Robertson, B.A.); Separate Lives (C/L: Bishop, Stephen); Prove Me Wrong (C/L: Pack, David; Howard, James Newton); Snake Charmer (C/L: Hiatt, John); Far Post (C/L: Plant, Robert; Blunt, Robbie; Woodroffe, Jezz); This Is Your Day (C/L: Rodgers, Nile); Say You Say Me (C/L: Richie, Lionel)

### 6798 ✦ WHITE SHADOWS IN THE SOUTH SEAS
Metro–Goldwyn–Mayer, 1928

**Musical Score**  Axt, William

**Director(s)**  Van Dyke, W.S.
**Screenwriter(s)**  Doyle, Ray; Cunningham, Jack
**Source(s)**  *White Shadows in the South Seas* (book) O'Brien, Frederick

**Cast**  Blue, Monte; Torres, Raquel; Anderson, Robert

**Song(s)**  Flower of Love (C: Axt, William; Mendoza, David; L: Ruby, Herman)

**Notes**    Direction was begun by Robert Flaherty but he was replaced. This was MGM's first sound film—synchronized sound and music. The first time Leo the Lion roared!

## 6799  ◆  WHITE WATER SUMMER
### Columbia, 1987

**Musical Score**    Boddicker, Michael

**Producer(s)**    Tarlov, Mark
**Director(s)**    Bleckner, Jeff
**Screenwriter(s)**    Starr, Manya; Kinoy, Ernest

**Cast**    Astin, Sean; Bacon, Kevin; Bleckner, Jeff; Ward, Jonathan; Martel, K.C.; Siebert, Charles

**Song(s)**    Hot Shot (C/L: Slamer, Mike; Ward, Roy; Luttrelle, John); Restless Heart (C/L: Slamer, Mike; Boals, Mark); Paradise [1] (C/L: Adams, Kaylee; Mitchell, Charles); Be Good to Yourself (C/L: Perry, Steve; Cain, Jonathan; Schon, Neal)

**Notes**    [1] Also in LITTLE NIKITA.

## 6800  ◆  WHITE WOMAN
### Paramount, 1933

**Composer(s)**    Revel, Harry
**Lyricist(s)**    Gordon, Mack

**Director(s)**    Walker, Stuart
**Screenwriter(s)**    Hoffenstein, Samuel; Loring, Jane; Lehman, Gladys

**Cast**    Lombard, Carole [1]; Laughton, Charles; Taylor, Kent; Bickford, Charles; Kilbride, Percy; Bell, James; Lawrence, Marc; Middleton, Charles; Griffies, Ethel

**Song(s)**    He's a Cute Little Brute (A Gentleman and a Scholar) [2]; Yes, My Dear; Rice Pounder's Song (C: Chase, Newell; Arensma, John)

**Notes**    [1] Lombard recorded the songs but it was decided to dub her voice by Miss Lowe. [2] Written for SITTING PRETTY but not used.

## 6801  ◆  WHO DONE IT?
### United Artists, 1956

**Musical Score**    Green, Philip
**Composer(s)**    Green, Philip
**Lyricist(s)**    Newell, Norman

**Producer(s)**    Relph, Michael; Dearden, Basil
**Director(s)**    Relph, Michael; Dearden, Basil
**Screenwriter(s)**    Clarke, T.E.B.

**Cast**    Hill, Benny; Kossoff, David; Shaw, Denis; Schiller, Frederick; Margo, George

**Song(s)**    Who Done It (L: Stellman, Marcel); To Know You Is to Love You; It's a Golden Afternoon

**Notes**    A British film from Ealing Studios.

## 6802  ◆  WHO KILLED COCK ROBIN
### Disney, 1935

**Song(s)**    Somebody Rubbed Out My Robin [1] (C: Churchill, Frank E.; L: Morey, Larry); Who Killed Cock Robin (C: Churchill, Frank E.; L: Morey, Larry)

**Notes**    Cartoon short. No credit sheet available. [1] Not used.

## 6803  ◆  WHO KILLED GAIL PRESTON?
### Columbia, 1938

**Composer(s)**    Oakland, Ben
**Lyricist(s)**    Drake, Milton

**Producer(s)**    Cohn, Ralph
**Director(s)**    Barsha, Leon
**Screenwriter(s)**    Kent, Robert E.; Taylor, Henry

**Cast**    Terry, Don; Hayworth, Rita [1]; Paige, Robert; Cahoon, Wyn; Morgan, Gene; Lawrence, Marc

**Song(s)**    The Greatest Attraction in the World; Twelve O'Clock and All's Not Well

**Notes**    Originally titled MURDER IN SWINGTIME. [1] Dubbed by Gloria Randolph.

## 6804  ◆  WHOOPEE!
### United Artists, 1930

**Composer(s)**    Donaldson, Walter [1]
**Lyricist(s)**    Kahn, Gus [1]
**Choreographer(s)**    Berkeley, Busby [1]

**Producer(s)**    Ziegfeld, Florenz [1]; Goldwyn, Samuel
**Director(s)**    Freeland, Thornton
**Screenwriter(s)**    Conselman, William
**Source(s)**    *Whoopee!* (musical) Kahn, Gus; Donaldson, Walter; McGuire, William Anthony

**Cast**    Cantor, Eddie [1]; Grable, Betty; Hunt, Eleanor; Gregory, Paul; Rutherford, John; Shutta, Ethel [1]; Charters, Spencer; Hackett, Albert; George Olsen and His Orchestra [1]; Marsh, Marian [2]

**Song(s)**    Making Whoopee; Stetson; My Baby Just Cares for Me; A Girl Friend of a Boy Friend of Mine; I'll Still Belong to You (C: Brown, Nacio Herb; L: Eliscu, Edward); The Song of the Setting Sun; Mission Number; Makin' Waffles; Come West Little Girl Come West

**Notes**    No cue sheet available. This is a fascinating almost too-faithful rendition of the Broadway success. [1] Repeating Broadway assignments. [2] Billed as Marilyn Morgan.

## 6805  ◆  WHOSE LIFE IS IT ANYWAY?
### Metro–Goldwyn–Mayer, 1981

**Musical Score**    Rubinstein, Arthur B.

**Producer(s)**    Bachmann, Lawrence P.
**Director(s)**    Badham, John

**Screenwriter(s)**   Clark, Brian; Rose, Reginald
**Source(s)**   *Whose Life Is It Anyway?* (play) Clark, Brian

**Cast**   Dreyfuss, Richard; Cassavetes, John; Lahti, Christine; Balaban, Bob; McMillan, Kenneth; Hunter, Kaki

**Song(s)**   Hospital Ladies (C/L: Rubinstein, Arthur B.)

**Notes**   No cue sheet available.

## 6806 ✦ WHO'S GOT THE ACTION?
### Paramount, 1962

**Musical Score**   Duning, George

**Producer(s)**   Rose, Jack
**Director(s)**   Mann, Daniel
**Screenwriter(s)**   Rose, Jack
**Source(s)**   *Four Horse-Players Are Missing* (novel) Rose, Alexander

**Cast**   Martin, Dean; Turner, Lana; Albert, Eddie; Talbot, Nita; McGiver, John; Margo; Albertson, Jack; Glass, Ned

**Song(s)**   Who's Got the Action? [1] (C: Duning, George; L: Brooks, Jack)

## 6807 ✦ WHO'S THAT GIRL
### Warner Brothers, 1987

**Musical Score**   Bray, Stephen
**Composer(s)**   Madonna; Bray, Stephen
**Lyricist(s)**   Madonna; Bray, Stephen

**Producer(s)**   Heller, Rosilyn; Williams, Bernard
**Director(s)**   Foley, James
**Screenwriter(s)**   Smith, Andrew; Finkleman, Ken

**Cast**   Madonna; Dunne, Griffin; Mills, John; Morris, Haviland; McMartin, John

**Song(s)**   Causing a Commotion; Turn It Up (C/L: Davidson, Michael; Mercier, Frederic); Best Thing Ever (C/L: Garthside, Green; Gamson, David); Can't Stop; I Could Go For You in a Big Way (C/L: Fairweather, Brian); El Coco Loco (So So Bad) (C/L: Mundi, Coati); 24 Hours (C/L: Kessler, Mary; Wilson, Joey); Step By Step (C/L: King, Jay; Foster, Denzil; McElroy, Thomas; Agent, David); The Look of Love (C/L: Madonna; Leonard, Patrick); Who's That Girl

**Notes**   All background vocals. Some were from records.

## 6808 ✦ WHO WAS THAT LADY?
### Columbia, 1960

**Musical Score**   Previn, Andre

**Producer(s)**   Sidney, George
**Director(s)**   Sidney, George
**Screenwriter(s)**   Krasna, Norman
**Source(s)**   *Who Was That Lady I Saw You With?* (play) Krasna, Norman

**Cast**   Curtis, Tony; Martin, Dean; Leigh, Janet; Whitmore, James; Nichols, Barbara; McIntire, John; Keating, Larry; Storch, Larry; Oakland, Simon; Lansing, Joi; Pollard, Snub

**Song(s)**   Who Was That Lady? (C: Van Heusen, James; L: Cahn, Sammy); Your Smile [1] (C: Previn, Andre; Langdon, Dory)

**Notes**   [1] Sheet music only.

## 6809 ✦ WHY BE GOOD?
### Warner Brothers–First National, 1929

**Director(s)**   Seiter, William A.
**Screenwriter(s)**   Wilson, Carey

**Cast**   Moore, Colleen; Hamilton, Neil; Martindel, Edward; Rosing, Bodil; St. Polis, John; Natheaux, Louis

**Song(s)**   I'm Thirsty for Your Kisses, Hungry For Love (C: Coots, J. Fred; L: Davis, Benny)

**Notes**   No cue sheet available. Jean Harlow made her motion picture debut as an extra in this film.

## 6810 ✦ WHY BRING THAT UP?
### Paramount, 1929

**Composer(s)**   Whiting, Richard A.
**Lyricist(s)**   Coslow, Sam; Robin, Leo

**Director(s)**   Abbott, George
**Screenwriter(s)**   Abbott, George

**Cast**   Moran, George; Mack, Charles; Brent, Evelyn; Green, Harry; Swor, Bert; Wood, Freeman; Leslie, Lawrence; Lynch, Helen

**Song(s)**   That's Just My Way of Forgeting You (C: Henderson, Ray; L: Brown, Lew; DeSylva, B.G.); Follow the Swallow [3] (C: Henderson, Ray; L: Dixon, Mort; Rose, Billy); Do I Know What I'm Doing While I'm in Love; Shoo Shoo Boogie Boo; Silvery Moonlight (Only a Moonbeam Dream) [1] (C: Tiomkin, Dimitri; L: Robin, Leo); Early Birds [2] (C: Coslow, Sam)

**Notes**   Formerly titled BACKSTAGE BLUES. [1] Used instrumentally only. [2] Not used. [3] Not written for this picture.

## 6811 ✦ WHY GIRLS LEAVE HOME
### Producers Releasing Corporation, 1945

**Musical Score**   Green, Walter
**Composer(s)**   Livingston, Jay; Evans, Ray
**Lyricist(s)**   Livingston, Jay; Evans, Ray

**Producer(s)**   Sax, Sam
**Director(s)**   Berke, William
**Screenwriter(s)**   Lawrence, Fanya Foss; Ropes, Bradford

**Cast**   Blake, Pamela; Leonard, Sheldon

**Song(s)**   Cat and Canary; What Am I Saying; Honey Won't You Call Me

## 6812 ◆ WHY LEAVE HOME?
Fox, 1929

**Composer(s)**   Gottler, Archie; Conrad, Con
**Lyricist(s)**   Mitchell, Sidney D.; Conrad, Con

**Producer(s)**   Boylan, Malcolm Stuart
**Director(s)**   Cannon, Raymond
**Screenwriter(s)**   Catlett, Walter
**Source(s)**   *The Cradle Snatchers* (play) Carr, Robert S.

**Cast**   Carol, Sue; Lee, Dixie; Bary, Jean; Stuart, Nick; Keene, Richard; Catlett, Walter; Prouty, Jed; Hamilton, Laura

**Song(s)**   Look What You've Done to Me [3]; Doing the Boom Boom; Home Sweet Home; Maudita [2]; Old Soldiers Never Die [1]

**Notes**   A remake of THE CRADLE SNATCHERS (1927). [1] Conrad based his music on the tune of "Old Soldiers Never Die" (1920) by Jack Foley. Part of the melody also came from "Kind Words Can Never Die" (1855) by Howard Waters. This number was later used in RACKETY RAX and might have been used in ANNABELLE'S AFFAIRS. [2] Some sources list this number as BONITA. [3] Also in DOUBLE CROSS ROADS and FOX MOVIETONE FOLLIES OF 1929.

## 6813 ◆ WHY ROCK THE BOAT
Nu–Image, 1977

**Musical Score**   Howe, John
**Composer(s)**   Howe, John
**Lyricist(s)**   Howe, John

**Producer(s)**   Weintraub, William
**Director(s)**   Howe, John
**Screenwriter(s)**   Weintraub, William
**Source(s)**   (novel) Weintraub, William

**Cast**   Gillard, Stuart; James, Ken; Leek, Tiiu; Beckman, Henry

**Song(s)**   Time Stood Still; Perhaps This Time; Lament; Love Is; Things Have Changed; It's Wild; One Regret

**Notes**   No cue sheet available.

## 6814 ◆ WHY WOULD I LIE?
Metro–Goldwyn–Mayer, 1980

**Musical Score**   Fox, Charles

**Producer(s)**   Kohner, Pancho
**Director(s)**   Peerce, Larry
**Screenwriter(s)**   Stone, Peter
**Source(s)**   *The Fabricator* (novel) Hodges, Hollis

**Cast**   Williams, Treat; Eichorn, Lisa; Heldfond, Susan; Byrne, Anne; Curtin, Valerie; Brando, Jocelyn; Coster, Nicolas; Darden, Severn; Davis, Sonny; Swann, Gabriel

**Song(s)**   Me and You and You (C/L: Goodrum, Randy)

## 6815 ◆ WICKED
Fox, 1931

**Director(s)**   Dwan, Allan

**Cast**   Landi, Elissa; McLaglen, Victor; Merkel, Una; Busch, Mae; Von Eltz, Theodore; Dinehart, Alan; Apfel, Oscar; Rich, Irene

**Song(s)**   Mon Coeur Est Comme un Nid (C/L: Landi, Elissa)

**Notes**   No screenplay credit.

## 6816 ◆ THE WICKED DREAMS OF PAULA SCHULTZ
United Artists, 1967

**Musical Score**   Haskell, Jimmie

**Producer(s)**   Whytock, Grant
**Director(s)**   Marshall, George
**Screenwriter(s)**   Styler, Burt; Lewin, Albert; Perrin, Nat

**Cast**   Sommer, Elke; Crane, Bob; Klemperer, Werner; Forman, Joey; Banner, John; Askin, Leon; Arthur, Maureen

**Song(s)**   Wicked Dreams (C: Haskell, Jimmie; L: Kaye, Buddy)

## 6817 ◆ WICKED, WICKED
Metro–Goldwyn–Mayer, 1973

**Musical Score**   Springer, Phil
**Composer(s)**   Springer, Phil
**Lyricist(s)**   Levine, Irwin

**Producer(s)**   Bare, Richard
**Director(s)**   Bare, Richard
**Screenwriter(s)**   Bare, Richard

**Cast**   Bailey, David; Roberts, Randolph; Bolling, Tiffany; Brady, Scott; Byrnes, Edward; McBain, Diane; Bowen, Roger; Sherwood, Madeleine; Danks, Indira; O'Connell, Arthur

**Song(s)**   Wicked, Wicked; I'll Be Myself

**Notes**   This film introduced Duo-Vision. The title read: "Simultaneous action through the use of a double screen . . . An experience that will challenge your imagination."

## 6818 ◆ A WICKED WOMAN (1934)
Metro–Goldwyn–Mayer, 1934

**Musical Score**   Axt, William
**Composer(s)**   Lane, Burton
**Lyricist(s)**   Adamson, Harold

**Producer(s)**   Rapf, Harry
**Director(s)**   Brabin, Charles R.
**Screenwriter(s)**   Ryerson, Florence; Sears, Zelda
**Source(s)**   (novel) Austin, Anne

**Cast** Christians, Mady; Parker, Jean; Bickford, Charles; Furness, Betty; Henry, William; Searl, Jackie; Taylor, Robert; Holloway, Sterling; Harvey, Paul; Sears, Zelda

**Song(s)** In Louisiana; In the Hash in the Stew

## 6819 ◆ WICKED WOMAN (1953)
United Artists, 1953

**Musical Score** Baker, Buddy

**Producer(s)** Greene, Clarence
**Director(s)** Rouse, Russell
**Screenwriter(s)** Rouse, Russell; Greene, Clarence

**Cast** Michaels, Beverly; Egan, Robert; Scott, Evelyn; Helton, Percy; Osterlob, Robert

**Song(s)** Wicked Woman (C: Baker, Buddy; L: Mullendore, Joseph); One Night in Acapulco [1] (C: Baker, Buddy; L: Mullendore, Joseph)

**Notes** [1] Used instrumentally only.

## 6820 ◆ WIFE, HUSBAND AND FRIEND
Twentieth Century–Fox, 1939

**Composer(s)** Pokrass, Sam
**Lyricist(s)** Hauser, Armand

**Producer(s)** Zanuck, Darryl F.
**Director(s)** Ratoff, Gregory
**Screenwriter(s)** Johnson, Nunnally
**Source(s)** *Career in C Major* (novel) Cain, James M.

**Cast** Young, Loretta; Baxter, Warner; Barnes, Binnie; Romero, Cesar; Barbier, George; Bromberg, J. Edward; Pallette, Eugene; Westley, Helen; Terry, Ruth; Dearing, Dorothy

**Song(s)** Pokrass Opera Sequence; Drink from the Cup of Tomorrow [1] (L: Bullock, Walter)

**Notes** Pokrass' opera was titled "Arlesiana." "Beyond the Blue Horizon" by Richard A. Whiting and W. Franke Harling was also used. [1] Walter Bullock not credited on cue sheet.

## 6821 ◆ THE WILBY CONSPIRACY
United Artists, 1975

**Musical Score** Myers, Stanley

**Producer(s)** Baum, Martin
**Director(s)** Nelson, Ralph
**Screenwriter(s)** Amateau, Rod; Nebenzal, Harold
**Source(s)** (novel) Driscoll, Peter

**Cast** Caine, Michael; Poitier, Sidney; Williamson, Nicol; Gee, Prunella

**Song(s)** Geliefde Man (C: Myers, Stanley; L: Taylor, Jeremy); All the Wishing in the World (C: Myers, Stanley; L: Black, Don)

## 6822 ◆ THE WILD AND THE INNOCENT
Universal, 1959

**Musical Score** Salter, Hans J.

**Producer(s)** Gomberg, Sy
**Director(s)** Sher, Jack
**Screenwriter(s)** Gomberg, Sy; Sher, Jack

**Cast** Murphy, Audie; Dee, Sandra; Dru, Joanne; Roland, Gilbert; Backus, Jim; Mitchell, George; Martin, Strother

**Song(s)** A Touch of Pink (C/L: Lampert, Diane; Loring, Richard)

## 6823 ◆ WILD AND WOOLLY
Twentieth Century–Fox, 1937

**Producer(s)** Stone, John
**Director(s)** Werker, Alfred
**Screenwriter(s)** Root, Lynn; Fenton, Frank

**Cast** Withers, Jane; Brennan, Walter; Moore, Pauline; Switzer, Carl "Alfalfa"; Searl, Jackie; Churchill, Berton; Chaney Jr., Lon

**Song(s)** Whoa Whoopee—Whoa Whippee (C: Akst, Harry; L: Clare, Sidney); When Did You Leave Heaven? [1] (C: Whiting, Richard A.; L: Bullock, Walter)

**Notes** [1] Also in SING BABY SING.

## 6824 ◆ WILD BILL HICKOK RIDES
Warner Brothers, 1942

**Musical Score** Steiner, Max; Jackson, Howard

**Producer(s)** Grainger, Edmund
**Director(s)** Enright, Ray
**Screenwriter(s)** Grayson, Charles; Smith, Paul Gerard; Schrock, Raymond

**Cast** Cabot, Bruce; Bennett, Constance; William, Warren; Bond, Ward; Brewer, Betty; Simpson, Russell; Wilcox, Frank; Da Silva, Howard; Bardette, Trevor; Emerson, Faye

**Song(s)** The Lady Got a Shady Deal (C: Jerome, M.K.; L: Newman, Charles)

## 6825 ◆ THE WILD BLUE YONDER
Republic, 1951

**Musical Score** Young, Victor

**Director(s)** Dwan, Allan
**Screenwriter(s)** Tregaskis, Richard

**Cast** Corey, Wendell; Ralston, Vera Hruba; Tucker, Forrest; Harris, Phil; Brennan, Walter

**Song(s)** The Thing (C/L: Grean, Charles R.); The Man Behind the Armor-Plated Desk (C: Traditional; L:

Dwan, Allan); The Heavy Bomber Song [1] (C: Young, Victor; L: Washington, Ned)

**Notes**   [1] Used instrumentally only.

## 6826 ✦ THE WILDCAT OF TUCSON
### Columbia, 1940

**Composer(s)**   Drake, Milton
**Lyricist(s)**   Drake, Milton

**Director(s)**   Hillyer, Lambert
**Screenwriter(s)**   Myton, Fred

**Cast**   Elliott, Bill; Young, Evelyn; Taylor, Dub; Brown, Stanley

**Song(s)**   Wild Bill; Looking Out Looking In

## 6827 ✦ WILDCATS
### Warner Brothers, 1986

**Composer(s)**   Wolinski, Hawk; Howard, James Newton
**Lyricist(s)**   Wolinski, Hawk; Howard, James Newton

**Producer(s)**   Sylbert, Anthea
**Director(s)**   Ritchie, Michael
**Screenwriter(s)**   Sacks, Ezra

**Cast**   Hawn, Goldie; Kurtz, Swoosie; Lively, Robyn; Gold, Brandy; Keach, James; Russell, Nipsey

**Song(s)**   Rock It; Penetration; Love Lies Alone; Razzle Dazzle; Sport of Kings (C/L: Smith, James Todd); Don't Wanna Be Normal (C/L: Leonard, Patrick; Wolinski, Hawk; Howard, James Newton; Pack, David; McDonald, Michael); Old Timer's Rap (C/L: Smith, James Todd); We Stand Alone (C/L: Wolinski, Hawk; Howard, James Newton; Cocker, Joe); Show Me How It Works (C/L: Wolinski, Hawk; Howard, James Newton; Pack, David); Good Hands; The First Game [1]; Hard to Say (C/L: Wolinski, Hawk; Howard, James Newton; Pack, David); Wildcats Football Rap [1] (C/L: Smith, James Todd; Ritchie, Michael; Snipes, Wesley; Thacker, Tab)

**Notes**   [1] Visual vocal. All others background vocals.

## 6828 ✦ WILD COMPANY
### Fox, 1930

**Producer(s)**   Rockett, Al
**Director(s)**   McCarey, Leo
**Screenwriter(s)**   King, Bradley
**Source(s)**   "Soft Shoulders" (story) Hurn, Philip

**Cast**   Albertson, Frank; Warner, H.B.; Lynn, Sharon; Compton, Joyce; McDowell, Claire; Lugosi, Bela

**Song(s)**   That's What I Like About You [1] (C: Monaco, James V.; L: Friend, Cliff); Joe! (C: Conrad, Con; L: Meskill, Jack)

**Notes**   [1] This song was registered for copyright under the film name ROADHOUSE. Fox produced a film of that name in 1928 though the registration was in 1930. ROADHOUSE might have been a working title for this film.

## 6829 ✦ THE WILDERNESS FAMILY, PART 2
### Pacific International, 1979

**Producer(s)**   Dubs, Arthur R.
**Director(s)**   Zuniga, Frank
**Screenwriter(s)**   Dubs, Arthur R.

**Cast**   Logan, Robert; Damante Shaw, Susan; Rattray, Heather

**Song(s)**   Snowflakes (C: Lackey, Douglas; Kauer, Gene; L: Bachman, Dennis)

**Notes**   No cue sheet available.

## 6830 ✦ WILD GEESE
### Allied Artists, 1978

**Musical Score**   Budd, Roy

**Producer(s)**   Lloyd, Euan
**Director(s)**   McLaglen, Andrew V.
**Screenwriter(s)**   Rose, Reginald
**Source(s)**   *Wild Geese* (novel) Carney, Daniel

**Cast**   Burton, Richard; Moore, Roger; Harris, Richard; Kruger, Hardy; Granger, Stewart; Watson, Jack; Ntshona, Winston; Kani, John

**Song(s)**   Flight of the Wild Geese (C/L: Armatrading, Joan)

**Notes**   No cue sheet available.

## 6831 ✦ WILD GEESE CALLING
### Twentieth Century–Fox, 1941

**Producer(s)**   Brown, Harry Joe
**Director(s)**   Brahm, John
**Screenwriter(s)**   McCoy, Horace
**Source(s)**   (novel) White, Stewart Edward

**Cast**   Fonda, Henry; Bennett, Joan; William, Warren; Munson, Ona; MacLane, Barton; Simpson, Russell; Adrian, Iris; Andrews, Stanley; Keane, Robert Emmett; Middleton, Charles

**Song(s)**   I've Taken a Fancy to You [1] (C: Pollack, Lew; L: Clare, Sidney)

**Notes**   [1] Also in FRONTIER MARSHALL (1939) and IN OLD CHICAGO.

## 6832 ✦ WILD GOLD
### Fox, 1934

**Composer(s)**   Gorney, Jay
**Lyricist(s)**   Clare, Sidney

**Producer(s)**    Wurtzel, Sol M.
**Director(s)**    Marshall, George
**Screenwriter(s)**    Cole, Lester; Johnson, Henry

**Cast**    Boles, John; Trevor, Claire; Green, Harry; Owsley, Monroe

**Song(s)**    I've Got You on the Top of My List [2]; Cute Little Rumba Rum-Ti-Di-Um-Ba Bay; She Is Fair and Lovely [1] (C/L: Boles, John)

**Notes**    [1] Only five bars long. [2] Also in BABY TAKE A BOW.

## 6833  ◆  WILD HARVEST
### Paramount, 1947

**Producer(s)**    Fellows, Robert
**Director(s)**    Garnett, Tay
**Screenwriter(s)**    Monks Jr., John

**Cast**    Lamour, Dorothy; Ladd, Alan; Preston, Robert; Nolan, Lloyd; Erdman, Richard; Jenkins, Allen; Sully, Frank

**Song(s)**    Money in My Clothes [1] (C: Fain, Sammy; Kahal, Irving)

**Notes**    Formerly titled THE BIG HAIRCUT. [1] Not written for the picture.

## 6834  ◆  WILD HORSE MESA
### RKO, 1947

**Musical Score**    Sawtell, Paul; Webb, Roy
**Composer(s)**    Sawtell, Paul
**Lyricist(s)**    Sawtell, Paul

**Producer(s)**    Schlom, Herman
**Director(s)**    Grissell, Wallace A.
**Screenwriter(s)**    Houston, Norman
**Source(s)**    *Wild Horse Mesa* (novel) Grey, Zane

**Cast**    Holt, Tim; Leslie, Nan; Martin, Richard; Powers, Richard; Robards, Jason; Barrett, Tony; Woods, Harry

**Song(s)**    Bonita Lolita Malone; Moon Is Low

## 6835  ◆  WILD HORSE RODEO
### Republic, 1937

**Producer(s)**    Siegel, Sol C.
**Director(s)**    Sherman, George
**Screenwriter(s)**    Drake, Oliver; Wright, Gilbert

**Cast**    Livingston, Bob; Corrigan, Ray; Terhune, Max; Martel, June; Miller, Walter; Snowflake

**Song(s)**    Ridin' High (C/L: Allan, Fleming); My Madonna of the Trail (C/L: Spencer, Leo; Spencer, Glenn); When the Round-Up Days Are Over [1] (C/L: Allan, Fleming)

**Notes**    [1] Sheet music only.

## 6836  ◆  WILD IN THE COUNTRY
### Twentieth Century–Fox, 1961

**Musical Score**    Hopkins, Kenyon
**Composer(s)**    Weisman, Ben
**Lyricist(s)**    Wise, Fred

**Producer(s)**    Wald, Jerry
**Director(s)**    Dunne, Philip
**Screenwriter(s)**    Odets, Clifford
**Source(s)**    *The Lost Country* (novel) Salamanca, J.R.

**Cast**    Presley, Elvis; Lange, Hope; Weld, Tuesday; Perkins, Millie; Johnson, Rafer; Ireland, John; Lockwood, Gary; Crawford, Christina

**Song(s)**    Wild in the Country (C: Weiss, George David; L: Peretti, Hugo; Creatore, Luigi); I Slipped, I Stumbled, I Fell; In My Way

## 6837  ◆  WILD IN THE STREETS
### American International, 1968

**Composer(s)**    Mann, Barry; Weil, Cynthia
**Lyricist(s)**    Mann, Barry; Weil, Cynthia

**Producer(s)**    Nicholson, James H.; Arkoff, Samuel Z.
**Director(s)**    Shear, Barry
**Screenwriter(s)**    Thom, Robert

**Cast**    Winters, Shelley; Jones, Christopher; Varsi, Diane; Holbrook, Hal; Perkins, Millie; Pryor, Richard; Freed, Bert

**Song(s)**    The Shape of Things to Come; Fifty-Two Per Cent; Listen to the Music; Sally LeRoy; Fourteen or Fight

**Notes**    No cue sheet available.

## 6838  ◆  WILD IS THE WIND
### Paramount, 1957

**Musical Score**    Tiomkin, Dimitri

**Producer(s)**    Wallis, Hal B.
**Director(s)**    Cukor, George
**Screenwriter(s)**    Schulman, Arnold
**Source(s)**    (story) Novarese, Vittorio Nino

**Cast**    Magnani, Anna; Quinn, Anthony; Franciosa, Anthony; Hart, Dolores; Calleia, Joseph; Valenty, Lily

**Song(s)**    Wild Is the Wind (C: Tiomkin, Dimitri; L: Washington, Ned); Scapricciatiello (C/L: Albano, Fernando; Vento, Pacifico)

## 6839  ◆  THE WILD NORTH
### Metro–Goldwyn–Mayer, 1951

**Musical Score**    Kaper, Bronislau
**Composer(s)**    Traditional
**Lyricist(s)**    Wolcott, Charles

**Producer(s)** Ames, Stephen
**Director(s)** Marton, Andrew
**Screenwriter(s)** Fenton, Frank

**Cast** Granger, Stewart; Corey, Wendell; Charisse, Cyd

**Song(s)** Winter Comes, Winter Goes; Northern Lights

## 6840 ✦ WILD ON THE BEACH
### Twentieth Century–Fox, 1965

**Musical Score** Haskell, Jimmie
**Composer(s)** Beverly, Bobby
**Lyricist(s)** Dunham, "By"

**Producer(s)** Dexter, Maury
**Director(s)** Dexter, Maury
**Screenwriter(s)** Spaulding, Harry

**Cast** Randall, Frankie; Jackson, Sherry; Jackie and Gayle; The Astronauts; Sonny and Cher; Malone, Cindy; Nelson, Sandy

**Song(s)** House on the Beach; It's Gonna Rain (C/L: Bono, Sonny); Run Away from Him; The Gods of Love; Yellow Haired Woman (C: Davis, Elaine); Pyramid Stomp (C: Haskell, Jimmie); Little Speedy Gonzales (L: Koss, Stan)

## 6841 ✦ THE WILD PARTY (1929)
### Paramount, 1929

**Director(s)** Arzner, Dorothy
**Screenwriter(s)** Sheldon, E. Lloyd

**Cast** Bow, Clara; March, Fredric; Oakie, Jack; Holmes, Phillips; Day, Marceline; Compton, Joyce

**Song(s)** My Wild Party Girl (C: Whiting, Richard A.; L: Robin, Leo)

## 6842 ✦ THE WILD PARTY (1976)
### American International, 1976

**Musical Score** Rosenthal, Laurence
**Composer(s)** Marks, Walter
**Lyricist(s)** Marks, Walter

**Producer(s)** Merchant, Ismail
**Director(s)** Ivory, James
**Screenwriter(s)** Marks, Walter
**Source(s)** (poem) March, Joseph Moncure

**Cast** Coco, James; King, Perry; Bolling, Tiffany; Dano, Royal; Dukes, David; Dietrich, Dena; Lewis, Bobo; Small, Marya; Welch, Raquel; Lawrence, Eddie

**Song(s)** The Wild Party; Queenie; Funny Man; Herbert Hoover Drag; Singapore Sally; Ain't Nothin' Bad About Feeling Good; Sunday Morning Blues

**Notes** No cue sheet available.

## 6843 ✦ WILD ROVERS
### Metro–Goldwyn–Mayer, 1971

**Musical Score** Goldsmith, Jerry

**Producer(s)** Edwards, Blake; Wales, Ken
**Director(s)** Edwards, Blake
**Screenwriter(s)** Edwards, Blake

**Cast** Holden, William; O'Neal, Ryan; Malden, Karl; Carlin, Lynn; Skerritt, Tom; Baker, Joe Don; French, Victor; Gunn, Moses; Roberts, Rachel; Carney, Alan

**Song(s)** The Melancholy Cowboy (C: Gelman, Harold; L: Traditional); Ballad of the Wild Rovers (C/L: Edwards, Blake; Andrews, Julie)

## 6844 ✦ THE WILD SEED
### Universal, 1964

**Musical Score** Markowitz, Richard

**Producer(s)** Ruddy, Albert S.
**Director(s)** Hutton, Brian G.
**Screenwriter(s)** Pine, Lester

**Cast** Parks, Michael; Kaye, Celia; Elliott, Ross; Chambliss, Woodrow

**Song(s)** That's Why (C: Markowitz, Richard; L: Markowitz, Richard; Ruddy, Albert S.; Hutton, Bryan)

**Notes** Originally titled FARGO.

## 6845 ✦ WILD WEST
### PRC, 1946

**Musical Score** Hajos, Karl
**Composer(s)** Rosoff, Charles; Cochran, Dorcas
**Lyricist(s)** Rosoff, Charles; Cochran, Dorcas

**Producer(s)** Tansey, Robert Emmett
**Director(s)** Tansey, Robert Emmett
**Screenwriter(s)** Kavanaugh, Frances

**Cast** Dean, Eddie; Ates, Roscoe; LaRue, Al "Lash"; Henry, Robert "Buzz"; Padden, Sarah

**Song(s)** Ride on the Tide of a Song [1]; Journey's End [1]; I Can Tell by the Stars; Elmer the Knock-Kneed Cowboy (C/L: Dean, Eddie; Herscher, Louis; Herscher, Ruth)

**Notes** [1] Also in PRAIRIE OUTLAWS (Eagle-Lion).

## 6846 ✦ THE WILD WESTERNERS
### Columbia, 1962

**Musical Score** DiMaggio, Ross

**Producer(s)** Katzman, Sam
**Director(s)** Rudolph, Oscar
**Screenwriter(s)** Adams, Gerald Drayson

**Cast** Philbrook, James; Kovack, Nancy; Eddy, Duane; Mitchell, Guy; Sanders, Hugh

**Song(s)** The Wild Westerners (C/L: Eddy, Duane; Hazlewood, Lee)

**Notes** No cue sheet available.

## 6847 ✦ WILD, WILD WINTER
Universal, 1965

**Musical Score** Long, Jerry
**Composer(s)** Capps, Al; Dean, Mary
**Lyricist(s)** Capps, Al; Dean, Mary

**Producer(s)** Patton, Bruce
**Director(s)** Weinrib, Lennie
**Screenwriter(s)** Malcolm, David

**Cast** Dick and Dee; Jay and the Americans; The Beau Brummels; Clarke, Gary; Noel, Chris; Edmonds, Don; Kaye, Suzie; Brown Jr., Les

**Song(s)** Our Love's Gonna Snowball; Just Wait and See (C/L: Elliott, Ron); Change of Heart (C/L: Pipkin, Chester; Gordon, Marc); Heartbeats; Two of a Kind (C/L: Bruno, Tony; Millrose, Victor); Wild Wild Winter [1] (C/L: Pipkin, Chester)

**Notes** [1] Used instrumentally only.

## 6848 ✦ WILLIE AND JOE IN BACK AT THE FRONT
Universal, 1952

**Musical Score** Mancini, Henry

**Producer(s)** Goldstein, Leonard
**Director(s)** Sherman, George
**Screenwriter(s)** Breslow, Lou; McGuire, Don; Brodney, Oscar
**Source(s)** "Willie and Joe" (cartoon) Mauldin, Bill

**Cast** Ewell, Tom; Lembeck, Harvey; Blanchard, Mari; Kelley, Barry; Long, Richard

**Song(s)** Bounce Me Brother with a Solid Four [1] (C: Prince, Hughie; L: Raye, Don)

**Notes** Also referred to as BACK TO THE FRONT. [1] Also in BUCK PRIVATES (1941) and ONE EXCITING WEEK (Republic).

## 6849 ✦ WILLIE DYNAMITE
Universal, 1973

**Musical Score** Johnson, J.J.

**Producer(s)** Zanuck, Richard D.; Brown, David
**Director(s)** Moses, Gilbert
**Screenwriter(s)** Cutler, Ron; Keyes Jr., Joe

**Cast** Orman, Roscoe; Walker, Joyce; Robinson, Robert; Donaldson, Norma; Sands, Diana; Rasulala, Thalmus; Wallace, Royce

**Song(s)** Willie D (C: Johnson, J.J.; Moses, Gilbert; L: Moses, Gilbert); King Midas (C/L: Moses, Gilbert); Keep on Movin' On (C/L: Moses, Gilbert)

## 6850 ✦ WILL PENNY
Paramount, 1967

**Musical Score** Raksin, David

**Producer(s)** Engel, Fred; Seltzer, Walter
**Director(s)** Gries, Tom
**Screenwriter(s)** Gries, Tom

**Cast** Heston, Charlton; Hackett, Joan; Pleasence, Donald; Majors, Lee; Dern, Bruce; Johnson, Ben; Pickens, Slim; James, Clifton; Zerbe, Anthony; Schallert, William; Francis, Jon

**Song(s)** Lonely Rider [1] (C: Raksin, David; L: Wells, Robert)

**Notes** [1] Used as background vocal only.

## 6851 ✦ WILL SUCCESS SPOIL ROCK HUNTER
Twentieth Century–Fox, 1957

**Producer(s)** Tashlin, Frank
**Director(s)** Tashlin, Frank
**Screenwriter(s)** Tashlin, Frank
**Source(s)** *Will Success Spoil Rock Hunter* (play) Axelrod, George

**Cast** Mansfield, Jayne; Randall, Tony; Drake, Betsy; Blondell, Joan; Williams, John; Hargitay, Mickey; Whittinghill, Dick

**Song(s)** You Got It Made (C/L: Troup, Bobby)

## 6852 ✦ WILLY
ABA Productions, 1963

**Musical Score** Carras, Nicholas

**Producer(s)** Buckhantz, Allan A.
**Director(s)** Buckhantz, Allan A.
**Screenwriter(s)** Rudorf, Guenter

**Cast** Persicke, Robert; Schroth, Hannelore; Schultze-Westrum, Edith

**Song(s)** Willy (C: Carras, Nicholas; L: Marlow, Ric)

**Notes** No cue sheet available.

## 6853 ✦ WILLY WONKA AND THE CHOCOLATE FACTORY
Paramount, 1971

**Musical Score** Scharf, Walter
**Composer(s)** Newley, Anthony; Bricusse, Leslie
**Lyricist(s)** Newley, Anthony; Bricusse, Leslie
**Choreographer(s)** Jeffrey, Howard

**Producer(s)** Margulies, Stan; Wolper, David L.
**Director(s)** Stuart, Mel
**Screenwriter(s)** Dahl, Roald
**Source(s)** "Charlie and the Chocolate Factory" (story) Dahl, Roald

**Cast** Wilder, Gene; Albertson, Jack; Ostrum, Peter; Kinnear, Roy; Cole, Julie Dawn; Stone, Leonard; Sowle, Diana [1]

**Song(s)** Candy Man; Cheer Up, Charlie; I've Got a Golden Ticket; Pure Imagination; Oompa-loompa-doompa-dee-doo; I Want It Now

**Notes** [1] Dubbed by Diana Lee.

---

**6854 ✦ THE WIND**
Metro–Goldwyn–Mayer, 1928

**Director(s)** Seastrom, Victor
**Screenwriter(s)** Marion, Frances
**Source(s)** The Wind by Scarborough, Dorothy

**Cast** Gish, Lillian; Hanson, Lars; Love, Montagu; Cumming, Dorothy; Earle, Edward; Orlamond, William; Ramon, Leon

**Song(s)** Love Brought the Sunshine (C: Axt, William; Mendoza, David; L: Dreyer, Dave; Ruby, Herman)

**Notes** No cue sheet available.

---

**6855 ✦ WIND ACROSS THE EVERGLADES**
Warner Brothers, 1958

**Musical Score** Sawtell, Paul; Shefter, Bert

**Producer(s)** Schulberg, Stuart
**Director(s)** Ray, Nicholas
**Screenwriter(s)** Schulberg, Budd
**Source(s)** "Across the Everglades" (story) Schulberg, Budd

**Cast** Ives, Burl; Plummer, Christopher; Lee, Gypsy Rose; Voskovec, George; Galento, Tony; Smith, Howard I.; Kelly, Emmett; Henning, Pat; Falk, Peter; Kantor, MacKinlay; Eden, Chana

**Song(s)** Empty Pocket Blues (C/L: Schulberg, Budd); Kissin' 'n Killin' (C: Brown, Toch; L: Ives, Burl); Lonely Boy Blues (C/L: Beachum, Rufus; Schulberg, Budd; Ray, Nicholas); Lostman's River (C/L: Brown, Toch); Shear 'Em Sheep, Shear 'Em (C/L: Brown, Toch)

---

**6856 ✦ WIND IN THE WILLOWS**
Disney, 1949

**Musical Score** Wallace, Oliver
**Composer(s)** Churchill, Frank E.
**Lyricist(s)** Morey, Larry

**Producer(s)** Sharpsteen, Ben
**Director(s)** Kinney, Jack; Geronimi, Clyde; Algar, James
**Screenwriter(s)** Penner, Erdman; Hibler, Winston; Rinaldi, Joe; Sears, Ted; Brightman, Homer; Reeves, Harry
**Source(s)** "The Story of Mr. Toad" (story) Grahame, Kenneth

**Voices** Rathbone, Basil; Blore, Eric; O'Malley, Pat; Ployardt, John; Campbell, Colin; Grant, Campbell; Allister, Claud

**Directing Animator(s)** Thomas, Franklin; Johnston, Ollie; Reitherman, Wolfgang; Kahl, Milt; Lounsbery, John; Kimball, Ward

**Song(s)** The Merrily Song (C: Churchill, Frank E.; Wolcott, Charles; L: Morey, Larry; Gilbert, Ray); Be a Stout Fellow [1]; The Bells of St. Bartholomew [1]; Galloping On Our Way [1]; Merry, Merry (Christmas Carol) [1] (C: Wolcott, Charles; L: Traditional); Tea-Time at Four O'Clock [1]; Wind in the Willows [1] (C: Wolcott, Charles; L: Gilbert, Ray)

**Notes** Animated cartoon. Part of THE ADVENTURES OF ICHABOD AND MR. TOAD. See also THE LEGEND OF SLEEPY HOLLOW. [1] Not used.

---

**6857 ✦ A WINDOW TO THE SKY**

See THE OTHER SIDE OF THE MOUNTAIN.

---

**6858 ✦ WINDY CITY**
Warner Brothers, 1984

**Musical Score** Nitzsche, Jack

**Producer(s)** Greisman, Alan
**Director(s)** Bernstein, Armyan
**Screenwriter(s)** Bernstein, Armyan

**Cast** Shea, John; Capshaw, Kate; Mostel, Josh; DeMunn, Jeffrey

**Song(s)** Hit and Run Lovers (C: Nitzsche, Jack; L: Sainte-Marie, Buffy)

**Notes** No cue sheet available.

---

**6859 ✦ WINGED VICTORY**
Twentieth Century–Fox, 1944

**Producer(s)** Zanuck, Darryl F.
**Director(s)** Cukor, George
**Screenwriter(s)** Hart, Moss
**Source(s)** *Winged Victory* (play) Hart, Moss

**Cast** McCallister, Lon; Crain, Jeanne; O'Brien, Edmond; Ball, Jane; Daniels, Mark; Dennison, Jo-Carroll; Taylor, Don; Holliday, Judy; Cobb, Lee J.; Hayes, Peter Lind; Buttons, Red; Nelson, Barry; Hultman, Sgt. Rune

**Song(s)** Gee Mom, I Want to Go Home (I Don't Want No More Army Life) (C/L: Kackley, Charlotte); Washout Blues (C/L: Rose, David); Wait for Me Mary (C/L: Tobias, Charles; Simon, Nat; Tobias, Harry); Pennsylvania Polka (C/L: Lee, Lester; Manners, Zeke); You're So Sweet to Remember [1] (C: Rose, David; L: Robin, Leo)

**Notes** It is not known if any of the above were written for this film. There are also other short vocals. [1] Sheet music only.

## 6860 ◆ WINGS
Paramount, 1929

**Musical Score** Zamecnik, J.S.

**Producer(s)** Hubbard, Lucien
**Director(s)** Wellman, William A.
**Screenwriter(s)** Loring, Hope; Lighton, Louis D.; Johnson, Julian

**Cast** Cooper, Gary; Bow, Clara; Rogers, Charles "Buddy"; Arlen, Richard; Ralston, Jobyna; Marchal, Arlette; Brendel, El; Smith, Gunboat; Tucker, Richard; Gordon, Julia Swayne; Walthall, Henry B.; Hopper, Hedda; Irving, George; De Brulier, Nigel

**Song(s)** Wings (C: Zamecnik, J.S.; L: Macdonald, Ballard)

**Notes** No cue sheet available. This is a silent picture with sound effects and a musical score.

## 6861 ◆ WINGS OF ADVENTURE
Tiffany, 1930

**Director(s)** Thorpe, Richard
**Screenwriter(s)** Fraser, Harry

**Cast** Lease. Rex; Armida; Cook, Clyde

**Notes** No cue sheet available.

## 6862 ◆ THE WINGS OF EAGLES
Metro–Goldwyn–Mayer, 1957

**Musical Score** Alexander, Jeff

**Producer(s)** Schnee, Charles
**Director(s)** Ford, John
**Screenwriter(s)** Fenton, Frank; Haines, William Wister
**Source(s)** life and writings by Wead, Frank W. "Spig"

**Cast** Wayne, John; Dailey, Dan; O'Hara, Maureen; Bond, Ward; Curtis, Ken; Lowe, Edmund; Tobey, Kenneth; Todd, James; Rumann, Sig; Jordan, Dorothy; McCrea, Jody; Marsh, Mae; McAvoy, May; Heydt, Louis Jean

**Song(s)** The Wings of Eagles [1] (C: Alexander, Jeff; L: Brooks, Jack); I'm Gonna Move that Toe (C/L: Dailey, Dan)

**Notes** [1] Used instrumentally only.

## 6863 ◆ WINGS OF THE NAVY
Warner Brothers, 1939

**Song(s)** Wings Over the Navy (C: Warren, Harry; L: Mercer, Johnny)

**Notes** No cue sheet available.

## 6864 ◆ WINNERS TAKE ALL
Apollo, 1987

**Musical Score** Timm, Doug
**Composer(s)** Richards, Deke; Martin Jr., Tony
**Lyricist(s)** Richards, Deke; Martin Jr., Tony

**Producer(s)** Knight, Christopher W.; Tatum, Tom
**Director(s)** Kiersch, Fritz
**Screenwriter(s)** Turner, Ed

**Cast** Paul, Don Michael; York, Kathleen; Krantz, Robert; Richter, Deborah; DeLuise, Peter

**Song(s)** Don't Look Back (C/L: Timm, Doug; Peterson, Randy); The Long Ride; Ladykiller; Love or Illusion (C/L: Richards, Deke; Lussier, Chris); When Your Old Man's Gone (C/L: Rubenhold, Leon); Skydance

**Notes** No cue sheet available.

## 6865 ◆ WINNIE THE POOH AND THE BLUSTERY DAY
Disney, 1967

**Musical Score** Baker, Buddy
**Composer(s)** Sherman, Richard M.; Sherman, Robert B.
**Lyricist(s)** Sherman, Richard M.; Sherman, Robert B.

**Director(s)** Reitherman, Wolfgang
**Screenwriter(s)** Clemmons, Larry; Wright, Ralph; Svendsen, Julius; Gerry, Vance
**Source(s)** Winnie the Pooh stories (stories) Milne, A.A.
**Voices** Cabot, Sebastian; Holloway, Sterling; Walmsley, Jon; Fiedler, John; Smith, Hal; Matthews, Junius; Luddy, Barbara; Morris, Howard; Howard, Clint; Winchell, Paul

**Song(s)** Heffalumps and Woozles [1]; Hip Hip Pooh-Ray [1]; The Rain, Rain, Rain Came Down, Down, Down [1]; A Rather Blustery Day [1]; The Wonderful Thing About Tiggers [1] [2]

**Notes** Animated cartoon. [1] Also in THE MANY ADVENTURES OF WINNIE THE POOH. [2] Also in WINNIE THE POOH AND TIGGER TOO.

## 6866 ◆ WINNIE THE POOH AND TIGGER TOO
Disney, 1974

**Musical Score** Baker, Buddy
**Composer(s)** Sherman, Richard M.; Sherman, Robert B.
**Lyricist(s)** Sherman, Richard M.; Sherman, Robert B.

**Producer(s)** Reitherman, Wolfgang
**Director(s)** Lounsbery, John
**Screenwriter(s)** Clemmons, Larry; Berman, Ted; Cleworth, Eric
**Source(s)** Winnie the Pooh stories (stories) Milne, A.A.
**Voices** Winchell, Paul; Holloway, Sterling; Cabot, Sebastian; Matthews, Junius; Fiedler, John; Luddy, Barbara; Whitaker, Dori; Turner, Timothy

**Directing Animator(s)** Kahl, Milt; Johnston, Ollie; Thomas, Franklin; Larson, Eric

**Song(s)** Rumbly in My Tumbly [1]; Winnie the Pooh; The Wonderful Thing About Tiggers [1] [2]

**Notes** Animated cartoon. [1] Also in THE MANY ADVENTURES OF WINNIE THE POOH. [2] Also in WINNIE THE POOH AND THE BLUSTERY DAY.

## 6867 ✦ WINNING OF THE WEST
Columbia, 1953

**Producer(s)** Schaefer, Armand
**Director(s)** Archainbaud, George
**Screenwriter(s)** Hall, Norman S.

**Cast** Autry, Gene; Burnette, Smiley; Davis, Gail; Crane, Richard; Livingston, Robert; Kirkwood, James; Champion

**Song(s)** Five Minutes Late and a Dollar Short (C/L: Unknown); Cowpoke Poking Along (C/L: Unknown); Cowboy Blues [1] (C/L: Walker, Cindy; Autry, Gene); Fetch Me Down My Trusty 45 [2] (C/L: Burnette, Smiley)

**Notes** No cue sheet available. [1] Also in TRAIL TO SAN ANTONE (Republic). [2] Also in Republic's RED RIVER VALLEY (1936).

## 6868 ✦ THE WINNING TEAM
Warner Brothers, 1952

**Musical Score** Buttolph, David

**Producer(s)** Foy, Bryan
**Director(s)** Seiler, Lewis
**Screenwriter(s)** Sherdeman, Ted; Lester, Seeleg; Gerard, Merwin
**Source(s)** "Alex the Great" (story) Lester, Seeleg; Gerard, Merwin

**Cast** Day, Doris; Reagan, Ronald; Lovejoy, Frank; Miller, Eve; Millican, James; Tamblyn, Russ; Jones, Gordon; Sanders, Hugh

**Song(s)** Ol' Saint Nicholas (C/L: James, Inez; Pepper, Buddy)

**Notes** It is not known if the song was written for the picture. There is also a rendition of "Take Me Out to the Ball Game" by Jack Norworth and Albert Von Tilzer.

## 6869 ✦ WINTER A GO-GO
Columbia, 1965

**Musical Score** Betts, Harry R.
**Composer(s)** Greenfield, Howard
**Lyricist(s)** Greenfield, Howard
**Choreographer(s)** Carson, Kay

**Producer(s)** Carell, Reno
**Director(s)** Benedict, Richard
**Screenwriter(s)** Kanter, Bob

**Cast** Stacy, James; Wellman Jr., William; Adams, Beverly; Hayes, Anthony; Donahue, Jill; Nardini, Tom; Parrish, Julie; Kanter, Bob; The Nooney Rickett Four; Lyman, Joni; The Reflections

**Song(s)** King of the Mountain; Winter A Go-Go; Ski City; Hip Square Dance (C/L: Venet, Steve; Boyce, Tommy; Hart, Bobby; Betts, Harry R.); I'm Sweet on You (C/L: Boyce, Tommy; Venet, Steve; Hart, Bobby); Do the Ski (with Me) (C/L: Venet, Steve; Boyce, Tommy; Hart, Bobby; Wine, Toni)

**Notes** No cue sheet available.

## 6870 ✦ WINTER CARNIVAL
United Artists, 1939

**Choreographer(s)** Freeman, Ned

**Producer(s)** Wanger, Walter
**Director(s)** Reisner, Charles
**Screenwriter(s)** Schulberg, Budd; Cole, Lester; Rapf, Maurice

**Cast** Sheridan, Ann; Carlson, Richard; Parrish, Helen; Lowry, Morton; Corner, James; Baldwin, Alan; Armstrong, Robert; Brodell, Joan [1]; Hunt, Marsha

**Song(s)** Winter Blossoms (C: Janssen, Werner; L: Gilbert, L. Wolfe)

**Notes** No cue sheet available. [1] Later known as Joan Leslie.

## 6871 ✦ WINTERHAWK
Howco International, 1976

**Musical Score** Holdridge, Lee

**Producer(s)** Pierce, Charles B.
**Director(s)** Pierce, Charles B.
**Screenwriter(s)** Pierce, Charles B.

**Cast** Dante, Michael; Erickson, Leif; Strode, Woody; Pyle, Denver; Cook Jr., Elisha; Wells, Dawn

**Song(s)** Winterhawk (C: Holdridge, Lee; L: Smith, Earl F.)

**Notes** No cue sheet available.

## 6872 ✦ WINTER OF OUR DREAMS
Satori, 1982

**Musical Score** Calcraft, Sharon

**Producer(s)** Mason, Richard
**Director(s)** Duigan, John
**Screenwriter(s)** Duigan, John

**Cast** Davis, Judy; Brown, Bryan; Mochrie, Peter

**Song(s)** Till Time Brings Change (C/L: Lowndes, Graham); Burning Bridges (C/L: Lowndes, Graham)

**Notes** No cue sheet available.

## 6873 ✦ WINTERTIME
### Twentieth Century–Fox, 1943

**Composer(s)** Brown, Nacio Herb
**Lyricist(s)** Robin, Leo
**Choreographer(s)** Williams, Kenny

**Producer(s)** LeBaron, William
**Director(s)** Brahm, John
**Screenwriter(s)** Moran, E. Edwin; Jevne, Jack; Starling, Lynn

**Cast** Henie, Sonja; Oakie, Jack; Romero, Cesar; Landis, Carole; Sakall, S.Z.; Wilde, Cornel; Woody Herman and His Orchestra; Reynolds, Helene

**Song(s)** I Like It Here; Wintertime; We Always Get Our Girl; Dancing in the Dawn; Later Tonight; Could It Be You [1] (L: Caesar, Irving); I'm All A-Twitter Over You [2]

**Notes** [1] Not used. Also not used in GREENWICH VILLAGE. [2] Not used.

## 6874 ✦ WISDOM
### Twentieth Century–Fox, 1986

**Musical Score** Elfman, Danny

**Producer(s)** Williams, Bernard
**Director(s)** Estevez, Emilio
**Screenwriter(s)** Estevez, Emilio

**Cast** Moore, Demi; Estevez, Emilio; Skerritt, Tom; Cartwright, Veronica; Young, William Allen; Minchenberg, Richard; Sheen, Charlie

**Song(s)** Home Again (C: Oingo Boingo; L: Elfman, Danny); Tears Run Down (C/L: Elfman, Danny)

**Notes** No cue sheet available.

## 6875 ✦ WISH YOU WERE HERE
### Atlantic, 1987

**Musical Score** Myers, Stanley

**Producer(s)** Radclyffe, Sarah
**Director(s)** Leland, David
**Screenwriter(s)** Leland, David

**Cast** Cavanagh, Trudy; Lloyd, Emily; Clifford, Clare; Durkin, Barbara

**Song(s)** Lost in a Dream (C: Myers, Stanley; L: Leland, David); Gentle Wind (C: Myers, Stanley; L: Leland, David)

**Notes** No cue sheet available.

## 6876 ✦ THE WISTFUL WIDOW OF WAGON GAP
### Universal, 1947

**Musical Score** Schumann, Walter

**Producer(s)** Arthur, Robert
**Director(s)** Barton, Charles T.

**Screenwriter(s)** Lees, Robert; Rinaldo, Frederic I.; Grant, John

**Cast** Abbott, Bud; Costello, Lou; Main, Marjorie; Young, Audrey; Cleveland, George; Jones, Gordon; Thompson, Peter; Ching, William

**Song(s)** Set 'Em Up Joe [1] (C: Fairchild, Edgar; L: Brooks, Jack)

**Notes** [1] Also in FRONTIER GAL and IDEA GAL.

## 6877 ✦ WITH A SONG IN MY HEART
### Twentieth Century–Fox, 1952

**Musical Score** Newman, Alfred
**Choreographer(s)** Daniels, Billy

**Producer(s)** Trotti, Lamar
**Director(s)** Lang, Walter
**Screenwriter(s)** Trotti, Lamar

**Cast** Hayward, Susan [1]; Calhoun, Rory; Wayne, David; Ritter, Thelma; Wagner, Robert; Westcott, Helen; Merkel, Una; Allan, Richard; Showalter, Max; Talbot, Lyle; Erickson, Leif; The Skylarks; The Modernaires; The Melody Men; The King's Men; The Starlighters; The Four Girlfriends

**Song(s)** Jim's Toasty Peanuts (C/L: Darby, Ken); The Right Kind [2] (C/L: George, Don; Newman, Lionel; Henderson, Charles); Montparnasse (C: Newman, Alfred; L: Daniel, Eliot); The Eight Links (C/L: Darby, Ken); Wonderful Home Sweet Home (C/L: Darby, Ken)

**Notes** Based on the life of Jane Froman. There are also vocals of "With a Song in My Heart" and "Blue Moon" by Richard Rodgers and Lorenz Hart; "That Old Feeling" by Sammy Fain and Lew Brown; "I'm Thru with Love" by Matt Malneck, Fud Livingston and Gus Kahn; "Get Happy" by Harold Arlen and Ted Koehler; "On the Gay White Way" by Ralph Rainger and Leo Robin; "Hoe That Corn" by Max Showalter and Jack Woodford; "Embraceable You" by George and Ira Gershwin; "Tea for Two" by Vincent Youmans and Irving Caesar; "It's a Good Day" by Peggy Lee and Dave Barbour; "They're Either Too Young or Too Old" by Arthur Schwartz and Frank Loesser; "I'll Walk Alone" by Jule Styne and Sammy Cahn; "Chicago (That Toddling Town)" by Fred Fisher; "California Here I Come" by Joseph Meyer, Al Jolson and B.G. DeSylva; "Carry Me Back to Old Virginny" by James A. Bland; "Indiana" by James F. Hanley and Ballard Macdonald; "Alabamy Bound" by Ray Henderson, B.G. DeSylva and Bud Green; "Deep in the Heart of Texas" by Don Swander and June Hershey; "I've Got a Feelin' Your Foolin'" by Arthur Freed and Nacio Herb Brown (also in BROADWAY MELODY OF 1936 and SINGING IN THE RAIN) and "America the Beautiful" by Katharine Lee Bates and Samuel A. Ward. [1] Dubbed by Jane Froman. [2] Also in ROAD HOUSE but without Lionel Newman credit.

## 6878 ◆ WITH BYRD AT THE SOUTH POLE
Paramount, 1930

**Musical Score**    Baer, Manny

**Screenwriter(s)**    Johnson, Julian; Gibbons, Floyd
**Narrator(s)**    Gibbons, Floyd

**Cast**    Byrd, Rear Adm. Richard E.; Alexander, Clair D.; Balchen, Bernt; Black, George H.; Blackburn, Quin A.; Bubier, Kennard F.; Braathen, Christopher; Bursey, Jacob

**Song(s)**    Back Home (C/L: Fain, Sammy; Kahal, Irving; Norman, Pierre)

**Notes**    No cue sheet available. This is a documentary about Byrd's reaching the Pole. The cast above are members of Byrd's expedition.

## 6879 ◆ WITH LOVE AND KISSES
Melody Pictures, 1937

**Director(s)**    Goodwins, Leslie
**Screenwriter(s)**    Lowe, Sherman

**Cast**    Tomlin, Pinky; Wing, Toby; Hopton, Russell; Housman, Arthur; Knight, Fuzzy; The Peters Sisters; Gray, Billy; Bergan, Jerry; Chelito and Gabriel

**Song(s)**    Don't Ever Lose It; I'm Right Back Where I Started (C/L: Tomlin, Pinky; Poe, Coy); The Trouble with Me Is You (C/L: Tomlin, Pinky; Tobias, Harry); Sweet (C/L: LeRoux, Buddy; Tomlin, Pinky; Heath, Al); With Love and Kisses (C/L: Lee, Connie); Sittin' on the Edge of My Chair (C/L: Parks, Paul; Poe, Coy; Tomlin, Pinky)

**Notes**    No cue sheet available.

## 6880 ◆ WITHOUT RESERVATIONS
RKO, 1946

**Musical Score**    Webb, Roy

**Producer(s)**    Lasky, Jesse L.
**Director(s)**    LeRoy, Mervyn
**Screenwriter(s)**    Solt, Andrew
**Source(s)**    *Thanks God! I'll Take It from Here* (novel) Allen, Jane; Livingston, Mae

**Cast**    Colbert, Claudette; Wayne, John; DeFore, Don; Triola, Anne; Brown, Phil; Puglia, Frank; Hall, Thurston; Drake, Dona; Parsons, Louella [1]

**Song(s)**    I'll Buy That Dream (C: Wrubel, Allie; L: Magidson, Herb); Negrita No Me Dejes [2] (C/L: Gonzales, Aaron)

**Notes**    [1] Billed as Miss Louella Parsons. [2] Also in FALCON IN MEXICO and MEXICAN SPITFIRE.

## 6881 ◆ WITHOUT YOU
Disney, 1946

**Song(s)**    Without You (C: Farres, Osvaldo; L: Farres, Osvaldo; Gilbert, Ray)

**Notes**    This cartoon is part of MAKE MINE MUSIC. See MAKE MINE MUSIC for other credits.

## 6882 ◆ WITH THEIR EYES ON THE STARS
Warner Brothers, 1964

**Composer(s)**    Stewart, John
**Lyricist(s)**    Stewart, John

**Song(s)**    With Their Eyes on the Stars; Let the Bullgine Run; A Song for Liberty; Do You Remember Their Names; There's Plenty of Gold; Many Thousand Gone; No, My Love, No; I'm Gonna Ride Railroad Bill; Hey, Up You Cattle; They've Gone Away (C/L: Stewart, Mike); The Road to Freedom; This Is the Next Frontier

**Notes**    Short subject.

## 6883 ◆ WITNESS
Paramount, 1985

**Musical Score**    Jarre, Maurice

**Producer(s)**    Feldman, Edward S.
**Director(s)**    Weir, Peter
**Screenwriter(s)**    Wallace, Earl W.; Kelley, William

**Cast**    Ford, Harrison

**Song(s)**    Party Down (C/L: Brackett, Alan; Shelly, Scott); Shocking Behavior (C/L: Chiten, Paul; Sheridan, Sue)

**Notes**    Both are background vocals only.

## 6884 ◆ THE WITNESS CHAIR
RKO, 1936

**Producer(s)**    Reid, Cliff
**Director(s)**    Nichols Jr., George
**Screenwriter(s)**    James, Rian; Purcell, Gertrude

**Cast**    Harding, Ann; Abel, Walter; Dumbrille, Douglass; Sage, Frances; Olsen, Moroni; Hamilton, Margaret

**Song(s)**    Isn't This a Night for Love [1] (C/L: Burton, Val; Jason, Will)

**Notes**    There are also vocals of "Tramp! Tramp! Tramp!" by George Frederick Root and "Take Me Back to My Boots and Saddle" by Samuels, Whitecup and Powell. [1] Also in MELODY CRUISE.

## 6885 ◆ WITNESS FOR THE PROSECUTION
United Artists, 1957

**Producer(s)**    Hornblow Jr., Arthur
**Director(s)**    Wilder, Billy
**Screenwriter(s)**    Wilder, Billy; Kurnitz, Harry
**Source(s)**    *Witness for the Prosecution* (play) Christie, Agatha

**Cast** Power, Tyrone; Dietrich, Marlene; Laughton, Charles; Lanchester, Elsa; Williams, John; Daniell, Henry; Wolfe, Ian; O'Connor, Una; Thatcher, Torin; Varden, Norma

**Song(s)** I May Never Go Home Anymore (C: Roberts, Ralph Arthur; L: Brooks, Jack)

**Notes** No cue sheet available.

## 6886 ✦ WITNESS TO MURDER
United Artists, 1954

**Musical Score** Gilbert, Herschel Burke

**Producer(s)** Erskine, Chester
**Director(s)** Rowland, Roy
**Screenwriter(s)** Erskine, Chester

**Cast** Stanwyck, Barbara; Merrill, Gary; Sanders, George

**Song(s)** Dark Is the Night (C/L: Gilbert, Herschel Burke)

## 6887 ✦ WIVES AND LOVERS
Paramount, 1963

**Musical Score** Murray, Lyn

**Producer(s)** Wallis, Hal B.
**Director(s)** Rich, John
**Screenwriter(s)** Anhalt, Edward

**Cast** Leigh, Janet; Johnson, Van; Winters, Shelley; Hyer, Martha; Walston, Ray; Slate, Jeremy

**Song(s)** Wives and Lovers [1] (C: Bacharach, Burt; L: David, Hal)

**Notes** [1] Written for exploitation only.

## 6888 ✦ WIVES NEVER KNOW
Paramount, 1936

**Producer(s)** Thompson, Harlan
**Director(s)** Nugent, Elliott
**Screenwriter(s)** Brennan, Frederick Hazlitt

**Cast** Ruggles, Charles; Boland, Mary; Menjou, Adolphe

**Song(s)** Moose-Bar (C: Boutelje, Phil; L: Brennan, Frederick Hazlett)

## 6889 ✦ THE WIZ
Universal, 1978

**Musical Score** Jones, Quincy
**Composer(s)** Smalls, Charlie
**Lyricist(s)** Smalls, Charlie
**Choreographer(s)** Johnson, Louis

**Producer(s)** Cohen, Rob
**Director(s)** Lumet, Sidney
**Screenwriter(s)** Schumacher, Joel
**Source(s)** *The Wiz* (musical) Smalls, Charlie

**Cast** Ross, Dorothy; King, Mabel; Horne, Lena; Jackson, Michael; Russell, Nipsey; Ross, Ted; Pryor, Richard; Merritt, Theresa; Carpenter, Thelma; Greene, Stanley; Barrett, Clyde, J.

**Song(s)** The Feeling that We Have; Can I Go On? (C/L: Jones, Quincy; Ashford, Nick; Simpson, Valerie); Give Her Time [1] (C/L: Jones, Quincy; Ashford, Nick; Simpson, Valerie); He's the Wizard; The Good Witch Glinda (C/L: Jones, Quincy; Ferraro, Ralph); March of the Munchkins (C/L: Jones, Quincy); Soon As I Get Home; You Can't Win; Ease on Down the Road; What Would I Do If I Could Feel?; Slide Some Oil to Me; (I'm a) Mean Ole Lion; Be a Lion; Emerald City Sequence (C/L: Jones, Quincy; Small, Charlie); So You Wanted to See the Wizard; Is This What Feeling Gets? (C/L: Jones, Quincy; Ashford, Nick; Simpson, Valerie); Don't Nobody Bring Me No Bad News; A Brand New Day (Everybody Rejoice) (C/L: Vandross, Luther); Believe in Yourself; Home

**Notes** The Charlie Small songs are from the Broadway original. [1] Instrumental use only.

## 6890 ✦ WIZARD
Universal, 1989

**Musical Score** Robinson, J. Peter
**Composer(s)** Neumann, Kurt; Llanas, Sam
**Lyricist(s)** Neumann, Kurt; Llanas, Sam

**Producer(s)** Chisholm, David; Topolsky, Ken
**Director(s)** Holland, Todd
**Screenwriter(s)** Chisholm, David

**Cast** Savage, Fred; Bridges, Beau; Slater, Christian; Lewis, Jenny; Edwards, Luke

**Song(s)** You Don't Get Much; Levin' on Your Mind (C/L: Walker, Wayne); Red River; Wheelin' Down the Road (C/L: Moulin, Mark; Moulin, Kirk); Send Me an Angel (C/L: Zatorski, Richard; Sterry, David); Hangin' Tough (C/L: Starr, Maurice); I Live by the Groove (C/L: Schwartz, Eddie; Carrack, Paul); Don't Be Cruel (C/L: Reed, Antonio; Edmonds, Kenneth; Simmons, Daryl); I Found My Way (C/L: Widelitz, Stacy; Cody, Lara)

## 6891 ✦ THE WIZARD OF BAGHDAD
Twentieth Century–Fox, 1960

**Musical Score** Gertz, Irving

**Producer(s)** Katzman, Sam
**Director(s)** Sherman, George
**Screenwriter(s)** Lasky, Jesse L.; Silver, Pat

**Cast** Shawn, Dick; Baker, Diane; Coe, Barry

**Song(s)** The Wizard of Baghdad (Eni Meni Geni) (C: Saxon, David; L: Lampert, Diane; Farrow, Peter); Doodyoo (C/L: Barer, Marshall; Fuller, Dean)

## 6892 ✦ THE WIZARD OF OZ
### Metro–Goldwyn–Mayer, 1939

**Musical Score** Stothart, Herbert
**Composer(s)** Arlen, Harold
**Lyricist(s)** Harburg, E.Y.
**Choreographer(s)** Connolly, Bobby

**Producer(s)** LeRoy, Mervyn
**Director(s)** Fleming, Victor
**Screenwriter(s)** Langley, Noel; Ryerson, Florence; Woolf, Edgar Allan
**Source(s)** *The Wizard of Oz* (novel) Baum, L. Frank

**Cast** Garland, Judy; Morgan, Frank; Bolger, Ray; Lahr, Bert; Haley, Jack; Burke, Billie; Hamilton, Margaret; Grapewin, Charley; The Singer Midgets

**Song(s)** Over the Rainbow; Munchkinland; Ding Dong the Witch Is Dead; We're Off to See the Wizard; If I Only Had a Brain [1] [3]; If I Only Had a Heart [1]; If I Only Had the Nerve [1]; Optimistic Voices; The Merry Old Land of Oz; If I Were King of the Forest; The Jitterbug [2]; March of the Winkies (C/L: Stothart, Herbert)

**Notes** Richard Thorpe was the first director. His footage was scrapped. Victor Fleming took over. Buddy Ebsen was the first Tinman but had an allergic reaction to his silver makeup. Ken Darby dubbed the mayor of Munchkin City and a lollipop guild member. Bud Linn dubbed the munchkin district attorney and another lollipop guild member. John Dodson dubbed the third lollipop guild member. The singing group the Three Debutantes dubbed the lullaby league. [1] Same music. [2] Cut from final print. [3] A significant portion of the dance accompanying this film was cut. The complete sequence is in THAT'S DANCING.

## 6893 ✦ WIZARDS
### Twentieth Century–Fox, 1977

**Musical Score** Belling, Andrew

**Producer(s)** Bakshi, Ralph
**Director(s)** Bakshi, Ralph
**Screenwriter(s)** Bakshi, Ralph
**Voices** Holt, Bob; Wells, Jesse; Romanus, Richard; Proval, David; Connell, James; Gravers, Steve

**Song(s)** Time Will Tell (C/L: Belling, Andrew)

**Notes** Animated feature.

## 6894 ✦ THE WOLF OF WALL STREET
### Paramount, 1929

**Director(s)** Lee, Rowland V.
**Screenwriter(s)** Anderson, Doris

**Cast** Bancroft, George; Baclanova, Olga; Carroll, Nancy; Lukas, Paul; Rankin, Arthur; Hurst, Brandon

**Song(s)** Love, Take My Heart (C: Meyer, Joseph; L: Christy, Harold); This Is the Moment [1] (C: Whiting, Richard A.; L: Robin, Leo)

**Notes** [1] The song was originally used in 1928 by Paramount. It was then adapted by Serge Malavsky. The number is based on a Russian folk song titled "Ia Tak Hochu Chtos Te Bel So Mriou" ("I Always Long for You to Be with Me") as adapted by Serge Malavsky. Also in THE VIRTUOUS SIN.

## 6895 ✦ WOLF SONG
### Paramount, 1929

**Composer(s)** Whiting, Richard A.
**Lyricist(s)** Robin, Leo

**Director(s)** Fleming, Victor
**Screenwriter(s)** Farrow, John; Thompson, Keene
**Source(s)** "Wolf Song" (story) Ferguson, Harvey

**Cast** Cooper, Gary; Velez, Lupe; Wolheim, Louis; Romanoff, Constantine; Vavitch, Michael; Columbo, Russ; Brody, Ann; Lopez, Augustina

**Song(s)** The Wolf Song; Fare Thee Well; Yo Te Amo (Means I Love You) (L: Bryan, Alfred); To Lola (L: Robin, Leo; Ferguson, Harvey); Mi Amado (C: Warren, Harry; L: Lewis, Sam M.; Young, Joe)

## 6896 ✦ THE WOMAN BETWEEN (1931)
### RKO, 1931

**Musical Score** Schertzinger, Victor

**Producer(s)** LeBaron, William
**Director(s)** Schertzinger, Victor
**Screenwriter(s)** Estabrook, Howard

**Cast** Damita, Lily; Vail, Lester; Heggie, O.P.; Heggie, Miriam; Louise, Anita; Weston, Ruth; Steadman, Lincoln; Hobbes, Halliwell

**Song(s)** Close to Me (C/L: Schertzinger, Victor)

## 6897 ✦ THE WOMAN BETWEEN (1937)

See THE WOMAN I LOVE.

## 6898 ✦ A WOMAN COMMANDS
### RKO, 1931

**Composer(s)** Brown, Nacio Herb
**Lyricist(s)** Clifford, Gordon

**Producer(s)** Rogers, Charles R.
**Director(s)** Stein, Paul
**Screenwriter(s)** Jackson, Horace

**Cast** Negri, Pola; Young, Roland; Rathbone, Basil; Warner, H.B.; Bushell, Anthony; Owen, Reginald; Boley, May; Reicher, Frank

**Song(s)** Promise You'll Remember Me (L: Whittaker, Charles); I'll Take You To Paradise; I Wanna Be Kissed

**Notes** The cue sheet doesn't differentiate between songs and vocals.

## 6899 ✦ THE WOMAN DISPUTED
### United Artists, 1928

**Musical Score** Riesenfeld, Hugo

**Director(s)** King, Henry; Taylor, Sam
**Screenwriter(s)** Sullivan, C. Gardner
**Source(s)** *The Woman Disputed* (play) Clift, Denison

**Cast** Talmadge, Norma; Roland, Gilbert; Kent, Arnold; De Fas, Boris; Vavitch, Michael; Von Seyffertitz, Gustav; Brockwell, Gladys; Soussanin, Nicholas

**Song(s)** Woman Disputed I Love You (C: Ward, Edward; L: Grossman, Bernie)

**Notes** No cue sheet available.

## 6900 ✦ THE WOMAN FOR JOE
### United Artists, 1955

**Musical Score** Arnold, Malcolm

**Producer(s)** Parkyn, Leslie
**Director(s)** O'Ferrall, George More
**Screenwriter(s)** Paterson, Neil

**Cast** Baker, George; Karoubi, Jimmy; Cilento, Diane

**Song(s)** A Fool and His Heart (C/L: Fishman, Jack)

## 6901 ✦ THE WOMAN I LOVE
### RKO, 1937

**Musical Score** Honneger, Arthur; Thiriet, Maurice
**Composer(s)** Shilkret, Nathaniel
**Lyricist(s)** Greene, Mort

**Producer(s)** Lewis, Albert
**Director(s)** Litvak, Anatole
**Screenwriter(s)** Borden, Ethel
**Source(s)** *L'Equipage* (novel) Kessel, Joseph

**Cast** Muni, Paul; Hayward, Louis; Hopkins, Miriam; Clive, Colin; Watson, Minor; Risdon, Elizabeth; Guilfoyle, Paul; Davis Jr., Owen; Holloway, Sterling

**Song(s)** See the Train; Duo D'Amour (C: Honneger, Arthur); I Give You This Bouquet; Happy Daddy (C: Thiriet, Maurice; L: Gilbert, L. Wolfe); Pomponette (C: Unknown; L: Gilbert, L. Wolfe); Song of the Rabbit (C: Honneger, Arthur; L: Gilbert, L. Wolfe); On Oublie Tout (C: Honneger, Arthur; L: Gilbert, L. Wolfe)

**Notes** Titled THE WOMAN BETWEEN internationally. Litvak had already directed a French version of the play. The Honneger and Thiriet score was used in that film also.

## 6902 ✦ THE WOMAN IN RED
### Orion, 1984

**Musical Score** Morris, John
**Composer(s)** Wonder, Stevie
**Lyricist(s)** Wonder, Stevie

**Producer(s)** Drai, Victor
**Director(s)** Wilder, Gene
**Screenwriter(s)** Wilder, Gene

**Cast** Wilder, Gene; Grodin, Charles; Bologna, Joseph; Ivey, Judith; Huddleston, Michael; Le Brock, Kelly; Radner, Gilda; Heffner, Kyle T.

**Song(s)** It's You; The Woman in Red; Moments Aren't Moments; Don't Drive Drunk; Love Light in Flight; Weakness; I Just Called to Say I Love You; Let's Just (C: Gittens, Larry; Bridges, Ben; L: Gittens, Larry)

**Notes** No cue sheet available. A remake of the French film UN ELEPHANT CA TROMPE ENORNEMENT (1975).

## 6903 ✦ A WOMAN OF AFFAIRS
### Metro–Goldwyn–Mayer, 1928

**Musical Score** Axt, William

**Director(s)** Brown, Clarence
**Screenwriter(s)** Meredyth, Bess; Ainslee, Marian; Cummings, Ruth
**Source(s)** *The Green Hat* (novel) Arlen, Michael

**Cast** Gilbert, John; Garbo, Greta; Stone, Lewis; Brown, Johnny Mack; Fairbanks Jr., Douglas; Sebastian, Dorothy; Bosworth, Hobart

**Song(s)** Love's First Kiss (C: Axt, William; Mendoza, David; L: Klages, Raymond)

## 6904 ✦ WOMAN OF THE TOWN
### United Artists, 1944

**Composer(s)** Lee, Lester
**Lyricist(s)** Seelen, Jerry

**Producer(s)** Rachmil, Lewis J.
**Director(s)** Archainbaud, George
**Screenwriter(s)** MacKenzie, Aeneas

**Cast** Trevor, Claire; Dekker, Albert; Sullivan, Barry

**Song(s)** The Tramp and the Millionaire; You Can't Blame Polly [1]

**Notes** [1] Not in FLAMING FEATHER (Paramount).

## 6905 ✦ THE WOMAN RACKET
### Metro–Goldwyn–Mayer, 1930

**Choreographer(s)** Lee, Sammy

**Director(s)** Ober, Robert; Kelley, Albert
**Screenwriter(s)** Le Vino, Albert Shelby

**Source(s)** *Night Hostess* (play) Dunning, Philip; Dunning, Frances

**Cast** Moore, Tom; Sweet, Blanche; Starr, Sally; Agnew, Robert; Miljan, John

**Song(s)** He's Good Enough for Me (C: Edwards, Gus; L: Goodwin, Joe); Call Me to Arms (C: Alter, Louis; L: Johnson, Howard); Just You, Just Me [1] (C: Greer, Jesse; L: Klages, Raymond)

**Notes** Titled LIGHTS AND SHADOWS internationally. [1] Also in MARIANNE.

## 6906 ✦ A WOMAN'S DEVOTION
Republic, 1956

**Musical Score** Baxter, Les

**Producer(s)** Bash, John
**Director(s)** Henreid, Paul
**Screenwriter(s)** Hill, Robert

**Cast** Meeker, Ralph; Rule, Janice; Henreid, Paul; Monteros, Rosenda; Schiller, Fanny

**Song(s)** A Woman's Devotion (C: Baxter, Les; L: Davis, Gwen)

## 6907 ✦ A WOMAN'S FACE
Metro–Goldwyn–Mayer, 1941

**Musical Score** Kaper, Bronislau
**Choreographer(s)** Matray, Ernst

**Producer(s)** Saville, Victor
**Director(s)** Cukor, George
**Screenwriter(s)** Stewart, Donald Ogden; Paul, Elliot
**Source(s)** *Il Etait une Fois* (play) de Croisset, Francis

**Cast** Crawford, Joan; Douglas, Melvyn; Veidt, Conrad; Massen, Osa; Basserman, Albert; Meek, Donald; Owen, Reginald; Main, Marjorie

**Song(s)** Chanson Triste (C: Kaper, Bronislau; L: Stewart, Donald Ogden); We Fill the Sky with Laughter (C: Kaper, Bronislau; L: Stewart, Donald Ogden)

**Notes** Ingrid Bergman had starred in a 1937 Swedish version of the play.

## 6908 ✦ WOMAN'S WORLD
Twentieth Century–Fox, 1954

**Producer(s)** Brackett, Charles
**Director(s)** Negulesco, Jean
**Screenwriter(s)** Binyon, Claude; Loos, Mary; Sale, Richard

**Cast** Webb, Clifton; Allyson, June; Heflin, Van; Bacall, Lauren; MacMurray, Fred; Dahl, Arlene; Wilde, Cornel; Reid, Elliott; Gillmore, Margalo; Reed, Alan

**Song(s)** It's a Woman's World (C: Mockridge, Cyril J.; L: Cahn, Sammy)

## 6909 ✦ THE WOMAN THEY ALMOST LYNCHED
Republic, 1953

**Musical Score** Wilson, Stanley

**Producer(s)** Dwan, Allan
**Director(s)** Dwan, Allan
**Screenwriter(s)** Fisher, Steve
**Source(s)** "The Woman They Almost Lynched" (story) Fessier, Michael

**Cast** Lund, John; Leslie, Joan; Donlevy, Brian; Totter, Audrey; Cooper, Ben; Davis, Jim; Savage, Ann; Corby, Ellen

**Song(s)** All My Life [1] (C: Stept, Sam H.; L: Mitchell, Sidney D.); How Strange (C: Young, Victor; L: Lee, Peggy)

**Notes** [1] Written in 1936.

## 6910 ✦ WOMAN TO WOMAN
Tiffany–Stahl, 1929

**Composer(s)** Whidden, Jay; May, Fred
**Lyricist(s)** Whidden, Jay; May, Fred

**Director(s)** Saville, Victor
**Screenwriter(s)** Fodor, Nicholas
**Source(s)** (play) Morton, Michael

**Cast** Compson, Betty; Barraud, George; Compton, Juliette; Chambers, Margaret

**Song(s)** Parisian Doll; Sunshine of My Heart; To You

**Notes** No cue sheet available.

## 6911 ✦ WOMAN TRAP
Paramount, 1929

**Director(s)** Wellman, William A.
**Screenwriter(s)** Cormack, Bartlett

**Cast** Morris, Chester; Brent, Evelyn; Skelly, Hal

**Song(s)** I'm All A-Twitter (And All A-Twirl) [1] (C: Whiting, Richard A.; L: Robin, Leo)

**Notes** [1] Also in CLOSE HARMONY.

## 6912 ✦ WOMAN WISE
Twentieth Century–Fox, 1936

**Composer(s)** Akst, Harry
**Lyricist(s)** Clare, Sidney

**Producer(s)** Wurtzel, Sol M.
**Director(s)** Dwan, Allan
**Screenwriter(s)** Markson, Ben

**Cast** Hudson, Rochelle; Whalen, Michael; Beck, Thomas; Dinehart, Alan; Fowley, Douglas; Hassell, George; Allwyn, Astrid; Chandler, Chick

**Song(s)** Over a Cup of Coffee [1]; You're a Knockout

**Notes** There is also a vocal of "Sing Baby Sing" by Lew Pollack and Jack Yellen. [1] Also in STAR FOR A NIGHT.

### 6913 ◆ THE WOMEN
Metro–Goldwyn–Mayer, 1939

**Musical Score** Ward, Edward; Snell, Dave

**Producer(s)** Stromberg, Hunt
**Director(s)** Cukor, George
**Screenwriter(s)** Loos, Anita; Murfin, Jane
**Source(s)** *The Women* (play) Boothe, Clare [2]

**Cast** Shearer, Norma; Crawford, Joan; Russell, Rosalind; Boland, Mary; Goddard, Paulette; Povah, Phyllis [1]; Fontaine, Joan; Weidler, Virginia; Watson, Lucile

**Song(s)** Forevermore (C: Ward, Edward; L: Wright, Bob; Forrest, Chet)

**Notes** [1] Also in Broadway cast. [2] Known later as Clare Boothe Luce.

### 6914 ◆ WOMEN EVERYWHERE
Fox, 1930

**Composer(s)** Kernell, William
**Lyricist(s)** Kernell, William

**Producer(s)** Marin, Ned
**Director(s)** Korda, Alexander
**Screenwriter(s)** Thompson, Harlan; Biro, Lajos

**Cast** Murray, J. Harold; D'Orsay, Fifi; Grossmith, George; Cook, Clyde; Dione, Rose; Kellard, Ralph

**Song(s)** I Do It with My Oo-La-La [1] (C: Monaco, James V.; L: Friend, Cliff); Good Bad Baby [1] (C: Klages, Raymond; L: Greer, Jesse); Women Everywhere; Good Time Fifi; Beware of Love; Bon Jour; One Day; Where Is Honky Tonk Town; Smile Legionnaire (C'est La Guerre) (L: Cadman, Charles Wakefield); One Day He'll Come Along; All in the Family [2] (L: Grossmith, George); Maxixe (Inst.)

**Notes** Originally titled HELLS BELLES. [1] Not used. [2] Used instrumentally only.

### 6915 ◆ WOMEN IN ROOM 13
Fox, 1932

**Composer(s)** Hanley, James F.

**Director(s)** King, Henry
**Screenwriter(s)** Bolton, Guy
**Source(s)** (play) Shipman, Samuel; Marcin, Max; Wilde, Percival

**Cast** Landi, Elissa; Bellamy, Ralph; Hamilton, Neil; Loy, Myrna

**Song(s)** Love at Dusk [1] (L: Browning, Robert); Harp with a Broken String (L: McCarthy, Joseph)

**Notes** [1] The lyric is based on the poem "In a Gondola."

### 6916 ◆ WOMEN LOVE ONCE
Paramount, 1931

**Director(s)** Goodman, Edward
**Screenwriter(s)** Akins, Zoe
**Source(s)** *Daddy's Gone A-Hunting* (play) Akins, Zoe

**Cast** Boardman, Eleanor; Lukas, Paul; Compton, Juliette

**Song(s)** Baby Bunting (C/L: King, Jack)

### 6917 ◆ WONDER BAR
Warner Brothers–First National, 1934

**Composer(s)** Warren, Harry
**Choreographer(s)** Berkeley, Busby

**Producer(s)** Foy, Bryan
**Director(s)** Bacon, Lloyd
**Screenwriter(s)** Baldwin, Earl
**Source(s)** *Wonder Bar* (musical) Herczeg, Geza; Farkas, Karl; Katscher, Robert

**Cast** Jolson, Al [3]; Francis, Kay; Del Rio, Dolores; Cortez, Ricardo; Powell, Dick; Kibbee, Guy; Donnelly, Ruth; Herbert, Hugh; Fazenda, Louise; D'Orsay, Fifi; Kennedy, Merna; LeRoy, Hal; O'Neill, Henry; Barrat, Robert; Kolker, Henry

**Song(s)** Why Do I Dream Those Dreams; Elizabeth [1] (C: Katscher, Robert; L: Caesar, Irving); Tango (Inst.) (C: Katscher, Robert); Vive La France; Don't Say Goodnight [4]; Wonder Bar; Goin' to Heaven on a Mule; You're So Divine [2]; All Washed Up [2]; Tango Del Rio (Inst.)

**Notes** There is also a vocal of "Dark Eyes" by Carol Raven and A. Fassio. [1] Instrumentals from the original score of Broadway musical. [2] Used instrumentally only. [3] From Broadway cast. [4] Also used in EVERY NIGHT AT EIGHT.

### 6918 ◆ WONDERFUL TO BE YOUNG
Paramount, 1962

**Musical Score** Black, Stanley
**Composer(s)** Myers, Peter; Cass, Ronnie
**Lyricist(s)** Myers, Peter; Cass, Ronnie
**Choreographer(s)** Ross, Herbert

**Producer(s)** Harper, Kenneth
**Director(s)** Furie, Sidney J.
**Screenwriter(s)** Myers, Peter; Cass, Ronnie

**Cast** Richard, Cliff; Morley, Robert; Gray, Carole; The Shadows

**Song(s)** Wonderful to Be Young! (C: Bacharach, Burt; L: David, Hal); Friday Night; Got a Funny Feeling

(C/L: Marvin, Hank B.; Welch, Bruce); Nothing's Impossible; The Young Ones (C/L: Tepper, Sid; Bennett, Roy C.); Lessons in Love (C: Soloway, Sy; L: Wolfe, Shirley); No-one for Me but Nicky; What D'You Know We've Got a Show; When the Girl In Your Arms Is the Girl in Your Heart (C/L: Tepper, Sid; Bennett, Roy C.); All for One; Mambo; We Say Yeah (C/L: Welch, Bruce; Marvin, Hank B.; Gormley, Peter)

## 6919 ✦ THE WONDERFUL WORLD OF THE BROTHERS GRIMM
### Metro–Goldwyn–Mayer, 1963

**Musical Score**  Harline, Leigh
**Composer(s)**  Merrill, Bob
**Lyricist(s)**  Merrill, Bob
**Choreographer(s)**  Romero, Alex

**Producer(s)**  Pal, George
**Director(s)**  Levin, Henry
**Screenwriter(s)**  Harmon, David P.; Beaumont, Charles; Roberts, William
**Source(s)**  *Die Bruder Grimm* (book) Gerstner, Dr. Hermann

**Cast**  Harvey, Laurence; Boehm, Karl; Bloom, Claire; Slezak, Walter; Eden, Barbara; Homolka, Oscar; Stang, Arnold; Hunt, Martita; Garde, Betty; Russell, Bryan; Wolfe, Ian; Marihugh, Tammy; Meredith, Cheerio; Rilla, Walter; Mimieux, Yvette; Tamblyn, Russ; Backus, Jim; Bondi, Beulah; Sundberg, Clinton; The Puppetoons; Brooke, Walter; Bettin, Sandra Gale; Foulk, Robert; Terry-Thomas; Hackett, Buddy; Kruger, Otto; Crawford Jr., Robert; Smith, Sydney

**Song(s)**  Dancing Princess; Ah-Oom; Christmas Land; Dee-Are-A-Gee-O-En; Singing Bone (L: Beaumont, Charles); The Wonderful World of the Brothers Grimm (Inst.); Above the Stars (Inst.); Gypsy Fire (Inst.)

**Notes**  Puppetoons directed by George Pal. Filmed in Cinerama.

## 6920 ✦ WONDER MAN
### RKO, 1945

**Musical Score**  Heindorf, Ray
**Composer(s)**  Fine, Sylvia
**Lyricist(s)**  Fine, Sylvia

**Producer(s)**  Goldwyn, Samuel
**Director(s)**  Humberstone, H. Bruce
**Screenwriter(s)**  Hartman, Don; Shavelson, Melville; Rapp, Philip

**Cast**  Kaye, Danny; Vera-Ellen; Mayo, Virginia; Woods, Donald; Sakall, S.Z.; Jenkins, Allen; Brophy, Edward S.; Kruger, Otto; Cochran, Steve; Gilmore, Virginia; Lane, Richard; Shafer, Natalie; Hall, Huntz

**Song(s)**  Bali Boogie; Palpably Inadequate; The Patter; So In Love (C: Rose, David; L: Robin, Leo); The Opera Sequence

## 6921 ✦ WONDER OF WOMEN
### Metro–Goldwyn–Mayer, 1929

**Director(s)**  Brown, Clarence
**Screenwriter(s)**  Meredyth, Bess
**Source(s)**  *The Wife of Stephan Tromholt* (novel) Sudermann, Hermann

**Cast**  Stone, Lewis; Wood, Peggy; Hyams, Leila; Meyers, Harry; Padden, Sarah; Frederici, Blanche

**Song(s)**  Ich Liebe Dich [1] (C: Broones, Martin; L: Fisher, Fred); At Close of Day [1] (C: Broones, Martin; L: Greer, Jesse)

**Notes**  [1] Cue sheet indicates instrumental use only. This is a part talkie.

## 6922 ✦ WON TON TON, THE DOG WHO SAVED HOLLYWOOD
### Paramount, 1976

**Musical Score**  Hefti, Neal

**Producer(s)**  Picker, David V.; Schulman, Arnold; Winner, Michael
**Director(s)**  Winner, Michael
**Screenwriter(s)**  Schulman, Arnold; Howard, Cy

**Cast**  Dern, Bruce; Kahn, Madeline; Carney, Art; Silvers, Phil; Garr, Teri; Leibman, Ron; Alda, Robert; Amsterdam, Morey; Archerd, Army; Arlen, Richard; Barty, Billy; Bergen, Edgar; Berle, Milton; Blair, Janet; Blondell, Joan; Calhoun, Rory; Carradine, John; Carter, Jack; Charisse, Cyd; Coogan, Jackie; Crawford, Broderick; Day, Dennis; De Carlo, Yvonne; De Haven, Gloria; Demarest, William; Devine, Andy; Faye, Alice; Feld, Fritz; Fetchit, Stepin; Fleming, Rhonda; Foy Jr., Eddie; Gabor, Zsa Zsa; Greene, Shecky; Hall, Huntz; Haymes, Dick; Holloway, Sterling; Hunter, Tab; Jessel, George; Lamas, Fernando; Lamour, Dorothy; LaRue, Jack; Lawford, Peter; Leeds, Phil; Luke, Keye; Madison, Guy; Mature, Victor; Mayo, Virginia; Mazurki, Mike; Merman, Ethel; Miller, Ann; Montalban, Ricardo; Morgan, Dennis; Morison, Patricia; Murray, Ken; Myers, Carmel; Nichols, Barbara; Norton, Cliff; Nye, Louis; Pidgeon, Walter; Ray, Aldo; The Ritz Brothers; Rutherford, Ann; Stockwell, Dean; Toomey, Regis; Vallee, Rudy; Vincent, Romo; Walker, Nancy; Weaver, Doodles; Weissmuller, Johnny; White, Jesse; Wilcoxon, Henry; Youngman, Henny

**Song(s)**  To Be Loved By You [1] (C: Hefti, Neal; L: Black, Don); They're Playing Our Song [2] (C: Hefti, Neal; L: Black, Don)

**Notes**  [1] Lyric added for exploitation only. From music titled "Theme from Won Ton Ton." [2] Lyric added for exploitation. From music titled "The Won Ton Ton Rag."

## 6923 ◆ WOODSTOCK
### Warner Brothers, 1970

**Producer(s)**  Maurice, Bob
**Director(s)**  Wadleigh, Michael

**Cast**  Havens, Richie; Crosby, Stills, Nash, and Young; Baez, Joan; Ten Years After; The Who; Sebastian, John; Crocker, Joe; Sha-Na-Na; Country Joe and the Fish; Santana; Guthrie, Arlo; Sly & the Family Stone; Hendrix, Jimi

**Song(s)**  Long Time Gone [1] (C/L: Crosby, David); Going Up the Country [1] (C/L: Wilson, Alan); Wooden Ships [1] (C/L: Crosby, David; Stills, Stephen); Handsome Johnny (C/L: Havens, Richie); Joe Hill (C: Robinson, Earl; L: Hayes, Alfred); Swing Low Sweet Chariot (C/L: Traditional); Go to the Mirror Boy (C/L: Townsend, Pete); Summertime Blues (C/L: Cochran, Eddie; Capehart, Jerry); At the Hop (C/L: Singer, Arthur; Medora, J.; White, P.); With a Little Help from My Friends (C/L: Lennon, John; McCartney, Paul); Rock and Soul Music (C/L: McDonald, Country Joe; Melton, Barry; Hirsch, Chicken; Barthol, Bruce; Cohen, David); Coming Into Los Angeles (C/L: Guthrie, Arlo); Sweet Judy Blue Eyes (C/L: Stills, Stephen); I'm Going Home (C/L: Lee, Alvin); Blue Suede Shoes (C/L: Perkins, Carl); Younger Generation (C/L: Sebastian, John); I Feel Like I'm Fixin' to Die Rag (C/L: McDonald, Country Joe); I Want to Take You Higher (C/L: Stewart, Sylvester); Purple Haze (C/L: Hendrix, Jimi); Woodstock [1] (C/L: Mitchell, Joni)

**Notes**  [1] Background vocal only. It is not known if any of these songs were written for the film.

## 6924 ◆ WOODY HERMAN'S VARIETIES
### Universal, 1951

**Composer(s)**  Rogers, Milton "Shorty"; Jackson, Danny
**Lyricist(s)**  Rogers, Milton "Shorty"; Jackson, Danny

**Cast**  Woody Herman and His Orchestra

**Song(s)**  We're Legitimate; Jivin' at the Drive In

**Notes**  This is one of a number of big band shorts made by Universal. It also contains a vocal of "Ninety Nine Guys" by Lou Carter, Herb Ellis and John Frigo.

## 6925 ◆ WORDS AND MUSIC (1929)
### Fox, 1929

**Composer(s)**  Stamper, Dave
**Lyricist(s)**  Thompson, Harlan
**Choreographer(s)**  Royce, Edward

**Producer(s)**  Sprague, Chandler
**Director(s)**  Tinling, James; Merlin, Frank [8]
**Screenwriter(s)**  Bennison, Andrew

**Cast**  Patricola, Tom; Percy, David; Twelvetrees, Helen; Albertson, Frank; Patterson, Elizabeth; Orlamond, William; Morrison, Duke; Bond, Ward; Keene, Richard [5]; The Biltmore Quartet [1]; The Collier Sisters; Gardner, Muriel [6]; Jordan, Dorothy [6]; Moran, Lois [6]; Parrish, Helen [6]; Percy, David [6]; Wade, Jack [6]; Gale, Vina [3]; Springer, Arthur [3]; Griffith, Harriet [4]; Griffith, John [4]; Huff, Charles [2]; Hunt, Helen [2]

**Song(s)**  Stepping Along (C/L: Kernell, William); Too Wonderful for Words [7] (C: Stamper, Dave; Kernell, William; L: Joseph, Edmund; Smith, Paul Gerard); Shadows (C/L: Mitchell, Sidney D.; Gottler, Archie; Conrad, Con); Good Old Mary Brown (C/L: Kernell, William); Hunting Song; Beauty Waltz; Yours Sincerely; Take a Little Tip

**Notes**  [1] Members include: Eddie Bush, Paul Gibbons, Bill Seckler and Ches Kirkpatrick. [2] Adagio dancers. [3] Adagio dancers. [4] Adagio dancers. [5] Singer in "Stepping Along." [6] Song and Dance principals. [7] Also in DOUBLE CROSS ROADS. [8] Credited with staging.

## 6926 ◆ WORDS AND MUSIC (1948)
### Metro–Goldwyn–Mayer, 1948

**Musical Score**  Hayton, Lennie
**Choreographer(s)**  Alton, Robert; Kelly, Gene

**Producer(s)**  Freed, Arthur
**Director(s)**  Taurog, Norman
**Screenwriter(s)**  Finklehoffe, Fred F.

**Cast**  Allyson, June; Garland, Judy; Horne, Lena; Kelly, Gene; Charisse, Cyd [1]; Torme, Mel; Vera-Ellen; Turnell, Dee; Rooney, Mickey; Sothern, Ann; Drake, Tom; Thompson, Marshall; Como, Perry; Garrett, Betty; Leigh, Janet; Nolan, Jeanette; Quine, Richard; Sundberg, Clinton; Antrim, Harry; Parnell, Emory; Earle, Edward; McLerie, Allyn Ann; The Blackburn Twins

**Notes**  Based on the lives and music of Richard Rodgers and Lorenz Hart. There are no original songs in this screenplay. All vocals were written by Rodgers and Hart. They included: "Lover," "Mountain Greenery," "Manhattan," "There's a Small Hotel," "Way Out West," "A Tree in the Park," "Where's That Rainbow," "On Your Toes," "Blue Room," "Someone Should Tell Them," "Thou Swell," "With a Song in My Heart," "Where or When," "Lady Is a Tramp," "I Wish I Were in Love Again," "Johnny One Note," "Blue Moon," "Spring Is Here," "My Heart Stood Still" and "With a Song in My Heart." Deleted from the final print were vocals of "You're Nearer," "This Can't Be Love," "The Poor Apache," "It Never Entered My Mind," "Lover (second vocal)," "It's Got to Be Love," "My Heart

Stood Still," "Falling in Love with Love," "You Took Advantage of Me" and "My Funny Valentine." "Way Out West" was filmed in a longer version but cut for release. [1] Dubbed by Eileen Wilson.

## 6927 ✦ WORKING GIRL
Twentieth Century–Fox, 1989

**Musical Score** Simon, Carly

**Producer(s)** Wick, Douglas
**Director(s)** Nichols, Mike
**Screenwriter(s)** Wade, Kevin

**Cast** Ford, Harrison; Weaver, Sigourney; Griffith, Melanie; Baldwin, Alec; Cusack, Joan; Bosco, Philip; Dunn, Nora; Platt, Oliver; Lally, James; Spacey, Kevin; Dukakis, Olympia; Lake, Ricki

**Song(s)** Let the River Run (C/L: Simon, Carly); Wall Street Rhythm [1] (C/L: Simon, Carly)

**Notes** [1] Not on cue sheet.

## 6928 ✦ WORK IS A FOUR LETTER WORD
Universal, 1968

**Musical Score** Woolfenden, Guy

**Producer(s)** Clyde, Thomas
**Director(s)** Hall, Peter
**Screenwriter(s)** Summers, Jeremy
**Source(s)** *Eh?* (play) Livings, Henry

**Cast** Warner, David; Black, Cilla; Spriggs, Elizabeth; Mohyeddin, Zia; Howard, Alan; Royle, Derek

**Song(s)** Work Is a Four Letter Word (C: Woolfenden, Guy; L: Black, Don)

**Notes** A Rank film.

## 6929 ✦ WORLD FOR RANSOM
Allied Artists, 1954

**Musical Score** De Vol, Frank

**Producer(s)** Aldrich, Robert; Tabakin, Bernard
**Director(s)** Aldrich, Robert
**Screenwriter(s)** Hardy, Lindsay

**Cast** Duryea, Dan; Lockhart, Gene; Knowles, Patric; Denny, Reginald; Bruce, Nigel; Carr, Marian; Dumbrille, Douglass; Luke, Keye

**Song(s)** Too Soon (C/L: Samuels, Walter G. G.)

## 6930 ✦ WORLD GONE WILD
Lorimar, 1988

**Musical Score** Juber, Laurence

**Producer(s)** Rosen, Robert L.
**Director(s)** Katzin, Lee H.
**Screenwriter(s)** Zamacona, Jorge

**Cast** Dern, Bruce; Pare, Michael; Stewart, Catherine Mary; Ant, Adam; Podell, Rick

**Song(s)** A World Gone Wild (C/L: Des Barres, Michael; Jones, Steve; Juber, Laurence)

**Notes** No cue sheet available.

## 6931 ✦ THE WORLD MOVES ON
Fox, 1934

**Producer(s)** Sheehan, Winfield
**Director(s)** Ford, John
**Screenwriter(s)** Berkeley, Reginald

**Cast** Carroll, Madeleine; Tone, Franchot; Denny, Reginald; Roulien, Raul

**Song(s)** Should She Desire Me Not (C: DeFrancesco, Louis E.; L: Berkeley, Reginald)

## 6932 ✦ THE WORLD OF SUZIE WONG
Paramount, 1960

**Musical Score** Duning, George

**Producer(s)** Perceval, Hugh
**Director(s)** Quine, Richard
**Screenwriter(s)** Patrick, John
**Source(s)** *The World of Suzie Wong* (play) Osborn, Paul; *The World of Suzie Wong* (novel) Mason, Richard

**Cast** Holden, William; Kwan, Nancy; Syms, Sylvia; Wilding, Michael; Chan, Jacqui; Naismith, Laurence

**Song(s)** Suzie Wong (The Cloud Song) (C: Van Heusen, James; L: Cahn, Sammy)

**Notes** Jean Negulesco was originally to be the director and Frances Nuyen was to be the star.

## 6933 ✦ THE WORLD OWES ME A LIVING
Republic, 1945

**Musical Score** May, Hans

**Producer(s)** Jackson, Louis H.
**Director(s)** Sewell, Vernon
**Screenwriter(s)** Sewell, Vernon; Reiner, Erwin
**Source(s)** (novel) Llewellyn-Rhys, John

**Cast** Farrar, David; Campbell, Judy; Dresdel, Sonia; Livesey, Jack

**Song(s)** We're a Bunch of Flying Fools (C/L: Barker, Jack)

**Notes** A British National picture.

## 6934 ✦ THE WORLD'S GREATEST ATHLETE
Disney, 1972

**Musical Score** Hamlisch, Marvin

**Producer(s)** Walsh, Bill
**Director(s)** Scheerer, Robert
**Screenwriter(s)** Gardiner, Gerald; Caruso, Dee

**Cast** Conway, Tim; Vincent, Jan-Michael; Amos, John; Browne, Roscoe Lee; Haddon, Dayle; De Wolfe, Billy; Walker, Nancy; Cosell, Howard; Gifford, Frank; McKay, Jim; Palmer, Bud; Kapp, Joe; Toomey, Bill; Muse, Clarence; Capers, Virginia

**Song(s)** Merrivale Fight Song (C: Hamlisch, Marvin; L: Gardner, Gerald; Caruso, Dee)

### 6935 ✦ WORLD'S GREATEST LOVER
Twentieth Century–Fox, 1977

**Musical Score** Morris, John

**Producer(s)** Wilder, Gene
**Director(s)** Wilder, Gene
**Screenwriter(s)** Wilder, Gene

**Cast** Wilder, Gene; Kane, Carol; DeLuise, Dom; Feld, Fritz; Ballantine, Carl; Collins, Matt; Gleason, James; Graham, Ronny; Huddleston, David

**Song(s)** Ain't It Kinda Wonderful (C/L: Wilder, Gene)

### 6936 ✦ THE WORLD, THE FLESH AND THE DEVIL
Metro–Goldwyn–Mayer, 1959

**Musical Score** Rozsa, Miklos

**Producer(s)** Englund, George
**Director(s)** MacDougall, Ranald
**Screenwriter(s)** MacDougall, Ranald

**Cast** Belafonte, Harry; Stevens, Inger; Ferrer, Mel

**Song(s)** I Don't Like It Here (C/L: Belafonte, Harry; MacDougall, Ranald); Gotta Travel On (C/L: Clayton, Paul; Ehrlich, Larry; Lazar, David; Six, Tom); Fifteen (C/L: Green, Alan; Nemiroff, Robert)

### 6937 ✦ THE WORST WOMAN IN PARIS
Fox, 1933

**Producer(s)** Lasky, Jesse L.
**Director(s)** Bell, Monta
**Screenwriter(s)** Brown, Martin

**Cast** Landi, Elissa; Manners, Adolphe; Chandler, Helen; Stephens, Harvey; Seddon, Margaret

**Song(s)** Love Passes Me By (C: Lange, Arthur; L: Burkhardt, Robert; Stuart, Allan)

### 6938 ✦ WRANGLER'S ROOST
Monogram, 1941

**Musical Score** Sanucci, Frank

**Producer(s)** Weeks, George W.
**Director(s)** Luby, S. Roy
**Screenwriter(s)** Blahos, John; Finkle, Robert

**Cast** King, John; Terhune, Ray; Corrigan, Ray; Taylor, Forrest; Gaze, Gwen; Chesebro, George; Shumway, Walter

**Song(s)** Joggin' (C/L: Whelan, Ekko; Romaro, Garet; Lohrman, Roger); Wrangler's Roost (C/L: Romaro, Garet; Lohrman, Roger)

### 6939 ✦ THE WRATH OF GOD
Metro–Goldwyn–Mayer, 1972

**Musical Score** Schifrin, Lalo

**Producer(s)** Gilmore Jr., William S.
**Director(s)** Nelson, Ralph
**Screenwriter(s)** Nelson, Ralph
**Source(s)** (novel) Graham, James

**Cast** Mitchum, Robert; Langella, Frank; Colicos, John; Buono, Victor; Hayworth, Rita

**Song(s)** Misa Criolla (C: Ramirez, Ariel; L: Mayol, Alejandro; Segde, Jesus G.; Catena, Osvaldo)

### 6940 ✦ THE WRECKER
Tiffany–Stahl, 1929

**Director(s)** Bolvary, G.M.
**Screenwriter(s)** McPhail, Angus
**Source(s)** (play) Didley, Arnold; Merivale, Bernard

**Cast** Hume, Benita; Hall, Winter; Striker, Joseph; Blackwell, Carlyle

**Song(s)** Are You Really Mine (C: Santley, Joseph; L: Caesar, Irving)

**Notes** This is a Gainsborough Production made in England as a silent film.

### 6941 ✦ THE WRECKING CREW
Columbia, 1968

**Musical Score** Montenegro, Hugo

**Producer(s)** Allen, Irving
**Director(s)** Karlson, Phil
**Screenwriter(s)** McGivern, William

**Cast** Martin, Dean; Sommer, Elke; Tate, Sharon; Kwan, Nancy; Green, Nigel; Louise, Tina

**Song(s)** House of 7 Joys (C: De Vol, Frank; L: David, Mack)

**Notes** No cue sheet available.

### 6942 ✦ WRITTEN ON THE WIND
Universal, 1956

**Musical Score** Skinner, Frank

**Producer(s)** Zugsmith, Albert
**Director(s)** Sirk, Douglas
**Screenwriter(s)** Zuckerman, George
**Source(s)** *Written on the Wind* (novel) Wilder, Robert

**Cast** Hudson, Rock; Stack, Robert; Malone, Dorothy; Keith, Robert; Bacall, Lauren; Williams, Grant; Platt, Edward; Shannon, Harry; Larch, John

**Song(s)** Written on the Wind (C: Young, Victor; L: Cahn, Sammy)

## 6943 ✦ WUSA
### Paramount, 1970

**Musical Score** Schifrin, Lalo

**Producer(s)** Newman, Paul; Foreman, John
**Director(s)** Rosenberg, Stuart
**Screenwriter(s)** Stone, Robert
**Source(s)** *A Hall of Mirrors* (novel) Stone, Robert

**Cast** Newman, Paul; Woodward, Joanne; Perkins, Anthony; Harvey, Laurence; Hingle, Pat; Gordon, Don; Cabot, Bruce; Leachman, Cloris; Gunn, Moses; Rogers, Wayne; James, Clifton; The Preservation Hall Jazz Band

**Song(s)** Glory Road [1] (C/L: Diamond, Neil); Today Is Where I Am [2] (C: Schifrin, Lalo; L: Hilton, Hermine)

**Notes** [1] It is not known if this was written for the picture. [2] Not used.

## 6944 ✦ W.W. AND THE DIXIE DANCEKINGS
### Twentieth Century–Fox, 1975

**Musical Score** Grusin, Dave

**Producer(s)** Canter, Stanley S.
**Director(s)** Avildsen, John G.
**Screenwriter(s)** Richman, Thomas

**Cast** Reynolds, Burt; Van Dyke, Conny; Reed, Jerry; Beatty, Ned; Tillis, Mel; Marshall, Mort; Lewis, Furry

**Song(s)** Hound Dog (C/L: Leiber, Jerry; Stoller, Mike); Send Me the Pillow You Dream On (C/L: Locklin, Hank); I'm In Love Again (C/L: Domino, Antoine "Fats"; Bartholomew, Dave); Bye Bye Love (C/L: Bryant, Felice; Bryant, Boudleaux); Blue Suede Shoes (C/L: Perkins, Carl); I'm Walkin' (C/L: Domino, Antoine "Fats"; Bartholomew, Dave); Goodnight It's Time to Go (C/L: Carter, Calvin; Hudson, James); Johnny B. Goode (C/L: Berry, Chuck); My Baby's Gone (C/L: Houser, Hazel); I Washed My Hands in Muddy Water (C/L: Babcock, Joe); Blues Stay Away from Me (C/L: Delmore, Alton; Delmore, Rabon; Raney, Wayne; Glover, Henry); The Losin' End (C/L: McDuffie, Ken); A Friend (C/L: Hubbard, Jerry R.)

**Notes** Obviously some of these weren't written for the film.

## 6945 ✦ WYNKEN, BLYNKEN AND NOD
### Disney, 1938

**Song(s)** Wynken, Blynken and Nod (C: Harline, Leigh; Grigor, Nico; L: Field, Eugene)

**Notes** No credit sheet available. Silly Symphony.

## 6946 ✦ WYOMING MAIL
### Universal, 1950

**Composer(s)** Shapiro, Dan; Lee, Lester
**Lyricist(s)** Shapiro, Dan; Lee, Lester
**Choreographer(s)** Belfer, Hal

**Producer(s)** Schenck, Aubrey
**Director(s)** LeBorg, Reginald
**Screenwriter(s)** Essex, Harry; Lee, Leonard

**Cast** McNally, Stephen; Smith, Alexis; Roberts, Roy; Da Silva, Howard; Begley, Ed; Riss, Dan; Bissell, Whit; Arness, James; Silvestre, Armando; Jaeckel, Richard; Darro, Frankie

**Song(s)** Take Me to Town [1]; Endlessly

**Notes** [1] Also in A DAY OF FURY and WYOMING MAIL.

# X

## 6947 ✦ XANADU
### Universal, 1980

**Musical Score**   De Vorzon, Barry
**Composer(s)**   Farrar, John
**Lyricist(s)**   Farrar, John
**Choreographer(s)**   Ortega, Kenny; Trent, Jerry

**Producer(s)**   Gordon, Lawrence
**Director(s)**   Greenwald, Robert
**Screenwriter(s)**   Danus, Richard Christian; Kane, Michael; Rubel, Marc Reid
**Voices**   Browne, Coral; Hyde-White, Wilfrid

**Cast**   Kelly, Gene; Beck, Michael; Newton-John, Olivia; Hanley, Sandra Katie; McCarren, Fred

**Song(s)**   I'm Alive (C/L: Lynne, Jeff); Magic (C/L: Farrar, John); Whenever You're Away from Me; Suddenly; Dancin'; Don't Walk Away (C/L: Lynne, Jeff); All Over the World (C/L: Lynne, Jeff); The Fall (C/L: Lynne, Jeff); Suspended in Time; Xanadu Chant; Fool; Xanadu Song (C/L: Lynne, Jeff)

**Notes**   There is also a vocal of "You Made Me Love You (I Didn't Want to Do It)" by Joseph McCarthy and James V. Monaco.

## 6948 ✦ XICA
### Unifilm/Embrafilme, 1982

**Musical Score**   Menescal, Roberto; Ben, Jorge

**Producer(s)**   Barbos, Jarbas
**Director(s)**   Diegues, Carlos
**Screenwriter(s)**   Diegues, Carlos; Dos Santos, Joao Felicio

**Cast**   Motta, Zeze; Chagas, Walmor; Wilker, Jose; Lima, Altair; Maravilha, Elke

**Song(s)**   Xica da Silva (C/L: Ben, Jorge)

**Notes**   No cue sheet available.

# Y

## 6949 ✦ THE YAKUZA
Warner Brothers, 1975

**Musical Score**  Grusin, Dave
**Composer(s)**  Grusin, Dave

**Producer(s)**  Pollack, Sydney; Hamilburg, Michael
**Director(s)**  Pollack, Sydney
**Screenwriter(s)**  Schrader, Paul; Towne, Robert

**Cast**  Mitchum, Robert; Keith, Brian; Ken, Takakura; Keiko, Kishi; Eiji, Okada; Shigeta, James; Edelman, Herb; Jordon, Richard

**Song(s)**  Only the Wind (L: Aku-Yu); Evening Sun, Morning Moon [1] (L: Bergman, Alan; Bergman, Marilyn)

**Notes**  [1] Used instrumentally only.

## 6950 ✦ YANKEE DOODLE DANDY
Warner Brothers, 1942

**Composer(s)**  Jerome, M.K.
**Lyricist(s)**  Scholl, Jack
**Choreographer(s)**  Prinz, LeRoy; Felix, Seymour

**Producer(s)**  Warner, Jack L.; Wallis, Hal B.
**Director(s)**  Curtiz, Michael
**Screenwriter(s)**  Buckner, Robert; Joseph, Edmund

**Cast**  Cagney, James; Leslie, Joan; Huston, Walter; Whorf, Richard; Manning, Irene; Tobias, George; De Camp, Rosemary; Cagney, Jeanne; Langford, Frances; Barbier, George; Sakall, S.Z.; Catlett, Walter; Foy Jr., Eddie; Croft, Douglas; Watson, Minor; Clute, Chester; Myrtil, Odette; Parsons, Patsy Lee; Young, Jack

**Song(s)**  Good Luck Johnny; Little Johnny Jones Special; Paddock Sequence Special; Finale Special; All Aboard for Old Broadway; Special Interlude #3

**Notes**  Based on the life of George M. Cohan. Many of these songs are briefly performed in medleys. Vocals include "The Dancing Master" by Jerry Cohan; "While Strolling Through the Park One Day" by Ed Haley; "Love Nest" by Louis A. Hirsch and Otto Harbach; "Jeepers Creepers" by Harry Warren and Johnny Mercer; "Off the Record" from I'D RATHER BE RIGHT by Richard Rodgers and Lorenz Hart and the following songs with music and lyrics by George M. Cohan: "I Was Born in Virginia," "The Warmest Baby in the Bunch," "Harrigan," "Yankee Doodle Boy," "Give My Regards to Broadway," "Oh You Wonderful Girl," "Blue Skies, Gray Skies," "The Belle of the Barber's Ball," "Mary's a Grand Old Name," "Forty-Five Minutes from Broadway," "So Long, Mary," "You're a Grand Old Flag," "Like the Wandering Minstrel," "Over There," "In a Kingdom of Our Own," "Nellie Kelly I Love You," "The Man Who Owns Broadway," "Molly Malone" and "Billie."

## 6951 ✦ YANKEE FAKIR
Republic, 1946

**Musical Score**  Laszlo, Alexander

**Producer(s)**  Wilder, W. Lee
**Director(s)**  Wilder, W. Lee
**Screenwriter(s)**  Conway, Richard S.

**Cast**  Fowley, Douglas; Woodbury, Joan; Bevans, Clem; Sherman, Ransom; Reicher, Frank; Bernard, Tommy; Dudgeon, Elspeth

**Song(s)**  Like a Poor Little Mouse in a Trap (C: Laszlo, Alexander; L: Robinson, J. Russel)

## 6952 ✦ A YANK IN LONDON
Twentieth Century–Fox, 1946

**Producer(s)**  Wilcox, Herbert
**Director(s)**  Wilcox, Herbert
**Screenwriter(s)**  Cowan, Maurice

**Cast**  Harrison, Rex; Neagle, Anna; Jagger, Dean; Morley, Robert; Manning, Irene; Darwell, Jane

**Song(s)**  Home (C/L: Manning, Irene)

**Notes**  Originally titled I LIVE IN GROSVENOR SQUARE.

## 6953 ✦ A YANK IN THE R.A.F.
Twentieth Century–Fox, 1941

**Composer(s)**  Rainger, Ralph
**Lyricist(s)**  Robin, Leo

**Producer(s)**  Zanuck, Darryl F.
**Director(s)**  King, Henry
**Screenwriter(s)**  Ware, Darrell; Tunberg, Karl

**Cast**   Power, Tyrone; Grable, Betty; Sutton, John; Gardiner, Reginald; Stuart, Donald

**Song(s)**   Hi-Ya Love; Another Little Dream Won't Do Us Any Harm

## 6954 ✦ YELLOW DUST
### RKO, 1936

**Producer(s)**   Reid, Cliff
**Director(s)**   Fox, Wallace W.
**Screenwriter(s)**   Hume, Cyril; Twist, John
**Source(s)**   *Mother Lode* (play) O'Neil, George; Totheroh, Dan

**Cast**   Dix, Richard; Hyams, Leila; Olsen, Moroni; Ralph, Jessie; Clyde, Andy

**Song(s)**   I'm in Love with the Golden West (C/L: Colombo, Alberto); I Live Just for Today (C/L: Colombo, Alberto)

## 6955 ✦ THE YELLOW ROLLS-ROYCE
### Metro–Goldwyn–Mayer, 1965

**Musical Score**   Ortolani, Riz
**Composer(s)**   Ortolani, Riz
**Lyricist(s)**   Newell, Norman

**Producer(s)**   de Grunwald, Anatole
**Director(s)**   Asquith, Anthony
**Screenwriter(s)**   Rattigan, Terence

**Cast**   Bergman, Ingrid; Harrison, Rex; Delon, Alain; Scott, George C.; Moreau, Jeanne; Sharif, Omar; MacLaine, Shirley; Carney, Art; Grenfell, Joyce; Cox, Wally; Lister, Moira; Purdom, Edmund; Hordern, Michael

**Song(s)**   Forget Domani; Now and Then; She's Just a Quiet Girl [1] (L: Vance, Paul)

**Notes**   [1] Sheet music only.

## 6956 ✦ YELLOW ROSE OF TEXAS
### Republic, 1944

**Producer(s)**   Grey, Harry
**Director(s)**   Kane, Joseph
**Screenwriter(s)**   Townley, Jack

**Cast**   Rogers, Roy; Evans, Dale; Haade, William; Cleveland, George; Heyburn, Weldon; Taliaferro, Hal; Sons of the Pioneers

**Song(s)**   Lucky Me, Unlucky You (C/L: Henderson, Charles); Song of the Rover (C/L: Nolan, Bob); Down in the Old Town Hall (C/L: Henderson, Charles); Western Wonderland (C: Carson, Hugh; L: Savage, Roy); The Timber Trail [3] (C/L: Spencer, Tim); Down Mexico Way [1] (C: Styne, Jule; L: Cherkose, Eddie; Meyer, Sol); Take It Easy [2] (C/L: Mizzy, Vic; Taylor, Vic; De Bru, Albert); Show Boat (C/L: Henderson, Charles); Two Seated Saddle and a One Gaited Horse [4] (C/L: Spencer, Tim)

**Notes**   [1] Also in DOWN MEXICO WAY, THE GOLDEN STALLION and HOME IN WYOMING. [2] Also in MEET MISS BOBBY SOCKS (Columbia) and BABES ON SWING STREET (Universal). [3] Also in TIMBER TRAIL. [4] Sheet music only.

## 6957 ✦ YELLOWSTONE CUBS
### Disney, 1963

**Musical Score**   Smith, Paul J.

**Producer(s)**   Hibler, Winston
**Screenwriter(s)**   Wright, Ralph; Speirs, Jack
**Narrator(s)**   Allen, Rex

**Song(s)**   Easy Livin' (C: Smith, Paul J.; L: George, Gil; Hibler, Winston)

## 6958 ✦ YELLOW SUBMARINE
### United Artists, 1968

**Musical Score**   Martin, George
**Composer(s)**   McCartney, Paul; Lennon, John
**Lyricist(s)**   McCartney, Paul; Lennon, John

**Producer(s)**   Brodax, Al
**Director(s)**   Dunning, George
**Screenwriter(s)**   Minoff, Lee; Brodax, Al; Mendelsohn, Jack; Segal, Erich
**Source(s)**   "Yellow Submarine" (song) McCartney, Paul; Lennon, John

**Song(s)**   Yellow Submarine; Eleanor Rigby; All Together Now; When I'm 64; Only a Northern Song (C/L: Harrison, George); With a Little Help from My Friends; Sgt. Pepper's Lonely Hearts Club Band; Lucy in the Sky with Diamonds; Nowhere Man; All You Need Is Love; It's All Too Much (C/L: Harrison, George); Toy Bulldog

**Notes**   Animated feature.

## 6959 ✦ YENTL
### MGM/UA, 1983

**Musical Score**   Legrand, Michel
**Composer(s)**   Legrand, Michel
**Lyricist(s)**   Bergman, Marilyn; Bergman, Alan
**Choreographer(s)**   Lynne, Gillian

**Producer(s)**   Streisand, Barbra; Lemorande, Rusty
**Director(s)**   Streisand, Barbra
**Screenwriter(s)**   Rosenthal, Jack
**Source(s)**   "Yentl, the Yeshiva Boy" (novella) Singer, Isaac Bashevis

**Cast**   Streisand, Barbra; Patinkin, Mandy; Irving, Amy; Persoff, Nehemiah; Hill, Steven; Goring, Ruth

**Song(s)**   A Piece of Sky; Where Is It Written?; Papa Can You Hear Me; Naztrov'eych; Yosheke, Yosheke; This Is One of Those Moments; No Wonder; The Way He Makes Me Feel; Tomorrow Night; Mein Shana Hadass;

Wedding Night Waltz; Will Someone Ever Look at Me that Way; No Matter What Happens

## 6960 ✦ YE OLDEN DAYS
Disney, 1933

**Musical Score** Churchill, Frank E.
**Composer(s)** Churchill, Frank E.
**Lyricist(s)** Churchill, Frank E.

**Song(s)** I'm a Wandering Minstrel; In Days of Old; Kingdom of Lapalooza; Duel Song

**Notes** Short subject. No credit sheets available. Songs are not indicated on the cue sheets.

## 6961 ✦ YES, GIORGIO
Metro–Goldwyn–Mayer, 1982

**Musical Score** Lewis, Michael J.

**Producer(s)** Fetterman, Peter
**Director(s)** Schaffner, Franklin J.
**Screenwriter(s)** Steinberg, Norman
**Source(s)** (novel) Piper, Anne

**Cast** Pavarotti, Luciano; Herrold, Kathryn; Albert, Eddie; Borboni, Paola; Hong, James; Mitchell, Leona; Adler, Kurt; Buckley, Emerston; Courage, Alexander

**Song(s)** If We Were in Love (C: Williams, John; L: Bergman, Alan; Bergman, Marilyn)

**Notes** There are also vocals of "Ave Maria" by F. Schubert; "Mattinata" by Ruggiero Leoncavallo; "Una Furtiva Lagrima" from L'ELISIR D'AMORE by Donizetti and Romani; "La Donna e Mobile" from RIGOLETTO by Verdi and Piave; "O Sole Mio" by Di Capua; "Cielo e Mar" from LA GIOCONDA by Ponchielli and Boito; "Funiculi, Funicula" by Luigi Denza; "I Left My Heart in San Francisco" by Douglas Cross and George Cory; "Santa Lucia" and "Donna Non Vidi Mai" from MANON LESCAUT by Puccini, Praga, Oliva and Illica; and "Turandot, Act I #3," and "Nessun Dorma" from TURANDOT by Puccini, Adami and Simoni.

## 6962 ✦ YES SIR, THAT'S MY BABY
Universal, 1949

**Composer(s)** Scharf, Walter
**Lyricist(s)** Brooks, Jack

**Producer(s)** Goldstein, Leonard
**Director(s)** Sherman, George
**Screenwriter(s)** Brodney, Oscar

**Cast** Coburn, Charles; O'Connor, Donald; De Haven, Gloria; Brown, Barbara; Shelley, Joshua; Lambert, Jack; Overman, Lynne; Spaulding, George

**Song(s)** Look At Me; They've Never Figured Out a Woman; Men Are Little Children

**Notes** There is also a vocal of "Yes Sir, That's My Baby" by Gus Kahn and Walter Donaldson.

## 6963 ✦ YOKEL BOY
Republic, 1942

**Producer(s)** North, Robert
**Director(s)** Santley, Joseph
**Screenwriter(s)** Dawn, Isabel
**Source(s)** *Yokel Boy* (musical) Brown, Lew; Tobias, Charles; Stept, Sam H.

**Cast** Dekker, Albert; Kean, Betty; Foy Jr., Eddie; Mowbray, Alan; Carver, Lynne; Karns, Roscoe; Rasumny, Mihkail; Dugan, Tom; Lawrence, Marc

**Song(s)** Jim [2] (C/L: Petrillo, Caesar; Ross, Edward; Shawn, Nelson); It's Me Again [1] (C: Stept, Sam H.; L: Brown, Lew; Tobias, Charles)

**Notes** Titled HITTING THE HEADLINES internationally. [1] From original Broadway musical. Other songs from the show are used instrumentally only. [2] Special lyrics by Paul Henning.

## 6964 ✦ YOLANDA AND THE THIEF
Metro–Goldwyn–Mayer, 1945

**Musical Score** Hayton, Lennie
**Composer(s)** Warren, Harry
**Lyricist(s)** Freed, Arthur
**Choreographer(s)** Loring, Eugene

**Producer(s)** Freed, Arthur
**Director(s)** Minnelli, Vincente
**Screenwriter(s)** Brecher, Irving

**Cast** Astaire, Fred; Bremer, Lucille; Morgan, Frank; Natwick, Mildred; Nash, Mary; Ames, Leon; Stossel, Ludwig

**Song(s)** This Is the Day for Love; Angel; Will You Marry Me; Yolanda; Coffee Time [3] [4]; By Candlelight [1]; Feminine Fashions [2]; Made in the U.S.A. [2]; Bananas [2]

**Notes** [1] Deleted from final print. [2] Not used. [3] Based on an instrumental number "Java Junction." [4] Also in THE SUBTERRANEANS with different lyrics.

## 6965 ✦ YOR—THE HUNTER FROM THE FUTURE
Columbia, 1983

**Musical Score** De Angelis, Guido; De Angelis, Maurizio

**Producer(s)** Marsala, Michele
**Director(s)** Dawson, Anthony M.
**Screenwriter(s)** Bailey, Robert; Dawson, Anthony M.
**Source(s)** *Yor* (novel) Zanetto, Juan; Collins, Ray

**Cast** Brown, Reb; Clery, Corinne; Steiner, John; Andre, Carole; Collins, Alan

**Song(s)** Yor's World (C: De Angelis, Guido; De Angelis, Maurizio; L: Antonia, Barbara; Hanna, Pauline; Duncan-Smith, Susan; De Natalie, Cesare)

## 6966 ✦ YOU AND ME
Paramount, 1938

**Composer(s)** Weill, Kurt
**Lyricist(s)** Coslow, Sam

**Producer(s)** Lang, Fritz
**Director(s)** Lang, Fritz
**Screenwriter(s)** Van Upp, Virginia

**Cast** Sidney, Sylvia; Raft, George; Cummings, Robert; Karns, Roscoe; MacLane, Barton; Carey, Harry; Stone, George E.; Hymer, Warren; Williams, Guinn "Big Boy"; Hayes, Bernadene; Compton, Joyce

**Song(s)** Song of the Cash Register (C: Weill, Kurt; Boutelje, Phil); The Right Guy for Me; We're the Kind of People Who Sing Lullabies (L: Burke, Johnny); The Song of the Lie (What Are You Doing) [1] [3] (L: Burke, Johnny); You and Me [1] [4] (C: Hollander, Frederick; L: Freed, Ralph); Five Years Ain't So Long [1] [2]

**Notes** Weill also wrote some incidental themes titled "Honeymoon Scene" and "Jiggaboo." [1] Not used. [2] Recorded. [3] Taken out after first sneak preview. [4] Not used though published.

## 6967 ✦ YOU ARE WHAT YOU EAT
Studio Unknown, 1968

**Musical Score** Simon, John

**Producer(s)** Yarrow, Peter; Feinstein, Barry
**Director(s)** Feinstein, Barry

**Cast** Tim, Tiny; Yarrow, Peter; Butterfield, Paul; McGuire, Barry; Boyd, Father Malcolm; The Electric Flag; Harper's Bizarre; Super Spade

**Song(s)** Memphis Tennessee (C/L: Berry, Chuck); Family Dog (C/L: Simon, John); You Are What You Eat (C/L: Simon, John; Yarrow, Peter); Moments of the Soft Persuasion (C/L: Yarrow, Peter); Silly Girl (C/L: Yarrow, Peter); The Wabe (C/L: Simon, John; Yarrow, Peter; Carroll, Lewis); Be My Baby (C/L: Barry, Jeff; Greenwich, Ellie; Spector, Phil); My Name Is Jack (C/L: Simon, John); Come to the Sunshine (C/L: Parks, Van Dyke); Don't Remind Me Now of Time (C/L: Yarrow, Peter); Teenage Fair (C/L: Simon, John; Yarrow, Peter); I Got You Babe (C/L: Bono, Sonny)

**Notes** Documentary. It is not known which, if any, of these were written for this film.

## 6968 ✦ YOU BELONG TO ME
Paramount, 1934

**Composer(s)** Coslow, Sam
**Lyricist(s)** Robin, Leo

**Producer(s)** Lighton, Louis D.
**Director(s)** Werker, Alfred
**Screenwriter(s)** De Leon, Walter

**Source(s)** "Fifty-two Weeks for Florette" (story) Alexander, Elizabeth

**Cast** Morgan, Helen; Tracy, Lee

**Song(s)** When He Comes Home to Me; Ain't That Marvelous My Baby Loves Me [2] (C/L: Hirsch, Walter; Bernie, Ben; Goering, Al); Laughing the Clouds Away [1]; I Ain't Gonna Carry No Torch [2] [3] (L: Coslow, Sam)

**Notes** Formerly titled FIFTY TWO WEEKS FOR FLORETTE. [1] Based on the Coslow song "Sweepin' the Clouds Away." [2] Not used. [3] Also not used in FOUR HOURS TO KILL, this was written for Helen Morgan.

## 6969 ✦ YOU BELONG TO MY HEART

See MR. IMPERIUM.

## 6970 ✦ YOU CAME ALONG
Paramount, 1945

**Producer(s)** Wallis, Hal B.
**Director(s)** Farrow, John
**Screenwriter(s)** Smith, Robert; Rand, Ayn

**Cast** Scott, Lizabeth; Cummings, Robert; DeFore, Don; Forrest, Helen

**Song(s)** You Came Along (Out of Nowhere) [1] (C: Green, Johnny; L: Heyman, Edward)

**Notes** Originally titled DON'T EVER GRIEVE ME. "Kiss the Boys Goodbye" by Frank Loesser and Victor Schertzinger; "My Ideal" by Leo Robin, Richard A. Whiting and Newell Chase; "A Stein Song" by Frederic Field Bullard and Richard Hovey and "One Dozen Roses" by Dick Jergens, Walter Donovan, Roger Lewis and Country Washburn are also given vocal treatments. [1] Also titled "Out of Nowhere." Not written for picture.

## 6971 ✦ YOU CAN'T BUY EVERYTHING
Metro–Goldwyn–Mayer, 1934

**Musical Score** Axt, William

**Producer(s)** Hubbard, Lucien
**Director(s)** Riesner, Charles F.
**Screenwriter(s)** Nichols, Dudley; Trotti, Lamar

**Cast** Robson, May; Parker, Jean; Stone, Lewis; Forbes, Mary; Mason, Reginald; Gillingwater, Claude

**Song(s)** You Can't Buy Everything (C: Stothart, Herbert; L: Freed, Ralph)

## 6972 ✦ YOU CAN'T DO THAT TO ME

See MAISIE GOES TO RENO.

**6973 ♦ YOU CAN'T HAVE EVERYTHING**
Twentieth Century–Fox, 1937

**Composer(s)** Revel, Harry
**Lyricist(s)** Gordon, Mack
**Choreographer(s)** Losee, Harry

**Producer(s)** Zanuck, Darryl F.
**Director(s)** Taurog, Norman
**Screenwriter(s)** Tugend, Harry; Yellen, Jack; Tunberg, Karl

**Cast** Faye, Alice; The Ritz Brothers; Ameche, Don; Andrews, Stanley; Treacher, Arthur; Martin, Tony; Brooks, Phyllis; Prouty, Jed; Prima, Louis; Blandick, Clara

**Song(s)** You Can't Have Everything; Long Underwear (C/L: Pokrass, Sam; Kuller, Sid; Golden, Ray); The Loveliness of You; Danger - Love at Work [1]; Afraid to Dream; Please Pardon Us - We're in Love; North Pole Sketch; Rhythm on the Radio (Inst.) (L: Prima, Louis); Danse Rubinoff (Inst.) (C: Rubinoff, Dave)

**Notes** [1] Also in DANGER—LOVE AT WORK.

**6974 ♦ YOU CAN'T RATION LOVE**
Paramount, 1944

**Composer(s)** Lee, Lester
**Lyricist(s)** Seelen, Jerry

**Producer(s)** MacEwen, Walter; Kraike, Michel
**Director(s)** Fuller, Lester
**Screenwriter(s)** Burton, Val; Fimberg, Hal

**Cast** Rhodes, Betty Jane; Johnston, Johnnie; Wilson, Marie

**Song(s)** Nothing Can Replace a Man; Look What You Did to Me; Love Is This; Ooh Ah Oh; How Did It Happen?; A Penny for Your Thoughts [1]

**Notes** There is also a vocal of "Louise" by Richard A. Whiting and Leo Robin. The song also appears in INNOCENTS OF PARIS and THE LOST WEEKEND. [1] Not used.

**6975 ♦ YOU CAN'T RUN AWAY FROM IT**
Columbia, 1956

**Musical Score** Duning, George
**Composer(s)** de Paul, Gene
**Lyricist(s)** Mercer, Johnny
**Choreographer(s)** Sidney, Robert

**Producer(s)** Powell, Dick
**Director(s)** Powell, Dick
**Screenwriter(s)** Binyon, Claude; Riskin, Robert
**Source(s)** "Night Bus" (story) Adams, Samuel Hopkins

**Cast** Allyson, June; Lemmon, Jack; Bickford, Charles; Kaye, Stubby; Gilbert, Paul; Backus, Jim; Youngman, Henny; Joslyn, Allyn

**Song(s)** You Can't Run Away from It; Old Reporters Never Die; Howdy Friends and Neighbors; Temporarily; Thumbin' a Ride; It Happened One Night [1]; What Cha Ma Call It [2]

**Notes** A musical remake of IT HAPPENED ONE NIGHT. [1] Not used. [2] Sheet music only.

**6976 ♦ YOU DON'T NEED PYJAMAS AT ROSIE'S**

See THE FIRST TIME.

**6977 ♦ YOU GOTTA STAY HAPPY**
Universal, 1948

**Producer(s)** Tunberg, Karl
**Director(s)** Potter, H.C.
**Screenwriter(s)** Tunberg, Karl
**Source(s)** magazine serial by Carson, Robert

**Cast** Fontaine, Joan; Stewart, James; Kilbride, Percy; Albert, Eddie; Young, Roland; Parker, Willard; McGuire, Marcy

**Song(s)** You Gotta Stay Happy (C: Alexander, Van; L: Brooks, Jack)

**6978 ♦ YOU HIT THE SPOT**
Paramount, 1945

**Producer(s)** Harris, Lou
**Director(s)** Templeton, George [1]

**Cast** Neill, Noel; Faylen, Frank; Coy, Johnny

**Song(s)** Turn on the Groove-Juice, Pappy (C: Wayne, Bernie; L: Raleigh, Ben)

**Notes** Short subject. [1] Billed as George (Dink) Templeton.

**6979 ♦ YOU LIGHT UP MY LIFE**
Columbia, 1977

**Musical Score** Brooks, Joseph

**Producer(s)** Brooks, Joseph
**Director(s)** Brooks, Joseph
**Screenwriter(s)** Brooks, Joseph

**Cast** Olfson, Ken; Conn, Didi [1]; Silver, Joe; Zaslow, Michael; Nathan, Stephen; Mayron, Melanie; Keller, Jerry; Reeves, Lisa; Brooks, Joseph [2]; Ciszk, Kasey [3]; Manning, Ruth; Pelish, Thelma

**Song(s)** You Light Up My Life (C/L: Brooks, Joseph)

**Notes** No cue sheet available. The recording of the hit song is by Debby Boone, singing to the original orchestral tracks. [1] Dubbed by Kasey Ciszk. [2] Played the creative director. [3] Appeared as a bridesmaid.

## 6980 ✦ YOU'LL FIND OUT
RKO, 1940

**Composer(s)** McHugh, Jimmy
**Lyricist(s)** Mercer, Johnny

**Producer(s)** Butler, David
**Director(s)** Butler, David
**Screenwriter(s)** Kern, James V.; Brice, Monte; Bennison, Andrew; Scott, R.T.M.

**Cast** Karloff, Boris; Babbitt, Harry; Kabibble, Ish; Mason, Sully; Kay Kyser and His Band; Simms, Ginny; Lorre, Peter; Parrish, Helen; O'Keefe, Dennis; Lugosi, Bela; Kruger, Alma

**Song(s)** You've Got Me This Way [1]; Like the Fella Once Said; I'd Know You Anywhere; I've Got a One-Track Mind; The Bad Humor Man; Don't Think This Ain't Been Charming [2]

**Notes** There is also a vocal of "Thinking of You" by Walter Donaldson and Paul Ash. [1] Also in WHEN WILLIE COMES MARCHING HOME (MGM). [2] Sheet music only.

## 6981 ✦ YOU'LL NEVER GET RICH
Columbia, 1941

**Composer(s)** Porter, Cole
**Lyricist(s)** Porter, Cole
**Choreographer(s)** Alton, Robert

**Producer(s)** Bischoff, Sam
**Director(s)** Lanfield, Sidney
**Screenwriter(s)** Fessier, Michael; Pagano, Ernest

**Cast** Astaire, Fred; Hayworth, Rita; Hubbard, John; Benchley, Robert; Inescort, Frieda; Williams, Guinn "Big Boy"; Shoemaker, Ann; Gateson, Marjorie; Sully, Frank; Massen, Osa; MacBride, Donald; Frost, Jack; Nazarro, Cliff

**Song(s)** Boogie Woogie Barcarolle (inst.); Dream Dancing [1]; Shootin' the Works for Uncle Sam; Since I Kissed My Baby Goodbye; So Near and Yet So Far; Wedding Cake Walk; A-stairable Rag (inst.)

**Notes** Originally titled HE'S MY UNCLE. [1] Performed instrumentally only, though recorded.

## 6982 ✦ YOU MUST BE JOKING!
Columbia, 1965

**Musical Score** Johnson, Laurie

**Producer(s)** Schneer, Charles H.
**Director(s)** Winner, Michael
**Screenwriter(s)** Hackney, Alan

**Cast** Callan, Michael; Jeffries, Lionel; Elliott, Denholm; Hyde-White, Wilfrid; Cribbins, Bernard; Bull, Peter; Licudi, Gabriella

**Song(s)** I'm with You (C: Bregman, Buddy; L: Shaper, Hal); I'll Be True to You Baby (C: Bregman, Buddy; L: Shaper, Hal)

**Notes** No cue sheet available.

## 6983 ✦ YOUNG AND BEAUTIFUL
Mascot, 1934

**Musical Score** Kay, Arthur

**Director(s)** Santley, Joseph
**Screenwriter(s)** Martin, Al; Clark, Colbert; Schary, Dore

**Cast** Malo, Gino; Garrick, John; Holloway, Stanley; Perrine, Stanley

**Song(s)** A Pretty Girl [1] (C/L: Fiorito, Ted; Tobias, Harry; Moret, Neil); Hush Your Fuss [1] (C: Snyder, Ted; L: Brennan, J. Keirn)

**Notes** [1] Used instrumentally only.

## 6984 ✦ YOUNG AND WILLING
Paramount, 1943

**Producer(s)** Griffith, Edward H.
**Director(s)** Griffith, Edward H.
**Screenwriter(s)** Van Upp, Virginia
**Source(s)** (play) Swann, Francis

**Cast** Holden, William; Bracken, Eddie; Hayward, Susan

**Song(s)** Beautiful Soup [1] (C: Tiomkin, Dimitri; Finston, Nat; L: Carroll, Lewis)

**Notes** Formerly titled OUT OF THE FRYING PAN. [1] Written for ALICE IN WONDERLAND.

## 6985 ✦ YOUNG AS YOU FEEL
Fox, 1931

**Director(s)** Borzage, Frank
**Screenwriter(s)** Burke, Edwin
**Source(s)** *Father and the Boys* (play) Ade, George

**Cast** Rogers, Will; D'Orsay, Fifi; Littlefield, Lucien; Murray, John T.

**Song(s)** The Cute Little Things You Do (C/L: Hanley, James F.)

**Notes** Originally titled CURE FOR THE BLUES.

## 6986 ✦ YOUNG AT HEART
Warner Brothers, 1955

**Producer(s)** Blanke, Henry
**Director(s)** Douglas, Gordon M.
**Screenwriter(s)** Epstein, Julius J.; Coffee, Lenore
**Source(s)** "Sister Act" (story) Hurst, Fannie

**Cast** Day, Doris; Sinatra, Frank; Young, Gig; Barrymore, Ethel; Malone, Dorothy; Keith, Robert;

Fraser, Elisabeth; Hale Jr., Alan; Chapman, Lonny; Ferguson, Frank; Bennett, Marjorie

**Song(s)** Young at Heart (C: Richards, Johnny; L: Leigh, Carolyn); Till My Love Comes to Me (C: Heindorf, Ray; L: Webster, Paul Francis); Hold Me in Your Arms (C: Heindorf, Ray; Pippin, Don; L: Henderson, Charles); You My Love (C: Van Heusen, Jimmy; L: Gordon, Mack); There's a Rising Moon for Every Falling Star [1] (C: Fain, Sammy; L: Webster, Paul Francis)

**Notes** It is not known if any of these songs were written for the picture. A remake of the 1938 film FOUR DAUGHTERS. There are also vocals of "Ready, Willing and Able" by Al Rinker, Floyd Huddleston and Dick Gleason; "Someone to Watch Over Me" by George and Ira Gershwin; "Just One of Those Things" by Cole Porter and "One for My Baby (And One More for the Road)" by Harold Arlen and Johnny Mercer. [1] Used instrumentally only.

## 6987 ✦ YOUNG BILL HICKOK
### Republic, 1940

**Producer(s)** Kane, Joseph
**Director(s)** Kane, Joseph
**Screenwriter(s)** Parker, Norton S.; Cooper, Olive

**Cast** Rogers, Roy; Hayes, George "Gabby"; Wells, Jacqueline; Miljan, John; Payne, Sally; Twitchell, Archie; Blue, Monte; Taliaferro, Hal

**Song(s)** I'll Keep on Singin' a Song (C/L: Rogers, Roy); When the Shadows Fall Across the Rockies (C/L: Tinturin, Peter); Up and Down the Prairie (C/L: Tinturin, Peter); Chollies Tamales (C: Kraushaar, Raoul; L: Cherkose, Eddie); I'm Gonna Have a Cowboy Weddin' [1] (C: Vincent, Nat; L: Sweet, Milo)

**Notes** [1] Also in MAN FROM OKLAHOMA.

## 6988 ✦ YOUNG BILLY YOUNG
### United Artists, 1969

**Musical Score** Manne, Shelly

**Producer(s)** Youngstein, Max E.
**Director(s)** Kennedy, Burt
**Screenwriter(s)** Kennedy, Burt
**Source(s)** *Who Rides with Wyatt* (novel) Henry, Will

**Cast** Mitchum, Robert; Dickinson, Angie; Walker, Robert; Carradine, David; Anderson, John

**Song(s)** Young Billy Young (C: Manne, Shelly; L: Sheldon, Ernie)

## 6989 ✦ YOUNGBLOOD (1978)
### American International, 1978

**Musical Score** Allen, Papa Dee; Brown, Harold; Dickerson, B.B.; Jordan, Lonnie; Miller, Charles; Oskar, Lee; Scott, Howard

**Producer(s)** Grillo, Nick; Riche, Alan
**Director(s)** Nosseck, Noel
**Screenwriter(s)** Harrison, Paul Carter

**Cast** Jacobs, Lawrence-Hilton; O'Dell, Bryan; Woods, Ren; Allen, Tony; Cannon, Vince; Evans, Art

**Song(s)** Youngblood Living in the Streets (C/L: Allen, Papa Dee; Brown, Harold; Dickerson, B.B.; Jordan, Lonnie; Miller, Charles; Oskar, Lee; Scott, Howard; Goldstein, Jerry)

**Notes** No cue sheet available.

## 6990 ✦ YOUNGBLOOD (1986)
### MGM/UA, 1986

**Musical Score** Orbit, William

**Producer(s)** Bart, Peter; Wells, Patrick
**Director(s)** Markle, Peter
**Screenwriter(s)** Markle, Peter

**Cast** Lowe, Rob; Gibb, Cynthia; Swayze, Patrick; Lauter, Ed; Youngs, Jim; Nesterenko, Eric; Finn, George; Flanagan, Fionnuala

**Song(s)** Ain't Gonna Walk the Line (C/L: Clark, Tena); I'm a Real Man (C/L: Hiatt, John); Soldier of Fortune (C/L: Jordan, Mark; Capek, John); Footsteps (C/L: Gilder, Nick; Silverman, Jeff); Something Real (C/L: Page, Richard; Lang, John; George, Steve); Don't Look Now (C: Orbit, William; L: Mayer, Laurie); Winning Is Everything (C/L: Plunkett, Steve; Lynch, Steve; Isham, Steve; Richards, Keni; Rand, Randy); Skate Time (C/L: Boradman, Chris); Get Ready (C/L: Robinson, William "Smokey"); Talk Me Into It (C/L: Warren, Diane); Cut You Down to Size (C/L: Chaquito, Craig; Thomas, Mickey); Stand in the Fire (C/L: Warren, Diane)

**Notes** It is not known if all these were written for this film.

## 6991 ✦ YOUNG BUFFALO BILL
### Republic, 1940

**Producer(s)** Kane, Joseph
**Director(s)** Kane, Joseph
**Screenwriter(s)** Jacobs, Harrison; Yost, Robert; Geraghty, Gerald

**Cast** Roger, Roy; Moore, Pauline; Hayes, George "Gabby"; Southern, Hugh; Pendleton, Gaylord; Chief Thundercloud

**Song(s)** Rollin' Down to Santa Fe (C/L: Samuels, Walter G.); Blow Breeze Blow (C/L: Tinturin, Peter)

## 6992 ✦ YOUNG EAGLES
### Paramount, 1930

**Director(s)** Wellman, William A.
**Screenwriter(s)** Jones, Grover; McNutt, William Slavens

**Source(s)** "The One Who Was Clever" (story) Springs, Elliott White; "Sky High" (story) Springs, Elliott White

**Cast** Rogers, Charles "Buddy"; Arthur, Jean; Lukas, Paul; Bruce, Virginia; Erwin, Stuart

**Song(s)** Love Here Is My Heart (C: Silesu, Leo; L: Adrian, Ross); The Sunrise and You (C/L: Penn, Arthur A.); Old Black Joe (C: Traditional; L: Gilbert, L. Wolfe)

## 6993 ✦ THE YOUNG GIRLS OF ROCHEFORT
### Warner Brothers, 1967

**Composer(s)** Legrand, Michel
**Lyricist(s)** Demy, Jacques
**Choreographer(s)** Maen, Norman

**Producer(s)** Bodard, Mag; de Goldschmidt, Gilbert
**Director(s)** Demy, Jacques
**Screenwriter(s)** Demy, Jacques

**Cast** Deneuve, Catherine [1]; Chakiris, George [3]; Kelly, Gene [12]; Darrieux, Danielle [13]; Dorleac, Francoise [2]; Piccoli, Michel [6]; Perrin, Jacques [5]; Dale, Grover [4]; Thenier, Genevieve [8]; Riberolles, Jacques [7]; Cremieux, Henri [13]; Hart, Pamela [9]; North, Leslie [10]; Jeantet, Patrick [11]

**Song(s)** Chanson des Jumelles; Chanson de Maxence; De Delphine a Lancien; Nous Voyageons de Ville en Ville; Chanson de Delphine; Chanson de Simon Dare; Marins, Amis, Amants ou Maris; Chanson d'Yvonne; Andy Amoureux; Chanson de Solange; Dans le Port de Hambourg; La Femme Coupee en Morceaux; Chant d'Andy; Les Rencontres; Chanson d'un Jour d'Ete; Toujours Jamais; Love Discover Me [14] (L: Shuman, Earl); To Love [14] (L: More, Julian; Brown, Earl); You Must Believe in Spring [14] (L: Bergman, Alan; Bergman, Marilyn)

**Notes** [1] Dubbed by Anne Germain. [2] Dubbed by Claude Parent. [3] Dubbed by Romauld. [4] Dubbed by Jose Bartel. [5] Dubbed by Jacques Revaux. [6] Dubbed by Georges Blanes. [7] Dubbed by Jean Stout. [8] Dubbed by Alice Herald. [9] Dubbed by Christiane Legrand. [10] Claudine Meunier. [11] Dubbed by Olivier Bonnet. [12] Dubbed by Donald Burke. [13] Not dubbed! [14] These are the English titles and lyricists. The film is in French.

## 6994 ✦ THE YOUNG GUNS
### Allied Artists, 1956

**Producer(s)** Heermance, Richard
**Director(s)** Band, Albert
**Screenwriter(s)** Garfinkle, Louis

**Cast** Tamblyn, Russ; Talbot, Gloria; Lopez, Perry; Marlowe, Scott; King, Wright

**Song(s)** Song of the Young Guns (C: Carpenter, Imogene; L: Adelson, Lenny)

**Notes** No cue sheet available. The song is sung on the soundtrack by Guy Mitchell.

## 6995 ✦ YOUNG GUNS OF TEXAS
### Twentieth Century–Fox, 1962

**Musical Score** Shefter, Bert; Sawtell, Paul

**Producer(s)** Dexter, Maury; Lippert, Robert L.
**Director(s)** Dexter, Maury
**Screenwriter(s)** Cross, Henry

**Cast** Mitchum, James; Ladd, Alana; McCrea, Jody; Wills, Chill; Conway, Gary

**Song(s)** Young Guns of Texas (C: Sawtell, Paul; Shefter, Bert; L: Herring, John)

## 6996 ✦ YOUNG JESSE JAMES
### Twentieth Century–Fox, 1960

**Producer(s)** Leewood, Jack
**Director(s)** Claxton, William F.
**Screenwriter(s)** Hampton, Orville H.; Sackheim, Jerry

**Cast** Stricklyn, Ray; Parker, Willard; Anders, Merry; Dix, Robert

**Song(s)** Young Jesse James (C: Gertz, Irving; L: Levy, Hal)

## 6997 ✦ THE YOUNG LAND
### Columbia, 1959

**Musical Score** Tiomkin, Dimitri

**Producer(s)** Ford, Patrick
**Director(s)** Tetzlaff, Ted
**Screenwriter(s)** Hall, Norman S.
**Source(s)** *Frontier Frenzy* (novel) Reese, John

**Cast** Wayne, Patrick; Craig, Yvonne; Hopper, Dennis; O'Herlihy, Dan; de la Madrid, Roberto; Ketchum, Cliff; Curtis, Ken

**Song(s)** The Young Land (C: Tiomkin, Dimitri; L: Unknown); Strange Are the Ways of Love (C: Tiomkin, Dimitri; L: Washington, Ned)

**Notes** No cue sheet available.

## 6998 ✦ THE YOUNG LOVERS
### Metro–Goldwyn–Mayer, 1966

**Musical Score** Kaplan, Sol
**Choreographer(s)** Nelson, Miriam

**Producer(s)** Goldwyn Jr., Samuel
**Director(s)** Goldwyn Jr., Samuel
**Screenwriter(s)** Garrett, George
**Source(s)** *The Young Lovers* (novel) Halevy, Julian

**Cast** Fonda, Peter; Hugueny, Sharon; Adams, Nick; Walley, Deborah; Straight, Beatrice; Campanella, Joseph

**Song(s)** The Young Lovers [1] (C: Kaplan, Sol; L: Russell, Bob)

**Notes** [1] Instrumental use only.

## 6999 ✦ YOUNG LUST
### Paramount, 1984

**Musical Score** Williams, Patrick

**Producer(s)** Stigwood, Robert; Van Noy, George
**Director(s)** Weis, Gary
**Screenwriter(s)** Menken, Robin; Wagner, Bruce

**Cast** Carvey, Dana; Gemignani, Rhoda; Kolb, Mina; Palmer, Peter; Wendt, George; Woronov, Mary

**Song(s)** Young Lust A Soap Opera [1] (C/L: Bugatti, Dominic; Musker, Frank); Don't Cry for Me Argentina [2] (C/L: Little, Russell; Procanada)

**Notes** [1] Does not appear on cue sheets but is on credits page. [2] Note that this is not the Webber/Rice song from EVITA. It is on screen for 19 seconds.

## 7000 ✦ YOUNG MAN OF MANHATTAN
### Paramount, 1930

**Composer(s)** Fain, Sammy; Norman, Pierre
**Lyricist(s)** Kahal, Irving

**Producer(s)** Bell, Monta
**Director(s)** Bell, Monta
**Screenwriter(s)** Reed, Daniel
**Source(s)** *Young Man of Manhattan* (novel) Brush, Katherine

**Cast** Rogers, Ginger; Colbert, Claudette; Foster, Norman; Ruggles, Charles; Four Aalbu Sisters

**Song(s)** (If You Could Just Forgive and Forget) I'd Fall in Love All Over Again; I've Got "It" (But It Don't Do Me No Good); Good 'n' Plenty; I'll Bob Up with the Bob-o-link (L: Kahal, Irving; Raskin, Willie) [1]

**Notes** [1] W. Raskin also credited on sheet music.

## 7001 ✦ YOUNG MAN OF MUSIC

See YOUNG MAN WITH A HORN.

## 7002 ✦ YOUNG MAN WITH A HORN
### Warner Brothers, 1950

**Producer(s)** Wald, Jerry
**Director(s)** Curtiz, Michael
**Screenwriter(s)** Foreman, Carl; North, Edmund
**Source(s)** *Young Man With a Horn* (novel) Baker, Dorothy

**Cast** Douglas, Kirk [1]; Bacall, Lauren; Day, Doris; Carmichael, Hoagy; Hernandez, Juano; Cowan, Jerome; Hughes, Mary Beth; Paiva, Nestor; Kindgren, Orley; Reed, Walter; Gerry, Alex

**Song(s)** Melancholy Rhapsody [2] (C: Heindorf, Ray; L: Cahn, Sammy)

**Notes** Released in Great Britain as YOUNG MAN OF MUSIC. Based on the life of Bix Beiderbecke. None of the songs were written for this film. Vocals include the traditional song "Sweet Bye and Bye;" "The Very Thought of You" by Ray Noble; "Lovin' Sam (The Shiek of Alabam')" by Milton Ager and Jack Yellen; "Too Marvelous for Words" by Richard A. Whiting and Johnny Mercer (also in DECEPTION and READY, WILLING AND ABLE); "I May Be Wrong but I Think You're Wonderful" by Harry Ruskin and Henry Sullivan (also in Universal's SWINGTIME JOHNNY and also in WALLFLOWER) and "With a Song in My Heart" (also in SPRING IS HERE) by Richard Rodgers and Lorenz Hart. [1] Trumpet playing dubbed by Harry James. [2] Sheet music only.

## 7003 ✦ YOUNG MAN WITH IDEAS
### Metro–Goldwyn–Mayer, 1952

**Musical Score** Rose, David

**Producer(s)** Wright, William H.
**Director(s)** Leisen, Mitchell
**Screenwriter(s)** Sheekman, Arthur

**Cast** Ford, Glenn; Roman, Ruth; Darcel, Denise; Foch, Nina; Corcoran, Donna

**Song(s)** Mon Cherie (C/L: Brent, Earl)

**Notes** There are also vocals of "I Don't Know Why" by Fred Ahlert and Roy Turk; "I've Got You Under My Skin" by Cole Porter and "M-O-T-H-E-R" by Theodore F. Morse and Howard Johnson.

## 7004 ✦ YOUNG PEOPLE
### Twentieth Century–Fox, 1940

**Composer(s)** Warren, Harry
**Lyricist(s)** Gordon, Mack
**Choreographer(s)** Castle, Nick; Sawyer, Geneva

**Producer(s)** Brown, Harry Joe
**Director(s)** Dwan, Allan
**Screenwriter(s)** Ettlinger, Don; Blum, Edwin

**Cast** Temple, Shirley; Oakie, Jack; Greenwood, Charlotte; Whelan, Arleen; Montgomery, George; Howard, Kathleen; Watson, Minor; Sully, Frank; Marsh, Mae; Bacon, Irving; Howard, Olin; Aylesworth, Arthur

**Song(s)** Mason Dixon Line; Fifth Avenue [1]; I Wouldn't Take a Million; Young People; Tra-La-La-La

**Notes** There are also vocals of "On the Beach at Waikiki" by Henry Kailikai and "Baby Take a Bow" by Lew Brown and Jay Gorney. [1] Also in I'LL GET BY with additional lyrics by Ken Darby.

## 7005 ✦ THE YOUNG RUNAWAYS
### Metro–Goldwyn–Mayer, 1968

**Musical Score** Karger, Fred

**Producer(s)** Katzman, Sam
**Director(s)** Dreifuss, Arthur
**Screenwriter(s)** Hampton, Orville H.

**Cast** Bundy, Brooke; Coughlin, Kevin; Bochner, Lloyd; McCormack, Patty; Dean, Quentin; Dreyfuss, Richard; Sargent, Dick; Bari, Lynn; Fell, Norman; Edwards, James; Sanford, Isabel; Vincent, Romo

**Song(s)** The Young Runaways (C: Karger, Fred; L: Coughlin, Kevin); Ophelia's Dream (C/L: Weatherly, James D.; Lobue, John D.; Russell, Leland); So Close to Love [1] (C/L: Karger, Fred; Weisman, Ben; Wayne, Sid); Blue Lou [1] (C/L: Karger, Fred; Weisman, Ben; Wayne, Sid)

**Notes** The song "Couldn't We" by James D. Weatherly, John D. Lobue and Leland Russell is listed in the credits but not the cue sheet. [1] Also in HOT RODS TO HELL.

### 7006 ♦ YOUNG SINNERS
Fox, 1931

**Composer(s)** Hanley, James F.
**Lyricist(s)** Hanley, James F.

**Director(s)** Blystone, John
**Screenwriter(s)** Conselman, William
**Source(s)** *Young Sinners* (play) Harris, Elmer

**Cast** Meighan, Thomas; Albright, Hardie; Jordan, Dorothy; Loftus, Cecilia

**Song(s)** You Called It Love; Better Wait Till You're Eighteen; Keep Doing It [1]

**Notes** [1] Sheet music only.

### 7007 ♦ THE YOUNG SWINGERS
Twentieth Century–Fox, 1964

**Musical Score** Levine, Hank

**Producer(s)** Dexter, Maury
**Director(s)** Dexter, Maury
**Screenwriter(s)** Spaulding, Harry

**Cast** Lauren, Rod; Bee, Molly; McDaniels, Gene; Larson, Jack

**Song(s)** Come to the Party (C: Levine, Hank; L: Dunham, "By"); Where Can Elijah Be (C/L: Dunham, "By"); Mad, Mad, Mad (C/L: Quickel, Susane C.; Baker, Bill); Watusi Surfer (C/L: Dunham, "By"); I Can't Get You Out of My Heart (C: Faith, Russell; L: Marcucci, Robert); Greenback Dollar (C/L: Axton, Hoyt; Ramsey, Kenneth R.); You Pass Me By (C/L: McKuen, Rod); Voice on the Mountain (C/L: Vars, Henry; L: Dunham, "By")

**Notes** Originally titled COME TO THE PARTY.

### 7008 ♦ YOU ONLY LIVE TWICE
United Artists, 1967

**Musical Score** Barry, John

**Producer(s)** Broccoli, Albert R.; Saltzman, Harry
**Director(s)** Gilbert, Lewis

**Screenwriter(s)** Dahl, Roald
**Source(s)** *You Only Live Twice* (novel) Fleming, Ian

**Cast** Connery, Sean; Pleasence, Donald; Hama, Mie; Wakabayashi, Akiko; Dor, Karin; Lee, Bernard; Maxwell, Lois

**Song(s)** You Only Live Twice (C: Barry, John; L: Bricusse, Leslie)

### 7009 ♦ YOUR CHEATIN' HEART
Metro–Goldwyn–Mayer, 1965

**Musical Score** Karger, Fred

**Producer(s)** Katzman, Sam
**Director(s)** Nelson, Gene
**Screenwriter(s)** Whitmore, Stanford

**Cast** Hamilton, George [1]; Oliver, Susan; Buttons, Red; O'Connell, Arthur; Marshall, Shary; Ingram, Rex; Crosby, Chris

**Song(s)** Poppin' that Shine (C/L: Karger, Fred; Whitmore, Stanford; Nelson, Gene)

**Notes** This is based on the life of Hank Williams. His son, Hank Williams Jr., recorded his father's songs for the soundtrack. There are also vocals of the following song with music and lyrics by Hank Williams: "Long Gone Lonesome Blues," "Just Waitin'" (written with Bob Gazzaway), "I Saw the Light," "I Can't Help It," "Cold Cold Heart," "Your Cheatin' Heart," "Jambalaya," "Hey Good Lookin" and "I'm So Lonesome I Could Cry." [1] Dubbed by Hank Williams Jr.

### 7010 ♦ YOU'RE A BIG BOY NOW
Warner Brothers, 1967

**Musical Score** Sebastian, John; Prince, Robert
**Composer(s)** Sebastian, John
**Lyricist(s)** Sebastian, John

**Producer(s)** Feldman, Phil
**Director(s)** Coppola, Francis Ford
**Screenwriter(s)** Coppola, Francis Ford

**Cast** Hartman, Elizabeth; Page, Geraldine; Harris, Julie; Kastner, Peter; Torn, Rip; Dunn, Michael; Bill, Tony; Black, Karen; Sweet, Dolph; O'Sullivan, Michael

**Song(s)** Girl, Beautiful Girl; Darling Be Home Soon; You're a Big Boy Now; Wash It Away

### 7011 ♦ YOU'RE A LUCKY FELLOW, MR. SMITH
Universal, 1943

**Producer(s)** Lilley, Edward
**Director(s)** Feist, Felix E.
**Screenwriter(s)** Riley, Lawrence; Barzman, Ben; Lantz, Louis

**Cast**  Jones, Allan; Ankers, Evelyn; Burke, Billie; Bruce, David; O'Connor, Patsy; Clements, Stanley; Alberni, Lula; Moreland, Mantan

**Song(s)**  Swing-A-Bye My Baby [1] (C: Berens, Norman; L: Brooks, Jack); On the Crest of a Rainbow (C/L: Sherman, Al; Tobias, Harry); Hup, Two Three Four Blues (C/L: Pepper, Buddy; James, Inez); You're a Lucky Fellow, Mr. Smith [2] (C: Prince, Hughie; Burke, Sonny; L: Raye, Don)

**Notes**  There are also vocals of "When You're Smiling" by Mark Fisher, Joe Goodwin and Larry Shay; "Three Little Men with Feathers" by Sam H. Stept; "What Is This Thing Called Love?" by Cole Porter and "You're Eyes Have Told Me So" by Gus Kahn, Egbert Van Alstyne and Walter Blaufuss. [1] Also in MELODY LANE (1942). [2] Also in ABBOTT & COSTELLO & DICK POWELL IN THE NAVY, HI 'YA CHUM and BUCK PRIVATES (1941).

## 7012 ◆ YOU'RE A SWEETHEART
Universal, 1938

**Composer(s)**  McHugh, Jimmy
**Lyricist(s)**  Adamson, Harold
**Choreographer(s)**  Randall, Carl; Rasch, Albertina

**Producer(s)**  DeSylva, B.G.
**Director(s)**  Butler, David
**Screenwriter(s)**  Brice, Monte; Grayson, Charles

**Cast**  Faye, Alice; Murphy, George; Winninger, Charles; Devine, Andy; Murray, Ken; Hunt, Frances; Gargan, William; Jenks, Frank; Meek, Donald; The Four Playboys; Malda and Ray; The Noville Brothers

**Song(s)**  You're a Sweetheart [1]; Broadway Jamboree; My Fine Feathered Friend; Scrapin' the Toast (C: Mencher, Murray; L: Tobias, Charles); So It's Love (C: Bring, Lou; Quenzer, Arthur; L: Bloom, Mickey); Oh, Oh, Oklahoma; Who Killed Maggie?

**Notes**  [1] Also used in HOW'S ABOUT IT and MEET DANNY WILSON. Universal used this song over and over and I only listed it when other songs also appeared in the score.

## 7013 ◆ YOU'RE IN THE ARMY NOW
Warner Brothers, 1941

**Musical Score**  Jackson, Howard

**Producer(s)**  Stoloff, Ben
**Director(s)**  Seiler, Lewis
**Screenwriter(s)**  Smith, Paul Gerard; Beatty, George

**Cast**  Durante, Jimmy; Wyman, Jane; Silvers, Phil; Toomey, Regis; McBride, Donald; Meeker, George; Sawyer, Joe; Haade, William

**Song(s)**  I'm Glad My Number Was Called (C/L: Adler, Charles; Kelly, George); I'm an Army Man (C/L: Durante, Jimmy); Whirlaway (C/L: Durante, Jimmy)

**Notes**  It is not known if any of these were written for the film.

## 7014 ◆ YOU'RE MY EVERYTHING
Twentieth Century–Fox, 1949

**Choreographer(s)**  Castle, Nick

**Producer(s)**  Trotti, Lamar
**Director(s)**  Lang, Walter
**Screenwriter(s)**  Trotti, Lamar; Hays, Will H., Jr.

**Cast**  Dailey, Dan; Baxter, Anne; Revere, Anne; Ridges, Stanley; Robinson, Shari; O'Neill, Henry; Royle, Selena; Mowbray, Alan; Arthur, Robert; Keaton, Buster

**Song(s)**  I Want to Be Teacher's Pet (C: Myrow, Josef; L: Gordon, Mack); (By) The White Magnolia Tree (C: Newman, Alfred; L: Darby, Ken); Lollypop Prelude (C/L: Gordon, Mack); Lollipop Interlude (C/L: Gordon, Mack); Sailor's Hornpipe (C: Traditional; L: Gordon, Mack)

**Notes**  There are also vocals of "The Varsity Drag" by B.G. DeSylva, Lew Brown and Ray Henderson; "You're My Everything" by Harry Warren, Mort Dixon and Joe Young; "Chicago (That Toddling Town)" by Fred Fisher; "California Here I Come" by Al Jolson, B.G. DeSylva and Joseph Meyer; "You Oughta Be in Pictures" by Dana Suesse and Edward Heyman; "I May Be Wrong (But I Think You're Wonderful)" by Henry Sullivan and Harry Ruskin; "Ain't She Sweet" by Milton Ager and Jack Yellen; "Chattanooga Choo Choo" by Harry Warren and Mack Gordon; "I Can't Begin to Tell You" by James V. Monaco and Mack Gordon; "Would You Like to Take a Walk" by Harry Warren, Mort Dixon and Billy Rose and "On the Good Ship Lollipop" by Richard A. Whiting and Sidney Clare.

## 7015 ◆ YOU'RE NEVER TOO YOUNG
Paramount, 1955

**Musical Score**  Scharf, Walter
**Composer(s)**  Schwartz, Arthur
**Lyricist(s)**  Cahn, Sammy
**Choreographer(s)**  Castle, Nick

**Producer(s)**  Jones, Paul
**Director(s)**  Taurog, Norman
**Screenwriter(s)**  Sheldon, Sidney
**Source(s)**  *Connie Goes Home* (play) Carpenter, Edward Childs

**Cast**  Lewis, Jerry; Martin, Dean; Lynn, Diana; Foch, Nina; Burr, Raymond; McCall, Mitzi; Borg, Veda Ann; Vincent, Romo; Kulp, Nancy

**Song(s)**  Relax-Ay-Voo; I Know Your Mother Loves You; Love Is All That Matters; You're Never Too Young; Simpatico; I Like to Hike; Every Day's a Happy Day [1]; Face the Music [1]

**Notes**  From a letter to Sammy Cahn: "I have been advised by Mr. Luraschi, who is head of the Foreign and

Censorship Departments, that your lyric "SIMPATICO" is not acceptable from a Latin point of view because of the manner in which the word "simpatico" is used. For example - "Your eyes are simpatico." [1] Sheet music only.

### 7016 ♦ YOU'RE ONLY YOUNG ONCE
Metro–Goldwyn–Mayer, 1938

**Director(s)**   Seitz, George B.
**Screenwriter(s)**   Van Riper, Kay
**Source(s)**   characters by Rouverol, Aurania

**Cast**   Stone, Lewis; Parker, Cecilia; Rooney, Mickey; Holden, Fay; Rutherford, Ann; Craven, Frank; Judels, Charles; Haden, Sara

**Song(s)**   You're Only Young Once [1] (C: Hyde, Alexander; L: Wright, Bob; Forrest, Chet)

**Notes**   [1] Used instrumentally only.

### 7017 ♦ YOU'RE THE ONE
Paramount, 1941

**Composer(s)**   McHugh, Jimmy
**Lyricist(s)**   Mercer, Johnny

**Producer(s)**   Markey, Gene
**Director(s)**   Murphy, Ralph
**Screenwriter(s)**   Markey, Gene

**Cast**   Baker, Bonnie; Tucker, Orrin; Dekker, Albert; Colonna, Jerry

**Song(s)**   You're the One for Me [3]; I Could Kiss You for That; Strawberry Lane; The Yogi (Who Lost His Will-Power); Gee, I Wish I Listened to My Mother [1]; Honor Bright [2]; P.S. I Got the Job [2]; This Is the Night of My Dreams [2]; It'll Get You—In the End [2]; In a Moment of Surrender [2]

**Notes**   The arrangements of "Strawberry Lane" and "The Yogi Who Lost His Will-Power" were written by Jule Styne. There are also vocals of "My Resistance Is Low" by Orrin Tucker and "Oh Johnny, Oh" by Abe Olman and Ed Rose. [1] Used briefly instrumentally only. [2] Not used. [3] Also in TIMBER QUEEN.

### 7018 ♦ YOURS AND MINE
Metro–Goldwyn–Mayer, 1935 unproduced

**Composer(s)**   Brown, Nacio Herb
**Lyricist(s)**   Freed, Arthur

**Song(s)**   Born to Dance; Busy Body; Yours and Mine

### 7019 ♦ YOURS, MINE AND OURS
United Artists, 1968

**Musical Score**   Karlin, Fred
**Composer(s)**   Karlin, Fred
**Lyricist(s)**   Sheldon, Ernie

**Producer(s)**   Blumofe, Robert F.
**Director(s)**   Shavelson, Melville
**Screenwriter(s)**   Shavelson, Melville; Lachman, Mort

**Cast**   Ball, Lucille; Fonda, Henry; Johnson, Van; Bosley, Tom; Leak, Jennifer; Shea, Eric; Matthieson, Timothy; Murphy, Ben

**Song(s)**   Yours, Mine and Ours; It's a Sometimes World

### 7020 ♦ YOURS SINCERELY

See SPRING IS HERE.

### 7021 ♦ YOUR UNCLE DUDLEY
Twentieth Century–Fox, 1935

**Producer(s)**   Lowe, Edward T.
**Director(s)**   Tinling, James; Forde, Eugene
**Screenwriter(s)**   Schary, Dore; Hoffman, Joseph

**Cast**   Horton, Edward Everett; Wilson, Lois; McGuire, John; Lawrence, Rosina; Dinehart, Alan; Gateson, Marjorie

**Song(s)**   When Twilight Comes [1] (C: Tandler, H.J.; L: Horne, Harold); I Sing of Spring (C: Sanders, Troy; L: Clare, Sidney)

**Notes**   [1] Not written for this picture.

### 7022 ♦ YOUTH ON PARADE
Republic, 1942

**Composer(s)**   Styne, Jule
**Lyricist(s)**   Cahn, Sammy
**Choreographer(s)**   Gould, Dave

**Producer(s)**   Cohen, Albert J.
**Director(s)**   Rogell, Albert S.
**Screenwriter(s)**   Brown, George Carleton; Gill, Frank, Jr.

**Cast**   Hubbard, John; Terry, Ruth; Driscoll, Martha [2]; Brown, Tom; Merrick, Lynn; Chandler, Chick; Simpson, Ivan L.; Smith, Charles; Bryant, Nana

**Song(s)**   Cotcha Too-Ta Mee (Alma Mater); If It's Love [4]; I'm on My Way to College; You're So Good to Me [5]; I've Heard That Song Before [3]; You Got To Study Buddy; Mad [1]

**Notes**   There is also a vocal of "Ah, So Pure" from MARTHA by Von Flotow. [1] Not used. [2] Dubbed by Margaret Whiting. [3] Also in PISTOL PACKIN' MAMA and SHANTYTOWN. [4] Also in SILENT PARTNER. [5] Also in HERE COMES ELMER and TELL IT TO A STAR.

### 7023 ♦ YOUTH ON PAROLE
Republic, 1937

**Musical Score**   Colombo, Alberto

**Producer(s)**   Rosen, Phil
**Director(s)**   Rosen, Phil
**Screenwriter(s)**   Rebaus, Herschel [1]

**Cast** Marsh, Marian; Oliver, Gordon; Dumont, Margaret; Shannon, Peggy; Mander, Miles; Boteler, Wade; Kornman, Mary; Songe, Milburn

**Song(s)** Dancing Under the Stars (C/L: Owens, Harry)

**Notes** [1] Pseudonym for Harry Sauber.

## 7024 ✦ YOUTH WILL BE SERVED
### Twentieth Century–Fox, 1940

**Composer(s)** Alter, Louis
**Lyricist(s)** Loesser, Frank
**Choreographer(s)** Castle, Nick

**Producer(s)** Hubbard, Lucien
**Director(s)** Brower, Otto
**Screenwriter(s)** Tuchock, Wanda

**Cast** Withers, Jane; Darwell, Jane; Brown Jr., Joe; Conway, Robert; Knox, Elyse; Qualen, John

**Song(s)** Youth Will Be Served; Hot Catfish and Corn Dodgers; With a Banjo on My Knee [1] (C: McHugh, Jimmy; L: Adamson, Harold)

**Notes** [1] Also in BANJO ON MY KNEE.

## 7025 ✦ YOU WERE MEANT FOR ME
### Twentieth Century–Fox, 1948

**Producer(s)** Kohlmar, Fred
**Director(s)** Bacon, Lloyd
**Screenwriter(s)** Davies, Valentine; Moll, Elick

**Cast** Crain, Jeanne; Dailey, Dan; Levant, Oscar; Lawrence, Barbara; Royle, Selena; Kilbride, Percy; Clark, Les; Barris, Harry

**Song(s)** Can't Sleep a Wink (C/L: Henderson, Charles)

**Notes** There are also vocals of "Crazy Rhythm" by Joseph Meyer, Roger Wolfe Kahn and Irving Caesar; "You Were Meant for Me" by Arthur Freed and Nacio Herb Brown; "I'll Get By (As Long As I Have You)" by Fred Ahlert and Roy Turk; "If I Had You" by Ted Shapiro, Jimmy Campbell and Reg Connelly; "Goodnight Sweetheart" by Ray Noble, Jimmy Campbell and Reg Connelly; "Ain't Misbehavin'" by Thomas "Fats" Waller, Harry Brooks and Andy Razaf; George Gershwin's "Concerto in F" (Inst.) and "Happy Days Are Here Again" and "Ain't She Sweet" by Milton Ager and Jack Yellen.

## 7026 ✦ YOU WERE NEVER LOVELIER
### Columbia, 1942

**Composer(s)** Kern, Jerome
**Lyricist(s)** Mercer, Johnny
**Choreographer(s)** Raset, Val

**Producer(s)** Edelman, Louis F.
**Director(s)** Seiter, William A.
**Screenwriter(s)** Fessier, Michael; Pagano, Ernest; Daves, Delmer
**Source(s)** "Los Martes Orquideas" (story) Olivari, Carlos A.; Rios, Sixto Pondal

**Cast** Hayworth, Rita [1]; Astaire, Fred; Menjou, Adolphe; Brooks, Leslie; Elsom, Isobel; Parks, Larry; Brown, Stanley; Howard, Kathleen; Cugat, Xavier

**Song(s)** Dearly Beloved; I'm Old Fashioned; Shorty George; Wedding in the Spring; You Were Never Lovelier; These Orchids; On the Beam [2]; Windmill Under the Stars [2]

**Notes** There is also a vocal of "Chiu, Chiu" by Nicanor Molinaire and Alan Surgal (also in Paramount's CHAMPAGNE FOR TWO). [1] Dubbed by Nan Wynn. [2] Not used.

## 7027 ✦ YUKON FLIGHT
### Criterion, 1940

**Composer(s)** Lange, Johnny
**Lyricist(s)** Porter, Lew

**Director(s)** Staub, Ralph
**Screenwriter(s)** Halperin, Edward
**Source(s)** "Renfrew of the Royal Mounted" (stories) Erskine, Laurie York

**Cast** Newill, James; Stanley, Louise; Hull, Warren; Pawley, William; O'Brien, Dave; Barcroft, Roy

**Song(s)** Mounted Men [1] (C/L: Laidlow, Betty; Lively, Robert); My Weakness Is Eyes of Blue; Mounted Men Are on Parade; The Old Grey Goose Is Dead

**Notes** [1] Also in CRASHING THRU, DANGER AHEAD, FIGHTING MAN, MURDER ON THE YUKON, RENFREW AND THE GREAT WHITE TRAIL and SKY BANDITS.

# Z

### 7028 ✦ ZABRISKIE POINT
Metro–Goldwyn–Mayer, 1969

**Composer(s)** Waters, Roger; Gilmour, David; Mason, Nick; Wright, Richard [1]

**Lyricist(s)** Waters, Roger; Gilmour, David; Mason, Nick; Wright, Richard [1]

**Producer(s)** Ponti, Carlo

**Director(s)** Antonioni, Michelangelo

**Screenwriter(s)** Antonioni, Michelangelo; Gardner, Fred; Guerra, Tonino; Shepard, Sam; Peploe, Clare

**Cast** Frechette, Mark; Halprin, Daria; Fix, Paul; Spradlin, G.D.; Garaway, Bill; Cleaver, Kathleen; Open Theater of Joe Chaikin; Taylor, Rod

**Song(s)** Heart Beat, Pig Meat; Brother Mary (C/L: Lindley, David); Crumbling Land; Come In Number 51, Your Time Is Up

**Notes** [1] Members of Pink Floyd. There are also vocals of "You Got the Silver" by Mick Jagger and Keith Richards; "Tennesse Waltz" by P.W. King and R. Stewart; "I Wish I Was a Single Girl Again" and "So Young" by Roy Orbison, Mike Curb and Roger Christian.

### 7029 ✦ ZAPPED!
Embassy, 1982

**Musical Score** Fox, Charles
**Composer(s)** Fox, Charles
**Lyricist(s)** Geyer, Stephen

**Producer(s)** Apple, Jeffrey D.
**Director(s)** Rosenthal, Robert J.
**Screenwriter(s)** Rubin, Bruce; Rosenthal, Robert J.

**Cast** Baio, Scott; Aames, Willie; Mandan, Robert; Schachter, Felice; Crothers, Benjamin "Scatman"; Langdon, Sue Ane

**Song(s)** Shoot the Moon; Just for Fun; Got to Believe in Magic; King and Queen of Hearts; Ready or Not

**Notes** No cue sheet available.

### 7030 ✦ ZAZA
Paramount, 1939

**Composer(s)** Hollander, Frederick
**Lyricist(s)** Loesser, Frank
**Choreographer(s)** Prinz, LeRoy

**Producer(s)** Lewin, Albert
**Director(s)** Cukor, George
**Screenwriter(s)** Akins, Zoe
**Source(s)** (play) Berton, Pierre; Simon, Charles

**Cast** Colbert, Claudette [3]; Lahr, Bert; Marshall, Herbert; Tobin, Genevieve; Cossart, Ernest; Catlett, Walter; Westley, Helen; O'Malley, Rex; Tree, Dorothy; Woolley, Monty; Collier, Constance

**Song(s)** Zaza; Hello My Darling; I'm the Stupidest Girl in the Class [1]; Street Song [1]; He Died of Love [1]; Forget Me [1]; Rain Song [2] (C/L: Boutelje, Phil)

**Notes** [1] Not used. [2] Recorded but used instrumentally only. [3] Recorded by her but finally dubbed by Martha Mears.

### 7031 ✦ ZEBRA IN THE KITCHEN
Metro–Goldwyn–Mayer, 1965

**Musical Score** Barker, Warren

**Producer(s)** Tors, Ivan
**Director(s)** Tors, Ivan
**Screenwriter(s)** Arthur, Art

**Cast** North, Jay; Milner, Martin; Devine, Andy; David, Jim; Meadows, Joyce; Green, Dorothy; Taylor, Vaughn; Weaver, Doodles

**Song(s)** Zebra in the Kitchen (C/L: Hopper, Hal)

### 7032 ✦ ZELIG
Orion, 1983

**Musical Score** Hyman, Dick
**Composer(s)** Hyman, Dick
**Lyricist(s)** Hyman, Dick

**Producer(s)** Rollins, Jack; Joffe, Charles H.
**Director(s)** Allen, Woody
**Screenwriter(s)** Allen, Woody

**Cast** Allen, Woody; Farrow, Mia; Buckwaiter, John; Wilson, Mary Louise; Rush, Deborah; Simmonds, Stanley; Holt, Will; Sontag, Susan; Howe, Irving; Bellow, Saul; Bricktop; Bettelheim, Dr. Bruno; Blum, Prof. John Morton; Lomita, Sol

**Song(s)** Doin' the Chameleon; Chameleon Days; You May Be Six People; Leonard the Lizard; Reptile Eyes

## 7033 ◆ ZERO HOUR
Paramount, 1958

**Musical Score**   Dale, Ted

**Producer(s)**   Champion, John
**Director(s)**   Bartlett, Hall
**Screenwriter(s)**   Hailey, Arthur; Bartlett, Hall;
Champion, John

**Cast**   Andrews, Dana; Darnell, Linda; Hayden, Sterling;
Hirsch, Elroy "Crazylegs"; Toone, Geoffrey; Paris, Jerry;
King, Peggy

**Song(s)**   Call It Loud (C/L: Dale, Ted); Zero Hour [1]
(C/L: Hamilton, Arthur)

**Notes**   [1] Used instrumentally only.


## 7034 ◆ ZIEGFELD FOLLIES
Metro–Goldwyn–Mayer, 1946

**Choreographer(s)**   Alton, Robert

**Producer(s)**   Freed, Arthur
**Director(s)**   Minnelli, Vincente [2]

**Cast**   Astaire, Fred; Ball, Lucille; Bremer, Lucille; Brice,
Fanny; Garland, Judy; Grayson, Kathryn; Horne, Lena;
Kelly, Gene; Melton, James; Moore, Victor; Skelton,
Red; Williams, Esther; Powell, William; Arnold, Edward;
Bunin's Puppets; Bell, Marion; Charisse, Cyd; Cronyn,
Hume; Frawley, William; Lewis, Robert; O'Brien,
Virginia; Wynn, Keenan

**Song(s)**   Here's to the Ladies (C: Edens, Roger; L:
Freed, Ralph); Bring on the Wonderful Men (C: Edens,
Roger; Brent, Earl; L: Brent, Earl); This Heart of Mine
(C: Warren, Harry; L: Freed, Arthur); Love [3] (C/L:
Martin, Hugh; Blane, Ralph); A Great Lady Has an
Interview (C/L: Edens, Roger; Thompson, Kay);
There's Beauty Everywhere (1) [1] (C: Warren, Harry;
L: Freed, Arthur); There's Beauty Everywhere (2) [1]
(C: Brent, Earl; L: Freed, Arthur); If Swing Goes I Go
Too [4] (C/L: Astaire, Fred); The Cocabola Tree [5]
(C/L: Blane, Ralph; Martin, Hugh); It's Getting Hot in
Tahiti [5] (C/L: Blane, Ralph; Martin, Hugh; Edens,
Roger); Shauny O'Shea [5] (C/L: Martin, Hugh; Blane,
Ralph)

**Notes**   The film was orignally produced in 1944 as
ZIEGFELD FOLLIES OF 1944. It was previewed and
the studio delayed the release. They deleted numbers and
filmed new numbers. The final version was released in
1946. Vocals also include "I'm an Indian" by Leo
Edwards and Blanche Merrill; "If You Knew Susie" by
B.G. DeSylva and Joseph Meyer; "Libiano" from LA
TRAVIATA by Verdi; "Limehouse Blues" by Philip
Braham and Douglas Furber (from British revue A TO Z
and American edition of ANDRE CHARLOT'S REVUE
OF 1924); "Knocked 'Em in the Old Kent Road" by
Charles Ingle and Albert Chevalier and "The Babbitt and
the Bromide" by George and Ira Gershwin.

Numbers which appeared in the 1944 preview print
but which were deleted from the 1946 print include: "If
Swing Goes, I Go Too" written and performed by Fred
Astaire and directed by George Sidney; Jimmy Durante
in "Start Off Each Day with a Song" directed by Charles
Walters; Fanny Brice in the sketch "Baby Snooks and the
Burglers" by Everett and Devery Freeman directed by
Roy Del Ruth; James Melton in "A Bit of the West"
directed by Merrill Pye; Lena Horne and Avon Long
singing the Gershwins' "Liza" directed by Minnelli and
staged by Eugene Loring; Esther Williams and James
Melton performing "We Will Meet Again in Honolulu"
by Nacio Herb Brown and Arthur Freed and directed by
Merrill Pye; "There's Beauty Everywhere" (see [1]
below) performed by Fred Astaire, Lucille Bremer, James
Melton, Cyd Charise and the ensemble directed by
Vincent Minnelli; and the sketch "Death and Taxes" by
David Freedman with Jimmy Durante and Edward
Arnold directed by Minnelli.

Prerecorded, but not photographed numbers include:
"Will You Love Me in Technicolor As You Do in Black
and White" with Judy Garland and Mickey Rooney.

Not used were: Fireside Chat with Judy Garland, Ann
Sothern and Lucille Ball; "Pass that Peace Pipe" by
Roger Edens, Hugh Martin and Ralph Blane with June
Allyson, Gene Kelly, Nancy Walker and the ensemble
(used in GOOD NEWS and in the score of the
unproduced HUCKLEBERRY FINN); David
Freedman's sketch "Reading of the Play" with Judy
Garland and Frank Morgan; Judy Garland and Mickey
Rooney performing the Edens, Martin and Blane song
"As Long as I Have My Art"; the sketch "Glorifying the
American Girl" with Lucille Ball, Marilyn Maxwell,
Lucille Bremer, Lena Horne and Elaine Shephard; the
sketch "A Trip to Hollywood" with Jimmy Durante,
Lucille Ball, Marilyn Maxwell and others; "Fairy Tale
Ballet" choreographed by Eugene Loring with Katharine
Hepburn, Margaret O'Brien and Jackie Jenkins; and
finally, the Dietz and Schwartz song "You're
Dreamlike."

The 1944 Film Daily Yearbook lists the songs
"Glorifying the American Girl" and "Goodbye, World"
as written by Sammy Fain and Ralph Freed for Ziegfeld
Follies.

[1] The cue sheet credits Earl Brent and Arthur Freed
as does Hirschhorn in his *Hollywood Musicals*. Kinkle
credits Warren and Freed as does Thomas' Harry Warren
biography, Fordin's Freed unit book and, most
importantly, the film's titles. Perhaps Brent wrote an
earlier version for the 1944 edition. [2] "Ziegfeld Days"
scene directed by Norman Taurog. "Here's to the
Ladies" directed by George Sidney. "This Heart of
Mine" directed by Merrill Pye. Number Please (by Peter
Barr) directed by Robert Lewis. "Pay the Two Dollars"
(by George White and William K. Wells) directed by
George Sidney. "A Sweepstakes Ticket" (by David
Freedman) directed by Roy Del Ruth and staged by
Charles Walters. "Love" directed by Lemuel Ayers.
"When Television Comes" (by Edna Skelton) directed by

George Sidney. All other numbers directed by Vincent Minnelli. [4] Deleted from final print. [5] Not used.

## 7035 ◆ ZIEGFELD GIRL
### Metro–Goldwyn–Mayer, 1941

**Composer(s)** Edens, Roger
**Lyricist(s)** Edens, Roger
**Choreographer(s)** Berkeley, Busby

**Producer(s)** Berman, Pandro S.
**Director(s)** Leonard, Robert Z.
**Screenwriter(s)** Roberts, Marguerite; Levien, Sonya

**Cast** Stewart, James; Garland, Judy; Lamarr, Hedy; Turner, Lana; Cooper, Jackie; Martin, Tony; Hunter, Ian; Winninger, Charles; Horton, Edward Everett; Dorn, Philip; Kelly, Paul; Arden, Eve; Dailey, Dan [1]; Shean, Al; Holden, Fay; Bressart, Felix; Hobart, Rose; Busch, Mae

**Song(s)** You Never Looked So Beautiful [2] (C: Donaldson, Walter; L: Adamson, Harold); Laugh? I Thought I'd Split My Sides; You Stepped Out of a Dream (C: Brown, Nacio Herb; L: Kahn, Gus); Caribbean Love Song (L: Freed, Ralph); Trinidad; Minnie from Trinidad; Ziegfeld Girls; You Gotta Pull Strings (C: Donaldson, Walter; L: Adamson, Harold); We Must Have Music [3] (C: Brown, Nacio Herb; L: Kahn, Gus); Too Beautiful to Last [4] (C: Lowe, Ruth; L: Symes, Marty)

**Notes** There are also vocals of "Whispering" by Malvin Schoenberger, Richard Coburn and John Schoenberger; "I'm Always Chasing Rainbows" by Harry Carroll and Joseph McCarthy; and "Mr. Gallagher and Mr. Shean" by Ed Gallagher and Al Shean. [1] Billed as Dan Dailey Jr. [2] Also in THE GREAT ZIEGFELD. [3] Recorded but not used. [4] Sheet music only.

## 7036 ◆ ZIG ZAG
### Metro–Goldwyn–Mayer, 1970

**Musical Score** Nelson, Oliver

**Producer(s)** Enders, Robert; Freeman, Everett
**Director(s)** Colla, Richard A.
**Screenwriter(s)** Kelley, John T.

**Cast** Kennedy, George; Jackson, Anne; Wallach, Eli; Ihnat, Steve; Marshall, William; Maross, Joe; Elcar, Dana; Brooke, Walter; O'Day, Anita

**Song(s)** Zigzag (C/L: Curb, Mike; Enders, Robert; Hemric, Guy)

**Notes** Titled FALSE WITNESS overseas. There is also a vocal of "On Green Dolphin Street" by Bronislau Kaper and Ned Washington.

## 7037 ◆ ZIS BOOM BAH
### Monogram, 1941

**Choreographer(s)** King, George

**Producer(s)** Katzman, Sam
**Director(s)** Nigh, William
**Screenwriter(s)** Gates, Harvey; Henley, Jack

**Cast** Hayes, Grace; Hayes, Peter Lind; Healy, Mary; Hall, Huntz; Wiley, Jan; Rubin, Benny; Elliot, Frank; Landon, Lois; Gallagher, Skeets; Sues, Leonard; Dupree, Roland

**Song(s)** Put Your Trust in the Moon (C: Callender, Charles R.; L: Baldwin, June); It Makes No Difference When You're in the Army (C/L: Lange, Johnny; Porter, Lew); Miss America (C/L: Ellon, Lee; Hammand, Earl); I've Learned to Smile Again (C/L: Fleeson, Neville); Good News Tomorrow (C/L: Fleeson, Neville); Annabelle (C/L: Lange, Johnny; Porter, Lew); Zis Boom Bah (C/L: Cannon, Elaine)

**Notes** No cue sheet available.

## 7038 ◆ ZOMBIES ON BROADWAY
### RKO, 1945

**Musical Score** Webb, Roy

**Producer(s)** Stoloff, Ben
**Director(s)** Douglas, Gordon M.
**Screenwriter(s)** Kimble, Lawrence

**Cast** Brown, Wally; Carney, Alan; Lugosi, Bela; Jeffreys, Anne; Leonard, Sheldon; Jenks, Frank; Hopton, Russell; Vitale, Joseph; Wolfe, Ian; Heydt, Louis Jean; Jones, Darby

**Song(s)** Que Chica [2] (C: Van Heusen, James; L: Burke, Johnny); Zombie Calypso Song [1] (C: Kimball, Lawrence; L: Bennett, Norman)

**Notes** [1] Used instrumentally only. [2] Also in PLAYMATES.

## 7039 ◆ ZORRO'S FIGHTING LEGION
### Republic, 1939

**Producer(s)** Beche, Bob
**Director(s)** Whitney, William; English, John
**Screenwriter(s)** Davidson, Ronald; Adreon, Frank; Cox, Morgan B.; Shor, Sol; Sarecky, Barney
**Source(s)** character by McCulley, Johnston

**Cast** Hadley, Reed; Darcy, Sheila

**Song(s)** We Ride (C: Lava, William; L: Cherkose, Eddie)

**Notes** A serial. The song was used as the "Main Title" for the series.